BJ
31
E 854
1997

Ethics in Practice

Blackwell Philosophy Anthologies

Motivated by the conviction that an education in philosophy involves exposure to and immersion in the classic and contemporary original texts, this outstanding new series provides comprehensive and authoritative selections of *the* essential primary readings of philosophy. Designed to complement and stand alongside the prestigious *Blackwell Companions to Philosophy* series, each volume represents an unparalleled resource in its own right, and will provide the ideal basis for course use.

1 Cottingham: *Western Philosophy: An Anthology*
2 Cahoone: *From Modernism to Postmodernism: An Anthology*
3 LaFollette: *Ethics in Practice: An Anthology*

Forthcoming

4 Goodin and Pettit: *Contemporary Political Philosophy: An Anthology*
5 Eze: *Africana Philosophy: An Anthology*
6 Kim and Sosa: *Metaphysics: An Anthology*
7 Sosa and Kim: *Epistemology: An Anthology*

Ethics in Practice
An Anthology

Edited by Hugh LaFollette
East Tennessee State University

BLACKWELL
Publishers

Chapter 22 copyright © Burton M. Leiser 1997, chapter 30 copyright © Robert E. Goodin 1997, chapter 34 copyright © John Arthur 1997, chapter 44 copyright © James Rachels 1997, chapter 46 copyright © Jeffrie G. Murphy 1997, chapter 53 copyright © Robert E. Goodin 1997, chapter 59 copyright © James P. Sterba 1997

First published 1997
2 4 6 8 10 9 7 5 3 1

Blackwell Publishers Inc.
238 Main Street
Cambridge, Massachusetts 02142
USA

Blackwell Publishers Ltd
108 Cowley Road
Oxford OX4 1JF
UK

Library of Congress Cataloging-in-Publication Data

Ethics in practice: an anthology/edited by Hugh LaFollette.
    p.   cm. — (Blackwell philosophy anthologies; 3)
    Includes bibliographical references and index.
    ISBN 1–55786–639–2 (hardcover: alk. paper). — ISBN 1–55786–640–6
(pbk.: alk. paper)
    1. Applied ethics.   2. Ethical problems.   I. LaFollette, Hugh, 1948– . II. Series.
BJ1031. E854   1997
170 — dc20   96–16025
                                                              CIP

British Library Cataloguing in Publication Data

A CIP catalogue record for this book is available from the British Library.

Commissioning Editor: Steve Smith
Desk Editor: Tony Grahame
Production Controller: Lisa Eaton

Typeset in 10 on 12 pt Ehrhardt
by Graphicraft Typesetters Ltd., Hong Kong
Printed in Great Britain by T. J. Press, Padstow, Cornwall

This book is printed on acid-free paper

Contents

"N" indicates a new essay, written specifically for this volume
"R" indicates a revised essay, revised specifically for this volume

Contents

Preface for Instructors

This anthology seeks to provide engagingly written, carefully argued philosophical essays, on a wide range of timely issues in practical ethics. When I had trouble finding essays that suited my purposes, I commissioned new essays – thirteen in all. I also invited a dozen philosophers to revise their "classic" essays. The result is a tasty blend of the old and the new, the familiar and the unfamiliar. I have organized the book into four large thematic parts and fourteen particular topics (sections) to give you the greatest flexibility to construct the course you want. When feasible, I begin or end sections with an essay that serves as a bridge to the preceding or following section. Finally, I have designed section introductions to give the volume a coherence too often lacking in introductory readers.

Although I have included essays that I think introductory students can read and comprehend, no one would believe me if I claimed all the essays are easy to read. We all know many students have trouble reading philosophical essays. That is not surprising. Many of these essays were written originally for other professional philosophers, not first-year undergraduates. Moreover, even when philosophers write expressly for introductory audiences, their ideas, vocabularies, and styles are often foreign to the reader. So I have included a brief introduction on READING PHILOSOPHY to advise students on how to read and understand philosophical essays.

I want this volume to be suitable for a variety of courses. The most straightforward way to use the text is to assign essays on six or seven of your favorite practical issues. If you want a more topical course, you could emphasize issues in one or more of the major thematic sections. You could also focus on one or more of the practical and theoretical issues that span the individual topics and major divisions of the book. If, for instance, you want to focus on gender, you could select most essays from five sections: ABORTION; FAMILY AND FRIENDS; SEXUALITY; SEXUAL AND RACIAL DISCRIMINATION, and AFFIRMATIVE ACTION, and combine these with some specific articles scattered throughout, e.g., Young's "Displacing the Distributive Paradigm" in the section on ECONOMIC JUSTICE. Finally, you can also give your course a decided theoretical flavor, by using essays that address, in diverse contexts, significant theoretical issues like the act/omission distinction, the determination of moral status, or the limits of morality, etc. At the end of this preface, I include a list of some of those theoretical issues, along with the number of some essays you could use to highlight them (see p. x).

Perhaps the most distinctive features of this anthology are the section introductions. Some anthologies do not include section introductions. Those that do, often use introductions simply to summarize the articles in that section. I have endeavored to do more: to craft introductions that will be more useful to students and faculty. The introductions outline the main thrust of the essays. That, however, is not their primary purpose.

Their purpose is (1) to focus students' attention on the theoretical issues at stake, and (2) to relate those issues to the discussion of the same or related issues in other sections. All too often students (and philosophers) see practical ethics as a hodgepodge of largely (or wholly) unrelated problems. The introductions should go some way toward remedying this tendency. They show students that practical questions are not discrete, but intricately connected with one another. Thinking carefully about any problem invariably illuminates (and is illuminated by) others. Thus, the overarching aim of these introductions is to give the book a coherence that many anthologies lack.

There are consequences of this strategy you might mention to your students. I organized the order of the papers within each section to maximize the students' understanding of that practical issue – nothing more. However, I wrote the introductions and organized the summaries to maximize the understanding of theoretical issues. Often the order of the discussion of essays in the introduction matches the order of essays in that section; occasionally, though, it does not. Moreover, I spend more time "summarizing" some essays than others. That in no way suggests I think these essays are more cogent or useful than the others. Rather, I found it easier to use these essays as *entrées* into the theoretical realm.

Finally, since I do not know which sections you will use, you should be aware that the introductions will be likely to refer to essays the student will not (have) read. When that happens, they will not realize part of the aim of the introductions. Part, but not all. For even if the student does not read the essays to which an introduction refers, she should still better appreciate the interconnections between issues. It might even have the delicious consequence of encouraging a student to read an essay that you did not assign.

One last note about the criteria for selecting essays. Many practical ethics anthologies include essays on opposing sides of every issue. For most topics I think that is a laudable aim that an editor can normally achieve. But not always. I include essays that discuss the issue as we currently frame and understand it. Sometimes that understanding precludes some positions that might have once been part of the debate. For instance, early practical ethics anthologies included essays that argued that an individual should always choose to prolong her life, by any medical means whatever. On this view, euthanasia of any sort and for any reason was immoral. Although that was once a viable position, virtually no one now advocates or even discusses it. The current euthanasia debate concerns *when* people might choose not to sustain their lives, and *how* they might carry out their wishes. Those are the questions addressed by these essays on euthanasia.

Likewise, I do not have any essays that argue that women and blacks ought to be relegated to the bedroom or to manual labor. Although everyone acknowledges that racism and sexism are still alive and well in the United States, few people openly advocate making blacks and women second-class citizens. No one seriously discusses these proposals in academic circles. Instead, I include essays that highlight current issues concerning the treatment of minorities and women (sexual harassment, date rape, etc.).

Some theoretical issues, and the numbers of the essays where they are discussed:

act/omission distinction – 2, 3, 5, 17, 40, 54, 55
autonomy – 1, 2, 3, 4, 5, 23, 27, 28, 29, 30
consequentialism – 3, 11, 54
deontology – 5, 7, 12, 16
equality – 6, 7, 9, 10, 11, 12, 15, 17, 33, 34, 35, 36, 37, 38, 39, 40, 41, 42, 43, 47, 48, 49, 50, 52, 53, 54, 55
freedom – 1, 2, 3, 4, 5, 27, 28, 29, 30, 31, 32, 33, 34, 35, 37, 47, 50, 52, 53, 55
groups, moral significance of – 10, 11, 12, 33, 34, 35, 36, 37, 38, 39, 40, 41, 42, 43, 60
institutions, moral significance of – 2, 3, 8, 13, 15, 18, 23, 25, 26, 27, 33, 35, 36, 37, 38, 39, 40, 43, 46, 56, 60
limits of morality – 5, 14, 16, 17, 24, 25, 26, 27, 29, 54, 55, 61
moral status – 5, 6, 7, 8, 9, 10, 11, 12, 13, 15, 36, 44, 46, 49, 56, 57, 58, 59, 60, 51, 62

Acknowledgments

The author and publishers wish to thank the following for permission to use copyright material:

J. Baird Callicott and Environmental Ethics for "Animal Liberation: A Triangular Affair," *Environmental Ethics*, 2, 4 (Winter 1980); and J. Baird Callicott for "Preface" to "A Triangular Affair" (1994).

Basic Books, a division of HarperCollins Publishers Inc., for Robert Nozick, "The Entitlement Theory of Justice" from *Anarchy, State and Utopia*. Copyright © 1974 by Basic Books Inc.

Blackwell Publishers for Tom Regan, "The Case for Animal Rights" from *In Defense of Animals*, ed. Peter Singer; and John Haldane and Anthony Harvey, "The Philosophy of State Compensation," *Journal of Applied Philosophy*, forthcoming. Copyright © Society for Applied Philosophy.

Commentary for James Q. Wilson, "Against the Legalization of Drugs," *Commentary*, February 1990.

Cornell University Press for material from James D. Wallace, *Virtues and Vices*, pp. 131–9. Copyright © 1978 by Cornell University.

R. G. Frey for "Moral Standing, the Value of Lives, and Speciesism," *Between the Species*, 4 (1988) pp. 191–201.

Robert E. Goodin for "Free Movement: If People were Money", from *Free Movement: Ethical Issues in the Transnational Migration of People and Money*, pp. 6–21, edited by Robert E. Goodin and Brian Barry. Copyright © Harvester Wheatsheaf. Revised especially for this volume.

Robert E. Goodin for "Permissible Paternalism: Saving Smokers from Themselves." Revised especially for this volume. Based on the article "Permissible Paternalism: In Defense of the Nanny State," in *The Responsible Community*, 1 (Summer, 1991), pp. 42–51.

Harvard University Press for material from John Rawls, *A Theory of Justice*, pp. 11–22, 60–5, 150–6. Copyright © 1971 by The President and Fellows of Harvard College; and Ronald Dworkin, "Do We Have a Right to Pornography?" from *A Matter of Principle*. Copyright © 1985 by the President and Fellows of Harvard College.

Lester H. Hunt and Reason Papers for "On Improving People by Political Means," *Reason Papers*, pp. 61–76 (1985).

Journal of Social Philosophy for Ann Cudd, "Oppression By Choice," *Journal of Social Philosophy*, 25, Special Anniversary Issue (1988) pp. 22–44; and Anita Superson, "Feminist Definition of Sexual Harassment," *Journal of Social Philosophy*, 24, 3 (Winter 1993) pp. 46–64.

Kluwer Academic Publishers B.V. for Lois Pineau, "Date Rape," *Law and Philosophy*, 8 (1989), pp. 217–43.

Rae Langton for "Pornography, Speech Acts, and Silence". This paper is an abridged version of "Speech Acts and Unspeakable Acts," which appeared first in *Philosophy and Public Affairs*, 22, pp. 293–330 (1993). Reprinted by permission of Princeton University Press. Italicization of quotations is the editor's.

Macmillan and Vincent C. Punzo for material from *Reflective Naturalism*. Copyright © 1969 by Macmillan.

Larry May and Robert Strikwerda and Hypatia for "Men in Groups: Collective Responsibility for Rape," *Hypatia*, vol. 9, n. 2 (Spring, 1994), pp. 134–51. Revised especially for this volume.

The Monist for Michael Levin, "Why Homosexuality is Abnormal," *The Monist*, 67, 2 (1984). Copyright © 1984 The Monist; and Thomas E. Hill, Jr., "Servility and Self-Respect," *The Monist*, 57, 1 (1974). Copyright © 1974 The Monist.

Jeffrie G. Murphy for "Repentence and Criminal Punishment". Reprinted with permission of the author. Revised especially for this volume. This essay originally appeared without footnotes in *The Responsible Community*, pp. 15–23 (Fall, 1995) with the title "Crime and Punishment: Where does Repentance Fit?"

The New York Review of Books for Ronald Dworkin, "The Rights of Allan Bakke," *New York Review of Books*, 10 November 1977. Copyright © 1977 Nyrev, Inc.

W.W. Norton and Company, for Barbara Katz Rothman, *Recreating Motherhood*, pp. 106–24. Copyright © 1988, W.W. Norton and Company.

Oxford University Press Inc. for material from Aldo Leopold, "Thinking Like a Mountain" from *A Sand County Almanac, with other essays on conservation from Round River*, pp. 129–33. Copyright © 1949, 1953, 1966, renewed 1977, 1981 by Oxford University Press, Inc.

Oxford University Press for material from Jane English, *Having Children*, pp. 351–6. Copyright © 1979 by Oxford University Press.

Prentice-Hall Inc. for John Arthur, "Rights and the Duty to Bring Aid" from *World Hunger and Moral Obligation*, ed. Aiken and LaFollette (1977) pp. 37–48.

Princeton University Press for material from Alan H. Goldman, "Plain Sex," *Philosophy and Public Affairs*, 6 (1977) pp. 158–67. Copyright © 1977 by Princeton University Press;

Judith Jarvis Thomson, "A Defense of Abortion," *Philosophy and Public Affairs*, 1 (1971) pp. 47–62, 65–6. Copyright © 1971 by Princeton University Press; Peter Singer, "Famine, Affluence, and Morality," *Philosophy and Public Affairs*, 1 (1972). Copyright © 1972 by Princeton University Press; and Iris Young, *Justice and the Politics of Difference* (1990), pp. 15–16, 18–30, 33–4, 37–8. Copyright © 1990 by Princeton University Press.

Public Affairs Quarterly for Ann E. Cudd, "Taking Drugs Seriously: Liberal Paternalism and the Rationality of Preferences," *Public Affairs Quarterly*, 4, 1, revised.

Routledge for revised material from Sandra Bartky, *Feminity and Domination*. Copyright © 1980 by Routledge. Revised especially for this volume.

Rowman and Littlefield Publishers for Pamela Foa, "What's Wrong with Rape?" from *Feminism and Philosophy*, ed. M. Vetterling-Braggin, F. Ellinston and Jane English (1977).

Rowman and Littlefield for revised material from Marilyn Friedman, *Political Correctness: For and Against*, pp. 1–6, 21–2, 26–30, 126–8. Copyright © 1995 Rowman and Littlefield. Revised especially for this volume.

Peter Singer for "All Animals Are Equal," *Philosophical Exchange*, 1 (Summer 1974).

Temple University Press for James Rachels, "Parents and Children" from *Person to Person*, ed. George Graham and Hugh Follette (1989), pp. 46–52. Copyright © 1989 Temple University.

Transaction Publishers for material from Michael Levin, "The Free Market and Feminism" from *Feminism and Freedom* (1987), pp. 369–80.

University of California Press for material from Michael Allen Fox, "The Moral Community" from *Case for Animal Experimentation: An Evolutionary and Ethical Perspective* (1986), pp. 49–63. Copyright © 1986 The Regents of the University of California; and Bernard Williams, "Persons, Character and Morality" from Amelie Rorty, *Identities of Persons* (1976), pp. 201, 211–15. Copyright © 1976 The Regents of the University of California.

University of Minnesota Press for Kwame Anthony Appiah, "Racisms" from *Anatomy of Racism*, ed. David Theo Goldberg (1990), pp. 3–17.

University of Wisconsin–Madison Archives and Nina Leopold Bradley for material from Aldo Leopold, "Some Fundamentals of Conservation in the Southwest."

Karen J. Warren and Environmental Ethics for "The Power and the Promise of Ecological Feminism," *Environmental Ethics*, 12, 2 (1990).

Mary Anne Warren and The Monist for "A Defense of Abortion," *The Monist*, 56, 1 (1973). Revised especially for this volume.

Every effort has been made to trace all the copyright holders but if any have been inadvertently overlooked the publishers will be pleased to make the necessary arrangement at the first opportunity.

General Introduction

All of us make choices. Some of our choices seem to concern only ourselves: what to wear, when to sleep, what to read, where to live, how to decorate our homes, and what to eat. Normally we do not think that choices that are purely personal – choices that affect only ourselves – are moral choices. Therefore, they will not be discussed in this book. Other choices demonstrably affect others: whether to prolong the life of our comatose grand-mother, when and with whom to have sex, and how to relate to people of different races. Choices that clearly affect others are moral choices, choices we should assess on moral grounds.

Upon close examination, however, we see that it is not so obvious which choices affect only us. If we choose to read or view pornography, are we supporting the degradation of women? When we choose to eat meat, are we supporting the inhumane treatment of animals or the depletion of resources that we could use to feed the starving? When we choose where to live, are we supporting practices that confine people of different races to inadequate housing? If so, then some choices that *seem* purely personal turn out to affect others in morally significant ways.

Thus, once we reflect carefully on our choices, we discover that many of them profoundly affect others, and therefore, that we ought to evaluate them morally. If I choose to buy a new stereo rather than send money for famine relief, children in India may starve. By choosing to support political candidates who oppose or support abortion, the death penalty, tough drug laws, affirmative action, or lax environmental protection, I have affected others in demonstrably significant ways. Of course knowing that our choices affect others does not prescribe how we should behave. It does, however, confirm that we should evaluate these choices, not least in part, by moral criteria.

Although many of our choices have undeniable moral dimensions, we are individually and collectively nearsighted. Many of us fail to see or appreciate the moral significance of our choices, thereby increasing the evil in the world. Often we talk as if evil resulted solely from the conscious choices of wholly evil people. My sense, though, is that evil more often results from ignorance and inattention: we just don't notice or attend to the significance of what we do. A central aim of this book is to provide glasses that refine our moral vision: to help us notice and comprehend the moral significance of what we do.

The primary means of achieving this end is to present essays that carefully and critically discuss a range of practical moral issues. These essays will supply information you do not have, and perspectives you probably have not considered. Many of you may find that your education has ill-prepared you to think carefully about these issues. Far too many public schools in the United States neither expect nor even permit students to think critically. Many of them will not have expected – or even wanted – you to develop and defend your own views. Instead, they may have demanded that you memorize the content of your texts and the assertions of your teachers.

In contrast, most philosophy professors do not want you to memorize what they say or someone else says. Still less will they want you to parrot them or the texts. They will require you to read what others have said, but not because they want you to recite it. Instead, they think that by critically reading the arguments of others, you will be better able to reach your own conclusions, based on the available evidence and the best arguments. Unfortunately, you may find that your high school education, with its premium on memorization and blind adherence to authority, will not have trained you to read philosophical essays. That is why I have included a brief section on READING PHILOSOPHY to help you comprehend the articles.

Finally, I include a brief introductory essay on ethical theorizing. Philosophers do not discuss practical issues in a vacuum. They strive to place their discussions in a larger context that clarifies and defines the particular issue. Thus, they discuss not only the details peculiar to the issue, but also more abstract, general features that are relevant to many practical moral quandaries. This introductory essay will explain the purpose of THEORIZING ABOUT ETHICS: the benefits of placing a practical question in a larger framework. The essay will also *briefly* describe some prominent ethical theories which you will encounter in these pages. (Some authors will provide more detailed explanations of these theories.)

To augment your understanding of theory, in the introductions to each section I will not only summarize the central themes of the essays in that section, but spotlight the general theoretical questions, and point out how these are relevant to a variety of other issues discussed in this volume. I want you to appreciate the myriad ways in which practical moral issues are woven together by common theoretical threads. Practical ethics is not a random collection of unconnected issues, but a systematic exploration of how we can most responsibly act in a variety of practical moral contexts.

Consequently, this is not a recipe book that answers all moral questions. Nor is it a primer of ethical theories. Rather, it is a chronicle of how a number of philosophers have thought about these significant practical moral issues. If you absorb the information the authors supply, attend to their arguments, and consider the diverse perspectives they offer, you will find, when the course is over, that you are better able to think carefully and critically about practical and theoretical moral issues.

Theorizing about Ethics

When deciding how to act, we are often faced with conflicting inclinations, desires, or interests. Sometimes conflicts arise when we are simply concerned about our self-interest. I may crave a scrumptious dessert, yet aspire to lose weight. I may need to write a paper, yet want to read the latest thriller. I may wish to watch the new blockbuster movie, yet pine for a hike in the mountains. Although such conflicts appear to concern only me, I may still not know how I should act. I may not know which action best promotes my self-interest. Or I may know precisely what is in my best long-term interest (e.g., losing weight), yet pursue my short-term interest (inhaling that delicious pie) instead. Despite these complications, what seems evident is that in these cases I can legitimately decide how to act based solely on what I take to be in my self-interest. After all, the action concerns only me.

However, many of our actions also concern others. Some actions may benefit others; some may harm them. I may benefit or harm another directly or indirectly, intentionally or unintentionally. I might push Joe because I am mad at him, or I might push him out of the way to take his place in line. In both cases I harm Joe directly, although I intended to harm him only in the first. In other situations, my actions may indirectly lead to harm. If I land the job for which Joe and I competed, then my action may damage his interests, although the damage is an indirect consequence of my getting that job. Also Joe might be offended by knowing that I engage in kinky sex. If so, my bedroom antics affect him, although only indirectly. Arguably it is inappropriate to say in these last two cases that I harmed Joe. Nonetheless, in all these situations, I choose to act knowing that my actions have consequences not only for me, but also for others. Knowing that, I am faced with a conflict between pursuing my self-interest and pursuing (or at least not harming) the interests of others. Occasionally I can find ways to promote everyone's interests. Occasionally, but not always. When my actions will harm others, then I should evaluate them using criteria of morality.

Morality, traditionally understood, involves primarily, and perhaps exclusively, behavior that affects others. I say perhaps, because people disagree about the scope of morality. For instance, I wish all of us would develop our talents, that we would become the best people we could be. However, are we morally obligated to do so? Some people think anyone who squanders her talents has done something morally wrong. For present purposes, though, we can leave this important question aside. For what everyone acknowledges is that actions which indisputably affect others fall within the moral arena.

Of course, we might disagree whether and to what extent actions which affect others only indirectly should be evaluated morally. We might also disagree about how to distinguish direct from indirect harm. Nonetheless, if someone's actions clearly and substantially affect others (either benefiting or harming them), then even if we do not yet know whether the actions are right or wrong, we can agree that they should be evaluated morally.

In fact, some moral "decisions" are easy to make. No one seriously debates whether morally she should drug a classmate so she can have sex with him, whether she should steal money from her co-workers to finance a vacation on the Riviera, or whether she should knowingly infect someone with AIDS. These are not the stuff of which moral disagreement and conflict are made. We must be careful, though, since we might think a decision is easy to make, when, in fact, it is not. Perhaps we even fail to see the moral conflict. For instance, we may not see how our actions affect the interests of others. And, in still other cases, we may understand precisely how our actions have an impact on others, but just don't care – the desire to promote our self-interest is just too strong. Finally, we may be so confident of our views that we do not acknowledge a conflict.

But these cases are the exception, not the rule. Just as we sometimes cannot decide how to best promote our self-interest, at other times we cannot decide whether an action is right or wrong. Moral conflict arises when we find ourselves pulled in different directions and we can find no straightforward way to resolve the conflict. We may be unable to decide which considerations are morally relevant, much less which ones are, in those circumstances, weightiest. The difficulty of resolving the conflict in these latter cases (or acknowledging it in the former ones) is heightened once we appreciate the ways in which our moral thinking is shaped by the outlook of our friends, family, church, and community. If we want to be our own masters – to make our own decisions and not merely ape the decisions of others – then we must find ways to ensure that our self-interest and the moral outlook of others do not control how we think and what we do.

The Need for Theory

By carefully reflecting on our thoughts, actions, and choices, we will see that our views are strongly influenced by others. We may think that an action is grossly immoral, but not really know why. Or we may think we know why, only to discover, upon careful examination, that we are just parroting the "reasons" offered by our friends, teachers, parents, or preachers. Of course there is nothing wrong with considering how others think and how they have decided tough moral questions. We would be fools not to benefit from the collective wisdom of others. Yet anyone who is historically sophisticated must acknowledge that collective wisdom, like individual wisdom, is sometimes mistaken. Our ancestors held slaves, denied women the right to vote, practiced genocide, and burned witches at the stake. They erred largely, I suspect, because they failed to be sufficiently self-critical. They didn't evaluate their own beliefs; they unquestioningly adopted the outlook of their ancestors and political leaders – a "sin" all of us have committed. The emphatic lesson of history is that we must scrutinize our beliefs, our choices, and our actions to ensure that we (a) are sufficiently informed, (b) are not unduly swayed by personal interest, and (c) are not governed by the views of others. Otherwise we may perpetrate evils we could avoid, evils for which future generations will rightly condemn us.

One way to critically evaluate our views is to theorize about ethics: to think about moral issues more abstractly, more coherently, and more consistently. Doing so will empower us to free ourselves from ill-conceived, uninformed, and irrelevant considerations. To explain what I mean, let's think about something dear to you: grades. My grading of student work can go awry in at least three different ways.

(1)   I might grade work inconsistently. That is, I might use different standards for different students: Joan gets an "A" because she has a pleasant smile; Ralph, because he works hard; Rachel, because her paper was exceptional. Of course, knowing that I should use a single grading standard does not tell me what grades the students should have received, or what standards I should have employed. Perhaps on purely academic grounds they all deserved the "A"s they received. However, it is not enough that I accidentally gave them the grades they deserved. I should have given them "A"s because they deserved them.

(2)   I might use improper grading standards. It is not enough that I have an invariant standard. After all, I might have a rotten standard, to which I adhere unwaveringly. For instance, I might consistently give students I like higher grades than students I dislike. If so, I grade the papers inappropriately, even if consistently.

(3)   I might apply the standards inappropriately. I might have appropriate and consistent grading standards, yet misapply them because I am ignorant, close-minded, exhausted, preoccupied, or inattentive.

I can make parallel "mistakes" in ethical deliberations. For instance:

1   I might apply ethical principles inconsistently.
2   I might use inappropriate moral standards.
3   I might apply moral standards inappropriately.

Let us look at each in more detail:

Consistency

We should treat two creatures the same unless they are relevantly different, that is, different in ways that justify treating them differently. Just as students expect teachers to grade consistently, we expect ourselves and others to make moral decisions consistently. The demand for consistency pervades our thinking about ethics. A common strategy for defending our moral views is to claim that they are consistent. A common strategy for criticizing another's views is to charge that they are inconsistent.

The argumentative role of consistency is nowhere more evident than in the abortion debate. Disputants spend considerable effort arguing that their positions are consistent, and that their opponents' positions are inconsistent. Each side labors to show why abortion is (or is not) relevantly similar to standard cases of murder. For example, most of those who think abortion is immoral (and probably all of those who think it should be illegal) claim abortion is relevantly similar to murder, while those who think abortion should be legal, claim it differs relevantly from murder. What we do not find are people who think abortion is murder – and wholly moral.

Consistency likewise plays a central role in debates over free speech and freedom of action. For instance, those opposed to censorship often argue that books, pictures, movies, plays, or sculptures which officials want to censor are relevantly similar to other art that most of us would not want censored. More specifically, those opposed to censoring pornography claim that pornography is a form of speech, and that if it can be prohibited because the majority finds it offensive, then consistency demands that we censor any speech – including political speech – that offends the majority. Conversely, those who claim we can legitimately censor pornography go to some pains to explain why pornography is relevantly different from other forms of speech we want to protect. Both sides want to show that their position is consistent and that their opponent's position is inconsistent.

Although consistency is generally recognized as a requirement of morality, in specific cases it is often difficult to detect if someone is (has been) (in)consistent. Someone may appear to act inconsistently, but only because we do not appreciate the complexity of her moral reasoning or because we fail to understand the relevant details of the situation. As we shall see shortly, determining what is and is not morally relevant is at the center of many moral debates. Nonetheless, what everyone would acknowledge is that *if* someone is being inconsistent, then that is a compelling reason to reject their position unless they can find some way to remove the inconsistency.

Correct principles

Consistency is not the only issue. We must also employ the appropriate guidelines, principles, or standards. Theorizing about ethics is one good way to discern the best (most defensible) standards or guidelines, to identify the morally relevant features of our actions. Later I discuss how we select these principles, how we determine what is morally relevant.

Correct "application"

Even when we "know" what is morally relevant, and even when we act consistently, we still make moral mistakes. Consider the ways I might misapply the "rules" that prohibit lying and harming another's feelings. Suppose my wife comes home wearing a gaudy sweater. She wants to know if I like it. What should I do? There are any number of ways in which I could act inappropriately. (1) *I may not see the alternatives*: I may assume, for example, that I must baldly lie or else substantially hurt her feelings. (2) *I may be insufficiently attentive to her needs and interests*: I may over- or under-estimate how much she will be hurt by my honesty (or lack of it). (3) *I may be unduly influenced by self-interest or personal bias*: I may lie not to protect her feelings, but because I don't want her to be angry with me. (4) *I may know precisely what I should do, but be insufficiently motivated to do it*: I may lie because I just don't want the hassle. (5) Or, *I may be motivated to act as I should, but lack the talent or skill to do it*: I may want to be honest, but lack the verbal and personal skills to be honest in a way that won't harm her.

These are all failings with practical significance. I would like to have the appropriate psychological tools to avoid these moral errors and to promote moral successes. Ultimately we should learn how to make ourselves more attentive, more informed, and better motivated. Although these are vitally important practical concerns, they are not the focus of these essays. What these authors do provide is relevant information, careful logical analysis, and a clear account of what they take to be the morally relevant features of practical ethical questions.

Is it just a matter of opinion?

Many of you may find talk of moral standards troubling. Thus, you will also find talk of the application of those standards equally troubling. You may think – certainly many people talk as if they think – that moral judgements are just a "matter of opinion." All of us have overheard people conclude a debate over a contentious moral issue (e.g., capital punishment) when one disputant says: "Well, it is all just a matter of opinion anyway!" What this claim signals is that the speaker wants to terminate the debate. Unfortunately this claim seems to imply more. It suggests that since moral judgements are just opinions, all opinions are equally good (or equally bad). It implies that we cannot criticize or rationally scrutinize our (or anyone else's) moral judgements. After all, if moral claims could be rationally evaluated, then why summarily suspend the debate?

For present purposes we need not decide exactly which judgements are best, or even how to evaluate moral judgements. I need only emphasize two significant practical points. First, even if no moral decisions are absolutely right, concluding that all moral opinions are equally reliable would be illogical. They are not. If a particular moral judgement is founded on misinformation, short-sightedness, lack of perception, or wholly bizarre moral principles, then we have reason to reject it. Such a judgement is demonstrably inferior to those based on full information, careful calculation, astute perception, and moral principles that have withstood the critical scrutiny of others.

Consider the following analogy: no grammatical or stylistic rules will determine precisely what my next sentence should be. However, from that we should not conclude that just any sentence will do. Some sentences would be complete gibberish; others would be comprehensible, but gaudy; still others might be reasonably precise, but bereft of style; while several (although perhaps not one I would pen) might be brilliant. In short, there may be a number of perfectly satisfactory sentences. No grammar book tells us specifically which ones are best. However, we do not need a divine grammatical rulebook to distinguish the trashy or the vague from the linguistically sublime.

Secondly, even if there is no uniquely appropriate moral judgement, circumstances often demand that we decide how to act. Can we assume, in practice, that all views are equal? Do we, for instance, standardly toss a coin to decide how to act? No! We (should) strive to make an informed decision. That demands a critical understanding of the relevant issues. In short, we don't have to decide if there is only one moral truth. We only need note that we must sometimes make decisions which profoundly affect others. To this extent we cannot escape making moral choices.

The Role of Theory

Even when people agree that an issue should be evaluated, at least partly, by criteria of morality, they often disagree about how to evaluate it. Or, to use the language of the previous section, people may disagree about what are the best principles; they may also disagree about how the same principles should be applied. Some may think the act is moral; others may think it is immoral. However, normally people do not baldly make moral judgements: they give, or are prepared to give, reasons for their respective conclusions (even if they are not that person's real reasons). Anti-abortionists argue that abortion is unjustified because the fetus has the same right to life as a normal adult, while pro-abortionists argue that abortion should be legal because the woman has the right to decide what happens in and to her body. Supporters of capital punishment argue that executions deter crime, while opponents argue that it is cruel and inhumane. Those who want to censor pornography claim that pornography degrades women, while supporters argue that it is a form of free speech that should be protected by law.

In giving reasons for their judgements, people usually cite some feature(s) of the action that are supposed to explain or undergird that evaluation. This function of reasons is not confined to ethical disagreements. I may justify my claim that "*Apollo 13* is a good movie" by claiming that it has well-defined characters, a gripping plot, and the appropriate dramatic tension. That is, I identify features of the movie that I think justify my evaluation. Notice, though, that the features I cite are not unique to this movie. In giving these reasons I imply that "having well-defined characters" or "having a gripping plot" or "having the appropriate dramatic tension" are important characteristics of good movies. That is not to say these are the only or the most important characteristics. However, it is to say that if a movie has any of these characteristics, then we have a reason to think it is a good movie.

There are three ways you can challenge my evaluation of the movie: you can challenge my criteria, my claim that the movie satisfies those criteria, or the weight I give those criteria. For instance, you could argue that having well-defined characters is not a relevant criterion, that I have given that criterion too much weight, or that *Apollo 13* does not have well-defined characters. In defense, I could explain why I think it is a relevant criterion, why I have given that criterion the appropriate weight, and why I think its characters are well developed. At this point we are discussing both a purely practical question about the evaluation of *Apollo 13*, and more theoretical questions about the appropriate criteria of good movies.

In like manner, when discussing practical ethical issues, we invariably engage in higher-level debates over underlying theoretical questions. We don't just want to know whether capital punishment deters crime. We also want to know just how important deterrence is. Ethical theories are simply formal and more systematic discussions of these theoretical questions. They are philosophers' efforts to identify the relevant moral criteria, to gauge the weight or significance of each criterion, and to provide some sense of how we could determine whether an action satisfies those criteria. At the end of this introduction I will *briefly* outline some more familiar ethical theories.

One warning. In thinking about ethical theories, we might be tempted to assume that people who hold the same theory will make the same practical ethical judgements, and that those who make the same practical ethical judgements will embrace the same theory. Not so. Two people with similar criteria for good movies, may have different reactions to *Apollo 13*, while two people who loved *Apollo 13* may have different criteria for good movies. Likewise, two people with different ethical theories may nonetheless agree that a specific action is morally permitted (or grossly immoral), while two adherents of the same moral theory may differently evaluate the same specific action. Knowing someone's theoretical commitments does not tell us precisely what actions that person thinks are right or wrong. It tells us only how she thinks about moral issues. Put more generally, moral theories do not dictate how we should act in all situations; rather, they offer different criteria of moral relevance. Each theory directs our moral attention to specific features of action. Normally different theories identify different criteria of relevance; they direct our attention to different features of action. Occasionally different theories employ the same criteria, but weigh those criteria differently.

Two Main Types of Theory

There are two broad classes of ethical theory: consequentialist and deontological. These two types have shaped most people's understanding of ethics. The first, consequentialism, states that we should choose the available action with the best overall consequences, while deontology states that we should act in ways circumscribed by moral rules or rights, and that these rules or rights are defined (at least partly) independently of consequences.

There are other theories as well. But these two are the most frequently mentioned in these essays. Let us look at each in turn. By necessity these descriptions will be oversimplified and vague. Vague, because even those who embrace these theories disagree about exactly how they should be interpreted. Oversimplified, because I do not have sufficient space to provide a complete account of each. However, you will find that several authors explicitly discuss one or more features of these theories.

Consequentialism

Consequentialists claim that we are obligated to act in ways that produce the best consequences. It is not difficult to see why this is an appealing theory. First, it relies on the same style of reasoning that we use in making purely prudential decisions. If you are trying to select a major, you will probably consider all the available options, judge the value of each option, and then predict which major would be most likely to lead to the best outcome. Using the best information possible, you would then select a major.

Consequentialism uses the same framework, but injects the interests of others into the "equation." When facing a moral decision, I should consider available alternative actions, trace the likely moral consequences of each of those alternatives, and then select the alternative with the best consequences for all concerned. When stated so vaguely, consequentialism is clearly an appealing moral theory. After all, it seems difficult to deny that achieving the best available outcome would be a good thing. The problem, of course, is in deciding which consequences we should consider and how much weight we should give to each. For, until we know that, we cannot know what we ought to do.

The most widely advocated form of consequentialism is utilitarianism. Utilitarians claim we should choose the option that maximizes "the greatest happiness of the greatest number." Of course we might disagree about exactly what that means and exactly how it is to be achieved. Thus, some utilitarians (act utilitarians) claim that we determine the morality of each action by deciding which action, in the particular circumstances, is more likely to promote the greatest happiness of the greatest number. Rule utilitarians, on the other hand, reject the idea that moral decisions should be decided case-by-case. They claim we should decide not whether a *particular* action is likely to promote the greatest happiness of the greatest number, but whether a particular *type* of action would, if done by most people, promote the greatest happiness of the greatest number.

Thus, some act utilitarian might decide that a lie, in a particular case, is justified because it maximizes the happiness of all those concerned, while the rule utilitarian might claim that since everyone's lying would diminish happiness, it would be best to adopt a rule against lying, even if, in some particular case, lying might appear to better promote the greatest happiness of the greatest number.

Deontological theory

Deontological theories are perhaps best understood in contrast to consequentialist theories. Whereas consequentialists claim we should always strive to promote the best consequences, deontologists claim that our moral obligations – whatever they are – are in some sense or to some degree independent of consequences. Thus, if I have obligations not to kill or steal or lie, those obligations are not justified simply on the ground that following such rules will always produce the best consequences.

That is one reason why deontological theories are so attractive. For instance, most of us would be offended if someone lied to us, even if the lie might produce the greatest happiness for the greatest number. I would certainly be offended if someone killed me, even if my death might produce the greatest happiness for the greatest number (you use my kidneys to save two people's lives, my heart so save someone else's life, etc.).

Instead, according to the deontologist, we can discover that some ways of acting just are right and others just are wrong, period. Of course there is considerable disagreement about how we should act and about how to decide in which ways we should act. Some deontologists claim abstract reason shows us how we should act (Kant), while others (McNaughton) claim intuitions are our guide, while still others talk about discovering principles that are justified in *reflective equilibrium* (Rawls, in the selection on ECONOMIC JUSTICE).

Conclusion

As you read the following essays, you will see how these different ways of thinking about ethics influence our deliberations about particular moral issues. Be alert to these theoretical differences. They will help you to better understand the essays. Also, pay close attention to the section introductions. These highlight the theoretical issues that play a central role within their section.

Further Reading

Hooker, B. (ed.) 1996: *Truth in Ethics*. Oxford: Blackwell.

Kant, I. *Grounding of the Metaphysics of Morals*. Indianapolis: Hackett.

LaFollette, H. 1991: "The Truth in Ethical Relativism." *Journal of Social Philosophy*: 146–54.

McNaughton, D. 1988: *Moral Vision*. Oxford: Blackwell.

Mill, J. 1861/1979: *Utilitarianism*. Indianapolis: Hackett.

Rachels, J. 1983: *The Elements of Moral Philosophy* (2nd edition). New York: McGraw-Hill.

Singer, P. (ed.) 1990: *A Companion to Ethics*. Oxford: Blackwell.

Smith, M. 1995: *The Moral Problem*. Oxford: Blackwell.

Reading Philosophy

Reading philosophy differs from reading science fiction or the daily newspaper. The subjects are different; the purposes are different; the styles are different. The newspaper purports to inform us of significant political, social, cultural, economic, and climatic events. Once we are informed we can presumably make better decisions about our leaders, our finances, and our social lives. Newspapers typically achieve their aims by a pithy style: short, simple sentences presumably designed to give us the facts, just the facts.

Science fiction attempts to transport us imaginatively to distant worlds: alien worlds of larger-than-life heroes and villains. Having taken us on a grand tour of fictional worlds, it redeposits us in our ordinary world populated by ordinary folks. Science fiction arguably has multiple aims: to entertain us, to divert us from the doldrums of our daily lives, or to empower us: having seen the glories or evils of worlds not yet experienced, we will (presumably) be better equipped to live in our undistinguished world. Science fiction achieves these aims through expressive language that evokes our imaginative powers.

Philosophers have neither the simple aims of the newspaper writer nor the airy aims of the science-fiction novelist: they do not aspire (primarily) to inform or to inspire. Moreover, their writing style is likely to be different from any with which you are familiar. Philosophers typically reject the simple style of the journalist and expressive style of the novelist. To make matters more difficult for the student, whereas the reporter and the novelist write for the public, philosophers usually write for each other.

Philosophical Language

Newspapers and (most) science fiction are written for an eighth-grade audience. Philosophers do not normally write for general audiences, but for those with university training. Thus, their vocabularies will be more robust than what you normally find in the local paper or the latest Asimov novel. Be prepared. Keep a dictionary handy to look up words you do not know. You may find "ordinary" words you have never seen. You will also find more familiar words with peculiar philosophical meanings. All academic disciplines have their own jargon: a set of specialized terms with meanings familiar only to other members of that discipline. Therefore, to understand philosophical writing, you will need to understand those words unique to philosophers – and not all philosophers use the same words in the same ways. Do not despair. We can explain most of these words in a clear, non-technical way. After identifying a technical term, try to discern its meaning from the context. It is likely you can. If, after doing your best, you still cannot understand its meaning, ask your instructor.

Moreover, philosophical writing is often more complex than the writings of reporters and novelists. Occasionally it is more complex than it needs to be: the author may not know how to write clearly. Sometimes the essay *seems* more complex because the author wrote it decades or even centuries ago, when the preferred style of writing featured long, intricate sentences. At still other times the writing appears convoluted because the author wrote in a different language and someone translated it into English. Often, though, the writing is complex simply because the ideas expressed are complex. We cannot always render profound thoughts into intellectual bouillon. In short, there is no easy way to cope with philosophical complexity. Sometimes you can break down long sentences into their component parts, e.g., by treating a semicolon as a period. In the end, though, the only sure solution is to read and reread the essay until you understand it.

Perhaps you will find the reading so difficult that you will be tempted to stop reading, to wait for the instructor to explain it. Don't stop. Press on. It is better to glean a general understanding of the essay on your own. Certainly it is more rewarding to figure it out for yourself. Think, for a moment, about what happens when someone "explains" a joke that you could (with time and effort) have understood on your own. It spoils the joke. It is better to "get it" on your own. It you persist, you will discover with time that it becomes easier to read these essays. Learning to read more complex essays requires practice. Nonetheless, the payoff is both immediate and enduring. You will better understand the day's reading assignment. You will also expand your vocabulary and hone your reading skills.

The Centrality of Argument

The writing may seem complex because it contains *arguments*. Philosophers are especially interested in arguments. They forward their own arguments and criticize (evaluate) the arguments of others. "Arguments," in this context, have a particular philosophical sense: Arguments are a connected series of statements with some central claim the writer is trying to defend (the conclusion), supported by evidence (the premise) the author offers for the conclusion. Within these essays, an argument is construed broadly as suggestions, ideas, empirical data, imaginative examples, etc. – anything that we can reasonably construe as reasons supporting one's conclusion.

Why, though, are philosophers so preoccupied with arguments? Here is a brief explanation: Each of us is constantly bombarded with claims. Some of these claims are true, some false. Some of these offer sage wisdom; some, devastating advice. How do we distinguish the true from the false, the wise from the stupid – especially when the topic concerns controversial moral, political, and social issues? How do we know the proper moral response to abortion, world hunger, homosexuality, and affirmative action?

One step toward formulating your own view is by listening to the views of others. The problem, of course, is that people on opposing sides of these debates often claim to know that their view is true, and not all these views can be true. So how do we choose between competing views? Do we just pick the one we like? The one our parents, preachers, teachers, friends, or society advocate? I hope not. Even a cursory study of history should convince even the most skeptical of us that many horrendous evils were committed by those who just *knew* they were right. Most Nazis, slave holders, and commanders of Russian Gulags did not think they were immoral; they thought they were doing the right thing. These perpetrators typically simply accepted their society's views – or the views of others – without subjecting them to rational scrutiny. That we should not do. At least not if we are responsible individuals. After all, people's lives, welfare, and happiness may depend on our decisions, and the decisions of people like us.

What is our option? We can look for claims supported by the best evidence. We should examine the *reasons* offered for alternative beliefs. Doing so will not ensure that we make the best decision, but it will increase the likelihood that we do. It will lessen the possibility that we make highly objectionable decisions – decisions we will later come to regret.

Most people are unaccustomed to scrutinizing arguments. Since most of us were taught to believe what our parents, our priests, our teachers, or even our pals told us, we are disinclined to consider the arguments of others seriously, especially if their views conflict with our own. If we have seen, heard, or even offered arguments ourselves, we have rarely done so with the care and depth that are the staples of good philosophy.

In the best of philosophy, the author attempts to provide rationally compelling arguments. That is, she aims to offer a clear, unambiguous conclusion supported by reasons that even those disinclined to believe her conclusions are likely to find persuasive. That is not to say that philosophers never make bad arguments or say stupid things. Of course they do. However, it *is* to say that the explicit aim of philosophy is a *clear, careful, assessment of the reasons for and against ours and others' views*.

Looking at Others' Views

Typically the philosopher will explain and defend her conclusion in a larger context that includes a discussion of other philosophers' arguments on the same subject. Thus, the philosopher not only provides (ideally) a strong argument for her view, but typically offers responses to arguments that might be forwarded against her view. So you will find, in most of these articles, that the author not only discusses her own view, but also compares and contrasts her view with the views of others. Sometimes the other views are advocated by a specific philosopher whose work is cited in the essay. Often, though, the view discussed is not that of any particular philosopher, but rather the view of some hypothetical representative. You will often find references to what "someone might say" about the issue. This "someone" is no one in particular, but rather a hypothetical spokesperson for either a *type* of position (e.g., conservatism or theism) or an alternative view that the author thinks plausible.

This is often double trouble for a student. You may be unfamiliar with the view being discussed. Perhaps you do not know if the view has been accurately represented, and therefore, do not know if the criticisms are telling. Worse, you may have trouble distinguishing the author's view from the views of those she discusses. Many students do. Sometimes you may be confused simply because you are unaccustomed to reading one author who explicitly discusses another author. Simply knowing that this is a common argumentative strategy should help lessen this problem.

At other times, though, the student may fail to understand the difference between the author's view and the view she is discussing, because the student has not read the essay carefully. Authors usually give argumentative road signs that show when they are arguing for a view, and when they are stating or discussing someone else's view. However, inattentive readers, like inattentive drivers, may miss their respective signs.

The student may miss these signs if she does not know what to look for. An American driving in Britain often has trouble seeing or understanding road signs and signals. Perhaps the American driver is unfamiliar with traffic circles or they expect stop lights to be hanging overhead rather than being mounted on a pole at the side of the street. Students unfamiliar with argumentative road signs may be similarly impeded.

For instance, when discussing another's views authors frequently use the third person to suggest that another person is speaking (or arguing). At other times the author may explicitly say something like "others may disagree . . ." and then go on to discuss someone else's view. In still other cases the distinction may be more subtle, likely to be picked up only after carefully reading the essay several times. In the end there is no single way to distinguish the author's view from other views the author is discussing. However, if you read the essays carefully, using the general strategy just outlined, you will increase the likelihood that you will not be confused.

The Rational Consequences of What we Say

The philosopher's discussion of examples or cases – especially fictional cases – sometimes confuses students. The use of such cases, though, builds upon a central pillar of philosophical argument, namely, that we should consider the implications or rational consequences of our beliefs and actions. The following fictional example explains what I mean. Suppose a teacher gives you an "A" because she likes you, and gives Robert – your worst enemy – an "F" because she dislikes him. You might be ecstatic that you received an "A"; you may also be thrilled to know that your worst enemy failed. However, would you want to say that what the teacher did was morally acceptable? No. There are implications of saying that, implications you would likely be unwilling to accept.

Were you to say that the teacher's *reason* for giving the grades was legitimate, you would be saying, in effect, that teachers should be able to give students they like good grades and students they dislike bad grades. Thus, you would be rationally committed to saying that if you had a teacher that disliked you, then she could legitimately fail you. That, of course, is a consequence you would likely be unwilling to accept. Therefore, you (and we) have reason to suspect that your original acceptance of the teacher's grading scheme was inappropriate. We see here a common argumentative strategy. Trace the implications – the rational consequences – of a person's reasons for action, and then see if they (or others) would be willing to accept the consequences of others' acting for similar reasons.

A Final Word

These suggestions will not make reading philosophical essays easy. Perhaps, though, they will make it easier. In the end, the key to success is practice. If you have never read philosophical arguments before, you are unlikely to be able simply to glance over an essay and understand the nuance of argument. You must read the assignments carefully, and more than once. Most are too difficult in style and content for you to grasp in a single reading. Not even most professional philosophers can do that.

Here is a good strategy: Read the essay once. Identify confusing or unusual terms. Try to get a general sense of the argument: what is the point the author wants to establish, what reason does she offer for this claim? What arguments does she discuss? After you have a general sense of the essay, reread it more carefully. Try to get a thorough sense of the argument. Come to class prepared to ask for help in clarifying the author's views. If you are accustomed to reading an assignment once – and then only quickly – this expectation will seem too demanding. Yet, it is important that you learn to read carefully and critically. Not only will you better understand the reading for this class – and so, do better on exams and papers – you will have acquired a valuable skill.

We accomplish few things of value effortlessly. Most require substantial work. Learning to read critically is no exception. Most of the world's great books are unaccessible to those with minimal reading and argumentative skills. Learning to read methodically, critically, and in depth will expand your mental horizons. It will increase your understanding of others' views. And it will enhance your ability to refine and defend your own views.

Part I

Life and Death

Euthanasia

Should individuals, especially terminally ill people in excruciating pain, be able to end their lives? If so, may they hasten their deaths only by refusing medical treatment designed to sustain their lives, or may they take active measures to kill themselves? If they can take measures to kill themselves, can they ask others to assist them? Who can they ask: their spouses? close friends? their doctors? Should they expect the law to support their decisions?

Many people think that (at least) terminally ill people have the moral authority to decide whether and how to end their lives. We can state the rationale for this view crisply: If people have the freedom to choose how to live, should they not also have the authority to choose how to die? The authors in this section think the answer to that question is a resounding – albeit differently qualified – "Yes." For them, respect for an individual's autonomy requires that everyone have this fundamental control over their lives.

Historically some people, especially some religious leaders, thought it was immoral for anyone to hasten her death, even if her life was, in some important sense, no longer worth living. On this view, taking one's (or another's) life is always wrong, whatever the reason. The authors in this section echo the current public sentiment against this categorical rejection of euthanasia. Most people now acknowledge that it is sometimes acceptable for an individual to act in ways (or to have others act in ways) which hasten her death. Nonetheless, there is still considerable disagreement about when, where, and how a person may hasten her death. Some claim only the terminally ill have the moral authority to end their lives, while others claim that anyone who finds her life no longer worth living may kill herself. Some people claim an individual can hasten her death only by refusing medical treatment that sustains her life, while others claim that an individual can legitimately kill herself. In short, many people disagree about the conditions under which a person may properly seek death, and about what such a person can legitimately do to achieve that end. However, most now agree that we have the autonomy to make fundamental decisions about our lives – and our deaths.

Most people acknowledge that autonomy is an important element of morality, an element that, as much as possible, the law should respect. They disagree profoundly, however, about the scope of autonomy, about the specific role it plays in a proper understanding of morality and the law. For instance, should law always respect our explicit wishes, even when we wish to act in a way that would normally be considered harmful – as killing oneself would most assuredly be? Or should we have autonomy to do only those things that society considers to be in our own best interests? Determining the scope of autonomy is centrally relevant to the debate over euthanasia – you can see its role in each essay in this section. Concern for autonomy, however, goes far beyond this issue. It is also a key to the discussion of DRUGS and paternalism in Section III. Should an individual be able to choose how she wants to live, even if others think those choices are detrimental to her? Suppose the action is demonstrably detrimental. For instance, we have compelling evidence that smoking is dangerous to smokers (forgetting the problem of second-hand smoke). Does that justify the state's forcing someone to give up smoking?

It would be a mistake to assume, though, that autonomy is the only relevant moral consideration. After all, we exercise autonomy, we make our personal choices, within a political, social, and economic environment that influences our choices and shapes their consequences. For instance, an individual may decide that her life is no longer worth living, perhaps because she is suffering from an extremely painful and debilitating disease. However, the disease may be especially painful and debilitating because she cannot afford the best medical care. Under these circumstances, death may be her best option. However, death may be the best option only because of the reigning political and economic structures. In a different economic and political world other options might be preferable.

Our decision to prolong or to end our lives also has dramatic consequences for our families. Suppose I decide to have doctors use every conceivable means to keep me alive. That choice does not affect only me. Family and friends must inevitably bear the emotional trauma of seeing me debilitated and in pain. Likely they must bear substantial financial costs as well. Often they must make considerable sacrifices of time since they would probably be expected – at least in our society – to care for me. In short, my decision to live or die substantially affects the interests of my friends and family. Should they therefore, as Hardwig argues, be centrally involved in making the decision about my death? Or should they, as Hooker argues, be explicitly excluded from making such decisions since they are likely to be biased precisely because their interests are so heavily affected?

It is useful to note that the disagreement between Hooker and Hardwig reflects a deep divide in ethical perspectives between individualists, who hold that personal autonomy is one of, and maybe the highest, moral good, and communitarians, who stress our relationships with others. Put differently, individualists focus on our separateness from (and often our conflicts with) others, while communitarians focus on our relationships with, dependence on, and responsibilities to others. This fundamental difference in moral outlook weaves through most of the issues discussed in this volume. Fesmire's essay in the section on VIRTUES discusses it explicitly.

Beauchamp and Hooker argue (for different reasons) that we must also be concerned about the broader effects of legalizing assisted suicide. What are the likely consequences of legally permitting physician-assisted suicide? Beauchamp is worried that it would damage the doctor–patient relationship; in particular, he fears it would make doctors less committed to saving life and less sensitive to their patients' pain. If this were a consequence of legalizing the practice, it would be a powerful reason to oppose its legalization. Pence, however, argues that such concerns are not empirically warranted.

The injection of the act/omission distinction further complicates the debate about euthanasia. Most people are inclined to think there is a fundamental moral difference between things we do, and things we permit. For instance, they think that killing Robert would be worse than failing to save Robert's life. That distinction undergirds the views of those who support passive euthanasia (the removal of medical measures sustaining a person's life), while opposing active euthanasia (an individual's – or some person acting for the individual – taking active steps to hasten her death). Most people opposed to active euthanasia usually rest their case on the moral significance of the act/omission distinction.

This distinction plays a central role not only in the current discussion, but in the discussion of most moral issues. For example although most people think that killing Indian children would be morally heinous, they think refusing to provide these same children with food and other assistance is not immoral (WORLD HUNGER). This distinction isolates a deep theoretical divide between deontological and consequentialist moral theories. Consequentialists, being more concerned with the outcome or consequences of actions, will not see any strong reason to think acts are fundamentally worse than omissions, at least morally. As Beauchamp argues, sometimes it appears that acts are worse than omissions. However, that is because some other difference explains the difference in moral evaluation. Hooker, for example, notes that if allowing involuntary active euthanasia would prompt some individuals not to seek necessary medical care, then that would be one reason, albeit perhaps not a decisive reason, against allowing involuntary active euthanasia. Thus, the consequentialists claim, acts and omissions are not fundamentally different.

Deontologists, on the other hand, are more likely to think the act/omission distinction is morally significant. Since they think the consequences of our actions are only a measure of the moral story, they are prone to put moral emphasis on what we explicitly do rather than on what we permit.

Further Reading

Beauchamp, T. (ed.) 1996: *Intending Death; The Ethics of Assisted Suicide and Euthanasia.* Englewood Cliffs, NJ: Prentice-Hall.

Pence, G. 1995; *Classic Cases in Medical Ethics,* chapter 1: "Comas: Karen Quinlan and Nancy Cruzan." McGraw-Hill.

Quill, T. 1991: " 'Death and Dignity' A Case of Individualized Decision Making." *New England Journal of Medicine,* 324: 690–4.

Quill, T. and Cassell, C. 1995: "Nonabandonment: A Central Obligation for Physicians." *Annals of Internal Medicine,* 122: 368–74.

Steinbock, B. 1980: *Killing and Letting Die.* Englewood Cliffs, NJ: Prentice-Hall.

Veatch, R. (ed.) 1989: *Medical Ethics.* Boston: Jones and Bartlett.

1

Why Physicians Should Aid the Dying

Gregory Pence

Background

Dying today is usually neither private nor easy to accomplish with dignity and without pain. For the typical person, dying today is a long, slow process of deterioration and dependence on others. It is exactly this dependence on others – on family, on physicians, and on nurses – that makes physician-assisted dying a moral issue.

What makes one issue a "moral issue" and not another? Actions that affect no one else are *personal*. Actions that may harm or help others, raise *moral* issues. Whether or not a physician helps a person die is a moral issue because it affects a very important interest of people: how and when they die.

Generally, physicians and patients see physician-assisted dying in different ways. Surveys of physicians repeatedly show that most *oppose* legalization of physician-assisted dying, while surveys of patients repeatedly show that most *endorse* legalization of physician-assisted dying (see *New York Times*, October 29, 1993, p. A7). This asymmetry creates the tension surrounding this moral issue.

Two Cases: Janet Adkins and "Diane"

In June of 1990, Jack Kevorkian, a retired pathologist, helped Janet Adkins, a 54-year-old Oregonian, kill herself. Janet had had an active life: she loved playing the piano, hiking, and playing tennis. When she developed Alzheimer's disease, the life she loved evaporated before her eyes. When she could no longer read sheet music or remember when she was supposed to play tennis, she decided her brain was being destroyed too quickly.

No treatment cures Alzheimer's and the experimental drug Tacrine did not help. So Mrs Adkins faced a "Catch 22" situation: kill herself while still in control of her declining life, or let her disease progress to the point where she would be incompetent and hence, incapable of deciding to die.

Because assisting in suicide was not illegal at the time in Michigan, Mrs Adkins's decision was honored by Dr Kevorkian. A year or so later, Dr Kevorkian was first successfully prosecuted for assisting in the death of his seventeenth patient, Thomas Hyde, a 30-year-old man in the last stages of Lou Gehrig's disease (amyotrophic lateral sclerosis). Medical experts testified that without Kevorkian's assistance in dying, Tom Hyde would have "strangled to death in his own saliva" (*New York Times*, April 28, 1994, p. A8). For a variety of reasons, including the belief that the law had no right to make terminally-ill patients suffer by forbidding physicians to help them die, the jury acquitted Dr Kevorkian (*New York Times*, May 5, 1994, pp. A1, 11).

In 1990, another physician, Timothy Quill, an internist in Rochester, New York, was asked by his patient "Diane" to help her die. As a young woman, Diane had survived vaginal cancer and overcome alcoholism. In 1990 at age 45, she developed acute myelomonocytic leukemia – one of the very worst kinds. Dr Quill explained to Diane that she had a 25 percent chance of long-term survival after treatment by two courses of chemotherapy and a bone-marrow transplant, but only if a well-matched bone-marrow donor could be found. Even with treatment, Diane had a 75 percent chance of being dead in several months, and because a good donor was not found, her chances of being dead in months with treatment were actually much higher. Moreover, the treatment would begin immediately and cause her last months to be marred with infections, hair loss, and nausea. Although the surgeons and oncologists pressured her into starting treatment "that very day," Diane waited and then decided not to undergo treatment.

After her decision, Dr Quill worried that a new "preoccupation with her fear of lingering death would interfere with her getting the most out of the time she had left." Having made sure that she was not irrationally depressed, he wrote her a prescription for barbiturates and told her how to use them for both sleep and suicide.

During the next three "tumultuous months," Diane's family provided constant support: her son stayed home from college and her husband worked at home. Several times she became weak or developed infections but bounced back. Near the end, she had two weeks of "relative calm," followed by rapid decline. Because she was now faced with what she feared most – "increasing discomfort, dependence, and hard choices" – Quill knew that her end had come:

> When we met, it was clear that she knew what she was doing, that she was sad and frightened to be leaving, but that she would be even more terrified to stay and suffer. In our tearful goodbye, she promised a reunion in the future at her favorite spot on the edge of Lake Geneva, with dragons swimming in the sunset.

Dr Quill published an account of Diane's death in the *New England Journal of Medicine* (1991: 691–4) and, soon thereafter, was prosecuted for murder. After hearing the district attorney's arguments, the grand jury refused to indict Dr Quill – in part because some members didn't agree with the law and believed that Diane both wanted to die and had the right to do so.

Between 1990 and 1995, Dr Kevorkian assisted 22 people to die and made physician-assisted dying a prominent, international moral issue. His cases, however, contrasted in several ways with those of Timothy Quill. Dr Quill knew Diane well and had treated her for a long time; he first offered her a course of treatment that might have allowed her to survive; he helped her to die privately and without publicity; he preserved her anonymity; he presented his account in an established medical forum; and he was not a "specialist" in assisted dying.

The point of comparing Dr Kevorkian and Dr Quill is this: some discussions of physician-assisted dying generalize from the eccentric personality and methods of Dr Kevorkian to the actions of average physicians, but Dr Quill is far closer to the average physician who might occasionally accept physician-assisted dying for his patients. Dr Quill was actually practicing medicine with real patients, whereas Dr Kevorkian, a retired pathologist, was not.

This is not necessarily to criticize Dr Kevorkian: he does not have a typical physician–patient relationship with his patients because they come to him after they feel they have been abandoned by all other physicians. But ideally, if such assistance was legal, dying patients would have a long-standing relationship with a personal physician who knew them well – like Dr Quill and Diane, and like physicians in Holland (see below).

When is Assisting in Death Wrong?

Throughout human history, most people have wanted to live as long as possible. That fact is less true today. Why? The answer is that our view of dying is different now because of the recent successes of medicine. Medicine has now largely cured the old, acute diseases that killed swiftly, and left us with chronic diseases that kill slowly, such as cancer and heart disease. In the past, people tried to live as long as possible because they never experienced the disability and dysfunction that came with chronic diseases, but we have now learned that if people live long enough, the quality of life diminishes. For most people, the quality of life is more important than the quantity of days lived.

Now let us specifically consider the morality of physician-assisted dying. When you help me accomplish what I want to do, you do a good thing, and morality encourages you to help me. When you prevent me from doing what I want to do, you hurt me and my interests, and morality regards you as immoral. Whether or not dying assisted by physicians is good or bad depends, not on what has traditionally been judged right or wrong, but on the dying patient and his desires. Similarly, whether physician-assisted dying is moral or immoral does not depend on whether it promotes or hinders mere life or death, but on whether the dying patient accepts it.

Someone might object that helping me do what I want is not a good thing if I want to do something immoral, and it is said, helping dying people die is immoral. But why should we accept the underlying premise that "Helping dying people die is immoral"? This begs the question, it is not an *argument against* a position to assume that it is wrong.

Faced with one who believes physician-assisted dying to be immoral, what do we do? No country advocates forced death, and that was the horror of what some Nazi physicians did. On the other hand, to forbid physicians from assisting dying patients will force many persons to prolong their pain and suffering unduly. From these patients' perspective, being forced to die in a way they do not like is little different from simply being forced to die. Both violate personal autonomy and destroy perhaps the most important choice a person ever makes.

People may disagree about whether they want to have a physician help them die more quickly. However, history has shown that democratic societies that allow citizens to make their own choices about such personal matters fare better than those that attempt to legislate one moral view on everybody.

Unfortunately, the debate over physician-assisted suicide has been defined so that the status quo (forbidding it) is conceived as one (and perhaps the) reasonable option. In fact, this is an extreme position, with the other extreme being forced death. The reasonable compromise is allowing each person to decide how and when she will die. To this extent the debate over physician-assisted suicide is like the debate over abortion: the real extremes are forced conception and forced abortion. The reasonable compromise is free choice.

Direct Arguments Against Physician-assisted Dying

The most general, direct argument against physician-assisted dying is that it is a kind of killing of innocent humans, conjoined with the claim that it is wrong to kill humans. Any time one human being consciously acts to end the life of another, a terrible evil is committed. Such an action goes, it is said, against the will of God.

This argument is not very good. First, and as argued previously, what is wrong is not "killing humans" but "killing humans who do not want to die." Secondly, it is not clear that God forbids aid-in-dying. After all, God presumably created a world with disease, God willed for each of us to die a mortal death, and God could save us if he chose to do so. Indeed, it is not even clear that God forbids suicide, since God allowed King Saul to fall on his sword, and allowed his own Son, Jesus, to go to Jerusalem when Jesus knew that there he would be crucified.

More important, no one thinks that dying patients commit suicide by not doing everything possible to stay alive – at least, no reasonable person, because dying patients are (and not to put too fine a point on it) *dying*. Moreover, is it reasonable to equate a physician helping a terminally-ill patient die with "killing" a patient? No. Again, to argue that "assisting the dying" is morally equivalent to "killing" is misleading because "killing" refers to taking the life of a person *who does not want to die*.

Let us end with another analogy. Suppose that a surgeon fixes a woman's deviated septum while she is under anesthesia for an operation on her knee, and without asking her permission. When she objects afterwards, he cannot claim that he has done nothing wrong because he has "healed" her nose. (Unknown to the surgeon, she was a promising singer and the operation permanently ruined the sound of her singing. He did not "heal" her; he ruined her.) So whether a particular operation is "healing" or "impairing," whether a particular act of assisted dying is "murder" or "compassion," depends on the desires and decisions of the patient in a particular circumstance.

Direct Arguments For Physician-assisted Dying

The argument from control of one's own life

Perhaps the strongest and simplest direct argument favoring physician-assisted dying is the Argument from Control of One's Own Life. This argument paradigmatically concerns a competent adult afflicted with a terminal illness. A fundamental principle in both moral and political life in civilized countries is that competent adults possess the right to make personal decisions. As John Stuart Mill argued famously in *On Liberty*, "The only part of the conduct of any one, for which [a citizen] is amenable to society, is that which concerns others. In the part which merely concerns himself, his independence is, of right, absolute. Over himself, over his own body and mind, the individual is sovereign."

A good law honors the ultimate choices that patients make because, at bottom, that is the point of living in a good society with democracy, the rule of law, and civilized attitudes. The State has no business telling people whether to make such choices, and consequently, telling a physician whether he can help a patient die more easily. Similarly, the government should not be able to prevent me from hiring a physician to help me die as I want.

Unfortunately, it is not so easy to kill oneself. The older one gets, the more difficult this becomes. Many elderly people become *gradually* infirm and weak, especially in their late 80s. When such people get a terminal illness, such as cancer or coronary artery disease, deterioration accelerates, but there rarely is a sudden death. A patient in the final stages of coronary artery disease may be so sick that, bedridden, he cannot even lift up his hand to wave. These patients and their families face more and more difficult tradeoffs as the disease progresses. They lose their physical health, their memory and their friends. So people at the end need a physician's help.

One tradeoff is between living as long as possible with an acceptable quality of life (but possibly losing control of one's own dying), and dying early (but exactly as one wants). The case of Janet Adkins shows this problem: because physicians now do not actively assist patients in dying, terminal patients sometimes die early to control their own fate.

Consider how different dying would be if physicians were to do what patients wanted. A patient could find a physician who would – at some indefinite point in the future – honor his or her request to die before pain became intolerable. Having made that "contract," the patient could then live as long as possible before intolerable pain began. When, and if, that point came (and an advantage of this approach is that sometimes it would not), the physician would do as the patient wanted. Under this vision of the future, patients would no longer need to guess about when pain "might" become impossible and then die before that happened.

So a related, direct argument for physician-assisted dying here is this: by legalizing it, medicine maximizes life for all those patients who now are forced to die early. Legalizing physician-assisted dying is life-enhancing for those not afraid to take control of their own dying.

The argument from mercy

Sometimes, medication cannot adequately control the pain associated with a disease. When this occurs with a family dog or cat, the veterinarian and owners mercifully do not make the animal suffer. When this occurs with a human, mercy is sometimes absent.

Some physicians deny that anyone need ever die in pain. But such claims must be carefully examined. Yes, it is possible to get someone out of pain if one totally sedates a patient, but most patients want to be conscious during their final weeks. But can dying patients stay conscious and be pain-free?

This is a question widely debated and with great disagreement over the answers. Some physicians deny that dying patients ever need be in intense pain and hence, ever need the "mercy" of physician-assisted death (Teno and Lynn, 1991: 827–30). Yet even they admit that most physicians are not adequately trained in pain relief, a point that champions of physician-assisted dying have been making for years. So most dying patients still have a physician who is not the best at pain control. Because that is so, some patients still die a horrible death in terrible pain. Is this a fact that a civilized society should tolerate? No, and so, some physicians should be legally allowed to heed the request of such patients for a speedier, painless death.

Critics of physician-assisted dying often say at this point, "We need better care of the dying, not physician-assisted dying. To legalize physician-assisted dying is to accept the failure of the present system to care well for the dying." Well, yes, this is not a perfect world, but what does that imply? What about the two million Americans who die each year? *They can't wait* for the system to improve. When the system gets perfect at some grand time in the future, we can reassess physician-assisted dying, but for the foreseeable future . . .

Moreover, it is not clear that the system will ever get very good for dying patients. Many physicians are not that comfortable with the process of dying. To them, it feels like failure on their part. Others don't like to empathize with the dying because it reminds them of their own death. As long as these statements are true, we need the legal option for some physicians to help patients who aren't getting adequate, compassionate care from their assigned physicians. Although it may seem odd, perhaps the idea of physicians who specialize in dying isn't such a bad idea after all.

The Argument from Empirical Precedent

Sometimes people argue moral issues in medicine and wish that there was some "ethics laboratory" where such issues could be tested empirically. Remarkably, there is. Holland is just such an "ethics lab," because Dutch citizens have almost totally legalized physician-assisted dying for over 25 years. In Holland, there are about a thousand assisted deaths each year (van Delden et al., 1993: 6) with this change.

What English-speaking people want is what Dutch patients have had for decades: a physician they have known for many years who makes house calls, not some impersonal specialist in a hospital who is a stranger. What people also want is what dying Dutch patients also have had for 25 years: a physician they trust to carry out their real wishes at the end.

Should we follow the Dutch example and legalize physician-assisted dying? Arguments against such legalization are generally "slippery slope" predictions: if we legalize one kind of dying, others will soon follow; if physicians are desensitized to killing one kind of patient, they will eventually kill others. At the most extreme, opponents claim that legalizing physician-assisted death will start us down a slippery slope to the kind of state-mandated killing of "undesirables" practiced in Nazi Germany.

I discuss examples of such arguments below, but for now, notice one thing: the predicted "descent" down the slope did not occur in Holland (some bad things may have occurred, but they don't qualify as a "descent" – see below). Put differently, terrible things were predicted to occur in Holland on a massive scale with legalization of physician-assisted dying. These terrible things have not occurred after a quarter-century of Dutch medical practice. So physician-assisted dying does not always lead down a slippery slope.

Indirect Arguments Against Physician-assisted Dying

The slippery slope

Most arguments against physician-assisted dying are indirect ones, such as the slippery slope. The phrase "slippery slope" actually covers many more ideas than is customarily noted in the literature and the use of this argument in practice is often quite sloppy. I discuss some variations below.

Slippery slope #1: Generalization to other kinds of cases
With legalization, the social practice of killing will snowball: once physicians become accustomed to killing competent, terminal patients, they will accept killing semi-competent and incompetent patients. In a famous article, Leo Alexander, a physician who witnessed the Nuremberg trials of Nazi physicians, wrote, "The destructive principle, once unleashed, is bound to engulf the whole personality and to occupy all its relationships. Destructive urges and destructive concepts arising there cannot remain limited or focused upon one subject or several subjects alone, but must inevitably spread and be directed against one's entire surrounding world . . ." (Alexander, 1949: 47).

A Right to Life spokesperson says in this context that if you "accept quality of life as the standard" then, "First you withdraw the respirators, then the food, and then you actively kill people. It's a straight line from one place to the others" (Bopp, as quoted in Specter, 1990). Vienna was shocked to discover in 1989 that a nursing aide had killed at least 49 elderly patients in an Austrian nursing home by lethal injection or by forcing water into their lungs (Protzman, 1989).

The answer to this "slope" argument is that not all change is unstoppable; not all change generalizes to everything. In essence, this slope claim argues that competent patients with terminal diseases are the easy, safe cases, but legalization of physician-assisted dying will inevitably spread to hard, murky, dangerous cases involving formerly-competent patients (e.g., Alzheimer's patients), then never-competent patients (severely retarded adults), and finally, as-yet-to-be competent patients (children with leukemia).

The evidence against this slope claim is impressive. The key slide is from competent to incompetent patients. It is easy for physicians and families to accept the wishes of a competent, adult, dying patient who repeatedly says, "Enough is enough!"

With formerly-competent and never-competent patients, the results are very different. It is one thing to decide for yourself to die because of low quality of life; it is quite another thing to decide that someone else's quality of life is so low that he or she should be "assisted" to find death. Spouses, families, judges, and legislatures are morally uncomfortable with, and hence have resisted, accelerating deaths for incompetent people judged to have a low quality of life. Indeed, surveys of families show that, while individuals want the right to die for themselves, they are very reluctant to force their view on someone else – even a family member they have known for many years.

Legally, different standards of evidence have often been erected to protect these different classes of patients. For example in America, the 1990 *Cruzan* decision by the US Supreme Court held that states may not pass laws restricting the rights of competent patients in any way to decline medical treatment and die. No "evidentiary" standard at all was necessary to prove that a physician here should do what a patient wanted. The same decision, however, said that a state may pass a much higher evidentiary standard to protect *incompetent* patients from overzealous attempts by families to end their lives. So the state of Missouri was permitted to apply the higher "clear and convincing evidence" standard and resist the efforts of Nancy Cruzan's parents to disconnect her feeding tube so her life could be ended (Pence, 1995). Similarly, many scholars and disability advocates believe that an even higher standard should be applied to ending the lives of never-competent patients, namely, the "beyond a reasonable doubt" standard. Only when ending the life of such a patient ended suffering and produced so much good that killing the person was good "beyond a reasonable doubt," could it be ordered.

Slippery slope #2: Unleashing the dark side of human nature
A second kind of slippery slope is also often predicted to occur with legalization of physician-assisted dying: with legalization, the worst motives of physicians and families will take over, and all decisions will be made for the sake of money or convenience of families, not for the best interests of the dying patient. Some fear that physicians will be pressured by skyrocketing medical costs into urging assisted dying on high-cost, low-benefit patients, mostly old and poor patients. Families can be financially crippled by the cost of supportive services for a dying or vegetative patient. Cost containment has become a driving force in the American health-care system; is it wise to institute "managed care" and physician-assisted dying at the same time?

Much of modern-day medical ethics evolved during times of economic prosperity, and bad times – such as a worldwide depression – might motivate individuals and communities to accept or demand euthanasia in more and more situations. (Was it not a crumbling economy that presaged the rise of the Nazis in Germany?) As medical historian Stanley Reiser says, "A good deal of the debate is about whether we could control all of the steps that might coerce or intimidate a patient" (Reiser, 1992: 13).

This is an important objection, perhaps more important than most citizens realize. American medicine is currently experiencing efforts to control its costs. More and more Americans are being enrolled in insurance plans where the physicians, not the company or the patients, assume the financial risk of keeping costs low.

If such massive change occurs, there is obviously a potential problem with physician-assisted suicide. If the financial momentum for physicians is also reversed, from maintaining life to ending life, what will then happen? No one really knows what will happen. Part of the (usually unspoken) worry here concerns what really motivates American physicians: will conscience hold firm when one's income is reduced by supporting the patient?

Some people say that the answer to this real problem is that some safeguards must be erected. Recognizing that financial gain may motivate some physicians, and that both physicians and families can have conflicts of interest *vis-à-vis* dying patients, devices must be created to prevent physicians from directly profiting on early deaths.

The problem with this discussion is that, at least in America, the current argument assumes that financial gain does not *already* motivate physicians to recommend treatment for patients that might benefit them financially. Where such temptation exists, a physician's ethics and conscience are supposed to prevent him from giving in. It is then bizarre for critics of physician-assisted dying to claim that, when it comes to dying patients, financial gain might be too tempting for physicians. Why isn't it too tempting in all the other areas of medicine *now*? Why isn't it financial gain that motivates physicians to *resist* physician-assisted dying?

Slippery slope #3: Consistency
What justifies one case of assisted death justifies other, similar cases. If it is justifiable to kill a 36-year-old dying leukemic in great misery, is it also justifiable to assist in the death of a 16-year-old? Or a spina bifida child with painful leukemia? In opposing physician-assisted dying, Daniel Callahan says that the logic of the case for assisted suicide will inevitably lead to its extension far beyond the cases of terminally-ill, competent adults. If relief of suffering

is critical, he says, "why should that relief be denied to the demented or the incompetent? (Callahan, as quoted in Steinfels, 1991).

There is some evidence that consistency has pulled Dutch physicians toward generalization of physician-assisted dying from the original class of competent patients, for some cases of incompetent patients. This problem is perhaps inevitable, given the pull of consistency. However, the Dutch people themselves do not think that the occasional abuse is an indictment against the whole system.

Nor is it clear that the pull of consistency is a bad thing. We just may not be ready for a perfectly consistent ethical system about life and death at this time. Practical ethics is not a logically perfect system. Lines must be drawn somewhere, and where the line is drawn is often somewhat arbitrary. The point is to have some cut-off point at all, not one that has some metaphysical anchor or logical perfection. It may be that, for a particular time in American history, we will draw the line about a moral issue at X and not Y. Then, 20 years later when conditions change, we may feel better about moving the line to Y, *even though Y may have been a more logically consistent point at the beginning.*

That is fine. The whole point of "drawing lines" is to stop a mindless run down a slippery slope as soon as some change occurs. We don't want to change everything at once because we need time to evaluate changes to see if they are producing good consequences. If they are not, we can reverse policies, just as Prohibition and the military draft were reversed.

In conclusion, considerations of consistency may tend to expand the cases covered under any criteria for physician-assisted dying. This pull can be resisted in statutes by legislatures that "draw the lines" of the laws of the land. If the passage of time shows that the lines need to be changed, either to permit more cases or to permit fewer, that is something that can be done.

The Role of Physicians

So far, we have been viewing the issue from the patient's side, but now we evaluate arguments frequently heard on the physician's side. Most are "slippery slope" arguments.

The physician–patient relationship

One line of worry about assisted dying is not about money but about the kind of relationship that exists between physician and patient in an assisted suicide. Dr Quill, who helped "Diane" die, argued that because Kevorkian had no long-term physician–patient relationship with those he helped, he had done a bad thing. Quill said of Kevorkian, "Suicide is the sole basis for the relationship he has with his patients, and that is frightening (*Newsweek*, March 8, 1993, p. 46).

Dutch physicians have an answer. Seeing a patient all his life and then doing nothing as he dies is not seen by them as good patient care. Instead it is seen as patient abandonment. Offering a continuity of care across a lifetime in a way unknown in modern America, Dutch physicians see helping patients die as the final step in a lifetime of intimate, personal medical care between physicians and their patients. It is true that coming to a stranger who was a "thanatologist" would be an undesirable way to die, but it need not be that way. Holland has shown us a better option.

The Argument from Medical Tradition

This argument asserts that physicians should not assist patients to die because physicians have not historically done so. This argument in itself carries little weight. Appeals to tradition always buttress such arguments against change, but they are question-begging. People who like tradition don't like change.

Tradition is only as good as its consequences. Western civilization practiced slavery for two thousand years, but the consequences of this practice were not good for most people.

The Argument from Tradition also implies that "tradition" has some collected moral wisdom embedded in it, as Tevye the dairyman implies in *Fiddler on the Roof* (possibly referring to the rabbinic moral teachings). But in medicine, tradition in the twentieth-century ethics does not always carry moral wisdom, especially when it comes to change.

Consider that American medicine in the twentieth century opposed the federal Medicare program for the elderly, which turned old age from terror of disease and resultant impoverishment to one of assured, good medical treatment. During the 1960s, medicine opposed telling cancer patients their true diagnosis, and opposed Elizabeth Kubler-Ross's attempt to identify dying patients as such and help them die comfortably in special hospices. Later, medicine opposed as "active euthanasia" the removal in the 1970s of respirators in comatose patients such as Karen Quinlan. After that and during the 1980s, it opposed removal of indwelling feeding tubes because to do so denied patients humane "food and water."

In all these cases, the public grew wise long before physicians and, as a result, it was the public who dragged medicine along with the new moral consensus. Thus, the argument – that medicine should not accept physician-assisted dying in the 1990s because it violates medical tradition – is. not a good argument. Medicine has rarely taken the lead in moral progress for patients' rights.

It should be noted too that medicine has not always resisted helping the dying. Ancient Greek physicians commonly helped the dying finish their days peacefully and with dignity. (Hippocrates was an exception who followed the sanctity-of-life ethic of Pythagoras.) It may be time for modern physicians to emulate the virtues of ancient Greek physicians.

The idea that the role of physicians does not permit killing is sometimes expressed in the saying that, "Physicians should be healers, not killers." This claim is frequently made, and as explained in the historical survey above about what patients want, this claim has been a good directive for most of human history. Today, however, it begs the question against patients by assuming, contrary to much evidence, that all patients do not want their physicians to help them die.

A related argument by opponents of physician-assisted dying concerns the role of physicians: If they are legally allowed to assist the dying, what reason do we have to suppose that they would not soon *recommend* dying? And once physicians began recommending assisted dying, how do we know that they – and others – would not try to make it *mandatory*?

This is a kind of scarey rhetorical argument that one sometimes hears, but it is a bad one. It is of exactly the same form as this: If we allow stores to sell cars to people who want one, soon the stores will make it mandatory to buy one (false). Giving people the choice to have something is not equivalent to, nor does it usually lead to, the same people being required to have that thing.

A related argument about the role of physicians is expressed in the idea that "killing will brutalize the medical profession." Again, this is a bad argument. First, physicians already have many experiences that could brutalize them, and so people who cannot stay compassionate around sick, dying, or paralyzed people should not be physicians. Whether or not a particular kind of experience brutalizes a physician depends on many things, including the patient's attitude to what is going on. Secondly, the status quo is already very "brutal" for both patients and physicians: to watch Janet Adkins lose her mind and then to maintain her mindless body for another decade is far more brutal on the Adkins family and attending physicians than to give her help in dying.

This point is relevant to the objection that, if we legalize physician-assisted dying, there will be some abuses by some physicians. That is true. No system is perfect. But what is overlooked is this: the slow, painful dying of many patients today, against their will, is just as much a kind of abuse. It is not as if the present system has no abuses.

Finally, some physicians argue that assisting terminal patients to die "doesn't feel right, and I have to go with my gut moral feelings." To this argument, it must be replied that pop psychology about feelings is not always correct. Feelings may be embedded in antiquated moral traditions, such as racist traditions, and so need to be re-evaluated. When incorrect, they need to be overcome by a decision to do what is morally right. If a physician's experience and reason tell her that the patient's best interest is to die quickly, then even if "it doesn't feel right" to assist, it still may be.

Conclusion

Jean-Paul Sartre made famous the idea that, "Not to choose is also a choice." Doing nothing to legalize physician-assisted dying is to choose to let millions upon millions of people pile up in advanced stages of senility, dysfunction, and mental vacuity. Doing nothing chooses to let millions upon millions of bodies continue to eke out an existence while the personalities that once inhabited them disintegrate. Doing nothing takes away the right of people to die who do not want their bodies to continue for decades after their minds are gone, or who do not want to live their final years in pain and misery.

We need not worry too much about slippery slopes and things getting out of control. Not all change is bad. People don't decide to die lightly. Let's face it: no one wants to die. To become so frail, so disoriented, so full of pain that death is preferable to life is to come to a very bad place. We need not fear help by physicians in getting out of that place. Instead of a danger, such help for some will be a blessing.

References

Alexander, L. 1949; "Medical Science Under Dictatorship," *New England Journal of Medicine*, 242: 47.

Pence, G. 1995: *Classic Cases in Medical Ethics*, chapter 1: "Comas: Karen Quinlan and Nancy Cruzan" (McGraw-Hill).

Protzman, F. 1989: "Killing of 49 Elderly Patients by Nurse Aides Stuns Austria," *New York Times*, April 18.

Quill, T. 1991: "'Death and Dignity' A Case of Individualized Decision Making," *New England Journal of Medicine*, 324: 691–4.

Reiser, S. 1992: "Physician-Assisted Dying: Historical Perspective – An Interview with Stanley J. Reiser," *Trends in Health Care, Law & Ethics*, 7: 13.

Specter, M. 1990: "Suicide Device Fuels Debate," *Washington Post*, June 8.

Steinfels, P. 1991: "Dutch Study is Euthanasia Vote Issue," *New York Times*, September 20.

Teno, J. and Lynn, J. 1991: "Voluntary Active Euthanasia: The Individual Case and Public Policy," *Journal of the American Geriatrics Society*, 39: 827–30.

van Delden, J. M. et al. 1993: "The Remmelink Study: Two Years Later," *Hastings Center Report*, 23: 6.

2

Justifying Physician-Assisted Deaths

Tom L. Beauchamp

Some recent developments in law encourage more discretion in the ways physicians are permitted to help patients die, despite traditional prohibitions in medicine against assisting in suicide and causing the death of patients. Among the most striking developments was the Canadian Supreme Court's decision in the case of Sue Rodriguez. She attempted to strike down section 241 of the Criminal Code of Canada, which prohibits physician–assisted suicide. The court did not find in her favor, but several justices delivered opinions that give strong support to the moral justifiability of Rodriguez's goal of dying with a physician's direct assistance.[1] A few legal developments in the United States have likewise suggested that prohibitions of assisted suicide are unconstitutional,[2] that certain acts of assistance in dying do not constitute manslaughter,[3] and that a physician's writing of a lethal prescription is acceptable.[4]

These legal developments encourage us to think of the primary moral questions about euthanasia as questions of legalization. The morality of what physicians do in particular cases is thereby demoted in importance, and it is left unclear whether the fundamental moral issue is the justification of *individual acts* of killing and letting-die or the justification of institutional rules and public laws – *policies* – that permit or prohibit such acts. In due course I will argue that certain acts by physicians in assisting persons to die are justified. This argument will not, however, be sufficient to support conclusions about the legalization of physician-assisted suicide or voluntary active euthanasia.

The Troubled Distinction between Killing and Letting-die

Those who claim that physician-assisted suicide is fundamentally wrong typically assume that there is a basic distinction between acts of killing and acts of merely letting-die. This distinction is troubled. The problem is illustrated by the many cases in which parents, surrogates, and physicians evaluate their intentional omissions of treatment as justifiable acts of *letting-die*, whereas their critics charge that they have unjustifiably *killed* by intentionally allowing to die. For example, in one recent case, Dr Gregory Messenger was charged with manslaughter after he terminated his own premature infant son's life support system by disconnecting the ventilator. In his view, he merely allowed his son to die.

Ordinary language, law, and traditional medical ethics afford no clear answer whether such cases should be described as "allowing to die" or "letting-die," rather than "killing." Moreover, in neither ordinary language nor law does the word "killing" entail a wrongful act or a crime or an intentional action. For example, we can say that persons are killed in accidental shootings and automobile collisions. In ordinary language, *killing* represents a set of related ideas whose central condition is causal intervention to bring about another's death, whereas *allowing to die* represents another family of ideas whose central condition is intentional avoidance of causal intervention so that disease, system failure, or injury causes death.

But if we are to retain this distinction between killing and letting-die, we need clearer, more precise meanings for these notions. For example, the term "killing" could be restricted entirely to circumstances in which one person *intentionally and unjustifiably* causes the death of another human being – a usage that limits and reconstructs the ordinary meaning of the term. "Killing" would then be morally loaded, so that *justified* acts of arranging for death in medicine logically could not be instances of killing; they would always be cases of allowing to die. Under this stipulative meaning of "killing," physicians logically cannot kill when they justifiably remove a life-sustaining treatment in accordance with a patient's refusal of treatment, and patients cannot kill themselves when they justifiably forgo treatment.

I want to resist this simple move to redefine "killing" – or at least to refine its meaning. It is little more than stipulation that evades the moral and conceptual problems. Although I am skeptical that there is or can be a morally neutral analysis of either "killing" or "letting-die," I prefer to start with the neutral assumption that the term "killing" refers only to certain ways in which death is caused.

When does a Role in Bringing About Death Constitute Killing?

Under this assumption, which captures more or less the ordinary sense of "killing," the justifiability of any particular type of killing is an open question and we cannot assert without looking at a particular case that killing is morally worse than allowing to die. That is, to apply the label "killing" or the label "letting-die" correctly (as morally neutral terms) to a set of events cannot determine whether one type of action is better or worse than the other, or whether either is acceptable or unacceptable.[5] Of course, killing may in most cases be worse than allowing to die, but this is not because of the meaning of the words. Some particular act of killing (a callous murder, say) may be morally worse than some particular act of allowing to die (forgoing treatment for a dying and comatose patient, say); but some act of letting-die (not resuscitating a patient who could easily be saved, but who has refused treatment because of a series of mistaken assumptions, say) also may be morally worse than some particular act of killing (mercy killing at the request of a seriously ill and suffering patient, say).

The point is this: Nothing about either killing or allowing to die, construed as morally neutral, entails judgments about the wrongness or rightness of either type of action, or about the acceptability of the intentions of the actor in performing the act. Rightness and wrongness depend exclusively on the merit of the justification underlying the action, not on the type of action it is. A judgment that an act of either killing or letting-die is justified or unjustified therefore entails that something else be known about the act besides its being an instance of killing or an instance of allowing to die. The actor's intention or motive (whether benevolent or malicious, for example), the patient's refusal of treatment or request of assistance, the balance of benefits over burdens to the patient, and the consequences of the act are all relevant to questions of justification, and some such additional factor is required to make a normative judgment.

Some writers who apparently accept the morally neutral character of "killing" have attempted to reach conclusions about the moral acceptability of letting-die, as follows:[6] They construe omission of treatment as letting-die rather than killing whenever an underlying disease or injury is the cause of death. By contrast, they argue, killings require that acts of persons be the causes of death. Accordingly, a natural death occurs when a respirator is removed, because natural conditions simply do what they would have done without the respirator. They conclude that one acts appropriately in many cases of intentionally allowing persons to die (one is no cause of death at all), but inappropriately in intentionally killing.

This argument does not support the moral conclusions that many draw from it. To make the argument plausible, one must add that the omission of treatment that allows a person to die is a *justified* omission. But what justifies an omission of treatment? The mere fact that a natural cause brings about death is not sufficient to justify not treating someone. To see why merely citing natural causes (of disease, etc.) is unsatisfactory without an additional justification, consider the following example: Mr Mafia comes into a hospital and maliciously detaches a patient, Mr Policeman, from a respirator. This act of detaching the patient from the respirator is causally no different from the acts physicians perform all the time in allowing patients to die. Some features in the circumstance other than omitting treatment, disconnecting the respirator, and the presence of disease or injury must be considered, to arrive at moral conclusions.

If Mr Mafia killed Mr Policeman – and he did – then physicians who do the same thing with their patients likewise kill their patients, unless we introduce a condition about the justifiability of the one omission of treatment and the unjustifiability of the other omission. Without some feature in the circumstances that renders their omissions of treatment justified, doctors cannot justifiably say "We do not kill our patients, only the underlying diseases and injuries do," any more than Mr Mafia can say, "It was the disease, not me, that killed him." An account of killing and letting-die restricted to omitting treatment, disconnecting machines, and disease-caused death leads to the absurd conclusion either that Mr Mafia did not kill the patient or that doctors always kill their patients when the patients die from such omissions of treatment. To solve this problem we must provide a more plausible account of justified omissions and justified actions.

Valid Refusal as the Basis of Letting-die

What justifies a physician's omission of treatment and disconnection of the respirator that does not justify Mr Mafia's "omission" of treatment and disconnection? Typically what validates the physician's omission is an *authoritative refusal of treatment* by a patient or authorized surrogate. It would be both immoral and illegal of the physician not to omit treatment in the face of a competent, authoritative refusal. It therefore seems attractive to say that what sorts the physician's act into the category of allowing to die rather than killing, and makes Mr Mafia's act one of killing rather than allowing to die, is nothing but the competent authoritative refusal of treatment present when the physician acts and absent when Mr Mafia and others act.

This claim has been defended by James L. Bernat, Bernard Gert, and R. Peter Mogielnicki.[7] They apparently believe that the type of action – killing or letting-die – depends on whether there is a valid refusal warranting an omission of treatment, rather than the validity of an omission of treatment (disconnection of the respirator, etc.) depending on the type of action it is. This clarification is insightful. Traditionally we have thought that the distinction between killing and letting-die is to be accounted for in terms of either the *intention* of persons (whether they intend someone's death) or the *causation* of persons (whether they cause someone's death). But the patient-refusal hypothesis provides a third way and demotes causation and intention in importance, giving the pivotal role to *valid refusal*.

A refusal is valid when the patient, who has rightful authority, autonomously refuses the proposed treatment (or an authorized surrogate does so). This account of the validity of a refusal is intimately tied to a larger account of the limits of professional authority and duty. The physician has a duty to follow an appropriate refusal and is required by society to do so; a bystander or someone like Mr Mafia has no comparable duty or social recognition. This duty and the corresponding limits of physician authority give us a reason for saying that the physician's actions *do not cause death*, whereas Mr Mafia's actions do cause death.

This theory shapes the meaning of the pivotal terms "killing" and "letting-die" in a way that protects the conventional moral thesis in law and medicine that it is justifiable to allow to die and unjustifiable to kill. This is exactly what Bernat, Gert, and Mogielnicki argue. But do they beg a central moral question by assuming that only letting-die, not killing, is justified? My own preference is to avoid this conclusion by independently looking at acts of killing to see if they can be justified on grounds other than a valid refusal. I believe we cannot decide the critical moral questions about physician-assisted suicide and euthanasia entirely by appeals to valid refusals and the letting-die–killing distinction. The critical question is whether there is an adequate justification for the action taken, whatever *type* of action it is and whether or not there has been a refusal of treatment.

I do agree with Bernat, Gert, and Mogielnicki that justification turns on having a valid *authorization*, but I would not limit the notion of a valid authorization to a valid refusal, and I would not make the account turn in any significant way on the distinction between killing and letting-die. I will now explain why.

Valid Refusals and Valid Requests

The problem with the analysis of Bernat, Gert, and Mogielnicki is not with their views about valid refusals, but with what they say about valid requests. They are correct in saying that a valid refusal of treatment always justifies a corresponding omission of the treatment, even if it is a refusal of hydration and nutrition that will result in death by starvation. Whenever valid refusals occur, how death occurs is not decisive, and it is never a moral offense to comply with a valid refusal. My disagreement with their analysis comes when they insist that a *request* for help by a competent patient has no legitimate role to play in the justification of an action of physician-assisted suicide or voluntary active euthanasia. They believe the moral and legal requirement to honor a refusal does not extend to honoring a request. My view, by contrast, is the following: (1) physicians are both morally and legally required to honor refusals; (2) they are not legally required to honor requests; (3) whether they are either morally required or morally permitted to honor requests depends on the nature of the request and the nature of the patient–physician relationship.

In some of the clearest cases of justified compliance with requests, the patient and the physician discuss what is in the patient's best interest, under the assumption that the physician will not abandon the patient or resist what they jointly decide to be in the patient's best interests. A physician with these professional commitments has made a moral commitment to help patients that differs from the commitment made by a physician who rigidly draws the line in opposition to any form of euthanasia or assistance in suicide.[8] In some cases, a patient both refuses to start or continue a possible treatment and requests help in dying in order that the death be less painful; refusal and request are combined as parts of a single plan, and, in many of these cases, the physician agrees with the plan. In this way assisted suicide or active euthanasia grows naturally out of a close patient–physician relationship.

In cases in which patients make reasonable requests for assistance in dying, it is a misconception to suppose that doctors can escape responsibility for their decisions if they refrain from helping their patients die. No physician can say "I am not responsible for outcomes when I choose not to act on a patient's request." There has long been a vague sense in the physician and legal community that if only the doctor lets nature take its course, then one is not responsible for the outcome of death. But a physician is always responsible for any decision taken and the consequent action or inaction. The physician who complies with a patient's request is therefore responsible in exactly the way physicians who refuse to comply with the request are responsible.

Physicians who refuse to comply with a request cannot magically pass responsibility to the patient's condition of disease. The only relevant matter is whether the path the physician chooses, including what is rejected and omitted, has an adequate justification. Doctors cannot evade responsibility for acting in the best interests of the patient, and they cannot turn their backs on what the patient believes to be in his or her best interests. Of course, doctors often reject courses of action requested by patients and have good and sufficient reasons for doing so. That is not in dispute. The question is whether the physician who conscientiously believes that the patient's request for assistance in dying is reasonable and justified and assumes responsibility for any assistance undertaken does wrong in complying with the request.

Bernat, Gert, and Mogielnicki will object that I am confusing moral obligations and (non-required) moral ideals. They regard the physicians I just described as moving beyond professional obligations of providing medical care, into the domain of optional moral ideals of assistance in dying. In important respects, I do not want to resist this classification of the physician's commitment as a moral ideal, but the distinction can be misleading without further qualification. As Gert himself has argued, moral ideals sometimes legitimately override moral obligations in cases of contingent conflict. This position will do well enough for our purposes. If a physician *justifiably* believes that his or her moral ideals of patient-assistance override all other moral obligations (to avoid killing, to not violate laws, etc.), this conclusion is all I need to support the argument in this section.

The Wrongness in Causing or Assisting in Death

But is the act the physician believes to be justified really justified? Could assistance in someone's self-requested death be wrong, even if the physician conscientiously believes it is right?

The only way to decide whether killing is wrong and letting-die not wrong in some cases, though wrong in others, is to determine what *makes* them wrong when they are wrong. By longstanding convention, a person is not guilty of a crime or a wrongful act merely because he or she killed someone. Legitimate defenses for killing (excusable homicide) include killing in self-defense and killing by misadventure (accidental and non-negligent killing while engaged in a lawful act). From a moral point of view, causing a person's death is wrong *when it is wrong* not because the death is *intended* or because it is *caused*, but because an unjustified harm or loss to the person occurs. Therefore, what makes a physician's act of killing or "assisting" in causing a death wrong, when it is wrong, is that a person is unjustifiably harmed – that is, unjustifiably suffers a setback to interests that the person otherwise would not have experienced.

The critical question for acts both of killing and of letting-die in medicine is whether an act of assisting persons in bringing about their deaths causes them a loss or, rather, provides a benefit. If a person chooses death and sees that event as a personal benefit, then helping that person bring about death neither harms nor wrongs the person and may provide a benefit or at least fulfill the person's last important goal.

This helping might harm society by setting back its interests, and therefore might be a reason against *legalization*, but this form of harm does not alter conclusions about the justifiability of the *act* of helping. Not helping persons of this description in their dying, on the analysis I have presented, can interrupt or frustrate their goals and, from their perspective, cause them harm, indignity, or despair – even if, at the same time, it protects society's interests.

The Key Argument in Defense of Euthanasia and Assisted Suicide

These conclusions can now be joined with the previous reflections on valid refusals and requests. If passive letting-die based on valid refusals does not harm or wrong persons or violate their rights, then how can assisted suicide and voluntary active euthanasia harm or wrong the person who dies? In both cases – active killing and passive letting-die – the person is, in effect, refusing to go on and is seeking the best means to the end of quitting life. The judgment is that the best obtainable information about the future indicates that continuing life is, on balance, worse than not continuing it. The person who attempts suicide, the person who seeks active euthanasia, and the person who forgoes life-sustaining treatment are identically situated except that they select different means to bring about the end of life. Each intends to quit life because of its bleak possibilities.[9] Therefore, those who believe it is morally acceptable to let people die when they refuse treatment, but not to take active steps to help them die when they request assistance, must give a different account of the wrongfulness of killing and letting-die than I have offered.

To insist on continued treatment (or even palliation, in many cases) while refusing to comply with a patient's request for assistance in dying is to burden rather than help the patient and, of course, to reject their autonomous wishes. As the autonomy interests in this choice increase on the scale of interests, denial of help to the patient increasingly burdens the patient; and to increase the burden is to increase the harm done to the person.

The core of the argument in favor of the moral justifiability of acts of physician-assisted suicide and voluntary active euthanasia is that relief from suffering and a voluntary request justify our doing what we otherwise would not do: implement a plan to end a human life. This action has its strongest defense when: (1) a condition is extremely burdensome and the burden outweighs any benefits, (2) pain management cannot be made adequate, (3) only a physician is capable of bringing relief, and (4) the patient makes an informed request.

Medicine and law seem now to say to many patients, "If you were on life-sustaining treatment, you could withdraw the treatment and we could let you die. But since you are not, we can only give you palliative care until you die a natural death." This position condemns the patient to live out a life he or she does not want – a form of cruelty that violates the patient's rights and prevents discharge of the fiduciary obligations of the physician. To use this argument is not to claim that physicians face large numbers of desperately ill patients. Pain management has made circumstances at least bearable for most of today's patients, but some patients still cannot be satisfactorily relieved, and, even if they could, questions would remain about the autonomy rights of patients: If there is a right to stop a medical treatment that sustains life, why is there not a right to stop one's life by arrangement with a physician?

Dr Kevorkian's "patients" raise profound questions about the lack of a support system in medicine or elsewhere for handling their problems. Having thought for over a year about her future, Adkins decided that her suffering would exceed the benefits of continuing to live. She apparently had firm views about what she wanted, and she carefully calculated both the costs and the benefits. She faced a bleak future from her perspective as a person who had lived an unusually vigorous life. She believed that her brain would be slowly destroyed, with progressive and devastating cognitive loss and confusion, fading memory, immense frustration, and lack of all capacity to take care of herself. She also believed that her family would have to assume the full burden of responsibility for her care. From her perspective, what Kevorkian offered was better than other physicians offered, which, to her, was no help at all.

Current social institutions, including the medical system, have not proved adequate for patients like Adkins. Dying persons often face inadequate counseling, emotional support, pain information, or pain control. Their condition is intolerable from their perspective, and without any avenue of hope. To maintain that these persons act immorally by arranging for death is a harsh judgment that needs to be backed by a more persuasive argument than I have seen.

If this argument is sound, then the burden of justification for proscriptions of acts of voluntary active euthanasia and physician-assisted suicide rests on those who refuse or hinder assistance to patients who express a competent and rational wish to die, rather than on those who would help them die. Associations of medical professionals in the US have, I believe, reversed the proper burden of justification by placing it on physicians who want to help patients.[10]

Justifying Policies and Justifying Acts

The argument thus far leads to the conclusion that physicians' acts of honoring valid refusals and complying with valid requests can both be justified under specifiable circumstances. However, I said at the beginning that my argument is not strong enough to show that *policies*, such as the law passed in Oregon, are justified. I want now to explain how one can consistently hold strong views about the justifiability of some acts of physician-assisted suicide and voluntary active euthanasia, while simultaneously having deep-seated reservations about revising public policies that prohibit these acts. The point is that one can consistently judge acts morally acceptable that one cannot support legalizing.

The backbone of the resistance to physician-assisted euthanasia and voluntary active euthanasia has long been an argument referred to as the wedge argument or "slippery slope" argument. It proceeds roughly as follows:[11] Although particular acts of assistance in dying might be morally justified on some occasions, the social consequences of sanctioning practices of killing would involve serious risks of abuse and misuse and, on balance, would cause more harm than benefit to society. Attitudes, not merely guidelines, can be eroded by shifts in public policy. Prohibitions are often symbolically important, and their removal could weaken the fabric of restraints and beneficial attitudes. The argument is not that these negative consequences will occur immediately after legalization, but that they will grow incrementally over time. Society might start with innocent beginnings by developing policies that carefully restrict the number of patients who qualify for assistance in suicide or euthanasia. Whatever restrictions are initially built into our policies will be revised and expanded over time, with ever-increasing possibilities in the system for unjustified killing. Unscrupulous persons will learn how to abuse the system, just as they do with methods of tax evasion that operate on the margins of the system of legitimate tax avoidance.

Slippery slope arguments depend on speculative predictions of a progressive erosion of moral restraints. If the dire and unmanageable consequences that they predict actually will flow from the legal legitimation of assisted suicide or voluntary active euthanasia, then slippery slope arguments do convincingly show that practices should be legally prohibited. But how good is the evidence that dire consequences will occur? Is there a sufficient reason to think that we cannot maintain control over and even improve public policy? Every reasonable person would agree that these difficult empirical questions are among the primary questions in the current moral controversy about euthanasia.

All that needs to be said here, I believe, is that even if slippery slope arguments provide solid reasons against legalization, they provide no moral basis for the conclusion that acts of euthanasia and physician-assisted suicide are morally wrong (unless one's only moral basis is identical to one's basis for opposing legalization). I will now explain why.

Slippery slope arguments conclude that patients such as Sue Rodriguez and the patrons of Jack Kevorkian cannot be justifiably helped by physicians because to help them, even if they deserve our help, would open the floodgates to killing persons who should not be killed. All patients should be denied help not because of anything they have done or because of any demerit in their cases or in their wishes, but because acts of assistance in dying would hurt others if legalized and therefore should not be tolerated under any circumstances.

There is something that seems both very right and very wrong about this slippery slope argument – right because the argument points to dangers of the most profound sort, wrong because at least some patients deserve to be helped and their physicians do nothing morally wrong in helping them. It may therefore be necessary to prohibit these acts of assistance in our public policies while acknowledging that there is nothing morally wrong with the acts other than their potentially far-reaching social consequences. They are truly "innocent beginnings."

In conclusion, I want to throw a final wrinkle into this already wrinkled picture. Despite my concerns about slippery slopes, I believe the legislation in Oregon is a promising development (which is not to say it is good legislation as it was passed), and I think that we should welcome some version of it. This suggestion may seem to contradict what I just argued about legalization, but concerns about slippery slopes ought not to be so paralyzing that we are not open to social experiments that will help us see whether empirical predictions are correct and which system works best.[12] The Oregon legislation could be viewed as a social experiment that gives us a good perspective on both risks and benefits – a trial that may or may not succeed. I would hope that research will be carried out to evaluate our experimental programs in upcoming years and that we will learn about the benefits and risks in a comprehensive, timely, and objective manner. Perhaps then we can be positioned to decide from evidence whether the slippery slope is as slippery as some fear it could be.

Notes

1 Supreme Court of Canada, *Sue Rodriguez* v. *Attorney General of Canada*, September 30, 1993, File No. 23476; on appeal from British Columbia Court of Appeal, *Rodriguez* v. *British Columbia (Attorney General)* [1993], B.C.J. No. 641 (Q.L.) (B.C.C.A.). In early 1994, with broad public support, Sue Rodriguez killed herself with the assistance of an anonymous physician.

2 *Compassion in Dying* v. *State of Washington*, 850 F. Supp. 1454 (W.D. Wash. 1994); overturned March 9, 1995, by the United States Court of Appeals for the Ninth Circuit in an opinion written by Judge John T. Noonan. *Compassion in Dying* v. *Washington*, No. 94–35534 (US App. March 9, 1995) (available March 1995, on LEXIS).

3 State of Michigan in the Circuit Court for the County of Oakland, *People of the State of Michigan* v. *Jack Kevorkian*, Case No. CR-92–115190-FC (July 21, 1992); Court of Appeals of Michigan, *Hobbins* v. *Attorney General* and *People of the State of Michigan* v. *Jack Kevorkian*, 518 N.W.2d 487 (Mich. App. 1994).

4 See *Oregon Death with Dignity Act* (1994). Under this Act, terminally ill adults are allowed to obtain lethal drugs from physicians in order to hasten death and escape unbearable suffering. This initiative, when scheduled to become law, faced legal challenges.

5 In effect, this proposal is made in James Rachels, "Active and Passive Euthanasia," *New England Journal of Medicine*, 292, No. 2 (January 9, 1975): 78–80; and Dan Brock, "Voluntary Active Euthanasia," *Hastings Center Report*, 22, No. 2 (March/April 1992): 10–22.

6 See: In the Matter of *Claire C. Conroy*, 190 N.J. Sup. 453, 464 A.2d 303 (App. Div. 1983); In the Matter of *Claire C. Conroy*, 486 A.2d 1209 (New Jersey Supreme Court, 1985), at 1222–3, 1236; *In re Estate of Greenspan*, 558 N.E.2d 1194, at 1203 (Ill. 1990); Daniel Callahan, "Vital Distinctions, Mortal Questions," *Commonweal*, 115 (July 15, 1988): 399–402; and several articles in Joanne Lynn (ed.), *By No Extraordinary Means* (Bloomington, IN: Indiana University Press, 1986), pp. 227–66.

7 James L. Bernat, Bernard Gert, and R. Peter Mogielnicki, "Patient Refusal of Hydration and Nutrition," *Archives of Internal Medicine*, 153 (1993): 2723–8; Bernard Gert, *Morality: A New Justification of the Moral Rules* (New York: Oxford University Press, 1988), pp. 294–300.

8 Cf. Sidney H. Wanzer, Daniel D. Federman, S. James Adelstein, et al., "The Physician's Responsibility toward Hopelessly Ill Patients: A Second Look," *New England Journal of Medicine*, 320 (March 30, 1989): 844–9.

9 For the extension to suicide, see Dan Brock, "Death and Dying," in *Medical Ethics*, ed. Robert M. Veatch (Boston: Jones and Bartlett, 1989), p. 345.

10 American Medical Association, Council on Ethical and Judicial Affairs, *Euthanasia: Report C*, in *Proceedings of the House of Delegates* (Chicago: American Medical Association, June 1988): 258–60 (and see *Current Opinions*, § 2.20, p. 13, 1989); "Decisions Near the End of Life," *Report B*, adopted by the House of Delegates (1991), pp. 11–15; and see the abridged version in "Decisions Near the End of Life," *Journal of the American Medical Association*, 267 (April 22/29, 1992): 2229–33.

11 Cf. Alan J. Weisbard and Mark Siegler, "On Killing Patients with Kindness: An Appeal for Caution," in J. Arras and N. Rhoden, *Ethical Issues in Modern Medicine*, 3rd edn (Mountain View, CA: Mayfield, 1989), esp. p. 218; Douglas Walton, *Slippery Slope Arguments* (Oxford: Clarendon Press, 1992); Trudy Govier, "What's Wrong with Slippery Slope Arguments?", *Canadian Journal of Philosophy*, 12 (June 1982): 303–16; Frederick Schauer, "Slippery Slopes," *Harvard Law Review*, 99 (1985): 361–83; and James Rachels, *The End of Life: Euthanasia and Morality* (Oxford: Oxford University Press, 1986), ch. 10.

12 Cf. Franklin G. Miller, Timothy Quill, Howard Brody, John C. Fletcher, Lawrence O. Gostin, and D. E. Meier, "Regulating Physician-Assisted Death," *New England Journal of Medicine*, 331 (1994): 119–23.

3

Rule-Utilitarianism and Euthanasia

Brad Hooker

1. Introduction

As scientific and technological advances enable the medical profession to keep people alive longer, the question arises whether this is always a good thing. Should those who could prolong life step back under certain conditions and allow a very ill person to die? And if allowing to die is sometimes right, then what about actively killing patients when this would be better for the patients than allowing them to die more slowly and painfully?

Such questions are debated under the heading of euthanasia. The term "euthanasia" derives from the Greek term for an easy, painless death. However, we often now hear the term "passive euthanasia", which refers to passing up opportunities to save an individual from death, out of concern for that individual. If passive euthanasia is indeed one kind of euthanasia, then "euthanasia" cannot mean "killing painlessly"; for to pass up an opportunity to save someone, i.e. passive euthanasia, is arguably not *killing*. Furthermore, the death involved in passive euthanasia is often *painful*. So let us take the term "euthanasia" to mean "either killing or passing up opportunities to save someone, out of concern for that person." (Note that, on this definition, what the Nazis called "euthanasia" was not euthanasia, because it was not done out of concern for the patients.)

Different moral theories will of course approach questions about the moral status of euthanasia in different ways, though some of these theories will end up with the same conclusions. This essay considers euthanasia from the perspective of just one moral theory. The theory is rule-utilitarianism. Rule-utilitarianism assesses possible rules in terms of their expected utility. It then tells us to follow the rules with the greatest expected utility. (Expected utility is calculated by multiplying the utility of each possible outcome by the probability that it will occur.)

In the next section, I explain what the term "utility" means. Then I outline another utilitarian theory – act-utilitarianism. I do this in order to contrast rule-utilitarianism with this perhaps more familiar theory. I then outline the distinctions between different kinds of euthanasia. The final sections of the paper consider the various factors that would go into a rule–utilitarian decision about euthanasia.

2. Utility

A moral theory is utilitarian if and only if it assesses acts and/or rules in terms of nothing but their utility. Classical utilitarianism took "utility" to refer to the well-being of sentient creatures. And classical utilitarianism took the well-being of sentient creatures to consist in pleasure and the absence of pain (Bentham, 1823; Mill, 1863; Sidgwick, 1874). On this view, people's level of well-being is determined *solely* by how much pleasure and pain they experience.

If anything is desirable for its own sake, pleasure is. But most utilitarians now think that pleasure, even if construed as widely as possible, is not the *only* thing desirable in itself, and pain not the *only* thing undesirable in itself (Moore, 1903, ch. 6; Hare, 1981, 101ff; Parfit, 1984, appendix I; Griffin, 1986, Part One; Goodin, 1991, p. 244; Harsanyi, 1993). Utilitarians can think that things that are desirable for their own sake include not only pleasure but also important knowledge, friendship, autonomy, achievement, and so on. Indeed, many utilitarians now construe utility just as the fulfillment of desire or the satisfaction of preferences, with relatively few restrictions on what the desires or preferences are for.

One reason most utilitarians have moved away from a version of utilitarianism that focuses exclusively on pleasure has to do with knowledge. Many of us care about certain things over and above the pleasure they typically bring, and one of these things is knowing the important truths (e.g. about the nature of the universe and about oneself), even if not knowing the truth would be more pleasant for us. Bliss isn't everything – for example, if purchased at the cost of ignorance. To be sure, knowledge does not always constitute a more significant addition to well-being than does pleasure. But sometimes it does.

People also care about autonomy, by which I mean control over one's own life. Many of us would be willing to trade away some pleasure for the sake of an increase in autonomy. Again, this is not to say that even a tiny increase in autonomy is more important than a great deal of pleasure; rather, the point is that pleasure is not always more important to our well-being than autonomy. Neither value is always more important than the other.

I agree with such convictions. Knowledge, autonomy, and other things can be beneficial to us, can increase our well-being, over and beyond whatever pleasure they directly or indirectly bring us. I shall presuppose this in what follows.

I shall also follow conventional philosophical opinion in supposing that it is possible to be in such a bad condition that death would be a welcome release. Severe pain can be unremitting, and indeed so overpowering that the person experiencing it can think of nothing else. If the rest of my life would consist of nothing but excruciating physical pain, then I might be better off dead. Indeed, if the rest of my life would consist wholly of intense psychological suffering, I'd be better off dead. Of course, we may argue about where to draw the line between being better off dead and being better off alive (Mitchell, 1995). But it seems deeply unreasonable to insist that there are never any instances of patients who would be better off dead.

Now, what about *divinely bestowed* benefits and harms? Most utilitarians, and all utilitarian writers of our era, have written as if there were no rewards or punishments granted by a god or gods. This is not to say that all utilitarians have been atheists. In fact, many have been religious believers (perhaps most notably, Bishop Berkeley, 1712). Nor would *any* utilitarians – theistic or agnostic or atheistic – hold that a person's religious beliefs are completely irrelevant to the morality of how he or she is treated. For any utilitarian would recognize that people's religious beliefs can have an effect on what brings them pleasure and on what preferences they form. So utilitarianism will favor, for example, freedom of religion and even the neutrality of the state with respect to religion.[1] But while utilitarians can think that people's religious beliefs are often relevant to moral argument about how these people should be treated, modern utilitarians eschew basing any moral argument on the *truth* of any religious belief. And this prohibition on assuming the truth of any religious belief applies to the belief that there are divinely bestowed benefits and harms.

That said, we must also note that utilitarianism is also often said to assume a god's-eye point of view. The main respect in which this is true is that the utilitarian approach prescribes a totally impartial calculation of well-being. To be more specific, in the calculation of utility, benefits or harms to any one person are to count for just as much as the same amount of benefit or harm to anyone else – that is, count the same without regard to race, religion, gender, social class, or the like.

It is a mistake to think that utilitarians hold that what benefits more people is *necessarily* better than what benefits fewer. Utilitarians focus on the greatest aggregate good. What results in the greatest aggregate good is sometimes not what benefits the majority. This is because the benefits to each of the smaller number may be large and the benefits to each of the greater number small. And large benefits to each of a minority can add up to more than small benefits to each of a majority. Thus, utilitarians will favor what benefits the minority if (but only if) what benefits the minority results in the greatest good overall.

On the other hand, many philosophers have pointed out that utilitarianism gives no intrinsic weight to how equally or fairly benefits are distributed. I myself accept that this is an important potential problem with utilitarianism. But because I don't think these worries about distribution are relevant to euthanasia, I shall ignore them in this paper.

3.   Act-utilitarianism

The most direct and most discussed form of utilitarianism is act-utilitarianism. There are different versions of this theory. One version holds that an act is right if and only if its *actual consequences* would contain at least as much utility as those of any other act open to the agent. Another version claims that an act is right if and only if its *expected* utility is at least as great as that of any alternative.

But there are many familiar counter-examples to both versions of act-utilitarianism. Some of these counter-examples have to do with moral prohibitions. For example, both versions of act-utilitarianism imply that killing an innocent person, or stealing, or breaking a promise would be morally right if the expected and actual utility of the act would be greater, even if just slightly greater, than that of any alternative act. We might think that normally prohibited acts could be right in very rare circumstances in which doing such acts is the only way to prevent something much worse. But we don't think such acts are permissible when the expected and actual utility of such an act would be only slightly greater than that of complying with the prohibition.

Another problem with act-utilitarianism is that it seems unreasonably demanding, requiring acts of self-sacrifice that seem beyond the call of duty. Think how much a middle-class individual in a relatively affluent country would have to give to CARE or Oxfam before further sacrifices on her part would constitute a larger loss to her than the benefit to the starving that CARE or Oxfam would produce with that contribution. Making sacrifices for strangers up to the point that act–utilitarianism requires would be saintly. But morality, most of us think, does not *require* sainthood.

4. Rule-utilitarianism

Rule-utilitarianism differs from act–utilitarianism in that rule–utilitarianism does *not* assess each act solely by its utility. Rather, rule–utilitarianism assesses acts in terms of rules, and rules in terms of their utility. Rule-utilitarianism holds that an act is morally permissible if and only if the rules with the greatest expected utility would allow it. The expected utility of rules is a matter of the utility of their "general" internalization, i.e., internalization by the overwhelming majority. For a code of rules to be internalized is for people to believe these rules justified and to be disposed to act and react in accordance with them. Assume I have internalized a rule against killing people against their will. If this assumption is correct, I will (a) think this kind of act wrong, (b) be disposed not to do this kind of act, and (c) be disposed to react negatively to those who I think have done it.

To say that rule-utilitarians focus on the consequences of the general internalization of rules does not mean that they consider only rules that existing people *already* accept. Rather, the question rule-utilitarians ask about each possible code is what the effects on utility would be of the code's being successfully inculcated in people who had no prior moral beliefs or attitudes. At least in principle, the code of rules best from a utilitarian point of view might be very different from those now accepted in any given society. (For developments of this sort of theory, see Brandt, 1963; 1967; 1979, part two; 1988; Harsanyi, 1982; Johnson, 1991; Barrow, 1991; Hooker, 1995; 1998.)

The intuitive attractions of rule-utilitarianism become clear as we notice the ways in which this theory seems superior to act–utilitarianism. For unlike act-utilitarianism, rule-utilitarianism agrees with common conviction that individual acts of murder, torture, promise-breaking, and so on can be wrong even when they produce somewhat more good than their omission would produce. For the general internalization of rules prohibiting murder, torture, promise-breaking, and the like would clearly result in more good than the general internalization of rules that did not prohibit such acts. Thus, on the rule-utilitarian criterion of moral permissibility, acts of murder, torture, and so on, can be impermissible even in rare cases where they really would produce better consequences than any alternative act.

Likewise, rule-utilitarianism will not require the level of self-sacrifice act-utilitarianism requires. For, crudely, rule-utilitarianism approaches this problem by asking how much each relatively well-off person would have to contribute in order for there to be enough to overcome world hunger and severe poverty. If *the overwhelming majority of the world's relatively well-off* made regular contributions to the most efficient famine relief organizations, no one would have to make severe self-sacrifices. Thus, rule-utilitarianism is not excessively demanding (Hooker, 1991; 1998; cf. Carson, 1991).

The advantages of rule-utilitarianism over act-utilitarianism are often construed as utilitarian advantages. In other words, some philosophers have argued that rule-utilitarianism will in fact produce more utility than act-utilitarianism (Brandt, 1979, pp. 271–7; Harsanyi, 1982, pp. 56–61; and Johnson, 1991, especially chs 3, 4, 9; Haslett, 1994, p. 21; but compare Hooker, 1995, section III). I am *not* running that argument. Instead, I am merely pointing out that rule-utilitarianism seems to have implications that are more intuitively acceptable than those of act-utilitarianism (Brandt, 1963; 1967).

5. Kinds of Euthanasia

We need to distinguish three different kinds of euthanasia, or rather three different ways euthanasia can be related to the will of the person killed. Suppose I ask you to either kill me or let me die should my medical condition get so bad that I am delirious and won't recover. If you then comply with my request, we have what is commonly called *voluntary euthanasia*. It is voluntary because the person killed asked that this be done.

Now suppose that I slip into an irreversible coma without ever telling anyone whether I wanted to be killed in such circumstances. If I am then killed or let die, we have what is commonly called *non-voluntary euthanasia*. The distinguishing characteristic of non-voluntary euthanasia is that it is euthanasia on someone who did not express a desire on the matter.

But what if I do express a desire not to be killed no matter how bad my condition gets? Then killing me would constitute what is called *involuntary euthanasia*. Quite apart from its moral status, involuntary euthanasia can seem puzzling. To be euthanasia, it must be done for the good of the person killed. Yet if the person concerned expresses a desire that it not be done, how can it be done for this person's own good? Well, involuntary euthanasia may be morally wrong (we will discuss why in a moment), but we must start by acknowledging that people are *not always* in the best position to know what is best for themselves. Someone could be mistaken even about whether he or she would be better off dead than alive in a certain state. And other people could think that the person in front of them had made just this kind of mistake. If they not only thought this but also were motivated to do what was best for this person, they might contemplate euthanasia. What they would then be contemplating would be involuntary euthanasia.

Another important distinction is the distinction between active and passive euthanasia. Active euthanasia involves actively killing someone out of a concern for that person's own good. Passive euthanasia involves passing up opportunities to prevent the death of someone out of concern for that person's own good.

The distinction between active and passive euthanasia cuts across the distinction between voluntary, non-voluntary, and involuntary euthanasia. In other words, either with my consent, or without knowing what my wishes are or were, or against my wishes, you might kill me. Likewise, either with my consent, or without knowing what my wishes are or were, or against my wishes, you might pass up an opportunity to keep me from dying. Thus we have:

Active Voluntary Euthanasia
Active Non-voluntary Euthanasia
Active Involuntary Euthanasia

Passive Voluntary Euthanasia
Passive Non-voluntary Euthanasia
Passive Involuntary Euthanasia

6. Law and Morality

We also need to distinguish between questions about law and questions about moral rightness, permissibility, and wrongness. Utilitarians, as well as moral philosophers of many other stripes, can think that there may be some moral requirements that the law should not try to enforce. A relatively uncontroversial example concerns the moral requirement forbidding breaking verbal promises to your spouse. There may be good utilitarian reasons for not bothering the law with such matters – to police the give and take of such relationships might be too difficult and too invasive. This isn't to deny that breaking verbal promises to spouses is usually morally wrong, only that the law shouldn't poke its nose into this matter.

So, initially at least, there is the potential for divergence in what the rule–utilitarian says about the law and about morality. There is less scope for this on rule–utilitarianism, however, than there is on some other theories. For both in the case of law and in the case of morality, the first thing rule–utilitarianism considers is the consequences of our *collective* compliance with rules. (See Mill, 1863, ch. 5.)

With respect to euthanasia, rule–utilitarianism is especially likely to take the same line on law as it does on morality. That is, if rule–utilitarians think that people's being allowed in certain circumstances to kill or let die would have generally good consequences, then they will think such acts are *morally* allowed in the specified circumstances. They will also think the *law* should allow them in the specified conditions. And if they think the consequences would be generally bad, then they will think morality does, and the law should, prohibit the acts in question.

Thus, in the following discussion of the rule–utilitarian approach to euthanasia, I will focus on just one realm and assume that the other follows suit. The realm on which I shall focus is the law. The question, then, is: what kinds of euthanasia (if any) should the law allow?

7. The Potential Benefits of Euthanasia

Perhaps the most obvious potential benefit of permitting euthanasia is that it could be used to prevent the unnecessary elongation of the suffering experienced by many terminally ill people and their families. What about painkilling drugs? Some kinds of pain cannot be eliminated with drugs, or at least not with drugs that leave the patient conscious and mentally coherent. And in addition to physical agony, there is often overwhelming emotional suffering for the patient, and derivatively for friends and family in attendance. All this could be shortened if euthanasia were allowed.

To the extent that the point is speedy termination of physical and emotional suffering, active rather than passive euthanasia can seem desirable. For passive euthanasia would often involve a slow and painful death, whereas active euthanasia could end the patient's suffering immediately. There may, however, be especially large costs associated with allowing active euthanasia. I shall consider these later.

Another advantage of permitting euthanasia – and again the advantage is even more pronounced in the case of permitting active euthanasia – concerns resource allocation. The resources, both economic and human, that are now devoted to keeping alive people who have incurable and debilitating diseases could often more cost-effectively be devoted to curing people of curable diseases, or to funding preventive medicine, or even just to feeding the starving. What I mean by saying that the change in resource allocation would be more cost effective is that this would increase average life-expectancy and quality of life.

For utilitarians who count personal autonomy as a value over and above whatever feelings of satisfaction it brings and frustration it prevents, there is an additional consideration. It is that *voluntary* euthanasia must increase personal autonomy, in that it gives people some control over *when* their lives end. And if active voluntary euthanasia were allowed, this would give people some control over *how* their lives end. Concern for people's autonomy obviously counts only in favor of *voluntary* euthanasia. It is irrelevant to the discussion of non-voluntary euthanasia of any kind, and opposes involuntary euthanasia of any kind.

8. The Potential Harms of Allowing Involuntary Euthanasia

A law permitting active *involuntary* euthanasia is likely to be strongly opposed by rule-utilitarians for other reasons as well. One such reason is that many people would be scared away from hospitals and doctors if they thought that they might be killed against their wishes. I cannot imagine how allowing involuntary euthanasia could generate benefits large enough even to begin to offset this loss. The last thing a public policy should do is scare people away from trained medical experts. A related point is that allowing involuntary euthanasia would terrify many people taken to a hospital while unconscious. Imagine waking up to find that you had been taken to a hospital where people can, *against your wishes*, kill you, as long as they (claim to) think this would be best for you.

Furthermore, to allow the killing of innocent people against their wishes would be difficult to square with other moral prohibitions of supreme importance. In particular, the general feeling of abhorrence for the killing of innocent people against their wishes is, as Hobbes (1651) insisted, the bedrock of social existence. Without communal acceptance of that prohibition, life would be precarious and insecure. No law should be passed which genuinely threatens to undermine people's commitment to the general prohibition on killing the innocent against their wishes.

At this point someone might say, "Ah, but we can distinguish between killing innocent people against their wishes but *for their own good*, and killing them *for some other reason*." True, we can make that distinction. But is it a distinction whose enshrinement in law would be felicitous? No, again because people would not feel secure in a society where they might be, against their wishes, killed for their own good.

These points about insecurity add up to a very persuasive rule-utilitarian argument against permitting *active* involuntary euthanasia. But do they count against *passive* involuntary euthanasia? In the case of passive euthanasia, there isn't such a risk that people will stay away from doctors and hospitals for fear of being made worse off than they are already. Suppose you had a serious illness and found yourself in a society where active involuntary euthanasia was neither permitted nor practiced, but passive involuntary euthanasia was permitted and practiced. Then, you would not need fear that going to the hospital would get you killed against your wishes. But you might worry that the doctors or hospital would, against your wishes, pass up opportunities to prolong your life. Yet you probably wouldn't live longer if you stayed out of the hospitals. Indeed, if you were under the care of a doctor, you would probably suffer less. Thus, you have less to lose by going into the hospital in a society were passive involuntary euthanasia is permitted than you do in a society were active involuntary euthanasia is permitted. If passive involuntary euthanasia only were legally and morally permitted, the consequence would not be that everyone who thought they had or might have a fatal disease would avoid doctors. So the disadvantages of allowing passive involuntary euthanasia are clearly less than the disadvantages of allowing active involuntary euthanasia.

The disadvantages of allowing passive involuntary euthanasia may nevertheless be enough to convince rule–utilitarians to oppose it. Utilitarians have long argued that their doctrine is generally anti-paternalistic (Mill, 1859). Grown-up human beings are generally the ones who know which of the ways their lives might unfold would be best for themselves, because they are generally the ones who know best their own aspirations, tastes, talents, sensitivities, vulnerabilities, etc. Of course there are general exceptions – e.g. people with permanent or temporary mental impairments. But, by and large, people are the best guardians of their own well-being.

As noted at the very end of the previous section, rule-utilitarians can have another reason for opposing involuntary euthanasia, passive just as much as active. This reason comes from the idea that autonomy is an important component of well-being. Indeed, this seems to be the strongest rule-utilitarian reason for disallowing passive involuntary euthanasia.

9. The Potential Harms of Allowing Voluntary and Non-voluntary Euthanasia

Turn now to the harms that voluntary and non-voluntary euthanasia might involve. Suppose the doctors tell Jones he has disease X. This disease almost immediately produces excruciating pain, dementia, and then death. Jones asks to be killed, or at least allowed to die, before the pain gets too severe. The doctors comply with Jones's wishes. Later, however, a post-mortem reveals that he didn't have disease X at all, but instead some curable condition. As this story illustrates, euthanasia can inappropriately take a life after a mistaken diagnosis.

And yet how often do medical experts misdiagnose a condition as a terminal illness when it isn't? And how wise is it now to go against expert medical opinion? And are there ways of minimizing the risk of the doctors' acting on misdiagnoses? Euthanasia could be restricted to cases where three independent medical experts – and I mean *real* experts – make the same diagnosis. With such a restriction, the worry about misdiagnoses seems overblown.

But closely associated with the point that doctors sometimes misdiagnose someone's condition is the point that doctors are sometimes wrong about what will happen to someone whose condition is correctly diagnosed. Suppose the doctors rightly believe that there is now no treatment known to prevent the disease some people have from bringing acute pain followed by a painful death. But a cure or more effective pain block might soon be discovered. If people are killed or allowed to die today and the medical breakthrough comes tomorrow, euthanasia will have amounted to giving up on those people too soon – with obviously tragic results.

However, again restrictions could be put in place to prevent the losses envisaged. One restriction could specify that euthanasia is completely out of the question until someone is fairly near the final stages of a disease, where new cures or treatments are very unlikely to be able to change the fatal path of the disease. (And one way of approximating this restriction would be to allow *passive* but not *active* euthanasia. But this seems an unnecessarily crude way of ensuring that people aren't killed before they could be cured.) Another restriction could specify that euthanasia be out of the question until after a thorough and disinterested investigation into the state of research on cures and treatments. When this investigation shows that the development of a cure or new treatment is a *realistic* possibility during the life of the patient, euthanasia would again be prohibited.

From a rule-utilitarian perspective, the points about mistaken diagnoses and future cures seem to mandate restrictions on when euthanasia would be considered, but they don't preclude euthanasia altogether – even active euthanasia. Something else, however, does threaten to add up to a conclusive case against allowing any kind of euthanasia, especially active euthanasia. This is the danger of intentional abuse.

Think of the people who might be in a hurry for some ill person's death. Some of these might be people who have to care for the ill person, or pay for the care and medicine the person receives. Another group, often overlapping with the first, is made up of the person's heirs. The heirs might even include the hospital in which the person lies. With so much to gain from an early death of the ill person, these people might easily convince themselves that the ill person would be better off dead. If it were left up to these people, many ill people might unnecessarily be killed or allowed to die. A system which allowed this would both result in unnecessary deaths and terrify the ill.

Even without these points about intentional abuse, rule-utilitarians have enough reason to disallow *involuntary* euthanasia. But do the points about intentional abuse add up to a compelling rule-utilitarian argument against *voluntary* euthanasia? Certainly they necessitate severe restrictions at the very least.

One sensible restriction would be that, with a single exception, the people given authority in the decision about euthanasia must be people with nothing to gain directly or indirectly from their decision. The single exception is of course the patient himself or herself. But heirs and those who stand to benefit from heirs could be denied any authoritative say in the matter. Thus if a hospital is itself an heir, its doctors could be precluded from having any role, including that of making or confirming the diagnosis. The law could be designed to ensure that the decision to perform euthanasia on a patient is made by people focusing on the wishes and best interests of the patient. Of course the patient may ask loved and trusted others, including heirs, what they think. But the law could insist that doctors with nothing to gain certify that the patient really would be, at the time of the euthanasia, better off dead. And the law could insist that the patient be asked on a number of occasions whether he or she really does want euthanasia. Patients will need the law to protect them against coercive pressures by family and other heirs (not that the law can ever entirely protect us from our families).

Focus now on *non-voluntary* euthanasia – euthanasia performed on people who have not indicated whether or not they want their lives to be prolonged. Some patients have never been in a position to give or withhold consent. This is true of individuals who never developed sufficient rationality to be capable of consenting. Any euthanasia performed on such people will be non-voluntary euthanasia. Rule-utilitarians might well think that a cost–benefit analysis of this sort of euthanasia would end up supporting it – given that the law is designed so as to ensure that the people making the final decision are experts with nothing but the best interests of the patient in mind.

But what about patients who were once rational enough to consent or withhold consent but never made their wishes known and now are incapable of prolonged rationality? Rule-utilitarians can think that to allow euthanasia would be best here too. A more important question, however, might be whether the law should require adults now in possession of their faculties to indicate formally whether they want euthanasia if they become terminally ill and are plagued by acute pain which can be mollified only by severely mind-altering drugs. It might actually increase autonomy to get people to decide whether they would want euthanasia for themselves before they are unable to make such decisions. Obviously, the system for doing this would have to involve informing people what they were being asked to decide about. It would also need to be designed so as to make sure people's decisions are their own, i.e., not the result of some sort of coercion. Furthermore, ideally the system would annually ask for confirmation that people haven't changed their minds (there could be a box to check on annual tax returns).

Some people will think that, no matter how clever rule-utilitarians are in adding safeguards to a law allowing euthanasia, there will be at least a few people who manage to subvert it, and so abuses will occur. Rule-utilitarians may grant this, but then ask how many such abuses there would be. Would there be so many abuses as to terrify the general population? These questions are ones of sociology and social psychology. If the answers to them are that the abuses would be extremely rare and the general population would not become paranoid over them, then a rule-utilitarian might be willing to accept that, if some abuse is inevitable, this cost of a few abuses would be worth the benefits of allowing euthanasia.

There is one more potential harm associated with allowing voluntary and non-voluntary *active* euthanasia. To allow them might seem to be a step onto a slippery slope to a very undesirable position. As I have already noted, the prohibition on killing the innocent against their will is an immensely valuable, indeed essential, prohibition. Would people slide away from a firm commitment to that prohibition if they came to accept the permissibility of voluntary and non-voluntary active euthanasia?

This question, like the question of whether the level of intentional abuse would be unacceptably high, is really one for social scientists. Any answers to such questions have to be partly speculative. We ought to know by now that large social, economic, or legal changes often have unexpected results. We cannot be *certain* what the results of allowing voluntary and non-voluntary active euthanasia would be. Rule-utilitarians have to make a judgment based on what they think the probabilities are. And with respect to the sorts of changes under discussion here, reasonable people can disagree about the probabilities. Thus, reasonable rule-utilitarians can come down on different sides about the permissibility of voluntary and non-voluntary active euthanasia.

But even where there is reasonable disagreement, there can be a right answer. The success of voluntary active euthanasia in Holland suggests that the worries about abuse and slippery slopes can be answered. Of course any law allowing euthanasia (especially, active euthanasia) would need to be very carefully drafted. And the law would have to be rigorously policed, to prevent abuse. Though not certain, I am confident these things could be done. And, undeniably, the benefits, mainly in terms of the decrease of suffering and the increase in autonomy, are potentially enormous.[2]

Notes

1 Though utilitarians may also favor some restrictions on this. I remember that in Tennessee in the 1960s there was a Christian sect using rattlesnakes in church services. As I remember, the government stopped the practice after it led to a few deaths, and the courts upheld that freedom of religion did not extend to persuading people to submit to lethal dangers during worship. These decisions could well be supported on utilitarian grounds.

2 Thanks to John Cottingham, Hugh LaFollette and Andrew Leggett for helpful comments on an earlier draft of this chapter.

References

Barrow, R., *Utilitarianism* (London: Edward Elgar, 1991).

Bentham, J., *An Introduction to the Principles of Morals and Legislation* (1823).

Berkeley, G., *Passive Obedience, or the Christian Doctrine of Not Resisting the Supreme Power, Proved and Vindicated upon the Principles of the Law of Nature* (1712).

Brandt, R. B., "Toward a Credible Form of Utilitarianism," *Morality and the Language of Conduct*, ed. H.-N. Castañeda and G. Nakhnikian (Detroit: Wayne State University Press, 1963), pp. 107–43.

——, "Some Merits of One Form of Rule-Utilitarianism," *University of Colorado Studies in Philosophy* (1967), pp. 39–65. Reprinted in Brandt, 1992, pp. 111–36.

——, *A Theory of the Good and the Right* (Oxford: Clarendon Press, 1979).

——, "Fairness to Indirect Optimific Theories in Ethics," *Ethics*, 98 (1988), 341–60. Reprinted in Brandt, 1992, pp. 137–57.

——, *Morality, Utilitarianism, and Rights* (New York: Cambridge University Press, 1992).

Carson, T., "A Note on Hooker's 'Rule Consequentialism'," *Mind*, 100 (1991), 117–21.

Goodin, R., "Utility and the Good," *A Companion to Ethics*, ed. P. Singer (Oxford: Blackwell, 1991), pp. 241–8.

Griffin, J., *Well-Being: Its Meaning, Measurement and Moral Importance* (Oxford: Clarendon Press, 1986).

Hare, R. M., *Moral Thinking* (Oxford: Clarendon Press, 1981).

Harsanyi, J., "Morality and the Theory of Rational Behaviour," *Utilitarianism and Beyond*, ed. A. Sen and B. Williams (Cambridge: Cambridge University Press, 1982), pp. 39–62.

——, "Expectation Effects, Individual Utilities, and Rational Desires," in Hooker, 1993, pp. 115–26.

Haslett, D. W., *Capitalism with Morality* (Oxford: Clarendon Press, 1994).

Hobbes, T., *Leviathan* (1651).

Hooker, B., "Rule-Consequentialism and Demandingness: Reply to Carson," *Mind*, 100 (1991), 270–76.

——(ed.), *Rationality, Rules, and Utility: New Essays on the Moral Philosophy of Richard Brandt* (Boulder, CO: Westview Press, 1993).

——, "Rule-Consequentialism, Incoherence, Fairness," *Proceedings of the Aristotelian Society*, 95 (1995), 19–35.

——, *The Ideal Code for the Real World: A Rule-Consequentialist Theory of Morality* (forthcoming 1998).

Johnson, C., *Moral Legislation* (New York: Cambridge University Press, 1991).

Mill, J. S., *On Liberty* (1859).

——, *Utilitarianism* (1863).

Mitchell, D., "The Importance of Being Important: Euthanasia and Critical Interests in Dworkin's *Life's Dominion*," *Utilitas*, 7 (1995), 301–14.

Moore, G. E., *Principia Ethica* (Cambridge: Cambridge University Press, 1903).

Parfit, D., *Reasons and Persons* (Oxford: Clarendon Press, 1984).

Sidgwick, H., *The Methods of Ethics* (London: Macmillan, 1874; 7th edition, 1907).

4

Dying at the Right Time: Reflections on (Un)assisted Suicide

John Hardwig

Let us begin with two observations about chronic illness and death:

1. Death does not always come at the right time. We are all aware of the tragedies involved when death comes too soon. We are afraid that it might come too soon for us. By contrast, we may sometimes be tempted to deny that death can come too late – wouldn't everyone want to live longer? But in our more sober moments, most of us know perfectly well that death can come too late.

2. Discussions of death and dying usually proceed as if death came only to hermits – or others who are all alone. But most of the time, death is a death in the family. We are connected to family and loved ones. We are sustained by these connections. They are a major part of what makes life worth living for most of us.

Because of these connections, when death comes too soon, the tragedy is often two-fold: a tragedy both for the person who is now dead and for those of us to whom she was connected. We grieve both for our loved one who is gone and for ourselves who have lost her. On one hand, there is the unrealized good that life would have been for the dead person herself – what she could have become, what she could have experienced, what she wanted for herself. On the other, there is the contribution she would have made to others and the ways *their* lives would have been enriched by her.

We are less familiar with the idea that death can come too late. But here, too, the tragedy can be two-fold. Death can come too late because of what living on means to the person herself. There are times when someone does not (or would not) want to live like this, times when she believes she would be better off dead. At times like these, suicide or assisted suicide becomes a perfectly rational choice, perhaps even the best available option for her. We are then forced to ask, "Does someone have a right to die?" Assisted suicide may then be an act of compassion, no more than relieving her misery.

There are also, sadly, times when death comes too late because *others* – family and loved ones – would be better off if someone were dead. (Better off overall, despite the loss of a loved one.) Since lives are deeply intertwined, the lives of the rest of the family can be dragged down, impoverished, compromised, perhaps even ruined because of what they must go through if she lives on. When death comes too late because of the effect of someone's life on her loved ones, we are, I think, forced to ask, "Can someone have a duty to die?" Suicide may then be an attempt to do what is right; it may be the only loving thing to do. Assisted suicide would then be helping someone do the right thing.

Most professional ethicists – philosophers, theologians, and bioethicists – react with horror at the very idea of a duty to die. Many of them even argue that euthanasia and physician-assisted suicide should not be legalized because then some people might somehow get the idea that they have a duty to die. To this way of thinking, someone who got that idea could only be the victim of vicious social pressure or perverse moral reasoning. But when I ask my classes for examples of times when death would come too late, one of the first conditions students always mention is: "when I become a burden to my family." I think there is more moral wisdom here than in the dismay of these ethicists.

Death does not always come at the right time. I believe there are conditions under which I would prefer not to live, situations in which I would be better off dead. But I am also absolutely convinced that I may one day face a duty or responsibility to die. In fact, as I will explain later, I think many of us will one day have this duty.

To my way of thinking, the really serious questions relating to euthanasia and assisted suicide are: Who would be better off dead? Who has a duty to die? *When* is the right time to die? And if my life should be over, who should kill me?[1] However, I know that others find much of what I have said here surprising, shocking, even morally offensive. So before turning to these questions that I want us to think about, I need to explain why I think someone can be better off dead and why someone can have a duty to die. (The explanation of the latter will have to be longer, since it is by far the less familiar and more controversial idea.)

When Someone would be Better Off Dead

Others have discussed euthanasia or physician-assisted suicide when the patient would be better off dead.[2] Here I wish to emphasize two points often omitted from discussion: (1) Unrelieved pain is not the only reason someone would be better off dead. (2) Someone can be better off dead even if she has no terminal illness.

(1)   If we think about it for even a little while, most of us can come up with a list of conditions under which we believe we would rather be dead than continue to live. Severe and unrelieved pain is one item on that list. Permanent unconsciousness may be another. Dementia so severe that we no longer recognize ourselves or our loved ones is yet another. There are some people who prefer not to live with quadriplegia. A future shaped by severe deterioration (such as that which accompanies MS, ALS, AIDS, or Huntington's chorea) is a future that some people prefer not to live out.

(Our lists would be different because our lives and values are different. The fact that some people would not or do not want to live with quadriplegia or AIDS, for example, does not mean that others should not want to live like that, much less that their lives are not worth living. That is very important. The point here is that almost all of us can make a list of conditions under which we would rather not live, and that uncontrolled pain is not the only item on most of our lists.)

Focusing the discussion of euthanasia and assisted suicide on pain ignores the many other varieties of suffering that often accompany chronic illness and dying: dehumanization, loss of independence, loss of control, a sense of meaninglessness or purposelessness, loss of mental capabilities, loss of mobility, disorientation and confusion, sorrow over the impact of one's illness and death on one's family, loss of ability even to recognize loved ones, and more. Often, these causes of suffering are compounded by the awareness that the future will be even bleaker. Unrelieved pain is simply not the only condition under which death is preferable to life, nor the only legitimate reason for a desire to end one's life.

(2)   In cases of terminal illness, death eventually offers the dying person relief from all her suffering. Consequently, things can be even worse when there is *NO* terminal illness, for then there is no end in sight. Both pain and suffering are often much worse when they are *not* accompanied by a terminal illness. People with progressive dementia, for example, often suffer much more if they are otherwise quite healthy. I personally know several old people who would be delighted to learn that they have a terminal illness. They feel they have lived long enough – long enough to have outlived all their loved ones and all sense of a purpose for living. For them, even daily existence is much worse because there is no end in sight.

Discussions of euthanasia and physician-assisted suicide cannot, then, be restricted to those with unrelieved pain and terminal illness. We must also consider requests made by those who have no untreatable pain and no terminal illness. Often, their case for relief is even more compelling.

Sometimes, a refusal of medical treatment will be enough to bring relief. Competent adults who are suffering from an illness have a well-established moral and legal right to decline any form of medical treatment, including life-prolonging medical treatment. Family members who must make medical decisions for incompetent people also have the right to refuse any form of medical treatment on their behalf, so long as they are acting in accordance with the known wishes or best interests of their loved one. No form of medical treatment is compulsory when someone would be better off dead.[3]

But those who would be better off dead do not always have terminal illnesses; they will not always need any form of medical treatment, not even medically-supplied food and water. The right to refuse medical treatment will not help these people. Moreover, death due to untreated illness can be agonizingly slow, dehumanizing, painful, and very costly, both in financial and emotional terms. It is often very hard. Refusing medical treatment simply will not always ensure a dignified, peaceful, timely death. We would not be having a national debate about physician-assisted suicide and euthanasia if refusal of medical treatment were always enough to lead to a reasonably good death. When death comes too late, we may need to do more than refuse medical treatment.

Religion and Ending a Life

Some people can easily see that there are people who would be better off dead. But they still cannot accept suicide or physician-assisted suicide because they believe we have a duty to God not to take our own lives. For them, human life is a gift from God and it remains a gift no matter how much pain and suffering it may bring. It is a sin or an offense against God, the giver of life, to take your own life or to help someone else end theirs. Such believers may also feel that no one should be allowed to end their lives – every life is a gift from God, even the lives of those who do not believe that this is so.

I do not understand this position for two reasons. First, it involves the assumption that it is possible to take a human life (our own or someone else's) *before* God wants it ended, but we cannot possibly preserve it *after* God wants it ended. For if we do not make that assumption, we face *two* dangers – the danger that we are prolonging human life beyond its divine purpose, as well as the danger that we are ending it too soon. If we can extend life longer than God intends, suicide and physician-assisted suicide may be more in accord with God's wishes than attempts to preserve that life.

I can understand the view that everyone dies at precisely the right time, the moment God intends. If that is so, people who commit suicide or who are intentionally killed by physicians also die at precisely the moment God wants them to die. I can also understand the view that we can take life before God wants it ended but we can also extend life longer than God wants it prolonged. But I cannot make sense of the view that we can end a human life too soon but not preserve it too long. Surely, God has given us both abilities or neither one.

I also have a second difficulty with this religious objection to suicide, assisted suicide and euthanasia. Suppose there is a right time to die, a divinely-ordained moment when God wants each life to end. Even so, we have no right to assume that God will "take my life" when it's the right time for me to die. In fact, we cannot even assume that God will send a terminal illness that will kill me at the right time. There could be a religious test – God may want me to take my own life and the question is whether I will meet this final challenge. Or a God who loves me might see that I would benefit spiritually from the process of coming to the conclusion that I should end my own life and then preparing to take it. That might be a fitting ending for me, the culminating step in my spiritual growth or development.

In short, a God not totally obsessed with the sheer quantity of our lives may well have purposes for us that are incompatible with longer life – even if we want to live longer. So, I think we should not believe that we always have a duty to God not to take our lives or to assist others in ending theirs. God may want me to step up and assume the responsibility for ending my own life or for seeing that someone else's suffering is ended. This observation leads to our next question: Can there be a responsibility or duty to die?

The Duty to Die

I may well one day have a duty to die, a duty most likely to arise out of my connections with my family and loved ones.[4] Sometimes preserving my life can only devastate the lives of those who care about me. I do not believe I am idiosyncratic, morbid or morally perverse in believing this. I am trying to take steps to prepare myself mentally and spiritually to make sure that I will be able to take my life if I should one day have such a duty. I need to prepare myself; it might be a very difficult thing for me to do.

Our individualistic fantasy about ourselves sometimes leads us to imagine that lives are separate and unconnected, or that they could be so if we chose. If lives were unconnected, then things that happen in my life would not or need not affect others. And if others were not (much) affected by my life, I would have no duty to consider the impact of my life on others. I would then be morally free to choose whatever life and death I prefer for myself. I certainly would have no duty to die when I would prefer to live.

Most discussions of assisted suicide and euthanasia implicitly share this individualistic fantasy: they just ignore the fact that people are connected and lives intertwined. As a result, they approach issues of life or death as if the only person affected is the one who lives or dies. They mistakenly assume the pivotal issue is simply whether the person *herself* prefers not to live like this and whether *she herself* would be better off dead.[5]

But this is morally obtuse. The fact is we are not a race of hermits – most of us are connected to family and loved ones. We prefer it that way. We would not want to be all alone, especially when we are seriously ill, as we age, and when we are dying. But being with others is not all benefits and pleasures; it brings responsibilities, as well. For then what happens to us and the choices we make can dramatically affect the lives of our loved ones. It is these connections that can, tragically, generate obligations to die, as continuing to live takes too much of a toll on the lives of those connected to us.[6]

The lives of our loved ones can, we know, be seriously compromised by caring for us. The burdens of providing care or even just supervision 24 hours a day, 7 days a week, are often overwhelming.[7] But it can also be emotionally devastating simply to be married to a spouse who is increasingly distant, uncommunicative, unresponsive, foreign and unreachable. A local newspaper tells the story of a woman with Alzheimer's who came running into her den screaming: "That man's trying to have sex with me! He's trying to have sex with me! Who *IS* that man?!" That man was her loving husband of more than 40 years who had devoted the past 10 years of his life to caring for her (Smith, 1995). How terrible that experience must have been for her. But how terrible those years must be for him, too.

We must also acknowledge that the lives of our loved ones can also be devastated just by having to *pay* for health care for us. A recent study documented the financial aspects of caring for a dying member of a family. Only those who had illnesses severe enough to give them less than a 50 percent chance to live six more months were included in this study. When these patients survived their initial hospitalization and were discharged, about one-third required considerable caregiving from their families; in 20 percent of cases a family member had to quit work or make some other major lifestyle change; almost one-third of these families lost all of their savings, and just under 30 percent lost a major source of income (Covinski et al., 1994).

A chronic illness or debilitating injury in a family is a misfortune. It is, most often, nobody's fault; no one is responsible for this illness or injury. But then we face choices about how we will respond to this misfortune. That is where the responsibility comes in and fault can arise. Those of us with families and loved ones always have a responsibility not to make selfish or self-centered decisions about our lives. We should not do just what we want or just what is best for *us*. Often, we should choose in light of what is best for all concerned.

Our families and loved ones have obligations to stand by us and to support us through debilitating illness and death. They must be prepared to make sacrifices to respond to an illness in the family. We are well aware of this responsibility and most families meet it rather well. In fact, families deliver more than 80 percent of the long-term care in the US, almost always at great personal cost.

But responsibility in a family is not a one-way street. When we become seriously ill or debilitated, we too may have to make sacrifices. There are limits to what we can ask our loved ones to do to support us, even in sickness. There are limits to what they should be prepared to do for us – only rarely and for a limited period of time should they do all they can for us.

Somehow we forget that sick, infirm, and dying adults also have obligations to their families and loved ones: a responsibility, for example, to try to protect the lives of loved ones from serious threats or greatly impoverished quality, or an obligation to avoid making choices that will jeopardize or seriously compromise their futures. Our obligations to our loved ones must be taken into consideration in making decisions about the end of life. It is out of these responsibilities that a duty to die can develop.

Tragically, sometimes the best thing you can do for your loved ones is to remove yourself from their lives. And the only way you can do that may be to remove yourself from existence. This is not a happy thought. Yet we must recognize that suicides and requests for assisted suicide may be motivated by love. Sometimes, it's simply the only loving thing to do.

Who has a Duty to Die?

Sometimes it is clear when someone has a duty to die. But more often, not. *WHO* has a duty to die? And *WHEN* – under what conditions? To my mind, these are the right questions, the questions we should be asking. Many of us may one day badly need answers to just these questions.

But I cannot supply answers here, for two reasons. In the first place, answers will have to be very particular and individualized . . . to the person, to the situation of her family, to the relationships within the family, etc. There will not be simple answers that apply to everyone.

Secondly and perhaps even more importantly, those of us with family and loved ones should not define our duties unilaterally. Especially not a decision about a duty to die. It would be isolating and distance-creating for me to decide without consulting them what is too much of a burden for my loved ones to bear. That way of deciding about my moral duties is not only atomistic, it also treats my family and loved ones paternalistically – *THEY* must be allowed to speak for themselves about the burdens my life imposes on them and how they feel about bearing those burdens.

I believe in family decision making. Important decisions for those whose lives are inter-woven should be made *together*, in a family discussion. Granted, a conversation about whether I have a duty to die would often be a tremendously difficult conversation. The temptations to be dishonest in such conversations could be enormous. Nevertheless, if we can, we should have just such an agonizing discussion – partly because it will act as a check on the information, perceptions and reasoning of all of us; but perhaps even more import-antly, because it affirms our connectedness at a critical juncture in our lives. Honest talk about difficult matters almost always strengthens relationships.

But many families seem to be unable to talk about death at all, much less a duty to die. Certainly most families could not have this discussion all at once, in one sitting. It might well take a number of discussions to be able to approach this topic. But even if talking about death is impossible, there are always behavioral clues – about your caregiver's tiredness, physical condition, health, prevailing mood, anxiety, outlook, over-all well-being etc. And families unable to talk about death can often talk about those clues. There can be conver-sations about how the caregiver is feeling, about finances, about tensions within the family resulting from the illness, about concerns for the future. Deciding whether you have a duty to die based on these behavioral clues and conversation about them is more relational than deciding on your own about how burdensome this relationship and care must be.[8]

For these two reasons, I cannot say when someone has a duty to die. But I can suggest a few ideas for discussion of this question. I present them here without much elaboration or explanation.

1. There is more duty to die when prolonging your life will impose greater burdens – emotional burdens, caregiving, disruption of life plans, and, yes, financial hardship – on your family and loved ones. This is the fundamental insight underlying a duty to die.
2. There is greater duty to die if your loved ones' lives have already been difficult or impoverished (not just financially) – if they have had only a small share of the good things that life has to offer.
3. There is more duty to die to the extent that your loved ones have already made great contributions – perhaps even sacrifices – to make your life a good one. Especially if you have not made similar sacrifices for their well-being.
4. There is more duty to die to the extent that you have *already* lived a full and rich life. You have already had a full share of the good things life offers.

5. Even if you have not lived a full and rich life, there is more duty to die as you grow older. As we become older, there is a diminishing chance that we will be able to make the changes that would now be required to turn our lives around. As we age, we will also be giving up less by giving up our lives, if only because we will sacrifice fewer years of life.

6. There is less duty to die to the extent that you can make a good adjustment to your illness or handicapping condition, for a good adjustment means that smaller sacrifice will be required of loved ones and there is more compensating interaction for them. (However, we must also recognize that some diseases – Alzheimer's or Huntington's chorea – will eventually take their toll on your loved ones no matter how courageously, resolutely, even cheerfully you manage to face that illness.)

7. There is more duty to die to the extent that the part of you that is loved will soon be gone or seriously compromised. There is also more duty to die when you are no longer capable of giving love. Part of the horror of Alzheimer's or Huntington's, again, is that it destroys the person we loved, leaving a stranger and eventually only a shell behind. By contrast, someone can be seriously debilitated and yet clearly still the person we love.

In an old person, "I am not ready to die yet" does not excuse one from a duty to die. To have reached the age of, say, 80 years without being ready to die is itself a moral failing, the sign of a life out of touch with life's basic realities.

A duty to die seems very harsh, and sometimes it is. But if I really do care for my family, a duty to protect their lives will often be accompanied by a deep desire to do so. I will normally *want* to protect those I love. This is not only my duty, it is also my desire. In fact, I can easily imagine wanting to spare my loved ones the burden of my existence more than I want anything else.

If I should be Dead, Who should Kill Me?

We need to reframe our discussions of euthanasia and physician-assisted suicide. For we must recognize that pleas for assisted suicide are sometimes requests for relief from pain and suffering, sometimes requests for help in fulfilling one's obligations, and sometimes both. If I should be dead for either of these reasons, who should kill me?

Like a responsible life, a responsible death requires that we think about our choices in the context of the web of relationships of love and care that surround us. We must be sensitive to the suffering as well as the joys we cause others, to the hardships as well as the benefits we create for them. So, when we ask, "Who should kill me?", we must remember that we are asking for a death that will reduce the suffering of *both* me and my family as much as possible. We are searching for the best ending, not only for me, but for *everyone concerned* – in the preparation for death, the moment of death, and afterwards, in the memory and on-going lives of loved ones and family.

Although we could perhaps define a new profession to assist in suicides – euthanasians?? – there are now really only three answers to the question, "Who should kill me?" (1) I should kill myself. (2) A loved one or family member should kill me. (3) A physician should kill me. I will consider these three possibilities. I will call these *unassisted* suicide, *family-* assisted suicide, and *physician-*assisted suicide.

(1)   *Unassisted suicide: I should kill myself*

The basic intuition here is that each of us should take responsibility for herself. I am primarily the one who wants relief from my pain and suffering, or it is fundamentally my own duty to die and *I* should be the one to do my duty. Moreover, intentionally ending a life is a very messy business – a heavy, difficult thing for anyone to have to do. If possible, I should not drag others into it. Often, I think, this is the right idea – I should be the one to kill myself.

But not always. We must remember that some people are physically unable to do so – they are too weak or incapacitated to commit suicide without assistance. Less persuasive perhaps are those who just can't bring themselves to do it. Without the assistance of someone, many lack the know-how or means to end their lives in a peaceful, dignified fashion. Finally, many attempted suicides – even serious attempts at suicide – fail or result in terrible deaths. Those who have worked in hospitals are familiar with suicide attempts that leave people with permanent brain damage or their faces shot off. There are also fairly common stories of people eating their own vomit after throwing up the medicine they hoped would end their lives.

Even more importantly, if I must be the one to kill myself, that may force me to take my life earlier than would otherwise be necessary. I cannot wait until I become physically debilitated or mentally incompetent, for then it will be too late for me to kill myself. I might be able to live quite comfortably for a couple more years, if I could count on someone else to take my life later. But if I cannot count on help from anyone, I will feel pressure to kill myself when unavoidable suffering for myself or my loved ones appears on the horizon, instead of waiting until it actually arrives.

Finally, many suicides are isolating – I can't die with my loved ones around me if I am planning to use carbon monoxide from automobile exhaust to end my life. For most of us, a meaningful end of life requires an affirmation of our connection with loved ones and so we do not want to die alone.

The social taboo against ending your own life promotes another type of isolation. The secrecy preceding many suicides creates conditions for misunderstanding or lack of under-standing on the part of loved ones – Why did she do it? Why didn't I see that she was going to kill herself? Why didn't I do something to help? Secrecy and lack of understanding often compound the suffering family and loved ones go through when someone ends their life.

Unassisted suicide – I should kill myself – is not always the answer. Perhaps, then, my loved ones should participate in ending my life.

(2) *Family-assisted suicide: A member of my family should kill me*

At times, we may have a moral obligation to help others end their lives, especially those close to us, those we love. I can easily imagine myself having an obligation to help a loved one end her life and I hope my family will come to my assistance if my death does not come at the right time. What should be the role of family and loved ones in ending a life?

They might help me get information about reliable and peaceful methods for ending my life. They might also be able to help me get the drugs I need, if that is the method I choose. Like most people, I would also very much want my loved ones to participate, at least to the extent of being there with me when I die.

For reasons already mentioned, I would hope I could talk over my plans with my loved ones, both to reassure myself and check on my reasoning, and also to help them work through some of the emotional reaction to my death. Some people believe that families should not be involved in decisions about the end of life because they are in the grips of powerful emotions that lead to wildly inappropriate decisions. (A familiar example is the difficulty many families have in deciding to withdraw medical treatment even when their loved one is clearly dying.) Families will always be gripped by powerful emotions over a death in the family. But appropriate decisions are not necessarily unemotional or uninvolved decisions. And I think inappropriate reactions or decisions stem largely from lack of the discussions I advocate or from an attempt to compress them into one, brief, pressure-packed conversation, often in the uncomfortable setting of a hospital.

So, a good death for all concerned would usually involve my family – the preparation for taking my life, at least, would be family-assisted. My loved ones should know; they should, if possible, understand. They should not be surprised. Hopefully my loved ones could come to agree with my decision. They should have had time to come to terms with the fact that I plan to end my life. Indeed, I should have helped them begin to deal emotionally with my death. All that would help to ease their suffering and also my concern about how my death will affect them. It would reaffirm our connectedness. It would also comfort me greatly to feel that I am understood and known by my loved ones as I take this important step.

More than this I cannot ask of them, for two related reasons. The first is that actually killing a loved one would usually be extremely difficult. It would be a searing and unforgettable experience that could well prove very hard to live with afterwards. Killing a loved one at her request *might* leave you feeling relieved – it could give you the satisfaction of feeling you had done what needed to be done. In cases of extreme debility or great suffering, family-assisted suicide might be experienced as a loving act of kindness, compassion and mercy. It would still be very hard. Much harder would be killing me because I have a duty to die, a duty to die because my life is too great a burden *for the one who now must kill me*. I cannot ask that of someone I love. I fear that they would suffer too much from taking my life.

I might be wrong about this, however. It might be that, though difficult indeed, being killed lovingly and with your consent by your spouse or your child would be a final testimonial to a solid, trusting, and caring relationship. There might be no more powerful reaffirmation of the strength of your relationship, even in the face of death. The traumatic experience for the family members who assist in the suicide might be a healing experience for them, as well. We know so little about family-assisted suicide.

But in any case, there is also a second reason: I cannot ask for family-assisted suicide because it is not legally protected – a loved one who killed me might well be charged with murder. I could not ask my family to subject themselves to such a risk. Moreover, unlike physician-assisted suicide, we would not want to legalize family-assisted suicide. The lives of families are just too complex and too often laced with strong negative emotions – guilt, resentment, hatred, anger, desire for revenge. Family members also often have multiple motives stemming from deeply conflicting interests. As a result, there would be just too many cases in which family-assisted suicide would be indistinguishable from murder.[9]

Finally, family members may also fail. They also may lack know-how or bungle the job. Caught in the compelling emotions of grief and/or guilt, they may be unable to end a life that should be ended.

All this notwithstanding, family-assisted suicide may be the right choice, especially if physician-assisted suicide is unavailable. But should it be unavailable?

(3) *Physician-assisted suicide: My doctor should kill me*

There are, then, important difficulties with both unassisted suicide and family-assisted suicide. These difficulties are arguments for physician-assisted suicide and euthanasia. If my death comes too late, a physician is often the best candidate to kill me . . . or at the very least, to help me kill myself.

Perhaps the main argument for physician-assisted suicide grows out of the physician's extensive knowledge of disease and of dying. If it is a medical condition that leads me to contemplate ending my life, a key question for determining *when* or even *whether* I should end my life is: What is the prognosis? To what extent can my illness be treated or at least alleviated? How long do I have to live with my condition? How much worse will it get and how soon? What will life with that condition be like for me and my family? Few besides physicians possess all this critical information. I will be more likely to reach the right decision at the right time if a trusted physician is in on my plans to end my life.

A related point is physicians' knowledge of and access to drugs. Few of us know what drugs to take and in what amounts without the advice of a physician. Often, only a physician will know what to do to ensure that I do not vomit up the "suicide pill" or what to do if it fails. Physicians also have a monopoly on access to drugs. If my physician were more closely involved in the process, I could be more certain – and thus reassured – that my death will be peaceful and dignified, a death that permits reaffirmation of my connections with family and close friends.

A second argument for physician-assisted suicide grows out of physicians' greater experience with death and dying. Physicians know what to expect; those of us outside the health professions often do not. Granted, few physicians nowadays will know *me* and *my* family. For this reason, physicians should seldom make unilateral decisions about assisted suicide. Still, most physicians could provide a rich source of information about death and about strategies to minimize the trauma, suffering, and agony of a death, both for the dying person and for the family.

Thirdly, physician-assisted suicide does not carry the same social stigma that unassisted suicide carries and physicians are not exposed to the legal risks involved in family-assisted suicide. Although many physicians are unwilling to take *any* risks to help someone end her life, there is really very little legal risk in physician-assisted suicide, especially if the family is in agreement. Physicians are also not morally censored the way family members would be for ending a life.

Finally, physicians ought not to abandon their patients, certainly not at the moment of death. Much has been made of the possibility that Americans would lose their trust in physicians if they knew that physicians sometimes kill. But many of us would trust our physicians *more* if we knew that we could count on them when death is needed or required (Quill and Cassell, 1995).

We have come, then, by a very round-about route to another argument for *physician-*assisted suicide. Often it is simply better – safer, more secure, more peaceful, less emotionally-damaging for others – than unassisted suicide or family-assisted suicide. If physicians refuse to assist or are not permitted to do so, families and seriously ill people will be forced back on their own resources. And many deaths will be much worse than they need to be. When death comes too late, a physician will often be the best candidate to kill me.

And yet, physician-assisted suicide is not always the answer, either. Many physicians take themselves to be sworn to preserve human life in all its forms. Also, many people want doctors who are sworn not to kill, for fear that physicians might start making presumptuous, single-handed decisions about when death comes too late. Moreover, in a time when most people lack a significant personal relationship with their physicians, physician-assisted suicide is often a death that is remote, isolated, disconnected from the relationships that gave meaning to life. It is not always the best death. At times, then, family-assisted suicide and unassisted suicide remain the best answers.

Conclusion

We have a long cultural tradition of attempts to deal with the problems of death that comes too soon. Modern medicine, with its dramatic high-tech rescue attempts in the emergency room and the intensive care unit, is our society's attempt to prevent death from coming too soon. On a more personal level, we are bombarded with advice about ways to avoid a death that would be too soon – sooner than we wished, before we were ready for it.

We have much less cultural wisdom about the problems of a death that comes too late. It is almost as if we had spent all our cultural resources trying to avoid deaths that come too soon, only to find that we then had no resources left to help us when death comes too late.

Deaths that come too soon usually raise no difficult moral problems, however difficult they may be in other ways. Such deaths normally occur despite our best attempts to prevent them. "There's nothing more we can do," we say to the dying person, her family, and ourselves. And there is ethical solace in this, despite the tragedy of the death itself. We admit our failure. But our failure is not a moral failure – we did what we could.

Deaths that come too late are ethically much more troubling. They call on us to assume responsibility – to make difficult decisions and to do difficult things. We can try to hide from this responsibility by claiming that we should always try to prolong life, no matter what. Or by not deciding anything. But we know that not to decide is to decide. And it is very often just not clear what we should do. The weight of life-or-death decision pushes down upon us.

The recognition that the lives of members of families are intertwined makes the moral problems of a death that comes too late even more difficult. For they deprive us of our easiest and most comfortable answers – "it's up to the individual," "whatever the patient wants." But we do know that measures to improve or lengthen one life often compromise the quality of the lives of those to whom that person is connected.

So, we are morally troubled by deaths that come too late. We don't know what to do. Beyond that, the whole idea is unfamiliar to us. But in other societies – primarily technologically primitive and especially nomadic societies – almost everyone knew that death could come too late. People in those cultures knew that if they managed to live long enough, death would come too late and they would have to do something about it. They were prepared by their cultural traditions to find meaning in death and to do what needed to be done.

We have largely lost those traditions. Perhaps we have supposed that our wealth and technological sophistication have purchased exemption for us from any need to worry about living too long, from any need to live less than every minute we enjoy living. For a while it looked that way. But we must now face the fact: deaths that come too late are only the other side of our miraculous life-prolonging modern medicine.

We have so far avoided looking at this dark side of our medical triumphs. Our modern medicine saves many lives and enables us to live longer. That is wonderful, indeed. But it thereby also enables more of us to survive longer than we are able to care for ourselves, longer than we know what to do with ourselves, longer than we even *are* ourselves. Moreover, if further medical advances wipe out many of today's "killer diseases" – cancers, AIDS, heart attacks, etc. – then most of us will one day find that death is coming too late. And there will be a very common duty to die.

Our political system and health-care reform (in the USA) are also moving in a direction that will put many more of us in the position of having a duty to die. Measures designed to control costs (for the government, and for employers who pay for retirement benefits and health insurance) often switch the burdens of care onto families. We are dismantling our welfare system and attempting to shift the costs of long-term health care onto families. One important consequence of these measures is that more of us will one day find ourselves a burden to our families and loved ones.[10]

Finally, we ourselves make choices that increase the odds that death will come too late. Patient autonomy gives us the right to make choices about our own medical treatment. We use that right to opt again and again for life-prolonging treatment – even when we have chronic illnesses, when we are debilitated, and as we begin to die. Despite this autonomy, we may feel we really have no choice, perhaps because we are unable to find meaning in death or to bring our lives to a meaningful close. But if we repeatedly opt for life-prolonging treatment, we thereby also increase the chances that death will come too late. This is the cost of patient autonomy, combined with powerful life-prolonging medical technology and inability to give meaning to death or even to accept it.

Death is very difficult for us. I have tried here to speak about it in plain language; I have used hard words and harsh tones to try to make us attend to troubling realities. We may question the arguments and conclusions of this paper. We should do so. But this questioning must not be fueled by denial or lead to evasion. For one thing seems very clear: we had better start learning how to deal with the problems of a death that comes too late. Some day, many of us will find that we should be dead or that one of our loved ones should be dead. What should we do then? We had better prepare ourselves – mentally, morally, culturally, spiritually, and socially. For many of us, if we are to die at the right time, it will be up to us.

Notes

I get by with a little help from my friends. I wish to thank Hilde and Jim Nelson, Mary English, Tom Townsend, and Hugh LaFollette for helpful comments on earlier versions of this paper. And more: these friends have been my companions and guides throughout my attempt to think through the meaning of love and family in our lives.

1 A note about language: I will be using "responsibility," "obligation," and "duty" interchangeably, despite significant differences in meaning. I generally use the word "duty" because it strikes me as a hard word for what can be a hard reality. (It also echoes Richard Lamm's famous statement: "Old people have a duty to die and get out of the way to give the next generation a chance.") Similarly, I use "kill" despite its connotations of destruction because I think we should not attempt to soften what we are doing. War and capital punishment have already taught us too much about how to talk in sweet and attractive ways about what we do. So I have resisted talking about "bringing my life to a close" and similar expressions. I have tried to use the plain, hard words.

2 There are many articles on this topic. Perhaps the classic article is Rachels (1975). It has been widely reprinted. A good collection of articles can be found in the *Journal of Medicine and Philosophy* (June 1993), which was devoted to the topic, "Legal Euthanasia: Ethical Issues in an Era of Legalized Aid in Dying." Recent anthologies include Beauchamp (1996) and Moreno (1995).

3 A few states in the US – currently (January 1996) New York, Missouri, Delaware, and Michigan – do require that family members be able to supply "clear and convincing evidence" that withdrawal of treatment is what their loved one would' have wanted. This can be hard to prove. So it is especially important for those who live in these states to put their wishes about the kind of treatment they would want (if they become unable to decide for themselves) in writing. For information about the laws that apply in your state, write to Choice in Dying, 200 Varick Street, New York, NY 10014, or call them at 212–366–5540.

4 I believe we may also have a duty to ourselves to die, or a duty to the environment or a duty to the next generation to die. But I think for most of us, the strongest duty to die comes from our connections to family and loved ones, and this is the only source of a duty to die that I will consider here.

5 Most bioethicists advocate a "patient-centered ethics" – an ethics which claims only the patient's interests should be considered in making medical treatment decisions. Most health-care professionals have been trained to accept this ethic and to see themselves as patient advocates. I have argued elsewhere that a patient-centered ethic is deeply mistaken. See Hardwig (1989) and Hardwig (1993).

6 I am considering only mentally competent adults. I do not think those who have never been competent – young children and those with severe retardation – can have moral duties. I do not know whether formerly competent people – e.g., those who have become severely demented – can still have moral duties. But if they cannot, I think some of us may face a duty to die even sooner – before we lose our moral agency.

7 A good account of the burdens of caregiving can be found in Brody (1990). To a large extent, care of the elderly is a women's issue. Most people who live to be 75 or older are women. But care for the elderly is almost always provided by women, as well – even when the person who needs care is the husband's parent.

8 Ultimately, in cases of deep and unresolvable disagreement between yourself and your loved ones, you may have to act on *your own* conception of your duty and your own conception of the burdens on them. But that is a fall-back position to resort to

when the better, more relational ways of arriving at a belief in a duty to die fail or are unavailable.

9 Although this is true, we also need to re-think our reactions to the motives of the family. Because lives are intertwined, if someone "wants Dad to be dead" and is relieved when he dies, this does not necessarily mean that she did not genuinely love him. Or that she is greedy, selfish, or self-centered. Her relief may stem from awareness of his suffering. It could also grow out of recognition of the sad fact that his life was destroying the lives of other family members whom she also loved.

10 Perhaps a more generous political system and a more equitable health-care system could counteract the trend toward a more and more common duty to die. For now, at least, we could pay for the care of those who would otherwise be a burden on their families. If we were prepared to do so, far fewer would face a duty to die. But we (in the US, at least) are not prepared to pay. Moreover, as medical advances enable more people to live longer (though also in various states of disability), it may be that the costs would overwhelm any society. Even if we could afford it, we should not continue to try to buy our way out of the problems of deaths that come too late. We would be foolish to devote all our resources to creating a society dedicated solely to helping all of us live just as long as we want.

References

Beauchamp, T. L. (ed.), *Intending Death: The Ethics of Assisted Suicide and Euthanasia* (Englewood Cliffs, NJ: Prentice-Hall, 1996).

Brody, Elaine M., *Women in the Middle: Their Parent-Care Years* (New York: Springer, 1990).

Covinsky, Kenneth E., Goldman, Less, et al., "The impact of serious illness on patients' families," *Journal of the American Medical Association*, 272 (1994), 1839–44.

Hardwig, John, "What about the family?," *Hastings Center Report*, 20 (March/April 1989), 5–10.

——, "The problem of proxies with interests of their own: toward a better theory of proxy

decisions," *Journal of Clinical Ethics*, 4 (Spring 1993), 20–27.

Moreno, Jonathan (ed.), *Arguing Euthanasia* (New York: Simon & Schuster, 1995).

Quill, Timothy E. and Cassell, Christine K., "Nonabandonment: a central obligation for physicians," *Annals of Internal Medicine*, 122 (1995), 368–74.

Rachels, James, "Active and passive euthanasia," *New England Journal of Medicine*, 292 (1975), 78–80.

Smith, V. P. [pen name of Val Prendergrast], "At home with Alzheimer's," *Knoxville Metro Pulse*, 5, no. 30 (1995), 7, 27.

Abortion

The public debate over abortion has intensified ever since the Supreme Court's decision in *Roe* v. *Wade* (410 U.S. 113, 1973). Advocates on each side of the debate often hint that we must select between two stark options: "Pro–life" and "Pro–choice." Strong pro-life advocates claim that abortion is immoral (except perhaps in a few cases) because the fetus is a human from the moment of conception, while strong pro-choice advocates claim women must have the legal right to determine what happens "in and to their bodies."

The authors in this section argue that although the common characterization of the debate is partly right, it also grossly over-simplifies the issues. For instance, both Warren, who defends abortion, and Marquis, who criticizes it, reject central tenets of each position, tenets that undergird the common characterization. Pro-lifers claim that abortion is immoral simply because the fetus is a human being. Warren and Marquis respond that calling a creature a "human being" is simply to identify its biological pedigree, not its moral status. On the other hand, pro-choicers claim that abortion should be legal simply because women want the right to choose what happens in their bodies. Warren and Marquis respond that this position illicitly ignores the status of the fetus. If the fetus has full moral status, they claim, then there is something profoundly wrong with abortion.

Although they agree that the pro-lifer's emphasis on biological humanity is misplaced, they disagree about how to determine if a creature has full moral status. Warren argues that "human being" is merely a biological description or category that is morally irrelevant. The proper moral question is not: "Is it human?" but "Is it a person?" Some creatures that are biologically human are not persons. For instance, we may say of someone in a persistent vegetative state: "She's a vegetable," thereby indicating that the body is no longer the person we once knew. Moreover, some non-humans might be persons. For instance, were we to find intelligent, caring, and sensitive aliens elsewhere in the universe, we should conclude they have full moral status.

Marquis accepts Warren's core insight: humanity is not the proper criterion of moral status. He does not, however, think the category of "person" does the moral trick. He proposes a different criterion. He claims we must first ascertain what it is about normal adult human beings that makes it wrong to kill them, and then determine if fetuses have those same characteristics. Killing a normal adult is wrong, he argues, because the adult is thereby deprived of a valuable future. Since fetuses have a *future like ours*, they, too, have moral status. Specifically, they have a right to life.

The need to establish criteria of moral status is not restricted to the issue of abortion. It is also essential for determining the proper treatment of non-human ANIMALS and of the ENVIRONMENT. Marquis explicitly mentions this connection between abortion and the treatment of animals. Since some animals have a *future like ours*, we should not kill them without compelling reasons. He thinks most people will share this conviction, and therefore be more inclined to adopt his proposed criterion of moral status. Marquis here employs a common strategy of philosophical argumentation, a strategy built upon the criterion of consistency, discussed in THEORIZING ABOUT ETHICS. Philosophers often support their arguments by showing how their views are consistent with widely held views on other moral topics.

Thomson challenges Marquis's and Warren's claim that we can settle the question of abortion by determining the moral status of the fetus. Even if we knew the fetus had full moral status and a serious right to life, abortion would still be morally – and should be legally – permissible. The central issue, according to Thomson, is not the status of the fetus, but whether the woman has an obligation to that fetus. Thomson claims a woman is not morally obliged to sustain the life of the fetus, not even if she became pregnant intentionally. We have obligations to help others only if we explicitly agree to help them. Since women do not explicitly agree to carry their fetuses to term, then they have no such obligations toward them.

We see here the nub of a broader moral question: under what circumstances (and how much) are we obligated to help others? If a fetus has a serious right to life, is that sufficient to show that a woman must carry it to term? Must she do so even if she is seriously inconvenienced, or if her health is threatened? Determining the origin, scope, and nature of our obligations to others is a theoretical question that pervades every practical ethical issue. For instance, I did not explicitly agree to feed starving children in China (WORLD HUNGER). Yet some people claim I should contribute to programs that help feed them. I did not explicitly agree to support, through my taxes, programs to care for needy children and aging seniors in my country (ECONOMIC JUSTICE). Yet many people claim I should financially assist them, at least through my taxes and perhaps through private contributions. This is a fundamental question of morality. Are we obligated only to help people we have specifically agreed to help? Or are we obligated to help others in need, simply because they are in need?

A different way of discussing these questions is to ask about the limits of morality, a question discussed explicitly by Williams and Rachels (FAMILY AND FRIENDS). Not surprisingly, these questions about the nature and limits of our obligations are complicated by the *act/omission* distinction, mentioned in the previous introduction. Why? Everyone acknowledges we have obligations not to harm others directly (even perfect strangers), even if fulfilling that obligation comes at considerable personal cost, and even if we did not explicitly assume these obligations. Thus, when people talk about the limits of morality, they are usually talking about the limits of our obligations to help or benefit others – not our obligations not to cause harm.

Additionally, the issue is not only what we, morally, *should* do, but what the state can properly force us to do, or prohibit us from doing. In the abortion debate, I frequently hear people say "Although I personally am opposed to abortion, I am also opposed to legally forbidding them." Even if you think this is an untenable position in the abortion debate, sometimes it is surely an appropriate response. There are many actions we morally should not do, but which the state should not punish. For instance, surely it is wrong to be callous to a grieving parent. However, most people would not want to see such callousness made a crime.

The problem, of course, is that although many people might agree that callousness should not be criminalized, other cases are not so clear. How can we reasonably distinguish actions that are immoral, but should not be criminalized, from actions that are immoral (e.g., murder), and should be criminalized? Clearly this is a central question of PUNISH-MENT. In slightly different form, it is also the question discussed by Hunt in "On Improving People by Political Means" (VIRTUES). Hunt acknowledges the importance of political authority. However, he argues that there are limits on whether and how we should use that authority to try to make people more virtuous.

Finally, we must be careful not to ask "loaded" moral questions that preclude viable answers. For instance, in asking someone "Have you stopped beating your wife?" I imply that he has, in fact, been beating his wife. That has been assumed, not established. Similarly, some ways of asking moral questions may inappropriately exclude sensible solutions. This can easily happen if people are ignorant of the history of and relevant empirical information about the issue under discussion. Rothman, for instance, argues that many people tend to ask the wrong questions about abortion. They ask about the status of the fetus, yet ignore the most important element, namely, women's lived experiences.

The preoccupation with the "fetus" began in the early 1960s, she argues, with the publication of a series of pictures of a fetus *in utero*. These pictures, first published in *Life*, do not show the woman in whose body the fetus resides. Thus, those who see the pictures are prone to conceive of the fetus as an entity, totally separate from and independent of the woman. The woman is transformed into a container for the fetus, rather than the creator of the fetus. This effectively eliminates the woman, her experiences, and her interests, from the debate about the morality of abortion.

Further Reading

Beckwith, F. 1993: *Politically Correct Death: Answering Arguments for Abortion Rights*. Grand Rapids, MI: Baker Books.

Feinberg, J. (ed.) 1973: *The Problem of Abortion*. Belmont, CA: Wadsworth.

Feldman, F. 1992: *Confrontations with the Reaper: A Philosophical Study of the Nature and Value of Death*. New York: Oxford University Press.

Pojman, L. and Beckwith, F. 1994: *The Abortion Controversy: A Reader*. Boston: Jones and Bartlett.

Rothman, B. 1989: *Recreating Motherhood: Ideology and Technology in a Patriarchal Society*. New York: W. W. Norton.

Steinbock, B. 1992: *Life Before Birth: The Moral and Legal Status of Embryos and Fetuses*. New York: Oxford University Press.

5

A Defense of Abortion

Judith Jarvis Thomson

Most opposition to abortion relies on the premise that the fetus is a human being, a person, from the moment of conception. The premise is argued for, but, as I think, not well. Take, for example, the most common argument. We are asked to notice that the development of a human being from conception through birth into childhood is continuous; then it is said that to draw a line, to choose a point in this development and say "before this point the thing is not a person, after this point it is a person" is to make an arbitrary choice, a choice for which in the nature of things no good reason can be given. It is concluded that the fetus is, or anyway we had better say it is, a person from the moment of conception. But this conclusion does not follow. Similar things might be said about the development of an acorn into an oak tree, and it does not follow that acorns are oak trees or that we had better say they are. Arguments of this form are sometimes called "slippery slope arguments" – the phrase is perhaps self-explanatory – and it is dismaying that opponents of abortion rely on them so heavily and uncritically.

I am inclined to agree, however, that the prospects for "drawing a line" in the development of the fetus look dim. I am inclined to think also that we shall probably have to agree that the fetus has already become a human person well before birth. Indeed, it comes as a surprise when one first learns how early in its life it begins to acquire human characteristics. By the tenth week, for example, it already has a face, arms and legs, fingers and toes; it has internal organs, and brain activity is detectable.[1] On the other hand, I think that the premise is false, that the fetus is not a person from the moment of conception. A newly fertilized ovum, a newly implanted clump of cells, is no more a person than an acorn is an oak tree. But I shall not discuss any of this. For it seems to me to be of great interest to ask what happens if, for the sake of argument, we allow the premise. How, precisely, are we supposed to get from there to the conclusion that abortion is morally impermissible? Opponents of abortion commonly spend most of their time establishing that the fetus is a person, and

Abridged from Judith Jarvis Thomson, "A Defense of Abortion," *Philosophy & Public Affairs*, 1, no. 1 (Fall 1971). Copyright © 1971 by Princeton University Press. Excerpts, pp. 47–62, 65–66, reprinted by permission of Princeton University Press.

hardly any time explaining the step from there to the impermissibility of abortion. Perhaps they think the step too simple and obvious to require much comment. Or perhaps instead they are simply being economical in argument. Many of those who defend abortion rely on the premise that the fetus is not a person, but only a bit of tissue that will become a person at birth; and why pay out more arguments than you have to? Whatever the explanation, I suggest that the step they take is neither easy nor obvious, that it calls for closer examination than it is commonly given, and that when we do give it this closer examination we shall feel inclined to reject it.

I propose, then, that we grant that the fetus is a person from the moment of conception. How does the argument go from here? Something like this, I take it. Every person has a right to life. So the fetus has a right to life. No doubt the mother has a right to decide what shall happen in and to her body; everyone would grant that. But surely a person's right to life is stronger and more stringent than the mother's right to decide what happens in and to her body, and so outweighs it. So the fetus may not be killed; an abortion may not be performed.

It sounds plausible. But now let me ask you to imagine this. You wake up in the morning and find yourself back to back in bed with an unconscious violinist. A famous unconscious violinist. He has been found to have a fatal kidney ailment, and the Society of Music Lovers has canvassed all the available medical records and found that you alone have the right blood type to help. They have therefore kidnapped you, and last night the violinist's circulatory system was plugged into yours, so that your kidneys can be used to extract poisons from his blood as well as your own. The director of the hospital now tells you, "Look, we're sorry the Society of Music Lovers did this to you – we would never have permitted it if we had known. But still, they did it, and the violinist now is plugged into you. To unplug you would be to kill him. But never mind, it's only for nine months. By then he will have recovered from his ailment, and can safely be unplugged from you." Is it morally incumbent on you to accede to this situation? No doubt it would be very nice of you if you did, a great kindness. But do you *have* to accede to it? What if it were not nine months, but nine years? Or longer still? What if the director of the hospital says, "Tough luck, I agree, but you've now got to stay in bed, with the violinist plugged into you, for the rest of your life. Because remember this. All persons have a right to life, and violinists are persons. Granted you have a right to decide what happens in and to your body, but a person's right to life outweighs your right to decide what happens in and to your body. So you cannot ever be unplugged from him." I imagine you would regard this as outrageous, which suggests that something really is wrong with that plausible-sounding argument I mentioned a moment ago.

In this case, of course, you were kidnapped; you didn't volunteer for the operation that plugged the violinist into your kidneys. Can those who oppose abortion on the ground I mentioned make an exception for a pregnancy due to rape? Certainly. They can say that persons have a right to life only if they didn't come into existence because of rape; or they can say that all persons have a right to life, but that some have less of a right to life than others, in particular, that those who came into existence because of rape have less. But these statements have a rather unpleasant sound. Surely the question of whether you have a right to life at all, or how much of it you have, shouldn't turn on the question of whether or not you are the product of a rape. And in fact the people who oppose abortion on the ground I mentioned do not make this distinction, and hence do not make an exception in case of rape.

Nor do they make an exception for a case in which the mother has to spend the nine months of her pregnancy in bed. They would agree that would be a great pity, and hard on the mother; but all the same, all persons have a right to life, the fetus is a person, and so on.

I suspect, in fact, that they would not make an exception for a case in which, miraculously enough, the pregnancy went on for nine years, or even the rest of the mother's life.

Some won't even make an exception for a case in which continuation of the pregnancy is likely to shorten the mother's life; they regard abortion as impermissible even to save the mother's life. Such cases are nowadays very rare, and many opponents of abortion do not accept this extreme view. All the same, it is a good place to begin: a number of points of interest come out in respect to it.

1. Let us call the view that abortion is impermissible even to save the mother's life "the extreme view." I want to suggest first that it does not issue from the argument I mentioned earlier without the addition of some fairly powerful premises. Suppose a woman has become pregnant, and now learns that she has a cardiac condition such that she will die if she carries the baby to term. What may be done for her? The fetus, being a person, has a right to life, but as the mother is a person too, so has she a right to life. Presumably they have an equal right to life. How is it supposed to come out that an abortion may not be performed? If mother and child have an equal right to life, shouldn't we perhaps flip a coin? Or should we add to the mother's right to life her right to decide what happens in and to her body, which everybody seems to be ready to grant – the sum of her rights now outweighing the fetus's right to life?

The most familiar argument here is the following. We are told that performing the abortion would be directly killing[2] the child, whereas doing nothing would not be killing the mother, but only letting her die. Moreover, in killing the child, one would be killing an innocent person, for the child has committed no crime, and is not aiming at his mother's death. And then there are a variety of ways in which this might be continued. (1) But as directly killing an innocent person is always and absolutely impermissible, an abortion may not be performed. Or, (2) as directly killing an innocent person is murder, and murder is always and absolutely impermissible, an abortion may not be performed.[3] Or, (3) as one's duty to refrain from directly killing an innocent person is more stringent than one's duty to keep a person from dying, an abortion may not be performed. Or, (4) if one's only options are directly killing an innocent person or letting a person die, one must prefer letting the person die, and thus an abortion may not be performed.[4]

Some people seem to have thought that these are not further premises which must be added if the conclusion is to be reached, but that they follow from the very fact that an innocent person has a right to life.[5] But this seems to me to be a mistake, and perhaps the simplest way to show this is to bring out that while we must certainly grant that innocent persons have a right to life, the theses in (1) through (4) are all false. Take (2), for example. If directly killing an innocent person is murder, and thus is impermissible, then the mother's directly killing the innocent person inside her is murder, and thus is impermissible. But it cannot seriously be thought to be murder if the mother performs an abortion on herself to save her life. It cannot seriously be said that she *must* refrain, that she *must* sit passively by and wait for her death. Let us look again at the case of you and the violinist. There you are, in bed with the violinist, and the director of the hospital says to you, "It's all most distressing, and I deeply sympathize, but you see this is putting an additional strain on your kidneys, and you'll be dead within the month. But you *have* to stay where you are all the same. Because unplugging you would be directly killing an innocent violinist, and that's murder, and that's impermissible." If anything in the world is true, it is that you do not commit murder, you do not do what is impermissible, if you reach around to your back and unplug yourself from that violinist to save your life.

The main focus of attention in writings on abortion has been on what a third party may or may not do in answer to a request from a woman for an abortion. This is in a way understandable. Things being as they are, there isn't much a woman can safely do to abort herself. So the question asked is what a third party may do; and what the mother may do, if it is mentioned at all, is deduced, almost as an afterthought, from what it is concluded that the third parties may do. But it seems to me that to treat the matter in this way is to refuse to grant to the mother that very status of person which is so firmly insisted on for the fetus. For we cannot simply read off what a person may do from what a third party may do. Suppose you find yourself trapped in a tiny house with a growing child. I mean a very tiny house, and a rapidly growing child – you are already up against the wall of the house and in a few minutes you'll be crushed to death. The child on the other hand won't be crushed to death; if nothing is done to stop him from growing he'll be hurt, but in the end he'll simply burst open the house and walk out a free man. Now I could well understand it if a bystander were to say, "There's nothing we can do for you. We cannot choose between your life and his, we cannot be the ones to decide who is to live, we cannot intervene." But it cannot be concluded that you too can do nothing, that you cannot attack it to save your life. However innocent the child may be, you do not have to wait passively while it crushes you to death. Perhaps a pregnant woman is vaguely felt to have the status of a house, to which we don't allow the right of self-defense. But if the woman houses the child, it should be remembered that she is a person who houses it.

I should perhaps stop to say explicitly that I am not claiming that people have a right to do anything whatever to save their lives. I think, rather, that there are drastic limits to the right of self-defense. If someone threatens you with death unless you torture someone else to death, I think you have not the right, even to save your life, to do so. But the case under consideration here is very different. In our case there are only two people involved, one whose life is threatened, and one who threatens it. Both are innocent: the one who is threatened is not threatened because of any fault, the one who threatens does not threaten because of any fault. For this reason we may feel that we bystanders cannot intervene. But the person threatened can.

In sum, a woman surely can defend her life against the threat to it posed by the unborn child, even if doing so involves its death. And this shows not merely that the theses in (1) through (4) are false; it shows also that the extreme view of abortion is false, and so we need not canvass any other possible ways of arriving at it from the argument I mentioned at the outset.

2.   The extreme view could of course be weakened to say that while abortion is permissible to save the mother's life, it may not be performed by a third party, but only by the mother herself. But this cannot be right either. For what we have to keep in mind is that the mother and the unborn child are not like two tenants in a small house which has, by an unfortunate mistake, been rented to both: the mother *owns* the house. The fact that she does adds to the offensiveness of deducing that the mother can do nothing from the supposition that third parties can do nothing. But it does more than this: it casts a bright light on the supposition that third parties can do nothing. Certainly it lets us see that a third party who says "I cannot choose between you" is fooling himself if he thinks this is impartiality. If Jones has found and fastened on a certain coat, which he needs to keep him from freezing, but which Smith also needs to keep him from freezing, then it is not impartiality that says "I cannot choose between you" when Smith owns the coat. Women have said again and again "This body is *my* body!" and they have reason to feel angry, reason to feel that it has been like shouting into the wind. Smith, after all, is hardly likely to bless us if we say to him, "Of

course it's your coat, anybody would grant that it is. But no one may choose between you and Jones who is to have it . . .".

3.   Where the mother's life is not at stake, the argument I mentioned at the outset seems to have a much stronger pull. "Everyone has a right to life, so the unborn person has a right to life." And isn't the child's right to life weightier than anything other than the mother's own right to life, which she might put forward as ground for an abortion?

This argument treats the right to life as if it were unproblematic. It is not, and this seems to me to be precisely the source of the mistake.

For we should now, at long last, ask what it comes to, to have a right to life. In some views having a right to life includes having a right to be given at least the bare minimum one needs for continued life. But suppose that what in fact *is* the bare minimum a man needs for continued life is something he has no right at all to be given? If I am sick unto death, and the only thing that will save my life is the touch of Henry Fonda's cool hand on my fevered brow, then all the same, I have no right to be given the touch of Henry Fonda's cool hand on my fevered brow. It would be frightfully nice of him to fly in from the West Coast to provide it. It would be less nice, though no doubt well meant, if my friends flew out to the West Coast and carried Henry Fonda back with them. But I have no right at all against anybody that he should do this for me. Or again, to return to the story I told earlier, the fact that for continued life that violinist needs the continued use of your kidneys does not establish that he has a right to be given the continued use of your kidneys. He certainly has no right against you that *you* should give him continued use of your kidneys. For nobody has any right to use your kidneys unless you give him such a right; and nobody has the right against you that you shall give him this right – if you do allow him to go on using your kidneys, this is a kindness on your part, and not something he can claim from you as his due. Nor has he any right against anybody else that *they* should give him continued use of your kidneys. Certainly he had no right against the Society of Music Lovers that they should plug him into you in the first place. And if you now start to unplug yourself, having learned that you will otherwise have to spend nine years in bed with him, there is nobody in the world who must try to prevent you, in order to see to it that he is given something he has a right to be given.

Some people are rather stricter about the right to life. In their view, it does not include the right to be given anything, but amounts to, and only to, the right not to be killed by anybody. But here a related difficulty arises. If everybody is to refrain from killing that violinist, then everybody must refrain from doing a great many different sorts of things. Everybody must refrain from slitting his throat, everybody must refrain from shooting him – and everybody must refrain from unplugging you from him. But does he have a right against everybody that they shall refrain from unplugging you from him? To refrain from doing this is to allow him to continue to use your kidneys. It could be argued that he has a right against us that *we* should allow him to continue to use your kidneys. That is, while he had no right against us that we should give him the use of your kidneys, it might be argued that he anyway has a right against us that we shall not now intervene and deprive him of the use of your kidneys. I shall come back to third-party interventions later. But certainly the violinist has no right against you that *you* shall allow him to continue to use your kidneys. As I said, if you do allow him to use them, it is a kindness on your part, and not something you owe him.

The difficulty I point to here is not peculiar to the right to life. It reappears in connection with all the other natural rights; and it is something which an adequate account of rights must deal with. For present purposes it is enough just to draw attention to it. But I would stress that I am not arguing that people do not have a right to life – quite to the contrary, it seems to me that the primary control we must place on the acceptability of an account of rights is that it should turn out in that account to be a truth that all persons have a right to life. I am arguing only that having a right to life does not guarantee having either a right to be given the use of or a right to be allowed continued use of another person's body – even if one needs it for life itself. So the right to life will not serve the opponents of abortion in the very simple and clear way in which they seem to have thought it would.

4.   There is another way to bring out the difficulty. In the most ordinary sort of case, to deprive someone of what he has a right to is to treat him unjustly. Suppose a boy and his small brother are jointly given a box of chocolates for Christmas. If the older boy takes the box and refuses to give his brother any of the chocolates, he is unjust to him, for the brother has been given a right to half of them. But suppose that, having learned that otherwise it means nine years in bed with that violinist, you unplug yourself from him. You surely are not being unjust to him, for you gave him no right to use your kidneys, and no one else can have given him any such right. But we have to notice that in unplugging yourself, you are killing him; and violinists, like everybody else, have a right to life, and thus in the view we were considering just now, the right not to be killed.

So here you do what he supposedly has a right you shall not do, but you do not act unjustly to him in doing it.

The emendation which may be made at this point is this: the right to life consists not in the right not to be killed, but rather in the right not to be killed unjustly. This runs a risk of circularity, but never mind: it would enable us to square the fact that the violinist has a right to life with the fact that you do not act unjustly toward him in unplugging yourself, thereby killing him. For if you do not kill him unjustly, you do not violate his right to life, and so it is no wonder you do him no injustice.

But if this emendation is accepted, the gap in the argument against abortion stares us plainly in the face: it is by no means enough to show that the fetus is a person, and to remind us that all persons have a right to life – we need to be shown also that killing the fetus violates its right to life, i.e., that abortion is unjust killing. And is it?

I suppose we may take it as a datum that in a case of pregnancy due to rape the mother has not given the unborn person a right to the use of her body for food and shelter. Indeed, in what pregnancy could it be supposed that the mother has given the unborn person such a right? It is not as if there were unborn persons drifting about the world, to whom a woman who wants a child says "I invite you in."

But it might be argued that there are other ways one can have acquired a right to the use of another person's body than by having been invited to use it by that person. Suppose a woman voluntarily indulges in intercourse, knowing of the chance it will issue in pregnancy, and then she does become pregnant; is she not in part responsible for the presence, in fact the very existence, of the unborn person inside her? No doubt she did not invite it in. But doesn't her partial responsibility for its being there itself give it a right to the use of her body? If so, then her aborting it would be more like the boy's taking away the chocolates, and less like your unplugging yourself from the violinist – doing so would be depriving it of what it does have a right to, and thus would be doing it an injustice.

And then, too, it might be asked whether or not she can kill it even to save her own life: If she voluntarily called it into existence, how can she now kill it, even in self-defense?

The first thing to be said about this is that it is something new. Opponents of abortion have been so concerned to make out the independence of the fetus, in order to establish that it has a right to life, just as its mother does, that they have tended to overlook the possible support they might gain from making out that the fetus is *dependent* on the mother, in order to establish that she has a special kind of responsibility for it, a responsibility that gives it rights against her which are not possessed by any independent person – such as an ailing violinist who is a stranger to her.

On the other hand, this argument would give the unborn person a right to its mother's body only if her pregnancy resulted from a voluntary act, undertaken in full knowledge of the chance a pregnancy might result from it. It would leave out entirely the unborn person whose existence is due to rape. Pending the availability of some further argument, then, we would be left with the conclusion that unborn persons whose existence is due to rape have no right to the use of their mothers' bodies, and thus that aborting them is not depriving them of anything they have a right to and hence is not unjust killing.

And we should also notice that it is not at all plain that this argument really does go even as far as it purports to. For there are cases and cases, and the details make a difference. If the room is stuffy, and I therefore open a window to air it, and a burglar climbs in, it would be absurd to say, "Ah, now he can stay, she's given him a right to the use of her house – for she is partially responsible for his presence there, having voluntarily done what enabled him to get in, in full knowledge that there are such things as burglars, and that burglars burgle." It would be still more absurd to say this if I had had bars installed outside my windows, precisely to prevent burglars from getting in, and a burglar got in only because of a defect in the bars. It remains equally absurd if we imagine it is not a burglar who climbs in, but an innocent person who blunders or falls in. Again, suppose it were like this: people-seeds drift about in the air like pollen, and if you open your windows, one may drift in and take root in your carpets or upholstery. You don't want children, so you fix up your windows with fine mesh screens, the very best you can buy. As can happen, however, and on very, very rare occasions does happen, one of the screens is defective; and a seed drifts in and takes root. Does the person-plant who now develops have a right to the use of your house? Surely not – despite the fact that you voluntarily opened your windows, you know-ingly kept carpets and upholstered furniture, and you knew that screens were sometimes defective. Someone may argue that you are responsible for its rooting, that it does have a right to your house, because after all you *could* have lived out your life with bare floors and furniture, or with sealed windows and doors. But this won't do – for by the same token anyone can avoid a pregnancy due to rape by having a hysterectomy, or anyway by never leaving home without a (reliable!) army.

It seems to me that the argument we are looking at can establish at most that there are *some* cases in which the unborn person has a right to the use of its mother's body, and therefore *some* cases in which abortion is unjust killing. There is room for much discussion and argument as to precisely which, if any. But I think we should sidestep this issue and leave it open, for at any rate the argument certainly does not establish that all abortion is unjust killing.

5. There is room for yet another argument here, however. We surely must all grant that there may be cases in which it would be morally indecent to detach a person from your body at the cost of his life. Suppose you learn that what the violinist needs is not nine years of your life, but only one hour: all you need do to save his life is to spend one hour in that bed with him. Suppose also that letting him use your kidneys for that one hour would not affect your health in the slightest. Admittedly you were kidnapped. Admittedly you did not give anyone permission to plug him into you. Nevertheless it seems to me plain you *ought* to allow him to use your kidneys for that hour – it would be indecent to refuse.

Again, suppose pregnancy lasted only an hour, and constituted no threat to life or health. And suppose that a woman becomes pregnant as a result of rape. Admittedly she did not voluntarily do anything to bring about the existence of a child. Admittedly she did nothing at all which would give the unborn person a right to the use of her body. All the same it might well be said, as in the newly emended violinist story, that she *ought* to allow it to remain for that hour – that it would be indecent in her to refuse.

Now some people are inclined to use the term "right" in such a way that it follows from the fact that you ought to allow a person to use your body for the hour he needs, that he has a right to use your body for the hour he needs, even though he has not been given that right by any person or act. They may say that it follows also that if you refuse, you act unjustly toward him. This use of the term is perhaps so common that it cannot be called wrong; nevertheless it seems to me to be an unfortunate loosening of what we would do better to keep a tight rein on. Suppose that box of chocolates I mentioned earlier had not been given to both boys jointly, but was given only to the older boy. There he sits, stolidly eating his way through the box, his small brother watching enviously. Here we are likely to say "You ought not to be so mean. You ought to give your brother some of those chocolates." My own view is that it just does not follow from the truth of this that the brother has any right to any of the chocolates. If the boy refuses to give his brother any, he is greedy, stingy, callous – but not unjust. I suppose that the people I have in mind will say it does follow that the brother has a right to some of the chocolates, and thus that the boy does act unjustly if he refuses to give his brother any. But the effect of saying this is to obscure what we should keep distinct, namely the difference between the boy's refusal in this case and the boy's refusal in the earlier case, in which the box was given to both boys jointly, and in which the small brother thus had what was from any point of view clear title to half.

A further objection to so using the term "right" that from the fact that A ought to do a thing for B, it follows that B has a right against A that A do it for him, is that it is going to make the question of whether or not a man has a right to a thing turn on how easy it is to provide him with it; and this seems not merely unfortunate, but morally unacceptable. Take the case of Henry Fonda again. I said earlier that I had no right to the touch of his cool hand on my fevered brow, even though I needed it to save my life. I said it would be frightfully nice of him to fly in from the West Coast to provide me with it, but that I had no right against him that he should do so. But suppose he isn't on the West Coast. Suppose he has only to walk across the room, place a hand briefly on my brow – and lo, my life is saved. Then surely he ought to do it, it would be indecent to refuse. Is it to be said "Ah, well, it follows that in this case she has a right to the touch of his hand on her brow, and so it would be an injustice in him to refuse"? So that I have a right to it when it is easy for him to provide it, though no right when it's hard? It's rather a shocking idea that anyone's rights should fade away and disappear as it gets harder and harder to accord them to him.

So my own view is that even though you ought to let the violinist use your kidneys for the one hour he needs, we should not conclude that he has a right to do so – we should say that if you refuse, you are, like the boy who owns all the chocolates and will give none away, self-centered and callous, indecent in fact, but not unjust. And similarly, that even supposing a case in which a woman pregnant due to rape ought to allow the unborn person to use her body for the hour he needs, we should not conclude that he has a right to do so; we should conclude that she is self-centered, callous, indecent, but not unjust, if she refuses. The complaints are no less grave; they are just different. However, there is no need to insist on this point. If anyone does wish to deduce "he has a right" from "you ought," then all the same he must surely grant that there are cases in which it is not morally required of you that you allow that violinist to use your kidneys, and in which he does not have a right to use them, and in which you do not do him injustice if you refuse. And so also for mother and unborn child. Except in such cases as where the unborn person has a right to demand it – and we were leaving open the possibility that there may be such cases – nobody is morally *required* to make large sacrifices, of health, of all other interests and concerns, of all other duties and commitments, for nine years, or even for nine months, in order to keep another person alive. . . .

6.   My argument will be found unsatisfactory on two counts by many of those who want to regard abortion as morally permissible. First, while I do argue that abortion is not impermissible, I do not argue that it is always permissible. I am inclined to think it a merit of my account precisely that it does *not* give a general yes or a general no. It allows for and supports our sense that, for example, a sick and desperately frightened fourteen-year-old schoolgirl, pregnant due to rape, may *of course* choose abortion, and that any law which rules this out is an insane law. And it also allows for and supports our sense that in other cases resort to abortion is even positively indecent. It would be indecent in the woman to request an abortion, and indecent in a doctor to perform it, if she is in her seventh month, and wants the abortion just to avoid the nuisance of postponing a trip abroad. The very fact that the arguments I have been drawing attention to treat all cases of abortion, or even all cases of abortion in which the mother's life is not at stake, as morally on a par ought to have made them suspect at the outset.

Secondly, while I am arguing for the permissibility of abortion in some cases, I am not arguing for the right to secure the death of the unborn child. It is easy to confuse these two things in that up to a certain point in the life of the fetus it is not able to survive outside the mother's body; hence removing it from her body guarantees its death. But they are importantly different. I have argued that you are not morally required to spend nine months in bed, sustaining the life of that violinist; but to say this is by no means to say that if, when you unplug yourself, there is a miracle and he survives, you then have a right to turn round and slit his throat. You may detach yourself even if this costs him his life; you have no right to be guaranteed his death, by some other means, if unplugging yourself does not kill him. There are some people who will feel dissatisfied by this feature of my argument. A woman may be utterly devastated by the thought of a child, a bit of herself, put out for adoption and never seen or heard of again. She may therefore want not merely that the child be detached from her, but more, that it die. Some opponents of abortion are inclined to regard this as beneath contempt – thereby showing insensitivity to what is surely a powerful source of despair. All the same, I agree that the desire for the child's death is not one which anybody may gratify, should it turn out to be possible to detach the child alive.

At this place, however, it should be remembered that we have only been pretending throughout that the fetus is a human being from the moment of conception. A very early abortion is surely not the killing of a person, and so is not dealt with by anything I have said here.

Notes

1 Daniel Callahan, *Abortion: Law, Choice and Morality* (New York, 1970), p. 373. This book gives a fascinating survey of the available information on abortion. The Jewish tradition

is surveyed in David M. Feldman, *Birth Control in Jewish Law* (New York, 1968), Part 5; the Catholic tradition in John T. Noonan, Jr, "An Almost Absolute Value in History," in *The Morality of Abortion*, ed. John T. Noonan, Jr (Cambridge, Mass., 1970).

2 The term "direct" in the arguments I refer to is a technical one. Roughly, what is meant by "direct killing" is either killing as an end in itself, or killing as a means to some end, for example, the end of saving someone else's life. See note 5, below, for an example of its use.

3 Cf. *Encyclical Letter of Pope Pius XI on Christian Marriage*, St Paul Editions (Boston, n.d.), p. 32: "however much we may pity the mother whose health and even life is gravely imperiled in the performance of the duty allotted to her by nature, nevertheless what could ever be a sufficient reason for excusing in any way the direct murder of the innocent? This is precisely what we are dealing with here." Noonan (*The Morality of Abortion*, p. 43) reads this as follows: "What cause can ever avail to excuse in any way the direct killing of the innocent? For it is a question of that."

4 The thesis in (4) is in an interesting way weaker than those in (1), (2), and (3): they rule out abortion even in cases in which both mother *and* child will die if the abortion is not performed. By contrast, one who held the view expressed in (4) could consistently say that one needn't prefer letting two persons die to killing one.

5 Cf. the following passage from Pius XII, *Address to the Italian Catholic Society of Midwives*: "The baby in the maternal breast has the right to life immediately from God. – Hence there is no man, no human authority, no science, no medical, eugenic, social, economic or moral 'indication' which can establish or grant a valid juridical ground for a direct deliberate disposition of an innocent human life, that is a disposition which looks to its destruction either as an end or as a means to another end perhaps in itself not illicit. – The baby, still not born, is a man in the same degree and for the same reason as the mother" (quoted in Noonan, *The Morality of Abortion*, p. 45).

6

On the Moral and Legal Status of Abortion

Mary Anne Warren

For our purposes, abortion may be defined as the act a woman performs in deliberately terminating her pregnancy before it comes to term, or in allowing another person to terminate it. Abortion usually entails the death of a fetus.[1] Nevertheless, I will argue that it is morally permissible, and should be neither legally prohibited nor made needlessly difficult to obtain, e.g., by obstructive legal regulations.[2]

Some philosophers have argued that the moral status of abortion cannot be resolved by rational means.[3] If this is so then liberty should prevail; for it is not a proper function of the law to enforce prohibitions upon personal behavior that cannot clearly be shown to be morally objectionable, and seriously so. But the advocates of prohibition believe that their position is objectively correct, and not merely a result of religious beliefs or personal prejudices. They argue that the humanity of the fetus is a matter of scientific fact, and that abortion is therefore the moral equivalent of murder, and must be prohibited in all or most cases. (Some would make an exception when the woman's life is in danger, or when the pregnancy is due to rape or incest; others would prohibit abortion even in these cases.)

In response, advocates of a right to choose abortion point to the terrible consequences of prohibiting it, especially while contraception is still unreliable, and is financially beyond the reach of much of the world's population. Worldwide, hundreds of thousands of women die each year from illegal abortions, and many more suffer from complications that may leave them injured or infertile. Women who are poor, under-age, disabled, or otherwise vulnerable, suffer most from the absence of safe and legal abortion. Advocates of choice also argue that to deny a woman access to abortion is to deprive her of the right to control her own body – a right so fundamental that without it other rights are often all but meaningless.

These arguments do not convince abortion opponents. The tragic consequences of prohibition leave them unmoved, because they regard the deliberate killing of fetuses as even more tragic. Nor do appeals to the right to control one's own body impress them, since they deny that this right includes the right to destroy a fetus. We cannot hope to persuade those who equate abortion with murder that they are mistaken, unless we can refute the standard antiabortion argument: that because fetuses are human beings, they have a right to life equal to that of any other human being. Unfortunately, confusion has prevailed with respect to the two important questions which that argument raises: (1) Is a human fetus really a human being at all stages of prenatal development? and (2) If so, what (if anything) follows about the moral and legal status of abortion?

John Noonan says that "the fundamental question in the long history of abortion is: How do you determine the humanity of a being?"[4] His antiabortion argument is essentially that of the Roman Catholic Church. In his words,

> . . . it is wrong to kill humans, however poor, weak, defenseless, and lacking in opportunity to develop their potential they may be. It is therefore morally wrong to kill Biafrans. Similarly, it is morally wrong to kill embryos.[5]

Noonan bases his claim that fetuses are human beings from the time of conception upon what he calls the theologians' criterion of humanity: that whoever is conceived of human beings is a human being. But although he argues at length for the appropriateness of this criterion of humanity, he does not question the assumption that if a fetus is a human being then abortion is almost always immoral.[6]

Judith Thomson has questioned this assumption. She argues that, even if we grant the antiabortionist the claim that a fetus is a human being with the same right to life as any other human being, we can still demonstrate that women are not morally obliged to complete every unwanted pregnancy.[7] Her argument is worth examining, because if it is sound it may enable us to establish the moral permissibility of abortion without having to decide just what makes an entity a human being, or what entitles it to full moral rights. This would represent a considerable gain in the power and simplicity of the pro-choice position.

Even if Thomson's argument does not hold up, her essential insight – that it requires *argument* to show that if fetuses are human beings then abortion is murder – is a valuable one. The assumption that she attacks is invidious, for it requires that in our deliberations about the ethics of abortion we must ignore almost entirely the needs of the pregnant woman and other persons for whom she is responsible. This will not do; determining what moral rights a fetus has is only one step in determining the moral status of abortion. The next step is finding a just solution to conflicts between whatever rights the fetus has, and the rights and responsibilities of the woman who is unwillingly pregnant.

My own inquiry will also have two stages. In Section I, I consider whether abortion can be shown to be morally permissible even on the assumption that a fetus is a human being with a strong right to life. I argue that this cannot be established, except in special cases. Consequently, we cannot avoid facing the question of whether or not a fetus has the same right to life as any human being.

In Section II, I propose an answer to this question, namely, that a fetus is not a member of the moral community – the set of beings with full and equal moral rights. The reason that a fetus is not a member of the moral community is that it is not yet a person, nor is it enough like a person in the morally relevant respects to be regarded the equal of those human beings who are persons. I argue that it is personhood, and not genetic humanity, which is the fundamental basis for membership in the moral community. A fetus, especially in the early stages of its development, satisfies none of the criteria of personhood. Consequently, it makes no sense to grant it moral rights strong enough to override the woman's moral rights to liberty, bodily integrity, and sometimes life itself. Unlike an infant who has already been born, a fetus cannot be granted full and equal moral rights without severely threatening the rights and well-being of women. Nor, as we will see, is a fetus's *potential* personhood a threat to the moral permissibility of abortion, since merely potential persons do not have a moral right to become actual – or none that is strong enough to override the fundamental moral rights of actual persons.

I

Judith Thomson argues that, even if a fetus has a right to life, abortion is often morally permissible. Her argument is based upon an imaginative analogy. She asks you to picture yourself waking up one day, in bed with a famous violinist, who is a stranger to you. Imagine that you have been kidnapped, and your bloodstream connected to that of the violinist, who has an ailment that will kill him unless he is permitted to share your kidneys for nine months. No one else can save him, since you alone have the right type of blood. Consequently, the Society of Music Lovers has arranged for you to be kidnapped and hooked up. If you unhook yourself, he will die. But if you remain in bed with him, then after nine months he will be cured and able to survive without further assistance from you.

Now, Thomson asks, what are your obligations in this situation? To be consistent, the antiabortionist must say that you are obliged to stay in bed with the violinist: for violinists are human beings, and all human beings have a right to life.[8] But this is outrageous; thus, there must be something very wrong with the same argument when it is applied to abortion. It would be extremely generous of you to agree to stay in bed with the violinist; but it is absurd to suggest that your refusal to do so would be the moral equivalent of murder. The violinist's right to life does not oblige you to do whatever is required to keep him alive; still less does it justify anyone else in forcing you to do so. A law which required you to stay in bed with the violinist would be an unjust law, since unwilling persons ought not to be required to be Extremely Good Samaritans, i.e., to make enormous personal sacrifices for the sake of other individuals towards whom they have no special prior obligation.

Thomson concludes that we can grant the antiabortionist his claim that a fetus is a human being with a right to life, and still hold that a pregnant woman is morally entitled to refuse to be an Extremely Good Samaritan toward the fetus. For there is a great gap between the claim that a human being has a right to life, and the claim that other human beings are morally obligated to do whatever is necessary to keep him alive. One has no duty to keep another human being alive *at great personal cost*, unless one has somehow contracted a special obligation toward that individual; and a woman who is pregnant may have done nothing that morally obliges her to make the burdensome personal sacrifices necessary to preserve the life of the fetus.

This argument is plausible, and in the case of pregnancy due to rape it is probably conclusive. Difficulties arise, however, when we attempt to specify the larger range of cases in which abortion can be justified on the basis of this argument. Thomson considers it a virtue of her argument that it does not imply that abortion is *always* morally permissible. It would, she says, be indecent for a woman in her seventh month of pregnancy to have an abortion in order to embark on a trip to Europe. On the other hand, the violinist analogy shows that, "a sick and desperately frightened fourteen-year-old schoolgirl, pregnant due to rape, may *of course* choose abortion, and that any law which rules this out is an insane law."[9] So far, so good; but what are we to say about the woman who becomes pregnant not through rape but because she and her partner did not use available forms of contraception, or because their attempts at contraception failed? What about a woman who becomes pregnant intentionally, but then re-evaluates the wisdom of having a child? In such cases, the violinist analogy is considerably less useful to advocates of the right to choose abortion.

It is perhaps only when a woman's pregnancy is due to rape, or some other form of coercion, that the situation is sufficiently analogous to the violinist case for our moral intuitions to transfer convincingly from the one case to the other. One difference between a pregnancy caused by rape and most unwanted pregnancies is that only in the former case is it perfectly clear that the woman is in no way responsible for her predicament. In the other cases, she *might* have been able to avoid becoming pregnant, e.g., by taking birth control pills (more faithfully), or insisting upon the use of high-quality condoms, or even avoiding heterosexual intercourse altogether throughout her fertile years. In contrast, if you are suddenly kidnapped by strange music lovers and hooked up to a sick violinist, then you are in no way responsible for your situation, which you could not have foreseen or prevented. And responsibility does seem to matter here. If a person behaves in a way which she could have avoided, and which she knows might bring into existence a human being who will depend upon her for survival, then it is not entirely clear that if and when that happens she may rightly refuse to do what she must in order to keep that human being alive.

This argument shows that the violinist analogy provides a persuasive defense of a woman's right to choose abortion only in cases where she is in no way morally responsible for her own pregnancy. In all other cases, the assumption that a fetus has a strong right to life makes it necessary to look carefully at the particular circumstances in order to determine the extent of the woman's responsibility, and hence the extent of her obligation. This outcome is unsatisfactory to advocates of the right to choose abortion, because it suggests that the decision should not be left in the woman's own hands, but should be supervised by other persons, who will inquire into the most intimate aspects of her personal life in order to determine whether or not she is entitled to choose abortion.

A supporter of the violinist analogy might reply that it is absurd to suggest that forgetting her pill one day might be sufficient to morally oblige a woman to complete an unwanted pregnancy. And indeed it is absurd to suggest this. As we will see, a woman's moral right to choose abortion does not depend upon the extent to which she might be thought to be morally responsible for her own pregnancy. But once we allow the assumption that a fetus has a strong right to life, we cannot avoid taking this absurd suggestion seriously. On this assumption, it is a vexing question whether and when abortion is morally justifiable. The violinist analogy can at best show that aborting a pregnancy is a deeply tragic act, though one that is sometimes morally justified.

My conviction is that an abortion is not always this deeply tragic, because a fetus is not yet a person, and therefore does not yet have a strong moral right to life. Although the truth of this conviction may not be self-evident, it does, I believe, follow from some highly plausible claims about the appropriate grounds for ascribing moral rights. It is worth examining these grounds, since this has not been adequately done before.

II

The question we must answer in order to determine the moral status of abortion is: How are we to define the moral community, the set of beings with full and equal moral rights? What sort of entity has the inalienable moral rights to life, liberty, and the pursuit of happiness? Thomas Jefferson attributed these rights to all *men*, and he may have intended to attribute them *only* to men. Perhaps he ought to have attributed them to all human beings. If so, then we arrive, first, at Noonan's problem of defining what makes an entity a human being, and second, at the question which Noonan does not consider: What reason is there for identifying the moral community with the set of all human beings, in whatever way we have chosen to define that term?

On the definition of "human"

The term "human being" has two distinct, but not often distinguished, senses. This results in a slide of meaning, which serves to conceal the fallacy in the traditional argument that, since (1) it is wrong to kill innocent human beings, and (2) fetuses are innocent human beings, therefore (3) it is wrong to kill fetuses. For if "human being" is used in the same sense in both (1) and (2), then whichever of the two senses is meant, one of these premises is question-begging. And if it is used in different senses then the conclusion does not follow.

Thus, (1) is a generally accepted moral truth,[10] and one that does not beg the question about abortion, only if "human being" is used to mean something like "a full-fledged member of the moral community, who is also a member of the human species." I will call this the *moral* sense of "human being." It is not to be confused with what I will call the *genetic* sense, i.e., the sense in which any individual entity that belongs to the human species is a human being, regardless of whether or not it is rightly considered to be an equal member of the moral community. Premise (1) avoids begging the question only if the moral sense is intended; while premise (2) avoids it only if what is intended is the genetic sense.

Noonan argues for the classification of fetuses with human beings by pointing, first, to the presence of the human genome in the cell nuclei of the human conceptus from conception onwards; and secondly, to the potential capacity for rational thought.[11] But what he needs to show, in order to support his version of the traditional antiabortion argument, is that fetuses are human beings in the moral sense – the sense in which all human beings have full and equal moral rights. In the absence of any argument showing that whatever is genetically human is also morally human – and he gives none – nothing more than genetic humanity can be demonstrated by the presence of human chromosomes in the fetus's cell nuclei. And, as we will see, the strictly potential capacity for rational thought can at most show that the fetus may later *become* human in the moral sense.

Defining the moral community

Is genetic humanity sufficient for moral humanity? There are good reasons for not defining the moral community in this way. I would suggest that the moral community consists, in the first instance, of all *persons*, rather than all genetically human entities.[12] It is persons who invent moral rights, and who are (sometimes) capable of respecting them. It does not follow from this that only persons can have moral rights. However, persons are wise not to ascribe to entities that clearly are not persons moral rights that cannot in practice be respected without severely undercutting the fundamental moral rights of those who clearly are.

What characteristics entitle an entity to be considered a person? This is not the place to attempt a complete analysis of the concept of personhood; but we do not need such an analysis to explain why a fetus is not a person. All we need is an approximate list of the most basic criteria of personhood. In searching for these criteria, it is useful to look beyond the set of people with whom we are acquainted, all of whom are human. Imagine, then, a space traveler who lands on a new planet, and encounters organisms unlike any she has ever seen or heard of. If she wants to behave morally toward these organisms, she has somehow to determine whether they are people and thus have full moral rights, or whether they are things that she need not feel guilty about treating, for instance, as a source of food.

How should she go about making this determination? If she has some anthropological background, she might look for signs of religion, art, and the manufacturing of tools, weapons, or shelters, since these cultural traits have frequently been used to distinguish our human ancestors from prehuman beings, in what seems to be closer to the moral than the genetic sense of "human being." She would be right to take the presence of such traits as evidence that the extraterrestrials were persons. It would, however, be anthropocentric of her to take the absence of these traits as proof that they were not, since they could be people who have progressed beyond, or who have never needed, these particular cultural traits.

I suggest that among the characteristics which are central to the concept of personhood are the following:

(1) *sentience* – the capacity to have conscious experiences, usually including the capacity to experience pain and pleasure;
(2) *emotionality* – the capacity to feel happy, sad, angry, loving, etc.;
(3) *reason* – the capacity to solve new and relatively complex problems;
(4) *the capacity to communicate*, by whatever means, messages of an indefinite variety of types; that is, not just with an indefinite number of possible contents, but on indefinitely many possible topics;
(5) *self-awareness* – having a concept of oneself, as an individual and/or as a member of a social group; and finally
(6) *moral agency* – the capacity to regulate one's own actions through moral principles or ideals.

It is difficult to produce precise definitions of these traits, let alone to specify universally valid behavioral indications that these traits are present. But let us assume that our explorer knows approximately what these six characteristics mean, and that she is able to observe whether or not the extraterrestrials possess these mental and behavioral capacities. How should she use her findings to decide whether or not they are persons?

An entity need not have *all* of these attributes to be a person. And perhaps none of them is absolutely necessary. For instance, the absence of emotion would not disqualify a being that was personlike in all other ways. Think, for instance, of two of the *Star Trek* characters, Mr Spock (who is half human and half alien), and Data (who is an android). Both are depicted as lacking the capacity to feel emotion; yet both are sentient, reasoning, communicative, self-aware moral agents, and unquestionably persons. Some people are unemotional; some cannot communicate well; some lack self-awareness; and some are not moral agents. It should not surprise us that many people do not meet all of the criteria of personhood. Criteria for the applicability of complex concepts are often like this: none may be logically necessary, but the more criteria that are satisfied, the more confident we are that the concept is applicable. Conversely, the fewer criteria are satisfied, the less plausible it is to hold that the concept applies. And if none of the relevant criteria are met, then we may be confident that it does not.

Thus, to demonstrate that a fetus is not a person, all I need to claim is that an entity that has *none* of these six characteristics is not a person. Sentience is the most basic mental capacity, and the one that may have the best claim to being a necessary (though not sufficient) condition for personhood. Sentience can establish a claim to moral considerability, since sentient beings can be harmed in ways that matter to them; for instance, they can be caused to feel pain, or deprived of the continuation of a life that is pleasant to them. It is unlikely that an entirely insentient organism could develop the other mental and behavioral capacities that are characteristic of persons. Consequently, it is odd to claim that an entity that is not sentient, and that has never been sentient, is nevertheless a person. Persons who have permanently and irreparably lost all capacity for sentience, but who remain biologically alive, arguably still have strong moral rights by virtue of what they have been in the past. But small fetuses, which have not yet begun to have experiences, are not persons yet and do not have the rights that persons do.

The presumption that all persons have full and equal basic moral rights may be part of the very concept of a person. If this is so, then the concept of a person is in part a moral one; once we have admitted that X is a person, we have implicitly committed ourselves to recognizing X's right to be treated as a member of the moral community.[13] The claim that X is a *human being* may also be voiced as an appeal to treat X decently; but this is usually either because "human being" is used in the moral sense, or because of a confusion between genetic and moral humanity.

If (1)–(6) are the primary criteria of personhood, then genetic humanity is neither necessary nor sufficient for personhood. Some genetically human entities are not persons, and there may be persons who belong to other species. A man or woman whose consciousness has been permanently obliterated but who remains biologically alive is a human entity who may no longer be a person; and some unfortunate humans, who have never had any sensory or cognitive capacities at all, may not be people either. Similarly, an early fetus is a human entity which is not yet a person. It is not even minimally sentient, let alone capable of emotion, reason, sophisticated communication, self-awareness, or moral agency.[14] Thus, while it may be greatly valued as a future child, it does not yet have the claim to moral consideration that it may come to have later.

Moral agency matters to moral status, because it is moral agents who invent moral rights, and who can be obliged to respect them. Human beings have become moral agents from social necessity. Most social animals exist well enough, with no evident notion of a moral right. But human beings need moral rights, because we are not only highly social, but also sufficiently clever and self-interested to be capable of undermining our societies through violence and duplicity. For human persons, moral rights are essential for peaceful and mutually beneficial social life. So long as some moral agents are denied basic rights, peaceful existence is difficult, since moral agents justly resent being treated as something less. If animals of some terrestrial species are found to be persons, or if alien persons come from other worlds, or if human beings someday invent machines whose mental and behavioral capacities make them persons, then we will be morally obliged to respect the moral rights of these nonhuman persons – at least to the extent that they are willing and able to respect ours in turn.

Although only those persons who are moral agents can participate directly in the shaping and enforcement of moral rights, they need not and usually do not ascribe moral rights only to themselves and other moral agents. Human beings are social creatures who naturally care for small children, and other members of the social community who are not currently capable of moral agency. Moreover, we are all vulnerable to the temporary or permanent loss of the mental capacities necessary for moral agency. Thus, we have self-interested as well as altruistic reasons for extending basic moral rights to infants and other sentient human beings who have already been born, but who currently lack some of these other mental capacities. These human beings, despite their current disabilities, are persons and members of the moral community.

But in extending moral rights to beings (human or otherwise) that have few or none of the morally significant characteristics of persons, we need to be careful not to burden human moral agents with obligations that they cannot possibly fulfill, except at unacceptably great cost to their own well-being and that of those they care about. Women often cannot complete unwanted pregnancies, except at intolerable mental, physical, and economic cost to themselves and their families. And heterosexual intercourse is too important a part of the social lives of most men and women to be reserved for times when pregnancy is an acceptable outcome. Furthermore, the world cannot afford the continued rapid population growth which is the inevitable consequence of prohibiting abortion, so long as contraception is neither very reliable nor available to everyone. If fetuses were persons, then they would have rights that must be respected, even at great social or personal cost. But given that early fetuses, at least, are unlike persons in the morally relevant respects, it is unreasonable to insist that they be accorded exactly the same moral and legal status.

Fetal development and the right to life

Two questions arise regarding the application of these suggestions to the moral status of the fetus. First, if indeed fetuses are not yet persons, then might they nevertheless have strong moral rights based upon the degree to which they *resemble* persons? Secondly, to what extent, if any, does a fetus's potential to *become* a person imply that we ought to accord to it some of the same moral rights? Each of these questions requires comment.

It is reasonable to suggest that the more like a person something is – the more it appears to meet at least some of the criteria of personhood – the stronger is the case for according it a right to life, and perhaps the stronger its right to life is. That being the case, perhaps the fetus gradually gains a stronger right to life as it develops. We should take seriously the suggestion that, just as "the human individual develops biologically in a continuous fashion . . . the rights of a human person . . . develop in the same way."[15]

A seven-month fetus can apparently feel pain, and can respond to such stimuli as light and sound. Thus, it may have a rudimentary form of consciousness. Nevertheless, it is probably not as conscious, or as capable of emotion, as even a very young infant is; and it has as yet little or no capacity for reason, sophisticated intentional communication, or self-awareness. In these respects, even a late-term fetus is arguably less like a person than are many nonhuman animals. Many animals (e.g., large-brained mammals such as elephants, cetaceans, or apes) are not only sentient, but clearly possessed of a degree of reason, and perhaps even of self-awareness. Thus, on the basis of its resemblance to a person, even a late-term fetus can have no more right to life than do these animals.

Animals may, indeed, plausibly be held to have some moral rights, and perhaps rather strong ones.[16] But it is impossible in practice to accord full and equal moral rights to all animals. When an animal poses a serious threat to the life or well-being of a person, we do not, as a rule, greatly blame the person for killing it; and there are good reasons for this species-based discrimination. Animals, however intelligent in their own domains, are generally not beings with whom we can reason; we cannot persuade mice not to invade our dwellings or consume our food. That is why their rights are necessarily weaker than those of a being who can understand and respect the rights of other beings.

But the probable sentience of late-term fetuses is not the only argument in favor of treating late abortion as a morally more serious matter than early abortion. Many – perhaps most – people are repulsed by the thought of needlessly aborting a late-term fetus. The late-term fetus has features which cause it to arouse in us almost the same powerful protective instinct as does a small infant.

This response needs to be taken seriously. If it were impossible to perform abortions early in pregnancy, then we might have to tolerate the mental and physical trauma that would be occasioned by the routine resort to late abortion. But where early abortion is safe, legal, and readily available to all women, it is not unreasonable to expect most women who wish to end a pregnancy to do so prior to the third trimester. Most women strongly prefer early to late abortion, because it is far less physically painful and emotionally traumatic. Other things being equal, it is better for all concerned that pregnancies that are not to be completed should be ended as early as possible. Few women would consider ending a pregnancy in the seventh month in order to take a trip to Europe. If, however, a woman's own life or health is at stake, or if the fetus has been found to be so severely abnormal as to be unlikely to survive or to have a life worth living, then late abortion may be the morally best choice. For even a late-term fetus is not a person yet, and its rights must yield to those of the woman whenever it is impossible for both to be respected.

Potential personhood and the right to life

We have seen that a presentient fetus does not yet resemble a person in ways which support the claim that it has strong moral rights. But what about its *potential*, the fact that if nurtured and allowed to develop it may eventually become a person? Doesn't that potential give it at least some right to life? The fact that something is a potential person may be a reason for not destroying it; but we need not conclude from this that potential people have a strong right to life. It may be that the feeling that it is better not to destroy a potential person is largely due to the fact that potential people are felt to be an invaluable resource, not to be lightly squandered. If every speck of dust were a potential person, we would be less apt to suppose that all potential persons have a right to become actual.

We do not need to insist that a potential person has no right to life whatever. There may be something immoral, and not just imprudent, about wantonly destroying potential people, when doing so isn't necessary. But even if a potential person does have some right to life, · that right could not outweigh the right of a woman to obtain an abortion; for the basic moral rights of an actual person outweigh the rights of a merely potential person, whenever the two conflict. Since this may not be immediately obvious in the case of a human fetus, let us look at another case.

Suppose that our space explorer falls into the hands of an extraterrestrial civilization, whose scientists decide to create a few thousand new human beings by killing her and using some of her cells to create clones. We may imagine that each of these newly created women will have all of the original woman's abilities, skills, knowledge, and so on, and will also have an individual self-concept; in short, that each of them will be a bona fide (though not genetically unique) person. Imagine, further, that our explorer knows all of this, and knows that these people will be treated kindly and fairly. I maintain that in such a situation she would have the right to escape if she could, thus depriving all of these potential people of their potential lives. For her right to life outweighs all of theirs put together, even though they are all genetically human, and have a high probability of becoming people, if only she refrains from acting.

Indeed, I think that our space traveler would have a right to escape even if it were not her life which the aliens planned to take, but only a year of her freedom, or only a day. She would not be obliged to stay, even if she had been captured because of her own lack of caution – or even if she had done so deliberately, knowing the possible consequences. Regardless of why she was captured, she is not obliged to remain in captivity for *any* period of time in order to permit merely potential people to become actual people. By the same token, a woman's rights to liberty and the control of her own body outweigh whatever right to life a fetus may have merely by virtue of its potential personhood.

The objection from infanticide

One objection to my argument is that it appears to justify not only abortion, but also infanticide. A newborn infant is not much more personlike than a nine-month fetus, and thus it might appear that if late-term abortion is sometimes justified, then infanticide must also sometimes be justified. Yet most people believe that infanticide is a form of murder, and virtually never justified.

This objection is less telling than it may seem. There are many reasons why infanticide is more difficult to justify than abortion, even though neither fetuses nor newborn infants are clearly persons. In this period of history, the deliberate killing of newborns is virtually never justified. This is in part because newborns are so close to being persons that to kill them requires a very strong moral justification – as does the killing of dolphins, chimpanzees, and other highly personlike creatures. It is certainly wrong to kill such beings for the sake of convenience, or financial profit, or "sport." Only the most vital human needs, such as the need to defend one's own life and physical integrity, can provide a plausible justification for killing such beings.

In the case of an infant, there is no such vital need, since in the contemporary world there are usually other people who are eager to provide a good home for an infant whose own parents are unable or unwilling to care for it. Many people wait years for the opportunity to adopt a child, and some are unable to do so, even though there is every reason to believe that they would be good parents. The needless destruction of a viable infant not only deprives a sentient human being of life, but also deprives other persons of a source of great satisfaction, perhaps severely impoverishing *their* lives.

Even if an infant is unadoptable (e.g., because of some severe physical disability), it is still wrong to kill it. For most of us value the lives of infants, and would greatly prefer to pay taxes to support foster care and state institutions for disabled children, rather than to allow them to be killed or abandoned. So long as most people feel this way, and so long as it is possible to provide care for infants who are unwanted, or who have special needs that their parents cannot meet without assistance, it is wrong to let any infant die who has a chance of living a reasonably good life.

If these arguments show that infanticide is wrong, at least in today's world, then why don't they also show that late-term abortion is always wrong? After all, third-trimester fetuses are almost as personlike as infants, and many people value them and would prefer that they be preserved. As a potential source of pleasure to some family, a fetus is just as valuable as an infant. But there is an important difference between these two cases: once the infant is born, its continued life cannot pose any serious threat to the woman's life or health, since she is free to put it up for adoption or to place it in foster care. While she might, in rare cases, prefer that the child die rather than being raised by others, such a preference would not establish a right on her part.

In contrast, a pregnant woman's right to protect her own life and health outweighs other people's desire that the fetus be preserved – just as, when a person's life or health is threatened by an animal, and when the threat cannot be removed without killing the animal, that person's right to self-defense outweighs the desires of those who would prefer that the animal not be killed. Thus, while the moment of birth may mark no sharp discontinuity in the degree to which an infant resembles a person, it does mark the end of the mother's right to determine its fate. Indeed, if a late abortion can be safely performed without harming the fetus, she has in most cases no right to insist upon its death, for the same reason that she has no right to insist that a viable infant be killed or allowed to die.

It remains true that, on my view, neither abortion nor the killing of newborns is obviously a form of murder. Perhaps our legal system is correct in its classification of infanticide as murder, since no other legal category adequately expresses the force of our disapproval of this action. But some moral distinction remains, and it has important consequences. When a society cannot possibly care for all of the children who are born, without endangering the survival of adults and older children, allowing some infants to die may be the best of a bad set of options. Throughout history, most societies – from those that lived by gathering and hunting to the highly civilized Chinese, Japanese, Greeks, and Romans - have permitted infanticide under such unfortunate circumstances, regarding it as a necessary evil. It shows a lack of understanding to condemn these societies as morally benighted for this reason alone, since in the absence of safe and effective means of contraception and abortion, parents must sometimes have had no morally better options.

Conclusion

I have argued that fetuses are neither persons nor members of the moral community. Furthermore, neither a fetus's resemblance to a person, nor its potential for becoming a person, provides an adequate basis for the claim that it has a full and equal right to life. At the same time, there are medical as well as moral reasons for preferring early to late abortion when the pregnancy is unwanted.

Women, unlike fetuses, are undeniably persons and members of the human moral community. If unwanted or medically dangerous pregnancies never occurred, then it might be possible to respect women's basic moral rights, while at the same time extending the same basic rights to fetuses. But in the real world such pregnancies do occur – often despite the woman's best efforts to prevent them. Even if the perfect contraceptive were universally available, the continued occurrence of rape and incest would make access to abortion a vital human need. Because women are persons, and fetuses are not, women's rights to life, liberty, and physical integrity morally override whatever right to life it may be appropriate to ascribe to a fetus. Consequently, laws that deny women the right to obtain abortions, or that make safe early abortions difficult or impossible for some women to obtain, are an unjustified violation of basic moral and constitutional rights.

Notes

1 Strictly speaking, a human conceptus does not become a fetus until the primary organ systems have formed, at about six to eight weeks gestational age. However, for simplicity I shall refer to the conceptus as a fetus at every stage of its prenatal development.

2 The views defended in this article are set forth in greater depth in my book *Moral Status*, which is forthcoming from Oxford University Press.

3 For example, Roger Wertheimer argues, in "Understanding the Abortion Argument," *Philosophy and Public Affairs*, 1 (Fall, 1971), that the moral status of abortion is not a question of fact, but only of how one responds to the facts.

4 John Noonan, "Abortion and the Catholic Church: A Summary History," *Natural Law Forum*, 12 (1967), p. 125.

5 John Noonan, "Deciding Who is Human," *Natural Law Forum*, 13 (1968), p. 134.

6 Noonan deviates from the current position

of the Roman Catholic Church in that he thinks that abortion is morally permissible when it is the only way of saving the woman's life. See "An Almost Absolute Value in History," in *Contemporary Issues in Bioethics*, edited by Tom L. Beauchamp and LeRoy Walters (Belmont, California: Wadsworth, 1994), p. 283.

7 Judith Jarvis Thomson, "A Defense of Abortion," *Philosophy and Public Affairs*, 1:1 (Fall, 1971), pp. 173–8.

8 Ibid., p. 174.

9 Ibid., p. 187.

10 The principle that it is always wrong to kill innocent human beings may be in need of other modifications, e.g., that it may be permissible to kill innocent human beings in order to save a larger number of equally innocent human beings; but we may ignore these complications here.

11 Noonan, "Deciding Who is Human," p. 135.

12 From here on, I will use "human" to mean "genetically human," since the moral sense of the term seems closely connected to, and perhaps derived from, the assumption that genetic humanity is both necessary and sufficient for membership in the moral community.

13 Alan Gewirth defends a similar claim, in *Reason and Morality* (University of Chicago Press, 1978).

14 Fetal sentience is impossible prior to the development of neurological connections between the sense organs and the brain, and between the various parts of the brain involved in the processing of conscious experience. This stage of neurological development is currently thought to occur at some point in the late second or early third trimester.

15 Thomas L. Hayes, "A Biological View," *Commonweal*, 85 (March 17, 1967), pp. 677–8; cited by Daniel Callahan, in *Abortion: Law, Choice, and Morality* (London: Macmillan, 1970).

16 See, for instance, Tom Regan, *The Case for Animal Rights* (Berkeley: University of California Press, 1983).

7

An Argument that Abortion is Wrong

Don Marquis

The purpose of this essay is to set out an argument for the claim that abortion, except perhaps in rare instances, is seriously wrong.[1] One reason for these exceptions is to eliminate from consideration cases whose ethical analysis should be controversial and detailed for clear-headed opponents of abortion. Such cases include abortion after rape and abortion during the first fourteen days after conception when there is an argument that the fetus is not definitely an individual. Another reason for making these exceptions is to allow for those cases in which the permissibility of abortion is compatible with the argument of this essay. Such cases include abortion when continuation of a pregnancy endangers a woman's life and abortion when the fetus is anencephalic. When I speak of the wrongness of abortion in this essay, a reader should presume the above qualifications. I mean by an abortion an action intended to bring about the death of a fetus for the sake of the woman who carries it. (Thus, as is standard on the literature on this subject, I eliminate spontaneous abortions from consideration.) I mean by a fetus a developing human being from the time of conception to the time of birth. (Thus, as is standard, I call embryos and zygotes, fetuses.)

The argument of this essay will establish that abortion is wrong for the same reason as killing a reader of this essay is wrong. I shall just assume, rather than establish, that killing you is seriously wrong. I shall make no attempt to offer a complete ethics of killing. Finally, I shall make no attempt to resolve some very fundamental and difficult general philosophical issues into which this analysis of the ethics of abortion might lead.

Why the Debate over Abortion seems Intractable

Symmetries that emerge from the analysis of the major arguments on either side of the abortion debate may explain why the abortion debate seems intractable. Consider the following standard anti-abortion argument: Fetuses are both human and alive. Humans have the right to life. Therefore, fetuses have the right to life. Of course, women have the right to control their own bodies, but the right to life overrides the right of a woman to control her own body. Therefore, abortion is wrong.

Thomson's view

Judith Thomson (1971) has argued that even if one grants (for the sake of argument only) that fetuses have the right to life, this argument fails. Thomson invites you to imagine that you have been connected while sleeping, bloodstream to bloodstream, to a famous violinist. The violinist, who suffers from a rare blood disease, will die if disconnected. Thomson argues that you surely have the right to disconnect yourself. She appeals to our intuition that having to lie in bed with a violinist for an indefinite period is too much for morality to demand. She supports this claim by noting that the body being used is *your* body, not the violinist's body. She distinguishes the right to life, which the violinist clearly has, from the right to use someone else's body when necessary to preserve one's life, which it is not at all obvious the violinist has. Because the case of pregnancy is like the case of the violinist, one is no more morally obligated to remain attached to a fetus than to remain attached to the violinist.

It is widely conceded that one can generate from Thomson's vivid case the conclusion that abortion is morally permissible when a pregnancy is due to rape (Warren, 1973, p. 49; and Steinbock, 1992, p. 79). But this is hardly a general right to abortion. Do Thomson's more general theses generate a more general right to an abortion? Thomson draws our attention to the fact that in a pregnancy, although a fetus uses a woman's body as a life-support system, a pregnant woman does not use a fetus's body as a life-support system. However, an opponent of abortion might draw our attention to the fact that in an abortion the life that is lost is the fetus's, not the woman's. This symmetry seems to leave us with a stand-off.

Thomson points out that a fetus's right to life does not entail its right to use someone else's body to preserve its life. However, an opponent of abortion might point out that a woman's right to use her own body does not entail her right to end someone else's life in order to do what she wants with her body. In reply, one might argue that a pregnant woman's right to control her own body doesn't come to much if it is wrong for her to take any action that ends the life of the fetus within her. However, an opponent of abortion can argue that the fetus's right to life doesn't come to much if a pregnant woman can end it when she chooses. The consequence of all of these symmetries seems to be a stand-off. But if we have the stand-off, then one might argue that we are left with a conflict of rights: a fetal right to life versus the right of a woman to control her own body. One might then argue that the right to life seems to be a stronger right than the right to control one's own body in the case of abortion because the loss of one's life is a greater loss than the loss of the right to control one's own body in one respect for nine months. Therefore, the right to life overrides the right to control one's own body and abortion is wrong. Considerations like these have suggested to both opponents of abortion and supporters of choice that a Thomsonian strategy for defending a general right to abortion will not succeed (Tooley, 1972; Warren, 1973; and Steinbock, 1992). In fairness, one must note that Thomson did not intend her strategy to generate a general moral permissibility of abortion.

Do fetuses have the right to life?

The above considerations suggest that whether abortion is morally permissible boils down to the question of whether fetuses have the right to life. An argument that fetuses either have or lack the right to life must be based upon some general criterion for having or lacking the right to life. Opponents of abortion, on the one hand, look around for the broadest possible plausible criterion, so that fetuses will fall under it. This explains why classic arguments against abortion appeal to the criterion of being human (Noonan, 1970; Beckwith, 1993). This criterion appears plausible: The claim that all humans, whatever their race, gender, religion or *age*, have the right to life seems evident enough. In addition, because the fetuses we are concerned with do not, after all, belong to another species, they are clearly human. Thus, the syllogism that generates the conclusion that fetuses have the right to life is apparently sound.

On the other hand, those who believe abortion is morally permissible wish to find a narrow, but plausible, criterion for possession of the right to life so that fetuses will fall outside of it. This explains, in part, why the standard pro-choice arguments in the philosophical literature appeal to the criterion of being a person (Feinberg, 1986; Tooley, 1972; Warren, 1973; Benn, 1973; Engelhardt, 1986). This criterion appears plausible: The claim that only persons have the right to life seems evident enough. Furthermore, because fetuses neither are rational nor possess the capacity to communicate in complex ways nor possess a concept of self that continues through time, no fetus is a person. Thus, the syllogism needed to generate the conclusion that no fetus possesses the right to life is apparently sound. Given that no fetus possesses the right to life, a woman's right to control her own body easily generates the general right to abortion. The existence of two apparently defensible syllogisms which support contrary conclusions helps to explain why partisans on both sides of the abortion dispute often regard their opponents as either morally depraved or mentally deficient.

Which syllogism should we reject? The anti-abortion syllogism is usually attacked by attacking its major premise: the claim that whatever is biologically human has the right to life. This premise is subject to scope problems because the class of the biologically human includes too much: human cancer-cell cultures are biologically human, but they do not have the right to life. Moreover, this premise also is subject to moral-relevance problems: the connection between the biological and the moral is merely assumed. It is hard to think of a good *argument* for such a connection. If one wishes to consider the category of "human" a moral category, as some people find it plausible to do in other contexts, then one is left with no way of showing that the fetus is fully human without begging the question. Thus, the classic anti-abortion argument appears subject to fatal difficulties.

These difficulties with the classic anti-abortion argument are well known and thought by many to be conclusive. The symmetrical difficulties with the classic pro-choice syllogism are not as well recognized. The pro-choice syllogism can be attacked by attacking its major premise: Only persons have the right to life. This premise is subject to scope problems because the class of persons includes too little: infants, the severely retarded, and some of the mentally ill seem to fall outside the class of persons as the supporter of choice understands the concept. The premise is also subject to moral-relevance problems: Being a person is understood by the pro-choicer as having certain psychological attributes. If the prochoicer questions the connection between the biological and the moral, the opponent of abortion can question the connection between the psychological and the moral. If one wishes to consider "person" a moral category, as is often done, then one is left with no way of showing that the fetus is not a person without begging the question.

Pro-choicers appear to have resources for dealing with their difficulties that opponents of abortion lack. Consider their moral-relevance problem. A pro-choicer might argue that morality rests on contractual foundations and that only those who have the psychological attributes of persons are capable of entering into the moral contract and, as a consequence, being a member of the moral community. [This is essentially Engelhardt's (1986) view.] The great advantage of this contractarian approach to morality is that it seems far more plausible than any approach the anti-abortionist can provide. The great disadvantage of this contractarian approach to morality is that it adds to our earlier scope problems by leaving it unclear how we can have the duty not to inflict pain and suffering on animals.

Contractarians have tried to deal with their scope problems by arguing that duties to some individuals who are not persons can be justified even though those individuals are not contracting members of the moral community. For example, Kant argued that, although we do not have direct duties to animals, we "must practice kindness towards animals, for he who is cruel to animals becomes hard also in his dealings with men" (Kant, 1963, p. 240). Feinberg argues that infanticide is wrong, not because infants have the right to life, but because our society's protection of infants has social utility. If we do not treat infants with tenderness and consideration, then when they are persons they will be worse off and we will be worse off also (Feinberg, 1986, p. 271).

These moves only stave off the difficulties with the pro-choice view; they do not resolve them. Consider Kant's account of our obligations to animals. Kantians certainly know the difference between persons and animals. Therefore, no true Kantian would treat persons as she would treat animals. Thus, Kant's defense of our duties to animals fails to show that Kantians have a duty not to be cruel to animals. Consider Feinberg's attempt to show that infanticide is wrong even though no infant is a person. All Feinberg really shows is that it is a good idea to treat with care and consideration the infants we intend to keep. That is quite compatible with killing the infants we intend to discard. This point can be supported by an analogy with which any pro-choicer will agree. There are plainly good reasons to treat with care and consideration the fetuses we intend to keep. This is quite compatible with aborting those fetuses we intend to discard. Thus, Feinberg's account of the wrongness of infanticide is inadequate.

Accordingly, we can see that a contractarian defense of the pro-choice personhood syllogism fails. The problem arises because the contractarian cannot account for our duties to individuals who are not persons, whether these individuals are animals or infants. Because the pro-choicer wishes to adopt a narrow criterion for the right to life so that fetuses will not be included, the scope of her major premise is too narrow. Her problem is the opposite of the problem the classic opponent of abortion faces.

The argument of this section has attempted to establish, albeit briefly, that the classic anti-abortion argument and the pro-choice argument favored by most philosophers both face problems that are mirror images of one another. A stand-off results. The abortion debate requires a different strategy.

The "Future Like Ours" Account of the Wrongness of Killing

Why do the standard arguments in the abortion debate fail to resolve the issue? The general principles to which partisans in the debate appeal are either truisms most persons would affirm in the absence of much reflection, or very general moral theories. All are subject to major problems. A different approach is needed.

Opponents of abortion claim that abortion is wrong because abortion involves killing someone like us, a human being who just happens to be very young. Supporters of choice claim that ending the life of a fetus is not in the same moral category as ending the life of an adult human being. Surely this controversy cannot be resolved in the absence of an account of what it is about killing us that makes killing us wrong. On the one hand, if we know what property we possess that makes killing us wrong, then we can ask whether fetuses have the same property. On the other hand, suppose that we do not know what it is about us that makes killing us wrong. If this is so, we do not understand even easy cases in which killing is wrong. Surely, we will not understand the ethics of killing fetuses, for if we do not understand easy cases, then we will not understand hard cases. Both pro-choicer and anti-abortionist agree that it is obvious that it is wrong to kill us. Thus, a discussion of what it is about us that makes killing us not only wrong, but seriously wrong, seems to be the right place to begin a discussion of the abortion issue.

Who is primarily wronged by a killing? The wrong of killing is not primarily explained in terms of the loss to the family and friends of the victim. Perhaps the victim is a hermit. Perhaps one's friends find it easy to make new friends. The wrong of killing is not primarily explained in terms of the brutalization of the killer. The great wrong to the victim explains the brutalization, not the other way around. The wrongness of killing us is understood in terms of what killing does to us. Killing us imposes on us the misfortune of premature death. That misfortune underlies the wrongness.

Premature death is a misfortune because when one is dead, one has been deprived of life. This misfortune can be more precisely specified. Premature death cannot deprive me of my past life. That part of my life is already gone. If I die tomorrow or if I live thirty more years my past life will be no different. It has occurred on either alternative. Rather than my past, my death deprives me of my future, of the life that I would have lived if I had lived out my natural life span.

The loss of a future biological life does not explain the misfortune of death. Compare two scenarios: In the former I now fall into a coma from which I do not recover until my death in thirty years. In the latter I die now. The latter scenario does not seem to describe a greater misfortune than the former.

The loss of our future conscious life is what underlies the misfortune of premature death. Not any future conscious life qualifies, however. Suppose that I am terminally ill with cancer. Suppose also that pain and suffering would dominate my future conscious life. If so, then death would not be a misfortune for me.

Thus, the misfortune of premature death consists of the loss to us of the future goods of consciousness. What are these goods? Much can be said about this issue, but a simple answer will do for the purposes of this essay. The goods of life are whatever we get out of life. The goods of life are those items toward which we take a "pro" attitude. They are completed projects of which we are proud, the pursuit of our goals, aesthetic enjoyments, friendships, intellectual pursuits, and physical pleasures of various sorts. The goods of life are what makes life worth living. In general, what makes life worth living for one person will not be the same as what makes life worth living for another. Nevertheless, the list of goods in each of our lives will overlap. The lists are usually different in different stages of our lives.

What makes the goods of my future good for me? One possible, but wrong, answer is my desire for those goods now. This answer does not account for those aspects of my future life that I now believe I will later value, but about which I am wrong. Neither does it account for those aspects of my future that I will come to value, but which I don't value now. What is valuable to the young may not be valuable to the middle-aged. What is valuable to the middle-aged may not be valuable to the old. Some of life's values for the elderly are best appreciated by the elderly. Thus it is wrong to say that the value of my future to me is just what I value now. What makes my future valuable to me are those aspects of my future that I will (or would) value when I will (or would) experience them, whether I value them now or not.

It follows that a person can believe that she will have a valuable future and be wrong. Furthermore, a person can believe that he will not have a valuable future and also be wrong. This is confirmed by our attitude toward many of the suicidal. We attempt to save the lives of the suicidal and to convince them that they have made an error in judgment. This does not mean that the future of an individual obtains value from the value that others confer on it. It means that, in some cases, others can make a clearer judgment of the value of a person's future *to that person* than the person herself. This often happens when one's judgment concerning the value of one's own future is clouded by personal tragedy. (Compare the views of McInerney, 1990, and Shirley, 1995.)

Thus, what is sufficient to make killing us wrong, in general, is that it causes premature death. Premature death is a misfortune. Premature death is a misfortune, in general, because it deprives an individual of a future of value. An individual's future will be valuable to that individual if that individual will come, or would come, to value it. We know that killing us is wrong. What makes killing us wrong, in general, is that it deprives us of a future of value. Thus, killing someone is wrong, in general, when it deprives her of a future like ours. I shall call this "an FLO."

Arguments in Favor of the FLO Theory

At least four arguments support this FLO account of the wrongness of killing.

The considered judgment argument

The FLO account of the wrongness of killing is correct because it fits with our considered judgment concerning the nature of the misfortune of death. The analysis of the previous section is an exposition of the nature of this considered judgment. This judgment can be confirmed. If one were to ask individuals with AIDS or with incurable cancer about the nature of their misfortune, I believe that they would say or imply that their impending loss of an FLO makes their premature death a misfortune. If they would not, then the FLO account would plainly be wrong.

The worst of crimes argument

The FLO account of the wrongness of killing is correct because it explains why we believe that killing is one of the worst of crimes. My being killed deprives me of more than does my being robbed or beaten or harmed in some other way because my being killed deprives me of all of the value of my future, not merely part of it. This explains why we make the penalty for murder greater than the penalty for other crimes.

As a corollary the FLO account of the wrongness of killing also explains why killing an adult human being is justified only in the most extreme circumstances, only in circumstances in which the loss of life to an individual is outweighed by a worse outcome if that life is not taken. Thus, we are willing to justify killing in self-defense, killing in order to save one's own life, because one's loss if one does not kill in that situation is so very great. We justify killing in a just war for similar reasons. We believe that capital punishment would be justified if, by having such an institution, fewer premature deaths would occur. The FLO account of the wrongness of killing does not entail that killing is always wrong. Nevertheless, the FLO account explains both why killing is one of the worst of crimes and, as a corollary, why the exceptions to the wrongness of killing are so very rare. A correct theory of the wrongness of killing should have these features.

The appeal to cases argument

The FLO account of the wrongness of killing is correct because it yields the correct answers in many life-and-death cases that arise in medicine and have interested philosophers.

Consider medicine first. Most people believe that it is not wrong deliberately to end the life of a person who is permanently unconscious. Thus we believe that it is not wrong to remove a feeding tube or a ventilator from a permanently comatose patient, knowing that such a removal will cause death. The FLO account of the wrongness of killing explains why this is so. A patient who is permanently unconscious cannot have a future that she would come to value, whatever her values. Therefore, according to the FLO theory of the wrongness of killing, death could not, *ceteris paribus*, be a misfortune to her. Therefore, removing the feeding tube or ventilator does not wrong her.

By contrast, almost all people believe that it is wrong, *ceteris paribus*, to withdraw medical treatment from patients who are temporarily unconscious. The FLO account of the wrongness of killing also explains why this is so. Furthermore, these two unconsciousness cases explain why the FLO account of the wrongness of killing does not include present consciousness as a necessary condition for the wrongness of killing.

Consider now the issue of the morality of legalizing active euthanasia. Proponents of active euthanasia argue that if a patient faces a future of intractable pain and wants to die, then, *ceteris paribus*, it would not be wrong for a physician to give him medicine that she knows would result in his death. This view is so universally accepted that even the strongest *opponents* of active euthanasia hold it. The official Vatican view (Sacred Congregation, 1980) is that it is permissible for a physician to administer to a patient morphine sufficient (although no more than sufficient) to control his pain even if she foresees that the morphine will result in his death. Notice how nicely the FLO account of the wrongness of killing explains this unanimity of opinion. A patient known to be in severe intractable pain is presumed to have a future without positive value. Accordingly, death would not be a misfortune for him and an action that would (foreseeably) end his life would not be wrong.

Contrast this with the standard emergency medical treatment of the suicidal. Even though the suicidal have indicated that they want to die, medical personnel will act to save their lives. This supports the view that it is not the mere *desire* to enjoy an FLO which is crucial to our understanding of the wrongness of killing. *Having* an FLO is what is crucial to the account, although one would, of course, want to make an exception in the case of fully autonomous people who refuse life-saving medical treatment. Opponents of abortion can, of course, be willing to make an exception for fully autonomous fetuses who refuse life support.

The FLO theory of the wrongness of killing also deals correctly with issues that have concerned philosophers. It implies that it would be wrong to kill (peaceful) persons from outer space who come to visit our planet even though they are biologically utterly unlike us. Presumably, if they are persons, then they will have futures that are sufficiently like ours so that it would be wrong to kill them. The FLO account of the wrongness of killing shares this feature with the personhood views of the supporters of choice. Classical opponents of abortion who locate the wrongness of abortion somehow in the biological humanity of a fetus cannot explain this.

The FLO account does not entail that there is another species of animals whose members ought not to be killed. Neither does it entail that it is permissible to kill any non-human animal. On the one hand, a supporter of animals' rights might argue that since some non-human animals have a future of value, it is wrong to kill them also, or at least it is wrong to kill them without a far better reason than we usually have for killing non-human animals. On the other hand, one might argue that the futures of non-human animals are not sufficiently like ours for the FLO account to entail that it is wrong to kill them. Since the FLO account does not specify which properties a future of another individual must possess so that killing that individual is wrong, the FLO account is indeterminate with respect to this issue. The fact that the FLO account of the wrongness of killing does not give a determinate answer to this question is not a flaw in the theory. A sound ethical account should yield the right answers in the obvious cases; it should not be required to resolve every disputed question.

A major respect in which the FLO account is superior to accounts that appeal to the concept of person is the explanation the FLO account provides of the wrongness of killing infants. There was a class of infants who had futures that included a class of events that were identical to the futures of the readers of this essay. Thus, reader, the FLO account explains why it was as wrong to kill you when you were an infant as it is to kill you now. This account can be generalized to almost all infants. Notice that the wrongness of killing infants can be explained in the absence of an account of what makes the future of an individual sufficiently valuable so that it is wrong to kill that individual. The absence of such an account explains why the FLO account is indeterminate with respect to the wrongness of killing non-human animals.

If the FLO account is the correct theory of the wrongness of killing, then because abortion involves killing fetuses and fetuses have FLOs for exactly the same reasons that infants have FLOs, abortion is presumptively seriously immoral. This inference lays the necessary groundwork for a fourth argument in favor of the FLO account that shows that abortion is wrong.

The analogy with animals argument

Why do we believe it is wrong to cause animals suffering? We believe that, in our own case and in the case of other adults and children, suffering is a misfortune. It would be as morally arbitrary to refuse to acknowledge that animal suffering is wrong as it would be to refuse to acknowledge that the suffering of persons of another race is wrong. It is, on reflection, suffering that is a misfortune, not the suffering of white males or the suffering of humans. Therefore, infliction of suffering is presumptively wrong no matter on whom it is inflicted and whether it is inflicted on persons or nonpersons. Arbitrary restrictions on the wrongness of suffering count as racism or speciesism. Not only is this argument convincing on its own, but it is the only way of justifying the wrongness of animal cruelty. Cruelty toward animals is clearly wrong. (This famous argument is due to Singer, 1979.)

The FLO account of the wrongness of abortion is analogous. We believe that, in our own case and the cases of other adults and children, the loss of a future of value is a misfortune. It would be as morally arbitrary to refuse to acknowledge that the loss of a future of value to a fetus is wrong as to refuse to acknowledge that the loss of a future of value to Jews (to take a relevant twentieth-century example) is wrong. It is, on reflection, the loss of a future of value that is a misfortune; not the loss of a future of value to adults or loss of a future of value to non-Jews. To deprive someone of a future of value is wrong no matter on whom the deprivation is inflicted and no matter whether the deprivation is inflicted on persons or nonpersons. Arbitrary restrictions on the wrongness of this deprivation count as racism, genocide or ageism. Therefore, abortion is wrong. This argument that abortion is wrong should be convincing because it has the same form as the argument for the claim that causing pain and suffering to non-human animals is wrong. Since the latter argument is convincing, the former argument should be also. Thus, an analogy with animals supports the thesis that abortion is wrong.

Replies to Objections

The four arguments in the previous section establish that abortion is, except in rare cases, seriously immoral. Not surprisingly, there are objections to this view. There are replies to the four most important objections to the FLO argument for the immorality of abortion.

The potentiality objection

The FLO account of the wrongness of abortion is a potentiality argument. To claim that a fetus *has* an FLO is to claim that a fetus now has the potential to be in a state of a certain kind in the future. It is not to claim that all ordinary fetuses *will* have FLOs. Fetuses who are aborted, of course, will not. To say that a standard fetus has an FLO is to say that a standard fetus either will have or would have a life it will or would value. To say that a standard fetus would have a life it would value is to say that it will have a life it will value if it does not die prematurely. The truth of this conditional is based upon the nature of fetuses (including the fact that they naturally age) and this nature concerns their potential.

Some appeals to potentiality in the abortion debate rest on unsound inferences. For example, one may try to generate an argument against abortion by arguing that because persons have the right to life, potential persons also have the right to life. Such an argument is plainly invalid as it stands. The premise one needs to add to make it valid would have to be something like: "If Xs have the right to Y, then potential Xs have the right to Y." This premise is plainly false. Potential presidents don't have the rights of the presidency; potential voters don't have the right to vote.

In the FLO argument potentiality is not used in order to bridge the gap between adults and fetuses as is done in the argument in the above paragraph. The FLO theory of the wrongness of killing adults is based upon the adult's potentiality to have a future of value. Potentiality is in the argument from the very beginning. Thus, the plainly false premise is not required. Accordingly, the use of potentiality in the FLO theory is not a sign of an illegitimate inference.

The argument from interests

A second objection to the FLO account of the immorality of abortion involves arguing that even though fetuses have FLOs, nonsentient fetuses do not meet the minimum conditions for having any moral standing at all because they lack interests. Steinbock (1992, p. 5) has presented this argument clearly:

> Beings that have moral status must be capable of caring about what is done to them. They must be capable of being made, if only in a rudimentary sense, happy or miserable, comfortable or distressed. Whatever reasons we may have for preserving or protecting nonsentient beings, these reasons do not refer to their own interests. For without conscious awareness, beings cannot have interests. Without interests, they cannot have a welfare of their own. Without a welfare of their own, nothing can be done for their sake. Hence, they lack moral standing or status.

Medical researchers have argued that fetuses do not become sentient until after 22 weeks of gestation (Steinbock, 1992, p. 50). If they are correct, and if Steinbock's argument is sound, then we have both an objection to the FLO account of the wrongness of abortion and a basis for a view on abortion minimally acceptable to most supporters of choice.

Steinbock's conclusion conflicts with our settled moral beliefs. Temporarily unconscious human beings are nonsentient, yet no one believes that they lack either interests or moral standing. Accordingly, neither conscious awareness nor the capacity for conscious awareness is a necessary condition for having interests.

The counter-example of the temporarily unconscious human being shows that there is something internally wrong with Steinbock's argument. The difficulty stems from an ambiguity. One cannot *take* an interest in something without being capable of caring about what is done to it. However, something can be *in* someone's interest without that individual being capable of caring about it, or about anything. Thus, life support can be *in* the interests of a temporarily unconscious patient even though the temporarily unconscious patient is incapable of *taking* an interest in that life support. If this can be so for the temporarily unconscious patient, then it is hard to see why it cannot be so for the temporarily unconscious (that is, nonsentient) fetus who requires placental life support. Thus the objection based on interests fails.

The problem of equality

The FLO account of the wrongness of killing seems to imply that the degree of wrongness associated with each killing varies inversely with the victim's age. Thus, the FLO account of the wrongness of killing seems to suggest that it is far worse to kill a five-year-old than an 89-year-old because the former is deprived of far more than the latter. However, we believe that all persons have an equal right to life. Thus, it appears that the FLO account of the wrongness of killing entails an obviously false view (Paske, 1994).

However, the FLO account of the wrongness of killing does not, strictly speaking, imply that it is worse to kill younger people than older people. The FLO account provides an explanation of the wrongness of killing that is sufficient to account for the serious presumptive wrongness of killing. It does not follow that killings cannot be wrong in other ways. For example, one might hold, as does Feldman (1992, p. 184), that in addition to the wrongness of killing that has its basis in the future life of which the victim is deprived, killing an individual is also made wrong by the admirability of an individual's past behavior. Now the amount of admirability will presumably vary directly with age, whereas the amount of deprivation will vary inversely with age. This tends to equalize the wrongness of murder.

However, even if, *ceteris paribus*, it is worse to kill younger persons than older persons, there are good reasons for adopting a doctrine of the legal equality of murder. Suppose that we tried to estimate the seriousness of a crime of murder by appraising the value of the FLO of which the victim had been deprived. How would one go about doing this? In the first place, one would be confronted by the old problem of interpersonal comparisons of utility. In the second place, estimation of the value of a future would involve putting oneself, not into the shoes of the victim at the time she was killed, but rather into the shoes the victim would have worn had the victim survived, and then estimating from that perspective the worth of that person's future. This task seems difficult, if not impossible. Accordingly, there are reasons to adopt a convention that murders are equally wrong.

Furthermore, the FLO theory, in a way, explains why we do adopt the doctrine of the legal equality of murder. The FLO theory explains why we regard murder as one of the worst of crimes, since depriving someone of a future like ours deprives her of more than depriving her of anything else. This gives us a reason for making the punishment for murder very harsh, as harsh as is compatible with civilized society. One should not make the punishment for younger victims harsher than that. Thus, the doctrine of the equal legal right to life does not seem to be incompatible with the FLO theory.

The contraception objection

The strongest objection to the FLO argument for the immorality of abortion is based on the claim that, because contraception results in one less FLO, the FLO argument entails that contraception, indeed, abstention from sex when conception is possible, is immoral. Because neither contraception nor abstention from sex when conception is possible is immoral, the FLO account is flawed.

There is a cogent reply to this objection. If the argument of the early part of this essay is correct, then the central issue concerning the morality of abortion is the problem of whether fetuses are individuals who are members of the class of individuals whom it is seriously presumptively wrong to kill. The properties of being human and alive, of being a person, and of having an FLO are criteria that participants in the abortion debate have offered to mark off the relevant class of individuals. The central claim of this essay is that having an FLO marks off the relevant class of individuals. A defender of the FLO view could, therefore, reply that since, at the time of contraception, there is no individual to have an FLO, the FLO account does not entail that contraception is wrong. The wrong of killing is primarily a wrong to the individual who is killed; at the time of contraception there is no individual to be wronged.

However, someone who presses the contraception objection might have an answer to this reply. She might say that the sperm and egg are the individuals deprived of an FLO at the time of contraception. Thus, there are individuals whom contraception deprives of an FLO and if depriving an individual of an FLO is what makes killing wrong, then the FLO theory entails that contraception is wrong.

There is also a reply to this move. In the case of abortion, an objectively determinate individual is the subject of harm caused by the loss of an FLO. This individual is a fetus. In the case of contraception, there are far more candidates (see Norcross, 1990). Let us consider some possible candidates in order of the increasing number of individuals harmed: (1) The single harmed individual might be the combination of the particular sperm and the particular egg that would have united to form a zygote if contraception had not been used. (2) The two harmed individuals might be the particular sperm itself, and, in addition, the ovum itself that would have physically combined to form the zygote. (This is modeled on the double homicide of two persons who would otherwise in a short time fuse. (1) is modeled on harm to a single entity some of whose parts are not physically contiguous, such as a university.) (3) The many harmed individuals might be the millions of *combinations* of sperm and the released ovum whose (small) chances of having an FLO were reduced by the successful contraception. (4) The even larger class of harmed individuals (larger by one) might be the class consisting of all of the individual sperm in an ejaculate and, in addition, the individual ovum released at the time of the successful contraception. (1) through (4) are all candidates for being the subject(s) of harm in the case of successful contraception or abstinence from sex. Which should be chosen? Should we hold a lottery? There seems to be no non-arbitrarily determinate subject of harm in the case of successful contraception. But if there is no such subject of harm, then no determinate thing was harmed. If no determinate thing was harmed, then (in the case of contraception) no wrong has been done. Thus, the FLO account of the wrongness of abortion does not entail that contraception is wrong.

Conclusion

This essay contains an argument for the view that, except in unusual circumstances, abortion is seriously wrong. Deprivation of an FLO explains why killing adults and children is wrong. Abortion deprives fetuses of FLOs. Therefore, abortion is wrong. This argument is based on an account of the wrongness of killing that is a result of our considered judgment of the nature of the misfortune of premature death. It accounts for why we regard killing as one of the worst of crimes. It is superior to alternative accounts of the wrongness of killing that are intended to provide insight into the ethics of abortion. This account of the wrongness of killing is supported by the way it handles cases in which our moral judgments are settled. This account has an analogue in the most plausible account of the wrongness of causing animals to suffer. This account makes no appeal to religion. Therefore, the FLO account shows that abortion, except in rare instances, is seriously wrong.

Note

1 This essay is an updated version of a view that first appeared in the *Journal of Philosophy* (1989). This essay incorporates attempts to deal with the objections of McInerney (1990), Norcross (1990), Shirley (1995), Steinbock (1992), and Paske (1994) to the original version of the view.

References

Beckwith, F. J., *Politically Correct Death: Answering Arguments for Abortion Rights* (Grand Rapids, Michigan: Baker Books, 1993).

Benn, S. I., "Abortion, infanticide, and respect for persons," *The Problem of Abortion*, ed. J. Feinberg (Belmont, California: Wadsworth, 1973), pp. 92–104.

Engelhardt, Jr, H. T., *The Foundations of Bioethics* (New York: Oxford University Press, 1986).

Feinberg, J., "Abortion," *Matters of Life and Death: New Introductory Essays in Moral Philosophy*, ed. T. Regan (New York: Random House, 1986).

Feldman, F., *Confrontations with the Reaper: A Philosophical Study of the Nature and Value of Death* (New York: Oxford University Press, 1992).

Kant, I., *Lectures on Ethics*, tr. L. Infeld (New York: Harper, 1963).

Marquis, D. B., "A future like ours and the concept of person: a reply to McInerney and Paske," *The Abortion Controversy: A Reader*, ed. L. P. Pojman and F. J. Beckwith (Boston: Jones and Bartlett, 1994), pp. 354–68.

——, "Fetuses, futures and values: a reply to Shirley," *Southwest Philosophy Review*, 11 (1995): 263–5.

——, "Why abortion is immoral," *Journal of Philosophy*, 86 (1989): 183–202.

McInerney, P., "Does a fetus already have a future like ours?," *Journal of Philosophy*, 87 (1990): 264–8.

Noonan, J., "An almost absolute value in history," in *The Morality of Abortion*, ed. J. Noonan (Cambridge, Massachusetts: Harvard University Press).

Norcross, A., "Killing, abortion, and contraception: a reply to Marquis," *Journal of Philosophy*, 87 (1990): 268–77.

Paske, G., "Abortion and the neo-natal right to life: a critique of Marquis's futurist argument," *The Abortion Controversy: A Reader*, ed. L. P. Pojman and F. J. Beckwith (Boston: Jones and Bartlett, 1994), pp. 343–53.

Sacred Congregation for the Propagation of the Faith, *Declaration on Euthanasia* (Vatican City, 1980).

Shirley, E. S., "Marquis' argument against abortion: a critique," *Southwest Philosophy Review*, 11 (1995): 79–89.

Singer, P., "Not for humans only: the place of nonhumans in environmental issues," *Ethics and Problems of the 21st Century*, ed. K. E. Goodpaster and K. M. Sayre (South Bend: Notre Dame University Press, 1979).

Steinbock, B., *Life Before Birth: The Moral and Legal Status of Embryos and Fetuses* (New York: Oxford University Press, 1992).

Thomson, J. J., "A defense of abortion," *Philosophy and Public Affairs*, 1 (1971): 47–66.

Tooley, M., "Abortion and infanticide," *Philosophy and Public Affairs*, 2 (1972): 37–65.

Warren, M. A., "On the moral and legal status of abortion," *Monist*, 57 (1973): 43–61.

8

Redefining Abortion

Barbara Katz Rothman

If pregnancy is a developing relationship, if a fetus is part of its mother's body, gradually becoming an other, then what is an abortion? For some women, and maybe for most women early on in pregnancy, an abortion is much the same as contraception: a way of not entering that relationship. And for some women, and maybe for most women as the pregnancy progresses, abortion is a way of ending a relationship, and with that, of stopping the growth of the other. The difference between avoiding and ending a relationship is not simply a matter of weeks of gestation. An abortion at, say, ten weeks may mean different things to different women, and different things to the same woman in different pregnancies. One woman schedules an abortion with less emotional involvement than she has in scheduling dental work. Another schedules an abortion and begins a lifelong grieving for the death of her baby.

Is this the contradiction it appears to be? No, not if we take a genuinely woman–centered view of pregnancy and of abortion, and recognize that abortion, like pregnancy itself, takes its meaning from the woman in whose body the pregnancy is unfolding.

Nor is it a contradiction that women take motherhood very seriously, and yet may have abortions relatively "casually." Abortion is one way a woman prevents herself from entering into an unwanted relationship, a way she can avoid the serious commitment of motherhood. Women understand motherhood to mean a lifetime commitment, a central relationship: we must have ways of avoiding such a commitment precisely because we do take it so seriously. In this way, the relation between abortion and motherhood is like the relation between divorce and marriage. In those societies that take marriage most seriously, that view the marital relationship as the central one in life, the divorce rate is the highest: people have to have a way out of such an important commitment. In those societies in which husband and wife are not expected to be all to each other, divorce is relatively rare: it matters less to whom you are married. If women took motherhood casually, abortion would be much less important. We could abandon, sell, or just ignore our children. Motherhood would not take over our lives.

But for the most part women do take motherhood seriously. And it is because of that, not in spite of that, that some abortions are easy, avoiding motherhood, while some are hard, ending motherhood. It is the meaning of a pregnancy for a woman that shapes the meaning an abortion holds for her.

A very young woman, after a few hurried sexual encounters in her boyfriend's car, finds her period two weeks late. All she wants is to get out of "trouble" and fast. Another woman weighs the hassles of an occasional abortion against the hassles of careful contraception, and decides to take her chances. Another woman chooses a diaphragm as the best compromise between safety and efficiency – and knows that this choice of contraception over her reproductive years could mean at least one and maybe several "accidental" pregnancies and abortions. A couple of abortions over the next twenty years are part of her contraceptive planning. And yet another woman learns that the baby she carries – a baby for whom she has rented a larger apartment, refused a job transfer, and knitted a receiving blanket – would be born with a fatal disease. She aborts, packs away the blanket, takes the job transfer after all, and mourns the death of her child.

Abortion truly is all of these things: the death of a wanted baby, a way out of trouble, a contraceptive technique. As part of contraception, abortion expresses an unwillingness to make a baby, stopping the division of self, stopping a bit of oneself from going on to become someone else. In this sense abortion is not fundamentally different from contraception. Each month that a woman ovulates she releases one particular egg, an egg with an already limited range of potential. This month's egg is capable of becoming a different baby than last month's, than next month's. The egg not fertilized when it comes forth in time for the new year is September's baby not to be. The egg that carried a particular dominant gene is a brown-eyed baby not to come. Let that egg be fertilized and then stopped, aborted rather than "contracepted" into nothingness, and it is a still more specific baby not to be.

Why do we make such an enormous distinction in modern society between abortion and contraception? One answer lies in certain philosophical premises about the nature of embryonic life. And yet some contraceptives – the IUD, some pills – are technically abortifacients. They do not prevent sperm from joining egg and creating a zygote, the genetically unique potential person, but prevent the very early embryo from implanting. So why is it that abortion planned and recognized by the woman, abortion deliberately controlled by the woman, is said to be distinct from, and less acceptable than, contraception?

The History of Abortion

The more pragmatic answer as to why abortion and contraception are perceived as being very different comes from a look at the historical development of contemporary abortion and contraception practices.

Women of ancient times have left few written records. Most of what we know about the early history of abortion comes from the responses of men. Early Greek and Roman law put restraints on abortion, both to protect women from mutilation and to guarantee that wives not deprive husbands of children. Jewish law is largely silent on the subject. In Christian thinking, Augustine in the fourth century concluded that the soul was not present until the time of quickening, when the woman felt movement. Abortion prior to that point was therefore not the destruction of a human life. In the thirteenth century Thomas Aquinas placed the presence of the soul at forty days after conception for a male, and eighty days for a female. It was not until the seventeenth century that the Roman Catholic Church crystallized its strong stand against abortion.[1]

The Catholic Church's current position is both internally consistent and, ironically, essentially the same as the argument I am making from the other side: abortion and contraception – and for that matter in vitro fertilization and artificial insemination – are fundamentally the *same*. But in contrast to what I am saying, the Church objects to all of these efforts to control our reproduction. Both the Church's position and mine focus on *control* rather than technique as the important issue, a control I value and the Church deplores.

In America, abortion has always been a personal problem for women, a problem of safety, access, and control, but as a political issue it dates back only to the mid-nineteenth century, when physicians used abortions as one more stepping stone toward gaining their professional status. Abortions were widely available in America at the time, advertised in newspapers and performed by people with a variety of backgrounds. In driving out the "quacks," physicians were in one sense doing what they were doing in other areas of practice. They replaced midwives at childbirth in the same way: by attempting to redefine the services provided as "medical" in nature. But with abortion, another dimension was added. Physicians argued that their knowledge of embryonic and fetal development, minimal as it truly was at the time, enabled them to know what the women having abortions presumably did not know: that the embryo was a baby. Having made this claim, doctors were able to say not only that the abortionists were incompetent, dirty, and backward – all the charges they leveled at the midwives and their other competition – but also that what they were doing was wrong and immoral, a kind of murder.

Physicians did not, however, want an absolute ban on abortions. What the doctors claimed, a contradiction highlighted in the work of Kristen Luker,[2] was that abortion was wrong, but physicians alone could determine when it was necessary. For example, abortion was necessary when the pregnancy threatened the life of the mother, a determination over which doctors claimed technical expertise. Thus there were two kinds of abortions: the ones the doctors did not do, which were "immoral," and the ones the doctors did do, which were both moral and, almost by definition, therapeutic.

The argument the physicians made, in sum, was that abortion was a crime against the fetus, the potential baby, made acceptable only when doctors thought it was necessary. But the standards of necessity the doctors applied were not the same standards that women – especially poor women without access to the sympathetic ear of a private physician – would necessarily apply.

Partly because of the lack of skill of the medical doctors themselves, and partly because the abortionists were indeed driven "underground," there was another powerful argument to be made against abortion: it was dangerous; it threatened the life and the health of the woman. Relatively early on in her crusade for available contraception, Margaret Sanger addressed this issue of the threat to women's health posed by abortion and the lack of contraception.

It is informative to look at her 1920 distinction between contraception and abortion: "If no children are desired, the meeting of the male sperm and the ovum must be prevented. When scientific means are employed to prevent this meeting, one is said to practice birth control. The means used is known as a contraceptive. If, however, a contraceptive is not used and the sperm meets the ovule and development begins, any attempt at removing it or stopping its further growth is called abortion."[3] There is no mention here of fetus, embryo, or unborn child, let alone murder, killing, or destruction – yet she is making a strong argument for the superiority of contraception over abortion.

There is, in the contemporary context, a striking lack of moral argument here: the superiority of contraception over abortion is presented as a safety issue, not a moral issue. "There is no doubt," Sanger wrote, "that women are apt to look upon abortion as of little consequence, and to treat it accordingly."[4] Here, one used to the 1980s' right-to-life rhetoric expects a condemnation of "unthinking, unfeeling women who abort casually." But no, Sanger is talking about the health and safety of the woman herself: "in an abortion there is always a very serious risk to the health and often to the life of the patient. It is only the women of wealth who can afford the best medical skill, care and treatment, both at the time of the operation and afterwards. In this way, they escape the usual serious consequences."[5] After reviewing the dangers of abortion, and its widespread practice in America at the time, she concluded: "There is the case in a nutshell. Family limitation will always be practiced as it is now being practiced – either by birth control or by abortion. We know that. The one means health and happiness – a stronger, better race. The other means disease, suffering, death."[6]

In the almost seventy years since Sanger's writing, the right to contraception has been widely accepted. We have gone beyond that, in fact, to think of contraception as more a *responsibility* than a right. Only immature, thoughtless, irresponsible people fail to use contraception, most Americans have come to think. Sanger's arguments about the relationship between too many mouths to feed and poverty have been accepted, and more. There is a film about children living in poverty that I often show to my undergraduate sociology students. Two of the three families depicted are small, just one or two children. One family is large, with both parents, eight children, and a grandchild. Students get angry at that: the other people are poor in spite of limiting family size, but these people are poor, it would seem, because they didn't use contraception. It's their own fault, self-righteous young students tell me. Why did they have those children if they couldn't afford them? Children, they believe, are luxuries you shouldn't indulge in, especially not in quantity, if you can't afford the upkeep.

So the idea of controlling fertility is now accepted as a moral good: for most Americans it is the responsible, mature, right way to behave.

But abortion – abortion is not just a way of controlling fertility, a form of "family limitation" to be compared with other forms on the basis of safety. Those same undergraduates get just as angry when we talk about women having repeated abortions. Abortion today is not just a less safe way of avoiding unwanted births. In fact, diaphragms with backup abortions are safer than the more effective contraceptives, the pill or the IUD. Safety is simply no longer the issue. The woman's life or health is not *seen* as threatened. The entire focus of the anti-abortion argument has shifted from the woman to the products of conception, the "life" for which they claim a right. It is not what she is doing to herself that the modern anti-abortion argument asks, but what she is doing to her embryo, to her fetus. And it is not her physical self or her safety that the pro–choice argument most often addresses, but her moral status, the issue of her moral agency, *her* right to life, to control her body, her motherhood, her self that is argued over and against the rights of the products of conception.

While Sanger and the birth–control activists won and birth control itself became widely available, the larger debate underlying the legalization of birth control did not get fully resolved. The underlying argument is about the relation between womanhood and motherhood: how much control over her motherhood a woman can exercise and still be acceptable as a woman. Much of this is now being argued out in the context of abortion. In 1920 Sanger wrote:

> Today . . . woman is rising in fundamental revolt. Even her efforts at mere reform are . . . steps in that direction. Underneath each of them is the feminine urge to complete freedom. Millions

of women are asserting their right to voluntary motherhood. They are determined to decide for themselves whether they shall become mothers, under what conditions, and when. This is the fundamental revolt referred to. It is for women the key to the temple of liberty.[7]

For our today, too, reproductive freedom often seems to be the fundamental revolt, the key to women's liberty. Abortion today, like contraception in 1920, is the touchstone for understanding motherhood, and womanhood. Is there a "new woman"? Is the experience of motherhood changing? In America today, abortion – the experience, the institution, the ethics, the *existence* of abortion – has become the starting and the stopping point for such discussion. People argue to and argue from abortion in their understanding of motherhood and of womanhood.

"But if a woman has the right . . . ," people say, and then argue toward or away from abortion. "Then what stops . . . ?" and "Then why can't . . . ?" they ask. Heated discussions of Baby M and Baby Doe, of birth control and controlling birth, of maternity leaves and paternity suits come back again and again to abortion as the point of reference.

And just what does abortion itself mean to modern America? Does it signify the two competing images of woman, the independent, person of the world on the one hand, and the nurturant, sacrificing, center of the home on the other?[8] Or is the competition not between the women a woman could be, but between the woman as real, flawed, genuine life in progress, and the fetus as fantasized, perfect, imagined life potential? Abortion signifies all of this and more, of course – individual and collective decision making, bodily autonomy and societal control, personal needs and social policy, rights and needs and responsibilities, connections and separations.

Constructing the Fetus

It is the separations that capture my attention: the separation of women from motherhood, of pregnancy from birth, of sexuality from reproduction, and of fetuses from mothers. The most fundamental change I hear between the arguments that Sanger and her contemporaries were making and today's debate is that the fetus has been brought into the discussion, the fetus not as part of its mother, but as separate, a little person lying in the womb. A woman's conflict about motherhood is not new; her need to balance the needs of her life as it is, her children that are, against those that are not yet, that too is not new. What is new is this cultural creation, the fetus, the "unborn child."

There is today, it seems, a cultural fascination with the fetus. Janet Gallagher compares it with whale watching[9] – the fetus, like the whale, symbolizes something pure, something of the world and innocent of the world. Both, fetuses and whales, have been made "real" for us by science, by an invasion of their watery worlds with recording equipment. People who live hundreds of miles from the sea can picture the sounding whale, see its smooth back, its spouting blowhole. And people who have never been pregnant, never shared anyone's pregnancy intimately, can visualize the fetal head shape, fetal hands, fetal movement in utero.

The ability to penetrate the hidden world of the fetus has been used – with great passion and power – on both sides of the abortion debate in the United States. "Right-to-life" advocates have used these techniques to make the fetus visible, real, a being who can capture our compassion. The most dramatic example of this is, of course, the film *The Silent Scream*, which purports to show via sonogram (an ultrasound picture) a twelve-week fetus during an abortion. With the use of special effects (dramatic slowing and speeding up of the film to make fetal movement appear to change in intensity) and powerfully suggestive language (the "child" in its "sanctuary") the audience is asked to share the identification with the fetus within, and to ignore entirely the woman – never shown – in whom it resides.

On the other hand, these same techniques are being marshaled in support of the right to abort. Women are being encouraged to have more and more prenatal screening tests to ascertain the condition of the fetus, and to abort when the medical determination is unsatisfactory. Abortions where the fetus would be "defective" are among the most socially acceptable of abortions in America. Fears of disability, extreme repugnance toward the mentally retarded, and firmly embedded cultural ideas about health combine to shape our attitude toward abortion for "fetal defect." These abortions, "selective" abortions, are also called "medically indicated" or "therapeutic" abortions. Like the old abortions to save the life of the mother, these are the abortions of which doctors approve. But this argument for legalized abortion, unlike the earlier one, focuses not on the woman, but on the fetus within.[10]

It is important to remember that not all arguments for legal abortion are feminist arguments. The feminist pro-choice voice has been only one of the forces for legalized abortion in America, and not, I think, necessarily the dominant one.

In fact, not everyone who is in favor of legalized abortion is necessarily pro-choice – that is, not all would have the decision to abort be entirely the decision of the woman herself. There are those who think a single woman or a married couple who want to have an abortion should be able to do so, but that a married woman whose husband wants the child should not have the individual freedom to abort. There are those who claim that it is morally wrong to bring to term a baby who would have some particular disease or suffer in some way. They are not speaking of a woman's right to choose, but of a moral obligation to abort. And there are those who would like to see "welfare mothers" be required to abort their third – or fifth, or twelfth – pregnancy and be forcibly sterilized.

One of the unresolved problems of the feminist reproductive-rights movement is what to do with these non-feminist allies in the abortion movement. This, too, is not a new problem, but one that the early birth-control movement faced. Sanger made her alliances with the eugenics movement and with the population-control movement. The contemporary feminist reproductive-rights movement does the same: making uneasy alliances with the new eugenics movement, which looks at embryos and fetuses as products suitable for quality-control testing, and with the population-control movement, with its often implicit classist and racist agenda. At the clinical level, the focus is on the fetus; at the policy level the focus is on the population. The woman is lost.

The Medicalization of Abortion

Sanger and the birth-control movement made alliances that were probably necessary, but there are costs, and we are still paying them. For Sanger, the most powerful allies were the doctors. The compromise she made was to give doctors control over contraception, to medicalize birth control. Fitting a diaphragm is no harder than fitting a shoe. Women can do it for themselves. Yet birth control for women was incorporated firmly into the practice of medicine – a diaphragm requires a prescription. Women coming for birth-control information and services are "patients."

So it is with abortion. The legalization of abortion in America has been as much a reaffirmation of the rights of doctors to practice medicine as they see fit as it has been an affirmation of women's rights to control their reproduction. Abortion, *Roe* v. *Wade* told us, is a decision between a woman *and her physician*.

For all of its power as metaphor, the actual practice of abortion is strangely stripped of its meaning. As experience and as institution, abortion is medicalized, constructed as a medical event, under medical control, and with the culture of medicine providing the meanings, defining women's experiences. Abortion occurs in clinics, in settings removed from women's lives, by people removed from women's lives. The medicalization of abortion – giving doctors absolute control over the procedure itself – means that "a woman's right to choose [abortion] is always circumscribed by the physician's right not to perform it."[11] By what the profession of medicine is and is not willing to do, doctors continue to shape the availability and the experience of abortion in America.

Doctors do not like to do abortions. That, Jonathan Imber, in a recent book on doctors and abortion, clearly demonstrates. Their objections are not primarily phrased as moral or ethical issues. Early abortions are boring; they have "low priority in terms of medical knowledge and technique." But late abortions? Here Imber shows us the contradiction in the doctors' positions: "Most doctors were unwilling to perform second trimester abortions precisely because of their technical challenge."[12] Obviously, something else is at stake here. Imber says it is an effort to avoid controversy. As one of the doctors he interviewed said: "But the real reason we try to avoid them is that I don't want to be known as the local abortionist. I want to be known as a doctor who loves mommies and their babies."[13]

For this doctor – and I think he speaks for many – there is a distinction to be made between the women who get abortions, whom he dislikes, and the "mommies" whom he loves. There are, of course, not two groups of women – those who have abortions and those who have babies. These are the same women at different moments of their lives.

Abortion to serve the needs of individual *women* is not a high priority for many doctors. Abortion for eugenics or for "social" reasons is. While at least one of the doctors Imber interviewed recognized the threat "not only Jews need worry about" of using abortion as a way to "keep the numbers of dirty, poor people down," others contended that "family planning services were reaching the wrong people," and that "the population problem is not caused by the offspring of young engineers or doctors." These views were, Imber says, "generously offered," a point of pride, an example of the medical profession serving the community.[14]

If doctors do not themselves want to do abortions, but tend to think some people ought to be having them, and if they don't want to be known as "abortionists," but some of the good mommies do come in with unwanted pregnancies, then what is the solution? As Imber convincingly demonstrates, it has been to move abortion outside of the private practice of medicine and into the clinic. Doctors do not do abortions – *clinics* do.

And what are the consequences of relying on referral to clinics as the solution? "Practitioners have reinforced the market stronghold that the larger clinics maintain over abortion," creating a system of mass-production abortion services.[15]

This solution, as it is practiced, is a very far cry from the feminist vision of abortion that was offered in the late 1960s and early 1970s, in which women's need for abortion was seen as connected to women's lives, as occurring in the context of who a woman is and how she lives her life. Abortion was a political issue, personally experienced, and a personal issue, politically ensnared. Clinics today revolve around the procedure of abortion, with the political work largely absent, and the counseling relegated from the heart of the event to a support service for medical staff. Counselors serve the clinic and the medical workers as much as or more than they serve the women – who themselves are relegated to the status of "patient."

Abortion has been legal in the United States since 1973; clinics have been part of the open, legal landscape for fewer than fifteen years as of this writing. For some people, that is just as good as forever – for the young teenagers now coming to abortion clinics, it truly is a lifetime. We now see the legacy of legalized, medicalized abortion, and it is a legacy that troubles many people.

In the past twenty years abortion counseling has shifted from illegal political work – work highly valued by the counterculture in which it was performed and strongly disdained by the society at large – to the more mundane work of easing women through legal and often profit-making clinics. What has this medicalization meant for the workers, and consequently for the women using the services? For an answer, let us compare what Carol Joffe found in a study of abortion counselors conducted shortly after legalization[16] with what Melinda Detlefs[17] and Wendy Simonds[18] saw in two separate and more recent studies of abortion-counseling services.

Very few of the current counselors have been doing abortion counseling for even as long as four years, so most of those working now entered the field long after the legalization and medicalization of abortion were settled issues. These women were not, unlike the earlier counselors, drawn into a political cause. Counselors Detlefs interviewed said they "stumbled" into it, got involved "accidentally." They feel, as one put it, "no real firm commitment" to doing abortion work. In marked contrast to the way it was seen by those interviewed by Joffe, abortion counseling today is more likely than not "just a job." The political commitment, the sense of doing something important for women, those feelings that motivated the counselors Joffe interviewed a decade ago, are strangely lacking now. One of the counselors Detlefs interviewed spoke almost longingly of how things were in the years before she entered the field, the years Joffe wrote about, when people were "adamant about it. And that's gone . . . after a while it's easy to start forgetting what's going on here and why you're doing it. . . . The awareness is gone, lost. At least here and a lot of places – now it's just shuffle, shuffle, shuffle the people."

What has happened in these intervening years to change things so? Some of the changes are the result of the work the early abortion counselors accomplished. In the early years, the activism, the energy, came from the pro-choice groups. But with the legalization of abortion, the energy shifted. These days, the pro-choice people are holding a defensive line at best – and doing a good job of it, as witness the response to the nomination of Robert Bork to the Supreme Court – but most of the activism comes from the right-to-life people. Joffe predicted that the pressure of the right-to-life movement would have the effect of stifling whatever discomfort counselors might feel about abortion. But that is not what happened. Counselors themselves are no longer uniformly pro-choice. Doubts come creeping in in two ways. Some of the people who "fell into" abortion counseling as "just a job" came without pro-choice feelings, certainly without strong pro-choice commitment. Others find themselves swayed by the right-to-life arguments, or just the right-to-life presence. As one counselor Detlefs interviewed said, "When you see people fighting so hard, you wonder."

And Wendy Simonds points to the conflicts the birth-control movement itself has created for attitudes toward abortion. Her research was done at a clinic which offered contraception and abortion services. There, she found, despite a stated insistence on value-free counseling, "The staff has definite views about abortion, and definite goals which it hopes to accomplish with each patient. . . . Though the guidebook (for counselor training) says that a counselor should 'help' the client choose a contraceptive, what is really expected of the counselor is that she impress upon the client the importance of contraception, which employees assume. Underneath the talk of objectivity, the organization exists to supply contraception." The clinic staff feels that abortion should not be used as contraception. Simonds says that when staff members talk about patients among themselves, they often whisper the word *abortion*, or call it "the procedure." They are dismayed by women coming for repeated abortions – for clinic workers these are contraceptive failures, not birth-control successes.

The medicalization of abortion has meant that medicine defines the meaning of the experience for all of those involved, for the other health workers as much as or more than for the women seeking abortions. What comes to be seen as being of significance is not a woman taking control over her life, making decisions for herself, but the medical procedure. The actual abortion, the physical act of suctioning, becomes the heart of what happens. The women counselors do the "people work" for the doctors and technicians, who do the "real work" of the clinic. The counselors mediate between the institution, which encourages a speedup to get the women on and off the tables as quickly as possible, and the human being who is being "processed." Rather than simply giving orders – sign on the dotted line, undress here, lie there, pay on your way out – the counselors are engaged in face-to-face interactions with the clients, easing them through the clinics. Even in nonprofit settings, the institutional goals of processing as many women as possible, of avoiding lawsuits, and of freeing doctors to do only highly valued technical work are met by having low-paid, nurturant women mediate between the client and the institution. The counselors are there, but the feminist goal of what the counselors were to do – helping a woman take charge of her life – has given way to the institutional goal of taking charge of the patients.

So the reproductive-rights feminists of the 1970s won, and abortion is available – just as the reproductive-rights feminists of the 1920s won, and contraception is available. But in another sense, we did not win. We did not win, could not win, because Sanger was right. What we really wanted was the fundamental revolt, the "key to the temple of liberty." A doctor's fitting for a diaphragm, or a clinic appointment for an abortion, is not the revolution. It is not even a woman-centered approach to reproduction.

Reconstructing Abortion

In 1965 *Life* magazine published the first photos of "life in the womb"[19] and we embarked on the cultural creation of the fetus. Now when we look at a pregnant woman, in our heads we look through her, to the fetus we know lies in there. If we were to look at the *woman*, at what she is *doing*, we could say that she is starting to make a baby. We could indeed think of her as a "little bit pregnant," as starting the pregnancy, beginning her entry into motherhood. But if we focus on the seed, focus on the fertilized egg, we come to think that the baby is there already, inside her, not the creation of her body but its captive. And then it comes to seem only reasonable, what ethicist Daniel Callahan calls a "balancing rights perspective,"[20] to weigh the rights of this fetus against the rights of *its mother*. But by creating this fetus, this unborn child as a social being, we turn this woman into "its mother" – defining her in terms of the fetus even as she seeks to avoid making a baby, avoid becoming a mother.

If women controlled abortion, controlled not only the clinics, but the values and the thinking behind abortion, would we make such a distinction between contraception, not letting this month's egg grow, and abortion, not letting this month's fertilized egg grow? Or could we put early abortion back together with contraception, into the larger idea of birth control, and say that until we feel we've made a baby, an abortion is stopping a baby from happening, not killing one? Seeing women as creators, not containers, means seeing abortion as refusing to create, not destroying that which we contain.

That standard, that there is a baby in there when the woman in whose body it exists feels it is a baby, is very close to the traditional cultural acceptance of quickening as the standard for abortion. Until a baby had quickened, that is, until the woman felt it move, abortion was her private business. Once the baby communicated itself to her, and through her to the society at large, then abortion was no longer generally acceptable. *Then* a "balancing" of rights was necessary.

A woman-centered understanding of abortion would return to a woman-centered standard. It would not look to the gestational age of the fetus, to its "viability," or to any other fetal standard for judging the meaning or the acceptability of an abortion. We would not feel obligated to counsel some women to take their abortions "more seriously," nor would we deny, or feel threatened by, the very real grief of other women. We could accept the fact that for one woman, in one pregnancy, an abortion is a minor inconvenience and a small price she expects to pay now and again for an active sex life and a safe barrier contraceptive; and that for another woman, or for the *same* woman in another pregnancy, an abortion is the death of a baby.

Notes

1   A brief history of abortion can be found in Hyman Rodman, Betty Sarvis, and Joy Bonar, 1987, *The Abortion Question* (New York: Columbia University Press).

2   Kristen Luker, 1984, *Abortion and the Polities of Motherhood* (Berkeley, California: University of California Press).

3   Margaret Sanger, 1920, *Women and the New Race* (New York: Blue Ribbon Books), p. 124.

4   Ibid.

5   Ibid., p. 125.

6   Ibid., pp. 128–129.

7   Ibid., p. 5.

8   This is the contrast Luker focuses on in her analysis of the abortion controversy.

9   Janet Gallagher, personal communication.

10 For a fuller discussion of the link between the abortion-rights movement and the eugenics movement, see Barbara Katz Rothman, 1986, *The Tentative Pregnancy: Prenatal Diagnosis and the Future of Motherhood* (New York: Viking Press).

11 Jonathan B. Imber, 1986, *Abortion and the Private Practice of Medicine* (New Haven: Yale University Press), p. xiv.

12 Ibid., p. 93.

13 Ibid., p. 68.

14 Ibid., pp. 49, 52.

15 Ibid., p. 120.

16 Carole Joffe, 1987, *The Regulation of Sexuality: Experiences of Family Planning Workers* (Philadelphia: Temple University Press).

17 Melinda Detlefs, 1986, unpublished masters thesis, Graduate School and University Center of the City University of New York.

18 Wendy Simonds, "At an Impasse: Inside an Abortion Clinic," unpublished paper.

19 Lennart Nilson, 1965, "Miracle in the Womb," *Life*, April 30.

20 Daniel Callahan, presentation at Hastings Center, September 9, 1987.

Animals

Many people think the morality of abortion hinges entirely on the nature of the fetus: that once we know its moral status, then we will know if abortion is moral and if it ought to be legal. Several authors in the previous section repudiated this rendition of the debate. Nonetheless, it is safe to say that the moral status of the fetus is *an element* of that debate. Parallel questions play an important, and probably a pivotal, role in determining our moral obligations, if any, to non-human animals. Do non-human animals have substantial or full moral status? If so, why? If not, why not? A central tenet of morality is that we should treat like cases alike. That is, morality requires that we should treat two creatures the same unless there is some general and relevant difference between them that morally justifies a difference in treatment. Thus, I can properly treat a pebble differently than I treat my friend George, because George and the pebble are relevantly different, different in ways that justify a difference in treatment.

We know there are serious moral limitations on how we should treat humans. We generally have no moral qualms about what we do to and with rocks. What about non-human animals? Are they more like the pebble or more like George? Are they sufficiently like us that they merit moral status? If so, how much status? Or are non-human animals sufficiently different from us that we can treat them as we wish – the way we might treat a pebble?

Of course, since not all animals are the same, it would be more precise to ask how we should treat those non-human animals (mostly mammals and birds) that we standardly use for food, for product and biomedical testing, and for their skins. At one time people assumed these animals had no moral worth – that we could morally do to them whatever we wanted, whenever we wanted, for any reason we wanted. For instance, nineteenth-century scientists would demonstrate the circulation of the blood by nailing a fully conscious dog to a large board, and then dissecting it. They cavalierly dismissed the dog's yelps as squeaks in the animal "machine."

Most philosophers, scientists, and laypeople have long since abandoned those views. Virtually everyone now agrees that it would be wrong to torture or kill (at least) a mammal or bird just for fun. Certainly all the authors in this section would agree. The issue for them is not whether these animals have moral status, but rather why and how much status they have. That is the rub.

In the section on ABORTION, the authors disagreed about the proper criteria for moral status. One strong strand of popular opinion holds that a fetus has moral status because it is a human being. In contrast, Warren thought only persons had moral status, while Marquis thought only creatures with a "future like ours" had moral status. Although the authors discussing animals do not use the same criteria of moral status, their criteria do resemble those used in the abortion debate.

For instance, Fox claims that only creatures who have rights and responsibilities can have full moral status, can be members of the moral community. Moreover, only creatures with critical self-awareness and the ability to manipulate complex concepts can have rights and responsibilities. That is why, on his view, humans – but not animals – are members of the moral community. Although his criteria of moral status are stronger than Warren's, they are conceptual kin.

Regan claims Warren's and Fox's criteria are too stringent. Were we to adopt such rigorous criteria of moral status, we would exclude many humans (infants and retarded adults, etc.) from the moral community. Regan claims, though, that infants and retarded adults have moral status although they are neither full persons (in Warren's sense) nor moral agents. Rather, they are moral patients – creatures who have morally significant interests, even if they cannot promote and protect those interests themselves. Moral patients must rely on others (moral agents) to protect their interests for them. On his view, animals, like infants and retarded humans, are moral patients.

Why, exactly, does Regan think animals are moral patients? They are, he claims, "subjects of a life": they have a life that matters to them. This criterion of moral status resembles Marquis's. Both philosophers claim that some creatures have serious moral status even if they do not have a hint of moral agency.

Although he does not employ the language of "moral status," Singer would claim that all the aforementioned criteria are too strict. Creatures deserve moral consideration, he claims, not because they can think, reason, envision a future, have obligations to others, or are subjects of a life, but simply because they suffer. Since many non-human animals can suffer, then they have moral status, they have interests we should morally consider. For him the central ethical question is: how heavily should we weigh their interests, how much moral status do they have? Do they have equal status with humans?

Suppose we can alleviate the suffering of only one of the following: a college professor, an infant, or an adult with Down's Syndrome. Whom should we assist? Singer would claim that even if we didn't know the best answer, we do know what would be a bad answer. It would be morally intolerable to favor the college professor simply because she is more intelligent, autonomous, or learned than the others. Equality demands that the similar suffering of each count similarly. That is true whether we are comparing the college professor with the infant, or whether we are comparing the college professor with a rat.

Frey acknowledges the moral importance of suffering and grants the importance of equality. Like Singer, he is an act utilitarian who claims we should maximize the greatest happiness of the greatest number. Animals as well as humans must be counted. Since non-human animals suffer, they deserve moral respect. "Higher" animals (mammals and birds) deserve additional moral respect because they have cognitive and emotional abilities. That explains why Frey thinks there are moral limits on what we can do to animals. They are not ours to use however we wish.

Nonetheless, Frey interprets the demands of equality rather differently than does Singer. Since animals are not as cognitively or emotionally sophisticated as (most) humans, then their lives are not as rich. The strength of a creature's moral status, Frey claims, is determined by the richness of its life. Since animals' lives are not as rich as the lives of (most) humans, equality does not require that we treat them all the same. Put differently, although they count morally, they do not count as much as normal humans.

Consequently, we can use non-human animals for our purposes, if the benefits of using them outweigh the costs. Of course, as a consistent utilitarian, Frey claims we could also use humans if the benefits were substantial enough, and the costs sufficiently slight. This vividly illustrates a profound difference between consequentialists and deontologists. Deontologists claim there are things we can't do to creatures with moral standing (usually humans) even if the action would have substantial benefits for others. Most consequentialists disagree. They claim there is no fundamental moral difference between acts and omissions (recall the discussion in the section on EUTHANASIA). If, by failing to act, I permit more evil than I would cause by acting, then I should act, no matter how objectionable that action might seem. For instance, if experimenting on a seriously retarded human would produce a cure for AIDS, and there is no other way to find that cure, then Frey would claim we should experiment on the human. If we do not experiment, then we will permit more evil than we would cause by doing it.

Earlier I mentioned that most people once believed we could do just anything we wanted to animals, for any reason whatever. For them the yelps of a dog were just squeaks of a machine. Now everyone thinks such a view is silly. Not one would seriously doubt that the dog's yelps are cries of pain. We have had a community-wide *gestalt* shift: we now interpret the same data differently (and presumably more correctly). Or so it seems. Gluck, though, claims that descendants of those old views about animals thrive in the animal-research community. Our educational system teaches prospective animal researchers that animals are tools, just like other laboratory tools. For most researchers, the animals have become invisible.

If, however, the researchers could come to see non-human animals as living creatures who can suffer and enjoy life – and not merely fleshy Petrie dishes – then they would be more likely to evaluate the practice of animal experimentation critically. That does not mean they would cease experiments. It does mean, however, that they would better control them. We have seen this idea before. It was the cornerstone of Rothman's argument on ABORTION. She claimed that the current characterization of the debate makes women invisible. Finally, we shall see this idea again, especially in Harris's and Narayan's discussion of AFFIRMATIVE ACTION and Crocker's essay on INTERNATIONAL JUSTICE AND WORLD HUNGER.

Further Reading

Carruthers, P. 1992: *The Animals Issue*. Cambridge: Cambridge University Press.

Clark, S. 1977: *The Moral Status of Animals*. Oxford: Oxford University Press.

Fox, M. 1986: *The Case for Animal Experimentation*. Berkeley: University of California Press.

Frey, R. 1983: *Rights, Killing, and Suffering*. Oxford: Blackwell.

——1980: *Rights and Interests*. Oxford: Oxford University Press.

LaFollette, H. and Shanks, N. 1996: *Brute Science: The Dilemmas of Animal Experimentation*. London: Routledge.

Rachels, J. 1990: *Created from Animals*. Oxford: Oxford University Press.

Singer, P. 1990: *Animal Liberation* (2nd edition). New York: Avon Books.

Regan, T. 1983: *The Case for Animal Rights*. Berkeley: University of California Press.

9

All Animals Are Equal

Peter Singer

In recent years a number of oppressed groups have campaigned vigorously for equality. The classic instance is the Black Liberation movement, which demands an end to the prejudice and discrimination that has made blacks second-class citizens. The immediate appeal of the Black Liberation movement and its initial, if limited, success made it a model for other oppressed groups to follow. We became familiar with liberation movements for Spanish-Americans, gay people, and a variety of other minorities. When a majority group – women – began their campaign, some thought we had come to the end of the road. Discrimination on the basis of sex, it has been said, is the last universally accepted form of discrimination, practiced without secrecy or pretense even in those liberal circles that have long prided themselves on their freedom from prejudice against racial minorities.

One should always be wary of talking of "the last remaining form of discrimination." If we have learnt anything from the liberation movements, we should have learnt how difficult it is to be aware of latent prejudice in our attitudes to particular groups until this prejudice is forcefully pointed out.

A liberation movement demands an expansion of our moral horizons and an extension or reinterpretation of the basic moral principle of equality. Practices that were previously regarded as natural and inevitable come to be seen as the result of an unjustifiable prejudice. Who can say with confidence that all his or her attitudes and practices are beyond criticism? If we wish to avoid being numbered amongst the oppressors, we must be prepared to re-think even our most fundamental attitudes. We need to consider them from the point of view of those most disadvantaged by our attitudes, and the practices that follow from these attitudes. If we can make this unaccustomed mental switch we may discover a pattern in our attitudes and practices that consistently operates so as to benefit one group – usually the one to which we ourselves belong – at the expense of another. In this way we may come to see that there is a case for a new liberation movement. My aim is to advocate that we make this mental switch in respect of our attitudes and practices towards a very large group of beings: members of species other than our own – or, as we popularly though misleadingly call them, animals. In other words, I am urging that we extend to other species the basic principle of equality that most of us recognize should be extended to all members of our own species.

All this may sound a little far-fetched, more like a parody of other liberation movements than a serious objective. In fact, in the past the idea of "The Rights of Animals" really has been used to parody the case for women's rights. When Mary Wollstonecraft, a forerunner of later feminists, published her *Vindication of the Rights of Women* in 1792, her ideas were widely regarded as absurd, and they were satirized in an anonymous publication entitled *A Vindication of the Rights of Brutes*. The author of this satire (actually Thomas Taylor, a distinguished Cambridge philosopher) tried to refute Wollstonecraft's reasonings by showing that they could be carried one stage further. If sound when applied to women, why should the arguments not be applied to dogs, cats, and horses? They seemed to hold equally well for these "brutes"; yet to hold that brutes had rights was manifestly absurd; therefore the reasoning by which this conclusion had been reached must be unsound, and if unsound when applied to brutes, it must also be unsound when applied to women, since the very same arguments had been used in each case.

One way in which we might reply to this argument is by saying that the case for equality between men and women cannot validly be extended to nonhuman animals. Women have a right to vote, for instance, because they are just as capable of making rational decisions as men are; dogs, on the other hand, are incapable of understanding the significance of voting, so they cannot have the right to vote. There are many other obvious ways in which men and women resemble each other closely, while humans and other animals differ greatly. So, it might be said, men and women are similar beings and should have equal rights, while humans and nonhumans are different and should not have equal rights.

The thought behind this reply to Taylor's analogy is correct up to a point, but it does not go far enough. There *are* important differences between humans and other animals, and these differences must give rise to *some* differences in the rights that each have. Recognizing this obvious fact, however, is no barrier to the case for extending the basic principle of equality to nonhuman animals. The differences that exist between men and women are equally undeniable, and the supporters of Women's Liberation are aware that these differ-. ences may give rise to different rights. Many feminists hold that women have the right to an abortion on request. It does not follow that since these same people are campaigning for equality between men and women they must support the right of men to have abortions too. Since a man cannot have an abortion, it is meaningless to talk of his right to have one. Since a pig can't vote, it is meaningless to talk of its right to vote. There is no reason why either Women's Liberation or Animal Liberation should get involved in such nonsense. The extension of the basic principle of equality from one group to another does not imply that we must treat both groups in exactly the same way, or grant exactly the same rights to both groups. Whether we should do so will depend on the nature of the members of the two groups. The basic principle of equality, I shall argue, is equality of consideration; and equal consideration for different beings may lead to different treatment and different rights.

So there is a different way of replying to Taylor's attempt to parody Wollstonecraft's arguments, a way which does not deny the differences between humans and nonhumans, but goes more deeply into the question of equality and concludes, by finding nothing absurd in the idea, that the basic principle of equality applies to so-called "brutes." I believe that we reach this conclusion if we examine the basis on which our opposition to discrimination on grounds of race or sex ultimately rests. We will then see that we would be on shaky ground if we were to demand equality for blacks, women, and other groups of oppressed humans while denying equal consideration to nonhumans.

When we say that all human beings, whatever their race, creed, or sex, are equal, what is it that we are asserting? Those who wish to defend a hierarchical, inegalitarian society have often pointed out that by whatever test we choose, it simply is not true that all humans are equal. Like it or not, we must face the fact that humans come in different shapes and sizes; they come with differing moral capacities, differing intellectual abilities, differing amounts of benevolent feeling and sensitivity to the needs of others, differing abilities to communicate effectively, and differing capacities to experience pleasure and pain. In short, if the demand for equality were based on the actual equality of all human beings, we would have to stop demanding equality. It would be an unjustifiable demand.

Still, one might cling to the view that the demand for equality among human beings is based on the actual equality of the different races and sexes. Although humans differ as individuals in various ways, there are no differences between the races and sexes *as such*. From the mere fact that a person is black, or a woman, we cannot infer anything else about that person. This, it may be said, is what is wrong with racism and sexism. The white racist claims that whites are superior to blacks, but this is false – although there are differences between individuals, some blacks are superior to some whites in all of the capacities and abilities that could conceivably be relevant. The opponent of sexism would say the same: a person's sex is no guide to his or her abilities, and this is why it is unjustifiable to discriminate on the basis of sex.

This is a possible line of objection to racial and sexual discrimination. It is not, however, the way that someone really concerned about equality would choose, because taking this line could, in some circumstances, force one to accept a most inegalitarian society. The fact that humans differ as individuals, rather than as races or sexes, is a valid reply to someone who defends a hierarchical society like, say, South Africa, in which all whites are superior in status to all blacks. The existence of individual variations that cut across the lines of race or sex, however, provides us with no defence at all against a more sophisticated opponent of equality, one who proposes that, say, the interests of those with I.Q. ratings above 100 be preferred to the interests of those with I.Q.s below 100. Would a hierarchical society of this sort really be so much better than one based on race or sex? I think not. But if we tie the moral principle of equality to the factual equality of the different races or sexes, taken as a whole, our opposition to racism and sexism does not provide us with any basis for objecting to this kind of inegalitarianism.

There is a second important reason why we ought not to base our opposition to racism and sexism on any kind of factual equality, even the limited kind which asserts that variations in capacities and abilities are spread evenly between the different races and sexes: we can have no absolute guarantee that these abilities and capacities really are distributed evenly, without regard to race or sex, among human beings. So far as actual abilities are concerned, there do seem to be certain measurable differences between both races and sexes. These differences do not, of course, appear in each case, but only when averages are taken. More important still, we do not yet know how much of these differences is really due to the different genetic endowments of the various races and sexes, and how much is due to environmental differences that are the result of past and continuing discrimination. Perhaps all of the important differences will eventually prove to be environmental rather than genetic. Anyone opposed to racism and sexism will certainly hope that this will be so, for it will make the task of ending discrimination a lot easier; nevertheless it would be dangerous to rest the case against racism and sexism on the belief that all significant differences are environmental in origin. The opponent of, say, racism who takes this line will be unable to avoid conceding that if differences in ability did after all prove to have some genetic connection with race, racism would in some way be defensible.

It would be folly for the opponent of racism to stake his whole case on a dogmatic commitment to one particular outcome of a difficult scientific issue which is still a long way from being settled. While attempts to prove that differences in certain selected abilities between races and sexes are primarily genetic in origin have certainly not been conclusive, the same must be said of attempts to prove that these differences are largely the result of environment. At this stage of the investigation we cannot be certain which view is correct, however much we may hope it is the latter.

Fortunately, there is no need to pin the case for equality to one particular outcome of this scientific investigation. The appropriate response to those who claim to have found evidence of genetically-based differences in ability between the races or sexes is not to stick to the belief that the genetic explanation must be wrong, whatever evidence to the contrary may turn up: instead we should make it quite clear that the claim to equality does not depend on intelligence, moral capacity, physical strength, or similar matters of fact. Equality is a moral ideal, not a simple assertion of fact. There is no logically compelling reason for assuming that a factual difference in ability between two people justifies any difference in the amount of consideration we give to satisfying their needs and interests. The principle of the equality of human beings is not a description of an alleged actual equality among humans: it is a prescription of how we should treat animals.

Jeremy Bentham incorporated the essential basis of moral equality into his utilitarian system of ethics in the formula: "Each to count for one and none for more than one." In other words, the interests of every being affected by an action are to be taken into account and given the same weight as the like interests of any other being. A later utilitarian, Henry Sidgwick, put the point in this way: "The good of any one individual is of no more importance, from the point of view (if I may say so) of the Universe, than the good of any other."[1] More recently, the leading figures in contemporary moral philosophy have shown a great deal of agreement in specifying as a fundamental presupposition of their moral theories some similar requirement which operates so as to give everyone's interests equal consideration – although they cannot agree on how this requirement is best formulated.[2]

It is an implication of this principle of equality that our concern for others ought not to depend on what they are like, or what abilities they possess – although precisely what this concern requires us to do may vary according to the characteristics of those affected by what we do. It is on this basis that the case against racism and the case against sexism must both ultimately rest; and it is in accordance with this principle that speciesism is also to be condemned. If possessing a higher degree of intelligence does not entitle one human to use another for his own ends, how can it entitle humans to exploit nonhumans?

Many philosophers have proposed the principle of equal consideration of interests, in some form or other, as a basic moral principle; but, as we shall see in more detail shortly, not many of them have recognized that this principle applies to members of other species as well as to our own. Bentham was one of the few who did realize this. In a forward-looking passage, written at a time when black slaves in the British dominions were still being treated much as we now treat nonhuman animals, Bentham wrote:

The day *may* come when the rest of the animal creation may acquire those rights which never could have been witholden from them but by the hand of tyranny. The French have already discovered that the blackness of the skin is no reason why a human being should be abandoned without redress to the caprice of a tormentor. It may one day come to be recognized that the number of the legs, the villosity of the skin, or the termination of the *os sacrum*, are reasons equally insufficient for abandoning a sensitive being to the same fate. What else is it that should trace the insuperable line? Is it the faculty of reason, or perhaps the faculty of discourse? But a full-grown horse or dog is beyond comparison a more rational, as well as a more conversable animal, than an infant of a day, or a week, or even a month, old. But suppose they were otherwise, what would it avail? The question is not, Can they reason? nor Can they *talk?* but, *Can they suffer?*[3]

In this passage Bentham points to the capacity for suffering as the vital characteristic that gives a being the right to equal consideration. The capacity for suffering – or more strictly, for suffering and/or enjoyment or happiness – is not just another characteristic like the capacity for language, or for higher mathematics. Bentham is not saying that those who try to mark "the insuperable line" that determines whether the interests of a being should be considered happen to have selected the wrong characteristic. The capacity for suffering and enjoying things is a prerequisite for having interests at all, a condition that must be satisfied before we can speak of interests in any meaningful way. It would be nonsense to say that it was not in the interests of a stone to be kicked along the road by a schoolboy. A stone does not have interests because it cannot suffer. Nothing that we can do to it could possibly make any difference to its welfare. A mouse, on the other hand, does have an interest in not being tormented, because it will suffer if it is.

If a being suffers, there can be no moral justification for refusing to take that suffering into consideration. No matter what the nature of the being, the principle of equality requires that its suffering be counted equally with the like suffering – in so far as rough comparisons can be made – of any other being. If a being is not capable of suffering, or of experiencing enjoyment or happiness, there is nothing to be taken into account. This is why the limit of sentience (using the term as a convenient, if not strictly accurate, shorthand for the capacity to suffer or experience enjoyment or happiness) is the only defensible boundary of concern for the interests of others. To mark this boundary by some characteristic like intelligence or rationality would be to mark it in an arbitrary way. Why not choose some other characteristic, like skin color?

The racist violates the principle of equality by giving greater weight to the interests of members of his own race, when there is a clash between their interests and the interests of those of another race. Similarly the speciesist allows the interests of his own species to override the greater interests of members of other species.[4] The pattern is the same in each case. Most human beings are speciesists. I shall now very briefly describe some of the practices that show this.

For the great majority of human beings, especially in urban, industrialized societies, the most direct form of contact with members of other species is at mealtimes: we eat them. In doing so we treat them purely as means to our ends. We regard their life and well-being as subordinate to our taste for a particular kind of dish. I say "taste" deliberately – this is purely a matter of pleasing our palate. There can be no defence of eating flesh in terms of satisfying nutritional needs, since it has been established beyond doubt that we could satisfy our need for protein and other essential nutrients far more efficiently with a diet that replaced animal flesh by soy beans, or products derived from soy beans, and other high-protein vegetable products.[5]

It is not merely the act of killing that indicates what we are ready to do to other species in order to gratify our tastes. The suffering we inflict on the animals while they are alive is perhaps an even clearer indication of our speciesism than the fact that we are prepared to kill them.[6] In order to have meat on the table at a price that people can afford, our society tolerates methods of meat production that confine sentient animals in cramped, unsuitable conditions for the entire durations of their lives. Animals are treated like machines that convert fodder into flesh, and any innovation that results in a higher "conversion ratio" is liable to be adopted. As one authority on the subject has said, "cruelty is acknowledged only when profitability ceases."[7] . . .

Since, as I have said, none of these practices cater for anything more than our pleasures of taste, our practice of rearing and killing other animals in order to eat them is a clear instance of the sacrifice of the most important interests of other beings in order to satisfy trivial interests of our own. To avoid speciesism we must stop this practice, and each of us has a moral obligation to cease supporting the practice. Our custom is all the support that the meat-industry needs. The decision to cease giving it that support may be difficult, but it is no more difficult than it would have been for a white Southerner to go against the traditions of his society and free his slaves: if we do not change our dietary habits, how can we censure those slaveholders who would not change their own way of living?

The same form of discrimination may be observed in the widespread practice of experimenting on other species in order to see if certain substances are safe for human beings, or to test some psychological theory about the effect of severe punishment on learning, or to try out various new compounds just in case something turns up. . . .

In the past, argument about vivisection has often missed the point, because it has been put in absolutist terms: Would the abolitionist be prepared to let thousands die if they could be saved by experimenting on a single animal? The way to reply to this purely hypothetical question is to pose another: Would the experimenter be prepared to perform his experiment on an orphaned human infant, if that were the only way to save many lives? (I say "orphan" to avoid the complication of parental feelings, although in doing so I am being overfair to the experimenter, since the nonhuman subjects of experiments are not orphans.) If the experimenter is not prepared to use an orphaned human infant, then his readiness to use nonhumans is simple discrimination, since adult apes, cats, mice, and other mammals are more aware of what is happening to them, more self-directing and, so far as we can tell, at least as sensitive to pain, as any human infant. There seems to be no relevant characteristic that human infants possess that adult mammals do not have to the same or a higher degree. (Someone might try to argue that what makes it wrong to experiment on a human infant is that the infant will, in time and if left alone, develop into more than the nonhuman, but one would then, to be consistent, have to oppose abortion, since the fetus has the same potential as the infant – indeed, even contraception and abstinence might be wrong on this ground, since the egg and sperm, considered jointly, also have the same potential. In any case, this argument still gives us no reason for selecting a nonhuman, rather than a human with severe and irreversible brain damage, as the subject for our experiments.)

The experimenter, then, shows a bias in favor of his own species whenever he carries out an experiment on a nonhuman for a purpose that he would not think justified him in using a human being at an equal or lower level of sentience, awareness, ability to be self-directing, etc. No one familiar with the kind of results yielded by most experiments on animals can have the slightest doubt that if this bias were eliminated the number of experiments performed would be a minute fraction of the number performed today.

Experimenting on animals, and eating their flesh, are perhaps the two major forms of speciesism in our society. By comparison, the third and last form of speciesism is so minor as to be insignificant, but it is perhaps of some special interest to those for whom this article was written. I am referring to speciesism in contemporary philosophy.

Philosophy ought to question the basic assumptions of the age. Thinking through, critically and carefully, what most people take for granted is, I believe, the chief task of philosophy, and it is this task that makes philosophy a worthwhile activity. Regrettably, philosophy does not always live up to its historic role. Philosophers are human beings, and they are subject to all the preconceptions of the society to which they belong. Sometimes they succeed in breaking free of the prevailing ideology: more often they become its most sophisticated defenders. So, in this case, philosophy as practiced in the universities today does not challenge anyone's preconceptions about our relations with other species. By their writings, those philosophers who tackle problems that touch upon the issue reveal that they make the same unquestioned assumptions as most other humans, and what they say tends to confirm the reader in his or her comfortable speciesist habits.

I could illustrate this claim by referring to the writings of philosophers in various fields – for instance, the attempts that have been made by those interested in rights to draw the boundary of the sphere of rights so that it runs parallel to the biological boundaries of the species *homo sapiens*, including infants and even mental defectives, but excluding those other beings of equal or greater capacity who are so useful to us at mealtimes and in our laboratories. I think it would be a more appropriate conclusion to this article, however, if I concentrated on the problem with which we have been centrally concerned, the problem of equality.

It is significant that the problem of equality, in moral and political philosophy, is invariably formulated in terms of human equality. The effect of this is that the question of the equality of other animals does not confront the philosopher, or student, as an issue itself – and this is already an indication of the failure of philosophy to challenge accepted beliefs. Still, philosophers have found it difficult to discuss the issue of human equality without raising, in a paragraph or two, the question of the status of other animals. The reason for this, which should be apparent from what I have said already, is that if humans are to be regarded as equal to one another, we need some sense of "equal" that does not require any actual, descriptive equality of capacities, talents or other qualities. If equality is to be related to any actual characteristics of humans, these characteristics must be some lowest common denominator, pitched so low that no human lacks them – but then the philosopher comes up against the catch that any such set of characteristics which covers *all* humans will not be possessed *only by humans*. In other words, it turns out that in the only sense in which we can truly say, as an assertion of fact, that all humans are equal, at least some members of other species are also equal – equal, that is, to each other and to humans. If, on the other hand, we regard the statement "All humans are equal" in some non-factual way, perhaps as a prescription, then, as I have already argued, it is even more difficult to exclude non-humans from the sphere of equality.

This result is not what the egalitarian philosopher originally intended to assert. Instead of accepting the radical outcome to which their own reasonings naturally point, however, most philosophers try to reconcile their beliefs in human equality and animal inequality by arguments that can only be described as devious.

As a first example, I take William Frankena's well-known article "The Concept of Social Justice." Frankena opposes the idea of basing justice on merit, because he sees that this could lead to highly inegalitarian results. Instead he proposes the principle that

> all men are to be treated as equals, not because they are equal, in any respect, but simply because they are human. They are human because they have emotions and desires, and are able to think, and hence are capable of enjoying a good life in a sense in which other animals are not.[8]

But what is this capacity to enjoy the good life which all humans have, but no other animals? Other animals have emotions and desires and appear to be capable of enjoying a good life. We may doubt that they can think – although the behavior of some apes, dolphins, and even dogs suggests that some of them can – but what is the relevance of thinking? Frankena goes on to admit that by "the good life" he means "not so much the morally good life as the happy or satisfactory life," so thought would appear to be unnecessary for enjoying the good life; in fact to emphasize the need for thought would make difficulties for the egalitarian since only some people are capable of leading intellectually satisfying lives, or morally good lives. This makes it difficult to see what Frankena's principle of equality has to do with simply being *human*. Surely every sentient being is capable of leading a life that is happier or less miserable than some alternative life, and hence has a claim to be taken into account. In this respect the distinction between humans and nonhumans is not a sharp division, but rather a continuum along which we move gradually, and with overlaps between the species, from simple capacities for enjoyment and satisfaction, or pain and suffering, to more complex ones.

Faced with a situation in which they see a need for some basis for the moral gulf that is commonly thought to separate humans and animals, but can find no concrete difference that will do the job without undermining the equality of humans, philosophers tend to waffle. They resort to high-sounding phrases like "the intrinsic dignity of the human individual";[9] they talk of the "intrinsic worth of all men" as if men (humans?) had some worth that other beings did not,[10] or they say that humans, and only humans, are "ends in themselves," while "everything other than a person can only have value for a person."[11]

This idea of a distinctive human dignity and worth has a long history; it can be traced back directly to the Renaissance humanists, for instance to Pico della Mirandola's *Oration on the Dignity of Man*. Pico and other humanists based their estimate of human dignity on the idea that man possessed the central, pivotal position in the "Great Chain of Being" that led from the lowliest forms of matter to God himself; this view of the universe, in turn, goes back to both classical and Judeo-Christian doctrines. Contemporary philosophers have cast off these metaphysical and religious shackles and freely invoke the dignity of mankind without needing to justify the idea at all. Why should we not attribute "intrinsic dignity" or "intrinsic worth" to ourselves? Fellow-humans are unlikely to reject the accolades we so generously bestow on them, and those to whom we deny the honor are unable to object. Indeed, when one thinks only of humans, it can be very liberal, very progressive, to talk of the dignity of all human beings. In so doing, we implicitly condemn slavery, racism, and other violations of human rights. We admit that we ourselves are in some fundamental sense on a par with the poorest, most ignorant members of our own species. It is only when we think of humans as no more than a small sub-group of all the beings that inhabit our planet that we may realize that in elevating our own species we are at the same time lowering the relative status of all other species.

The truth is that the appeal to the intrinsic dignity of human beings appears to solve the egalitarian's problems only as long as it goes unchallenged. Once we ask *why* it should be that all humans – including infants, mental defectives, psychopaths, Hitler, Stalin, and the rest – have some kind of dignity or worth that no elephant, pig, or chimpanzee can ever achieve, we see that this question is as difficult to answer as our original request for some relevant fact that justifies the inequality of humans and other animals. In fact, these two questions are really one: talk of intrinsic dignity or moral worth only takes the problem back one step, because any satisfactory defence of the claim that all and only humans have intrinsic dignity would need to refer to some relevant capacities or characteristics that all and only humans possess. Philosophers frequently introduce ideas of dignity, respect, and worth at the point at which other reasons appear to be lacking, but this is hardly good enough. Fine phrases are the last resource of those who have run out of arguments.

In case there are those who still think it may be possible to find some relevant characteristic that distinguishes all humans from all members of other species, I shall refer again, before I conclude, to the existence of some humans who quite clearly are below the level of awareness, self-consciousness, intelligence, and sentience, of many nonhumans. I am thinking of humans with severe and irreparable brain damage, and also of infant humans. To avoid the complication of the relevance of a being's potential, however, I shall henceforth concentrate on permanently retarded humans.

Philosophers who set out to find a characteristic that will distinguish humans from other animals rarely take the course of abandoning these groups of humans by lumping them in with the other animals. It is easy to see why they do not. To take this line without rethinking our attitudes to other animals would entail that we have the right to perform painful experiments on retarded humans for trivial reasons; similarly it would follow that we had the right to rear and kill these humans for food. To most philosophers these consequences are as unacceptable as the view that we should stop treating nonhumans in this way.

Of course, when discussing the problem of equality it is possible to ignore the problem of mental defectives, or brush it aside as if somehow insignificant.[12] This is the easiest way out. What else remains? My final example of speciesism in contemporary philosophy has been selected to show what happens when a writer is prepared to face the question of human equality and animal inequality without ignoring the existence of mental defectives, and without resorting to obscurantist mumbo-jumbo. Stanley Benn's clear and honest article "Egalitarianism and Equal Consideration of Interests"[13] fits this description.

Benn, after noting the usual "evident human inequalities," argues, correctly I think, for equality of consideration as the only possible basis for egalitarianism. Yet Benn, like other writers, is thinking only of "equal consideration of human interests." Benn is quite open in his defence of this restriction of equal consideration:

> . . . not to possess human shape *is* a disqualifying condition. However faithful or intelligent a dog may be, it would be a monstrous sentimentality to attribute to him interests that could be weighed in an equal balance with those of human beings . . . if, for instance, one had to decide between feeding a hungry baby or a hungry dog, anyone who chose the dog would generally be reckoned morally defective, unable to recognize a fundamental inequality of claims.
>
> This is what distinguishes our attitude to animals from our attitude to imbeciles. It would be odd to say that we ought to respect equally the dignity or personality of the imbecile and of the rational man . . . but there is nothing odd about saying that we should respect their interests equally, that is, that we should give to the interests of each the same serious consideration as claims to considerations necessary for some standard of well-being that we can recognize and endorse.

Benn's statement of the basis of the consideration we should have for imbeciles seems to me correct, but why should there be any fundamental inequality of claims between a dog and a human imbecile? Benn sees that if equal consideration depended on rationality, no reason could be given against using imbeciles for research purposes, as we now use dogs and guinea pigs. This will not do: "But of course we do distinguish imbeciles from animals in this regard," he says. That the common distinction is justifiable is something Benn does not question; his problem is how it is to be justified. The answer he gives is this:

> . . . we respect the interests of men and give them priority over dogs not *insofar* as they are rational, but because rationality is the human norm. We say it is *unfair* to exploit the deficiencies of the imbecile who falls short of the norm, just as it would be unfair, and not just ordinarily dishonest, to steal from a blind man. If we do not think in this way about dogs, it is because we do not see the irrationality of the dog as a deficiency or a handicap, but as normal for the species. The characteristics, therefore, that distinguish the normal man from the normal dog make it intelligible for us to talk of other men having interests and capacities, and therefore

claims, of precisely the same kind as we make on our own behalf. But although these characteristics may provide the point of the distinction between men and other species, they are not in fact the qualifying conditions for membership, or the distinguishing criteria of the class of morally considerable persons; and this is precisely because a man does not become a member of a different species, with its own standards of normality, by reason of not possessing these characteristics.

The final sentence of this passage gives the argument away. An imbecile, Benn concedes, may have no characteristics superior to those of a dog; nevertheless this does not make the imbecile a member of "a different species" as the dog is. *Therefore* it would be "unfair" to use the imbecile for medical research as we use the dog. But why? That the imbecile is not rational is just the way things have worked out, and the same is true of the dog – neither is any more responsible for their mental level. If it is unfair to take advantage of an isolated defect, why is it fair to take advantage of a more general limitation? I find it hard to see anything in this argument except a defence of preferring the interests of members of our own species because they are members of our own species. To those who think there might be more to it, I suggest the following mental exercise. Assume that it has been proven that there is a difference in the average, or normal, intelligence quotient for two different races, say whites and blacks. Then substitute the term "white" for every occurrence of "men" and "black" for every occurrence of "dog" in the passage quoted; and substitute "high I.Q." for "rationality" and when Benn talks of "imbeciles" replace this term by "dumb whites" – that is, whites who fall well below the normal white I.Q. score. Finally, change "species" to "race." Now re-read the passage. It has become a defence of a rigid, no-exceptions division between whites and blacks, based on I.Q. scores, *not withstanding an admitted overlap* between whites and blacks in this respect. The revised passage is, of course, outrageous, and this is not only because we have made fictitious assumptions in our substitutions. The point is that in the original passage Benn was defending a rigid division in the amount of consideration due to members of different species, despite admitted cases of overlap. If the original did not, at first reading, strike us as being as outrageous as the revised version does, this is largely because although we are not racists ourselves, most of us are speciesists. Like the other articles, Benn's stands as a warning of the ease with which the best minds can fall victim to a prevailing ideology.

Notes

1 Henry Sidgwick, *The Methods of Ethics* (7th edn), p. 382.
2 For example, R. M. Hare, *Freedom and Reason* (Oxford, 1963), and J. Rawls, *A Theory of Justice* (Harvard, 1972); for a brief account of the essential agreement on this issue between these and other positions, see R. M. Hare, "Rules of War and Moral Reasoning," *Philosophy and Public Affairs*, vol. 1, no. 2 (1972).
3 Jeremy Bentham, *Introduction to the Principles of Morals and Legislation*, ch. XVII.
4 I owe the term *speciesism* to Richard Ryder.
5 In order to produce 1 lb of protein in the form of beef or veal, we must feed 21 lbs of protein to the animal. Other forms of livestock are slightly less inefficient, but the average ratio in the United States is still 1:8. It has been estimated that the amount of protein lost to humans in this way is equivalent to 90 percent of the annual world protein deficit. For a brief account, see Frances Moore Lappé, *Diet for a Small Planet* (Friends of The Earth/Ballantine, New York, 1971), pp. 4–11.
6 Although one might think that killing a being is obviously the ultimate wrong one can do to it, I think that the infliction of

suffering is a clearer indication of speciesism because it might be argued that at least part of what is wrong with killing a human is that most humans are conscious of their existence over time and have desires and purposes that extend into the future – see, for instance, M. Tooley, "Abortion and Infanticide," *Philosophy and Public Affairs*, vol. 2, no. 1 (1972). Of course, if one took this view one would have to hold – as Tooley does – that killing a human infant or mental defective is not in itself wrong and is less serious than killing certain higher mammals that probably do have a sense of their own existence over time.

7   Ruth Harrison, *Animal Machines* (Stuart, London, 1964). For an account of farming conditions, see my *Animal Liberation* (New York Review Company, 1975).

8   In R. Brandt (ed.), *Social Justice* (Prentice-Hall, Englewood Cliffs, 1962), p. 19.

9   William Frankena, "The Concept of Social Justice," in R. Brandt, *Social Justice*, p. 23.

10 H. A. Bedau, "Egalitarianism and the Idea of Equality," in *Nomos IX: Equality*, ed. J. R. Pennock and J. W. Chapman (New York, 1967).

11 G. Vlastos, "Justice and Equality," in Brandt, *Social Justice*, p. 48.

12 For example, Bernard Williams, "The Idea of Equality," in *Philosophy, Politics, and Society* (2nd series), ed. P. Laslett and W. Runciman (Blackwell, Oxford, 1962), p. 118; J. Rawls, *A Theory of Justice*, pp. 509–10.

13 *Nomos IX: Equality*; the passages quoted are on pp. 62ff.

10

The Moral Community

Michael Allen Fox

... Another view that is currently popular among spokespersons for animal welfare is that which endorses the notion of animal rights. To different individuals, the ascription of rights to animals means different things. To some, it is a way of expressing their conviction that animals' lives have intrinsic value or value to themselves. I have already shown [. . .] that no meaning can be attached to the notion of anything's having totally self-contained value; and as animals cannot reflectively examine their lives to arrive at qualitative assessments about them, their lives also cannot have intrinsic value or value to themselves. Others seem to think that granting rights to animals is like waving a magic wand or uttering incantations, as if by doing so they could change overnight the attitudes and behavior of their fellow human beings.

The origin of the idea of animal rights is not easy to trace. One view is that this notion is a natural spin-off or even a logical extension of the civil rights and women's rights movements; another is that it represents nothing more than another symptom of the tendency, particularly prevalent in the United States, to couch all demands for change in the language of rights. Arthur L. Caplan has referred to this contemporary phenomenon as the "hortatory or political usage of rights," remarking on "rights language . . . as a politically expedient device to focus social concern on any ethical or political question."[1] Thus we hear daily of employees' rights, students' rights, the right to die with dignity, a bill of rights for nonsmokers, the right to work, the right to strike, tenants' rights, landlords' rights, the right to a safe environment, prisoners' rights, gay rights, the rights of future generations, the rights of the handicapped, and so on. Lately, even the rights of left-handers and the right of parents to spank their children have been defended in the media! Some of these rights claims are surely legitimate. But there is little doubt that the concept of rights has been much abused, having been stretched almost beyond recognition and frequently invoked when other terminology would do just as well or when basic constitutional or civil rights could be cited instead. In any event, a sizable and growing number of people think that animals have (or should have) rights, such as the right to life, the right not to suffer, and the right to a certain minimum quality of life, and that it makes perfectly good sense to talk this way.

I think it can be shown that both the utilitarian position on animals and the advocacy of animal rights are fundamentally mistaken. To see why and to develop a sensible alternative position on the moral status of animals, it is necessary to examine the foundations of our system of moral beliefs. This in turn requires that we consider the nature of a moral community, for only within such a social organization can the basic concepts and principles of morality arise.

Foundations of the Moral Community: Preliminaries

Few people will dispute the statement that we all belong to a moral community, though we may have different ideas about the nature of such a community (for example, whether it is rooted in religion or in purely secular precepts) and its scope (such as whether morality is relative to a given culture or is universal; whether it includes only human beings or other species as well). What, then, is a moral community? Most generally, it is a group of beings that shares certain characteristics and whose members are or consider themselves to be bound to observe certain rules of conduct in relation to one another because of their mutual likeness. These rules create what we call obligations and derive in some intimate way from the characteristics which the beings composing the moral community have in common. Thus a moral community is a society in the broadest sense of the word, and the beings belonging to it are related by natural bonds, whereas their conduct is regulated by bonds of obligation – that is, the beings in question possess certain salient characteristics, are capable of recognizing these in other, similar beings, and acknowledge possession by other beings of the characteristics in question as grounds for following certain rules of conduct toward them.

Note, however, that not all people who are members of a moral community necessarily accept that they are bound to follow specifiable standard rules of conduct even by virtue of recognizing and acknowledging that others share important characteristics with them. Sociopaths and terrorists, for instance, do not. Most moral theorists, however (as well as most laypersons), would argue that such exceptions do not seriously undermine our moral community or threaten to destroy the bond of association that holds it together, any more than the occasional act of anarchism or civil disobedience harmfully erodes the basic principles of political obligation and community.

Membership in the Moral Community

Now what sorts of beings do actually belong to a moral community such as I have just described? Clearly, they must be beings that, by their nature, are capable of functioning within one. This means, in effect, that they must possess the sorts of characteristics that we have already discussed: critical self-awareness; the ability to manipulate complex concepts and to use a sophisticated language (especially for the purpose of communicating wishes, desires, needs, decisions, choices, and so on);[2] and the capacity to reflect, plan, deliberate, choose, and accept responsibility for acting. The importance of these attributes in humans' evolutionary adaptation and in establishing their uniqueness has already been stressed. What we need to emphasize here is that these characteristics make humans autonomous or self-directing and capable of functioning as rational moral agents. It is because they are capable of long-range planning, anticipating consequences, choosing among alternative courses of action, taking responsibility, making and following rules, and the like that humans can engage in moral behavior, or behavior that affects others as well as themselves and that is subject to moral appraisal. Furthermore, the possession of these characteristics, plus the capacity to recognize them in others and to care about others, goes a long way toward explaining what we mean by speaking of ourselves as *persons*. Thus it appears that a moral community is a social group composed of interacting autonomous beings where moral concepts and precepts can evolve and be understood. It is also a social group in which the mutual recognition of autonomy and personhood exists. The latter feature is equally important and indeed inseparable from the former, since the development of moral institutions (such as promise keeping, truth telling, making contractual agreements, and giving mutual aid in emergencies) is contingent on recognition of and respect for persons.

A number of animal-protectionist authors have attempted to refute the approach I have followed here, claiming that when we examine critically each of the characteristics differentiating humans from animals, which I have identified as morally relevant differences, we find that none of them succeeds in establishing the moral superiority of humans.[3] But I am not arguing that any one of these characteristics taken in isolation establishes the moral superiority of humans (or better, of autonomous agents or persons), rather that all of them do, when taken together. This is a crucial point: It is the whole cluster of interrelated capacities, and this alone, that constitutes the nature of an autonomous being. The piecemeal approach taken by animal welfarists to undermine, as they suppose, the position advocated here simply succeeds in trivializing the claim being advanced on behalf of autonomy as the focus of full moral status and discourse. Their argument amounts in fact to an illicit *reductio*, much like one that might be offered, say, to "prove" that there is no politically relevant difference between democracy and other forms of government and hence no superiority of the former over the latter. We could imagine such an argument, cast in Socratic form, to run as follows: "'Does freedom of speech, which you claim to be a politically relevant difference between democracy and other forms of government, establish the superiority of democracy over these other forms?' 'No, not taken by itself.' 'Well, then, what about freedom of assembly?' 'Also inadequate taken by itself.' 'Freedom from arbitrary arrest?' 'Not by itself.' 'The right to vote?' 'No.' 'It appears, then, that democracy is not superior to other forms of government because under examination each of its essential characteristics shows itself to be a politically irrelevant difference.'" But, of course, no one would think to defend democracy by placing the entire weight of the argument on one isolated feature. In like manner, no one would seek to support the claim that autonomous beings are morally superior by building the case on a single characteristic of such beings.

On Rights

I wish to argue now that only within the context of a moral community do rights and obligations (duties) arise at all. This is so first of all because rights are possessed solely by persons. As a preliminary, I want to stress that I am speaking here of basic moral rights as distinct from legal rights. Defenders of animal rights are often unclear in their own minds, as well as in the presentation of their case to the public, whether they are endorsing moral or legal rights for animals or indeed both. This is an important distinction to which I return in the final chapter. For the moment, however, let us concentrate on moral rights. Why are moral rights possessed only by persons? The short answer is that rights are accorded to persons (that is, reflectively self-valuing beings) by other persons in recognition of their inherent independence, dignity, and worth *as persons* (rather than as individuals who have attained or failed to attain some level of moral development in their lives).

Much has been written over the past few centuries on the subject of rights, and a good deal of this literature has mystified rather than clarified the concept. Probably the principal factor in this mystification lies in the traditional doctrine of natural rights. Natural rights are "rights we are alleged to have in a state of nature, independently of human institutions and conventions, simply by virtue of our humanity (or some other set of attributes). Such rights are typically indefeasible, that is, they cannot be overridden (except maybe in great catastrophes . . .)."[4] Now the idea of a "state of nature" is notoriously vague, and for all we know one may never have existed, at least in the way envisioned by natural-rights theorists, since *Homo sapiens* and their ancestral hominids have always been highly social creatures. In addition, it has never been made plain what it means to say that we possess rights "by virtue of our humanity." Some have claimed that rights are God-given, others that no grounds can be given for the possession of rights; it is simply self-evident that all humans have them. Still others have asserted both, as in the famous passage from the Declaration of Independence of the United States of America, which reads, "We hold these truths to be self-evident, that all men are created equal, that they are endowed by their Creator with certain unalienable Rights, that among these are Life, Liberty and the pursuit of Happiness."

Because of these and other difficulties with the notion of rights, many philosophers have become convinced that talk of rights, although useful in a civil libertarian (that is, legal) context, has no value in moral theory and in fact should be avoided altogether in our discussion of moral issues. Some have also said that the British libertarian/egalitarian tradition in morality and the law does not depend on a strong conception of rights and that the American system is the exception, rights have been initially enshrined in the Declaration and then later in the Bill of Rights. However, in my view the idea of basic moral rights lies at the core of our system of moral beliefs and is an essential feature of the moral community. In an article on "Rights, Human Rights, and Racial Discrimination," Richard Wasserstrom observes that if the question be raised

> why ought anyone have a right to anything? or why not have a system in which there are not rights at all? the answer is that such a system would be a morally impoverished one . . . [for] one ought to be able to claim as entitlements those minimal things without which it is impossible to develop one's capabilities and to live a life as a human being.[5]

Wasserstrom helps to bring out here the crucial role that rights have to play by indicating that they serve to express the moral equality of autonomous beings, each of which has an equal claim to be provided the conditions necessary for self-development as a being of that kind. Rights also serve in this context to protect the interests of each in having certain goods and services on which self-development depends, and this sets the stage for the many compromises and trade-offs that society must assure are justly arrived at and implemented. Some additional points may also be worth noting here.

First, the fact that scores of nations are signatories to the Universal Declaration of the Rights of Man, on which the United Nations was founded, indicates, prima facie at least, that the concept of rights is understandable and significant to people of diverse experience and cultural backgrounds. This remains true in spite of the egregious and often shocking violations of human rights in all parts of the globe that are characteristic of our era. Whether people in general live up to their moral precepts or only pay lip service to them is surely independent of considerations of their validity and significance, for moral beliefs as such are not invalidated by immoral behavior, however widespread.

Second, it seems highly unlikely that an account of fundamental legal or otherwise institutionalized rights (such as the rights of habeas corpus, trial by jury, suffrage, freedom of speech and assembly, and property) could even be formulated if there were no moral rights on which they could rest. One kind of legal right in fact serves the sole function of guaranteeing the exercise of basic moral rights in society and establishes grounds for protecting individuals against violations of their moral rights (in essence, their persons) in practical situations. In other words, this subclass of legal rights gives concrete definition to moral rights within a political framework. (Bills of rights and guarantees of civil liberties are of this type.)

Third, it is questionable whether morality can dispense with a strong assertion of rights. Persistent violation of persons' autonomy in some countries could be said to underscore the necessity of ascribing rights to individuals to serve as a declaration of the dignity and inviolability of the person, as well as some kind of protection against the arbitrary use of power over the person and as a foundation for international laws to protect individuals everywhere against such abuses.

With these points in mind, then, I wish to consider what it means to ascribe moral rights to human beings.

The idea of basic moral rights (the rights to life, liberty, happiness or well-being, freedom from suffering, and the like) need not remain a mystery, because it is possible to retain the attractive features of the traditional natural-rights theory while avoiding its pitfalls. To begin with, the possession of those characteristics that make humans members of a moral community also makes them the possessors of rights. It would be a mistake, however, to construe this as simply another way of expressing the natural-rights theorist's claim that rights are possessed by virtue of our being humans. Whereas I have endorsed the view that the possession of certain *attributes* is crucial to both autonomy and having rights, there are two important differences between the position I am defending and the traditional natural-rights theory. One is that having rights and ascribing them to others are functions of the mutual recognition that occurs within a social group of autonomous beings, that is, of the recognition that they manifest the sorts of characteristics that identify them as autonomous agents. In other words, members of the social group recognize and acknowledge, either explicitly or tacitly, that others in the group, like themselves, possess the prerequisites for autonomous, rational behavior and hence for moral personhood. The ascription of rights, then, is an act signifying the recognition that others are beings of this sort and expresses in symbolic form the resolve that they shall be treated in a manner appropriate to the autonomy and personhood thus perceived. Among other things, this resolve means that each undertakes to guarantee everyone else adequate scope for independent self-expression, responsibility, self-determination, and an equal opportunity to develop to his or her fullest potential. From the standpoint of the individual, rights may be seen, inversely, as claims on others to be recognized and respected in accordance with one's natural capacities, autonomy, and personhood.[6]

Thus rights belong to beings because they are moral agents functioning within a community of which responsibility and accountability are central features and where they are acknowledged to be such. Rights therefore do not need to be thought of as arising in some nebulous "state of nature, independently of human institutions and conventions, simply by virtue of our humanity," even though they do require that we conceive of them by reference to the possession of a certain set of attributes. Nor do rights need to be described or defended as God-given or as self-evidently attached to being a member of the genus *Homo sapiens* or even as self-evidently attached to manifestations of autonomy, personhood, and agency (although they are so attached). As we have seen, criteria for the assignment and possession of rights can be specified, so that religious and intuitionist considerations are unnecessary to give substance to the notion of universal moral rights, as belonging properly to a certain class of beings.

The second principal difference between the position put forward here and traditional natural-rights theory is that I have generally avoided speaking of humans or referring to "our humanness" in considering the notions of moral community and rights, opting instead for speaking in more species-neutral terms – of "beings" of a certain type (autonomous beings). In discussing such questions as the comparative moral status of humans and animals, we should try to avoid the sort of species chauvinism or narrow anthropocentrism argued against [. . .]. Many scientists now believe it is very probable that intelligent life exists elsewhere in the universe. If so, we may well come into contact some day with extra-terrestrial forms of intelligent life with which we can communicate and interact at a high level of complexity. We have no reason to suppose that such extraterrestrials would belong to our own or a similar species or even resemble anything with which we are familiar.[7] But by the same token, there appears to be no good reason to assume that they would not share the same sorts of aspirations and have many of the same fundamental needs and interests as we or that they would be instinctively hostile to us. We should therefore recast our moral precepts in a form that could be extended to such creatures, which might very well be like us in all morally relevant respects.

Another reason for framing our moral precepts more cautiously has to do with other species that inhabit the earth. Though I do not think anyone can honestly assert, on the basis of the evidence available, that it is at all likely we shall learn to communicate at a high level with any terrestrial animals (such as chimpanzees, whales, or dolphins), it is at least possible. It is possible too that they are so very similar to us in all important respects that we should be prepared to extend our moral community to include them as equals if this turned out to be the case. However remote these prospects may be, it would be foolishly shortsighted to exclude animals from the moral community merely as a matter of principle or definition. Speaking of "beings" rather than "humans" avoids just these problems.[8]

The argument thus far has been that human beings have basic moral rights because they are beings of the requisite kind, that is, autonomous beings, persons, or moral agents. Even though other species have not been systematically excluded from possible membership in the moral community, I have not hesitated to characterize the central concepts that define the moral community in human or humanly understandable terms. For this I offer no apology. Since the only species we know of that has developed the notions of rights and obligations (and the institutions associated with them) is *Homo sapiens*, there must be something about this peculiar sort of social being that accounts for the phenomenon in question. My claim is that the attributes of humans that explain why they have developed such concepts and institutions are humans' possession of a particular kind of reflexive consciousness, unique cognitive and linguistic abilities, and the capacity to comprehend, undertake, and carry out obligations and to expect the same of similarly constituted beings. Furthermore, it is important to note that autonomous beings have certain types of interests which these institutions exist to ensure are recognized and respected. Only in this manner can such agents' well-being be protected and facilitated.

Autonomy and Rights

Why do only autonomous beings have rights? The answer can now be given quite briefly: (1) Autonomous beings are capable of free (self-determining, voluntary), deliberative, responsible action and have the sort of awareness necessary to see this kind of action as essential to their nature, well-being, and development as individuals. (2) Autonomous beings are capable of recognizing autonomy in others and of full participation in the moral community, as already described.[9] It is not arbitrary to hold that all and only such beings qualify for the possession of rights. Once we demystify the notion of natural rights, we can see that the ascription of rights to other beings and to ourselves is the keystone of the mutual recognition process on which the moral community is founded. Assigning rights to others and claiming them for oneself is tantamount to issuing a declaration of nonintervention in the self-governing lives of others, by acknowledging the sort of being they are, and acquiring mutual guarantees of this type by tacit agreement (that is, "All things being equal, I agree to recognize your autonomy and not interfere with its free expression and development if you agree to do the same for me").

This is why philosophers have generally regarded rights and obligations as logically connected or correlative. If I have a right, then others are deemed to have a duty to respect that right, which means either to refrain from interfering with my free exercise of it or to assist me in attaining what I have a right to, as the case may be and as the circumstances require and permit. It does not follow, of course, that all such rights are absolute, inalienable, or indefeasible, and here the present account departs once more from traditional natural-rights theory. Normally, basic moral rights cannot be forfeited, compromised, suspended, or overridden by the acts of others or even of oneself. Under exceptional conditions, such as self-defense, imprisonment for crimes, or declarations of legal incompetence, certain rights justifiably may be abrogated. In addition, conflicts between individuals are commonplace in society and moral principles and institutions have to be evolved to deal with them in ways that are fair to those concerned. (A good deal of our political machinery serves just this function.)

The Position of Animals *vis-à-vis* the Moral Community

The conclusion to be drawn from the foregoing discussion, so far as it pertains to animals, is that lacking in various degrees the possession of capacities on which moral autonomy or agency depends, animals fail to meet the conditions specified for full membership in the moral community and likewise fail to qualify for having rights. Joel Feinberg has, I believe, stated fairly clearly why this is so with particular reference to dogs, but his point is generalizable to all animals.

Well-trained dogs sometimes let their masters down; they anticipate punishment or other manifestations of displeasure; they grovel and whimper, and they even make crude efforts at redress and reconciliation. But do they feel remorse and bad conscience? They have been conditioned to associate manifestations of displeasure with departures from a norm, and this is a useful way of keeping them in line, but they haven't the slightest inkling of the *reasons* for the norm. They don't *understand* why departures from the norm are wrong, or why their masters become angry or disappointed. They have a concept perhaps of the *mala prohibita* – the act that is wrong because it is prohibited, but they have no notion of the *mala in se* – the act that is prohibited because it is wrong. Even in respect to the *mala prohibita* their understanding is grossly deficient, for they have no conception of rightful authority. For dogs, the only basis of their master's "right" to be obeyed is his *de facto* power over them. Even when one master steals a beast from another, or when an original owner deprives it of its natural freedom in the wild, the animal will feel no moralized emotion, such as outraged propriety or indignation. These complex feelings involve cognitive elements beyond an animal's ken. Similarly, to suffer a guilty conscience is to be more than merely unhappy or anxious; it is to be in such a state because one has violated an "internalized standard," a principle of one's own, the rationale of which one can fully appreciate and the correctness of which one can, but in fact does not, doubt.[10]

Since animals could not begin to function as equals in a society of autonomous beings, they cannot be counted within the bond of association that makes morality and its institutions viable and gives them vitality. It should be apparent by now that the intent of this sort of judgment is not to portray the moral community as an exclusive club for membership within which "no animals need apply." Rather, it is to take a realistic look at the considerations that are relevant to regarding a being as having (or lacking) full moral status.

It should also be evident that any attempt to equate the "animal liberation" movement, which claims that animals and humans have equal moral status, with the civil rights and feminist movements is preposterous and indeed insulting to those who have worked long and hard to advance the cause of blacks and women (and children and other underprivileged groups). Blacks and women have been systematically denied full and equal moral status with whites and men. In effect, they have been prevented from enjoying the full membership in the moral community that is their due, on the basis of morally irrelevant differences – skin color and sex. It is precisely this sort of discrimination that we describe as unjust treatment. Animals, however, are denied full and equal moral status (and hence full membership in the moral community) for reasons that *are* morally relevant, namely, their lack of autonomy and moral agency. When women and blacks are granted their rights, these are not invented or "given" to them; rather, granting their rights is simply belatedly acknowledging that women and blacks are the sorts of beings that should have been perceived as autonomous all along and that therefore can claim to have been oppressed.

The characteristics on which this judgment or admission is made do not reduce merely to the capacity to experience pleasure and to suffer but are much more complex, as we have seen. If these characteristics are lacking in animals, then it makes no sense to speak of animals as "oppressed" and as deserving of equal moral concern. Failure to apprehend this crucial difference between animals and humans not only displays moral insensitivity but also denigrates and, by introducing conceptual confusion, weakens the legitimate case of those who genuinely are oppressed by trivializing it and making it appear ridiculous.[11]

I have tried to show why it is inappropriate to think of animals in terms that have meaningful application only to persons and to argue for this position rather than make a stand on faith or dogma. We may now turn to other issues to arrive at a resolution of the question of animals' proper moral status.

The Position of Deficient Humans *vis-à-vis* the Moral Community

Before we can make any progress on defining animals' moral status, however, we must face an extremely difficult question that is raised by the foregoing analysis and immediately presses itself on our attention. This is the problem of how to classify in relation to the moral community those beings that fall short of autonomy but which we should still consider candidates for rights and therefore to which we have obligations. Examples here would include infants, the severely mentally retarded, and those who are senile, autistic, mentally ill, badly brain damaged, comatose, and so on. Any theory linking full moral status to the possession of rights and the possession of rights in turn to autonomy is bound to encounter this issue and to stand or fall by how well it comes to terms with it.[12] This problem is also relevant because some might contend that certain animals are among those beings that fall short of autonomy but possess in varying degrees at least some of the capacities believed essential to autonomy. If deficient humans qualify for rights in spite of what they lack, it may then be asked, why not also higher animals? The difficulty is aggravated by the previous admission that it is not necessary to membership in the moral community that one be a member of the genus *Homo sapiens*; and if the stress falls on the possession of certain crucial traits, then it would seem that it is also not sufficient for membership that one be human.

Do human beings deficient in autonomy fail to qualify for rights, and do we as a result cease to have moral obligations toward them? Some antivivisectionists maintain that under-developed or deficient humans are no more and often less similar to normal humans in morally relevant respects than healthy and mature members of certain other species. Thus, it is claimed, a fully developed horse may be more reflective than a brain-damaged child; a chimpanzee more skilled in language than a newborn infant; a cat better able to reason than a comatose accident victim. It has even been suggested that to be consistent we should consider ourselves morally bound not to use such animals for any purpose for which we would not feel equally justified in using an underdeveloped or deficient human being.[13] However, this line of reasoning seems to me to betray a degree of moral insensitivity which we should all wish to reject.

If, as most would agree, natural emotional responses to and feelings of kinship with other species are allowed to count as factors in shaping our assessment of their moral status, then such responses and feelings should count equally in our dealings with members of our own species. We must also acknowledge differences among the sorts of cases under considera-tion. Infants are appropriately related to as potential fully autonomous beings, possessing in latency those attributes that will later (typically at maturity, given normal development) find expression, whereas those who are senile, comatose, mentally ill, or incapacitated by disease or accident are generally individuals who have achieved autonomy but whose full function-ing is now blocked by conditions or circumstances beyond their control. In the case of children who are severely retarded, autistic, and so on, however, we are dealing with people who may never achieve a semblance of autonomy. In deciding how we ought to look on all these classes of individuals, a reasonable position to take would seem to be that here membership in our own species ought to count for something, in the sense in which a charitable attitude toward those less developed or less fortunate than ourselves, for whom we feel some especially close kinship, is particularly compelling to a morally mature person. Just as our untutored moral sense tells us that we have very strong obligations to members of our immediate families, so it seems that preferential treatment should, under certain circumstances, accordingly be granted to members of the human family.[14]

John Passmore, writing on the subject of our obligations to future generations, has argued that "a chain of love and concern" extends from our children and grandchildren to our grandchildren's grandchildren, and that it also embraces the "places, institutions and forms of activity" that shape our daily life. As Passmore notes, "Such links are sufficiently com-mon and persistent to lend continuity to a civilization" and to explain sacrificing for future human beings.[15] Such a "chain" surely accounts for our concern for those among us who are severely handicapped or grievously disadvantaged. This is not to deny, of course, that a similar chain connects us to the animals, but the latter is not, I think, naturally so strong, direct, or morally compelling. (I have more to say on this important topic later in this chapter.)

Admittedly, for many it is not an easy matter to feel a close kinship to those less fortunate or often even to see them as human. Many cannot even establish an empathetic relationship with a normal, healthy human infant. Probably almost all of us would prefer and choose to spend time with responsive, sociable animals than with humans whose faculties are severely compromised. But none of these facts obviates the responsibility of each of us (whether religious or not) to develop and incorporate into our moral outlook the spirit behind the old saying, "There, but for the grace of God, go I." Let us say, then, that although underdeveloped or deficient humans are also, like animals, not full members of the moral community because they lack autonomy, they must nevertheless fall within the most immediate extension of the moral community and as such are subject to its protection. This sensibility is indeed a cornerstone of civilized society, for failure to cultivate and preserve this frail thread leaves the way open to systematic abuses of the dignity and rights of those designated as second-class citizens. Under certain all-too-common circumstances, it may also lead to Nazilike genocidal campaigns to eliminate "undesirables," "defectives," or "unworthy lives."

We might add that it is also a matter of prudence that we cultivate such a sentiment; for each of us knows that under certain unforeseeable circumstances he or she might suffer an injury or illness that could severely limit or even terminate his or her autonomy.

Membership in the moral community is not a cut-and-dried matter. How many and what kinds of affinities with ourselves a creature must exhibit before being counted as autonomous is not something that can be decided in the abstract but rather has to be examined on a case-by-case basis. Just as animals cannot be looked on as an undifferentiated or virtually identical collection of beings, so too there is no uniform class of underdeveloped or deficient human beings. Because of this, a comparison of such individuals would array them variably according to the presence or absence in them of capacities that are essential for autonomy. At one end of the scale would be those whom we sometimes (less than charitably) identify as hopeless "human vegetables" or "basket cases," whereas at the other end could be found normal infants, less severe retardates, and others who manifest to a greater or lesser degree psychological attributes that are typical of personhood.

To add further complexity to this already very difficult issue, we must bear in mind that conditions considered irremediable at present may yield to scientific inroads with astonishing suddenness. Autism is a case in point. Once considered completely impervious to all therapies and treatments, techniques have been devised in the past few years that promise to give autistic children a semblance of a normal life.[16] This sort of breakthrough, of course, does not happen as often as some try to make out. A cure is not just around the corner for every severe handicap. But the examples that can be cited should give us pause when we feel inclined to lump together as without hope a whole range of diverse conditions affecting normal human functioning and autonomy.

In view of this, it appears that drawing a line to separate human beings who are full members of the moral community from those who are not is probably not only an impossible task but also, even if feasible, extremely dangerous and unwise. If we must nevertheless give a rule that will rationalize including such borderline cases within the framework of the moral community, it might reasonably take the following form:

> All underdeveloped, deficient, or seriously impaired human beings are to be considered members of an immediately extended moral community and therefore as deserving of equal moral concern. To whatever degree seems reasonable, they should be treated according to either (a) their potential for full agency (and hence as potentially full participants in the moral community, taking into account their past participation, if any) or (b) the degree to which their behavior and capacities approximate what is generally considered to be characteristically human (that is,

typically the case at maturity, given normal development) and the extent to which their behavior and capacities permit full participation in the moral community.

This benefit-of-the-doubt principle might be looked on by critics as speciesist, but it seems to me that charity, benevolence, humaneness, and prudence require such an extension and that it is not inconsistent with a theory of morality that makes rights and autonomy central or, more important, with the way we in fact treat such cases in everyday life. Finally, dealing with these cases in the way I have suggested here, if properly labeled speciesist at all, is not unacceptably so; for extending the moral community to take account of exceptional cases does not exclude other species in principle from being treated in a similar manner or bar them from full membership in the moral community if they so qualify. So-called borderline cases or marginal humans – those where we are unsure whether to call something a human being or person or where our moral principles come under severe strain – are notoriously difficult to deal with. There seems to be no justification, however, for condemning a theory holding persons (not species) to be the central focus of moral concern on the grounds that it favors *Homo sapiens* over other known species in fringe areas where the applicability of our usual moral categories is bound to be far from clear-cut.

Notes

1 Arthur L. Caplan, "Rights Language and the Ethical Treatment of Animals," in Laurence B. McCullough and James Polk Morris, III, eds., *Implications of History and Ethics to Medicine – Veterinary and Human* (College Station, Texas: Centennial Academic Assembly, Texas A & M University, 1978), 129.

2 Cf. H. J. McCloskey, "The Right to Life," *Mind* 84 (1975), 413.

3 This strategy is followed by Bernard E. Rollin in *Animal Rights and Human Morality* (Buffalo, N.Y.: Prometheus Books, 1981), pt. 1; but it is also a central feature of Singer's *Animal Liberation* and of other works. Indeed, the archetype of the argument is Bentham's frequently cited remark which I too have quoted at the beginning of this chapter.

4 Christopher W. Morris, "Comments on 'Rights and Autonomy,' by David Richards, and 'Autonomy and Rights: A Case for Ethical Socialism,' by Michael McDonald," paper presented to Conference on Human Rights, University of Waterloo, Waterloo, Ontario, April 17–19, 1980, 2.

5 Richard Wasserstrom, "Rights, Human Rights, and Racial Discrimination," in A. I. Melden, ed., *Human Rights* (Belmont, Calif.: Wadsworth, 1970), 104, 105.

As Alan Goldman has written, rights "carve out a moral space in which persons can develop as distinct individuals free from the constant intrusion of demands from others" ("The Source and Extent of a Patient's Right to the Truth," *Queen's Quarterly* 91 [1984], 126).

6 It may be objected that agents' autonomy is protected by the traditional right to liberty and that therefore there is no reason why animals should not be seen as possessing other rights, such as the right not to suffer or the right to live. (I owe this objection to Christine Pierce.) But the argument offered here is that rights only arise and make sense within a framework in which mutual recognition and accountability are typical characteristics of relationships, and it is clear that animals have no place in such a conceptual environment.

7 Carl Sagan, *The Cosmic Connection: An Extraterrestrial Perspective* (New York: Dell, 1975); John W. Macvey, *Interstellar Travel: Past, Present, and Future* (New York: Stein and Day, 1977).

8 For more on this interesting subject, see Roland Puccetti, *Persons: A Study of Possible Moral Agents in the Universe* (London: Macmillan, 1968), chap. 4.

9 A largely psychogenetic account has been

given here of the reasons why the possession of autonomy or personhood (and only this) confers moral rights on a being or entitles it to respect and equal moral concern; that is, the ascription of rights to such beings has been explained in terms of the conditions under which autonomous beings are disposed to ascribe rights to themselves and to other like beings. It may be argued therefore that a clinching philosophical argument for such ascriptions has not been provided; that it has not been shown why the possession of autonomy is a peculiarly relevant consideration, whereas possession of other characteristics, such as the capacity to suffer, are not.

I am not sure this kind of argument can be supplied, though I think that further reflections on the nature of autonomy, like those that occupy much of the rest of this chapter, go a good distance toward satisfying this demand. The reason such an argument cannot be given is that here we are up against the same problem of the fact–value gap that plagues all moral theories. By the same token, for instance, utilitarians cannot defend their key claim that the capacity to suffer is the singularly relevant criterion for the assignment of rights or the entitlement to respect and equal moral concern.

10 Joel Feinberg, "Human Duties and Animal Rights," in Morris and Fox, *On the Fifth Day*, 50 (author's italics).

11 For reasons of this sort, some critics of animal liberation have denied that speciesism constitutes a form of immorality comparable to racism and sexism – indeed, that it is immoral at all. For good arguments against the claim that speciesism is immoral, see the following: Leslie Pickering Francis and Richard Norman, "Some Animals Are More Equal Than Others," *Philosophy* 53, no. 206 (October 1978), 507–527; Cigman, "Death, Misfortune, and Species Inequality"; Meredith Williams, "Rights, Interests, and

Moral Equality," *Environmental Ethics* 2 (1980), 149–161; Richard A. Watson, "Self-Consciousness and the Rights of Nonhuman Animals and Nature," *Environmental Ethics* 1 (1979), 99–129; Michael Wreen, "In Defense of Speciesism," *Ethics and Animals* 5, no. 3 (September 1984), 47–60.

12 Any alternative moral theory will have to confront the same problem; for since no society's resources are unlimited, the interests of disadvantaged individuals must always be weighed against those of everyone else.

13 For example, Singer, *Animal Liberation*, 80 f.

14 For a closer look at the family-of-man argument and a perceptive discussion, from a different perspective, of its bearing on the ethical problem of according preferential treatment to defective humans over animals, see Vinit Haksar, *Equality, Liberty, and Perfectability* (Oxford: Oxford University Press, 1979), 38–45, 71–79. See also Wreen, "In Defense of Speciesism," 53; United States Congress, Office of Technology Assessment, *Alternatives to Animal Use in Testing, Research, and Education* (Washington, D.C.: US Government Printing Office, 1985), chap. 4.

15 Passmore, *Man's Responsibility for Nature*, 88–89.

16 See Helen Kohl, "The Strange Ones," *Canadian Magazine*, April 7, 1979, pp. 10–12, 14; Laura Schreibman and Robert L. Koegel, "Autism: A Defeatable Horror," *Psychology Today* 8, no. 10 (March 1975), 61–67; O. Ivar Lovaas, "Behavioral Treatment of Autistic Children," in Janet T. Spence et al., eds., *Behavioral Approaches to Therapy* (Morristown, N. J.: General Learning Press, 1976), 185–201. The techniques described by Kohl and others, it should be noted, are based largely on knowledge about the efficacy of rewards and punishments in learning acquired initially through animal experiments.

11

Moral Standing, the Value of Lives, and Speciesism

R. G. Frey

The question of who or what has moral standing, of who or what is a member of the moral community, has received wide exposure in recent years. Various answers have been extensively canvassed; and though controversy still envelops claims for the inclusion of the inanimate environment within the moral community, such claims on behalf of animals (or, at least, the "higher" animals) are now widely accepted. Morally, then, animals count. I do not myself think that we have needed a great deal of argument to establish this point; but numerous writers, obviously, have thought otherwise. In any event, no work of mine has ever denied that animals count. In order to suffer, animals do not have to be self-conscious, to have interests or beliefs or language, to have desires and desires related to their own future, to exercise self-critical control of their behaviour, or to possess rights; and I, a utilitarian, take their sufferings into account, morally. Thus, the scope of the moral community, at least so far as ("higher") animals are concerned, is not something I contest. I may disagree with some particular way of trying to show that animals possess moral standing, e.g., by ascribing them some variant of moral rights, but I have no quarrel with the general claim that they possess such standing. Indeed, my reformist position with respect to vegetarianism, vivisection, and our general use of animals in part turns upon this very fact.

As I have indicated in my two books and numerous articles on animal issues,[1] my reservations come elsewhere. Some of these doubts and criticisms I have explored and developed in a recent series of articles.[2] There, I have focused upon the comparative value of human and animal life; I have taken the notion of autonomy to be central to this issue, since the exercise of autonomy by normal adult humans is the source of an immense part of the value of their lives. Here, I want to sketch one way this concern with the comparative value of human and animal life comes to have importance and to interact with the charge of speciesism.

I

Those who concern themselves with the moral considerability of animals may well be tempted to suppose that their work is finished, once they successfully envelop animals within the moral community. Yet, to stop there is never *per se* to address the issue of the value of animal life and so never to engage the position that I, and others, hold on certain issues. Thus, I am a restricted vivisectionist,[3] not because I think animals are outside the moral community but because of views I hold about the value of their lives. Again, I think it is permissible to use animal parts in human transplants,[4] not because I think animals lack moral standing but because I think animal life is less valuable than human life. (As some readers may know, I argue that experiments upon animals and the use of animal parts in human transplants are only permissible if one is prepared to sanction such experiments upon, and the use of, certain humans. I think the benefits to be derived from these practices are *sometimes* substantial enough to compel me to endorse the practices in the human case, unless the side-effects of any such decision offset these benefits.[5] I return to this matter of our use of humans below.)

I have written of views that I hold; the fact is, I think, that the vast majority of people share my view of the differing value of human and animal life. This view we might capture in the form of three propositions:

1. Animal life has some value;
2. Not all animal life has the same value;
3. Human life is more valuable than animal life.

Very few people today would seem to believe that animal life is without value and that, therefore, we need not trouble ourselves morally about taking it. Equally few people, however, would seem to believe that all animal life has the same value. Certainly, the lives of dogs, cats, and chimps are very widely held to be more valuable than the lives of mice, rats, and worms, and the legal protections we accord these different creatures, for example, reflect this fact. Finally, whatever value we take the lives of dogs and cats to have, most of us believe human life to be more valuable than animal life. We believe this, moreover, even as we oppose cruelty to animals and acknowledge value – in the case of some animals, considerable value – to their lives. I shall call this claim about the comparative value of human and animal life the unequal-value thesis. A crucial question, obviously, is whether we who hold this thesis can defend it.

Many "animal rightists" themselves seem inclined to accept something like the unequal-value thesis. With respect to the oft-cited raft example, in which one can save a man or a dog but not both, animal rightists often concede that, other things being equal, one ought to save the man. To be sure, this result only says something about our intuitions and about those *in extremis*; yet, what it is ordinarily taken to say about them – that we take human life to be more valuable than animal life – is not something we think in extreme circumstances only. Our intuitions about the greater value of human life seem apparent in and affect all our relations with animals, from the differences in the ways we regard, treat, and even bury humans and animals to the differences in the safeguards for their protection that we construct and the differences in penalties we exact for violation of those safeguards.

In a word, the unequal-value thesis seems very much a part of the approach that most of us adopt towards animal issues. We oppose cruelty to animals as well as humans, but this does not lead us to suppose that the lives of humans and animals have the same value. Nor is there any entailment in the matter: one can perfectly consistently oppose cruelty to all sentient creatures without having to suppose that the lives of all such creatures are equally valuable.

We might note in passing that if this is right about our intuitions, then it is far from clear that it is the defender of the unequal-value thesis who must assume the burden of proof in the present discussion. Our intuitions about pain and suffering are such that if a theorist today suggested that animal suffering did not count morally, then he would quickly find himself on the defensive. If I am right about our intuitions over the comparative value of human and animal life, why is the same not true in the case of the theorist who urges or assumes that these lives are of equal value? If, over suffering, our intuitions force the exclusion of the pains of animals to be defended, why, over the value of life, do they not force an *equal*-value thesis to be defended? In any event, I have not left this matter of the burden of proof to chance in my other work (see also below), where I have *argued* for the unequal-value thesis. Here, I want only to stress that our intuitions *do not obviously endorse*, as it were, a starting-point of equality of value in the lives of humans and animals.[6] On the strength of this consideration alone, we seem justified in at least treating sceptically arguments and claims that proceed from or implicitly rely upon some initial presumption of equal value, in order to undermine the unequal-value thesis from the outset.

Where pain and suffering are the central issue, most of us tend to think of the human and animal cases in the same way; thus, cruelty to a child and cruelty to a dog are wrong and wrong for the same reason.[7] Pain is pain; it is an evil, and the evidence suggests that it is as much an evil for dogs as for humans.[8] Furthermore, autonomy or agency (or the lack thereof) does not seem a relevant factor here, since the pains of non-autonomous creatures count as well as the pains of autonomous ones. Neither the child nor the dog is autonomous, at least in any sense that captures why autonomy is such an immensely important value; but the pains of both child and dog count and affect our judgements of rightness and wrongness with respect to what is done to them.

Where the value of life is the central issue, however, we do not tend to think of the human and animal cases alike. Here, we come down in favour of humans, as when we regularly experiment upon and kill animals in our laboratories for (typically) human benefit; and a main justification reflective people give for according humans such advantage invokes directly a difference in value between human and animal life. Autonomy or agency is now, moreover, of the utmost significance, since the exercise of autonomy by normal adult humans is one of the central ways they make possible further, important dimensions of value to their lives.

Arguably, even the extended justification of animal suffering in, say, medical research may make indirect appeal to the unequal-value thesis. Though pain remains an evil, the nature and size of some benefit determines whether its infliction is justified in the particular cases. Nothing precludes this benefit from accruing to human beings, and when it does, we need an independent defence of the appeal to benefit in this kind of case. For the appeal is typically invoked in cases where those who suffer are those who benefit, as when we go to the dentist, and in the present instance human beings are the beneficiaries of animal suffering. Possibly the unequal-value thesis can provide the requisite defence: what justifies the infliction of pain, if anything does, is the appeal to benefit; but what justifies use of the appeal in those cases where humans are the beneficiaries of animal suffering is, arguably, that human life is more valuable than animal life. Thus, while the unequal-value thesis cannot alter the character of pain, which remains an evil, and cannot directly, independently of benefit, justify the infliction of pain, it can, the suggestion is, anchor a particular use of the appeal to benefit.

I do not have space to discuss what constitutes a benefit, the magnitude of benefit required in order to justify the infliction of pain, and some principle of proportionality that rejects even a significant benefit at a cost of immense and excruciating suffering. In general, my views on these matters favour animals, especially when further commercial products are in question but also even when much medical/scientific research is under consideration. More broadly, I think a presumption, not in favour of, but against the use of animals in medical/scientific research would be desirable. Its intended effect would be to force researchers as a matter of routine to argue in depth a case for animal use.[9] Such a presumption coheres with my earlier remarks. The unequal-value thesis in no way compels its adherents to deny that animal lives have value; the destruction or impairment of such lives, therefore, needs to be argued for, which a presumption against use of animals would force researchers to do.

Clearly, a presumption against use is not the same thing as a bar; I allow, therefore, that researchers can make a case. That they must do so, that they must seek to justify the destruction or impairment of lives that have value, is the point.

II

How might we defend the unequal-value thesis? At least the beginnings of what I take to be the most promising option in this regard can be briefly sketched.

Pain is one thing, killing is another, and what makes killing wrong – a killing could be free of pain and suffering – seems to be the fact that it consists in the destruction of something of value. That is, killing and the value of life seem straightforwardly connected, since it is difficult to understand why taking a particular life would be wrong if it had no value. If few people consider animal life to be without value, equally few, I think, consider it to have the same value as normal (adult) human life. They need not be speciesists as a result: in my view, normal (adult) human life is of a much higher quality than animal life, not because of species, but because of richness; and the value of a life is a function of its quality.

Part of the richness of our lives involves activities that we have in common with animals but there are as well whole dimensions to our lives – love, marriage, educating children, jobs, hobbies, sporting events, cultural pursuits, intellectual development and striving, etc. – that greatly expand our range of absorbing endeavours and so significantly deepen the texture of our lives. An impoverished life for *us* need not be one in which food or sex or liberty is absent; it can equally well be a life in which these other dimensions have not taken root or have done so only minimally. When we look back over our lives and regret that we did not make more of them, we rarely have in mind only the kinds of activities that we share with animals; rather, we think much more in terms of precisely these other dimensions of our lives that equally go to make up a rich, full life.

The lives of normal (adult) humans betray a variety and richness that the lives of rabbits do not; certainly, we do not think of ourselves as constrained to live out our lives according to some (conception of a) life deemed appropriate to our species. Other conceptions of a life for ourselves are within our reach, and we can try to understand and appreciate them and to choose among them. Some of us are artists, others educators, still others mechanics; the richness of our lives is easily enhanced through developing and moulding our talents so as to enable us to live out these conceptions of the good life. Importantly, also, we are not condemned to embrace in our lifetimes only a single conception of such a life; in the sense intended, the artist can choose to become an educator and the educator a mechanic. We can embrace at different times different conceptions of how we want to live.

Choosing among conceptions of the good life and trying to live out such a conception are not so intellectualized a set of tasks that only an elite few can manage them. Some reflection upon the life one wants to live is necessary, and some reflection is required in order to organize one's life to live out such a conception; but virtually all of us manage to engage in this degree of reflection. (One of the tragic aspects of Alzheimer's disease is how it undoes a person in just this regard, once it has reached advanced stages.) Even an uneducated man can see the choice between the army and professional boxing as one that requires him to sit down and ponder what he wants to do, whether he has the talents to do it, and what his other, perhaps conflicting desires come to in strength. Even an habitual street person, if free long enough from the influence of drink or drugs to be capable of addressing himself to the choice, can see the life the Salvation Army holds out before him as different in certain respects, some appealing, others perhaps not, from his present life. Choosing how one will live one's life can often be a matter of simply focusing upon these particulars and trying to gauge one's desires with respect to them.

Now, in the case of the rabbit the point is not that the activities which enrich an adult human's life are different from those which enrich its life; it is that the scope or potentiality for enrichment is truncated or severely diminished in the rabbit's case. The quality of a life is a function of its richness, which is a function of its scope or potentiality for enrichment; the scope or potentiality for enrichment in the rabbit's case never approaches that of the human. Nothing we have ever observed about rabbits, nothing we know of them, leads us to make judgements about the variety and richness of their life in anything even remotely comparable to the judgements we make in the human case. To assume as present in the rabbit's life dimensions that supply the full variety and richness of ours, only that these dimensions are hidden from us, provides no real answer, especially when the evidence we have about their lives runs in the other direction.

Autonomy is an important part of the human case. By exercising our autonomy we can mould our lives to fit a conception of the good life that we have decided upon for ourselves; we can then try to live out this conception, with all the sense of achievement, self-fulfilment, and satisfaction that this can bring. Some of us pursue athletic or cultural or intellectual endeavours; some of us are good with our hands and enjoy mechanical tasks and manual labour; and all of us see a job – be it the one we have or the one we should like to have – as an important part of a full life. (This is why unemployment affects more than just our incomes.) The emphasis is upon agency: we can *make* ourselves into repairmen, pianists, and accountants; by exercising our autonomy, we can *impose* upon our lives a conception of the good life that we have for the moment embraced. We can then try to live out this conception, with the consequent sense of fulfilment and achievement that this makes possible. Even failure can be part of the picture: a woman can try to make herself into an Olympic athlete and fail; but her efforts to develop and shape her talents and to take control of and to mould her life in the appropriate ways can enrich her life. Thus, by exercising our autonomy and trying to live out some conception of how we want to live, we make possible further, important dimensions of value to our lives.

We still share certain activities with rabbits, but no mere record of those activities would come anywhere near accounting for the richness of our lives. What is missing in the rabbit's case is the same scope or potentiality for enrichment; and lives of less richness have less value.

The kind of story that would have to be told to make us think that the rabbit's life *was* as rich as the life of a normal (adult) human is one that either postulates in the rabbit potentialities and abilities vastly beyond what we observe and take it to have, or lapses into a rigorous scepticism. By the latter, I mean that we should have to say either that we know nothing of the rabbit's life (and so can know nothing of that life's richness and quality) or that what we know can never be construed as adequate for grounding judgements about the rabbit's quality of life.[10] Such sceptical claims, particularly after Ryle and Wittgenstein on the one hand and much scientific work on the other, may strike many as misplaced, and those who have recourse to them, at least in my experience, have little difficulty in pronouncing pain and suffering, stress, loss of liberty, monotony, and a host of other things to be detrimental to an animal's quality of life. But the real puzzle is how this recourse to scepticism is supposed to make us think that a rabbit's life is as varied and rich as a human's life. If I can know nothing of the rabbit's life, presumably because I do not live that life and so cannot experience it from the inside (this whole way of putting the matter sets ill with a post-Ryle, post-Wittgenstein understanding of psychological concepts and inner processes), then how do I know that the rabbit's life is as rich as a human's life? Plainly, if I cannot know this, I must for the argument's sake assume it. But why should I do this? Nothing I observe and experience leads me to assume it; all the evidence I have about rabbits and humans seems to run entirely in the opposite direction. So, why make this assumption? Most especially, why assume animal lives are as rich as human lives, when we do not even assume, or so I suggest below, that all human lives have the same richness?

III

I have taken autonomy to be or to imply agency, and I have elsewhere considered two ways animal rightists might try to move on this issue. On the one hand, I have in my paper "The Significance of Agency and Marginal Cases" considered attempts to work animals into the class of the autonomous by appeal to (i) some distinction between potential and actual autonomy, (ii) some notion of impaired autonomy, (iii) some attempt to loosen the requirements for possessing one or more of the components of agency, and (iv) some notion of proxy agency. On the other hand, both in that paper and in "Autonomy and the Value of Animal Life", I have considered the attempt, notably by Tom Regan,[11] to sever autonomy from agency altogether. Both paths I have argued against and tried to show why they will not substantiate the claims that animal lives are as rich as human lives and that animal lives have roughly the same value as human lives. In Regan's case in particular, I have been concerned to show that any sense of autonomy that severs the concept from agency has been drained of virtually all the significance for the value of a life that we take autonomy to have.

Agency matters to the value of a life, and animals are not agents. Thus, we require some argument to show that their lack of agency notwithstanding, animals have lives of roughly equal richness and value to the lives of normal (adult) humans. The view that they are members of the moral community will not supply it, the demand is compatible with acknowledging that not all life has the same value; and as we shall see, the argument from the value of the lives of defective humans will not supply it. Any *assumption* that they have lives of equal richness and value to ours seems to run up against, quite apart from the evidence we take ourselves to have about the lives of animals, the fact that, as we shall see, not all human lives have the same richness and value.

Most importantly, it will not do to claim that the rabbit's life is as valuable as the normal (adult) human's life because it is the only life each has. This claim does not as yet say that the rabbit's life has any particular value. If the rabbit and man are dead, they have no life which they can carry on living, at some quality or other; but this *per se* does not show that the lives of the man and the rabbit have a particular value as such, let alone that they have the same value. Put differently, both creatures must be alive in order to have a quality of life, but nothing at all in this shows that they have the same richness and quality of life and, therefore, value of life.[12] I am not disputing that animals can have *a* quality of life and that their lives, as a result, can have value; I am disputing that the richness, quality, and value of their lives is that of normal (adult) humans.

IV

Not all members of the moral community have lives of equal value. Human life is more valuable than animal life. That is our intuition, and as I have assumed, we must defend it. How we defend it is, however, a vitally important affair. For I take the charge of speciesism – the attempt to justify either different treatment or the attribution of a different value of life by appeal to species membership – very seriously. In my view, if a defence of the unequal-value thesis is open to that charge, then it is no defence at all.

As a result, one's options for grounding the unequal-value thesis become limited; no ground will suffice that appeals, either in whole or in part, to species membership. Certainly, some ways of trying to differentiate the value of human from animal life in the past seem pretty clearly to be speciesist. But not all ways are; the important option set out above – one that construes the value of a life as a function of its quality, its quality as a function of its richness, and its richness as a function of its capacity of enrichment – does not use species membership to determine the value of lives. Indeed, it quite explicitly allows for the possibility that some animal life may be more valuable than some human life.

To see this, we have only to realize that the claim that not all members of the moral community have lives of equal value encompasses not only animals but also some humans. Some human lives have less value than others. An infant born without a brain, or any very severely handicapped infant, seems a case in point, as does an elderly person fully in the grip of Alzheimer's disease or some highly degenerative brain, nervous, or physiological disorder. In other words, I think we are compelled to admit that some human life is of a much lower quality and so value than normal (adult) human life. (This is true as well of infants generally, though readers may think in their cases, unlike the cases of seriously defective infants and adults, some argument from potentiality may be adduced to place them in a separate category. The fact remains, however, that the lives of normal (adult) humans betray a variety and richness that the lives of animals, defective humans, and infants do not.)

Accordingly, we must understand the unequal-value thesis to claim that normal (adult) human life is more valuable than animal life. If we justify this claim by appeal to the quality and richness of normal (adult) human life and if we at the same time acknowledge that some human life is of a much lower quality and value than normal (adult) human life, then it seems quite clear that we are not using species membership to determine the value of a life.

Moreover, because some human lives fall drastically below the quality of life of normal (adult) human life, we must face the prospect that the lives of some perfectly healthy animals have a higher quality and greater value than the lives of some humans. And we must face this prospect, with all the implications it may have for the use of these unfortunate humans by others, at least if we continue to justify the use of animals in medical/scientific research by appeal to the lower quality and value of their lives.[13]

What justifies the medical/scientific use of perfectly healthy rabbits instead of humans with a low quality of life? If, for example, experiments on retinas are suggested, why use rabbits or chimps instead of defective humans with otherwise excellent retinas? I know of nothing that cedes human life of any quality, however low, greater value than animal life of any quality, however high. If, therefore, we are going to justify medical/scientific uses of animals by appeal to the value of their lives, we open up directly the possibility of our having to envisage the use of humans of a lower quality of life in preference to animals of a higher quality of life. It is important to bear in mind as well that other factors then come under consideration, such as (i) the nature and size of benefit to be achieved, (ii) the side-effects that any decision to use humans in preference to animals may evoke, (iii) the degree to which education and explanation can dissipate any such negative side-effects, and (iv) the projected reliability of animal results for the human case (as opposed to the projected reliability of human results for the human case). All these things may, in the particular case, work in favour of the use of humans.

The point, of course, is not that we *must* use humans; it is that we cannot invariably use animals in preference to humans, if appeal to the quality and value of lives is the ground we give for using animals. The only way we could justifiably do this is if we could cite something that always, no matter what, cedes human life greater value than animal life. I know of no such thing.

Always in the background, of course, are the benefits that medical/scientific research confers: if we desire to continue to obtain these benefits, are we prepared to pay the price of the use of defective humans? The answer, I think, must be positive, at least until the time comes when we no longer have to use either humans or animals for research purposes. Obviously, this deliberate use of some of the weakest members of our society is distasteful to contemplate and is not something, in the absence of substantial benefit, that we could condone; yet, we presently condone the use of perfectly healthy animals on an absolutely massive scale, and benefit is the justification we employ.

I remain a vivisectionist, therefore, because of the benefits medical/scientific research can bestow. Support for vivisection, however, exacts a cost: it forces us to envisage the use of defective humans in such research. Paradoxically, then, to the extent that one cannot bring oneself to envisage and consent to their use, to that extent, in my view, the case for anti-vivisectionism becomes stronger.

V

The fact that not even all human life has the same value explains why some argument from marginal cases, one of the most common arguments in support of an equal-value thesis, comes unstuck. Such an argument would only be possible if human life of a much lower quality were ceded equal value with normal (adult) human life. In that case, the same concession could be requested for animal life, and an argument from marginal or defective humans could get underway. On the account of the value of a life set out above, however, the initial concession is not made; it is not true that defective human life has the same quality and value as normal (adult) human life. Nor is this result unfamiliar to us today; it is widely employed in much theoretical and practical work in medical ethics.

This fate of the argument from marginal cases matters; for unless one adopts a reverence-for-life principle (a possibility that I considered and rejected in *Rights, Killing, and Suffering*[14]) or adopts some form of holistic ethic, the supposed equal value of human and animal life, if it is not to be merely assumed, is often made to turn upon some variant of the argument from marginal cases.

As for an holistic account of value, wherein the value of the parts of an eco-system turns upon the value of the whole, this is much too large an issue for me to address here. Suffice it to say that I have elsewhere expressed doubts about any such account.[15] I have no very clear idea of exactly how one sets about uncovering the value of an entire eco-system, in order to arrive at some view of the value of humans and animals within it, or how one knows one has ascertained that value correctly. There seems no touchstone of error in any such uncovering; that is, there seems no clear way to contest one's claim that some eco-system in some particular state has whatever value one says it has.

This leaves the argument from marginal cases to try to force the admission of the equal value of human and animal life. Tom Regan has long relied upon this argument, and though I have given my objections to his position in another place,[16] a word on his use of the argument may help in part to clarify why I reject it.

In a recent article Regan wonders what could be the basis for the view that human life is more valuable than animal life and moves at once to invoke the argument from marginal cases to dispel any such possibility:

> What could be the basis of our having more inherent value than animals? Their lack of reason, or autonomy, or intellect? Only if we are willing to make the same judgment in the case of humans who are similarly deficient. But it is not true that some humans – the retarded child, for example, or the mentally deranged – have less inherent value than you or I.[17]

Regan provides no argument for this claim (and, for that matter, no analysis of "inherent value"), but it seems at least to involve, if not to depend upon, our agreeing that human life of any quality, however low, has the same value as normal (adult) human life. I can see no reason whatever to accept this. Some human lives are so very deficient in quality that we would not wish those lives upon anyone, and there are few lengths to which we would not go in order to avoid such lives for ourselves and our loved ones. I can see little point in pretending that lives which we would do everything we could to avoid are of equal value to those normal (adult) human lives that we are presently living.

Of course, it is always possible to draw up, say, six different senses in which lives may be said to be valuable and to try to make out that deficient human life is as valuable as normal (adult) human life in four or five of them. I suspect that most of us, however, would see such an exercise as just that. For in however many senses human lives may be said to be valuable, the fact remains that we would do everything we could to avoid a life of severe derangement or mental enfeebleness or physical paralysis. It is hard to believe, as a result, that normal (adult) humans would consider such a life to be as valuable as their present life or to be a life – think of a life in the advanced stages of AIDS – that they would even remotely regard as a life as desirable to live as their present one.

So far as I can see, the quality of some lives can plummet so disastrously that those lives can cease to have much value at all, can cease to be lives, that is, that are any longer worth living. I acknowledge the difficulty in determining in many cases when a life is no longer worth living; in other cases, however, such as an elderly person completely undone by Alzheimer's disease or an infant born with no or only half a brain, the matter seems far less problematic.

VI

Is an involved defence of the unequal-value thesis, however, really necessary? Is there not a much more direct and uncomplicated defence readily to hand? I have space for only a few words on several possibilities in this regard.

The defence of the unequal-value thesis that I have begun to sketch, whether in its positive or negative aspect, does not make reference to religion; yet, it is true that certain religious beliefs seem to favour the thesis. The doctrine of the sanctity of life has normally been held with respect to human life alone; the belief in human dominion over the rest of creation has traditionally been held to set humans apart; and the belief that humans but not animals are possessed of an immortal soul seems plainly to allude to a further dimension of significance to human life. I am not myself religious, however, and I do not adopt a religious approach to questions about the value of lives. Any such approach would seem to tie one's defence of the unequal-value thesis to the adequacy of one's theological views, something which a non-religious person can scarcely endorse. I seek a defence of the unequal-value thesis, whatever the status of God's existence or the adequacy of this or that religion or religious doctrine. I do not pre-judge the issue of whether a religious person can accept a quality-of-life defence of the sort I have favoured; my point is simply that that defence does not rely upon theological premises.

It may be asked, however, why we need anything quite so sophisticated as a *defence* of the unequal-value thesis at all. Why can we not just express a preference for our own kind and be done with the matter? After all, when a father gives a kidney to save his daughter's life, we perfectly well understand why he did not choose to give the kidney to a stranger *in preference to* his daughter. This "natural bias" we do not condemn and do not take to point to a moral defect in the father. Why, therefore, is not something similar possible in the case of our interaction with animals? Why, that is, can we not appeal to a natural bias in favour of members of our own species? There are a number of things that can be said in response, only several of which I shall notice here.

There is the problem, if one takes the charge of speciesism seriously, of how to articulate this bias in favour of members of our species in such a way as to avoid that charge. Then there is the problem of how to articulate this preference for our own kind in such a way as to exclude interpretations of "our own kind" that express preferences for one's own race, gender, or religion. Otherwise, one is going to let such preferences do considerable work in one's moral decision-making. I do not wish to foreclose all possibilities in these two cases, however; it may well be that a preference for our own kind *can* be articulated in a way that avoids these and some other problems.

Even so, I believe that there is another and deeper level of problem that this preference for our own kind encounters. On the one hand, we can understand the preference to express a bond we feel with members of our own species *over and above* the bond that we (or most of us) feel with ("higher") animals. Such a bond, if it exists, poses no direct problem, if its existence is being used to explain, for example, instances of behaviour where we obviously exhibit sympathy for human beings. (We must be careful not to *under-value* the sympathy most people exhibit towards animals, especially domesticated ones.) On the other hand, we can understand this preference for our own kind to express the claim that we stand in a special moral relationship to members of our own species. This claim does pose a problem, since, if we systematically favour humans over animals on the basis of it, it does considerable moral work – work, obviously, that would not be done if the claim were rejected. I have elsewhere commented on this claim;[18] a word on one facet of it must suffice here.

I cannot see that species membership is a ground for holding that we stand in a special moral relationship to our fellow humans. The father obviously stands in such a relationship to his daughter, and his decision to marry and to have children is how he comes to have or to stand in that relationship. But how, through merely being born, does one come to stand in a special moral relationship to humans generally? Typically, I can step in and out of special moral relationships; in the case of species membership, that is not true. In that case, so long as I live, nothing can change my relationship to others, so long as they live. If this were true, my morality would to an extent no longer express my view of myself at large in a world filled with other people but would be something foisted upon me simply through being born.

Since we do not choose our species membership, a special moral relationship I am supposed to stand in to humans generally would lie outside my control; whereas it is precisely the voluntary nature of such relationships that seems most central to their character. And it is precisely because of this voluntary nature, of, as it were, our ability to take on and shed such relationships, that these relationships can be read as expressing *my* view of myself at large in a world filled with other people.

We often do stand in special moral relationships to others; but mere species membership would have us stand in such a relationship to all others. There is something too sweeping about this, as if birth alone can give the rest of human creation a moral hold over me. In a real sense, such a view would sever me from my morality; for my morality would no longer consist in expressions of how I see myself interacting with others and how I choose to interact with them. My own choices and decisions have no effect upon species membership and so on a moral relationship that I am supposed to stand in to each and every living, human being. Such a view is at odds not only with how we typically understand special moral relationships but also with how we typically understand our relationship to our own morality.

VII

It may well be tempting, I suppose, to try to develop another sense of "speciesism" and to hold that a position such as mine is speciesist in that sense. I have space here for only a few comments on one such sense.

If to be a *direct* speciesist is to discriminate among the value of lives solely on the basis of species membership, as it is, for example, for Peter Singer, then I am not, as I have tried to show, a direct speciesist. But am I not, it might be suggested, an *indirect* speciesist, in that, in order to determine the quality and value of a life, I use human-centred criteria as if they were appropriate for assessing the quality and value of all life? Thus, for instance, when I emphasize cultural and artistic endeavours, when I emphasize autonomy and mental development and achievement, when I emphasize making choices, directing one's life, and selecting and living out conceptions of the good life, the effect is to widen the gulf between animals and humans by using human-centred criteria for assessing the quality and value of a life as if they were appropriate to appreciating the quality and value of animal life. And this will not do; for it amounts to trying to judge animals and animal lives by human standards. What one should do, presumably, is to judge the quality and value of animal life by criteria appropriate to each separate species of animals.

I stress again that the argument of this paper is not about whether rabbits have lives of value (I think that they do) but rather about whether they have lives of equal value to normal (adult) human life. It is unclear to me how the charge of indirect speciesism addresses this argument.

We must distinguish this charge of an indirect speciesism from the claim, noted earlier, that we can know nothing of animal lives and so nothing about their quality and value; indeed, the two claims may conflict. The point behind the speciesism charge is that I am not using criteria appropriate to a species of animal for assessing its quality of life, which presumably means that there *are* appropriate criteria available for selection. Knowledge of appropriate criteria seems to require that we know something of an animal's life, in order to make the judgement of appropriateness. Yet, the whole point behind the lack-of-knowledge claim is that we can know nothing of an animal's life, nothing of how it experiences the world, nothing, in essence, about how well or how badly its life is going. It would seem, therefore, as if the two views can conflict.

The crucial thing here about both claims, however, is this: both are advanced against my defence of the unequal-value thesis and on behalf of the equality of value of human and animal life without it being in any wise clear how they show this equality.

The ignorance claim would seem to have it that, because we can know nothing of the animal case, we must assume that animal and human life have the same value. But why should we fall in with this assumption? The ignorance claim would have us start from the idea, presumably, that all life, irrespective of its level of development and complexity, has the same value; but why should we start from that particular idea? Surely there must be some *reason* for thinking all life whatever has the same value. It is this reason that needs to be stated and assessed.

The indirect speciesist claim would seem to have it that, were we only to select criteria for assessing the quality and value of life appropriate to animals' species, we must agree that animal and human life are of equal value. The temptation is to inquire after what these criteria might be in rabbits, but any such concern must be firmly understood in the light of the earlier discussion of the richness of our lives. What the unequal-value thesis represents is our quest to gain some understanding of (i) the capacities of animals and humans, (ii) the differences among these various capacities, (iii) the complexity of lives, (iv) the role of agency in this complexity, and (v) the way agency enables humans to add further dimensions of value to their lives. The richness of our lives encompasses these multi-faceted aspects of our being and is a function of them. The point is not that a rabbit may not have a keener sense of smell than we do and may not derive intense, pleasurable sensations through that sense of smell; it is that we have to believe that something like this, augmented, perhaps, by other things we might say in the rabbit's case of like kind, suffices to make the rabbit's life as rich and as full as ours. If one thinks of our various capacities and of the different levels on which they operate, physical, mental, emotional, imaginative, then pointing out that rabbits can have as pleasurable sensations as we do in certain regards does not meet the point.

When we say of a woman that she has "tasted life to the full", we do not make a point about (or solely about) pleasurable sensations; we refer to the different dimensions of our being and to the woman's attempt to develop these in herself and to actualize them in the course of her daily life. And an important aspect in all this is what agency means to the woman: in the sense intended, she is not condemned to live the life that all of her ancestors have lived; she can mould and shape her life to "fit" her own conception of how she should live, thereby enabling her to add further dimensions of value to her life. It is this diversity and complexity in us that needs to be made good in the rabbit's case and that no mere catalogue of its pleasures through the sense of smell seems likely to accomplish.

Again, it is not that the rabbit cannot do things that we are unable to do and not that it has capacities which we lack; what has to be shown is how this sort of thing, given how rabbits behave and live out their days, so enriches their lives that the quality and value of them approach those of humans. And what is one going to say in the rabbit's case that makes good the role agency plays in ours? The absence of agency from a human life is a terrible thing; it deeply impoverishes a life and forestalls completely one's making one's life into the life one wants to live. Yet, this must be the natural condition of rabbits. It is this gulf that agency creates, the gulf between living out the life appropriate to one's species and living out a life one has chosen for oneself and has moulded and shaped accordingly, that is one of the things that it is difficult to understand what rabbits can do to overcome.

VIII

In sum, I think the unequal-value thesis is defensible and can be defended even as its adherent takes seriously the charge of speciesism. And it is the unequal-value thesis that figures centrally in the justification of our use of animals in medical and scientific research. If, as I have done here, we assume that the thesis must be defended, then the character of that defence, I think, requires that *if* we are to continue to use animals for research purposes, then we must begin to envisage the use of some humans for those same purposes. The cost of holding the unequal-value thesis, and most of us, I suggest, do hold it, is to realize that, upon a quality-of-life defence of it, it encompasses the lives of some humans as well as animals. I cannot at the moment see that any other defence of it both meets the charge of speciesism and yet does indeed amount to a defence.[19]

Notes

1 See especially my books *Interests and Rights: The Case Against Animals* (Oxford: Clarendon Press, 1980), and *Rights, Killing, and Suffering* (Oxford: Basil Blackwell, 1983). These give a reasonably full listing of my articles relevant to the subject of this paper, when taken together with those articles mentioned below.

2 "Autonomy and The Value of Animal Life", *The Monist* (1986); "The Significance of Agency and Marginal Cases", *Philosophica* (1986); "Autonomy and Conceptions of the Good Life", in L. W. Sumner, T. Attig, D. Callen (eds), *Values and Moral Standing* (Bowling Green Studies in Applied Philosophy, 1986); and "Animal Parts, Human Wholes: On the Use of Animals as a Source of Organs for Human Transplants", in J. Humber, R. Almeder (eds), *Biomedical Reviews 1987* (New Jersey: Humana Press, 1988).

3 See my "Vivisection, Medicine, and Morals", *Journal of Medical Ethics* (1983), and *Rights, Killing, and Suffering*, op. cit., ch. 12.

4 See "Animal Parts, Human Wholes", op. cit.

5 For a brief discussion of these side-effects, see my "Vivisection, Medicine, and Morals", op. cit.

6 One might want to advance some vast generality here, of the order, for example, that all living things, just because and to the extent that they are living, have value and, perhaps, even equal value; but this generality will need argument in its support. I have heard such a generality advanced often in discussion, almost always, it eventually turned out, as a fundamental assumption about value; but I have not come across any good reason to grant such an assumption. Besides, most of us are going to need convincing that the lives of "lower" animals, such as agricultural pests, are as valuable as human lives. This whole way of talking, however, is alien to the discussion of the value of a life I advance below, in which richness and quality of life figure prominently.

7 This is not to say, of course, that there may not be ways in which normal (adult) humans can suffer that animals do not.

8 Suffering is a wider notion than pain; but I drop the distinction here, since it is not relevant to what follows.

9 In Britain, such a presumption increasingly receives support among the public, scientific bodies, and government, where the use of animals in medical/scientific research is on

the whole already subject to more severe examination than in the United States. And the matter is under continuous review. I am at present part of a working party in the Institute of Medical Ethics in London that is examining the ethics of our use of animals in medical research. The members come from government, industry, the medical establishment, academia, religious organizations, and animal-welfare societies, and our aim is to produce a report that will assist and perhaps even direct discussion on all levels about our present, simply massive use of animals in medical research.

10 Something along these sceptical lines has been suggested to me by S. F. Sapontzis, a line of argument that doubtless his book *Morals, Reason, and Animals* (Philadelphia: Temple University Press, 1987) will pursue. (I have only now, May 1988, received Sapontzis' book for review.)

11 Tom Regan, *The Case for Animal Rights* (Berkeley: University of California Press, 1983).

12 For a discussion of this point, see *Rights, Killing, and Suffering, op. cit.*, p. 110.

13 I discuss this matter of our use of humans, in the context of a discussion of xenograph, in some detail in "Animal Parts, Human Wholes", *op. cit.* See also my "Vivisection, Medicine, and Morals", *op. cit.*, and *Rights, Killing, and Suffering, op. cit.*, chapter 12.

14 *Rights, Killing, and Suffering, op. cit.*, chapter 12.

15 See *Rights, Killing, and Suffering, op. cit.*, chapter 14. This discussion is preliminary only and does not fully address a worked-out, holistic theory, if there be such.

16 See "Autonomy and The Value of Animal Life", *op. cit.*

17 Tom Regan, "The Case for Animal Rights", in Peter Singer (ed.), *In Defence of Animals* (Oxford: Basil Blackwell, 1985), p. 23. This article mirrors some central claims of Regan's book of the same name.

18 See "Animal Parts, Human Wholes", *op. cit.*

19 An earlier version of this paper was read in 1986 as my contribution to a debate with Stephen R. L. Clark, in a Wolfson College, Oxford, debate series on *Animal Rights and Wrongs*. It was especially pleasing to be able to join my old friend and colleague in starting off the series.

12

The Case for Animal Rights

Tom Regan

How to proceed? We begin by asking how the moral status of animals has been understood by thinkers who deny that animals have rights. Then we test the mettle of their ideas by seeing how well they stand up under the heat of fair criticism. If we start our thinking in this way, we soon find that some people believe that we have no duties directly to animals, that we owe nothing to them, that we can do nothing that wrongs them. Rather, we can do wrong acts that involve animals, and so we have duties regarding them, though none to them. Such views may be called *indirect duty views*. By way of illustration: suppose your neighbor kicks your dog. Then your neighbor has done something wrong. But not to your dog. The wrong that has been done is a wrong to you. After all, it is wrong to upset people, and your neighbor's kicking your dog upsets you. So you are the one who is wronged, not your dog. Or again: by kicking your dog your neighbor damages your property. And since it is wrong to damage another person's property, your neighbor has done something wrong – to you, of course, not to your dog. Your neighbor no more wrongs your dog than your car would be wronged if the windshield were smashed. Your neighbor's duties involving your dog are indirect duties to you. More generally, all of our duties regarding animals are indirect duties to one another – to humanity.

How could someone try to justify such a view? Someone might say that your dog doesn't feel anything and so isn't hurt by your neighbor's kick, doesn't care about the pain since none is felt, is as unaware of anything as is your windshield. Someone might say this, but no rational person will, since, among other considerations, such a view will commit anyone who holds it to the position that no human beings feel pain either – that human beings also don't care about what happens to them. A second possibility is that though both humans and your dog are hurt when kicked, it is only human pain that matters. But, again, no rational person can believe this. Pain is pain wherever it occurs. If your neighbor's causing you pain is wrong because of the pain that is caused, we cannot rationally ignore or dismiss the moral relevance of the pain that your dog feels.

Philosophers who hold indirect duty views – and many still do – have come to understand that they must avoid the two defects just noted: that is, both the view that animals don't feel anything as well as the idea that only human pain can be morally relevant. Among such thinkers the sort of view now favored is one or another form of what is called *contractarianism*.

Here, very crudely, is the root idea: morality consists of a set of rules that individuals voluntarily agree to abide by, as we do when we sign a contract (hence the name contractarianism). Those who understand and accept the terms of the contract are covered directly; they have rights created and recognized by, and protected in, the contract. And these contractors can also have protection spelled out for others who, though they lack the ability to understand morality and so cannot sign the contract themselves, are loved or cherished by those who can. Thus young children, for example, are unable to sign contracts and lack rights. But they are protected by the contract nonetheless because of the sentimental interests of others, most notably their parents. So we have, then, duties involving these children, duties regarding them, but no duties to them. Our duties in their case are indirect duties to other human beings, usually their parents.

As for animals, since they cannot understand contracts, they obviously cannot sign; and since they cannot sign, they have no rights. Like children, however, some animals are the object of the sentimental interest of others. You, for example, love your dog or cat. So those animals that enough people care about (companion animals, whales, baby seals, the American bald eagle), though they lack rights themselves, will be protected because of the sentimental interests of people. I have, then, according to contractarianism, no duty directly to your dog or any other animal, not even the duty not to cause them pain or suffering; my duty not to hurt them is a duty I have to those people who care about what happens to them. As for other animals, where no or little sentimental interest is present – in the case of farm animals, for example, or laboratory rats – what duties we have grow weaker and weaker, perhaps to the vanishing point. The pain and death they endure, though real, are not wrong if no one cares about them.

When it comes to the moral status of animals, contractarianism could be a hard view to refute if it were an adequate theoretical approach to the moral status of human beings. It is not adequate in this latter respect, however, which makes the question of its adequacy in the former case, regarding animals, utterly moot. For consider: morality, according to the (crude) contractarian position before us, consists of rules that people agree to abide by. What people? Well, enough to make a difference – enough, that is, *collectively* to have the power to enforce the rules that are drawn up in the contract. That is very well and good for the signatories but not so good for anyone who is not asked to sign. And there is nothing in contractarianism of the sort we are discussing that guarantees or requires that everyone will have a chance to participate equally in framing rules of morality. The result is that this approach to ethics could sanction the most blatant forms of social, economic, moral, and political injustice, ranging from a repressive caste system to systematic racial or sexual discrimination. Might, according to this theory, does make right. Let those who are the victims of injustice suffer as they will. It matters not so long as no one else – no contractor, or too few of them – cares about it. Such a theory takes one's moral breath away . . . as if, for example, there would be nothing wrong with apartheid in South Africa if few white South Africans were upset by it. A theory with so little to recommend it at the level of the ethics of our treatment of our fellow humans cannot have anything more to recommend it when it comes to the ethics of how we treat our fellow animals.

The version of contractarianism just examined is, as I have noted, a crude variety, and in fairness to those of a contractarian persuasion, it must be noted that much more refined, subtle, and ingenious varieties are possible. For example, John Rawls, in his *A Theory of Justice*, sets forth a version of contractarianism that forces contractors to ignore the accidental features of being a human being – for example, whether one is white or black, male or female, a genius or of modest intellect. Only by ignoring such features, Rawls believes, can we ensure that the principles of justice that contractors would agree upon are not based on bias or prejudice. Despite the improvement a view such as Rawls's represents over the cruder forms of contractarianism, it remains deficient: it systematically denies that we have direct duties to those human beings who do not have a sense of justice – young children, for instance, and many mentally retarded humans. And yet it seems reasonably certain that, were we to torture a young child or a retarded elder, we would be doing something that wronged him or her, not something that would be wrong if (and only if) other humans with a sense of justice were upset. And since this is true in the case of these humans, we cannot rationally deny the same in the case of animals.

Indirect duty views, then, including the best among them, fail to command our rational assent. Whatever ethical theory we should accept rationally, therefore, it must at least recognize that we have some duties directly to animals, just as we have some duties directly to each other. The next two theories I'll sketch attempt to meet this requirement.

The first I call the cruelty–kindness view. Simply stated, this says that we have a direct duty to be kind to animals and a direct duty not to be cruel to them. Despite the familiar, reassuring ring of these ideas, I do not believe that this view offers an adequate theory. To make this clearer, consider kindness. A kind person acts from a certain type of motive – compassion or concern, for example. And that is a virtue. But there is no guarantee that a kind act is a right act. If I am a generous racist, for example, I will be inclined to act kindly towards members of my own race, favoring their interests above those of others. My kindness would be real and, so far as it goes, good. But I trust it is too obvious to require argument that my kind acts may not be above moral reproach – may, in fact, be positively wrong because rooted in injustice. So kindness, notwithstanding its status as a virtue to be encouraged, simply will not carry the weight of a theory of right action.

Cruelty fares no better. People or their acts are cruel if they display either a lack of sympathy for or, worse, the presence of enjoyment in another's suffering. Cruelty in all its guises is a bad thing, a tragic human failing. But just as a person's being motivated by kindness does not guarantee that he or she does what is right, so the absence of cruelty does not ensure that he or she avoids doing what is wrong. Many people who perform abortions, for example, are not cruel, sadistic people. But that fact alone does not settle the terribly difficult question of the morality of abortion. The case is no different when we examine the ethics of our treatment of animals. So, yes, let us be for kindness and against cruelty. But let us not suppose that being for the one and against the other answers questions about moral right and wrong.

Some people think that the theory we are looking for is *utilitarianism*. A utilitarian accepts two moral principles. The first is that of equality: everyone's interests count, and similar interests must be counted as having similar weight or importance. White or black, American or Iranian, human or animal – everyone's pain or frustration matters, and matters just as much as the equivalent pain or frustration of anyone else. The second principle a utilitarian accepts is that of utility: do the act that will bring about the best balance between satisfaction and frustration for everyone affected by the outcome.

As a utilitarian, then, here is how I am to approach the task of deciding what I morally ought to do: I must ask who will be affected if I choose to do one thing rather than another, how much each individual will be affected, and where the best results are most likely to lie – which option, in other words, is most likely to bring about the best results, the best balance between satisfaction and frustration. That option, whatever it may be, is the one I ought to choose. That is where my moral duty lies.

The great appeal of utilitarianism rests with its uncompromising *egalitarianism*: everyone's interests count and count as much as the like interests of everyone else. The kind of odious discrimination that some forms of contractarianism can justify – discrimination based on race or sex, for example – seems disallowed in principle by utilitarianism, as is speciesism, systematic discrimination based on species membership.

The equality we find in utilitarianism, however, is not the sort an advocate of animal or human rights should have in mind. Utilitarianism has no room for the equal rights of different individuals because it has no room for their equal inherent value or worth. What has value for the utilitarian is the satisfaction of an individual's interests, not the individual whose interests they are. A universe in which you satisfy your desire for water, food, and warmth is, other things being equal, better than a universe in which these desires are frustrated. And the same is true in the case of an animal with similar desires. But neither you nor the animal have any value in your own right. Only your feelings do.

Here is an analogy to help make the philosophical point clearer: a cup contains different liquids, sometimes sweet, sometimes bitter, sometimes a mixture of the two. What has value is the liquids: the sweeter the better, the bitterer the worse. The cup, the container, has no value. It is what goes into it, not what it goes into, that has value. For the utilitarian, you and I are like the cup; we have no value as individuals and thus no equal value. What has value is what goes into us, what we serve as receptacles for; our feelings of satisfaction have positive value, our feelings of frustration negative value.

Serious problems arise for utilitarianism when we remind ourselves that it enjoins us to bring about the best consequences. What does this mean? It doesn't mean the best consequences for me alone, or for my family or friends, or any other person taken individually. No, what we must do is, roughly, as follows: we must add up (somehow!) the separate satisfactions and frustrations of everyone likely to be affected by our choice, the satisfactions in one column, the frustrations in the other. We must total each column for each of the options before us. That is what it means to say the theory is aggregative. And then we must choose that option which is most likely to bring about the best balance of totalled satisfactions over totalled frustrations. Whatever act would lead to this outcome is the one we ought morally to perform – it is where our moral duty lies. And that act quite clearly might not be the same one that would bring about the best results for me personally, or for my family or friends, or for a lab animal. The best aggregated consequences for everyone concerned are not necessarily the best for each individual.

That utilitarianism is an aggregative theory – different individuals' satisfactions or frustrations are added, or summed, or totalled – is the key objection to this theory. My Aunt Bea is old, inactive, a cranky, sour person, though not physically ill. She prefers to go on living. She is also rather rich, I could make a fortune if I could get my hands on her money, money she intends to give me in any event, after she dies, but which she refuses to give me now. In order to avoid a huge tax bite, I plan to donate a handsome sum of my profits to a local children's hospital. Many, many children will benefit from my generosity, and much joy will be brought to their parents, relatives, and friends. If I don't get the money rather soon, all these ambitions will come to naught. The once-in-a-lifetime opportunity to make a real killing will be gone. Why, then, not kill my Aunt Bea? Oh, of course I *might* get caught. But I'm no fool and, besides, her doctor can be counted on to cooperate (he has an eye for the same investment and I happen to know a good deal about his shady past). The deed can be done . . . professionally, shall we say. There is *very* little chance of getting caught. And as for my conscience being guiltridden, I am a resourceful sort of fellow and will take more than sufficient comfort – as I lie on the beach at Acapulco – in contemplating the joy and health I have brought to so many others.

Suppose Aunt Bea is killed and the rest of the story comes out as told. Would I have done anything wrong? Anything immoral? One would have thought that I had. Not according to utilitarianism. Since what I have done has brought about the best balance between totalled satisfaction and frustration for all those affected by the outcome, my action is not wrong. Indeed, in killing Aunt Bea the physician and I did what duty required.

This same kind of argument can be repeated in all sorts of cases, illustrating, time after time, how the utilitarian's position leads to results that impartial people find morally callous. It *is* wrong to kill my Aunt Bea in the name of bringing about the best results for others. A good end does not justify an evil means. Any adequate moral theory will have to explain why this is so. Utilitarianism fails in this respect and so cannot be the theory we seek.

What to do? Where to begin anew? The place to begin, I think, is with the utilitarian's view of the value of the individual – or, rather, the lack of value. In its place, suppose we consider that you and I, for example, do have value as individuals – what we'll call *inherent value*. To say we have such value is to say that we are something more than, something different from, mere receptacles. Moreover, to ensure that we do not pave the way for such injustices as slavery or sexual discrimination, we must believe that all who have inherent value have it equally, regardless of their sex, race, religion, birthplace, and so on. Similarly to be discarded as irrelevant are one's talents or skills, intelligence and wealth, personality or pathology, whether one is loved and admired or despised and loathed. The genius and the retarded child, the prince and the pauper, the brain surgeon and the fruit vendor, Mother Teresa and the most unscrupulous used-car salesman – all have inherent value, all possess it equally, and all have an equal right to be treated with respect, to be treated in ways that do not reduce them to the status of things, as if they existed as resources for others. My value as an individual is independent of my usefulness to you. Yours is not dependent on your usefulness to me. For either of us to treat the other in ways that fail to show respect for the other's independent value is to act immorally, to violate the individual's rights.

Some of the rational virtues of this view – what I call the *rights view* – should be evident. Unlike (crude) contractarianism, for example, the rights view *in principle* denies the moral tolerability of any and all forms of racial, sexual, or social discrimination; and unlike utilitarianism, the view *in principle* denies that we can justify good results by using evil means that violate an individual's rights – denies, for example, that it could be moral to kill my Aunt Bea to harvest beneficial consequences for others. That would be to sanction the disrespectful treatment of the individual in the name of the social good, something the rights view will not – categorically will not – ever allow.

The rights view, I believe, is rationally the most satisfactory moral theory. It surpasses all other theories in the degree to which it illuminates and explains the foundation of our duties to one another – the domain of human morality. On this score it has the best reasons, the best arguments, on its side. Of course, if it were possible to show that only human beings are included within its scope, then a person like myself, who believes in animal rights, would be obliged to look elsewhere.

But attempts to limit its scope to humans only can be shown to be rationally defective. Animals, it is true, lack many of the abilities humans possess. The can't read, do higher mathematics, build a bookcase, or make *baba ghanoush*. Neither can many human beings, however, and yet we don't (and shouldn't) say that they (these humans) therefore have less inherent value, less of a right to be treated with respect, than do others. It is the *similarities* between those human beings who most clearly, most noncontroversially have such value (the people reading this, for example), not our differences, that matter most. And the really crucial, the basic similarity is simply this: we are each of us the experiencing subject of a life, a conscious creature having an individual welfare that has importance to us whatever our usefulness to others. We want and prefer things, believe and feel things, recall and expect things. And all these dimensions of our life, including our pleasure and pain, our enjoyment and suffering, our satisfaction and frustration, our continued existence or our untimely death – all make a difference to the quality of our life as lived, as experienced, by us as individuals. As the same is true of those animals that concern us (the ones that are eaten and trapped, for example), they too must be viewed as the experiencing subjects of a life, with inherent value of their own.

Some there are who resist the idea that animals have inherent value. "Only humans have such value," they profess. How might this narrow view be defended? Shall we say that only humans have the requisite intelligence, or autonomy, or reason? But there are many, many humans who fail to meet these standards and yet are reasonably viewed as having value above and beyond their usefulness to others. Shall we claim that only humans belong to the right species, the species *Homo sapiens*? But this is blatant speciesism. Will it be said, then, that all – and only – humans have immortal souls? Then our opponents have their work cut out for them. I am myself not ill-disposed to the proposition that there are immortal souls. Personally, I profoundly hope I have one. But I would not want to rest my position on a controversial ethical issue on the even more controversial question about who or what has an immortal soul. That is to dig one's hole deeper, not to climb out. Rationally, it is better to resolve moral issues without making more controversial assumptions than are needed. The question of who has inherent value is such a question, one that is resolved more rationally without the introduction of the idea of immortal souls than by its use.

Well, perhaps some will say that animals have some inherent value, only less than we have. Once again, however, attempts to defend this view can be shown to lack rational justification. What could be the basis of our having more inherent value than animals? Their lack of reason, or autonomy, or intellect? Only if we are willing to make the same judgment in the case of humans who are similarly deficient. But it is not true that such humans – the retarded child, for example, or the mentally deranged – have less inherent value than you or I. Neither, then, can we rationally sustain the view that animals that are like them in being the experiencing subjects of a life have less inherent value. *All* who have inherent value have it *equally*, whether they be human animals or not.

Inherent value, then, belongs equally to those who are the experiencing subjects of a life. Whether it belongs to others – to rocks and rivers, trees and glaciers, for example – we do not know and may never know. But neither do we need to know, if we are to make the case for animal rights. We do not need to know, for example, how many people are eligible to vote in the next presidential election before we can know whether I am. Similarly, we do not need to know how many individuals have inherent value before we can know that some do. When it comes to the case for animal rights, then, what we need to know is whether the animals that, in our culture, are routinely eaten, hunted, and used in our laboratories, for example, are like us in being subjects of a life. And we do know this. We do know that many – literally, billions and billions – of these animals are the subjects of a life in the sense explained and so have inherent value if we do. And since, in order to arrive at the best theory of our duties to one another, we must recognize our equal inherent value as individuals, reason – not sentiment, not emotion – reason compels us to recognize the equal inherent value of these animals and, with this, their equal right to be treated with respect.

That, *very* roughly, is the shape and feel of the case for animal rights. Most of the details of the supporting argument are missing. They are to be found in the book that bears the same title as this essay.[1] Here, the details go begging, and I must, in closing, limit myself to two final points.

The first is how the theory that underlies the case for animal rights shows that the animal rights movement is a part of, not antagonistic to, the human rights movement. The theory that rationally grounds the rights of animals also grounds the rights of humans. Thus those involved in the animal rights movement are partners in the struggle to secure respect for human rights – the rights of women, for example, or minorities, or workers. The animal rights movement is cut from the same moral cloth as these.

Secondly, having set out the broad outlines of the rights view, I can now say why its implications for farming and science, among other fields, are both clear and uncompromising. In the case of the use of animals in science, the rights view is categorically abolitionist. Lab animals are not our tasters; we are not their kings. Because these animals are treated routinely, systematically as if their value were reducible to their usefulness to others, they are routinely, systematically treated with a lack of respect, and thus are their rights routinely, systematically violated. This is just as true when they are used in trivial, duplicative, unnecessary or unwise research as it is when they are used in studies that hold out real promise of human benefits. We can't justify harming or killing a human being (my Aunt Bea, for example) just for these sorts of reason. Neither can we do so even in the case of so lowly a creature as a laboratory rat. It is not just refinement or reduction that is called for, not just larger, cleaner cages, not just more generous use of anesthesia or the elimination of multiple surgery, not just tidying up the system. It is complete replacement. The best we can do when it comes to using animals in science is – not to use them. That is where our duty lies, according to the rights view.

As for commercial animal agriculture, the rights view takes a similar abolitionist position. The fundamental moral wrong here is not that animals are kept in stressful close confinement or in isolation, or that their pain and suffering, their needs and preferences are ignored or discounted. All these *are* wrong, of course, but they are not the fundamental wrong. They are symptoms and effects of the deeper, systematic wrong that allows these animals to be viewed and treated as lacking independent value, as resources for us – as, indeed, a renewable resource. Giving farm animals more space, more natural environments, more companions does not right the fundamental wrong, any more than giving lab animals more anesthesia or bigger, cleaner cages would right the fundamental wrong in their case. Nothing less than the total dissolution of commercial animal agriculture will do this, just as, for similar reasons I won't develop at length here, morality requires nothing less than the total elimination of hunting and trapping for commercial and sporting ends. The rights view's implications, then, as I have said, are clear and uncompromising.

Note

Reprinted by permission from *In Defense of Animals* (Oxford, England: Basil Blackwell). Paper presented at the national conference, "Animals and Humans: Ethical Perspectives," Moorhead State University, Moorhead, MN, April 21–23, 1986.

1 *The Case for Animal Rights* (Berkeley: University of California Press, 1983).

13

Learning to See the Animals Again

John P. Gluck

The Conduct of Science

The conduct of science contains a number of conflicting demands. Among them on the one hand is that the process in its best form requires focused curiosity, imaginative and unrestrained thinking, and boundary-stretching creativity. On the other hand, the conduct of specific experiments, once designed, calls for compulsive attention to detail and unwavering conformity to established procedure and technique. Intellectual flexibility and methodological obedience must find a way to coexist. Often however they do not coexist and complement. Rather, one may dominate to the detriment of the other and of the whole process (see Campbell and Stanley, 1963, for a classic treatment of the problems of experimental validity). When undisciplined imagination and flexibility overly dominate, the results can be fascinating theories and sloppy, inconclusive, supportive experiments. When the structure of technique governs, the experiments are tightly controlled and largely uninteresting, extremely limited in focus and perhaps irrelevant to the larger experimental question.

This situation is further complicated by the fact that experimental procedures, which are the ways research ideas are transformed into concrete action, are not always freshly developed for each new experiment. Rather, procedures and methods are often borrowed, adapted, or transported from previous experimental uses to present needs. The particular evolution and historical context that led to the development of those procedures may in fact be unknown to contemporary users. In other words, some experimental procedures can take on a meaning and importance of their own, cease being just one way of asking questions with specific strengths and limitations, and become identified with the process of science itself. They can become seen as "The" way to ask and answer a question. When this occurs, the so-called "standardized" procedure may become a blinder rather than a source of light and clarification; a blinder because the strengths and limitations which are embedded in the history of their development may no longer be seen or appreciated. The techniques have become simply the way research is done. In fact, experimental questions may be shaped just so that they will fit into the structure of a particular method (see Underwood, 1957).

The use of animals and the ways in which animals are tested in research can certainly fall prey to these same types of blinders. If an individual researcher is trained and experienced in the use of animals and has ready access to an animal laboratory, research ideas considered are likely to be those that fit into that scheme of experience and "resource." I have seen this pattern operate in my own professional activities and now recognize it to have important ethical implications.

Personal Reflection

While I was a graduate student in psychology during the late 1960s, I developed a strong interest in the learning capacities of nonhuman primates and the developmental variables that affect them. This interest emerged from a more general fascination by the evolution of intelligence which had been stimulated in several courses that I had taken as an undergraduate. This interest had been further reinforced by the fact that there had been in psychology a recurring critique that too much research on topics like learning had been limited to the study of rodents (Beach, 1950; Hodos and Campbell, 1969). If psychology was to be a truly comprehensive behavioral science the selection of species studied would also have to be comprehensive, or so went the argument. There was substantial encouragement to study many more animal types, nonhuman primates in particular because of their evolutionary relationship to humans. In other words, the study of primates seemed to have a sort of built-in relevance that other animal species lacked.

Therefore, as I pursued graduate education I tried to position myself experience-wise so that I could continue this special interest. I had taken seriously the preparation required to enable me to continue to pursue this interest once I had graduated, when I would not have the staff of technical experts that was available to me on a daily basis as a student. On the academic side, I studied the rich variety of psychological theories that attempted to explain the learning process. I took the time to become practically experienced in the use of a variety of methods typically used to conduct research on learning with those animals. I had worked to learn the basic skills of electronics, programming, and apparatus construction. I did these things so that I would be able to recreate the housing, apparatus, and procedures necessary to do my own tests. Finally, although I did not have formal veterinary training, I became familiar with the diagnosis and treatment of the diseases common in monkeys when they lived in laboratories. Although at one level I recognized that the array of dysenteries, trauma injuries, and cage paralyses that I learned about were primarily confinement-induced stress conditions, I relieved and assured myself that living in the wild would certainly have been harder on these animals than the confines of the clean, stainless steel and temperature-controlled laboratory. At the end of my graduate education I felt confident that I knew how to manage a learning laboratory and a "captive colony" of monkeys.

My first job offer out of graduate school came substantially because I had these skills. It was clear to me that I would improve my chances of success in the university if I demonstrated to my new colleagues that I was able to quickly establish and run a general primate research facility and an active laboratory devoted to the study of learning. I gladly took on that challenge: after all, this is what I had been preparing to do.

Upon arrival at this position I wasted no time and quickly became engaged with the realities of setting up a laboratory. I negotiated for space and start-up funds and began interviewing applicants for laboratory-technician positions. I had also been permitted by my advisor to take a supply of retired equipment and a small group of monkeys to help me get started (Gluck, 1984). However, the central task that remained was the process of securing grant funds to support the research program at the level required by such a facility. As was the typical mode of operation for young professors, I looked to the sources of government funding to determine the topics currently of interest to the granting agencies and find out where my interests and expertise would fit. After a review of these possibilities, a colleague experienced in psychopharmacology and I decided to submit for a grant to study the effects of marihuana intoxication on the short-term memory of the monkey. In the application we pointed to the developing concern about marihuana use among adolescents and adults and to the unknown and perhaps dangerous consequences of its use on the activities of daily life. We argued for the value of the research and that the rhesus monkey was an ideal experimental model. We emphasized our experience in the study of learning and memory in monkeys, hoping to convince the eventual reviewers that we possessed the skill to determine what marihuana actually did to the short-term memory of rhesus monkeys and, by inference, human beings. Also important was the fact that I was already in the process of establishing a colony of monkeys and a laboratory that would be equipped with the necessary testing apparatus that could be pressed into the service of the proposed project immediately. We were careful to emphasize that rhesus monkeys were from the same biological order as humans, were a highly social species like humans, had recognized complex learning and memory abilities, and adapted well to laboratory housing arrangements. We made the case that using monkeys would allow generalization to the human condition in ways that the more familiar studies which utilized laboratory rats could not. It was time for this research to go beyond the "lowly" rat. I acknowledge now that the same enumeration of monkey virtues could also be used as an argument in favor of their moral standing and against their use, but that frankly was not a prominent thought I had at that time. My sense then was that monkeys were to be used. They were a means, a tool, a resource and not a primary object of ethical consideration. That is not to say that I didn't have feelings about monkeys as monkeys. Actually, during my studies I had come to admire the intellectual abilities of monkeys and apes and took great joy in regaling classes with data and laboratory anecdotes which emphasized these qualities.

With respect to my own experiences with primates, I especially enjoyed talking about H89, a 5-year-old stumptail macaque (*Macaca arctoides*) who had been born in the laboratory breeding colony while I was a graduate student and had been released to me when I graduated. Stumptails are members of a very diverse group of "old world" monkeys whose natural range encompasses most of Southeast Asia. They have a chunky body type (they are sometimes referred to as "bear" monkeys), redish brown coats, a small stubby two-inch tail, colorful brown, black and red splotchy faces, and a distinctive pungent odor. Unlike the close relative and more commonly used rhesus macaque (*Macaca mulatta*), stumptails tend to be less aggressive to humans, are more accepting of direct human handling, and are just generally easier to manage. Due to her proven cleverness and intelligence, I had come to regularly enlist H89 to pretest new experimental procedures and problem types. She could quickly indicate to us whether the problems we had selected were too difficult or too easy and what loopholes in procedure we had inadvertently created. In one of these experiments, H89 was tested in an apparatus which was a small test cage with vertical bars on the front wall through which she could extend her arms and hands. In front of that wall she was presented with a series of two three-dimensional wooden objects that differed from one another only slightly in terms of shape (see Harlow, 1949, for a discussion of the procedure). One of the objects of each pair was randomly selected as "correct." The objects were presented on a sliding tray which was moved to within her reach by an experimenter when the trial was to begin. H89 was trained to make her choice by pushing one of the objects to the side. If she chose the correct object, a small piece of food which had been hidden behind a visual barrier before the trial, would be revealed beneath it in a small shallow well. The food was then quickly eaten or stored in the monkey's large-capacity cheek pouches to be consumed at another time. The position of the correct object would be changed at random from one side of the tray to the other. Each separate problem would be presented for a fixed number of trials. As easily can be seen, on the first trial of a new problem with two new objects H89 could have no knowledge of which of the two objects had been designated as correct, and she was required to "guess."

The difficulty I encountered was that H89 virtually never made an error, even on the first trial of a new problem! Either she had developed a form of extrasensory perception, or I was inadvertently cuing her about the identity of the correct object in a manner similar to the well-known case of Clever Hans (see Candland, 1993, chapter 6, for a discussion of this case). I did everything I could do to eliminate the cues that I believed I was providing. I asked experienced testers to observe my technique and had some of those testers run the experiment themselves. The results were the same. H89 did not make errors. After weeks of sleuthing we eventually figured out the key to her success. In fact, it was one of the laboratory maintenance people that discovered the problem. H89 had learned a way to spy on me as I was hiding the small pieces of food under the "correct" objects behind what I thought was a secure visual barrier. I discovered that as I baited the objects she watched my reflection in a fragment of broken reflecting glass that had been left innocently on a shelf in the corner of the testing room. Using the reflection in this glass required that she contort her body and hang upside down so that she could glimpse the glass through a small crack in the side wall of the testing cage. She then had to reverse the appearance of the image to determine the proper location of the correct object.

I liked to tell this story to students because I felt that it illustrated the fact that monkeys were intentional and clever animals who seemed at times to solve problems the hard way because it brought them pleasure to challenge and befuddle their human experimenters. The point was that they were far from furry machines that behaved according to some computer-like program. The image of their intentionality, planning, and deceptions always gave me a bit of pause. After telling the H89 story or one similar, I recall that I often felt a little tightness in my throat that I didn't quite understand. I now appreciate that a fragment of an ethical question was forming. Did the existence of these characteristics require a different consideration of their treatment? Unfortunately, I was prepared neither intellectually nor emotionally either to recognize the question or to evaluate its features. Ethical questions were rarely discussed during my professional training and I was quietly ignorant of their importance where animals were concerned. Instead I would force myself to return to the functional view that portrayed monkeys and their abilities as a cabinet of laboratory supplies that were meant to be pulled off the shelf when the proper need arose. Nonetheless, when a colleague offered to purchase H89 for use as a subject in a brain lesion experiment, I rejected his offer without the slightest hesitation. I knew that this wasn't the right end for "Stumpy" but failed to appreciate the more general ethical implications nested in my decision.

Eventually the grant for the study of marihuana use was funded, the project was begun, and another subjective shift occurred. Yes, H89's cleverness amused and impressed me, but as time went on and the achievement of the proposed experimental goals became more important, I became less amused when the animals refused to "play" my experimental games according to my rules. Their resistance became seen as an impediment to a goal and lost the status of something important in and of itself.

From Animal to Object

The goal–oriented mind set transformed the reality of the animals from an entity with an individual and species psychology to a laboratory "preparation." When an animal subject becomes a method it begins to stop being an animal and starts to become an object. The meaning and function of its existence become tied to its use and may become one and the same. The animal, as an independent entity, may no longer be seen. It becomes incorporated, perhaps entirely, by the experimental goal. From this perspective it is difficult to experience the animal as a subject worthy of ethical concern. This is easily recognized as potentially dangerous moral territory, but I assert that it is also dangerous scientific territory. Let me illustrate the point.

Removing the Animal from the Animal

In one of the central experiments designed for marihuana study, monkeys were placed in a test cage and presented with a display that had three illuminating panels centered at eye level on one wall. The procedure involved illuminating the panels in various sequences, and then, after a delay, determining if the monkeys could repeat the sequence they had seen by touching the panels in the identical order. The time between the presentation of the sample sequence and the opportunity for the monkey to repeat it could be varied from several seconds to several minutes. In addition, the length and difficulty of the sequence to be repeated could also be varied. The task was very similar to "Simon," the popular child's electronic toy where sequences are presented that the child tries to repeat, getting an off-key buzzing sound when they miss. Beneath the three panels was a small cup into which bite-size pieces of food could be dropped by an automatic mechanism when an animal had correctly repeated the sequence. As the intervals and sequences got longer, it was assumed that short-term memory functions would be engaged. It was these functions in particular that we hypothesized would be affected by marihuana intoxication.

It was, to our standards, a very sophisticated apparatus that automated many of the functions normally conducted by human testers. Problems were selected and presented and correct and incorrect responses were controlled and recorded, all automatically by computer. We built several of these chambers so that we could test many more animals per day than would have been permitted by the traditional manual approaches. Human testers no longer had to directly observe and interact with the monkeys. Instead, all that was necessary was that the animals be removed from their home cage environments and be delivered to the test chambers. When the tests were complete, the testers needed only to return the animals and file the computer printouts.

In earlier work, it was unnecessary to deprive the monkeys of food in order to get them to work on related types of problem. Instead, as long as solutions were rewarded with highly preferred food items like raisins and sweet breakfast cereals, the monkeys persistently worked on the problems. At the end of the testing session the animals would receive their standard food ration (Purina Monkey Chow) when they were returned to their home cage. Therefore, before initiating testing each animal was evaluated in order to determine its favorite food items. Although this was the first time we were using an automated testing situation (the earlier work was accomplished using an apparatus and procedure described previously in the anecdote about H89), we assumed that food deprivation would also be unnecessary in the new testing situation: an apparatus is an apparatus.

It was our intention to look at the effect of different dosages of synthetic marihuana on the accuracy of the monkeys' performance on the sequencing. But before we could test the drug we needed to know which problems were solvable by the monkeys in the absence of the drug. There were difficulties from the start. This time, however, the problems were the opposite of the difficulties we had had with H89: the monkeys would not consistently attempt to solve the problems. They would on occasion repeat a short sequence after a brief delay but little more. Observations of the animals while they were inside the test chambers showed that they tended to sit quietly grooming themselves or to curl up and sleep until the end of the session. In response to these problems we changed a number of factors in hopes of improving the situation. For example, we increased the brightness of the displays, darkened the inside of the test chamber, lit up the food receptacle when food was discharged into it, and added more reward choices such as peanuts and grapes. These changes failed to substantially influence performance and only added to our disappointment.

During a lab meeting it was suggested that we begin to food deprive the monkeys prior to testing. Perhaps this change would result in increased interest on the part of the monkeys. The procedure recommended was a standard procedure for investigators who studied learning in rodents and was commonly applied to many different species of animals (Underwood, 1966, p. 344). It was agreed that we would try reducing the monkeys first to 90 percent of their base weight and then retest. Instead of raisins and grapes, the monkeys would now receive small pieces of the basic Monkey Chow diet when they responded correctly. Again, the procedures used for rats involved reducing the weight generally over a one to two week period. We followed a similar procedure. Once the new weights were attained, testing was renewed. The performance results were only slightly improved. While the monkeys seemed more active during testing, often pacing in tight circles inside the chambers, the overall performance on the problems was still quite limited. As our frustration increased so did our worry. We were beginning to be concerned that we were not going to be able to achieve the experimental goals we had set forth in the research plan for the grant.

The next step involved reducing the monkeys to 80 percent of their base weights, which took approximately another ten days. While the monkeys were far from being skinny, their appearances were obviously changed. "Leaner and meaner," we thought. I remember thinking that the monkeys reminded me of the changes I saw in several of my chubby boyhood friends after they had returned from Marine boot camp. An image that certainly deflected concern for the animals. The effect of this change had promise. When placed into the chambers the monkeys were now keenly interested in the food that was available. They were at times very active and ate the food with a noticeable urgency. They licked their fingers and hands cleanly after each handling of a food reward. Even so, their performances were erratic because at other times they appeared disinterested in both the task and the availability of food. The fact was that even if the monkeys failed to earn food rewards during the testing situation they would receive their full daily ration when they were returned to their home cage. It was suggested that perhaps one more 5 percent decrease in weight would do the trick. We rationalized that the monkeys were really quite overweight at the beginning of the deprivation schedule.

As the next round of weight reductions were being discussed, a sophomore undergraduate student working in the lab raised a quiet but recognizable objection. This young woman, who had been working directly with the monkeys, was concerned about how thin the monkeys had become during the previous weeks. She was additionally concerned because several of them were not acting "like themselves." I tried to reassure her that they were fine and she need not worry, but this "novice" was unmoved. In order to keep peace it was decided to schedule them all for physical exams before we proceeded with the next round of weight reductions.

The medical school veterinarian who answered the request had recently joined the staff of the animal resource facility after completing a fellowship in microbiology. I liked the fact that he had a research background in addition to clinical experience; it would be easier to communicate with him. During the exams he drew blood samples for analysis, checked teeth, and paid particular attention to the distribution of fat deposits. As he worked on the animals, I discussed with him our plan to further reduce the weights of the monkeys. He looked concerned. I explained to him that the previous reductions, along with the current plan, were all quite "standard" procedures in experiments like these. I showed him the test chambers and discussed the details of the research plan and its goals. I was trying to enlist his general support for the project by illustrating the importance of the research questions and demonstrating our research sophistication.

After examining the animals and listening to our presentation, he asked a series of very direct questions. There was a simplicity to the questions that belied the depth of their importance. Specifically, he asked me to consider what it meant that I had to go to such deep levels of food deprivation in order to get the monkeys to work on these particular problems. Might not one of the possibilities be that the test of short-term memory was just not very good? He went on to suggest that it seemed to him that I was asking the monkeys to do something that didn't make sense to them as monkeys, and this was why they were "refusing" to work on the problems. The procedure and task design might make sense in the abstract terms of the basic science and the information I wanted to gather, but it didn't appear to make sense to the monkeys. Was I asking questions in an experimental language that the monkeys didn't understand? Was I listening to the monkeys and taking to heart what was in effect their criticism of my procedure? By instituting the strict deprivation schedules was I creating an animal that was so desperate to eat that it was operating at a very primitive level of psychological functioning? Was that what I wanted to do? By depriving the animals to such a level, we were not only creating a level of distress and suffering that wasn't being considered or justified, I was also essentially taking the monkey out of the monkey, thereby undercutting one of the reasons for using monkeys in the first place. Finally, he asked me to wonder what it would be like to be forced to lose 20 percent of my body weight in a less than two-month period. These questions, all asked in a collegial and professional way, left me stunned and defensive. The thoughts circulating in my mind continued to hang on to the notion that everything that I was doing had a long history of experimental precedence. But that was the basic problem.

All of the issues had the same thread: I had not considered the work from the perspective of the animal. This had led both to poor treatment of the animals and to inferior science. By virtue of the reflexive emphasis on the application of "standard procedure" we had lost sight of the animal and ignored the messages they repeatedly presented. Instead of listening, we instituted procedures which overrode normal behavioral patterns. This move damaged the scientific validity of the experiment and robbed us of the knowledge of the animals' distress and our obligation to work it through in the light of our values and the potential benefits of the research.

Summary

As I reflect on this project of 20 years ago, I can see the following process operating. The context was that I was trained as a primate researcher, a "monkey man." That was an important part of my scientific, research, and even personal identity. I controlled a colony of monkeys and a test apparatus, and I possessed substantial procedural know-how ready to be utilized. In reality, the question we had addressed was less, how do I best study drug effects on memory? And more, how can I study the effects of drugs on memory with the intellectual and physical resources available to me? If I was going to study drugs and memory, it was going to be with monkeys and it was going to make use of the methods with which I was already familiar. In other words, my commitment to the methods preceded my commitment to the relevant question, reducing the animals to objects.

An animal is more than an object. An animal expresses and is an expression of a kind of life that characterizes its unique make-up. It has a place in the world and the world has a place in it. This place has come to exist by virtue of its own acts and the actions of evolution. Appreciation of this should give us pause when we consider "using" an animal and lead to a sense of ambivalence. Maintaining an ambivalent attitude toward the use of animals in research is essential (Gluck and Kubacki, 1991). Research, in general and with animals and humans in particular, is more than just an encounter with nature. It is also a moral encounter which requires an attentiveness not illuminated by typical science-training programs that stress fact and technique.

Some scientists hold the belief, covertly or overtly, that an emphasis on the ethical concerns regarding research subjects impedes scientific inquiry. On the contrary, while such consideration may eventually alter our patterns of animal use, recognition and respect for each animal and species and consideration of their moral standing can increase the sophistication of our research and extend the limits of its application by forcing us to go beyond what has become "standard procedure."

References

Beach, F. A. (1950). "The snark was a boojum." *American Psychologist*, 5: 115–24.

Campbell, D. T. and Stanley, J. C. (1963). *Experimental and Quasi-experimental Designs for Research* (Chicago: Rand McNally).

Candland, D. C. (1993). *Feral Children and Clever Animals* (New York: Oxford).

Gluck, J. P. (1984). "Harry Harlow: lessons on explanations, ideas, and mentorship." *American Journal of Primatology*, 7: 139–46.

Gluck, J. P. and Kubacki, S. (1991). "Animals in biomedical research: the undermining effect of the rhetoric of the besieged." *Ethics and Behavior*, 1(3): 157–73.

Harlow, H. F. (1949). "The formation of learning sets." *Psychological Review*, 56: 51–65.

Hodos, W. and Campbell, C. B. G. (1969). "Scala naturae." *Psychological Review*, 76: 337–50.

Underwood, B. J. (1957). *Psychological Research* (New York: Appleton, Century and Crofts).

——(1966). *Experimental Psychology* (New York: Appleton, Century and Crofts).

Part II

The Personal Life

Family and Friends

For most of us, relationships with family and friends are among the most important, most valuable elements of our lives. Although they can be the source of anguish and pain, they also infuse our lives with meaning and fill us with joy. When relationships with friends, family, and lovers are flourishing, it is difficult to envision life without them. At those times we aren't concerned about what we owe our friends, or what they owe us. We care for them, we seek to promote their interests; they do likewise. In this idyllic world of friendship and family, ordinary moral principles have no clear function. Our culture has few principles for morally evaluating close relationships, and then only in tightly prescribed circumstances. We condemn incest and child or spousal abuse. Otherwise, we do not normally seek to evaluate these relationships in moral terms.

English maintains that this is as it should be. If those who claim to be friends or spouses were to constantly harp about their rights, and remind significant others of their duties, we would begin to wonder if these people were, in fact, intimate. True, we may speak loosely of "filial obligations," but these are not obligations as we ordinarily conceive of them. They are not something we "owe" people, at least not in the sense that we owe a bank money. If I obtain a bank loan, the bank explicitly agrees to provide the money I desire, and I explicitly agree to repay the loan, with interest. In making the loan, the bank is not being generous, nor does it care for me. In repaying the loan, I am not being generous or exhibiting my love for the bank. By making the loan, bank officials were merely promoting their interests; by repaying the loan I am simply promoting mine.

However, we usually do things for our friends and family, not to promote our interests, but rather, to promote theirs. Friendship and love are like gifts, and, in giving a gift, we do not expect them to be reciprocated. That explains why, English claims, grown children do not owe anything to their parents. Healthy family relationships are not governed by moral rules, but by care. Of course if parents had a good relationship with their children, then we would anticipate that the children will care for and help their ailing parents. However, that is a prediction of how we think the children will act; it in no way implies that the children are obligated to help.

In his discussion of generosity (VIRTUES), Wallace explores the distinction between what we owe others and what we may, out of generosity, give them. This distinction plays a pivotal role in determining the proper response to WORLD HUNGER. Arthur claims that although it would be nice of us to assist the starving, we are not strongly obligated to help them. Singer, on the other hand, claims we owe more to the starving than mere generosity. We are obligated to help them: we *should* help them, even if we don't want to. If we do not help them, we have done something wrong – we are not merely tight-fisted. Many people will think Singer's position is too exacting; they will suggest a different way to distinguish duty from generosity. However, it is clear that the distinction between what we are morally required to do, no matter what our desires, and what it would be nice or decent or generous for us to do, is a central theoretical distinction with substantial practical import.

Although personal relationships are not normally judged by criteria of morality, occasionally relationships are so exploitative that we are compelled to so judge them. According to Bartky, relationships between men and women are often exploitative, and, in particular, emotionally exploitative. Although most men want and expect emotional sustenance and care from the women around them (their intimates, their kin, and their colleagues), many men fail to give such support in return. Such exploitation is evil, Bartky argues, because it disempowers women, it deprives women of control over their lives. The disempowerment of women is discussed in more detail by K. Warren (ENVIRONMENT).

Some people (probably mostly men) who read Bartky's essay will think she is off the mark, while others (mostly women) will think she has clearly articulated an obvious truth. For present purposes we needn't decide if she is correct. What her essay does highlight, however, is the central role that gender plays in our society, and, therefore, the prominent role it will play in the discussion of many moral issues. In our society, gender is essential to the way we understand ourselves and others. When a child is born, the first question people invariably ask is: "Is it a boy or a girl?" When we mention others (friends, teachers, politicians, businesspeople, etc.), frequently we mention their gender. Why? When a newscaster identifies "the female Senator from California," he is not informing his listeners about the Senator's genitalia, or identifying her as the possible object of sexual interest, but rather suggesting something about her interests, abilities, personality, and political stance.

The issue is not whether gender is central to how we describe and understand ourselves and others. That is a given. The question is, are there important biological differences between women and men, and, if so, should these influence public policy or shape how we personally treat or relate to others? Questions about the nature, scope, and moral relevance of differences in gender are addressed by many essays throughout this book. Some essays directly discuss these questions, for example, the essays in the sections on SEXUAL AND RACIAL DISCRIMINATION and AFFIRMATIVE ACTION.

In other sections the authors address the questions more indirectly, as in several essays on FREE SPEECH. Does (some) pornography harm women? If so, should we prohibit it? Here we see a dramatic clash between an action that seemingly harms women, and the "right to free speech." We see a similar clash in the debate over speech codes. Several universities have adopted codes that prohibit "hate speech," especially speech that demeans women and minorities. Should we have such codes? How do we balance competing interests or values: here, an interest in free speech and an interest in not being denigrated? The clash between competing values will play a prominent role in the discussion of many of these moral issues.

Williams, in fact, claims that concern for our personal relationships often clashes with the demands of morality. When they do conflict, our personal commitments usually take precedence. Morality has its place, Williams claims, albeit a limited place. Rachels disagrees. He argues that morality takes precedence over purely personal commitments. Morality does not require that we abandon our personal relationships. A proper understanding of morality permits close friendships and familial relationships. However, morality does not permit us to favor our friends and family in trivial ways – at least not if doing so means others are substantially worse off.

This argument by Rachels resembles Singer's discussion of our obligation to feed the starving (WORLD HUNGER). Both philosophers deny, among other things, that there is a fundamental moral distinction between acts and omissions. A failure to care for needy children when we can easily do so is morally equivalent to directly harming those children. Conversely, Williams's position resembles Arthur's view on WORLD HUNGER. Arthur claims we can legitimately take a special interest in ourselves and in those we love.

This disagreement between Williams and Rachels (and Arthur and Singer) has implications for virtually every moral issue. Determining whether an action is purely personal, or whether we should evaluate it by criteria of morality, pervades the discussions of ABORTION, SEXUALITY, DRUGS, FREE SPEECH, as well as WORLD HUNGER.

Further Reading

Bartky, S. 1990: *Femininity and Domination: Studies in the Phenomenology of Oppression*. New York: Routledge.

Graham, G. and LaFollette, H. (eds) 1989: *Person to Person*. Philadelphia: Temple University Press.

LaFollette, H. 1996: *Personal Relationships: Love, Identity, and Morality*. Oxford: Blackwell.

Noddings, N. 1984: *Caring: A Feminine Approach to Ethics and Moral Education*. Berkeley: University of California Press.

O'Neill, O. and Ruddick, W. 1979: *Having Children: Philosophical and Legal Reflections on Parenthood*. New York: Oxford University Press.

Williams, B. 1985: *Ethics and the Limits of Philosophy*. London: Williams Collins & Sons.

14

What do Grown Children Owe their Parents?

Jane English

What do grown children owe their parents? I will contend that the answer is "nothing." Although I agree that there are many things that children *ought* to do for their parents, I will argue that it is inappropriate and misleading to describe them as things "owed." I will maintain that parents' voluntary sacrifices, rather than creating "debts" to be "repaid," tend to create love or "friendship." The duties of grown children are those of friends and result from love between them and their parents, rather than being things owed in repayment for the parents' earlier sacrifices. Thus, I will oppose those philosophers who use the word "owe" whenever a duty or obligation exists. Although the "debt" metaphor is appropriate in some moral circumstances, my argument is that a love relationship is not such a case.

Misunderstandings about the proper relationship between parents and their grown children have resulted from reliance on the "owing" terminology. For instance, we hear parents complain, "You owe it to us to write home (keep up your piano playing, not adopt a hippie lifestyle), because of all we sacrificed for you (paying for piano lessons, sending you to college)." The child is sometimes even heard to reply, "I didn't ask to be born (to be given piano lessons, to be sent to college)." This inappropriate idiom of ordinary language tends to obscure, or even to undermine, the love that is the correct ground of filial obligation.

1. Favors Create Debts

There are some cases, other than literal debts, in which talk of "owing," though metaphorical, is apt. New to the neighborhood, Max barely knows his neighbor, Nina, but he asks her if she will take in his mail while he is gone for a month's vacation. She agrees. If, subsequently, Nina asks Max to do the same for her, it seems that Max has a moral obligation to agree (greater than the one he would have had if Nina had not done the same for him), unless for some reason it would be a burden far out of proportion to the one Nina bore for him. I will call this a *favor*: when A, at B's request, bears some burden for B, then B incurs an obligation to reciprocate. Here the metaphor of Max's "owing" Nina is appropriate. It is not literally a debt, of course, nor can Nina pass this IOU on to heirs, demand payment in the form of Max's taking out her garbage, or sue Max. Nonetheless, since Max ought to perform one act of similar nature and amount of sacrifice in return, the term is suggestive. Once he reciprocates, the debt is "discharged" – that is, their obligations revert to the condition they were in before Max's initial request.

Contrast a situation in which Max simply goes on vacation and, to his surprise, finds upon his return that his neighbor has mowed his grass twice weekly in his absence. This is a voluntary sacrifice rather than a favor, and Max has no duty to reciprocate. It would be nice for him to volunteer to do so, but this would be supererogatory on his part. Rather than a favor, Nina's action is a friendly gesture. As a result, she might expect Max to chat over the back fence, help her catch her straying dog, or something similar – she might expect the development of a friendship. But Max would be chatting (or whatever) out of friendship, rather than in repayment for mown grass. If he did not return her gesture, she might feel rebuffed or miffed, but not unjustly treated or indignant, since Max has not failed to perform a duty. Talk of "owing" would be out of place in this case.

It is sometimes difficult to distinguish between favors and non-favors, because friends tend to do favors for each other, and those who exchange favors tend to become friends. But one test is to ask how Max is motivated. Is it "to be nice to Nina" or "because she did x for me"? Favors are frequently performed by total strangers without any friendship developing. Nevertheless, a temporary obligation is created, even if the chance for repayment never arises. For instance, suppose that Oscar and Matilda, total strangers, are waiting in a long checkout line at the supermarket. Oscar, having forgotten the oregano, asks Matilda to watch his cart for a second. She does. If Matilda now asks Oscar to return the favor while she picks up some tomato sauce, he is obligated to agree. Even if she had not watched his cart, it would be inconsiderate of him to refuse, claiming he was too busy reading the magazines. He may have had a duty to help others, but he would not "owe" it to her. But if she has done the same for him, he incurs an additional obligation to help, and talk of "owing" is apt. It suggests an agreement to perform equal, reciprocal, canceling sacrifices.

2.   The Duties of Friendship

The terms "owe" and "repay" are helpful in the case of favors, because the sameness of the amount of sacrifice on the two sides is important; the monetary metaphor suggests equal quantities of sacrifice. But friendship ought to be characterized by *mutuality* rather than reciprocity: friends offer what they can give and accept what they need, without regard for the total amounts of benefits exchanged. And friends are motivated by love rather than by the prospect of repayment. Hence, talk of "owing" is singularly out of place in friendship.

For example, suppose Alfred takes Beatrice out for an expensive dinner and a movie. Beatrice incurs no obligation to "repay" him with a goodnight kiss or a return engagement. If Alfred complains that she "owes" him something, he is operating under the assumption that she should repay a favor, but on the contrary his was a generous gesture done in the hopes of developing a friendship. We hope that he would not want her repayment in the form of sex or attention if this was done to discharge a debt rather than from friendship. Since, if Alfred is prone to reasoning in this way, Beatrice may well decline the invitation or request to pay for her own dinner, his attitude of expecting a "return" on his "invest-ment" could hinder the development of a friendship. Beatrice should return the gesture only if she is motivated by friendship.

Another common misuse of the "owing" idiom occurs when the Smiths have dined at the Joneses' four times, but the Joneses at the Smiths' only once. People often say, "We owe them three dinners." This line of thinking may be appropriate between business acquaintances, but not between friends. After all, the Joneses invited the Smiths not in order to feed them or to be fed in turn, but because of the friendly contact presumably enjoyed by all on such occasions. If the Smiths do not feel friendship toward the Joneses, they can decline future invitations and not invite the Joneses; they owe them nothing. Of course, between friends of equal resources and needs, roughly equal sacrifices (though not necessarily roughly equal dinners) will typically occur. If the sacrifices are highly out of proportion to the resources, the relationship is closer to servility than to friendship.[1]

Another difference between favors and friendship is that after a friendship ends, the duties of friendship end. The party that has sacrificed less owes the other nothing. For instance, suppose Elmer donated a pint of blood that his wife Doris needed during an operation. Years after their divorce, Elmer is in an accident and needs one pint of blood. His new wife, Cora, is also of the same blood type. It seems not only that Doris does not "owe" Elmer blood, but that she should actually refrain from coming forward if Cora has volunteered to donate. To insist on donating not only interferes with the newlyweds' friendship, but it belittles Doris and Elmer's former relationship by suggesting that Elmer gave blood in hopes of favors returned instead of simply out of love for Doris. It is one of the heart-rending features of divorce that it attends to quantity in a relationship previously characterized by mutuality. If Cora could not donate, Doris's obligation is the same as that for any former spouse in need of blood; it is not increased by the fact that Elmer similarly aided her. It *is* affected by the degree to which they are still friends, which in turn may (or may not) have been influenced by Elmer's donation.

In short, unlike the debts created by favors, the duties of friendship do not require equal quantities of sacrifice. Performing equal sacrifices does not cancel the duties of friendship, as it does the debts of favors. Unrequested sacrifices do not themselves create debts, but friends have duties regardless of whether they requested or initiated the friendship. Those who perform favors may be motivated by mutual gain, whereas friends should be motivated by affection. These characteristics of the friendship relation are distorted by talk of "owing."

3. Parents and Children

The relationship between children and their parents should be one of friendship characterized by mutuality rather than one of reciprocal favors. The quantity of parental sacrifice is not relevant in determining what duties the grown child has. The medical assistance grown children ought to offer their ill mothers in old age depends upon the mothers' need, not upon whether they endured a difficult pregnancy, for example. Nor do one's duties to one's parents cease once an equal quantity of sacrifice has been performed, as the phrase "discharging a debt" may lead us to think.

Rather, what children ought to do for their parents (and parents for children) depends upon (1) their respective needs, abilities, and resources and (2) the extent to which there is an ongoing friendship between them. Thus, regardless of the quantity of childhood sacrifices, an able, wealthy child has an obligation to help his needy parents more than does a needy child. To illustrate, suppose sisters Cecile and Dana are equally loved by their parents, even though Cecile was an easy child to care for, seldom ill, while Dana was often sick and caused some trouble as a juvenile delinquent. As adults, Dana is a struggling artist living far away, while Cecile is a wealthy lawyer living nearby. When the parents need visits and financial aid, Cecile has an obligation to bear a higher proportion of these burdens than her sister. This results from her abilities, rather than from the quantities of sacrifice made by the parents earlier.

Sacrifices have an important causal role in creating an ongoing friendship, which may lead us to assume incorrectly that it is the sacrifices that are the source of obligation. That the source is the friendship instead can be seen by examining cases in which the sacrifices occurred but the friendship, for some reason, did not develop or persist. For example, if a woman gives up her newborn child for adoption, and if no feelings of love ever develop on either side, it seems that the grown child does not have an obligation to "repay" her for her sacrifices in pregnancy. For that matter, if the adopted child has an unimpaired love relationship with the adoptive parents, he or she has the same obligations to help them as a natural child would have.

The filial obligations of grown children are a result of friendship, rather than owed for services rendered. Suppose that Vance married Lola despite his parents' strong wish that he marry within their religion, and that as a result, the parents refuse to speak to him again. As the years pass, the parents are unaware of Vance's problems, his accomplishments, the birth of his children. The love that once existed between them, let us suppose, has been completely destroyed by this event and thirty years of desuetude. At this point, it seems, Vance is under no obligation to pay his parents' medical bills in their old age, beyond his general duty to help those in need. An additional, filial obligation would only arise from whatever love he may still feel for them. It would be irrelevant for his parents to argue, "But look how much we sacrificed for you when you were young," for that sacrifice was not a favor but occurred as part of a friendship which existed at the time but is now, we have supposed, defunct. A more appropriate message would be, "We still love you, and we would like to renew our friendship."

I hope this helps to set the question of what children ought to do for their parents in a new light. The parental argument, "You ought to do x because we did y for you," should be replaced by, "We love you and you will be happier if you do x," or "We believe you love us, and anyone who loved us would do x." If the parents' sacrifice had been a favor, the child's reply, "I never asked you to do y for me," would have been relevant; to the revised parental remarks, this reply is clearly irrelevant. The child can either do x or dispute one of the parents' claims: by showing that a love relationship does not exist, or that love for someone does not motivate doing x, or that he or she will not be happier doing x.

Seen in this light, parental requests for children to write home, visit, and offer them a reasonable amount of emotional and financial support in life's crises are well founded, so long as a friendship still exists. Love for others does call for caring about and caring for them. Some other parental requests, such as for more sweeping changes in the child's lifestyle or life goals, can be seen to be insupportable, once we shift the justification from debts owed to love. The terminology of favors suggests the reasoning, "Since we paid for your college education, you owe it to us to make a career of engineering, rather than becoming a rock musician." This tends to alienate affection even further, since the tuition payments are depicted as investments for a return rather than done from love, as though the child's life goals could be "bought." Basing the argument on love leads to different reasoning patterns. The suppressed premise, "If A loves B, then A follows B's wishes as to A's lifelong career" is simply false. Love does not even dictate that the child adopt the parents' values as to the desirability of alternative life goals. So the parents' strongest available argument here is, "We love you, we are deeply concerned about your happiness, and in the long run you will be happier as an engineer." This makes it clear that an empirical claim is really the subject of the debate.

The function of these examples is to draw out our considered judgments as to the proper relation between parents and their grown children, and to show how poorly they fit the model of favors. What is relevant is the ongoing friendship that exists between parents and children. Although that relationship developed partly as a result of parental sacrifices for the child, the duties that grown children have to their parents result from the friendship rather than from the sacrifices. The idiom of owing favors to one's parents can actually be destructive if it undermines the role of mutuality and leads us to think in terms of quantitative reciprocal favors.

Note

1 *Cf.* Thomas E. Hill, Jr, "Servility and Self-respect," *Monist* 57 (1973). Thus, during childhood, most of the sacrifices will come from the parents, since they have most of the resources and the child has most of the needs. When children are grown, the situation is usually reversed.

15

Emotional Exploitation

Sandra Lee Bartky

(Male) culture was (and is) parasitical, feeding on the emotional strength of women without reciprocity.[1]

I

What does a man want? What, in the conflict-ridden arena of current heterosexual relations, does a man want from a woman? Men want, among other things, emotional support, something they are typically unwilling to provide in return. In short, many men emotionally exploit women with whom they have established some intimacy. To understand the nature of this exploitation, we must first understand what it is to give someone "emotional support."

Emotional support is best understood using metaphors of sustenance, of keeping the Other from falling. To support someone emotionally is to keep up his spirits, to keep him from sinking under the weight of burdens that are his to bear. To sink would be to fail to cope at all, to be paralyzed or in despair; in less extreme cases, to cope poorly. To give such support then is to tend to a person's state of mind so that he is less likely to sink; it is to comfort him, typically by bandaging his emotional wounds and by offering him sustenance, typically by feeding his self-esteem. The aim of this support and sustenance is to convince him of the value of his chosen projects, and therefore, of his own intrinsic value.

It is the quality of a caregiver's attention that can bolster the Other's confidence. This caregiver may directly praise the Other's character and accomplishments. Or she may send him a variety of verbal signals ("conversational cheerleading") that encourage him to continue speaking, hence reassuring him of the importance of what he is saying. Or she may bolster his confidence non-verbally, e.g., by leaning toward him, maintaining eye contact, cocking her head to the side, or by smiling as he speaks.

The caregiver may emotionally heal the Other in a myriad of verbal ways. She may express indignation at what the boss has said about him, or she may construct elaborate rationales that aim, by reconceptualizing the boss's comments, to make the Other's failures and disappointments less terrible. She may also heal him non-verbally, by compassionately squeezing his hand, hugging him, sympathetically furrowing her brow, or sighing distressfully.

The work of emotional repair – the bandaging of wounds, the bolstering of confidence, and the feeding of egos – overlaps in many ways. A sustained sympathetic listening conveys to the speaker the importance of what he is saying, hence the suggestion that he himself is important. Moreover, a willingness to listen is comforting. Hurts – if hurts there are – sting less when we can share them. To enter feelingly and without condescension into another's distress affirms that person's worth, though an affirmation of someone's worth need not require any particular effort at emotional restoration. Spouses most often support one another emotionally through simple affection. Although a stranger on a train in whom I decide to confide may provide some emotional support, the forms of emotional caregiving I have described are among the most common ways we show affection, especially when the caregiving is underscored by loving endearments.

In our society, most women are expected to provide emotional service to men, and many chafe at the failure of men to provide such service in return. Lillian Rubin's sensitive study of working-class marriage demonstrates that a concern for relationship and intimacy, once thought to be the province of the middle class, is equally important to other socio-economic groups.[2] The wives in Rubin's study complain that their men are emotionally unavailable in tones reminiscent of those sounded by the professional therapists who write popular-psychology relationship manuals for a middle-class audience. Such complaints are strikingly absent from what was for years the landmark study of working-class couples, Mirra Komarovsky's *Blue Collar Marriage* (1962).[3] Since the working class is increasingly mobile, many families have lost the network of kin that once supported them. Thus, working-class couples are thrown increasingly onto their own emotional resources. Such families are also under the powerful cultural sway of middle-class values and styles of life. Together these factors bring new demands and, with them, new discontents.

Black women have frequently been singled out for failing to provide their men with "female tenderness." Some black men have laid part of their troubles at the door of the black woman: she is too critical, too aggressive, too hard, a castrator who not only fails to "stand behind her man," but actively undermines him.[4] These charges, fueled by the relative economic independence of the black woman, became particularly virulent during the emergence, in the late sixties, of the Black Power movement and of various black nationalist and separatist movements. This led to an extended and acrimonious discussion among politically conscious black women and men.[5] Though far poorer than white women, as a group black women tend to be less economically dependent on men and are more likely to be heads of their own households. Black women often face unusual economic hardships, yet they are often self-assertive and refuse to submit to domestic tyranny. This should be seen as female strength. However, the frequent complaints about black females' assertive-ness suggest that women of whatever color are expected to provide unidirectional emotional support for their men.

Someone may emotionally care for another because she loves him. She may also care for her Other as part of her job. Both forms of emotional caregiving include the feeding of egos and the nursing of wounds. However, commercial caregiving is significantly different from caring between intimates. In a detailed study of flight attendants, Arlie Hochschild provides an illuminating account of the "commercialization of human feeling."[6] These mostly female workers are paid to show commercial affection for passengers: to create an atmosphere of warmth, cheerfulness, and friendly attention. The demand that they be relentlessly cheerful was always difficult; the speed-up associated with airline deregulation has made the difficult, impossible. The attendant's emotional care must be expended on many more passengers per flight; moreover, many passengers are stressed from waiting in longer lines, lost baggage, and late flights.[7]

Attendants must manage their own feelings as well as those of their passengers. They must work to "induce or suppress feeling in order to sustain the outward countenance that produces the proper state of mind in others."[8] Although this is surely work, "to show that the enjoyment takes effort is to do the job poorly."[9] A commercial logic penetrates "deeper and deeper into what we used to think of as a private, psychological, sacred part of a person's self and soul."[10] What often results is a flight attendant's feeling of falseness or emptiness, an estrangement from her own feeling self, even a confusion about what she is feeling or whether she is feeling anything at all. The flight attendant's sense of inauthenticity, worsened by the physical and psychological effects of speed-up generally, can contribute to situational depression, insomnia, alcoholism, and drug-abuse.[11] In short, attendants are disempowered by having to provide constant emotional caregiving.

However, the emotional sustenance women give men in relationships of intimacy resembles commercial caregiving only superficially. True, the flight attendant, like the good wife, must feed egos and heal wounds; she is supposed to make every passenger feel wanted and important and to deal with whatever distress is occasioned by the stresses of travel. However, one relationship is casual and brief; the other, more enduring and profound. Intimate relationships require more complex sensitivities and engage more aspects of the self. A woman intimately related to a man feels deep affection for him: she sincerely provides care and support; she loses herself in her work. Of course caregiving in intimate relationships can sometimes come to *feel* just as mechanical as it does for the flight attendant in speed-up, a performance from which the woman herself feels increasingly remote. However, intimate relationships in which this happens are surely in trouble; indeed, any relationship in which this occurs consistently hardly qualifies as an intimate relationship at all.

We can well understand how the routine emotional work of flight attendants may become disempowering, leading as it often does to self-estrangement, an inability to identify one's own emotional states, even to drug-abuse or alcoholism. But how can the provision of affectionate regard and the sympathetic tending of psychic wounds – activities that require the exercise of such virtues as loving kindness and compassion – be disempowering too? Surely, the opportunity to attend to the Other in these ways must be morally empowering for it gives us the chance not merely to be good by doing good, but to become morally better through the cultivation and exercise of important moral qualities. And are we not privileged, too, in being allowed entrée into the deepest psychological recesses of another, in being released, if only temporarily, from the burden of isolation and loneliness that each of us must bear? The claim that women in intimacy are disempowered in their provision of emotional support to men may begin to seem not merely mistaken, but perverse. But let us look more closely.

II

Many feminist theorists have treated women's unequal provision of emotional caregiving to men as a zero-sum game: they assume men are empowered and women disempowered in roughly equal proportion. Metaphors of filling and emptying are often used to describe this state of affairs: women fill men with our energies; this filling strengthens men and depletes ourselves. Moreover, the psychic benefits men gain from women's caregiving make them fitter to rule; in dispensing these benefits, women only make themselves fitter to obey.

There is no quarreling with the claim that men as a group receive direct psychological benefits from women's emotional sustenance: this seems obvious. But in my opinion, the standard view errs on two counts. First, I suspect that people overestimate the efficacy of female nurturance. Secondly, I believe that the standard view underestimates the subjectively disempowering effects of unreciprocated caregiving on women. I will examine this latter claim in Sections III and IV below. In the balance of this section, I explore whether women's emotional caregiving really sustains men.

Hegel says that no man can be a hero to his valet. Surely, though, many men are heroes to their wives. However, although it is good to have one's importance affirmed, even by an underling, affirmation by one's social inferior is of limited value. Women have too little prestige ourselves to be a source of much prestige for men. Most men determine their status and seek personal affirmation from other men. When such affirmation is not forthcoming, the tender concern of women may offer some consolation, but how much?

After all, many men survive for long periods without the emotional support of women, for example, if in prison or in the army. In an absorbing study of the current social and psychological dimensions of friendship, Lillian Rubin claims that even though men's relationships with other men do not typically include features of deep intimacy – verbal disclosure of feeling and significant emotional display – they nonetheless bond with each other in ways that emotionally support them. Bonding, she says,

> . . . can live quite robustly without intimacy – an emotional connection that ties two people together in important and powerful ways. At the most general level, the shared experience of maleness – of knowing its differences from femaleness, of affirming those differences through an intuitive understanding of each other that needs no words – undoubtedly creates a bond between men. It's often a primitive bond, a sense of brotherhood that may be dimly understood, one that lives side by side with the more easily observable competitive strain that exists in their relations as well.[12]

Rubin's research suggests that competition among men is *not* always a source of male emotional distress that requires female caregiving. In fact, it may be a powerful impetus to male bonding and a profound source of male self-esteem. Consider the comments of one of her respondents: "It's not that I don't feel comfortable with women, but I enjoy men in a special way. I enjoy competing with men. I don't like to compete with women: there's no fun in it."[13] When Rubin asks him what precisely he enjoys about competition, he replies:

> (Laughing) Only a woman would ask that. (Then more seriously) It's hard to put into words. I can strut my stuff, let myself go all the way really get off on that; its exciting. It doesn't make much difference whether it's some sport or getting an account, I'm playing to win. I can show off just how good I am.[14]

This further suggests that some men must suffer from emotional anemia: they *refuse* even to accept sustenance from their women. Tough guys, confined since childhood to a narrow range of acceptable masculine emotion, cannot easily become emotionally expressive – even with a woman. But perhaps this way of formulating the situation is misleading. It suggests a dualism: the appearance of invulnerability without; the reality of a rich, suffering and needy emotional life within. It is likelier that a taboo on the display of emotion prevents men from even feeling these emotions. Men apparently have psychological mechanisms that tend, quite independently of female emotional nurturance, to control potentially destabilizing emotions such as resentment, grief, and frustration. Even if we did assume that such emotions have not been anaesthetized, but are only simmering below the surface, there is no evidence that emotionally inexpressive men are more rebellious than their less repressed counterparts.

Some cite the better mental and physical health of married men as evidence that men receive very significant benefits from women's emotional caregiving. If we assume that some measure of emotional sustenance is a factor in marriage, this may explain why married men live longer than single men and score lower on standard indices of psychopathology.[15] But even here, some scepticism is in order. The greater longevity of married men, for example, may be due as much to better physical care (regular meals, better nutrition, more urging from the wife to seek medical help) as to wives' provision of emotional care. Moreover, it isn't clear whether the superior mental health of married men is due to female emotional caretaking or whether marriage as an institution selects men who are sufficiently stable to receive these benefits in the first place. Even in relatively permanent relationships, there are tragic cases in which every resource of a woman's loving attention is ineffective against what are arguably the effects of the stressful circumstances of her man's life – alcoholism, drug addiction, depression, or suicide.

All these considerations, I think, tell somewhat against the claim that men are emotionally rescued by female caregiving from the pressures of competition. While there is no doubt that men receive benefits from women's provision of emotional sustenance and while it is conceivable that this sustenance may to some extent keep the lid on male discontent, these effects are not likely to be extensive or significant. It is unlikely that women's disempowerment is proportional either to the emotional benefits that men receive, or to whatever stabilization men's psychological repair may lend to an oppressive political and economic system. I suggest instead that we look for a disempowerment that is more subtle and oblique, one rooted in the subjective and deeply interiorized effects *upon women ourselves*.

III

Love, affection, and the affectionate dispensing of emotional sustenance may seem to be purely private transactions that have nothing to do with the macrosocial domain of status. But this is false. The sociologist Theodore Kemper maintains that "a love relationship is one in which at least one actor gives (or is prepared to give) extremely high status to another actor."[16] "Status accord" he defines as "the voluntary compliance with the needs, wishes or interests of the other."[17] But which needs, wishes, or interests? Another sociologist of love, R. C. Centers, proposes a list of needs whose satisfaction generates an "affectionate response": sexual satisfaction; affectionate intimacy; maintenance and enhancement of sexual identity and role; interpersonal security and self-esteem.[18] Women's provision of emotional sustenance to men through the feeding of egos and the tending of wounds, satisfies all or most of these needs. To build a man's self-esteem is very frequently just to maintain and enhance his sexual identity and role. The provision of sexual satisfaction and the loving endearments of "affectionate intimacy" may have the same effect.

Women's emotional caregiving thus confers status on men. The verbal and non-verbal behavior of women encourages their intimates to continue their recitals. The women's behaviors are identical to forms of deference displayed in hierarchies of status.[19] Here status is not mutual. The gendered division of emotional labor does not require of men what it requires of women. Thus, women's caregiving is, in effect, a collective genuflection by women to men, an affirmation of male importance that is unreciprocated. The consistent giving of what we don't get in return is a performative acknowledgment of male supremacy, and thus a contribution to our own social demotion. Yet many women rarely see or appreciate this. A woman sincerely cares about her man's emotional needs. This reinforces in her own mind the importance of his little dramas of daily life. Moreover, he thinks he is entitled to her attention, while she is not entitled to his. When he fails to attend to her needs, he confirms for both of them her inferior position in the hierarchy of gender.

Given the companionate ideal that now holds sway, women yearn for recognition from the men with whom they are intimate. When men withhold such recognition, it is painful, especially since in the larger society men have the power to give or to withhold social recognition.[20] Wishing that he would notice; waiting for him to ask: how familiar this is to women, how like waiting for a sovereign to notice a subject, or a rich man, a beggar. Indeed, we sometimes find ourselves begging for his attention – and few things are as disempowering as having to beg.

Women have responded in many ways to men's refusal of recognition. A woman may merge with her man psychologically to such an extent that she just claims as her own his joys and sorrows. She no longer needs to resent his indifference to her doings, since his doings have *become* her doings. After eight years of seeing it, we recall the picture easily: Ronald Reagan at the podium; Nancy, a bit behind her husband, fixing upon him a trance-like gaze of total admiration and utter absorption. Here is the perfect visual icon of the attempt to merge one's consciousness with the consciousness of the Other.

Psychologists such as Nancy Chodorow and Dorothy Dinnerstein claim that women's style of feeling and our more "permeable ego boundaries" arise because girls, unlike boys, are not currently expected to sever their original identification with the maternal caretaker.[21] Hence, the phenomenon that I am describing may be "overdetermined" by psychological factors. Nevertheless, it is worth wondering to what extent the merging of the consciousness of the woman with the target of her emotional care may be a strategy adopted in adult life to avoid the anger and the disruption of relationship that might otherwise follow the refusal of recognition.

Women sometimes demand that men perform ritualized gestures of concern – the re-membering of a birthday or anniversary, a Valentine's day card. These are signs of a caring that is largely absent from everyday life. The ferocity with which some women insist on these ritual observances is a measure, I believe, of our sense of deprivation. If the man fails to give her some object – a present, a valentine – that cultural rituals have defined as visible and material symbols of esteem, then a lack felt privately may be turned into a public affront. Women's preoccupation with such things, without an understanding of what this preoccupation means, has gained us a reputation for capriciousness and superficiality, a reputation that in itself, is disempowering. "Why can't a woman be more like a man?" sings the exasperated Professor Henry Higgins. "If I forgot your silly birthday, would you fuss? / ... Why can't a woman be like us?"[22]

Neither of these strategies – minimalism or merger – really works. The woman who accepts these ritualized and perfunctory gestures in exchange for the emotional caregiving she provides regularly, has made a bad bargain. On the other hand, if she psychologically overidentifies with her man, she engages in a self-deceived attempt to deny her pain and to avoid the consequences of her anger. To attempt such merger is to practice magic or to have a try at self-hypnosis. A woman who is economically dependent on a man may have every reason to identify with his interests: economic dependence feeds the tendency to overidentify. However, given the frequency of divorce and the regular conflicts that arise within ongoing relationships, prudence requires that a woman regard the coincidence of her interests with those of her partner as if they were merely temporary.

IV

Unreciprocated caregiving may easily become both epistemically and ethically disempowering. While caretaking, a woman may be tempted to adopt morally questionable attitudes and standards of behavior. These kinds of disempowerment are hardly inevitable, but they are certainly risks, occupational hazards that attend the dispensing of "female tenderness."

First, there is the epistemic risk, i.e., the risk that the woman will accept uncritically "the world according to him" and that she will have corresponding difficulty constructing the world according to herself. How does this happen? To support and succor a person is, typically, to enter feelingly into that person's world; it is to see things from his point of view, to enter imaginatively into what he takes to be real and true.[23] Nel Noddings expresses it well: to adopt a caring attitude toward another is to become "engrossed" in that other: it is "a displacement of interest from my own reality to the reality of the other [whereby] . . . I set aside my temptation to analyze and to plan. I do not project; I receive the other into myself, and I see and feel with the other."[24] Hence caring "involves stepping out of one's own personal frame of reference into the other's."[25] Here is merger of another sort, one not motivated by a failure of recognition but by the very character of emotional caregiving itself.

A woman need not always merge epistemically with the man she is sustaining. Occasionally she will reject his version of things, either to his face or to herself. However, if a caregiver *consistently* questions the values and beliefs of the one to whom she is supposed to be offering sustenance, her caregiving will suffer. She is caught in the following paradox: if she keeps her doubts to herself, she may become distant and unauthentic as do those who must provide care in commercial settings. If she articulates her doubts, it is as likely as not she will be seen as rejecting him or as being disloyal. Either way, her relationship will suffer. Professional therapists are required to develop a "hermeneutic of suspicion"; our intimates are not. We have the eminently reasonable expectation that our friends and intimates will support our struggles and share our allegiances, rejoice in our victories and mourn our defeats, in a word, that they will see things – at least the big things in our lives – as we see them. That is part of the caregiver's job.

There will be many occasions on which his version of things will be the same as her own best version, his picture of things as much a reflection of her interests as his own. For example, black women and men who struggle in common against racism must share an understanding of the society in which their struggle takes place. But unless we posit a *general* identity of interest between men and women, there will be occasions, indeed countless occasions, on which a man's version of what is real and true will simply reflect his more privileged social location.

Women in our society lack epistemic authority,[26] in large part because historically males monopolized social interpretation and communication. Yet some feminist "standpoint theorists" have argued that the special social location of women, especially the work we do (including, of course, our emotional work), gives us a view of the world that is more reliable and less distorted than the view of things available to men.[27] There is much truth in this claim. Nevertheless women's emotional caregiving in heterosexual intimacy – when we do it with conviction and in long-term relationships – tends to underscore, not undermine, the perspective of men.

Unreciprocated caregiving also endangers women's ethical development. Hegel claimed that women's ethical perfectibility lay in the family, a position echoed by recent conservative Christian writers.[28] With more perspicacity, John Stuart Mill claimed that the patriarchal family morally corrupts both men and women. Women are often encouraged to lie, to be hypocritical and self-abasing. These, Mill claims, are the principal dangers for women.[29] Yet there are other dangers, ones that involve neither lying nor self-abasement. These arise from sincere and committed caregiving.

To affirm a man's sense of reality is also to affirm his values. "Stand by your man": what else can this mean? Male psychologists Cowan and Kinder claim men do not want high ethical principles in a woman, but rather "female tenderness."[30] Tenderness may involve compassion and forgiveness, clearly virtues under some circumstances and certainly excellences in a caregiver. But there are situations in which virtues such as forgiveness lead to moral blindness or outright complicity:

> Behind every great man is a woman, we say, but behind every monster there is a woman too, behind each of those countless men who stood astride their narrow worlds and crushed other human beings, causing them hideous suffering and pain. There she is in the shadows, a vague female silhouette, tenderly wiping blood from their hands.[31]

This is vividly seen with Teresa Stangl, wife of Fritz Stangl, Kommandant of Treblinka. Teresa, anti-Nazi and a devout Catholic, was appalled by what she knew of her husband's work. Nevertheless she maintained home and hearth as a safe harbor to which he returned when he could; she "stood behind her man." Few of us would take female tenderness to these lengths, but many of us, I suspect, have been morally silenced or morally compromised in small ways because we thought it more important to provide emotional support than to keep faith with our own principles. When that happens, there is tension between our commitments and what we think it is prudent to express. More corrosive is a danger that inheres in the nature of intimate caregiving – the danger of an ethical perspective that may rob the caregiver of a place to stand.

Although the emotional caregiving provided by the "good wife" or her equivalent is similar in some ways to caregiving furnished by the "good mother," it is importantly different as well. In so far as a mother is interested in the preservation, growth, and social acceptability of her child, she must be attentive to the child's moral development. She must be capable of "shaping a child according to moral restraints."[32] Yet a woman's adult partner is not a child, no matter how childishly he may behave; she will be judged by society more for her loyalty than for his morality. A husband – or lover – does not want and will not easily tolerate ethical training from his wife; what he wants instead is her approval and acceptance. William James expressed it most candidly: what the "average American" wants is a wife who will provide him with a "tranquil spot"

> where he shall be valid absolutely and once for all; where, having been accepted, he is secure from further criticism, and where his good aspirations may be respected no less than if they were accomplished realities.[33]

Women and men seek intimacy, a "haven in a heartless world" where the damage sustained elsewhere can be repaired. Nevertheless, here, as elsewhere, men's needs are not only likelier to be satisfied but satisfied at women's expense. The epistemic and ethical dangers tied to emotional caregiving are borne disproportionately by women. Men get the benefits; women run the risks.

V

Women's unreciprocated caregiving disempowers them. But this is only part of the story. In this section I will identify some countertendencies, ways in which women's provision of emotional sustenance to men may *feel* empowering and hence contradict, on a purely phenomenal level, what may be its objectively disempowering character.

When we give others emotional support, we tend to their wounds. This suggests that the man appears injured and vulnerable to his female caregiver. Many men, when not engaging in competitive displays of masculinity, will exhibit fear and insecurity. These are aspects of men's lives that women know well. To the woman who tends him, this fellow is not only no colossus who bestrides the world, but he may bear little resemblance to the patriarchal oppressor of feminist theory. The man may indeed belong to a more powerful caste; no matter, this isn't what he *seems* to her at the moment. One imagines Frau Stangl's tender clucks of sympathy as the harried Fritz rehearses, greatly edited, the trials and tribulations of his day at work: how put upon he is from above and below, how he suffers!

This phenomenon partially explains why some women aren't feminists. Feminism tells a tale of female injury. But the average woman in heterosexual intimacy knows that men are injured too, as indeed they are. This average woman may grant that men overall have more power than women. This fact, though, is *abstract*, while the man of flesh and blood who stands before her is *concrete*. His hurts are real, his fears palpable. Like those heroic doctors on the Late Show who work tirelessly through the epidemic although they may be fainting from fatigue, the woman may set her own needs to one side to better attend to his. She does this not because she is "chauvinized," or has "false consciousness," but because *this is what the work requires*. Indeed, she may even excuse the man's abuse of her, having glimpsed the great reservoir of pain and rage from which it issues. Here is a further way in which women's caregiving may ethically disempower them: women in these situations are tempted to collude in their own ill-treatment.[34]

An apparent reversal has taken place: the man, her superior in the hierarchy of gender, now appears before the woman as the weaker before the stronger, the patient before his nurse. The woman senses within herself a great power of healing. She imagines herself to be a great reservoir of restorative power. She gains a sense of agency and of personal efficacy that she may not find elsewhere. We read that one of Kafka's mistresses, Milena Jesenka, "believed she could cure Kafka of all his ills and give him a sense of well-being simply by her presence – if only he wanted it."[35]

While women suffer from our relative lack of power in the world and often resent it, certain dimensions of this powerlessness seem abstract and remote. We know, for example, that we rarely get to make the laws or direct the major financial institutions. However, Wall Street and the US Congress are far away. The power a woman feels in herself to heal and sustain, on the other hand – "the power of love" – is concrete. It is a field of force emanating from within herself.

Thus, here, as elsewhere, within a unified act women are affirmed in some ways and diminished in others. The woman who gives a man largely unreciprocated emotional sustenance accords him status and pays him homage; she agrees to the unspoken proposition that his life deserves much more attention than her own. Yet although this implies man's supremacy, the man reveals himself to be vulnerable and insecure. While she may be ethically and epistemically disempowered by the care she provides, this caregiving gives her an immediate sense of power.

Yet those men who seek female tenderness do not abandon their superordinate position nor do they relinquish their male privilege. Conversely, feeling that one's love is a mighty force for good in the life of the beloved doesn't make it so, as Milena Jesenka found, to her sorrow. The *feeling* of outflowing personal power so characteristic of the caregiving woman is quite different from the *having* of any actual power in the world. Doubtless this sense of personal efficacy partially compensates for the extra-domestic power women are denied: if one cannot be a king oneself, being a confidante of kings is the next best thing. But just as we make a bad bargain in accepting an occasional valentine in lieu of the sustained attention we deserve, we are ill-advised to settle for a mere sense of power, however heady and intoxicating it may be, in place of the effective power to which we have every right.

VI

We may think of relationships of emotional support as lying along a continuum. At one end are the perfunctory and routinized relationships of commercial caregiving in which the caregiver feels no genuine concern for the object of her attention and where, in the worst case, the doing of her job requires that she manipulate, suppress, and falsify her own feelings. At the other end of the continuum lies absolutely sincere caregiving. Here, there is no sense that that caregiver has some ulterior motive nor an inner reservation that might compromise her wholehearted acceptance of the Other. Most provisions of emotional support fall somewhere between. I have chosen to focus on sincere caregiving since I think that its risks have not been fully appreciated. We take this kind of non-commercial caregiving as a norm; we measure ourselves by it and blame ourselves when we fall short. It is sobering to consider the extent to which the Victorian ideal of the woman as "angel in the house" has survived. The dispensing of "female tenderness" is still seen, even by writers who declare themselves sympathetic to the aims of the women's movement, as crucial to the manifestation and enactment of femininity.

Yet women run real risks of exploitation in heterosexual caregiving. Typically, women are disempowered by the inequalities that characterize the exchange itself. This disempowerment, I have argued, lies in women's active and affective assimilation of the world according to men; it lies, too, in certain satisfactions of caregiving. The risks to women will vary from one case to the next; they may be a function of a woman's age or her degree of economic or emotional dependence, or the presence or absence of resources with which to construct a picture of the world according to herself.

Many feminist theorists have characterized this disempowerment in metaphors of filling and emptying: women fill men with their energies, thereby strengthening them and depleting ourselves. This depletion should be measured not only in an increase of male energies or in a reduction in male tensions, but in subtle affective and ideational changes in women ourselves that, taken *in toto*, tend to keep us in a position of subservience.

Conservatives argue, in essence, that women's caregiving may be properly exchanged for men's economic support. This view is not defensible. The classic bargain so lauded by conservatives – economic support in return for domestic and emotional labor – has broken down under the weight of economic necessity. Many millions of women must work outside the home. The continuing needs of these women for men's economic patronage is a measure of the undervaluation of women's labor in the waged sector. To this superexploitation at work is added a disproportionate share of domestic labor, childcare and emotional labor; women in this situation are quadruply exploited. Nor should we forget the growing number of single women, some single mothers as well, who give emotional support to men in relationships of shorter or longer duration, but receive absolutely no economic recompense at all. But even in the dwindling number of cases in which men are willing and able to offer economic patronage to women, it would be difficult to show how such support could compensate a woman for the epistemic decentering, ethical damage, and general mystification that put us at risk in unreciprocated caregiving.

Recently, conservatives have been joined by many feminist theorists in the celebration of female nurturance. These thinkers differ from conservatives: they want to raise women's status by properly valuing our emotional work and to see this quality of caring extended to the formal domains of commerce and politics. I applaud these aims. However, many feminist thinkers who extol women's nurturance, like most conservatives, have just ignored the possibility that women may suffer moral damage by doing emotional labor.[36] Clearly, the development of any ethics of care needs to be augmented by a careful analysis of the pitfalls and temptations of caregiving itself.

Notes

1 Shulamith Firestone, *Dialectic of Sex* (New York: Bantam Books, 1971), p. 127.

2 Lillian Rubin, *Worlds of Pain: Life in the Working Class Family* (New York: Basic Books, 1976).

3 Mirra Komarovsky, *Blue Collar Marriage* (New York: Random House, 1962).

4 Robert Staples, a noted sociologist of black sex roles, acknowledges that these attitudes are widespread among black men, in "The Myth of Black Macho: A Response to Angry Black Feminists," in *The Black Scholar*, March/April 1979.

5 See, for example, the exchange in *The Black Scholar*, May/June 1979; also Bell Hooks, *Ain't I a Woman: Black Women and Feminism* (Boston: South End Press, 1981), esp. pp. 79 and 181–7; and *Feminist Theory from Margin to Center* (Boston: South End Press, 1984).

6 Arlie Hochschild, *The Managed Heart: The Commercialization of Human Feeling* (Berkeley, CA: University of California Press, 1983).

7 Ibid., p. 122.

8 Ibid., p. 7.

9 Ibid., p. 8.

10 Arlie Hochschild, "Smile Wars, Counting the Casualties of Emotional Labor," *Mother Jones*, December 1983, p. 40.

11 Hochschild, *The Managed Heart*, p. 131.

12 Lillian Rubin, *Just Friends* (New York: Harper and Row, 1985), p. 69.

13 Ibid., p. 90.

14 Ibid., p. 90.

15 Jesse Bernard, "The Paradox of the Happy Marriage," in *Woman in Sexist Society*, ed. Vivian Gornick and Barbara K. Moran (New York: Basic Books, 1971).

16 Theodore Kemper, *A Social Interactional Theory of Emotions* (New York: John Wiley and Sons, 1978), p. 285.

17 Ibid., p. 96.

18 R. C. Centers, "Attitude Similarity–Dissimilarity as a Correlate of Heterosexual Attraction and Love," *Journal of Personality*, 39 (1975), pp. 303–18.

19 See Hochschild, *The Managed Heart*, p. 168. See also Nancy Henley, *Body Politics* (New York: Simon and Schuster, 1977), esp. chapters 6, 9 and 10.

20 "Since giving and according status are, by definition, at the heart of love relationships and only one sex is particularly expected to be competent in the performance of this attribute – *although both sexes require it* if the mutuality of the relationship is to be maintained – it is likely that the deficit of affection and love given by men to women will have devastating effects on the relationship. Wives in troubled marriages do in fact report more often than their husbands a lack of demonstrated affection, tenderness and love . . . This is precisely what we would have expected from an examination of the sex-linked differential in standards for status conferral that is an obvious feature of our culture." Kemper, *A Social Interactional Theory of Emotions*, p. 320.

21 Dorothy Dinnerstein, *The Mermaid and the Minotaur* (New York: Harper and Row, 1977); and Nancy Chodorow, *The Reproduction of Mothering: Psychoanalysis and the Sociology of Gender* (Berkeley: University of California Press, 1978).

22 "A Hymn to Him," Lerner and Lowe, *My Fair Lady*.

23 Given the context, my use of masculine pronouns is deliberate.

24 Nel Noddings, *Caring: A Feminine Approach*

to Ethics and Moral Education (Berkeley: University of California Press, 1984), pp. 14 and 30.

25 Ibid., p. 24.

26 See, for example, Mary Field Belenky, Blythe McVicker Clinchy, Nancy Rule Goldberger, Jill Mattuck Garule, *Women's Ways of Knowing: The Development of Self, Voice and Mind* (New York: Basic Books, 1986).

27 Alison Jaggar, *Feminist Politics and Human Nature* (Totowa, NJ: Rowman and Allanheld, 1983), p. 370. Jaggar makes the point, however, that women's special social location only makes possible a clearer understanding of social reality; it does not produce it. The proper standpoint of women can be gained only through critical analysis in the course of "a collective process of political and scientific struggle" (p. 371).

28 Hegel, *The Phenomenology of Spirit*, trans. A. V. Miller (London: Oxford University Press, 1977), pp. 267–79; see also Judith M. Miles, *The Feminine Principle* (Minneapolis: Bethany Fellowship, 1975).

29 John Stuart Mill, *The Subjection of Women*, in *Essays on Sex Equality*, ed. Alice S. Rossi (Chicago: University of Chicago Press, 1970).

30 Connell Cowan and Mervyn Kinder, *Smart Women, Foolish Choices* (1985), p. 229.

31 Jill Tweedie, *In the Name of Love* (London: Jonathan Cape, 1979), p. 49.

32 Sara Ruddick, "Maternal Thinking," in *Women and Values: Readings in Recent Feminist Philosophy*, ed. Marilyn Pearsall (Belmont, CA: Wadsworth, 1986), p. 342.

33 William James, A review of Horace Bucknell, *Women's Suffrage and Reform Against Nature* (New York: Scribner, 1869), and John Stuart Mill, *The Subjection of Women* (New York: Appleton, 1869), *North American Review*, October 1869, pp. 562–3. Cited in Linda A. Bell, "Does Marriage Require a Head? Some Historical Arguments," *Hypatia*, vol. 4, no. 1 (Spring 1989), p. 148.

34 I think that this may be true only for occasional or non-serious abuse. Women stay with chronic abusers either because of the serious emotional injury done them in long-term abusive situations – impairment of judgment, "learned helplessness," disablingly low self-esteem or fear of worse abuse if they try to leave – or else for largely economic reasons. See Susan Schechter, *Women and Male Violence: The Struggles of the Battered Women's Movement* (Boston: South End Press, 1982).

35 Nahum N. Glatzer, *The Loves of Franz Kafka* (New York: Schocken Books, 1986), p. x.

36 Nell Nodding's otherwise impressive book contains no analysis of the effects on the moral agent of uncompensated caring. Nor is this a significant theme on the part of contributors to *Women and Moral Theory*, ed. Eva Feder Kittay and Diana T. Meyers (Totowa, NJ: Rowman and Littlefield, 1987), a book of essays on the philosophical implications of Carol Gilligan's research on gender differences in moral reasoning – research that has been a central source for theorizing about an ethics of care. Claudia Card's "Gender and Moral Luck" (unpublished, 1989) is a notable exception. Two classic papers on the wrongness of female deference that present approaches somewhat different than my own are Thomas E. Hill, Jr, "Servility and Self-Respect," *Monist*, vol. 57, no. 1 (January 1973), pp. 87–104; and Marilyn Friedman, "Moral Integrity and the Deferential Wife," *Philosophical Studies*, vol. 47 (1985), pp. 141–50.

16

The Priority of Personal Interests

Bernard Williams

An individual person has a set of desires, concerns or, as I shall often call them, projects, which help to constitute a *character*. . . . The point is that he wants these things, finds his life bound up with them, and that they propel him forward; thus they give him, in a certain sense, a reason for living his life. But that is compatible with these drives, and this life, being much like others'; it gives him, distinctively, a reason for living this life, in the sense that he has no desire to give up and make room for others, but it does not require him to lead a *distinctive* life. While this is so, people do have dissimilar characters and projects; our *general* view of these matters, and the significance given to individuality in our own and others' lives, would certainly change if there were not between persons indefinitely many differences which are important to us. The level of description is of course also vital for determining what is the same or different; a similar description can be given of two people's dispositions, but the concrete detail be perceived very differently – and it is a feature of our experience of persons that we can perceive and be conscious of an indefinitely fine degree of difference in concrete detail (though it is only in certain connections and certain cultures that one spends much time rehearsing it).

One area in which *difference* of character directly plays a role in the concept of moral individuality is that of personal relations, and I shall close with some remarks in this connection. Differences of character give substance to the idea that individuals are not inter-substitutable. As I have just argued, a particular man so long as he is propelled forward does not need to assure himself that he is unlike others, in order not to feel substitutable; but in his personal relations to others the idea of difference can (even if it is not essential) certainly make a contribution, in more than one way – to the thought that his friend cannot just be equivalently replaced by another friend, is added both the thought that he cannot just be replaced himself, and also the thought that he and his friend are different from each other. This last thought is important to us as part (though of course a qualified one) of our view of friendship, a view thus set apart from Aristotle's opinion that a good man's friend was a duplication of himself. This I suspect to have been an Aristotelian, and not generally a Greek, opinion; and it is connected with another feature of his views which seems even stranger to us, at least with regard to any deeply committed friendship, namely that friendship for him has to be minimally *risky*, and one of his problems is indeed to reconcile the role of friendship with his unappetizing ideal of self-sufficiency. Once one agrees that a three-dimensional mirror would not represent the ideal of friendship, one can begin to see both how some degree of difference can play an essential role; and also, how a commitment or involvement with a particular other person might be one of the kinds of project which figured basically in a man's life in the ways already sketched – something which would be mysterious or even sinister on an Aristotelian account.

For Kantians, personal relations at least presuppose moral relations, and some are rather disposed to go further and regard them as a *species* of moral relations, as in the richly moralistic account given by Richards[1] of one of the four main principles of supererogation which would be accepted in "the Original Position" (that is to say, adopted as a moral limitation):

> a principle of mutual love requiring that people should not show personal affection and love to others on the basis of arbitrary physical characteristics alone, but rather on the basis of traits of personality and character related to acting on moral principles.

This righteous absurdity is no doubt to be traced to a feeling that love, even love based on "arbitrary physical characteristics", is something which has enough power and even authority to conflict badly with morality unless it can be brought within it from the beginning; and evidently that is a sound feeling, though it is an optimistic Kantian who thinks that much will be done about that by the adoption of this principle in the Original Position. The weaker view, that love and similar relations presuppose moral relations, in the sense that one could love someone only if one also had to them the moral relations one has to all people, is less absurd, but also wrong. It is of course true that loving someone involves some relations of the kind that morality requires or imports more generally, but it does not follow from that that one cannot have them in a particular case unless one has them generally in the way the moral man does; thus a man might be concerned about the interests of this person, and even about carrying out promises he made to this person, while not very concerned about these things with other persons. In general: to the extent (whatever it may be) that loving someone involves showing some of the same concerns in relation to them that the moral man shows, or at least thinks he ought to show, elsewhere, the lover's relations will be examples of moral relations, or at least resemble them; but this does not have to be because they are *applications to this case* of relations which the lover, *qua* moral man, more generally enters into. (That might not be the best description of the situation even if he *is* a moral man who enters into such relations more generally.)

However, once morality is there, and also personal relations to be taken seriously, so is the possibility of conflict. This of course does not mean that if there is some friendship with which his life is much involved, then a man must prefer any possible demand of that over other, impartial, moral demands: that would be absurd, and also a pathological kind of friendship, since both parties exist in the world and it is part of the sense of their friendship that it exists in the world.

But the possibility is there of conflict, not only, in the outcome, with substantial moral claims of others, but also with moral demands on how the outcome is arrived at: the situation may not have been subjected to an impartial process of resolution, and this fact itself may cause unease to the impartial moral consciousness. There is an example of such unease in a passage by Fried. After an illuminating discussion of the question why, if at all, we should give priority of resources to actual and present sufferers over absent or future ones, he writes:

> surely it would be absurd to insist that if a man could, at no risk or cost to himself, save one of two persons in equal peril, and one of those in peril was, say, his wife, he must treat both equally, perhaps by flipping a coin. One answer is that where the potential rescuer occupies no office such as that of captain of a ship, public health official or the like, the occurrence of the accident may itself stand as a sufficient randomizing event to meet the dictates of fairness, so he may prefer his friend, or loved one. Where the rescuer does occupy an official position, the argument that he must overlook personal ties is not unacceptable.[2]

The most striking feature of this passage is the direction in which Fried implicitly places the onus of proof: the fact that coin-flipping would be inappropriate raises some question to which an "answer" is required, while the resolution of the question by the rescuer's occupying an official position is met with what sounds like relief (though it remains unclear what that rescuer does when he "overlooks personal ties" – does *he* flip a coin?). The thought here seems to be that it is unfair to the second victim that, the first being the rescuer's wife, they never even get a chance of being rescued; and the answer (as I read the reference to the "sufficient randomizing event") is that at another level it is sufficiently fair – although in this disaster this rescuer has a special reason for saving the other person, it might have been another disaster in which another rescuer had a special reason for saving them. But, apart from anything else, that "might have been" is far too slim to sustain a reintroduction of the notion of fairness. The "random" element in such events, as in certain events of tragedy, should be seen not so much as affording a justification, in terms of an appropriate application of a lottery, as being a reminder that some situations lie beyond justifications.

But has anything yet shown that? For even if we leave behind thoughts of higher-order randomization, surely *this* is a justification on behalf of the rescuer, that the person he chose to rescue was his wife? It depends on how much weight is carried by "justification": the consideration that it was his wife is certainly, for instance, an explanation which should silence comment. But something more ambitious than this is usually intended, essentially involving the idea that moral principle can legitimate his preference, yielding the conclusion that in situations of this kind it is at least all right (morally permissible) to save one's wife. (This could be combined with a variety of higher-order thoughts to give it a rationale; rule-Utilitarians might favour the idea that in matters of this kind it is best for each to look after his own, like house insurance.) But this construction provides the agent with one thought too many: it might have been hoped by some (for instance, by his wife) that his motivating thought, fully spelled out, would be the thought that it was his wife, not that it was his wife and that in situations of this kind it is permissible to save one's wife.

Perhaps others will have other feelings about this case. But the point is that somewhere (and if not in this case, where?) one reaches the necessity that such things as deep attachments to other persons will express themselves in the world in ways which cannot at the same time embody the impartial view, and that they also run the risk of offending against it.

They run that risk if they exist at all; yet unless such things exist, there will not be enough substance or conviction in a man's life to compel his allegiance to life itself. Life has to have substance if anything is to have sense, including adherence to the impartial system; but if it has substance, then it cannot grant supreme importance to the impartial system, and that system's hold on it will be, at the limit, insecure.

It follows that moral philosophy's habit, particularly in its Kantian forms, of treating persons in abstraction from character is not so much a legitimate device for dealing with one aspect of thought, but is rather a misrepresentation, since it leaves out what both limits and helps to define that aspect of thought. Nor can it be judged solely as a theoretical device: this is one of the areas in which one's conception of the self, and of oneself, most importantly meet.

Notes

1 D. A. J. Richards, *A Theory of Reasons for Action* (Oxford: Oxford University Press, 1971), p. 94.

2 Charles Fried, *An Anatomy of Value* (Cambridge, MA: Harvard University Press, 1970), p. 227.

17

Morality, Parents, and Children

James Rachels

The Problem

At about the same time Socrates was being put to death for corrupting the youth of Athens, the great Chinese sage Mo Tzu was also antagonizing his community. Unlike the Confucianists, who were the social conservatives of the day, Mo and his followers were sharply critical of traditional institutions and practices. One of Mo's controversial teachings was that human relationships should be governed by an "all-embracing love" that makes no distinctions between friends, family, and humanity at large. "Partiality," he said, "is to be replaced by universality" (Fung, 1960, 92). To his followers, these were the words of a moral visionary. To the Confucianists, however, they were the words of a man out of touch with moral reality. In particular, Mo's doctrine was said to subvert the family, for it recommended that one have as much regard for strangers as for one's own kin. Meng Tzu summed up the complaint when he wrote that "Mo Tzu, by preaching universal love, has repudiated the family" (Rubin, 1976, 36). Mo did not deny it. Instead, he argued that universal love is a higher ideal than family loyalty, and that obligations within families can be properly understood only as particular instances of obligations to all mankind.

This ancient dispute has not disappeared. Do parents have special obligations to their own children? Or, to put the question a bit differently: Do they have obligations to their own children that they do not have to other children, or to children in general? Our instincts are with the Confucianists. Surely, we think, parents do have a special obligation to care for their own. Parents must love and protect their children; they must feed and clothe them; they must see to their medical needs, their education, and a hundred other things. Who could deny it? At the same time, we do not believe that we have such duties toward strangers. Perhaps we do have a general duty of beneficence toward them, but that duty is not nearly so extensive or specific as the duties we have toward our own young sons and daughters. If faced with a choice between feeding our own children and sending food to orphans in a foreign country, we would prefer our own, without hesitation.

Yet the Mohist objection is still with us. The idea that morality requires us to be impartial, clearly articulated by Mo Tzu, is a recurring theme of Western moral philosophy. Perhaps the most famous expression of this idea was Bentham's formula, "Each to count for one and none for more than one." Mill's formulation was less memorable but no less emphatic: He urged that, when weighing the interests of different people, we should be "as strictly impartial as a disinterested and benevolent spectator" (Mill, 1957, 22). Utilitarianism of the kind espoused by Bentham and Mill has, of course, often been criticized for conflicting with common-sense morality, and so it will probably come as no great surprise that utilitarian notions clash with the common-sense idea of special parental obligations. However, the idea that morality requires impartiality is by no means exclusively a utilitarian doctrine. It is common ground to a considerable range of theories and thinkers.[1]

The problem, in its most general form, is this. As moral agents, we cannot play favorites – at least, not according to the conception of morality as impartiality. But as parents, we do play favorites. Parental love is partial through and through. And we think there is nothing wrong with this; in fact, we normally think there is something wrong with the parent who is *not* deeply partial where his own children are concerned. Therefore, it would seem, one or the other of these conceptions has to be modified or abandoned.

Of course, exactly the same is true of our relations with friends, spouses, and lovers. All these relationships, and others like them, seem to include, as part of their very nature, special obligations. Friends, spouses, and lovers are not just members of the great crowd of humanity. They are all special, at least to the one who loves them. The problem is that the conception of morality as impartiality seems to conflict with *any* kind of loving personal relationship. Mo Tzu notwithstanding, it seems to conflict with love itself.[2] In this essay I discuss only the question of parental obligations to children, but it should be kept in mind that the deeper issue has to do with personal relationships in general.

Possible Solutions

There are three obvious approaches to solving our problem: first, we might reject the idea of morality as impartiality; second, we might reject the idea of special parental obligations; or third, we might try to find some way of understanding the two notions that would make them consistent. The first approach has recently attracted some support among philosophers, who think that although the conception of morality as impartiality seems plausible when stated abstractly, it is refuted by such counter-examples as parental obligation. Their thought is that we should reject this conception and look for a new theory of morality, one that would acknowledge from the outset that personal relationships can be the source of special obligations.

Rejecting the idea of impartiality has a certain appeal, for it is always exciting to learn that some popular philosophical view is no good and that there is interesting work to be done in formulating an alternative. However, we should not be too quick here. It is no accident that the conception of morality as impartiality has been so widely accepted. It seems to express something deeply important that we should be reluctant to give up. It is useful, for example, in explaining why egoism, racism, and sexism are morally odious, and if we abandon this conception we lose our most natural and persuasive means of combating those doctrines. (The idea of morality as impartiality is closely connected to modern thoughts about human equality. That humans are in some sense equals would never have occurred to the Confucianists, which perhaps explains why they saw nothing plausible in Mo's teaching.) Therefore, it seems desirable to retain the notion of moral impartiality in some form. The question is, can we find some way of keeping both ideas – morality as impartiality, and special parental obligations? Can we understand them in a way that makes them compatible with one another?

As it turns out, this is not a difficult task. It is fairly easy to interpret impartiality in such as way that it no longer conflicts with special parental obligations. We can say, for example, that impartiality requires us to treat people in the same way *only when there are no relevant differences between them*. This qualification is obviously needed, quite apart from any considerations about parents and children. For example, it is not a failure of impartiality to imprison a convicted criminal, while innocent citizens go free, because there is a relevant difference between them (one has committed a crime; the others have not) to which we can appeal to justify the difference in treatment. Similar examples come easily to mind. But once we have admitted the need for this qualification, we can make use of it to resolve our problem about parental obligations: We can say that there is a relevant difference between one's own children and other children that justifies treating one's own children better. The difference will have something to do with the fact that they are one's own.

We might call this the compromise view. It is appealing because it allows us to retain the plausible idea of morality as impartiality, without having to give up the equally plausible idea that we have special obligations to our own children. Having found this solution to our problem, we might be tempted to stop here. That, however, would be premature. There is a further issue that needs to be addressed, and when we do address it, the compromise view will begin to look less attractive.

We are not free to call just any differences between individuals relevant. Suppose a racist claimed that there is a relevant difference between blacks and whites that justifies treating whites better – the difference being that they are members of different races. We would think this mere bluster and demand to know why *that* difference should count for anything. Similarly, it is only hand-waving to say that there is a relevant difference between one's own children and others that justifies treating one's own better – the difference being that they are one's own. We need to ask why *that* difference matters.

Why Should it Matter that a Child is One's Own?

Why should it matter, from a moral point of view, that a child is one's own? Our natural tendency is to assume that it *does* matter and to take it as a mere philosophical puzzle to figure out why. Why should anyone want to resist this tendency? The feeling that our own children have a superior natural claim on our attention is among the deepest moral instincts we have. Can it possibly be doubted? I believe there is a powerful reason for doubting that this feeling is morally legitimate – the fact that a child is one's own may *not* matter, or at least it may not matter nearly as much as we usually assume. That reason has to do with luck.

The point about luck can be brought out like this. Suppose a parent believes that, when faced with a choice between feeding his own children and feeding starving orphans, he should give preference to his own. This is natural enough. But the orphans need the food just as much, and they are no less deserving. It is only their bad luck that they were not born to affluent parents; and why should luck count, from a moral point of view? Why should we think that a moral view is correct, if it implies that some children should be fed, while others starve, for no better reason than that some were unlucky in the circumstances of their birth? This seems to me to be an extremely important matter – important enough, perhaps, that we should take seriously the possibility that a child's being one's own does not have the moral importance that we usually assume it has.

With this in mind, let us look at some of the arguments that support the Compromise View. The idea that one's own children have a superior claim to one's care might be defended in various ways. Let us consider the three arguments that seem most important.

1. *The argument from social roles*

The first line of reasoning begins with some observations about social roles. It is not possible for an isolated individual to have anything resembling a normal human life. For that, a social setting is required. The social setting provides roles for us to fill – thus in the context of society we are able to be citizens, friends, husbands and wives, hospital patients, construction workers, scientists, teachers, customers, sports fans, and all the rest. None of us (with rare heroic exceptions) creates the roles we play; they have evolved over many centuries of human life, and we encounter them as simply the raw materials out of which we must fashion our individual lives.

These roles define, in large measure, our relations with other people. They specify how we should behave toward others. Teachers must wisely guide their students; friends must be loyal; husbands should be faithful; and so on. To the extent that you fail in these respects, you will be an inferior teacher, a bad friend, a poor husband. You can avoid these obligations by declining to enter into these roles: Not everyone will be a teacher, not everyone will marry, and some unfortunate people will not even have friends. But you can hardly avoid *all* social roles, and you cannot fill a social role without at the same time acknowledging the special responsibilities that go with it.

Now, parenthood is a social role, and like other such roles it includes special duties as part of its very nature. You can choose not to have children, or, having had a child, you may give it up for adoption. But if you *are* a parent, you are stuck with the responsibilities that go with the role. A parent who doesn't see to his children's needs is a bad parent, just as a disloyal friend is a bad friend, and an unfaithful husband is a poor husband. And that is why (according to this argument) we have obligations to our own children that we do not have to other children.

The argument from social roles is plausible; but how far should we be persuaded by it? The argument has at least four apparent weaknesses.

(i) We need to distinguish two claims: first, that our obligations to our own children *have a different basis* from our obligations to other children; and second, that our obligations to our own children *are stronger than* (take precedence over) our obligations to other children. If successful, the argument from social roles would show only that our obligations to our own children are based on different considerations than are our obligations to other children. We have a social relationship with our own children that is the basis of our obligation to them, while our obligations to other children are based on a general duty of beneficence. The argument would not show that the former obligations are *stronger*. Thus a critic of the idea of special parental obligations could continue the dispute at another level. It could be argued that, even if one's duties to one's own children have a different basis, they nevertheless are *no stronger than* one's duties to other children.

(ii) The second point is related to the first. The argument from social roles trades on the notion of what it means to be a bad father or a bad mother. Now, suppose we admit that a man who ignores the needs of his own children is a bad father. It may also be observed that a man who ignores the cries of orphans, when he could help, is a bad *man* – a man lacking a proper regard for the needs of others. While it is undesirable to be a bad father (or mother), it is also undesirable to be a bad man (or woman). So, once again, the argument from social roles does nothing to show that our obligations to other children are weaker.

(iii) Third, there is the point about luck that I have already mentioned. The system of social roles acknowledged in our society makes special provision for children lucky enough to live in homes with parents. This system favors even more those lucky enough to have affluent parents who can provide more for them than less affluent parents are able to provide. Even granting this, we can still ask: Is it a morally decent system? The system itself can be subject to criticism.

We do not have to look far to find an obvious objection to the system. The system does well enough in providing for some children; but it does miserably where others are concerned. There is no social role comparable to the parent–child relationship that targets the interests of orphans, or the interests of children whose parents are unable or unwilling to provide for them. Thus in this system luck plays an unacceptably important part.

(iv) Finally, students of social history might find the argument from social roles rather naïve. The argument draws much of its strength from the fact that contemporary American and European ideals favor families bound together by love. Anyone who is likely to read these words will have been influenced by that ideal – consider how the reader will have passed over the second paragraph of this essay, with its easy talk of parents loving and protecting their children, without a pause. Yet the cozy nuclear family, nourished by affectionate relationships, is a relatively recent development. The norm throughout most of Western history has been very different.

In his acclaimed book *The Family, Sex and Marriage in England 1500–1800*, Lawrence Stone points out that as recently as the seventeenth century affectionate relations between husbands and wives were so rare as to be virtually nonexistent, and certainly were not expected within normal marriages. Among the upper classes, husbands and wives occupied separate stations within large households and rarely saw one another in private. Children were sent away immediately after birth to be looked after by wet-nurses for 12 to 18 months; then, returning home, they would be raised largely by nurses, governesses, and tutors. Finally they would be sent away to boarding school when they were between 7 and 13, with 10 the commonest age (Stone, 1979, 83–4). The children of the poor were of course worse off: they would leave home at an equally early age, often to go and work in the houses of the rich. Stone writes,

> About all that can be said with confidence on the matter of emotional relations within the sixteenth- and early seventeenth-century family at all social levels is that there was a general psychological atmosphere of distance, manipulation, and deference. . . . Family relationships were characterized by interchangeability, so that substitution of another wife or another child was easy. . . . It was a structure held together not by affective bonds but by mutual economic interests. (Stone, 1979, 88)

And what of parental duties? Of course there has always been a recognition of *some* special parental duties, but in earlier times these were much more restricted and were not associated with bonds of affection. Until some time in the eighteenth century, it seems, the emphasis in European morals was almost entirely on the duties owed by children to parents, rather than the other way around. Children were commonly said to owe their parents absolute obedience, in gratitude for having been given life. The French historian Jean

Flandrin notes that "In Brittany the son remained subject to the authority of his father until the age of sixty, but marriage contracted with the father's consent emancipated him" (Flandrin, 1979, 130). Pity the man whose father lived to a ripe old age and refused consent for marriage – his only emancipation would be to flee. Both Stone and Flandrin make it clear that, while parental *rights* is an old idea, the idea of extensive parental *obligations* is a notion of much more recent vintage. (The debate between Mo Tzu and the Confucianists was also conducted in such terms – for them, the primary issue was whether children had special duties to their fathers, not the other way around.)

These observations about social history should be approached with care. Of course they do not refute the idea of special parental obligations. However, they do go some way toward undermining our easy confidence that present-day social arrangements only institutionalize our natural duties. That is the only moral to be drawn from them, but it is an important one. In this area, as in so many others, what seems natural just depends on the conventions of one's society.

2. *The argument from proximity*

The second argument goes like this. It is reasonable to accept a social arrangement in which parents are assigned special responsibility for their own children because parents are *better situated* to look after their own. Granted, all children need help and protection. But other children are remote, and their needs are less clear, while a parent's own children live in the same house, and the parent is (or ought to be) intimately familiar with their needs. Other things being equal, it makes sense to think that A has a greater responsibility for helping B than for helping C, if A is better situated to help B. This is true in the case of helping one's own children versus helping other children; therefore, one's obligation in the first instance is greater.

This argument is plausible if we concentrate on certain kinds of aid. Children wake up sick in the middle of the night; someone must attend to them, and that someone is usually Mother or Father. The parents are in a position to do so, and (most of the time) no one else is. The complaint that you nursed your own children, but you didn't help the other children who woke up sick elsewhere in the world, is obviously misguided. The same goes for countless other ways that parents assist their children: by making them take their medicine, by stopping them from playing in the roadway, by bundling them up against the cold, and so on. These are all matters of what we might call *day-to-day care*.

Day-to-day care involves a kind of personal attention that a parent *could not* provide for many others, because it is physically impossible. The importance of physical proximity is that it makes these kinds of caring behaviors possible; the impossibility of doing the same for other children is just the impossibility of being in two places at once. So if there is partiality here, it is a partiality that we need not worry about because it cannot be avoided. There is little doubt, then, that parents are normally in a better position to provide day-to-day care for their own children than for others.

This type of argument is less plausible, however, when we consider more general, fundamental needs, such as food. Is a parent in a better position to feed his own children than to provide for others? At one time this might have been the case. Before the advent of modern communications and transportation, and before the creation of efficient relief agencies, people might have been able to say that while they could feed their own, they were unable to do much about the plight of children elsewhere. But that is no longer true. Today, with relief agencies ready to take our assistance all over the world, needing only sufficient resources to do so, it is almost as easy to provide food for a child in Africa as to provide for one's own. The same goes for providing basic medical care: international relief agencies carry medical assistance around the world on the same basis.

Therefore, the argument from proximity is, at best, only partially successful. Some forms of assistance (such as getting up in the middle of the night to attend to sick children) do require proximity but others (such as providing food) do not. The argument might show that, where day-to-day care is concerned, parents have special duties. But the same cannot be said for the provision of fundamental needs.

3. *The argument from personal goods*

The third argument hinges on the idea that loving relationships are personal goods of great importance: To love other people and be loved in return are part of what is involved in having a rich and satisfying human life. A loving relationship with one's children is, for many parents, a source of such happiness that they would sacrifice almost anything else to preserve it. But as we have already observed, love necessarily involves having a special concern for the well-being of the loved one, and so it is not impartial. An ethic that required absolute impartiality would therefore require forgoing a great personal good.

The intuitive idea behind this argument may seem plain enough. Nevertheless, it is difficult to formulate the argument with any precision. Why, exactly, is a loving relationship with another person such a great good? Part of the answer may be that pacts of mutual assistance enable all of us to fare better. If A and B have this sort of relationship, then A can count on B's assistance when it is needed, and vice versa. They are both better off. Of course, deals of this kind could be made between people who are not joined by bonds of affection, but affection makes the arrangement more dependable: People who love one another are more apt to remain faithful when the going is hard. But there is more. Bonds of affection are more than just instrumentally good. To be loved is to have one's own value affirmed; thus it is a source of self-esteem. This is important for all of us, but especially for children, who are more helpless and vulnerable than adults. Moreover, there is, at a deep level, a connection between love and the meaning of life (although I cannot go into this very deeply here). We question whether our lives have meaning when we find nothing worth valuing, when it seems to us that "all is vanity." Loving relationships provide individuals with things to value, and so give their lives this kind of meaning. That is why parents who love their children, and who strive to see that they do well, can find, in this, meaning for their lives.

These are important points, but they do not prove as much as they are sometimes taken to prove. In the first place, there is a lot about parental love that *is* consistent with a large measure of impartiality. Loving someone is not only a matter of preferring their interests. Love involves, among other things, intimacy and the sharing of experiences. A parent shows his love by listening to the child's jokes, by talking, by being a considerate companion, by praising, and even by scolding when that is needed. It may be objected that these kinds of behavior also show partiality, since the parent does not do these things for all children. But these are only further instances of the day-to-day care that requires proximity; again, if this is partiality, it is partiality that cannot be avoided. And there is another difference between these kinds of support and such things as providing food and medical care. The companionship, the listening, the talking, and the praising and scolding are what make personal relationships *personal*. That is why the psychic benefits that accompany such relationships are more closely associated with these matters than with such relatively impersonal things as being fed.

Moreover, it is not necessary, in order to have a loving relationship with one's children and to derive from it the benefits that the argument from personal goods envisions, to regard their interests as *always* having priority, especially when the interests in question are not comparable. One could have a loving relationship that involves all the intimacies of day-to-day care and the provision of life's necessities, while acknowledging at the same time that when it comes to choosing between luxuries for them and food for orphans, the orphans' needs should prevail. At the very least, there is nothing in the argument from personal goods that rules out such an approach.

The Moral Point of Utopian Thinking

There is another approach to our problem, favored by the Mohists, that we have not yet considered: Clinging to the ideal of impartiality, we could simply reject the idea of special parental duties. This goes against our intuitions, and it is opposed by the (partially successful) arguments we have just examined. Nevertheless, we may ask whether there is anything to be said in favor of this approach.

In fact, there is a lot that might be said in its favor. Suppose we forget, for a moment, the imperfections of actual human life, and try to imagine what it would be like if everyone behaved in a morally blameless manner. What would relations between adults and children be like in such a utopia? Here is one plausible picture of such a world. In it, children with living parents able to provide for them would be raised by their parents, who would give them all the love and care they needed. Parents who through no fault of their own were unable to provide for their children would be given whatever assistance they needed. Orphans would be taken in by families who would raise and love them as their own. The burdens involved in such adoptions would be shared by all.

It is fair to say that, in such a world, the ideal of impartiality is realized. In this world people do not act as if any child is more deserving than any other: one way or another, equal provision is made for the needs of all. Moreover, luck plays no part in how children will fare: the orphans' needs are satisfied too. When it is said by the Mohists that "love is universal," or by their modern counterparts, the utilitarians, that we should "promote impartially the interests of everyone alike," this might be the point: In the morally best world, we would not recognize many of the distinctions that we do recognize in the real world we inhabit.

But the idea of special obligations has crept back in. In the utopian world I have sketched, some special obligations are acknowledged, because particular adults (most often parents) are assigned special responsibility for looking after particular children. However, two points need to be emphasized: First, the *reason* for this arrangement is consistent with the principle of impartiality (and inconsistent with the thought that one's own children somehow have a natural superior claim on one's attention); the reason is that this is the best way to see that the needs of all children are satisfied. Second, the recognition of some special obligations might be *welcomed*, even in utopia; it need not be merely something that is grudgingly admitted. The arguments we have already considered suggest that there are special benefits to be derived from a social system in which particular adults are assigned responsibility for particular children – the benefits that go with loving personal relationships. This gives us reason to think that such an assignment would be part of the best social system – a system that would at the same time make adequate provision for all.

Of course we do not live in a utopia, and it might be objected that, in the real world we inhabit, it would be either silly or disastrous to start telling parents to stop favoring their own children – silly because no one would listen, or disastrous because if some did, their children would suffer greatly. (There might be, in current terms, a coordination problem: It might not be wise for some to adopt the best strategy unless all do.) So what is the point of thinking about utopia? I suggest this: A picture of utopia gives us an idea, not only of what we should strive for, but of what is in one sense objectively right and wrong. Conditions may exist in our own world that make it wrong, in some circumstances, to act as though we lived in utopia. But that is only because in our world human behavior is flawed. It may nevertheless be true that, in a deep sense, the utopian behavior is morally best.

Let me try to make this clearer by giving a different sort of example. It has been argued by many philosophers that there is nothing immoral in mercy-killing, when it is requested by a dying person as a humane alternative to a slow, painful death. Others have objected that if mercy-killing were permitted it would lead to further killings that we would not want – we might begin by killing people at their own request to put them out of misery, it is said, but then we would begin to pressure sick people into making such requests, and that would lead to killing old people who have not requested it (for their own good, of course), and then we would go on to killing the feeble-minded, and so on. I do not believe these things would happen.[3] But suppose they would. What would follow? It would not follow that mercy-killing is immoral in the original case. The objection would show, paradoxically, that there are good reasons why we should not perform actions that *are* moral and humane. Those reasons would have to do with the imperfections of human beings – the claim is that people are so flawed that they would slide down the slippery slope from the (moral) practice of euthanasia to the additional (immoral) practices described.

This suggests that moral philosophy might be idealistic in a way that applied ethics is not. Moral philosophy describes the ideals that motivate perfect conduct, the conduct of people in utopia.[4] In utopia, as Thomas More observed in his book of that name, euthanasia would be accepted (More, 1965, 102), and the slippery-slope argument would be irrelevant because people in utopia do not abuse humane practices. Applied ethics, however, takes into account the messy details of the real world, including the prejudices, faults, and vices of real human beings, and recommends how we should behave considering all *that* as well as the ideals of perfect conduct.

What does this mean for the question of special parental obligations? It means that there is a point to the philosophical insistence that all children are equal, even if in the real world it would be unwise to urge particular parents to stop providing preferential care for their own. The practical question is, therefore, how nearly we can expect to approach the ideal system in the real world and what specific recommendations should be made, in light of this, to particular parents.

Practical Implications

How should parents, living not in utopia but in our society, who are concerned to do what is morally best, conceive of the relation between their obligations to their own children and their obligations to other children? Here are three contrasting views; each is implausible, but for different reasons.

1. *Extreme bias*

On this view, parents have obligations to provide for their own children, but they have *no obligations at all* to other children. Anything done for other children is at best supererogatory

– good and praiseworthy if one chooses to do it, but in no way morally mandatory. On this view, parents may provide not only necessities but also luxuries for their own children, while other children starve, and yet be immune from moral criticism.

Extreme bias is not plausible, because it makes no provision whatever for a duty of general beneficence. It is hard to believe that we do not have *some* obligation to be concerned with the plight of the starving, whoever they are, even if that obligation is less extensive than our obligations to our own kin.[5] Thus it will not be surprising if this view turns out to be unacceptable.

2. *Complete equality*

The opposite view seems to be implied by the idea of morality as impartiality – the view that all children are equal and that there is no difference at all between one's moral obligations toward one's own children and one's moral obligations toward other children. This view denies that there are any good moral grounds for preferring to feed one's own child rather than an orphan in a foreign country. In our society anyone who accepted and acted on such a view would seem to his neighbors to be morally deranged, for doing so would seem to involve a rejection of one's children – a refusal to treat them with the love that is appropriate to the parent–child relationship.

3. *The most common view*

What, in fact, do people in our society seem to believe? Most people seem to believe that one has an obligation to provide the necessities of life for other children only after one has already provided a great range of luxuries for one's own. On this view, it is permissible to provide one's own children with virtually everything they need in order to have a good start in life – not only food and clothing, but, if possible, a good education, opportunities for travel, opportunities for enjoyable leisure, and so forth. In the United States children of affluent families often have TV sets, stereos, and now computers, all laid out in their own rooms. They drive their own cars to high school. Few people seem to think there is anything wrong with this – parents who are unable to provide their children with such luxuries nevertheless aspire to do so.

The most common view imposes *some* duty regarding other children, but not much. In practical terms, it imposes a duty only on the very rich, who have resources left over even after they have provided ample luxuries for their own children. The rest of us, who have nothing left after doing as much as we can for our own, are off the hook. It takes only a little reflection to see that this view is also implausible. How can it be right to spend money on luxuries for some children, even one's own – buying them the latest trendy toys, for example – while others do not have enough to eat? Perhaps, when confronted with this, many people might come to doubt whether it is correct. But certainly most affluent people act as if it were correct.

Is there a better alternative? Is there a view that escapes the difficulties of extreme bias, complete equality, and the most common view, and is consistent with the various other points that have been made in our discussion? I suggest the following.

4. *Partial bias*

We might say that, while we do have a substantial obligation to be concerned about the welfare of all children, our own nevertheless come first. This vague thought needs to be sharpened. One way of making it more precise is this. When considering similar needs, you may permissibly prefer to provide for the needs of your own children. For example, if you were faced with a choice between feeding your own children or contributing the money to provide food for other children, you could rightly choose to feed your own. But if the choice were between some relatively trivial thing for your own and necessities for other children, preference should be given to helping the others. Thus if the choice were between providing trendy toys for your own already well-fed children or feeding the starving, you should feed the starving.

This view will turn out to be more or less demanding, depending on what one counts as a "relatively trivial thing." We might agree that buying trendy toys for some children, even for one's own, while other children starve is indefensible. But what about buying them nice clothes? Or a college education? Am I justified in sending my children to an expensive college? Clearly, the line between the trivial and the important can be drawn at different places. (One will be pushed toward a more demanding interpretation as one takes more seriously the point about the moral irrelevance of luck.) Nevertheless, the intuitive idea is plain enough. On this view, you may provide the necessities for your own children first, but you are not justified in providing them luxuries while other children lack necessities. Even in a fairly weak form, this view would still require much greater concern for others than the view that is most common in our society.

From the point of view of the various arguments we have considered, partial bias clearly stands out as the superior view. It is closer to the utopian ideal than either extreme bias or the most common view; it is morally superior in that it makes greater provision for children who have no loving parents; it is consistent with the arguments we have considered concerning the benefits to be derived from loving relationships; and it is perhaps as much as we could expect from people in the real world. It is not, in fact, very far from the utopian ideal. If we begin with complete equality, and then modify it in the ways suggested in our discussion of utopia, we end up with something very much like partial bias.

What would the adoption of partial bias mean for actual families? It would mean that parents could continue to provide loving day-to-day care for their own children, with all that this involves, while giving them preferential treatment in the provision of life's necessities. But it would also mean preferring to provide the necessities for needier children, rather than luxuries for their own. Children in such families would be worse off, in an obvious sense, than the children of affluent parents who continued to live according to the dictates of extreme bias or the most common view. However, we might hope that they would not regard themselves as deprived, for they might learn the moral value of giving up their luxuries so that the other children do not starve. They might even come to see their parents as morally admirable people. That hope is itself utopian enough.

Notes

1   "The good of any one individual is of no more importance, from the point of view (if I may say so) of the Universe, than the good of any other," says Sidgwick (1907, 382). "We [must] give equal weight in our moral deliberations to the like interests of all those affected by our actions," says Singer (1972, 197). "Moral rules must be for the good of everyone alike," says Baier (1958, 200). "A rational and impartial sympathetic spectator is a person who takes up a general perspective: he assumes a position where his own interests are not at stake and he possesses all the requisite information and powers of reasoning. So situated he is equally responsive and sympathetic to the desires and satisfactions of everyone affected

by the social system. . . . Responding to the interests of each person in the same way, an impartial spectator gives free reign to his capacity for sympathetic identification by viewing each person's situation as it affects that person," says Rawls (1971, 186). In an interesting discussion, R. M. Hare argues that virtually all the major moral theories incorporate a requirement of impartiality and adds that his own "universal prescriptivism" is no exception.

2 The point is a familiar one that pops up in all sorts of philosophical contexts. For example: In his recent book *On the Plurality of Worlds*, David Lewis discusses an ethical objection to his thesis that all possible worlds are equally real, a thesis he calls modal realism. The objection is that, if modal realism is true, then our actions will have no effect whatever on the total amount of good or evil that exists. If we prevented an evil from occurring in *this* world, it would still exist in some *other* world. As Lewis puts it, "The sum total of good throughout the plurality of worlds is non-contingently fixed and depends not at all on what we do." Thus we might as well forget about trying to maximize the good. Lewis comments, "But if modal realism subverts only a 'truly universalistic ethics,' I cannot see that

as a damaging objection. What collapses is a philosopher's invention, no less remote from common sense than modal realism itself. An ethics of our own world is quite universalistic enough. Indeed, I dare say that it is already far too universalistic; it is a betrayal of our particular affections" (1986, 128).

3 For a complete discussion see Rachels (1986, chap. 10).

4 On this point I am following Richard Brandt, although he does not put it in just this way. Brandt writes: "What I mean by 'is objectively wrong' or 'is morally unjustified' is 'would be prohibited by the set of moral rules which a rational person would prefer to have current or subscribed to in the consciences of persons in the society in which he expected to live a whole life, as compared with any other set of moral rules or none at all'" (1975, 367). Clearly, this is a set of rules appropriate for a utopia, where it is assumed that people will actually live according to the rules. In the real world we can make no such assumption, and sometimes this will mean we should do things that, according to this definition, would be objectively wrong.

5 For arguments concerning the extensiveness of our obligations toward others, see Singer (1972) and Rachels (1979).

References

Baier, Kurt. 1958. *The Moral Point of View* (Ithaca: Cornell University Press).

Brandt, Richard B. 1975. "The Morality and Rationality of Suicide." In James Rachels (ed.) *Moral Problems* (New York: Harper & Row).

Flandrin, Jean. 1979. *Families in Former Times.* trans. Richard Southern (Cambridge: Cambridge University Press).

Fung Yu-lan. 1960. *A Short History of Chinese Philosophy* (New York: Macmillan).

Hare, R. M. 1972. "Rules of War and Moral Reasoning." *Philosophy and Public Affairs*, 1, 166–81.

Lewis, David. 1986. *On the Plurality of Worlds* (Oxford: Blackwell).

Mill, John Stuart. 1957. *Utilitarianism* (Indianapolis: Bobbs-Merrill). This work, first published in 1861, is today available in many editions.

More, Thomas. 1965. *Utopia* (Harmondsworth: Penguin). This work, first published in Latin in 1516, is today available in many editions. The Penguin translation is by Paul Turner.

Rachels, James. 1979. "Killing and Starving to Death." *Philosophy*, 54, 159–71.

——. 1986. *The End of Life: Euthanasia and Morality* (Oxford: Oxford University Press).

Rawls, John. 1971. *A Theory of Justice* (Cambridge: Harvard University Press).

Rubin, Vitaly A. 1976. *Individual and State in Ancient China* (New York: Columbia University Press).

Sidgwick, Henry. 1907. *The Methods of Ethics*, 7th edn (London: Macmillan).

Singer, Peter. 1972. "Famine, Affluence, and Morality." *Philosophy and Public Affairs*, 1, 229–43.

——. 1978. "Is Racial Discrimination Arbitrary?" *Philosophia*, 8, 185–203.

Stone, Lawrence. 1979. *The Family, Sex and Marriage in England 1500–1800* (New York: Harper & Row).

Sexuality

A few readers may be surprised to see essays discussing animals, the environment, smoking, immigration, and the virtues, included in this volume. They may not think all these are moral issues, at least not especially important or interesting ones. However, everyone recognizes sex is a morally significant issue. In fact, people sometimes talk as if sex were the only moral issue. They imply that the most important moral issue is "with whom shall I sleep, and when?" This view is not restricted to laypeople or preachers; I also find it in academics. Recently a respected professor at this university listed what he saw as a dozen pressing moral issues. Nine of them were related to sex.

Such a view of morality is unacceptably narrow. The scope of morality is much broader. Nonetheless, sex does raise important moral questions, which some essays in this section explore. Some of these are familiar moral fare, for instance, "Should people have sex only if they love one another?" and "Is homosexuality moral?" However, the section begins in a different vein. Foa's essay on rape exhorts us to re-examine the nature and role of sexuality in our society. She claims that in our society rape is not the antithesis of sex, but its model.

How could this be? The answer emerges, she argues, once we understand that rape is embedded within a social environment in which men generally hold power and expect that women will be subservient. Within that environment, women are not encouraged or allowed to state their preferences openly, and even when they do, men often do not hear them. Specifically, most women have learned not to trust their own sexuality, and many men have learned to interpret a woman's "No" as a sexual turn-on.

Her emphasis on the social conditions that shape our choices and our moral deliberations is reminiscent of Rothman's portrayal of the ABORTION debate and Bartky's discussion of emotional exploitation within personal relationships (FAMILY AND FRIENDS). These are themes we will see again in discussions of SEXUAL AND RACIAL DISCRIMINATION, AFFIRMATIVE ACTION, and pornography (FREE SPEECH). Many of these authors aver that moral issues are inexplicable in a historical vacuum. We can understand the issues only when we see the history and continuing character of men's power over and discrimination toward women.

Here we see the nub of a raging debate within ethics, political philosophy, and the public arena. Are moral principles independent of the specific context in which they are used? Or do moral judgements make sense only in the larger social–political–historical context in which we make them? Some philosophers argue that these two positions are compatible: that moral principles can be independent of particular historical circumstances, even though their application is sensitive to those circumstances. However, even if these two positions are compatible, many people talk as if they were not. Many philosophers are prone to discuss moral issues abstractly, as if we could understand them ahistorically, while others focus almost exclusively on the particular social–cultural–political and historical circumstances in which these problems arise and within which we make decisions. Pay attention to this difference in philosophical style. It will help you better to grasp the views developed in this volume.

For instance, Punzo uses a similar strategy in defending conventional sexual morality. He claims that sexual intercourse should be limited to living, committed relationships. However, most people today fail to see the wisdom of this view because they see the world through the lens of the "acquisitive society." Our social–political environment encourages us to think of having sex with someone in the same way we think about going out to dinner with them. If I ask you to dinner and you agree, then there is nothing morally wrong with our sharing dinner. Likewise if I ask you to have sex and you agree, then there is nothing wrong with sharing our bodies.

Punzo argues that this is a perverted conception of sex. In a healthier, non-acquisitive environment, we would see that sex is more than just physical contact. It is a unique physical union, "the most intimate physical expression of themselves." To treat sex as a simple exchange, as people in our society are wont to do, is to misunderstand its nature and role.

Goldman disagrees. He claims that sex is just the desire for a certain kind of physical contact with another's body. Sex is concerned with giving and receiving certain kinds of pleasure, nothing more. Perhaps sex is better between two people who love one another. Nevertheless, he might say, a fine dinner is also better when shared by two people who love one another. However, no one thinks only people who are in love should share dinner. So why should we think that only people who are in love (or still less, only people who are married) should share sex?

Goldman rejects any definition of "sex" that seeks to settle moral issues by fiat. For instance, if we define "sex" as "a form of physical interaction between people who have committed, long-term relationships," then, according to that definition, "casual sex" is a contradiction. Perhaps casual sex is not as meaningful as sex between people who deeply love one another. Nonetheless, that is something we should not settle by definition. We must first understand what sex is. Then, and only then, can we morally evaluate it.

Not surprisingly, this explains why Goldman thinks no analysis of "sex" can show that homosexuality is immoral. The last two authors explicitly discuss this theme. Levin claims homosexuality is biologically unnatural. That is, he argues that homosexuality is not the result of evolution, it is not conducive to the survival of the organism or of the species. Although he does not think this shows that homosexuality is immoral, it does explain the "almost universal revulsion" toward the practice. That explains why we can legitimately discriminate against homosexuals – especially male homosexuals – even though they are not immoral. Leiser, on the other hand, claims that homosexuality is not unnatural, at least not in any sense that would lead us to conclude that it is immoral. Thus, we have no reason to think it is immoral, and no reason to discriminate against anyone who is homosexual.

No matter how we resolve this issue, the debate between Levin and Leiser raises a fascinating theoretical question. Does an action's biological nature determine (or even influence) its morality? Some people, e.g., Sterba (ENVIRONMENT), claim that humans are biologically inclined to favor humans over non-human animals. Suppose Sterba is correct. Does that morally justify favoring humans over non-human ANIMALS? Many authors (e.g., Frey) say "No." These authors argue that moral discussion may be informed by, but not entirely settled by, biological facts. Thus, we should not discriminate against animals, even if we are biologically prone to do so. Warren and Marquis (ABORTION) would agree. Both argue (although from different sides of the abortion debate) that we cannot determine that a fetus has moral status, simply by knowing its species. Rather, we must determine what are morally relevant characteristics, and then decide if fetuses have them. For instance, we are likely to have some biological or natural tendency to favor our family, friends, and neighbors, over strangers. Some philosophers, like Williams (FAMILY AND FRIENDS), claim that such favoritism is not only justified, but essential for a fully moral life. Rachels, in the same section, argues that such favoritism would be immoral.

We see a similar dispute at play in the debate between Singer and Arthur over WORLD HUNGER. Arthur argues, similarly to Williams, that we may reasonably favor family and friends, while Singer, like Rachels, thinks we must embrace the principle of equality, even if it means we cannot treat family with the sort of favoritism we might like. Again we have confronted questions about the scope and limits of morality.

Further Reading

Baker, R. and Elliston, F. (eds) 1984: *Philosophy and Sex*. Buffalo, NY: Prometheus Books.

Mohr, R. 1988: *Gays/Justice: A Study of Ethics, Society, and Law*. New York: Columbia University Press.

Soble, A. (ed.) 1980: *The Philosophy of Sex: Con-temporary readings*. Totowa, NJ: Littlefield, Adams.

Taylor, R. 1982: *Having Loving Affairs*. Buffalo, NY: Prometheus Books.

Vannoy, R. 1980: *Sex without Love: A Philosophical Exploration*. Buffalo, NY: Prometheus Books.

18

What's Wrong with Rape

Pamela Foa

It is clear that rape is wrong. It is equally clear that the wrongness of rape is not completely explained by its status as a criminal assault. Dispute begins, however, when we attempt to account for the special features of rape, the ways in which its wrongness goes beyond its criminal character. I shall argue against those who maintain that the special wrongness of rape arises from and is completely explained by a societal refusal to recognize women as *people*. I shall offer a different explanation: The special wrongness of rape is due to, and is only an exaggeration of, the wrongness of our sexual interactions in general. Thus, a clear analysis of the special wrongness of rape will help indicate some of the essential features of healthy, non-rapine sexual interactions.

1. The Wrongness of Rape Goes Beyond its Criminality

It is to be expected during this period of resurgent feminism that rape will be seen primarily as a manifestation of how women are mistreated in our society. For example, consider these remarks of Simone de Beauvoir:

> All men are drawn to B[rigitte] B[ardot]'s seductiveness, but that does not mean that they are kindly disposed towards her.... They are unwilling to give up their role of lord and master.... Freedom and full consciousness remain their [the men's] right and privilege.... In the game of love BB is as much a hunter as she is a prey. The male is an object to her, just as she is to him. And that is precisely what wounds the masculine pride. In the Latin countries where men cling to the myth of "the woman as object," BB's naturalness seems to them more perverse than any possible sophistication. It is to assert that one is man's fellow and equal, to recognize that between the woman and him there is a mutual desire and pleasure....
>
> But the male feels uncomfortable if, instead of a doll of flesh and blood, he holds in his arms a conscious being who is sizing him up. "You realize," an average Frenchman once said to me, "that when a man finds a woman attractive, he wants to be able to pinch her behind." A ribald gesture reduces a woman to a thing that a man can do with as he pleases without worrying about what goes on in her mind and heart and body.[1]

And rape is apparently the quintessential instance of women being viewed as objects, of women being treated as entities other than, and morally inferior to, men. It is implicit in this object-view that if men, and therefore society, viewed women as full moral equals, rape would be an assault no different in kind than any other. Thus, it is a consequence of this view that the special wrongness of rape is to be found in the nonsexual aspects of the act.

To this end, Marilyn Frye and Carolyn Shafer suggest in their paper "Rape and Respect" that the wrongness of rape is two-fold: first, it is the use of a person without her consent in the performance of an act or event which is against her own best interests; and second, it is a social means of reinforcing the status of women as kinds of entities who lack and ought to lack the full privileges of personhood – importantly, the freedom to move as they will through what is rightfully their domain.[2] What is good about this account is that it provides one way of understanding the sense of essential violation of one's *person* (and not mere sexual abuse), which seems to be the natural concomitant of rape.

This account, further, gives one explanation for the continuous social denial of the common fact of criminal rape. On this view, to recognize rape as a criminal act, one must recognize the domains of women. But if domains are inextricably connected with personhood – if personhood, in fact, is to be analyzed in terms of domains – then it ought to be obvious that where there is no domain there can be no criminal trespass of domain; there can only be misperceptions or misunderstandings. To recognize domains of consent is to recognize the existence of people at their centers. Without such centers, there can be no rape.

Unfortunately, I do not believe that this kind of account can serve as an adequate explanation of what is wrong with rape. I find irrelevant its emphasis on the ontological status of women as persons of the first rank. It is granted that in any act of rape a person is used without proper regard to her personhood, but this is true of every kind of assault. If there is an additional wrongness to rape, it must be that more is wrong than the mere treatment of a person by another person without proper regard for her personhood. Later in this paper, I shall show that there is no need to differentiate ontologically between victim and assailant in order to explain the special wrongness of rape. However, it is important to recognize that rape is profoundly wrong even if it is not an act between ontological equals.

The special wrongness of rape cannot be traced to the fact that in this act men are not recognizing the full array of moral and legal rights and privileges which accrue to someone of equal status. Rape of children is at least as heinous as rape of adults, though few actually believe that children have or ought to have the same large domain of consent adults (male and female) ought to have. In part, this is what is so disturbing about a recent English decision I shall discuss in a moment: it seems to confuse the ontological with the moral. Men's wishes, intentions, and beliefs are given a different (and more important) weight, just because they are (wrongly in this case, perhaps rightly in the case of children) viewed as different kinds of entities than women.

But even if one thinks that women are not people, or that all people (for example, children) do not have the same rights or, prima facie, the same domains of consent, it seems that rape is still especially horrible, awful in a way that other assaults are not. There is, for example, something deeply distressing, though not necessarily criminal, about raping one's pet dog. It is disturbing in ways no ordinary assault, even upon a person, seems to be disturbing. It may here be objected that what accounts for the moral outrage in these two cases is that the first is an instance of pedophilia, and the second of bestiality. That is, the special wrongness of these acts is due to the "unnatural" direction of the sexual impulse, rather than to the abusive circumstances of the fulfillment of a "natural" sexual impulse.

I would argue in response that outrage at "unnatural" acts is misdirected and inappropriate.

The notion that acting "against" nature is immoral stems from the false belief that how things are in the majority of cases is, morally speaking, how things always ought to be. Acting unnaturally is not acting immorally unless there is a moral design to the natural order – and there is no such structure to it. This means, then, that if it is reasonable to feel that something very wrong has occurred in the above two cases, then it must be because they are rapes and not because they are "unnatural acts." However, even if this argument is not conclusive, it must be agreed that the random raping of a mentally retarded adult is clearly wrong even though such an individual does not, in our society, have all the legal and moral rights of normal people.[3]

Of course, another very reasonable point to make here may well be that it is not just people who have domains, and that what is wrong with rape is the invasion by one being into another's domain without consent or right. But if something like this were true, then rape would be wrong because it was an "incursion" into a domain. This would make it wrong in the same way that other assaults are wrong. The closer the incursion comes to the center of a person's identity, the worse the act.

The problem here is that such an argument suggests that rape is wrong in the same way, and only the same way, that other assaults are wrong. And yet the evidence contradicts this. There is an emotional concomitant to this assault, one that is lacking in nonsexual criminal assaults. What must be realized is that when it comes to sexual matters, people – in full recognition of the equal ontological status of their partners – treat each other abominably. Contrary to the Frye/Shafer theory, I believe that liberated men and women – people who have no doubts about the moral or ontological equality of the sexes – can and do have essentially rape-like sexual lives.

The following case is sufficient to establish that it is not just the assault upon one's person, or the intrusion into one's domain, that makes for the special features of rape. In New York twenty or so years ago, there was a man who went around Manhattan slashing people with a very sharp knife. He did not do this as part of any robbery or other further bodily assault. His end was simply to stab people. Although he was using people against their own best interests, and without their consent – that is, although he was broadly violating domains – to be the victim of the Mad Slasher was not to have been demeaned or dirtied as a person in the way that the victim of rape is demeaned or dirtied. It was not to be wronged or devalued in the same way that to be raped is to be wronged or devalued. No one ever accused any of the victims of provoking, initiating, or enjoying the attack.

Yet the public morality about rape suggests that unless one is somehow mutilated, broken, or killed in addition to being raped, one is suspected of having provoked, initiated, complied in, consented to, or even enjoyed the act. It is this public response, the fear of such a response and the belief (often) in the rationality of such a response (even from those who do unequivocally view you as a person) that seems to make rape especially horrible.

Thus, what is especially bad about rape is a function of its place in our society's sexual views, not in our ontological views. There is, of course, nothing necessary about these views, but until they change, no matter what progress is made in the fight for equality between the sexes, rape will remain an especially awful act.

2. Sex, Intimacy, and Pleasure

Our response to rape brings into focus our inner feelings about the nature, purpose, and morality of all sexual encounters and of ourselves as sexual beings. Two areas which seem immediately problematic are the relation between sex and intimacy and the relation between sex and pleasure.

Our Victorian ancestors believed that sex in the absence of (at least marital) intimacy was morally wrong and that the only women who experienced sexual pleasure were nymphomaniacs.[4] Freud's work was revolutionary in part just because he challenged the view of "good" women and children as asexual creatures.[5] Only with Masters and Johnson's work, however, has there been a full scientific recognition of the capacity of ordinary women for sexual pleasure.[6] But though it is now recognized that sexual pleasure exists for all people at all stages of life and is, in its own right, a morally permissible goal, this contemporary attitude is still dominated by a Victorian atmosphere. It remains the common feeling that it is a kind of pleasure which should be experienced only in private and only between people who are and intend to be otherwise intimate. Genital pleasure is private not only in our description of its physical location, but also in our conception of its occurrence or occasion.

For the rape victim, the special problem created by the discovery of pleasure in sex is that now some people believe that *every* sex act must be pleasurable to some extent, including rape.[7] Thus, it is believed by some that the victim in a rape must at some level be enjoying herself – and that this enjoyment in a non-intimate, non-private environment is shameful. What is especially wrong about rape, therefore, is that it makes evident the essentially sexual nature of women, and this has been viewed, from the time of Eve through the time of Victoria, as cause for their humiliation. Note that on this view the special evil of rape is due to the feminine character and not to that of her attacker.[8]

The additional societal attitude that sex is moral only between intimates creates a further dilemma in assessing the situation of the rape victim. On the one hand, if it is believed that the sex act itself creates an intimate relationship between two people, then, by necessity, the rape victim experiences intimacy with her assailant. This may incline one to deny the fact of the rape by pointing to the fact of the intimacy. If one does not believe that sex itself creates intimacy between the actors, but nonetheless believes that sex is immoral in the absence of intimacy, then the event of sex in the absence of an intimate relationship, even though involuntary, is cause for public scorn and humiliation. For the rape victim, to acknowledge the rape is to acknowledge one's immorality. Either way, the victim has violated the social sexual taboos and she must therefore be ostracized.

What is important is no longer that one is the victim of an assault, but rather that one is the survivor of a social transgression. This is the special burden that the victim carries.

There is support for my view in Gary Wills's review of Tom Wicker's book about the Attica prisoners' revolt.[9] What needs to be explained is the apparently peculiar way in which the safety of the prisoners' hostages was ignored in the preparations for the assault on the prison and in the assault itself. What strikes me as especially important in this event is that those outside the prison walls treated the *guards* exactly like the *prisoners*. The critical similarity is the alleged participation in taboo sexual activity, where such activity is seen as a paradigm of humiliating behavior. In his review Wills says,

Sexual fantasy played around Attica's walls like invisible lightning. Guards told their families that all the inmates were animals. . . .

When the assault finally came, and officers mowed down the hostages along with the inmates, an almost religious faith kept faked stories alive against all the evidence – that the hostages were found castrated; that those still living had been raped. . . . None of it was true, but the guards knew what degradation the prisoners had been submitted to, and the kind of response that might call for. . . .

One has to go very far down into the human psyche to understand what went on in that placid town. . . . The bloodthirsty hate of the local community was so obvious by the time of the assault that even Rockefeller . . . ordered that no correction personnel join the attack. . . . [Nonetheless] eleven men managed to go in. . . . Did they come to save the hostages, showing more care for them than outsiders could? Far from it. They fired as early and indiscriminately as the rest. Why? I am afraid Mr Wicker is a bit too decent to understand what was happening, though his own cultural background gives us a clue. Whenever a white girl was caught with a black in the old South, myth demanded that a charge of rape be brought and the "boy" be lynched. But a shadowy ostracism was inflicted on the girl. Did she fight back? Might she undermine the myth with a blurted tale or a repeated episode? At any rate, she was tainted. She had, willed she or nilled she, touched the untouchable and acquired her own evil halo of contamination. Taboos take little account of "intention." In the same way, guards caught in that yard were tainted goods. . . . They were an embarrassment. The white girl may sincerely have struggled with her black assailant; but even to imagine that resistance was defiling – and her presence made people imagine it. She was a public pollution – to be purged. Is this [comparison] fanciful? Even Wicker . . . cannot understand the attitude of those in charge who brought no special medical units to Attica before the attack began. . . . The lynch mob may kill the girl in its urgency to get at the boy – and it will regret this less than it admits.[10]

Accounts like the one offered by Frye and Shafer might explain why the *prisoners* were treated so callously by the assaulting troops, but they cannot explain the brutal treatment of the hostages. Surely they cannot say that the guards who were hostages were not and had never been viewed as people, as ontological equals, by the general society. And yet there was the same special horror in being a hostage at Attica as there is for a woman who has been raped. In both cases the *victim* has acquired a "halo of contamination" which permanently taints. And this cannot be explained by claiming that in both cases society is denying personhood or domains of consent to the victim.

The victim in sexual assault cases is as much a victim of our confused beliefs about sex as of the assault itself. The tremendous strains we put on such victims are a cruel result of our deep confusion about the place of, and need for, sexual relationships and the role of pleasure and intimacy in those relationships.

In spite of the fact, I believe, that as a society we share the *belief* that sex is only justified in intimate relationships, we act to avoid real intimacy at almost any cost. We seem to be as baffled as our predecessors were about the place of intimacy in our sexual and social lives. And this is, I think, because we are afraid that real intimacy creates or unleashes sexually wanton relationships, licentious lives – and this we view as morally repugnant. At the same time, we believe that sex in the absence of an intimate relationship is whoring and is therefore also morally repugnant. It is this impossible conflict which I think shows us that we will be able to make sense of our response to rape only if we look at rape as the model of all our sexual interactions, not as its antithesis.

3. The Model of Sex: Rape

Though we may sometimes speak as though sexual activity is most pleasurable between friends, we do not teach each other to treat our sexual partners as friends. Middle-class children, whom I take to be our cultural models, are instructed from the earliest possible time to ignore their sexual feelings. Long before intercourse can be a central issue, when children are prepubescent, boys are instructed to lunge for a kiss and girls are instructed to permit nothing more than a peck on the cheek. This encouragement of miniature adult sexual behavior is instructive on several levels.

It teaches the child that courting behavior is rarely spontaneous and rarely something which gives pleasure to the people involved – that is, it is not like typical playing with friends. It gives the child a glimpse of how adults do behave, or are expected to behave, and therefore of what is expected in future life and social interactions. Importantly, boys are instructed *not* to be attentive to the claims of girls with respect to their desires and needs. And girls are instructed *not* to consult their feelings as a means of or at least a check on what behavior they should engage in.

Every American girl, be she philosopher-to-be or not, is well acquainted with the slippery-slope argument by the time she is ten. She is told that if she permits herself to become involved in anything more than a peck on the cheek, anything but the most innocent type of sexual behavior, she will inevitably become involved in behavior that will result in intercourse and pregnancy. And such behavior is wrong. That is, she is told that if she acquiesces to any degree to her feelings, then she will be doing something immoral.

Meanwhile, every American boy is instructed, whether explicitly or not, that the girls have been given this argument (as a weapon) and that therefore, since everything that a girl says will be a reflection of this argument (and not of her feelings), they are to ignore everything that she says.

Girls are told never to consult their feelings (they can only induce them to the edge of the slippery slope); they are always to say "no." Boys are told that it is a sign of their growing manhood to be able to get a girl way beyond the edge of the slope, and that it is standard procedure for girls to say "no" independently of their feelings. Thus, reasonably enough, boys act as far as one can tell independently of the explicit information they are currently receiving from the girl.

For women, it is very disconcerting to find that from the age of eight or nine or ten, one's reports of one's feelings are no longer viewed as accurate, truthful, important, or interesting. R. D. Laing, the English psychiatrist and theorist, claims that it is this type of adult behavior which creates the environment in which insanity best finds its roots.[11] It is clear, at least, that such behavior is not a model of rationality or health. In any event, rape is a case where only the pretense of listening has been stripped away. It is the essence of what we have all been trained to expect.

In a sexually healthier society, men and women might be told to engage in that behavior which gives them pleasure as long as that pleasure is not (does not involve actions) against anyone's will (including coerced actions) and does not involve them with responsibilities they cannot or will not meet (emotional, physical, or financial).

But as things are now, boys and girls have no way to tell each other what gives them pleasure and what not, what frightens them and what not; there are only violence, threats of violence, and appeals to informing on one or the other to some dreaded peer or parental group. This is a very high-risk, high-stake game, which women and girls, at least, often feel may easily become rape (even though it is usually played for little more than a quick feel in the back seat of the car or corner of the family sofa). But the ultimate consequences of this type of instruction are not so petty. Consider, for example, the effects of a recent English high-court decision:

Now, according to the new interpretation, no matter how much a woman screams and fights, the accused rapist can be cleared by claiming he believed the victim consented, even though his belief may be considered unreasonable or irrational.

On a rainy night seven months ago, a London housewife and mother of three claims she was dragged into this dilapidated shed. Annie Baker says she screamed for help and she fought but she was raped. Mrs Baker lost her case in court because the man claimed he thought when she said no, she meant yes.

One member of Parliament [predicts juries will] "now have the rapist saying that the woman asked for what she got and she wanted what they [*sic*] gave her."

However, the Head of the British Law Society maintains, "Today juries are prepared to accept that the relationship between the sexes has become much more promiscuous, and they have to look much more carefully to see whether the woman has consented under modern conditions. . . . One mustn't readily assume that a woman did not consent, because all indications are that there is a greater willingness to consent today than there was thirty years ago."[12]

"The question to be answered in this case," said Lord Cross of Chelsea, "as I see it, is whether, according to the ordinary use of the English language, a man can be said to have committed rape if he believed that the woman was consenting to the intercourse. I do not think he can."[13]

This is the most macabre extension imaginable of our early instruction. It is one which makes initially implausible and bizarre any suggestion that the recent philosophical analyses of sexuality as the product of a mutual desire for communication – or even for orgasm or sexual satisfaction – bear any but the most tangential relation to reality.[14]

As we are taught, sexual desires are desires women ought not to have and men must have. This is the model which makes necessary an eternal battle of the sexes. It is the model which explains why rape is the prevalent model of sexuality. It has the further virtue of explaining the otherwise puzzling attitude of many that women will cry "rape" falsely at the slightest provocation. It explains, too, why men believe that no woman can be raped. It is as though what was mildly unsatisfactory at first (a girl's saying "no") becomes, over time, increasingly erotic, until the ultimate turn-on becomes a woman's cry of "rape!"

4. An Alternative: Sex between Friends

Understanding what's wrong with rape is difficult just because it is a member of the most common species of social encounter. To establish how rape is wrong is to establish that we have *all* been stepping to the wrong beat. Rape is only different in degree from the quintessential sexual relationship: marriage.

As Janice Moulton has noted, recent philosophical attention to theories of sexuality seems primarily concerned with sex between strangers.[15] On my view, we can explain this primary interest by noticing that our courting procedures are structured so that the couple must remain essentially estranged from each other. They do not ever talk or listen to each other with the respect and charity of friends. Instead, what is taken as the height of the erotic is sex without intimacy.

As long as we remain uncertain of the legitimacy of sexual pleasure, it will be impossible to give up our rape model of sexuality. For it can only be given up when we are willing to talk openly to each other without shame, embarrassment, or coyness about sex. Because only then will we not be too afraid to listen to each other.

Fortunately, to give this up requires us to make friends of our lovers.[16] Once we understand that intimacy enlarges the field of friendship, we can use some of the essential features of friendship as part of the model for sexual interaction, and we can present the pleasures of friendship as a real alternative to predatory pleasures.

I am not here committing myself to the view that the correct model for lovers is that of friends. Though I believe lovers involved in a healthy relationship have a fairly complex friendship, and though I am at a loss to find any important feature of a relationship between lovers which is not also one between friends, it may well be that the two relationships are merely closely related and not, in the end, explainable with the identical model.

It remains an enormously difficult task to throw over our anachronistic beliefs, and to resolve the conflict we feel about the sexual aspects of ourselves. But once this is done, not only will there be the obvious benefits of being able to exchange ignorance and denial of ourselves and others for knowledge, and fear for friendship, but we will also be able to remove the taboo from sex – even from rape. There will be no revelation, no reminder in the act of rape which we will need so badly to repress or deny that we must transform the victim into a guilt-bearing survivor. An act of rape will no longer remind us of the "true" nature of sex or our sexual desires.

Where there is nothing essentially forbidden about the fact of our sexual desires, the victim of rape will no longer be subject to a taboo or be regarded as dirty and in need of societal estrangement. The victim can then be regarded as having been grievously insulted, without simultaneously and necessarily having been permanently injured.

Further, if the model of sexual encounters is altered, there will no longer be any motivation for blaming the victim of rape. Since sex and rape will no longer be equated, there will be no motive for covering our own guilt or shame about the rapine nature of sex in general by transferring our guilt to the victim and ostracizing her. Rape will become an unfortunate aberration, the act of a criminal individual, rather than a symbol of our systematic ill-treatment and denial of each other.

Notes

1 Simone de Beauvoir, *Brigitte Bardot and the Lolita Syndrome* (London: New English Library, 1962), pp. 28, 30, 32.

2 Frye and Shafer characterize a domain as "where . . . a person . . . lives. . . . Since biological life and health are prerequisites for the pursuit of any other interests and goals, . . . everything necessary for their maintenance and sustenance evidently will fall very close to the center of the domain. Anything which exerts an influence on . . . a person's will or dulls its intelligence or affects its own sense of its identity . . . also comes very near the center of the domain. Whatever has a relatively permanent effect on the person, whatever affects its relatively constant surroundings, whatever causes it discomfort or distress – in short, whatever a person has to live with – is likely to fall squarely within its domain" ("Rape and Respect," in *Feminism and Philosophy*, ed. Mary Vetterling-Braggin, Frederick Elliston, and Jane English (Totowa, NJ: Littlefield-Adams, 1977).

3 This societal attitude, however, that the mentally retarded are not the equals of normal people is not one with which I associate myself.

4 Françoise Basch, *Relative Creatures: Victorian Women in Society and the Novel* (New York: Schocken Books, 1974), pp. 8–9, 270–71.

5 See *The Basic Writings of Sigmund Freud*, ed. A. A. Brill (New York: Random House, 1948), pp. 553–633.

6 William H. Masters and Virginia E. Johnson, *Human Sexual Response* (Boston: Little, Brown, 1966).

7 It may well be that Freud's theory of human sexuality is mistakenly taken to support this view. See Sigmund Freud, *A General Introduction to Psychoanalysis* (New York: Washington Square Press, 1962), pp. 329–47.

8 What is a complete non sequitur, of course, is that the presence of such pleasure is sufficient to establish that no criminal assault has occurred. The two events are completely independent.

9 Tom Wicker, *A Time to Die* (New York: Quadrangle Books, 1975).

10 Gary Wills, "The Human Sewer," *New York Review of Books*, 3 April 1975, p. 4.

11 See, for example, R. D. Laing and A. Esterson, *Sanity, Madness and the Family* (Baltimore: Penguin, Pelican Books, 1970).

12 CBS Evening News with Walter Cronkite, 22 May 1975.

13 *New American Movement Newspaper*, May 1975, p. 8.

14 See R. C. Solomon, "Sex and Perversion," Tom Nagel, "Sexual Perversion," and Janice Moulton, "Sex and Reference," in *Philoso-phy and Sex*, ed. Robert Baker and Frederick Elliston (Buffalo, NY: Prometheus Books, 1975).

15 Janice Moulton, "Sex and Sex," unpublished manuscript.

16 See Lyla O'Driscoll, "On the Nature and Value of Marriage," in *Feminism and Philosophy*, ed. Mary Vetterling-Braggin, Frederick Elliston, and Jane English (Totowa, NJ: Littlefield-Adams, 1977).

19

Morality and Human Sexuality

Vincent C. Punzo

If one sees man's moral task as being simply that of not harming anyone, that is if one sees this task in purely negative terms, he will certainly not accept the argument to be presented in the following section. However, if one accepts the notion of the morality of aspiration, if one accepts the view that man's moral task involves the positive attempt to live up to what is best in man, to give reality to what he sees to be the perfection of himself as a human subject, the argument may be acceptable.

Sexuality and the Human Subject

[Prior discussion] has left us with the question as to whether sexual intercourse is a type of activity that is similar to choosing a dinner from a menu. This question is of utmost significance in that one's view of the morality of premarital intercourse seems to depend on the significance that one gives to the sexual encounter in human life. Those such as [John] Wilson and [Eustace] Chesser who see nothing immoral about the premarital character of sexual intercourse seem to see sexual intercourse as being no different from myriad other purely aesthetic matters. This point is seen in Chesser's questioning of the reason for demanding permanence in the relationship of sexual partners when we do not see such permanence as being important to other human relationships.[1] It is also seen in his asking why we raise a moral issue about premarital coition when two people may engage in it, with the resulting social and psychological consequences being no different than if they had gone to a movie.[2]

Wilson most explicitly makes a case for the view that sexual intercourse does not differ significantly from other human activities. He holds that people think that there is a logical difference between the question "Will you engage in sexual intercourse with me?" and the question "Will you play tennis with me?" only because they are influenced by the acquisitive character of contemporary society.[3] Granted that the two questions may be identical from the purely formal perspective of logic, the ethician must move beyond this perspective to a consideration of their content. Men and women find themselves involved in many different relationships: for example, as buyer–seller, employer–employee, teacher–student, lawyer–client, and partners or competitors in certain games such as tennis or bridge. Is there any morally significant difference between these relationships and sexual intercourse? We cannot examine all the possible relationships into which a man and woman can enter, but we will consider the employer–employee relationship in order to get some perspective on the distinctive character of the sexual relationship.

A man pays a woman to act as his secretary. What rights does he have over her in such a situation? The woman agrees to work a certain number of hours during the day taking dictation, typing letters, filing reports, arranging appointments and flight schedules, and greeting clients and competitors. In short, we can say that the man has rights to certain of the woman's services or skills. The use of the word "services" may lead some to conclude that this relationship is not significantly different from the relationship between a prostitute and her client in that the prostitute also offers her "services."

It is true that we sometimes speak euphemistically of a prostitute offering her services to a man for a sum of money, but if we are serious about our quest for the difference between the sexual encounter and other types of human relationships, it is necessary to drop euphemisms and face the issue directly. The man and woman who engage in sexual intercourse are giving their bodies, the most intimate physical expression of themselves, over to the other. Unlike the man who plays tennis with a woman, the man who has sexual relations with her has literally entered her. A man and woman engaging in sexual intercourse have united themselves as intimately and as totally as is physically possible for two human beings. Their union is not simply a union of organs, but is as intimate and as total a physical union of two selves as is possible of achievement. Granted the character of this union, it seems strange to imply that there is no need for a man and a woman to give any more thought to the question of whether they should engage in sexual intercourse than to the question of whether they should play tennis.

In opposition to Wilson, I think that it is the acquisitive character of our society that has blinded us to the distinction between the two activities. Wilson's and Chesser's positions seem to imply that exactly the same moral considerations ought to apply to a situation in which a housewife is bartering with a butcher for a few pounds of pork chops and the situation in which two human beings are deciding whether sexual intercourse ought to be an ingredient of their relationship. So long as the butcher does not put his thumb on the scale in the weighing process, so long as he is truthful in stating that the meat is actually pork, so long as the woman pays the proper amount with the proper currency, the trade is perfectly moral. Reflecting on sexual intercourse from the same sort of economic perspective, one can say that so long as the sexual partners are truthful in reporting their freedom from contagious venereal diseases and so long as they are truthful in reporting that they are interested in the activity for the mere pleasure of it or to try out their sexual techniques, there is nothing immoral about such activity. That in the one case pork chops are being exchanged for money whereas in the other the decision concerns the most complete and intimate merging of one's self with another makes no difference to the moral evaluation of the respective cases.

It is not surprising that such a reductionistic outlook should pervade our thinking on sexual matters, since in our society sexuality is used to sell everything from shave cream to underarm deodorants, to soap, to mouthwash, to cigarettes, and to automobiles. Sexuality has come to play so large a role in our commercial lives that it is not surprising that our sexuality should itself come to be treated as a commodity governed by the same moral rules that govern any other economic transaction.

Once sexuality is taken out of this commercial framework, once the character of the sexual encounter is faced directly and squarely, we will come to see that Doctor Mary

Calderone has brought out the type of questions that ought to be asked by those contemplating the introduction of sexual intercourse into their relationships: "How many times, and how casually, are you willing to invest a portion of your total self, and to be the custodian of a like investment from the other person, without the sureness of knowing that these investments are being made for keeps?"[4] These questions come out of the recognition that the sexual encounter is a definitive experience, one in which the physical intimacy and merging involves also a merging of the nonphysical dimensions of the partners. With these questions, man moves beyond the negative concern with avoiding his or another's physical and psychological harm to the question of what he is making of himself and what he is contributing to the existential formation of his partner as a human subject.

If we are to make a start toward responding to Calderone's questions we must cease talking about human selfhood in abstraction. The human self is an historical as well as a physical being. He is a being who is capable of making at least a portion of his past an object of his consciousness and thus is able to make this past play a conscious role in his present and in his looking toward the future. He is also a being who looks to the future, who faces tomorrow with plans, ideals, hopes, and fears. The very being of a human self involves his past and his movement toward the future. Moreover, the human self is not completely shut off in his own past and future. Men and women are capable of consciously and purposively uniting themselves in a common career and venture. They can commit themselves to sharing the future with another, sharing it in all its aspects – in its fortunes and misfortunes, in its times of happiness and times of tragedy. Within the lives of those who have so committed themselves to each other, sexual intercourse is a way of asserting and confirming the fullness and totality of their mutual commitment.

Unlike those who have made such a commitment and who come together in the sexual act in the fullness of their selfhood, those who engage in premarital sexual unions and who have made no such commitment act as though they can amputate their bodily existence and the most intimate physical expression of their selfhood from their existence as historical beings. Granting that there may be honesty on the verbal level in that two people engaging in premarital intercourse openly state that they are interested only in the pleasure of the activity, the fact remains that such unions are morally deficient because they lack existential integrity in that there is a total merging and union on a physical level, on the one hand, and a conscious decision not to unite any other dimension of themselves, on the other hand. Their sexual union thus involves a "depersonalization" of their bodily existence, an attempt to cut off the most intimate physical expression of their respective selves from their very selfhood. The mutual agreement of premarital sex partners is an agreement to merge with the other not as a self, but as a body which one takes unto oneself, which one possesses in a most intimate and total fashion for one's own pleasure or designs, allowing the other to treat oneself in the same way. It may be true that no physical or psychological harm may result from such unions, but such partners have failed to existentially incorporate human sexuality, which is at the very least the most intimate physical expression of the human self, into the character of this selfhood.

In so far as premarital sexual unions separate the intimate and total physical union that is sexual intercourse from any commitment to the self in his historicity, human sexuality, and consequently the human body, have been fashioned into external things or objects to be handed over totally to someone else, whenever one feels that he can get possession of another's body, which he can use for his own purposes.[5] The human body has thus been treated no differently from the pork chops spoken of previously or from any other object or commodity which human beings exchange and haggle over in their day-to-day transactions. One hesitates to use the word that might be used to capture the moral value that has been sacrificed in premarital unions because in our day the word has taken on a completely negative meaning at best, and, at worst, it has become a word used by "sophisticates" to mock or deride certain attitudes toward human sexuality. However, because the word "chastity" has been thus abused is no reason to leave it in the hands of those who have misrepresented the human value to which it gives expression.

The chaste person has often been described as one intent on denying his sexuality. The value of chastity as conceived in this section is in direct opposition to this description. It is the unchaste person who is separating himself from his sexuality, who is willing to exchange human bodies as one would exchange money for tickets to a baseball game – honestly and with no commitment of self to self. Against this alienation of one's sexuality from one's self, an alienation that makes one's sexuality an object, which is to be given to another in exchange for his objectified sexuality, chastity affirms the integrity of the self in his bodily and historical existence. The sexuality of man is seen as an integral part of his subjectivity. Hence, the chaste man rejects depersonalized sexual relations as a reduction of man in his most intimate physical being to the status of an object or pure instrument for another. He asserts that man is a subject and end in himself, not in some trans-temporal, nonphysical world, but in the historical–physical world in which he carries on his moral task and where he finds his fellow man. He will not freely make of himself in his bodily existence a thing to be handed over to another's possession, nor will he ask that another treat his own body in this way. The total physical intimacy of sexual intercourse will be an expression of total union with the other self on all levels of their beings. Seen from this perspective, chastity is one aspect of man's attempt to attain existential integrity, to accept his body as a dimension of his total personality.

In concluding this section, it should be noted that I have tried to make a case against the morality of premarital sexual intercourse even in those cases in which the partners are completely honest with each other. There is reason to question whether the complete honesty, to which those who see nothing immoral in such unions refer, is as a matter of fact actually found very often among premarital sex partners. We may well have been dealing with textbook cases which present these unions in their best light. One may be pardoned for wondering whether sexual intercourse often occurs under the following conditions: "Hello, my name is Josiah. I am interested in having a sexual experience with you. I can assure you that I am good at it and that I have no communicable disease. If it sounds good to you and if you have taken the proper contraceptive precautions, we might have a go at it. Of course, I want to make it clear to you that I am interested only in the sexual experience and that I have no intention of making any long-range commitment to you." If those who defend the morality of premarital sexual unions so long as they are honestly entered into, think that I have misrepresented what they mean by honesty, then they must specify what they mean by an honest premarital union. . . .

Marriage as a Total Human Commitment

The preceding argument against the morality of premarital sexual unions was not based on the view that the moral character of marriage rests on a legal certificate or on a legal or religious ceremony. The argument was not directed against "preceremonial" intercourse, but against premarital intercourse. Morally speaking, a man and woman are married when they make the mutual and total commitment to share the problems and prospects of their historical existence in the world. . . .

. . . A total commitment to another means a commitment to him in his historical existence.

Such a commitment is not simply a matter of words or of feelings, however strong. It involves a full existential sharing on the part of two beings of the burdens, opportunities, and challenges of their historical existence.

Granted the importance that the character of their commitment to each other plays in determining the moral quality of a couple's sexual encounter, it is clear that there may be nothing immoral in the behavior of couples who engage in sexual intercourse before participating in the marriage ceremony. For example, it is foolish to say that two people who are totally committed to each other and who have made all the arrangements to live this commitment are immoral if they engage in sexual intercourse the night before the marriage ceremony. Admittedly this position can be abused by those who have made a purely verbal commitment, a commitment which will be carried out in some vague and ill-defined future. At some time or other, they will unite their two lives totally by setting up house together and by actually undertaking the task of meeting the economic, social, legal, medical responsibilities that are involved in living this commitment. Apart from the reference to a vague and amorphous future time when they will share the full responsibility for each other, their commitment presently realizes itself in going to dances, sharing a box of popcorn at Saturday night movies, and sharing their bodies whenever they can do so without taking too great a risk of having the girl become pregnant.

Having acknowledged that the position advanced in this section can be abused by those who would use the word "commitment" to rationalize what is an interest only in the body of the other person, it must be pointed out that neither the ethician nor any other human being can tell two people whether they actually have made the commitment that is marriage or are mistaking a "warm glow" for such a commitment. There comes a time when this issue falls out of the area of moral philosophy and into the area of practical wisdom. . . .

The characterization of marriage as a total commitment between two human beings may lead some to conclude that the marriage ceremony is a wholly superfluous affair. It must be admitted that people may be morally married without having engaged in a marriage ceremony. However, to conclude from this point that the ceremony is totally meaningless is to lose sight of the social character of human beings. The couple contemplating marriage do not exist in a vacuum, although there may be times when they think they do. Their existences reach out beyond their union to include other human beings. By making their commitment a matter of public record, by solemnly expressing it before the law and in the presence of their respective families and friends and, if they are religious people, in the presence of God and one of his ministers, they sink the roots of their commitment more deeply and extensively in the world in which they live, thus taking steps to provide for the future growth of their commitment to each other. The public expression of this commitment makes it more fully and more explicitly a part of a couple's lives and of the world in which they live. . . .

Notes

1 Eustace Chesser, *Unmarried Love* (New York: Pocket Books, 1965), p. 29.

2 *Ibid.*, pp. 35–6, see also p. 66.

3 John Wilson, *Logic and Sexual Morality* (Baltimore, MD: Penguin Books, 1965). See footnote 1, p. 67.

4 Mary Steichen Calderone, "The Case for Chastity," *Sex in America*, ed. Henry Anatole Grunwald (New York: Bantam Books, 1964), p. 147.

5 The psychoanalyst Rollo May makes an excellent point in calling attention to the tendency in contemporary society to exploit the human body as if it were only a machine. Rollo May, "The New Puritanism," *Sex in America*, pp. 161–4.

Plain Sex

Alan H. Goldman

I

Before we can get a sensible view of the relation of sex to morality, perversion, social regulation, and marriage, we require a sensible analysis of the concept itself; one which neither understates its animal pleasure nor overstates its importance within a theory or system of value. I say "before," but the order is not quite so clear, for questions in this area, as elsewhere in moral philosophy, are both conceptual and normative at the same time. Our concept of sex will partially determine our moral view of it, but as philosophers we should formulate a concept that will accord with its proper moral status. What we require here, as elsewhere, is "reflective equilibrium," a goal not achieved by traditional and recent analyses together with their moral implications. Because sexual activity, like other natural functions such as eating or exercising, has become imbedded in layers of cultural, moral, and superstitious superstructure, it is hard to conceive it in its simplest terms. But partially for this reason, it is only by thinking about plain sex that we can begin to achieve this conceptual equilibrium.

I shall suggest here that sex continues to be misrepresented in recent writings, at least in philosophical writings, and I shall criticize the predominant form of analysis which I term "means–end analysis." Such conceptions attribute a necessary external goal or purpose to sexual activity, whether it be reproduction, the expression of love, simple communication, or interpersonal awareness. They analyze sexual activity as a means to one of these ends, implying that sexual desire is a desire to reproduce, to love or be loved, or to communicate with others. All definitions of this type suggest false views of the relation of sex to perversion and morality by implying that sex which does not fit one of these models or fulfill one of these functions is in some way deviant or incomplete.

The alternative, simpler analysis with which I will begin is that sexual desire is desire for contact with another person's body and for the pleasure which such contact produces; sexual activity is activity which tends to fulfill such desire of the agent. Whereas Aristotle and Butler were correct in holding that pleasure is normally a byproduct rather than a goal of purposeful action, in the case of sex this is not so clear. The desire for another's body is, principally among other things, the desire for the pleasure that physical contact brings. On the other hand, it is not a desire for a particular sensation detachable from its causal context, a sensation which can be derived in other ways. This definition in terms of the general goal of sexual desire appears preferable to an attempt to more explicitly list or define specific sexual activities, for many activities such as kissing, embracing, massaging, or holding hands may or may not be sexual, depending upon the context and more specifically upon the purposes, needs, or desires into which such activities fit. The generality of the definition also represents a refusal (common in recent psychological texts) to overemphasize orgasm as the goal of sexual desire or genital sex as the only norm of sexual activity. . . .

Central to the definition is the fact that the goal of sexual desire and activity is the physical contact itself, rather than something else which this contact might express. By contrast, what I term "means–end analyses" posit ends which I take to be extraneous to plain sex, and they view sex as a means to these ends. Their fault lies not in defining sex in terms of its general goal, but in seeing plain sex as merely a means to other separable ends. I term these "means–end analyses" for convenience, although "means–separable-end ana-lyses," while too cumbersome, might be more fully explanatory. The desire for physical contact with another person is a minimal criterion for (normal) sexual desire, but is both necessary and sufficient to qualify normal desire as sexual. Of course, we may want to express other feelings through sexual acts in various contexts; but without the desire for the physical contact in and for itself, or when it is sought for other reasons, activities in which contact is involved are not predominantly sexual. Furthermore, the desire for physical contact in itself, without the wish to express affection or other feelings through it, is sufficient to render sexual the activity of the agent which fulfills it. Various activities with this goal alone, such as kissing and caressing in certain contexts, qualify as sexual even without the presence of genital symptoms of sexual excitement. The latter are not therefore necessary criteria for sexual activity.

This initial analysis may seem to some either over- or underinclusive. It might seem too broad in leading us to interpret physical contact as sexual desire in activities such as football and other contact sports. In these case, however, the desire is not for contact with another body per se, it is not directed toward a particular person for that purpose, and it is not the goal of the activity – the goal is winning or exercising or knocking someone down or displaying one's prowess. If the desire is purely for contact with another specific person's body, then to interpret it as sexual does not seem an exaggeration. A slightly more difficult case is that of a baby's desire to be cuddled and our natural response in wanting to cuddle it. In the case of the baby, the desire may be simply for the physical contact, for the pleasure of the caresses. If so, we may characterize this desire, especially in keeping with Freudian theory, as sexual or protosexual. It will differ nevertheless from full-fledged sexual desire in being more amorphous, not directed outward toward another specific person's body. It may also be that what the infant unconsciously desires is not physical contact per se but signs of affection, tenderness, or security, in which case we have further reason for hesitating to characterize its wants as clearly sexual. The intent of our response to the baby is often the showing of affection, not the pure physical contact, so that our definition in terms of action which fulfills sexual desire *on the part of the agent* does not capture such actions, whatever we say of the baby. (If it is intuitive to characterize our response as sexual as well, there is clearly no problem here for my analysis.) The same can be said of signs of affection (or in some cultures polite greeting) among men or women: these certainly need not be homo-sexual when the intent is only to show friendship, something extrinsic to plain sex although valuable when added to it.

Our definition of sex in terms of the desire for physical contact may appear too narrow in that a person's personality, not merely her or his body, may be sexually attractive to another, and in that looking or conversing in a certain way can be sexual in a given context without bodily contact. Nevertheless, it is not the contents of one's thoughts per se that are sexually appealing, but one's personality as embodied in certain manners of behavior. Furthermore, if a person is sexually attracted by another's personality, he or she will desire not just further conversation, but actual sexual contact. While looking at or conversing with someone can be interpreted as sexual in given contexts it is so when intended as preliminary to, and hence parasitic upon, elemental sexual interest. Voyeurism or viewing a porno-graphic movie qualifies as a sexual activity, but only as an imaginative substitute for the real thing (otherwise a deviation from the norm as expressed in our definition). The same is true of masturbation as a sexual activity without a partner.

That the initial definition indicates at least an ingredient of sexual desire and activity is too obvious to argue. We all know what sex is, at least in obvious cases, and do not need philosophers to tell us. My preliminary analysis is meant to serve as a contrast to what sex is not, at least, not necessarily. I concentrate upon the physically manifested desire for another's body, and I take as central the immersion in the physical aspect of one's own existence and attention to the physical embodiment of the other. One may derive pleasure in a sex act from expressing certain feelings to one's partner or from awareness of the attitude of one's partner, but sexual desire is essentially desire for physical contact itself: it is a bodily desire for the body of another that dominates our mental life for more or less brief periods. Traditional writings were correct to emphasize the purely physical or animal aspect of sex; they were wrong only in condemning it. This characterization of sex as an intensely pleasurable physical activity and acute physical desire may seem to some to capture only its barest level. But it is worth distinguishing and focusing upon this least common denominator in order to avoid the false views of sexual morality and perversion which emerge from thinking that sex is essentially something else.

II

We may turn then to what sex is not, to the arguments regarding supposed conceptual connections between sex and other activities which it is necessary to conceptually distin-guish. The most comprehensible attempt to build an extraneous purpose into the sex act identifies that purpose as reproduction, its primary biological function. While this may be "nature's" purpose, it certainly need not be ours (the analogy with eating, while sometimes overworked, is pertinent here). While this identification may once have had a rational basis which also grounded the identification of the value and morality of sex with that applicable to reproduction and childrearing, the development of contraception rendered the connec-tion weak. Methods of contraception are by now so familiar and so widely used that it is not necessary to dwell upon the changes wrought by these developments in the concept of sex itself and in a rational sexual ethic dependent upon that concept. In the past, the ever present possibility of children rendered the concepts of sex and sexual morality different from those required at present. There may be good reasons, if the presence and care of both mother and father are beneficial to children, for restricting reproduction to marriage. Inso-far as society has a legitimate role in protecting children's interests, it may be justified in giving marriage a legal status, although this question is complicated by the fact (among others) that children born to single mothers deserve no penalties. In any case, the point here is simply that these questions are irrelevant at the present time to those regarding the morality of sex and its potential social regulation. (Further connections with marriage will be discussed below.)

It is obvious that the desire for sex is not necessarily a desire to reproduce, that the psychological manifestation has become, if it were not always, distinct from its biological roots. There are many parallels, as previously mentioned, with other natural functions. The pleasures of eating and exercising are to a large extent independent of their roles in nourishment or health (as the junk-food industry discovered with a vengeance). Despite the obvious parallel with sex, there is still a tendency for many to think that sex acts which can be reproductive are, if not more moral or less immoral, at least more natural. These categories of morality and "naturalness," or normality, are not to be identified with each other, as will be argued below, and neither is applicable to sex by virtue of its connection to reproduction. The tendency to identify reproduction as the conceptually connected end of sex is most prevalent now in the pronouncements of the Catholic church. There the assumed analysis is clearly tied to a restrictive sexual morality according to which acts become immoral and unnatural when they are not oriented toward reproduction, a morality which has independent roots in the Christian sexual ethic as it derives from Paul. However, the means–end analysis fails to generate a consistent sexual ethic: homosexual and oral–genital sex is condemned while kissing or caressing, acts equally unlikely to lead in themselves to fertilization, even when properly characterized as sexual according to our definition, are not.

III

Before discussing further relations of means–end analyses to false or inconsistent sexual ethics and concepts of perversion, I turn to other examples of these analyses. One common position views sex as essentially an expression of love or affection between the partners. It is generally recognized that there are other types of love besides sexual, but sex itself is taken as an expression of one type, sometimes termed "romantic" love.[1] Various factors again ought to weaken this identification. First, there are other types of love besides that which it is appropriate to express sexually, and "romantic" love itself can be expressed in many other ways. I am not denying that sex can take on heightened value and meaning when it becomes a vehicle for the expression of feelings of love or tenderness, but so can many other usually mundane activities such as getting up early to make breakfast on Sunday, cleaning the house, and so on. Secondly, sex itself can be used to communicate many other emotions besides love, and, as I will argue below, can communicate nothing in particular and still be good sex.

On a deeper level, an internal tension is bound to result from an identification of sex, which I have described as a physical–psychological desire, with love as a long-term, deep emotional relationship between two individuals. As this type of relationship, love is permanent, at least in intent, and more or less exclusive. A normal person cannot deeply love more than a few individuals even in a lifetime. We may be suspicious that those who attempt or claim to love many love them weakly if at all. Yet, fleeting sexual desire can arise in relation to a variety of other individuals one finds sexually attractive. It may even be, as some have claimed, that sexual desire in humans naturally seeks variety, while this is obviously false of love. For this reason, monogamous sex, even if justified, almost always represents a sacrifice or the exercise of self-control on the part of the spouses, while monogamous love generally does not. There is no such thing as casual love in the sense in which I intend the term "love." It may occasionally happen that a spouse falls deeply in love with someone else (especially when sex is conceived in terms of love), but this is relatively rare in comparison to passing sexual desires for others; and while the former often indicates a weakness or fault in the marriage relation, the latter does not.

If love is indeed more exclusive in its objects than is sexual desire, this explains why those who view sex as essentially an expression of love would again tend to hold a repressive or restrictive sexual ethic. As in the case of reproduction, there may be good reasons for reserving the total commitment of deep love to the context of marriage and family – the normal personality may not withstand additional divisions of ultimate commitment and allegiance. There is no question that marriage itself is best sustained by a deep relation of love and affection; and even if love is not naturally monogamous, the benefits of family units to children provide additional reason to avoid serious commitments elsewhere which weaken family ties. It can be argued similarly that monogamous sex strengthens families by restricting and at the same time guaranteeing an outlet for sexual desire in marriage. But there is more force to the argument that recognition of a clear distinction between sex and love in society would help avoid disastrous marriages which result from adolescent confusion of the two when sexual desire is mistaken for permanent love, and would weaken damaging jealousies which arise in marriages in relation to passing sexual desires. The love and affection of a sound marriage certainly differs from the adolescent romantic variety, which is often a mere substitute for sex in the context of a repressive sexual ethic.

In fact, the restrictive sexual ethic tied to the means–end analysis in terms of love again has failed to be consistent. At least, it has not been applied consistently, but forms part of the double standard which has curtailed the freedom of women. It is predictable in light of this history that some women would now advocate using sex as another kind of means, as a political weapon or as a way to increase unjustly denied power and freedom. The inconsistency in the sexual ethic typically attached to the sex–love analysis, according to which it has generally been taken with a grain of salt when applied to men, is simply another example of the impossibility of tailoring a plausible moral theory in this area to a conception of sex which builds in conceptually extraneous factors.

I am not suggesting here that sex ought never to be connected with love or that it is not a more significant and valuable activity when it is. Nor am I denying that individuals need love as much as sex and perhaps emotionally need at least one complete relationship which encompasses both. Just as sex can express love and take on heightened significance when it does, so love is often naturally accompanied by an intermittent desire for sex. But again love is accompanied appropriately by desires for other shared activities as well. What makes the desire for sex seem more intimately connected with love is the intimacy which is seen to be a natural feature of mutual sex acts. Like love, sex is held to lay one bare psychologically as well as physically. Sex is unquestionably intimate, but beyond that the psychological toll often attached may be a function of the restrictive sexual ethic itself, rather than a legitimate apology for it. The intimacy involved in love is psychologically consuming in a generally healthy way, while the psychological tolls of sexual relations, often including embarrassment as a correlate of intimacy, are too often the result of artificial sexual ethics and taboos. The intimacy involved in both love and sex is insufficient in any case in light of previous points to render a means–end analysis in these terms appropriate. . . .

I have now criticized various types of analysis sharing or suggesting a common means–end form. I have suggested that analyses of this form relate to attempts to limit moral or natural sex to that which fulfills some purpose or function extraneous to basic sexual desire.

The attempts to brand forms of sex outside the idealized models as immoral or perverted fail to achieve consistency with intuitions that they themselves do not directly question. The reproductive model brands oral–genital sex a deviation, but cannot account for kissing or holding hands. . . .

The sex–love model makes most sexual desire seem degrading or base. These views condemn extramarital sex on the sound but irrelevant grounds that reproduction and deep commitment are best confined to family contexts. The romanticization of sex and the confusion of sexual desire with love operate in both directions: sex outside the context of romantic love is repressed; once it is repressed, partners become more difficult to find and sex becomes romanticized further, out of proportion to its real value for the individual.

What all these analyses share in addition to a common form is accordance with and perhaps derivation from the Platonic–Christian moral tradition, according to which the animal or purely physical element of humans is the source of immorality, and plain sex in the sense I defined it is an expression of this element, hence in itself to be condemned. All the analyses examined seem to seek a distance from sexual desire itself in attempting to extend it conceptually beyond the physical. The love and communication analyses seek refinement or intellectualization of the desire; plain physical sex becomes vulgar, and too straightforward sexual encounters without an aura of respectable cerebral communicative content are to be avoided. Solomon explicitly argues that sex cannot be a "mere" appetite, his argument being that if it were, subway exhibitionism and other vulgar forms would be pleasing.[2] This fails to recognize that sexual desire can be focused or selective at the same time as being physical. Lower animals are not attracted by every other member of their species, either. Rancid food forced down one's throat is not pleasing, but that certainly fails to show that hunger is not a physical appetite. Sexual desire lets us know that we are physical beings and, indeed, animals; this is why traditional Platonic morality is so thorough in its condemnation. Means–end analyses continue to reflect this tradition, sometimes unwittingly. They show that in conceptualizing sex it is still difficult, despite years of so-called revolution in this area, to free ourselves from the lingering suspicion that plain sex as physical desire is an expression of our "lower selves," that yielding to our animal natures is subhuman or vulgar.

VI

Having criticized these analyses for the sexual ethics . . . they imply, it remains to contrast my account along these lines. To the question of what morality might be implied by my analysis, the answer is that there are no moral implications whatever. Any analysis of sex which imputes a moral character to sex acts in themselves is wrong for that reason. There is no morality intrinsic to sex, although general moral rules apply to the treatment of others in sex acts as they apply to all human relations. We can speak of a sexual ethic as we can speak of a business ethic, without implying that business in itself is either moral or immoral or that special rules are required to judge business practices which are not derived from rules that apply elsewhere as well. Sex is not in itself a moral category, although like business it invariably places us into relations with others in which moral rules apply. It gives us opportunity to do what is otherwise recognized as wrong, to harm others, deceive them or manipulate them against their wills. Just as the fact that an act is sexual in itself never renders it wrong or adds to its wrongness if it is wrong on other grounds (sexual acts towards minors are wrong on other grounds, as will be argued below), so no wrong act is to be excused because done from a sexual motive. If a "crime of passion" is to be excused, it would have to be on grounds of temporary insanity rather than sexual context (whether insanity does constitute a legitimate excuse for certain actions is too big a topic to argue here). Sexual motives are among others which may become deranged, and the fact that they are sexual has no bearing in itself on the moral character, whether negative or exculpatory, of the actions deriving from them. Whatever might be true of war, it is certainly not the case that all's fair in love or sex.

Our first conclusion regarding morality and sex is therefore that no conduct otherwise immoral should be excused because it is sexual conduct, and nothing in sex is immoral unless condemned by rules which apply elsewhere as well. The last clause requires further clarification. Sexual conduct can be governed by particular rules relating only to sex itself. But these precepts must be implied by general moral rules when these are applied to specific sexual relations or types of conduct. The same is true of rules of fair business, ethical medicine, or courtesy in driving a car. In the latter case, particular acts on the road may be reprehensible, such as tail-gating or passing on the right, which seem to bear no resemblance as actions to any outside the context of highway safety. Nevertheless their immorality derives from the fact that they place others in danger, a circumstance which, when avoidable, is to be condemned in any context. This structure of general and specifically applicable rules describes a reasonable sexual ethic as well. To take an extreme case, rape is always a sexual act and it is always immoral. A rule against rape can therefore be considered an obvious part of sexual morality which has no bearing on nonsexual conduct. But the immorality of rape derives from its being an extreme violation of a person's body, of the right not to be humiliated, and of the general moral prohibition against using other persons against their wills, not from the fact that it is a sexual act.

The application elsewhere of general moral rules to sexual conduct is further complicated by the fact that it will be relative to the particular desires and preferences of one's partner (these may be influenced by and hence in some sense include misguided beliefs about sexual morality itself). This means that there will be fewer specific rules in the area of sexual ethics than in other areas of conduct, such as driving cars, where the relativity of preference is irrelevant to the prohibition of objectively dangerous conduct. More reliance will have to be placed upon the general moral rule, which in this area holds simply that the preferences, desires, and interests of one's partner or potential partner ought to be taken into account. This rule is certainly not specifically formulated to govern sexual relations; it is a form of the central principle of morality itself. But when applied to sex, it prohibits certain actions, such as molestation of children, which cannot be categorized as violations of the rule without at the same time being classified as sexual. I believe this last case is the closest we can come to an action which is wrong *because* it is sexual, but even here its wrongness is better characterized as deriving from the detrimental effects such behavior can have on the future emotional and sexual life of the naive victims, and from the fact that such behavior therefore involves manipulation of innocent persons without regard for their interests. Hence, this case also involves violation of a general moral rule which applies elsewhere as well.

Aside from faulty conceptual analyses of sex and the influence of the Platonic moral tradition, there are two more plausible reasons for thinking that there are moral dimensions intrinsic to sex acts per se. The first is that such acts are normally intensely pleasurable. According to a hedonistic, utilitarian moral theory they therefore should be at least prima facie morally right, rather than morally neutral in themselves. To me this seems incorrect and reflects unfavorably on the ethical theory in question. The pleasure intrinsic to sex acts is a good, but not, it seems to me, a good with much positive moral significance. Certainly

I can have no duty to pursue such pleasure myself, and while it may be nice to give pleasure of any form to others, there is no ethical requirement to do so, given my right over my own body. The exception relates to the context of sex acts themselves, when one partner derives pleasure from the other and ought to return the favor. This duty to reciprocate takes us out of the domain of hedonistic utilitarianism, however, and into a Kantian moral framework, the central principles of which call for just such reciprocity in human relations. Since independent moral judgments regarding sexual activities constitute one area in which ethical theories are to be tested, these observations indicate here, as I believe others indicate elsewhere, the fertility of the Kantian, as opposed to the utilitarian, principle in reconstructing reasoned moral consciousness.

It may appear from this alternative Kantian viewpoint that sexual acts must be at least prima facie wrong in themselves. This is because they invariably involve at different stages the manipulation of one's partner for one's own pleasure, which might appear to be prohibited on the formulation of Kant's principle, which holds that one ought not to treat another as a means to such private ends. A more realistic rendering of this formulation, however, one which recognizes its intended equivalence to the first universalizability principle, admits no such absolute prohibition. Many human relations, most economic transactions for example, involve using other individuals for personal benefit. These relations are immoral only when they are one-sided, when the benefits are not mutual, or when the transactions are not freely and rationally endorsed by all parties. The same holds true of sexual acts. The central principle governing them is the Kantian demand for reciprocity in sexual relations. In order to comply with the second formulation of the categorical imperative, one must recognize the subjectivity of one's partner (not merely by being aroused by her or his desire, as Nagel describes). Even in an act which by its nature "objectifies" the other, one recognizes a partner as a subject with demands and desires by yielding to those desires, by allowing oneself to be a sexual object as well, by giving pleasure or ensuring that the pleasures of the acts are mutual. It is this kind of reciprocity which forms the basis for morality in sex, which distinguishes right acts from wrong in this area as in others. (Of course, prior to sex acts one must gauge their effects upon potential partners and take these longer-range interests into account.)

VII

I suggested earlier that in addition to generating confusion regarding the rightness or wrongness of sex acts, false conceptual analyses of the means–end form cause confusion about the value of sex to the individual. My account recognizes the satisfaction of desire and the pleasure this brings as the central psychological function of the sex act for the individual. Sex affords us a paradigm of pleasure, but not a cornerstone of value. For most of us it is not only a needed outlet for desire but also the most enjoyable form of recreation we know. Its value is nevertheless easily mistaken by being confused with that of love, when it is taken as essentially an expression of that emotion. Although intense, the pleasures of sex are brief and repetitive rather than cumulative. They give value to the specific acts which generate them, but not the lasting kind of value which enhances one's whole life. The briefness of these pleasures contributes to their intensity (or perhaps their intensity makes them necessarily brief), but it also relegates them to the periphery of most rational plans for the good life.

By contrast, love typically develops over a long-term relation; while its pleasures may be less intense and physical, they are of more cumulative value. The importance of love to the individual may well be central in a rational system of value. And it has perhaps an even deeper moral significance relating to the identification with the interests of another person, which broadens one's possible relationships with others as well. Marriage is again important in preserving this relation between adults and children, which seems as important to the adults as it is to the children in broadening concerns which have a tendency to become selfish. Sexual desire, by contrast, is desire for another which is nevertheless essentially self-regarding. Sexual pleasure is certainly a good for the individual, and for many it may be necessary in order for them to function in a reasonably cheerful way. But it bears little relation to those other values just discussed, to which some analyses falsely suggest a conceptual connection.

Notes

1 Even Bertrand Russell, whose writing in this area was a model of rationality, at least for its period, tends to make this identification and to condemn plain sex in the absence of love: "sex intercourse apart from love has little value, and is to be regarded primarily as experimentation with a view to love." *Marriage and Morals* (New York: Bantam, 1959), p. 87.

2 Robert Solomon, "Sex and Perversion," *Philosophy and Sex*, ed. R. Baker and F. Elliston (Buffalo: Prometheus, 1975), p. 285.

Why Homosexuality is Abnormal

Michael Levin

1. Introduction

This paper defends the view that homosexuality is abnormal and hence undesirable – not because it is immoral or sinful, or because it weakens society or hampers evolutionary development, but for a purely mechanical reason. It is a misuse of bodily parts. Clear empirical sense attaches to the idea of *the use* of such bodily parts as genitals, the idea that they are *for* something, and consequently to the idea of their misuse. I argue on grounds involving natural selection that misuse of bodily parts can with high probability be connected to unhappiness. I regard these matters as prolegomena to such policy issues as the rights of homosexuals, the rights of those desiring not to associate with homosexuals, and legislation concerning homosexuality, issues which I shall not discuss systematically here. However, I do in the last section draw a seemingly evident corollary from my view that homosexuality is abnormal and likely to lead to unhappiness. . . .

2. On "Function"

To bring into relief the point of the idea that homosexuality involves a misuse of bodily parts, I will begin with an uncontroversial case of misuse, a case in which the clarity of our intuitions is not obscured by the conviction that they are untrustworthy. Mr Jones pulls all his teeth and strings them around his neck because he thinks his teeth look nice as a necklace. He takes puréed liquids supplemented by intravenous solutions for nourishment. It is surely natural to say that Jones is misusing his teeth, that he is not using them for what they are for, that indeed the way he is using them is incompatible with what they are for. Pedants might argue that Jones's teeth are no longer part of him and hence that he is not misusing any bodily parts. To them I offer Mr Smith, who likes to play "Old MacDonald" on his teeth. So devoted is he to this amusement, in fact, that he never uses his teeth for chewing – like Jones, he takes nourishment intravenously. Now, not only do we find it perfectly plain that Smith and Jones are misusing their teeth, we predict a dim future for them on purely physiological grounds; we expect the muscles of Jones's jaw that are used for – that *are* for – chewing to lose their tone, and we expect this to affect Jones's gums. Those parts of Jones's digestive tract that are for processing solids will also suffer from disuse. The net result will be deteriorating health and perhaps a shortened life. Nor is this all. Human beings enjoy chewing. Not only has natural selection selected in muscles for chewing and favored creatures with such muscles, it has selected in a tendency to find the use of those muscles reinforcing. Creatures who do not enjoy using such parts of their bodies as deteriorate with disuse will tend to be selected out. Jones, product of natural selection that he is, descended from creatures who at least tended to enjoy the use of such parts. Competitors who didn't simply had fewer descendants. So we expect Jones sooner or later to experience vague yearnings to chew something, just as we find people who take no exercise to experience a general listlessness. Even waiving for now my apparent reification of the evolutionary process, let me emphasize how little anyone is tempted to say "each to his own" about Jones or to regard Jones's disposition of his teeth as simply a deviation from a statistical norm. This sort of case is my paradigm when discussing homosexuality. . . .

3. Applications to Homosexuality

The application of this general picture to homosexuality should be obvious. There can be no reasonable doubt that one of the functions of the penis is to introduce semen into the vagina. It does this, and it has been selected in because it does this. . . . Nature has consequently made this use of the penis rewarding. It is clear enough that any proto–human males who found unrewarding the insertion of penis into vagina have left no descendants. In particular, proto–human males who enjoyed inserting their penises into each other's anuses have left no descendants. This is why homosexuality is abnormal, and why its abnormality counts prudentially against it. Homosexuality is likely to cause unhappiness because it leaves unfulfilled an innate and innately rewarding desire. And should the reader's environmentalism threaten to get the upper hand, let me remind him again of an unproblematic case. Lack of exercise is bad and even abnormal not only because it is unhealthy but also because one feels poorly without regular exercise. Nature made exercise rewarding because, until recently, we had to exercise to survive. Creatures who found running after game unrewarding were eliminated. Laziness leaves unreaped the rewards nature has planted in exercise, even if the lazy man cannot tell this introspectively. If this is a correct description of the place of exercise in human life, it is by the same token a correct description of the place of heterosexuality.

It hardly needs saying, but perhaps I should say it anyway, that this argument concerns tendencies and probabilities. Generalizations about human affairs being notoriously "true by and large and for the most part" only, saying that homosexuals are bound to be less happy than heterosexuals must be understood as short for "Not coincidentally, a larger proportion of homosexuals will be unhappy than a corresponding selection of the heterosexual population." There are, after all, genuinely jolly fat men. To say that laziness leads to adverse affective consequences means that, because of our evolutionary history, the odds are relatively good that a man who takes no exercise will suffer adverse affective consequences. Obviously, some people will get away with misusing their bodily parts. Thus, when evaluating the empirical evidence that bears on this account, it will be pointless to cite cases of well-adjusted homosexuals. I do not say they are non-existent; my claim is that, of biological necessity, they are rare.

My argument might seem to show at most that heterosexual behavior is (self-)reinforcing, not that homosexuality is self-extinguishing – that homosexuals go without the built-in rewards of heterosexuality, but not that homosexuality has a built-in punishment. This distinction, however, is merely verbal. They are two different ways of saying that homosexuals will find their lives less rewarding than will heterosexuals. Even if some line demarcated happiness from unhappiness absolutely, it would be irrelevant if homosexuals were all happily above the line. It is the comparison with the heterosexual life that is at issue. A lazy man might count as happy by some mythic absolute standard, but he is likely to be less happy than someone otherwise like him who exercises. . . .

Talk of what is "in the genes" inevitably provokes the observation that we should not blame homosexuals for their homosexuality if it is "in their genes." True enough. Indeed, since nobody decides what he is going to find sexually arousing, the moral appraisal of sexual object "choice" is entirely absurd. However, so saying is quite consistent with regarding homosexuality as a misfortune, and taking steps – this being within the realm of the will – to minimize its incidence, especially among children. Calling homosexuality involuntary does not place it outside the scope of evaluation. Victims of sickle-cell anemia are not blameworthy, but it is absurd to pretend that there is nothing wrong with them. Homosexual activists are partial to genetic explanations and hostile to Freudian environmentalism in part because they see a genetic cause as exempting homosexuals from blame. But surely people are equally blameless for indelible traits acquired in early childhood. And anyway, a blameless condition may still be worth trying to prevent. (Defenders of homosexuality fear Freud at another level, because his account removes homosexuality from the biological realm altogether and deprives it of whatever legitimacy adheres to what is "in the genes.")

My sociobiological scenario also finds no place for the fashionable remark that homosexuality has become fitness-enhancing in our supposedly overpopulated world. Homosexuality is said to increase our species' chances by easing the population pressure. This observation, however correct, is irrelevant. Even if homosexuality has lately come to favor species survival, this is no part of how homosexuality is created. Salvation of the human species would be at best a fortuitous by-product of behavior having other causes. It is not easy, moreover, to see how this feature of homosexuality could get it selected in. If homosexuality enhances inclusive fitness precisely because homosexuals don't reproduce, the tendency to homosexuality cannot get selected for by a filtering process when it is passed to the next generation – it doesn't get passed to the next generation at all. The same applies, of course, to any tendency to find homosexuality rewarding.

The whole matter of the survival advantage of homosexuality is in any case beside the point. Our organs have the functions and rewards they do because of the way the world was, and what favored survival, many millions of years ago. *Then*, homosexuality decreased fitness and heterosexuality increased it; an innate tendency to homosexuality would have gotten selected out if anything did. We today have the tendencies transmitted to us by those other ancestors, whether or not the race is going to pay a price for this. That 50 years ago certain self-reinforcing behavior began to threaten the race's future is quite consistent with the behavior remaining self-reinforcing. Similarly, widespread obesity and the patent enjoyment many people experience in gorging themselves just show that our appetites were shaped in conditions of food scarcity under which gorging oneself when one had the chance was a good policy. Anyway, the instability created by abundance is, presumably, temporary. If the current abundance continues for 5000 generations, natural gluttons will almost certainly disappear through early heart disease and unattractiveness to the opposite sex. The ways in which the populous human herd will be trimmed are best left to speculation.

I should also note that nothing I have said shows bisexuality or sheer polymorphous sexuality to be unnatural or self-punishing. One might cite the Greeks to show that only exclusive homosexuality conflicts with our evolved reinforcement mechanism. But in point of fact bisexuality seems to be a quite rare phenomenon – and animals, who receive no cultural conditioning, seem instinctively heterosexual in the vast majority of cases. Clinicians evidently agree that it is possible for a person to be homosexual at one period of his life and heterosexual at another, but not at the same time. . . .

Utilitarians must take the present evolutionary scenario seriously. The utilitarian attitude toward homosexuality usually runs something like this: even if homosexuality is in some sense unnatural, as a matter of brute fact homosexuals take pleasure in sexual contact with members of the same sex. As long as they don't hurt anyone else, homosexuality is as great a good as heterosexuality. But the matter cannot end here. Not even a utilitarian doctor would have words of praise for a degenerative disease that happened to foster a certain kind of pleasure (as sore muscles uniquely conduce to the pleasure of stretching them). A utilitarian doctor would presumably try just as zealously to cure diseases that feel good as less pleasant degenerative diseases. A pleasure causally connected with great distress cannot be treated as just another pleasure to be toted up on the felicific scoreboard. Utilitarians have to reckon with the inevitable consequences of pain-causing pleasure.

Similar remarks apply to the question of whether homosexuality is a "disease." A widely-quoted pronouncement of the American Psychiatric Association runs:

> Surely the time has come for psychiatry to give up the archaic practice of classifying the millions of men and women who accept or prefer homosexual object choices as being, by virtue of that fact alone, mentally ill. The fact that their alternative life-style happens to be out of favor with current cultural conventions must not be a basis in itself for a diagnosis.

Apart from some question-begging turns of phrase, this is right. One's taste for mutual anal intercourse is nothing "in itself" for one's psychiatrist to worry about, any more than a life of indolence is anything "in itself" for one's doctor to worry about. In fact, in itself there is nothing wrong with a broken arm or an occluded artery. The fact that my right ulna is now in two pieces is just a fact of nature, not a "basis for diagnosis." But this condition is a matter for medical science anyway, because it will lead to pain. Permitted to persist, my fracture will provoke increasingly punishing states. So if homosexuality is a reliable sign of present or future misery, it is beside the point that homosexuality is not "by virtue of that fact alone" a mental illness. High rates of drug addiction, divorce and illegitimacy are in themselves no basis for diagnosing social pathology. They support this diagnosis because of what else they signify about a society which exhibits them. Part of the problem here is the presence of germs in paradigm diseases, and the lack of a germ for homosexuality (or psychosis). . . . Whether homosexuality is a disease is a largely verbal issue. If homosexuality is a self-punishing maladaptation, it hardly matters what it is called.

4. Evidence and Further Clarification

I have argued that homosexuality is "abnormal" in both a descriptive and a normative sense because – for evolutionary reasons – homosexuals are bound to be unhappy. In Kantian terms, I have explained how it is possible for homosexuality to be unnatural even if it violates no cosmic purpose or such purposes as we retrospectively impose on nature. What is the evidence for my view? For one thing, by emphasizing homosexual unhappiness, my view explains a ubiquitous fact in a simple way. The fact is the universally acknowledged unhappiness of homosexuals. Even the staunchest defenders of homosexuality admit that, as of now, homosexuals are not happy. . . .

The usual environmentalist explanation for homosexuals' unhappiness is the misunderstanding, contempt and abuse that society heaps on them. But this not only leaves unexplained why society has this attitude, it sins against parsimony by explaining a nearly universal phenomenon in terms of variable circumstances that have, by coincidence, the same upshot. Parsimony urges that we seek the explanation of homosexual unhappiness in the nature of homosexuality itself, as my explanation does. Having to "stay in the closet" may be a great strain, but it does not account for all the miseries that writers on homosexuality say are the homosexual's lot. . . .

One crucial test of my account is its prediction that homosexuals will continue to be unhappy even if people altogether abandon their "prejudice" against homosexuality. This prediction, that homosexuality being unnatural homosexuals will still find their behavior self-punishing, coheres with available evidence. It is consistent with the failure of other oppressed groups, such as American Negroes and European Jews, to become warped in the direction of "cruising," sado-masochism and other practices common in homosexual life. It is consistent as well with the admission by even so sympathetic an observer of homosexuality as Rechy that the immediate cause of homosexual unhappiness is a taste for promiscuity, anonymous encounters and humiliation. It is hard to see how such tastes are related to the dim view society takes of them. Such a relation would be plausible only if homosexuals courted multiple anonymous encounters *faute de mieux*, longing all the while to settle down to some sort of domesticity. But, again, Europeans abhorred Jews for centuries, but this did not create in Jews a special weakness for anonymous, promiscuous sex. Whatever drives a man away from women, to be fellated by as many different men as possible, seems independent of what society thinks of such behavior. It is this behavior that occasions misery, and we may expect the misery of homosexuals to continue.

In a 1974 study, Weinberg and Williams found no difference in the distress experienced by homosexuals in Denmark and the Netherlands, and in the US, where they found public tolerance of homosexuality to be lower. This would confirm rather strikingly that homosexual unhappiness is endogenous, unless one says that Weinberg's and Williams's indices for public tolerance and distress – chiefly homosexuals' self-reports of "unhappiness" and "lack of faith in others" – are unreliable. Such complaints, however, push the social causation theory toward untestability. Weinberg and Williams themselves cleave to the hypothesis that homosexual unhappiness is entirely a reaction to society's attitudes, and suggest that a condition of homosexual happiness is positive endorsement by the surrounding society. It is hard to imagine a more flagrantly *ad hoc* hypothesis. Neither a Catholic living among Protestants nor a copywriter working on the great American novel in his off hours asks more of a society than tolerance in order to be happy in his pursuits.

It is interesting to reflect on a natural experiment that has gotten under way in the decade since the Weinberg–Williams study. A remarkable change in public opinion, if not private sentiment, has occurred in America. For whatever reason – the prodding of homosexual activists, the desire not to seem like a fuddy-duddy – various organs of opinion are now hard at work providing a "positive image" for homosexuals. Judges allow homosexuals to adopt their lovers. The Unitarian Church now performs homosexual marriages. Hollywood produces highly sanitized movies like *Making Love* and *Personal Best* about homosexuality. Macmillan strongly urges its authors to show little boys using cosmetics. Homosexuals no longer fear revealing themselves, as is shown by the prevalence of the "clone look." Certain products run advertising obviously directed at the homosexual market. On the societal reaction theory, there ought to be an enormous rise in homosexual happiness. I know of no systematic study to determine if this is so, but anecdotal evidence suggests it may not be. The homosexual press has been just as strident in denouncing pro-homosexual movies as in denouncing Doris Day movies. Especially virulent venereal diseases have very recently appeared in homosexual communities, evidently spread in epidemic proportions by unabating homosexual promiscuity. One selling point for a presumably serious "gay rights" rally in Washington, DC, was an "all-night disco train" from New York to Washington. What is perhaps most salient is that, even if the changed public mood results in decreased homo-sexual unhappiness, the question remains of why homosexuals in the recent past, who suffered greatly for being homosexuals, persisted in being homosexuals.

But does not my position also predict – contrary to fact – that any sexual activity not aimed at procreation or at least sexual intercourse leads to unhappiness? First, I am not sure this conclusion is contrary to the facts properly understood. It is universally recognized that, for humans and the higher animals, sex is more than the insertion of the penis into the vagina. Foreplay is necessary to prepare the female and, to a lesser extent, the male. Ethologists have studied the elaborate mating rituals of even relatively simple animals. Sexual intercourse must therefore be understood to include the kisses and caresses that necessarily precede copulation, behaviors that nature has made rewarding. What my view does predict is that exclusive preoccupation with behaviors normally preparatory for inter-course is highly correlated with unhappiness. And, so far as I know, psychologists do agree that such preoccupation or "fixation" with, e.g., cunnilingus is associated with personality traits independently recognized as disorders. In this sense, sexual intercourse really is virtually necessary for well-being. Only if one is antecedently convinced that "nothing is more natural than anything else" will one confound foreplay as a prelude to intercourse with "foreplay" that leads nowhere at all. One might speculate on the evolutionary advantages of foreplay, at least for humans; by increasing the intensity and complexity of the pleasures of intercourse, it binds the partners more firmly and makes them more fit for child-rearing. In fact, such analyses of sexual perversion as Nagel's, which correctly focus on the interruption of mutuality as central to perversion, go wrong by ignoring the evolutionary role and built-in rewards of mutuality. They fail to explain why the interruption of mutuality is disturbing.

It should also be clear that my argument permits gradations in abnormality. Behavior is the more abnormal, and the less likely to be rewarding, the more its emission tends to extinguish a genetic cohort that practices it. The less likely a behavior is to get selected out, the less abnormal it is. Those of our ancestors who found certain aspects of foreplay reinforcing might have managed to reproduce themselves sufficiently to implant this strain in us. There might be an equilibrium between intercourse and such not directly reproduc-tive behavior. It is not required that any behavior not directly linked to heterosexual intercourse lead to maximum dissatisfaction. But the existence of these gradations provides no entering wedge for homosexuality. As no behavior is more likely to get selected out than rewarding homosexuality – except perhaps an innate tendency to suicide at the onset of puberty – it is extremely unlikely that homosexuality can now be unconditionally reinforc-ing in humans to any extent.

Nor does my position predict, again contrary to fact, that celibate priests will be unhappy. My view is compatible with the existence of happy celibates who deny themselves as part of a higher calling which yields compensating satisfactions. Indeed, the very fact that one needs to explain how the priesthood can compensate for the lack of family means that people do regard heterosexual mating as the natural or "inertial" state of human relations. The comparison between priests and homosexuals is in any case inapt. Priests do not simply give up sexual activity without ill-effect; they give it up for a reason. Homosexuals have hardly given up the use of their sexual organs, for a higher calling or anything else. Homosexuals continue to use them, but, unlike priests, they use them for what they are not for. . . .

5.   On Policy Issues

Homosexuality is intrinsically bad only in a prudential sense. It makes for unhappiness. However, this does not exempt homosexuality from the larger categories of ethics – rights, duties, liabilities. Deontic categories apply to acts which increase or decrease happiness or expose the helpless to the risk of unhappiness.

If homosexuality is unnatural, legislation which raises the odds that a given child will become homosexual raises the odds that he will be unhappy. The only gap in the syllogism is whether legislation which legitimates, endorses or protects homosexuality does increase the chances that a child will become homosexual. If so, such legislation is *prima facie* objectionable. The question is not whether homosexual elementary school teachers will molest their charges. Pro-homosexual legislation might increase the incidence of homosexuality in subtler ways. If it does, and if the protection of children is a fundamental obligation of society, legislation which legitimates homosexuality is a dereliction of duty. I am reluctant to deploy the language of "children's rights," which usually serves as one more excuse to interfere with the prerogatives of parents. But we do have obligations to our children, and one of them is to protect them from harm. If, as some have suggested, children have a right to protection from a religious education, they surely have a right to protection from homosexuality. So protecting them limits somebody else's freedom, but we are often willing to protect quite obscure children's rights at the expense of the freedom of others. There is a movement to ban TV commercials for sugar-coated cereals, to protect children from the relatively trivial harm of tooth decay. Such a ban would restrict the freedom of advertisers, and restrict it even though the last clear chance of avoiding the harm, and thus the responsibility, lies with the parents who control the TV set. I cannot see how one can consistently support such legislation and also urge homosexual rights, which risk much graver damage to children, in exchange for increased freedom for homosexuals. (If homosexual behavior is largely compulsive, it is falsifying the issue to present it as balancing risks to children against the freedom of homosexuals.) The right of a homosexual to work for the Fire Department is not a negligible good. Neither is fostering a legal atmosphere in which as many people as possible grow up heterosexual.

It is commonly asserted that legislation granting homosexuals the privilege or right to be firemen endorses not homosexuality, but an expanded conception of human liberation. It is conjectural how sincerely this can be said in a legal order that forbids employers to hire whom they please and demands hours of paperwork for an interstate shipment of hamburgers. But in any case legislation "legalizing homosexuality" cannot be neutral because passing it would have an inexpungeable speech-act dimension. Society cannot grant unaccustomed rights and privileges to homosexuals while remaining neutral about the value of homosexuality. Working from the assumption that society rests on the family and its consequences, the Judaeo-Christian tradition has deemed homosexuality a sin and withheld many privileges from homosexuals. Whether or not such denial was right, for our society to grant these privileges to homosexuals *now* would amount to declaring that it has rethought the matter and decided that homosexuality is not as bad as it had previously supposed. And unless such rethinking is a direct response to new empirical findings about homosexuality, it can only be a revaluing. Someone who suddenly accepts a policy he has previously opposed is open to the same interpretation: he has come to think better of the policy. And if he embraces the policy while knowing that this interpretation will be put on his behavior, and if he knows that others know that he knows they will so interpret it, he is acquiescing in this interpretation. He can be held to have intended, meant, this interpretation. A society that grants privileges to homosexuals while recognizing that, in the light of generally known history, this act can be interpreted as a positive re-evaluation of homosexuality, is signalling that it now thinks homosexuality is all right. Many commentators in the popular press have observed that homosexuals, unlike members of racial minorities, can always "stay in the closet" when applying for jobs. What homosexual rights activists really want, therefore, is not access to jobs but legitimation of their homosexuality. Since this is known, giving them what they want will be seen as conceding their claim to legitimacy. And since legislators know their actions will support this interpretation, and know that their constituencies know they know this, the Gricean effect or symbolic meaning of passing anti-discrimination ordinances is to declare homosexuality legitimate.

Legislation permitting frisbees in the park does not imply approval of frisbees for the simple reason that frisbees are new; there is no tradition of banning them from parks. The legislature's action in permitting frisbees is not interpretable, known to be interpretable and so on, as the reversal of long-standing disapproval. It is because these Gricean conditions are met in the case of abortion that legislation – or rather judicial fiat – permitting abortions and mandating their public funding are widely interpreted as tacit approval. Up to now, society has deemed homosexuality so harmful that restricting it outweighs putative homosexual rights. If society reverses itself, it will in effect be deciding that homosexuality is not as bad as it once thought.

Postscript Added 1995

I now see the foregoing argument as defective in two ways.

First, it is biased toward environmental explanations of homosexuality. Recent evidence from neuroanatomy and behavioral genetics has confirmed a significant biological factor in sexual orientation. The region of the hypothalamus which controls sexual arousal has been found to be twice as large in heterosexual as homosexual males. Identical twins reared apart are more concordant for homosexuality than fraternal twins reared apart or together, and, within families, concordance for homosexuality is greater than chance for males related on the mother's side but not the father's, suggesting sex-linkage.

However, a genetic basis for homosexuality does *not* imply that homosexuality is normal, for it does not imply that homosexuality has an adaptive function. The ostensible maladaptiveness of homosexuality suggests, rather, that the (poly)gene for homosexuality survives through *pleiotropy*, expression in more than one phenotype. The (poly)gene that codes for homosexuality presumably also codes for some other trait(s) that strongly enhance(s) fitness, although no-one now knows what that trait might be. But whatever version of the pleiotropy hypothesis may prove correct, it still counts homosexuality itself as abnormal, or at least non-normal. If the homosexual phenotype survives through an adaptive correlate, homosexuality would not explain the survival of the gene that codes for it – the gene would survive by expressing the correlate – and would therefore serve no function. Homosexuality would be a side-effect fatal to any gene that coded for it alone, resembling genetic diseases like sickle-cell anemia, which has survived because its gene also confers immunity to malaria. Homosexuality would also retain its negative aspect, on the pleiotropy hypothesis, since maladaptive side-effects are not expected to be reinforcing. Enjoyment of homosexuality would not increase fitness, so there would not have been selection for its being reinforcing.

My second error was to misconstrue the normative issues involved in the homosexuality debate. In effect I attacked an Equal Rights Amendment for homosexuals, defending some legal classifications based on sexual orientation on the grounds that overturning them would signal social acceptance of homosexuality and increase its prevalence. On one hand, emphasizing genes undercuts this argument; if homosexuality is largely biological in origin, this worry is empty. (I should add, however, that, if the central role of reproduction in society's continued existence gives the state a say in sexual relations, the state may and should reserve the privileges of marriage for heterosexuals.)

Ironically, the more ambitious goals of current homosexual liberationists make a biology *more* relevant than it was fifteen years ago. What is now being demanded is civil rights for homosexuals, that is, a legal ban on *private* discrimination based on sexual object choice.

This demand is often based upon the idea that it is wrong to discriminate on the basis of immutable traits, and homosexuality is involuntary and immutable if genetic. I contest the major premise: we discriminate every day on the basis of immutable traits. Reflex speed is unchosen, but the quickest shortstop makes the team. Going on the offensive, civil rights for homosexuals violates freedom of association, which, it seems to me, is an immediate corollary of the categorical imperative. It will be replied that, on my view, civil rights for blacks and women are also illicit; that indeed is my view, although, because others will find it a reductio, it is important to stress the difference between blacks and women, on one hand, and homosexuals on the other. There is nothing *abnormal* about being a black or a woman, and no-one is made as profoundly uncomfortable by members of the opposite sex or other races as many people are made by homosexuals. This antipathy to homosexuals – which is not "hate," a desire to harm, but merely a desire to avoid – may itself have a biological basis. This being so, it strikes me as profoundly wrong to force association with homosexuals on anyone who does not want it.

These views are developed at length in "Homosexuality, Abnormality, and Civil Rights," to appear in *Public Affairs Quarterly*, which expresses my current thinking on the subject.

Michael Levin
September 10, 1995

Homosexuality, Morals, and the Law of Nature

Burton M. Leiser

Philosophers and others have insisted for centuries that homosexuality is immoral. The Bible proclaims that it is an abomination (e.g., Leviticus 18:22), but in ancient Greece and in some other societies, homosexuality was accepted as a normal form of sexual activity. In our own time, some nations have repealed laws discriminating against homosexuals and others have given legal recognition to homosexual relationships.

Arguments in support of the thesis that homosexual behavior is immoral and ought to be outlawed run the gamut from utilitarian arguments – that homosexuality causes harm to innocent persons or to society as a whole – to those based on the theory that homosexual relations are contrary to the laws of nature. In addition to these attempts to justify an anti-gay stance on philosophical grounds, substantial numbers of people have powerful emotional reactions to the very thought of homosexual relations, while others, relying upon Scripture or religious tradition as the source of their moral judgments, need no philosophical justifications for their feelings.

This article will critically examine the principal arguments that have been advanced in favor of the proposition that homosexuality is wrong. It will then consider some of the responsibilities that gays and lesbians have in relation to others who may be associated with them, as well as the responsibilities that others have toward gays and lesbians; and finally, some of the moral issues that have arisen as a result of recent attitudes and developments in this area.

I. Utilitarian Arguments against Homosexuality

The Greeks and Romans of ages past believed that earthquakes and volcanic eruptions were often brought about by homosexual behavior. Readers of the biblical book of Genesis might infer from the story of the destruction of Sodom and Gomorra that entire cities could be engulfed in fire and their inhabitants annihilated by homosexual activities. If homosexual relations were likely to cause fire and brimstone to descend upon a city's inhabitants, convulsing the earth and inducing it to open up and swallow innocent human beings alive, that would certainly be an excellent reason for condemning such behavior and enacting the most rigid legal prohibitions against it. But no one with a scintilla of scientific training could reasonably believe that there is any such causal connection between homosexuality and volcanic eruptions or earthquakes.

Nevertheless, there is ample reason to believe that unprotected anal intercourse (a form of sexual behavior that is often engaged in by homosexual males) contributes to the spread of the HIV virus that causes the Auto-Immune Deficiency Syndrome (AIDS), an incurable, invariably fatal disease that has caused the deaths of countless victims since it was first discovered less than two decades ago. Anyone – whatever his or her sexual orientation – who engages in such sexual behavior knowing that there is a significant risk of spreading the disease, and fails to take appropriate measures to protect against infection, is rightly held to be morally, if not legally, culpable for recklessly endangering the lives of others. It may be argued, with some legitimacy, that homosexual sex has not only contributed immensely to human suffering and misery, but has also robbed the world of the services of some extraordinarily talented, creative persons whose contributions might have enhanced the quality of life for vast numbers of other people.

It has also been argued that homosexual relations are a threat to the integrity of vital social institutions and are inconsistent with the moral perceptions of ordinary people. In an influential essay he prepared for the British House of Lords long before the AIDS epidemic, Sir Patrick Devlin, one of England's most respected legal experts, responded to a committee that had been charged with recommending legislation on homosexual relations. The committee (known as the Wolfenden Committee) had concluded that consensual sodomy (that is, anal or oral intercourse to which the parties consent – assuming that they are of age and are mentally competent to make such decisions for themselves) should be legalized. Lord Devlin concluded that the committee's conclusion was erroneous, and that the British Parliament should adhere to the traditions of the past, under which homosexual behavior was legally forbidden and violators were subject to severe penalties. The law is not designed solely for the protection of the individual, he said, but for the protection of society. So-called victimless crimes, or crimes to which the "victim" has consented, are criminal nevertheless, for *society as a whole* is the victim in every such case. A murderer who acts with the consent of his victim, or even at the victim's request, is still a murderer, because the purpose of the law is the preservation of "one of the great moral principles upon which society is based, . . . the sanctity of human life." Thus, acts committed in private and with consent, such as dueling, suicide, and incest, may nevertheless be criminal.

The institution of marriage, Devlin argued, is one of the moral foundations of society. Consequently, adultery is not merely a private matter. It is a concern of the public as well, for it strikes at the very heart of the institution of marriage. The same is true of homosexuality, he said, for no society can exist without a shared sense of morals and ethics – common bonds of thought that constitute the glue that holds a society together. A common morality, he argued, is part of the price we pay to live in a civil society, for a society can be as readily destroyed from within, by the destruction of its moral standards, a loosening of its moral bonds, as it can from without. Therefore, he concluded, the suppression of vice is very much the law's business, and it is perfectly reasonable to prohibit homosexual relations.

But what criterion ought to be employed in determining what ought to be the moral standards upon which such legislation should rest? The test of a society's morals, Devlin said, is the standard of the ordinary man in the street. Immorality, he said, is what "every right-minded person is presumed to consider immoral." When ordinary people feel a deep sense of reprobation and disgust, and there is evidence that the practice in question is injurious to society, then, according to Devlin, we have reached the outer limits of toleration, the point at which the practice may be outlawed.

Devlin does not consider the possibility that a society's moral standards, as measured by "the ordinary man" test, might change or that they might differ from place to place, as they clearly do in various regions of the United States. In a very real sense, that "community of ideas" that is fundamental to Devlin's thesis simply does not exist in the vast, multicultural society that stretches across an entire continent and encompasses communities as diverse as Boise, Idaho, Anita, Iowa, New York City, and San Francisco. Nor, for that matter, is it likely to exist in any part of the industrialized world where the government does not impose severe restrictions on movement or the free exchange of ideas. The ordinary person on the streets of the Bronx is likely to have rather different attitudes from his or her counterpart in Charleston, South Carolina, and those differences are likely to be reflected in the persons elected to the state legislature, to Congress, and to the courts.

The community of interests that Devlin supposes must exist in a given society may not be very evident in the diverse societies with which we are familiar, at least in the areas of ethics and social mores. So far as the United States is concerned, the Supreme Court held as recently as 1986 that the prosecution of homosexuals for private, consensual acts is not inconsistent with the Constitution. Although some states have considered allowing homosexuals to enter into marriage or some relationship comparable to it, most have refused to remove statutes forbidding homosexual relations. Some states have explicitly refused to recognize the right of homosexuals to be treated as entitled to the rights that have been extended to women and members of racial and ethnic minorities who have been perceived as having been discriminated against in the past. Colorado voters adopted an amendment to the State Constitution in 1992 that specifically provided that neither the state nor any state agency or subdivision could adopt any statute, regulation, or policy under which homosexuals, lesbians, or bisexuals would have the status of or be permitted to claim to be a protected minority. The Colorado Supreme Court subsequently held that the amendment violated the United States Constitution. The United States Supreme Court has upheld this decision on the grounds that it violates the equal protection of rights of homosexuals. The vote of the people of Colorado suggests, however, that a substantial number of persons in the United States believe that homosexuals are unworthy of the protections that have been accorded, for example, to racial, religious, and ethnic minorities and to women.

II.   Other Reasons for Condemning Homosexual Behavior

Philosophers, theologians, and social critics have come up with a number of other reasons for condemning homosexuality. None of them, however, seems to hold up under critical analysis. Most, in fact, would apply equally to heterosexuals, if the logic were consistently carried to its ultimate conclusion.

It has been argued, for example, that homosexuals tend to molest children, and that once a young person has been seduced by a gay or lesbian individual, he or she is likely to be initiated irreversibly into that way of life. But the offense being denounced is not homosexuality as such, but pedophilia – having sexual relations with minors. Persons guilty of pedophilia should be strongly denounced and their behavior should remain punishable under criminal statutes. The law has always presumed that minors are not capable of giving meaningful consent to sexual relations with adults, since they are not mature enough or well enough informed to understand the full implications of what they are doing. Criminal sanctions have been imposed upon adults who take advantage of their greater age and authority to seduce youngsters who are under the age of consent, regardless of the alleged willingness of the youngster to participate in such sexual conduct. Thus, an adult who has sexual relations with a 14-year-old may be tried and convicted of statutory rape despite the youngster's express willingness to enter into a sexual liaison with him. There should be no distinction, however, between homosexual and heterosexual relations of this type. Indeed, heterosexuals are guilty of far more acts of pedophilia than homosexuals.

The critics claim that homosexuals are afflicted by such serious psychological problems as feelings of guilt, insecurity, and constant fear of disgrace and ruin, and that homosexuality itself is a psychological problem. There is some truth to this, but as homosexuals "come out of the closet," becoming more open about their sexual preferences, it is becoming less so. One who has openly exposed his or her sexual preferences need no longer fear exposure. One who proudly claims to be a homosexual has conquered much, if not all, of the guilt that he or she might once have felt. The fear of disgrace and ruin is predicated entirely upon the judgment that the critics make: that homosexuals are bad people and that their sexual orientation renders them unfit for a bank loan, for the jobs they hold, or for the homes in which they live. However, if society – or, more specifically, banks, employers, and landlords – abandons its negative judgment on homosexuals and bases individual judgments upon the record of an individual's performance, gays and lesbians would have no more reason to fear exposure or feel insecure than "straight" individuals.

As for homosexual orientation being a psychological "problem," a condition is a problem only when the individual who has it feels that it is one, or when it objectively interferes with the achievement of that individual's goals in life. If homosexuals do not see their sexual preferences as problematic, but (as many evidently do) as liberating, then they are simply *not* problems, psychological or otherwise. And if those preferences do not interfere with the achievement of a homosexual's goals, except to the extent that society, its institutions, and the individuals who run them stand in the way because of an emotional need to condemn people who are different, then the "problem" is not a psychological one, but a social, political, and legal one that must be addressed as those problems are customarily addressed: through the political process.

The charge that homosexuals are unreliable and are poor security risks is true only if society perceives homosexuality to be evil or imposes criminal or social sanctions on those who are homosexual. A person cannot be blackmailed if the threat is exposure of a trait or practice that is deemed by all concerned to be socially acceptable. The fear that a teacher or scoutmaster might sexually abuse his or her charges is no more and no less rational in the case of a homosexual than it is in the case of a "straight" person. Pedophilia, not homosexuality, is the issue.

Homosexuals who engage in tasteless public displays of affection, cross-dressing, and solicitation or street walking for purposes of prostitution may appropriately be censured, reproached, or, where the offense is particularly egregious, punished. But the same is true of heterosexuals who engage in similarly crude and unseemly behavior in public.

III. Homosexual Behavior and the Law of Nature

By far the most interesting of the reasons offered by philosophers, theologians, and legal thinkers for declaring that homosexuality is wrong is the claim that it is contrary to the laws of nature. Homosexuals, it is said, violate natural law when they misuse their genital organs in ways that frustrate nature's intention that they be employed exclusively for purposes of reproduction. The critics claim that this violation of nature's laws and of God's design deserves the most severe reprobation. Indeed, many of the statutes that criminalize homo-sexual relations refer to them as the "infamous crime against nature."

Whether they believe that homosexual behavior should be punishable by law or not, many people seem to feel that anal intercourse, for example, is "unnatural." It takes a bit of a jump to infer that because something is *unnatural* or *contrary to the laws of nature*, it is wicked or wrong. A careful analysis of these concepts will reveal that the inference is completely unwarranted.

Descriptive laws of nature

To begin, consider the concept of *law*. In the ordinary sense of the word, laws have the following characteristics:

- They are social conventions, differing from one society to another, and sometimes between various groups within a society.
- They are *prescriptive*. That is, they prescribe or command that people engage in certain forms of behavior, that they either do or refrain from doing certain things. (For example, the law in the United States commands that every resident file an income tax return on the fifteenth of April, that no one assault anyone else, and that no government agency interfere with the free exercise of religion.)
- It is possible to violate them. (A person may fail to file an income tax return; he may assault his neighbor in defiance of the law; and a municipality may pass an ordinance that interferes with religious freedom.)
- Violators may be subject to penalties or other sanctions.
- Penalties or sanctions are imposed and carried out formally by government or institu-tional officials, or informally by members of the community.
- The laws of a state are not discovered by its citizens. Rather, the citizens are expected to *know* them so that they can obey them. People learn of the state's laws by being informed about them after they have been promulgated.
- The laws of a state may be abolished or modified by suitable governmental enactments.

Now consider what scientists call the laws of nature – i.e., such laws as the law of gravity, Boyle's Law, or Newton's laws of motion.

- They are not mere conventions, and are not variable from one society to another or from one place to another, but are universal.
- They are *descriptive*. That is, they merely *describe* what actually happens and do not command or order anything or anyone. (See the discussion that follows.)
- It is impossible to violate them. A person may not violate the law of gravity, for example. Anyone who attempts to "defy" that law by leaping from the observation deck of the Empire State Building will be treated, within a few seconds, to a dramatic proof of this fact. Astronauts who fly to the moon and balloonists who float above the trees and soar to great heights do not violate the law of gravity or any other natural law, but act in full accordance with them.
- Since it is impossible to violate a law of nature, there are no penalties for doing so. There are *consequences*, however, some of which are perfectly predictable. The hard landing

that a person who leaps from a tall building makes on the concrete below is not a punishment, but a predictable consequence of his action. The force of his impact and the speed with which he will strike the concrete are easily calculable by any high school student of physics who is given the height of the building and the weight – or more properly, the mass – of the jumper.

- The laws of nature cannot be abolished by any government. Nor can any government enact a natural law. The laws of nature are *discovered*. They are not created by men.

A simple example of a natural law is Boyle's Law, discovered over three hundred years ago by Robert Boyle. The law states simply that if a given quantity of a gas is kept under constant temperature, its volume will be inversely proportional to the pressure exerted upon it. Thus, an air bubble rising from deep in the ocean to the surface will expand as it rises because the pressure exerted upon it is constantly decreasing as it moves closer to the surface. A helium-filled balloon, lifting from the surface of the earth, will expand as it climbs to ever greater altitudes, because the pressure diminishes as it ascends toward the stratosphere. Eventually, the balloon will burst because the expansion of the gases within it will be greater than the thin skin of the balloon is able to withstand. When the balloon bursts, it is not being punished for "violating" Boyle's Law. It is simply undergoing the inevitable consequences of "obedience" (if we can call it that) to Boyle's Law. Scuba divers must bear in mind a vitally important practical application of Boyle's Law: A diver who has descended to any significant depth at all (even six feet) must not hold her breath as she returns to the surface, for her lungs will act like the balloon just described. As she rises closer to the surface of the water, the pressure diminishes very rapidly, and the volume of the air in her lungs will increase correspondingly, causing severe injury or death. To prevent this from happening, she must exhale, or continue to breathe normally during the ascent in order to relieve the pressure within her lungs. A diver who fails to follow this procedure and suffers serious lung damage has not been *punished* for failing to obey Boyle's Law. The air in her lungs has acted completely in accordance with Boyle's Law, and she has simply suffered the inevitable tragic consequences.

Note that at the beginning of the last paragraph, I wrote that Robert Boyle "discovered" the law that was named after him. He did not create it, but through scientific methods of observation and experimentation, he formulated the general rule as to how gases behave under certain conditions.

None of this is remotely like the sort of thing that critics of homosexuality have in mind when they say that it is wrong because it violates the laws of nature. It is simply not possible to violate a law of nature: A gas cannot help but expand when the pressure on it is relieved, and when support is pulled out from under a stone or a person, neither of them can avoid moving toward the center of the earth (what we call "falling"). Since the descriptive laws of nature cannot be violated, it is sheer nonsense to say that homosexual behavior is wrong because it violates such laws.

All is not lost, however, since there are several other senses in which one might interpret the meaning of the claim that "homosexual behavior is wrong because it violates the laws of nature."

What is artificial is unnatural

When we speak of something as being unnatural or not natural, we sometimes mean that it is artificial or synthetic, that it is the product of human artifice.

In recent years, for example, chains of stores have grown up promoting what they call "natural" foods, and cosmetics that they claim are made of "natural ingredients." The implication is that there is something unnatural, or contrary to nature, in the foods and cosmetics that are sold in other stores or under different labels. The difference, presumably, is to be found in the fact that "natural" foods are grown and treated with substances that are found in nature rather than with substances that are manufactured or compounded artificially. Manure would be a natural fertilizer under this definition, since it is collected directly from the source – a farmer's herd of cattle, for example – while powders that the farmer purchases from a chemical manufacturer for the same purpose would be regarded as unnatural because they are synthetic. Similarly, a farmer who fights the insects that attack his crops with praying mantises or ladybugs might call his crops "natural," while one who applies commercial insecticides might not, inasmuch as the compounds he applies are artificial or synthetic, having been created out of a variety of ingredients ranging from petroleum to gases extracted from the air.

There may be some benefits, ecologically and otherwise, to the "organic" or "natural" approach to the production of products such as foods and cosmetics. However, it is a considerable leap from that to the conclusion that non-organic or artificial substances are harmful or – to go to the ultimate extreme – evil. On the contrary, many artificial, synthetic substances and products are vital to life as we know it. The only alternatives might be quite unappealing, if we thought about them.

If I were to walk into my classroom one day in a completely natural state, without any of the artificial garments that I ordinarily wear, I am confident not only that my students and colleagues would be quite shocked and offended, but that my job would be in jeopardy. Consider what you are wearing as you read these words: your clothes undoubtedly consist in large part of synthetic materials, such as nylon, orlon, and rayon, created in the very chemical plants that manufacture the farmer's fertilizers and insecticides, in more or less the same manner and out of the same raw materials. The metals that went into making the rivets, zippers, and buckles you wear were mined, smelted, and formed using techniques that must all be deemed to be artificial. It is obvious that the clothes we wear are not found in nature, but must all be manufactured. If you wear corrective lenses, as I do, you are probably as grateful as I am for the optician's art and for the brilliance of the scientists and engineers who have created the substances out of which our plastic lenses and frames are formed. The artificial fillings in our teeth are certainly superior to the only "natural" way of dealing with toothache – having the offending teeth pulled out. The synthetic substances we take to cure our headaches – whether aspirin or Tylenol – are certainly to be preferred over doing nothing at all for them, or employing unproved, possibly ineffective, and potentially harmful "natural" remedies. And the very book you are reading is an artificial object whose existence was made possible only because of the technological expertise of many people who formulated the artificial inks, papers, and glues that went into its production, and the printing presses and other machines that printed and folded and bound it.

In short, industry and its products are not evil, even though they are "unnatural" in this sense of the word. Nor is interference with nature evil or wrong. On the contrary, we are free of many diseases, and can be cured of many others, only because we have interfered with nature in many ways. Only our ability to turn nature's laws to our own advantage has enabled us to escape the diseases, the insects, the ravages of floods and cold and heat that would otherwise make our lives miserable.

Homosexual behavior simply cannot be considered unnatural in this sense. There is nothing *artificial* about it. On the contrary, to those who engage in it, it is the most natural thing in the world. Even if it *were* unnatural in this sense, it is difficult to see how that would justify calling it wrong.

The uncommon or abnormal is unnatural

It may be suggested that homosexuality should be condemned because it is "unnatural" in the sense of being uncommon or "abnormal" (i.e., not usual). But this proves no more to the point than the previous suggestions. Many of our most esteemed scientists, artists, musicians, and scholars do things that are quite out of the ordinary, but we don't scorn them for that. Of all the thousands of students who have attended my classes during the years I have been teaching, only one, so far as I can recall, played the harp, and one other played the oboe. Both of them engaged in uncommon or unusual behavior, but the fact that they did so simply set them apart as having unusual interests and uncommon talent. The geniuses like Thomas Alva Edison, Albert Einstein, and Jonas Salk, who gave the world the phonograph and the electric light bulb, the theory of relativity, and a vaccine that has saved millions of people from the ravages of polio, deserve praise rather than condemnation for their extraordinary (i.e., abnormal or uncommon) contributions. If homosexuality is wrong, it cannot be because it is "unnatural" in this sense of the word.

The use of an organ or instrument in a way that is contrary to its principal purpose or function is unnatural

Screwdrivers are admirably suited for their intended function: driving screws; hammers for pounding nails; the eyes for seeing; the teeth for chewing. Abuse of any of these instruments or organs can lead to trouble. One who uses a screwdriver to pound a nail may get hurt, and one who uses his teeth to pry the cap from a beer bottle is likely to end up with less than a full set of teeth. By the same token, it has been suggested that it is inconsistent with the proper function or purpose of one's sex organs to use them for anything but reproduction, that any such use (or abuse) is unnatural, and that it is therefore wrong and worthy of condemnation.

In the absence of technology capable of cloning people from cells scraped from inside their cheeks, it appears that the only way for people to reproduce is via the more or less traditional methods associated with the genital organs. Even though it is now possible to fertilize an ovum in a test tube without either the mother or the father having sexual intercourse, the resulting embryo will die unless it is transplanted into the uterus of a woman who is willing to carry it and nurture it until it has reached a stage of development at which it can exist more or less on its own. The sperm cells and the ova must in any event be collected from men and women who are willing to donate them. Therefore, although medical technology has developed so far that human reproduction can take place without actual sexual intercourse, the human sexual apparatus is still essential for its successful achievement.

Because the sex organs are obviously and uniquely designed for the purpose of procreation, it is argued, any use of them for any other purpose is abusive, abnormal, unnatural, and therefore wrong. Masturbation, homosexual relations, and heterosexual intercourse that deliberately frustrates the design of the sex organs are therefore deemed to be perversions that are or ought to be prohibited in any right-thinking society.

But the matter is not so straightforward. Both tools and body organs *can* be used for a multitude of tasks which we ordinarily consider to be perfectly acceptable. Although a screwdriver's original purpose might have been to drive screws, it is not considered a misuse of such a tool, much less a perversion, to use it to pop the cap from a soda bottle or as a wedge or a lever, or for any number of other useful purposes. Teeth seem to be well designed for chewing, to be sure; but they can also be quite attractive, and add considerably to the beauty of a smile or the ferocity of a threatening glare. A person's ears are uniquely adapted for hearing. If a comedian wiggles his ears in order to draw a laugh from his audience, only an utterly humorless crank would accuse him of being perverse and wicked for using his ears to entertain his neighbors when they were designed for hearing.

The sex organs seem to be well suited, not only for reproduction, but also for the production of intense pleasure in oneself and in others. Their being so well suited for that purpose would seem to be utterly inconsistent with calling anyone who uses them merely to produce pleasure, either in himself or in another, while ignoring or frustrating procreation, perverse or wicked simply on the ground that he or she has committed an "unnatural" act. Since sex organs fulfill the function of producing pleasure so admirably, employing them for that purpose scarcely seems to be perverse or wicked on that account alone.

Moreover, it is quite obvious that human sex organs are used to express, in the deepest and most intimate way, the love of one person for another. Even those who most ardently oppose "unfruitful" intercourse concede this point, in practice if not in words, when they permit older married people who are beyond the age of reproduction to have sexual intercourse with one another. Similarly, when a woman is pregnant and thus incapable of becoming pregnant, she and her husband are nevertheless permitted to engage in sexual relations with one another without the slightest thought that what they are doing is perverse or "unnatural" because it is sure to be unfruitful. Under these circumstances, no one thinks that it is perverse or unnatural to engage in sexual relations that one knows will not lead to pregnancy. Sex organs, like other things that we are capable of manipulating, can be put to many uses. In themselves, those uses do not seem to be wicked, perverse, or unnatural, though some may be more common than others, at least in some societies or among some groups within a given society.

The fact that people *are* condemned for using their sex organs for their own pleasure or profit, or for that of others, reveals a great deal about the prejudices and irrational taboos of our society. The assumption that any organ has one and only one "proper" function is indefensible. The identification of such a "proper" or "natural" use when there are others is arbitrary and without foundation in scientific fact. To say that any use of an organ that is contrary to its principal purpose or function is unnatural and therefore evil or depraved proves nothing, for it merely begs the question.

That which is natural is good, and whatever is unnatural is bad

We asked at the beginning what definition of "unnatural" might reasonably lead to the conclusion that homosexual behavior, being unnatural, was therefore evil or wrong. Perhaps this is the key to the solution of our problem. Other senses of the word "unnatural" do not work: some "unnatural" things, such as artificial or synthetic things, are quite good and highly desirable; others, such as the uncommon or "abnormal," may also be good and praiseworthy. In other senses of the word, the unnatural simply cannot exist: the descriptive laws of nature admit of no exceptions. Therefore, nothing can be unnatural if that word is understood to refer to what is contrary to or inconsistent with the laws of nature.

But perhaps there is a sense of the word "unnatural" which simply *means* that which is wrong, perverse, depraved, or wicked. Then if homosexuality is unnatural, it would logically follow that it is wrong, perverse, depraved, or wicked!

But this is not very helpful, for it explains nothing at all. This is what it amounts to:

> Whatever is unnatural is, by definition, wicked, wrong, perverse, and depraved.
> Now, why is homosexuality wicked, wrong, perverse, and depraved?
> Because it is unnatural.

Now let's substitute the *definition* of "unnatural" for the *word* "unnatural" in this sentence: **Homosexuality is wicked, wrong, perverse, and depraved because it is *unnatural*.**

And we come up with the result: **Homosexuality is wicked, wrong, perverse, and depraved because it is *wicked, wrong, perverse, and depraved*.**

What is the end result? A tautology – a sentence that is true by definition, but is completely worthless since it communicates no information about anything whatever. In other words, if "unnatural" means wicked, wrong, perverse, and depraved, then it provides no support whatever for the argument that homosexuality is wicked, wrong, perverse, and depraved *because* it is unnatural. The argument is question-begging, and should be completely unconvincing to anyone who is at all familiar with elementary logic.

IV. Is Homosexuality Immoral?

Upon careful analysis, we have seen that those arguments that are advanced most often with the intention of supporting the thesis that homosexuality is wrong simply do not hold up. We have not established that *no* valid argument exists to support that thesis. But a diligent search of the literature fails to discover one.

For some people, the fact that the Bible expresses very strong disapproval of homosexuality is sufficient to establish the fact that it is wicked. For them, no further argument is needed. Others are so disgusted by what they consider to be gross practices, more or less on the same level as bestiality or the consumption of rats or insects, that no intellectual arguments are likely to overcome their powerful emotional reactions. But such reasons are not philosophical, and are not likely to persuade anyone who chooses to base her moral judgments on reason rather than on ancient authority or pure emotionalism.

Despite the weight of tradition, the burden is on those who advocate the ostracism of homosexuals to demonstrate that there are cogent reasons for so punishing human beings whose only crime, if it is one, is to engage in the only form of love-making that they feel capable of. Nor is there any intellectually acceptable justification for the imposition of civil or criminal sanctions against gays and lesbians, or depriving them of the benefits of legal privileges that are available to people whose sexual inclinations are more in accordance with the views of most other people – such privileges as the right to inherit, to enjoy tax relief that is open to married couples, and perhaps to adopt children. (I say "perhaps" because further considerations may be relevant to that policy issue.) Some adult gays and lesbians have adopted their lovers, with their lovers' consent, in order to establish a kind of family relationship that would be recognized by the law. That they have had to resort to this rather strange use of adoption laws is an unfortunate consequence of the law's refusal to recognize long-term, stable relationships between them. Legislatures have generally refused to change the law to make it more favorable to homosexual relationships because many legislators and their constituents view homosexuality as immoral and are unwilling to confer legal recognition upon it.

V. Homosexuals: Rights and Responsibilities

The moral issues surrounding homosexuality are not exhausted, however, by this discussion. Even if our communities recognize the rights of gays and lesbians to pursue their way of life without legal interference, there remain exceedingly delicate questions of the relations of gays and lesbians with their families and associates, and the moral dimensions of some of those relationships. Since none of the philosophical arguments against homosexuality holds up under critical analysis, it would seem to be reasonable to conclude that there remains no cogent justification for discriminating against homosexuals, either legally or in social relations. At the same time, however, it is reasonable to expect homosexuals to behave responsibly toward others, including those who – for whatever reason – find their way of life unacceptable.

Gays and lesbians who have demonstrated in St Patrick's Cathedral in New York City, for example, disrupting services by raucous chanting designed to draw attention to their displeasure with the Church's policies toward people with their orientation, seem to have overstepped the bounds of decency and propriety. The gay and lesbian organization "Act Up" has mounted numerous rowdy demonstrations and marches, protesting what its participants see as injustices perpetrated against homosexuals. Far from winning sympathy for their cause, such incidents are likely to drive potential supporters away. But there is a larger question of the moral propriety of their behavior.

The American legal tradition exempts religious institutions from governmental control. The public policy behind this tradition derives from the theory that private associations should be free to determine their own policies, so long as they do not seriously jeopardize the fundamental rights of others. That principle implies that religious institutions, and other private associations, should be free to change their ancient strictures against homosexuality if their leaders choose to do so; but that they ought also to be free to *refuse* to abandon those practices and restrictions, as they see fit. Neither the First Amendment nor liberal views on free speech sanction the disruption of religious services, however worthy the cause. Nor do they authorize gays and lesbians to appoint themselves as censors to delete Biblical passages that unequivocally condemn homosexuality, however hurtful those passages might be.

Consider a man who pays surreptitious visits to a married woman, sends her flowers, writes amorous notes to her, and frequently calls her on the phone when her husband is out. These attentions threaten the integrity and stability of her marriage and the happiness of her husband and children, even if the relationship never develops into an overtly sexual one. Substitute a woman for the man (i.e., the third party) in this example, so that the outsider, a woman, is paying loving attention to the wife, and the morality of the situation undergoes no change at all. If the affection that develops between them becomes so deep and passionate that it alienates the married party from her spouse, then it is wrong – whether the new relationship is heterosexual or not. And if the new relationship becomes a sexual one, then it appears to be adulterous, whatever the sexual orientation of the parties. Although we gave up prosecuting adulterers and adulteresses long ago, and no longer permit people to sue for the damage done to them and their families through what the law used to call criminal conversation – adulterous cohabitation – or alienation of a spouse's affections, moral reprobation would seem to be appropriate in such cases, considering the hurt and the damage that they cause. What is true of heterosexuals seems no less true of homosexuals.

Many gays and lesbians, having been hurt by others, may have become callous toward persons who do not share their views on sexuality. Intent on pursuing their own inclinations – perhaps with justification – they may fail to realize how much hurt they cause to others in the process. No doubt it can be extremely painful for the traditional parents of a gay person to accept the strange (to them) way of life that their son or daughter has adopted. The natural desire of the gay son or daughter to be accepted by his or her parents should, one would think, be accompanied by an understanding of the difficulty the parents must have in accepting what must seem to them to be an outrageous, immoral way of life.

On the other hand, it is difficult to think of anything more cruel and heartless than the utter abandonment of a dying AIDS victim by his or her family because of self-righteousness, religious zealotry, or disapproval of homosexuality. Too many victims of that awful disease have withered, suffered, and died with no one to comfort them but their lovers, who are often weakened by the same affliction. Those who should be closest to them – their fathers and mothers, brothers and sisters – may be so preoccupied with nursing their own anger, their hurts, and their grievances that they have lost the capacity to be understanding or compassionate toward those to whom they have the closest possible biological connections. In some ways, this is one of the most grievous moral afflictions of our time. If there were a law of nature, one might wish that it would teach us, if not incline us, to care for our sons and daughters, despite our disagreements with them over matters that touch us deeply, particularly when they are suffering. Some have, indeed, responded to that call in heroic measure. But all too many have not.

Like every real human problem, the issues surrounding homosexual relations are complex and fraught with deep emotions. Philosophers may be able to shed some light on the arguments, but in the final analysis, only compassion and good will on all sides will lead to the kind of understanding and acceptance that may ultimately lead to a resolution of the most painful of them.

Virtues

Although William Bennett's *The Book of Virtues* (Simon and Schuster, 1993) has reinjected the language of virtue into the public arena, many people don't think much about the virtues – virtues just aren't a central part of our culture's currency. When most people do think about them, they primarily think of quaint virtues like chastity and humility, virtues possessed by the few – and usually the puritan. Some people have a more robust catalogue of virtues that includes honesty, integrity, and generosity. Even so, these people tend to conceive of virtues as private possessions reflecting personal purity ("He is a virtuous person"), rather than habits of action with profound social and political consequences.

Perhaps some virtues are primarily private. Most, though, are not private either in origin or influence. Generosity is a clear example. We assume generous people will benefit others within and without their community. We would not be surprised to learn that Generous George regularly contributes to organizations working to alleviate WORLD HUNGER. However, we would think it ludicrous to call George "generous" if he never contributed to charity. Generous people act generously: they directly benefit others.

Social environments also support, even spawn, certain virtues (and vices). I suspect some virtues (vices) are impossible except in particular social environments. It is difficult to see how generosity (or stinginess) could flourish, or even be possible, in a world where everyone had everything they wanted. Nor could we understand how chastity could be a virtue (or promiscuity a vice) in a wholly asexual world.

However, we need not rely on highly fictional examples. With a bit of thought we will realize that we usually develop or downplay virtues (or vices) in response to social and political circumstances. Hill argues, for example, that the vice of servility, and the virtue of self-respect, are more likely to emerge and to be of profound moral concern in a society with a long history of oppression. Slaves were often servile: they did not claim their rights. Probably they didn't recognize or appreciate their own moral worth. That is neither surprising nor objectionable. Prudent slaves were usually deferential or self-deprecating since their lives and the lives of their families depended on it. In such an oppressive environment, servility was not a vice. Perhaps it is a misnomer to call it "servility." Rather, it was disguised prudence.

Although the oppression of women has not been quite so dramatic, Hill claims, most women in our society have learned to defer to their husbands: not just to grant their husbands' wishes, but actually preferring that their husbands' desires and interests be satisfied over their own. This suggests that Hill would agree with Bartky's claim that men often emotionally exploit the women in their lives (FAMILY AND FRIENDS).

Although prudence once required that blacks and women be servile, it does so no longer. In the current environment, servility is a vice that blacks and women should eliminate. Indeed, it is vitally important that the victims of systematic discrimination now cultivate the virtue of self-respect: to see themselves as valuable people whom others should respect. People with the appropriate self-respect will, among other things, claim their rights, even if – and perhaps especially if – others would prefer that they be silent. Thus, self-respecting blacks must be willing to claim their rights, especially in the face of persistent racism. Likewise, self-respecting women must claim their rights, especially in the face of gross sexism. Otherwise, by their silence, they imply that the dominant group's attitude toward them is justified.

This appears to be at odds with Leiser's suggestion that homosexuals should respect the views of others, including (and perhaps especially) the views of those who condemn homosexuality (SEXUALITY). I suspect Hill would argue, instead, that homosexuals should claim their rights, especially against those who condemn them. Otherwise, by their silence they imply that they think they are inferior to heterosexuals.

Although Hunt acknowledges that society and education shape individual virtues, he thinks it is misleading, and probably dangerous, to assume that political systems are the best means for making people more virtuous. The law can require citizens to comply with pre-established rules and norms. However, virtuous people do not simply follow prescribed rules. What matters is not only what a person does, but why she does it. The truly virtuous does not simply mimic virtuous action. She understands why she acts virtuously. That requires, Hunt says, that she respect others. And law cannot require that we respect others. In trying to legislate virtue, the state not only fails to promote virtue, it hinders its development.

Hunt's general description of virtue is consistent with Wallace's specific account of generosity. Since an act is generous only if it goes beyond what we expected of a person, then, by definition, we cannot legislate generosity. It is especially interesting to note the parallel between Hunt's claim that respect for others is the cornerstone of virtuous action and Hill's claim that only a person who respects herself can be virtuous. Taken together these claims suggest that acknowledgment of personal worth – whether one's own or of others – is the key to becoming virtuous, to becoming a full moral person.

Fesmire disagrees with Hunt, at least in part. Whereas Hunt denigrates the power of political means to make people virtuous, Fesmire claims that social and political arrangements not only can promote individual virtues, but are essential for virtues. Contrary to popular opinion, virtues are never purely individual. To assume they are is to assume that humans are atomistic, individualistic, and fundamentally non-social. They are not, Fesmire claims. Rather, humans are inevitably social. Our social environment shapes our language, thoughts, beliefs, virtues, and vices. Although virtues are usually associated with particular individuals ("Sue is courageous," or "James is conscientious"), virtues are never the sole possession of any individual, but only of that individual within a society.

These questions about the nature and origin of virtues are intricately connected to our understanding of individual responsibility. If we choose our characters (virtuous and vicious), then naturally we are responsible for all our actions. Conversely if our environment significantly shapes our character, then our individual responsibility will be more diffuse. That does not mean that we are not responsible for what we do. I suspect it means we are more, but differently, responsible. On this ecological view, we are responsible not only for what we do directly, but also for our role in supporting and sustaining social conditions which shape and maintain the character of others.

How we resolve these questions has clear implications for our system of criminal PUNISHMENT. According to Rachels and Murphy, the criminal justice system requires that we hold individuals responsible for their actions. That is, Rachels claims, the system of criminal punishment rests on the idea that we should give criminals what they deserve, and what they deserve is determined by what they choose to do. Yet if who I am and what I do is determined by society, then in what sense am I responsible for my actions? For, on this supposition, it seems as if I could not have acted differently than I did. Many critics of the criminal-justice punishment raise just this objection. For instance, it underlies Pasquerella's misgivings about the current tendency to make criminal PUNISHMENT more severe.

Murphy also rejects any attempt to relieve individuals of responsibility for their actions. However, he develops his view rather differently. He argues that repentance should play a central role in an ideal system of punishment. Repentance, though, would be inappropriate if we were not responsible for our actions. Yet sociological evidence suggests that society strongly influences how we think and act. Does that mean we must jettison all talk about character, virtues, and personal responsibility from our language? I don't think so. According to Fesmire, if we recognize the social basis of character, we will alter our notion of individual responsibility, but we will not relinquish it. Nonetheless, it is a fascinating theoretical question how we should understand and explain individual responsibility if individuals are shaped, as they seem to be, by social forces.

Further Reading

Baier, A. 1985: *Postures of the Mind*. Minneapolis: University of Minnesota Press.

Flanagan, O. and Rorty, A. 1993: *Identity, Character, and Morality*. Cambridge, MA: MIT Press.

Foot, P. 1978: *Virtues and Vices*. Berkeley: University of California Press.

French, P., Uehling, T., Weitstein, H. 1988: *Ethical Theory: Character and Virtue*. Notre Dame, IN: University of Notre Dame Press.

MacIntyre, A. 1981: *After Virtue*. Notre Dame, IN: University of Notre Dame Press.

Sabini, J. and Silver, M. 1982: *Moralities of Everyday Life*. New York: Oxford University Press.

Slote, M. 1983: *Goods and Virtues*. Oxford: Oxford University Press.

Sommers, C. and Sommers, F. 1989: *Vice and Virtue in Everyday Life: Introductory Readings in Ethics* (2nd edition). New York: Harcourt, Brace, Jovanovich.

Wallace, J. 1978: *Virtues and Vices*. Ithaca, NY: Cornell University Press.

23

Servility and Self-Respect

Thomas E. Hill, Jr.

Several motives underlie this paper. In the first place, I am curious to see if there is a legitimate source for the increasingly common feeling that servility can be as much a vice as arrogance is. There seems to be something morally defective about the Uncle Tom and the submissive housewife; and yet, on the other hand, if the only interests they sacrifice are their own, it seems that we should have no right to complain. Secondly, I have some sympathy for the now unfashionable view that each person has duties to himself as well as to others. It does seem absurd to say that a person could literally violate his own rights or owe himself a debt of gratitude, but I suspect that the classic defenders of duties to oneself had something different in mind. If there are duties to oneself, it is natural to expect that a duty to avoid being servile would have a prominent place among them. . . .

I

Three examples may give a preliminary idea of what I mean by *servility*. Consider, first, an extremely deferential black, whom I shall call the *Uncle Tom*. He always steps aside for white men; he does not complain when less qualified whites take over his job; he gratefully accepts whatever benefits his all-white government and employers allot him, and he would not think of protesting its insufficiency. He displays the symbols of deference to whites, and of contempt toward blacks: he faces the former with bowed stance and a ready "Sir" and "Ma'am"; he reserves his strongest obscenities for the latter. Imagine, too, that he is not playing a game. He is not the shrewdly prudent calculator, who knows how to make the best of a bad lot and mocks his masters behind their backs. He accepts without question the idea that, as a black, he is owed less than whites. He may believe that blacks are mentally inferior and of less social utility, but that is not the crucial point. The attitude which he displays is that what he values, aspires for, and can demand is of less importance than what whites value, aspire for, and can demand. He is far from the picture book's carefree, happy servant, but he does not feel that he has a right to expect anything better.

Another pattern of servility is illustrated by a person I shall call the *Self-deprecator*. Like the Uncle Tom, he is reluctant to make demands. He says nothing when others take unfair advantage of him. When asked for his preferences or opinions, he tends to shrink away as if what he said should make no difference. His problem, however, is not a sense of racial inferiority but rather an acute awareness of his own inadequacies and failures as an individual. These defects are not imaginary: he has in fact done poorly by his own standards and others'. But, unlike many of us in the same situation, he acts as if his failings warrant quite unrelated maltreatment even by strangers. His sense of shame and self-contempt makes him content to be the instrument of others. He feels that nothing is owed him until he has earned it and that he has earned very little. He is not simply playing a masochist's game of winning sympathy by disparaging himself. On the contrary, he assesses his individual merits with painful accuracy.

A rather different case is that of the *Deferential Wife*. This is a woman who is utterly devoted to serving her husband. She buys the clothes *he* prefers, invites the guests *he* wants to entertain, and makes love whenever *he* is in the mood. She willingly moves to a new city in order for him to have a more attractive job, counting her own friendships and geographical preferences insignificant by comparison. She loves her husband, but her conduct is not simply an expression of love. She is happy, but she does not subordinate herself as a means to happiness. She does not simply defer to her husband in certain spheres as a trade-off for his deference in other spheres. On the contrary, she tends not to form her own interests, values, and ideals; and, when she does, she counts them as less important than her husband's. She readily responds to appeals from Women's Liberation that she agrees that women are mentally and physically equal, if not superior, to men. She just believes that the proper role for a woman is to serve her family. As a matter of fact, much of her happiness derives from her belief that she fulfills this role very well. No one is trampling on her rights, she says; for she is quite glad, and proud, to serve her husband as she does.

Each one of these cases reflects the attitude which I call servility.[1] It betrays the absence of a certain kind of self-respect. What I take this attitude to be, more specifically, will become clearer later on. It is important at the outset, however, not to confuse the three cases sketched above with other, superficially similar cases. In particular, the cases I have sketched are not simply cases in which someone refuses to press his rights, speaks disparagingly of himself, or devotes himself to another. A black, for example, is not necessarily servile because he does not demand a just wage; for, seeing that such a demand would result in his being fired, he might forbear for the sake of his children. A self-critical person is not necessarily servile by virtue of bemoaning his faults in public; for his behavior may be merely a complex way of satisfying his own inner needs quite independent of a willingness to accept abuse from others. A woman need not be servile whenever she works to make her husband happy and prosperous; for she might freely and knowingly choose to do so from love or from a desire to share the rewards of his success. If the effort did not require her to submit to humiliation or maltreatment, her choice would not mark her as servile. There may, of course, be grounds for objecting to the attitudes in these cases; but the defect is not servility of the sort I want to consider. It should also be noted that my cases of servility are not simply instances of deference to superior knowledge or judgment. To defer to an expert's judgment on matters of fact is not to be servile; to defer to his every wish and whim is. Similarly the belief that one's talents and achievements are comparatively low does not, by itself, make one servile. It is no vice to acknowledge the truth, and one may in fact have achieved less, and have less ability, than others. To be servile is not simply to hold certain empirical beliefs but to have a certain attitude concerning one's rightful place in a moral community.

II

Are there grounds for regarding the attitudes of the Uncle Tom, the Self-deprecator, and the Deferential Wife as morally objectionable? Are there moral arguments we could give them to show that they ought to have more self-respect? None of the more obvious replies is entirely satisfactory.

One might, in the first place, adduce utilitarian considerations. Typically the servile person will be less happy than he might be. Moreover, he may be less prone to make the best of his own socially useful abilities. He may become a nuisance to others by being overly dependent. He will, in any case, lose the special contentment that comes from standing up for one's rights. A submissive attitude encourages exploitation, and exploitation spreads misery in a variety of ways. These considerations provide a *prima facie* case against the attitudes of the Uncle Tom, the Deferential Wife, and the Self-deprecator, but they are hardly conclusive. Other utilities tend to counterbalance the ones just mentioned. When people refuse to press their rights, there are usually others who profit. There are undeniable pleasures in associating with those who are devoted, understanding, and grateful for whatever we see fit to give them – as our fondness for dogs attests. Even the servile person may find his attitude a source of happiness, as the case of the Deferential Wife illustrates. There may be comfort and security in thinking that the hard choices must be made by others, that what I would say has little to do with what ought to be done. Self-condemnation may bring relief from the pangs of guilt even if it is not deliberately used for that purpose. On balance, then, utilitarian considerations may turn out to favor servility as much as they oppose it.

For those who share my moral intuitions, there is another sort of reason for not trying to rest a case against servility on utilitarian considerations. Certain utilities seem irrelevant to the issue. The utilitarian must weigh them along with others, but to do so seems morally inappropriate. Suppose, for example, that the submissive attitudes of the Uncle Tom and the Deferential Wife result in positive utilities for those who dominate and exploit them. Do we need to tabulate *these* utilities before conceding that servility is objectionable? The Uncle Tom, it seems, is making an error, a moral error, quite apart from consideration of how much others in fact profit from his attitude. The Deferential Wife may be quite happy; but if her happiness turns out to be contingent on her distorted view of her own rights and worth as a person, then it carries little moral weight against the contention that she ought to change that view. Suppose I could cause a woman to find her happiness in denying all her rights and serving my every wish. No doubt I could do so only by nonrational manipulative techniques, which I ought not to use. But is this the only objection? My efforts would be wrong, it seems, not only because of the techniques they require but also because the resultant attitude is itself objectionable. When a person's happiness stems from a morally objectionable attitude, it ought to be discounted. That a sadist gets pleasure from seeing others suffer should not count even as a partial justification for his attitude. That a servile person derives pleasure from denying her moral status, for similar reasons, cannot make her attitude acceptable. These brief intuitive remarks are not intended as a refutation of utilitarianism, with all its many varieties; but they do suggest that it is well to look elsewhere for adequate grounds for rejecting the attitudes of the Uncle Tom, the Self-deprecator, and the Deferential Wife.

III

Why, then, is servility a moral defect? There is, I think, another sort of answer which is worth exploring. The first part of this answer must be an attempt to isolate the objectionable features of the servile person; later we can ask why these features are objectionable. As a step in this direction, let us examine again our three paradigm cases. The moral defect in each case, I suggest, is a failure to understand and acknowledge one's own moral rights. I assume, without argument here, that each person has moral rights. Some of these rights may be basic human rights; that is, rights for which a person needs only to be human to qualify. Other rights will be derivative and contingent upon his special commitments, institutional affiliations, etc. Most rights will be *prima facie* ones; some may be absolute. Most can be waived under appropriate conditions; perhaps some cannot. Many rights can be forfeited; but some, presumably, cannot. The servile person does not, strictly speaking, violate his own rights. At least in our paradigm cases he fails to acknowledge fully his own moral status because he does not fully understand what his rights are, how they can be waived, and when they can be forfeited.

The defect of the Uncle Tom, for example, is that he displays an attitude that denies his moral equality with whites. He does not realize, or apprehend in an effective way, that he has as much right to a decent wage and a share of political power as any comparable white. His gratitude is misplaced; he accepts benefits which are his by right as if they were gifts. The Self-deprecator is servile in a more complex way. He acts as if he has forfeited many important rights which in fact he has not. He does not understand, or fully realize in his own case, that certain rights to fair and decent treatment do not have to be earned. He sees his merits clearly enough, but he fails to see that what he can expect from others is not merely a function of his merits. The Deferential Wife *says* that she understands her rights vis-à-vis her husband, but what she fails to appreciate is that her consent to serve him is a valid waiver of her rights only under certain conditions. If her consent is coerced, say, by the lack of viable options for women in her society, then her consent is worth little. If socially fostered ignorance of her own talents and alternatives is responsible for her consent, then her consent should not count as a fully legitimate waiver of her right to equal consideration within the marriage. All the more, her consent to defer constantly to her husband is not a legitimate setting aside of her rights if it results from her mistaken belief that she has a moral duty to do so. (Recall: "The *proper* role for a woman is to serve her family.") If she believes that she has a *duty* to defer to her husband, then, whatever she may say, she cannot fully understand that she has a *right* not to defer to him. When she says that she freely gives up such a right, she is confused. Her confusion is rather like that of a person who has been persuaded by an unscrupulous lawyer that it is legally incumbent on him to refuse a jury trial but who nevertheless tells the judge that he understands that he has a right to a jury trial and freely waives it. He does not really understand what it is to have and freely give up the right if he thinks that it would be an offense for him to exercise it.

Insofar as servility results from moral ignorance or confusion, it need not be something for which a person is to blame. . . . Suppose, however, that our servile persons come to know their rights but do not substantially alter their behavior. Are they not still servile in an objectionable way?

The answer, I think, should depend upon why the deferential role is played. If the motive is a morally commendable one, or a desire to avert dire consequences to oneself, or even an ambition to set an oppressor up for a later fall, then I would not count the role player as servile. The Uncle Tom, for instance, is not servile in my sense if he shuffles and bows to keep the Klan from killing his children, to save his own skin, or even to buy time while he plans the revolution. Similarly, the Deferential Wife is not servile if she tolerates an abusive husband because he is so ill that further strain would kill him, because protesting would deprive her of her only means of survival, or because she is collecting atrocity stories for her book against marriage. If there is fault in these situations, it seems inappropriate to call it *servility*. The story is quite different, however, if a person continues in his deferential role just from laziness, timidity, or a desire for some minor advantage. He shows too little concern for his moral status as a person, one is tempted to say, if he is willing to deny it for a small profit or simply because it requires some effort and courage to affirm it openly. A black who plays the Uncle Tom merely to gain an advantage over other blacks is harming them, of course; but he is also displaying disregard for his own moral position as an equal among human beings. Similarly, a woman throws away her rights too lightly if she continues to play the subservient role because she is used to it or is too timid to risk a change. A Self-deprecator who readily accepts what he knows are violations of his rights may be indulging his peculiar need for punishment at the expense of denying something more valuable. In these cases, I suggest, we have a kind of servility independent of any ignorance or confusion about one's rights. The person who has it may or may not be blameworthy, depending on many factors; and the line between servile and nonservile role-playing will often be hard to draw. Nevertheless, the objectionable feature is perhaps clear enough for present purposes: it is a willingness to disavow one's moral status, publicly and systematically, in the absence of any strong reason to do so.

IV

The objectionable feature of the servile person, as I have described him, is his tendency to disavow his own moral rights either because he misunderstands them or because he cares little for them. The question remains: why should anyone regard this as a moral defect? After all, the rights which he denies are his own. He may be unfortunate, foolish, or even distasteful; but why *morally* deficient? One sort of answer, quite different from those reviewed earlier, is suggested by some of Kant's remarks. Kant held that servility is contrary to a perfect nonjuridical duty to oneself.[2] To say that the duty is perfect is roughly to say that it is stringent, never overridden by other considerations (e.g., beneficence). To say that the duty is nonjuridical is to say that a person cannot legitimately be coerced to comply. Although Kant did not develop an explicit argument for this view, an argument can easily be constructed from materials which reflect the spirit, if not the letter, of his moral theory. The argument which I have in mind is prompted by Kant's contention that respect for persons, strictly speaking, is respect for moral law.[3] If taken as a claim about all sorts of respect, this seems quite implausible. If it means that we respect persons only for their moral character, their capacity for moral conduct, or their status as "authors" of the moral law, then it seems unduly moralistic. My strategy is to construe the remark as saying that at least one sort of respect for persons is respect for the rights which the moral law accords them. If one respects the moral law, then one must respect one's own moral rights; and this amounts to having a kind of self-respect incompatible with servility.

   The premises for the Kantian argument, which are all admittedly vague, can be sketched as follows:

First, let us assume, as Kant did, that all human beings have equal basic human rights. Specific rights vary with different conditions, but all must be justified from a point of view under which all are equal. Not all rights need to be earned, and some cannot be forfeited. Many rights can be waived but only under certain conditions of knowledge and freedom. These conditions are complex and difficult to state; but they include something like the condition that a person's consent releases others from obligation only if it is autonomously given, and consent resulting from underestimation of one's moral status is not autonomously given. Rights can be objects of knowledge, but also of ignorance, misunderstanding, deception, and the like.

Second, let us assume that my account of servility is correct; or, if one prefers, we can take it as a definition. That is, in brief, a servile person is one who tends to deny or disavow his own moral rights because he does not understand them or has little concern for the status they give him.

Third, we need one formal premise concerning moral duty, namely, that each person ought, as far as possible, to respect the moral law. In less Kantian language, the point is that everyone should approximate, to the extent that he can, the ideal of a person who fully adopts the moral point of view. Roughly, this means not only that each person ought to do what is morally required and refrain from what is morally wrong but also that each person should treat all the provisions of morality as valuable – worth preserving and prizing as well as obeying. One must, so to speak, take up the spirit of morality as well as meet the letter of its requirements. To keep one's promises, avoid hurting others, and the like, is not sufficient; one should also take an attitude of respect towards the principles, ideals, and goals of morality. A respectful attitude towards a system of rights and duties consists of more than a disposition to conform to its definite rules of behavior; it also involves holding the system in esteem, being unwilling to ridicule it, and being reluctant to give up one's place in it. The essentially Kantian idea here is that morality, as a system of equal fundamental rights and duties, is worthy of respect, and hence a completely moral person would respect it in word and manner as well as in deed. And what a completely moral person would do, in Kant's view, is our duty to do so far as we can.

The assumptions here are, of course, strong ones, and I make no attempt to justify them. They are, I suspect, widely held though rarely articulated. In any case, my present purpose is not to evaluate them but to see how, if granted, they constitute a case against servility. The objection to the servile person, given our premises, is that he does not satisfy the basic requirement to respect morality. A person who fully respected a system of moral rights would be disposed to learn his proper place in it, to affirm it proudly, and not to tolerate abuses of it lightly. This is just the sort of disposition that the servile person lacks. If he does not understand the system, he is in no position to respect it adequately. This lack of respect may be no fault of his own, but it is still a way in which he falls short of a moral ideal. If, on the other hand, the servile person knowingly disavows his moral rights by pretending to approve of violations of them, then, barring special explanations, he shows an indifference to whether the provisions of morality are honored and publicly acknowledged. This avoidable display of indifference, by our Kantian premises, is contrary to the duty to respect morality. The disrespect in this second case is somewhat like the disrespect a religious believer might show towards his religion if, to avoid embarrassment, he laughed congenially while nonbelievers were mocking the beliefs which he secretly held. In any case, the servile person, as such, does not express disrespect for the system of moral rights in the obvious way by violating the rights of others. His lack of respect is more subtly manifested by his acting before others as if he did not know or care about his position of equality under that system.

The central idea here may be illustrated by an analogy. Imagine a club, say, an old German dueling fraternity. By the rules of the club, each member has certain rights and responsibilities. These are the same for each member regardless of what titles he may hold outside the club. Each has, for example, a right to be heard at meetings, a right not to be shouted down by the others. Some rights cannot be forfeited: for example, each may vote regardless of whether he has paid his dues and satisfied other rules. Some rights cannot be waived: for example, the right to be defended when attacked by several members of the rival fraternity. The members show respect for each other by respecting the status which the rules confer on each member. Now one new member is careful always to allow the others to speak at meetings; but when they shout him down, he does nothing. He just shrugs as if to say, "Who am I to complain?" When he fails to stand up in defense of a fellow member, he feels ashamed and refuses to vote. He does not deserve to vote, he says. As the only commoner among illustrious barons, he feels that it is his place to serve them and defer to their decisions. When attackers from the rival fraternity come at him with swords drawn, he tells his companions to run and save themselves. When they defend him, he expresses immense gratitude – as if they had done him a gratuitous favor. Now one might argue that our new member fails to show respect for the fraternity and its rules. He does not actually violate any of the rules by refusing to vote, asking others not to defend him, and deferring to the barons, but he symbolically disavows the equal status which the rules confer on him. If he ought to have respect for the fraternity, he ought to change his attitude. Our servile person, then, is like the new member of the dueling fraternity in having insufficient respect for a system of rules and ideals. The difference is that everyone ought to respect morality whereas there is no comparable moral requirement to respect the fraternity.

The conclusion here is, of course, a limited one. Self-sacrifice is not always a sign of servility. It is not a duty always to press one's rights. Whether a given act is evidence of servility will depend not only on the attitude of the agent but also on the specific nature of his moral rights, a matter not considered here. Moreover, the extent to which a person is responsible, or blameworthy, for his defect remains an open question. Nevertheless, the conclusion should not be minimized. In order to avoid servility, a person who gives up his rights must do so with a full appreciation for what they are. A woman, for example, may devote herself to her husband if she is uncoerced, knows what she is doing, and does not pretend that she has no decent alternative. A self-contemptuous person may decide not to press various unforfeited rights but only if he does not take the attitude that he is too rotten to deserve them. A black may demand less than is due to him provided he is prepared to acknowledge that no one has a right to expect this of him. Sacrifices of this sort, I suspect, are extremely rare. Most people, if they fully acknowledged their rights, would not auto-nomously refuse to press them.

An even stronger conclusion would emerge if we could assume that some basic rights cannot be waived. . . .

Even if there are no specific rights which cannot be waived, there might be at least one formal right of this sort. This is the right to some minimum degree of respect from others. No matter how willing a person is to submit to humiliation by others, they ought to show him some respect as a person. By analogy with self-respect, as presented here, this respect owed by others would consist of a willingness to acknowledge fully, in word as well as action, the person's basically equal moral status as defined by his other rights. To the extent that a person gives even tacit consent to humiliations incompatible with this respect, he will be acting as if he waives a right which he cannot in fact give up. To do this, barring special explanations, would mark one as servile.

Kant suggests that duties to oneself are a precondition of duties to others. On our account of servility, there is at least one sense in which this is so. Insofar as the servile person is ignorant of his own rights, he is not in an adequate position to appreciate the rights of others. Misunderstanding the moral basis for his equal status with others, he is necessarily liable to underestimate the rights of those with whom he classifies himself. On the other hand, if he plays the servile role knowingly, then, barring special explanation, he displays a lack of concern to see the principles of morality acknowledged and respected and thus the absence of one motive which can move a moral person to respect the rights of others. In either case, the servile person's lack of self-respect necessarily puts him in a less than ideal position to respect others. Failure to fulfill one's duty to oneself, then, renders a person liable to violate duties to others. This, however, is a consequence of our argument against servility, not a presupposition of it.

Notes

1   Each of the cases is intended to represent only one possible pattern of servility. I make no claims about how often these patterns are exemplified, nor do I mean to imply that only these patterns could warrant the labels "Deferential Wife," "Uncle Tom," etc. All the more, I do not mean to imply any comparative judgments about the causes or relative magnitude of the problems of racial and sexual discrimination. One person, e.g. a self-contemptuous woman with a sense of racial inferiority, might exemplify features of several patterns at once; and, of course, a person might view her being a woman the way an Uncle Tom views his being black, etc.

2   See Immanuel Kant, *The Doctrine of Virtue*, Part II of *The Metaphysics of Morals*, ed. M. J. Gregor (New York: Harper & Row, 1964), pp. 99–103; Prussian Academy edition, vol. VI, pp. 434–7.

3   Immanuel Kant, *Groundwork of the Metaphysics of Morals*, ed. H. J. Paton (New York: Harper & Row, 1964), p. 69; Prussian Academy edition, vol. IV, p. 401; *The Critique of Practical Reason*, ed. Lewis W. Beck (New York: Bobbs-Merrill, 1956), pp. 81, 84; Prussian Academy edition, vol. V, pp. 78, 81. My purpose here is not to interpret what Kant meant but to give a sense to his remark.

24

Generosity

James D. Wallace

Economic Generosity

Generosity is concerned with giving, and different kinds of generosity can be distinguished according to the kind of things given. Aristotle said that generosity (*eleutheriotēs*) has to do with giving and taking of things whose value is measured in money. There is a virtue called generosity, the actions fully characteristic of which are meritorious, which has to do with freely giving things that have a *market value* – freely giving goods and services of a type that normally are exchanged on the open market. This sort of generosity I call "economic generosity" to distinguish it from other varieties. One can be generous in the judgments one makes about the merits and demerits of others, and one can be generous in forgiving those who trespass against one. "Generous-mindedness" and "generous-heartedness," as these other kinds of generosity might be called, do not involve being generous with things whose value is measured in money. These are like economic generosity in certain ways, but they also differ in important respects, as I shall try subsequently to show. Unless otherwise indicated, however, by generosity I mean economic generosity.

A generous person is one who has a certain attitude toward his own things, the value of which is measured in money, and who also has a certain attitude toward other people. Generosity, like other forms of benevolence, in its primary occurrence, involves as one of its constituents a concern for the happiness and well-being of others. The actions fully characteristic of generosity have as their goal promoting someone else's well-being, comfort, happiness, or pleasure – someone else's good. In *primary generosity*, the agent is concerned directly about the good of another. Thus, an action fully characteristic of generosity might be done to please someone or to help someone, with no further end in view beyond pleasing or helping. "I just wanted to do something nice for them" or "I just wanted her to have it" are typical explanations of generous acts.

That an act fully characteristic of *the virtue* generosity, is motivated in this way by a direct concern for the good of another is not immediately obvious, because we sometimes call giving "generous" and mean only that the giver is giving more than someone in his situation normally gives. Thus, the host is being generous with the mashed potatoes when he unthinkingly heaps unusually large portions on the plates. Or perhaps he does not do it unthinkingly. It might be that he is giving such generous portions because he wants to use up all the potatoes to prevent them from spoiling. Being generous in this way – giving a lot for reasons such as these – would not tend to show that the host is a *generous person*, even if he did so frequently. If we restrict ourselves to the kind of generous action that is fully characteristic of a generous person, then in every case, the agent's giving will be motivated by a direct concern for the good (in the broad sense) of another. I shall say in such cases that the agent intends to *benefit* the recipient.

There is a further complication. The virtue generosity, in its *primary occurrence*, I have said, involves a sort of direct concern for the good of others, as do other forms of benevolence. Someone who is deficient in such concern or who lacks it altogether might admire generous people for their generosity and want as far as he can to be like them. He might then want to do in certain situations what a generous person would do. Acting as a generous person would act because one regards generosity as a virtue, and wants, therefore, to emulate the generous person is meritorious, and it reflects credit upon the agent. It is, however, a secondary sort of generosity. It depends, for its merit, upon the fact that primary generosity *is* a virtue and is thus a worthy ideal at which to aim. I will concentrate, therefore, upon primary generosity, which does involve a direct concern for the good of another. An account of why this is a virtue is easily extended to explain why a generous person is worthy of emulation.

A certain sort of attitude on the part of the agent toward what he gives is also a feature of actions fully characteristic of the virtue of generosity. In acting generously, one must give something that one values – something that one, therefore, has some reason to keep rather than discard or abandon. If, for example, one is about to throw away an article of clothing, and on the way to the trash barrel one meets someone who would like to have it, it would not be *generous* of one to give it to him. What disqualifies such giving from being generous is neither the giver's motive nor the nature of what is given but rather the fact that the giver himself does not value the object enough. Similarly, when we do favors for one another, giving matches or coins for parking meters, often what is given is too insignificant for the giving of it to be generous. One may be being kind in giving things that one does not particularly value, but for the giving to be generous, one must value the thing given for some reason. I may have acquired a particularly repulsive piece of primitive art that I have no desire to keep. Still, I might generously give it to a museum if it were a valuable piece – one I could sell or exchange for something I really want. How *generous* one is being in giving something generally depends upon how much one values the thing given, how much one is giving up.

Usually, the giver must give in excess of what he is required to give by morality or custom, if his giving is to be generous. Where there exists a generally recognized moral obligation to give, or where giving is customary, then normally one's giving is not generous even though it is prompted by a direct concern for the good of the recipient. If one were certain of a more than ample and continuing supply of food, so that it would clearly be wrong not to give some food to a neighbor who would otherwise go hungry, giving the neighbor a portion of food would not be generous. Similarly, to give a person a gift when one is expected to do so, because it is customary to exchange gifts (for example birthdays, Christmas, weddings, etc.), is normally not a matter of generosity, even though one aims to please the recipient. If one gives *more* than what is expected in such cases, then the giving might be generous. A generous person is one who exceeds normal expectations in giving, and one who gives no more than what is generally expected in the circumstances is not apt to be cited for generosity.

A special problem arises in cases of the following sort. Although it would clearly be wrong for a certain person *not* to give, he does not see this. Nevertheless, he does give on a generous impulse. Suppose, for example, that a certain person is a social Darwinist, convinced that it is wrong to give the necessities of life to people in need, because this enables the weak to survive, thus weakening the species. She encounters a starving family, and touched by their plight, she provides food for them, though not without a twinge of social Darwinist guilt. Assuming that what she gives is not insignificant to her, but that it is no more than what the family needs to keep them alive, is her giving generous? On the one hand, she is really doing no more than the minimum required of her by the duty to help people in distress, and this makes one hesitate to say that she is being generous. On the other hand, *she* does not recognize any moral obligation here, and it is the kind and generous side of her nature that overcomes her cruel principles and leads her to give. This seems to support the view that she is being generous.

An act fully characteristic of generosity will normally have the following features.

(1) The agent, because of his direct concern for the good of the recipient, gives something with the intention of benefiting the recipient.
(2) The agent gives up something of his that has a market value and that he has some reason to value and, therefore, to keep.
(3) The agent gives more than one is generally expected, because of moral requirements or custom, to give in such circumstances.

In normal cases, an act that meets these three conditions will be a generous act, and a generous act will have these three features. These are, however, abnormal cases – cases in which the agent has, concerning the circumstances mentioned in the three conditions, a false belief or an unusual or eccentric attitude. The case of the social Darwinist is such a case. She thinks she is morally required *not* to give, when in fact she is required to give. If one accepts *her* view of the situation, her act is generous. In fact, however, the third condition is not satisfied. In another sort of abnormal case, the agent values what he gives, but in fact the gift is utterly worthless – it is literally trash. Here it is not clear that the second condition is fulfilled, but from the agent's odd point of view, the act is generous. The very rich often give to charity sums of money that are large in comparison with what others give, and their gifts seem generous. These sums, however, which are substantial, may be relatively insignificant to the donors, and one may wonder whether condition (2) is satisfied in such a case. Does the donor, who has so much, in fact have reason to value and keep what he gives, or is his "gift" analogous to an ordinary person's giving away a book of matches? In a rather different sort of case, someone might be convinced that he is morally required to give away nearly all he has to the poor. For this reason, he divests himself of a substantial fortune. In such cases, it may be that condition (1) is not satisfied. The agent believes, in effect, that condition (3) is not satisfied, since he believes that he is required to do this. These circumstances will make one hesitate to call his giving generous, although other features of the case incline one toward the view that he is being generous.

In these cases involving unusual beliefs or attitudes, one is pulled simultaneously in two different directions. The way the agent sees the situation and the way one expects him to see the situation diverge. Crucial conditions are satisfied from one way of regarding the case and unsatisfied from the other. It is not surprising that one is reluctant to say simply that the act is (or is not) fully characteristic of the virtue generosity. Any such statement must be qualified, and the actual consequences of the qualification may or may not be important, depending upon the case. Normally, of course, the agent's beliefs about the features in (1)– (3) will not be grossly mistaken nor will his attitudes toward those things be unusual or eccentric. In such cases, if the three conditions are satisfied, the act is unqualifiedly generous, and vice versa.

A generous person is one who has a tendency to perform actions that meet these conditions. The stronger the tendency, the more generous the person.

Generous-mindedness

The conditions in the preceding section are meant as an account of actions that are fully characteristic of *economic generosity* – generosity that involves giving things whose value is measured in money. Another kind of generosity, however, has to do with making judgments about the merits and failings of other people. This too is a virtue, which sometimes is called *generous-mindedness*.[2] I will try briefly to indicate some similarities and differences between this virtue and economic generosity.

Generous-mindedness is shown by seeing someone else's merit (technical, moral, etc.) in cases where it is difficult to see because the facts of the case admit of other, not unreasonable interpretations, or because the situation is complex and the merit is not immediately apparent. Generous-mindedness is also shown by seeing that a derogatory judgment is not called for in cases where the facts might not unreasonably be taken to indicate a derogatory judgment. Many of us actually dislike to find that others are as good or better than we are, so that we have some desire to find grounds for derogatory judgments. It is plausible to think that people of otherwise fair judgment are sometimes led to think less of others than they should because they do not want to think well of them or because they want to think ill of them. They do not purposely close their eyes to merit; rather because they do not wish to find it, they do not try hard enough to find it. This may involve a certain amount of self-deception, but I suspect that in many cases the matter is more straightforward. If someone wants to find another inferior to himself in some respect, then where he sees some (prima facie) grounds for such a judgment, he is apt to be quick to seize upon it and regard the matter as settled. A generous-minded person is one who wants to think well of other people, so that in such cases he will look and find the merit that might otherwise go overlooked. Of course, it is possible to be too generous-minded ¬ to overlook demerit because one does not want to find it.

If someone exhibits generous-mindedness in his judgment on a particular occasion, his act of judgment will not fulfill the conditions for an act of economic generosity. It will have features, however, that can be seen as analogous to the features characteristic of economic generosity. If an individual is well-disposed toward other people, then besides wanting to benefit them by giving them things, he will wish them well. He will tend to want their undertakings to succeed and to reflect well on them. If he wants to think well of others, he will be apt to look harder for merit, and he will, therefore, be more likely to find it. Generous-mindedness seems properly regarded as a manifestation of good will toward others that shows a direct concern for the well-being of others.

Economic generosity generally involves giving more than is required or customary, and there is a counterpart to this in generous-mindedness. The generous-minded person sees merit where a competent evaluator might miss it, where it would be reasonable (though incorrect) to find that there is no such merit. In this way, one might say that generous-mindedness leads a person to go beyond what is required of an evaluator. . . .

For generous-mindedness not to distort one's judgment – for it not to lead one to incorrect evaluations – an individual must be a competent evaluator and be conscientious about reaching a correct judgment. Also, it does seem that if one has sufficiently good judgment and is sufficiently concerned to make the right judgment, then this by itself should lead one to see merit when it is present just as well as would the desire *to find merit*. The strong desire to make favorable judgments, moreover, *may* distort one's judgment. It may lead one to overlook defects and to find merit where it is not. A strong desire to make *the correct evaluation* cannot distort one's judgment in this way. Generous-mindedness should not be regarded as a primary virtue of evaluators. It can counteract an inclination to build oneself up by tearing others down, but so too can a strong desire to evaluate correctly. Generous-mindedness is a manifestation of the sort of concern for others that is characteristic of all forms of benevolence. It derives the greatest part of its merit from this concern. . . .

Notes

1   *Nicomachean Ethics*, IV, 1, 1119b21–27.

2   I am indebted to David Shwayder for bringing this topic to my attention.

25

On Improving People by Political Means

Lester H. Hunt

> *Some writers have so confounded society with government, as to leave little or no distinction between them; whereas, they are not only different, but have different origins. Society is produced by our wants, and government by our wickedness; the former promotes our happiness positively by uniting our affections, the latter negatively by restraining our vices. . . . The first is a patron, the last is a punisher.*
>
> Thomas Paine, Common Sense[1]

Clearly, there are a number of ways in which one might think that Thomas Paine's remarks restrict too narrowly the ends that laws can legitimately be framed to serve. I will be concerned with one of them. It has been said that the law may be used not only to restrain our vices but to increase our virtue as well: it can make better people of us and thereby positively promote – if not our happiness, necessarily, then – what might be called "the quality of life." Perhaps the most familiar statement of this notion of the legislator as a moral educator is Aristotle's:

> . . . we become just by the practice of just actions, self-controlled by exercising self-control, and courageous by performing acts of courage. This is corroborated by what happens in states. Lawgivers make the citizens good by inculcating habits in them, and this is the aim of every lawgiver; if he does not succeed in doing that, his legislation is a failure.[2]

In other words, the law makes us good by compelling us to act as a good person acts. More specifically, I assume that Aristotle is putting forward the following position:[3] To be a good person is to possess certain virtues, such as courage. To each of these traits there corresponds a certain class of actions, such as courageous actions. The law instills these traits by making us perform the acts that correspond to them. This it does, I assume, by declaring what must be done and offering, by specifying punishments for noncompliance, some extra incentive for doing as it says. In complying with such declarations we gradually form certain habits that either are virtues or are naturally transformed into virtues when we reach a certain level of maturity and enlightenment.

Needing a name for it, I will call this model of how virtues arise "the Aristotelian paradigm." Since the method of moral education it recommends is perhaps the most obvious way in which the state might accomplish this aim, I will call it "the political means of improving character" or "the political means" for short. In what follows, I will argue that the Aristotelian paradigm is an incorrect picture of how character is changed for the better. I will also try to show that, for the same reasons, the political means suffers from certain crippling deficiencies as a means of imparting precisely those virtues it seems most likely to impart. These deficiencies should at least inspire caution in legislators who contemplate using it. If I am right, it is in some contexts misleading to call it an instrument of moral education at all.

I will not claim that what I call the political means is the only way in which the law and the state could possibly make us better.[4] Nor will I claim that it must not play a role in any program of moral education whatsoever. In this way, the case I will make will arrive at a less sweeping conclusion than the most familiar arguments against the political means, which always take the form of showing that the political means should never be used. We shall soon see that these arguments are inadequate, and the need to overcome the most obvious difficulties they encounter will take us directly to one of the most difficult questions of moral psychology: the question of how excellence of character is in fact instilled. Such arguments assume some answer to this question and, as we shall see, it is only by offering a true one that the political means can be plausibly criticized as a pedagogical method. I will offer an alternative answer in which something like the work the Aristotelian paradigm assigns to the state will be performed instead by what Paine called "society." As I do so, I will also offer reasons for rejecting a third alternative, which might be called "the Kantian paradigm," the notion that moral education is accomplished largely by means of the student's own purely autonomous insight. As far as specific policy recommendations are concerned, the case I will make will be unspectacular, but if I manage to shed light on the nature of moral education I think no one should complain.

Some Familiar Arguments

One objection to the political means is perhaps more obvious and more often heard than the others. A straightforward example of it may be found in the writings of the American anarchist Albert J. Nock.[5] According to Nock, to control human behavior by means of law is to control it "by force, by some form of outside compulsion." Thus it is incompatible with freedom. Freedom, however, is a necessary condition of "responsibility," because to be responsible, Nock believes, means "to rationalize, construct and adhere to a code of one's own." Responsibility, in turn, is a necessary condition of virtue. Thus the effort to create virtue by law destroys the very thing it is intended to bring about. The political means is therefore simply self-defeating.

This line of reasoning poses a number of problems, not the least of which arises from the remarkably narrow conception of responsibility it employs. If this is what responsibility is, it is surely practiced by very few of the people who actually exist in this world: most people do not live by a code they have constructed themselves, nor even by one they have thought about critically to any large extent. For the most part they accept the principles they live by as social conventions; that is, they accept them because they are accepted by others, who have accepted them for the same reason.[6] This fact presents anyone who holds Nock's position with a dilemma. On the one hand, if this is what responsibility is, social convention is at least as incompatible with it as law is. Thus if Nock's reasoning shows anything about the law it shows that social convention as such prevents people from being responsible. Since such conventions are in large part the basis of human life as we know it, this would seem to mean that most people are not responsible and, presumably, that they have no moral worth. Since such a conclusion must surely seem too harsh even to most cynics, it is a good reason for abandoning this notion of responsibility. But this would destroy the argument as a critique of attempts to create virtue by making it legally obligatory. The argument therefore proves both too much and too little.

We encounter a problem similar to the one confronting Nock's remarks in what is surely the most famous critique of the idea that virtue can be created by enforcing it legally. This is the "fugitive and cloistered virtue" passage in John Milton's *Areopagitica*. In it, he says:

> As therefore the state of man now is, what wisdom can there be to choose, what continence to forbear without the knowledge of evil? He that can apprehend and consider vice with all her baits and seeming pleasures, and yet abstain, and yet distinguish, and yet prefer that which is truly better, he is the true warfaring Christian. I cannot praise a fugitive and cloistered virtue, unexercised and unbreathed.... Assuredly we bring not innocence into the world, we bring impurity rather: that which purifies us is trial, and trial is by what is contrary.[7]

Like Nock's argument, Milton's assumes a moral theory: virtue requires a certain sort of knowledge, and this knowledge must include acquaintance with models of bad thought and conduct. Thus, it is precisely by attempting to "banish all objects of lust"[8] from the community that law defeats the purpose proposed by Aristotle, which is to make us more virtuous. Milton's alternative is the one expressed in the form of a paradox by the "revised motto" of Mark Twain's "The Man That Corrupted Hadleyburg": "Lead us into temptation."

Milton's argument suffers from a rather serious shortcoming. He wants to say, not merely that the political means of promoting virtue is a bad one, but that at least in some circumstances there is a better one. "Impurity and remissness, for certain, are the bane of a commonwealth; but there the great art lies, to discern in what the law is to bid restraint and punishment, and in what things persuasion only is to work."[9] But why is persuasion ever any better than the law in this respect? To the extent that it works at all, it eliminates temptation from our lives and will presumably produce the same problem he believes to be generated by the law. Indeed, Milton's argument settles on the one characteristic that *all* means to ethical improvement have in common, to the extent that they are successful.[10] If it proves anything about the law it therefore proves the same thing about all of them. It gives no reason for preferring one successful method over another. Since neither Milton nor anyone else wants to oppose all of them, his argument is at best incomplete. Those who like it as far as it goes can only use it as a criticism of the political means if, at least, they find some feature of some alternative, such as convention, which compensates for the effect exposed by Milton, making it a superior method.[11]

A little reflection will show that the remarks of Nock and Milton indicate a problem that confronts any attempt to criticize the political means of improving character. It is obvious that social conventions resemble laws in a number of ways. Any attempt to criticize the political means is in some danger of going too far and opposing reliance on social convention as well. Perhaps, as I have suggested, we can only avoid this danger by indicating some relevant difference between these two ways of controlling behavior. I will try to indicate such a difference in what follows, but first I will attempt to diminish the plausibility of the paradigm suggested by Aristotle's remarks.

Virtuous Action

First, it is not difficult to see at least that actions (including abstentions from action) that are done because the law requires them are different in kind from virtuous actions. Whether an action is virtuous or not depends partly on the reason for which it is done: to give something to someone in order to curry their favor is not to be generous. When a lawgiver gives us a law requiring some action that was previously not required by law, he gives us two new reasons for performing that action, and it is for these reasons that it will be performed more frequently than before. First, laws that require us to act in certain ways are widely seen as commands issued by a body of persons having the authority to do so, and thus those who see it this way will see the fact that the law requires something of them as by itself a reason for doing what it requires. Second, such laws bring with them penalties that make it less desirable to omit the required action than it was before.

It is easy to see that neither of these reasons by themselves can make what we do virtuous. Consider the first one. Suppose that I am a member of a mass movement, an admirer of its charismatic leader. One day our leader issues an order that all members of the movement must give all they have to those in need, and I immediately begin to do it. If this makes me a generous person, then by the same token if my leader cancels his order and forbids us to give to the needy then I immediately cease being a generous person. If he replaces the order with another commanding that we fight the enemies of the movement in spite of the danger involved, I become courageous: if he reverses himself again and commands extreme prudence I become something else. Obviously, virtues – and vices – do not change as easily as authoritative directives do. Such traits are what Aristotle called *hexeis*, relatively permanent dispositions to act in certain ways. Obedience can give one a disposition to act in the same ways, but the disposition is apparently different in kind from those that constitute one's character. Obedience to authority does not generate any virtues by itself.

This is if anything more obvious in the case of the second reason for doing as the laws enjoin. Giving things to people in order to avoid a penalty is no more generous than doing it in order to curry favor.

Separately, neither obedience nor fear of retribution are the sort of reason that virtue requires and they will be equally insufficient when they are combined, as they often are, when one does something because the law requires it. What is perhaps more interesting is that what we have seen so far suggests that, in a limited way, Nock was right: virtue does seem to rest on a certain minimal sort of autonomy, if not on the extreme kind he describes. To have a trait like courage or generosity is to act on the basis of one's own notions about the right and the good. This would explain why virtue does not change as easily as the behavior of an obedient person: such notions are themselves relatively fixed characteristics of a person.[12] In acting obediently one acts on the basis of the directives of others, which change much more readily than one's own principles do.

The fact that virtuous conduct is quite different from actions that are done because the law requires them is not fatal to the Aristotelian paradigm. Aristotle himself, in fact, seems to recognize the difference between them.[13] But if authoritative commands and the penalties attached to them can make us better persons by making us act as better persons act, then they must, by making us act that way, teach us the notions about what is right and good that make us better people. By considering an example, we can see that, in a way, such methods do teach us ideas of this sort, but we can also see that it does not appear to be true in the way that the Aristotelian paradigm requires.

Let us take an extreme case. Mary's son, Peter, is five years old and no more concerned with the welfare of others than most boys his age. She decides that he will not grow up to be a truly charitable person unless she guides him in that direction. She lays down a rule to the effect that he must give his best toy to any needy child he meets. She knows he is a good boy and generally does what she tells him to do, but to help make sure of it she hints that he will be punished if he disobeys. Eventually he forms a painful habit of doing what the rule says. Before long, though, something unforeseen happens: he conceives a powerful disliking for children who have something "wrong" with them. Children who are lame or blind or sick become more odious to him than broccoli or spinach. This odium is in a way quite rational in the present circumstances and is based on something he has learned: namely, that people with disabilities are bad. He has learned this because his mother *has made it true*. She has altered his situation in such a way that people with disabilities have become bad in the sense that they are now *bad for him*, like poison. Even if, due to a certain natural sympathy with the sufferings of others, he minds sacrificing his interests to theirs less than he would have without it, it remains true that they are destructive of his interests. Since all the most powerfully visible evidence he has on the matter leads to this conclusion, it would actually be irrational of him not to draw it. In a way, he has learned the principle she meant him to learn. She meant to teach him that he should act in a certain way and he has learned it. But she also wanted him to learn that others are worthy of respect and concern. This is shown by the fact that she wanted him to be a charitable person and not simply a compulsive giver. But somehow he has learned virtually the opposite of this.

In the Aristotelian paradigm, the formation of a virtue is the formation of a certain habit. We can see now that this is at best only part of the story of how such traits are formed. Mary has given Peter precisely that habit she would be giving him in teaching him to be charitable, but she has not taught him to be charitable. Peter consistently gives to those in need, but he does so with a resentful, teeth-gritting attitude which, as Aristotle tells us, is inconsistent with virtuous giving.[14] What is missing from this sort of account is an explanation of how the moral educator is to impart to the student an understanding, in terms of notions of what is right or good, of the *point* of the activity in which he is being drilled. Any activity, in order to qualify as a form of education, must give the instructor a certain measure of control over how the student sees things after the activity is completed. I have described Mary as using educational resources – namely, authoritative commands and punishments – which are precisely the ones that the political means employs. As I have described the situation so far, the control that the instructor exercises over how the point is taken seems very poor.

The problem remains even if we alter my admittedly extreme example in ways that make it more realistic. We might suppose, for instance, that Mary attempts to impart a rule about giving that is more reasonable than the one I have her trying to instill. But any rule which requires giving to others would ensure that to some extent Peter's interests come into conflict with the interests of others, thus opening the possibility of his drawing the conclusions I have him drawing. Again, we might introduce into the example the familiar fact that moral education proceeds by precept as well as habituation – that authoritative commands and punishments are not the only means employed. That is, we might have Mary telling her son that the point of all this is that others have dignity and importance as well as oneself, and that their welfare thus merits our concern. But why would he believe this? It is true that her – to him – awesome parental authority helps to make her pronouncements credible, but all the *facts* she presents him with lead in another direction. So far, she does not seem to have an even minimally reliable method of influencing which way he will go. What is worse, nothing in all this suggests how he is even to understand what such precepts mean. Such assertions are not self-explanatory, and this one conflicts with all the palpable facts she has presented him with, since they point to the conclusion that others are dangerous to him and therefore to be avoided insofar as they need his concern.

Notice, finally, that the story I have told does not in any way assume that Peter possesses an ineradicable, natural instinct to be "selfish." I have made two psychological assumptions about him, neither of which commits me to a controversial theory about human nature. First, I have assumed that he has certain desires – whatever their nature and wherever they come from – which run contrary to the rule he has learned. If this were not so, there would be no point in laying down the rule at all. Second, I have assumed that he really believes the rule he has learned. Due to the regard he has for his mother's authority, he may even be quite incapable of doubting the correctness of the rule. Consequently, he believes that he really ought to give his toys to needy children he meets. This is precisely why they have become so odious to him: whenever one of them appears, he thinks he really must do something that is painful to him, something that is peculiarly painful because he does not see the point of it. Though he believes the rule he must, so far, find it more or less meaningless and even, in a way, absurd.

Rules and Understanding

So far, my efforts to undermine the Aristotelian paradigm rather obviously have something in common with the arguments I considered earlier. I have tried to show that the educational efficacy of the law is limited to the extent that its resources are those singled out by the theory I have attributed to Aristotle. It is already obvious, however, that the same resources are employed in the sort of instruction that occurs in the home, in which we make our initial acquaintance with social conventions. The problem I have posed for the law seems to afflict social convention as well. This is so despite the fact that I have applied a requirement of autonomous moral understanding that is considerably less drastic than the one applied by Nock. Later I will attempt to show that, in fact, such conventions make certain other resources available, in the home and elsewhere, which do meet my less drastic requirement while the political means does not. First, however, I will need to describe in somewhat more detail the problem I have posed.

Both law and social norms serve primarily to regulate our relations with others. Both contain rules which, like the one laid down by Mary in my example, propose that we promote the interests of others. Both also include rules that in various ways require us to refrain from doing things which damage the interests of others. It might be supposed that the difficulties encountered by Mary arise from the fact that she was teaching the first sort of rule, but in fact problems of the same kind are raised by the second sort as well. Rules that prevent us from harming others always either require that we forgo goods we could otherwise secure (by picking pockets, and so forth), or else they require us to give up some good we might otherwise keep (for instance, by refusing to pay our bills). On the whole, it costs us a great deal to observe such rules. In a way, they present other people as threats and obstacles to the pursuit of our own interests. Perhaps even a child can see that we are nonetheless all better off if we all obey rules of this sort. Yet it is rather more obvious that he can see that there is another situation in which he is still better off – namely, that in which everyone else obeys them and he does not. The rules are a help if others follow them and a hindrance if he does.

What is interesting, though, is the fact that, while this is in a way what the rules of morality are like, a moral person does not *see* them that way. If he believes in a rule prohibiting theft, he does not see it as an obstacle to his enriching himself by stealing the purse of the woman standing next to him at the subway station. To see a rule as an obstacle is, in itself, perfectly consistent with believing in the rightness of the rule. I can believe that I really ought to stop for all stop signs and yet be very irritated when one delays me in meeting an important appointment. Why does a moral person not see persons and the moral rules that protect them from harm in this light? The answer suggested by my remarks on the case of Peter is that he "respects" persons in a way that we do not normally "respect" stop signs. Yet the rules themselves do not support any positive attitude toward persons at all, while they do support a certain negative attitude – namely, seeing others as obstructions. On the other hand, while they do not *support* respect, they do *require* it. If we are to acquire any of the virtues expressed by following these rules – honesty, considerateness, and the like – we must somehow acquire respect for others.[15]

It appears that any institution that instills the virtues which both the law and social convention can most plausibly be thought to give us must somehow teach us respect for others. What we need, then, is some insight into what this respect amounts to and how such institutions might teach it. To this end, it will help to draw a distinction – an informal one will be sufficient – between two kinds of rules, one of which I have thus far ignored.

So far, I have treated social norms that are examples of a class of rules that also includes the kind of laws the political means employs: these are rules which tell us what to do and what not to do. In all the examples I have cited, they also, in one way or another, determine the distribution of various goods which, of course, exist independently of the rules that distribute them. Such rules, which might be called "substantive rules," can be contrasted with what I will call "ceremonial rules."[16] Ceremonial rules do not declare who shall have goods of this kind. Indeed, they do not even tell us what to do or not to do. They only specify *ways* in which we can engage in certain activities if we wish or need to. We are quite familiar with such rules in virtue of having observed them. We begin an encounter with others by saying "Hello" and asking how they are, we end it by saying "Goodbye." We make requests and ask permissions; if granted them, we give thanks. If we do not do such things at the time or place which some substantive rule requires, we make apologies and give excuses. As these examples suggest, the activities these rules might be said to regulate would not exist if rules of this kind did not exist. When we say "Hello" we are engaging in an activity called a "salutation" and, if it were not for the rule which says that we can accomplish it by saying "Hello," and other rules like it, there would be no such thing as a salutation. The same is true of making requests, giving thanks, and all other activities of this sort. Further, these activities are important to us only because of their expressive function and, although it is not always easy to say just what they express, it always has something to do with the agent's appreciation of the person to whom they are done. The lesson of ceremonial observances seems to be that others must be approached gingerly and left with a benediction: we must not assume too much or handle them too roughly.

It is not difficult to see how a child can be brought to learn this lesson by being taught to follow ceremonial rules. Consider the following story. Young Paul wants to play with a pair of binoculars belonging to his uncle John. John has let him use them in the past and, thinking that John wouldn't object to his having them now, Paul takes them. But his mother, Martha, makes it clear to him that this is not the way one goes about getting what someone else has already got: you must ask him for it first, and say "please." Paul asks his uncle if he can please use the binoculars and is immediately told he has done it wrong: one says "may," not "can." If your request is granted, you say "thank you." He soon masters these rules well enough. He cannot doubt their correctness, since he has them on the infallible authority of his mother. He even possesses evidence of their correctness: somehow, people become angry and unpleasant if you take something they have, even if they have no objection to giving it to you, without first saying words like "may," "please," and "thank you." If you say the words, however, they are soothed and happy. There are many ways in which one must avoid jarring people's feelings, and this is one of them. He has learned his lesson.

Yet Paul is really in more or less the same position that Peter was in after Mary laid down her new rule: he has faith in certain principles but does not understand them. Why do people have such volatile feelings about such things in the first place, and why do these words have the apparently magic power to soothe these feelings? If Paul had the sophisticated intellectual resources of a social scientist or a philosopher there would be many answers he could give to these questions. For instance, he might suppose that people are proud of the things they possess because such things show that they have the power it takes to accumulate them. Thus, they hate to have things taken from them because it is a challenge to their power: they would rather give or lend things than have them taken, since giving or lending shows that they have the power to dispose of what they have according to their whims and without any hindrance. Alternatively, Paul might think that people simply want to keep in their possession as many things as possible, and that they insist on the practice of asking permission because it enables them to say "no," so that they can maintain the size of their hoard. Because he is only a child, however, Paul cannot indulge in such imaginative speculations. Fortunately, though, he does not need to. It is obvious to him that Martha and John understand the rules he has learned; for him, to understand them is simply to know how adults understand them.

This method of understanding rules, unlike the method in which one relies on one's own imagination, can only lead to one conclusion. These principles are related in definite ways to other ideas that adults use, including especially the notions of "yours" and "mine." The practices of asking, granting, and refusing permission are among those which mark the boundaries between what is yours and what is mine. Paul is aware that he need not seek permission to use something that already belongs to him; he also knows that he need not seek permission in order to come into possession of something which he is being given as a gift, or which he is taking in trade.

Sometimes, though, Paul wants to get to use, on his own initiative, something that is not his and for which he offers nothing in trade. The practices concerning permissions make it possible to accomplish this without simply taking what he wants. The use of this complicated apparatus makes sense to him when he realizes that it is one indication of the fact that, in the adult world, people are ordinarily seen as having a *right* to determine what happens to the things they possess: this is part of what it means to say that these things are *their* things. Asking permission is a practice that makes it possible for Paul to acquire something possessed by someone else without violating that right, which he would be violating if he were to simply take it. If he understands this, he can understand the moves in the game he has been taught in the way that adults understand them. By saying "may" rather than "can" he signifies that he is asking that a right be transferred from someone else to him rather than asking for information. By saying "please" and "thank you" he expresses an appreciation for the fact that the thing he is asking for is not already his by right – that it comes to him, if it does, as a gift. The entire activity, then, expresses a respect for the boundaries between "mine" and "yours" – it expresses a respect for the rights of others.[17] If he comes to see and to pursue the activity in this way, he has acquired in some degree the respect for others that I have said underlies decent relations between people.

The kind of training Paul has undergone is a more effective form of moral instruction than the sort to which Peter was subjected. It is possible, on the basis of what I have said, to explain this fact. The rule Peter learned was one of the substantive rules that regulate our relations with others. It was an example of the sort of substantive rule that governs the distribution of things which, independently of these rules, are regarded as good. Rules of this sort always require that we forgo or relinquish such goods. Consequently, they have a certain tendency to make us see others as threats or obstacles to the promotion of our interests. It was precisely what Peter could see in light of his rule that prevented him from grasping what respect is.

In a limited way, Paul's circumstances were like Peter's; they also involved a substantive rule requiring him to forgo or relinquish something antecedently regarded as good. This is the rule prohibiting one from simply taking things which do not belong to oneself. But of course it was not from this rule that Paul learned respect. He learned it from a ceremonial rule and not from a substantive one. Ceremonial rules in general are relatively costless to follow.[18] It is not in itself against one's interest to ask permission (rather the contrary, in fact). This is true even if one knows in advance that the request will probably be refused. These rules make possible an activity which obviously expresses something, and which is quite mysterious to someone in Paul's position because he does not yet understand what it expresses. As such it *invites* him to try to understand it. We have seen that the practice he is confronted with, and others associated with it, provide him with the materials he needs to succeed. Once he understands it, he also understands substantive rules like the one that prohibits him from simply taking things that do not belong to him: once he comes to see others as having rights, he can appreciate rules that specify what rights others have, and that is what rules like this one do. We have also seen that to understand this practice is, in part, to understand what it is to regard others with respect; it is also clear from what I have said that to come to understand such respect under the influence of a certain sort of authority is, to some extent, to come to possess it.

Conclusion

It is time to stop and review the argument I have laid down so far, to see what it has come to. Early on, I said Nock's argument has certain undesirable consequences because of a rather extreme assumption he makes regarding the sort of autonomy required for virtue. These consequences can be avoided if one replaces this assumption with the much more reasonable one that one must act on principles which one understands. The political means however cannot reliably impart this kind of understanding because of the nature of the class of rules of which the relevant kinds of laws are instances: such rules, in general, place barriers in the way of achieving this sort of understanding. There are certain conventions, however, which do have the capacity to impart this sort of understanding. This capacity is sufficient to deliver us from the difficulties that I said were entailed by the assumptions behind Milton's familiar criticism of the political means. It shows that not all ways of promoting decent behavior are equal in this respect; there is one that has virtues which compensate to some extent for whatever limitations they might have in common.

What may we conclude concerning the relative merits of these two kinds of rules as instruments of moral education? It is perhaps important to notice the difference here between what follows and what does not. What follows is that, if they are considered separately, one of them has the character of an instrument of education and the other does not: one tends to lead to the required sort of understanding and the other is apt to block it. However, it is obvious that such instruments are not used separately in the world we live in. As far as what I have said is concerned, it is possible that substantive rules can acquire such a character when they work in the context of a whole system of educational means. It is possible that such rules could contribute something worthwhile to such a system, while other parts of the system overcome the bad effects which, as I have claimed, they are likely to produce. Indeed, we have good reason to believe that such a system is possible, because the one we use to raise our children seems to be precisely of this sort: their behavior is held in place by all sorts of substantive rules while other means of moral education do their work. This is how I have described the case of Paul earlier. It is part of the value of the practices having to do with making requests that they enable Paul to understand certain substantive rules such as the one which prohibits him from simply taking what he wants. Presumably, by helping him to grasp the point of such rules it also enables him to follow them with greater alacrity than before.

As I said at the outset, my argument does not imply that the political means ought never to be used.[19] However, it does imply several other things which were not obvious in the beginning. First, even in the context of the sort of system I have just imagined, the political means has a rather peculiar status: if the system works, it is because the other means function as adequate *antidotes* to the political means. They overcome its ill effects. This in turn suggests a second point. If a legislator is pressing for a new use of the political means, if he is trying to pass a new law to instill a virtue that will improve the way his subjects treat one another, it is not enough for him to claim that the actions enjoined by the proposed law are indeed those which would spring from the neglected virtue itself. The measure he proposes is apt to have effects that run counter to his own purpose and they will be overcome, if at all, by a complex system of beliefs and practices over which he has little control. He must claim the undesirable effects of this measure are not too weighty to be overcome by this system. This is a kind of claim which is obviously capable of being false. It would be false, for instance, if it were made of the rule that I have imagined Mary laying down for Peter. The difficulties involved in making such a claim may not be serious in the parent–child relationship, where it is possible to see all the important effects and easy to change the rule if it does not appear to be a good one. For legislators, who in most states control the behavior of millions of people they can never know, they are much more likely to be formidable. Whether they can be surmounted or not, they should not be ignored.

What I have said here also implies a third and more metaphysical point, one which concerns the relative positions of society and the state in the foundations of the moral life. The Aristotelian paradigm, as I have defined it, depicts the process by which virtue is taught as being fundamentally like the one in which a drill instructor teaches his soldiers to march. I have tried to show that part of the process of acquiring the other-regarding virtues which the law seems most likely to instill is more like learning a language than it is like learning to march or stand at attention, and that ceremonial rules provide the materials for this crucial aspect of moral education. They provide the expressive actions the meaning of which the student must grasp. This suggests that legislators in fact cannot originate such rules. It is impossible for the same reason that it is impossible for the law to originate a new language. The resources of the political means – authoritative commands and punishments – can make people do what the legislator wants them to do, but they cannot make them mean what the legislator wants them to mean by what they do.

To the extent that what people mean is not a product of individual fiat, it seems to arise from social conventions like those which govern the use of language. We do not need to have a theory showing precisely how such rules originate in order to know that they are not made by a specialized social organ which, like the state, imposes its rules on those outside it. They appear to arise somehow from voluntary relations among individuals. In a way, the position I have taken here can be seen as a variant of the theme, which appeared above, that virtue depends on freedom. But it is rather widely different from the variants I considered there. Specifically, I have avoided the assumption that virtue can only arise from purely autonomous individual insight. I have avoided suggesting that the individual must devise his principles himself (by deriving them, perhaps, from the dictates of pure practical reason), or even that he must subject them to critical examination. However, I have supposed that he must *understand* them, and I have tried to show that here the individual relies on the social background of his actions. On this point, Aristotle, with his insistence that man is a social being (*zoon politikon*), seems closer to the truth than an extreme individualist like Kant.[20]

Notes

1 In Merrill Jensen (ed.), *Tracts of the American Revolution* (Indianapolis: Bobbs–Merrill, 1977), pp. 402–3.

2 Aristotle, *Nicomachean Ethics*, trans. Martin Ostwald (Indianapolis: Bobbs–Merrill, 1962), 110362–5.

3 This is not an essay in Aristotle scholarship, and I do not insist that this is Aristotle's position. It seems attractive enough to be worth discussing on its own merits, even if he did not hold it.

4 For examples of other possible ways, see Aristotle's *Politics*, 7, chaps 13–15 and 17. I have argued elsewhere that the criminal law produces an effect of this kind by removing opportunities for vengeful thoughts and feelings on the part of the victims of crime. But this happens by means of a process that bears no resemblance to what I am now calling the political means. See "Punishment, Revenge, and the Minimal Functions of the State," in *Understanding Human Emotions*, ed. Fred D. Miller, Jr, and Thomas W. Attig (Bowling Green, Ohio: Applied Philosophy Program, 1979).

5 All quotations in this paragraph are from his short essay, "On Doing the Right Thing," reprinted as an appendix to his *Our Enemy the State* (New York: Free Life Editions, 1973), pp. 93–9.

6 For a more complete account of what social conventions are and how they work, see my "Some Advantages of Social Control: An Individualist Defense," in *Public Choice*, 36 (1981): 3–16.

7 *Areopagitica*, in *John Milton: Complete Poems and Major Prose*, ed. Merrit Y. Hughes (New York: Odyssey, 1957), p. 728.

8 Ibid., p. 733.

9 Ibid.

10 It is worth noticing that, in Mark Twain's story, convention has precisely the effects Milton says the law has. It creates a sort of virtue which is not genuine and is easily corruptible, simply because it works too well in eliminating temptation. The virtue of Hadleyburg is exemplary only because it has never been subjected to a trial, but this means it is only apparent virtue, because it will fail any genuine trial it meets.

11 Perhaps I should point out in passing that the issue dealt with in these remarks of Nock and Milton is distinct from that of "the enforcement of morals" as it is presented in the writings of J. F. Stephen and Patrick Devlin, although the two issues are connected in a way. Someone who believes in the enforcement of morals could conceivably agree with Nock and Milton that the law actually makes us worse – he might think for instance that, if we obey the strictures of morality because it is the law, we are doing it for *reasons* which are vicious rather than virtuous. Yet he might think that immoral *acts* are so horrible as such that it is worthwhile to debase people somewhat in order to reduce the frequency with which such acts are done. Where victimless crimes are concerned, this may be an uncomfortable position to hold, but it is not contradictory. It is possible to hold that "morals" should always be enforced while admitting that this would not improve anyone's character.

12 See my "Character and Thought," *American Philosophical Quarterly* (July 1978), where I argue at length that both virtues and vices rest on such notions. I also attempt to show that beliefs about the right and the good are in fact more difficult to change than other beliefs are.

13 See *Nicomachean Ethics*, 1144a13–18 and 1105a18–1105b18.

14 *Nicomachean Ethics*, 1120a30–31.

15 In addition, respect seems essential to the value we place upon having these rules observed by others in their conduct toward us. It is obvious that both laws and social norms serve to protect the conditions of our well-being – our property, our health, our "territories," and so forth – against destructive acts on the part of others. It has been pointed out, though, that damage of this kind is not the only evil we perceive in the offenses thus discouraged. Adam Smith remarked that "what chiefly enrages us against the man who injures or insults us, is the little account which he seems to make of us. . . ." We read offenses against us as expressive acts in which the offender shows that "he seems to imagine, that other people may be sacrificed at any time, to his convenience or his humour." Adam Smith, *The Theory of Moral Sentiments* (Indianapolis: Liberty Press, 1969), p. 181. A large part of the value of living in a community in which our rights are observed is the fact that it seems to show that our rights are *respected*. It may be possible for the social and political apparatus to secure such observance solely through fear of the penalties it imposes, but order obtained in this way, even if it were perfect, would be hollow and flat.

16 This distinction is a reformulation of one made by Emile Durkheim. See chapter 2 of Erving Goffman's *Interaction Ritual* (Garden City, NY: Doubleday, 1967). The account of ceremonial norms in this paragraph is largely drawn from Goffman. See also his *Relations in Public* (New York: Harper, 1971), chaps 2 and 4.

17 Paul can come to this conclusion because it explains a coherent system of practices of which this activity is a part. His reaching this conclusion is an instance of what Gilbert Harman calls an inference to the best explanation.

18 Of course, this generalization has exceptions, but since the activities these rules make possible are important only because of their expressive function, the exceptions can only be cases in which the meaning of the act is one that one finds unpleasant to express. An obvious case of this is the activity of apologizing, in which we express a conviction that we have wronged the person to whom the activity is directed. Also, in some cultures, there are conventions for greeting religious and political leaders by performing intrinsically self-abasing gestures, like banging one's forehead on the ground. In addition, there may be some conventions that some people find abasing while others do not. It is conceivable, for instance, that some people find it unpleasant to say thank you because it includes an acknowledgment that people other than themselves have rights. If this sort of unpleasantness were a common feature of ceremonial observances then, naturally, the account of moral education I am offering would be no good. However, I doubt that, in our culture at least, they are very common.

19 It seems obvious that such a position could only be a sensible one if applied to adults. It may turn out that it can only be adequately supported by an argument that is not pedagogical, like mine, but *moral*. It can perhaps only be supported by defending a principle like the one which H. L. Mencken called "Mencken's Law": "When A annoys or injures B on the pretense of saving or improving X, A is a scoundrel." *Newspaper Days: 1899–1906* (New York: Knopf, 1941), pref. This is the sort of argument John Locke gives throughout the *First Letter Concerning Toleration*.

20 This paper was improved by comments from acquaintances, colleagues, and students too numerous to thank by name, but I should mention that Charles King, John Kekes, Gilbert Harman, Amelie Rorty, Michael Stocker, Morton Winston, and James D. Wallace were good enough to provide comments in writing. An earlier version was presented at the April 1980 Liberty Fund Conference on Virtue and Political Freedom. A fellowship from the Mellon Foundation made writing it much easier than it would have been otherwise.

26

The Social Basis of Character: An Ecological Humanist Approach

Steven Fesmire

I. The Ecological Self

It is common knowledge in the biological sciences that organic beings, far from existing in isolation, live as integral parts of larger ecological systems. Although it is helpful to speak of localized individuals like *this* flower or *that* bee, these individuals are intelligible only when understood in their interrelations with other parts of the systems they inhabit.

Charles Darwin reported, for example, that there exists a species of flowering clover in England, the population of which depends in some measure on the population of *cats* in a region. Does this seem a bit far-fetched? Not from an ecological perspective. Many flowering plants require pollination (removal of pollen that results in fertilization) if they are to produce seeds enabling them to reproduce and thereby survive as a species. With this English clover, pollination is accomplished by "humble bees" (we call them "bumble bees"). Darwin inferred the following: An increase in a region's humble bee population results in a proportional increase in the region's clover population, while a decrease in bees results in a decrease in clover.

The plot thickens: "The number of humble-bees in any district," Darwin writes, "depends in a great measure upon the number of field-mice, which destroy their combs and nests."[1] Thus, other factors remaining the same, an increase in the ravenous field-mice population results in a *decrease* in the bee population accompanied by a decrease in the under-pollinated clover population. Contrariwise, a decrease in field-mice results in an increase in both bees and clover. If a drought were drastically to reduce the clover population, many bees would starve and die for want of pollen. This decrease in bees would deprive the field-mice of a primary food source thus drastically reducing the mouse population.

So how do cats fit into this story? Cats of course eat the field-mice, so that an increase in the number of cats results in fewer mice, more bees, and more clover. Darwin concludes: "Hence it is quite credible that the presence of a feline animal in large numbers in a district might determine, through the intervention first of mice and then of bees, the frequency of certain flowers in that district!"[2]

The "moral" of this story is that individual organisms or species – like mice, bees, *or humans* – may initially *appear* to be self-sufficing and isolated, but observation, experimentation, and reflection reveal that they are situated in a web of interdependencies. This notion of an "ecological system" is applicable to more than biological systems. Complex organisms may live not only as parts of biological systems, but also as integral parts of socio-cultural and even family systems. ("Ecology" is from the Greek *oiko*, house, a study of our home in the *broadest* sense.)

A human creature is no exception to this. One thing unique about humans – aside from having larger brains that have stirred up both more mischief and more art than have the brains of non-human animals – is that they are creatures of *culture* to a far greater extent than any other organic being. That is, humans are creatures who grow into social organizations that have complex sets of shared habits or "customs" that enable them to communicate so that an uncertain future may be anticipated and created together. These "social habits" (e.g., symbol systems, values, etc.), as they are referred to in what follows, are communal circuits that are in place prior to the development of a particular individual.

The reader may pause to reflect for a moment that she is reading an essay written in a language she did not consciously choose as an infant to read or speak ("I believe I shall communicate in . . . English!"). Although the author is writing in the privacy of his study, he legitimately expects these American English symbols to be more or less readily comprehended because he *shares* a culture with his readers. We *inherit* (mostly unconsciously) our language from our social surroundings, and this language structures not only our public communication with others but also our innermost private thoughts. After all, as the philosopher and sociologist George Herbert Mead (1863–1931) observes, our thoughts are for the most part inner conversations.[3]

To inherit the language (i.e., linguistic social habits) of a culture is to inherit its drawbacks as well as its benefits. The American linguistic inheritance encourages us, for example, to think of ourselves as self-sufficing, atomic, enclosed individuals. But as we are beginning to see, this radically individualistic inheritance is incompatible with the actualities of shared experience.

In a recent news broadcast, a man in his thirties was interviewed at a Chicago post office during the holiday season. He was responding with personal gifts to a handful of the thousands of "Dear Santa" letters the post office receives each year, often from impoverished children. When asked about his motives, this obviously caring man replied: "Because it makes me feel good inside. When I give gifts to these children it's really just a Christmas gift to myself." This is what he *said*, but were his actions motivated exclusively or even primarily by a thirst for selfish gratification? His motives were probably less arbitrary, but America's individualistic language did not provide him with the "tools" requisite for telling the whole story.[4] He could not articulate that he was responding to an overall *situation* that involved the needs and desires of *others* interwoven with his own.

This language – what a recent sociological study called "the first language of American individualism"[5] – has roots in early pioneer days, when interpersonal interactions on the "frontier" were kept to a minimum. This pioneer individualism was combined with a pre-scientific Greek and Christian view of the self as a metaphysically enclosed entity or substantive "soul." Thus were laid the foundations of "rugged individualism" in America.[6] Note the irony of this cherished delusion: individualism is itself a cultural phenomenon.

What are some moral implications of this dissonance between the *fact* (not an ethical "ought") that humans are social organisms and the *fact* that Americans have inherited a view of themselves as self-sufficing atoms? Social and material conditions in America have changed dramatically since pioneer days so that associated life has become a far more complex and interconnected affair. We need increased rather than diminished cooperation. Consequently, this extreme individualism, fossilized in our culture's language and customs, has become appallingly destructive. Our individualistic inheritance is woefully maladapted to current social realities, and this leaves our social concerns and commitments arbitrary and unintelligible. Like any other "tool," our language needs to be well adapted to the work at hand. Radically individualistic language "fits" the work of getting along with others in about the way a tire iron fits the job of tuning a guitar. The American philosopher, psychologist, and social reformer John Dewey (1859–1952) observes that such individualism leads to

> aloofness and indifference. It often makes an individual so insensitive in his relations to others as to develop an illusion of being really able to stand and act alone – an unnamed form of insanity which is responsible for a large part of the remediable suffering of the world.[7]

Although a cultivated individuality is paramount for value-rich lives and healthy communities, proclaiming a wholly autonomous "I" is no more sensible than one of the aforementioned bees proclaiming its independence from the ecological system of which it is part. "Tell that to the mice," one is inclined to respond to such a hubristic humble bee.

You are no less (or more) a feather in nature's cap than a clover, bee, or mouse. Indeed, during your prolonged infancy, you were far more needful than a young bee or mouse, whose instinctive tendencies developed far more rapidly than did your own. A human infant is helpless without established adult social habits. Dewey explains this thoroughgoing dependence:

> An individual begins life as a baby, and babies are dependent beings. Their activities could continue at most for only a few hours were it not for the presence and aid of adults with their formed habits. And babies owe to adults more than procreation, more than the continued food and protection which preserve life. They owe to adults the opportunity to express their native activities in ways which have meaning. Even if by some miracle original activity could continue without assistance from the organized skill and art of adults, it would not amount to anything. It would be mere sound and fury.[8]

The true opposite of a *social* human is a *dead* human rather than a radically individual one.

Even if a baby could be imagined to have its physiological needs miraculously met without interaction with established social habits, the level of *meaning* (either qualitative or semiotic) attained would be minimal. In short, the meaning of human activities is acquired through "interaction with a matured social medium."[9] The practical difference between humans and other living organisms is that humans, by employing the interpretive tools of culture, are capable of *recognizing* their ecological situatedness (natural, physical, cultural, and interpersonal) so that they may deliberately adjust their responses accordingly.

II. The Community Without and Within

Moral theorists from the eighteenth century to the present, and Western religious traditions for over two millennia, have typically supposed the fundamental fact of morality to be our capacity to discern unchanging and universally applicable moral laws or rules. As a result, we tend to suppose that there is a single "right thing to do" in every moral situation and that this "right" course of action can be ascertained by proper application of settled moral criteria.

The work of John Dewey stands in stark contrast to this tradition. On a Deweyan view, moral principles (e.g., "the Golden Rule") may and often do provide fruitful *guidance* as rules-of-thumb, but insofar as we solidify them into moral "laws" and allow them to *govern* or dictate our actions, we fall short of the mark. This is because morality is far more a matter of finely textured sensitivity and immersion in concrete situations than insight into ultimate universal rules. To be moral is to feel one's way through a tangled web of relationships with a discerning eye for possible ways in which this web may be artfully woven. There are no fixed and settled rules for such moral artistry - nothing to specify a single "Right" thing to do. This implies that morality is a complex affair of imaginatively discerning *better* and *worse* alternatives for action. It is not a black and white affair of distinguishing absolute *Right* from *Wrong*.

The capacity for moral discernment described here is a socialized (i.e., educated) capacity; there is no such thing as someone who is "born" a saint or savage. Dewey observes that the *habits* (a term to be examined presently) that constitute our *characters* (defined as "the interpenetration of habits") are products of interactions with our social environments rather than being isolated, individual attainments. In short, as children inherit the languages of their culture and sub-cultures (and family systems), they simultaneously inherit the beliefs and values of these systems, defects and all. Adherence to "virtues" (like generosity) and avoidance of "vices" (like mean-spiritedness) are *socialized* behaviors ("vice" meaning a deviation from recognized custom).[10]

Moral maturation, for Dewey, is a process whereby these inherited customs become intelligently reconstructed in light of changing circumstances rather than championed in blind conformity *or* dismissed in reactionary defiance. In contrast, moral growth is not a matter of *transcending* cultural values by employing "universal human rationality"[11] so that we can follow absolutely binding "moral laws," as the moral philosophy of Immanuel Kant supposes.

Nonetheless, the "self" is popularly thought to exist in some way separate from its social environment, in part a legacy of the metaphysical assumption that humans have "souls." One day our patchwork of inherited beliefs may include recognition that moral character is *encultured* rather than *en-souled*. Were we to take all of the components that constitute our identity – culture, biological make-up, historical period, family, formal education, work, friendship, etc. – and toss them into a test tube in a chemist's centrifuge, we mistakenly imagine that a pure solution of "self," an "I am," would remain when all of these "incidental" residual components had been filtered out. But in fact, the mixture would yield no distillates.

To put this differently, if we "peel" away what is socio-cultural, biological, and historical from our "selves," at the end of the day we find that we have been peeling an onion. The skins lie at our feet with no "core" remaining to gratify our mis-placed longings. Whether we "ought" to agree with Kant about the importance of "obeying the moral law" is thus a moot question. Kant was articulating the still popular assumption that moral reflection is a-cultural, a-historical, and disembodied. But, for all its merit, this is incompatible with the stubborn biological and psychological facts.

In order to provide a stronger empirical basis for these claims, we begin with one very simple example of *linguistic* habits we inherit from our social environment.[12] Recent work in cognitive science reveals the operations of such social habits as conventional (i.e., shared) *metaphors* (a mode of thinking and experiencing whereby one thing, usually more abstract, is understood in terms of another, usually more concrete and accessible). This work offers sustained treatments of the social nature of human imagination, meaning, and reason.[13]

In our culture, time is money. Carefully consider some expressions in American English: Time can be "wasted," "saved," "spent," "spared," "given," "budgeted," "squandered," and "invested." We can live on "borrowed time," and we can "run out of time."[14] We can "give" our time to others by "paying attention." It is an annoyance when someone "takes up our time" with trivialities. And we are gratified when those whom we deeply respect "set aside" or "allot" time to "spend" with us.

Read the following remarks carefully:

> If you are able to spare time to read this, you may find it worth your while and finish feeling that it was time well spent. You should invest many hours paying attention to social habits – surely a profitable use of time. It may save time if we start with a simple example of social habits.

Now re-read the remarks again to find seven instances, frequently used, of the "Time as Money" metaphor: "spare time," "worth your while," "time well spent," "invest hours," "paying attention," "profitable use of time," and "save time."

The "Time as Money" metaphor is a tiny portion of what *you* are as a member of this culture. As a member of a non-industrialized culture in which time and monetary exchange are not closely conjoined (a culture without hourly wages, etc.), you would understand *and* experience time differently.

There is a cultural reservoir from which each of us drinks, and this reservoir is permeated with metaphors. Ironically, these linguistic habits are cloaked from us in part *because* they are so indispensable and familiar; examining them is somewhat like trying to glance at our own eyes without the aid of a mirror. We seldom recognize the linguistic habits that form our capacities for communicating with others and making sense of the world.[15] More generally, we recognize very few of the social customs that co-author our characters. This helps to explain why moral education in our culture has been on the whole an arbitrary rather than an artfully directed process.

Social habits or customs, we have said, are shared and stable interpretive structures (e.g., symbol systems, metaphors and other imaginative structures, beliefs, values, virtues, gestures, prejudices) that we inherit as we form personal habits. Social habits are, as the philosopher Maurice Merleau-Ponty observes in *The Phenomenology of Perception*, our "stable organs and pre-established circuits."[16] It is through these structures that possibilities for an enriched life are opened or closed for us. These structures range in value-for-life from the apex of civilization down to what Mary Pipher, a psychologist writing about anorexic and bulimic adolescent girls literally dying from our cultural obsession with the "perfect figure," aptly calls "junk values of mass culture."[17]

That human conduct is socially saturated is put forth as a testable theory about facts. That our habits "should" be social is as moot a point as that we "should" communicate by means of language or that we "should" feel erotic desire. Dewey explains: "It is not an ethical 'ought' that conduct *should* be social. It *is* social, whether bad or good."[18] Private deliberations, as a matter of inescapable fact (regardless of the fact's desirability), begin with public tools.

"Virtues" are thus not radically private possessions or ethereal saintly attainments, and "vices" do not merely result from "weak wills" or "sinful natures." Virtuous and vicious habits (courage and cowardice, honesty and deceit, love and malice, tolerance and bigotry, and the like) are products of interaction between the make-up of an individual on the one hand and objective elements of the social world on the other.

Recognition of the fact that virtue and vice are functions of social conditions enables individuals to act intelligently for social progress by reconstructing social arrangements. Dewey explains the practical upshot of this recognition:

> Our individual habits are links in forming the endless chain of humanity. Their significance depends upon the environment inherited from our forerunners, and it is enhanced as we foresee the fruits of our labors in the world in which our successors live.[19]

III.　Habits and Human Conduct

It is by now apparent that a conception of "social habits" must play a central role in any adequate theory of moral character. But the pivotal notion of a "habit" at work here remains unacceptably vague. The remainder of this essay fleshes out this crucial concept in order better to illuminate the structure of human conduct.

What, then, is a "habit"? In *Human Nature and Conduct*, Dewey discusses his use of the term. He proposes:

> We need a word to express that kind of human activity which is influenced by prior activity and in that sense acquired; which contains within itself a certain ordering or systematization of minor elements of action; which is projective, dynamic in quality, ready for overt manifestation; and which is operative in some subdued subordinate form even when not obviously dominating activity.[20]

A capsule summary will focus our discussion. (1) Habits emerge through interaction with a physical and social environment. (2) Habits are "plastic" or flexible. (3) Change of habit necessitates change of environment. (4) Habits have "propulsive power," though most are formed unconsciously. (5) Habits, especially social habits, constitute our characters.

1.　*Habits are functions of organic interaction with a natural and social environment*

We observed that humans are not private and atomic; we are not separated either as a sack of skin or as a disembodied "mind" or "soul" from our surroundings. Our purpose has been to interpret this fact in terms of our social surroundings, but it may help to consider this on analogy with simple physical interactions. For example, breathing is an interaction of air and lungs, digestion an interaction of food and stomach, and walking an interaction of ground and legs. Air, food, and ground are *incorporated* into our habits of breathing, eating, and walking through interaction with lungs, stomach, and legs.[21] All habits likewise incorporate part of our objective environment within themselves.

Just as an artist's medium (canvas, brushes, pigments, etc.) has definite features and *resists* being given just any form, and the good artist is one whose habits are coordinated with these objective features, so our objective environment is recalcitrant. We must strive to assimilate this environment into our habits so that our surroundings support us rather than destroy us.

This is why no set of moral laws, rules, or commandments can perfectly adapt us to our environment. Neither our habits nor our laws can incorporate the entire ever-changing environment. Because the world is in perpetual flux, we can never be certain that the outcomes of our actions will satisfy our original expectations.[22] We can only speak of "tendencies" toward certain outcomes or "probabilities in the long run." A virtuous disposition is no guarantee of a good outcome. Chance, unforeseeable contingencies, can "carry an act one side of its usual effect."[23]

The book of human history is a co-authored work; it is not already written prior to our experiences. Consequently, the fact of *change* must be central to an adequate conception of habit. Habits *will* be frustrated, so they must be flexible and open to intelligent reconstruction. Far from being mere mechanisms for blind routine, habits themselves are dynamic, growing patterns. This *plasticity* of habit is a necessary condition for moral growth.

2. *Habits are plastic*

In *Democracy and Education*, Dewey explains the "plasticity" of habit as something distinct from the pliability of wax or putty. "Plasticity" signifies "the ability to learn from experience; the power to retain from one experience something which is of avail in coping with the difficulties of a later situation."[24] Habits are not nor should they be fixed and permanent; they are open to intelligent reconstruction.

Unfortunately, our religious, educational, and political institutions have tended to turn a deaf ear to the need for changing rigid and maladapted past customs. Past designs that may be ill-suited to managing current problems are nonetheless the dominant models for "molding" the young. Dewey criticizes this tendency to allow habits to control us rather than us controlling them:

> That plasticity also means power to change prevailing custom is ignored. . . . The inert, stupid quality of current customs perverts learning into a willingness to follow where others point the way, into conformity, constriction, surrender of scepticism and experiment.[25]

Because a bundle of habits made a life virtuous hundreds or thousands of years ago does not entail that latter twentieth-century Americans should strive to imitate every feature of that life. Indeed, it is even conceivable that my own virtuous habits of yesterday *may* be vices today. "What makes a habit bad," Dewey observes, "is enslavement to old ruts." This is true regardless of how "good" we take those ruts to be. We must not identify morality "with what *was* sometime rational, possibly in some prior experience of one's own, but more probably in the experience of some one else who is now blindly set up as a final authority."[26] Being satisfied with habits merely because they were effective once upon a time is a way of being careless about intelligently coping with problems of the insistent present.

3. *Habit-change demands a change in environment*

Habits, we have seen, are coordinated conjunctions with environing conditions. Consequently, to think that we can simply "will" a change of habit is to believe in "moral magic." Direct mental action cannot operate for an extended period in opposition to a habit any more than ordering a fire to stop burning will make it go out.[27] Try, for example, to change a habit of posture simply by "willing" it. You will find that a change of circumstances is required.

Thus the futility of puritanical condemnation. Self-righteously calling a prostitute a sinner does not alter the social conditions that give rise to her trade.[28] The politician who promises to "get tough on crime" merely by building more prisons for "born criminals" does nothing to transform the social and material conditions that make crime inevitable. Likewise, the campaign to combat drug use by asking people to "Just Say No" may edify shallow philanthropic sentiment, but it contributes little toward curbing the social problem of drug addiction.

4. Habits have "propulsive power," though most are not deliberately formed

Dewey highlights this propulsive or "projectile power" – the force of habit – by focusing on bad habits, like compulsive gambling and drug addiction. Because we would not intentionally have formed such habits, we tend to reject our bad habits as being not who we *really* are. But we are in these cases deluded. We *are* our habits. A "self" is a conglomeration of habits, and the only way to start becoming the self we wish to be is to own up to bad habits.

5. Habits are horizonal and social, and they form our characters

Three aspects of this will be addressed: (a) habit is synonymous with will; (b) habits form our character; (c) habits are horizonal rather than focal.

a. Habit is synonymous with will

Traditionally, the key concept of moral theory has been "will." This is reflected in popular moral discourse when people say, for example, "She chose to do that as an act of free will." As long as "will" is meant concretely, as a synonym for "habit," Dewey agrees with the tradition. "In any intelligible sense of the word will, they [habits] *are* will."[29]

But orthodox moralists cringe at the thought of collapsing the cherished distinction between the ever-changing world of "prudence" (everyday problem-solving) where habit is important, and a supposed unchanging moral realm of "free will" where worldly habits are irrelevant and transcendental rationality reigns. Nevertheless, Dewey's notion of habit accommodates and clarifies what is of practical relevance in the traditional notions of "will" and "choice," minus the dubious notion that we have an unchanging mental power of "free will."

b. Habits form our characters

Dewey defines character as "the interpenetration of habits."[30] Because we are bundles of habits, we can meaningfully say: "X is the *kind of person* who acts, thinks, or feels in a certain way." X acts according to a stable, foreseeable pattern of behavior. Martin Luther was the *kind of person* who, at the diet of Worms, could "do no other." Socrates was the *kind of person* who would not break the laws of the polis.[31] They acted according to a pattern set by prior habits, habits that continued to operate in all their actions. If habits did not have this stability, there could be no such thing as character.

c. Habits are horizonal

The habits that form our characters are horizonal, not focal, in our experience, and are mostly unconscious. This helps to explain how our social habits comprise the framework for our moral deliberations. They constitute a "horizon" of possibilities for action beyond which we cannot see, enabling what we misleadingly call an "intuitive sense" of the probable consequences of projected lines of behavior. Moral deliberation (an imaginative survey of alternative futures) is thus a function of our habits marking out a limited range of viable courses of action.[32]

From this, we see that habits are the fundamental instrumentalities of human conduct.

Even more than the hammer for carpentry or the utensils for eating, the *habits* of hammering and utensil-using are instrumental. More fundamental than the kiss, for expressing affection, is knowing and feeling when and how and why to kiss, and this depends on one's stock of habits.

IV. Conclusion

If an oak tree sprang from the ground and proclaimed its independence from interactions with soil, water, and air, we would chide it for its plain lack of forethought. We would implore that the tree cease this behavior that will inevitably lead to its withering death. The same advice must of course be given to the hubristic bee who we imagined to declare its absolute independence.

Analogously, we are born into communities and traditions whose social roles and practices cannot be detached from our characters. Without the inheritance of established social habits we would very literally wither and die. (Of course, without reformation of defective social habits we may be little better off.) As the contemporary philosopher Alasdair MacIntyre forcefully writes: "I am born with a past."[33]

> We are never more (and sometimes less) than the co-authors of our own narratives. Only in fantasy do we live what story we please. . . . We enter upon a stage which we did not design and we find ourselves part of an action that was not of our making. Each of us being a main character in his own drama plays subordinate parts in the dramas of others, and each drama constrains the others.[34]

A person is not an isolated entity set over and against a social world.

Human relationships, then, may be understood in terms of co-authored dramas in which dramatic narratives (or "life-stories") interlock with one another.[35] If our moral lives are to be coherent, we must attend to the constraints imposed by other dramas enacted on the same stage. In our deliberations about how to act, not only must we forecast consequences for ourselves, we must also take on the standpoint or role of others whose lives interlace with our own. We must imaginatively project ourselves into the emerging dramas of *their* lives to discover how their life-stories may be meaningfully continued alongside our own.

Notes

1   Charles Darwin, *On the Origin of Species*, vol. 11 of *The Harvard Classics* (New York: P. F. Collier & Son, 1909), 87–8. Originally published in 1859.

2   Ibid., 88.

3   George Herbert Mead, "The Social Self," in *Selected Writings*, ed. Andrew J. Reck (University of Chicago Press, 1964), 146.

4   For further insight into the problem of radical individualism in America, see Robert Bellah et al.'s now classic *Habits of the Heart* (University of California Press, 1985), vi–26.

5   The "first language of American individualism" is a phrase borrowed from Bellah's *Habits of the Heart*.

6   See Dewey's *Individualism, Old and New* (1930) for a sustained treatment of this theme. The opposite extreme may be illustrated with an anecdote from a friend who recently taught English in Japan. When she first asked a student "What do you think the answer is?" this American teacher expected the student to reply "*I* think . . .". It intrigued her when the student immediately consulted with the rest of the class and proceeded to report the findings of their joint inquiry.

7   John Dewey, *Democracy and Education*, The Middle Works, vol. 9 of *The Collected Works of John Dewey*, ed. J. A. Boydston (Carbondale: SIU Press), 49.

8   John Dewey, *Human Nature and Conduct*, The Middle Works, vol. 14 of *The Collected Works of John Dewey*, ed. J. A. Boydston (Carbondale: SIU Press), 65.

9   Ibid., 65. For a recent psychological account of the emergence of the self in infancy compatible with Dewey's work, see Daniel Stern's *The Interpersonal World of the Infant* (New York: Basic Books, 1985).

10 In an honorific sense, a "virtue" is a fruitful custom – a habit with a tendency toward beneficial outcomes. An individual has a "virtuous" character, then, insofar as her or his habits are conducive to fruitfully mediating problematic moral situations. A "vicious" character has the contrary tendencies. Understood in this way, it is possible for a socially sanctioned custom to be a vice mistaken for a virtue. Numerous puritans in seventeenth-century America believed in the virtue of religious *in*tolerance, and racism is construed a virtue by the Ku Klux Klan. Tolerance and egalitarianism would be deemed "vices" in these sub-cultures. Because these are examples of habits that are not in fact conducive to fruitful outcomes (if one takes a broader, more inclusive perspective), we can conclude that, although virtues are "relative" to cultures, they are not *radically* relative. We can adjudicate between better and worse values. It is not the case that "anything goes so long as a culture sanctions it."

11 It is not possible here fully to explain the notion of "universal human rationality," but the following is a thumbnail sketch. According to this view, human rationality is: (a) disembodied (ontologically separated from the body - i.e., separated from the body and thus from the brain "in the very nature of things"); (b) dispassionate (able to be separated from feelings and bodily inclinations); (c) a-cultural (able to be separated from any cultural conditioning); (d) a-temporal and a-historical (transcending time and not conditioned by the history of what went before); and (e) radically individual (at its best when detached from a community of co-investigators). Although each of these claims has been powerfully critiqued by philosophers in the twentieth century (perhaps most notably by Dewey), our primary focus in this essay is on (c) above.

12 Linguistic evidence is one among many ways to bolster the claim that we are social selves. Evidence from such fields as biology, anthropology, sociology, and psychology are equally crucial.

13 For example, see George Lakoff and Mark Johnson's *Metaphors we Live By* (University of Chicago Press, 1980); George Lakoff's *Women, Fire and Dangerous Things* (University of Chicago Press, 1987); Mark Johnson's *The Body in the Mind* (University of Chicago Press, 1987); and Mark Johnson's *Moral Imagination* (University of Chicago Press, 1993).

14 Lakoff and Johnson, *Metaphors we Live By*, 8.

15 To take another brief example, consider the everyday metaphor "Ideas are Food." For example: "There are too many facts here for me to *digest* them all." "I just can't *swallow* that claim." "That's *food for thought*." "He *devoured* the book." "He's a *voracious* reader." In Lakoff and Johnson, *Metaphors we Live By*, 46–7.

16 Maurice Merleau-Ponty, *The Phenomenology of Perception*, trans. Colin Smith (New Jersey: Humanities Press, 1962), 87. Quoted in Thomas Alexander, *John Dewey's Theory of Art, Experience and Nature* (SUNY Press, 1987), 143.

17 Mary Pipher, *Reviving Ophelia: Saving the Selves of Adolescent Girls* (New York: Ballantine Books, 1994), 23. See also *Hunger Pains: The American Woman's Tragic Quest for Thinness* (Lincoln: Barking Gator Press, 1982).

18 Dewey, *Human Nature and Conduct*, 16.

19 Ibid., 19.

20 Ibid., 31.

21 Ibid., 15.

22 As Plato observes in the *Statesman*: [Law] is like a self-willed, ignorant man who lets no one do anything but what he has ordered and forbids all subsequent questioning of his orders even if the situation has shown some marked improvement on the one for which he originally legislated (294ac).

23 Dewey, *Human Nature and Conduct*, 37.

24 Dewey, *Democracy and Education*, 49.

25 Dewey, *Human Nature and Conduct*, 47.

26 Ibid., 48.

27 Ibid., 24–5.

28 See George Herbert Mead, "The Philosophical Basis of Ethics," *Selected Writings*, 92. Acknowledgment is due here to Heather E. Keith for a paper presentation at the 1995 meeting of the "Society for the Advancement of American Philosophy."

29 Ibid., 21.

30 Ibid., 29.

31 These examples are drawn from a public lecture given by John E. Smith at Millsaps College in 1989.

32 Dewey conceives deliberation as an imaginative "dramatic rehearsal" (see, e.g., *Human Nature and Conduct*, ch. 16). When problematic situations arise, we "try on" in our imaginations various possibilities for acting. We do this in search of a path that will integrate competing desires and restore equilibrium to our experience. In a manner analogous to the creative imagination of the fiction writer or playwright, we run through a dramatic scene in our imaginations and thereby discover mediating courses that may temper our original impulses. A refined imagination discloses an expansive horizon of possibilities and fosters a capacity for choosing actions that will meaningfully continue our life-dramas.

33 Alasdair MacIntyre, *After Virtue* (University of Notre Dame Press, 1984), 221.

34 Ibid., 213.

35 Ibid., 213. As MacIntyre observes, "the narrative of any life is part of an interlocking set of narratives" (218).

Part III

Liberty and Equality

Drugs

When discussing how much freedom an individual should have, there is no better place to begin than by reading John Stuart Mill. Mill's *On Liberty* is the classic defense of individual liberty. Arguably it is still the best. He clearly states the liberal credo: "that the sole end for which mankind are warranted, individually or collectively, in interfering with the liberty of action of any of their number is . . . to prevent harm to others." Interfering with the liberty of a rational person, merely to prevent her from harming herself, is never legitimate. Thus, on Mill's view there are no "victimless crimes." If an action has no victim, then it cannot be a crime.

Of course, as I noted in THEORIZING ABOUT ETHICS, we sometimes have difficulty deciding whether an action harms someone other than the agent. Virtually every action we do affects others to some degree or in some fashion. If nothing else, someone may be put in a position where they are bothered, upset, or offended by our actions. As mentioned earlier, the bare knowledge that I engage in kinky sexual behavior might offend you. Does that mean that my actions harm you in ways the law and society should recognize? Should the state legally prohibit me from pursuing my peculiar sexual behavior? Should society criticize me if I continue? Not according to Mill. In setting social policy we should give no weight to such reactions. Otherwise, we unduly stretch the notion of harm.

It appears that Arthur, in his discussion of hate speech (FREE SPEECH), would agree. He claims that an action harms others only if it negatively affects their long-term interests. That is why we should not have speech codes. It would also explain why, on his view, we should not legally prohibit pornography. If Arthur is correct, then many actions people consider harmful are not, in fact, harmful, at least not in any sense that should concern the law. For instance, saying that your mere knowledge that I engage in non-standard sexual practices harms your interests would be absurd. Other writers will find Arthur's account of harm too restrictive. Clearly much is at stake. Exactly how we define "harm" has momentous practical consequences.

Until now I have been discussing harm to others. However, the essays in this section focus on harm to oneself, particularly harm caused by using chemical substances. Evidence suggests that using drugs like heroin is dangerous. According to Wilson, that justifies the state's decision to continue making the possession and sale of heroin (and similar drugs) against the law. These laws will limit the drugs' use, thereby protecting potential users from harm. Although Wilson's primary focus is on the harm done to users, he also argues that drug use harms others as well. People who use (certain) drugs are more likely to abuse their children and less likely to fulfill their familial and social obligations. Consequently, he argues, drug use is not a victimless crime.

One important aside. Wilson – like most people who oppose legalization of drugs – argues both that these restrictive laws prevent harm to the users *and* that they prevent harm to others. That is odd. If we had compelling evidence that drug use harmed others, then that would be sufficient reason to restrict their use. There would be no need to claim that such laws prevent harm to users. To even raise the paternalistic argument only muddies the political and moral waters. The problem, though, is that we do not have overwhelming evidence that drug use harms others.

The question, then, is whether we can legitimately prohibit drug use because some drug users sometimes harm others. Mill's discussion of drunkenness (included in this section) suggests he would not think we should. If, for example, a policeperson gets drunk and fails to discharge her duties, then we should punish her. But we should punish her for failing to do her duty, not for drinking. Likewise, Mill would claim we should punish drug users who steal and kill, but we should punish them because they steal and kill, not because they use drugs.

To that extent Mill's views seem similar to Cudd's. Cudd argues that we should legalize many drugs that are currently illegal: heroin, crack, marijuana, etc. Why? Because, she claims, the use of those drugs does not really harm others. On the other hand, we can legitimately prohibit the use of anabolic steroids. Why? Because, she argues, in the competitive world of athletics, legalizing steroids would effectively force many athletes to use steroids against their will. Here's why. Athletes participating in some sports, for example, football, take steroids to build up their muscles. Using these drugs quickly builds up their body mass. However, it also does serious, long-term damage to the body.

If given a genuine choice, most prudent athletes would decide not to use steroids. However, they also know that if they don't use steroids while others do, then they will be substantially disadvantaged. Thus, if they seriously want to compete, then they will feel compelled to use steroids. Thus, she argues, we should prohibit the use of steroids not because they are dangerous to the user, but because in these particular circumstances, many people will be forced to do things they don't really want to do. Even if this reasoning does not convince you, you should recognize a familiar theme: the ways in which social, political, and economic conditions make certain behaviors more (or less) likely. It is a theme you will see again in May's and Strikwerda's essay on male responsibility for rape (SEXUAL AND RACIAL DISCRIMINATION).

In the absence of these pressures, however, we must respect an individual's decision to use drugs – even if those drugs demonstrably harm her. Autonomy demands it. Most of the authors writing on EUTHANASIA argued that autonomy was exceedingly important. However, as I noted in that introduction, autonomy is a slippery notion. Most of us have no trouble deciding that a careful and seemingly reasonable choice by an unstressed, intelligent adult is fully autonomous. Nor do we have trouble deciding that the desire of a two-year-old to put her hand on a hot stove is not. Nonetheless, there are many cases about which we are far less sure.

The entire discussion is further complicated once we realize that we can interpret "autonomy" both descriptively and prescriptively. To say that a decision is *descriptively* autonomous is to say that an individual has made an informed choice, based on a rational assessment of the evidence. On the other hand, if we say that a law would violate a person's *prescriptive* autonomy, we are simply saying that the law would inappropriately restrict a choice that that person ought to be able to make – even if the choice is demonstrably irrational. Classical liberals like Mill claim that an individual has prescriptive autonomy, i.e., that she should be able to act as she pleases, even if, in some particular case, her choice is uninformed or silly.

The only time we can legitimately force someone to act against her express will is if we think she does not comprehend the consequences of her action, and will, after the fact, be glad that we coerced her. For instance, if I am about to cross a bridge that you – but not I – know is dangerous, you can legitimately stop me because: (a) you assume I do not know that the bridge is dangerous, and (b) once I fully understand the facts, I will be glad that you stopped me.

Goodin employs this reasoning to explain why he thinks some forms of paternalism are permissible. He shares Cudd's disdain for paternalistic laws that force rational adults to act against their will simply because someone else (the state) decides that an action would be in the citizen's best interests. However, Goodin argues, we cannot ignore the fact that most humans do not have only one preference, and that the preferences they do have change over time. Most of us have multiple preferences, and some of these preferences conflict with others.

For instance, someone may want to smoke (because they enjoy it) *and* want to stop (because they know it is bad for them). In other cases someone may currently have only the first preference (to continue smoking), yet we have good reason to think they will later develop the second (to stop). Consequently, forcing people to stop smoking – or passing laws that make smoking less likely (by increasing the cost) or less attractive (by banning advertisements) – will be likely to clash with their immediate stated preferences. Nonetheless, if, as seems plausible, we can safely infer that most smokers have mixed preferences or will later develop different preferences, then using legal means to restrict or forbid smoking is not crassly paternalistic. After all, the action is justified by the smokers' current or future preferences. In this way, Goodin claims to respect individual autonomy without sacrificing people's long-term interests on its altar.

Further Reading

Dworkin, R. 1977: *Taking Rights Seriously*. Cambridge, MA: Harvard University Press.

Feinberg, J. 1984: *The Moral Limits of the Criminal Law: Harm to Others*. New York: Oxford University Press.

Feinberg, J. 1984: *The Moral Limits of the Criminal Law: Harm to Self*. New York: Oxford University Press.

Goodin, R. 1989: *No Smoking: The Ethical Issues*. Chicago and London: University of Chicago Press.

Luper-Foy, S. and Brown, C. (eds) 1994: *Drugs, Morality, and the Law*. New York: Garland Press.

Mill, J. S. 1859/1978: *On Liberty*. Indianapolis, IN: Hackett.

Sartorious, R. 1983: *Paternalism*. Minneapolis: University of Minnesota Press.

27

Freedom of Action[1]

John Stuart Mill

The object of this Essay is to assert one very simple principle . . . to govern absolutely the dealings of society with the individual. . . . [It is to govern the] control [over individuals], whether the means used be physical force in the form of legal penalties, or the moral coercion of public opinion. That principle is, that the sole end for which mankind are warranted, individually or collectively in interfering with the liberty of action of any of their number, is self-protection. [T]he only purpose for which power can be rightfully exercised over any member of a civilized community, against his will, is to prevent harm to others. His own good, either physical or moral, is not a sufficient warrant. He cannot rightfully be compelled to do or forbear because it will be better for him to do so, because it will make him happier, because, in the opinions of others, to do so would be wise, or even right. These are good reasons for remonstrating with him, or reasoning with him, or persuading him, or entreating him, but not for compelling him, or visiting him with any evil, in case he do otherwise. To justify that, the conduct from which it is desired to deter him must be calculated to produce evil to some one else. The only part of the conduct of any one, for which he is amenable to society, is that which concerns others. In the part which merely concerns himself, his independence is, of right, absolute. Over himself, over his own body and mind, the individual is sovereign. . . .

No society in which these liberties are not on the whole respected, is free, whatever may be its form of government; and none is completely free in which they do not exist absolute and unqualified. The only freedom which deserves the name, is that of pursuing our own good in our own way, so long as we do not attempt to deprive others of theirs, or impede their efforts to obtain it. . . . Mankind are greater gainers by suffering each other to live as seems good to themselves, than by compelling each to live as seems good to the rest. . . .

[Of course] no one pretends that actions should be as free as opinions. On the contrary, even opinions lose their immunity, when the circumstances in which they are expressed are . . . a positive instigation to some mischievous act. An opinion that corndealers are starvers of the poor, or that private property is robbery, ought to be unmolested when simply circulated through the press, but may justly incur punishment when delivered orally to an excited mob assembled before the house of a corndealer, or when handed about among the same mob in the form of a placard. Acts of whatever kind, which, without justifiable cause, do harm to others, may be, and in the more important cases absolutely require to be, controlled by the unfavourable sentiments, and, when needful, by the active interference of mankind. The liberty of the individual must be thus far limited; he must not make himself a nuisance to other people. But if he refrains from molesting others in what concerns them, and merely acts according to his own inclination and judgment in things which concern himself, [then] . . . he should be allowed, without molestation, to carry his opinions into practice at his own cost.

[A]s it is useful that while mankind are imperfect there should be different opinions, so is it that there should be different experiments of living. [We should give] free scope . . . to varieties of character, short of injury to others. [T]he worth of different modes of life should be proved practically, when any one thinks fit to try them. It is desirable, in short, that in things which do not primarily concern others, individuality should assert itself. Where not the person's own character, but the traditions of customs of other people are the rule of conduct, there is wanting one of the principal ingredients of human happiness, and quite the chief ingredient of individual and social progress.

[I]f it were felt that the free development of individuality is one of the leading essentials of well-being; that it is not only a coordinate element with all that is designated by the terms civilization, instruction, education, culture, but is itself a necessary part and condition of all those things; there would be no danger that liberty should be undervalued, and the adjustment of the boundaries between it and social control would present no extraordinary difficulty. But the evil is that individual spontaneity is hardly recognized by the common modes of thinking as having any intrinsic worth, or deserving any regard on its own account. The majority, being satisfied with the ways of mankind as they now are (for it is they who make them what they are), cannot comprehend why those ways should not be good enough for everybody. [W]hat is more, spontaneity forms no part of the ideal of the majority. . . .

[However,] no one's idea of excellence in conduct is that people should do absolutely nothing but copy one another. No one would assert that people ought not to put into their mode of life, and into the conduct of their concerns, any impress whatever of their own judgment, or of their own individual character. On the other hand, it would be absurd to pretend that people ought to live as if nothing whatever had been known in the world before they came into it; as if experience had as yet done nothing towards showing that one mode of existence, or of conduct, is preferable to another. Nobody denies that people should be so taught and trained in youth, as to know and benefit by the ascertained results of human experience. But it is the privilege and proper condition of a human being, arrived at the maturity of his faculties, to use and interpret experience in his own way. It is for him to find out what part of recorded experience is properly applicable to his own circumstances and character.

The traditions and customs of other people are, to a certain extent, evidence of what their experience has taught them . . . and as such, have a claim to this deference. [However,] their experience may be too narrow; or they may not have interpreted it rightly. [Moreover] their interpretation of experience may be correct but unsuitable to him. Customs are made for customary circumstances, and customary characters: and his circumstances or his character may be uncustomary. [Finally] though the customs be both good as customs, and suitable to him, yet to conform to custom, merely as custom, does not educate or develop in him any of the qualities which are the distinctive endowment of a human being. The human faculties of perception, judgment, discriminative feeling, mental activity, and even moral preference, are exercised only in making a choice. He who does anything because it is the custom, makes no choice. He gains no practice either in discerning or in desiring what is best. The mental and moral, like the muscular powers, are improved only by being used.

He who lets the word, or his own portion of it, choose his plan of life for him, has no need of any other faculty than the ape-like one of imitation. He who chooses his plan for himself, employs all his faculties. He must use observation to see, reasoning and judgment to foresee, activity to gather materials for decision, discrimination to decide, and when he has decided, firmness and self-control to hold to his deliberate decision. And these qualities he requires and exercises exactly in proportion as the part of his conduct which he determines according to his own judgment and feelings is a large one. It is possible that he might be guided in some good path, and kept out of harm's way, without any of these things. But what will be his comparative worth as a human being? It really is of importance, not only what men do, but also what manner of men they are that do it. Among the works of man, which human life is rightly employed in perfecting and beautifying, the first in importance surely is man himself. . . . Human nature is not a machine to be built after a model, and set to do exactly the work prescribed for it, but a tree, which requires to grow and develop itself on all sides, according to the tendency of the inward forces which make it a living thing. . . .

It is not by wearing down into uniformity all that is individual in themselves, but by cultivating it and calling it forth, within the limits imposed by the rights and interests of others, that human beings become a noble and beautiful object of contemplation. [A]s the works partake the character of those who do them, by the same process human life also becomes rich, diversified, and animating. [Such a life furnishes] more abundant aliment to high thoughts and elevating feelings, and strengthens the tie which binds every individual to the race. [B]y making the race infinitely better worth belonging to [by developing] his individuality, each person becomes more valuable to himself, and is therefore capable of being more valuable to others. There is a greater fulness of life about his own existence, and when there is more life in the units there is more in the mass which is composed of them. As much compression as is necessary to prevent the stronger specimens of human nature from encroaching on the rights of others, cannot be dispensed with. [F]or this there is ample compensation even in the point of view of human development. The means of development which the individual loses by being prevented from gratifying his inclinations to the injury of others, are chiefly obtained at the expense of the development of other people. . . .

. . . It will not be denied by anybody, that originality is a valuable element in human affairs. There is always need of persons not only to discover new truths, and point out when what were once truths are true no longer, but also to commence new practices, and set the example of more enlightened conduct, and better taste and sense in human life. This cannot well be gainsaid by anybody who does not believe that the world has already attained perfection in all its ways and practices. It is true that this benefit is not capable of being rendered by everybody alike: there are but few persons, in comparison with the whole of mankind, whose experiments, if adopted by others, would be likely to be any improvement on established practice. But these few are the salt of the earth; without them, human life would become a stagnant pool. Not only is it they who introduce good things which did not before exist; it is they who keep the life in those which already existed. If there were nothing new to be done, would human intellect cease to be necessary? . . .

Persons of genius, it is true, are, and are always likely to be, a small minority; but in order to have them, it is necessary to preserve the soil in which they grow. Genius can only breathe freely in an atmosphere of freedom. Persons of genius are . . . more individual than any other people – less capable, consequently, of fitting themselves, without hurtful compression, into any of the small number of moulds which society provides in order to save its members the trouble of forming their own character. If from timidity they consent to be forced into one of these moulds, and to let all that part of themselves which cannot expand under the pressure remain unexpanded, society will be little the better for their genius. . . .

I insist thus emphatically on the importance of genius. [We must allow it] to unfold itself freely both in thought and in practice, being well aware that no one will deny the position in theory, but knowing also that almost every one, in reality, is totally indifferent to it. People think genius a fine thing if it enables a man to write an exciting poem, or paint a picture. But in its true sense, that of originality in thought and action, though no one says that it is not a thing to be admired, nearly all, at heart, think they can do very well without it. Unhappily this is too natural to be wondered at. Originality is the one thing which unoriginal minds cannot feel the use of. They cannot see what it is to do for them: how should they? If they could see what it would do for them, it would not be originality. The first service which originality has to render them, is that of opening their eyes: which being once fully done, they would have a chance of being themselves original. . . .

In sober truth, whatever homage may be professed, or even paid, to real or supposed mental superiority, the general tendency of things throughout the world is to render mediocrity the ascendant power among mankind. . . . Those whose opinions go by the name of public opinion, are not always the same sort of public: in America, they are the whole white population; in England, chiefly the middle class. But they are always a mass, that is to say, collective mediocrity. And what is still greater novelty, the mass do not now take their opinions from dignitaries in Church or State, from ostensible leaders, or from books. Their thinking is done for them by men much like themselves, addressing them or speaking in their name, on the spur of the moment, through the newspapers.

I am not complaining of all this. I do not assert that anything better is compatible, as a general rule, with the present low state of the human mind. But that does not hinder the government of mediocrity from being mediocre government. No government by a democracy or a numerous aristocracy, either in its political acts or in the opinions, qualities, and tone of mind which it fosters, ever did or could rise above mediocrity, except in so far as the sovereign Many have let themselves be guided (which in their best times they always have done) by the counsels and influence of a more highly gifted and instructed One or Few. . . .

I have said that it is important to give the freest scope possible to uncustomary things, in order that it may in time appear which of these are fit to be converted into customs. But independence of action, and disregard of custom are not solely deserving of encouragement for the chance they afford that better mode of action. [C]ustoms more worthy of general adoption, may be struck out; nor is it only persons of decided mental superiority who have a just claim to carry on their lives in their own way. There is no reason that all human existences should be constructed on some one, or some small number of patterns. If a person possesses any tolerable amount of common sense and experience, his own mode of laying out his existence is the best, not because it is the best in itself, but because it is his own mode. Human beings are not like sheep; and even sheep are not undistinguishably alike. A man cannot get a coat or a pair of boots to fit him, unless they are either made to his measure, or he has a whole warehouseful to choose from: and is it easier to fit him with a life than with a coat, or are human beings more like one another in their whole physical and spiritual conformation than in the shape of their feet? If it were only that people have diversities of taste that is reason enough for not attempting to shape them all after one model. But different persons also require different conditions for their spiritual development; and can no more exist healthily in the same moral, than all the variety of plants can in the same physical atmosphere and climate.

The same things which are helps to one person towards the cultivation of his higher nature, are hindrances to another. The same mode of life is a healthy excitement to one, keeping all his faculties of action and enjoyment in their best order, while to another it is a distracting burden, which suspends or crushes all internal life. Such are the differences among human beings in their sources of pleasure, their susceptibilities of pain, and the operation on them of different physical and moral agencies, that unless there is a corresponding diversity in their modes of life, they neither obtain their fair share of happiness, nor grow up to the mental, moral, and aesthetic stature of which their nature is capable. . . .

The despotism of custom is everywhere the standing hindrance to human advancement, being in unceasing antagonism to that disposition to aim at something better than customary, which is called, according to circumstances, the spirit of liberty, or that of progress or improvement. . . .

[Nonetheless] every one who receives the protection of society owes a return for the benefit, and the fact of living in society renders it indispensable that each should be bound to observe a certain line of conduct towards the rest. This conduct consists, first, in not injuring the interests of one another; or rather certain interests, which, either by express legal provision or by tacit understanding, ought to be considered as rights; and secondly, in each person's bearing his share (to be fixed on some equitable principle) of the labors and sacrifices incurred for defending the society or its members from injury and molestation. These conditions society is justified in enforcing, at all costs to those who endeavour to withhold fulfilment. Nor is this all that society may do. The acts of an individual may be hurtful to others, or wanting in due consideration for their welfare, without going the length of violating any of their constituted rights. The offender may then be justly punished by opinion, though not by law.

As soon as any part of a person's conduct affects prejudicially the interests of others, society has jurisdiction over it, and the question whether the general welfare will or will not be promoted by interfering with it, becomes open to discussion. But there is no room for entertaining any such question when a person's conduct affects the interests of no persons besides himself, or needs not affect them unless they like (all the persons concerned being of full age, and the ordinary amount of understanding). In all such cases there should be perfect freedom, legal and social, to do the action and stand the consequences. . . .

Note

1   Abridged and edited from chapters 1 and 3 of
    On Liberty.

28

Against the Legalization of Drugs

James Q. Wilson

In 1972, the President appointed me chairman of the National Advisory Council for Drug Abuse Prevention. Created by Congress, the Council was charged with providing guidance on how best to coordinate the national war on drugs. (Yes, we called it a war then, too.) In those days, the drug we were chiefly concerned with was heroin. When I took office, heroin use had been increasing dramatically. Everybody was worried that this increase would continue. Such phrases as "heroin epidemic" were commonplace.

That same year, the eminent economist Milton Friedman published an essay in *Newsweek* in which he called for legalizing heroin. His argument was on two grounds: as a matter of ethics, the government has no right to tell people not to use heroin (or to drink or to commit suicide); as a matter of economics, the prohibition of drug use imposes costs on society that far exceed the benefits. Others, such as the psychoanalyst Thomas Szasz, made the same argument.

We did not take Friedman's advice. (Government commissions rarely do.) I do not recall that we even discussed legalizing heroin, though we did discuss (but did not take action on) legalizing a drug, cocaine, that many people then argued was benign. Our marching orders were to figure out how to win the war on heroin, not to run up the white flag of surrender.

That was 1972. Today, we have the same number of heroin addicts that we had then – half a million, give or take a few thousand. Having that many heroin addicts is no trivial matter, these people deserve our attention; but not having had an increase in that number for over fifteen years is also something that deserves our attention. What happened to the "heroin epidemic" that many people once thought would overwhelm us?

The facts are clear: a more or less stable pool of heroin addicts has been getting older, with relatively few new recruits. In 1976 the average age of heroin users who appeared in hospital emergency rooms was about twenty-seven; ten years later it was thirty-two. More than two-thirds of all heroin users appearing in emergency rooms are now over the age of thirty. Back in the early 1970s, when heroin got onto the national political agenda, the typical heroin addict was much younger, often a teenager. Household surveys show the same thing – the rate of opiate use (which includes heroin) has been flat for the better part of two decades. More fine-grained studies of inner-city neighborhoods confirm this. John Boyle and Ann Brunswick found that the percentage of young blacks in Harlem who used heroin fell from 8 percent in 1970–71 to about 3 percent in 1975–76.

Why did heroin lose its appeal for young people? When the young blacks in Harlem were asked why they stopped, more than half mentioned "trouble with the law" or "high cost" (and high cost is, of course, directly the result of law enforcement). Two-thirds said that heroin hurt their health; nearly all said they had had a bad experience with it. We need not rely, however, simply on what they said. In New York City in 1973–75, the street price of heroin rose dramatically and its purity sharply declined, probably as a result of the heroin shortage caused by the success of the Turkish government in reducing the supply of opium base and of the French government in closing down heroin-processing laboratories located in and around Marseilles. These were short-lived gains for, just as Friedman predicted, alternative sources of supply – mostly in Mexico – quickly emerged. But the three-year heroin shortage interrupted the easy recruitment of new users.

Health and related problems were no doubt part of the reason for the reduced flow of recruits. Over the preceding years, Harlem youth had watched as more and more heroin users died of overdoses, were poisoned by adulterated doses, or acquired hepatitis from dirty needles. The word got around: heroin can kill you. By 1974 new hepatitis cases and drug-overdose deaths had dropped to a fraction of what they had been in 1970.

Alas, treatment did not seem to explain much of the cessation in drug use. Treatment programs can and do help heroin addicts, but treatment did not explain the drop in the number of *new* users (who by definition had never been in treatment) nor even much of the reduction in the number of experienced users.

No one knows how much of the decline to attribute to personal observation as opposed to high prices or reduced supply. But other evidence suggests strongly that price and supply played a large role. In 1972 the National Advisory Council was especially worried by the prospect that US servicemen returning to this country from Vietnam would bring their heroin habits with them. Fortunately, a brilliant study by Lee Robins of Washington University in St Louis put that fear to rest. She measured drug use of Vietnam veterans shortly after they had returned home. Though many had used heroin regularly while in Southeast Asia, most gave up the habit when back in the United States. The reason: here, heroin was less available and sanctions on its use were more pronounced. Of course, if a veteran had been willing to pay enough – which might have meant traveling to another city and would certainly have meant making an illegal contact with a disreputable dealer in a threatening neighborhood in order to acquire a (possibly) dangerous dose – he could have sustained his drug habit. Most veterans were unwilling to pay this price, and so their drug use declined or disappeared. . . .

Back to the Future

Now cocaine, especially in its potent form, crack, is the focus of attention. Now as in 1972 the government is trying to reduce its use. Now as then some people are advocating legalization. Is there any more reason to yield to those arguments today than there was almost two decades ago?[1]

I think not. If we had yielded in 1972 we almost certainly would have had today a permanent population of several million, not several hundred thousand, heroin addicts. If we yield now we will have a far more serious problem with cocaine.

Crack is worse than heroin by almost any measure. Heroin produces a pleasant drowsiness and, if hygienically administered, has only the physical side effects of constipation and sexual impotence. Regular heroin use incapacitates many users, especially poor ones, for any productive work or social responsibility. They will sit nodding on a street corner, helpless but at least harmless. By contrast, regular cocaine use leaves the user neither helpless nor harmless. When smoked (as with crack) or injected, cocaine produces instant, intense, and short-lived euphoria. The experience generates a powerful desire to repeat it. If the drug is readily available, repeat use will occur. Those people who progress to "bingeing" on cocaine become devoted to the drug and its effects to the exclusion of almost all other considerations — job, family, children, sleep, food, even sex. Dr Frank Gawin at Yale and Dr Everett Ellinwood at Duke report that a substantial percentage of all high-dose, binge users become uninhibited, impulsive, hypersexual, compulsive, irritable, and hyperactive. Their moods vacillate dramatically, leading at times to violence and homicide.

Women are much more likely to use crack than heroin, and if they are pregnant, the effects on their babies are tragic. Douglas Besharov, who has been following the effects of drugs on infants for twenty years, writes that nothing he learned about heroin prepared him for the devastation of cocaine. Cocaine harms the fetus and can lead to physical deformities or neurological damage. Some crack babies have for all practical purposes suffered a disabling stroke while still in the womb. The long-term consequences of this brain damage are lowered cognitive ability and the onset of mood disorders. Besharov estimates that about 30,000 to 50,000 such babies are born every year, about 7,000 in New York City alone. There may be ways to treat such infants, but from everything we now know the treatment will be long, difficult, and expensive. Worse, the mothers who are most likely to produce crack babies are precisely the ones who, because of poverty or temperament, are least able and willing to obtain such treatment. In fact, anecdotal evidence suggests that crack mothers are likely to abuse their infants.

The notion that abusing drugs such as cocaine is a "victimless crime" is not only absurd but dangerous. Even ignoring the fetal drug syndrome, crack-dependent people are, like heroin addicts, individuals who regularly victimize their children by neglect, their spouses by improvidence, their employers by lethargy, and their co-workers by carelessness. Society is not and could never be a collection of autonomous individuals. We all have a stake in ensuring that each of us displays a minimal level of dignity, responsibility, and empathy. We cannot, of course, coerce people into goodness, but we can and should insist that some standards must be met if society itself — on which the very existence of the human personality depends — is to persist. Drawing the line that defines those standards is difficult and contentious, but if crack and heroin use do not fall below it, what does? . . .

Have We Lost?

Many people who agree that there are risks in legalizing cocaine or heroin still favor it because, they think, we have lost the war on drugs. "Nothing we have done has worked" and the current federal policy is just "more of the same." Whatever the costs of greater drug use, surely they would be less than the costs of our present, failed efforts.

That is exactly what I was told in 1972 — and heroin is not quite as bad a drug as cocaine. We did not surrender and we did not lose. We did not win, either. What the nation accomplished then was what most efforts to save people from themselves accomplish: the problem was contained and the number of victims minimized, all at a considerable cost in law enforcement and increased crime. Was the cost worth it? I think so, but others may disagree. What are the lives of would-be addicts worth? I recall some people saying to me then, "Let them kill themselves." I was appalled. Happily, such views did not prevail. . . .

It took about ten years to contain heroin. We have had experience with crack for only about three or four years. Each year we spend perhaps $11 billion on law enforcement (and some of that goes to deal with marijuana) and perhaps $2 billion on treatment. Large sums, but not sums that should lead anyone to say, "We just can't afford this any more."

The illegality of drugs increases crime, partly because some users turn to crime to pay for their habits, partly because some users are stimulated by certain drugs (such as crack or PCP) to act more violently or ruthlessly than they otherwise would, and partly because criminal organizations seeking to control drug supplies use force to manage their markets. These also are serious costs, but no one knows how much they would be reduced if drugs were legalized. Addicts would no longer steal to pay black-market prices for drugs, a real gain. But some, perhaps a great deal, of that gain would be offset by the great increase in the number of addicts. These people, nodding on heroin or living in the delusion-ridden high of cocaine, would hardly be ideal employees. Many would steal simply to support themselves, since snatch-and-grab, opportunistic crime can be managed even by people unable to hold a regular job or plan an elaborate crime. Those British addicts who get their supplies from government clinics are not models of law-abiding decency. Most are in crime, and though their per-capita rate of criminality may be lower thanks to the cheapness of their drugs, the total volume of crime they produce may be quite large. Of course, society could decide to support all unemployable addicts on welfare, but that would mean that gains from lowered rates of crime would have to be offset by large increases in welfare budgets.

Proponents of legalization claim that the costs of having more addicts around would be largely if not entirely offset by having more money available with which to treat and care for them. The money would come from taxes levied on the sale of heroin and cocaine.

To obtain this fiscal dividend, however, legalization's supporters must first solve an economic dilemma. If they want to raise a lot of money to pay for welfare and treatment, the tax rate on the drugs will have to be quite high. Even if they themselves do not want a high rate, the politicians' love of "sin taxes" would probably guarantee that it would be high anyway. But the higher the tax, the higher the price of the drug, and the higher the price the greater the likelihood that addicts will turn to crime to find the money for it and that criminal organizations will be formed to sell tax-free drugs at below-market rates. If we managed to keep taxes (and thus prices) low, we would get that much less money to pay for welfare and treatment and more people could afford to become addicts. There may be an optimal tax rate for drugs that maximizes revenue while minimizing crime, bootlegging, and the recruitment of new addicts, but our experience with alcohol does not suggest that we know how to find it. . . .

The Benefits of Illegality

. . . We are now investing substantially in drug-education programs in the schools. Though we do not yet know for certain what will work, there are some promising leads. But I wonder how credible such programs would be if they were aimed at dissuading children from doing something perfectly legal. We could, of course, treat drug education like smoking education: inhaling crack and inhaling tobacco are both legal, but you should not do it because it is bad for you. That tobacco is bad for you is easily shown: the Surgeon General has seen to that. But what do we say about crack? It is pleasurable, but devoting yourself to so much pleasure is not a good idea (though perfectly legal)? Unlike tobacco, cocaine will not give you cancer or emphysema, but it will lead you to neglect your duties to family, job, and neighborhood? Everybody is doing cocaine, but you should not?

Again, it might be possible under a legalized regime to have effective drug-prevention programs, but their effectiveness would depend heavily, I think, on first having decided that cocaine use, like tobacco use, is purely a matter of practical consequences; no fundamental moral significance attaches to either. But if we believe – as I do – that dependency on certain mind-altering drugs *is* a moral issue and that their illegality rests in part on their immorality, then legalizing them undercuts, if it does not eliminate altogether, the moral message.

That message is at the root of the distinction we now make between nicotine and cocaine. Both are highly addictive, both have harmful physical effects. But we treat the two drugs differently, not simply because nicotine is so widely used as to be beyond the reach of effective prohibition, but because its use does not destroy the user's essential humanity. Tobacco shortens one's life, cocaine debases it. Nicotine alters one's habits, cocaine alters one's soul. The heavy use of crack, unlike the heavy use of tobacco, corrodes those natural sentiments of sympathy and duty that constitute our human nature and make possible our social life. To say, as does Nadelmann, that distinguishing morally between tobacco and cocaine is "little more than a transient prejudice" is close to saying that morality itself is but a prejudice.

The Alcohol Problem

Now we have arrived where many arguments about legalizing drugs begin: is there any reason to treat heroin and cocaine differently from the way we treat alcohol?

There is no easy answer to that question because, as with so many human problems, one cannot decide simply on the basis either of moral principles or of individual consequences; one has to temper any policy by a common-sense judgment of what is possible. Alcohol, like heroin, cocaine, PCP, and marijuana, is a drug – that is, a mood-altering substance – and consumed to excess it certainly has harmful consequences: auto accidents, barroom fights, bedroom shootings. It is also, for some people, addictive. We cannot confidently compare the addictive powers of these drugs, but the best evidence suggests that crack and heroin are much more addictive than alcohol.

Many people, Nadelmann included, argue that since the health and financial costs of alcohol abuse are so much higher than those of cocaine or heroin abuse, it is hypocritical folly to devote our efforts to preventing cocaine or drug use. But as Mark Kleiman of Harvard has pointed out, this comparison is quite misleading. What Nadelmann is doing is showing that a *legalized* drug (alcohol) produces greater social harm than *illegal* ones (cocaine and heroin). But of course. Suppose that in the 1920s we had made heroin and cocaine legal and alcohol illegal. Can anyone doubt that Nadelmann would now be writing that it is folly to continue our ban on alcohol because cocaine and heroin are so much more harmful? . . .

If I am Wrong . . .

No one can know what our society would be like if we changed the law to make access to cocaine, heroin, and PCP easier. I believe, for reasons given, that the result would be a sharp increase in use, a more widespread degradation of the human personality, and a greater rate of accidents and violence.

I may be wrong. If I am, then we will needlessly have incurred heavy costs in law enforcement and some forms of criminality. But if I am right, and the legalizers prevail anyway, then we will have consigned millions of people, hundreds of thousands of infants, and hundreds of neighborhoods to a life of oblivion and disease. To the lives and families destroyed by alcohol we will have added countless more destroyed by cocaine, heroin, PCP, and whatever else a basement scientist can invent.

Human character is formed by society; indeed, human character is inconceivable without society, and good character is less likely in a bad society. Will we, in the name of an abstract doctrine of radical individualism, and with the false comfort of suspect predictions, decide to take the chance that somehow individual decency can survive amid a more general level of degradation?

I think not. The American people are too wise for that, whatever the academic essayists and cocktail-party pundits may say. But if Americans today are less wise than I suppose, then Americans at some future time will look back on us now and wonder, what kind of people were they that they could have done such a thing?

Note

1 I do not here take up the question of marijuana. For a variety of reasons – its widespread use and its lesser tendency to addict – it presents a different problem from cocaine or heroin. For a penetrating analysis, see Mark Kleiman, *Marijuana: Costs of Abuse, Costs of Control* (Greenwood Press, 217 pp., $37.95).

29

Taking Drugs Seriously: Liberal Paternalism and the Rationality of Preferences*

Ann E. Cudd

> . . . it is clear that it is a Good Thing for the individual to have what he prefers. This is not a question of satisfaction, but freedom . . . But drug-fiends should be cured; children should go to school. How do we decide what preferences should be respected and what restrained unless we judge the preferences themselves?
>
> (Robinson, 1963, p. 49)

The War on Drugs has made very pertinent (though curiously taboo) the question of whether people ought to have the legal right to take drugs. The War targets all and only the already illegal drugs as targets in its war. The reasons are hazy and anecdotal, but backed up by the very real threat of prison. Presumably, drug use should be illegal only if it is immoral or at least irrational. However, the claim that it is immoral or irrational to take drugs is neither obviously right nor wrong, and since it involves some interesting problems for the theory of rationality, as well as for those who are inclined to indulge in the use of drugs, it is worthy of serious consideration by philosophers.

1. Liberal Paternalism and Drugs

In this essay I argue that in a liberal society citizens have the right to take most drugs. In my view the infringement of that right for almost all drugs is legitimate in a liberal society only under special circumstances, namely those circumstances in which what I call "liberal paternalism" is justified. However, there is only a small and very special class of drugs which fall under this category. My argument analyses choices from the perspective of rational choice theory, in an attempt to specify precisely the senses in which a choice to take drugs may be irrational. I shall consider all questionable uses of drugs, not only illegal ones (marijuana, opiates, psychedelics, etc.), but also legal drugs such as "designer drugs", and abused prescription drugs, as well as alcohol and nicotine. They all have two things in common that make them interesting test cases for theories of rationality and liberalism: they may, in at least some uses, cause significant problems for the user, and they may, in at least some uses, provide significant satisfaction for the user.

On a plausible conception of liberal paternalism, interference with a person's liberty is justified when the person acts irrationally, either because she miscalculates the consequences of her actions, or she acts on irrational desires or (to use the rational choice theorists' word) preferences. It would be impossible to have irrational preferences on a Humean view of desire, since on that view preferences are uncriticizable; it is not *irrational* to "prefer the destruction of the whole world to the scratching of my finger" (Hume, 1978, p. 216). I maintain with Joan Robinson that, *pace* Hume, preferences can be rationally criticized, but that the preference for taking drugs is not irrational in every case, and that the society at large is not in a proper position to sort out individual cases.

I assume, for the purposes of this essay, the Millian liberal principle that individuals have the right to do whatever they want, provided that they are not thereby failing to take normal care to avoid physically harming another, nor failing to perform their legal contracts, nor failing to perform their legal duties as parents or citizens (excepting, for now, the taking of drugs, of course). Liberals hold that there are purely self-regarding acts, and that society may not determine whether or not individuals may perform them. The requirements of morality may go further than the liberal principle. For example, we may want to say that friends are morally required to come to each other's aid. This moral requirement goes beyond what liberal states can legitimately require of people, since it has to do with personal relations. What counts as a personal matter is, of course, debatable. But we won't carry on that debate here. For the purposes of this essay we will not be interested in the moral issues that go beyond the simple right to take drugs in a liberal society.

I will assume that taking drugs is permissible if there are no grounds for liberal paternalism, as long as one is not operating a car or performing some other licensed or sensitive duty. In other words I assume that there is no significant harm-to-others issue here. There are arguments one could marshall against this claim, such as that taking drugs causes (a sufficiently high proportion of) users to do anything necessary to ensure a future supply of drugs, and hence is a cause of violence, or that taking drugs illegitimately increases the tax burden on the rest of society by raising the probability that one will require emergency medical care. But in the first instance one could argue that the *criminalization* of drugs is largely to blame, and in the second, football would face the same objection. If I am wrong about this, however, it will not affect my argument about outlawing drugs *on grounds of liberal paternalism*. So I assume for now that we could defend the right to take (at least most) drugs against these harm-to-others objections, as a full defence would take us too far afield here.

It is not beyond the bounds of liberalism, however, to require that people behave (more or less) rationally. John Stuart Mill justifies liberalism by arguing that each individual's plan for her life is the best plan because it is hers (Mill, 1978, p. 64). He makes two claims here: that individuals have privileged information with respect to their own desires, and that autonomy is to be valued in itself. Mill thought there should be an exception to our freedom to choose: we may not sell ourselves into slavery since that is a renunciation of all future autonomy (Mill, 1978, p. 101). I would argue that another exception he would have to admit is that one may be prevented from choosing if one is clearly irrational, since one cannot then act autonomously. Ronald Dworkin's justification of liberalism is that it is a consequence of the requirement that government have equal concern for all persons (Dworkin, 1977). If a person is irrational, incompetent, or infirm then the requirement of equal concern entails that the government provide her with some care. Thus the liberal principle does not prohibit paternalism on the part of the state when an individual is judged incapable of making a rational choice.

I am not proposing to argue for a particular conception of liberal paternalism here, rather I am concerned with how the drug issue is resolved on one plausible understanding of liberal paternalism. In this paper, then, I will assume that *for liberals, paternalism is justified to prevent people from making choices which are clearly and necessarily irrational, or in which rational people would agree to a constraint on their liberty*. Rational choices are, minimally, choices which give the individual a satisfactory (to her) level of expected utility in the situation. So desires that are self-defeating, in the sense that if one were to satisfy them one would thereby lower one's expected utility level, are irrational. Rationality may involve more than this, however. We may want to argue that there are certain desires which rationally cannot be held. It is then a further question to ask whether we want to prohibit acting on these desires. I shall assume that if we can show that an action is necessarily irrational then it legitimately may be controlled by the state. I proceed by analysing the ways in which drug taking is arguably irrational, and hence susceptible to liberal paternalist objections.

2. Strategic Irrationality

One way that a choice may be irrational is if it leads to a socially and individually suboptimal outcome. In this case law may be useful to coordinate actions to bring about an optimal outcome. Legal restrictions on actions that do not cause harm to others can be divided into two categories: (1) laws that coerce individual self-regarding actions for special strategic considerations that rational agents accept; and (2) paternalistic laws, or laws that coerce an individual's actions for that individual's good. The rational liberal accepts all laws that are clearly of the first kind. She can accept some paternalistic laws too; remember, even Mill claimed that we may not sell ourselves into slavery. But she can accept the second kind of laws only when they amount to a *liberal* paternalism. Do drug laws constitute liberal paternalism or illegitimate interference?

Of the actions which liberal laws coerce for special strategic considerations there seem to be three cases. The most well discussed case consists of laws to prevent free-rider problems. It may be argued that drug users are "free-riding" on the social benefits of other people's refraining from using drugs. Given the harms to all of us from massive free-riding, we ought, rationally, all to agree to punish harshly any free-rider. But this assumes that there will be massive drug use without laws against it. Furthermore, at worst it is the same sort of free-riding that anyone who does not develop her talents commits, and liberals typically assume that self-development is too personal to interfere with.

The second case consists of laws that serve to coordinate social actions for a socially and individually better outcome. Insofar as they are justified by promoting the individual's own good, they are paternalist. An example of this (presented by Thomas Schelling in 1984) was the NHL hockey players who refused to wear helmets because they thought they would not look tough enough if they were wearing them. As long as there were some who would not wear the helmets, or even as long as they thought others might not wear them, no one wanted to look like a wimp, even if it meant a great risk to their well being. However, all of them, according to Schelling, preferred to be required to wear helmets, since in that case they would not appear to be wimps for wearing the helmets, and they could protect their heads. The situation where there is no rule can be represented by the familiar *assurance game* matrix as shown, where the numbers represent Mario's and Wayne's respective ordinal rankings of the situation.

Wayne

	helmet	no helmet
helmet	1,1	4,3
no helmet	3,4	2,2

Mario

The problem of the assurance game is that there are two equilibria, i.e., two choice combinations that are each player's best response to the other's choice, but one (both wear helmets) is clearly better than the other (both wear no helmets). If there is a rule that strictly prohibits not wearing helmets, then the situation changes to one where both prefer wearing helmets no matter what the other does. Since the rule just gives them the security to do what they both really want to do in the absence of the rule, it does not violate their autonomy.

If it is only rational to do what one prefers, then laws that solve assurance-game problems in this way are legitimate liberal paternalist laws. Peer pressure, causing people to choose to perform actions for reputation effects of the action rather than for any intrinsic value of the action, is an assurance game situation. So if we suppose that people take drugs only because others do, and that they would prefer not to take drugs if others also refrained, then this would be a case in which the liberal would accept laws against drugs. Since we assume that peer pressure might very well be the motivation for children and especially teenagers to take drugs, it would be justifiable for a liberal state to take coercive measures to prevent them from doing so. This analysis is appealing to the liberal, since any rational person in this situation would voluntarily choose the coercive measures, and, unlike in the prisoner's dilemma (which I discuss below), would have no reason to cheat. However, we cannot assume that the payoffs to drug taking commonly present this pattern. Too many people seem to choose drug taking apart from others, in spite of the risks, even the risk of censure by their peers, as in a case we will examine in the next section. Thus we cannot suppose that in general people's preferences for taking drugs constitute an assurance game.

The third case consists of the laws which prevent prisoner's dilemmas from arising. The use of anabolic steroids in athletics constitutes a prisoner's dilemma. The pressures and incentives to succeed in athletics cause some athletes to seek advantage in every possible way, even if it requires some sacrifice of present or future health. Anabolic steroids clearly increase an athlete's chances of success. In the absence of an effective law against it each player has a *dominant strategy* to take the drug. That is, they do better by pursuing that strategy no matter what the other does, as in the matrix shown.

Ben

Carl		use steroid	don't use
	use steroid	3,3	4,1
	don't use	1,4	2,2

The dilemma is that if they could somehow manage it, the players would prefer to both not use than to both use. It is then rational for them to agree to have a coercive power that will *force* them to both not use. Thus, this is also a case of paternalist intervention to which rational players would agree. In this case it is legitimate for a liberal society to pass laws against the athletic use of steroids, provided that there is a reasonably effective enforcement mechanism.

There appears to be only one kind of drug, then, which a liberal state can outlaw for adults on grounds of its strategic considerations alone, and that is anabolic steroids used by athletes. All other paternalist drug laws are to be justified, if they are justifiable at all, by the claim that it is individually irrational to take them. Thus the question I will be addressing in the rest of this essay is whether taking drugs (which we shall henceforth understand to exclude steroid use by athletes) is irrational, and so, whether it can on those grounds be made illegal in a liberal society.

3. The Insanity Plea

People don't come equipped with rationality indicators, and it is notoriously difficult to attribute irrationality to someone with any certainty. Rational choices depend holistically on beliefs and desires, so that if an action appears to be irrational given one set of beliefs and desires it may be rational given another set. Since we can never be sure of another's beliefs and desires, it is difficult to attribute irrationality to someone. One *prima facie* example of irrational behaviour would be intentionally inflicting serious non-fatal wounds on oneself; one cannot rationally desire to hurt oneself, since it reduces one's utility now and into the future. If we agree that wounding oneself is irrational, then it would be legitimate, though perhaps unnecessary, for our liberal state to take some actions to prevent it.

Now one might want to say that taking drugs is a kind of self-inflicted wound. But it seems that there may be significant advantages to the person taking the drugs which do not exist in the case of self-inflicted physical wounds. There are effects which we can inter-subjectively identify, and agree that they are positive. For example, many artists have found drugs to be an aid to creativity. (Ken Kesey and Alan Ginsberg immediately spring to mind.) Also, since so many people desire the effects of drugs, while we do not find many people intentionally inflicting wounds on themselves, we should not be so quick to find the cases analogous.

Taking drugs sometimes has the result of making people temporarily or permanently insane. Might we want to outlaw it on these grounds alone? Surely a liberal society would not want to do so on the grounds that it may make one insane, since there are many things which also increase the chances that one will become insane which we would not want to outlaw. For example, becoming a psychiatrist, or taking up a competitive and stressful occupation, working hard, moving to a new place, trying new things, taking up a cult religion, having children, or watching too much television, all have the potential for making one crazy, even certifiably so. Yet these are all clear cases of things a liberal society would not want to outlaw, since liberals believe that the right of people to make their own choices overrules the right of the state to be paternal in all but the most clear-cut cases of irrationality. The case of taking drugs, I would argue, is similar to these examples; though one may increase one's chances of mental health problems, the right of the individual clearly overrides any right of the society to protect its citizens from themselves.

One might claim that it is necessarily irrational to take drugs *in order* to make oneself insane. But it is not true that one should prefer to be rational all the time. Derek Parfit (1984, pp. 12–13) argues that one can rationally choose to make oneself irrational, with an example in which a person takes a drug to make himself insane in order to make himself immune to the threats of a robber, showing that it can even be rational to relinquish one's sanity. One might object that this case is too far-fetched, but it is not far-fetched to suppose that one might want others to think one is so crazy that one will carry out a suboptimal threat. (This is the idea behind the "mutual assured destruction" strategy, after all.) It is more likely that in many instances it is nice to see life from a different perspective. Drugs are often taken because they make us perceive reality differently. But isn't that also the case with art or with philosophy?

One might argue that the examples I have given all have the potential for making one's life better, even for increasing the probability of long-term mental health. Taking drugs may also have this effect. Imagine the life of a person trapped in a depressing social situation from which there is no realistic chance of escape, such as a member of a discriminated class who cannot find meaningful work and who has no realistic chance of ever doing so. Taking drugs may allow that person an escape from the daily drudgery that nothing else, short of suicide or insanity, could. In such a case taking drugs would be conducive of better long-term mental health than would any feasible alternative. One might respond that there is no such situation which cannot be overcome given sufficient diligence: the illiterate can learn to read, the uneducated can become educated, the inexperienced can work their way up the work ladder, the uninspired can inspire themselves. We should not allow people to make second best choices when their mental health is at stake. This response violates the spirit of liberalism in two ways. The liberal principle entails that there exist acts that no one can be legally required to perform. Furthermore, liberals may not require one to take the best possible care of oneself, or even good care of oneself. To require that the person in our example pull himself up by his bootstraps is to require not only that he take good care of himself, but also that he work harder at it than most people would have to, since his social situation makes his boots that much heavier. Hence there is no direct argument from the fact that drugs may make one insane to the conclusion that taking drugs may be made illegal in a liberal society.

4. Narrow Individual Irrationality

A better argument for the proponent of drug laws is to argue that the preference for taking drugs is necessarily irrational. This might be argued for in two ways. One might argue that taking drugs is self-defeating in the sense that one can only decrease one's utility, now and into the future, by action on a desire to take drugs. Or one might argue that the desire to take drugs, while not self-defeating, is irrational on other grounds. We will examine these possibilities in turn.

Is the desire to take drugs directly self-defeating? One way of construing this question is this: is there an intransitivity in the preference to take drugs? To say that there is an intransitivity in someone's preferences is to say that the person ranks a set of options {a,b,c} such that a is preferred to b (aPb), bPc, and cPa. The well known problem with such a set of preferences is that they lead one to become a money pump, i.e., to pay to trade b for a, then c for b, then a for c continuously until one is pumped out of money; this is irrational no matter what else one prefers.

Taking drugs, it might be argued, has the same problem. In the short run you realize some satisfaction, but in the long run you end up with the same problems with less money and time (and perhaps lost health). Now you are able to satisfy fewer of your desires than before, hence taking drugs is self-defeating. But this assumes that one gets nothing out of the experience of the drug high, and that is a bad assumption for many people. Just as some people will pay a great deal for a meal in a restaurant with very good food and special ambience for the sake of the experience, some may want to spend a good deal of money and time, and even risk ill health, for a good drug experience. This does not show that no one's preferences for taking drugs are intransitive, just as it doesn't show that no one's preferences for fancy restaurants are intransitive. It does suggest the possibility of transitive preferences for taking drugs, and so taking drugs is not necessarily irrational on these grounds.

The possibility of addiction to drugs, however, raises more difficult problems for a defence of the right to take drugs. Since addiction often comes with a sort of schizophrenic preference for the drug on the one hand, and for freedom from the drug on the other, it leads to intransitive preferences of the worst kind: taking x to mean "having drugs" and y to mean "not having drugs", xPy and yPx. But addiction does not lead to straightforward intransitivities, since it makes one have ever stronger preferences for the drugs at the time one prefers them, so that it is not the case that one holds xPy and yPx *at the same time*. Furthermore, the addict may not actually hold that yPx, but rather yPx^1, where x^1 means "being addicted to drugs". Thus one does not, at those times when one prefers the drug, prefer anything else to the drug. An addict's preferences may oscillate rapidly over time, however, in which case the addict's preferences, while not intransitive, are not perfectly reasonable either. We shall return to the problem of addiction in the next section.

To this point I have been assuming a particularly narrow conception of rationality. On this conception rational preferences are simply consistent preferences, there are no substantive requirements about the content of the preferences. A belief in the supernatural is as rational as the belief in tables and chairs, so long as these beliefs are consistent with other beliefs one holds. And as we just saw, there are no requirements concerning the way preferences develop over time. On this conception of rationality it is not too surprising that preferences for taking drugs are not necessarily irrational. But this is not the only conception of rationality consistent with liberalism, and on other, more substantive conceptions it may turn out that the desire to take drugs is an irrational desire.

5. Broad Individual Rationality

Jon Elster (1985, p. 22) provides what he calls a "broad conception of the rationality of desires". He argues that desires should be evaluated by considering the way in which they are shaped. Respectable preferences must be *autonomous*, which means that they must have been formed through a process over which the agent had sufficient, and the right kind of, control. Elster discusses several non-autonomous preference-formation processes. I shall discuss just the two processes which are directly relevant to the drug case: *adaptive preference formation* and *wishful thinking*.

Adaptive preferences change with changes in the feasible set, or the states of affairs the agent considers achievable for him. Adaptive preference formation is the phenomenon of "sour grapes", which makes anything outside the feasible set seem undesirable. The case of taking drugs may involve adaptations to the feasible set by causing the person to prefer those states of affairs in which one could be a drug taker. Now if one is an addict, then one's feasible set is considerably different from what it would be if one were not an addict; one could not also be in positions of responsibility for others and one would have to have some secure source of drugs and money to buy them, for instance. An addict might come to prefer those states of affairs, and ask that the state respect his preference. Does this constriction of the feasible set make being an addict irrational? Or, can one rationally choose a course of action which restricts one's feasible set? We can think of the alternatives in one's feasible set as the opportunities one has, and the restrictions on those alternatives as opportunity costs. Choices always have opportunity costs. When one decides on a particular career one rules out many others as life choices, or when one decides to commit oneself (monogamously) to another person one rules out other potential mates. Thus we have at most a difference of degree to which the feasible set is altered between addiction and other choices.

Elster claims that there are other problems with adaptive preference formation which make the preferences formed in this way less respectable. First, it is a causal process which goes on behind the back of the person who is choosing and over which she therefore has little control. Many other causes operate on us to form our preferences without our conscious approval. For example, I suspect that there is something causal and uncontrollable about the forces that helped me to form my preference for eating chocolate, but I don't resent it, nor do I think it is less worthy of respect than most preferences I and others have. Secondly, adaptive preferences typically downgrade the inaccessible options, and this does not increase utility. Elster holds that this is irrational because one could choose instead to upgrade the available options, thereby increasing one's overall utility. But the states of affairs which are downgraded here are, by hypothesis, infeasible, and so one will not lose any utility by rating those states of affairs lower. Furthermore, this may make the available options more attractive and even more valuable, which means that one will actually get more satisfaction from what one can achieve after the adaptation process. It seems to me that anything which helps one to be happier with one's lot in life is worth having. Elster points out that this sort of preference change is essentially a by-product; the fox cannot *choose* to believe the grapes are sour. But that does not mean that the process is irrational – since one rationally should want to choose it if one could – rather it is at worst non-rational.

Wishful thinking involves mistakes in the conception of the feasible set itself. It occurs when one fails to consider the steps necessary to bring about the preferred state of affairs. One may then come to have a preference over some state of affairs which is impossible, or one may just fail sufficiently to realize what bringing about that state of affairs would entail. To come to recognize these preferences as mere pipe dreams one needs to go through a thought experiment to see if the fully imagined intermediate states of affairs involved in getting what one wants are possible and desirable.

Many people argue that it is wishful thinking to believe that one can take drugs without becoming addicted to them. If the only rational preference for taking drugs involves this belief, then one could argue that these preferences are irrational. If, on the other hand, one knows that drug use usually leads to addiction and one still prefers it, then the preference is not irrational on these grounds. I take it that there are drug users who fall under this category. Of course, there are many people who incorrectly estimate the likelihood or pain of addiction, and for the sake of these people a good society and their friends ought to educate them and lead them to perform the required thought experiments which would make clear to them what life as an addict might be like. But we cannot condemn as irrational the preferences of those who have made the thought experiments, because we can imagine circumstances under which rational people would choose addiction over abstinence.

Elster's objection to non-autonomous preferences in general is that one is less free when one is manipulated by a causal process. Lack of freedom does not mean that a preference is irrational. However, the claim forces us to ask whether liberalism demands that our preferences be autonomous. Elster's claims about the non-autonomy of preferences challenge the foundation of liberalism itself. Liberalism holds the individual to be the final arbiter of what she wants, and gives her the maximal liberty consistent with equal liberty for others to achieve her desires. If individuals' preferences are not autonomously formed, but rather formed by some causal process operating behind their backs, then by allowing the agents' preferences to be the ultimate guide for individuals the society is allowing these causal mechanisms to manipulate them. It is plausible to suggest that autonomy is what Mill wanted to respect when he claimed that we could not sell ourselves into slavery. One might say that whether the master is another human being or some other source of non-autonomy, we must not be allowed to become a slave to it.

According to Elster, autonomous preferences do not change when one's feasible set changes. The formal condition for autonomous preferences is:

If S_1 and S_2 are two feasible sets, with preference rankings R_1 and R_2, then for no x or y (in the global set) should it be the case that xP_1y and yP_2x.

In other words, one cannot have autonomous preferences which reverse themselves in two different feasible sets (Elster, 1985, p. 131). I want to argue that this condition is too strong as a condition on respectable preferences.

Suppose that David is a talented and kind-hearted professor. In world w David has a small family and is married to a woman who works part-time and takes primary care of their two children. In w David prefers working long hours at his office and spending many days away from home giving papers rather than working at home and rarely travelling. In world w* David is married to a successful athlete, who must be on the road often for competitions, and they have two children. In w* David prefers working at home and rarely travelling and having a wife who travels to competitions, rather than working long hours at his office and giving many papers at distant schools and having a wife who stays home. Suppose that from w to w* at least one item of the feasible sets has changed: in w David could have an exciting lifestyle, a fulfilled wife, and children who were well taken care of by a parent, in w* this is infeasible. Suppose also that David's preferences changed with the change in his feasible set, so that his preferences are non-autonomous by Elster's condition. Would we have to say that David is manipulated by his circumstances?

There is certainly a sense in which the answer is yes, but this is not a very disturbing sense of "manipulated". We are all in that sense manipulated by our circumstances: everyone would prefer something different if they had some different feasible alternatives. But our feasible alternatives provide the constraints within which we build our lives. David is not a victim; we might even imagine that he is happy in either world. The point is simply that he has re-evaluated his preferences in the light of what is feasible for him. Our feasible alternatives certainly constrain our freedom, but if preferences are suspect whenever this condition holds, then everyone's preferences are suspect. The conditions of one's life, including one's conception of the options one has, inevitably affect the formation of one's preferences. One might even argue that it would be irrational not to do what one can to alter one's preferences in the face of different feasible sets, because in the face of severe limitations preferences for great performances would set one up for bitter defeat. If avoiding such pain requires allowing or encouraging adaptive preferences to form, that too is rational.

The notion that there is a clear distinction between autonomous and non-autonomous preferences is, I think, a mistake. All preferences come about in a social and physical environment and have causal and other forces acting on them, or are traceable to some causal force. Many of our preferences come at mother's knee, and many others are trained into or out of us as we go to school and make friends and gradually become part of the larger society. Peer pressure is a strong force in the formation of preference, as are many other uncontrollable causal forces. Only a relatively small number of our preferences come as a result of our conscious control, such as learning to dislike meat when deciding to become a vegetarian. And even these can usually be traced to some non-autonomous preference, such as wanting to impress one's friends. Autonomy, in Elster's sense, cannot be a condition on respectable preferences.

The real problem with addiction is that it seems to restrict one's future choices and abilities in a way that just doesn't seem prudent. Thomas Nagel (1970) presents the *timelessness principle* for evaluating preferences as to their prudence. On his view we are rationally required to regard each moment of our lives as equally real in evaluating actions. We can rationally have some preferences for the present over the future, but only because we are uncertain about when we might die; rationally I should discount the future according to my best estimate of the probability that I shall be alive. If, when all future times are considered, discounting appropriately for the possibility of death, the overall utility effect of taking drugs is negative, then one rationally should not take drugs. The timelessness principle asserts a duty to one's future selves. It seems that, in order properly to evaluate the utility effects, one has to evaluate the counterfactual utility function representing the utility that future selves would have enjoyed had one not taken the drugs. In other words if one's future selves' utility given that one has taken drugs is less than their utility if one were not to take drugs, then one should not take drugs.

Evaluating the drug case one might argue that addiction leads to exactly this situation. The problem with taking drugs seems to be that they reduce people's possibilities for fulfilment in the future. But we have difficulty determining whether this violates timelessness with any degree of certainty, since there is nothing less law-abiding (in the sense of scientific law) than the course of human lives. This uncertainty has important implications for social and political theories. It is part of the justification of liberalism that each individual is in the best position to determine what course of action she will take to realize her plans. That is, liberalism assumes that we are in the best position to know our own future selves' desires. If *the present individual* recognizes that the future utility will be reduced, then she is irrational to take drugs, but whether the condition holds must finally be up to her to decide. Friends and fellow citizens may want to argue the point with her, but since we can imagine situations in which future utility would not be lessened by taking drugs, a liberal must hold that the individual is the final court of appeals on this decision.

6. Concluding Remarks

In the cases of anabolic steroids and peer pressure among young people to take drugs we saw that there is an important strategic consideration which makes laws necessary for people to be able to get what they really want. Namely, these are situations in which people's preferences interfere with what they would choose in the absence of others; the situation is one of mutual harm. Thus liberals can allow that such laws are legitimate.

When there are no such strategic considerations, however, laws prohibiting the use of drugs restrict people's rights to do what they may rationally prefer when they do not thereby harm others. We can imagine a situation in which one would believe that addiction to a drug was better than the alternatives. The example of the person who is trapped in the horrible social or economic situation is just such a case in which someone might believe this. It is also true that many people may wrongly believe that the life of an addict is better than his or her alternatives either because they misunderstand the miseries of addiction or because they incorrectly estimate the alternatives. For this reason kind and gentle liberal societies ought to provide good education for all, and counselling for those who wish to explore alternative lifestyles. And among friends we should examine and question desires to perform risky actions, such as taking drugs. But because some people can rationally evaluate the alternative of drug use as preferable, it should not be made illegal. It is not wrong to say that preferences can be rationally criticized, but the individual who has the preferences is the final judge of which criticisms are good ones, and what her preferences ought to be.

Thus a liberal society cannot legitimately or consistently outlaw the taking of drugs, other than anabolic steroids, on paternalist grounds. Perhaps the reader will respond that that is a *reductio* on liberalism.

Note

* I would like to thank Neal Becker, Ed Green, Jean Hampton, Tamara Horowitz, Paul Hurley, the Ethicists for Lunch group at the University of Pittsburgh, and the University of Kansas Philosophy Club for comments on earlier drafts of this essay.

References

Dworkin, R.: *Taking Rights Seriously* (Cambridge, MA: Harvard University Press, 1977).

Elster, J.: *Sour Grapes: Studies in the Subversion of Rationality* (Cambridge: Cambridge University Press, 1985).

Hume, D.: *A Treatise of Human Nature* (Oxford: Oxford University Press, 1978).

Mill, J. S.: *On Liberty* (Indianapolis: Hackett, 1978).

Nagel, T.: *The Possibility of Altruism* (Oxford: Oxford University Press, 1970).

Parfit, D.: *Reasons and Persons* (Oxford: Oxford University Press, 1984).

Robinson, J.: *Economic Philosophy* (Chicago: Aldine, 1963).

Sartorius, R.: *Paternalism* (Minneapolis: University of Minnesota Press, 1983).

30

Permissible Paternalism: Saving Smokers from Themselves

Robert E. Goodin

Paternalism is desperately out of fashion. Nowadays notions of "children's rights" severely limit what even parents may do to their own offspring, in their children's interests but against their will. What public officials may properly do to adult citizens, in their interests but against their will, is presumably even more tightly circumscribed. So the project I have set for myself – carving out a substantial sphere of morally permissible paternalism – might seem simply preposterous in present political and philosophical circumstances.

Here I shall say no more about the paternalism of parents toward their own children. My focus will instead be upon ways in which certain public policies designed to promote people's interests might be morally justifiable even if those people were themselves opposed to such policies.

Neither shall I say much more about notions of rights. But in focusing upon people's interests rather than their rights, I shall arguably be sticking closely to the sorts of concerns that motivate rights theorists. Of course, what it is to have a right is itself philosophically disputed; and on at least one account (the so-called "interest theory") to have a right is nothing more than to have a legally protected interest. But on the rival account (the so-called "choice theory") the whole point of rights is to have a legally protected choice. There, the point of having a right is that your choice in the matter will be respected, even if that choice actually runs contrary to your own best interests.

It is that understanding of rights which leads us to suppose that paternalism and rights are necessarily at odds, and there are strict limits in the extent to which we might reconcile the two positions. Still, there is some substantial scope for compromise between the two positions.

Those theorists who see rights as protecting people's choices rather than promoting their interests would be most at odds with paternalists who were proposing to impose upon people what is judged to be *objectively* good for them. That is to say, they would be most at odds if paternalists were proposing to impose upon people outcomes which are judged to be good for those people, whether or not there were any grounds for that conclusion in those people's own subjective judgments of their own good.

Rights theorists and paternalists would still be at odds, but less at odds, if paternalists refrained from talking about interests in so starkly objective a way. Then, just as rights command respect for people's choices, so too would paternalists be insisting that we respect choices that people themselves have or would have made. The two are not quite the same, to be sure, but they are much more nearly the same than the ordinary contrast between paternalists and rights theorists would seem to suggest.

That is precisely the sort of conciliatory gesture that I shall here be proposing. In paternalistically justifying some course of action on the grounds that it is in someone's interests, I shall always be searching for some warrant in that person's own value judgments for saying that it is in that person's interests.

"Some warrant" is a loose constraint, to be sure. Occasionally will we find genuine cases of what philosophers call "weakness of will": people being possessed of a powerful, conscious present desire to do something that they nonetheless just cannot bring themselves to do. Then public policy forcing them to realize their own desire, though arguably paternalistic, is transparently justifiable even in terms of people's own subjective values. More often, though, the subjective value to which we are appealing is one which is present only in an inchoate form, or will only arise later, or can be appreciated only in retrospect.

Paternalism is clearly paternalistic in imposing those more weakly-held subjective values upon people in preference to their more strongly held ones. But, equally clearly, it is less offensively paternalistic thanks to this crucial fact: at least it deals strictly in terms of values that are or will be subjectively present, at some point or another and to some extent or another, in the person concerned.

I. The Scope of Paternalism

When we are talking about public policies (and maybe even when we are talking of private, familial relations), paternalism surely can only be justified for the "big decisions" in people's lives. No one, except possibly parents and perhaps not even they, would propose to stop you from buying candy bars on a whim, under the influence of seductive advertising and at some marginal cost to your dental health.

So far as public policy is concerned, certainly, to be a fitting subject for public paternalism a decision must first of all involve high stakes. Life-and-death issues most conspicuously qualify. But so do those that substantially shape your subsequent life prospects. Decisions to drop out of school or to begin taking drugs involve high stakes of roughly that sort. If the decision is also substantially irreversible – returning to school is unlikely, the drug is addictive – then that further bolsters the case for paternalistic intervention.

The point in both cases is that people would not have a chance to benefit by learning from their mistakes. If the stakes are so high that losing the gamble once will kill you, then there is no opportunity for subsequent learning. Similarly, if the decision is irreversible, you might know better next time but be unable to benefit from your new wisdom.

II. Evaluating Preferences

The case for paternalism, as I have cast it, is that the public officials might better respect your own preferences than you would have done through your own actions. That is to say that public officials are engaged in evaluating your (surface) preferences, judging them according to some standard of your own (deeper) preferences.

Public officials should refrain from paternalistic interference, and allow you to act without state interference, only if they are convinced that you are acting on:

- *relevant* preferences;
- *settled* preferences;
- *preferred* preferences; and, perhaps,
- *your own* preferences.

In what follows, I shall consider each of those requirements in turn. My running example will be the problem of smoking and policies to control it. Nothing turns on the peculiarities of that example, though. There are many others like it in relevant respects.

It often helps, in arguments like this, to apply generalities to particular cases. So, in what follows, I shall further focus in on the case of one particular smoker, Rose Cipollone. Her situation is nowise unique – in all the respects that matter here, she might be considered the proto-typical smoker. All that makes her case special is that she (or more precisely her heir) was the first to win a court case against the tobacco companies whose products killed her.

In summarizing the evidence presented at that trial, the judge described the facts of the case as follows.

> Rose . . . Cipollone . . . began to smoke at age 16, . . . while she was still in high school. She testified that she began to smoke because she saw people smoking in the movies, in advertisements, and looked upon it as something "cool, glamorous and grown-up" to do. She began smoking Chesterfields . . . primarily because of advertising of "pretty girls and movie stars," and because Chesterfields were described . . . as "mild." . . .
>
> Mrs. Cipollone attempted to quit smoking while pregnant with her first child . . . , but even then she would sneak cigarettes. While she was in labor she smoked an entire pack of cigarettes, provided to her at her request by her doctor, and after the birth . . . she resumed smoking. She smoked a minimum of a pack a day and as much as two packs a day.
>
> In 1955, she switched . . . to L&M cigarettes . . . because . . . she believed that the filter would trap whatever was "bad" for her in cigarette smoking. She relied upon advertisements which supported that contention. She . . . switched to Virgina Slims . . . because the cigarettes were glamorous and long, and were associated with beautiful women – and the liberated woman. . . .
>
> Because she developed a smoker's cough and heard reports that smoking caused cancer, she tried to cut down her smoking. These attempts were unsuccessful. . . .
>
> Mrs. Cipollone switched to lower tar and nicotine cigarettes based upon advertising from which she concluded that those cigarettes were safe or safer . . . [and] upon the recommendation of her family physician. In 1981 her cancer was diagnosed, and even though her doctors advised her to stop she was unable to do so. She even told her doctors and her husband that she had quit when she had not, and she continued to smoke until June of 1982 when her lung was removed. Even thereafter she smoked occasionally – in hiding. She stopped smoking in 1983 when her cancer had metasized and she was diagnosed as fatally ill.

This sad history contains many of the features that I shall be arguing makes paternalism most permissible.

Relevant preferences

The case against paternalism consists in the simple proposition that, morally, we ought to respect people's own choices in matters that affect themselves and by-and-large only themselves. But there are many questions we first might legitimately ask about those preferences, without in any way questioning this fundamental principle of respecting people's autonomy.

One is simply whether the preferences in play are genuinely *relevant* to the decision at hand. Often they are not. Laymen often make purely factual mistakes in their means–ends reasoning. They think – or indeed, as in the case of Rose Cipollone, are led by false advertising to suppose – that an activity is safe when it is not. They think that an activity like smoking is glamorous, when the true facts of the matter are that smoking may well cause circulatory problems requiring the distinctly unglamorous amputation of an arm or leg.

When people make purely factual mistakes like that, we might legitimately override their surface preferences (the preference to smoke) in the name of their own deeper preferences (to stay alive and bodily intact). Public policies designed to prevent youngsters from taking up smoking when they want to, or to make it harder (more expensive or inconvenient) for existing smokers to continue smoking when they want to, may be parternalistic in the sense of running contrary to people's own manifest choices in the matter. But this overriding of their choices is grounded in their own deeper preferences, so such paternalism would be minimally offensive from a moral point of view.

Settled preferences

We might ask, further, whether the preferences being manifested are "settled" preferences or whether they are merely transitory phases people are going through. It may be morally permissible to let people commit euthanasia voluntarily, if we are sure they really want to die. But if we think that they may subsequently change their minds, then we have good grounds for supposing that we should stop them.

The same may well be true with smoking policy. While Rose Cipollone herself thought smoking was both glamorous and safe, youngsters beginning to smoke today typically know better. But many of them still say that they would prefer a shorter but more glamorous life, and that they are therefore more than happy to accept the risks that smoking entails. Say what they may at age sixteen, though, we cannot help supposing that they will think differently when pigeons eventually come home to roost. The risk-courting preferences of youth are a characteristic product of a peculiarly dare-devil phase that virtually all of them will, like their predecessors, certainly grow out of.

Insofar as people's preferences are not settled – insofar as they choose one option now, yet at some later time may wish that they had chosen another – we have another ground for permissible paternalism. Policy-makers dedicated to respecting people's own choices have, in effect, two of the person's own choices to choose between. How such conflicts should be settled is hard to say. We might weigh the strength or duration of the preferences, how well they fit with the person's other preferences, and so on.

Whatever else we do, though, we clearly ought not privilege one preference over another just because it got there first. Morally, it is permissible for policy-makers to ignore one of a person's present preferences (to smoke, for example) in deference to another that is virtually certain later to emerge (as was Rose Cipollone's wish to live, once she had cancer).

Preferred preferences

A third case for permissible paternalism turns on the observation that people have not only multiple and conflicting preferences but also preferences for preferences. Rose Cipollone wanted to smoke. But, judging from her frequent (albeit failed) attempts to quit, she also wanted *not to want* to smoke.

In this respect, it might be said, Rose Cipollone's history is representative of smokers more generally. The US Surgeon General reports that some 90 percent of regular smokers have tried and failed to quit. That recidivism rate has led the World Health Organization to rank nicotine as an addictive substance on a par with heroin itself.

That classification is richly confirmed by the stories that smokers themselves tell about their failed attempts to quit. Rose Cipollone tried to quit while pregnant, only to end up smoking an entire pack in the delivery room. She tried to quit once her cancer was diagnosed, and once again after her lung was taken out, even then only to end up sneaking an occasional smoke.

In cases like this – where people want to stop some activity, try to stop it but find that they cannot stop – public policy that helps them do so can hardly be said to be paternalistic in any morally offensive respect. It overrides people's preferences, to be sure. But the preferences which it overrides are ones which people themselves wish they did not have.

The preferences which it respects – the preferences to stop smoking (like preferences of reformed alcoholics to stay off drink, or of the obese to lose weight) – are, in contrast, preferences that the people concerned themselves prefer. They would themselves rank those preferences above their own occasional inclinations to backslide. In helping them to implement their own preferred preferences, we are only respecting people's own priorities.

Your own preferences

Finally, before automatically respecting people's choices, we ought to make sure that they are really their *own* choices. We respect people's choices because in that way we manifest respect for them as persons. But if the choices in question were literally someone else's – the results of a post-hypnotic suggestion, for example – then clearly there that logic would provide no reason for our respecting those preferences.

Some people say that the effects of advertising are rather like that. No doubt there is a certain informational content to advertising. But that is not all there is in it. When Rose Cipollone read the tar and nicotine content in advertisements, what she was getting was information. What she was getting when looking at the accompanying pictures of movie stars and glamorous, liberated women was something else altogether.

Using the power of subliminal suggestion, advertising implants preferences in people in a way that largely or wholly by-passes their judgment. Insofar as it does so, the resulting preferences are not authentically that person's own. And those implanted preferences are not entitled to the respect that is rightly reserved for a person's authentic preferences, in consequence.

Such thoughts might lead some to say that we should therefore ignore altogether advertising-induced preferences in framing our public policy. I demur. There is just too much force in the rejoinder that, "Wherever those preferences came from in the first instance, they are mine now." If we want our policies to respect people by (among other things) respecting their preferences, then we will have to respect all of those preferences with which people now associate themselves.

Even admitting the force of that rejoinder, though, there is much that still might be done to curb the preference-shaping activities of, for example, the tobacco industry. Even those who say "they're my preferences now" would presumably have preferred, ahead of time, to make up their own minds in the matter. So there we have a case, couched in terms of people's own (past) preferences, for severely restricting the advertising and promotion of products – especially ones which people will later regret having grown to like, but which they will later be unable to resist.

III. Conclusions

What, in practical policy terms, follows from all that? Well, in the case of smoking, which has served as my running example, we might ban the sale of tobacco altogether or turn it into a drug available only on prescription to registered users. Or, less dramatically, we might make cigarettes difficult and expensive to obtain – especially for youngsters, whose purchases are particularly price-sensitive. We might ban all promotional advertising of tobacco products, designed as it is to attract new users. We might prohibit smoking in all offices, restaurants, and other public places, thus making it harder for smokers to find a place to partake and providing a further inducement for them to quit.

All of those policies would be good for smokers themselves. They would enjoy a longer life expectancy and a higher quality of life if they stopped smoking. But that is to talk the language of interests rather than of rights and choices. In those latter terms, all those policies clearly go against smokers' manifest preferences, in one sense or another. Smokers want to keep smoking. They do not want to pay more or drive further to get their cigarettes. They want to be able to take comfort in advertisements constantly telling them how glamorous their smoking is.

In other more important senses, though, such policies can be justified even in terms of the preferences of smokers themselves. They do not want to die, as a quarter of them eventually will (and ten to fifteen years before their time) of smoking-related diseases; it is only false beliefs or wishful thinking that make smokers think that continued smoking is consistent with that desire not to avoid a premature death. At the moment they may think that the benefits of smoking outweigh the costs, but they will almost certainly revise that view once those costs are eventually sheeted home. The vast majority of smokers would like to stop smoking but, being addicted, find it very hard now to do so.

Like Rose Cipollone, certainly in her dying days and intermittently even from her early adulthood, most smokers themselves would say that they would have been better off never starting. Many even agree that they would welcome anything (like a workplace ban on smoking) that might now make them stop. Given the internally conflicting preferences here in play, smokers also harbor at one and the same time preferences pointing in the opposite direction; that is what might make helping them to stop seem unacceptably paternalistic. But in terms of other of their preferences – and ones that deserve clear precedence, at that – doing so is perfectly well warranted.

Smoking is unusual, perhaps, in presenting a case for permissible paternalism on all four of the fronts here canvassed. Most activities might quality under only one or two of the headings. However, that may well be enough. My point here is not that paternalism is always permissible but merely that it may always be.

In the discourse of liberal democracies, the charge of paternalism is typically taken to be a knock-down objection to any policy. If I am right, that knee-jerk response is wrong. When confronted with the charge of paternalism, it should always be open to us to say, "Sure, this proposal is paternalistic – but is the paternalism in view permissible or impermissible, good or bad?" More often than not, I think we will find, paternalism might prove perfectly defensible along the lines sketched here.

Further Reading

Goodin, Robert E. "The Ethics of Smoking." *Ethics*, 99 (April 1989), 575–624.

Goodin, Robert E. *No Smoking: The Ethical Issues* (Chicago and London: University of Chicago Press, 1989).

Free Speech

Should we be morally and legally permitted to say whatever we want, whenever we want? Or are there moral – and should there be legal – limits on the views that we can publicly express? As in the previous section, we begin with a selection from John Stuart Mill's *On Liberty*. Mill argues that we are never justified in silencing the expression of an opinion, even if the view is patently false. We can, however, control when and how someone expresses an opinion. If the opinion is expressed at a time or in a way that is likely to harm another, for instance, by prompting third parties to attack that person violently, then we can legitimately constrain the speech. In all other circumstances, restricting speech is inappropriate. In fact, Mill argues, we should actively encourage and promote the expression of diverse views.

Is Mill correct? Is it legitimate to restrict speech only when that speech demonstrably harms others? Many people speak as if they agree with Mill. But we know better. Although few people openly denounce free speech, many people loathe free and open discussion. How can this be? There are two answers – one psychological and one logical. The psychological explanation is simple: never underestimate the power of self-deception. Some individuals sincerely believe they are staunch advocates of individual liberty while seeking every available opportunity to squelch speech they dislike. Somehow they are blind to what they do – and why they do it.

The logical explanation is more interesting and more complex. Many people agree that we should suppress speech only when it harms others. However, they have radically different views about when speech in fact harms others. Therefore they disagree about when speech can be limited or prohibited. Mill thinks speech can rarely harm others, and therefore, we can only rarely restrict it. Other people think speech frequently harms others, and therefore, is often fair game for the legal system. This disagreement about the criteria for harm was central to the discussion about DRUGS. Those authors had widely divergent views about what constitutes harm to oneself. In this section the authors are sharply divided about what harms others.

This is an interesting maneuver in ethical debate, a maneuver worth stressing. We tend to think of ethical disagreements as disagreements over principles. Often, though, moral disagreements are not so much disagreements over fundamental principles, but disagreements about their application to a particular practical problem. This exhibits a feature I identified in THEORIZING ABOUT ETHICS. We should not assume all deontologists or all consequentialists will reach the same moral conclusions about a particular moral problem. Ethical theories do not determine exactly how an advocate will evaluate any particular moral issue. Instead, they accent what that person takes to be morally relevant, morally significant.

Disagreements over the meaning and application of the harm principle infuse the debate over free speech. Virtually no one contends we should cavalierly restrict speech. Instead, everyone carefully explains how some speech they wish to restrict harms others. For instance, the authors of the recent Telecommunications Bill in the United States balk at the suggestion that their Bill blithely restricts free speech on the Internet. According to their version of events, the Bill restricts only demonstrably harmful speech.

This best describes the disputes between the authors in this section. All of them would claim to be champions of Millean liberalism. Nonetheless, since they disagree dramatically about whether any particular speech really does harm others, they disagree about whether that speech can be legally forbidden. Should the state restrict the showing of sexually explicit movies? A sizeable minority of people say "Yes." Those who support legal restrictions on pornography usually fall into two camps. The most politically powerful opponents of "a right to pornography" are (typically religious) folk who are offended by public depictions of sex. The second group comprises feminists who are not especially concerned about the idea of public displays of sex. However, they are concerned about the ways that pornography apparently harms women. Most so-called pornography, these feminists say, is not primarily a depiction of sex, but rather a glorification of the rape of and violence toward women. Thus, pornography harms women not by portraying explicit sex, but by encouraging the abuse of and violence toward women.

We can thus see that both fundamentalists and feminists see themselves as embracing the Millean framework. We should restrict speech only if it harms others. Since pornography harms others, then we can restrict it. On the other hand, they radically disagree about whom it harms and how it harms them.

Dworkin thinks both fundamentalists and feminists are mistaken. If pornography demonstrably caused harm, he claims, then we would have a compelling reason to prohibit or at least constrain it. However, the claim that it causes harm is merely idle "academic speculation." Notice, though, that it is not merely or even primarily that these authors disagree about what constitutes harm. They also disagree about how strong the evidence of harm must be before the state can legitimately intervene. Dworkin apparently thinks the evidence of harm must be compelling and overwhelming, while feminists and fundamentalists disagree either about what counts as harm, or over the evidence required to establish harm, or over how much harm must be wrought before the state can legitimately intervene.

Thus, *pace* Dworkin, Langton claims there is abundant evidence that pornography harms women. The problem is that Dworkin is looking for the wrong kind of evidence, and he is looking for it in the wrong place. Pornography, Langton argues, harms women by silencing them. This harm is not simply the causal result of pornography. Rather, pornography is, in this culture, an authoritative statement – a speech act – which silences (and thus disempowers) women. Men and women learn that a woman's saying "No" to sex is not authoritative. Many men don't hear it, believe it, or heed it. That is why rape is so common. Langton's suggestion here resembles that made earlier by Foa (SEXUALITY), and will be repeated later by Pineau (SEXUAL AND RACIAL DISCRIMINATION).

Langton's argument provides a theoretical framework that illuminates many arguments in this volume, especially arguments in the following section. Since men are generally in power, we assume their statements are authoritative, i.e., others heed them. Conversely, we rarely see the statements of women, who generally have less power, as authoritative. Since we fail to understand how males have controlled speech in this society, then we fail to understand the ways in which pornography is a form of speech that silences women.

Langton's argument could also be applied to the discussion of hate speech. Derogatory comments about women and blacks are, at least in this culture, powerful ways in which white males silence blacks and women. Over the past ten years several universities have instituted "speech codes" forbidding inflammatory speech aimed at members of racial, sexual, national, or religious groups. Arthur says that although he is sympathetic to the aims of speech codes, there is no evidence that hate speech harms anyone. Hence such codes cannot be justified. An action is only harmful if it interferes with someone's future interests. Hate speech, as uncomfortable as it might be, does not harm anyone's future interests.

Friedman shares Arthur's misgivings about speech codes. However, she thinks that the virulent objections to speech codes heard in the public press are often not so much aimed at protecting speech, as they are thinly veiled attacks on feminists and other leftists. For example, she claims that most outspoken critics of speech codes would not lift a finger to defend other forms of free speech. So why do they attack speech codes? Because, she says, their targets are not the codes, but the feminists who advocate them. Thus, although she does not favor the codes, she suggests that, in abandoning them, we should not forget that hate speech, even if protected by law, is nonetheless an abomination, symbolic of the ways in which women are often demeaned in this society.

Further Reading

Altmann, A. 1993: 'Liberalism and Campus Hate Speech.' *Ethics*, 103.

Arthur, J. and Shapiro, A. (eds) 1995: *Campus Wars: Multi-culturalism and the Politics of Difference*. Boulder, CO: Westview Press.

Berger, F. (ed.) 1980: *Freedom of Expression*. Belmont, CA: Wadsworth.

Copp, D. and Wendell, S. (eds) 1983: *Pornography and Censorship*. Bufflao, NY: Prometheus Books.

Donnerstein, E., Linz, D., and Penrod, S. (eds) 1987: *The Question of Pornography: Research Findings and Policy Implications*. New York: Free Press.

Faludi, S. 1991: *Backlash: The Undeclared War against American Women*. New York: Crown.

MacKinnon, C. 1987: *Feminism Unmodified*. Cambridge, MA: Harvard University Press.

31

Freedom of Thought and Discussion[1]

John Stuart Mill

. . . If all mankind minus one, were of one opinion, and only one person were of the contrary opinion, mankind would be no more justified in silencing that one person, than he, if he had the power, would be justified in silencing mankind. Were an opinion a personal possession of no value except to the owner; if to be obstructed in the enjoyment of it were simply a private injury, it would make some difference whether the injury was inflicted only on a few persons or on many. But the peculiar evil of silencing the expression of an opinion is that it is robbing the human race. . . . [It robs] those who dissent from the opinion, still more than those who hold it. (1) If the opinion is right, they are deprived of the opportunity of exchanging error for truth: (2) if wrong, they lose, what is almost as great a benefit, the clearer perception and livelier impression of truth, produced by its collision with error. . . .

It is necessary to consider separately these two . . . [options], each of which has a distinct branch of the argument corresponding to it. We can never be sure that the opinion we are endeavouring to stifle is a false opinion; and if we were sure, stifling it would be an evil still.

First: the opinion which it is attempted to suppress by authority may possibly be true. Those who desire to suppress it, of course deny its truth; but they are not infallible. They have no authority to decide the question for all mankind, and exclude every other person from the means of judging. To refuse a hearing to an opinion, because they are sure that it is false, is to assume that their certainty is the same thing as absolute certainty. All silencing of discussion is an assumption of infallibility. Its condemnation may be allowed to rest on this common argument, not the worse for being common.

Unfortunately for the good sense of mankind, the fact of their fallibility is far from carrying the weight in their practical judgment, which is always allowed to it in theory. . . . [W]hile every one well knows himself to be fallible, few think it necessary to take any precautions against their own fallibility. [Neither do they] admit the supposition that any opinion of which they feel very certain, may be one of the examples of the error to which they acknowledge themselves to be liable. . . .

[How can we take precautions against our own fallibility?] [T]he source of everything respectable in man, either as an intellectual or as a moral being, . . . [is] that his errors are corrigible. He is capable of rectifying his mistakes by discussion and experience. [However, we cannot correct ourselves] by experience alone. There must be discussion, to show how experience is to be interpreted. Wrong opinions and practices gradually yield to fact and argument: but facts and arguments, to produce any effect on the mind, must be brought before it. Very few facts are able to tell their own story, without comments to bring out their meaning. The whole strength and value, then, of human judgment, depends [on its being able to be] set right when it is wrong. . . . [R]eliance can be placed on it only when the means of setting it right are kept constantly at hand.

In the case of any person whose judgment is really deserving of confidence, how has it become so? Because he has kept his mind open to criticism of his opinions and conduct. Because it has been his practice to listen to all that could be said against him; to profit by as much of it as was just, and expound to himself, and upon occasion to others, the fallacy of what was fallacious. Because he has felt that the only way in which a human being can make some approach to knowing the whole of a subject is by hearing what can be said about it by persons of every variety of opinion, and studying [them all]. No wise man ever acquired his wisdom in any mode but this; nor is it in the nature of human intellect to become wise in any other manner. . . .

. . . [Thus] the beliefs which we have most warrant for, have no safeguard to rest on, but a standing invitation to the whole world to prove them unfounded. If the challenge is not accepted, or is accepted and the attempt fails, we are far enough from certainty still; but we have done the best that the existing state of human reason admits of; we have neglected nothing that could give the truth a chance of reaching us. . . . This is the amount of certainty attainable by a fallible being, and this the sole way of attaining it.

Strange it is, that men should admit the validity of the arguments for free discussion, but object to their being "pushed to an extreme"; not seeing that unless the reasons are good for an extreme case, they are not good for any case. Strange that they should imagine that they are not assuming infallibility when they acknowledge that there should be free discussion on all subjects which can possibly be doubtful, but think that some particular principle or doctrine should be forbidden to be questioned because it is so certain, that is, because they are certain that it is certain. To call any proposition certain, while there is any one who would deny its certainty if permitted, but who is not permitted, is to assume that we ourselves, and those who agree with us, are the judges of certainty, and judges without hearing the other side. . . .

Let us now pass to the second division of the argument. . . . [L]et us assume [the received options] to be true. [Let us] examine into the worth of the manner in which they are likely to be held, when their truth is not freely and openly canvassed. However unwillingly a person who has a strong opinion may admit the possibility that his opinion may be false, he ought to be moved by the consideration that however true it may be, if it is not fully, frequently, and fearlessly discussed, it will be held as a dead dogma, not a living truth. . . .

. . . He who knows only his own side of the case, knows little of that. His reasons may be good, and no one may have been able to refute them. But if he is equally unable to refute the reasons on the opposite side; if he does not so much as know what they are, he has no ground for preferring either opinion. The rational position for him would be suspension of judgment, and unless he contents himself with that, he is either led by authority, or adopts, like the generality of the world, the side to which he feels most inclination.

Nor is it enough that he should hear the arguments of adversaries from his own teachers, presented as they state them, and accompanied by what they offer as refutations. This is not the way to do justice to the arguments, or bring them into real contact with his own mind. He must be able to hear them from persons who actually believe them; who defend them in earnest, and do their very utmost for them. He must know them in their most plausible and persuasive form; he must feel the whole force of the difficulty ... else he will never really possess himself of the portion of truth which meets and removes that difficulty.

Ninety-nine in a hundred of what are called educated men are in this condition, even of those who can argue fluently for their opinions. Their conclusion may be true, but it might be false for anything they know: they have never thrown themselves into the mental position of those who think differently from them, and considered what such persons may have to say; and consequently they do not, in any proper sense of the word, know the doctrine which they themselves profess.... All that part of the truth which turns the scale, and decides the judgment of a completely informed mind, they are strangers to; nor is it ever really known, but to those who have attended equally and impartially to both sides, and endeavoured to see the reasons of both in the strongest light. So essential is this discipline to a real understanding of moral and human subjects, that if opponents of all important truths do not exist, it is indispensable to imagine them and supply them with the strongest arguments which the most skilful devil's advocate can conjure up....

[Consider] the manner in which the majority of believers hold the doctrines of Christianity. By Christianity I here mean what is accounted such by all churches and sects – the maxims and precepts contained in the New Testament. These are considered sacred, and accepted as laws, by all professing Christians. Yet it is scarcely too much to say that not one Christian in a thousand guides or tests his individual conduct by reference to those laws.

The standard to which he does refer it, is the custom of his nation, his class, or his religious profession. He has thus, on the one hand, a collection of ethical maxims, which he believes to have been vouchsafed to him by infallible wisdom as rules for his government; and on the other, a set of every-day judgments and practices, which go a certain length with some of those maxims, not so great a length with others, stand in direct opposition to some, and are, on the whole, a compromise between the Christian creed and the interests and suggestions of worldly life. To the first of these standards he gives his homage; to the other his real allegiance. All Christians believe that the blessed are the poor and humble, and those who are ill-used by the world; that it is easier for a camel to pass through the eye of a needle than for a rich man to enter the kingdom of heaven; that they should judge not, lest they be judged; that they should swear not at all; that they should love their neighbour as themselves; that if one take their cloak, they should give him their coat also; that they should take no thought for the morrow; that if they would be perfect, they should sell all that they have and give it to the poor.

[Christians] are not insincere when they say that they believe these things. They do believe them, as people believe what they have always heard lauded and never discussed. But in the sense of that living belief which regulates conduct, they believe these doctrines just up to the point to which it is usual to act upon them. The doctrines in their integrity are serviceable to pelt adversaries with; and it is understood that they are to be put forward (when possible) as the reasons for whatever people do that they think laudable. But any one who reminded them that the maxims require an infinity of things which they never even think of doing would gain nothing but to be classed among those very unpopular characters who affect to be better than other people. The doctrines have no hold on ordinary believers – are not a power in their minds. They have an habitual respect for the sound of them, but no feeling which spreads from the words to the things signified, and forces the mind to take them in, and make them conform to the formula. Whenever conduct is concerned, they look round for Mr A and B to direct them how far to go in obeying Christ.

Now we may be well assured that the case was not thus, but far otherwise, with the early

Christians. Had it been thus, Christianity never would have expanded from an obscure sect of the despised Hebrews into the religion of the Roman Empire. When their enemies said, "See how these Christians love one another" (a remark not likely to be made by anybody now), they assuredly had a much livelier feeling of the meaning of their creed than they have ever had since. And to this cause, probably, it is chiefly owing that Christianity now makes so little progress in extending its domain, and after eighteen centuries, is still nearly confined to Europeans and the descendants of Europeans. . . . The sayings of Christ coexist passively in their minds, producing hardly any effect beyond what is caused by mere listening to words so amiable and bland.

There are many reasons, doubtless, why doctrines which are the badge of a sect retain more of their vitality than those common to all recognized sects, and why more pains are taken by teachers to keep their meaning alive; but one reason certainly is, that the peculiar doctrines are more questioned, and have to be oftener defended against open gainsayers. Both teachers and learners go to sleep at their post, as soon as there is no enemy in the field. . . .

Before quitting the subject of freedom of opinion, it is fit to take notice of those who say that the free expression of all opinions should be permitted, on condition that the manner be temperate, and do not pass the bounds of fair discussion. Much might be said on the impossibility of fixing where these supposed bounds are to be placed. [I]f the test be offence to those whose opinion is attacked, I think experience testifies that this offence is given whenever the attack is telling and powerful, and that every opponent who pushes them hard, and whom they find it difficult to answer, appears to them, if he shows any strong feeling on the subject, an intemperate opponent. [T]his, though an important consideration in a practical point of view, merges in a more fundamental objection. Undoubtedly the manner of asserting an opinion, even though it be a true one, may be very objectionable, and may justly incur severe censure. But the principal offences of the kind are such as it is mostly impossible, unless by accidental self-betrayal, to bring home to conviction. The gravest of them is, to argue sophistically, to suppress facts or arguments, to misstate the elements of the case, or misrepresent the opposite opinion. [I]t is rarely possible on adequate grounds conscientiously to stamp [this kind of] misrepresentation as morally culpable; and still less could law presume to interfere with this kind of controversial misconduct.

With regard to what is commonly meant by intemperate discussion, namely, invective, sarcasm, personality, and the like, the denunciation of these weapons would deserve more sympathy if it were ever proposed to interdict them equally to both sides; but it is only desired to restrain the employment of them against the prevailing opinion: against the unprevailing they may not only be used without general disapproval, but will be likely to obtain for him who uses them the praise of honest zeal and righteous indignation. Yet whatever mischief arises from their use, is greatest when they are employed against the comparatively defenceless; and whatever unfair advantage can be derived by any opinion from this mode of asserting it, accrues almost exclusively to received opinions. . . .

[Hence, since we should not restrict speech if the opinion to be repressed is false or if it is true, then we should not repress speech.]

Note

1 Abridged and edited from chapter 2 of *On Liberty*.

32

Do We Have a Right to Pornography?

Ronald Dworkin

Goals

The Williams strategy

It is an old problem for liberal theory how far people should have the right to do the wrong thing. Liberals insist that people have the legal right to say what they wish on matters of political or social controversy. . . . The majority of people in both countries [the United States and the United Kingdom] would prefer (or so it seems) substantial censorship, if not outright prohibition, of "sexually explicit" books, magazines, photographs, and films, and this majority includes a considerable number of those who are themselves consumers of whatever pornography is on offer. (It is part of the complex psychology of sex that many of those with a fixed taste for the obscene would strongly prefer that their children, for example, not follow them in that taste.) If we assume that the majority is correct, and that people who publish and consume pornography do the wrong thing, or at least display the wrong sort of character, should they nevertheless have the legal right to do so?

Some lawyers and political philosophers consider the problem of pornography to be only . . . the problem of freedom to speak unpopular or wicked thoughts. But we should be suspicious of that claim, because the strongest arguments in favor of allowing *Mein Kampf* to be published hardly seem to apply in favor of the novel *Whips Incorporated* or the film *Sex Kittens*. No one, I think, is denied an equal voice in the political process, however broadly conceived, when he is forbidden to circulate photographs of genitals to the public at large, or denied his right to listen to argument when he is forbidden to consider these photographs at his leisure. If we believe it wrong to censor these forms of pornography, then we should try to find the justification for that opinion elsewhere than in the literature celebrating freedom of speech and press. . . .

Rights

Consider the following suggestion. People have the right not to suffer disadvantage in the distribution of social goods and opportunities, including disadvantage in the liberties permitted to them by the criminal law, just on the ground that their officials or fellow-citizens think that their opinions about the right way for them to lead their own lives are ignoble or wrong. I shall call this (putative) right the right to moral independence, and in this part I shall consider what force this right would have on the law of pornography if it were recognized. In the next part I shall consider what grounds we might have to recognize it.

The right to moral independence is a very abstract right (or, if you prefer, the statement of the right I gave is a very abstract statement of the right) because this statement takes no account of the impact of competing rights. It does not attempt to decide whether the right can always be jointly satisfied for everyone, or how conflicts with other rights, if they arise, are to be settled. These further questions, along with other related questions, are left for more concrete statements of the right. Or (what comes to the same thing) for statements of the more concrete rights that people have in virtue of the abstract right. Nevertheless, the questions I wish to put may usefully be asked even about the abstract statement or the abstract right.

Someone who appeals to the right of moral independence in order to justify a legal regime permissive of obscenity does not suppose that the community will be better off in the long run (according to some description of what makes a community better off, like, for example, the description offered in the Williams strategy) if people are free to look at obscene pictures in private. He does not deny this. His argument is in the conditional mood: even if conditions will not then be so suitable for human flourishing as they might be, for example, nevertheless the right must be respected. But what force does the right then have? When does the government violate that right?

It violates the right, we may say, at least in this case: when the only apparent or plausible justification for a scheme of regulation of pornography includes the hypothesis that the attitudes about sex displayed or nurtured in pornography are demeaning or bestial or otherwise unsuitable to human beings of the best sort, even though this hypothesis may be true. It also violates that right when that justification includes the proposition that most people in the society accept that hypothesis and are therefore pained or disgusted when other members of their own community, for whose lives they understandably feel special responsibility, do read dirty books or look at dirty pictures. The right is therefore a powerful constraint on the regulation of pornography, or at least so it seems, because it prohibits giving weight to exactly the arguments most people think are the best arguments for even a mild and enlightened policy of restriction of obscenity. What room is left, by the apparently powerful right, for the government to do anything at all about pornography?

Suppose it is discovered that the private consumption of pornography does significantly increase the danger of crimes of violence, either generally, or specifically crimes of sexual violence. Or suppose that private consumption has some special and deleterious effect on the general economy, by causing great absenteeism from work, for example, as drink or breakfast television is sometimes said to do. Then government would have, in these facts, a justification for the restraint and perhaps even for the prohibition of pornography that does not include the offending hypothesis either directly, by the assumption that the hypothesis is true, or indirectly, in the proposition that many people think it true.

But this is, in any case, only academic speculation, because there is no reason to suppose a sufficiently direct connection between crime and either *Sex Kittens* or *Hamlet* to provide a ground for banning either one as private entertainment. But what about public display [of sex]? Can we find a plausible justification for restricting the display of pornography that does not violate the right of moral independence? We can, obviously, construct a certain argument in that direction, as follows. "Many people do not like to encounter genital displays on the way to the grocer. This taste is not, nor does it necessarily reflect, any adverse view of the character of those who do not mind such encounters. Someone who would not like to find pornography in his ordinary paths may not even object to finding it elsewhere. . . . Or he . . . may find or believe, for example, that his own delight in other peoples' bodies is lessened or made less sharp and special if nakedness becomes either too familiar to him or less peculiar to those occasions in which it provides him special pleasure, which may be in museums or his own bedroom or both. Or that sex will come to be different and less valuable for him if he is too often or too forcefully reminded that it has different, more commercial or more sadistic, meaning for others. Or that his goal that his children develop certain similar tastes and opinions will be thwarted by the display or advertising that he opposes. None of these different opinions and complaints *must* be the product of some conviction that those with other opinions and tastes are people of bad character, any more than those who hope that state-supported theater will produce the classics exclusively must think that those who prefer experimental theater are less worthy people.

This picture of the motives people might have for not wanting to encounter pornography on the streets is a conceivable picture. But I suspect . . . that it is far too crude and one-dimensional as a picture of what these motives actually are. The discomfort many people find in encountering blatant nudity on the hoardings is rarely so independent of their moral convictions as those various descriptions suggest. It is at least part of the offense, for many people, that they detest themselves for taking the interest in the proceedings that they do. It is a major part of the offense, for others, that they are so forcefully reminded of what their neighbors are like and, more particularly, of what their neighbors are getting away with. People object to the display of naked men and women in erotic poses, that is, even when these displays occur (as for commercial reasons they inevitably do) in those parts of cities that would be in no sense beautiful or enlightening even without the pornography. Even if we took the descriptions of peoples' motives in the argument I set out at face value, moreover, we should be forced to recognize the substantial influence of moral convictions just in those motives, for someone's sense of what he wants his own attitudes toward sex to be, and certainly his sense of what attitudes he hopes to encourage in his children, are not only influenced by, but constitute, his moral opinions in the broad sense.

We therefore encounter, in peoples' motives for objecting to the advertising or display of pornography, at least a mix and interaction of attitudes, beliefs, and tastes that rule out any confident assertion that regulation justified by appeal to these motives would not violate the right to moral independence. We do not know whether, if we could disentangle the different strands of taste, ambition, and belief, so as to winnow out those that express moral condemnation or would not exist but for it, the remaining strands would justify any particular scheme of regulation of display. This is not just a failure of information that would be expensive to obtain. The problem is more conceptual than that: the vocabulary we use to identify and individuate motives – our own as well as those of others – cannot provide the discrimination we need.

A society anxious to defend the abstract right to moral independence in the face of this complexity has two options at least. It might decide that if popular attitudes toward a minority or a minority practice are mixed in this way, so that the impact of adverse moral convictions can be neither excluded nor measured, then these attitudes should all be deemed to be corrupted by such convictions, and no regulation is permissible. Or it might decide that the case of mixed attitudes is a special kind of case in the administration of the abstract right, so that more concrete statements of what people are entitled to have under the right must take the fact of mixed attitudes into account. It might do this, for example, by stipulating, at the more concrete level, that no one should suffer *serious* damage through legal restraint when this can only be justified by the fact that what he proposes to do will frustrate or defeat preferences of others that we have reason to believe are mixed with or are consequences of the conviction that people who act in that way are people of bad character. This second option, which defines a concrete right tailored to the problem of mixed preferences, is not a relaxation or compromise of the abstract right, but rather a (no doubt controversial) application of it to that special situation. . . .

If society takes the second option just described in the case of pornography (as I think it should, for reasons I describe later), then its officials must undertake to decide what damage to those who wish to publish or read pornography is serious and what is trivial. Once again reasonable and honest officials will disagree about this, but we are trying to discover, not an algorithm for a law of obscenity, but rather whether a plausible concrete conception of a plausible abstract right will yield a sensible scheme of regulation. We should therefore consider the character of the damage that would be inflicted on consumers of pornography by, say, a scheme of zoning that requires that pornographic materials be sold and films shown only in particular areas, a scheme of advertising that prohibits in public places advertisements that would widely be regarded as indecent, and a scheme of labeling so that those entering cinemas or shops whose contents they might find indecent would be warned. There are three main heads of damage that such a regime might inflict on consumers: inconvenience, expense, and embarrassment. Whether the inconvenience is serious will depend on the details of, for example, the zoning. But it should not be considered serious if shoppers for pornography need travel on average only as far as, say, shoppers for stereo equipment or diamonds or secondhand books need travel to find the centers of such trade. How far this scheme of restriction would increase the price of pornography is harder to predict. Perhaps the constraint on advertising would decrease the volume of sales and therefore increase unit costs. But it seems unlikely that this effect would be very great, particularly if the legal ban runs to the character not to the extent of the advertising, and permits, as it should, not only stark "tombstone" notices, but the full range of the depressingly effective techniques through which manufacturers sell soap and video cassette recorders. . . .

I conclude that the right to moral independence, if it is a genuine right, requires a permissive legal attitude toward the consumption of pornography in private, but that a certain concrete conception of that right nevertheless permits a scheme of restriction. . . . It remains to consider whether that right and that conception can themselves be justified in political theory. . . .

Equality

A trump over utility

Rights, I have argued elsewhere, are best understood as trumps over some background justification for political decisions that states a goal for the community as a whole. If someone has a right to moral independence, this means that it is for some reason wrong for officials to act in violation of that right, even if they (correctly) believe that the community as a whole would be better off if they did. . . .

We need rights, as a distinct element in political theory, only when some decision that injures some people nevertheless finds *prima facie* support in the claim that it will make the community as a whole better off on some plausible account of where the community's general welfare lies. But the most natural source of any objection we might have to such a decision is that, in its concern with the welfare or prosperity or flourishing of people on the whole, or in the fulfillment of some interest widespread within the community, the decision pays insufficient attention to its impact on the minority; and some appeal to equality seems a natural expression of an objection from that source. We want to say that the decision is wrong, in spite of its apparent merit, because it does not take the damage it causes to some into account in the right way and therefore does not treat these people as equals entitled to the same concern as others.

33

Pornography, Speech Acts, and Silence

Rae Langton

Pornography is speech. So the courts declared in judging it protected by the First Amendment. Pornography is a kind of act. So Catherine MacKinnon declared in arguing for feminist laws against it. Put these together and we have: pornography is a kind of *speech act*.

If pornography is speech, what does it say? If pornography is a kind of act, what does it do? Judge Frank Easterbrook, accepting the premises of anti-pornography legislation, gave an answer. Pornography is speech that depicts subordination. Pornography depicts women "dehumanized as sexual objects, things or commodities; enjoying pain or humiliation or rape; being tied up, cut up, mutilated, bruised, or physically hurt; in postures of sexual submission or servility or display; reduced to body parts, penetrated by objects or animals, or presented in scenarios of degradation, injury, torture; shown as filthy or inferior; bleeding, bruised or hurt in a context which makes these conditions sexual" (MacKinnon, 1987, p. 176). Pornography is a kind of act that has certain effects: depictions of subordination, said Easterbrook, "tend to perpetuate subordination. The subordinate status of women in turn leads to affront and lower pay at work, insult and injury at home, battery and rape on the streets." Easterbrook's conclusion was that pornography should be protected, since this effect "simply demonstrates the power of pornography as speech".[1] Pornography, on this view, depicts subordination, and causes it. A closer look at the feminist ordinance shows us that MacKinnon is saying something more. Before describing what pornography depicts, the ordinance begins: "We define pornography as the graphic sexually explicit subordination of women in pictures or words . . .". Besides depicting and causing subordination, pornography *is*, in and of itself, a form of subordination.

This aspect of the feminist legislation irritated judges and philosophers. When the drafters of the ordinance said that pornography actually *is* subordination, they were tricksters, guilty of "a certain sleight of hand", said Judge Barker.[2] They were guilty of conceptual confusion, and their claim was "philosophically indefensible", said William Parent (1990). It is all very well to talk about what pornography depicts; and it is all very well to talk about the effects it has on the lives of women. Those ideas are not, at least, incoherent. But MacKinnon wants to say something more: she wants to attend, not simply to the *content* of pornographic speech, nor simply to its *effects*, but to the *actions* constituted by it.

What she says may strike a chord of recognition amongst those who recall a philosopher who said that "to say something is to *do* something". In *How to Do Things with Words*, J. L. Austin complained of a "constant tendency in philosophy" to overlook something important: a tendency to consider the content of speech, and its effects on hearers, but to overlook the action constituted by it. Words, he said, are used to perform all kinds of *actions* (warning, promising, marrying . . .) which philosophers have blithely ignored.

To say something is to do quite a few different things. Here is an imaginary example (adapted from Austin, 1962, p. 101). Two men stand beside a woman. The first turns to the second, and says "Shoot her". The second man looks shocked, then raises a gun and shoots the woman. You witness the scene, and you describe it later (perhaps to the police): "The first man said to the second, 'Shoot her' meaning by 'shoot' to shoot with a gun, and referring by 'her' to the woman nearby." That report describes one aspect of what was done with those words: it captures what Austin called the *locutionary* act. To perform a locutionary act is to utter a sentence that has a particular meaning, or content. However, there is more to what you witnessed, so you describe the scene again: "By saying 'Shoot her', the first man *shocked* the second; by saying 'Shoot her', the first man *persuaded* the second to shoot the woman." That report describes what was done *by* saying those words, the *effects* of what was said: it captures what Austin called the *perlocutionary* act. But if you stop there, you will still have left something out. You will have left out what the first man did *in* saying what he said. In saying "Shoot her", was he making a *suggestion*? giving a word of *advice*? *ordering* the second man to shoot? You describe the scene yet again: "In saying 'Shoot her', the first man *ordered* the second to shoot." That report describes what Austin called the *illocutionary* act, the action performed in saying those words.

The actions listed earlier – warning, promising, marrying – are illocutionary acts. Nearly every time we say something, we do things with our words in all three ways that Austin described: we say something that has a certain content (the locution), has a certain effect (the perlocution), and is a certain act (the illocution). Austin's complaint was that the illocutionary aspect of speech is often ignored: that there is "a tendency in philosophy to elide [illocutions] in favour of the other two" (p. 103).

Now pornography is not always done with words. Yet Easterbrook's description fits the tendency of which Austin complained. Pornography depicts subordination, and causes it. That is to describe its locutionary and perlocutionary aspects. When MacKinnon says that pornography *is* an act of subordination, she supplies what is missing in Easterbrook's description: she describes its *illocutionary* force. Like Austin, MacKinnon wants to undermine the division between word and action. "Which is saying 'kill' to a trained guard dog, a word or an act?" she asks, in a passage that echoes Austin's example (MacKinnon, 1987, p. 156; cf. 1993, pp. 12, 21). MacKinnon has something in common with Austin, as she acknowledges (1993, p. 121), and in this paper I draw on Austin to illuminate and defend her feminist work.

I focus on two claims. First is the claim we just saw, that pornography *subordinates* women. Second is a claim that pornography *silences* women. This idea has an important role to play in a feminist reply to the traditional "free speech" defence of pornography. "[The] free speech of men silences the free speech of women. It is the same social goal, just other *people*," says MacKinnon (1987, p. 156), arguing that if the law protects free speech, it should protect the speech of women. This second claim, that pornography silences women, has also been regarded as problematic: its detractors describe it as "dangerous confusion", while even sympathizers have reservations, conceding that the silence in question is "figurative", "metaphorical" (Dworkin, 1991, p. 103; Michelman, 1989, p. 294). But I want to show that the silence is literal, and that the second feminist claim is as defensible as the first.

If pornography subordinates women, it determines women's inferior civil status. Seen this way, anti-pornography legislation poses a conflict between liberty and equality: the liberty of men to produce and consume pornography, and the rights of women to equal civil status. That is how the case was seen by the courts. The claim that pornography silences women expresses a different conflict, within liberty itself. Seen this way, the ordinance poses a conflict between the liberty of men to produce and consume pornography, and the liberty of women to speak.

One liberal philosopher, Ronald Dworkin, says that only the latter feminist approach has any chance of success. Showing that pornography silences women is the only way to justify censorship, in a legal system that "assigns a preeminent place to free speech" (Dworkin, 1991, p. 108). He thinks that the feminist "silencing" argument doesn't work – it is a "confusion". I will show that it is not a confusion. Nor is the silencing argument the only possible feminist argument – there are other ways of arguing for censorship than by saying pornography silences women.

Indeed, Dworkin's own liberal theory provides a way to build a different argument for censorship, as I have shown elsewhere (Langton, 1990). We can give what Dworkin calls an argument of principle, a rights-based argument, for the conclusion that pornography ought to be prohibited. It goes something like this. A policy that permits pornography relies on the fact that many people like pornography, and would like to be able to read and watch it. (Remember that we are talking about the pornography of MacKinnon's definition, that depicts women "dehumanized as sexual objects, things, or commodities; enjoying pain or humiliation or rape", etc.) These preferences for pornography are what Dworkin would call "external" preferences, because they are preferences that depend on views about the inferior worth of other people, in particular, women. Dworkin says that when a policy relies on external preferences, the policy violates the rights of those other people. So women have rights against a policy that permits pornography. Although Dworkin himself says porno-graphy should be permitted (1981; 1991), his own principles apparently imply that porno-graphy should be prohibited.

My strategy in this paper is different, and it divides into two parts, addressing the two feminist claims about subordination and silence. What I propose, in a nutshell, is this. Once we think of pornographic images and texts as speech acts, these feminist claims are intelli-gible and even (on certain assumptions) plausible. Understanding how pornographic utter-ances are speech acts will help us understand how pornography might subordinate. Understanding how potential speech acts can be made unspeakable for women will help us understand how pornography might silence. If pornography subordinates women, it presents a conflict between liberty and equality. If pornography silences women, it presents a conflict between liberty and liberty: the free speech of men, and that of women.

I. "Pornography Subordinates"

Before seeing whether pornographic speech acts can subordinate, we need to think about speech acts, and whether they can subordinate. Our interest is in the illocutionary speech act: the action performed in saying something. A perlocutionary act (by contrast) is the action performed (not *in* but) *by* saying something: the utterance considered in terms of its effects. Austin took care to distinguish illocutions from perlocutions, and he thought that the phrases "in saying" and "by saying" were typical – though not infallible – markers of the two. Recall the earlier example. *In saying* "Shoot her", the first man *ordered* the second to shoot: that was the illocutionary act. *By saying* "Shoot her", he *shocked* the second man, and *persuaded* him to shoot: those are some of the perlocutionary acts. Another example: *In saying* "I do" I was marrying; *by saying* "I do" I greatly distressed my mother. Saying "I do" in the right context counts as, constitutes, marrying: that is the illocutionary act. It does not count as distressing my mother, even if it has that effect: that is the perlocutionary act.

Austin said that an utterance has illocutionary force of a certain kind when it satisfies certain conditions for success: he called them *felicity conditions*. Whether or not in saying "I do" the speaker is marrying depends on the felicity conditions of marriage: that the speaker intends to marry, the utterance takes place in a conventional procedure, with appropriate participants (e.g. adult heterosexual couple, unmarried, plus priest or registrar). And the hearers should *recognize* that an illocution of a certain kind is being performed; Austin called this recognition necessary for the illocution, the *uptake*.

Speech acts sometimes go wrong. What we do, and what we aim to do, are not always the same. Speech acts can misfire, and they misfire when their conditions are not satisfied. Things would go wrong if the marriage ceremony were not completed, or if the celebrant turned out to be an actor in priestly garb, or the prospective spouse was a monkey (Austin, 1962, p. 24). Intending to marry is not enough. You have to get it right, not just by saying the right words ("I do"), and intending to marry, but by making sure the other conditions are satisfied as well. These ways that speech can go wrong will be relevant later to how we think about silence.

Can speech acts subordinate? People after all do all kinds of things with words. Besides advising, warning and marrying one another, people also hurt and oppress one another. A child may chant that "sticks and stones may break my bones, but names will never hurt". Names do hurt, though. That is why she chants. Words can break bones. "Shoot her!" might break a few, as perlocutionary act at any rate. ("By saying 'Shoot her' he caused her skull to be fractured.") Speech can do more than break bones. Perhaps it can determine civil status. MacKinnon says that to subordinate someone is to put them in a position of inferiority or loss of power, or to demean or denigrate them (1987, p. 176). Can speech be an illocutionary act that subordinates?

Yes, surely. Consider this utterance: "Blacks are not permitted to vote." Imagine that it is uttered by a legislator in Pretoria, in the context of enacting apartheid legislation. It is a locutionary act ("Blacks" refers to blacks, etc.). It is a perlocutionary act: it will have the effect, for example, that blacks stay away from polling booths. But it is, first and foremost, an illocutionary act: it makes it the case that blacks are not permitted to vote. It subordinates blacks. So does this utterance: "Whites Only". It too is a locutionary act ("Whites" refers to whites, etc.). It has some important perlocutionary effects (keeps blacks away from white areas, etc.). But it is also an illocutionary act: it orders blacks away, welcomes whites, permits whites to act in a discriminatory way towards blacks. It is an illocutionary act that subordinates blacks. If this is right, then there is no sleight of hand, no philosophical mistake, in the idea that speech can be an illocutionary act of subordination (cf. MacKinnon, 1987, p. 202; 1993, pp. 12–14).

The speech acts of apartheid subordinate because of (at least) the following three features. They *rank* blacks as having inferior worth. They *legitimate* discriminatory behaviour on the part of whites. And they *deprive* blacks of some important powers: the power to go to certain places, the power to vote. Not all acts of ranking people, legitimating behaviour, and depriving people of powers, are acts of subordination. Someone might rank an athlete as the fastest; legitimate beer drinking on campus; deprive a drink-driver of his licence. These are not acts of subordination. The speech acts of apartheid *are* acts of subordination: they unfairly rank people as inferior; they legitimate discriminatory behaviour; and they unjustly deprive people of powers. We can be glad that the example is now anachronistic.

Speech acts of this kind belong to an important subset of speech acts, *authoritative illocutions.* Some illocutions involve the authoritative delivery of a finding: for example, actions of ranking, valuing, giving a verdict. Imagine an umpire calls "Fault" at a tennis match. What does he do, in saying that word? He describes the world as he sees it. But he does more: he gives his *verdict.* Imagine a mere bystander says "Fault". He describes the world as he sees it. He says the same thing as the umpire says: they perform the same locutionary act. But the bystander's word makes no difference to the score. The umpire's does. The umpire can do more things with his words. Other authoritative illocutions confer powers and rights on people, or deprive people of powers and rights. Actions of ordering, permitting, prohibiting, enacting law, firing an employee are illocutions of this kind. You can't order someone, or fire someone, unless you have authority. The authority of the speaker gives an utterance an illocutionary force which would be otherwise absent (cf. Austin, 1962, pp. 152–6).

It is because of their authority that the speech acts of apartheid subordinate. As MacKinnon herself puts it, "*authoritatively saying* someone is inferior is largely how structures of status and differential treatment are demarcated and actualized" (MacKinnon, 1993, p. 31, emphasis added). This already tells us something about subordinating speech acts: they are speech acts whose conditions for success (felicity conditions) require that the speaker has authority. Sometimes that authority is officially recognized, in written laws and regulations. That is true of the legislator enacting the laws of apartheid; it is true of the umpire giving verdict on a fault. Sometimes the authority may be less explicitly recognized, but we can expect the principle to be the same.

We can turn now to the main question. Pornography is said to subordinate women. It is also said to rank women as sex objects, "defined on the basis of [their] looks . . . [their] availability for sexual pleasure", and to represent degrading and abusive sexual behaviour "in such a way as to *endorse* the degradation" (MacKinnon, 1987, p. 173; Longino, 1980, p. 29). MacKinnon herself provides a range of additional illocutionary verbs:

> Pornography sexualizes rape, battery, sexual harassment . . . and child sexual abuse; it . . . *celebrates, promotes, authorizes* and *legitimates* them. (MacKinnon, 1987, p. 171, emphasis added)

These descriptions are relevant to the claim that pornography subordinates.

Recall why the speech acts of apartheid subordinate. They *rank* certain people as inferior; they *legitimate* discriminatory behaviour towards them; and they *deprive* them of some important powers and rights. The feminists just quoted say pornography has some of these features: pornography ranks women as sex objects, legitimates sexual violence. Feminists think of sexual violence not simply as harm, but as a kind of discrimination. If pornography ranks women as sex objects, and legitimates discriminatory behaviour, it is an illocutionary act of subordination. So the claim that *pornography subordinates women* makes sense: it is not confused, not "sleight of hand", not "philosophically indefensible". It makes good sense: but is it true?

There is disagreement – to put it mildly – about whether the feminist descriptions are correct. Disagreements about illocutions can be hard to resolve. Austin said that disputed speech acts need to have "a construction put upon them by judges" (p. 114), and I discuss elsewhere some different methods for resolving disagreement (Langton, 1993). However, if the argument so far is right, then we know that subordinating speech is a kind of authoritative speech. Whether you can perform authoritative speech acts depends on the authority you have. The umpire, not the bystander, can call a fault. The government, not the private citizen, can enact law that ranks people and legitimates discriminatory behaviour. So one way to help answer the question: "Does pornography subordinate?" is to ask whether it has authority. If it does, then at least one crucial felicity condition is satisfied: pornographic speech acts may then be authoritative illocutions that rank women as inferior, legitimate violence, and thus subordinate.

This question about authority may well be at the heart of the controversy about pornography. Some think pornography is the speech of a powerless minority, vulnerable to moralistic persecution. Then it seems odd to say pornographic speech is authoritative. But some think the voice of pornography is the voice of the ruling power. MacKinnon says, "the power of pornography is more like the power of the state" (1993, p. 39). Then it seems obvious that pornographic speech is authoritative – that the authors of pornographic speech are not mere bystanders to the game, but speakers whose verdict counts.

Does pornographic speech have authority? This is not really a question to be settled from the philosopher's armchair. To answer it we need to know about the role pornographers occupy as authoritative speakers about the "facts" of sex. What is important is not whether pornographic speech is generally respected, but whether it is authoritative in the domain of speech about sex. What is important is whether it is authoritative for the hearers that count: people, men, boys, who want (among other things) to discover how to act, want to know which moves in the sexual game are legitimate. What is important is whether it is authoritative for those hearers who somehow learn that violence is sexy and coercion legitimate: those who "think it is okay for a man to rape a woman if he is sexually aroused by her", who say they have raped a woman on a date, who say that they enjoy the conquest part of sex, who rank faces of women displaying pain and fear to be more sexually attractive than faces showing pleasure (Warshaw, 1988, pp. 93, 120; Wolf, 1990, pp. 162–8). In this domain, and for these hearers, perhaps pornography has the authority of a monopoly. If, as a matter of fact, pornography has authority, then the claim that pornography subordinates may be not only intelligible, but true.

II. "Pornography Silences"

If speech is action, then silence is failure to act. If pornography silences women, it prevents women from doing things with their words. Before thinking about whether pornography silences women, we need to think about how speech acts may be silenced, and whether speech acts can silence.

The ability to perform speech acts can be a measure of political power. Those who use the words "Blacks are not permitted to vote" to *prohibit* are the ones with authority. One mark of powerlessness is an inability to perform speech acts one might otherwise like to perform. We can distinguish three kinds of silence, since (following Austin) there are three kinds of act one may fail to perform.

At a first and basic level, members of a powerless group may be silent because they are intimidated. They do not protest, because they think protest is futile. They do not vote, because they fear the guns. In such cases no words are uttered at all. Speakers fail to perform even a *locutionary* act. Sometimes, however, people speak, and what they say fails to achieve the intended effects: such speakers fail to perform their intended perlocutionary act. Silencing of this second kind (perlocutionary frustration) is a common fact of life: you argue, but persuade no-one; you invite, but no-one comes to the party; you vote, hoping to oust the government, but in vain.

There is a third kind of silence: you speak, you utter words, and you fail to perform the illocutionary act that you intend. Things go wrong: your speech misfires. Silencing of this third kind I call *illocutionary disablement*.

Example (1): Warning

This example is from the philosopher Donald Davidson (1984, p. 269).

> Imagine this: the actor is acting a scene in which there is supposed to be a fire . . . It is his role to imitate as persuasively as he can a man who is trying to warn others of a fire. "Fire!" he screams. And perhaps he adds, at the behest of the author, "I mean it! Look at the smoke!" etc. And now a real fire breaks out, and the actor tries vainly to warn the real audience. "Fire!" he screams. "I mean it! Look at the smoke!" etc.

The actor says words appropriate for warning. He gets the locutionary act exactly right. He intends to warn. But he does not warn. Something about the role he occupies prevents his utterance from counting as a warning. Something, perhaps, about the conventions of theatre constrains the speech acts he can make. The same words said with the same intentions by a member of the audience *would* count as a warning. The actor, though, has been silenced. The act of warning has been made unspeakable for him.

Example (2): Marriage

To say "I do" is, in the right circumstances, to marry. But suppose both parties intending to marry are male. They intend to marry. The speaker uses the right words. The priest is no mere actor. The ceremony is performed by the book. The speaker satisfies all the felicity conditions: all but one. Something about who he is, and who his partner is, prevents him from satisfying one crucial condition. The act of marrying misfires. The act of marriage is not speakable for homosexual couples. The power to marry is not available to them.

Example (3): Voting

A white in apartheid South Africa makes marks on a piece of paper in a polling booth. A black makes marks that look the same. Their intentions are the same. But the former has done something significant. He has voted. The latter has not. Something about *who he is* prevents him from satisfying a crucial felicity condition. The law prevents his utterance from counting as a vote. Voting is, for him, an unspeakable act. He lacks an important political power available to other citizens.

Example (4): Divorce

To say "*Mutallaqa, mutallaqa, mutallaqa*" (literally "Divorced, divorced, divorced") is to perform the illocutionary act of divorce in a country where Islamic law is in force, provided the felicity conditions are met. Pronounced by a husband to his wife, it is an act of divorce. Not so if it is pronounced by the wife to her husband (Bahadur, 1898, p. 47). No matter how hard she tries, a woman cannot, in saying those words, divorce her spouse. Divorce of that kind is an act that is unspeakable for women.

If we are interested in the silence of illocutionary disablement, we can ask about its source. When speech misfires because speakers fail to satisfy certain conditions, we can ask how those conditions came to be. MacKinnon says there can be "*words that set conditions*" (1987, p. 228), and Austin would agree. Felicity conditions can be set by other speech acts. Laws are enacted that specify the felicity conditions for marriage, voting, divorce. Some illocutionary acts fix the range and scope of other illocutionary acts. Some speech acts build and limit a space for other speech acts, making it possible for some people to marry, vote, divorce – and impossible for other people to marry, vote, divorce. Speech can thus silence by making speech acts, illocutionary acts, unspeakable.

For more informal illocutions (warning, advising, etc.) there are no enactments of legislation to "set conditions". But perhaps here too, conditions can be set by speech: by informal practices of communication that set informal rules about what counts as, for example, a warning. Here too, perhaps, there can be speech that builds and limits the space for potential speech acts, and silences those who do not satisfy the conditions.

Let us consider, now, some different examples of silence.

Example (5): Refusal

Think about the utterance "No." We know how to do things with this word. We use it, typically, to disagree, refuse, prohibit. In sexual contexts a woman sometimes uses it to refuse sex. However, in sexual contexts a woman sometimes tries to use the "No" locution to refuse sex, and it does not work. It does not work for the women who are date raped, or for the girls who are sexually forced (Wolf, 1990, pp. 166–7; Caputi, 1987, p. 119). Saying "No" sometimes doesn't work. But perhaps there are two ways in which it can fail to work. Sometimes the woman's hearer recognizes the action she performs: recognizes that she is refusing. In saying "No", she really does refuse. By saying "No", she intends to stop her hearer from continuing his advances. But the hearer goes ahead, and forces sex on her. She prohibits, but he fails to obey. She fails to achieve the (perlocutionary) goal of her refusal: her refusal is frustrated. ("Perlocutionary frustration" is too academic a label: this is simple rape.) Sometimes, perhaps, there is a different silencing. Sometimes "No", when spoken by a woman, does not *count* as the act of refusal. The hearer fails to recognize the utterance as a refusal: uptake is not secured. In saying "No" she may well intend to refuse. By saying "No" she intends to prevent sex, but she is far from doing as she intends. Since illocutionary force depends, in part, on uptake being secured, the woman fails to refuse. She is like the actor in Davidson's story, silenced as surely as the actor is silenced. He shouts "Fire!" He says the right words. He means what he says. He intends to warn. But what he says misfires. Something about him, something about the role he occupies, prevents him from warning the audience. She says "No". She says the right words. She means what she says. She intends to refuse. But what she says misfires. Something about her, something about the role she occupies, prevents her from voicing refusal. Refusal – in that context – has become unspeakable for her.

Example (6): Protest

The following appeared in a mail-order catalogue advertising "Adult Reading", flanked by such titles as "426. *Forbidden Sexual Fantasies*" and "428. *Orgy: an Erotic Experience*".

> No. 427   ORDEAL: an autobiography by Linda Lovelace. With M. McGrady. The star of *Deep Throat* tells the shocking story of her enslavement in the pornographic underworld, a nightmarish ordeal of savage violence and unspeakable perversion, of thrill-seeking celebrities and sadistic criminals. For Sale to Adults Over 21 Only.

Ordeal is a book that has been cited by feminists who oppose pornography. The author, Linda Marchiano (alias Lovelace), tells the story of the making of the film *Deep Throat*.

Austin remarked (p. 118) that you can perform the illocutionary act of protest a number of different ways: you can shout; you can hurl a tomato. You can also write a book in protest. *Ordeal* is an act of protest, a denunciation of the industry in which Marchiano says she was forced to perform. One can see why it is cited by anti-pornography feminists. As locutionary act *Ordeal* depicts the subordination of a woman: it depicts a woman "in scenarios of degradation, injury and torture". But it does not "endorse the degradation"; it does not "celebrate, promote, authorize and legitimate" the sexual violence. It does not appear to have pornography's illocutionary force.

Why is *Ordeal* in a mail-order catalogue, flanked by ordinary pornographic titles? Perhaps because *it is pornography after all*: here, in this context, for these intended hearers, the uptake secured is that of pornography. Marchiano says words appropriate for an act of protest. She uses the right locutions, words that graphically depict her own past subordination. She intends to protest. But her speech misfires. Something about who she is, or the role she occupies, prevents her from satisfying protest's felicity conditions, at least here. Though the threats and gags are gone, there is silence of another kind. She too is like the actor. Warning was unspeakable for him. Protest is unspeakable for her, in this context. What he tries to say comes out as "merely acted". What she tries to say comes out as pornography. Her protest has been disabled.

We can ask about the origins of the illocutionary disablement in examples (5) and (6): the disablement of the rape victim whose attempted refusal is not recognized as a refusal; the disablement of an author whose attempted protest is not recognized as protest. These misfires betray the presence of structural constraints on women's speech. The felicity conditions for refusal, for protest, are, somehow, not met. Something is robbing the speech of its intended force. Intending to refuse, intending to protest, is not enough. Pornography may be responsible for this illocutionary disablement. For if women's speech is disabled, and we ask how the disabling conditions came to be, we can reflect that felicity conditions for illocutions can be set by other speech acts. And when MacKinnon says there can be "words that set conditions", she means that *the felicity conditions for women's speech acts are set by the speech acts of pornography*.

Consider how this might apply to (5). Pornography might legitimate rape, and silence refusal, by doing something other than eroticizing refusal itself. It may simply leave no space for the refusal move in its depictions of sex. In pornography of this kind there would be all kinds of words the women depicted could use to make the consent move. "Yes" is one. "No" is just another. Here the refusal move is not eroticized: it is absent altogether. Consent is the *only* thing a woman can do with her words, in this game. Someone learning the rules from this kind of pornography might not recognize an attempted refusal. Refusal, here, would be disabled. Refusal would be made unspeakable for a woman.

How common is silencing of this kind, and the rape which accompanies it? It is hard to tell, because so few rapes are reported (and these least of all). Studies about sexual violence say that men often "refuse to take no for an answer". Perhaps they recognize the refusal, and persist in spite of it, or because of it (matching the first pattern in example (5)). Or perhaps there is something else: Naomi Wolf says (1990, p. 167)

> . . . boys rape and girls get raped *as a normal course of events*. The boys may even be unaware that what they are doing is wrong; violent sexual imagery may well have raised a generation of young men who can rape women without even knowing it.

If young men can rape without knowing it, then women sometimes fail to secure uptake for their attempted refusals. This is the silence of disablement.

Refusal, prohibition, is an authoritative illocution. To satisfy its felicity conditions, you need to have authority in the relevant domain. A government that prohibits has authority over a large domain; a parent who prohibits has authority within the local domain of the family; a patient who prohibits treatment has authority within the local domain of his own body. A woman who prohibits sexual advances has authority within the local domain of her own body. If she cannot prohibit, cannot refuse, the authority is absent. If she is disabled from speaking refusal, it shows that her body is, in a sense, not her own. If pornography prevents her from refusing, then pornography destroys her authority as it twists her words.

The story about *Ordeal* shows the same phenomenon. Marchiano tries to protest, but only succeeds in making more pornography. The pornographers know how to do things with her words: stories of "savage violence" and "enslavement in the pornographic underworld" are pornography to readers for whom violence has been legitimated as sex. And there is ironic truth in what the pornographers say: the violence is indeed "unspeakable" for Marchiano. If you are a woman using sexually explicit speech, describing the savage sexual violence you have suffered, and especially if you are a famous pornography star, what you say counts as pornography. Too bad if you want it to count as something else. It is an effective way to silence: not simply by depriving her speech of its intended illocutionary force, but by replacing it with a force that is its antithesis. That story is not an isolated anecdote. If MacKinnon is right, it is comparable to a similar disablement encountered by women who give testimony in court about rape and sexual harassment, and whose testimony, and descriptions of their experience, achieve the uptake appropriate to a description of "normal" sex.

If pornography sets up the rules in the language games of sex in a way that disables and silences women, then it belongs in the class of speech acts that removes powers. This, recall, was part of what it meant to be subordinating speech: so we come full circle. If pornography silences, it subordinates. And if pornography silences, it is authoritative speech. So the second feminist claim, like the first, depends on a premise about the authority of pornography – it depends on that premise for its plausibility, but not for its coherence.

For the claim that pornography silences women is neither "metaphorical", nor a "confusion". It can be taken literally. One might object that the silencing I have described is not literal silencing because pornography does not literally prevent women from uttering words. It does not usually prevent women from performing locutionary acts. But to think that way is to exhibit the tendency of which Austin complained: to be preoccupied with the content of what is said, at the expense of the action performed. One way of being silent is to make no noise. Another way of being silent – literally silent – is to perform no speech act. Locutions on their own are nothing. Words are there to be used. Words are tools. Words are for doing things with. There is little point in giving someone tools if they cannot do things with them. And there is little point in allowing women words if we cannot do things with them.

The claim is not metaphor; it is not confusion either. Dworkin says (1991, p. 108) it is a "confusion" to suppose that pornography silences women, because it is a confusion to "characterize certain ideas as silencing ideas". But the feminist claim is not that ideas are silencing ideas, but that acts can be silencing acts. That is no confusion. People do all kinds of thing with words: advise, warn, marry – and also silence one another. They silence by preventing other speakers from doing things with words. They can silence simply, by ordering, or threatening; they can silence by frustrating a speaker's perlocutionary acts; they can silence by disabling a speaker's illocutionary acts, and this latter silence has been the special focus of our attention.

The claim that pornography silences is not really about ideas at all, but about people and what they do. It is common to cast ideas as the heroes of the free speech story. Free speech is a good thing, because it provides a free-market marketplace for ideas, where the best and truest ideas can win out in the end. To say that some speech silences is to describe a shopping problem: some ideas which could be on the market are not. This too is the tendency of which Austin complained: a focus on content, while ignoring the speech act performed. The claim that pornography silences women is not about ideas, but about people. Free speech is a good thing because it *enables people to act*, lets people do things with words: argue, protest, question, answer. Speech that silences is bad, not – or not just – because it restricts the ideas available on the shelves, but because it constrains people's actions. Perhaps women do have trouble developing new ideas about themselves, about sexuality, about life, when pornography has market monopoly. The market is missing out on some good ideas. But that is not the point. The point is that a woman's liberty to speak the *actions* she wants to speak has been thwarted: a woman's liberty to protest against pornography and rape, refuse sex when she wants to, argue about violence in court. The point is that while pornography sets the conditions of women's speech, women cannot do things with words, even when we think we know how. And if speech itself is more than "only words", then free speech is as well.

Notes

1   *American Booksellers, Inc.* v. *Hudnut*, 771 F2nd 329 (7th Cir. 1985).

2   *Hudnut*, 598 F. Supp. 136 (1984).

References

Austin, J. L.: *How to Do Things with Words* (London: Oxford University Press, 1962).

Bahadur, Mahomed Yusoof Khan: *Mahomedan Law*, vol. III (Calcutta: Thacker, Spink & Co., 1898).

Caputi, J.: *The Age of Sex Crime* (London: The Women's Press, 1987).

Davidson, Donald: "Communication and Convention" (1982), in *Inquiries into Truth and Interpretation* (Oxford: Oxford University Press, 1984).

Donnerstein, E., D. Linz, and S. Penrod: *The Question of Pornography: Research Findings and Policy Implications* (New York: Free Press; London: Collier Macmillan, 1987).

Dworkin, R.: "Do we have a Right to Pornography?", *Oxford Journal of Legal Studies*, I (1981), 177–212; reprinted in *A Matter of Principle* (Cambridge, MA: Harvard University Press, 1985), pp. 335–72.

——: "Two Concepts of Liberty", in *Isaiah Berlin: A Celebration*, ed. Edna and Avishai Margalit (London: Hogarth Press, 1991).

Habermas, Jürgen: *The Theory of Communicative Action* (Beacon Press, 1984), vol. I.

Hodkinson, K: *Muslim Family Law* (London: Croom Helm, 1984).

Hornsby, Jennifer: "Illocution and its Significance", *Foundations of Speech Act Theory: Philosophical and Linguistic Perspectives*, ed. S. L. Tsohatzidis (London and New York: Routledge, 1994).

——: "Speech Acts and Pornography", *Women's Philosophy Review*, 10 (1993), 38–45; reprinted in *The Problem of Pornography*, ed. Sue Dwyer (Belmont, CA: Wadsworth, 1995).

Jacobson, D.: "Freedom of Speech Acts? A Response to Langton", *Philosophy and Public Affairs*, 24 (1995), 64–79.

Langton, Rae: "Speech Acts and Unspeakable Acts", *Philosophy and Public Affairs*, 22 (1993), 293–330.

——: "Whose Right? Ronald Dworkin, Women and Pornographers", *Philosophy and Public Affairs*, 19 (1990), 311–59.

Longino, H. E.: "Pornography, Oppression and

Freedom: A Closer Look", in *Take Back the Night: Women on Pornography*, ed. Laura Lederer (New York: William Morrow, 1980).

Lovelace, L. with M. McGrady: *Ordeal* (Secaucus, NJ: Citadel Press, 1980).

MacKinnon, Catherine: *Feminism Unmodified* (Cambridge, MA: Harvard University Press, 1987).

——: *Only Words* (Cambridge, MA: Harvard University Press, 1993).

Michelman, F.: "Conceptions of Democracy in American Constitutional Argument: The Case of Pornography Regulation", *Tennessee Law Review*, 56 (1989).

Parent, W. A.: "A Second Look at Pornography and the Subordination of Women", *Journal of Philosophy*, 87 (1990), 205–11.

Tribe, Laurence: *American Constitutional Law* (2nd edn) (Mineola, NY: Foundation Press, 1988), chapter 12.

Vadas, Melinda: "A First Look at the Pornography/Civil Rights Ordinance: Could Pornography be the Subordination of Women?", *Journal of Philosophy*, 84 (1987), 487–511.

Warshaw, R.: *I Never Called it Rape* (New York: Harper and Rowe, 1988).

Wolf, Naomi: *The Beauty Myth* (New York: Vintage, 1990).

34

Sticks and Stones

John Arthur

A recent *New York Times* article described the intense controversy surrounding a German court's decision that a bumper-sticker proclaiming "soldiers are murderers" is constitutionally protected, just as it would be under the First Amendment to the United States Constitution. Chancellor Helmut Kohl characterized himself as "outraged" at the court's decision, saying that "We cannot and must not stand by while our soldiers are placed on the same level with criminals." A leading German newspaper editorialized that "In a democracy, criticism of war and the military is naturally not forbidden. But among reasonable people, it must be done in a civilized way and not with brutal insults like 'murderers.' " And the judge in the case, who said he regretted having to decide as he did, complained that earlier decisions of the Constitutional Court "are steadily placing freedom of speech ahead of the protection of people's honor" (*New York Times*, January 15, 1996, p. A-5). As this event shows, hate speech occurs in a wide array of contexts; it can also be directed at many different targets, not just racial groups. It is also unclear, of course, whether and in what form hate speech should be censored.

Proponents of limiting hate speech on college campuses and elsewhere have generally taken one of two approaches. One is to pass a "speech code" that identifies which words or ideas are banned, the punishment that may be imposed, and (as at the University of Michigan) an interpretive "Guide" meant to explain how the rules will be applied. The other approach has been to treat hate speech as a form of harassment. Here the censorship is justified on anti-discrimination grounds: hate speech, it is argued, subjects its victims to a "hostile" work environment, which courts have held constitutes job discrimination (*Meritor Savings Bank* v. *Vinson*, 1986).

Advocates of banning hate speech do not usually include all expressions of hatred, however devastating and humiliating they may be. Few would ban such criticism of the military, for example. And words directed at another person because of what he has done are also not normally included: "You bastard, you murdered my father!" is not thought of as "hate speech," nor is an attack on a person simply for being stupid or incompetent. Rather than censoring all expressions of hatred, advocates of banning hate speech use the term narrowly, to refer to speech directed at people *in virtue of their membership in a (usually historically disadvantaged) racial, religious, ethnic, sexual or other group.*

Such a conception can be criticized, of course, on the ground that it arbitrarily narrows the field to one form of hate speech. Perhaps, however, there is reason to focus on a limited problem: if it turns out, for example, that hate speech directed against such groups is especially harmful, then it may seem reasonable to have created this special usage of the term. In this paper I consider some of the important issues surrounding hate speech and its regulation: the political and legal importance of free speech; the types of harm that might be attributed to it; and whether, even if no harm results, causing emotional distress and offense is by itself sufficient to warrant censorship.

1. Why Protect Freedom of Speech?

Respecting freedom of speech is important for a variety of reasons. First, as J. S. Mill argued long ago, free and unfettered debate is vital for the pursuit of truth. If knowledge is to grow, people must be free to put forth ideas and theories they deem worthy of consideration, and others must be left equally free to criticize them. Even false ideas should be protected, Mill argued, so that the truth will not become mere dogma, unchallenged and little understood. "However true [an opinion] may be," he wrote, "if it is not fully, frequently, and fearlessly discussed, it will be held as a dead dogma, not a living truth" (Mill, 1978, p. 34). It helps, of course, if the competition among ideas is fair and all sides have an equal opportunity to have their ideas expressed. Censorship is therefore only one of the dangers to the marketplace of ideas; unequal access to the media is another.

Free speech is also an essential feature of democratic, efficient and just government. Fair, democratic elections cannot occur unless candidates are free to debate and criticize each other's policies, nor can government be run efficiently unless corruption and other abuses can be exposed by a free press. But beyond that, there is an important sense in which freedom of speech provides a necessary pre-condition for the protection of other rights and therefore for justice. Free and open debate about the nature and limits of other rights – to privacy, religion, equal treatment and the rest – is vital if society is to reach sound and fair decisions about when and how those other rights must be defined and respected. We cannot expect sound political deliberation, including deliberation about rights themselves, without first securing freedom of speech.

A third value, individual autonomy, is also served by free speech. In chapter III of *On Liberty*, "Of Individuality, as One of the Elements of Well Being," Mill writes that "He who lets the world, or his own portion of it, choose his plan of life for him, has no need of any other faculty than the ape-like one of imitation. . . . Among the works of man, which human life is rightly employed in perfecting and beautifying, the first in importance surely is man himself" (Mill, 1978, p. 56). Mill's suggestion is that the best life does not result from being forced to live a certain way, but instead is freely chosen without coercion from outside. But if Mill is right, then freedom of speech as well as action are important to achieve a worthwhile life. Free and open discussion helps people exercise their capacities of reasoning and judgment, capacities that are essential for autonomous and informed choices.

Besides these important social advantages of respecting free speech, including learning the truth, securing efficient, democratic and just government, and promoting individual autonomy, freedom of expression is important for its own sake, because it is a basic human right. Not only does free speech *promote* autonomy, as Mill argued, but it is also a *reflection* of individual autonomy and of human equality. Censorship denigrates our status as equal, autonomous persons by saying, in effect, that some people simply cannot be trusted to make up their own minds about what is right or true. Because of the ideas they hold or the subjects they find interesting, they need not be treated with the same respect as other citizens with whom they disagree; only we, not they, are free to believe as we wish. Viewed that way, denying free speech is much like establishing an official religion: it says to some citizens that because of their beliefs they are less than equal members of society. So, unlike the previous arguments, which see speech as an instrument to realize other important values, here the claim is that free speech must be protected out of respect for the fact that each adult in the community is entitled to be treated as an equal among others (Dworkin, 1996, chapter 8).

Because it serves important social goals, and also must be respected in the name of equal citizenship, the right to speak and write freely is perhaps the most important of all rights. But beyond that, two further points also need to be stressed. Free speech is fragile, in two respects. The first is the chilling effect that censorship poses. Language banning hate speech will inevitably be vague and indeterminate, at least to some extent: words like "hate" and "denigrate" and "victimize," which often occur in such rules, are not self-defining. When such bans bring strict penalties, as they sometimes do, they risk sweeping too broadly, capturing valuable speech in their net along with the speech they seek to prohibit. Criminal or civil penalties therefore pose a threat to speech generally, and the values underlying it, as people consider the potential risks of expressing their opinions while threatened by legal sanctions. Censorship risks having a chilling effect.

The second danger of censorship, often referred to as the "slippery slope," begins with the historical observation that unpopular minorities and controversial ideas are always vulnerable to political repression, whether by authoritarian regimes hoping to remain in power, or elected officials desiring to secure re-election by attacking unpopular groups or silencing political opponents. For that reason, it is important to create a high wall of constitutional protection securing the right to speak against attempts to limit it. Without strong, politically resistant constraints on governmental efforts to restrict speech, there is constant risk – demonstrated by historical experience – that what begins as a minor breech in the wall can be turned by governmental officials and intolerant majorities into a large, destructive exception.

Protecting speech is essential if society is to protect truth, autonomy, efficiency, democracy, and justice; it also must be protected if we are to show equal respect for others with whom we differ. Censorship is also risky, I have argued, given the dangers of chilling effects and slippery slopes. Given all this, it is not surprising that the United States Supreme Court has sought ways to protect freedom of speech. So before considering hate-speech regulations, it will be helpful to look briefly at how the US Supreme Court has understood the First Amendment's guarantee of freedom of speech.

2. Free Speech and the Constitution

The Supreme Court has not always interpreted the First Amendment's free speech and press clauses in a manner consistent with speech's importance. Early in the twentieth century people were often jailed, and their convictions upheld, for expressing unpopular political views, including distributing pamphlets critical of American military intervention in the Russian revolution (*Abrams* v. *United States*, 1919). Then, in the McCarthy era of the 1950s, government prosecuted over a hundred people for what was in effect either teaching Marxism or belonging to the Communist Party (*Dennis* v. *United States*, 1951). Beginning in the 1960s, however, the US Supreme Court changed direction, interpreting the Constitution's command that government not restrict freedom of speech as imposing strict limits on governmental power to censor speech and punish speakers.

Pursuing this goal, the first defined "speech" broadly, to include not just words but other forms of expression as well. Free speech protection now extends to people who wear arm bands, burn the flag, and peaceably march. The Court has also made a critically important distinction, between governmental regulations aimed at the *content* or *ideas* a person wishes to convey and content-neutral restrictions on the *time, place, and manner* in which the speech occurs. Thus, government is given fairly wide latitude to curtail speakers who use bull-horns at night, spray-paint their ideas on public buildings, or invade private property in order to get their messages across. But when governmental censors object not to how or where the speech occurs, but instead to the content itself, the Constitution is far more restrictive. Here, the Supreme Court has held, we are at the very heart of the First Amendment and the values it protects. Indeed, said the Court, there is "no such thing as a false idea" under the US Constitution (*Gertz. v. Robert Welch, Inc.*, 1974).

Wary of the chilling effect and the slippery slope, the Supreme Court has therefore held that government cannot regulate the content of speech unless it falls within certain narrowly defined categories. These constitutionally "unprotected categories" include libel (but criticisms of public officials must not only be false but uttered "maliciously" to be libelous), incitement to lawlessness (if the incitement is "immanent," such as yelling "Let's kill the capitalist!" in front of an angry mob), obscenity (assuming that the speech also lacks substantial social value), and "fighting words" (like "fascist pig" that are uttered in a face-to-face context likely to injure or provoke immediate, hostile reaction). In that way, each of these unprotected categories is precisely defined so as not to endanger free expression in general. Like Ulysses tying himself to the mast, the Supreme Court uses the unprotected-categories approach to reduce the chance that we will return to a time when constitutional protections were vaguely defined and government was left free to issue vaguely worded sedition statutes, stifle dissent and lock up critics. Harmless advocacy of revolution, for example, is now constitutionally protected, as is virtually all criticism of public officials.

Applying these principles, the Supreme Court held in 1989 that a "flag desecration" is constitutionally protected (*Texas* v. *Johnson*, 1989). Texas's statute had defined "desecration" in terms of the tendency to "offend" someone who was likely to know of the act. But, said the Court in striking down the statute, not only does flag burning involve ideas, the statute is not viewpoint neutral. Because it singled out one side of a debate – those who are critical of government – the law must serve an especially clear and important purpose. Mere "offense," the justices concluded, was insufficiently important to warrant intrusion into free expression.

In light of this constitutional history, it is not surprising that attempts to ban hate speech have fared poorly in American courts. Responding to various acts of racist speech on its campus, the University of Michigan passed one of the most far-reaching speech codes ever attempted at an American university; it prohibited "stigmatizing or victimizing" either individuals or groups on the basis of "race, ethnicity, religion, sex, sexual orientation, creed, national origin, ancestry, age, marital status, handicap or Vietnam-era veteran status." According to a "Guide" published by the University to help explain the code's meaning, conduct that violates the code would include a male student who "makes remarks in class like 'Women just aren't as good in this field as men,' thus creating a hostile learning atmosphere for female classmates." Also punishable under the code were "derogatory" comments about a person's or group's "physical appearance or sexual orientation, or their cultural origins, or religious beliefs" (*Doe* v. *University of Michigan*, 1989, pp. 857–8). To almost nobody's surprise, the Michigan Code was rejected as unconstitutional, on grounds that it violated rights both to free speech and to due process of law. The case was brought by a psychology instructor who feared that his course in developmental psychology, which discussed biological differences between males and females, might be taken by some to be "stigmatizing and victimizing." The Court agreed with the professor, holding that the Michigan code was both "over-broad" and "unconstitutionally vague." A second code at the University of Wisconsin soon met a similar fate, even though it banned only slurs and epithets (*UMV Post* v. *Board of Regents of the University of Wisconsin*, 1991).

Confirming these lower court decisions, the Supreme Court in 1992 ruled unconstitutional a city ordinance making it a misdemeanor to place on public or private property any "symbol, object, appellation, characterization or graffiti" that the person knows or has reasonable grounds for knowing will arouse "anger, alarm or resentment" on the basis of race, color, creed, religion or gender (*R.A.V.* v. *City of St Paul*, 1992, p. 2541). In overturning a juvenile's conviction for placing a burning cross on a black family's lawn, the majority held that even if the statute were understood very narrowly, to limit only "fighting words," it was nonetheless unconstitutional because it punished only some fighting words and not others. In so doing, argued one justice, the law violated the important principle of content neutrality: it censored some uses of fighting words, namely those focusing on race, color, creed, religion or gender, but not others. It prescribed political orthodoxy. Other justices emphasized that no serious harm had been identified that could warrant restrictions on speech. The law, wrote Justice White, criminalizes conduct that "causes only hurt feelings, offense, or resentment, and is protected by the First Amendment" (*R.A.V.* v. *City of St. Paul*, 1992, p. 2559).

Perhaps, however, the Court has gone too far in protecting hate speech. Advocates of banning hate speech commonly claim it harms its victims. "There is a great difference," writes Charles Lawrence, "between the offensiveness of words that you would rather not hear because they are labelled dirty, impolite, or personally demeaning and the injury [of hate speech]" (Lawrence, 1990, p. 74). Elsewhere he describes hate speech as "aimed at an entire group with the effect of causing significant *harm* to individual group members" (Lawrence, 1990, p. 57, emphasis added). Richard Delgado similarly claims that it would be rare for a white who is called a "dumb honkey" to be in a position to claim legal redress since, unlike a member of an historically oppressed group, it would be unlikely that a white person would "suffer *harm* from such an insult" (Delgado, 1982, p. 110, emphasis added).

But are these writers correct that various forms of hate speech cross the boundary from the distressing and offensive to the genuinely harmful? To weigh their claim, we will first ask how we are to understand the concept of harm. Once that is clear, we can then proceed to the question of whether hate speech is in fact harmful, and then to whether it should be banned on other grounds.

3. Harm and Offense

To claim that someone has been harmed is different from claiming she has been wronged. I can break into your house undetected, do no damage, and leave. While I have wronged you, I might not have harmed you, especially if you didn't know about it and I didn't take anything.

What then must be the case for wronging somebody to also constitute a harm? First, to be harmed is not merely to experience a minor irritation or hurt, nor is it simply to undergo an unwanted experience. Though unwanted, the screech of chalk on the blackboard, an unpleasant smell, a pinch or slap, a brief but frightening experience, and a revolting sight are not harms. Harms are significant events. Following Joel Feinberg, I will assume that harms occur not when we are merely hurt or offended, but when our "interests" are frustrated, defeated or set back (Feinberg, 1984, pp. 31–51). By interests he means something in which we have a stake – just as we may have a "stake" in a company. So while many of our interests are obviously tied to our wants and desires, a mere want does not constitute an interest. A minor disappointment is not a frustration of interests in the relevant sense. Feinberg thus emphasizes the "directional" nature of interests that are "set back" when one is harmed, pointing out that the interests are "ongoing concerns" rather than temporary wants. Genuine harms thus impede or thwart people's future objectives or options, which explains why the unpleasant memory or smell and the bite's itch are not harms while loss of a limb, of freedom, and of health are. Harms can therefore come from virtually any source: falling trees, disease, economic or romantic competitors, and muggers are only a few examples.

It seems clear therefore why government is concerned about harm and its prevention. Whether caused by other people or by nature, to be harmed is never trivial; it involves a set-back or frustration of an interest of a person. For government to ignore genuinely harmful acts requires justification; sometimes such a justification is easy to see, as when competition causes economic harm or a person injures another in self-defense. But, absent such a justification, there is a *prima facie* case that harmful actions should not be allowed.

We now turn to the question of whether hate speech causes harm. In discussing this, we will consider various types of harm that might result, as well as making important distinctions between group and individual harm, between cumulative and individual harm and between direct and indirect harm.

4. Group Harm

One typical form of hate speech is directed not at any particular individual but at a group: fliers attacking racial and religious minorities are typical examples. But why might it be thought that attacks on groups are harmful? Here are some possibilities.

Larry May argues that attacks on groups harm people "vicariously." Because people care about others in their group, an attack on any one of them is in effect an attack on them all. He terms this state "solidarity." "If people are in a state of solidarity," he writes, "in which they identify the interests of others as their own interests, then . . . vicarious harm is possible" (May, 1987, p. 115). But that seems wrong: even assuming people are in a state of solidarity and identify strongly with the interests of others in the group, and also assuming that the hate speech harms the interests of its specific subject in some way, it still does not follow that others in the group are harmed by such an attack. Even such an attack on a family member might not result in such vicarious *harm*, though it could surely cause distress, anger, and resentment. Attacks on group members cause harm only if they also frustrate others' interests, understood as limiting on-going objectives or options. But group "solidarity" is not normally like that; no doubt other group members are often distressed, but to suffer distress is not, by itself, a harm.

Perhaps, however, the harm caused by attacks aimed at a racial or other group is to the group itself rather than to any particular individual. But what sense can be made of such a claim, that the group itself is somehow harmed? It may seem that groups are not the sort of thing that *can* be harmed, only individual members. But consider corporations. Not only do they have duties and rights (they can sue and be sued, be held legally liable, and be fined) but they also have goals and objectives (namely to make a profit or to achieve some charitable goal if they are not-for-profit corporations). Nor is the corporation's goal reducible to the interests of its members: individuals involved with the corporation may care little or nothing about whether the corporation makes a profit, worrying instead about their salary, job security, work conditions, status among others, or whatever. So because corporations have independent goals, it seems that corporations can also be harmed. Exxon corporation, for example, was probably harmed by the Alaskan oil spill, and certainly US auto makers were harmed by competition from the Japanese in the 1980s.

It is far from clear, however, how the analogy with corporations can be extended to religious, racial, or other groups. Consider the group of people on board an airplane. *Individuals* on the airplane can be harmed, of course, but it makes little sense to ask after a crash whether, in addition to all the deaths, the *group* itself was harmed. One reason that some groups, like corporations, can be harmed while others, such as people on airplanes, cannot is that corporations exist in a legal environment that provides them with their own, independent goal: both their charter and the legal context in which they function define their purpose as making profits for share-holders. A second point, besides legally defined purpose, is that corporations have an organizational structure whose purpose is to achieve the goal. For these reasons, sense can be made of a corporation being harmed in its pursuit of its goals. The situation is different, however, for racial, religious, ethnic, or cultural groups. These groups are socially, not legally created, and obviously do not have a charter defining their goals; nor do they have the organizational structures that allowed us to make sense of a corporation's goals. Lacking a purpose, they therefore cannot be harmed in its pursuit.

It might be argued in response, however, that at least some groups, like religious ones, *can* have defined goals: The goal of the Jewish people, it is sometimes said, is to be a "light unto the nations," and that of Evangelical Christians, to preach salvation. But again it is unclear how to make sense of these "group" goals without assuming there is somebody else, God, who has established the purpose for the groups. But then it would be God, and not the group itself, that has the goal. On the other hand, if God has not established such a purpose then it seems reasonable to think of the goal as residing in individual members, not in the group itself. Similarly, a people or nation are sometimes said to have goals such as creating "socialist man" or achieving "manifest destiny," but again this depends on an organizational structure, usually a government, that represents the people and pursues the objective. Take that structure away, and the "group" goal dissolves.

The claim that hate speech harms a racial, religious, or ethnic group is therefore best not taken literally. Group harm is best understood as a shorthand way of suggesting individual members have been harmed. What sort of harm is then at issue, exactly? And how might hate speech cause it?

5. Cumulative versus Individual Harm

To give this argument its due, we must first distinguish between harms flowing from *individual* actions and *cumulative* harms. Often what is a singly harmless act can be damaging when added to other similar acts. One person walking across a lawn does little damage, but constant walking will destroy the lawn. Indeed the single act might be entirely without negative effect. Pollution, for instance, is often harmful only cumulatively, not singly. Though one car battery's lead may do no harm to those who drink the water downstream, when added to the pollution of many others the cumulative harm can be disastrous.

Further, the fact that it was singly harmless is no justification for performing the act. The complete response to a person who insists that he had a right to pollute since his action did no damage is that if everyone behaved that way great harm would follow: once a legal scheme protecting the environment is in place, criminal law is rightly invoked even against individually harmless acts on grounds of cumulative harm.

It might then be argued that even if individual hate speech acts do not cause harm, it should still be banned because of its cumulatively harmful effects. What might that harm consist in? Defending hate speech codes, Mari J. Matsuda writes that "As much as one may try to resist a piece of hate propaganda, the effect on one's self-esteem and sense of personal security is devastating. To be hated, despised, and alone is the ultimate fear of all human beings. . . . [R]acial inferiority is planted in our minds as an idea that may hold some truth" (Matsuda, 1989, p. 25). Besides the distress caused by the hate speech, Matsuda is suggesting, hate speech victims may also be harmed in either of two ways: reduced self-esteem or increased risk of violence and discrimination. I will begin with self-esteem, turning to questions of violence and discrimination in the next section.

6. Cumulative Harm to Self-esteem

What then is self-esteem? Following Rawls, let us assume that by "self-esteem" or "self-respect" we mean the sense both that one's goals and life-plan are worthwhile and that one has talents and other characteristics sufficient to make their accomplishment possible (Rawls, 1971, pp. 440–6). Loss of self-esteem might therefore constitute harm because it reduces motivation and willingness to put forth effort. If hate-speech victims believe they have little or no chance of success, their future options will be reduced, rather as former slaves are sometimes said to have had their futures foreclosed as a result of the attitudes they inherited from slavery.

Assuming loss of self-esteem is a harm, how plausible is Matsuda's suggestion that hate speech has the (cumulative) effect of reducing it? Many factors can reduce self-esteem. Demeaning portrayals of one's group in the media, widespread anti-social behavior of others in the group, family breakdown, poor performance in school and on the job, drugs, and even well intended affirmative-action programs all may lessen self-esteem. Indeed, I suggest that, absent those other factors, simply being subject to hate speech would not significantly reduce self-esteem. An otherwise secure and confident person might be made angry (or fearful) by racial or other attacks, feeling the speaker is ignorant, rude, or stupid. But without many other factors it is hard to see that hate speech by itself would have much impact on self-esteem. Gerald Gunther, who as a Jew was subjected to some of the worst hate speech imaginable, nevertheless opposes speech codes. While writing eloquently of the distress such speech caused, there is no suggestion that the speech had an impact on the self-esteem of an otherwise self-confident person (Gunther, 1990).

But even assuming hate speech does reduce self-esteem to some degree, notice how far the argument has strayed from the original, robust claim that hate speech should be banned because it causes harm. First each individual act must be added to other acts of hate speech, but then it must also be added to the many other, more important factors that together reduce self-esteem. Given the importance of protecting speech I discussed earlier, and the presumption it creates against censorship, Matsuda's argument that it reduces self-esteem seems far too speculative and indirect to warrant criminalizing otherwise protected speech.

7. Discrimination and Violence as Indirect Harms

But surely, it may be objected, the real issue is simply this: hate speech should be banned because it increases racial or other forms of hatred, which in turn leads to increased violence and discrimination – both of which are obviously harmful. That is a serious claim, and must be taken seriously. Notice first, however, that this effect of hate speech, if it exists, is only indirect; hate speech is harmful only because of its impact on others who are then led in turn to commit acts of violence or discrimination. The claim is not that the speech itself directly caused the harm, but instead that it encouraged attitudes in people who then, on their own, acted wrongly and harmed others.

There are important problems with this as an argument for banning hate speech. One, epistemological problem is whether we really know that the link exists between hate speech, increased hatred, and illegal acts. Suppose we discovered a close correlation between reading hate speech and committing acts of violence – what have we proved? Not, as might be thought, that hate speech causes violence. Rather, we would only know that *either* (A) reading such material increases hatred and violence, *or* (B) those who commit hate crimes also tend to like reading hate speech. The situation with respect to hate speech mirrors arguments about violence and pornography: the observation that rapists subscribe in greater proportion to pornographic magazines than do non-rapists does not show we can reduce rape by banning pornography. Maybe people who rape just tend also to like pornography. Similarly, reduction in hate speech might, or might not, reduce hate-related crime, even assuming that those who commit hate crimes are avid readers of hate literature.

Nor is it clear that hate speech has the effect on people's attitudes that the argument assumes. Consider an example reported recently in Mizzoula, Montana, where a vandal threw a brick through a window of the house of a Jewish family that had put a Menorah in their window to celebrate Hanukkah. In response, much of that overwhelmingly Christian city simply put pictures of a Menorah in their own windows, published in the local newspaper. Far from encouraging anti-Jewish hatred, this act seemed to have the opposite effect. Indeed it seems clear that members of groups who hate-speech regulations are aimed to protect are themselves aware that hate speech can sometimes be beneficial. At my university alone, we have had two incidents in which acts of hate speech were perpetrated by members of the attacked group itself. Evidently, those students believed that rather than increasing hatred they could use hate speech to call attention to problems of racism and anti-semitism and increase people's sympathy, just as occurred in Mizzoula. We cannot assume, therefore, that censoring hate speech would reduce hatred. The reaction in Mizzoula, to meet racist speech with more speech, not only avoided censorship but also allowed people to make a powerful statement of their feelings about the importance of respecting the rights of others in their community.

It is unclear, I am suggesting, that regulating hate speech really would reduce hatred, let alone reduce hate crimes. And that uncertainty matters in the case of speech. Pollution, walking on the grass, and other activities that are less important than speech, and less threatened by governmental regulation, can be restricted without clear demonstration of their harmful effects. We need not wait to see for certain that a product is toxic to ban it; sometimes only a reasonable suspicion is enough if the product is relatively unimportant and the risks it may pose are significant. But speech, I have argued, is not like that. Freedom of expression is of great social value, enjoys the status as a basic right, and is in real danger due to slippery slopes and chilling effects.

There is a further problem, in addition to the epistemological one we have been discussing, with the argument that, by increasing hatred, hate speech in turn leads to more violence and discrimination. Any accused criminal, including one whose acts were motivated by racial or group hatred, must be shown to have *mens rea* or "guilty mind" in order to be convicted. That means, roughly, that the accused must have been aware of the nature of the act, aware that it was illegal or wrong, and was *able to have complied with the law*. But if the person could have complied with the law, then it follows that despite having read or heard the hate speech, and (we are now assuming) thereby had his hatred increased, he must still have been able to ask himself whether he wished to *act* on the basis of that attitude. Between the desire and the action comes the decision. Criminals are not zombies, controlled by their desires and unable to reflect on the nature and quality of their actions. It is no excuse that the criminal acted on a strong desire, whether it was to be wealthy without earning money, have sex without another's consent, or express hatred of a group through violent acts or discrimination.

This means, then, that we have on hand two different ways of dealing with acts of violence and discrimination motivated by hatred: by using government censorship in an effort at thought control, trying to eliminate hatred and prejudice, or by insisting that whether people like somebody or not they cannot assault them or discriminate against them. My suggestion is that passing and vigorously enforcing laws against violence and discrimination themselves is a better method of preventing indirect harm than curtailing speech. Government should not be in the business of making people like each other; it should, however, insist that we treat each other fairly and respect each other's rights. Indeed, using the power of government to persuade people how they should live and whom they should like seem quite incompatible with Mill's claim, discussed earlier, that individual autonomy and freedom are part of the valuable life. Even if we could, through government, force people to share our attitudes it is not clear we should try.

8. Offensive Expression and Epithets

I have argued that hate speech should not be banned on the ground of preventing harm. But government often restricts behavior that is not strictly speaking harmful: it prevents littering, for instance, and limits how high we build our buildings, the drugs we take and the training our doctors receive, to mention only a few examples. Some of these restrictions are controversial, of course, especially ones that seem designed only to keep us from harming ourselves. But others, for example limiting alterations of historic buildings and preventing littering, are rarely disputed. Government also limits various forms of public behavior that are grossly offensive, revolting or shocking. An assault on the sense of smell and hearing, unusual or even common sexual activities in public, extreme provocations of anger, or threats that generate great anxiety or fear, are generally regarded as examples of behavior that can be restricted although they do not cause genuine harm.

Charles Lawrence suggests that this argument also applies to hate speech. The experience of being called "nigger," "spic," "Jap," or "kike," he writes, "is like receiving a slap in the face. The injury is instantaneous" (Lawrence, 1990, pp. 68–9). He describes the experience of a student who was called a "faggot" on a subway: "He found himself in a state of semishock, nauseous, dizzy, unable to muster the witty, sarcastic, articulate rejoinder he was accustomed to making" (Lawrence, 1990, p. 70).

Sometimes, of course, hate speech can be banned, even speech about important public issues. A Nazi yelling about the virtues of Fascism in a public bus or library, for example, can be asked to stop by a policeman. But that is not *content* regulation, unless somebody yelling just as loudly about the virtues of patriotism or of the Republican Party would be permitted to remain. Neutral regulations that prevent people from disturbing others, without regard to what is being said, do not raise the same constitutional and political issues as does content regulation of political speech.

But because of speech's critical importance and government's tendency to regulate and limit political discussion to suit its own ends, I have argued, it is important to limit governmental censorship to narrowly and precisely defined unprotected categories. This provides a more secure protection of speech than allowing officials to balance, case by case, the relative costs and benefits of individual laws government might wish to pass limiting free speech. Assuming that we might wish to keep this unprotected-categories approach, how might offensive hate speech be regulated? One possibility is to allow government to ban speech that "causes substantial distress and offense" to those who hear it. Were we to adopt such a principle, however, we would effectively gut the First Amendment. All kinds of political speech, including much that we would all think must be protected, is offensive to somebody somewhere. "Fuck the draft" is but one of many examples of constitutionally protected offensive speech (*Cohen* v. *California*, 1971); burning the American Flag is another (*Texas* v. *Johnson*, 1989).

Nor would it work to limit the unprotected category to all speech that is distressing and offensive to members of historically stigmatized groups, for that too would sweep far too broadly. Speech critical of peoples, nations, and religious institutions and practices often offends group members, as do discussions of differences between the races and sexes. Social and biological scientists sometimes find themselves confronted by people who have been deeply wounded by their words, as the instructor who got in trouble at the University of Michigan over his comments about sex-linked abilities illustrates. Or what about psychologists who wish to do research into group IQ differences? Should only those who reach conclusions that are not offensive be allowed to publish? Or should we perhaps simply ban research into any topic that offends? Such examples can be repeated endlessly, of course; it is virtually impossible to predict what might be taken as offensive. Even Malcolm X's autobiography might be punishable; he says at one point that "I'd had too much experience that women were only tricky, deceitful, untrustworthy flesh" (Malcolm X, 1964, p. 226).

Others, however, have suggested another, less sweeping approach: why not at least ban racial or other *epithets* since they are a unique form of "speech act" that does not deserve protection. Unlike other forms of protected speech, it is claimed that epithets and name calling are constitutionally useless; they constitute acts of "subordination" that treat others as "moral inferiors" (Altmann, 1993). Racial, religious and ethnic epithets are therefore a distinct type of speech act in which the speaker is subordinating rather than claiming, asserting, requesting, or any of the other array of actions we accomplish with language. So (it is concluded) while all the other types of speech acts deserve protection, mere epithets and slurs do not.

The problem with this argument, however, is that epithets are *not* simply acts of subordination, devoid of social and political significance or meaning, any more than burning a flag is simply an act of heating cloth. Besides "subordinating" another, epithets can also express emotion (anger or hatred, for example) or defiance of authority. And like burning or refusing to salute the flag (both protected acts), epithets also can be seen to express a political message, such as that another person or group is less worthy of moral consideration or is receiving undeserved preferences. That means, then, that however objectionable the content of such epithets is they go well beyond mere acts of "subordination" and therefore must be protected.

It is worth emphasizing, however, that although people have a political and constitutional *right* to use such language, it does not follow that they *should* use it or that they are behaving decently or morally when they exercise the right. A wrong remains a wrong, even if government may for good reason choose not to punish it. I am therefore in no way defending on moral grounds those who utter hate speech – an impossible task, in my view – but instead have tried to show why meeting hatred with more speech, as was done in Mizzoula, is a better response than governmental censorship. Nor is it correct to think that because government allows people to speak it is thereby condoning either the speech or the speaker. Government doesn't condone Christians, Jews, Muslims and atheists by merely allowing them to exercise their religious freedom, as it would if it established and financed one religion. In religious matters, as well as in the case of speech, government's job is to remain neutral.

What, finally, should be said when a university is seeking to prevent harassment by limiting speech that creates a "hostile" environment for faculty and students? Clearly, a university could on aesthetic grounds prevent people from hanging banners or other material from their windows and doors, or pasting billboards on public walls. But again such a regulation must be content neutral; a state university cannot ban some messages while leaving other students, with different, less controversial and offensive views, to express themselves. (Private universities, since they are not run by government and therefore not bound by the First Amendment, are free to impose whatever orthodoxy they choose.)

More than most places, a university is committed to scholarship and the pursuit of knowledge. Freedom of inquiry is its life-blood. That means, however, that nobody can be guaranteed never to be offended or upset. (How often are students in a religion class deeply offended by what they hear? Or conservative Christians by openly gay, or pro-choice speech?) Being forced to confront people with widely different views and attitudes, including those whom we dislike and who dislike us, is rarely easy or pleasant; but it can also be an important part of acquiring an education. Once it is admitted that for purposes of regulating speech *content* there is no such thing as a false idea, Nazi marches have as much constitutional value as civil rights marches, swastikas as much value as anti-war or Israeli symbols, and emotionally charged speeches by members of the Klan as much value as Martin Luther King's "I Have a Dream" speech. Indeed, it is rare that hate speech is merely expressive and does not have at least some political or social content. However offensive and stupid Louis Farrakhan's description of Jews as "blood-sucking" may be, it is more than contentless expression of emotion.

None of this implies, however, that genuine harassment, whether in the workplace or university, should be protected. But harassment is not hate speech. For one thing, to suffer harassment requires more than hearing an offensive remark. Genuine harassment requires a pattern of behavior, not just a single event, and must occur in a context in which its intended victim(s) are made to feel sufficiently intimidated or distressed that their ability to perform is impeded. Nor would verbal harassment be limited to "hate speech" directed at women and racial or ethnic minorities. Vulgar, sexually explicit language directed at a religiously conservative white male could be part of a pattern of harassment of him, for example, as could verbal attacks aimed at people for being short, or in a fraternity, or long haired, or even (a personal concern of mine) being bald. Nor, finally, are acts of harassment limited to speech; other actions (making late-night noise or dumping litter, for example) would also have to be included under a genuine anti-harassment regulation. The point, then, is not that people have a free speech right to harass others. Rather, it is that a ban on harassment would be both broader and narrower than a ban on hate speech. To avoid the charge that they are disguised censorship, harassment regulations must ban more than hate speech as well as avoid treating hate speech per se as harassment.

But how, then, should others respond to those, on a university or off, who are offended and distressed when others exercise their right to speak? When children call each other names and cruelly tease each other, the standard adult response is to work on both sides of the problem. Teasers are encouraged to be more sensitive to others' feelings, and victims are encouraged to ignore the remarks. "Sticks and stones can break my bones, but names can never hurt me" was a commonplace on the playground when I was a child. A minimum of self-assurance and toughness can be expected of people, including students at college.

Like the sexual freedoms of homosexuals, freedom of speech is often the source of great distress to others. I have argued, however, that because of the risks and costs of censorship there is no alternative to accepting those costs, or more precisely to imposing the costs on those who find themselves distressed and offended by the speech. Like people who are offended by homosexuality or inter-racial couples, targets of hate speech can ask why *they* should have to suffer distress. The answer is the same in each case: nobody has the right to demand that government protect them against distress when doing so would violate others' rights. Many of us believe that racists would be better people and lead more worthwhile lives if they didn't harbor hatred, but that belief does not justify restricting their speech, any more than the Puritans' desire to save souls would warrant religious intolerance, or Catholics' moral disapproval of homosexuality justify banning homosexual literature.

References

Abrams v. *United States*, 250 US 616 (1919).

Altmann, A.: "Liberalism and Campus Hate Speech," *Ethics*, 103 (1993).

Cohen v. *California*, 403 US 15 (1971).

Delgado, R.: "Words that Wound: A Tort Action for Racial Insults, Epithets, and Name Calling," 17, *Harvard Civil Rights – Civil Liberties Law Review*, 133 (1982); reprinted in Matsuda et al. (1993).

Dennis v. *United States*, 341 US 494 (1951).

Doe v. *University of Michigan*, 721 F. Supp. 852 (E. D. Mich. 1989).

Dworkin, R.: *Freedom's Law: The Moral Reading of the American Constitution* (Cambridge, MA: Harvard University Press, 1996).

Feinberg, J.: *The Moral Limits of the Criminal Law*, Volume I: *Harm to Others* (New York: Oxford University Press, 1984).

——: *The Moral Limits of the Criminal Law*, Volume II: *Offense to Others* (New York: Oxford University Press, 1985).

Gertz. v. *Robert Welch, Inc.*, 418 US 323, 339 (1974).

Gunther, G.: "Good Speech, Bad Speech – No," *Stanford Lawyer*, 24 (1990).

Lawrence, C.: "If He Hollers Let Him Go: Regulating Racist Speech on Campus," *Duke Law Journal*, 431 (1990); reprinted in Matsuda et al. (1993).

Malcolm X., and Haley, A.: *The Autobiography of Malcolm X* (New York: Grove Press, 1964).

Matsuda, M.: "Public Response to Racist Speech: Considering the Victim's Story," *Michigan Law Review*, 87 (1989); reprinted in Matsuda et al. (1993).

Matsuda, M., Lawrence, C. R., Delgado, R., and Crenshaw, K. W.: *Words that Wound: Critical Race Theory, Assaultive Speech, and the First Amendment* (Boulder, CO: Westview Press, 1993).

May, L.: *The Morality of Groups: Collective Responsibility, Group-Based Harm, and Corporate Rights* (Notre Dame: University of Notre Dame Press, 1987).

Meritor Savings Bank v. *Vinson*, 477 US 57 (1986).

Mill, J. S.: *On Liberty* (Indianapolis, IN: Hackett, 1978).

Rawls, J.: *A Theory of Justice* (Cambridge, MA: Harvard University Press, 1971).

Texas v. *Johnson*, 491 US 397 (1989).

UMV Post v. *Board of Regents of the University of Wisconsin*, 774 F. Supp. 1163 (1991).

Acknowledgments

Earlier versions of this paper were read at the American Philosophical Association Pacific Meetings, St Andrews College, Mansfield University, the University of Glasgow and St Andrews University. I am grateful for the many helpful comments I received on all those occasions, and especially to Jacqueline Mariña and Amy Shapiro.

35

Speech Codes and Feminism

Marilyn Friedman

In the fall of 1990, "political correctness" in the academy emerged as a national news media preoccupation. Political correctness (PC) comprises a host of academic reforms and attitudes that, according to their critics, are destroying higher education and threatening national survival.

The alleged culprit is the academic left, a group encompassing feminists, multiculturalists, Marxists, and deconstructionists. In their teaching and scholarship, these leftist academics are supposed to have launched a full-scale attack on Western civilization. They have replaced the classical works of Western culture with third world, anti-Western trash and have forsaken standards of truth, objectivity, and merit of any sort. They have consolidated their academic power by smuggling unqualified women and minorities into positions of vast academic power and by ruthlessly quashing dissenting voices. Their multicultural machinations will soon surely fragment the United States into an intellectual Yugoslavia.

From the standpoint of the left, however, the picture is quite different. The reforms in question are intended to revamp a host of traditional academic practices and attitudes that constitute the *real* malaise of higher education. The real correctness to worry about, from a leftist perspective, is the "rectitude" of those traditionalists who resist the growing cultural diversity of academia today. The policies of the critics of political correctness would return us to the deplorably homogeneous and exclusionary educational world of yesterday.

Speech Codes

The left has, accordingly, raised critical questions about the quality of everything academic, from esoteric scholarly research to the interpersonal dynamics of daily campus life. Of special concern are campus climates that are often inhospitable to students who are not white, not male, and not heterosexual. In such a climate, offensive comments referring to someone's race, sex, or sexual preference are not an uncommon phenomenon.

In order to deal with the problem of offensive speech, a number of academic institutions have recently tried to implement a novel sort of student behavior code. The codes in question penalize students who use racist, sexist, or homophobic "hate speech" to insult other students. Schools that have experimented with these codes include Stanford University, the University of Michigan, and the University of Wisconsin. The codes have been drafted in an attempt to protect from verbal harassment certain groups of students who are otherwise vulnerable to taunts and insults. The intent of the codes is thus salutary. Nevertheless, they have been widely challenged as unjustified infringements on the First Amendment guarantee of freedom of speech.

Some of the challenges have taken legal form and speech codes have not fared well in the courts. In the fall of 1991, for example, the University of Wisconsin code was overturned by a US district court that held that the code violated the constitutional guarantee of freedom of expression (*UMV Post* v. *Board of Regents of the University of Wisconsin System*, No. 90-C328, Oct. 11, 1991). In 1992, the Supreme Court overturned a St Paul, Minnesota, ordinance that similarly attempted to regulate racial and sexual epithets (*R.A.V.* v. *City of St. Paul* (1992) 112 S.Ct. 2538).

Defenders of speech codes have tried to argue that the insults in question do not merit First Amendment protection because they are a variety of what the Supreme Court has called "fighting words." As defined by the Court in 1942, fighting words are those insults "which by their very utterance inflict injury or tend to incite an immediate breach of the peace" (*Chaplinsky* v. *New Hampshire*, 315 US 568, 569 (1942), at 571–72). In recent years, this court doctrine has been greatly modified but not entirely eliminated. Fighting words can still be penalized provided they pose the "clear and present danger" of a breach of the peace: for instance, a violent reaction by the insulted party (Smolla, 1992, p. 162).

Unfortunately for the codes, court doctrine requires that an immanent danger be demonstrated in each and every case; no particular type of language can be declared punishable in advance. Nevertheless, in its 1992 decision regarding the St Paul, Minnesota, ordinance, the Supreme Court allowed that fighting words could be banned provided the ban was not restricted to certain categories of insults, such as those focusing only on sex or race (Jaschik, 1992, p. A19). Thus, academic speech codes, if carefully drafted, may yet survive their court challenges.

The codes have, nevertheless, faced strong opposition. Regrettably, code critics too often seem far more bothered by requirements *not to express* racism, sexism, and homophobia in public than they are by the prevalence of those attitudes. In this context, however, I will not be defending academic speech codes as such. My concern focuses instead on some disturbing features in the campaign that has been waged against the codes by some of their critics.

First of all, code critics suggest that speech codes are being used to suppress criticism of policies such as affirmative action and abortion rights by treating such criticism as if it were racist or sexist language (Hentoff, 1992, pp. 217–18). To my knowledge, this suggestion is incorrect. Speech codes have been neither designed nor implemented to suppress genuine debate over controversial issues. During the University of Wisconsin's brief period of speech code enforcement, students were penalized for calling other students such obscenities as "fucking bitch" and "fat-ass nigger" (Fineman, 1992, 17). If speech codes were used to punish criticism of, say, abortion or affirmative action, then that would be misuse of the codes. Misuse, however, does not show that codes against racist or sexist insults are themselves wrong. The real issue is whether or not it is legally and morally appropriate for an academic institution to penalize genuine group-based insults used by some students against other students (Fish, 1992).

A second problem with the campaign being waged against speech codes is its occasional hypocrisy. Code critics insistently invoke the constitutional and moral halo of a right to freedom of expression, or free speech. There have been a variety of threats to free speech in recent years, however, and someone who really wants to protect that right should have challenged all of them. Code critics have not always been so consistent.

A genuine defender of free speech would have objected to President George Bush's executive order that prohibited employees in federally funded health clinics from counseling their patients about abortion services. This order was upheld by the US Supreme Court (*Rust* v. *Sullivan* (1991) 111 S.Ct. 1759), although it was subsequently rescinded by the Clinton administration. A genuine defender of free speech should have been just as concerned at the time about the abortion "gag rule" as she was about campus speech codes. The morality of abortion was not at issue; the question was one of free speech – in this case, the freedom of a health care worker to tell a client about a legally available medical service.

Now, someone might try to justify an abortion "gag rule" by arguing that it is all right to curb the speech of anyone who is even partly supported by tax dollars if the taxpayers object to what is being said. Antiabortion taxpayers do not want their tax dollars used to support even the merest mention of abortion. Remember, however, that opinion polls show repeatedly that only a minority of US taxpayers are flatly opposed to abortion under any circumstances (Rodman et al., 1987, p. 137). The relevant principle would have to be something like this: speech that is otherwise legal may be suppressed when it is partly supported by tax money and conflicts with the values of some taxpayers.

That principle, however, condones campus speech codes just as readily as it condones the abortion gag rule. Some taxpayers – I, for one – do not want our tax dollars going to support public universities in which some students may with impugnity call other students "niggers," "bitches," and "faggots." Thus, using the gag rule as a model, college administrators at publicly funded universities are entitled to implement codes that penalize hate speech, as long as at least some of the taxpayers in that state oppose it. The same argument would hold by analogy for private universities whose financial supporters oppose hate speech on their campuses.

On the other hand, if it is wrong for universities to stifle racial and sexual insults, even when their financial supporters oppose such speech, then gag rules are also wrong that prevent health care workers from using polite speech to describe legally available medical services. Consistency calls for the opponents of speech codes to condemn abortion gag rules in the same breath in which they condemn the codes (Smolla, 1992, pp. 216–19). In the case of those who have not done so, it is legitimate to wonder whether they are really defending all free speech or merely speech of a certain sort, in this case, racist, sexist, or homophobic insults.

The third problem with the opposition to speech codes is that it sometimes blurs the issues and switches to a different target. Speech code critics sometimes try to make it seem as if leftist advocacy by itself is as much a violation of free speech rights as are the formal codes. Criticizing speech codes thereby becomes a vehicle for covertly denouncing leftist expression as such without having to respond to its content.

Nat Hentoff, for example, a journalist and veteran free speech proponent, complains that students who advocate leftist views in the classroom create a "chilling atmosphere" that leads other students to censor themselves. According to Hentoff, on one occasion at New York University Law School, a "sizable number" of leftist law students challenged the use of a case that was assigned for moot court competition. The case involved a divorced father who was trying to gain custody of his children because their mother, his ex-wife, had become a lesbian. The students who objected to using the case in moot court apparently thought that lesbian and gay students in the class might be offended by someone arguing on behalf of the father. A chilling atmosphere resulted, according to Hentoff, in which those students who wanted to discuss the case "censored themselves" from saying so (Hentoff, 1992, pp. 218–19).

Why, we should ask, is Hentoff upset about this? Those leftist students who challenged the case were merely exercising their rights to free speech. On the basis of Hentoff's own principles, the fact that some students were chilled by the expression of this view is irrelevant. In a context of virtually unrestricted freedom in the expression of ideas, some people will sometimes say what others find to be chilling. Unrestricted freedom of speech is not a protection merely for those who want to insult women, minorities, lesbians, and gays.

Hentoff opposes speech codes because he does not think that black, female, lesbian, or gay students should be "insulated from barbed language." They should have to learn to respond to language they do not like "with more and better language of their own." On this subject, Hentoff quotes approvingly the words of Gwen Thomas, a "black community college administrator from Colorado." Thomas opposes speech codes on the grounds that students should have to learn "how to deal with adversarial situations" (Hentoff, 1992, pp. 221, 224).

Evidently, Hentoff thinks that non-leftist students should *not* have to learn how to deal with adversarial situations. They should not have to learn to respond, with more and better language of their own, to the leftist views that chill the atmosphere for them.

The problem of free speech is that when a view is expressed by a majority of those present, or even a vocal minority, it may well suppress those who think differently. Rather than being part of the speech-code framework, however, this group pressure is precisely the result of having no prohibitions on the relevant speech. Facing virtually no restrictions, majority opinion or outspoken minority opinion will range wherever it can, and exert the pressures that it exerts. Sometimes the most vocal opinions will be leftist, and when this happens, conservatives and other nonleftists are the ones who will feel a bit of a chill.

If Hentoff really cares about freedom of *all* speech, he should gallantly accept the chilling effects exerted by vocal leftists no less than the chilling effects exerted by conservatives, racists, and bigots of all sorts as the price to be paid for whatever value we gain from freedom of speech. Why should blacks, women, and certain others have to devote extra time responding to chilling or adversarial speech against them if students who dissent from leftist views are permitted to enjoy the luxury of not having to respond to their adversaries? After all, leftist students are entitled to exercise their own vaunted free speech rights, too.

I do not promote speech codes. I do support values of mutual respect, civility, and courtesy wherever possible – and most of the time, a university is a place where upholding these values is eminently possible. Ideally, the members of our academic citizenries (and of our societies at large) should regard hate speech as so morally intolerable that they object to it vocally and point out the bigoted attitudes manifested by such speech. My recommendation, then, is to avoid the use of formal speech codes but to make sure that the issue of offensive speech does not die with the codes.

Antifeminist Backlash Reconsidered

One of the problems with offensive speech is that it can block the sort of thoughtful reflection that we need on urgent issues of the day. Feminism is a collection of viewpoints that has been especially targeted for such suppression. Instead of reasoned discussion of feminist issues, we are more likely to find feminist views being misrepresented and feminist individuals insulted outright.

Feminist women, it seems, have become the females we all love to hate. They are the school marm surrogates of the nineties, at whom we defiantly aim our verbal sling-shots. Nasty fictional women, such as *Fatal Attraction*'s Alex Forrest or *The Last Seduction*'s "Wendy Kroy," conveniently reinforce the stereotypes that rationalize widespread feminist-bashing (Faludi, 1991). And why not bash feminists? For over two decades, they have been challenging deeply rooted conventions of social and cultural life. Surely it is time to strike back.

Mass media promote stereotypes that make it easy to ridicule feminists. The media caricature of a feminist hates the family, hates men, and hates sex. She has nothing but contempt for women who are full-time mothers and homemakers. She is a belligerent shrew or a whining victim (depending on what the audience most detests), yet she has clawed her way to the apex of professional power. Virtually omnipotent, she has caused every contemporary US ill from the collapse of the family to the decline of our global economic preeminence.

It seems as if many people have a perennial need to belittle some group of women or another, to make some women the targets of witch-hunts and the brunt of comic routines. If we did not have feminists to hate, we would have to draft some other category of women into scapegoat service. Women in general should be grateful to feminists for shielding them from the wife- and mother-in-law-bashing that used to be a cultural passtime. ("Family values," perhaps?)

These attacks on feminists, however, are misguided. Feminism has always sought to improve the quality of women's lives by diminishing the exploitations, abuses, and oppressions that afflict various women and by promoting diverse forms of female flourishing. Frivolous attacks on feminism can only serve to undermine the energy and motivation needed to sustain these important social projects. The cost of suppressing feminism will be the loss of real improvements in the lives of many women.

What are some of the improvements that feminism has struggled to achieve? They include ending workpalce discrimination against women; increasing women's participation in government and economy; securing women's reproductive freedom; reducing violence against women; combating the multiple oppressions of minority women; fostering a female-centered eroticism; achieving equal rights for lesbians; curtailing the sexual objectification of women; eliminating cultural misogyny; correcting the scientific misunderstandings of women's health, physiology, and psychology; promoting honesty about marriage and mothering; and ending the sexual exploitation of women.

So why all the fuss? Why is feminism under attack if its goals are exemplary and its value is so great?

One of the striking features of the current campaign against feminism is its anti-intellectual slant and the fact that much of the war is being waged in mass media where a flair for glib wisecracks and an eccentric personality can score more points than thoughtful analysis. The consumers of mass media are busy with their own lives and do not have the time, energy, or inclination to plod through the complicated issues involved. Radio talk show host Rush Limbaugh is a striking example. Consider this idea from his first book: "Feminazi Trading Cards," with "all the vital statistics" on the back, including waist and hip measurements and "number of abortions" (Limbaugh, 1993, p. 204).

Culture critic Camille Paglia is another illustrative example. *Time* magazine recently dubbed Paglia "The Bête Noire of Feminism" and celebrated Paglia's "contempt for modern feminists", which, *Time* unabashedly admitted, has "drawn the media with magnetic force" (Duffy, 1992, pp. 62–3). It is Paglia's personal insults against feminists that seem to attract journalists the most – Germaine Greer is a "drone," Diana Fuss's output is "junk," the feminists concerned with date rape are "sex-phobic, irrational, borderline personalities" (quoted in Duffy, 1992, p. 62; and Chin, 1992, p. 126). Without the empty epithets, Paglia's actual criticisms of feminism are usually rather pedestrian – with a few bizarre exceptions, such as this: "Feminism, with its solemn Carrie Nation repressiveness, does not see what is for men the eroticism or fun element in rape, especially the wild, infectious delirium of gang rape" (Paglia, 1993, p. 64). Is this what Harvard government professor Harvey Mansfield, Jr, had in mind when he hailed Paglia's "fearlessness," her tendency to say "what you're not supposed to" and "tell off the boss" (quoted by Chin, 1992, p. 129)?

Just who is this sex-phobic boss, blind to the delights of gang rape, whom the critics are so busy telling off, and why is everyone so worried about her? The stereotypic feminist, you recall, hates the family, hates men, hates sex, and is contemptuous of full-time mothers and homemakers. What truth is there to this caricature? Frankly very little.

Let us consider feminism's supposed hostility to "the family." The first question to ask is "what do you mean by 'family'"? Social commentators who praise "family values" usually have in mind the values of the so-called "traditional family." The traditional family is a nuclear family consisting of a legally married heterosexual couple and their children, in which the man is the principal breadwinner and head of the household and the woman is responsible for all, or nearly all, the domestic work and child care. As early as 1977, however, this family form comprised only 16 percent of all US households, according to the US Census Bureau (Thorne with Yalom, 1982, p. 5; see also Coontz, 1992).

A family is, generically speaking, any group of persons who together form a household based at least partly on some sort of enduring interpersonal commitment. Legally or religiously sanctioned marriage is one example of such a commitment but it is not the only one. The concept of an enduring household captures the core idea of family life, and it has the credibility of having appeared in dictionary definitions of "family" even before the recent wave of the feminist movement (Funk and Wagnalls, 1965, p. 457).

The notion of an enduring household does not resonate with greeting-card sentimentality, however – and that is its distinct theoretical advantage. The point of the conception is to serve as an analytical category to enable understanding of the institution. To understand contemporary families in their diversity, we need a generic concept of family life that does not presuppose any norms about who is supposed to do what. Family norms should be debated as separately as possible from the relevant descriptive categories.

Defining family generically as any enduring household based on interpersonal commitment allows us to acknowledge the familyness of all sorts of domestic relationships. We already know (although some of us mindlessly forget) that families by *adoption* are genuine families and, thus, that biological links between parents and children are not necessary for family life. It is now high time to give social recognition and support to families comprised of heterosexual couples who are not married (with or without children), heterosexual couples who do not abide by traditional gender roles in domestic tasks or child rearing, lesbian and gay couples (with or without children), and single parents with children.

Any stable and nonoppressive domestic relationship will constitute a better family environment if it is, in turn, sustained by a respectful and supportive community that grants it all the privileges of family life. Feminists work to support nontraditional families, which sadly still receive substantially fewer of the privileges reserved for traditionally correct families (privileges such as inheritance rights and family health insurance) and which suffer a great deal of social stigma instead. In supporting nontraditional families, feminists promote family life more extensively and more thoroughly than our opponents who otherwise intone family values. Feminists, thus, do not oppose family life as such. Far from it. We are just as concerned as anyone else that the familial dimensions of our lives and our various enduring domestic relationships satisfy the needs and promote the flourishing of their participants – all of their participants. It is society at large, not feminists, that, by neglecting or denying the needs of *nontraditional* families, is currently forsaking family life.

When feminists criticize family life, our targets are usually male family dominance and the female dependency that it promotes and enforces. It is patently obvious that to criticize this form of family life is not to oppose family life as such.

It is also patently obvious that to criticize male-dominant families for the risks and oppressions that they pose for women is not to criticize the women who choose such arrangements. Rather, it is to challenge uncritical and overly romantic cultural images of those male-dominant marriage and family forms. Women, depending on their circumstances, might well derive satisfactions within male-dominated marriages and families – but at what cost? The fact that some people are content with certain social arrangements is hardly a conclusive reason to avoid questioning those arrangements.

Some critics have, nevertheless, tried to undermine feminist challenges to *male-dominated* family life by claiming that such families are beneficial for women and that women secretly recognize this. The philosopher and social critic Alan Bloom has argued this line.

Bloom has the candor to admit that the "old family arrangements" were not entirely good for women. He concedes that because of economic changes and the recognition of injustices, "the feminist case [against the old family arrangements] is very strong indeed." The problem, in Bloom's view, is that there are no "viable substitutes." Macho men can be "softened" but they cannot be made caring, sensitive, or nurturant. Men will make positive contributions to family life only in the old-fashioned families in which they can exercise power and protectiveness over "weak," "modest," "blushing" women (Bloom's words). Women's independence, however, diminishes men's motivations for staying thus married and providing for children. And women's premarital sexual independence reduces men's motivations for getting married in the first place. "Women can say they do not care" about this loss of men's interest in them, warns Bloom, "but everyone, and they best of all, knows that they are being, at most, only half truthful with themselves" (Bloom, 1987, pp. 129–32).

This antifeminist theme has a cunning seductiveness to it. It avoids the argument that feminism is bad because it hurts men, an argument that, we must admit, will not necessarily deter women from joining the ranks. Bloom argues instead that feminism *hurts women*. If the very people who might be attracted to feminism can be convinced that feminism is bad *for them*, then there is some chance of stopping the spread of this contagion. The argument hinges on two claims: first, by becoming feminist (too independent, too self-reliant), women will lose male love and male commitment to marriage and family; and secondly, women *really want* male love and commitment more than we want independence – *regardless of what we might think*.

Telling women that feminism will hurt *us* is not a new tactic in the public debate over women's issues. Barbara Ehrenreich found examples of it written over two decades ago by Taylor Caldwell in John Birch Society literature (Ehrenreich, 1983, pp. 158–61). Caldwell argued in 1970 that, over the centuries, women had entrapped and hung on to men both by avoiding opportunities to earn their own incomes and by faking dependent personalities. By encouraging female independence, feminism threatens to undermine this "con." In the years since 1970, certain economic realities have made it harder to persuade women to give up our incomes. Alan Bloom prudently ignores income but the rest of the argument remains unchanged: if women act too independently, we will lose male love and the opportunity for (heterosexual) marriage and family, which, Bloom says, we really want more than anything else.

This message is reminiscent of age-old clichés that warn women not to be too sensible or too self-reliant in our habits. Not too long ago, women were routinely admonished: "men don't make tracks for girls who wear slacks," and "men don't make passes at girls who wear glasses." (In the days before contact lenses, the latter meant giving up clear sightedness in order to please men.) Since our cultural traditions give so little public recognition or esteem to love and friendship among women ourselves, the threat of a woman's being unloved by a man has the public meaning of being unloved, period. What women, other than lesbians, would not be made a little anxious by these sorts of messages?

Challenging male dominance is one of the most explosive of feminist positions. The target is men's ultimate power over traditional family life, which most feminists regard as a material peril and a moral adversity for women and their children. In the mildest forms of male dominance, husbands/fathers love and protect their wives and children with wisdom and kindness. Mild male dominance is benevolent paternalism. In the most virulent forms of male dominance, husbands beat up their wives and children and generally tyrannize over their households.

Many people will concede that tyrannical husbands are a nasty lot. Despite this concession, however, traditional social practices and institutions have often shamefully tolerated such men (Klein, 1982). Part of the feminist fight against male family domination has been the uphill struggle to make social institutions more punitive toward such abuses as wife-battering, marital rape, and incest.

Feminists have also argued that even seemingly benevolent male family domination is a problem for women. There is no reason why a woman should relinquish to her husband her own autonomous selfhood or an equal share of legitimate authority and control over what is, after all, her home and family as much as his. The philosophical tradition is rich with praise for self-determination and the importance of being a "free man." Until the recent decades of contemporary feminism, however, the ideals of liberty and autonomy were *never* applied by conventional (usually male) philosophers to female roles. At stake is the legitimacy of women following our own considered judgments about what is worth valuing and pursuing in our family lives. It is no less than a question of women's moral integrity.

If a woman is economically dependent on her husband or male partner, then male family dominance threatens more than a woman's moral integrity. It also threatens her material well-being and that of her children (Okin, 1989, ch. 7). For financial reasons alone, she, much more than he, needs the relationship to persist. Her financial standard of living would be likely to plummet after divorce or break-up while his would almost certainly rise. She thus has more need to please and defer to him than vice versa in those inevitable situations in which their desires or values conflict. One overriding concern that keeps many battered women tied to their violent husbands is the fear of losing financial support, a paramount consideration when children are involved.

To be sure, there have always been some women who were strong and independent enough to stand up to their husbands for the views and values to which they were committed. There have also, fortunately, been men who did not avail themselves of the power provided by their breadwinning status and legitimized by masculine ideals of forcefulness and aggressiveness. There are, in other words, genuinely good men.

Such men, however, run the risk of being socially stigmatized as "wimps." The comic, though often sympathetic, figure of the "hen-pecked husband" only makes sense against a background presumption that men ought to prevail in their marriages and heterosexual relationships. "Taming" the "shrew" is, after all, part of the Western canon (Shakespeare, 1928). The rooster-pecked wife, by contrast, is not even a recognized category. Remember that it was *his* castle, not hers, the place where he was supposed to rule supreme.

If women are to choose their ways of life with some measure of autonomy and wisdom, then they should understand the risks inherent in the available options. Offensive speech that dismisses feminist concerns by mere ridicule and personal insults makes careful and reasoned public debate about the issues almost impossible. Such speech is a profound offense against all women.

References

Bloom, Alan: *The Closing of the American Mind* (New York: Simon & Schuster, 1987).

Chaplinsky v. *New Hampshire*, 315 US 568, 569 (1942).

Chin, Paula: "Street fighting woman," *People* (April 20, 1992), pp. 125–7.

Coontz, Stephanie: *The Way We Never Were: American Families and the Nostalgia Trap* (New York: Basic Books, 1992).

Duffy, Martha: "The bête noire of feminism," *Time* (January 13, 1992), pp. 62–3.

Ehrenreich, Barbara: *The Hearts of Men: American Dreams and the Flight from Commitment* (New York: Doubleday, 1983).

Faludi, Susan: *Backlash: The Undeclared War against American Women* (New York: Crown, 1991).

Fineman, Martha Albert: "Who pays for free speech?", *Women's Review of Books*, 9, no. 5 (1992), p. 17.

Fish, Stanley: "There's no such thing as free speech and it's a good thing, too," *Debating P.C.*, ed. Paul Berman (New York: Dell, 1992), pp. 231–45.

Funk & Wagnalls: *Standard Dictionary of the English Language* (Chicago: Encyclopaedia Britannica, 1965).

Hentoff, Nat: "'Speech codes' on the campus and problems of free speech," *Debating P.C.*, ed. Paul Berman (New York: Dell, 1992), pp. 215–24. Reprinted from *Dissent* (Fall 1991).

Jaschik, Scott: "Campus 'hate speech' code in doubt after high court rejects a city ordinance," *Chronicle of Higher Education*, July 1, 1992, pp. A19, A22.

Klein, Dorie: "The dark side of marriage: battered wives and the domination of women," *Judge, Lawyer, Victim, Thief: Women, Gender Roles, and Criminal Justice* (Boston: Northeastern University Press, 1982), pp. 83–107.

Limbaugh, Rush: *The Way Things Ought to Be* (New York: Simon & Schuster, 1993).

Okin, Susan Moller: *Justice, Gender, and the Family* (New York: Basic Books, 1989).

Paglia, Camille: "It's a jungle out there so get used to it!", *Utne Reader*, January/February 1993, pp. 61–5.

R.A.V. v. *City of St Paul* (1992) 112 S.Ct. 2538.

Rodman, Hyman; Sarvis, Betty; and Bonar, Joy Walker: *The Abortion Question* (New York: Columbia University Press, 1987).

Rust v. *Sullivan* (1991) 111 S.Ct. 1759.

Shakespeare, William: *The Taming of the Shrew* (Cambridge: Cambridge University Press, 1928).

Smolla, Rodney A.: *Free Speech in an Open Society* (New York: Alfred A. Knopf, 1992).

Thorne, Barrie with Marilyn Yalom, eds: *Rethinking the Family: Some Feminist Questions* (New York: Longman, 1982).

UMV post v. *Board of Regents of the University of Wisconsin System*, No. 90-C328, Oct. 11, 1991.

Sexual and Racial Discrimination

Several times in this volume I have pointed out that even when people embrace the same general moral principle, they may disagree dramatically over practical moral questions. For instance, in the previous section I explained that although most people assert that we should limit speech only if it demonstrably harms others, they often disagree about what counts as harm and whether particular actions do harm others. Thus, at the more abstract level of principles it appears most people hold the same moral view, while at the practical level people often hold profoundly different views.

In this section we see a similar gap between abstract principles and concrete behavior. Few people unabashedly champion racism or sexism – and those that do, rarely populate courses like this one. That does not mean, however, that everyone agrees about how we should treat people of different races and genders. Anything but. Only the most naive person would think that we are not still a racist and sexist society. Many of us see within ourselves, much to our chagrin, remnants of our racist and sexist past. We all occasionally see those tendencies in others. Thus, the real questions are not whether we are or should be racist or sexist, but (1) exactly what we mean by "racism" and "sexism," (2) just how pervasive racism and sexism are, and (3) how, precisely, should people of different races and different genders relate?

This explains why I have not included any essays advocating racism or sexism. These are not now positions intelligent people openly advocate. That just isn't where the current debate is being waged. The real debates center on a range of practical issues about discrimination toward people of different races and different genders. The essays in this section discuss some of those debates.

Appiah's discussion of racism not only illuminates the forms racism takes in our culture, he also focuses our attention on important theoretical questions: (1) the extent to which we define ourselves and others by group membership, and (2) the nature and power of subconscious forces that lead people to discriminate against others, even when they claim to be neither racists or sexists. Appiah's discussion of the first question will inform debates about the moral status of groups, debates that played a key role in the essays by Langton and

Arthur in the previous section (FREE SPEECH). The second question is pivotal for understanding discrimination in our culture. Few people openly recommend racism and sexism, yet we are, individually and collectively, racists and sexists. How could that be? The answer must be found in the powerful role that subconscious forces play in our lives. We react and behave as racists and sexists, but are unaware (or only marginally aware) of what we do. Only by attending to these forces can we have any hope of understanding and controlling them.

Although the remainder of these selections focus on sexual discrimination, the authors discuss these issues in ways that will illuminate racial discrimination. For instance, Cudd asks whether some women choose to be oppressed, and, if so, whether that makes their oppression less morally objectionable. Although she focuses on women's choices, her analysis has clear implications for racism. One common objection to programs like AFFIRMATIVE ACTION is that since minorities have chosen their current lifestyles ("if they wanted to escape poverty, they could"), then they neither need nor deserve affirmative action.

The central concern of Cudd's paper is how to distinguish free choices from coerced choices. There is a temptation to think that an individual is free as long as she selects among available options. The question, though, according to Cudd, is whether her options were inappropriately limited by the actions of others. If she chooses among five options, yet men have excluded all the attractive options, then she is not free. Since institutional structures and the actions of individuals have limited the options available to most women, then their choices are coerced, not wholly free. Thus, although their choices might be prudent given their options, that does not alter the fact that they were oppressed.

Whether you agree with Cudd that women's options have been unjustly limited, the underlying issue is crucial: under what conditions are we really free? Answering this question will have bearing on many practical issues, including the discussion of AFFIRMATIVE ACTION in the following section. For if women or blacks have been inappropriately forced into their current economic and social niches, does society now have an obligation to give them recompense for previous treatment or to improve their competitive advantage for jobs or placement in educational institutions?

The final three selections discuss issues on the borders of sexism and SEXUALITY. The first topic – sexual harassment – has been widely discussed in the popular press. The issue gained prominence during the confirmation hearings for Clarence Thomas, a nominee to the United States Supreme Court. A former employee of Thomas's, Anita Hill, claimed he had sexually harassed her on numerous occasions. This case highlights all the relevant questions: what, exactly, is sexual harassment, and why is it so bad? Thomas's main line of defense was that he did not intend to harass anyone, and that many women who worked with him did not interpret his behavior as harassing. Thomas thus embraced what Superson calls the "subjective view of harassment" – the view that an action is harassment only if it, in fact, bothers the women. She argues we should supplant this view with an "objective view of harassment," which holds that an action is harassment if it helps perpetuate the view that men are superior to, and should have control over, women.

That explains why she thinks sexual harassment is not a wrong merely to the specific women being harassed. Instead, it wrongs all women. The underlying idea here is that women, as a group, have interests that we can harm – or promote. This view contrasts with Arthur's rejection of the claim that groups can be harmed (FREE SPEECH). We have seen this debate over the moral status of groups before. We will see it again in May's and Strikwerda's paper later in this section. They argue not merely that the actions of others can harm groups, but that groups can be responsible for harms perpetuated by individual members of their group. Almost certainly Arthur would also find this claim unreasonable. However, this disagreement emphasizes again the significance of determining whether groups have moral status.

The paper by Pineau discusses a topic widely discussed on university campuses: date rape. Available evidence suggests that date rape is far more common than we would like to admit. Several significant court cases in the United States – the trials of William Kennedy Smith (the nephew of former US President John Kennedy) and of heavyweight fighter Michael Tyson – made citizens vividly aware of this phenomenon. These cases accent some conceptual and moral quandaries about date rape. Virtually everyone agrees that rape is bad, even if, and perhaps especially if, the perpetrator and the victim know one another.

However, people disagree vehemently about how, in particular cases, to distinguish consensual sex from date rape. We can all agree about paradigm cases of consensual sex – when it is clear to everyone that both parties are eager participants. We can also agree about paradigm cases of forced rape – when a woman is taken forcibly from her home, physically assaulted, and raped. However, in the two aforementioned cases, the public was not so sure. Neither defendant denied that he had had sex with the victim. Both defended themselves by arguing that the woman had consented to sex. Kennedy's jurors believed his account of events and acquitted him, while Tyson's jurors did not believe him, and convicted him of rape. Admittedly the facts of the cases differ, but I suspect the different verdicts reflect the public's confusion about when sex is consensual, and when it is rape.

The problems in deciding if date rape has occurred are twofold. Criminal law, which we discuss in the following section (PUNISHMENT), typically holds that we should punish a person for a crime only if he has the appropriate *mens rea* or "guilty mind." If a person does not have a guilty mind, then we should not punish him. On this view, a man charged with rape who sincerely believes that the woman consented would not have a guilty mind, and therefore would not be guilty of rape. However, Pineau claims that the relevant question is not whether the man thought she consented, but whether his belief was reasonable. To this extent, Pineau advocates an "objective view of rape" not unlike Superson's "objective view of sexual harassment."

The second (related) issue is what must a woman do to show (especially in court) that she did not consent. The legal assumption, at least for people who know each other (as in date rape), is that the woman must give clear and strong evidence that she did not consent. Lacking such evidence, jurors will be likely to construe the fact that she dated the man as *prima facie* evidence that she did, in fact, consent. Pineau rejects this presumption, which, she claims, is founded on a series of myths about women, sex, and rape.

Further Reading

Card, C. (ed.) 1991: *Feminist Ethics*. Lawrence, KA: University of Kansas Press.

Friedman, M. and May, L. 1985: "Harming Women as a Group," *Social Theory and Practice*, 11: 208–34.

Griffin, S. 1971: "Rape: The All-American Crime." *Ramparts*: 26–35.

Jaggar, A. 1983: *Feminist Politics and Human Nature*. Totowa, NJ: Rowman and Allenheld.

Kittay, E. and Myers, D. (eds) 1987: *Women and Moral Theory*. Totowa, NJ: Rowman and Allenheld.

Levin, M. 1987: *Feminism and Freedom*. New Brunswick, NJ: Transaction Books.

Mill, J. S. 1988: *On the Subjection of Women*. Indianapolis: Hackett.

Scully, D. 1990: *Understanding Sexual Violence*. Boston: Unwin Hyman.

Vetterling-Braggin, M., Elliston, F., and English, J. (eds) 1978: *Feminism and Philosophy*. Totowa, NJ: Rowman and Allenheld.

West, C. 1993: *Race Matters*. Boston: Beacon Press.

36

Racisms

Kwame Anthony Appiah

If the people I talk to and the newspapers I read are representative and reliable, there is a good deal of racism about. People and policies in the United States, in Eastern and Western Europe, in Asia and Africa and Latin America are regularly described as "racist." Australia had, until recently, a racist immigration policy; Britain still has one; racism is on the rise in France; many Israelis support Meir Kahane, an anti-Arab racist; many Arabs, according to a leading authority, are anti-Semitic racists;[1] and the movement to establish English as the "official language" of the United States is motivated by racism. Or, at least, so many of the people I talk to, and many of the journalists with the newspapers I read, believe.

But visitors from Mars – or from Malawi – unfamiliar with the Western concept of racism could be excused if they had some difficulty in identifying what exactly racism was. We see it everywhere, but rarely does anyone stop to say what it is, or to explain what is wrong with it. Our visitors from Mars would soon grasp that it had become at least conventional in recent years to express abhorrence for racism. They might even notice that those most often accused of it – members of the South African Nationalist party, for example – may officially abhor it also. But if they sought in the popular media of our day – in newspapers and magazines, on television or radio, in novels or films – for an explicit definition of this thing "we" all abhor, it is very likely they would be disappointed.

Now, of course, this would be true of many of our most familiar concepts. *Sister, chair, tomato* – none of these gets defined in the course of our daily business. But the concept of racism is in worse shape than these. For much of what we say about it is, on the face of it, inconsistent.

It is, for example, held by many to be racist to refuse entry to a university to an otherwise qualified "Negro" candidate, but not to be so to refuse entry to an equally qualified "Caucasian" one. But "Negro" and "Caucasian" are both alleged to be names of races, and invidious discrimination on the basis of race is usually held to be a paradigm case of racism. Or, to take another example, it is widely believed to be evidence of an unacceptable racism to exclude people from clubs on the basis of race; yet most people, even those who think of "Jewish" as a racial term, seem to think that there is nothing wrong with Jewish clubs, whose members do not share any particular religious beliefs, or Afro-American societies, whose members share the juridical characteristic of American citizenship and the "racial" characteristic of being black.

I say that these are inconsistencies "on the face of it," because, for example, affirmative action in university admissions is importantly different from the earlier refusal to admit blacks or Jews (or other "Others") that it is meant, in part, to correct. Deep enough analysis may reveal it to be quite consistent with the abhorrence of racism; even a shallow analysis suggests that it is intended to be so. Similarly, justifications can be offered for "racial" associations in a plural society that are not available for the racial exclusivism of the country club. But if we take racism seriously we ought to be concerned about the adequacy of these justifications.

In this essay, then, I propose to take our ordinary ways of thinking about race and racism and point up some of their presuppositions. And since popular concepts are, of course, usually fairly fuzzily and untheoretically conceived, much of what I have to say will seem to be both more theoretically and more precisely committed than the talk of racism and racists in our newspapers and on television. My claim is that these theoretical claims are required to make sense of racism as the practice of reasoning human beings. If anyone were to suggest that much, perhaps most, of what goes under the name "racism" in our world cannot be given such a rationalized foundation, I should not disagree; but to the extent that a practice cannot be rationally reconstructed it ought, surely, to be given up by reasonable people. The right tactic with racism, if you really want to oppose it, is to object to it rationally in the form in which it stands the best chance of meeting objections. The doctrines I want to discuss can be rationally articulated; and they are worth articulating rationally in order that we can rationally say what we object to in them.

Racist Propositions

There are at least three distinct doctrines that might be held to express the theoretical content of what we call "racism." One is the view – which I shall call *racialism*[2] – that there are heritable characteristics, possessed by members of our species, that allow us to divide them into a small set of races, in such a way that all the members of these races share certain traits and tendencies with each other that they do not share with members of any other race. These traits and tendencies characteristic of a race constitute, on the racialist view, a sort of racial essence; and it is part of the content of racialism that the essential heritable characteristics of what the nineteenth century called the "Races of Man" account for more than the visible morphological characteristics – skin color, hair type, facial features – on the basis of which we make our informal classifications. Racialism is at the heart of nineteenth-century Western attempts to develop a science of racial difference; but it appears to have been believed by others – for example, Hegel, before then, and many in other parts of the non-Western world since – who have had no interest in developing scientific theories.

Racialism is not, in itself, a doctrine that must be dangerous, even if the racial essence is thought to entail moral and intellectual dispositions. Provided positive moral qualities are distributed across the races, each can be respected, can have its "separate but equal" place. Unlike most Western-educated people, I believe – and I have argued elsewhere[3] – that racialism is false; but by itself, it seems to be a cognitive rather than a moral problem. The issue is how the world is, not how we would want it to be.

Racialism is, however, a presupposition of other doctrines that have been called "racism," and these other doctrines have been, in the last few centuries, the basis of a great deal of human suffering and the source of a great deal of moral error.

One such doctrine we might call "extrinsic racism": extrinsic racists make moral distinctions between members of different races because they believe that the racial essence entails certain morally relevant qualities. The basis for the extrinsic racists' discrimination between people is their belief that members of different races differ in respects that *warrant* the differential treatment, respects – such as honesty or courage or intelligence – that are uncontroversially held (at least in most contemporary cultures) to be acceptable as a basis for treating people differently. Evidence that there are no such differences in morally relevant characteristics – that Negroes do not necessarily lack intellectual capacities, that Jews are not especially avaricious – should thus lead people out of their racism if it is purely extrinsic. As we know, such evidence often fails to change an extrinsic racist's attitudes substantially, for some of the extrinsic racist's best friends have always been Jewish. But at this point – if the racist is sincere – what we have is no longer a false doctrine but a cognitive incapacity, one whose significance I shall discuss later in this essay.

I say that the *sincere* extrinsic racist may suffer from a cognitive incapacity. But some who espouse extrinsic racist doctrines are simply insincere intrinsic racists. For *intrinsic racists*, on my definition, are people who differentiate morally between members of different races because they believe that each race has a different moral status, quite independent of the moral characteristics entailed by its racial essence. Just as, for example, many people assume that the fact that they are biologically related to another person – a brother, an aunt, a cousin – gives them a moral interest in that person,[4] so an intrinsic racist holds that the bare fact of being of the same race is a reason for preferring one person to another. (I shall return to this parallel later as well.)

For an intrinsic racist, no amount of evidence that a member of another race is capable of great moral, intellectual, or cultural achievements, or has characteristics that, in members of one's own race, would make them admirable or attractive, offers any ground for treating that person as he or she would treat similarly endowed members of his or her own race. Just so, some sexists are "intrinsic sexists," holding that the bare fact that someone is a woman (or man) is a reason for treating her (or him) in certain ways.

There are interesting possibilities for complicating these distinctions: some racists, for example, claim, as the Mormons once did, that they discriminate between people because they believe that God requires them to do so. Is this an extrinsic racism, predicated on the combination of God's being an intrinsic racist and the belief that it is right to do what God wills? Or is it intrinsic racism because it is based on the belief that God requires these discriminations because they are right? (Is an act pious because the gods love it, or do they love it because it is pious?) Nevertheless, the distinctions between racialism and racism and between two potentially overlapping kinds of racism provide us with the skeleton of an anatomy of the propositional contents of racial attitudes.

Racist Dispositions

Most people will want to object already that this discussion of the propositional content of racist moral and factual beliefs misses something absolutely crucial to the character of the psychological and sociological reality of racism, something I touched on when I mentioned that extrinsic racist utterances are often made by people who suffer from what I called a "cognitive incapacity." Part of the standard force of accusations of racism is that their objects are in some way *irrational*. The objection to Professor Shockley's claims about the intelligence of blacks is not just that they are false; it is rather that Professor Shockley seems, like many people we call "racist," to be unable to see that the evidence does not support his factual claims and that the connection between his factual claims and his policy prescriptions involves a series of non sequiturs.

What makes these cognitive incapacities especially troubling – something we should respond to with more than a recommendation that the individual, Professor Shockley, be offered psychotherapy – is that they conform to a certain pattern: namely, that it is especially where beliefs and policies are to the disadvantage of nonwhite people that he shows the sorts of disturbing failure that have made his views both notorious and notoriously unreliable. Indeed, Professor Shockley's reasoning works extremely well in some other areas: that he is a Nobel Laureate in physics is part of what makes him so interesting an example.

This cognitive incapacity is not, of course, a rare one. Many of us are unable to give up beliefs that play a part in justifying the special advantages we gain (or hope to gain) from our positions in the social order – in particular, beliefs about the positive characters of the class of people who share that position. Many people who express extrinsic racist beliefs – many white South Africans, for example – are beneficiaries of social orders that deliver advantages to them by virtue of their "race," so that their disinclination to accept evidence that would deprive them of a justification for those advantages is just an instance of this general phenomenon.

So too, evidence that access to higher education is as largely determined by the quality of our earlier educations as by our own innate talents, does not, on the whole, undermine the confidence of college entrants from private schools in England or the United States or Ghana. Many of them continue to believe in the face of this evidence that their acceptance at "good" universities shows them to be intellectually better endowed (and not just better prepared) than those who are rejected. It is facts such as these that give sense to the notion of false consciousness, the idea that an ideology can prevent us from acknowledging facts that would threaten our position.

The most interesting cases of this sort of ideological resistance to the truth are not, perhaps, the ones I have just mentioned. On the whole, it is less surprising, once we accept the admittedly problematic notion of self-deception, that people who think that certain attitudes or beliefs advantage them or those they care about should be able, as we say, to "persuade" themselves to ignore evidence that undermines those beliefs or attitudes. What is more interesting is the existence of people who resist the truth of a proposition while thinking that its wider acceptance would in no way disadvantage them or those individuals about whom they care – this might be thought to describe Professor Shockley; or who resist the truth when they recognize that its acceptance would actually advantage them – this might be the case with some black people who have internalized negative racist stereotypes; or who fail, by virtue of their ideological attachments, to recognize what is in their own best interests at all.

My business here is not with the psychological or social processes by which these forms of ideological resistance operate, but it is important, I think, to see the refusal on the part of some extrinsic racists to accept evidence against the beliefs as an instance of a widespread phenomenon in human affairs. It is a plain fact, to which theories of ideology must address themselves, that our species is prone both morally and intellectually to such distortions of judgment, in particular to distortions of judgment that reflect partiality. An inability to change your mind in the face of appropriate[5] evidence is a cognitive incapacity: but it is one that all of us surely suffer from in some areas of belief; especially in areas where our own interests or self-images are (or seem to be) at stake.

It is not, however, as some have held, a tendency that we are powerless to resist. No one, no doubt, can be impartial about everything – even about everything to which the notion of partiality applies; but there is no subject matter about which most sane people cannot, in the end, be persuaded to avoid partiality in judgment. And it may help to shake the convictions of those whose incapacity derives from this sort of ideological defense if we show them how their reaction fits into this general pattern. It is, indeed, because it generally *does* fit this pattern that we call such views "racism" – the suffix "-ism" indicating that what we have in mind is not simply a theory but an ideology. It would be odd to call someone brought up in a remote corner of the world with false and demeaning views about white people a "racist" if that person gave up these beliefs quite easily in the face of appropriate evidence.

Real live racists, then, exhibit a systematically distorted rationality, the kind of systematically distorted rationality that we are likely to call "ideological." And it is a distortion that is especially striking in the cognitive domain: extrinsic racists, as I said earlier, however intelligent or otherwise well informed, often fail to treat evidence against the theoretical propositions of extrinsic racism dispassionately. Like extrinsic racism, intrinsic racism can also often be seen as ideological; but since scientific evidence is not going to settle the issue, a failure to see that it is wrong represents a cognitive incapacity only on controversially realist views about morality. What makes intrinsic racism similarly ideological is not so much the failure of inductive or deductive rationality that is so striking in someone like Professor Shockley but rather the connection that it, like extrinsic racism, has with the interests – real or perceived – of the dominant group.[6] Shockley's racism is in a certain sense directed *against* nonwhite people: many believe that his views would, if accepted, operate against their objective interests, and he certainly presents the black "race" in a less than flattering light.

I propose to use the old-fashioned term "racial prejudice" in the rest of this essay to refer to the deformation of rationality in judgment that characterizes those whose racism is more than a theoretical attachment to certain propositions about race.

Racial Prejudice

It is hardly necessary to raise objections to what I am calling "racial prejudice"; someone who exhibits such deformations of rationality is plainly in trouble. But it is important to remember that propositional racists in a racist culture have false moral beliefs but may not suffer from racial prejudice. Once we show them how society has enforced extrinsic racist stereotypes, once we ask them whether they really believe that race in itself, independently of those extrinsic racist beliefs, justifies differential treatment, many will come to give up racist propositions, although we must remember how powerful a weight of authority our arguments have to overcome. Reasonable people may insist on substantial evidence if they are to give up beliefs that are central to their cultures.

Still, in the end, many will resist such reasoning; and to the extent that their prejudices are really not subject to any kind of rational control, we may wonder whether it is right to treat such people as morally responsible for the acts their racial prejudice motivates, or morally reprehensible for holding the views to which their prejudice leads them. It is a bad thing that such people exist; they are, in a certain sense, bad people. But it is not clear to me that they are responsible for the fact that they are bad. Racial prejudice, like prejudice generally, may threaten an agent's autonomy, making it appropriate to treat or train rather than to reason with them.

But once someone has been offered evidence both (1) that their reasoning in a certain domain is distorted by prejudice, and (2) that the distortions conform to a pattern that suggests a lack of impartiality, they ought to take special care in articulating views and proposing policies in that domain. They ought to do so because, as I have already said, the phenomenon of partiality in judgment is well attested in human affairs. Even if you are not immediately persuaded that you are yourself a victim of such a distorted rationality in a certain domain, you should keep in mind always that this is the usual position of those who suffer from such prejudices. To the extent that this line of thought is not one that itself falls within the domain in question, one can be held responsible for not subjecting judgments that *are* within that domain to an especially extended scrutiny; and this is *a fortiori* true if the policies one is recommending are plainly of enormous consequence.

If it is clear that racial prejudice is regrettable, it is also clear in the nature of the case that providing even a superabundance of reasons and evidence will often not be a successful way of removing it. Nevertheless, the racist's prejudice will be articulated through the sorts of theoretical propositions I dubbed extrinsic and intrinsic racism. And we should certainly be able to say something reasonable about why these theoretical propositions should be rejected.

Part of the reason that this is worth doing is precisely the fact that many of those who assent to the propositional content of racism do not suffer from racial prejudice. In a country like the United States, where racist propositions were once part of the national ideology, there will be many who assent to racist propositions simply because they were raised to do so. Rational objection to racist propositions has a fair chance of changing such people's beliefs.

Extrinsic and Intrinsic Racism

It is not always clear whether someone's theoretical racism is intrinsic or extrinsic, and there is certainly no reason why we should expect to be able to settle the question. Since the issue probably never occurs to most people in these terms, we cannot suppose that they must have an answer. In fact, given the definition of the terms I offered, there is nothing barring someone from being both an intrinsic and an extrinsic racist, holding both that the bare fact of race provides a basis for treating members of his or her own race differently from others and that there are morally relevant characteristics that are differentially distributed among the races. Indeed, for reasons I shall discuss in a moment, *most* intrinsic racists are likely to express extrinsic racist beliefs, so that we should not be surprised that many people seem, in fact, to be committed to both forms of racism.

The Holocaust made unreservedly clear the threat that racism poses to human decency. But it also blurred our thinking because in focusing our attention on the racist character of the Nazi atrocities, it obscured their character as atrocities. What is appalling about Nazi racism is not just that it presupposes, as all racism does, false (racialist) beliefs – not simply that it involves a moral incapacity (the inability to extend our moral sentiments to all our fellow creatures) and a moral failing (the making of moral distinctions without moral differences) – but that it leads, first, to oppression and then to mass slaughter. In recent years, South African racism has had a similar distorting effect. For although South African racism has not led to killings on the scale of the Holocaust – even if it has both left South Africa judicially executing more (mostly black) people per head of population than most other countries and led to massive differences between the life chances of white and nonwhite South Africans – it *has* led to the systematic oppression and economic exploitation of people who are not classified as "white," and to the infliction of suffering on citizens of all racial classifications, not least by the police state that is required to maintain that exploitation and oppression.

Part of our resistance, therefore, to calling the racial ideas of those, such as the Black Nationalists of the 1960s, who advocate racial solidarity, by the same term that we use to describe the attitudes of Nazis or of members of the South African Nationalist party, surely resides in the fact that they largely did not contemplate using race as a basis for inflicting harm. Indeed, it seems to me that there is a significant pattern in the modern rhetoric of race, such that the discourse of racial solidarity is usually expressed through the language of *intrinsic* racism, while those who have used race as the basis for oppression and hatred have appealed to *extrinsic* racist ideas. This point is important for understanding the character of contemporary racial attitudes.

The two major uses of race as a basis for moral solidarity that are most familiar in the West are varieties of Pan-Africanism and Zionism. In each case it is presupposed that a "people," Negroes or Jews, has the basis for shared political life in the fact of being of the same race. There are varieties of each form of "nationalism" that make the basis lie in shared traditions; but however plausible this may be in the case of Zionism, which has in Judaism, the religion, a realistic candidate for a common and nonracial focus for nationality, the peoples of Africa have a good deal less in common culturally than is usually assumed. I discuss this issue at length in *In My Father's House: Essays in the Philosophy of African Culture*, but let me say here that I believe the central fact is this: what blacks in the West, like secularized Jews, have mostly in common is that they are perceived – both by themselves and by others – as belonging to the same race, and that this common race is used by others as the basis for discriminating against them. "If you ever forget you're a Jew, a goy will remind you." The Black Nationalists, like some Zionists, responded to their experience of racial discrimination by accepting the racialism it presupposed.[7]

Although race is indeed at the heart of Black Nationalism, however, it seems that it is the fact of a shared race, not the fact of a shared racial character, that provides the basis for solidarity. Where racism is implicated in the basis for national solidarity, it is intrinsic, not (or not only) extrinsic. It is this that makes the idea of fraternity one that is naturally applied in nationalist discourse. For, as I have already observed, the moral status of close family members is not normally thought of in most cultures as depending on qualities of character: we are supposed to love our brothers and sisters in spite of their faults and not because of their virtues. Alexander Crummell, one of the founding fathers of Black Nationalism, literalizes the metaphor of family in these startling words:

> Races, like families, are the organisms and ordinances of God: and race feeling, like family feeling, is of divine origin. The extinction of race feeling is just as possible as the extinction of family feeling. Indeed, a race *is* a family.[8]

It is the assimilation of "race feeling" to "family feeling" that makes intrinsic racism seem so much less objectionable than extrinsic racism. For this metaphorical identification reflects the fact that, in the modern world (unlike the nineteenth century), intrinsic racism is acknowledged almost exclusively as the basis of feelings of community. We can surely, then, share a sense of what Crummell's friend and co-worker Edward Blyden called "the poetry of politics," that is, "the feeling of race," the feeling of "people with whom we are connected."[9] The racism here is the basis of acts of supererogation, the treatment of others better than we otherwise might, better than moral duty demands of us.

This is a contingent fact. There is no logical impossibility in the idea of racialists whose moral beliefs lead them to feelings of hatred for other races while leaving no room for love of members of their own. Nevertheless most racial hatred is in fact expressed through extrinsic racism: most people who have used race as the basis for causing harm to others have felt the need to see the others as independently morally flawed. It is one thing to espouse fraternity without claiming that your brothers and sisters have any special qualities that deserve recognition, and another to espouse hatred of others who have done nothing to deserve it.[10]

Many Afrikaners – like many in the American South until recently – have a long list of extrinsic racist answers to the question why blacks should not have full civil rights. Extrinsic racism has usually been the basis for treating people worse than we otherwise might, for giving them less than their humanity entitles them to. But this too is a contingent fact. Indeed, Crummell's guarded respect for white people derived from a belief in the superior moral qualities of the Anglo-Saxon race.

Intrinsic racism is, in my view, a moral error. Even if racialism were correct, the bare fact that someone was of another race would be no reason to treat them worse – or better – than someone of my race. In our public lives, people are owed treatment independently of their biological characters: if they are to be differently treated there must be some morally relevant difference between them. In our private lives, we are morally free to have aesthetic preferences between people, but once our treatment of people raises moral issues, we may not make arbitrary distinctions. Using race in itself as a morally relevant distinction strikes most of us as obviously arbitrary. Without associated moral characteristics, why should race provide a better basis than hair color or height or timbre of voice? And if two people share all the properties morally relevant to some action we ought to do, it will be an error – a failure to apply the Kantian injunction to universalize our moral judgments – to use the bare facts of race as the basis for treating them differently. No one should deny that a common ancestry might, in particular cases, account for similarities in moral character. But then it would be the moral similarities that justified the different treatment.

It is presumably because most people – outside the South African Nationalist Party and the Ku Klux Klan – share the sense that intrinsic racism requires arbitrary distinctions that they are largely unwilling to express it in situations that invite moral criticism. But I do not know how I would argue with someone who was willing to announce an intrinsic racism as a basic moral idea: the best one can do, perhaps, is to provide objections to possible lines of defense of it.

De Gustibus

It might be thought that intrinsic racism should be regarded not so much as an adherence to a (moral) proposition as the expression of a taste, analogous, say, to the food prejudice that makes most English people unwilling to eat horse meat, and most Westerners unwilling to eat the insect grubs that the !Kung people find so appetizing. The analogy does at least this much for us, namely, to provide a model of the way that *extrinsic* racist propositions can be a reflection of an underlying prejudice. For, of course, in most cultures food prejudices are rationalized: we say insects are unhygienic and cats taste horrible. Yet a cooked insect is no more health-threatening than a cooked carrot, and the unpleasant taste of cat meat, far from justifying our prejudice against it, probably derives from that prejudice.

But there the usefulness of the analogy ends. For intrinsic racism, as I have defined it, is not simply a taste for the company of one's "own kind," but a moral doctrine, one that is supposed to underlie differences in the treatment of people in contexts where moral evaluation is appropriate. And for moral distinctions we cannot accept that "de gustibus non est disputandum." We do not need the full apparatus of Kantian ethics to require that public morality be constrained by reason.

A proper analogy would be with someone who thought that we could continue to kill cattle for beef, even if cattle exercised all the complex cultural skills of human beings. I think it is obvious that creatures that shared our capacity for understanding as well as our capacity for pain should not be treated the way we actually treat cattle – that "intrinsic speciesism" would be as wrong as racism. And the fact that most people think it is worse to be cruel to chimpanzees than to frogs suggests that they may agree with me. The distinction in attitudes surely reflects a belief in the greater richness of the mental life of chimps. Still, I do not know how I would *argue* against someone who could not see this; someone who continued to act on the contrary belief might, in the end, simply have to be locked up.

The Family Model

I have suggested that intrinsic racism is, at least sometimes, a metaphorical extension of the moral priority of one's family: it might, therefore, be suggested that a defense of intrinsic racism could proceed along the same lines as a defense of the family as a center of moral interest. The possibility of a defense of family relations as morally relevant – or, more precisely, of the claim that one may be morally entitled (or even obliged) to make distinctions between two otherwise morally indistinguishable people because one is related to one and not to the other – is theoretically important for the prospects of a philosophical defense of intrinsic racism. This is because such a defense of the family involves – like intrinsic racism – a denial of the basic claim, expressed so clearly by Kant, that from the perspective of morality, it is as rational agents *simpliciter* that we are to assess and be assessed. For anyone who follows Kant in this, what matters, as we might say, is not who you are but how you try to live. Intrinsic racism denies this fundamental claim also. And, in so doing, as I have argued elsewhere, it runs against the mainstream of the history of Western moral theory.[11]

The importance of drawing attention to the similarities between the defense of the family and the defense of the race, then, is not merely that the metaphor of family is often invoked by racism; it is that each of them offers the same general challenge to the Kantian stream of our moral thought. And the parallel with the defense of the family should be especially appealing to an intrinsic racist, since many of us who have little time for racism would hope that the family is susceptible to some such defense.

The problem in generalizing the defense of the family, however, is that such defenses standardly begin at a point that makes the argument for intrinsic racism immediately implausible: namely, with the family as the unit through which we live what is most intimate, as the center of private life. If we distinguish, with Bernard Williams, between ethical thought, which takes seriously "the demands, needs, claims, desires, and generally, the lives of other people,"[12] and morality, which focuses more narrowly on obligation, it may well be that private life matters to us precisely because it is altogether unsuited to the universalizing tendencies of morality.

The functioning family unit has contracted substantially with industrialization, the disappearance of the family as the unit of production, and the increasing mobility of labor, but there remains that irreducible minimum: the parent or parents with the child or children. In this "nuclear" family, there is, of course, a substantial body of shared experience, shared attitudes, shared knowledge and beliefs; and the mutual psychological investment that exists within this group is, for most of us, one of the things that gives meaning to our lives. It is a natural enough confusion – which we find again and again in discussions of adoption in the popular media – that identifies the relevant group with the biological unit of *genitor*, *genetrix*, and *offspring* rather than with the social unit of those who share a common domestic life.

The relations of parents and their biological children are of moral importance, of course, in part because children are standardly the product of behavior voluntarily undertaken by their biological parents. But the moral relations between biological siblings and half-siblings cannot, as I have already pointed out, be accounted for in such terms. A rational defense of the family ought to appeal to the causal responsibility of the biological parent and the common life of the domestic unit, and not to the brute fact of biological relatedness, even if the former pair of considerations defines groups that are often coextensive with the groups generated by the latter. For brute biological relatedness bears no necessary connection to the sorts of human purposes that seem likely to be relevant at the most basic level of ethical thought.

An argument that such a central group is bound to be crucially important in the lives of most human beings in societies like ours is not, of course, an argument for any specific mode of organization of the "family": feminism and the gay liberation movement have offered candidate groups that could (and sometimes do) occupy the same sort of role in the lives of those whose sexualities or whose dispositions otherwise make the nuclear family uncongenial; and these candidates have been offered specifically in the course of defenses of a move toward societies that are agreeably beyond patriarchy and homophobia. The central thought of these feminist and gay critiques of the nuclear family is that we cannot continue to view any one organization of private life as "natural," once we have seen even the broadest outlines of the archaeology of the family concept.

If that is right, then the argument for the family must be an argument for a mode of organization of life and feeling that subserves certain positive functions; and however the details of such an argument would proceed it is highly unlikely that the same functions could be served by groups on the scale of races, simply because, as I say, the family is attractive in part exactly for reasons of its personal scale.

I need hardly say that rational defenses of intrinsic racism along the lines I have been considering are not easily found. In the absence of detailed defenses to consider, I can only offer these general reasons for doubting that they can succeed: the generally Kantian tenor of much of our moral thought threatens the project from the start; and the essentially unintimate nature of relations within "races" suggests that there is little prospect that the defense of the family – which seems an attractive and plausible project that extends ethical life beyond the narrow range of a universalizing morality – can be applied to a defense of races.

Conclusions

I have suggested that what we call "racism" involves both propositions and dispositions. The propositions were, first, that there are races (this was *racialism*) and, second, that these races are morally significant either (a) because they are contingently correlated with morally relevant properties (this was *extrinsic racism*) or (b) because they are intrinsically morally significant (this was *intrinsic racism*).

The disposition was a tendency to assent to false propositions, both moral and theoretical, about races – propositions that support policies or beliefs that are to the disadvantage of some race (or races) as opposed to others, and to do so even in the face of evidence and argument that should appropriately lead to giving those propositions up. This disposition I called "racial prejudice."

I suggested that intrinsic racism had tended in our own time to be the natural expression of feelings of community, and this is, of course, one of the reasons why we are not inclined to call it racist. For, to the extent that a theoretical position is not associated with irrationally held beliefs that tend to the *dis*advantage of some group, it fails to display the *directedness* of the distortions of rationality characteristic of racial prejudice. Intrinsic racism may be as irrationally held as any other view, but it does not *have* to be directed *against* anyone.

So far as theory is concerned I believe racialism to be false: since theoretical racism of both kinds presupposes racialism, I could not logically support racism of either variety. But even if racialism were true, both forms of theoretical racism would be incorrect. Extrinsic racism is false because the genes that account for the gross morphological differences that underlie our standard racial categories are not linked to those genes that determine, to whatever degree such matters are determined genetically, our moral and intellectual characters. Intrinsic racism is mistaken because it breaches the Kantian imperative to make moral distinctions only on morally relevant grounds – granted that there is no reason to believe that race, *in se*, is morally relevant, and also no reason to suppose that races are like families in providing a sphere of ethical life that legitimately escapes the demands of a universalizing morality.

Notes

1   Bernard Lewis, *Semites and Anti-Semites* (New York: Norton, 1986).

2   I shall be using the words "racism" and "racialism" with the meanings I stipulate: in some dialects of English they are synonyms, and in most dialects their definition is less than precise. For discussion of recent biological evidence see M. Nei and A. K. Roychoudhury, "Genetic Relationship and Evolution of Human Races," *Evolutionary Biology*, vol. 14 (New York: Plenum, 1983), pp. 1–59; for useful background see also M. Nei and A. K. Roychoudhury, "Gene Differences between Caucasian, Negro, and Japanese Populations," *Science*, 177 (August 1972), pp. 434–5.

3   See my "The Uncompleted Argument: Du Bois and the Illusion of Race," *Critical Inquiry*, 12 (Autumn 1985); reprinted in Henry Louis Gates (ed.), *"Race," Writing, and Difference* (Chicago: University of Chicago Press, 1986), pp. 21–37.

4   This fact shows up most obviously in the assumption that adopted children intelligibly make claims against their natural siblings: natural parents are, of course, causally responsible for their child's existence and that could be the basis of moral claims, without any sense that biological relatedness entailed rights or responsibilities. But no such basis exists for an interest in natural *siblings*; my sisters are not causally responsible for my existence. See "The Family Model," later in this essay.

5   Obviously what evidence should *appropriately* change your beliefs is not independent of your social or historical situation. In mid-nineteenth-century America, in New England quite as much as in the heart of Dixie, the pervasiveness of the institutional support for the prevailing system of racist belief – the fact that it was reinforced by religion and state, and defended by people in the universities and colleges, who had the greatest

cognitive authority – meant that it would have been appropriate to insist on a substantial body of evidence and argument before giving up assent to racist propositions. In California in the 1980s, of course, matters stand rather differently. To acknowledge this is not to admit to a cognitive relativism; rather, it is to hold that, at least in some domains, the fact that a belief is widely held – and especially by people in positions of cognitive authority – may be a good prima facie reason for believing it.

6   Ideologies, as most theorists of ideology have admitted, standardly outlive the period in which they conform to the objective interests of the dominant group in a society; so even someone who thinks that the dominant group in our society no longer needs racism to buttress its position can see racism as the persisting ideology of an earlier phase of society. (I say "group" to keep the claim appropriately general; it seems to me a substantial further claim that the dominant group whose interests an ideology serves is always a class.) I have argued, however, in "The Conservation of 'Race,'" that racism continues to serve the interests of the ruling classes in the West; in *Black American Literature Forum*, 23 (Spring 1989), pp. 37–60.

7   As I argued in "The Uncompleted Argument: Du Bois and the Illusion of Race." The reactive (or dialectical) character of this move explains why Sartre calls its manifestations in Négritude an "antiracist racism"; see "Orphée Noir," his preface to Senghor's *Anthologie de la nouvelle poésie nègre et malagache de langue française* (Paris: PUF, 1948). Sartre believed, of course, that the synthesis of this dialectic would be transcendence of racism; and it was his view of it as a

stage – the antithesis – in that process that allowed him to see it as a positive advance over the original "thesis" of European racism. I suspect that the reactive character of antiracist racism accounts for the tolerance that is regularly extended to it in liberal circles; but this tolerance is surely hard to justify unless one shares Sartre's optimistic interpretation of it as a stage in a process that leads to the end of all racisms. (And unless your view of this dialectic is deterministic, you should in any case want to play an argumentative role in moving to this next stage.)

For a similar Zionist response see Horace Kallen's "The Ethics of Zionism," *Maccabean*, August 1906.

8   Alexander Crummell, "The Race Problem in America," in Brotz's *Negro Social and Political Thought* (New York: Basic Books, 1966), p. 184.

9   *Christianity, Islam and the Negro Race* (1887; reprinted Edinburgh: Edinburgh University Press, 1967), p. 197.

10   This is in part a reflection of an important asymmetry: loathing, unlike love, needs justifying; and this, I would argue, is because loathing usually leads to acts that are *in se* undesirable, whereas love leads to acts that are largely *in se* desirable – indeed, supererogatorily so.

11   See my "Racism and Moral Pollution," *Philosophical Forum*, 18 (Winter–Spring 1986–87), pp. 185–202.

12   Bernard Williams, *Ethics and the Limits of Philosophy* (Cambridge, MA: Harvard University Press, 1985), p. 12. I do not, as is obvious, share Williams's skepticism about morality.

37

Oppression by Choice

Ann E. Cudd

I. The Problem

This paper presents a solution to two related puzzles concerning the nature of oppression: (1) can a social structure be oppressive if the situation that is alleged to be oppressive comes about as the result of the voluntary, informed, rational choice of the allegedly oppressed, and (2) why do oppressed people sometimes appear to join in their own oppression and reinforce it? Although there are several oppressed groups for whom these are interesting questions, I shall focus on the oppression of women, a group for whom these questions are often voiced in the form of accusations or justifications for unequal treatment.

On the face of it, the answer to question (1) seems to be no, since one of the criteria of oppression (so I shall argue) is that one suffer harm as a result of coercion. It may be asked, is it really oppression at all if the situation we call oppressive results from the voluntary, informed, rational choice of the purportedly oppressed? Michael Levin (1987) presents the skeptical position, claiming that any situation that results from choice or preferences vitiates the charge of oppression or discrimination.

> [The assignment of sex roles] is not an oppressive device if it came about because men and women for the most part innately prefer things the way they are, or as an unintended consequence of preferences. . . . A charge of discrimination is rebuttable by showing (for instance) that the numerical preponderance of men in positions of power came about through individual choices. (Levin, 1987, p. 31)

This claim coupled with the following charge from economist Victor Fuchs would entail that women choose their economic oppression, and that nothing ought to be done to alter the situation.

> On average women have a stronger demand for children than men do and have more concern for children after they are born. In short, there is a difference on the side of preferences, and this difference is a major source of women's economic disadvantage. (Fuchs, 1989, p. 38)

Levin could be read as charging that a person is not oppressed by a feature of society if it is the unintended result of *her* choices. Similar arguments are made often by libertarians and neo-classical economists to show that there is nothing oppressive about capitalism if property rights are properly enforced (e.g., Nozick, 1974). For both Levin and libertarians, "unintended consequences of (individual) preferences" are unobjectionable. I shall argue, though, that oppression operates by means of apparently voluntary choices, and that the oppression of women in contemporary US society is an example of choice under oppression. Because their choices are coerced, their choosing does not justify the conditions that result from their choices.

The conclusion I shall argue for is uncontroversial to some social theorists. Marxists argue for a similar conclusion, namely, that the working class is exploited or oppressed through its limited choices. Traditional Marxist theory holds that the members of the working class make these choices because they are under the sway of false consciousness; they have been fooled into thinking that the relative wealth and status in society is just or inevitable. Likewise a central claim of the second wave of the women's movement in the US has been that women are shaped by society to see their situation as natural, inevitable, and sometimes even preferable. This argument would bring about the same conclusion that I wish to draw, that the conditions of women are unjustifiable, but it does so at an unacceptably high price. The problem with the argument is that it is only a part of the story, and telling only that part encourages a rather disrespectful attitude toward women, claiming that they are mere victims rather than survivors who have had to make some hard choices. The argument also implies that women have no responsibility for their choices, since their choices are not rational. If I can show that all rational agents who are in the kind of objective circumstances that women in contemporary society often find themselves would make the same decisions, then I will substantiate the claim that there is more to oppression of women than erecting an ideology and keeping women enraptured by it. I will also have made a powerful argument, without appealing to any essential nature that is peculiar to women, that there is a social injustice that needs to be remedied.

I begin by setting out four criteria of oppression. In order to make clear the final criterion of oppression, coercion, I shall defend a moralized theory of coercion that accounts for institutional coercion. Then I present a model to explain a typical feature of women's oppression as the result of rational choices of the women, and show that it is oppressive by my criteria. My aim in this paper is to show that coercion can be the result of a special kind of constrained rational choice, that a common feature of oppression is that the oppressed make such rational but coerced choices, and that women in particular are oppressed by them.

II. Criteria of Oppression

"Oppression" picks out a special kind of harm done to groups of persons by other groups of persons. To claim that a group is oppressed entails that its members face decreased options and diminished futures *vis-à-vis* other members of the society, and it implies that there is a serious social disorder. The charge of oppression carries with it a deep moral claim against those responsible for the oppression, or those who are responsible for maintaining the oppressive status quo. Oppression is *prima facie* injustice, and to oppress someone is morally wrong. There are, of course, some injustices which cannot be rectified or compensated without creating greater injustice. I ignore these balancing problems for now. To see when it is an appropriate charge, I begin by positing four necessary and jointly sufficient criteria of oppression.

First, oppression must involve some sort of physical or psychological harm, though it need not be recognized as harm by the ones who are oppressed. People can be harmed by things of which they are not aware: one can get cancer from some imperceptible chemicals, or one can be prevented from getting an education by a system whose unfairness one does not discern. One kind of harm that is typical of oppression, and important for the oppression that I will focus on, is limited freedom of choice relative to others in one's society. Not all harm is oppression, and not all limitations on one's freedom of choice oppress, though. People who are killed in airplane accidents or people who make poor investment decisions and lose their shirts are not, in suffering those harms, oppressed.

The second feature of oppression is that it applies in the first instance to groups who are identifiable independently of their oppressed status. Oppression is a kind of harm that individual members of groups suffer by virtue of their membership in that group. To say that a person is oppressed means that she belongs to a group that is oppressed and that she suffers some oppressive harms. Oppression is a special kind of harm, a harm that comes to persons because they belong to a group that they closely identify with, so that the harm attaches to their very self-image (Friedman and May, 1985). If "oppression" is to pick out something interesting about our social structure, then it has to refer to harm done to structural groups in the society, and not just to arbitrary sets of persons.

Thirdly, oppression implies that some persons benefit from the oppression. A stronger criterion than this is sometimes required, namely, that there be an identifiable oppressor class. For a group to be an oppressor group its members must intentionally oppress another group. But having the intention to oppress requires that one understand the relevant effects of one's actions, and in many cases of oppression such detailed knowledge of the social fabric is not widely available. Many typical cases of oppression involve persons who reinforce the status quo social norms without thereby intending to harm anyone else, or even without being aware that upholding the status quo could harm others. These persons lack the moral knowledge to be held morally responsible for their actions. Since the term "oppressor" implies moral responsibility, it is best reserved for those who know the results of their action.

Could it be the case that no one benefits from oppression? Since oppression is a phenomenon that happens to a group that is a proper subset of the population, those who are not oppressed gain (at least) to whatever extent social rewards are zero sum. There are zero sum aspects to many social interactions: excluding Blacks from some jobs makes more job opportunities for whites, the lower wage that women earn redistributes the social product toward men. Thus where there is oppression there is a group who suffers and a group who benefits. The persons who are most likely to be the ones enforcing the coercion that brings about the oppression are those who benefit most from it, but this is not always the case. Overseers of slaves are sometimes slaves themselves.

Fourthly, oppression must involve some coercion or force. In order for the oppressed to be able to complain that they are wronged, it must be that they are coerced into the situation in which they suffer the oppressive harm. While in some circumstances choice negates the claim of oppression, the claim of coercion negates the voluntariness of the choice, and re-establishes the claim of oppression. Coercion, as I shall argue, can be subtle and unrecognized by the one who suffers it, although it is typically recognized by its victims. One suspects coercion whenever a bad outcome is inescapable for its victims, but I will say more about coercion in the next section.

This paper is meant to be complementary to other analyses of oppression; it highlights the fact that barriers can arise for all as a result of the choices of some, that the choices can be motivated by a vicious cycle in the individual's case. I examine one specific feature of oppressed groups – the apparently freely chosen collaboration in their oppression – which is especially acute in the case of women, although present in other examples of oppression as well. My purpose is not to argue that this feature of oppression, which I call *oppression by choice*, is the most important feature, or that it is a necessary condition of oppression, or that it is the most harmful aspect of oppression. But it is critical to examine oppression by choice in order to counter the argument implied by the quotes from Levin and Fuchs, and to do so without chalking it all up to the false consciousness of the victims.

III. Coercion and Voluntary Choice

A necessary condition of coercion is that one lacks a choice, but one has to lack choice in the right way to be coerced. Choices may be voluntary or involuntary, freely made or forced. To be coerced to act is still to act, that is, to exercise some choice. Even when you get mugged (a paradigm case of coercion) you have a choice in the sense of having two options: give the mugger your money or refuse and risk losing your life. But a coerced choice is different from a voluntary choice psychologically and morally. Psychologically, coerced persons feel that they are compelled to act as they do by the unacceptability of their other options; one says in such circumstances that one had "no choice" but to act as one did. Morally, coercion is a *prima facie* wrong because it violates justice and the autonomy of its victim. Also, the degree of voluntariness of a choice determines whether one can be held responsible for one's action or whether one can receive moral credit for it. When someone is coerced her actions may be justified or excused. Coercion is not the absence of all choice, but a lack of the right kind of choices, namely, voluntary choices.

There are two competing philosophical accounts of coercion in the literature, an empirical account and a moralized account. An empirical account "maintains that the truth of a coercion claim rests, at its core, on ordinary facts: will B be worse off than he now is if he fails to accept A's proposal? Is there great psychic pressure on B? Does B have any 'reasonable' alternative?" (Wertheimer, 1987, p. 7). Empirical accounts ask about the allegedly coerced agent's state of mind, about whether he feels that his choice is voluntary, or made under conditions of duress. They are parallel to psychological theories of freedom, and do not require a prior normative theory. A moralized theory "holds that we cannot determine whether A coerces B without answering the following sorts of questions: Does A have the right to make his proposal? Should B resist A's proposal? Is B entitled to recover should he succumb to A's proposal?" (Wertheimer, 1987, p. 7). Moralized theories of coercion claim that the state of mind of the allegedly coerced person is irrelevant to the question of whether she is coerced, and that the only relevant matter is whether the agent is denied some choice that she ought morally to have. Thus moralized theories are embedded within a moral theory, typically a theory of rights or entitlement.

Many Marxist arguments for the claim that workers are coerced in capitalism employ empirical accounts of force and coercion. G. A. Cohen (1988) argues that workers are forced to make contracts that exploit them, or that subject them to hazardous conditions, because they have no "acceptable alternative" to making these contracts. He argues that the proletariate is unfree because they are forced to work for capitalists who exploit them. Their only alternatives to working for the wages proposed by the capitalist are starvation, or begging, or going on the public dole, and these are not acceptable alternatives because they involve death or serious disenfranchisement from society. Hence workers are forced to make exploitative contracts. This is an empirical account of force since it simply examines the alternatives open to the persons, not whether the options are deserved.

However, Cohen's theory faces a dilemma that threatens to sneak a moral theory into his account. If an alternative is unacceptable because the agent *feels* that it is, then the theory is not moralized, but it threatens to leave us with the view that all hard choices are forced. If, on the other hand, an alternative counts as unacceptable because it is undeserved or unusually unfair in one's society, then the theory of force is moralized after all. According to Cohen, an alternative B is unacceptable compared with A if and only if B is not worse than A or B is not thoroughly bad, where "thoroughly bad" is understood in an absolute sense in expected utility terms (Cohen, 1988, p. 282). He claims that by taking "thoroughly bad" as "absolute *in some sense*" we avoid the conclusion that rational persons are always forced to do what they do, since they always do the utility maximizing thing. But Cohen's understanding of unacceptable alternatives leads to the conclusion that all *hard* choices are forced choices. Perhaps survival is an objective criterion of acceptability, but it is difficult to see what else is objectively unacceptable in the absence of a moral theory, and survivability is too weak as a criterion of acceptability. Furthermore, Cohen's understanding does not allow choices to be forced when the options are not so "thoroughly bad," but when they are unfair, unequal, or undeserved. Suppose that a person has a choice between two mediocre and uninspired high schools, but is denied the option of attending a very good high school in her neighborhood because she is Black. This is a case where we would want to say that she is forced to choose the school she chooses, even though it is not "thoroughly bad," since it is morally unacceptable that she should be prevented from attending the good school on grounds of race.

Like most Marxists, Cohen argues that force, oppression, and exploitation are *objective* circumstances of workers in capitalism. That claim seems to me to be right when understood as saying that oppression goes deeper than the mere feelings of the workers, that oppression involves their physical circumstances. This explains how workers can be oppressed even when they do not feel as though they are: they could be in objectively bad circumstances and believe that they deserve them and so deny that they are oppressed. It is a mistake to take the claim of objectivity to imply that oppression is therefore non-normative, however. We can make sense of a moralized theory of force as objectively determinable *by an objective moral theory*, where the theory of force is moralized, and we can require that the harms suffered by the forced or coerced persons be objective harms. Thus we can agree that force, coercion, and oppression are objective, while maintaining that those theories are moralized theories.

Robert Nozick (1974) argues that only a moralized account of coercion supports the moral force of a coercion claim. On his view, one cannot claim to be coerced simply because one has bad alternatives, but only if one had the *right* to better ones. "A person's choice among differing degrees of unpalatable alternatives is not rendered nonvoluntary by the fact that others voluntarily chose and acted within their rights in a way that did not provide him with a more palatable alternative" (Nozick, 1974, p. 264). The example he uses to argue this point is choice of marriage partners among men and women who have the same preference orderings over the members of the other gender as all the other members of their own. Suppose that there are 26 of each, with names A–Z for men and A^1–Z^1 for women, and suppose that they are rank ordered by each member of the opposite gender in alphabetical order, so that A is preferred to B is preferred to C, etc. by women and A^1 is preferred to B^1 is preferred to C^1, etc. by men. Suppose that their preferences are transitive and that they prefer anyone of the other gender to remaining unmarried. Then if they are perfectly free to accept or reject any other partner, A will marry A^1, B will marry B^1, and so forth. In this situation B's options limit him to selecting from among B^1-Z^1, C's options are limited to C^1-Z^1, etc. Are they coerced into marrying their partners? On an empirical account of coercion they must be. But it is clear to Nozick that they are not, since each of the women who the men could not marry had the *right* to choose another partner to marry, and thus limit the men's choices. To say that this is coercive is to say that these men are owed some remedy, and the only possible remedy would be to violate the women's rights and coerce them into marrying men whom they do not wish to marry. Thus, the choices that these people make are not coerced.

On Nozick's view, coercion claims must be judged against a theory of rights. Cohen denies this, pointing out that Nozick's view "has the absurd upshot" that the criminal who is imprisoned justly is therefore not *forced* to be in prison (Cohen, 1988, p. 256). Clearly there are two senses of "force" being used here: in Cohen's use P is forced to A whenever P finds the alternatives to A unacceptable or physically impossible to resist, while in Nozick's use force arises only when P's rights are being violated by someone's denying her another alternative. The issue concerning the use of "force" would be entirely semantic but for the fact that each is trying to derive a moral conclusion from them. In Nozick's case the conclusion comes immediately: being forced to do A means that one's rights are being violated and thus one is being wronged. In Cohen's case the moral conclusion comes down the road a bit: if P is forced to A then P is unfree, but since the lacked freedom is not a *moral* freedom, the moral implication arises only when one shows that it is unjust for P to be unfree, and that has to do with the fairness of P's situation as compared with that of her fellows. In deciding on the fairness of P's situation, Cohen may not appeal to the fact that P is forced, for no moral conclusion can follow from it, as the marriage case or even the prison case clearly show. "Force" has no normative force unless it appeals to a background moral theory when determining what counts as an acceptable alternative, either a theory of freedom that tells us when it is obstructed immorally, or a theory of justice. Thus Cohen's account of force is either normatively impotent or it appeals to a background moral theory after all.

Hence, I agree with Nozick that coercion claims are to be judged against a background moral theory. On my account of it, oppression claims themselves are *prima facie* moral claims for remedy or redress. The coercion requirement in my account of oppression transmits the *prima facie* moral claim, and only a moralized concept of coercion can do this. To accept a moralized account of coercion, however, is not necessarily to accept Nozick's account. First, one may reject Nozick's theory of rights as historically grounded. Moreover, I shall argue that coercion claims must be judged against a broader moral theory than the theory of property rights. As in Nozick's account of voluntary choice, I take coercion to be a non-voluntary choice where the voluntariness of the choice is moralized, and where a choice that is involuntary yet beyond human control is also uncoerced. But where Nozick discusses only violations of rights as the requirement of involuntariness, I argue that the moral background should be broadened to a theory of justice. Here's why. Rights are formulated within social institutions and norms that are taken for granted (Martin, 1993). Within a set of social practices, which normally appear to be determined prior to moral or legal systems, rights may be justified as fair and just rules for interactions among individuals. The emphasis on rights tends to obscure the contingent nature of the social practices and the way that background social institutions and practices rig the competition for the gains from social cooperation in favor of some and against others.

While seeing that rights must be morally justified for a system, political philosophers tend to take their own social practices, or the ancestors of those practices, for granted. For example, consider a Nozickean world where two persons have the same rights but where the parents of one are wealthy and generous to their child and the parents of the other are poor. Clearly they have differential access to the gains from social cooperation. On Nozick's theory there can be no more moral consideration of the situation than whether the line of succession of the property rights is unbroken by force or fraud. But it is arbitrary to restrict moral consideration to property rights as they have been protected and enforced by the state powers in that historical chain. These powers have also denied women and serfs and slaves the rights even to seek to own property, for instance, and every person now living has some of these disenfranchised persons in their past. Even if the men who have owned property had the right to acquire the property and treated no one else unjustly in acquiring it, there were many others who were prevented from competing with them for a claim to it. Since owning property enables one more easily to acquire more property, those who were denied the right to own property were not competing on an equal or fair basis even once they were given those rights. Thus there have been violations of justice, if not of property rights *per se*, in the transmission of every claim to property ownership. Since social institutions define the available options in favor of some groups and to the disadvantage of others, and since this advantage and disadvantage is sometimes unjust but not a violation of rights, we need a broader moral theory as the background moral theory in our account of coercion. Specifically, we need a moral theory that can recognize injustice in social institutions.

To further illustrate the problem, let us reconsider Nozick's marriage example. Suppose again that the men and the women each have preference rankings of all the members of the opposite gender, and that these rankings are transitive (i.e., if A is preferred to B and B to C, then A is preferred to C) and strict (for any two choices A and B either A is preferred to B or B to A), but we need not suppose that the rankings are exactly the same for each member of the two groups. Now suppose that the men are allowed to propose to their favorite women and the women are allowed only to accept or reject the proposals and not to propose, and again suppose that everyone is free to refuse to marry anyone whom they would rather not marry. In such a situation it can be shown that: (1) a stable set of marriages will form, in the sense that no one will be paired with someone who they like worse than someone else who likes her better than their partner; (2) the men (the proposers) are systematically advantaged over the women (the group who can only accept or reject), in the sense that (a) all the men are happier or at least as happy with this match as they would be with the one that would have arisen from the match made by women acting as proposers and men as the group who could only accept or reject, and (b) all the women like their match less than the alternative match in which they get to propose (Roth and Sotomayor, 1990, ch. 2). That is, the men are benefited as a group by this matchmaking arrangement and have a common interest in maintaining it, even while they compete with each other within it and it gives both men and women *equal rights* to reject any proposed partner. This marriage market shows that the norms that govern proposals in marriage can seriously disadvantage one group, even while they are voluntary and equal under the law. The case of marriage is especially important to the overall theme of this paper, since it is a case where apparently arbitrary and innocent gender distinctions solidify into one gender's disadvantage. Exactly how unjust this disadvantage is depends on whether there is systematic disadvantage for that gender in many other institutions, i.e., whether the disadvantage is avoidable.

Nozick's model of force is an agent-to-agent model; the marriage market example shows that force can also be applied by institutions on agents, and thus that Nozick's model is too limited. Social practices, institutions, and norms give persons power (or differential access to burdens and benefits) in relationships, and sometimes they do so by differentiating between persons on account of gender or race. In the marriage market example the power to propose enforced the best possible outcome for men within the confines of a stable matchmaking institution that allowed women the right to reject any suitor. Social institutions thus create unequal power in relationships among individuals of different groups.

The agent-to-agent model conceals the force relationships between persons with unequal power. What we need, then, is a moralized theory of coercion that reveals these relationships and determines when they are unjust. Thus we need a model of institutional coercion that takes a theory of fairness and justice as its background moral theory. I propose the following definition of institutional coercion:

> An institution (norm, legal system) is **coercive** if the institution unfairly limits the choices of some group of persons relative to other groups in society.

There are two issues that arise immediately with this definition: (1) What theory of fairness or justice should we apply? (2) What counts as a group? I dealt earlier in this paper with the definition of social group, and the definition provided there answers this question adequately for my purposes here. As for (1), this paper is hardly the place to develop a theory of justice, however any acceptable theory of justice (I have in mind a broadly contractarian view, e.g., Rawls, 1971) would claim that no social institutions would be permitted to benefit men at the expense of women, white persons at the expense of persons of color, straight persons at the expense of gay or lesbian ones, or make any of the other humiliating discriminations against groups that I discussed in the previous section. First, such discriminations lead to instability in resulting institutions because they violate dignity, which is held dear by all persons. By signifying that they are morally inferior for features of themselves over which they have no control, discriminating against persons in this way will cause them to resist those institutions that maintain the discrimination. Since a just society is a stable one, such institutions cannot exist in a just society. Secondly, they violate the autonomy of persons by restricting their choices for reasons that would not be agreed upon by equals. To be agreed upon by free and equal persons, a social institution cannot violate autonomy.

To summarize the argument of this section: the account of coercion that will support the claim that oppression is *prima facie* unjust is a moralized account of coercion, including institutional coercion. Such an account of coercion allows us to claim that coercion negates the aspect of choice that makes plausible Levin's view that choice negates oppression; choice negates oppression, then, only when the choice is uncoerced. The background moral theory, in order to account for institutional coercion, must go beyond a theory of property rights, even beyond a theory of moral or human rights, and must be a complete theory of justice of social institutions. Armed with this fuller account of coercion, let us return to the claim that women are oppressed by the apparently voluntary choices they make.

IV. Vicious Cycles

There is a loaded query aimed at feminists that goes something like this: Didn't she *choose* to stay home with the kids? The quotes by Levin and Fuchs illustrate the point of the question: if she chose her situation how can anyone call it oppression? The question is rhetorical; it is supposed to absolve society of any guilt for putting her, or women generally, into a disadvantageous position *vis-à-vis* men. The question presupposes an analysis of oppression that says that a society in which persons may choose their occupations is free (at least in this sphere), and if the society is free then there is no oppression (in that sphere), no matter what results from their choices. If someone freely chooses her situation, she is responsible for its consequences, and if she was rational when making her choice, then she must want, all things considered, whatever she expected to be its consequences. That is, choice confers responsibility.

Contemporary western society is commonly thought to be free in this sense (among others). There is anecdotal evidence for this belief: the ranks of the owners of business and leaders of government and education include people who raised themselves from the bottom of the socio-economic ladder to near the top, and their stories, appealing as they are, become well known. Since there are those who do succeed in climbing the ladder in their chosen field, many infer that it is possible for all to do so. And they further infer that this implies free choice of occupation, subject only to the constraints of native talent. There is also an *a priori* argument that economists give for the claim that there is no discrimination on the part of business against any particular racial group or gender. Since businesses are out to maximize profits, and indeed (so the argument goes) cannot survive if they don't, they must seek to hire the most talented individuals regardless of race or gender. Thus they do not discriminate on the basis of race or gender, since those who would discriminate would tend to go out of business (Bergmann, 1986).

At the same time, women who are employed in the outside labor force in the US continue to earn about 64 percent of what men earn. This proportion is roughly equal at all levels of education, that is, women with less than high school education earn approximately 64 percent of what men with less than high school education earn, and women with more than 4 years of college earn approximately 64 percent of what men with more than 4 years of college earn (Bergmann, 1986, pp. 405–13).

The wage gap sets women up for a vicious cycle that is an important feature of their oppression. What makes it particularly insidious is that the cycle is the result of apparently *rational* choices of individual women themselves. Susan Moller Okin explains how women are caught in "*a cycle of socially caused and distinctly asymmetric vulnerability*" (Okin, 1989, p. 138). Okin argues that society is unjust because it creates this asymmetric vulnerability. She too makes the point that rational individual choice can play a role in this cycle, yet argues that "since the maldistribution of wages and jobs between the sexes in our society is largely out of women's control, even *seemingly nonconflictual* decisions made on this basis cannot really be considered fully voluntary on the part of wives" (Okin, 1989, p. 154). What I mean to do here is to explain how the choices can be rational, nonconflictual, and coerced. First I need a model of how such decisions are made, and for this I shall borrow heavily from Okin's own illustrations. The explanation I shall give of why the wage gap persists is an *invisible foot explanation*: the individually rational choices, taken by large numbers of individuals, lead to socially suboptimal outcomes. To show this I build a simple rational-choice model of a man and a woman of the same age with exactly equal talents, education, and work experience. Let us suppose that these two, call them Larry and Lisa, have decided to marry and to have children together. In the beginning they have equal power in the relationship to enforce their individual intentions for collective action. Suppose that they harbor no prejudices about "men's" or "women's" work, and that with the exception of the specific tasks of impregnation, conception, childbearing, and lactation, they are equally capable, and believe themselves to be equally capable, of all childrearing and domestic tasks. Suppose that they also believe that one parent ought to take primary care of the children, that neither socialized childcare nor equally shared care by both parents is as good as care by one parent who specializes in the children's care. Then if there is a wage gap between men and women, and Larry and Lisa have rational expectations about their relative earning potential, and if they consider only family income in their decision, they will decide that Lisa should specialize in childcare and Larry in wage work.

This decision has enormous implications for their future and the relative share of power in the family. In staying home, it will be rational for Lisa to take on the burden of the greater share of other domestic work as well, and she will come to have greater skill for it. Her skills for outside employment will become less valuable, and, especially relative to Larry, she will become even less valuable as a wage worker for the family. Lisa will become the domestic specialist and Larry the specialist in wage work. Even later, when the children are grown to the point where both parents feel they can work outside the home, her value as a domestic worker will be on the whole greater than Larry's, and his greater value as a wage worker will guarantee that he need never take on a large share of domestic tasks.

This division of labor could be neutral with respect to power in some societies, but not in societies such as our own in which wealth determines power, domestic work is unpaid, and divorce laws do not evenly divide wealth. In a relationship the relative power of the partners is determined largely by the opportunities available to each should the relationship end. While Lisa's value as a domestic worker does not increase much since it is unpaid work, Larry's value increases with experience. He builds what economists call "human capital." If their relationship ends then Larry has the human capital to guarantee that his income will continue the same, while Lisa, whose skills and value as a wage worker have atrophied since she took on the domestic work, will see her income fall appreciably. Even if divorce laws evenly divide the accumulated wealth between them, the difference in their future incomes as a result of their uneven human capital will be greater the longer the marriage (and hence her domestic specialization) has lasted. Furthermore, Lisa still faces the wage gap, which was the reason that she specialized in domestic work to begin with. Thus Lisa's prospects are considerably dimmer than Larry's if the relationship ends. And this means that she has less power in the ongoing relationship.

Her lack of power might be manifested in many ways in the marriage. He can demand that she work more hours than he does, that she continue to serve him after each has put in a day of work. He may demand, if she gets a job outside the home, that she sacrifice her job to meet family needs and emergencies, that she take time from work to care for sick children or household repairs. He may demand more leisure time, or refuse to share his wages with her. He may beat or rape her with much less risk of punishment than if they held power equally.

If Larry and Lisa represent typical men and women in society, then there are serious consequences for all men and women arising from the typical individually rational choices about work and family. If it is the case that women typically make the decision to subordinate career and work to family and domestic tasks, then women will be seen as the domestic workers of the society and as unreliable wage workers. There is evidence, statistical and anecdotal, showing that this is indeed a significant obstacle to equality of opportunity for women in the workforce. Employers tend not to trust that women will stay with their careers, or assume that if they do, they will not devote the kind of time and energy to them that men will. Women are poorer risks, and so employers will not invest in specialized training for them as easily as for men, and women will not be promoted as quickly as men. The supposed unreliability of women, on average, counteracts the *a priori* argument that purports to show that employers ought not to discriminate against women. If women are less reliable workers, then it makes sense for employers to do whatever they can to skirt the laws that demand equal treatment for men and women, for statistically speaking women are poor risks for jobs that require mobility, independence, and devotion. But these are, typically, the more highly paid (not to mention more interesting) positions. This means that women will on average earn less for the same skill level as men. But it was this fact, the wage gap, that forced women (and men) to make the choices that led to this outcome. Thus the cycle is complete. It is a vicious cycle because the opportunities for women are lowered, or at best remain stagnant, as a result of each revolution. Where the result in the market is an invisible hand that allocates goods efficiently, the result of individual rational choice in a vicious cycle is an invisible foot that grinds down the social position of women.

If the outcome for Lisa looks so bleak, then why does she agree to the original division of labor? Is it really a rational choice for women themselves? Suppose that Larry and Lisa can unproblematically come to a joint decision. The choices that they face are for each to work for wages or to do domestic work. They cannot both choose domestic work in their society and still make a living. If they choose to both do wage work, then because of the wage gap Lisa will still have less power in the relationship, since her income is lower, and their children are less well cared for (in their view, by hypothesis). If they choose to have Larry do domestic work and Lisa do wage work, then their children are properly cared for but they have a lower income than before. The share of power is indeterminate in this case; it depends on how much she gains in human capital and how much he loses by not working, and whether the wage gap is offset by her gain and his loss. Under some conditions it will be optimal for Larry and Lisa to divide the domestic and wage work as I hypothesized; the frequency of this division in our society suggests that the conditions necessary are normal conditions. Now suppose that they have to bargain over the division of labor. Larry is bound to get what he wants in the negotiation, since his no-agreement outcome is better than hers. Even if they break up he will gain more by virtue of the wage gap. She will resist his demands only if her outcome after a break-up would be better than his demand, that is, if she expects that her life as the domestic worker with him will be worse than her life without him and working for wages or as a domestic worker married to someone else.

The Larry and Lisa model shows how a vicious cycle can result from simply an initial social inequality and subsequent rational, apparently voluntary, choices. Even the maintenance of the social inequality is the rational result of the choices made by individuals, given an initial social inequality. This in itself tells us little more than Levin and Fuchs could tell us. Levin goes on to draw the moral conclusion from this freedom of choice that society is absolved from its responsibility for changing the situation, even if it appears unjust when viewed ahistorically. But does this freedom of choice so absolve society? Is a society in which vicious cycles exist just?

V.   Oppression, Coercion, and Choice

To answer these questions we have to examine whether vicious cycles are oppressive and therefore unjust. We can apply the criteria of oppression from section II to see that vicious cycles can be manifestations of oppression, and that the vicious cycle in the Larry and Lisa example is an example of an oppressive vicious cycle. A cycle is vicious only if it is harmful. In the Larry and Lisa example I argued that women's employment opportunities are continually degraded both for the individuals and for women as a group, and this is clearly a harm. Some people, namely the Larrys of the world, benefit from the vicious cycle that the Lisas face. This is true even for those Larrys who regret the cycle, since their wages are relatively better than the wages of the Lisas. Thus the cycle is harmful for one social group and benefits another social group. So criteria 1–3 are satisfied.

We come then to the coercion criterion. The vicious-cycle phenomenon we examined has the character of coercion because it leads to fewer and worse life choices for women than they would have were it not for the vicious cycle, both on the individual level and at the level of the wage gap for all women. This lack of choice has no redeeming aspect that leads to greater freedom either. One just cannot argue that women have more freedom as a result of the wage gap, or of their lack of social power. The option for Lisa in the model is to eschew traditional domestic roles, either by not marrying, by not having children, by not raising children as they would have them raised, or to get Larry to do the domestic work. Each of these thwarts Lisa's desires, except the last one. That option, though, requires agreement by Larry and results in lower living standards for the family as a whole, because of the original wage gap. Relative to the choices men face, relative to what the situation would be if there were no original wage gap, these are bad options. More importantly, they are unfair. Women's freedom of choice here is like that of the marriage market at the end of section III: women's freedom is complete only within an unjust framework for their options. Any acceptable background moral theory would regard this fundamental asymmetry in the available life choices and power as unfair. Thus women are coerced in making the choice to eschew economic power and status for domestic servitude. So I conclude that the vicious cycle is coercive. This implies that women are oppressed by the vicious–cycle phenomenon, and thus, by means of their own individually rational choices.

References

Bergmann, B. R.: *The Economic Emergence of Women* (New York: Basic Books, 1986).

Cohen, G. A.: *History, Labour, and Freedom: Themes from Marx* (Oxford: Clarendon Press, 1988).

Friedman, M. and May, L.: "Harming women as a group," *Social Theory and Practice*, 11 (Summer 1985), 208–34.

Frye, M.: *The Politics of Reality: Essays in Feminist Theory* (Trumansburg, NY: The Crossing Press, 1983).

Fuchs, V. R.: "Women's quest for economic equality," *Journal of Economic Perspectives*, 3 (1989), 25–41.

Levin, M.: *Feminism and Freedom* (New Brunswick: Transaction Books, 1987).

Martin, R.: *A System of Rights* (Oxford: Clarendon Press, 1993).

Mill, J. S.: *On the Subjection of Women* (Indianapolis: Hackett, 1988).

Nozick, R.: *Anarchy, State, and Utopia* (New York: Basic Books, 1974).

Okin, S. M.: *Justice, Gender, and the Family* (New York: Basic Books, 1989).

Rawls, J.: *A Theory of Justice* (Cambridge: Harvard University Press, 1971).

Roth A. E. and Sotomayor, M. A. O.: *Two-Sided Matching: A Study in Game-theoretic Modeling and Analysis* (Cambridge: Cambridge University Press, 1990).

Wertheimer, A.: *Coercion* (Princeton: Princeton University Press, 1987).

38

Sexual Harassment[1]

Anita M. Superson

I.   Introduction

By far the most pervasive form of discrimination against women is sexual harassment (SH). Women in every walk of life are subject to it, and I would venture to say, on a daily basis. Even though the law is changing to the benefit of victims of SH, the fact that SH is still so pervasive shows that there is too much tolerance of it, and that victims do not have sufficient legal recourse to be protected.

The main source for this problem is that the way SH is defined by various Titles and other sources does not adequately reflect the social nature of SH, or the harm it causes all women. As a result, SH comes to be defined in subjective ways. One upshot is that when subjective definitions infuse the case law on SH, the more subtle but equally harmful forms of SH do not get counted as SH and thus are not afforded legal protection. . . .

II.   The Social Nature of Sexual Harassment

Sexual harassment, a form of sexism, is about domination, in particular, the domination of the group of men over the group of women.[2] Domination involves control or power which can be seen in the economic, political, and social spheres of society. Sexual harassment is not simply an assertion of power, for power can be used in beneficial ways. The power men have over women has been wielded in ways that oppress women. The power expressed in SH is oppression, power used wrongly.

Sexual harassment is integrally related to sex roles. It reveals the belief that a person is to be relegated to certain roles on the basis of her sex, including not only women's being sex objects, but also their being caretakers, motherers, nurturers, sympathizers, etc. In general, the sex roles women are relegated to are associated with the body (v. mind) and emotions (v. reason).

When A sexually harasses B, the comment or behavior is really directed at the group of all women, not just a particular woman, a point often missed by the courts. After all, many derogatory behaviors are issued at women the harasser does not even know (e.g., scanning a stranger's body). Even when the harasser knows his victim, the behavior is directed at the particular woman because she happens to be "available" at the time, though its message is for all women. For instance, a catcall says not (merely) that the perpetrator likes a woman's body, but that he thinks women are at least primarily sex objects and he – because of the power he holds by being in the dominant group – gets to rate them according to how much pleasure they give him. The professor who refers to his female students as "chicks" makes a statement that women are intellectually inferior to men as they can be likened to non-rational animals, perhaps even soft, cuddly ones that are to serve as the objects of (men's) pleasure. Physicians' using Playboy centerfolds in medical schools to "spice up their lectures" sends the message that women lack the competence to make it in a "man's world" and should perform the "softer tasks" associated with bearing and raising children.[3]

These and other examples make it clear that SH is not about dislike for a certain person; instead, it expresses a person's beliefs about women as a group on the basis of their sex, namely, that they are primarily emotional and bodily beings. Some theorists – Catherine MacKinnon, John Hughes and Larry May – have recognized the social nature of SH. Hughes and May claim that women are a disadvantaged group because (1) they are a social group having a distinct identity and existence apart from their individual identities, (2) they occupy a subordinate position in American society, and (3) their political power is severely circumscribed.[4] They continue:

> Once it is established that women qualify for special disadvantaged group status, all practices tending to stigmatize women as a group, or which contribute to the maintenance of their subordinate social status, would become legally suspect.[5]

This last point, I believe, should be central to the definition of SH.

Because SH has as its target the group of all women, this *group* suffers harm as a result of the behavior. Indeed, when any one woman is in any way sexually harassed, all women are harmed. The group harm SH causes is different from the harm suffered by particular women as individuals: it is often more vague in nature as it is not easily causally tied to any particular incident of harassment. The group harm has to do primarily with the fact that the behavior reflects and reinforces sexist attitudes that women are inferior to men and that they do and ought to occupy certain sex roles. For example, comments and behavior that relegate women to the role of sex objects reinforce the belief that women *are* sex objects and that they *ought to* occupy this sex role. Similarly, when a female professor's cogent comments at department colloquia are met with frowns and rolled eyes from her colleagues, this behavior reflects and reinforces the view that women are not fit to occupy positions men arrogate to themselves.

The harm women suffer as a group from any single instance of SH is significant. It takes many forms. A Kantian analysis would show what is wrong with being solely a sex object. Though there is nothing wrong with being a caretaker or nurturer, etc., *per se*, it is sexist – and so wrong – to assign such roles to women. In addition, it is wrong to assign a person to a role she may not want to occupy. Basically women are not allowed to decide for themselves which roles they are to occupy, but this gets decided for them, no matter what they do. Even if some women occupy important positions in society that men traditionally occupy, they are still viewed as being sex objects, caretakers, etc., since all women are thought to be more "bodily" and emotional than men. This is a denial of women's autonomy, and degrading to them. It also contributes to women's oppression. The belief that women must occupy certain sex roles is both a cause and an effect of their oppression. It is a cause because women are believed to be more suited for certain roles given their association with body and emotions. It is an effect because once they occupy these roles and are victims of oppression, the belief that they *must* occupy these sex roles is reinforced.

Women are harmed by SH in yet another way. The belief that they are sex objects, caretakers, etc., gets reflected in social and political practices in ways that are unfair to women. It has undoubtedly meant many lost opportunities that are readily available to men. Women are not likely to be hired for jobs that require them to act in ways other than the ways the sex roles dictate, and if they are, what is expected of them is different from what is expected of men. Mothers are not paid for their work, and caretakers are not paid well in comparison with people in jobs traditionally held by men. Lack of economic reward is paralleled by lack of respect and appreciation for those occupying such roles. Certain rights granted men are likely not to be granted women (e.g., the right to bodily self-determination, and marriage rights).

Another harm SH causes all women is that the particular form sex stereotyping takes promotes two myths: (1) that male behavior is normally and naturally predatory, and (2) that females naturally (because they are taken to be primarily bodily and emotional) and even willingly acquiesce despite the appearance of protest.[6] Because the behavior perpetuated by these myths is taken to be normal, it is not seen as sexist, and in turn is not counted as SH.

The first myth is that men have stronger sexual desires than women, and harassment is just a natural venting of these desires which men are unable to control. The truth is, first, that women are socialized *not* to vent their sexual desires in the way men do, but this does not mean these desires are weaker or less prevalent. Masters and Johnson have "decisively established that women's sexual requirements are no less potent or urgent than those of men."[7] But secondly, SH has nothing to do with men's sexual desires, nor is it about seduction; instead, it is about oppression of women. Indeed, harassment generally does not lead to sexual satisfaction, but it often gives the harasser a sense of power.

The second myth is that women either welcome, ask for, or deserve the harassing treatment. Case law reveals this mistaken belief. In *Lipsett* v. *Rive-Mora*[8] (1987), the plaintiff was discharged from a medical residency program because she "did not react favorably to her professor's requests to go out for drinks, his compliments about her hair and legs, or to questions about her personal and romantic life."[9] The court exonerated the defendant because the plaintiff had initially reacted favorably by smiling when shown lewd drawings of herself and when called sexual nicknames as she thought she had to appease the physician. The court said that "given the plaintiff's admittedly favorable responses to these flattering comments, there was no way anyone could consider them as 'unwelcome.'"[10] The court in *Swentek* v. *US Air*[11] (1987) reacted similarly when a flight attendant who was harassed with obscene remarks and gestures was denied legal recourse because previously she had used vulgar language and openly discussed her sexual encounters. The court concluded that "she was the kind of person who could not be offended by such comments and therefore welcomed them generally."[12]

The idea that women welcome "advances" from men is seen in men's view of the way women dress. If a woman dresses "provocatively" by men's standards, she is said to welcome or even deserve the treatment she gets. One explanation harassing professors give for their behavior is that they are bombarded daily with the temptation of physically desirable young women who dress in what they take to be revealing ways.[13] When the case becomes public, numerous questions arise about the attractiveness of the victim, as if she were to blame for being attractive and the consequences thereof. Catcallers often try to justify their behavior by claiming that the victim should expect such behavior, given her tight-fitting dress or shorts, low-cut top, high heels, etc. This way of thinking infests discussions of rape in attempts to establish that women want to be raped, and it is mistaken in that context, too. The myth that women welcome or encourage harassment is designed "to keep women in their place" as men see it. The truth of the matter is that the perpetrator alone is at fault.

Both myths harm all women as they sanction SH by shifting the burden onto the victim and all members of her sex: women must either go out of their way to avoid "natural" male behavior, or establish conclusively that they do not in any way want the behavior. Instead of the behavior being seen as sexist, it is seen as women's problem to rectify.

Last, but certainly not least, women suffer group harm from SH because they come to be stereotyped as victims.[14] Many men see SH as something they can do to women, and in many cases, get away with. Women come to see themselves as victims, and come to believe that the roles they *can* occupy are only the sex roles men have designated for them. Obviously these harms are quite serious for women, so the elimination of all forms of SH is warranted.

I have spoken so far as if it is only men who can sexually harass women, and I am now in a position to defend this controversial view. When a woman engages in the very same harassing behavior men engage in, the underlying message implicit in male-to-female harassment is missing. For example, when a woman scans a man's body, she might be considering him to be a sex object, but all the views about domination and being relegated to certain sex roles are absent. She cannot remind the man that he is inferior because of his sex, since given the way things are in society, he is not. In general, women cannot harm or degrade or dominate men *as a group*, for it is impossible to send the message that one dominates (and so cause group harm) if one does not dominate. Of course, if the sexist roles predominant in our society were reversed, women *could* sexually harass men. The way things are, any bothersome behavior a woman engages in, even though it may be of a sexual nature, does not constitute SH because it lacks the social impact present in male-to-female harassment. Tort law would be sufficient to protect against this behavior, since it is unproblematic in these cases that tort law fails to recognize group harm.

III.   Subjective v. Objective Definitions of Sexual Harassment

Most definitions of "sexual harassment" make reference to the behavior's being "unwelcome" or "annoying" to the victim. *Black's Law Dictionary* defines "harassment" as a term used "to describe words, gestures and actions which tend to annoy, alarm and abuse (verbally) another person."[15] The *American Heritage Dictionary* defines "harass" as "to disturb or irritate persistently," and states further that "[h]arass implies systematic persecution by besetting with annoyances, threats, or demands."[16] The EEOC *Guidelines* state that behavior constituting SH is identified as "unwelcome sexual advances, requests for sexual favors, and other verbal or physical conduct of a sexual nature."[17] In their philosophical account of SH, Hughes and May define "harassment" as "a class of annoying or unwelcome acts undertaken by one person (or group of persons) against another person (or group of persons)."[18] And Rosemarie Tong takes the feminists' definition of noncoercive SH to be that which "denotes sexual misconduct that merely annoys or offends the person to whom it is directed."[19]

The criterion of "unwelcomeness" or "annoyance" is reflected in the way the courts have handled cases of SH, as in *Lipsett*, *Swentek*, and *Meritor*, though in the latter case the court said that the voluntariness of the victim's submission to the defendant's sexual conduct did not mean that she welcomed the conduct.[20] The criterion of unwelcomeness or annoyance present in these subjective accounts of harassment puts the burden on the victim to establish that she was sexually harassed. There is no doubt that many women *are* bothered by this behavior, often with serious side-effects including anything from anger, fear, and guilt,[21] to lowered self-esteem and decreased feelings of competence and confidence,[22] to anxiety disorders, alcohol and drug abuse, coronary disturbances, and gastro-intestinal disorders.[23]

Though it is true that many women are bothered by the behavior at issue, I think it is seriously mistaken to say that whether the victim is bothered determines whether the behavior constitutes SH. This is so for several reasons.

First, we would have to establish that the victim was bothered by it, either by the victim's complaints, or by examining the victim's response to the behavior. The fact of the matter is that many women are quite hesitant to report being harassed, for a number of reasons. Primary among them is that they fear negative consequences from reporting the conduct. As is often the case, harassment comes from a person in a position of institutional power, whether he be a supervisor, a company president, a member of a dissertation committee, the chair of the department, and so on. Unfortunately for many women, as a review of the case law reveals, their fears are warranted.[24] Women have been fired, their jobs have been made miserable, forcing them to quit, professors have handed out unfair low grades, and so on. Worries about such consequences mean that complaints are not filed, or are filed years after the incident, as in the *Anita Hill* v. *Clarence Thomas* case. But this should not be taken to imply that the victim was not harassed.

Moreover, women are hesitant to report harassment because they do not want anything to happen to the perpetrator, but just want the behavior to stop.[25] Women do not complain because they do not want to deal with the perpetrator's reaction when faced with the charge. He might claim that he was "only trying to be friendly." Women are fully aware that perpetrators can often clear themselves quite easily, especially in tort law cases where the perpetrator's intentions are directly relevant to whether he is guilty. And most incidents of SH occur without any witnesses – many perpetrators plan it this way. It then becomes the harasser's word against the victim's. To complicate matters, many women are insecure and doubt themselves. Women's insecurity is capitalized upon by harassers whose behavior is in the least bit ambiguous. Clever harassers who fear they might get caught or be reported often attempt to get on the good side of their victim in order to confuse her about the behavior, as well as to have a defense ready in case a charge is made. Harassers might offer special teaching assignments to their graduate students, special help with exams and publications, promotions, generous raises, and the like. Of course, this is all irrelevant to whether he harasses, but the point is that it makes the victim less likely to complain. On top of all this, women's credibility is very often questioned (unfairly) when they bring forth a charge. They are taken to be "hypersensitive." There is an attitude among judges and others that women must "develop a thick skin."[26] Thus, the blame is shifted off the perpetrator and onto the victim. Given this, if a woman thinks she will get no positive response – or, indeed, will get a negative one – from complaining, she is unlikely to do so.

Further, some women do not recognize harassment for what it is, and so will not complain. Sometimes this is because they are not aware of their own oppression, or actually seem to endorse sexist stereotypes. I recall a young woman who received many catcalls on the streets of Daytona Beach, Florida, during spring break, and who was quite proud that her body could draw such attention. Given that women are socialized into believing their bodies are the most important feature of themselves, it is no surprise that a fair number of them are complacent about harassing behavior directed at them. Sandra Bartky provides an interesting analysis of why every woman is not a feminist, and I think it holds even for women who understand the issue.[27] Since for many women having a body felt to be "feminine" is crucial to their identity and to their sense of self "as a sexually desiring and desirable subject," feminism "may well be apprehended by a woman as something that threatens her with desexualization, if not outright annihilation."[28] The many women who resist becoming feminists are not likely to perceive harassing behavior as bothersome. It would be incorrect to conclude that the behavior is not harassment on the grounds that such victims are not bothered. What we have is a no-win situation for victims: if the behavior bothers a woman she often has good reason not to complain; and if it does not bother her, she will not complain. Either way, the perpetrator wins. So we cannot judge whether women are bothered by the behavior on the basis of whether they *say* they are bothered.

Moreover, women's *behavior* is not an accurate indicator of whether they are bothered. More often than not, women try to ignore the perpetrator's behavior in an attempt not to give the impression they are encouraging it. They often cover up their true feelings so that the perpetrator does not have the satisfaction that his harassing worked. Since women are taught to smile and put up with this behavior, they might actually appear to enjoy it to some extent. Often they have no choice but to continue interacting with the perpetrator, making it very difficult to assert themselves. Women often make up excuses for not "giving in" instead of telling the perpetrator to stop. The fact that their behavior does not indicate they are bothered should not be used to show they were not bothered. In reality, women are fearful of defending themselves in the face of men's power and physical strength. Given the fact that the courts have decided that a lot of this behavior should just be tolerated, it is no wonder that women try to make the best of their situation.

It would be wrong to take a woman's behavior to be a sign that she is bothered also because doing so implies the behavior is permissible if she does not seem to care. This allows the *perpetrator* to be the judge of whether a woman is harassed, which is unjustifiable given the confusion among men about whether their behavior is bothersome or flattering. Sexual harassment should be treated no differently than crimes where harm to the victim is assessed in some objective way, independent of the perpetrator's beliefs. To give men this power in the case of harassment is to perpetuate sexism from all angles.

An *objective* view of SH avoids the problems inherent in a subjective view. According to the objective view defended here, what is decisive in determining whether behavior constitutes SH is not whether the victim is bothered, but whether the behavior is an instance of a practice that expresses and perpetuates the attitude that the victim and members of her sex are inferior because of their sex. Thus the Daytona Beach case counts as a case of SH because the behavior is an instance of a practice that reflects men's domination of women in that it relegates women to the role of sex objects.[29]

The courts have to some extent tried to incorporate an objective notion of SH by invoking the "reasonable person" standard. The EEOC *Guidelines*, as shown earlier, define SH partly as behavior that "has the purpose or effect of *unreasonably* interfering with an individual's work performance . . . ".[30] The *Restatement of Torts*, referring to the tort of intentional infliction of emotional distress, states that the emotional distress must be "so severe that no *reasonable* man could be expected to endure it."[31]

In various cases the courts have invoked a reasonable man (or person) standard, but *not* to show that women who are not bothered still suffer harassment. Instead, they used the standard to show that even though a particular woman *was* bothered, she would have to tolerate such behavior because it was behavior a reasonable person would not have been affected by. In *Rabidue* v. *Osceola Refining Co.*[32] (1986), a woman complained that a co-worker had made obscene comments about women in general and her in particular. The court ruled that "a reasonable person would not have been significantly affected by the same or similar circumstances,"[33] and that "women must expect a certain amount of demeaning conduct in certain work environments."[34]

But the reasonable man standard will not work, since men and women perceive situations involving SH quite differently. The reasonable person standard fares no better as it becomes the reasonable man standard when it is applied by male judges seeing things through male eyes. Studies have shown that sexual overtures that men find flattering are found by women to be insulting. And even when men recognize behavior as harassment, they think women will be flattered by it.[35] The difference in perception only strengthens my point about the group harm that SH causes all women: unlike women, men can take sexual overtures directed at them to be complimentary because the overtures do not signify the stereotyping that underlies SH of women. A reasonable man standard would not succeed as a basis upon which to determine SH, as its objectivity is outweighed by the disparity found in the way the sexes assess what is "reasonable."

Related to this last topic is the issue of the harasser's intentions. In subjective definitions this is the counterpart to the victim's being bothered. Tort law makes reference to the injuror's intentions: in battery tort, the harasser's intent to contact, in assault tort, the harasser's intent to arouse psychic apprehension in the victim, and in the tort of intentional emotional distress, the harasser's intent or recklessness, must be established in order for the victim to win her case.

But like the victim's feelings, the harasser's intentions are irrelevant to whether his behavior is harassment. As I just pointed out, many men do not take their behavior to be bothersome, and sometimes even mistakenly believe that women enjoy crude compliments about their bodies, ogling, pinching, etc. From perusing cases brought before the courts, I have come to believe that many men have psychological feelings of power over women, feelings of being in control of their world, and the like, when they harass. These feelings might be subconscious, but this should not be admitted as a defense of the harasser. Also, as I have said, many men believe women encourage SH either by their dress or language, or simply by the fact that they tolerate the abuse without protest (usually out of fear of repercussion). In light of these facts, it would be wrongheaded to allow the harasser's intentions to count in assessing harassment, though they might become relevant in determining punishment. I am arguing for an objective definition of SH: it is the attitudes embedded and reflected *in the practice* the behavior is an instance of, not the attitudes or intentions *of the perpetrator*, that makes the behavior SH.

Yet the idea that the behavior must be directed at a certain person in order for it to count as harassment, seems to suggest that intentions *do* count in assessing harassment. This feature is evident both in my definition, as well as in that found in *Black's Law Dictionary*, which takes harassment to be conduct directed against a specific person causing substantial emotional distress. If conduct is directed at a particular individual, it seems that the person expressing himself must be intentionally singling out that individual, wanting to cause her harm.

I think this is mistaken. Since the harasser can subconsciously enjoy the feeling of power harassing gives him, or might even consider his behavior to be flattering, his behavior can be directed at a specific person (or group of persons) without implying any ill intention on his part. By "directed at a particular individual," I mean that the behavior is in some way observed by a particular person (or persons). This includes, for example, sexist comments a student hears her professor say, pornographic pictures a worker sees, etc. I interpret it loosely enough to include a person's overhearing sexist comments even though the speaker has no idea the person is within earshot (sometimes referred to as "nondirected behavior"). But I interpret it to exclude the bare knowledge that sexist behavior is going on (e.g., female employees knowing that there are pornographic pictures hidden in their boss's office). If it did not exclude such behavior it would have to include knowledge of *any* sexist behavior, even if no person who can be harmed by it ever observes it (e.g., pornographic magazines strewn on a desert island). Though such behavior is sexist, it fails to constitute SH.

IV. Implications of the Objective Definition

One implication of my objective definition is that it reflects the correct way power comes into play in SH. Traditionally, SH has been taken to exist only between persons of unequal power, usually in the workplace or an educational institution. It is believed that SH in universities occurs only when a professor harasses a student, but not *vice versa*. It is said that students can cause "sexual hassle," because they cannot "destroy [the professor's] self-esteem or endanger his intellectual self-confidence," and professors "seldom suffer the complex psychological effects of sexual harassment victims."[36] MacKinnon, in her earlier book, defines SH as "the unwanted imposition of sexual requirements in the context of a relationship of unequal power."[37]

Though it is true that a lot of harassment occurs between unequals, it is false that harassment occurs *only* between unequals: equals and subordinates can harass. Indeed, power is irrelevant to tort law, and the courts now recognize harassment among co-workers under Title VII.

The one sense in which it is true that the harasser must have power over his victim is that men have power – social, political, and economic – over women as a group. This cannot be understood by singling out individual men and showing that they have power over women or any particular woman for that matter. It is power that all men have, in virtue of being men. Defining SH in the objective way I do allows us to see that *this* is the sense in which power exists in SH, in *all* of its forms. The benefit of not restricting SH to cases of unequal institutional power is that *all* victims are afforded protection.

A second implication of my definition is that it gives the courts a way of distinguishing SH from sexual attraction. It can be difficult to make this distinction, since "traditional courtship activities" are often quite sexist and frequently involve behavior that is harassment. The key is to examine the practice the behavior is an instance of. If the behavior reflects the attitude that the victim is inferior because of her sex, then it is SH. Sexual harassment is not about a man's attempting to date a woman who is not interested, as the courts have tended to believe; it is about domination, which might be reflected, of course, in the way a man goes about trying to get a date. My definition allows us to separate cases of SH from genuine sexual attraction by forcing the courts to focus on the social nature of SH.

Moreover, defining SH in the objective way I do shifts the burden and the blame off the victim. On the subjective view, the burden is on the victim to prove that she is bothered significantly enough to win a tort case; or under Title VII, to show that the behavior unreasonably interfered with her work. In tort law, where the perpetrator's intentions are allowed to figure in, the blame could easily shift to the victim by showing that she in some way welcomed or even encouraged the behavior, thereby relinquishing the perpetrator from responsibility. By focusing on the practice the behavior is an instance of, my definition has nothing to do with proving that the victim responds a certain way to the behavior, nor does it in any way blame the victim for the behavior.

Finally, defining SH in a subjective way means that the victim herself must come forward and complain, as it is her response that must be assessed. But given that most judges, law enforcement officers, and even superiors are men, it is difficult for women to do so. They are embarrassed, afraid to confront someone of the same sex as the harasser, who is likely not to see the problem. They do not feel their voices will be heard. Working with my definition will, I hope, assuage this. Recognizing SH as a group harm will allow women to come to each other's aid as co-complainers, thereby alleviating the problem of reticence. Even if the person the behavior is directed at does not feel bothered, other women can complain, as they suffer the group harm associated with SH.

V. Conclusion

The definition of SH I have defended in this paper has as its main benefit that it acknow-ledges the group harm SH causes all women, thereby getting to the heart of what is wrong with SH. By doing so, it protects all victims in all cases from even the most subtle kinds of SH, since all cases of SH have in common group harm.

Of course, as with any definition, problems exist. Though space does not allow that I deal with them, a few are worth mentioning. One is that many behaviors will count as SH, leading perhaps to an unmanageable number of claims. Another is that it will still be a matter of interpretation whether a given behavior meets the criteria for SH. Perhaps the most crucial objection is that since so many kinds of behavior count as SH, the right to free speech will be curtailed in unacceptable ways.[38]

I believe there are at least partial solutions to these problems. My proposal is only programmatic, and a thorough defense of it would include working through these and other problems. Such a defense will have to wait.

Notes

1 I would like to thank John Exdell and Lois Pineau for helpful discussions and many insightful comments on an earlier draft of this paper.

2 This suggests that only men can sexually harass women. I will defend this view later in the paper.

3 Frances Conley, a 50-year-old distinguished neurophysician at Stanford University, recently came forward with this story. Conley resigned after years of putting up with sexual harassment from her colleagues. Not only did they use Playboy spreads during their lectures, but they routinely called her "hon," invited her to bed, and fondled her legs under the operating table. *Chicago Tribune*, Sunday, June 9, 1991, Section 1, p. 22.

4 Hughes, J. and May, L. "Sexual Harassment," *Social Theory and Practice*, vol. 6, no. 3 (Fall 1980), pp. 264–5.

5 Ibid., p. 265.

6 These same myths surround the issue of rape. This is discussed fruitfully by Lois Pineau in "Date Rape: A Feminist Analysis," *Law and Philosophy*, vol. 8 (1989), pp. 217–43.

7 Catherine MacKinnon, *Sexual Harassment of Working Women: A Case of Sex Discrimi-nation* (New Haven: Yale University Press, 1979), p. 152.

8 *Lipsett* v. *Rive-Mora*, 669 F. Supp. 1188 (D. Puerto Rico 1987).

9 Dawn D. Bennett-Alexander, "Hostile Environment Sexual Harassment: A Clearer View," *Labor Law Journal*, vol. 42, no. 3 (March 1991), p. 135.

10 *Lipsett*, ibid., Sec. 15.

11 *Swentek* v. *US Air*, 830 F. 2d 552 (4th Cir. 1987).

12 *Swentek* v. *US Air*, ibid., 44 EPd at 552.

13 Billie Wright Dziech and Linda Weiner, *The Lecherous Professor: Sexual Harassment on Campus* (Boston: Beacon Press, 1984), p. 63.

14 This harm is similar to the harm Ann Cudd finds with rape. Since women are the victims of rape, "they come to be seen as in need of protection, as weak and passive, and available to all men." See Ann E. Cudd, "Enforced Pregnancy, Rape, and the Image of Woman," *Philosophical Studies*, vol. 60 (1990), pp. 47–59.

15 *Black's Law Dictionary* (6th edn) (St Paul, MN: West Publishing, 1990), p. 717.

16 *American Heritage Dictionary of the English Language* (New York: American Heritage Publishing, 1973), p. 600.

17 EEOC *Guidelines on Discrimination because of Sex*, 29, C.F.R. Sec 1604.11(a) (1980).

18 Hughes and May, "Sexual Harassment," p. 250.

19 Rosemarie Tong, *Women, Sex, and the Law* (Savage, MD: Rowman & Littlfield, 1984), p. 67.

20 *Meritor Savings Bank, FSB* v. *Vinson*, 477 US 57 (1986). 1113–16.

21 MacKinnon, *Sexual Harassment of Working Women*, p. 83.

22 Stephanie Riger, "Gender Dilemmas in Sexual Harassment Policies and Procedures," *American Psychologist*, vol. 46 (1991), pp. 497–505.

23 Martha Sperry, "Hostile Environment Sexual Harassment and the Imposition of Liability Without Notice: A Progressive Approach to Traditional Gender Roles and Power Based Relationships," *New England Law Review*, vol. 24 (1980), p. 942, fns. 174 and 175.

24 See Catherine MacKinnon, *Feminism Unmodified: Discourses on Life and Law* (Cambridge: Harvard University Press, 1987), chapter 9, for a nice discussion of the challenges women face in deciding whether to report harassment. See also Ellen Frankel Paul, "Sexual Harassment as Sex Discrimination: A Defective Paradigm," *Yale Law & Policy Review*, vol. 8, no. 2 (1990) for an excellent summary of the case law on sexual harassment.

25 MacKinnon, *Sexual Harassment of Working Women*, p. 83.

26 See Frankel Paul, "Sexual Harassment," pp. 333–65. Frankel Paul wants to get away from the "helpless victim syndrome," making women responsible for reporting harassment, and placing the burden on them to develop a tough skin so as to avoid being seen as helpless victims (pp. 362–3). On the contrary, what Frankel Paul fails to understand is that placing these additional burdens on women *detracts* from the truth that they *are* victims, and implies that they deserve the treatment if they do not develop a "tough attitude."

27 Sandra Bartky, "Foucault, Femininity, and the Modernization of Patriarchal Power," in Sandra Bartky, *Femininity and Domination: Studies in the Phenomenology of Oppression* (New York: Routledge, Chapman, and Hall, 1990), pp. 63–82. See especially pp. 77–8.

28 Ibid., p. 77.

29 This case exemplifies my point that the behavior need not be persistent in order to constitute harassment, despite the view of many courts. One catcall, for example, will constitute SH if catcalling is shown to be practice reflecting domination.

30 EEOC *Guidelines*, Sec. 1604.11(a), my emphasis.

31 *Restatement (Second) of Torts*, Sec. 146, (1965), comment i, my emphasis.

32 *Rabidue* v. *Osceola Refining Co.*, 805 F2d (1986), Sixth Circuit Court.

33 Ibid., at 662.

34 Ibid., at 620–22.

35 Stephanie Riger, "Gender Dilemmas in Sexual Harassment Policies and Procedures," *American Psychologist*, vol. 46, no. 5 (May 1991), p. 499, is where she cites the relevant studies.

36 Wright Dziech and Weiner, *The Lecherous Professor*, p. 24.

37 MacKinnon, *Sexual Harassment of Working Women*, p. 1. It is actually not clear that MacKinnon endorses this definition throughout this book, as what she says seems to suggest that harassment can occur at least between equals. In her most recent book, she recognizes that harassment "also happens among coworkers, from third parties, even by subordinates in the workplace, men who are women's hierarchical inferiors or peers." Catherine A. MacKinnon, *Feminism Unmodified: Discourses on Life and Law* (Cambridge: Harvard University Press, 1987), p. 107.

38 For an excellent analysis on sexist speech and the limits of free speech as guaranteed by the Constitution, see March Strauss, "Sexist Speech in the Workplace," *Harvard Civil Rights and Civil Liberties Law Review*, vol. 25 (1990), pp. 1–51. She cites the relevant case law concerning sexist speech that is not protected by First Amendment rights. She defends the view that the Constitution can prohibit speech demanding or requesting sexual relationships, sexually explicit speech directed at the woman, and degrading speech directed at the woman, but not sexually explicit or degrading speech that the woman employee knows exists in the workplace, even though it is not directed at her (p. 43). She employs an interesting and useful distinction between speech that discriminates, and speech that merely advocates discrimination, recognizing that the state has an interest in regulating the former, given the harm it can cause.

39

Date Rape

Lois Pineau

Date rape is nonaggravated sexual assault, nonconsensual sex that does not involve physical injury, or the explicit threat of physical injury. But because it does not involve physical injury, and because physical injury is often the only criterion that is accepted as evidence that *actus reas* is nonconsensual, what is really sexual assault is often mistaken for seduction. The replacement of the old rape laws with the new laws on sexual assault have done nothing to resolve this problem.

Rape, defined as nonconsensual sex, usually involving penetration by a man of a woman who is not his wife, has been replaced in some criminal codes with the charge of sexual assault. This has the advantage both of extending the range of possible victims of sexual assault, the manner in which people can be assaulted, and replacing a crime which is exclusive of consent, with one for which consent is a defence. But while the consent of a woman is now consistent with the conviction of her assailant in cases of aggravated assault, nonaggravated sexual assault is still distinguished from normal sex solely by the fact that it is not consented to. Thus the question of whether someone has consented to a sexual encounter is still important, and the criteria for consent continue to be the central concern of discourse on sexual assault.

However, if a man is to be convicted, it does not suffice to establish that the *actus reas* was nonconsensual. In order to be guilty of sexual assault a man must have the requisite *mens rea*, i.e., he must have believed either that his victim did not consent or that she was probably not consenting. In many common law jurisdictions a man who sincerely believes that a woman consented to a sexual encounter is deemed to lack the required *mens rea*, even though the woman did not consent, and even though his belief is not reasonable. Recently, strong dissenting voices have been raised against the sincerity condition, and the argument made that *mens rea* be defeated only if the defendant has a reasonable belief that the plaintiff consented. The introduction of legislation which excludes "honest belief" (unreasonable sincere belief) as a defence, will certainly help to provide women with greater protection against violence. But while this will be an important step forward, the question of what constitutes a reasonable belief, the problem of evidence when rapists lie, and the problem of the entrenched attitudes of the predominantly male police, judges, lawyers, and jurists who handle sexual assault cases, remains.

The criteria for *mens rea*, for the reasonableness of belief, and for consent are closely related. For although a man's sincere belief in the consent of his victim may be sufficient to defeat *mens rea*, the court is less likely to believe his belief is sincere if his belief is unreasonable. If his belief is reasonable, they are more likely to believe in the sincerity of his belief. But evidence of the reasonableness of his belief is also evidence that consent really did take place. For the very things that make it reasonable for *him* to believe that the defendant consented are often the very things that incline the court to believe that she consented. What is often missing is the voice of the woman herself, an account of what it would be reasonable for *her* to agree to, that is to say, an account of what is reasonable from *her* standpoint.

Thus, what is presented as reasonable has repercussions for four separate but related concerns: (1) the question of whether a man's belief in a woman's consent was reasonable; (2) the problem of whether it is reasonable to attribute *mens rea* to him; (3) the question of what could count as reasonable from the woman's point of view; (4) the question of what is reasonable from the court's point of view. These repercussions are of the utmost practical concern. In a culture which contains an incidence of sexual assault verging on epidemic, a criterion of reasonableness which regards mere submission as consent fails to offer persons vulnerable to those assaults adequate protection.

The following statements by self-confessed date rapists reveal how our lack of a solution for dealing with date rape protects rapists by failing to provide their victims with legal recourse:

> All of my rapes have been involved in a dating situation where I've been out with a woman I know. . . . I wouldn't take no for an answer. I think it had something to do with my acceptance of rejection. I had low self-esteem and not much self-confidence and when I was rejected for something which I considered to be rightly mine, I became angry and I went ahead anyway. And this was the same in any situation, whether it was rape or it was something else.

> When I did date, when I was younger, I would pick up a girl and if she didn't come across I would threaten her or slap her face then tell her she was going to fuck – that was it. But that's because I didn't want to waste time with any come-ons. It took too much time. I wasn't interested because I didn't like them as people anyway, and I just went with them just to get laid. Just to say that I laid them.

There is, at this time, nothing to protect women from this kind of unscrupulous victimization. A woman on a casual date with a virtual stranger has almost no chance of bringing a complaint of sexual assault before the courts. One reason for this is the prevailing criterion for consent. According to this criterion, consent is implied unless some emphatic episodic sign of resistance occurred, and its occurrence can be established. But if no episodic act occurred, or if it did occur, and the defendant claims that it didn't, or if the defendant threatened the plaintiff but won't admit it in court, it is almost impossible to find any evidence that would support the plaintiff's word against the defendant. This difficulty is exacerbated by suspicion on the part of the courts, police, and legal educators that even where an act of resistance occurs, this act should not be interpreted as a withholding of consent, and this suspicion is especially upheld where the accused is a man who is known to the female plaintiff.

In Glanville Williams's classic textbook on criminal law we are warned that where a man is unknown to a woman, she does not consent if she expresses her rejection in the form of an episodic and vigorous act at the "vital moment". But if the man is known to the woman she must, according to Williams, make use of "all means available to her to repel the man". Williams warns that women often welcome a "mastery advance" and present a token resistance. He quotes Byron's couplet,

> A little still she strove, and much repented
> And whispering 'I will ne'er consent' – consented

by way of alerting law students to the difficulty of distinguishing real protest from pretence. Thus, while in principle a firm unambiguous stand, or a healthy show of temper ought to be sufficient, if established, to show nonconsent, in practice the forceful overriding of such a stance is apt to be taken as an indication that the resistance was not seriously intended, and that the seduction had succeeded. The consequence of this is that it is almost impossible to establish the defendant's guilt beyond a reasonable doubt.

Thus, on the one hand, we have a situation in which women are vulnerable to the most exploitive tactics at the hands of men who are known to them. On the other hand, almost nothing will count as evidence of their being assaulted, including their having taken an emphatic stance in withholding their consent. The new laws have done almost nothing to change this situation. Yet clearly, some solution must be sought. Moreover, the road to that solution presents itself clearly enough as a need for a reformulation of the criterion of consent. It is patent that a criterion that collapses whenever the crime itself succeeds will not suffice. . . .

The reasoning that underlies the present criterion of consent is entangled in a number of mutually supportive mythologies with see sexual assault as masterful seduction, and silent submission as sexual enjoyment. Because the prevailing ideology has so much informed our conceptualization of sexual interaction, it is extraordinarily difficult for us to distinguish between assault and seduction, submission and enjoyment, or so we imagine. At the same time, this failure to distinguish has given rise to a network of rationalizations that support the conflation of assault with seduction, submission and enjoyment. . . .

Rape Myths

The belief that the natural aggression of men and the natural reluctance of women somehow makes date rape understandable underlies a number of prevalent myths about rape and human sexuality. These beliefs maintain their force partly on account of a logical compulsion exercised by them at an unconscious level. The only way of refuting them effectively, is to excavate the logical propositions involved, and to expose their misapplication to the situations to which they have been applied. In what follows, I propose to excavate the logical support for popular attitudes that are tolerant of date rape. These myths are not just popular, however, but often emerge in the arguments of judges who acquit date rapists, and policemen who refuse to lay charges.

The claim that the victim provoked a sexual incident, that "she asked for it", is by far the most common defence given by men who are accused of sexual assault. Feminists, rightly incensed by this response, often treat it as beneath contempt, singling out the defence as an argument against it. On other fronts, sociologists have identified the response as part of an overall tendency of people to see the world as just, a tendency which disposes them to conclude that people for the most part deserve what they get. However, an inclination to see the world as just requires us to construct an account which yields this outcome, and it is just such an account that I wish to examine with regard to date rape.

The least sophisticated of the "she asked for it" rationales, and in a sense, the easiest to deal with, appeals to an injunction against sexually provocative behaviour on the part of women. If women should not be sexually provocative, then, from this standpoint, a woman who is sexually provocative deserves to suffer the consequences. Now it will not do to respond that women get raped even when they are not sexually provocative, or that it is men who get to interpret (unfairly) what counts as sexually provocative. The question should be: Why shouldn't a woman be sexually provocative? Why should this behaviour warrant any kind of aggressive response whatsoever?

Attempts to explain that women have a right to behave in sexually provocative ways without suffering dire consequences still meet with surprisingly tough resistance. Even people who find nothing wrong or sinful with sex itself, in any of its forms, tend to suppose that women must not behave sexually unless they are prepared to carry through on some fuller course of sexual interaction. The logic of this response seems to be that at some point a woman's behaviour commits her to following through on the full course of a sexual encounter as it is defined by her assailant. At some point she has made an agreement, or formed a contract, and once that is done, her contractor is entitled to demand that she satisfy the terms of that contract. Thus, this view about sexual responsibility and desert is supported by other assumptions about contracts and agreement. But we do not normally suppose that casual nonverbal behaviour generates agreements. Nor do we normally grant private persons the right to enforce contracts. What rationale would support our conclusion in this case?

The rationale, I believe, comes in the form of a belief in the especially insistent nature of male sexuality, an insistence which lies at the foot of natural male aggression, and which is extremely difficult, perhaps impossible to contain. At a certain point in the arousal process, it is thought, a man's rational will gives way to the prerogatives of nature. His sexual need can and does reach a point where it is uncontrollable, and his natural masculine aggression kicks in to ensure that this need is met. Women, however, are naturally more contained, and so it is their responsibility not to provoke the irrational in the male. If they do go so far as that, they have both failed in their responsibilities, and subjected themselves to the inevitable. One does not go into the lion's cage and expect not to be eaten. Natural feminine reluctance, it is thought, is no protection against a sexually aroused male.

This belief about the normal aggressiveness of male sexuality is complemented by common knowledge about female gender development. Once, women were taught to deny their sexuality and to aspire to ideals of chastity. Things have not changed so much. Women still tend to eschew conquest mentalities in favour of a combination of sex and affection. Insofar as this is thought to be merely a cultural requirement, however, there is an expectation that women will be coy about their sexual desire. The assumption that women both want to indulge sexually, and are inclined to sacrifice this desire for higher ends, gives rise to the myth that they want to be raped. After all, doesn't rape give them the sexual enjoyment they *really* want, at the same time that it relieves them of the responsibility for admitting to and acting upon what they want? And how then can we blame men, who have been socialized to be aggressively seductive precisely for the purpose of overriding female reserve? If we find fault at all, we are inclined to cast our suspicions on the motives of the woman. For it is on her that the contradictory roles of sexual desirer and sexual denier have been placed. Our awareness of the contradiction expected of her makes us suspect her honesty. In the past, she was expected to deny her complicity because of the shame and guilt she felt at having submitted. This expectation persists in many quarters today, and is carried over into a general suspicion about her character, and the fear that she might make a false accusation out of revenge, or some other low motive.

But if women really want sexual pleasure, what inclines us to think that they will get it through rape? This conclusion logically requires a theory about the dynamics of sexual pleasure that sees that pleasure as an emergent property of overwhelming male insistence. For the assumption that a raped female experiences sexual pleasure implies that the person who rapes her knows how to cause that pleasure independently of any information she might convey on that point. Since her ongoing protest is inconsistent with requests to be touched in particular ways in particular places, to have more of this and less of that, then we must believe that the person who touches her knows these particular ways and places instinctively, without any directives from her.

Thus, we find, underlying and reinforcing this belief in incommunicative male prowess, a conception of sexual pleasure that springs from wordless interchanges, and of sexual success that occurs in a place of meaningful silence. The language of seduction is accepted as a tacit language: eye contact, smiles, blushes, and faintly discernible gestures. It is, accordingly, imprecise and ambiguous. It would be easy for a man to make mistakes about the message conveyed, understandable that he should mistakenly think that a sexual invitation has been made, and a bargain struck. But honest mistakes, we think, must be excused.

In sum, the belief that women should not be sexually provocative is logically linked to several other beliefs, some normative, some empirical. The normative beliefs are (1) that people should keep the agreements they make, (2) that sexually provocative behaviour, taken beyond a certain point, generates agreements, (3) that the peculiar nature of male and female sexuality places such agreements in a special category, one in which the possibility of retracting an agreement is ruled out, or at least made highly unlikely, (4) that women are not to be trusted, in sexual matters at least. The empirical belief, which turns out to be false, is that male sexuality is not subject to rational and moral control.

Dispelling the Myths

The "she asked for it" justification of sexual assault incorporates a conception of a contract that would be difficult to defend in any other context and the presumptions about human sexuality which function to reinforce sympathies rooted in the contractual notion of just deserts are not supported by empirical research.

The belief that a woman generates some sort of contractual obligation whenever her behaviour is interpreted as seductive is the most indefensible part of the mythology of rape. In law, contracts are not legitimate just because a promise has been made. In particular, the use of pressure tactics to extract agreement is frowned upon. Normally, an agreement is upheld only if the contractors were clear on what they were getting into, and had sufficient time to reflect on the wisdom of their doing so. Either there must be a clear tradition in which the expectations involved in the contract are fairly well known (marriage), or there must be an explicit written agreement concerning the exact terms of the contract and the expectations of the persons involved. But whatever the terms of a contract, there is no private right to enforce it. So that if I make a contract with you on which I renege, the only permissible recourse for you is through due legal process.

Now it is not clear whether sexual contracts can be made to begin with, or if so, what sort of sexual contracts would be legitimate. But assuming that they could be made, the terms of those contracts would not be enforceable. To allow public enforcement would be to grant the State the overt right to force people to have sex, and this would clearly be unacceptable. Granting that sexual contracts are legitimate, state enforcement of such contracts would have to be limited to ordering nonsexual compensation for breaches of contract. So it makes no difference whether a sexual contract is tacit or explicit. There are no grounds whatsoever that would justify enforcement of its terms.

Thus, even if we assume that a woman has initially agreed to an encounter, her agreement does not automatically make all subsequent sexual activity to which she submits legitimate. If during coitus a woman should experience pain, be suddenly overcome with guilt or fear of pregnancy, or simply lose her initial desire, those are good reasons for her to change her mind. Having changed her mind, neither her partner nor the State has any right to force her to continue. But then if she is forced to continue she is assaulted. Thus, establishing that consent occurred at a particular point during a sexual encounter should not exclusively establish the legitimacy of the encounter. What is needed is a reading of whether she agreed throughout the encounter.

If the "she asked for it" contractual view of sexual interchange has any validity, it is because there is a point at which there is no stopping a sexual encounter, a point at which that encounter becomes the inexorable outcome of the unfolding of natural events. If a sexual encounter is like a slide on which I cannot stop halfway down, it will be relevant whether I enter the slide of my own free will, or am pushed.

But there is no evidence that the entire sexual act is like a slide. While there may be a few seconds in the "plateau" period just prior to orgasm in which people are "swept" away by sexual feelings to the point where we could justifiably understand their lack of heed for the comfort of their partner, the greater part of a sexual encounter comes well within the bounds of morally responsible control of our own actions. Indeed, the available evidence shows that most of the activity involved in sex has to do with building the requisite level of desire, a task that involves the proper use of foreplay, the possibility of which implies control over the form that foreplay will take. Modern sexual therapy assumes that such control is universally accessible, and so far there has been no reason to question that assumption. Sexologists are unanimous, moreover, in holding that mutual sexual enjoyment requires an atmosphere of comfort and communication, a minimum of pressure, and an ongoing check-up on one's partner's state. They maintain that different people have different predilections, and that what is pleasurable for one person is very often anathema to another. These findings show that the way to achieve sexual pleasure, at any time at all, let alone with a casual acquaintance, decidedly does not involve overriding the other person's express reservations and providing them with just any kind of sexual stimulus. And while we do not want to allow science and technology a voice in which the voices of particular women are drowned, in this case science seems to concur with women's perception that aggressive incommunicative sex is not what they want. But if science and the voice of women concur, if aggressive seduction does not lead to good sex, if women do not like it, or want it, then it is not rational to think that they would agree to it. Where such sex takes place, it is therefore rational to presume that the sex was not consensual.

The myth that women like to be raped, is closely connected, as we have seen, to doubt about their honesty in sexual matters, and this suspicion is exploited by defence lawyers when sexual assault cases make it to the courtroom. It is an unfortunate consequence of the presumption of innocence that rape victims who end up in court frequently find that it is they who are on trial. For if the defendant is innocent, then either he did not intend to do what he was accused of, or the plaintiff is mistaken about his identity, or she is lying. Often the last alternative is the only plausible defence, and as a result, the plaintiff's word seldom goes unquestioned. Women are frequently accused of having made a false accusation, either as a defensive mechanism for dealing with guilt and shame, or out of a desire for revenge.

Now there is no point in denying the possibility of false accusation, though there are probably better ways of seeking revenge on a man than accusing him of rape. However, we can now establish a logical connection between the evidence that a woman was subjected to high-pressure aggressive "seduction" tactics, and her claim that she did not consent to that encounter. Where the kind of encounter is not the sort to which it would be reasonable to consent, there is a logical presumption that a woman who claims that she did not consent is telling the truth. Where the kind of sex involved is not the sort of sex we would expect a woman to like, the burden of proof should not be on the woman to show that she did not consent, but on the defendant to show that contrary to every reasonable expectation she did consent. The defendant should be required to convince the court that the plaintiff persuaded him to have sex with her even though there are not visible reasons why she should.

In conclusion, there are no grounds for the "she asked for it" defence. Sexually provocative behaviour does not generate sexual contracts. Even where there are sexual agreements, they cannot be legitimately enforced either by the State, or by private right, or by natural prerogative. Secondly, all the evidence suggests that neither women nor men find sexual enjoyment in rape or in any form of noncommunicative sexuality. Thirdly, male sexual desire is containable, and can be subjected to moral and rational control. Fourthly, since there is no reason why women should not be sexually provocative, they do not "deserve" any sex they do not want. This last is a welcome discovery. The taboo on sexual provocativeness in women is a taboo both on sensuality and on teasing. But sensuality is a source of delight, and teasing is playful and inspires wit. What a relief to learn that it is not sexual provocativeness, but its enemies, that constitute a danger to the world. . . .

In thinking about sex we must keep in mind its sensual ends, and the facts show that aggressive high-pressure sex contradicts those ends. Consensual sex in dating situations is presumed to aim at mutual enjoyment. It may not always do this, and when it does, it might not always succeed. There is no logical incompatibility between wanting to continue a sexual encounter, and failing to derive sexual pleasure from it.

But it seems to me that there is a presumption in favour of the connection between sex and sexual enjoyment, and that if a man wants to be sure that he is not forcing himself on a woman, he has an obligation either to ensure that the encounter really is mutually enjoyable, or to know the reasons why she would want to continue the encounter in spite of her lack of enjoyment. A closer investigation of the nature of this obligation will enable us to construct a more rational and more plausible norm of sexual conduct.

Onora O'Neill has argued that in intimate situations we have an obligation to take the ends of others as our own, and to promote those ends in a non-manipulative and non-paternalistic manner. Now it seems that in honest sexual encounters just this is required. Assuming that each person enters the encounter in order to seek sexual satisfaction, each person engaging in the encounter has an obligation to help the other seek his or her ends. To do otherwise is to risk acting in opposition to what the other desires, and hence to risk acting without the other's consent.

But the obligation to promote the sexual ends of one's partner implies that obligation to know what those ends are, and also the obligation to know how those ends are attained. Thus, the problem comes down to a problem of epistemic responsibility, the responsibility to know. The solution, in my view, lies in the practice of a communicative sexuality, one which combines the appropriate knowledge of the other with respect for the dialectics of desire. . . .

Cultural Presumptions

Now it may well be that we have no obligation to care for strangers, and I do not wish to claim that we do. Nonetheless, it seems that O'Neill's point about the special moral duties we have in certain intimate situations is supported by a conceptual relation between certain kinds of personal relationships and the expectation that it should be a communicative relation. Friendship is a case in point. It is a relation that is greatly underdetermined by what we usually include in our sets of rights and obligations. For the most part, rights and obligations disappear as terms by which friendship is guided. They are still there, to be called upon, in case the relationship breaks down, but insofar as the friendship is a friendship, it is concerned with fostering the quality of the interaction and not with standing on rights. Thus, because we are friends, we share our property, and property rights between us are not invoked. Because we are friends, privacy is not an issue. Because we are friends we may see to each other's needs as often as we see to our own. The same can be said for relations between lovers, parents and dependent children, and even between spouses, at least when interaction is functioning at an optimal level. When such relations break down to the point that people must stand on their rights, we can often say that the actors ought to make more of an effort, and in many instances fault them for their lack of charity, tolerance, or benevolence. Thus, although we have a right to end friendships, it may be a reflection on our lack of virtue that we do so, and while we cannot be criticized for violating other people's rights, we can be rightfully deprecated for lacking the virtue to sustain a friendship.

But is there a similar conceptual relation between the kind of activity that a date is, and the sort of moral practice that it requires? My claim is that there is, and that this connection is easily established once we recognize the cultural presumption that dating is a gesture of friendship and regard. Traditionally, the decision to date indicates that two people have an initial attraction to each other, that they are disposed to like each other, and look forward to enjoying each other's company. Dating derives its implicit meaning from this tradition. It retains this meaning unless other aims are explicitly stated, and even then it may not be possible to alienate this meaning. It is a rare woman who will not spurn a man who states explicitly, right at the onset, that he wants to go out with her solely on the condition that he have sexual intercourse with her at the end of the evening, and that he has no interest in her company apart from gaining that end, and no concern for mutual satisfaction.

Explicit protest to the contrary aside, the conventions of dating confer on it its social meaning, and this social meaning implies a relationship which is more like friendship than the cutthroat competition of opposing teams. As such, it requires that we do more than stand on our rights with regard to each other. As long as we are operating under the auspices of a dating relationship, it requires that we behave in the mode of friendship and trust. But if a date is more like a friendship than a business contract, then clearly respect for the dialectics of desire is incompatible with the sort of sexual pressure that is inclined to end in date rape. And clearly, also, a conquest mentality which exploits a situation of trust and respect for purely selfish ends is morally pernicious. Failure to respect the dialectics of desire when operating under the auspices of friendship and trust is to act in flagrant disregard of the moral requirement to avoid manipulative, coercive, and exploitive behaviour.

Respect for the dialectics of desire is *prima facie* inconsistent with the satisfaction of one person at the expense of the other. The proper end of friendship relations is mutual satisfaction. But the requirement of mutuality means that we must take a communicative approach to discovering the ends of the other, and this entails that we respect the dialectics of desire.

But now that we know what communicative sexuality is, and that it is morally required, and that it is the only feasible means to mutual sexual enjoyment, why not take this model as the norm of what is reasonable in sexual interaction. The evidence of sexologists strongly indicates that women whose partners are aggressively uncommunicative have little chance of experiencing sexual pleasure. But it is not reasonable for women to consent to what they have little chance of enjoying. Hence it is not reasonable for women to consent to aggressive noncommunicative sex. Nor can we reasonably suppose that women have consented to sexual encounters which we know and they know they do not find enjoyable. With the communicative model as the norm, the aggressive contractual model should strike us as a model of deviant sexuality, and sexual encounters patterned on that model should strike us as encounters to which *prima facie* no one would reasonably agree. But if acquiescence to an encounter counts as consent only if the acquiescence is reasonable, something to which a reasonable person, in full possession of knowledge relevant to the encounter, would agree, then acquiescence to aggressive noncommunicative sex is not reasonable. Hence, acquiescence under such conditions should not count as consent.

Thus, where communicative sexuality does not occur, we lack the main ground for believing that the sex involved was consensual. Moreover, where a man does not engage in communicative sexuality, he acts either out of reckless disregard, or out of wilful ignorance. For he cannot know, except through the practice of communicative sexuality, whether his partner has any sexual reason for continuing the encounter. And where she does not, he runs the risk of imposing on her what she is not willing to have. All that is needed then, in order to provide women with legal protection from "date rape" is to make both reckless indifference and wilful ignorance a sufficient condition of *mens rea* and to make communicative sexuality the accepted norm of sex to which a reasonable woman would agree. Thus, the appeal to communicative sexuality as a norm for sexual encounters accomplishes two things. It brings the aggressive sex involved in "date rape" well within the realm of sexual assault, and it locates the guilt of date rapists in the failure to approach sexual relations on a communicative basis.

40

Men in Groups: Collective Responsibility for Rape

Larry May and Robert Strikwerda

As teenagers, we ran in a crowd that incessantly talked about sex. Since most of us were quite afraid of discovering our own sexual inadequacies, we were quite afraid of women's sexuality. To mask our fear, of which we were quite ashamed, we maintained a posture of bravado, which we were able to sustain through mutual reinforcement when in small groups or packs. Riding from shopping mall to fast food establishment, we would tell each other stories about our sexual exploits, stories we all secretly believed to be pure fictions. We drew strength from the camaraderie we felt during these experiences. Some members of our group would yell obscenities at women on the street as we drove by. Over time, conversation turned more and more to group sex, especially forced sex with women we passed on the road. To give it its proper name, our conversation turned increasingly to rape. At a certain stage, we tired of it all and stopped associating with this group of men, or perhaps they were in most ways still boys. The reason we left was not that we disagreed with what was going on but, if this decision to leave was reasoned at all, it was that the posturing (the endless attempts to impress one another by our daring ways) simply became very tiresome. Only much later in life did we think that there was anything wrong, morally, socially, or politically, with what went on in that group of adolescents who seemed so ready to engage in rape. Only later still did we wonder whether we shared in responsibility for the rapes that are perpetrated by those men who had similar experiences to ours.

This is a paper about the relationship between the shared experiences of men in groups, especially experiences that make rape more likely in western culture, and the shared responsibility of men for the prevalence of rape in that culture. The claim of the paper is that in some societies men are collectively responsible for rape in that most if not all men contribute in various ways to the prevalence of rape, and as a result, these men should share in responsibility for rape.

Most men do very little at all to oppose rape in their societies; does this make them something like co-conspirators with the men who rape? In Canada, a number of men have founded the "White Ribbon Campaign." This is a program of fund-raising, consciousness raising, and symbolic wearing of white ribbons during the week ending on December 6th, the anniversary of the murder of 14 women at a Montreal engineering school by a man shouting "I hate feminists." Should men in US society start a similar campaign? If they do not, do they deserve the "co-conspirator" label? If they do, is this symbolic act enough to diminish their responsibility? Should men be speaking out against the program of rape in the war in Bosnia? What should they tell their sons about such rapes, and about rapes that occur in their home towns? If men remain silent, are they not complicitous with the rapists?

We will argue that insofar as male bonding and socialization in groups contributes to the prevalence of rape in western societies, men in those societies should feel responsible for the prevalence of rape and should feel motivated to counteract such violence and rape. In addition, we will argue that rape should be seen as something that men, as a group, are collectively responsible for, in a way which parallels the collective responsibility of a society for crimes against humanity perpetrated by some members of their society. Rape is indeed a crime against humanity, not merely a crime against a particular woman. And rape is a crime perpetrated by men as a group, not merely by the individual rapist.

To support our claims we will criticize four other ways to understand responsibility for rape. First, it is sometimes said that only the rapist is responsible since he alone intentionally committed the act of rape. Secondly, it is sometimes said that no one is responsible since rape is merely a biologically oriented response to stimuli that men have little or no control over. Thirdly, it is sometimes said that everyone, women and men alike, contribute to the violent environment which produces rape so both women and men are equally responsible for rape, and hence it is a mistake to single men out. Fourthly, it is sometimes said that it is "patriarchy," rather than individual men or men as a group, which is responsible for rape. After examining each of these views we will conclude by briefly offering our own positive reasons for thinking that men are collectively responsible for the prevalence of rape in western society.

I. The Rapist as Loner or Demon

Joyce Carol Oates has recently described the sport of boxing, where men are encouraged to violate the social rule against harming one another, as "a highly organized ritual that violates taboo."

> The paradox of the boxer is that, in the ring, he experiences himself as a living conduit for the inchoate, demonic will of the crowd: the expression of their collective desire, which is to pound another human being into absolute submission. (Oates, 1992, p. 60)

Oates makes the connection here between boxing and rape. The former boxing heavyweight champion of the world, Mike Tyson, epitomizes this connection both because he is a convicted rapist, and also because, according to Oates, in his fights he regularly used the pre-fight taunt "I'll make you into my girlfriend," clearly the "boast of a rapist" (Oates, 1992, p. 61).

Just after being convicted of rape, Mike Tyson gave a twisted declaration of his innocence.

> I didn't rape anyone. I didn't hurt anyone – no black eyes, no broken ribs. When I'm in the ring, I break their ribs, I break their jaws. To me, that's hurting someone. (St Louis Post Dispatch, 1992)

In the ring, Tyson had a license to break ribs and jaws; and interestingly he understood that this was a case of hurting another person. It was just that in the ring it was acceptable. He knew that he was not supposed to hurt people outside the ring. But since he didn't break any ribs or jaws, how could anyone say that he hurt his accuser, Desiree Washington?

Having sex with a woman could not be construed as having hurt her, for Tyson apparently, unless ribs or jaws were broken.

Tyson's lawyer, attempting to excuse Tyson's behavior, said that the boxer grew up in a "male-dominated world." And this is surely true. He was plucked from a home for juvenile delinquents and raised by boxing promoters. Few American males had been so richly imbued with male tradition, or more richly rewarded for living up to the male stereotype of the aggressive, indomitable fighter. Whether or not he recognized it as a genuine insight, Tyson's lawyer points us toward the heart of the matter in American culture: misbehavior, especially sexual misbehavior of males toward females is, however mixed the messages, something that many men condone. This has given rise to the use of the term "the rape culture" to describe the climate of attitudes that exists in the contemporary American male-dominated world (see Griffin, 1971).

While noting all of this, Joyce Carol Oates ends her *Newsweek* essay on Tyson's rape trial by concluding that "no one is to blame except the perpetrator himself." She absolves the "culture" at large of any blame for Tyson's behavior. Oates regards Tyson as a sadist who took pleasure in inflicting pain both in and out of the boxing ring. She comes very close to demonizing him when, at the end of her essay, she suggests that Tyson is an outlaw or even a sociopath. And while she is surely right to paint Tyson's deed in the most horrific colors, she is less convincing when she suggests that Tyson is very different from other males in our society. In one telling statement in her essay, however, Oates opens the door for a less individualistic view of rape by acknowledging that the boxing community had built up in Tyson a "grandiose sense of entitlement, fueled by the insecurities and emotions of adolescence" (Oates, 1992, p. 61).

Rape is normally committed by individual men; but, in our view, rape is not best understood in individualistic terms. The chief reasons for this are that individual men are more likely to engage in rape when they are in groups, and men receive strong encouragement to rape from the way they are socialized as men, that is, in the way they come to see themselves as instantiations of what it means to be a man. Both the "climate" that encourages rape and the "socialization" patterns which instill negative attitudes about women are difficult to understand or assess when one focuses on the isolated individual perpetrator of a rape. There are significant social dimensions to rape that are best understood as group-oriented.

As parents, we have observed that male schoolchildren are much more likely to misbehave (and subsequently to be punished by being sent to "time out") than are female schoolchildren. This fact is not particularly remarkable, for boys are widely believed to be more active than girls. What is remarkable is that school teachers, in our experience, are much more likely to condone the misbehavior of boys than the misbehavior of girls. "Boys will be boys" is heard as often today as it was in previous times. (See Robert Lipsyte's essay about the Glen Ridge, New Jersey rape trial where the defense attorney used just these words to defend the star high school football players who raped a retarded girl.) From their earliest experience with authority figures, little boys are given mixed signals about misbehavior. Yes, they are punished, but they are also treated as if their misbehavior is expected, even welcome. It is for some boys, as it was for us, a "badge of honor" to be sent to detention or "time out." From older boys and from their peers, boys learn that they often will be ostracized for being "too goody-goody." It is as if part of the mixed message is that boys are given a license to misbehave.

And which of these boys will turn out to be rapists is often as much a matter of luck as it is a matter of choice. The data on date rape suggest that young men in our society engage in much more rape than anyone previously anticipated. It is a serious mistake in psychological categorization to think that all of these rapes are committed by sadists. (Studies by Amir, cited in Griffin, 1971, p. 178, show that the average rapist is not psychologically "abnormal.") Given our own experiences and similar reports from others, it is also a serious mistake to think that those who rape are significantly different from the rest of the male population. (Studies by Smithyman, cited in Scully, 1990, p. 75, indicate that rapists "seemed not to differ markedly from the majority of males in our culture.") Our conclusion is that the typical rapist is not a demon or sadist, but, in some sense, could have been many men.

Most of those who engage in rape are at least partially responsible for these rapes, but the question we have posed is this: are those who perpetrate rape the *only* ones who are responsible for rape? Contrary to what Joyce Carol Oates contends, we believe that it is a serious mistake to think that only the perpetrators are responsible. The interactions of men, especially in all-male groups, contribute to a pattern of socialization that also plays a major role in the incidence of rape. In urging that more than the individual perpetrators be seen as responsible for rape, we do not mean to suggest that the responsibility of the perpetrator be diminished. When responsibility for harm is shared it need not be true that the perpetrators of harm find their responsibility relieved or even diminished. Rather, shared responsibility for harms merely means that the range of people who are implicated in these harms is extended. (More will be said on this point in the final section.)

II.   The Rapist as Victim of Biology

The most recent psychological study of rape is that done by Randy Thornhill and Nancy Wilmsen Thornhill (1992). In this work, any contention that coercion or rape may be socially or culturally learned is derisively dismissed, as is any feminist argument for changing men's attitudes through changing especially group-based socialization. The general hypothesis they support is that:

> sexual coercion by men reflects a sex-specific, species-typical psychological adaptation to rape: Men have certain psychological traits that evolved by natural selection specifically in the context of coercive sex and made rape adaptive during human evolution. (p. 363)

They claim that rape is an adaptive response to biological differences between men and women.

Thornhill and Thornhill contend that the costs to women to engage in sex ("nine months of pregnancy") greatly exceed the costs to men ("a few minutes of time and an energetically cheap ejaculate"). As a result women and men came very early in evolutionary time to adapt quite differently sexually.

> Because women are more selective about mates and more interested in evaluating them and delaying copulation, men, to get sexual access, must often break through feminine barriers of hesitation, equivocation, and resistance. (p. 366)

Males who adapted by developing a proclivity to rape and thus who "solved the problem" by forcing sex on a partner, were able to "out-reproduce" other more passive males and gain an evolutionary advantage.

In one paragraph, Thornhill and Thornhill dismiss feminists who support a "social learning theory of rape" by pointing out that males of several "species with an evolutionary history of polygyny" are also "more aggressive, sexually assertive and eager to copulate." Yet, in "the vast majority of these species there is no sexual training of juveniles by other members of the group." This evidence, they conclude, thoroughly discredits the social learning theory and means that such theories "are never alternatives to evolutionary hypotheses about psychological adaptation" (p. 364). In response to their critics, Thornhill and Thornhill go so far as to say that the feminist project of changing socialization patterns is pernicious.

> The sociocultural view does seem to offer hope and a simple remedy in that it implies that we need only fix the way that boys are socialized and rape will disappear. This naive solution is widespread. . . . As Hartung points out, those who feel that the social problem of rape can be solved by changing the nature of men through naive and arbitrary social adjustments should "get real about rape" because their perspective is a danger to us all. (p. 416)

According to the Thornhills, feminists and other social theorists need to focus instead on what are called the "cues that affect the use of rape by adult males" (p. 416).

The evolutionary biological account of rape we have rehearsed above would seemingly suggest that no one is responsible for rape. After all, if rape is an adaptive response to different sexual development in males and females, particular individuals who engage in rape are merely doing what they are naturally adapted to do. Rape is something to be controlled by those who control the "cues" that stimulate the natural rapist instincts in all men. It is for this reason that the Thornhills urge that more attention be given to male arousal and female stimulation patterns in laboratory settings (p. 375). Notice that even on the Thornhills' own terms, those who provide the cues may be responsible for the prevalence of rape, even if the perpetrators are not. But Thornhill and Thornhill deny that there are any normative conclusions that follow from their research, and criticize those who wish to draw out such implications as committing the "naturalistic fallacy" (p. 407).

In contrast to the Thornhills, a more plausible sociobiological account is given by Lionel Tiger. Tiger is often cited as someone who attempted to excuse male aggression. In his important study he defines aggression as distinct from violence, but nonetheless sees violence as one possible outcome of the natural aggressive tendencies, especially in men.

> Aggression occurs when an individual or group see their interest, their honor, or their job bound up with coercing the animal, human, or physical environment to achieve their own ends rather than (or in spite of) the goals of the object of their action. Violence may occur in the process of interaction. (Tiger [1969] 1984, pp. 158–9)

For Tiger, aggression is intentional behavior which is goal-directed and based on procuring something which is necessary for survival. Aggression is a " 'normal' feature of the human biologically based repertoire" (p. 159). Violence, "coercion involving physical force to resolve conflict" (p. 159), on the other hand, is not necessarily a normal response to one's environment, although in some circumstances it may be. Thus, while human males are evolutionarily adapted to be aggressive, they are not necessarily adapted to be violent.

Tiger provided an account that linked aggression in males with their biological evolution.

> Human aggression is in part a function of the fact that hunting was vitally important to human evolution and that aggression is typically undertaken by males in the framework of a unisexual social bond of which participants are aware and with which they are concerned. It is implied, therefore, that aggression is "instinctive" but also must occur within an explicit social context varying from culture to culture and to be learned by members of any community. . . . Men in continuous association aggress against the environment in much the same way as men and women in continuous association have sexual relations. (pp. 159–60)

And while men are thus predisposed to engage in aggression, in ways that women are not, it is not true in Tiger's view that a predisposition to engage in violent acts is a normal part of this difference.

Thornhill and Thornhill fail to consider Tiger's contention that men are evolutionarily adapted to be aggressive, but not necessarily to be violent. With Tiger's distinction in mind it may be said that human males, especially in association with other males, are adapted to aggress against women in certain social environments. But this aggressive response need not lead to violence, or the threat of violence, of the sort epitomized by rape; rather it may merely affect non-coercive mating rituals. On a related point, Tiger argues that the fact that war has historically been "virtually a male monopoly" (p. 81) is due to both male bonding patterns and evolutionary adaptation. Evolutionary biology provides only part of the story since male aggressiveness need not result in such violent encounters as occur in war or rape. After all, many men do not rape or go to war; the cultural cues provided by socialization must be considered at least as important as evolutionary adaptation.

We side with Tiger against the Thornhills in focusing on the way that all-male groups socialize their members and provide "cues" for violence. Tiger has recently allied himself with feminists such as Catherine MacKinnon and others who have suggested that male attitudes need to be radically altered in order to have a major impact on the incidence of rape. (See the preface to the second edition of Tiger [1969] 1984.) One of the implications of Tiger's research is that rape and other forms of male aggressive behavior are not best understood as isolated acts of individuals. Rather than simply seeing violent aggression as merely a biologically predetermined response, Tiger places violent aggressiveness squarely into the group dynamics of men's interactions – a result of his research not well appreciated.

In a preface to the second edition of his book, Tiger corrects an unfortunate misinterpretation of his work.

> One of the stigmas which burdened this book was an interpretation of it as an apology for male aggression and even a potential stimulus of it – after all, boys will be boys. However I clearly said the opposite: "This is not to say that . . . hurtful and destructive relations between groups of men are inevitable . . . It may be possible, as many writers have suggested, to alter social conceptions of maleness so that gentility and equivocation rather than toughness and more or less arbitrary decisiveness are highly valued." (p. 191)

If Tiger is right, and the most important "cues" are those which young boys and men get while in the company of other boys and men, then the feminist project of changing male socialization patterns may be seen as consistent with, rather than opposed to, the sociobiological hypotheses. Indeed, other evidence may be cited to buttress the feminist social-learning perspective against the Thornhills. Different human societies have quite different rates of rape. In her anthropological research among the Minangkabau of West Sumatra, Peggy Reeves Sanday has found that this society is relatively rape-free. Rape does occur, but at such a low rate – 28 per 3 million in 1981–82 for example – as to be virtually nonexistent (Sanday, 1986, p. 85; also see Sanday, 1990, and Lepowsky, 1990). In light of such research, men, rather than women, are the ones who would need to change their behavior. This is because it is the socialization of men by men in their bonding-groups, and the view of women that is engendered, that provides the strongest cues toward rape. Since there may indeed be something that males could and should be doing differently that would affect the prevalence of rape, it does not seem unreasonable to continue to investigate the claim that men are collectively responsible for the prevalence of rape.

III. The Rapist as Victim of Society

It is also possible to acknowledge that men are responsible for the prevalence of rape in our society but nonetheless to argue that women are equally responsible. Rape is often portrayed as a sex crime perpetrated largely by men against women. But importantly, rape is also a crime of violence, and many factors in our society have increased the prevalence of violence. This prevalence of violence is the cause of both rape and war in western societies. Our view, that violence of both sorts is increased in likelihood by patterns of male socialization, which then creates collective male responsibility, may be countered by pointing out that socialization patterns are created by both men and women, thereby seemingly implicating both men and women in collective responsibility for rape and war.

Sam Keen has contended that it is violence that we should be focusing on rather than sex or gender, in order to understand the causes and remedies for the prevalence of rape. According to Keen,

> Men are violent because of the systematic violence done to their bodies and spirits. Being hurt they become hurters. In the overall picture, male violence toward women is far less than male violence toward other males . . . these outrages are a structural part of a warfare system that victimizes both men and women. (Keen, 1991, p. 47)

Keen sees both men and women conspiring together to perpetuate this system of violence, especially in the way they impart to their male children an acceptance of violence.

Women are singled out by Keen as those who have not come to terms with their share of responsibility for our violent culture. And men have been so guilt-tripped on the issue of rape that they have become desensitized to it. Keen thinks that it is a mistake to single out men, and not women also, as responsible for rape.

> Until women are willing to weep for and accept equal responsibility for the systematic violence done to the male body and spirit by the war system, it is not likely that men will lose enough of their guilt and regain enough of their sensitivity to accept responsibility for women who are raped. (p. 47)

Even though women are equally responsible for the rape culture, in Keen's view, women should be singled out because they have not previously accepted their share of responsibility for the creation of a violent society.

Keen is at least partially right insofar as he insists that issues of rape and war be understood as arising from the same source, namely the socialization of men to be violent in western cultures. We agree with Keen that rape is part of a larger set of violent practices that injure both men and women. He is right to point out that men are murdering other men in our society in increasing numbers, and that this incidence of violence probably has something to do with the society's general condoning, even celebrating, of violence, especially in war.

Keen fails to note though that it is men, not women, who are the vast majority of both rapists and murderers in our society. And even if some women do act in ways which trigger violent reactions in men, nevertheless, in our opinion this pales in comparison with the way that men socialize each other to be open to violence. As Tiger and others have suggested, aggressive violence results primarily from male-bonding experiences. In any event, both fathers and mothers engage in early childhood socialization. Men influence the rape culture both through early childhood socialization and through male-bonding socialization of older male children. But women only contribute to this culture, when they do, through individual acts of early childhood socialization. For this reason Keen is surely wrong to think that women share responsibility *equally* with men for our rape culture.

In our view, some women could prevent some rapes; and some women do contribute to the patterns of socialization of both men and women that increase the incidence of rape. For these reasons, it would not be inappropriate to say that women share responsibility for rape as well as men. But we believe that it is a mistake to think that women share equally in this responsibility with men. For one thing, women are different from men in that they are, in general, made worse off by the prevalence of rape in our society. As we will next see, there is a sense in which men, but not women, benefit from the prevalence of rape, and this fact means that men have more of a stake in the rape culture, and hence have more to gain by its continued existence.

In general, our conclusion is that women share responsibility, but to a far lesser extent than men, for the prevalence of rape. We do not support those who try to "blame the victim" by holding women responsible for rape because of not taking adequate precautions, or dressing seductively, etc. Instead, the key for us is the role that women, as mothers, friends and lovers, play in the overall process of male socialization that creates the rape culture. It should come as no surprise that few members of western society can be relieved of responsibility for this rape culture given the overwhelming pervasiveness of that culture. But such considerations should not deter us from looking to men, first and foremost, as being collectively responsible for the prevalence of rape. The women who do contribute to aggressive male-socialization do so as individuals; women have no involvement parallel to the male-bonding group.

IV. The Rapist as Group Member

Popular literature tends to portray the rapist as a demonic character, as the "Other". What we find interesting about the research of Thornhill and Thornhill is that it operates unwittingly to support the feminist slogan that "all men are rapists," that the rapist is not male "Other" but male "Self." What is so unsettling about the tens of thousands of rapes in Bosnia is the suggestion that what ordinary men have been doing is not significantly different from what the "sex-fiends" did. The thesis that men are adapted to be predisposed to be rapists, regardless of what else we think of the thesis, should give us pause and make us less rather than more likely to reject the feminist slogan. From this vantage point, the work of Tiger as well as Thornhill and Thornhill sets the stage for a serious reconsideration of the view that men are collectively responsible for rape.

There are two things that might be meant by saying that men are collectively responsible for the prevalence of rape in western culture. First, seeing men as collectively responsible may mean that men as a group are responsible in that they form some sort of super-entity that causes, or at least supports, the prevalence of rape. When some feminists talk of "patriarchy," what they seem to mean is a kind of institution that operates through, but also behind the backs of, individual men to oppress women. Here it may be that men are collectively responsible for the prevalence of rape and yet no men are individually responsible. We call this nondistributive collective responsibility. Second, seeing men as collectively responsible may mean that men form a group in which there are so many features that the members share in common, such as attitudes or dispositions to engage in harm, that what holds true for one man also holds true for all other men. Because of the common features of the members of the group men, when one man is responsible for a particular harm, other men are implicated. Each member of the group has a share in the responsibility for a harm such as rape. We call this distributive collective responsibility. (See May, 1992, especially chapter 2.) In what follows we will criticize the first way of understanding men's collective responsibility, and offer reasons to support the second.

When collective responsibility is understood in the first (nondistributive) sense, this form of responsibility is assigned to those groups that have the capacity to act. Here there are two paradigmatic examples: the corporation and the mob. (See May, 1987, especially chapters 2 and 4.) The corporation has the kind of organizational structure that allows for the group to form intentions and carry out those intentions, almost as if the corporation were itself a person. Since men, qua men, are too amorphous a group to be able to act in an organized fashion, we will not be interested in whether they are collectively responsible in this way. But it may be that men can act in the way that mobs act, that is, not through a highly organized structure but through something such as like-mindedness. If there is enough commonality of belief, disposition and interest of all men, or at least all men within a particular culture, then the group may be able to act just as a mob is able to respond to a commonly perceived enemy.

It is possible to think of patriarchy as the oppressive practices of men coordinated by the common interests of men, but not organized intentionally. It is also productive to think of rape as resulting from patriarchy. For if there is a "collective" that is supporting or creating the prevalence of rape it is not a highly organized one, since there is nothing like a corporation that intentionally plans the rape of women in western culture. If the current Serbian army has engaged in the systematic and organized rape of Muslim women as a strategy of war, then this would be an example of nondistributive responsibility for rape. But the kind of oppression characterized by the prevalence of rape in most cultures appears to be systematic but not organized. How does this affect our understanding of whether men are collectively responsible for rape?

If patriarchy is understood merely as a system of coordination that operates behind the backs of individual men, then it may be that no single man is responsible for any harms that are caused by patriarchy. But if patriarchy is understood as something which is based on common interests, as well as common benefits, extended to all or most men in a particular culture, then it may be that men are collectively responsible for the harms of patriarchy in a way which distributes out to all men, making each man in a particular culture at least partially responsible for the harms attributable to patriarchy. This latter strategy is consistent with our own view of men's responsibility for rape. In the remainder of this essay we will offer support for this conceptualization of the collective responsibility of men for the prevalence of rape.

Our positive assessment, going beyond our criticism of the faulty responses in earlier sections of our paper, is that men in western culture are collectively responsible in the distributive sense, that is, they each share responsibility, for the prevalence of rape in that culture. This claim rests on five points. (1) Insofar as most perpetrators of rape are men, then these men are responsible, in most cases, for the rapes they committed. (2) Insofar as some men, by the way they interact with other (especially younger) men, contribute to a climate in our society where rape is made more prevalent, then they are collaborators in the rape culture and for this reason share in responsibility for rapes committed in that culture. (3) Also, insofar as some men are not unlike the rapist, since they would be rapists if they had the opportunity to be placed into a situation where their inhibitions against rape were removed, then these men share responsibility with actual rapists for the harms of rape. (4) In addition, insofar as many other men could have prevented fellow men from raping, but did not act to prevent these actual rapes, then these men also share responsibility along with the rapists. (5) Finally, insofar as some men benefit from the existence of rape in our society, these men also share responsibility along with the rapists.

It seems to us unlikely that many, if any, men in our society fail to fit into one or another of these categories. Hence, we think that it is not unreasonable to say that men in our society are collectively responsible (in the distributive sense) for rape. We expect some male readers to respond as follows:

I am adamantly opposed to rape, and though when I was younger I might have tolerated rape-conducive comments from friends of mine, I don't now, so I'm not a collaborator in the rape culture. And I would never be a rapist whatever the situation, and I would certainly act to prevent any rape that I could. I'm pretty sure I don't benefit from rape. So how can I be responsible for the prevalence of rape?

In reply we would point out that nearly all men in a given western society meet the third and fifth conditions above (concerning similarity and benefit). But women generally fail to meet either of these conditions, or the first. So, the involvement of women in the rape culture is much less than is true for men. In what follows we will concentrate on the benefit issue.

We believe that Lionel Tiger's work illustrates the important source of strength that men derive from the all-male groups they form. There is a strong sense in which men benefit from the all-male groups that they form in our culture. What is distinctly lacking is any sense that men have responsibility for the social conditions, especially the socialization of younger men which diminishes inhibitions toward rape, that are created in those groups. Male bonding is made easier because there is an "Other" that males can bond "against." And this other is the highly sexualized stereotype of the "female." Here is a benefit for men in these groups – but there is a social cost: from the evidence we have examined there is an increased prevalence of rape. Men need to consider this in reviewing their own role in a culture that supports so much rape.

There is another sense in which benefit is related to the issue of responsibility for rape. There is a sense in which many men in our society benefit from the prevalence of rape in ways of which many of us are quite unaware. Consider this example:

> Several years ago, at a social occasion in which male and female professors were present, I asked off-handedly whether people agreed with me that the campus was looking especially pretty at night these days. Many of the men responded positively. But all of the women responded that this was not something that they had even thought about, since they were normally too anxious about being on campus at night, especially given the increase in reported rapes recently.

We men benefited in that, relative to our female colleagues, we were in an advantageous position *vis-à-vis* travel around campus. And there were surely other comparative benefits that befell us as a result of this advantage concerning travel, such as our ability to gain academically by being able to use the library at any hour we chose.

In a larger sense, men benefit from the prevalence of rape in that many women are made to feel dependent on men for protection against potential rapists. It is hard to overestimate the benefit here for it potentially affects all aspects of one's life. One study found that 87 percent of women in a borough of London felt that they had to take precautions against potential rapists, with a large number reporting that they never went out at night alone (Radford, 1987, p. 33). Whenever one group is made to feel dependent on another group, and this dependency is not reciprocal, then there is a strong comparative benefit to the group that is not in the dependent position. Such a benefit, along with the specific benefits mentioned above, supports the view that men as a group have a stake in perpetuating the rape culture in ways that women do not. And just as the benefit to men distributes throughout the male population in a given society, so the responsibility should distribute as well.

V. Conclusions

The feminist slogan "all men are rapists" seems much stronger than the claim "all men contribute to the prevalence of rape." Is the feminist slogan merely hyperbole? It is if what is meant is that each time a rape occurs, every man did it, or that only men are ever responsible for rape. But, as we have seen, each time a rape occurs, there is a sense in which many men could have done it, or made it more likely to have occurred, or benefited from it. By direct contribution, or by negligence or by similarity of disposition, or by benefiting, most if not all men do share in each rape in a particular society. This is the link between being responsible for the prevalence of rape and being responsible, at least to some extent, for the harms of each rape.

The purpose of these arguments has been to make men aware of the various ways that they are implicated in the rape culture in general as well as in particular rapes. And while we believe that men should feel some shame for their group's complicity in the prevalence of rape, our aim is not to shame men but rather to stimulate men to take responsibility for changing the socialization of boys and men. How much should any particular man do? Answering this question would require another paper, although participating in the Canadian White Ribbon Campaign, or in anti-sexism education programs, would be a good first step. Suffice it to say that the status quo, namely doing nothing, individually or as a group, is not satisfactory, and will merely further compound our collective and shared responsibility for the harms caused by our fellow male members who engage in rape.

References

Griffin, Susan. 1971. "Rape: The All-American Crime." *Ramparts*, September: 26–35. Reprinted in *Women and Values: Readings in Feminist Philosophy*, ed. Marilyn Pearsall (Belmont, CA: Wadsworth, 1986), pp. 176–88.

Keen, Sam. 1991. *Fire in the Belly* (New York: Bantam Books).

Lepowsky, Maria. 1990. "Gender in an Egalitarian Society." In *Beyond the Second Sex*, ed. Peggy Reeves Sanday and Ruth Gallagher Goodenough (Philadelphia: University of Pennsylvania Press).

Lipsyte, Robert. 1993. "An Ethics Trial: Must Boys Always be Boys." *New York Times*, March 12: B-11.

May, Larry. 1987. *The Morality of Groups* (Notre Dame, IN: University of Notre Dame Press).

——. 1992. *Sharing Responsibility* (Chicago: University of Chicago Press).

Oates, Joyce Carol. 1992. "Rape and the Boxing Ring." *Newsweek*, February 24: 60–61.

Radford, Jill. 1987. "Policing Male Violence, Policing Women." In *Women, Violence and Social Control*, ed. Jalna Hanmer and Mary Maynard (Atlantic Highlands, NJ: Humanities Press).

St Louis Post Dispatch, March 22, 1992: 20A.

Sanday, Peggy Reeves. 1986. "Rape and the Silencing of the Feminine." In *Rape: An Historical and Social Enquiry*, ed. Sylvana Tomaselli and Roy Porter (Oxford: Basil Blackwell).

——. 1990. "Androcentric and Matrifocal Gender Representation in Minangkabau Ideology." In *Beyond the Second Sex*, ed. Peggy Reeves Sanday and Ruth Gallagher Goodenough (Philadelphia: University of Pennsylvania Press).

Scully, Diana. 1990. *Understanding Sexual Violence* (Boston: Unwin Hyman).

Thornhill, Randy and Nancy Wilmsen Thornhill. 1992. "The Evolutionary Psychology of Men's Coercive Sexuality." *Behavioral and Brain Sciences*, vol. 15: 363–75.

Tiger, Lionel. [1969] 1984. *Men in Groups* (New York: Marion Boyars Publishers).

Affirmative Action

Affirmative action – the practice of giving special consideration to minorities and women in hiring and school placement – once enjoyed widespread support in the United States. Now many people think the practice, if it had ever been justified, no longer serves a useful purpose. In fact, many people see affirmative action of any form as a positive evil that we must purge from public life. As I write this introduction, Californians, once thought to be the consummate liberals, are discussing a proposal that would ban affirmative action in their state.

Michael Levin articulates the standard objections to the practice. Although his arguments focus on affirmative action for women, most of these arguments are frequently raised against all affirmative-action programs. He argues, as do most opponents of affirmative action, that such programs are unfair to more qualified white males who are passed over because of their sex or race. These programs disadvantage males and whites who are not themselves responsible for the harm historically done to women and blacks. Finally, he claims that these programs deprive employers of the right to hire the most competent person for a job.

The case against affirmative action thus rests on two theoretical moral claims. The first denies that groups have any moral status. That is, individuals are responsible only for acts that they, as specific individuals do, and, as a corollary we should compensate individuals only for wrongs that they specifically suffered. The second asserts that a society should distribute its goods according to merit. That is, we should always give jobs and school positions to the persons with "the best qualifications."

Dworkin explicitly disavows both principles. Group membership – in this case race or gender – can have moral significance. If some individuals have been mistreated because of their membership in a group, then we must now compensate them because they are members of that group. According to Dworkin we have no alternative. However, as we have seen, there is considerable disagreement about the moral status of groups. Arthur (FREE SPEECH) explicitly rejects the idea that groups have moral status or significance, while May and Strikwerda (SEXUAL AND RACIAL DISCRIMINATION) argue not only that members of groups can be responsible for the actions of members of their group, but that, in fact, all males share collective responsibility for rape. And Appiah, in that same section, argues that group membership is, at least in our society, central to how we define ourselves. Finally, several authors in later sections will discuss whether we are, because of our group membership, responsible to those in economic need (ECONOMIC JUSTICE and INTERNATIONAL JUSTICE AND WORLD HUNGER).

Dworkin likewise rejects the second lynchpin of Levin's argument: Levin implies that employers should hire (and school officials should admit) the "best qualified" candidates. In discussing the case of Allan Bakke, a white male who successfully challenged an affirmative-action program at the University of California–Davis Medical School, Dworkin disagrees. He argues that no one has a right to be judged on their merits – at least not in any sense that would support Bakke's case. The problem, he claims, is that there is no such thing as merit *per se*. Having high grades in college chemistry does not automatically mean that I am the most qualified prospective medical student – or that I would be a better doctor than some student with less stellar grades. Nor does it justify the claim that I deserve a seat in medical school. Rather, an individual "deserves" the seat if school officials decide that she could be the best doctor they think we need. For instance, if, in the school officials' best judgement, we need to increase the number of blacks and female physicians (perhaps because blacks and women are more likely to seek medical care from someone of the same race and sex), then race and sex are now qualifications for that post, and someone who is black is, in fact, better qualified.

Although Harris and Narayan challenge Levin's conclusions, they reject Dworkin's arguments as well. That is, even though they think affirmative action is justified, they think Dworkin's arguments for that conclusion are seriously flawed. More than flawed, positively dangerous. Calling affirmative action "preferential treatment" suggests that we give blacks and women some benefit withheld from whites and males. However, they argue, affirmative action does not involve any form of preference. Rather, it is a program to promote equality of opportunity for people who have been, and continue to be, victims of systematic discrimination.

Discrimination was not merely a relic of past civilizations. Blacks and women continue to suffer the effects of past discrimination. Moreover, they argue, they continue to be effectively excluded from many jobs, simply because of their race or gender. Therefore, the purpose of affirmative action is not to discriminate against whites and men, nor is it to bestow benefits on blacks and women. Rather, the aim of affirmative action is to level the playing field, to provide genuine equality of opportunity.

Of course not everyone agrees that equality is desirable. Still less do people agree about what we must do to guarantee "equality of opportunity." Clearly, though, this is a significant theoretical concern that weaves through most practical issues discussed in this volume. It underlines every essay in the section on SEXUAL AND RACIAL DISCRIMINATION – after all, discrimination is, by definition, an unjust denial of equal treatment. Equality likewise plays a pivotal role in determining what is an equal PUNISHMENT for an equal crime. Are all murders equal? Should we punish them equally? Or are some murders (say, the torture and killing of a young child) sufficiently different from others (a fight between two drunks) that we should punish the first more severely?

Questions about equality were also central in the discussion about ANIMALS. Humans and non-human animals are indisputably different. The question, though, is: Are they different in ways that justify their being treated differently? Finally, we will see the issue discussed in the later sections on ECONOMIC JUSTICE and INTERNATIONAL JUSTICE AND WORLD HUNGER. Does equality require that we financially help those in need, whether they be residents of our country or foreigners?

Additionally, if we are to think carefully about affirmative action, we must attend to the ways in which institutional structures constrain our choices and shape our moral understanding. Defenders of affirmative action claim that discrimination is not simply, or even primarily, a result of conscious choice. Most racists and sexists do not consciously advocate discrimination. Many of them would vehemently deny they are racists or sexists. Therefore, most discrimination toward, and mistreatment of, minorities and women is probably best explained as the result of well-entrenched institutional structures. These structures have a life of their own: they undermine the opportunities of blacks and women even when no one actively tries to discriminate against them. Perhaps that explains why white males passed over by such programs feel wronged by this system: since they have not intentionally discriminated against minorities or women, they don't feel at all responsible for their plight. This explanation fits with Fesmire's discussion of the way that culture shapes our moral understanding (VIRTUES).

Finally, Harris and Narayan explicitly reject the model of compensation on which Dworkin – and many supporters of affirmative action – rest their case. They claim that by focusing on compensation, we put undue emphasis on particular individuals whom we have harmed, rather than on the harm caused to members of the entire group, in virtue of their being members of that group. We will explore the issue of compensatory justice again in the section on PUNISHMENT. There Haldane and Harvey argue that the state should compensate some victims of crime although we are in no way responsible for the crime.

Further Reading

Cohen, M., Nagel, T., and Scanlon, T. (eds) 1977: *Equality and Preferential Treatment*. Princeton: Princeton University Press.

Glazer, N. 1978: *Affirmative Discrimination: Ethnic Inequality and Public Policy*. New York: Basic Books.

Goldman, A. 1979: *Justice and Reverse Discrimination*. Princeton: Princeton University Press.

Wasserstrom, R. 1977: "Racism, Sexism, and Preferential Treatment: An Approach to the Topics." *UCLA Law Review*: 581–682.

41

Affirmative Action

Michael Levin

The Free Market and Feminism

Judged historically, the free market is the most successful economic arrangement. Permitting people to trade and associate freely for productive purposes has created unparalleled prosperity, along with support for the democratic institutions on which other forms of individual liberty have been found to depend. It is inevitable that feminists reject the free market, however, because they must interpret the expressions of sex differences facilitated by the freedom of the market as products of adverse socialization and discrimination.

Certainly, the observed differences between male and female labor-market behavior are not in dispute; men and women do different sorts of work, and women earn lower average wages. It is also widely agreed that the immediate causes of these differences are differences in the motives which lead men and women into the labor market. Most married working women work to supplement their husband's income, which is regarded as the mainstay of the family budget.[1] Working mothers are expected to care for their children as well, or at any rate to supervise the arrangements for their care, an expectation that does not fall nearly so heavily upon fathers. Unmarried women often see work as an interregnum between school and marriage. For these reasons, women gravitate to jobs permitting easy entry, exit and re-entry to and from the workforce. Nor, finally, is it seriously questioned that men tend to seek (although of course not always find) more prestigious jobs and to try to "get ahead" more than women do. In short, men and women invest their human capital differently.[2]

As always, the question is why these things are so. Feminist theory takes them to be consequences of oppression. In the words of the Committee on Women's Employment and Related Social Issues of the National Research Council of the National Science Foundation:

> to the extent that sex segregation in the workplace connotes the inferiority of women or contributes to maintaining women as men's inferiors, it has great symbolic significance. To this extent, we believe it is fundamentally at odds with the established goals of equal opportunity and equality under the law in American society.[3]

This theory is contradicted by the close match between many of the major differences in skills brought by men and women to the workplace and a number of the innate differences. Together with the greater innate dominance-aggression of men, which manifests itself economically as greater competitiveness, this match strongly suggests that differences in workplace behavior are not best explained as products of the denial of equal opportunity. While it is somewhat artificial to divide the effects of gender on job-seeking behavior from its effects on wage-seeking behavior, I focus on workplace segregation in the present chapter.

In 1980, the National Opinion Research Center administered the Armed Services Vocational Aptitude Battery of ten tests of 12,000 randomly selected males and females between the ages of eighteen and twenty-three.[4] The ASVAB was then factored into four composite tests for "mechanical," "electronic," "administrative," and "general" aptitudes.[5] It was found that men scored considerably higher than women in mechanical and electronic aptitude, and slightly higher in general aptitude, while women exhibited greater administrative aptitude.[6] (On the individual tests, men for instance did considerably better on mechanical comprehension and women did considerably better on coding speed.[7]) These differences in aptitude were constant at all educational levels. Since the average female has 11.9 years of schooling to the average male's 11.8, these differences do not represent an educational deficit.[8] One might still wish to explain these aptitude differences in terms of socialization, but however they are explained they show that occupational segregation is not wholly the result of employer discrimination working on a homogeneous population of men and women.

Some innate sex differences correlate closely with aptitude for specific occupations, many of them prestigious, remunerative, and important in industrial society. Spatial ability is requisite for pipe fitting, technical drawing, and wood working,[9] and is the most important component of mechanical ability.[10] Only about 20 percent of girls in the elementary grades reach the average level of male performance on tests of spatial ability, and, according to the US Employment Service, all classes of engineering and drafting as well as a high proportion of scientific and technical occupations require spatial ability in the top 10 percent of the US population.[11] While one should normally be chary of explaining any social phenomenon *directly* in terms of some innate gender dimorphism, male domination of the technical and engineering professions is almost certainly due to the male's innate cognitive advantage rather than to a culturally induced female disadvantage.[12] Proportionally fewer women enter the technical fields than there are women in the population with the requisite raw skills, to be sure, but this is most plausibly attributed to the Goldberg feedback effect which selectively discourages women with marginal levels of skill – an injustice, perhaps, but one also borne by men with atypical skills. In any case, the sex segregation of the workforce is essentially the result of innate sex differences and unmanipulated expectations.

However, if one assumes that women would, given the opportunity, be as interested in and as suited for virtually the same work as men, one is compelled to interpret the continuing statistical segregation of the workforce as evidencing discrimination. And, as the 1964 Civil Rights Act outlawed sex discrimination in all phases of employment, the claim that discrimination not only persists but is so pervasive as to demand extraordinary remedies must involve an unusual construction of "discrimination." One such construction prominent in government research on the question, is that women's own preferences obstruct equality of opportunity. A study by the Labor Department, *Women in Traditionally Male Jobs*, cites "the lack of female interest in many blue-collar jobs" as a "ubiquitous problem" in achieving "equal opportunity goals."[13] The Congressional Office of Technology Assessment cites "sex discrimination and sex stereotyping" as the barriers to women entering science and engineering:

As long as women expect to assume the major role in housekeeping and child-rearing, and to sacrifice their professional interests to those of their husbands, they will be less likely than men to select occupations like science and engineering that require major educational and labor force commitment.[14]

The Case for Quotas

There are three basic arguments for quotas, yielding as corollaries the three basic arguments for gender quotas. I cannot demonstrate that every argument that anyone might offer for quotas falls under one of these three, but if these three fail, it seems extremely unlikely that any entirely new argument is going to be successful.

Quotas create role models

"Role models" are needed in unusual jobs to let women know that their options are wider than prevalent sex stereotypes now permit them to realize. A self-sustaining influx of women into nontraditional jobs will be triggered once enough women – a number never specified – are in place. The VERA Institute of justice argues that the lower felony arrest rate for female officers shows the need for more female officers to create an atmosphere in which females feel comfortable enough to do a better job.[15] Janet Richards puts the argument clearly:

> What we want to achieve is . . . *an improvement of the position of women until society is fair to them*, and as a matter of fact probably the best way to achieve this is to appoint to positions of importance women who are rather less good at the work than the men who are in competition with them. As long as they are not such hopeless failures as to confirm everyone's ideas that women are not capable of any serious work, their holding those positions will be enough to make others set their sights higher, and make people in general more used to seeing women in former male preserves and expecting more of them.[16]

A variant of this argument in the NOW amicus brief in *Rostker* v. *Goldberg*[17] claimed that registering and conscripting women would improve their image and decrease the incidence of rape.

Advocates of gender quotas have not pressed this argument with great enthusiasm. It rather conspicuously ignores the possible consequences of inserting less-than-the-best candidates into positions on which lives depend (like surgery or piloting commercial airliners). It seems to assume that the differences between incompetence, competence, and excellence are for the most part trivial, and that most people could do most things pretty well if given the chance.

Properly understood, furthermore, this argument has nothing to do with equality of opportunity. The creation of role models is not intended to guarantee women freedom equal to men's to pursue the occupations they wish, which is how equality of opportunity is usually understood, but to induce women to want to pursue occupations they do not want (and whose pursuit would allegedly make them happier than they are now). Not that there is any evidence for a role model effect of the appropriate sort; psychologists coined "role model" to refer to the function performed by parents in influencing the ego ideals of very young children, and ego ideals are formed before the age of five.

But the most serious difficulty with the role model argument is this: Even if there were a demonstrable role model effect, and women would be happier (if not freer) attempting nontraditional pursuits, *and* the damage done by placing incompetent women in important jobs was tolerable, the question would remain whether quotas were fair to the individual males bypassed in the process, males not themselves responsible for women's currently constricted aspirations. If quotas do men an injustice, the role model defense is unpersuasive.

Quotas as preventive measures

This argument maintains that discrimination is, while illegal, so subtle, pervasive, and vicious that it must be stopped in advance:

> Another depressing topic at [the Congressional Black Caucus] was the Administration's late-August announcement that it would sharply decrease the enforcement of federal affirmative-action regulations designed to prevent discrimination against women and against blacks and other minorities – a curtailment Representative Charles Rangel . . . charged would be a signal to those in the private sector that they "need no longer worry about the government looking over their shoulders" and would in most cases be free to go back to indulging in the prejudices and biases that come naturally to many Americans.[18]

It is frequently added that discrimination is too difficult to prove to be attacked on an individual, case-wise basis.

This argument, too, founders on the question of justice. Preventive coercion is justified only in emergencies. It is generally agreed that the government may prevent grave wrongs clearly about to be done (it can disrupt conspiracies) and more remote but potentially catastrophic possibilities, but must otherwise act after the fact. It would be regarded as impermissibly unfair to reduce the felony rate by incarcerating all eighteen-year-old males, since males who were never going to attack anyone would inevitably be swept along. To be sure, sex discrimination is sometimes described as an evil of sufficient magnitude to warrant preventive measures too extreme to be developed elsewhere, but this supplementary argument must also await consideration of the issue of justice.

The argument from preemption is also empirically vulnerable. To stop discrimination before it occurs by enforcing the outcome that would obtain without discrimination presupposes knowledge of what the nondiscriminatory outcome would be, and if that outcome is taken to be statistical proportionality, it is being assumed that the only possible causes of aggregate differences in outcomes are malign forces. This is the complete environmentalism which we have seen to be wholly untenable.

There is a close connection between quotas conceived as preventive detention and the concept of institutional discrimination. Quotas are necessary, it is argued, because the very structure of institutions and the unconscious assumptions that accompany them result in minorities and women being excluded from certain activities. Still, in order for quotas to be an appropriate response, it must be demonstrated that the *particular Blacks and women* who gain admission to otherwise structurally discriminatory institutions would have been excluded but for quotas. After all, it cannot be assumed that structural discrimination discriminates against absolutely every member of every unprotected class. Similarly, it must be somehow demonstrated that the particular White males penalized by preventive quotas are just those who would have benefited from institutional discrimination – we cannot just assume that *every* White male so benefits. Even if there is such a phenomenon as institutional discrimination, it does not follow that quotas are consistent with justice.

Quotas as indemnification

We come to the *nervus probandi*: quotas are not only unjust, they are demanded by justice, for they give today's Blacks and women the jobs they would have gotten had there been no sexual or racial discrimination in the past. Judging today's Blacks and women by sex-blind and race-blind merit standards unfairly disadvantages them by allowing past discrimination to perpetuate itself. Quotas make whole today's Blacks and women by "neutralizing the *present* competitive disadvantages caused by those past privations";[19] quotas compensate Blacks and women for the competitive abilities they would have had had their ancestors been treated properly. Reserving jobs for less qualified women and Blacks is fair to the bypassed, better-qualified White males, who would not have been better qualified in a non-discriminatory world. To let better-qualified White males claim those jobs is to let them profit from wrong-doing, even if not their own. As for which White males have profited from the mistreatment of which Blacks and females, it must be assumed that every male enjoys an unfair advantage over every Black and female:

> Surely every white person, however free of direct implication in victimizing non-whites, is still a daily beneficiary of white dominance – past and present. . . . Though, of course, there are obvious and important differences, women too have been victimized as a group.[20]

This final phase of the argument may seem gratuitous paranoia, but it is actually crucial. To use any other indicator of victimhood which merely correlates with race or sex as a basis for preference – poverty, let us say – will entitle a poor White male, although a relatively rarer specimen, to the same preference as an equally poor Black woman. (And to call for affirmative action for Blacks or women to attack poverty, without claiming the support of justice, is still to call for the equally special treatment of equally poor Whites, Blacks, men, and women.) Unless race and sex are in themselves the stigmata of victimhood, racial and gender quotas are inappropriate instruments of compensation. . . .

Compensatory Quotas for Women

A compensation claim is a thought experiment in which we return the world to the moment when a wrong was done and imagine how the world would have evolved had the wrong not bee done. What the injured party would have possessed in this ideal world is what he *should* possess in the real world; the difference between his two positions in the two worlds is what the wrong cost the injured party and what the tort-feasor owes him. Despite the obvious uncertainties that beset such reasoning, the courts are able to carry it out in limited contexts – but not merely by observing the truism that people deserve what they wrongfully lost. Five specific conditions must be met to establish a compensation claim: (1) injury must be shown; (2) the injured party must be identified; (3) the cost to the injured party must be established; (4) those who inflicted or profited from the injury must be identified. The complainant's loss cannot be restored at the expense of the innocent. Moreover, while those who do not inflict a wrong may be compensatorily liable if they profit from it, they must profit from it *directly*. If a terrorist bomb detonated a half-mile away loosens a treasure hidden in someone's ceiling, he does not owe the treasure to the terrorist's victim. (5) Restitution must be feasible, and feasibility constraints may dictate the replacement of what has been lost by an equivalent. Since the dancer cannot get back his mangled toe, the jury awards him compensatory damages in the amount he would have earned in performance fees had the moving man not clumsily dropped the piano on his foot. Indemnificatory quotas fail all five conditions; gender quotas far more completely than racial quotas.

Was injury done?
The beginnings of a case for compensating contemporary Blacks can be based on the injuries done to their ancestors by slavery, segregation, and the lynch mob. No remotely

comparable injuries have been done to women. Rape is occasionally cited as such an injury, but there is no evidence that rape adversely affects female acquisition of job skills. Because no palpable, physical injuries have been done to women, advocates of gender quotas are forced back on psychological injury supposedly done by sex role stereotyping. The most able defender of the compensation argument known to me is able to marshal only the following evidence of injury to women: "The feminist movement has convincingly documented the ways in which sexual bias is built into the information received by the young."[21]

It scarcely needs repeating that sex stereotypes are no more than reports of the inevitable manifestations of innate sex differences. Stereotypes are true, and possess little independent power. But even supposing sex stereotypes baseless, it is moral lunacy to equate them with racial animosity. Within living memory, a Black man risked a beating or far worse for drinking from a Whites-only fountain. The feelings of an employer uncomfortable about putting a woman on the assembly line bears no resemblance to the hatred that led to what newspapers of the nineteenth century shamelessly called "negro barbecues." No matter how frequently it is repeated, the comparison of the sufferings of women to those of Blacks remains offensive to reason.

Who was injured? Who inflicted the injury? Who benefited?

That Blacks were actually injured in the past does not justify racial quotas today. The perpetrators of those wrongs have died, and it is impossible to trace in detail the effects of those wrongs. It is therefore impossible to determine which particular Blacks are worse off than they should have been, or by how much, or which Whites are better off. Slavery cannot be said, by the standards of law, science, or common sense, to have benefited today's second-generation Greek-American. It is if anything more speculative to claim that a particular White man has benefited from the wrongs which have disadvantaged a particular Black man. It simply cannot be determined whether every Black promoted over Brain Weber would have been his senior had there been no discrimination.

That the basic showing of injury cannot be sustained for women makes it superfluous to ask how the women injured by sexist discrimination, and the men who have benefited from this injury, are to be identified. Janet Richards writes: "The only men excluded [from jobs] on this principle would be the ones who, as far as we could tell, would not have succeeded anyway if the situation had been fair."[22] This merely restates the problem without some account of how one *is* to tell which men these are and what net advantage they enjoy over particular women.

Current Black disadvantages at least *appear* traceable to past wrongs because Blacks form a coherent subgroup within the general population. It is clear that parents may transmit handicaps to their children within coherent subpopulations (although this effect is attenuated by the social mobility characteristic of industrial democracies). Whatever slight support this transmission of handicaps may lend to the case for racial quotas, it is entirely inappropriate for women. Women do not form an autonomous subpopulation within which norms and traditions are transmitted. Women's ancestors are *everybody*. To the extent that a person's competitive position reflects that of his parents, the average woman must be assumed to have gained as much from her father's ill-gotten advantages as she has lost from her mother's undeserved handicaps. What is particularly ludicrous about the comparison of Blacks and females in the workforce is that *women marry men* whereas Blacks do not typically marry Whites. For most practical purposes a wife has full use of her husband's assets. If the average man is better off than he should have been because the average woman is worse off, they pool their resources and split the difference when they marry. Since virtually all men and women marry, gender quotas harm virtually all women. If compensatory quotas harmed a Black for every Black they helped, they would defeat their own purpose. But whenever a man loses a job, promotion or training to a woman, just because he is a man, another woman, namely the man's wife, is deprived of precisely what the quota beneficiary gained. Gender quotas self-defeatingly compensate some members of the allegedly victimized group by depriving others.

So far as I know, this self-evident point has been overlooked in the literature on quotas. This oversight is due in part to the central role played in the case for gender quotas by the young woman seeking a nontraditional career, a woman less likely than average to be married. A more fundamental cause of this oversight is the repeated portrayal of men and women as competing groups. The motif of woman-as-outsider is a staple of feminist rhetoric;[23] as I mentioned, even feminist evolutionary biology treats men and women as competitors.[24] In addition to the ambitious career woman, much attention has been given to the single mother who must support her family alone and would benefit from an affirmative-action boost to a high salary job. Quite apart from the irrelevance of her plight to the justification of affirmative action – men also have families to support, and a single mother is not usually single because of the actions of the men against whom she is competing for jobs – the single mother does not make men and women disparate groups.

What was lost?

"Lost competitive ability" is too obscure to justify compensation, although again its application to race must be distinguished from its application to sex. Compensation theory emphasizes the need for tangible criteria of loss, some *goods* lost, since the career of a physical object can be relatively easily traced. If you steal my car, it is possible many years later to identify it as what I lost. There are limits even on the use of physical objects and sums of money as guides to compensation, since the identity of a (stolen) physical object can be blurred by the contributions of subsequent recipients and bystanders. The common law will not dispossess the current holders of land that has been transferred in good faith for a number of generations, despite proof from a claimant that the land was stolen from his ancestors; too much honest labor is now part of the land.

Even in the racial case, "inability to compete" fails the test of identifiability. No Black can point to a successful White and claim that he would have had just *that* much competitive ability had the world been fair. Allan Bakke, a White denied admission to the University of California medical school under a racial quota system, had an undergraduate grade point average of 3.8 out of a possible 4, while the Blacks chosen over him had averages no higher than 2.38.[25] If competitive ability is operationalized as college average, defenders of the University of California quota must be prepared to claim that the Blacks selected over Bakke would have had grade averages at least 1.42 points higher had the world been fair. It is not clear how anyone could know this. And if competitive ability is not operationalized in some such way, it is not clear what advocates of compensatory quotas have in mind when they speak of it.

In marked contrast, no detours into the metaphysics of compensation are needed to see how much less substantial is the corresponding claim about women's "lost competitive abilities." Dominance-aggression, the ability most crucial for success in competitive situations, is physiologically determined and could not have been shared more equally by women in any physiologically possible world, however just it might be. Blacks and Whites want to get to the top equally badly, but Blacks lack some of the skills possessed by Whites. There is this much sense to talk of Black/White competitive abilities being discrepant. The difference between men and women is that women do not want to get to the top as badly as men do and men do not want to do the things women prefer intensely to do.

The basic trouble with speculating about the abilities people would have had in a better world is that it ignores the constitutive contribution of competitive abilities to the human personality and indeed to personal identity. Intelligence, persistence, a sense of detachment toward setbacks – all make a person who he is. Failure to recognize this is the profound error of the shackled runner analogy. We understand what real shackles cost a shackled runner because it is easy to imaginatively remove the shackles and speculate about how *he* would perform without them. Competitive traits are not so easily prised off their possessors. One cannot "unshackle" an ordinary person from his ordinariness by imagining him brilliant, decisive, and unquenchably ambitious; it would not be the same person. You are imagining somebody else who looks to your mind's eye like the man you thought you were imagining. Compensation arguments which posit far more gifted counterparts, for various actually existing people, are describing *replacements*, whose hypothetical performances imply nothing about the entitlements of anybody who actually exists.[26]

Is rectification feasible?

Quotas require the award of jobs to individuals who by hypothesis are not the best able to perform them and are in some cases absolutely unable to perform them. Quotas thus violate feasibility constraints that normally limit compensation. The dancer crippled by the careless piano mover does not ask the moving company to hire him to perform *Swan Lake*, for the dancer's complaint, after all, is that – thanks to the moving company's negligence – he can no longer dance very well. He asks for the monetary equivalent of his lost skill, not the right to perform actions for which the lost skill is necessary. (There are reidentification problems even in this case, and perhaps an element of convention enters into the jury's determination of what the dancer would have earned over a lifetime had his skill level remained unimpaired by negligence; these difficulties show that estimates of lost higher-order abilities, like the ability to compete, are even less well founded than I suggested above.) It is therefore odd that compensation for Blacks and women, assuming it to be deserved, should take the form of jobs, when the grounds for compensating them is their lack of the skills necessary for those jobs. The normal mode of reparation in such cases is monetary. If, instead of money, Blacks and women deserve the very jobs they should have been but are not able to fill, if no substitutes are acceptable, Black and female students deserve the grades they should have but are not able to earn. If no substitutes are acceptable, why not allow a free felony, one major crime without punishment, to compensate each Black for all the undeserved punishments inflicted on his ancestors by a legal system once unjust to Blacks? In fact, there *are* government-mandated grading quotas. The US State Department awards five extra points to Blacks taking its Foreign Service, and girls in the Australian Capital Territory receive five extra points on their college entrance examinations.

Feasibility constraints are disregarded when the subject is quotas, I suspect, because discrimination is taken to be morally special, not just one wrong among many others all competing for rectification, but the worst wrong imaginable, a sin. The world must be remade just as it would have been had this blot on humanity never happened at all. It is this assumption that elicits defense of preventive discrimination from people who would not think of preventively detaining potential murderers. Sin is a theological doctrine which cannot profitably be judged by an unbeliever, but it might be instructive to ask the actual victims of a variety of wrongs which one they think worse and in more urgent need of remedy. Would the average Black man prefer to lose a job because of his skin color, or be murdered? Would the average woman prefer to be robbed at knifepoint or be told that driving a truck is unladylike? Which does she want back first, her freedom to realize herself, or her pocketbook?

Racial discrimination seems special because people tend to reify races into entities in their own right, and think of the race itself, not merely the particular victims of discriminatory practices, as having suffered. This is a mistake in its own right – only individuals can suffer – and leads to the further mistake of forgetting that particularly grave discriminatory acts, like lynching, are grave precisely because they fall under nonracial headings like intimidation and murder. No doubt the female sex has also been reified into a victim by the ontologically careless, but, again, it remains crazy to compare the "romantic paternalism"[27] with which may nineteenth-century American males may have viewed women to the racial hatred endured by Blacks. . . .

The Trouble with Reverse Discrimination

Quotas deny benefits and impose burdens on individuals not responsible for any wrongs. They cannot be justified as compensation, inspiration, or prevention, and they decrease economic efficiency. So much alone suffices to close the case against them, but it does not clarify why quotas strike most people as *unfair*. Quotas burden innocent, well-qualified White males – But what is wrong with that?

The usual explanations are unsatisfactory. Quotas cannot sin against the right of the best qualified to a job, since, as far as I can see, there is no such right. The rights and correlative obligations that control employment are created by the mutual agreements of employers and employees. If every individual has a right to refuse to enter agreements with anyone he pleases, an employer may refuse to enter an agreement with anyone, including the person best able to perform a job the employer wants done. If the employer has no right to refuse an offer the best-qualified individual makes him, the employer is to that extent his slave, and has no right to associate *or not* with other people as he pleases. The employer may be irrational in refusing to deal with the best-qualified individual, but the employer does not *harm* him. The employer is simply *refusing to help* that individual (and himself).

For similar reasons, I do not see how White males or anyone else can have a right to be "free from discrimination."[28] Private discrimination is not a force that attacks White males (or anyone else) minding their own business. A White male is discriminated against in employment when, after he offers his services to an employer, the employer turns him down for no other reason than his sex and skin color. It was the White male who initiated proceedings. The potential employer, who was minding his own business, has simply refused to enter a mutually beneficial arrangement with the White male; the White male has been made no worse off than he was before proceedings began. If the employer has no right not to bargain with White males as such, White males to that extent *own* him.

There is no injustice in discriminating against White males, *just as, in logical consistency, there is no injustice in discriminating against Black males, females, or members of any other group.* Favoritism, injustice, and moral arbitrariness enter when the government permits and demands preference for one group while forbidding preference toward another. If, as the Supreme Court held in *Weber*, preference for Blacks is a legitimate exercise of an employer's freedom of association, preference for Whites must also, in consistency, be considered a legitimate exercise of the same freedom. The unfairness of the present quota system lies in the government's disadvantaging White males by permitting – and encouraging and requiring – employer discrimination against them while forbidding employer discrimination against non-White males. The government thereby denies to White males a protection it extends to Blacks, Hispanics, females and other populations.

There are two ways to restore symmetry. It might be argued that, since there are utilitarian reasons to forbid private discrimination,[29] the government should impartially forbid preference of any sort. (If the government rejects the "right" not to be discriminated against but forbids discrimination for the general good, it might wish to rethink the equation of Blacks and women when redrawing the limits of permissible favoritism.) On the other hand, it might be argued that the government should leave freedom of association unlimited, and impartially permit preference of any sort. In the latter case, employers persuaded by the arguments for quotas would be free to treat Blacks and females preferentially; employers persuaded of the virtues of merit criteria would be free to use pure merit criteria; and employers persuaded that by now White males deserve some reverse reverse discrimination would be free to prefer White males. The government would revert to a neutral, nondiscriminatory stance under either alternative.

As for the government's own hiring policies, it is clearly impermissible for the state to confer benefits like employment on the basis of race alone, and state action could easily be race blind, so long as proportionality was not the test of race blindness. It is not so clear that the state could ever be blind to sex. The state will always have to impose the burden of defense on men, which is a form of discrimination against them (unless it is argued that combat positions open to male volunteers are a public benefit discriminatorily denied woman – an argument which must be withdrawn whenever the shooting starts). It is unthinkable that the state could pursue its functions without taking some account of biological sex differences.

Notes

1   Donna Shalala estimates that 80 percent of full-time working women work out of perceived economic necessity (presentation to the National Convention of the Council on Foundations, Detroit, April 29, 1982). According to a survey conducted by *Newsweek*, 56 percent of working women say they work "for money" ("A Mother's Choice." *Newsweek* [March 31, 1986]: 51). Presumably, the figure is much higher for working mothers. For the economist, no one (except perhaps those facing imminent starvation) "has" to work; work is preferred to not working. Let us say that a woman has to work if she would not work were her husband's salary increased by an amount equal to her own (or, if she is unmarried, she suddenly acquired a suitably salaried husband).

2   On male and female commitment to employment, see June O'Neill and Rachel Braun, *Women and the Labor Market: A Survey of Issues and Policies in the United States* (Washington, DC: Urban Institute, 1981).

3   Barbara F. Reskin and Heidi I. Hartmann (eds), *Women's Work, Men's Work: Sex Segregation on the Job* (Washington, DC: National Academy Press, 1985). Cited in *The Women's Rights Issues of the 1980s*, undated pamphlet distributed by National Academy Press.

4   *Profile of American Youth: 1980 National Administration of Armed Services Vocational Aptitude Battery* (Department of Defense, Office of the Assistant Secretary of Defense for Manpower, March 1982). The ten ASVAB subtests are: Arithmetic Reasoning, Numerical Operations, Paragraph Comprehension, Word Knowledge, Coding Speed, General Science, Mathematics Knowledge, Electronics Information, Mechanical Comprehension, and Automotive-Shop Information.

5   Mechanical includes: Mechanical Comprehension, Automotive-Shop Information, and General Science. Administrative includes: Coding Speed, Numerical Operations, Paragraph Comprehension, and Word Knowledge. General includes: Arithmetical Reasoning, Paragraph Comprehension, and Word Knowledge. Electronics includes:

Arithmetic Reasoning, Electronics Information, General Science, and Mathematics Knowledge (ibid., p. 27, table 13).

6 Expressed in mean percentiles (so that a score of *n* for a group means that the average member of the group scored as well as *n* percent of the population): Mechanical–Male, 51; Mechanical–Female, 26; Administrative–M, 44; Administrative–F, 51; General–M, 52; General–F, 48; Electronics–M, 53; Electronics–F, 41 (ibid., p. 32).

7 Ibid., p. 90, table C-14.

8 Ibid., tables C-10–C-13, pp. 86–9.

9 See I. Smith, *Spatial Ability* (San Diego: R. R. Knopp, 1964), pp. 135–55.

10 See L. M. Terman and Leona Tyler, "Psychological Sex Differences," in *Manual of Child Psychology*, 2nd edn, ed. L. Charmichael (New York: Wiley, 1954), pp. 1064–1114.

11 *Estimates of Worker Trait Requirements for 4000 Jobs* (Washington, DC: US Government Printing Office, 1957).

12 For a survey of occupationally relevant sex differences, see F. L. Schmidt, "Sex Differences in Some Occupationally Relevant Traits: The Viewpoint of an Applied Differential Psychologist," manuscript (Washington, DC: Office of Personnel Management, 1972).

13 *Women in Traditionally Male Jobs: The Experience of Ten Public Utility Companies*, Deprtment of Labor Research and Development Monograph 65 (Washington, DC: US Government Printing Office, 1978), p. 117.

14 "Panel Report Sex Disparity in Engineering," *New York Times*, December 16, 1985: A15.

15 *Women on Patrol: A Pilot Study of Police Performance in New York City* (New York: VERA Institute, 1978).

16 *The Sceptical Feminist*, p. 111.

17 *Rostker* v. *Goldberg* 101 SCE 2646, 453 US 57 (1981).

18 "Around City Hall," *New York* (September 18, 1981): 161.

19 George Sher, "Justifying Reverse Discrimination in Employment," *Philosophy and Public Affairs*, 4 (Winter 1975): 163.

20 Haywood Burns, "The Bakke Case and Affirmative Action: Some Implications for the Future," *Freedomways* (First Quarter 1978): 6.

21 Sher, n. 6.

22 Janet Richards, *The Sceptical Feminist* (Boston: Routledge & Kegan Paul, 1980), p. 118.

23 "I am not real to my civilization. I am not real to the culture that has spawned me and made use of me" (Vivian Gornick, "Woman as Outsider," in *Woman in Sexist Society*, ed. Vivian Gornick and Betty Moran (New York: Mentor, 1971), p. 114).

24 [See chapter 4, fn. 15].

25 *Bakke* v. *University of California Regents*, 438 US 265 (1978), in which the Supreme Court approved race-conscious admissions policies.

26 For further discussion of these points, see Michael Levin, "Reverse Discrimination, Shackled Runners, and Personal Identity," *Philosophical Studies*, 37 (1980): 139–49. It is sometimes argued that the biologically determined differential success rates of men and women are unjust since, had women been treated fairly over the millennia, the market would have evolved to reward female talents as much as it now rewards male talents. Trying to substantiate a conditional to this counterfactual is like trying to determine whether Julius Caesar would have used atomic weapons had they been available 2,000 years ago.

27 US Commission on Civil Rights, 1980, p. 9.

28 John Bunzel speaks of "the right to be free of discrimination" in "Rescuing Equality," in *Sidney Hook*, ed. Paul Kurtz (Buffalo, NY: Prometheus, 1983), p. 179. "Mr Celler: The bill seeks simply to protect the right of American citizens to be free from racial and religious discrimination." *Legislative History of Title*, VII, p. 3283.

29 This position is defended in Kent Greenawalt, *Discrimination and Reverse Discrimination* (New York: Borzoi, 1983).

42

The Rights of Allan Bakke

Ronald Dworkin

On October 12, 1977 the Supreme Court heard oral argument in the case of *The Regents of the University of California* v. *Allan Bakke*. No lawsuit has ever been more widely watched or more thoroughly debated in the national and international press before the Court's decision. Still, some of the most pertinent facts set before the Court have not been clearly summarized.

The medical school of the University of California at Davis has an affirmative action program (called the "task force program") designed to admit more black and other minority students. It sets sixteen places aside for which only members of "educationally and economically disadvantaged minorities" compete. Allan Bakke, white, applied for one of the remaining eighty-four places; he was rejected but, since his test scores were relatively high, the medical school has conceded that it could not prove that he would have been rejected if the sixteen places reserved had been open to him. Bakke sued, arguing that the task force program deprived him of his constitutional rights. The California Supreme Court agreed, and ordered the medical school to admit him. The university appealed to the Supreme Court.

The Davis program for minorities is in certain respects more forthright (some would say cruder) than similar plans now in force in many other American universities and professional schools. Such programs aim to increase the enrollment of black and other minority students by allowing the fact of their race to count affirmatively as part of the case for admitting them. Some schools set a "target" of a particular number of minority places instead of setting aside a flat number of places. But Davis would not fill the number of places set aside unless there were sixteen minority candidates it considered clearly qualified for medical education. The difference is therefore one of administrative strategy and not of principle.

So the constitutional question raised by *Bakke* is of capital importance for higher education in America, and a large number of universities and schools have entered briefs *amicus curiae* urging the Court to reverse the California decision. They believe that if the decision is affirmed then they will no longer be free to use explicit racial criteria in any part of their admissions programs, and that they will therefore be unable to fulfill what they take to be their responsibilities to the nation.

It is often said that affirmative action programs aim to achieve a racially conscious society divided into racial and ethnic groups, each entitled, as a group, to some proportionable share of resources, careers, or opportunities. That is a perverse description. American society is currently a racially conscious society; this is the inevitable and evident consequence of a history of slavery, repression, and prejudice. Black men and women, boys and girls, are not free to choose for themselves in what roles – or as members of which social groups – others will characterize them. They are black, and no other feature of personality or allegiance or ambition will so thoroughly influence how they will be perceived and treated by others, and the range and character of the lives that will be open to them.

The tiny number of black doctors and professionals is both a consequence and a continuing cause of American racial consciousness, one link in a long and self-fueling chain reaction. Affirmative action programs use racially explicit criteria because their immediate goal is to increase the number of members of certain races in these professions. But their long-term goal is to *reduce* the degree to which American society is over-all a racially conscious society.

The programs rest on two judgments. The first is a judgment of social theory: that America will continue to be pervaded by racial divisions as long as the most lucrative, satisfying, and important careers remain mainly the prerogative of members of the white race, while others feel themselves systematically excluded from a professional and social elite. The second is a calculation of strategy: that increasing the number of blacks who are at work in the professions will, in the long run, reduce the sense of frustration and injustice and racial self-consciousness in the black community to the point at which blacks may begin to think of themselves as individuals who can succeed like others through talent and initiative. At that future point the consequences of nonracial admissions programs, whatever these consequences might be, could be accepted with no sense of racial barriers or injustice.

It is therefore the worst possible misunderstanding to suppose that affirmative action programs are designed to produce a balkanized America, divided into racial and ethnic subnations. They use strong measures because weaker ones will fail; but their ultimate goal is to lessen not to increase the importance of race in American social and professional life.

According to the 1970 census, only 2.1 percent of US doctors were black. Affirmative action programs aim to provide more black doctors to serve black patients. This is not because it is desirable that blacks treat blacks and whites treat whites, but because blacks, for no fault of their own, are now unlikely to be well served by whites, and because a failure to provide the doctors they trust will exacerbate rather than reduce the resentment that now leads them to trust only their own. Affirmative action tries to provide more blacks as classmates for white doctors, not because it is desirable that a medical school class reflect the racial makeup of the community as a whole, but because professional association between blacks and whites will decrease the degree to which whites think of blacks as a race rather than as people, and thus the degree to which blacks think of themselves that way. It tries to provide "role models" for future black doctors, not because it is desirable for a black boy or girl to find adult models only among blacks, but because our history has made them so conscious of their race that the success of whites, for now, is likely to mean little or nothing for them.

The history of the campaign against racial injustice since 1954, when the Supreme Court decided *Brown* v. *Board of Education*, is a history in large part of failure. We have not succeeded in reforming the racial consciousness of our society by racially neutral means. We are therefore obliged to look upon the arguments for affirmative action with sympathy and an open mind. Of course, if Bakke is right that such programs, no matter how effective they may be, violate his constitutional rights then they cannot be permitted to continue. But we must not forbid them in the name of some mindless maxim, like the maxim that it cannot be right to fight fire with fire, or that the end cannot justify the means. If the strategic claims for affirmative action are cogent, they cannot be dismissed simply on the ground that racially explicit tests are distasteful. If such tests are distasteful it can only be for reasons that make the underlying social realities the programs attack more distasteful still.

The New Republic, in a recent editorial opposing affirmative action, missed that point. "It is critical to the success of a liberal pluralism," it said, "that group membership itself is not among the permissible criteria of inclusion and exclusion." But group membership is in fact, as a matter of social reality rather than formal admission standards, part of what determines inclusion or exclusion for us now. If we must choose between a society that is in fact liberal and an illiberal society that scrupulously avoids formal racial criteria, we can hardly appeal to the ideals of liberal pluralism to prefer the latter.

Professor Archibald Cox of Harvard Law School, speaking for the University of California in oral argument, told the Supreme Court that this is the choice the United States must make. As things stand, he said, affirmative action programs are the only effective means of increasing the absurdly small number of black doctors. The California Supreme Court, in approving Bakke's claim, had urged the university to pursue that goal by methods that do not explicitly take race into account. But that is unrealistic. We must distinguish, as Cox said, between two interpretations of what the California court's recommendation means. It might mean that the university should aim at the same immediate goal, of increasing the proportion of black and other minority students in the medical school, by an admissions procedure that on the surface is not racially conscious.

That is a recommendation of hypocrisy. If those who administer the admissions standards, however these are phrased, understand that their immediate goal is to increase the number of blacks in the school, then they will use race as a criterion in making the various subjective judgments the explicit criteria will require, because that will be, given the goal, the only right way to make those judgments. The recommendation might mean, on the other hand, that the school should adopt some nonracially conscious goal, like increasing the number of disadvantaged students of all races, and then hope that that goal will produce an increase in the number of blacks as a by-product. But even if that strategy is less hypocritical (which is far from plain), it will almost certainly fail because no different goal, scrupulously administered in a nonracially conscious way, will in fact significantly increase the number of black medical students.

Cox offered powerful evidence for that conclusion, and it is supported by the recent and comprehensive report of the Carnegie Council on Policy Studies in Higher Education. Suppose, for example, that the medical school sets aside separate places for applicants "disadvantaged" on some racially neutral test, like poverty, allowing only those disadvantaged in that way to compete for these places. If the school selects these from that group who scored best on standard medical school aptitude tests, then it will take almost no blacks, because blacks score relatively low even among the economically disadvantaged. But if the school chooses among the disadvantaged on some basis other than test scores, just so that more blacks will succeed, then it will not be administering the special procedure in a nonracially-conscious way.

So Cox was able to put his case in the form of two simple propositions. A racially conscious test for admission, even one that sets aside certain places for qualified minority applicants exclusively, serves goals that are in themselves unobjectionable and even urgent. Such programs are, moreover, the only means that offer any significant promise of achieving these goals. If these programs are halted, then no more than a trickle of black students will enter medical or other professional schools for another generation at least.

If these propositions are sound, then on what ground can it be thought that such programs are either wrong or unconstitutional? We must notice an important distinction between two different sorts of objections that might be made. These programs are intended, as I said, to decrease the importance of race in the United States in the long run. It may be objected, first, that the programs will in fact harm that goal more than they will advance it. There is no way now to prove that that is so. Cox conceded, in his argument, that there are costs and risks in these programs.

Affirmative action programs seem to encourage, for example, a popular misunderstanding, which is that they assume that racial or ethnic groups are entitled to proportionate shares of opportunities, so that Italian or Polish ethnic minorities are, in theory, as entitled to their proportionate shares as blacks or Chicanos or American Indians are entitled to the shares the present programs give them. That is a plain mistake: the programs are not based on the idea that those who are aided are entitled to aid, but only on the strategic hypothesis that helping them is now an effective way of attacking a national problem. Some medical schools may well make that judgment, under certain circumstances, about a white ethnic minority. Indeed it seems likely that some medical schools are even now attempting to help white Appalachian applicants, for example, under programs of regional distribution.

So the popular understanding is wrong, but so long as it persists it is a cost of the program because the attitudes it encourages tend to a degree to make people more rather than less conscious of race. There are other possible costs. It is said, for example, that some blacks find affirmative action degrading; they find that it makes them more rather than less conscious of prejudice against their race as such. This attitude is also based on a misperception, I think, but for a small minority of blacks at least it is a genuine cost.

In the view of the many important universities who have such programs, however, the gains will very probably exceed the losses in reducing racial consciousness over-all. This view is hardly so implausible that it is wrong for these universities to seek to acquire the experience that will allow us to judge whether they are right. It would be particularly silly to forbid these experiments if we know that the failure to try will mean, as the evidence shows, that the status quo will almost certainly continue. In any case, this first objection could provide no argument that would justify a decision by the Supreme Court holding the programs unconstitutional. The Court has no business substituting its speculative judgment about the probable consequences of educational policies for the judgment of professional educators.

So the acknowledged uncertainties about the long-term results of such programs could not justify a Supreme Court decision making them illegal. But there is a second and very different form of objection. It may be argued that even if the programs *are* effective in making our society less a society dominated by race, they are nevertheless unconstitutional because they violate the individual constitutional rights of those, like Allan Bakke, who lose places in consequence. In the oral argument Reynold H. Colvin of San Francisco, who is Bakke's lawyer, made plain that his objection takes this second form. Mr Justice White asked him whether he accepted that the goals affirmative action programs seek are important goals. Mr Colvin acknowledged that they were. Suppose, Justice White continued, that affirmative action programs are, as Cox had argued, the only effective means of seeking such goals. Would Mr Colvin nevertheless maintain that the programs are unconstitutional? Yes, he insisted, they would be, because his client has a constitutional right that the programs be abandoned, no matter what the consequences.

Mr Colvin was wise to put his objections on this second ground; he was wise to claim that his client has rights that do not depend on any judgment about the likely consequences of affirmative action for society as a whole, because if he makes out that claim then the Court must give him the relief he seeks.

But can he be right? If Allan Bakke has a constitutional right so important that the urgent goals of affirmative action must yield, then this must be because affirmative action violates some fundamental principle of political morality. This is not a case in which what might be called formal or technical law requires a decision one way or the other. There is no language in the Constitution whose plain meaning forbids affirmative action. Only the most naïve theories of statutory construction could argue that such a result is required by the language of any earlier Supreme Court decision or of the Civil Rights Act of 1964 or of any other congressional enactment. If Mr Colvin is right it must be because Allan Bakke has not simply some technical legal right but an important moral right as well.

What could that right be? The popular argument frequently made on editorial pages is that Bakke has a right to be judged on his merit. Or that he has a right to be judged as an individual rather than as a member of a social group. Or that he has a right, as much as any black man, not to be sacrificed or excluded from any opportunity because of his race alone. But these catch phrases are deceptive here, because, as reflection demonstrates, the only genuine principle they describe is the principle that no one should suffer from the prejudice or contempt of others. And that principle is not at stake in this case at all. In spite of popular opinion, the idea that the *Bakke* case presents a conflict between a desirable social goal and important individual rights is a piece of intellectual confusion.

Consider, for example, the claim that individuals applying for places in medical school should be judged on merit, and merit alone. If that slogan means that admissions committees should take nothing into account but scores on some particular intelligence test, then it is arbitrary and, in any case, contradicted by the long-standing practice of every medical school. If it means, on the other hand, that a medical school should choose candidates that it supposes will make the most useful doctors, then everything turns on the judgment of what factors make different doctors useful. The Davis Medical School assigned to each regular applicant, as well as to each minority applicant, what it called a "benchmark score." This reflected not only the results of aptitude tests and college grade averages, but a subjective evaluation of the applicant's chances of functioning as an effective doctor, in view of society's present needs for medical service. Presumably the qualities deemed important were different from the qualities that a law school or engineering school or business school would seek, just as the intelligence tests a medical school might use would be different from the tests these other schools would find appropriate.

There is no combination of abilities and skills and traits that constitutes "merit" in the abstract; if quick hands count as "merit" in the case of a prospective surgeon, this is because quick hands will enable him to serve the public better and for no other reason. If a black skin will, as a matter of regrettable fact, enable another doctor to do a different medical job better, then that black skin is by the same token "merit" as well. That argument may strike some as dangerous; but only because they confuse its conclusion – that black skin may be a socially useful trait in particular circumstances – with the very different and despicable idea that one race may be inherently more worthy than another.

Consider the second of the catch phrases I have mentioned. It is said that Bakke has a right to be judged as an "individual," in deciding whether he is to be admitted to medical school and thus to the medical profession, and not as a member of some group that is being judged as a whole. What can that mean? Any admissions procedure must rely on generalizations about groups that are justified only statistically. The regular admissions process at Davis, for example, set a cutoff figure for college grade-point averages. Applicants whose averages fell below that figure were not invited to any interview, and were therefore rejected out of hand.

An applicant whose average fell one point below the cutoff might well have had personal qualities of dedication or sympathy that would have been revealed at an interview, and that would have made him or her a better doctor than some applicant whose average rose one point above the line. But the former is excluded from the process on the basis of a decision taken for administrative convenience and grounded in the generalization, unlikely to hold true for every individual, that those with grade averages below the cutoff will not have other qualities sufficiently persuasive. Indeed, even the use of standard Medical College Aptitude Tests (MCAT) as part of the admissions procedure requires judging people as part of groups because it assumes that test scores are a guide to medical intelligence, which is in turn a guide to medical ability. Though this judgment is no doubt true statistically, it hardly holds true for every individual.

Allan Bakke was himself refused admission to two other medical schools, not because of his race but because of his age: these schools thought that a student entering medical school at the age of thirty-three was likely to make less of a contribution to medical care over his career than someone entering at the standard age of twenty-one. Suppose these schools relied, not on any detailed investigation of whether Bakke himself had abilities that would contradict the generalization in his specific case, but on a rule of thumb that allowed only the most cursory look at applicants over (say) the age of thirty. Did these two medical schools violate his right to be judged as an individual rather than as a member of a group?

The Davis Medical School permitted whites to apply for the sixteen places reserved for members of "educationally or economically disadvantaged minorities," a phrase whose meaning might well include white ethnic minorities. In fact several whites have applied, though none has been accepted, and the California Court found that the special committee charged with administering the program had decided, in advance, against admitting any. Suppose that decision had been based on the following administrative theory: it is so unlikely that any white doctor can do as much to counteract racial imbalance in the medical professions as a well-qualified and trained black doctor can do that the committee should for reasons of convenience proceed on the presumption no white doctor could. That presumption is, as a matter of fact, more plausible than the corresponding presumption about medical students over the age of thirty, or even the presumption about applicants whose grade-point averages fall below the cutoff line. If the latter presumptions do not deny the alleged right of individuals to be judged as individuals in an admissions procedure, then neither can the former.

Mr Colvin, in oral argument, argued the third of the catch phrases I mentioned. He said that his client had a right not to be excluded from medical school because of his race alone, and this as a statement of constitutional right sounds more plausible than claims about the right to be judged on merit or as an individual. It sounds plausible, however, because it suggests the following more complex principle. Every citizen has a constitutional right that he not suffer disadvantage, at least in the competition for any public benefit, because the race or religion or sect or region or other natural or artificial group to which he belongs is the object of prejudice or contempt.

That is a fundamentally important constitutional right, and it is that right that was systematically violated for many years by racist exclusions and anti-Semitic quotas. Color bars and Jewish quotas were not unfair just because they made race or religion relevant or because they fixed on qualities beyond individual control. It is true that blacks or Jews do not choose to be blacks or Jews. But it is also true that those who score low in aptitude or admissions tests do not choose their levels of intelligence. Nor do those denied admission because they are too old, or because they do not come from a part of the country underrepresented in the school, or because they cannot play basketball well, choose not to have the qualities that made the difference.

Race seems different because exclusions based on race have historically been motivated not by some instrumental calculation, as in the case of intelligence or age or regional distribution or athletic ability, but because of contempt for the excluded race or religion as such. Exclusion by race was in itself an insult, because it was generated by and signaled contempt.

Bakke's claim, therefore, must be made more specific than it is. He says he was kept out of medical school because of his race. Does he mean that he was kept out because his race is the object of prejudice or contempt? That suggestion is absurd. A very high proportion of those who were accepted (and, presumably, of those who run the admissions program) were members of the same race. He therefore means simply that if he had been black he would have been accepted, with no suggestion that this would have been so because blacks are thought more worthy or honorable than whites.

That is true: no doubt he would have been accepted if he were black. But it is also true, and in exactly the same sense, that he would have been accepted if he had been more intelligent, or made a better impression in his interview, or, in the case of other schools, if he had been younger when he decided to become a doctor. Race is not, in *his* case, a different matter from these other factors equally beyond his control. It is not a different matter because in his case race is not distinguished by the special character of public insult. On the contrary the program presupposes that his race is still widely if wrongly thought to be superior to others.

In the past, it made sense to say that an excluded black or Jewish student was being sacrificed because of his race or religion; that meant that his or her exclusion was treated as desirable in itself, not because it contributed to any goal in which he as well as the rest of society might take pride. Allan Bakke is being "sacrificed" because of his race only in a very artificial sense of the word. He is being "sacrificed" in the same artificial sense because of his level of intelligence, since he would have been accepted if he were more clever than he is. In both cases he is being excluded not by prejudice but because of a rational calculation about the socially most beneficial use of limited resources for medical education.

It may now be said that this distinction is too subtle, and that if racial classifications have been and may still be used for malign purposes, then everyone has a flat right that racial classifications not be used at all. This is the familiar appeal to the lazy virtue of simplicity. It supposes that if a line is difficult to draw, or might be difficult to administer if drawn, then there is wisdom in not making the attempt to draw it. There may be cases in which that is wise, but those would be cases in which nothing of great value would as a consequence be lost. If racially conscious admissions policies now offer the only substantial hope for bringing more qualified black and other minority doctors into the profession, then a great loss is suffered if medical schools are not allowed voluntarily to pursue such programs. We should then be trading away a chance to attack certain and present injustice in order to gain protection we may not need against speculative abuses we have other means to prevent. And such abuses cannot, in any case, be worse than the injustice to which we would then surrender.

We have now considered three familiar slogans, each widely thought to name a constitutional right that enables Allan Bakke to stop programs of affirmative action no matter how effective or necessary these might be. When we inspect these slogans, we find that they can stand for no genuine principle except one. This is the important principle that no one in our society should suffer because he is a member of a group thought less worthy of respect, as a group, than other groups. We have different aspects of that principle in mind when we say that individuals should be judged on merit, that they should be judged as individuals, and that they should not suffer disadvantages because of their race. The spirit of that fundamental principle is the spirit of the goal that affirmative action is intended to serve. The principle furnishes no support for those who find, as Bakke does, that their own interests conflict with that goal.

It is of course regrettable when any citizen's expectations are defeated by new programs serving some more general concern. It is regrettable, for example, when established small businesses fail because new and superior roads are built; in that case people have invested more than Bakke has. And they had more reason to believe their businesses would continue than Bakke had to suppose he could have entered the Davis Medical School at thirty-three even without a task-force program.

There is, of course, no suggestion in that program that Bakke shares in any collective or individual guilt for racial injustice in America; or that he is any less entitled to concern or respect than any black student accepted in the program. He has been disappointed, and he must have the sympathy due that disappointment, just as any other disappointed applicant – even one with much worse test scores who would not have been accepted in any event – must have sympathy. Each is disappointed because places in medical schools are scarce resources and must be used to provide what the more general society most needs. It is hardly Bakke's fault that racial justice is now a special need – but he has no right to prevent the most effective measures of securing that justice from being used.

43

Affirmative Action as Equalizing Opportunity: Challenging the Myth of "Preferential Treatment"

Luke Charles Harris and Uma Narayan

Introduction

Affirmative action is an issue on which there has been considerable public debate. We think, however, that it is a policy that has often been misunderstood and mischaracterized, not only by those opposed to it, *but even by its defenders* (Harris and Narayan, 1994). In this essay, we intend to describe these misconceptions, to explain why we consider them misconceptions, and to offer a much stronger defense of affirmative action policies than is usually offered. In the first section, we examine and challenge prevalent misrepresentations of the *scope* of affirmative action policies – misconceptions about the groups of people these policies are designed to benefit, and about the benefits they are intended to achieve. In the second section, we address misunderstandings about the *rationale* for affirmative action policies, and take issue with those who regard affirmative action as bestowing "preferential treatment" on its beneficiaries. We argue that affirmative action policies should be understood as attempts to *equalize opportunity* for groups of people who confront ongoing forms of institutional discrimination and a lack of equal opportunity. In the third and fourth sections respectively, we take issue with those who defend affirmative action on the grounds that it is a form of *compensation*, and with those who defend it on the grounds that it promotes *diversity* and a range of other long-term goals. We argue that such rationales mischaracterize affirmative action as providing justifiable "preferences" to its beneficiaries. In the final section, we argue that the "stigma argument" against affirmative action dissolves if affirmative action is understood as equalizing opportunities, and not as *bestowing preferences*.

Clarifying the Scope of Affirmative Action Policies

The debate on affirmative action often misrepresents the scope of these policies in several important ways. The most perturbing of these misrepresentations is the widespread tendency to construe these policies as *race-based policies alone*, and further, to talk about African

Americans as the only racial group they are intended to benefit. This picture of affirmative action policies is, to put it bluntly, false. Even when these policies were first initiated, they were designed to benefit members of other disadvantaged racial minorities besides African Americans. For example, almost two-thirds of the students admitted under the affirmative action program of the Davis Medical School that was challenged in the landmark *Bakke* case in 1978 were Latino or Asian American. Nonetheless, almost the entire public debate surrounding the case discussed it in terms of Blacks and Whites only. Even more oddly, the opinions of the Justices of the Supreme Court that considered this case – the majority opinions as well as the dissenting opinions – discussed affirmative action only as benefiting African Americans. In the context of the racial politics of the United States, we believe such a misrepresentation of the scope of these policies is not only false, but also dangerous since it is easier to negatively stereotype these policies when African Americans are viewed as their only beneficiaries.

Thus, even at their inception, when affirmative action policies were predominantly race-based, they were designed to remedy the institutional exclusion of *a number of racially-disadvantaged groups*. In many institutional contexts, they have long since expanded to cover other grounds on which groups of people face discrimination and unequal opportunity. A great many educational institutions, professions and trades have opened their doors to *women* as a result of affirmative action, promoting the entry of women into a range of formerly male domains, from law schools to corporations to police departments. This has benefited not only women of color, but many middle-class White women. Affirmative action policies in some institutions such as professional schools have also promoted the entry of working-class applicants, including working-class White men, a fact that is seldom discussed and little known. Derrick Bell points out that "special admissions criteria have been expanded to encompass disadvantaged but promising White applicants," and that, for example, the open admissions program of New York's City University system, which was initiated by minority pressure, has benefited even greater numbers of lower-middle-class and working-class Whites than Blacks (Bell, 1979).

We need to remember that the world in which affirmative action policies were initiated was a world where a great many prestigious institutions and professions were almost exclusively enclaves of upper-class White men, and where many of the blue-collar trades were predominantly the preserve of White working-class men. Affirmative action has been crucial in opening up the former to women, to members of racial minorities, and to working-class Whites, and in opening up the latter to women and members of racial minorities. We are not arguing that each and every instance of affirmative action does or should consider each category of class, race, and gender. Which factors should be considered depends on the patterns of exclusion within a particular occupation and institution. For instance, affirmative action policies in the blue-collar trades and police and fire departments need to affirmatively promote the entry of women of all races and of minority men, since they were the groups who faced obstacles to entry, not White working-class men. On the other hand, student admissions policies at institutions that used to be women's colleges attended predominantly by White upper-class women such as our institution, Vassar College, should seek to affirmatively recruit students of color and students from working-class backgrounds, including White working-class men. What we are arguing is that, taken as a whole, affirmative action policies in many contexts have long operated on multiple criteria of inclusion, even though they continue to be portrayed as policies that either only benefit or principally benefit African Americans.

The prevalent failure to consider the range of people that affirmative action policies have benefited breeds a number of misplaced objections to these policies. For instance, many people argue that affirmative action policies should be class-based instead of race-based, since they believe that middle-class African Americans do not need or "deserve" affirmative action (Carter, 1991). This view is problematic in a number of ways. First, many proponents of this view pose the issue as *a choice between race and class*, ignoring the fact that affirmative action policies have been *both* class-based and race-based. Secondly, proponents of this view believe that middle-class Blacks do not suffer from the effects of discrimination despite substantial evidence to the contrary.

In 1985, independent studies by the Grier Partnership and the Urban League revealed striking disparities in the employment levels of Blacks and Whites in Washington, DC, an area that constitutes one of the "best markets" for Blacks (Pyatt, 1985). Both studies cite racial discrimination as the major factor that accounts for this difference. A 1991 study by the Urban Institute examined employment practices in the Chicago and Washington, DC areas by sending equally qualified and identically dressed White and Black applicants to newspaper-advertised positions. The testers were also matched for speech patterns, age, work experience, physical build and personal characteristics. The study found repeated discrimination that increased with the level of the advertised position, and revealed that Whites received job offers three times more often than *equally qualified* Blacks (Turner, et al., 1991).

Finally, the limitation of the view that middle-class Blacks do not suffer racial discrimination becomes clear when we attend to gender-based affirmative action policies. No one has seriously suggested that the sexism and gender-based discrimination women face in a variety of institutions is merely a product of their class status, or that middle-class status shields White women from these effects. Just as affirmative action policies that attend only to class disadvantages are unlikely to remedy the institutional exclusions faced by women, they would surely fail to remedy race-based exclusions faced by members of several racial minority groups. In short, the effects of gender and race bias would be only partially curtailed by purely class-based policies. Indeed, purely class-based policies would mostly benefit working-class White men, whose race and gender are not the sources of invidious discrimination. As some recent feminist works teach us, we must, therefore, pay particular attention to the inter-connected ways in which factors such as class, race, gender and sexual orientation work together to sustain disparities between different groups of Americans in a variety of institutional and social contexts.

There is, then, no need to pit class against race (or against gender) as the only valid basis for affirmative action. An array of factors that contribute to institutional discrimination – such as class, race, gender and disability – should be taken into account. When several factors intersect and jointly contribute to a process of discrimination, as in the case of a working-class Black woman, each factor should be considered. When only one aspect of a person's identity adversely affects his or her opportunities in a given setting – for instance, class status in the case of working-class White men, or race in the case of middle-class Black men – then only that factor should be taken into account.

Another prevalent objection to affirmative action policies that seems connected to misunderstanding its actual scope is the objection that *truly disadvantaged* poor Blacks have not benefited from these policies. The impression that affirmative action benefits only the Black middle class and that few working-class or poor Blacks benefit from these programs is mistaken. For the vast majority of Blacks were working-class prior to the Civil Rights Era and the promulgation of civil rights laws and affirmative action initiatives. These efforts have combined to play a major role in the creation of the Black middle class that exists today. Bob Blauner points out that due to occupational mobility that is in part a product of affirmative action, nearly 25 percent of Black families had incomes of more than $25,000 (in constant dollars) in 1982, compared with 8.7 percent in 1960. Moreover, the proportion of employed Blacks who hold middle-class jobs rose from 13.4 percent in 1960 to 37.8 percent in 1981. The number of Black college students rose from 340,000 in 1966 to more than one million in 1982 (Blauner, 1989). From sanitation departments to university departments, from the construction industry to corporate America, these programs have helped to open doors once tightly sealed.

An empirically accurate assessment of affirmative action policies shows that they have not only benefited poor and working-class Blacks, but poor and working-class people of all races, including some White working-class men and women. White working-class people's opposition to these policies based on the belief that they are "victims" of such programs is based on a mistake, a mistake facilitated by discussions of these policies that portray them as only benefiting Blacks.

Lastly, some people also argue against affirmative action on the grounds that it has not solved a host of problems pertaining to poverty, the inner-city and the "underclass" (Shelby Steele, 1990). It is entirely true that affirmative action has not solved these problems. Neither has it solved problems such as rape, domestic violence and sexual harassment. However, we do not think these are legitimate objections, since they more obviously over-inflate the scope of what these policies were intended to accomplish. Affirmative action polices cannot be, and were not intended to be, a magic solution to *all* our social problems; indeed no single policy can solve every social problem we confront. Their purpose is a limited though important one – to partially counter the ways in which factors such as class, race, gender and disabilities function in our society to impede equal access and opportunity, thereby promoting greater inclusion of diverse Americans in a range of institutions and occupations. They have clearly succeeded in this goal, and should not be condemned for failing to solve problems they were not intended to solve.

Re-envisioning the Rationale for Affirmative Action: from "Preferential Treatment" to "Equal Opportunity"

We believe that many mistaken views about affirmative action result from misunderstand-ings about the justification or rationale for such policies. Unfortunately, the debate on affirmative action has largely been a dialogue between two broadly characterizable positions. On the one hand, its critics describe it as a form of "reverse discrimination" that bestows "undeserved preferences" on its beneficiaries. On the other hand, its defenders continue to characterize the policy as "preferential treatment," but argue that these preferences are justified, either as "compensation" or on grounds of "social utility." Few question the assumption that affirmative action involves the "bestowal of preferences," or challenge the premise that it marks a sudden deviation from a system that, until its advent, operated strictly and clearly on the basis of merit. Setting out a view of affirmative action that rejects these ideas is our central task here.

In our view, affirmative action is not a matter of affording "preferential treatment" to its beneficiaries. Our position is that affirmative action is best understood as an attempt to promote *equality of opportunity* in a social context marked by pervasive inequalities, one in which many institutional criteria and practices work to impede a fair assessment of the capabilities of those who are working-class, women or people of color. Thus, affirmative action is an attempt to equalize opportunity for people who continue to face institutional obstacles to equal consideration and equal treatment. These obstacles include not only continuing forms of blatant discrimination, but, more importantly, a variety of subtle institutional criteria and practices that unwarrantedly circumscribe mobility in contemporary America. These criteria and practices are often not deliberately designed to discriminate and exclude; the fact remains, however, that they nevertheless function to do so, as our subsequent examples demonstrate. Thus, in countering such forms of discrimination, affirmative action policies attempt only to "level the playing field." They do not "bestow preferences" on their beneficiaries; rather, they attempt to undo the effects of institutional practices and criteria that, however unintentionally, amount in effect to "preferential treatment" for Whites.

Those who believe that affirmative action constitutes "preferential treatment" assume (a) that the criteria and procedures generally used for admissions and hiring are neutral indicators of "merit," unaffected by factors such as class, race, or gender, and (b) that such criteria are fairly and impartially applied to all individuals at each of the stages of the selection process. In the rest of this section, we will try to show why these two assumptions are seriously open to question.

Although test scores on standardized tests are often "taken as absolute by both the public and the institutions that use the scores in decision making," there is ample evidence that they do not predict equally well for men and women. A study of three college admissions tests (the SAT, the PSAT/NMSQT, and the ACT) reveals that although women consistently earn better high school and college grades, they receive lower scores on all three tests. Rosser argues that "if the SAT predicted equally well for both sexes, girls would score about 20 points higher than the boys, not 61 points lower" (Rosser, 1987). Standardized test scores adversely affect women's chances for admission to colleges and universities, their chances for scholarships, and entry into "gifted" programs, as well as their academic self-perceptions. Similarly, James Crouse and Dale Trusheim argue, on the basis of statistical evidence, that the scores are not very useful indicators for helping to "admit black applicants who would succeed and reject applicants who would fail" (Crouse and Trusheim, 1988).

The literature on such standardized tests demonstrates that they are often inaccurate indicators even with respect to their *limited stated objective* of predicting students' first-year grades in college and professional school. Yet, they are often used as if they measured a person's overall intelligence and foretold long-term success in educational institutions and professional life. As a result of these unsupported beliefs, affirmative action policies that depart from strict considerations of these test scores are often taken to constitute the strongest evidence for institutional deviation from standards of merit, and constitutive elements of the "preference" thought to be awarded to women and minority applicants.

There are also many other examples of established rules, practices and policies of institutions that, no matter how benign their intention, have the effect of discriminating against the members of relatively marginalized groups. For instance, word-of-mouth recruitment where the existing labor pool is predominantly White male reduces the chances of women or people of color applying for the jobs in question, as do unions that influence or control hiring in well-paid jobs in the construction, transportation and printing industries when they recruit through personal contacts. A 1990 study reports that over 80 percent of executives find their jobs through networking, and that about 86 percent of available jobs do not appear in the classifieds (Ezorsky, 1991). "Last hired, first fired" rules make more recently hired women and minorities more susceptible to lay-offs. The "old boy network" that results from years of social and business contacts among White men, as well as racially or sexually segregated country clubs or social organizations, often paid for by employers, also have discriminatory impacts on women and minorities. Furthermore, stereotyped beliefs about women and minorities often justify hiring them for low-level, low-paying jobs, regardless of their qualifications for higher-level jobs (Kantor and Stein, 1976).

Indeed, some empirical studies show that many Black candidates for jobs are rated more negatively than White candidates with identical credentials. Other studies demonstrate that the same résumé with a woman's name on it receives a significantly lower rating than when it has a man's name on it, showing that gender-bias operates even when there is no direct contact with the persons evaluated. Still other problematic practices include evaluations where subjective assessments of factors such as "fitting in," "personality," and "self-confidence" serve class, race and gender prejudice.

Personal interviews, job evaluations, and recommendations all have an inescapable subjective element which often works in the favor of better-off White men. As Lawrence A. Blum writes:

> Persons can fail to be judged purely on ability because they have not gone to certain colleges or professional schools, because they do not know the right people, because they do not present themselves in a certain way. And, again, sometimes this sort of discrimination takes place without either those doing the discriminating or those being discriminated against realizing it. . . . Often these denials of equal opportunity have a lot to do with class background, as well as race or sex, or with a combination of these.

Interview processes that precede being selected or hired are often not as "neutral" as assumed. A two-step experiment done at Princeton University began with White undergraduates interviewing both White and Black job applicants. Unknown to the interviewers, the applicants in the first stage of the experiment were all confederates of the experimenters and were trained to behave consistently from interview to interview. This study reported that interviewers spent less time with Black applicants and were less friendly and outgoing than with the White applicants. In the second stage of the experiment, confederates of the experimenters were trained to approximate the two styles of interviewing observed during the first stage of the study when they interviewed two groups of White applicants. A panel of judges who reviewed tapes of these interviews reported that White applicants subjected to the style previously accorded Blacks performed noticeably worse in the interviews than other White applicants. In this respect, there is also substantial evidence that women are asked inappropriate questions and subject to discrimination in interviews.

None of the discriminatory institutional structures and practices we have detailed above necessarily involve conscious antipathy toward women and minorities or the operation of conscious sexist or racist stereotypes. Some discriminatory structures and practices involve unconscious stereotypes at work, from which women and people of color are hardly immune in their evaluations of other women and minorities. Many of the examples we discuss involve practices central to hiring and promotion that work to disadvantage many marginalized Americans even when all persons involved sincerely believe themselves to be fair and impartial. Because the processes of getting through an educational program, or being hired, retained and promoted in a job involve the possibility, for example, of women and minority applicants being subject to a variety of such practices, it seems likely that few, if any, women or people of color are apt to escape the cumulative adverse effects of these practices. In the context of these structures and practices that systematically disadvantage some Americans, it would be naive, at best, to believe that our society is a well-functioning meritocracy.

The problem is far more complicated than is captured by the common perspective that working-class people, women and minorities have generally not had equal advantages and opportunities to acquire qualifications that are on par with those of their better-off, White male counterparts, and so we should compensate them by awarding them preferences even though they are less well qualified. Their qualifications, in fact, tend to be under-valued and under-appraised in many institutional contexts. Moreover, many of the criteria that are unquestioningly taken to be important impartial indicators of people's competencies, merit and potential, such as test scores, not only fail to be precise measurements of these qualities, but systematically stigmatize these individuals within institutions in which these tests function as important criteria of admission.

We do not however wish to deny that factors such as class, race and gender often impede persons from acquiring qualifications. A 1981 study, for instance, showed that Black school districts received less funding and inferior educational resources compared with similar White districts, often as a result of decision-making by Whites. There is also increasing evidence of disadvantaging practices in the pre-college advising offered to minority students. Evidence suggests that teachers often interpret linguistic and cultural differences as indications of low potential or a lack of academic interests on the part of minority students; and guidance counselors often steer female and minority students away from "hard" subjects, such as mathematics and science, which are often paths to high-paying jobs.

In such contexts, even if the criteria used to determine admission and hiring were otherwise unproblematic, it is not at all clear that taking them simply "at face value" would fairly or accurately gauge the talents and potential of disparate individuals. When some candidates have to overcome several educational and social obstacles that others do not, similarity of credentials may well amount to a significant difference in talent and potential. Thus, treating identical credentials as signs of identical capabilities and effort may, under prevailing conditions of inequality, significantly devalue the worth of credentials obtained in the teeth of such obstacles. We would argue that individuals who obtained their credentials in the face of severe obstacles are likely to do better than those who have similar or even somewhat better credentials obtained without coping with such obstacles, especially over a period of years, where they have opportunities to remedy their handicaps. Affirmative action policies with respect to admissions and hiring recruit individuals for positions where "success" depends on the nature of one's performance over several years. Such recruitment should rightly concern itself with a person's evidenced *potential* for success rather than simply assess what their capabilities appear to be, based on the comparison of credentials acquired by individuals under distinctly different circumstances.

We are not arguing, however, that affirmative action policies are, or can be, magical formulas that help us determine with perfect precision in every case the exact weights that must be accorded a person's class background, gender, and minority status so as to afford him or her perfect equality of opportunity. Particular institutions must use practical wisdom and good-faith efforts to determine the exact measures that they will undertake to promote equality within their frameworks, as well as monitor and periodically reassess the parameters and scope of their institutional policies. Nor do we wish to deny that some persons recruited as a result of affirmative action policies might turn out to be incompetent or demonstrate significant limitations in their ability to meet requirements. After all, the same incompetencies and limitations are manifested by some who are recruited by "regular" channels. No recruitment policies are immune to these problems. What we do argue is that in contexts where, for example, class, race, and gender operate to impede equality of opportunity, affirmative action policies have enabled many talented and promising individuals to have their talent and promise more fairly evaluated by the institutions in question than would otherwise have been the case.

The Limitations of the Compensation Rationale for Affirmative Action

Affirmative action has frequently been defended on the grounds that it provides preferential treatment to members of marginalized groups as reparation or compensation for injustices they have suffered. The term *compensation* draws heavily on the model of recompense or payment of damages that is found in tort law. In the context of tort remedies, the particular agent who is responsible for injuring another compensates the specific person injured by paying what is judged to be an appropriate sum of money for the actual extent of the injury he or she has caused. This rationale tends to raise a number of questions precisely at those points where affirmative action policies seem to differ from the practice of tort-based compensation. Some argue that those who are "paying the price" for affirmative action have no direct responsibility for any harms or injuries suffered by any of its beneficiaries. Others raise the question of why the specific form of payment involved – construed as preferences for jobs or preferential entry to educational institutions – is the appropriate form of compensation, rather than monetary awards. Such critics reinforce these arguments by pointing out that affirmative action policies do not seem to be the most equitable form of compensation because those who have been most injured are probably not the ones receiving the compensation since their injuries have resulted in their not having "the qualifications even to be considered."

There have been attempts to defend the compensation rationale against these objections (Boxhill, 1978). However, we believe that it remains an inadequate and problematic rationale for affirmative action. In suggesting that affirmative action compensates individuals for damage done by phenomena such as racism or sexism, this rationale implies that the problem is one of "damaged individuals" rather than a problem due to structures, practices and institutional criteria within our institutions that continue to impede a fair assessment of the capabilities of some Americans. We have argued in the previous section that there is ample evidence to show that many prevalent criteria and procedures do not fairly gauge the capabilities of members of marginalized groups. The compensation model, however, does not question the normative criteria used by our institutions or encourage critical reflection about the processes of assessment used to determine these "qualifications"; and, as a result, it fails to question the view that affirmative action involves "preferential treatment." We consider this a serious weakness, since it does not challenge the view that affirmative action policies promote the entry of "less qualified" individuals. Rather it merely insists that "preferences" bestowed on less qualified individuals are justified as a form of compensation.

The compensation literature also conflates the rationale for race- and gender-based affirmative action policies with that for policies that promote institutional access for veterans. Policies based on veteran status may indeed be understood as compensation for their risks, efforts, and injuries sustained in the service of the nation, which may also have impeded or detracted from their employment or educational goals. However, it does not necessarily follow that a rationale that works best to explain one type of special assistance program works equally well to explain all others. In this respect, not only is a person's veteran status usually less visible than their race or gender, veteran status *per se* does not very often render persons targets of prejudice and institutional discrimination.

The Limitations of the Social Utility Rationales for Affirmative Action

We believe that our rationale for affirmative action is stronger than the "social utility" arguments that have been proffered in its defense. To illuminate our perspective, we will focus on one of the best known of such defenses, that offered by Ronald Dworkin. Dworkin understands affirmative action to involve "preferential treatment" and discusses affirmative action policies only as pertaining to Blacks. His argument can be summarized as follows. First, he argues that affirmative action policies that "give preferences" to minority candidates do not violate the "right to equal treatment" or the "right to equal consideration and respect" of White male applicants. Dworkin argues that these rights would be violated if a White male suffers disadvantage when competing with Blacks because his race is "the object of prejudice or contempt," but that this is not the case with affirmative action policies. Secondly, Dworkin argues that the "costs" that White male applicants suffer as a result of affirmative action policies are justified because such policies promote several beneficial social ends, the most important of which is their long-term impact in making us a less race-conscious society. Other beneficial social ends that Dworkin argues are served by affirmative action include providing role models for Blacks, providing more professionals such as doctors and lawyers willing to serve the Black community, reducing the sense of frustration and injustice in the Black community, and alleviating social tensions along racial lines.

Whereas Dworkin focuses on the negative claim that affirmative action policies do not violate the right to treatment as an equal, or the right to equal consideration and respect for the interests of White men, we make the positive and much stronger claim that affirmative action policies are justified because *they are necessary to ensure the right to treatment as an equal for the members of marginalized groups*, in a social context where a variety of social structures and institutional practices conspire to deny their interests equal consideration and respect. While we have no quarrel with Dworkin's claims about the social benefits of affirmative action, we do not rest our case for affirmative action on such *consequentialist arguments* about its long-term effects, arguments that are notoriously vulnerable to counter-arguments that project a set of more negative consequences as the long-term results. Since we do not believe that affirmative action bestows "preferential treatment" on its beneficiaries or imposes "costs" on White male applicants, as Dworkin does, we do not need to rely on Dworkin-type arguments that the long-term social "benefits" of these "preferences" justify imposing these "costs."

Our rationale for affirmative action also differs from social utility arguments that justify these policies on the ground that they contribute to a greater diversity of backgrounds and perspectives within academic institutions, thereby enhancing the learning process. First, "diversity" on a campus can be enhanced by admitting people from a wide variety of backgrounds, and with a wide range of special talents. A commitment to "diversity" *per se* could justify policies that promoted the recruitment of students from abroad, from remote areas of the country, and those with artistic skills or unusual interests. While there might well be institutional reasons for, and benefits from, promoting diversity in these forms, none of these students need necessarily have suffered from the systematic effects of social and institutional forms of discrimination within the United States. Thus, many students who would provide "diversity" would not qualify for affirmative action, even though there might be other reasons for admitting them. Secondly, while admitting greater numbers of working-class people, women, and minorities into institutions in which they are significantly underrepresented would also increase institutional diversity in meaningful ways, we see such beneficial consequences as supplemental benefits of affirmative action rather than its central goal.

While we believe affirmative action has in fact had beneficial consequences in making many areas of work and education more integrated along class, race and gender lines, we see these consequences as the results of treating people more equally, and not as benefits that have resulted from "imposing costs" on non-beneficiaries of affirmative action. Our central objection to both the "compensation" and "social utility" rationales for affirmative action is that neither questions the related assumptions that affirmative action "bestows preferences" on some, and imposes "costs" on others, even as they regard these "preferences" and "costs" as justified. In short, we insist that affirmative action policies that attempt to foster equal treatment do not constitute "preferential treatment" and that such attempts to undo the effects of institutional practices and criteria that privilege the capacities of some people over others are not "costs" that need to be justified by pointing to the "benefits" of the long-term consequences of these policies.

Challenging the "Stigma" of Affirmative Action

Affirmative action has been criticized on the grounds that it "stigmatizes" its participants because both they themselves as well as others regard the beneficiaries of affirmative action as "less qualified" than non-beneficiaries. Affirmative action policies are also criticized on the grounds that they cause resentment among the "more qualified" people who are denied entry as a result of these policies and thereby forced to pay its "costs." We believe that both criticisms are often the results of failing to accurately understand the rationale for affirmative action. Furthermore, we believe that these arguments about "stigma" and "resentment" are unwittingly reinforced by those who defend affirmative action on the basis of the "compensation" or "social utility" arguments, since these arguments fail to challenge the claims that affirmative action promotes the "less qualified" and imposes "costs" on those who are "better qualified" for the positions in question. Instead they merely insist that such "preferences" and "costs" are justified either as "compensation" or as a means to promote a range of long-term goals.

Our view of affirmative action as a policy to foster equality of opportunity rejects the claim that its beneficiaries are "less qualified." We argue instead that there is good reason to believe that their capabilities are not *accurately gauged or fairly evaluated* by prevailing selection criteria and procedures. Without affirmative action policies, as we see it, those who are its beneficiaries would not be given equal consideration, or have their qualifications and capabilities assessed fairly. Given our rationale for affirmative action, the "stigma problem" disappears since we see nothing demeaning or stigmatizing in being given equal consideration or in being treated as fairly as one's peers. Thus, from our perspective, not only do the beneficiaries of affirmative action have no valid reason to feel "inferior," the non-beneficiaries of it have no good reason to regard themselves as "more qualified" than affirmative action beneficiaries.

Our account of affirmative action, then, also helps to illuminate why resentment by non-beneficiaries is unjustified. We believe that such resentment is based on the *false* belief that the "better qualified" are being burdened by having to bear the "costs" of "preferences" bestowed on others, a sentiment reinforced by views that see affirmative action as preferential treatment. Since we do not believe affirmative action bestows preferences we do not think that affirmative action imposes any corresponding costs or burdens on non-beneficiaries. On the contrary, we believe that it should be understood as an attempt to counteract a variety of procedures and criteria that work to *unfairly privilege* those who are middle-class, White and male. We believe that the only costs to non-beneficiaries that result from affirmative action policies are the loss of these privileges, privileges that are the results of a lack of fairness to and opportunity for others.

Neither affirmative action policies, nor a fair and judicious assessment of the performance of their various beneficiaries, are the central causes of the prevailing negative stereotypes about the competencies of women, working-class people, or people of color. Critiques of affirmative action along these lines often suggest that the world was once a fairer place, which has only recently become tainted with new stereotypes about the capabilities of women or members of racial minorities as a result of affirmative action policies infusing large numbers of its "underqualified" and "unqualified" beneficiaries into American institutions. Such critiques suggest that affirmative action has exacerbated the old negative stereotypes about women and people of color which had begun to wane. In fact, however, it was racist and sexist stereotypes, and the institutional practices that worked to perpetuate and reinforce them, that made affirmative action policies necessary.

One of the ways in which racist and sexist stereotypes function is to obstruct our ability to see women and people of color as individuals. Thus, an individual woman or minority person's inadequacies can be generalized and seen as signs of the incompetence of whole groups, whereas the failures of White men remain personal limitations. Moreover, success stories involving women or minorities often tend to be interpreted as exceptions, and not as examples of the capabilities of women or people of color generally (Harris, 1994). Much of the discourse on affirmative action reveals this pattern: instances of women and people of color who have failed to meet the requirements of a profession or institution are taken to be testimony to the grand failure of affirmative action policies and the incompetence of the bulk of its beneficiaries. No nuanced account is given of the possible causes of these failures. The fact that no set of admissions or promotion criteria can guarantee that everyone who manifests potential for success will in fact succeed gets lost amidst anxious rumors of incompetence. Seldom dwelt upon are the numerous stories of those who have succeeded as a result of affirmative action.

As far back as the debate over the admission of minority applicants to the Davis Medical School in the *Bakke* case, little attention was paid to the success stories of people admitted as a result of affirmative action. Yet four years after the admission of the sixteen "affirmative action" candidates to Davis in 1978, thirteen had graduated in good standing, several had excelled, and one of their number had earned the school's most prestigious senior class award for "the qualities most likely to produce an outstanding physician." Much of the debate in 1978, however, *presumed*, just as it does now, that affirmative action's departure from the traditional admissions criteria represented a departure from objective criteria of "excellence."

There are a number of additional troublesome assumptions that underlie the stigma arguments. For example, for decades, almost all of our elite institutions and professions, as well as many non-elite career paths, were domains that permitted entry to a very small, and extremely privileged segment of the population. Yet there were millions of equally talented individuals who, because they were working-class, or women, or members of racial minority groups, were deprived of the chances to develop their talents and capabilities, which may well have exceeded those of many of their privileged White male counterparts. Rarely, if ever, in all these decades, have privileged White men who benefited from such "undeserved privileges" ever castigated themselves or publicly expressed the feeling that they were not "really talented" or "really deserving of their positions" because they had acquired them in a context that had eliminated most of their fellow citizens, including the female members of their own families, from the competitive pool. We are unaware of a body of literature from these individuals filled with anxiety and self-doubt about their capabilities and merit. Indeed, one of the unnerving effects of privilege is that it permits the privileged to feel so entitled to their privileges that they often fail to see them as privileges at all. In such a setting, it is more than a little ironic that the beneficiaries of affirmative action programs designed to counteract the effect of institutional discrimination are now expected to wear the hair-shirt of "stigma."

Many who complain about the preferential treatment they believe affirmative action accords to women and minorities in academia assume that everyone other than its beneficiaries is admitted purely as a result of merit. Yet, paradoxically, policies that favor relatives of alumni, and children of faculty members or donors to the university, have not created a storm of legal or social controversy, or even been objected to. Perhaps this is because such policies tend to benefit predominantly White middle-class individuals. Our point is not simply to claim, however, that people who accept preferential policies that benefit middle-class Whites are often outraged by "preferences" rooted in affirmative action policies. Our point is in fact a much stronger one that hinges on the profound differences between affirmative action and these other policies. Policies that favor children of alumni or donors are policies that may serve some useful goals for a particular institution, but they are genuinely "favors" or "preferences" with respect to the individuals admitted, in that such policies are in no way intended to equalize the opportunities of those thus admitted. We therefore insist on a conceptual distinction between affirmative action and policies that are genuinely tantamount to bestowing preferences.

Our point, however, is not to endorse a "purely meritocratic society" as the ideal society, but rather to highlight the reality that many existing institutional structures not only fail to function as pure meritocracies, but also serve to systematically disadvantage whole groups of people including working-class people, women, and people of color. To those strongly committed to traditional meritocratic ideals, we suggest that when close attention is paid to the systematically disadvantaging effects of many institutional procedures, they may have reason to see affirmative action policies as conducive to their ideal rather than as deviations from it.

Conclusion

The intellectual confusion surrounding affirmative action transcends ideological categories. Critics and supporters, of all political stripes, have underestimated the significance of these policies, collaborated in equating affirmative action with "preferential treatment," and permitted important assumptions about how institutions function, to lie unchallenged. We argue that affirmative action policies do not involve preferential treatment but should rather be understood as attempts to promote fairness, equality and full citizenship by affording members of marginalized groups a fair chance to enter significant social institutions.

The fact that formal legal equality seems commonplace and obviously justified to many today, should not obscure how recently formal equality has been a reality for many nor the struggles it took to make it a reality. More importantly, we should not imagine that the achievement of formal legal equality erased the consequences of centuries of inequality, making the promise of equality and full citizenship an immediate reality for those previously excluded. The institutional consequences of such historically group-based exclusions in significant domains of occupational and social life still remain. Class, race, and gender, for example, continue to deprive people of the opportunities to participate in numerous forms of association and work that are crucial to the development of talents and capabilities that enable people to contribute meaningfully to, and benefit from, the collective possibilities of national life.

Only since the latter part of the nineteenth century and the early decades of the twentieth century have some democratic political communities, such as the United States, sought to embrace the members of certain marginalized groups they had once excluded from the rights and privileges of citizenship. Only in the latter part of the twentieth century has there dawned the recognition that laws and policies that promote formal equality do not necessarily ensure substantive equality or genuine equal opportunity for all citizens to participate in all spheres of American life. In this respect, affirmative action policies are a significant historic achievement, for they constitute an attempt to transform our legacy of unequal treatment with respect to certain marginalized groups of Americans. They symbolize our political commitment to ensuring substantive participation in all domains of life for various groups of our diverse citizenry. Thus, we believe that affirmative action programs warrant a much more favorable evaluation, both as an historic achievement and in terms of their positive effects within contemporary American institutions, than they are usually accorded.

References

Derrick A. Bell, Jr, "Bakke, Minority Admissions and the Usual Price of Racial Remedies," 67 q. L. Rev. 3, 13 (1979).

Lawrence A. Blum. "Opportunity and Equality of Opportunity," *Public Affairs Quarterly* (1988).

Leslie Bennets, "Carnegie Study Finds Status, Not Brains, Makes a Child's Future," in *Racism and Sexism: An Integrated Study*, ed. Paula Rothenberg (1988), pp. 54, 55.

Robert Blauner, *Black Lives, White Lives: Three Decades of Race Relations* (1989).

Bernard R. Boxhill, "The Morality of Preferential Hiring," 7 *Phil. and Pub. Aff.* 246 (1978).

Stephen L. Carter, *Reflections of an Affirmative Action Baby* (1991).

James Crouse and Dale Trusheim, *The Case Against the SAT* (1988).

Ronald Dworkin, "Why Bakke Has No Case," in *Today's Moral Problems*, ed. Richard Wasserstrom (1985), pp. 138, 145–6.

Gertrude Ezorsky, *Racism and Justice: The Case for Affirmative Action* (1991), p. 72.

Luke Charles Harris, "Affirmative Action and the White Backlash: Notes from a Child Apart-

heid," in *Picturing Us: African American Identity in Photography*, ed. Deborah Willis (1994).

Luke Charles Harris and Uma Narayan, "Affirmative Action and the Myth of Preferential Treatment: A Transformative Critique of the Terms of the Affirmative Action Debate," 11, *Harvard BlackLetter Law Journal*, 1 (1994).

R. M. Kantor and B. A. Stein, "Making a Life at the Bottom," in *Life in Organizations, Workplaces as People Experience Them* (1976), pp. 176–90.

Rudolf A. Pyatt, Jr, "Significant Job Studies," *Washington Post*, April 30, 1985, at D1–D2 (cited in Tom Beauchamp, "Goals and Quotas in Hiring and Promotion," in *Ethical Theory and Business*, eds Tom Beauchamp and Norman E. Borire (1993), p. 384.

Margery Austin Turner et al., *Opportunities Denied, Opportunities Diminished: Racial Discrimination in Hiring* (1991), pp. 91–9.

Rosser et al., *Sex Bias in College Admissions Tests: Why Women Lose Out* (2nd edn 1987).

S. Steele, *The Content of our Character: A New Vision of Race in America* (1990).

Part IV

Justice

Punishment

Public opinion polls suggest that people in the Western World are increasingly worried about crime. In the United States the public thinks crime is out of control, and that it is out of control because the state has not punished criminals as often or as severely as it should. Thus, for many people, deciding what to do about crime is not a minor technical problem criminologists or the police should solve. It is a practical problem with momentous consequences. However, we should be responsible citizens. We should not let fear lead us to embrace immoral policies. Harming another person without compelling reasons is wrong, and criminal punishment most assuredly harms the person punished. Therefore, before we blindly embrace a "get tough" policy toward criminals, we should be confident that our system is morally justified. That is, (1) we must determine the circumstances under which the state can justifiably deprive someone of her life or liberty, and (2) we must decide what the morally appropriate punishment would be.

Historically there have been three dominant theories of punishment: deterrence, retribution; and rehabilitation. The deterrence theorist holds that the overriding reason to punish someone is to deter future crime. Thus, the deterrence theory is primarily forward looking: it is concerned about what will happen in the future, not what has happened in the past.

In contrast, the retributive theory is backward looking: it emphasizes not the deterrence of future crimes, but punishment for past actions. Punishing people for their crimes may deter future crimes. However, if it does deter, that is an unexpected benefit of retributive punishment, not its justification.

Finally, the rehabilitative theory, like the deterrence theory, is forward looking. However, unlike the deterrence theory, its primary aim is not to prevent future crime, but to rehabilitate criminals so that they can return to society as responsible and productive citizens. Of course, rehabilitated criminals are less likely to commit further crimes. Nonetheless, although that may be a desirable consequence of rehabilitation, it is not its purpose.

All three theories often lead to the same practical conclusions. Normally they would agree about whom we should punish, and about how severely we should punish them. For instance, severely punishing an armed robber may be, from the retributivist standpoint, exactly what the criminal deserves, and, for the deterrence theorist, the action most likely to prevent future crime. Moreover, if we carry out the punishment correctly, we might also expect that the criminal would be rehabilitated.

It would be a mistake, however, to infer that since these theories often offer the same practical advice, they are really the same theory dressed up differently. Despite their similarities, they will at least sometimes disagree over whether, when, and how we should punish someone. The severity of punishment required to deter a criminal (and others) is, I suspect, often greater (or less) than what we might, on retributive grounds, think the criminal deserves. Perhaps the person has committed a monstrous crime (torture), yet we know that this criminal and others would probably be deterred by only a few months in prison. Or, conversely, someone may have committed an insignificant crime (jaywalking), which we could deter only by a severe punishment (chopping off the offender's legs).

Moreover, even when these theorists do agree about whom we should punish (and how severely we should punish them), they will disagree about why we should punish them. The difference in rationale is likely to lead to important, though perhaps barely perceptible, differences in punishment. Even if both retributive and deterrence theorists conclude that we should send a child molester to prison for twenty years, we will be likely to communicate something different to the criminal (and to others) if we think we are giving the criminal what he deserves, or if we think we are deterring potential child molesters.

It is illuminating to note the striking parallels between these theories of punishment and the conseqentialist and deontological ethical theories. Consequentialist theories are forward looking; deontological theories tend to be backward looking. Even when both tell us to refrain from lying, to feed our starving neighbors, or to care for our ailing parents, their reasons for so acting invariably differ. We tend to think different ethical theories give different practical advice. Sometimes they do, sometimes they don't. What they invariably do is direct us to attend to different features of an action, or to evaluate those features differently. They disagree about which features of an action are morally relevant. Likewise, the principal difference between deterrence and retributive theories is not necessarily that they disagree about whom we should punish, or how we should punish them, but rather *why* we should punish them. Put differently, these theories identify different features of action that we should consider.

Rachels provides a plausible rationale for adopting a backward-looking stance toward punishment. He argues that the key to our ordinary moral understanding is that we should give people what they deserve, and that what people deserve is based on their freely chosen actions. If you work hard, you deserve to get that promotion. If you perform well in school, you deserve good grades. Conversely, if you are a slacker, you do not deserve either a promotion or good grades. This premium on individual responsibility undergirds the retributive theory of punishment. It may also undergird one of Levin's objections to AFFIRMATIVE ACTION, namely, that white males may deserve the jobs these programs have distributed to blacks and women.

Rawls agrees that punishment must be based on what the criminal has done. Nonetheless, the overarching goal of the criminal justice system is to deter crime, to make citizens safe. Although these seemingly disparate goals appear to be at odds, we can accommodate them, he claims, if we distinguish between justifying the institution of punishment, and justifying the punishment of a particular person. We adopt the institution because it deters crime, but we punish particular individuals only if they have committed a crime.

Murphy thinks Rachels and Rawls accurately describe the current aims of punishment. However, he thinks these philosophers overlook a crucial element of morally legitimate punishment: repentance. Punishment should aim to improve criminals morally. That is, we should have a system that makes it increasingly likely that criminals will come to regret their actions and seek to transform themselves – with the aid of the state – into productive and morally responsible citizens. Of course, criminals who repent would be unlikely, upon release, to commit future crimes. However, that is not the aim of punishment, but a fortunate consequence.

Repentance is possible, however, only if the criminal understands that she has harmed the community, feels sorry for what she has done, and wishes to re-establish a relationship with that community. Unfortunately, many people in our society, and especially those most likely to commit crimes, do not see themselves as part of the larger community. Hence, they are unlikely to repent. From that we should not conclude, however, that this is not the appropriate aim of punishment. Instead, we should see this as compelling evidence why we should transform our society, why we should create a community that embraces all our citizens.

Murphy notes that there is a conflict between the aims of repentance and the current trend toward harsh punishment. Harsh punishments rarely improve criminals. Instead, they make criminals resentful. They are subsequently less likely to repent. After all, why should they want to re-establish a relationship with the community that hurt them? Of course, since many criminals do not feel part of the community, harsh punishments may be required to deter crime. If so, we can see a disturbing flaw in our society. If criminals wanted to be part of the larger community, then merely removing them from that community and placing them in penitentiaries would be a sufficiently severe punishment to deter them from future crime.

Pasquerella echoes many of Murphy's worries about the trend toward harsh punishments. She argues that we cannot justify getting tough with criminals, either on deterrence or retributive grounds. After all, most people we incarcerate did not freely choose to be criminals, at least not in the strong sense of "free choice" discussed by Cudd (SEXUAL AND RACIAL DISCRIMINATION). Thus, saying that criminals deserve harsh punishment is inappropriate.

Haldane and Harvey raise a different question about the criminal justice system. They argue that we should compensate victims of crime. Of course just as we have difficulty determining if AFFIRMATIVE ACTION is an appropriate compensation for past discrimination, we will also have trouble determining exactly how much compensation a victim deserves. Nonetheless, they argue, on any acceptable theory of punishment, the state should compensate victims of crime. One of their arguments parallels one of Murphy's arguments for thinking repentance should be a centerpiece of the criminal justice system. Murphy claims that criminals are more likely to repent if we have a strong sense of community. In a similar vein, Haldane and Harvey argue that an important reason for compensating victims of crime is "Social Solidarity." This echoes a theme seen earlier, e.g., by Fesmire (VIRTUES), that our social, political, and economic environment may make the development of some virtues more (or less) likely.

Further Reading

Duff, A. 1986: *Trials and Punishments*. Cambridge: Cambridge University Press.

Gorr, M. and Harwood, S. (eds) 1995: *Crime and Punishment*. Boston: Jones and Bartlett.

Gross, H. 1979: *Theory of Criminal Punishment*. New York: Oxford University Press.

Hart, H. 1968: *Punishment and Responsibility*. New York: Oxford University Press.

Hondrerich, T. 1984: *Punishment: The Supposed Justification*. New York: Penguin.

Morris, H. 1981: "A Paternalistic Theory of Punishment." *American Philosophical Quarterly*.

Murphy, J. (ed.) 1995: *Punishment and Rehabilitation* (3rd edition). Belmont, CA: Wadsworth Press.

44

Punishment and Desert

James Rachels

When someone who delights in annoying and vexing peace-loving folk receives at last a right good beating, it is certainly an ill, but everyone approves of it and considers it as good in itself, even if nothing further results from it.

Immanuel Kant, Critique of Practical Reason (1788)[1]

Retributivism – the idea that wrongdoers should be "paid back" for their wicked deeds – fits naturally with many people's feelings. They find it deeply satisfying when murderers and rapists "get what they have coming," and they are infuriated when villains "get away with it." But others dismiss these feelings as primitive and unenlightened. Sometimes the complaint takes a religious form. The desire for revenge, it is said, should be resisted by those who believe in Christian charity. After all, Jesus himself rejected the rule of "an eye for an eye,"[2] and St Paul underscored the point, saying that we should not "return evil for evil" but we should "overcome evil with good."[3] To those who adopt this way of thinking, whether on secular or religious grounds, vengeance cannot be an acceptable motive for action.

This objection is, for the most part, misguided. The idea that wrongdoers should be "paid back" for their wickedness is not merely a demand for primitive vengeance. It is part of a moral view with a subtle and complicated structure, that can be supported by a surprisingly strong array of arguments. The key idea is that people deserve to be treated in the same way that they voluntarily choose to treat others. If this were only a view about punishment, it would not be very compelling. But the idea that people should be treated according to their deserts is a central component of our general moral understanding. It has applications in many areas of life. Retributivism is just the application of this idea to the special case of punishment.

In what follows we will begin by asking what it means to treat people as they deserve. What does the practice of "treating people as they deserve" involve? We can describe this practice without making any judgment about whether it is a good thing. Then we will consider, as a separate matter, the normative question: Should we treat people as they deserve? Are there any compelling reasons in favor of such a practice? Finally, we will turn to the special case of punishment.

Treating People as They Deserve

Desert and past actions

What people deserve always depends on what they have done in the past. The familiar lament, "What have I done to deserve this?" is not just an idle remark; when desert is at issue, it asks exactly the right question. Consider this case:

> *The two candidates for promotion.* The owner of a small business must decide which of two employees to promote. The first is a man who has been a loyal and hard-working member of the staff for many years. He has frequently taken on extra work without complaint, and in the company's early days, when its future was in doubt, he would put in overtime without demanding extra pay. His efforts are one reason that the company survived and prospered. The other candidate is a man who has always done the least he could get by with, avoiding extra duties and quitting early whenever he could. We may call them Worker and Slacker. Which should the owner promote?

Clearly, Worker deserves the promotion. He has earned it and Slacker has not.

Deserving the promotion is not the same as needing it or wanting it. Both Worker and Slacker might benefit from the promotion; perhaps both could use the extra money and status it would bring. But this has nothing to do with desert. Although Slacker might benefit just as much from being promoted, he does not have the same claim to it as Worker because he has not earned it in the same way.

Nor is the question of desert the same as the question of who would perform better in the new position. Obviously there is reason to think Worker would do better, because he has shown himself to be more diligent. But again, that is not the basis of Worker's claim. Even if we knew that Slacker would reform and do just as well in the new position – the promotion may be just the prod he needs – Worker would still have an independent claim on the promotion, based simply on his past performance.

Does anything other than past performance affect what a person deserves? Sometimes it is assumed that people deserve things because of their superior native endowments. If Slacker is naturally smarter or more talented than Worker, it might be suggested that this makes him deserving of the promotion. This sort of idea was once commonplace, but it is no longer very popular among those who systematically study ethics. It has fallen into disrepute since the publication of John Rawls's *A Theory of Justice*. Rawls writes that:

> Perhaps some will think that the person with greater natural endowments deserves those assets and the superior character that made their development possible. Because he is more worthy in this sense, he deserves the greater advantages that he could achieve with them. This view, however, is surely incorrect. It seems to be one of the fixed points of our considered judgments that no one deserves his place in the distribution of native endowments, any more than one deserves one's initial starting place in society.[4]

Rawls refers to "our considered judgments," but there is something more here than an appeal to our beliefs. There is also an implicit argument, namely that native endowments are not deserved because no one *does anything* to deserve them: they are the result of a "natural lottery" over which we have no control. If you are naturally smarter or more talented than other people, you are just luckier; and you do not deserve better merely on that account. This fits well with the idea that people deserve things because and only because of their past actions.

What else might plausibly be thought to provide a basis for desert? It has sometimes been suggested that *achievements* are pertinent. It may be argued that Slacker could deserve the promotion, despite Worker's greater effort, if Slacker had succeeded in contributing more to the company. (Maybe Slacker's puny efforts had a big payoff.) But achievements are only the products of native endowments combined with work – often with a good bit of luck thrown in – and if one cannot deserve things because of one's native endowments, neither can one deserve things because of the achievements that those endowments make possible. To see what someone deserves we have to separate the two components (native endowments and work) and identify the contribution made by each. The maximally deserving man or woman is not simply the one who achieves the most, but the one who achieves the most he or she can given the abilities with which he or she is endowed. The key idea, as far as desert is concerned, is "doing the best you can with what you have."

Moral deserts

Moral deserts are deserts that one has, not in virtue of one's performance in a special type of activity (such as working at a job), but in virtue of one's more general way of dealing with other people. We can choose to treat others well or badly, and what we deserve from them in return depends on the choice we make. Consider this example:

> *The ride to work.* Suppose you, Smith, and Jones all work at the same place. One morning your car won't start and you need a ride to work, so you call Smith and ask him to come by for you. But Smith refuses. It is clear that he could do it, but he doesn't want to be bothered, so he makes up some excuse. Then you call Jones, and he gives you the ride you need. A few weeks later, you get a call from Smith. Now he is having car trouble and he asks you for a ride. Should you accommodate him?

Perhaps you will think you should help Smith, despite his own unhelpfulness – after all, it would be little trouble for you, and by helping him you might teach him a lesson in generosity. But if we focus on what he *deserves* a different answer seems obvious: he deserves to be left to fend for himself. Jones, on the other hand, is an entirely different matter. If Jones should ask you for a ride, you have every reason to give it: not only will it help him, he deserves it. This is especially clear when we consider the case of a forced choice:

> *The simultaneous requests.* Smith calls and asks for a ride. Meanwhile, Jones is on the other line also needing a ride. But they live in opposite directions, so it is impossible for you to help both. Which do you help?

If we did not concede that Jones's past conduct makes him more deserving, we would be hard put to explain why it seems so obvious that helping Jones is the mandatory choice.

Particular people may be especially obligated in this way. If someone has done you a favor, *you* are indebted to them and you specifically owe it to them to return the favor. It is you, and not someone else, who owes Jones the ride. Sometimes this is thought to end the matter: if someone has helped you, it is said, you are indebted to them; otherwise you have no obligation. But it is short-sighted to view things in this way. Anyone at all can justifiably take it as a good reason for treating someone well if that person has treated others well. Suppose Jones is habitually helpful to people, while Smith is not; but you personally have never had much interaction with either of them. Now suppose you must choose which to help, and you cannot help both. Surely their respective histories is a reason, even for you, to prefer Jones. Thus we have:

> *The principle of desert.* People deserve to be treated in the same way that they have (voluntarily) treated others. Those who have treated others well deserve to be treated well in return, while those who have treated others badly deserve to be treated badly in return.

This principle has both a positive and a negative side. Those with a generous temperament may find one appealing but recoil from the other: they may like the idea that some people deserve good treatment but dislike the companion idea that others deserve bad treatment. After all, it seems ungrateful to say that someone who has treated others well does not deserve to be treated well in return; but to say that someone deserves to be treated badly seems, on the face of it, mean-spirited and unsympathetic. So it might be suggested that we keep the idea of positive desert and discard the idea of negative desert.

But this won't work. If we jettison one we will surely have to jettison the other. Superficially it may appear that we could split them apart. We could *say* that some people deserve good treatment but that no one ever deserves ill, and if we go no further this might seem consistent. But the inconsistency would emerge when we tried to provide a rationale for this combination of beliefs. What reasoning could justify holding that good performance merits a positive response that would not also imply that bad performance merits a negative response? The answer, so far as I can tell, is none.

Why People Should Be Treated as They Deserve

So far we have merely described, in a rough-and-ready way, what it means to treat people as they deserve. But we have given no reason whatever for thinking this is a good thing. Should we treat people as they deserve? Or, having seen what the practice involves, should we reject the whole business? There are at least three reasons for treating people according to their deserts. Together they add up to a compelling case.

First, acknowledging deserts is a way of granting people the power to determine their own fates. Because we live together in mutually cooperative societies, how each of us fares depends not only on what we do but on what others do as well. So, if we are to flourish, we need to obtain the good treatment of other people. A system of understandings in which desert is acknowledged gives us a way of doing that. Thus, if you want to be promoted, you may earn it by working hard at your job; and if you want others to treat you decently, you can treat them decently.

Absent this, what are we to do? We might imagine a system in which the only way for a person to secure good treatment by others is somehow to coerce that treatment from them – Worker might try threatening his employer. Or we might imagine that good treatment always comes as charity – Worker might simply hope the employer will be nice to him. But the practice of acknowledging deserts is different. The practice of acknowledging deserts gives people control over whether others will treat them well or badly, by saying to them: if you behave well, you will be *entitled* to good treatment from others because you will have earned it. Without this control people would be impotent, unable to affect how others will treat them and dependent on coercion or charity for any decent treatment they might receive.

I believe this is the deepest reason why desert is important, but there are others. A second reason is connected with the egalitarian idea that social burdens and benefits should be equally distributed. In working harder, Worker had to forgo benefits that Slacker was able to enjoy. While Worker was tied down on the job, Slacker was free to do things that Worker might have liked to do but was unable to. (This, of course, will be typical of any situation in which one person chooses to expend time and effort on a disagreeable task, while another person – faced with the same choice – opts for a more enjoyable alternative.) This suggests a simple argument for rewarding the harder worker: Slacker has had a benefit (more leisure time) that Worker has not had, while Worker has had a burden (more work) that Slacker has not had. Giving Worker a benefit now (the promotion) may therefore be seen as nothing more than righting the balance. Contrary to superficial appearances, then, giving Worker the promotion does not make their respective situations less equal. On the contrary, it alters things in the direction of greater equality. This is a reason why even egalitarians might favor treating people according to their deserts.

These arguments apply equally well to moral deserts. Acknowledging moral desert permits people, who are after all largely dependent for their welfare on what other people do, to control their own fates by allowing them to earn good treatment at the hands of others. They do not have to rely on coercion or charity. Moreover, those who treat others well will have, in the course of doing so, forgone benefits for themselves. There are costs involved in helping others – in giving you the ride, Jones was inconvenienced in a way that Smith was not. So once again, reciprocating is a way of making the distribution of burdens and benefits more nearly equal.

To these reasons a third may be added. Morality includes (some would say it consists in) how we choose to treat other people in our myriad interactions with them. But if reciprocity could not be expected, the morality of treating others well would come to occupy a less important place in people's lives. Morality would have no reward, and immorality would have no bad consequences; so there would be less reason for one to be concerned with it. If people were perfectly benevolent, of course, such incentives would not be needed. But for imperfectly benevolent beings such as ourselves the acknowledgment of deserts provides the reason for being moral that is required for the whole system to be effective.

Punishment

Retributivism is the application of the Principle of Desert to the special case of criminal punishment: it is the view that people who commit crimes such as murder and rape deserve to be punished and that this alone is sufficient to justify punishing them. It is not merely that punishing them satisfies certain sorts of vengeful feelings. On the contrary, it is a violation of justice if murderers and rapists are allowed to walk away as if they had done nothing wrong. It is a matter of justice for the same reason that promoting Worker is a matter of justice or that preferring to help Jones rather than Smith is a matter of justice.

As we have seen, acknowledging deserts is part of a moral system that allows people, by their own behavior, to determine how others will respond to them. Those who treat others well elicit good treatment in return, while those who treat others badly provoke ill treatment in return. That is why, when a criminal is punished, it may be said that "He brought it on himself." The argument concerning equality is also commonly invoked when punishment is at issue. There are costs associated with law-abidance. Law-abiding people bear a burden – inconvenient constraints on their conduct – that the lawbreaker has not shouldered. Meanwhile the lawbreaker has had benefits denied to others (assuming that his illegal conduct was not entirely irrational, and that there was profit of *some* kind in it for him). Punishment corrects things in the direction of greater equality.[5] That is why it is commonly said that crime "upsets the scales of justice" and that punishing wrongdoers "restores the balance."

But the charge that retributivism is a mere rationalization of vengeful feelings is not the only objection that has been made against it. Philosophers have faulted retributivism on other, weightier grounds. Bentham, who believed that social policies should promote the general welfare, noted that retributivism approves of *increasing the amount of suffering in the world* – if a miscreant harms someone, and we "pay him back" by harming him in return, we have only added to the total misery. Bentham did not see how this could be right. In his *Principles of Morals and Legislation*, published only one year after Kant's remark about the "right good beating," Bentham wrote: "All punishment is mischief: all punishment in itself is evil." Therefore, he concluded, "if it ought at all to be admitted, it ought only to be admitted in as far as it promises to exclude some greater evil."[6]

How can punishment "exclude some greater evil"? The obvious answer is by preventing crime. If there were no rules against murder, assault, and theft, no one would be safe; we would live in a Hobbesian State of Nature in which life would be "solitary, poor, nasty, brutish, and short." To avoid this, it is not enough to ask people politely if they would mind behaving themselves. Murder, theft, and the like cannot be left as matters of individual discretion. So, to ensure compliance with such rules, we attach sanctions to them. We do not say "Please do not murder"; we say "You must not murder, *or else.*"

The idea that punishment is justified as a means of preventing crime is so natural and appealing that we might expect it would dominate social-scientific thinking about the criminal justice system. Surprisingly, however, it has not been that influential. During the past 150 years a different sort of conception has prevailed. In the latter half of the nineteenth century it was argued that, if we are serious about preventing crime, we should try to identify its causes and do something about them. Crime, it was said, results from poverty, ignorance, and unemployment; therefore, social energy should be directed toward eliminating those blights. Moreover, when individuals commit crimes, rather than simply punishing them, we should address the problems that caused their aberrant behavior. People turn to crime because they are uneducated, lack job skills, and have emotional problems. So they should be educated, trained, and treated, with an eye to making them into "productive members of society" who will not repeat their offenses. In enlightened circles this came to be regarded as the only sensible approach. As Bertrand Russell once put it,

> No man treats a motorcar as foolishly as he treats another human being. When the car will not go, he does not attribute its annoying behavior to sin; he does not say, "You are a wicked motorcar, and I shall not give you any more petrol until you go." He attempts to find out what is wrong and to set it right.[7]

Today people are often skeptical about efforts to rehabilitate criminals. Those efforts have not been notably successful, and there is reason to doubt whether they could be successful

– for one thing, we do not know nearly enough about the individual causes of crime or the nature of personality or motivation to design effective ways to control them. Nevertheless, rehabilitationist ideas have been the single most important force in shaping the modern criminal justice system.[8] In the United States prisons are not even called prisons; they are called "correctional facilities," and the people who work in them are called "corrections officers."

Here, then, are three theories about punishment: retributivism, deterrence, and rehabilitation. What are we to make of them? We have already seen that retributivism is more plausible than its critics suppose. But the other theories are also plausible. As for the deterrence theory, there is no doubt that sanctions are useful. They ensure massive, if imperfect, compliance with the social rules. That would probably be enough to justify punishment even if there was no other argument available. Moreover, it is hard to deny that rehabilitating criminals would be a good thing, if only we knew how to do it. Yet it can still be argued that the criminal justice system should not be designed primarily to promote deterrence or rehabilitation. Rather, it should be designed along lines suggested by the retributive theory.

The argument for this is that a system of punishment based on retributive principles is fairer and more just than systems fashioned after those other ideas. This may be shown by considering the following four principles:

1. *Guilt*: Only the guilty may be punished.

This is perhaps the most fundamental of all rules of justice: if you have committed no crime, the law should leave you alone.

2. *Equal Treatment*: People who have committed the same crime should get the same punishment.

It is not fair for one person to be sent to prison for five years, while another is incarcerated for only eighteen months, if they are charged and convicted for exactly the same offense.

3. *Proportionality*: The punishment should be proportional to the crime.

Sometimes it is not easy to say what punishment "fits" a particular crime; nevertheless, the basic idea is clear enough. Serious crimes merit severe punishments, while minor infractions should receive only mild punishments. People should not be sent to prison for jay-walking; nor should they be fined five dollars for murder.

4. *Excuses*: People who have good excuses should not be punished, or at the very least, they should not be punished as severely as if they had no excuse.

Excuses include, for example, accident (the child ran in front of the car and there was no way the driver could stop), coercion (the man was forced to help the criminals because they were holding a gun to his head), and ignorance of fact (that nurse had been told by the child's mother that the child was not allergic to penicillin). In each case, if there was no excuse (the driver deliberately ran over the child, the man willingly participated in the crime, the nurse knowingly gave the child a harmful drug), the person would be fully blameworthy. But the excuse relieves the person of responsibility and so he or she should not be punished.

Any system of punishment is unjust if it departs from these four principles. But now suppose we were to design a system of punishment with deterrence in mind – that is to say, suppose we were to give the system just those features it would need to motivate people not to break the law. Would such a system satisfy these four principles?

(1) *Guilt* – No. There is no reason, if we are concerned only with deterrence, to punish only the guilty. As far as deterrence is concerned, what matters is not whether the person punished is guilty, but whether he or she is generally *believed* to be guilty. If people believe she is guilty, the deterrent effect will be the same as if she really were guilty. Moreover, from this point of view, it would be much better to convict an innocent person (who is generally believed to be guilty) than for the crime to go "unsolved," because when crimes are unsolved people get the idea that the law is ineffective and the deterrent effect of the law is diminished.

(2) *Equal Treatment* – Yes. A system of punishment designed solely to maximize the deterrent effect would need to be consistent in meting out similar punishments for similar crimes. This would be necessary to assure people who are tempted to violate the law that they will also get the full penalty. If in some cases lesser penalties had been imposed, then they might reasonably hope for the lesser penalty, and the deterrent effect would thereby be diminished.

(3) *Proportionality* – No. How severe should punishments be? If we are concerned only to deter crime, we will want to make penalties severe enough that the unlawful behavior really will be discouraged. This is a very different standard from the idea that punishments should "fit the crime." For example, a penalty that would actually stop people from jay-walking might have to be much more severe than we would think appropriate given the trivial nature of the offense.

(4) *Excuses* – No. For purposes of deterrence, it is best to have a "no excuses accepted" policy. If excuses are allowed, people might hope to avoid punishment by pleading special circumstances. A system that relentlessly punishes all offenders will offer less hope of avoiding punishment and so will have greater deterrent power.

A deterrence-based system of punishment will therefore violate three of the four principles. What about a system of rehabilitation? Rehabilitation fares no better.

(1) *Guilt* – No. The basic aim of such a system is to transform people who are inclined to commit crimes into people who are not inclined to commit crimes. The fact that someone *has* committed a crime is simply the best evidence we currently have of the inclination. But if it were possible to identify such people in advance, why should we wait until a crime has actually been committed? Why not go ahead and pick up individuals who are deemed likely to commit crimes and subject them to the rehabilitative routines? Of course this seems unjust, but there is nothing in the basic idea of such a system to preclude bringing people who have not committed crimes within its grasp.

(2) *Equal Treatment* – No. In a system designed to rehabilitate, individuals who have committed similar crimes will not receive similar treatments. What will happen to a particular lawbreaker will depend on his or her particular circumstances. Typically, a convicted person will be sentenced to prison for an indefinite period of time – say, "not less than ten nor more than twenty years" – and then he or she will be released when the authorities (the prison officials, a parole board) decide they are "ready" to be released. Since it takes people different amounts of time to be rehabilitated, the amount of time served will vary from prisoner to prisoner.

As we have already noted, the American criminal justice system has largely been shaped by the rehabilitationist ideal, in theory if not in fact. The widespread use of indefinite sentencing, the parole system, and the like, are manifestations of this. But the rehabilitationist character of the system has implications that are frequently misunderstood. Often critics point out that an affluent white offender is likely to serve less time in prison than a black kid from the ghetto, even if they have committed the same crime (say, a drug-related crime); and this disparity is attributed to racism. Racism no doubt has something to do with it. But it should not be overlooked that the prevailing rehabilitationist ideology also contributes decisively to such outcomes. When a "white-collar criminal" is well-educated, psychologically healthy, and has a good job, there's not much for a rehabilitationist system to do with him. He may as well be given an early release. But a surly, uneducated kid with no job skills is another matter – he is just the sort of person for whom the system is designed.

(3) *Proportionality* – No. It should now be clear why a rehabilitative system will not respond proportionately to the crimes committed. It will respond instead to the offender's psychological or educational needs. More concretely, in most US jurisdictions today, the length of one's stay in prison will depend on a parole board's judgment about when one is ready to be released, not on the seriousness of one's offense.

(4) *Excuses* – Yes. This is the only one of our four principles with which the rehabilitationist ideology is in accord. People need to be rehabilitated only if something in their character inclines them to commit crimes. But if someone violated the law only because of an unavoidable accident, coercion, or the like, then they do not need to be rehabilitated – or at least, the fact that they violated the law in this manner provides no evidence of it. So, in a rehabilitationist scheme, offenders with a good excuse would be let off the hook.

Once again, three of our four principles are violated.

When we turn to retributivism, however, things are entirely different. Retributivism incorporates all four principles in the most natural way possible. (1) Only the guilty should be punished, because innocent people have not done anything to deserve punishment. (2) People who committed the same crime should receive the same punishment, because what one deserves depends only on what one has done. It is a trivial consequence of the Principle of Desert that those who have behaved in the same way deserve the same response. (3) The Principle of Desert also requires proportionate responses, because what people deserve depends on how well, or how badly, they have behaved. A murderer has treated another person very badly indeed, and so deserves a very severe response. (That is why retributivists are inclined to support capital punishment in principle, although they might have other reasons for opposing it in practice.) A thief, on the other hand, has done something less wicked, and so deserves a more moderate response. (4) Finally, a retributivist system of punishment would have to accept excuses, because what people deserve depends only on their *voluntary* behavior. Acceptable excuses show that behavior was not voluntary; that is why the demonstration that one was coerced, or that it was all an unavoidable accident, and the like, gets one off the hook.

We have now asked a number of questions about the three theories and four principles, and we might summarize our results as is shown in the table. The upshot is that retribution is the only idea that provides the basis of a just system of punishment. The other ideas do not even come close.

Does all this mean that Kant was right? Unlike Bentham, who believed that, to be justified, the pains of punishment must "exclude some greater evil," Kant believed that a villain's punishment is "good in itself, even if nothing further results from it." The argu-

	Deterrence	Rehabilitation	Retribution
Guilt	No	No	Yes
Equal Treatment	Yes	No	Yes
Proportionality	No	No	Yes
Excuses	No	Yes	Yes

ments we have examined seem to support Kant, but they do so only up to a point. To justify punishing someone, we may refer simply to what he or she has done – we may point out that they deserve it. But when we examine the arguments that support the general practice of treating people as they deserve, it turns out that those arguments all refer to ways in which people are *better off* under such a practice. So, at least as far as anything said here is concerned, the ultimate justifications could all be utilitarian.

Thus we might understand our overall situation as follows. The best social practices are the ones that maximize welfare. The practice of treating people as they deserve is like this – people are on the whole better off if deserts are taken into account than if decisions are made solely on other grounds. One consequence of this is that we end up with a retributive understanding of punishment. Our feelings – our sense of justice, which requires that the four principles be satisfied, and our retributive feelings, which cause us to be happy when villains are punished and outraged when they are not – are useful because they reinforce the useful social practice. So Kant's description of our attitudes is correct: when the annoying fellow gets at last a right good beating, we approve of it even if there are no further results. But in the larger accounting, it is a good thing that we have such attitudes only because they reinforce social practices that do have further results.

Notes

1. Immanuel Kant, *Critique of Practical Reason*, translated by Lewis White Beck (Chicago: University of Chicago Press, 1949; but originally published in 1788), p. 170.
2. Matthew 5: 38–41.
3. Romans 12: 17, 21.
4. John Rawls, *A Theory of Justice* (Cambridge, MA: Harvard University Press, 1971), pp. 103–4.
5. Philosophical discussions of justice frequently distinguish "retributive justice" from "distributive justice" and treat them as altogether different topics. But if this argument is correct, the two are closely related.
6. Jeremy Bentham, *An Introduction to the Principles of Morals and Legislation* (New York: Hafner, 1948; but first published in 1789), p. 170.
7. Bertrand Russell, *Why I Am Not a Christian* (New York: Simon and Schuster, 1967), p. 40.
8. *Struggle for Justice: A Report on Crime and Punishment in America*, by the American Friends Service Committee (New York: Hill & Wang, 1971), is still one of the best discussions of the rehabilitationist idea ever produced.

45

Two Concepts of Rules

John Rawls

In this paper I want to show the importance of the distinction between justifying a practice[1] and justifying a particular action falling under it, and I want to explain the logical basis of this distinction and how it is possible to miss its significance. While the distinction has frequently been made,[2] and is now becoming commonplace, there remains the task of explaining the tendency either to overlook it altogether, or to fail to appreciate its importance.

To show the importance of the distinction I am going to defend utilitarianism against those objections which have traditionally been made against it in connection with punishment and the obligation to keep promises. I hope to show that if one uses the distinction in question then one can state utilitarianism in a way which makes it a much better explication of our considered moral judgments than these traditional objections would seem to admit.[3] Thus the importance of the distinction is shown by the way it strengthens the utilitarian view regardless of whether that view is completely defensible or not.

To explain how the significance of the distinction may be overlooked, I am going to discuss two conceptions of rules. One of these conceptions conceals the importance of distinguishing between the justification of a rule or practice and the justification of a particular action falling under it. The other conception makes it clear why this distinction must be made and what is its logical basis.

The subject of punishment, in the sense of attaching legal penalties to the violation of legal rules, has always been a troubling moral question.[4] The trouble about it has not been that people disagree as to whether or not punishment is justifiable. Most people have held that, freed from certain abuses, it is an acceptable institution. Only a few have rejected punishment entirely, which is rather surprising when one considers all that can be said against it. The difficulty is with the justification of punishment: various arguments for it have been given by moral philosophers, but so far none of them has won any sort of general acceptance; no justification is without those who detest it. I hope to show that the use of the aforementioned distinction enables one to state the utilitarian view in a way which allows for the sound points of its critics.

For our purposes we may say that there are two justifications of punishment. What we may call the retributive view is that punishment is justified on the grounds that wrongdoing merits punishment. It is morally fitting that a person who does wrong should suffer in proportion to his wrongdoing. That a criminal should be punished follows from his guilt, and the severity of the appropriate punishment depends on the depravity of his act. The state of affairs where a wrongdoer suffers punishment is morally better than the state of affairs where he does not: and it is better irrespective of any of the consequences of punishing him.

What we may call the utilitarian view holds that on the principle that bygones are bygones and that only future consequences are material to present decisions, punishment is justifiable only by reference to the probable consequences of maintaining it as one of the devices of the social order. Wrongs committed in the past are, as such, not relevant considerations for deciding what to do. If punishment can be shown to promote effectively the interest of society it is justifiable, otherwise it is not.

I have stated these two competing views very roughly to make one feel the conflict between them: one feels the force of *both* arguments and one wonders how they can be reconciled. From my introductory remarks it is obvious that the resolution which I am going to propose is that in this case one must distinguish between justifying a practice as a system of rules to be applied and enforced, and justifying a particular action which falls under these rules; utilitarian arguments are appropriate with regard to questions about practices, while retributive arguments fit the application of particular rules to particular cases.

We might try to get clear about this distinction by imagining how a father might answer the question of his son. Suppose the son asks, "Why was *J* put in jail yesterday?" The father answers, "Because he robbed the bank at *B*. He was duly tried and found guilty. That's why he was put in jail yesterday." But suppose the son had asked a different question, namely, "Why do people put other people in jail?" Then the father might answer, "To protect good people from bad people" or "To stop people from doing things that would make it uneasy for all of us, for otherwise we wouldn't be able to go to bed at night and sleep in peace." There are two very different questions here. One question emphasizes the proper name: It asks why *J* was punished rather than someone else, or it asks what he was punished for. The other question asks why we have the institution of punishment: Why do people punish one another rather than, say, always forgiving one another?

Thus the father says in effect that a particular man is punished, rather than some other man, because he is guilty, and he is guilty because he broke the law (past tense). In his case the law looks back, the judge looks back, the jury looks back, and a penalty is visited upon him for something he did. That a man is to be punished, and what his punishment is to be, is settled by its being shown that he broke the law and that the law assigns that penalty for the violation of it.

On the other hand we have the institution of punishment itself, and recommend and accept various changes in it, because it is thought by the (ideal) legislator and by those to whom the law applies that, as a part of a system of law impartially applied from case to case arising under it, it will have the consequence, in the long run, of furthering the interests of society.

One can say, then, that the judge and the legislator stand in different positions and look in different directions: one to the past, the other to the future. The justification of what the judge does, *qua* judge, sounds like the retributive view; the justification of what the (ideal) legislator does, *qua* legislator, sounds like the utilitarian view. Thus both views have a point (this is as it should be since intelligent and sensitive persons have been on both sides of the argument): and one's initial confusion disappears once one sees that these views apply to persons holding different offices with different duties, and situated differently with respect to the system of rules that make up the criminal law.[5]

One might say, however, that the utilitarian view is more fundamental since it applies to a more fundamental office, for the judge carries out the legislator's will so far as he can determine it. Once the legislator decides to have laws and to assign penalties for their violation (as things are there must be both the law and the penalty) an institution is set up which involves a retributive conception of particular cases. It is part of the concept of the criminal law as a system of rules that the application and enforcement of these rules in particular cases should be justifiable by arguments of a retributive character. The decision whether or not to use law rather than some other mechanism of social control, and the decision as to what laws to have and what penalties to assign, may be settled by utilitarian arguments; but if one decides to have laws then one has decided on something whose working in particular cases is retributive in form.[6]

The answer, then, to the confusion engendered by the two views of punishment is quite simple: One distinguishes two offices, that of the judge and that of the legislator, and one distinguishes their different stations with respect to the system of rules which make up the law; and then one notes that the different sorts of considerations which would usually be offered as reasons for what is done under the cover of these offices can be paired off with the competing justifications of punishment. One reconciles the two views by the time-honored device of making them apply to different situations.

But can it really be this simple? Well, this answer allows for the apparent intent of each side. Does a person who advocates the retributive view necessarily advocate, as an *institution*, legal machinery whose essential purpose is to set up and preserve a correspondence between moral turpitude and suffering? Surely not.[7] What retributionists have rightly insisted upon is that no man can be punished unless he is guilty, that is, unless he has broken the law. Their fundamental criticism of the utilitarian account is that, as they interpret it, it sanctions an innocent person's being punished (if one may call it that) for the benefit of society.

On the other hand, utilitarians agree that punishment is to be inflicted only for the violation of law. They regard this much as understood from the concept of punishment itself.[8] The point of the utilitarian account concerns the institution as a system of rules: utilitarianism seeks to limit its use by declaring it justifiable only if it can be shown to foster effectively the good of society. Historically it is a protest against the indiscriminate and ineffective use of the criminal law.[9] It seeks to dissuade us from assigning to penal institutions the improper, if not sacrilegious, task of matching suffering with moral turpitude. Like others, utilitarians want penal institutions designed so that, as far as humanly possible, only those who break the law run afoul of it. They hold that no official should have discretionary power to inflict penalties whenever he thinks it for the benefit of society; for on utilitarian grounds an institution granting such power could not be justified.[10]

The suggested way of reconciling the retributive and the utilitarian justifications of punishment seems to account for what both sides have wanted to say. There are, however, two further questions which arise, and I shall devote the remainder of this section to them.

First, will not a difference of opinion as to the proper criterion of just law make the proposed reconciliation unacceptable to retributionists? Will they not question whether, if the utilitarian principle is used as the criterion, it follows that those who have broken the law are guilty in a way which satisfies their demand that those punished deserve to be punished? To answer this difficulty, suppose that the rules of the criminal law are justified on utilitarian grounds (it is only for laws that meet his criterion that the utilitarian can be held responsible). Then it follows that the actions which the criminal law specifies as offenses are such that, if they were tolerated, terror and alarm would spread in society. Consequently, retributionists can only deny that those who are punished deserve to be punished if they deny that such actions are wrong. This they will not want to do.

The second question is whether utilitarianism doesn't justify too much. One pictures it as an engine of justification which, if consistently adopted, could be used to justify cruel and arbitrary institutions. Retributionists may be supposed to concede that utilitarians *intend* to reform the law and to make it more humane; that utilitarians do not *wish* to justify any such thing as punishment of the innocent; and that utilitarians may appeal to the fact that punishment presupposes guilt in the sense that by punishment one understands an institution attaching penalties to the infraction of legal rules, and therefore that it is logically absurd to suppose that utilitarians in justifying *punishment* might also have justified punishment (if we may call it that) of the innocent. The real question, however, is whether the utilitarian, in justifying punishment, hasn't used arguments which commit him to accepting the infliction of suffering on innocent persons if it is for the good of society (whether or not one calls this punishment). More generally, isn't the utilitarian committed in principle to accepting many practices which he, as a morally sensitive person, wouldn't want to accept? Retributionists are inclined to hold that there is no way to stop the utilitarian principle from justifying too much except by adding to it a principle which distributes certain rights to individuals. Then the amended criterion is not the greatest benefit of society *simpliciter* [simply], but the greatest benefit of society subject to the constraint that no one's rights may be violated. Now while I think that the classical utilitarians proposed a criterion of this more complicated sort, I do not want to argue that point here.[11] What I want to show is that there is *another* way of preventing the utilitarian principle from justifying too much, or at least of making it much less likely to do so: namely, by stating utilitarianism in a way which accounts for the distinction between the justification of an institution and the justification of a particular action falling under it.

I begin by defining the institution of punishment as follows: a person is said to suffer punishment whenever he is legally deprived of some of the normal rights of a citizen on the ground that he has violated a rule of law, the violation having been established by trial according to the due process of law, provided that the deprivation is carried out by the recognized legal authorities of the state, that the rule of law clearly specifies both the offense and the attached penalty, that the courts construe statutes strictly, and that the statute was on the books prior to the time of the offense.[12] This definition specifies what I shall understand by punishment. The question is whether utilitarian arguments may be found to justify institutions widely different from this and such as one would find cruel and arbitrary.

This question is best answered, I think, by taking up a particular accusation. Consider the following from Carritt:

> . . . the utilitarian must hold that we are justified in inflicting pain always and only to prevent worse pain or bring about greater happiness. This, then, is all we need to consider in so-called punishment, which must be purely preventive. But if some kind of very cruel crime becomes common, and none of the criminals can be caught, it might be highly expedient, as an example, to hang an innocent man, if a charge against him could be so framed that he were universally thought guilty; indeed this would only fail to be an ideal instance of utilitarian "punishment" because the victim himself would not have been so likely as a real felon to commit such a crime in the future; in all other respects it would be perfectly deterrent and therefore felicific.[13]

Carritt is trying to show that there are occasions when a utilitarian argument would justify taking an action which would be generally condemned; and thus that utilitarianism justifies too much. But the failure of Carritt's argument lies in the fact that he makes no distinction between the justification of the general system of rules which constitutes penal institutions and the justification of particular applications of these rules to particular cases by the various officials whose job it is to administer them. This becomes perfectly clear when one asks who the "we" are of whom Carritt speaks. Who is this who has a sort of absolute authority on particular occasions to decide that an innocent man shall be "punished" if everyone can be convinced that he is guilty? Is this person the legislator, or the judge, or the body of private citizens, or what? It is utterly crucial to know who is to decide such matters, and by what authority, for all of this must be written into the rules of the institution. Until one knows these things one doesn't know what the institution is whose justification is being challenged; and as the utilitarian principle applies to the institution one doesn't know whether it is justifiable on utilitarian grounds or not.

Once this is understood it is clear what the countermove to Carritt's argument is. One must describe more carefully what the *institution* is which his example suggests, and then ask oneself whether or not it is likely that having this institution would be for the benefit of society in the long run. One must not content oneself with the vague thought that, when it's a question of *this* case, it would be a good thing if *somebody* did something even if an innocent person were to suffer.

Try to imagine, then, an institution (which we may call "telishment") which is such that the officials set up by it have authority to arrange a trial for the condemnation of an innocent man whenever they are of the opinion that doing so would be in the best interests of society. The discretion of officials is limited, however, by the rule that they may not condemn an innocent man to undergo such an ordeal unless there is, at the time, a wave of offenses similar to that with which they charge him and telish him for. We may imagine that the officials having the discretionary authority are the judges of the higher courts in consultation with the chief of police, the minister of justice, and a committee of the legislature.

Once one realizes that one is involved in setting up an *institution*, one sees that the hazards are very great. For example, what check is there on the officials? How is one to tell whether or not their actions are authorized? How is one to limit the risks involved in allowing such systematic deception? How is one to avoid giving anything short of complete discretion to the authorities to telish anyone they like? In addition to these considerations, it is obvious that people will come to have a very different attitude toward their penal system when telishment is adjoined to it. They will be uncertain as to whether a convicted man has been punished or telished. They will wonder whether or not they should feel sorry for him. They will wonder whether the same fate won't at any time fall on them. If one pictures how such an institution would actually work, and the enormous risks involved in it, it seems clear that it would serve no useful purpose. A utilitarian justification for this institution is most unlikely.

It happens in general that as one drops off the defining features of punishment one ends up with an institution whose utilitarian justification is highly doubtful. One reason for this is that punishment works like a kind of price system: By altering the prices one has to pay for the performance of actions, it supplies a motive for avoiding some actions and doing others. The defining features are essential if punishment is to work in this way; so that an institution which lacks these features, for example, an institution which is set up to "punish" the innocent, is likely to have about as much point as a price system (if one may call it that) where the prices of things change at random from day to day and one learns the price of something after one has agreed to buy it.[14]

If one is careful to apply the utilitarian principle to the institution which is to authorize particular actions, then there is *less* danger of its justifying too much. Carritt's example gains plausibility by its indefiniteness and by its concentration on the particular case. His argument will only hold if it can be shown that there are utilitarian arguments which justify an institution whose publicly ascertainable offices and powers are such as to permit officials to exercise that kind of discretion in particular cases. But the requirement of having to build the arbitrary features of the particular decision into the institutional practice makes the justification much less likely to go through.

Notes

1   I use the word "practice" throughout as a sort of technical term meaning any form of activity specified by a system of rules which defines offices, roles, moves, penalties, defenses, and so on, and which gives the activity its structure. As examples one may think of games and rituals, trials and parliaments.

2   The distinction is central to Hume's discussion of justice in *A Treatise of Human Nature*, bk. III, pt. ii, esp. secs 2–4. It is clearly stated by John Austin in the second lecture of *Lectures on Jurisprudence* (4th edn, London, 1873), I, 116ff (1st edn, 1832). Also it may be argued that J. S. Mill took it for granted in *Utilitarianism*; on this point cf. J. O. Urmson, "The Interpretation of the Moral Philosophy of J. S. Mill," *Philosophical Quarterly*, vol. III (1953). In addition to the arguments given by Urmson there are several clear statements of the distinction in *A System of Logic* (8th edn, London, 1872), bk. VI, chapter xii, pars 2, 3, 7. The distinction is fundamental to J. D. Mabbott's important paper, "Punishment," *Mind*, n.s., vol. XLVIII (April 1939). More recently the distinction has been stated with particular emphasis by S. E. Toulmin in *The Place of Reason in Ethics* (Cambridge, 1950), see esp. chapter xi, where it plays a major part in his account of moral reasoning. Toulmin doesn't explain the basis of the distinction, nor how one might overlook its importance, as I try to in this paper, and in my review of this book (*Philosophical Review*, vol. LX [October 1951]); as some of my criticisms show, I failed to understand the force of it. See also H. D. Aiken, "The Levels of Moral Discourse," *Ethics*, vol. LXII (1952). A. M.

Quinton, "Punishment," *Analysis*, vol. XIV (June 1954), and P. H. Nowell-Smith, *Ethics* (London, 1954), pp. 236–9, 271–3.

3   On the concept of explication see the author's paper, *Philosophical Review*, vol. LX (April 1951).

4   While this paper was being revised, Quinton's appeared; see note 2, above. There are several respects in which my remarks are similar to his. Yet as I consider some further questions and rely on somewhat different arguments, I have retained the discussion of punishment and promises together as two test cases for utilitarianism.

5   Note the fact that different sorts of arguments are suited to different offices. One way of taking the differences between ethical theories is to regard them as accounts of the reasons expected in different offices.

6   In this connection see Mabbott, *op. cit.*, pp. 163–4.

7   On this point see Sir David Ross, *The Right and the Good* (Oxford, 1930), pp. 57–60.

8   See Hobbes's definition of punishment in *Leviathan*, chapter xxvii; and Bentham's definition in *The Principle of Morals and Legislation*, chapter xii, par. 36, chapter xv, par. 28; and in *The Rationale of Punishment* (London, 1830), bk. I, chapter 1. They could agree with Bradley that "Punishment is punishment only when it is deserved. We pay the penalty, because we owe it, and for no other reason; and if punishment is inflicted for any other reason whatever than because it is merited by wrong, it is a gross immorality, a crying injustice, an abominable crime, and not what it pretends to be." *Ethical Studies* (2nd edn, Oxford, 1927), pp. 26–7. Certainly by definition it isn't what it pretends

to be. The innocent can only be punished by mistake, deliberate "punishment" of the innocent necessarily involves fraud.

9 Cf. Leon Radzinowicz, *A History of English Criminal Law: The Movement for Reform, 1750–1833* (London, 1948), esp. chapter xi on Bentham.

10 Bentham discusses how corresponding to a punitory provision of a criminal law there is another provision which stands to it as an antagonist and which needs a name as much as the punitory. He calls it, as one might expect, the *anaetiosostic*, and of it he says "The punishment of guilt is the object of the former one: the preservation of innocence that of the latter."

11 By the classical utilitarians I understand Hobbes, Hume, Bentham, J. S. Mill, and Sidgwick.

12 All these features of punishment are mentioned by Hobbes, cf. *Leviathan*, chapter xxviii.

13 *Ethical and Political Thinking* (Oxford, 1947), p. 65.

14 The analogy with the price system suggests an answer to the question how utilitarian considerations ensure that punishment is proportional to the offense. It is interesting to note that Sir David Ross, after making the distinction between justifying a penal law and justifying a particular application of it, and after stating that utilitarian considerations have a large place in determining the former, still holds back from accepting the utilitarian justification of punishment on the grounds that justice requires that punishment be proportional to the offense, and that utilitarianism is unable to account for this. Cf. *The Right and the Good*, pp. 61–2. I do not claim that utilitarianism can account for this requirement as Sir David might wish, but it happens nevertheless that if utilitarian considerations are followed, penalties will be proportional to offenses in this sense, the order of offenses according to seriousness can be paired off with the order of penalties according to severity. Also the absolute level of penalties will be as low as possible. This follows from the assumption that people are rational (i.e., that they are able to take into account the "prices" the state puts on actions), the utilitarian rule that a penal system should provide a motive for preferring the less serious offense, and the principle that punishment as such is an evil. All this was carefully worked out by Bentham in *The Principles of Morals and Legislation*, chs xiii–xv.

46

Repentance and Criminal Punishment

Jeffrie G. Murphy

As the millennium (in at least one sense of that word) approaches, the newspapers are filled with talk of repentance. Pope John Paul has suggested that the Catholic Church repent for some of the injustices against non-Catholics to which it has been party during its history; the American Southern Baptist Convention has publicly repented its role in American slavery and racism; and French President Jacques Chirac has attempted to express, for France, repentance for its cooperative role in the Nazi extermination of French Jews. The government of Japan has struggled with developing a public response to its Second World War atrocities against other Asian nations – some officials advocating full repentance and others more cautious expressions of sorrow or regret – and the government of Argentina is still struggling with the nature and degree of its public response to the atrocities committed against its own citizens in the "dirty war" during the regime of the Generals. America, though taking a qualified public stand of repentance with respect to its wartime internment of Japanese Americans in concentration camps, has so far not taken such a stand with respect to slavery, genocide against Native Americans, or the terror-obliteration bombing of German and Japanese cities during World War II. All of these possible acts of repentance have been advocated, however, by some voices of influence in American politics and opinion.

In sharp contrast to this talk about what might be called *collective* or *group* repentance (and all the logical and moral problems in which such talk is immersed), we rarely hear much talk these days about *individual* repentance. These two facts may, of course, be related, since a stress on collective responsibility could well have a tendency to weaken feelings of individual responsibility. Living (at least in America) in what some have called a "culture of victims," we have seen in recent years the development of various strategies to allow wrongdoers to avoid responsibility for their wrongdoing by claiming victim status for themselves, and a world without responsibility is a world in which repentance lacks logical space.

Gone, it seems, are the days in which we could comfortably refer to prisons as *penitentiaries* – as places to which we would send responsible wrongdoers in order to encourage their repentance: their remorseful acceptance of responsibility for their wrongful actions, their repudiation of the aspects of character that generated those actions, their resolve to extirpate those aspects of character, and their resolve to atone or make amends for what they had done. We simply do not value this rich notion of individual repentance the way we once did; and the world has, in my view, suffered a loss thereby. Perhaps we see repentance as some vestigial relic of a religious worldview to which most people now, at most, pay only lip service. Or perhaps, even if we accept the value of repentance in certain contexts, we do not see an important place for the concept in a system of criminal law and punishment organized around secular values. It is even possible – given the realities of crime and punishment in America – that we cannot in honesty see our prisons as anything more than fortresses in which we warehouse an alienated underclass that is perceived, often quite accurately, as highly dangerous to the stability of ordinary life.

A Return to Plato

It was not always this way, of course. Plato, although he made some place for deterrence and incapacitation in his account of punishment in his great dialogue *Laws*, rejected retribution (which he could not distinguish from vengeance) as utterly barbaric.[1] He offered instead, as the dominant value that should govern criminal punishment, the value of *moral improvement* – punishment as a means of transforming the character of the criminal from a state of vice to a state of virtue. The goal of punishment is future oriented, but not mainly as a device for securing future compliance to law. Compliance is not the primary aim of punishment but will rather be secured as a by-product of the value that is the primary aim: instilling in the criminal, not just a fear based in self-interest, but rather a true sense of justice – a desire to do the right thing for the right reason. The goal is to confer upon the criminal a good (the greatest good: a good character), and this is why the theory is sometimes referred to as a "paternalistic" theory of punishment.

This Platonic theory, until recently rejected by legal philosophers as quite implausible, has now been powerfully resurrected – particularly in the recent writings of R. A. Duff, Herbert Morris, and Jean Hampton.[2] Repentance has a central role to play in such a theory – particularly in the version presented by Duff in his book *Trials and Punishments* – and it merits our serious consideration.

First of all, however, it is worth considering why – for a long time – the theory that punishment may function to generate repentance was understandably rejected as implausible. There are several reasons. The most obvious is that our primary methods of punishment are so brutal as to make repentance either impossible or unlikely. (In spite of Dr Johnson's quip that the prospect of being hanged tends to focus the mind, the death penalty and incarceration in the pest-hole of the modern prison seem primarily to brutalize all those who come in contact with the system.) Also, contemporary criminal law (at least in America) tends toward radical overcriminalization – punishing many offenses with absurd excess and regarding some actions as crimes that, since their moral wrongness is doubtful, are also doubtful objects of repentance. The Georgia penal code, for example, provides that consensual homosexual sodomy may be punished by up to 20 years in prison, but it is by no means obvious that the homosexual has done evil of a kind for which repentance may legitimately be demanded by a secular community. Also, the criminal process will sometimes result in the conviction of persons who are actually innocent. To demand repentance of such persons is simply to add insult to the injury that they suffer from being unjustly punished. Consider finally the crimes (e.g., criminal trespass, unlawful assembly) that may be committed by persons whose motives are those of non-violent civil disobedience. Do we really want to seek repentance from the Martin Luther Kings and Gandhis of the world?

The answer to these worries is, I think, to insist that the paternalistic theory of punishment is an *ideal* theory – not a description of the world in which we live but rather the portrait of a world to which we should aspire. A state or community properly using the criminal law to provoke repentance would have only just laws (laws organized around a respect for fundamental human rights) and would use only methods of punishment that would assist genuine moral rebirth and not simply reflex conformity or terrified submission. Thus the fact that most of our present penal practices are not of this nature will be seen – by someone committed to the paternalistic theory – as a condemnation of those practices and not as a refutation of the paternalistic theory itself. The Chinese demand for criminal repentance under the regime of Mao was morally disgusting, not because it sought repentance, but because the system of values upon which the demand for repentance was based contained much evil and the means used to secure repentance were degrading.

Even as an ideal theory, however, the paternalistic theory is open to serious challenge. Punishments that are not brutal and inhumane must still, if they are truly to be called punishments, inflict some serious deprivation – some hard treatment – on offenders. (Otherwise how would punishment be distinguished from reward or from psychiatric therapy as a means of reform?) But when people hurt us we tend to get angry and resentful, not repentant, and this fact generates a very puzzling question: How is the hard treatment that is necessarily a part of punishment to be justified as a step toward repentance and reform?

There is, of course, an obvious connection between repentance and suffering. Repentant people feel *guilty*, and a part of feeling guilty is a sense that one ought to suffer punishment. Thus guilty and repentant people may well seek out, or at least accept willingly, the punishment that is appropriate for their wrongdoing.

This connection, by itself, will not yield the paternalistic theory, however. For the connection thus far establishes only that repentance will naturally lead to an accepting of punishment (or other penance). The paternalistic theory requires that the connection go in the other direction – i.e., that punishment itself will produce repentance. How could this be so?

Evoking Repentance

There is a traditional answer here, but it is not one that is likely to appeal to the contemporary mind. A certain kind of Platonist, committed to soul/body dualism, might argue that tendencies to wrongdoing arise from the desires of the body when those desires are not under the proper control of the rational soul. St Paul was no doubt under the influence of this kind of Platonism when, in Romans 7: 23, he described his own moral failings by saying "I see another law in my members, warring against the law of my mind, and bringing me into captivity to the law of sin which is in my members." If one accepts this kind of dualism, of course, it is not difficult to imagine that the infliction of suffering that mortifies the body might well cause one to grow to hate the body and focus more upon the soul and the life of virtue that the soul makes possible – a thought that permeates the Christian ascetic tradition and is expressed by such figures as Pascal.

Such an account is, however, highly problematic. It is hard for the contemporary mind to embrace a sharp soul/body dualism and even harder to accept the claim that wrongdoing typically arises from desires of the body. (This may work for rape, but it seems highly implausible for treason.) Some vice is highly intellectual in nature and results far more from a corrupt mind or will than from slavery to the body. Thus, if one wants a theory that follows in Plato's spirit without embracing the metaphysics of his letter, one might see the infliction of punishment as reforming – not merely by subjecting the body – but by curtailing the power of whatever aspect of the personality is responsible for vice.[3] As Herbert Fingarette has argued, the wrongdoer has assumed a power greater than is his right to assume, and thus it is important that he have his will humbled. Punishment makes him suffer (in the sense of *endure*), and such suffering not only gives him what he deserves but also provides him with an important lesson in the legitimate scope of his power.[4]

But how does punishment itself make the lesson *take*? Unless we can imagine a plausible mechanism to explain how the infliction of suffering itself generates repentance and reform, it looks as though we will at most be able to claim that punishment provides us with an *opportunity* to do *something else* to a person (provide therapy, education, religious instruction, etc.) that might be reformative. But then we would be justifying punishment, not in terms of its own reformative potential, but simply in terms of the opportunities that it provides – hardly the challenging promise originally held out by the paternalistic theory.

R. A. Duff is sensitive to this problem and makes a very promising start toward salvaging the paternalistic theory from the many objections that have been raised against it. He makes no pretense that punishment can guarantee repentance and reform. (Neither, of course, can other interventions – e.g., psychotherapy – that also aim at reform.) In this sense he would agree that punishment can do no more than offer criminals an opportunity for moral rebirth. In his view, however, the opportunity is presented by the punishment itself and not by some other devices that might be employed while punishment is being endured.

How could this be? It is, claims Duff, because punishment must be understood in communitarian terms – as an *act of communication* between the community and a person who has flouted one of that community's shared norms. The suffering endured is that of separation from a valued community – a community which the criminal values (perhaps without realizing it until he experiences its loss) and to which he would like to return – and communicates to the wrongdoer the judgment that his actions have made him, at least temporarily, unworthy of full participation in the life of the community. It requires that he experience the pain of separation so that he can come to see, in his heart, the appropriateness of that separation and thus seek, with the appropriate humility, reconciliation with the community that he has wronged. In other words, the hope is that a kind of compulsory penance will be replaced by a voluntary penance. Voluntary penance is a sincere act of reattachment or allegiance to community values – an act that will allow the wrongdoer to be welcomed again and reintegrated into community life. And what makes this paternalistic? Simply this: Punishment on such terms will benefit the wrongdoer because severance from a community – if it is a *just* and *decent* community – is a genuine harm to the individual who is isolated, and reintegration is a genuine good for him. The *right sort* of prison may help him to achieve this good because, as Duff says, it "removes the criminal from his corrupting peers, and provides the opportunity for and the stimulus to a reflective self-examination which will [ideally] induce repentance and self-reform." Also worth considering are such alternatives to prison as community service and restitution.

Duff's theory is rich and in many ways compelling. It cannot be the whole story on the justification of punishment, but it is – in my judgment – an important and largely neglected part of the story. It may, of course, be highly unrealistic to attempt an application of the theory to the crime problem in a society such as that found in contemporary America. It is not at all clear to what degree there is a genuine community of values in our society; and, even where there may be a community of values, it is sometimes the case that those who flout those values feel so alienated (perhaps because of poverty or racial injustice or cultural exclusion) that they could not reasonably see reintegration into the community as a good to be secured by their punishment because they never felt truly integrated into the community in the first place.[5] However, if the paternalistic theory really is a compelling ideal theory, then even a serious gap between theory and practice will not be a legitimate ground for rejecting the theory. Rather it will be an occasion for mourning the community that we have lost and for seeking to regain it – or for seeking to create it if we have never had it. Those committed to the paternalistic view will argue that we should work to create a community of mutual concern and respect wherein punishment, if needed at all, could – without self-deception or hypocrisy – be defended on paternalistic grounds.

But suppose that we are sufficiently charmed by the paternalistic theory that we want to get started now and not wait for the ideal world. How might we proceed? Perhaps the best arena in which initially to attempt to apply the theory is to be found, not in the adult criminal law, but in the law dealing with juvenile offenders. Juvenile offenders are probably more open to radical character transformations than are adults. Also, as David Moore has suggested, the more informal and discretionary proceedings might allow – in encounters between offender (and family) and victim (and family) – the use of empathy to build a sense of community that more abstract and formal proceedings might mask.[6]

It is also possible that one might be able to draw on subcommunities in ways that would ultimately benefit the larger community by developing in juvenile offenders a sense of self-worth through "belonging." For example, a state court in Washington recently placed the punishment of two Tlingit teenagers guilty of robbery and assault in the hands of a tribal court – a court that banished the teenagers for 18 months to separate uninhabited Alaskan islands in the hope that the necessity of surviving on their own, with only traditional tools and folkways to guide them, would build their characters and allow them reintegration into the community. Ideally, of course, one would want all citizens to feel a sense of belonging in the larger national community. One has to start somewhere, however, and – since self-esteem cannot grow in an asocial vacuum – why not (before gangs come in and assume the role) take advantage of the opportunities offered by particular cultural subgroups? Such experiments are surely worth a try.[7]

Sentencing and Pardon

For the most part, however, we will no doubt continue to employ a system of criminal punishment that is driven by a variety of different values. Even if we seek to introduce paternalistic concerns as one of our justifications, concerns with crime control (deterrence, both special and general, and incapacitation) will also loom large. So too will concerns with retribution. A demand for retribution can be based on either a belief that people deserve to suffer for the badness of their characters (character retributivism) or a belief that victims and the community, having been wronged by the criminal, are owed a debt that can be paid only when the criminal suffers appropriate punishment (grievance retributivism). Both versions of retributivism have played a role in the justification for punishment in our society, and they – along with a deep concern with crime control – will no doubt retain an important role for the foreseeable future.

To the degree that the system is driven by these important but generally non-paternalistic values, even full repentance on the part of the criminal will often be seen as not sufficient to remove the need for punishment. Punishing even the fully repentant, though having no special deterrence value, might well serve general deterrence values; and punishment will sometimes be demanded by crime victims who believe, on grievance retributive grounds, that the injuries that they have suffered require a response that is proportional to the wrongs that have produced those injuries. Repentant wrongdoers may have better characters than unrepentant wrongdoers (and thus may deserve less punishment on the theory of character retributivism), but victims might well think that the legitimate grievances they have against wrongdoers are a function of the violations they have suffered, violations that do not cease to matter simply because the person who caused them is now sorry.[8]

If repentance is to play any role at all in our present system of criminal punishment, then, it will probably be as one reason bearing on whatever *discretion* officials are allowed within a punitive range that satisfies the legitimate demands of crime control and grievance retribution. If, for example, we have grounds for believing that society's legitimate general deterrence and retributive objectives with respect to a specific offense could be satisfied by any punishment within a particular range (e.g., 3 to 8 years), then sincere repentance could provide an authority with discretion (normally a sentencing judge or an executive with the power of pardon) with a good reason for choosing a punishment at the lower rather than the higher end of the range.

A truly repentant wrongdoer is recommitted to community values, requires no additional special deterrence, and even – at least on a theory of retribution that bases criminal desert on character rather than victim grievance – deserves less punishment than a wrongdoer who is unrepentant. When one could promote the goods represented by these considerations without compromising the legitimate crime control and grievance retribution purposes of the law, it would seem irrational – even cruel – not to do so.

It is, of course, important that any system that rewards repentance (and thus, like our present system of plea bargaining, gives defendants strong incentives to fake it) develop safeguards against counterfeit repentance. As Montaigne observed in his essay *Of Repentance*, "These men make us believe that they feel great regret and remorse within, but of amendment and correction or interruption they show us no sign. . . . I know of no quality so easy to counterfeit as piety."

Legitimate caution here, however, should not lead one to adopt the radical skeptic or cynical view that we can *never* have reasonable grounds for thinking that repentance is genuine. It is indeed hard to know another's mental states or states of character; but, as our reasonably comfortable use of *mens rea* (e.g., a requirement of intention) in the criminal law illustrates, we do not generally regard it as impossible.

A Final Thought on Collective Repentance

When one thinks of repentance in connection with criminal punishment, one tends to think that all demands for repentance must be addressed to the criminal. But surely the community – through its patterns of abuse, neglect and discrimination – sometimes creates a social environment that undermines the development of virtuous character and makes the temptations to crime very great – greater than many of us might have been able to resist if similarly situated. The idea here is not that criminals, if they are from social groups that are poor or despised or abused or discriminated against, are not to any degree responsible for their criminality. They are. As a part of their dignity as human beings, they must be seen as responsible agents and not merely as helpless victims. But their responsibility is, in my view, sometimes *shared* with those of us in the larger community. In these cases, we too may be legitimately called upon for repentance and atonement – attitudes of mind that should prevent us from thinking of criminals as totally other and should thus moderate our tendencies to respond to them with smug and self-righteous viciousness. The wise and forgiving view that Felicia (in William Trevor's novel *Felicia's Journey*) came to adopt toward the man who tried to murder her surely admits of a wider application: "Lost within a man who murdered, there was a soul like any other soul, purity itself it surely once had been."

Notes

1   The two best discussions of Plato's philosophy of punishment are Mary Margaret Mackenzie's *Plato on Punishment* (Berkeley: University of California Press, 1981); and Trevor J. Saunders's *Plato's Penal Code* (Oxford: Oxford University Press, 1991).

2   Herbert Morris, "A Paternalistic Theory of Punishment," *American Philosophical Quarterly*, volume 18, number 4 (October 1981); Jean Hampton, "The Moral Education Theory of Punishment," *Philosophy and Public Affairs*, volume 13 (1984); R. A. Duff, *Trials and Punishments* (Cambridge: Cambridge University Press, 1986). Although emphasizing punishment as a means of educating and reforming character, Duff, Morris and Hampton – unlike Plato – make room for retributive values as well. For an argument that the values of both retribution and moral education may be in tension with a liberal theory of the state, see my "Retribution, Moral Education and the Liberal State," *Criminal Justice Ethics* (Winter/Spring 1985), and "Legal Moralism and Liberalism," *Arizona Law Review*, volume 37, number 1 (Spring 1995).

3   Plato only sometimes (e.g., in parts of *Phaedo*) relies on a simplistic soul/body dualism to explain wrongdoing. At other times (e.g., in *Republic*) he offers a more complex picture of the nature of motivation.

4   Herbert Fingarette, "Punishment and Suffering," American Philosophical Association Presidential Address, 1977.

5   For a discussion of the ways in which social inequality can undermine the application of theories of punishment, see my "Marxism and Retribution," *Philosophy and Public Affairs*, volume 2, number 3 (Spring 1973).

6   David B. Moore, "Shame, Forgiveness, and Juvenile Justice," *Criminal Justice Ethics*, Winter/Spring 1993.

7   According to the *New York Times* (September 11, 1995), the Tlingit experiment was unfortunately undermined by interference from friends and family and was not allowed to run its full course.

8   Should the self-imposed suffering experienced by the sincerely repentant wrongdoer count as relevant toward the amount of suffering that the state might legitimately inflict as legal punishment? I explore this question – and defend a qualified answer of "yes" – in the expanded version of this essay. ("Repentance, Punishment, and Mercy," in *The Quality of Mercy*, ed. A. Brien. Rodopi Press, 1997.)

47

Making Hard Time Even Harder

Lynn Pasquerella

Introduction

The most brutal and shocking cases of violent crime, brought home to us in the daily headlines or on the evening news, remind each of us of our own vulnerability. It is perhaps not surprising, then, that in spite of the fact the crime rate has remained relatively stable over the past few years, there has been a rise in public fear and outrage at the perceived nature and frequency of violent crime in America (Kaminer, 1995, p. 226). Indeed, public concern over crime, accompanied by doubts about the effectiveness of our criminal justice system, has led to a flurry of renewed calls for penal reform. In response, hard-line legislative proposals, fueled by media attention, have included provisions for a wide range of harsher sentences, from stiffer minimum penalties to "three-time loser laws" that impose mandatory sentences of from 25 years to life on those convicted of more than two violent felonies.

With approximately one million criminals already in prison and another three million on probation or parole, such sentencing reform is likely to increase the number of people who will remain in prison for longer durations. From a public policy perspective, these proposals require evaluation in relation to inevitable financial constraints that will place limits on how many inmates can be housed long-term. Realizing this, a growing number of law-makers, distressed by the notion that prisons provide a life of luxury for many rather than a deterrent to crime, hope to make prisons a place "you don't want to go."

Thus, the legislatures in several states have recently introduced bills that would lead to the creation of "no frills prisons." For example, law-makers in Louisiana, Wisconsin, and Florida are among those who have proposed legislation that would ban inmates' access to such amenities as televisions, tape players, computers, air conditioners, weight-training rooms, martial arts, and pornographic reading material. Officials in Alabama and Arizona have succeeded in their attempts to reinstate chain gangs. New Jersey and Connecticut have begun charging inmates for medical care that used to be paid for by taxpayers, while New York has discontinued a 17-year program that paid tuition for college-degree programs behind bars. Perhaps the most extreme example of this movement, however, can be found on death row at the Oklahoma State Penitentiary. Prisoners there spend 23 hours of every weekday and the entire weekend in a concrete cell with no sunlight, no view of the outside world, and no physical contact with visitors or guards. Inmates have no access to vocational programs or even the prison library. Though Amnesty International has condemned these conditions as inhumane, there has been little criticism from taxpayers.

The legislative trend underlying each of these proposed measures and policies reveals a popular "get tough" attitude designed to discourage repeat offenders and make sure that people who break the law get what they deserve. In what follows, I will explore the legal and philosophical challenges raised by these current trends in punishment and overall criminal justice policy. For purposes here, my focus will be on attempts to justify making hard time even harder through the removal of amenities and the imposition of hard labor on prisoners. In the end, whether these policies are deemed wise, or even justified, will partially depend upon what one considers to be the legitimate aims and purposes of punishment. Certainly, an acceptance of the punitive and deterrent functions of incarceration over rehabilitation may well lead one to regard these measures as removing privileges that promote the coddling of inmates, as opposed to "limiting civil liberties" by infringing upon prisoners' constitutional rights. In fact, the current trends in criminal justice, perhaps reflective of popular opinion in society that removal of all rights from prisoners is exactly what criminals deserve, are grounded in certain philosophical theories related to punishment. For this reason, we will begin by considering these theories and their implications for the nature and extent of our obligations to those in prison.

Differing Perspectives on the Aims and Purposes of Punishment

Punishment, by its very nature, involves the intentional infliction of pain on an individual by an authorized agent of the state in response to some crime committed by the person being punished. Because the act of punishment entails the imposition of suffering through the loss of liberty, and sometimes life – acts which are themselves ordinarily considered to be wrong – the act of punishment requires moral justification.

In general, there are two distinct, contrasting theories appealed to by those concerned with the attempt to justify punishment. These theories are retributivism and utilitarianism respectively. Retributivism, also known as retributionism, is a theory of punishment characterized by the notion that we are justified in punishing criminals as a means of exacting the debt they owe to society in virtue of their criminal wrongdoing. The most famous proponent of the retributivist theory of punishment is the eighteenth-century German philosopher Immanuel Kant. According to Kant:

> Judicial punishment can never be used merely as a means to promote some other good for the criminal himself or for civilized society, but instead it must in all cases be imposed on him only on the ground that he has committed a crime. . . . He must first be found to be deserving of punishment before any consideration is given to the utility of punishment for himself or for his fellow citizens.
>
> What kind and what degree of punishment does public legal justice adopt as its principle and standard? None other than the principle of equality (illustrated by the pointer on the scales of justice), that is the principle of not treating one side more favorably than the other. Accordingly, any undeserved evil that you inflict on someone else . . . is one that you do to yourself. If you

vilify him, you vilify yourself; if you kill him, you kill yourself. Only the law of retribution (*jus talionis*) can determine exactly the kind of punishment. . . . All other standards . . . cannot be compatible with the principle of pure and strict legal justice. (Kant, 1965, pp. 100–101)

As the passage above indicates, at the basis of a Kantian retributivism are two principles: the *principle of desert* and the *principle of proportionality*. The principle of desert dictates that a person be punished if and only if he or she deserves to be punished. Not only is it wrong to punish someone who is innocent and so does not deserve punishment, but it is also wrong to fail to punish someone who is deserving of punishment. The second principle, that of proportionality, is highlighted by the retributivists' claim that the punishment must fit the crime. The more serious the crime, the more severe should be the punishment. In fact, it is morally wrong to punish an individual more or less severely than the wrongdoer deserves.

Because retributivism justifies punishment solely on the basis of what has happened in the past, it is known as a *backward looking* theory of punishment. The fact that a person is guilty of a crime is sufficient to justify a punishment in proportion to the severity of the crime, regardless of any future consequences that might result. Central to this view is the attitude that the criminal has brought the punishment on him or herself. By treating the criminal as a moral agent who is responsible for the actions following from his or her free choices, we accord the individual respect. Thus, some philosophers have referred to a criminal's "right to be punished" under retributivism. A failure to punish a criminal in this scheme denies the criminal the opportunity to pay back a debt to society owed as a result of the violation of criminal law. This repayment is necessary in order to restore moral equilibrium to the society in which someone has reaped the benefits of social order without paying the price of conformity to the law.

Indeed, Kant believed in universal consent by members of society to abide by the rules. By breaking the law, criminals have gained an unfair advantage over others who relinquish some freedom to do as they choose in order to live in a civil society. When a criminal fails to suppress the will to break the law, the individual becomes a "free rider" while the others pay the price of compliance with the rule of the law. Such a person is worthy of social condemnation, the loss of liberty, and at times, Kant believed, the loss of life.

An alternative to the retributivist position on punishment is the utilitarian perspective. Utilitarianism, developed by Jeremy Bentham and his student John Stuart Mill, presumes that acts are right if and only if they produce the greatest good for the greatest number of people. Whereas retributivists regard the guilt of the criminal as sufficient to justify punishment, utilitarians, in a forward-looking approach to punishment, weigh the consequences of punishment before concluding that the act would be justified. For utilitarians, a penalty should impose a degree of pain in excess of the degree of pleasure derived from committing the crime. Furthermore, the act of punishment, insofar as it involves the intentional infliction of pain on the wrongdoer, is regarded as an evil that can be justified only through an appeal to the social good punishment may produce.

The aims and purposes of punishment consistent with the utilitarian perspective are *prevention, deterrence*, and *rehabilitation*. Prevention refers to the incapacitation of the criminal through imprisonment or execution. Acts of punishment may be justified if they serve to prevent further crimes from being committed by the individual who is punished. The second goal, deterrence, shifts the emphasis from the person who has committed the crime to other potential criminals. Punishment sometimes serves the function of providing other members of society with the motive for not committing similar offenses for fear of suffering the same punishment. Under the broad heading of deterrence, some philosophers and sociologists distinguish further between *general deterrence*, which refers to the psychological effect punishment will likely have on others, and *specific deterrence*, which deals with the persuasive effect punishment will have on the one who suffers it by providing the motive to steer clear of any future wrongdoing. Finally, utilitarians appeal to the rehabilitative function of punishment. A criminal is rehabilitated when the desire to commit crimes no longer exists. This lack of criminal intent is not due to fear of being punished, but due rather to a personality change brought about by the therapeutic effects of punishment.

It is important to note that while retributivists and utilitarians differ in their approaches to justifying punishment, they do not necessarily disagree with respect to whether punishment and the form it should take are justified in a given case. Consider, for instance, the jury's rejection of the death penalty for Susan Smith, the infamous South Carolina mother who drowned her two young sons in October 1994 by rolling her car into a lake with the boys strapped into their car-seats, and later blamed the crime on an imaginary black carjacker. From a retributivist perspective, the jury needed to take into account whether punishment was deserved, and if so, the severity of the punishment. In our judicial system, a crime is made up of two components, a bad act (*actus reus*) and a guilty mind (*mens rea*). There was no doubt that Smith committed the act of killing her sons, yet there was a great deal of controversy surrounding her mental state at the time of the killing. Past experiences in her own life, which included her parents' divorce and her father's subsequent suicide when she was a young girl, sexual abuse by her step-father that began when she was a teenager, leading to a sexual relationship that continued until the time she killed her children, her own depression and attempts at suicide as a teen, combined with her mother's refusal to press charges or allow Smith to receive psychological counseling after being sexually abused out of fear of destroying the family's reputation, Smith's divorce from the boys' father, who had an affair during their marriage, and rejection from a boyfriend who did not want responsibility for Smith's children, each served to create a pattern whereby Smith's mental culpability was mitigated. Since desert is comprised of both the act and the mental state, Smith was viewed as not deserving of the most severe punishment, though by no means considered devoid of responsibility.

A utilitarian analysis might well lead to the same conclusion regarding the appropriateness of the punishment. Susan Smith is not the sort of criminal we usually fear. Her case was domestic, meaning she killed people in her own family. Society does not need protection from Smith, though she may need to be protected from herself and others. Potential murderers in similar situations are not likely to be deterred by the threat of punishment Smith receives, because of the unique and desperate circumstances surrounding the case. Treatment, with the aim of rehabilitation, may be a legitimate goal in Smith's case and certainly this purpose could not be achieved through execution.

Just as we can appeal to both utilitarian and retributivist reasoning to support the jury's conclusion in the Smith case, we can use both theories to champion a wide range of policies, including those that advocate harsher conditions of confinement for prison inmates. This notion that utilitarian and retributivist analyses can be reconciled has been defended quite persuasively by contemporary moral philosopher John Rawls. In his highly influential article "Two Concepts of Rules," Rawls makes the argument that any satisfactory account of punishment *must* include components from both utilitarianism and retributivism. Specifically, he contends that considerations of social utility must be invoked to justify the institution of punishment as a whole, whereas retributivist considerations are necessary to justify various practices within the institution – for instance, justifying why a particular defendant was put in jail (Rawls, 1995, pp. 3–13). How might these theories be applied in an effort to justify attempts at making hard time even harder?

To begin with, proponents of such policies and practices have argued along retributivist lines that punishment in prison is not severe enough. They claim the amount of deprivation inmates are suffering in prison is disproportionate to the severity of the crimes many of them have committed, suggesting that prisons are no longer capable of serving the function of punishing those who have broken the law. Their contention is that incarceration cannot possibly meet the goal of making the criminal pay when life in prison is often better than life on the street. In fact, in February 1995, the US House of Representatives, incensed that taxpayers are subsidizing what are perceived as vacations for murderers, rapists, and muggers, passed a bill requiring federal prison officials to "provide prisoners the least amount of amenities and personal comforts consistent with constitutional requirements and good order and discipline" (Peterson, 1995, p. B7). Representative Dick Zimmer from New Jersey, who proposed the legislation, argued, "When you break the law of the land, you should pay the price for your crime, not be rewarded with a vacation watching premium cable on your personal television" (ibid.).

The amendment was just one part of a broader law that would require prisoners to work at least forty hours a week toward their support and payment of restitution to victims. The law would also mandate federally supported corrections systems to provide "living conditions and opportunities to prisoners within its prisons that are not more luxurious than those conditions and opportunities the average prisoner would have experienced if such prisoner were not incarcerated" (ibid.). The sentiments expressed by Representative Zimmer echo a hard-line retributivism and are reminiscent of a principle in criminology known as the *principle of less eligibility*. According to the principle of less eligibility, conditions for those in prison should be no better than the living conditions of those law-abiding citizens who are the least well off of those among us in the working class.

Yet, as we can see, this principle has not only retributivist overtones, but utilitarian ones as well. For not only does the principle suggest that those in prison don't deserve to be better off than those on the outside, but it claims that prison cannot serve as a deterrent if the standard of living in prison is an improvement over what criminals had on the outside. This is crucial, since behind many of the proposals for cutting amenities from prisons is the desire to deter criminals and prevent crimes. Thus, as one member of the Law Enforcement Alliance, an organization which pushes for harsher prison conditions, has said, "Prisons have become mini-resorts and it's disgusting to crime victims. We strongly believe that prison is meant to be punishment, a deterrent and a prevention tool, not a resort experience" (ibid.).

Assessment of Retributivist and Utilitarian Arguments in Support of Harsher Prisons

While we have seen that both retributivist and utilitarian analyses can be used to support no-frills prisons and the further restriction of prisoners' rights, there are objections that must be addressed before we conclude that the proposed policies making prison life harsher are worthy of our support philosophically. To begin with, recall the retributivist contention that the criminal owes a debt in virtue of having shirked the responsibility of abiding by the law in exchange for reaping the benefits of living in a civil society. Some philosophers, such as Richard Delgado, reject the idea of consent to the community and a debt owed in virtue of benefits reaped within contemporary society as being seriously flawed. There is no doubt that some members of society, especially those in impoverished urban or extreme rural areas, are completely disenfranchised. With little or no access to health care, insurance, police or fire protection, these individuals will be at a loss when trying to identify the benefits that have been heaped upon them. Thus, as Delgado points out, "it is not much of a burden to the economically powerful to obey the laws, nor is it a "benefit" to the powerless to live in a community which is indifferent to them" (Delgado, 1995, p. 263).

Though seemingly inconsistent with America's resurgence of "get tough" policies on crime, Delgado's view has received increasing tacit recognition in the judicial system, burnished by what some experts have termed the "Oprahization of the courtroom" (Gregory, 1994, p. 30). Signaling the influence of television talk shows in generating sympathy for defendants, this phrase is used to help explain juries' excusing defendants from responsibility by delving into how past negative experiences may have caused them to commit their crimes. Indeed, "urban survival syndrome," "black rage" and "post-traumatic stress disorder" have become familiar phrases in the courts, used by attorney's seeking defenses of "diminished capacity" for their clients by explaining how easily the victimized become the victimizers under such circumstances. While we may be loath to excuse the heinous acts that arise under these conditions, we are perhaps given insight into the reasons why, for instance, a ten-year-old and eleven-year-old boy would drop a five-year-old from the window of a high-rise tenement because he refused to steal candy for them.

Under the present circumstances then, is it truly justifiable on retributivist grounds to punish excluded individuals on the basis of a debt owed to the community? While it may be possible in principle, under retributivism, to support harsher forms of punishment in a perfectly just society, applying a retributivist analysis to contemporary society appears enigmatic. Comprised of vast differences grounded in race, class, and gender as to the benefits conferred and burdens shouldered by society, retributivists will have an onerous task attempting to justify harsher punishment for many of the repeat offenders they claim aren't getting what they deserve because life in prison is better for them than what they have experienced in their own communities.

Yet, what of those criminals who have not experienced the "rotten social background" to which Delgado refers? Can retributivists justify harsher prison conditions for these individuals? If we focus solely on the notion of a debt owed to the community, perhaps harsher punishment is justified in certain cases. We must remember, however, that even the most ardent retributivists accept the position that some punishments are to be rejected as inconsistent with human dignity. As a consequence, retributivists fail to advocate the rape of rapists and torture of torturers. Because there are no fixed retributivist guidelines for determining whether or not a punishment in most cases truly fits the crime, it is not clear that the punishments proposed in policies promoting hard time are, in fact, consistent with a retributivist analysis. This will be the case even after we discount the sociological and economic factors some would offer as an excuse for criminal behavior.

Further challenges associated with the retributivists' proportionality requirement can be understood by considering recent policies reinstating chain gangs. The harsher punishment they inflict on criminals might initially be welcomed by retributivists as giving criminals what they deserve, but are likewise subject to challenge on these same grounds. The central problem with the justification of chain gangs revolves around the fact that selection for them often has little to do with the severity of the crime committed and more to do with racism. Thus, in South Carolina, past presiding judges have been given complete discretion over the alternative of sentencing prisoners to a county chain gang, local jail, or state penitentiary. As a consequence, two people found guilty of having committed the same crime and sentenced to the same number of years might have vastly different penalties to pay. Sending certain prisoners to the penitentiary where rehabilitative services are available and others to chain gangs where there are none counts as denial of the equal protection clause of the Fourteenth Amendment. For this reason, chain gangs have been considered excessive in relation to the penalty paid by others for similar crimes both inside and outside of the same jurisdiction.

Injustice involved in the application of the punishment can, of course, be remedied by making the penalty mandatory for everyone convicted of a certain crime, regardless of the jurisdiction. But even if the retributivist could determine that this punishment is actually befitting of certain crimes, it would still remain to be seen for the retributivist whether the penalty of chaining people together to perform hard labor is consistent with respect for human dignity.

The retributivists are not alone in facing challenges to their attempts at justifying harsher conditions of confinement. Utilitarian attempts are also subject to substantial criticism, starting with the utilitarian goal of deterrence. Deterrence is the primary purpose cited by many officials for the proposed measures making hard time harder. The science of deterrence is complex and involves a number of presumptions, including the notion that prospective offenders are in a position to make rational choices in weighing the benefits of crime against the pain of punishment. But, as Al Brownstein, 1995's director of the American Civil Liberties Union's National Prison Project argues, this notion is faulty. Brownstein reveals, "Study after study has told us that people who commit crimes never think about the consequences beforehand. They think they'll never be caught" (Curriden, 1995, p. 75). This is especially true when dealing with certain types of crimes, such as crimes of passion. In fact, with only 3.8 percent of all crimes actually being prosecuted, the risk of apprehension is very low. So even if the average criminal who has a 7.7 percent chance of being arrested undertook a thoughtful analysis, the outcome would not be favorable for deterrence theorists (Walker, 1994, p. 103).

Suppose we were able to crack down on crime and guarantee arrest. Would deterrence theory be more plausible under these circumstances? The evidence suggests otherwise. Consider, for example, high-rate offenders who do tend to contemplate the likelihood that they will be caught, given that most eventually find themselves arrested and imprisoned repeatedly. In their cases, repeated arrest, conviction, and imprisonment seem to do nothing by way of producing a deterrent effect. This conclusion follows from a study done by James Q. Wilson and Allan Abrahams in which they analyzed Rand Inmate Survey data revealing that "prisoners believe that crime in general is very likely to lead to arrest, imprisonment, and even death." Nevertheless, they continue to commit crimes (ibid.).

Hence, while prison sanctions continue to be perceived by those in criminal law and the public consciousness as an effective deterrent to criminal behavior, empirical evidence does not support the assumption that we can reduce crime even by increasing the severity of punishment (Weisburd, 1995, p. 589). In fact, no matter how harsh prison conditions become, for many, the risks associated with criminal behavior are likely to be outweighed by the benefits. And while certain defenders of harsher prison conditions contend that the statistics would change in a system where punishment were administered with swiftness, certainty, and increased severity, their response appears to ignore social realities and the genuine limits of both the deterrence model and the principle of less eligibility. Proposing that we confront these limits, criminologist Jonathan Simon asserts, "Individual sanctions can be applied effectively only in a context that provides a viable normative framework for choice. In the long run we can control crime only if we can restore the context of economic opportunity and common political destiny against which modern punishment has been intelligible and manageable" (Simon, 1993, p. 267). Thus, Simon challenges the utilitarian reasoning upon which the less eligibility principle is based. He does so by noting that the utilitarian focus on the choices of individuals who must decide between crime and the available alternatives is increasingly incoherent and destructive in the context of a society in which involvement with the criminal justice system is a virtual certainty for those trapped by "hardened urban poverty" (ibid., p. 265).

Equally questionable, under the same reasoning, is the efficacy of punishment involving shame, guilt, and harassment, proposed by some policy makers as an alternative to traditional approaches that have failed to deter. These theorists would support the increased stigmatization involved in such practices as Alabama's chain gangs. Little attention has been paid to this approach thus far, and there is no evidence that they will prove to be any more effective as deterrent factors. Moreover, we need to consider, in advance, the possibility that these practices may actually turn out to produce the opposite effect. Making prisoners wear stripes and serve in chain gangs breaking rocks is certainly stigmatizing, but isn't going to provide inmates with the economic means for survival on the outside that Simon believes we should emphasize. Instead, opponents such as Brownstein admonish, "These people advocating the return of the chain gangs are saying they want to treat prisoners like wild animals. Unfortunately, it may become a self-fulfilling prophecy" (Curriden, 1995, p. 5).

Further, without conclusive evidence to support the claim that chain gangs, like other "shock incarceration" techniques, are effective in deterring criminals, it is not clear that the increased punishment entailed serves any legitimate penological purpose. As the Southern Poverty Law Center has argued in the courts, the infliction of pain under these circumstances should be viewed as wanton, and therefore in violation of the Eighth Amendment's prohibition against cruel and unusual punishment. In fact, this leads to one of the most formidable challenges for utilitarians to overcome, namely that their theory allows for the possibility that the guilty are punished more or less severely than they deserve if doing so will serve an overriding social purpose. Utilitarians may be able to justify such disproportionately harsh punishments, but at the cost of what some consider to be essential principles of justice and fairness.

Another objection for the utilitarian to address follows from the fact that such practices deny opportunities for rehabilitation, a central component of the utilitarian justification for punishment. While the rehabilitative ideal was once popular, it has all but been abandoned in the 1990s. Diminished confidence in this goal has led to reduced funding for programs in prison, thwarting efforts to provide treatment for criminals. Rather, prisons are so fraught with drug traffic, gang violence, and sexual assault, that they often do little more than shift the victims of violence from those on the outside to those on the inside. Nevertheless, it should be noted that if rehabilitation remains a theoretical if not practical goal of incarceration, it certainly is not going to be achieved in the chain gangs or in institutions where there is gross deprivation and diminished opportunity for acquiring the skills necessary to survive on the outside.

Finally, while these measures were introduced in part to reduce the costs of incarcerating prisoners, they may actually end up costing states more money due to a flood of lawsuits filed from prison cells. During 1993 alone, the most recent year for which statistics are available, more than 34,000 such suits were filed. As a result, proposals to make prison life increasingly austere have been accompanied by changes in laws to limit inmates' abilities to sue state governments over prison conditions and make it more difficult for federal judges to intervene in how prisons are run (Curriden, 1995, p. 74). Worsening conditions of confinement and at the same time restricting inmates' access to the courts provides a solution that utilitarians need to assess carefully.

Apart from the philosophical analysis that must be undertaken when assessing the justification for these policies, there are questions of jurisprudence that must be addressed as well. Whether or not these changes in conditions of confinement will ultimately prove to be legal remains to be seen. However, we can begin to understand the issues underlying the debate that is likely to ensue by outlining the evolution of prisoners' rights within our judicial system and applying the standards set forth to diminishing conditions of confinement.

A Brief History of Prisoners' Rights

Prior to the 1960s, prisoners in our judicial system were considered "slaves of the state," with minimal enforceable rights. Reflecting this outlook, the courts adopted a "hands off" policy concerning conditions of confinement, allowing solely prison officials to regulate prison conditions and the enforcement of control within prisons. Coinciding with the civil rights movement, however, was a recognition that even while incarcerated, prisoners retain certain constitutional protections. The emerging conception of prisoners' rights during this time allowed prisoners to gain access to the federal courts, resulting in a subsequent consideration of whether conditions of confinement could be challenged by inmates on the grounds that they violate the Eighth Amendment's prohibition against cruel and unusual punishment.

While historically there has been widespread disagreement concerning the precise meaning of the phrase "cruel and unusual punishment," the Supreme Court has determined that included among punishments proscribed by the Eighth Amendment are those deemed excessive either by inflicting unnecessary pain or by being grossly disproportionate to the severity of the crime and, therefore, that fail to meet the constitutional requirement that the penalty comport with the "dignity of man" (*Trop* v. *Dulles*, 356 US 86, 1958, p. 100). Moreover, the court has remained steadfast in its insistence that "punishment must take place within the limits of civilized standards" and that an assessment of whether a punishment is cruel and unusual "must draw its meaning from the evolving standards of decency that mark the progress of a maturing society" (ibid., p. 101). Taken together, these principles have served as the background for inquiries into whether prison conditions could be rightly challenged as cruel and unusual punishment.

The Supreme Court explicitly addressed the question of whether the scope of the Eighth Amendment extended to conditions of confinement for the first time in 1978, in *Hutto* v. *Finney* (437 US 1122, 1978, p. 685). Here the court ruled that prison conditions *are* a form of punishment that could be challenged as cruel and unusual under the Eighth Amendment. At the time, however, the court failed to propose a standard for determining whether prison conditions were indeed in violation of the Constitution.

A standard was finally offered three years later in *Rhodes* v. *Chapman*, a case involving the constitutionality of "doubling up" inmates in 6 × 8-foot cells. In *Rhodes*, the Supreme Court maintained that all prison conditions, "alone or in combination," that deprive inmates of "the minimal civilized measures of life's necessities" are to be regarded as cruel and unusual (*Rhodes* v. *Chapman*, 452 US 337, 1981, p. 347). Yet, while *Rhodes* provided a standard by which courts could judge prisoners' claims regarding conditions of confinement, the problems with the decision should be obvious. Though the court concluded that prison conditions which are not cruel and unusual under contemporary standards of decency are constitutional, the justices failed to define what counts as minimal civilized measures of life's necessities or to specify what criteria must be met and what evidence needs to be offered by prisoners attempting to establish a claim of cruel and unusual punishment.

At least one of these objections was addressed in a later Supreme Court decision, *Wilson* v. *Seiter*. This decision set the standard of proof for establishing whether conditions of confinement were to be regarded as cruel and unusual. As we will see, however, the standard set forth in *Wilson* raises as many questions as did previous decisions concerning the scope of prisoners' rights. For in this case, the court held prisoners to a poorly framed double burden of proof concerning claimed constitutional violations. The first requires a prisoner to demonstrate that the disputed prison condition deprives the inmate of a "single, identifiable human need" such as food, warmth, or exercise. The second requirement for the prisoner is to show that the prison administration acted with "deliberate indifference" to the needs of the prisoner (*Wilson* v. *Seiter*, 501 US 294, 1991, p. 294). In applying this dual standard, we need to know not only what counts as a basic human need, but also what evidence the prisoner can and must offer to prove the subjective element of "deliberate indifference."

For instance, if there is a long history of failure to attend to the needs of an inmate, but the administration wasn't aware of the need through inattention, is this deliberate indifference? What if the administration is aware, but believes the services necessary to meet the inmate's needs are too costly and would jeopardize the standard of living for all other inmates if addressed? Such questions are a natural consequence of a subjective standard requiring the inmate to delve into the mental state of prison authorities. Even after these questions have been answered, however, there remains the issue of how harmful a deprivation must be in order to constitute cruel and unusual punishment.

The courts' failure to resolve these issues led to a new challenge in the 1993 case of *Helling* v. *McKinney* (113 S. Ct., 1993, p. 2475). *Helling* extended the scope of prisoners' rights significantly by expanding the range of basic human needs to which inmates are constitutionally entitled. William McKinney, a convicted felon in the Nevada state prison system, challenged the conditions of his confinement as cruel and unusual on the grounds that prison administrators, acting with deliberate indifference, exposed him to levels of environmental tobacco smoke that posed an unreasonable risk of serious damage to his future health. Confined to a 6×8-foot, poorly ventilated cell with a chain-smoker who went through five packs of cigarettes a day, McKinney began to develop nosebleeds, headaches, lethargy, shortness of breath, and chest pains. Because smoking was also permitted in the prison classrooms and law library, McKinney was continuously exposed to environmental tobacco smoke. In an effort to avoid the involuntary exposure, McKinney made repeated requests to be housed with a nonsmoker or to be moved to a single cell.

After several years of legal battles, the Supreme Court agreed to hear McKinney's case. At the center of controversy was whether the Eighth Amendment provides protection against prison conditions that merely threaten to cause future health problems. In the end, the court acknowledged that the Eighth Amendment does protect inmates from the risk of future harm, and reaffirmed the requirement that the alleged harm must be serious. In doing so, they set forth three criteria that must be met by prisoners seeking relief from dangerous prison conditions. First, the court retained the subjective standard set forth in *Wilson* v. *Seiter*, which compels the prisoner to offer proof that prison officials intended, or were deliberately indifferent to, the harm inflicted on the prisoner. Next, the court held the prisoner to standards of evidence requiring the production of objective statistical and scientific data supporting the alleged risk of harm. This meant that the prisoner must prove the likelihood that exposure to the alleged harm would cause injury. Last, the court ruled that the prisoner must demonstrate that no individual in contemporary American society would choose to tolerate the purported risk. This was signified by the court's enjoinder that the risk in question must be so severe that it would violate "contemporary standards of decency to expose anyone unwillingly to such a risk" (ibid., p. 2482).

When assessing prisoners' claims against corrections officials, recent courts have applied a standard for reviewing prison regulations, known as "reasonable relation." According to this standard, "When a prison regulation impinges on inmates' constitutional rights, the regulation is valid if it is reasonably related to legitimate penological interests" (*Turner* v. *Safley*, 482 US 78, 1987). In weighing challenges brought by inmates, then, the courts must consider: (1) whether there is a rational connection between the prison regulation in question and the legitimate government interest put forward to justify it; (2) whether there is some alternative means of allowing the prisoner to exercise the claimed constitutional right; (3) whether accommodating the right will adversely affect guards, other inmates, and the general allocation of prison resources; and (4) whether there is an obvious alternative to the prison regulation that would accommodate the prisoner's rights at *de minimus* cost to the penological interest. As we can see from *Helling*, though, the considerable burden remains on the prisoner to demonstrate that the restriction or condition imposed by the prison administration is an unreasonable one.

The Implications for Making Hard Time Even Harder

What are the implications of these decisions for the court challenges likely to be brought in response to current policies removing amenities from prison? It is doubtful whether the creation of "no frills" prisons will be the subject of a successful constitutional challenge. This is because, in most cases, the perceived amenities being withdrawn do not count as basic human needs. And as Justice Lewis Powell said, "The Constitution does not mandate comfortable prisons" (*Rhodes* v. *Chapman*, 452 US, 1981, p. 349). Nevertheless, these "no frills" policies could result in environments that place inmates at risk of significant future harm. Prisons are already inherently dangerous and risky places. The imposition of increasingly harsh living conditions and the deletion of control mechanisms, such as time in the weight room for good behavior, are feared by many prison administrators as likely to promote loss of control over inmates (Gavzer, 1995, p. 7). Tension throughout correctional facilities has the potential for erupting into violence among inmates and between inmates and correctional officers, which in turn may increase the likelihood of physical brutality.

Tension is already palpable in the maximum security prisons in the state of New York, following their legislature's adoption of a bill that would allow "doubling up" in 810 of the 20,000 maximum security cells there. The advantage for the state is that taxpayers avoid having to pay for a new 100 million-dollar facility. Inmates, however, have responded to the policy with hunger strikes, work stoppages, and "silent protests" in which they refuse to speak to guards. Guards, in turn, have filed suit in the state's Supreme Court, insisting that the policy creates an unsafe working environment. In their suit they argue that not only do these conditions create inmate on inmate violence and forced sexual activity, but they also breed highly communicable diseases like tuberculosis. Thus, one consequence of making hard times harder is likely to be increased tension and violence within prisons. As a result, these policies, especially when taken together with the elimination of education and training programs to cut costs and the cessation of drug treatment programs, might be challenged as posing a risk of significant future harm. Inadequate opportunities for rehabilitation, tension, and anxiety contribute to both mental and physical deterioration. Nevertheless, while the decision in *Helling* extended the scope of prisoners' rights under the Eighth Amendment to future harm, it imposes standards that are quite stringent and in the final analysis may be insurmountable for those prisoners seeking to challenge their conditions of confinement on this basis.

Moreover, as the proposals intended to limit law suits from prisoners indicate, not everyone agrees that prisoners retain the degree of constitutional rights granted to them by the courts. Justice Clarence Thomas, in his dissent from the majority in *Helling*, criticized the notion that conditions of confinement and deprivation within prisons count as punishment for purposes of interpreting the Eighth Amendment. Thomas believes that punishment refers only to the penalty imposed through a sentence or statute, and not the circumstances or conditions inflicted upon prisoners by prison officials. Indeed, he goes even further by maintaining that neither historical evidence nor precedent in the courts give any indication that harsh prison conditions can count as cruel and unusual punishment.

Critics of Thomas appeal to the courts' consistent reference to contemporary standards of decency to justify what they perceive as advancements the courts have made in weighing prisoners' claims regarding conditions of confinement. Such appeals may ultimately be unpersuasive, however. Since it was first introduced, questions have persisted regarding how we determine such a standard. While the Supreme Court has become the barometer for contemporary standards of decency based on its own experience and perceptions, if the standard were set by public sentiment, the behavior that has led to court-ordered improvement of conditions of confinement for inmates might well be permitted.

Conclusion

The "no frills" prison bill was just a small part of the "Taking Back Our Streets Act" of 1995, contained in the Republicans' Contract with America. The act embraces provisions for more prisons, police, and penalties and, at the same time, includes the elimination of virtually all funding for prevention programs. An additional component, the "Stop Turning Out Prisoners Act," substantially limits the power of federal courts to grant relief in conditions of confinement cases and automatically voids all court orders governing prison conditions within two years, whether or not constitutional violations still exist (Taifa, 1995, p. 22).

This shift in the public mood toward harsher punishment signifies fear and disillusionment on the part of Americans. Yet, while the trend toward tougher prison policies represents the will of the people weighing concerns over both public safety and the economy, there is no evidence that these policies will achieve the stated purpose of reduced recidivism. Nor, as we have seen, do the philosophical theories that underlie advocates' appeals to these policies do the work of justifying them.

As financial burdens for the criminal justice system continue to mount, overcrowding in prisons will increase and the public will be forced to reassess current trends. Lengthy mandatory prison terms in "no frills" prisons may satisfy the emotional needs and political aspirations of those supporting these policies, but will lead to prisons filled with unruly inmates who have nothing to lose. This prospect frightens many correctional officers, prison administrators, and others who are more familiar with the realities of prison life than are the legislators on Capitol Hill who are proposing these measures (Curriden, 1995, p. 77).

Legal concerns regarding these policies must be addressed as well. In the past, successful constitutional challenges were limited to conditions of confinement that "shocked the conscience." While "no frills" prisons and hard labor may fail to meet this standard, *Helling* opened up the possibility for challenges based on the risk of both future psychological and physiological harm. Deprivation, overcrowding, and forced hard labor may indeed comprise affronts to human dignity that call for constitutional redress. However, even if we accept Justice Thomas's rather extreme contention that prisoners have no constitutional right to certain conditions of confinement, we still have a moral obligation to treat fellow human beings with a basic respect for human dignity. Hence, the lack of any legitimate claim by prisoners based on an appeal to legal rights does thereby relieve us of all moral responsibility toward those we incarcerate.

For these reasons, we ought to consider alternative proposals which include sentencing wisely and strictly supervised probation, in combination with drug treatment and job training for nonviolent offenders. Though less championed by legislators in their political fervor, this would also cut back on the prison population. In the case of violent offenders who must remain in custody, there is no denying that maintaining them in prison is expensive. There is nothing wrong with a proposal making prisoners work to help meet these expenses. But when work is used solely to punish, there is no need for it to be interesting or to teach job skills and habits consistent with rehabilitation. An alternative approach calls for the system implemented in the Northwest by prisoners who are responsible for the production of blue jeans called "Prison Blues." Inmates earn up to two thousand dollars a month from production and sales, with the proceeds going toward support of their families, restitution to victims, their own maintenance while in prison, and mandatory savings for when they are released. Prisoners are allowed to keep any money that is left over. In the process, inmates are acquiring valuable skills through their employment.

If we can achieve the goal of reducing recidivism through community support and by providing people with skills they can use once released from prison, adherence to policies imposing harsh prison conditions and hard labor without training do little more than satisfy people's desire for vengeance. Focusing on deprivation rather than rehabilitation and training is not only inhumane, but bound to frustrate the correctional goals aimed at by those who wish to make hard time even harder.

References

Curriden, Mark. "Hard Time." *ABA Journal* (July 1995): 72–8.

Delgado, Richard. " 'Rotten Social Back': Should the Criminal Law Recognize a Defense of Severe Environmental Deprivation?" in Jeffrie G. Murphy (ed.), *Punishment and Rehabilitation*, 3rd edition (Belmont, CA: Wadsworth Press, 1995).

Gavzer, Bernard. "Life Behind Bars." *Parade Magazine* (August 13, 1995): 4–7.

Gregory, Sophronia Scott. "Oprah! Oprah in the Court!" *Time* (June 6, 1994): 30–1.

Helling v. *McKinney*, 113 S. Ct. 2475 (1993).

Hutto v. *Finney*, 437 US 1122 (1978).

Kaminer, Wendy. *It's All the Rage* (Reading, MA: Addison Wesley, 1995).

Kant, Immanuel. *The Metaphysical Elements of Justice* (Indianapolis, IN: Bobbs-Merrill, 1965).

Peterson, Iver. "Cutting Down on Amenities to Achieve No-Frills Jails." *New York Times* (July 10, 1995): B7.

Rawls, John. "Two Concepts of Rules." *Philosophical Review*, 44 (1995): 3–13.

Rhodes v. *Chapman*, 452 US 337 (1981).

Simon, Jonathan. *Poor Discipline: Parole and the Social Control of the Underclass, 1890–1990* (Chicago: University of Chicago Press, 1993).

Taifa, Nkechi. "The Taking Back Our Streets Act of 1995, Criminal Justice Provisions in the Republican Contract with America." *National Bar Association Magazine* (March/April 1995): 21–6.

Trop v. *Dulles*, 356 US 86 (1958).

Turner v. *Safley*, 482 US 78 (1987).

Weisburd, David, Elin Waring, Ellen Chayet. "Specific Deterrence in a Sample of Offenders Convicted of White-Collar Crimes." *Criminology*, 33 (November 1995): 587–607.

Walker, Samuel. *Sense and Nonsense about Crime and Drugs: A Policy Guide* (Belmont, CA: Wadsworth Press, 1994).

Wilson v. *Seiter*, 501 US 294 (1991).

48

The Philosophy of State Compensation[1]

John Haldane and Anthony Harvey

I

That the state has a responsibility for the victims of violent crime is a proposition which has only recently come to be accepted by governments. The first comprehensive compensation scheme was enacted in New Zealand in 1964; a few months later a scheme was instituted in the United Kingdom, and during the following decade similar schemes were adopted in the United States, Canada, Australia and some member states of the European Community. In 1983 a European Convention on the Compensation of Victims of Violent Crime was adopted, drawing attention to the "need" to compensate victims and declaring it "necessary" for governments to make provision to do so.

What has happened to bring the needs of victims, which appear for so long to have been almost totally ignored by governments, into recent prominence? If society has a duty to provide compensation to the victims of violent crime, this duty might be thought to rest on fundamental principles of equity and social responsibility, which were surely just as valid in earlier times as they are today. This may be so; but state compensation for the victims of crime requires the expenditure of public money, and in earlier times a sense of responsibility for the plight of such victims was not felt sufficiently strongly in the public at large to warrant any government to pursue the matter. In the years after the Second World War, however, the moral conscience of the West became increasingly preoccupied with the needs and legitimate claims of the socially disadvantaged. The UN Declaration of Human Rights of 1948, which was motivated principally by the concern to prevent any repetition of the atrocities committed by the Nazi regime, was subsequently adopted as a charter for protection against discrimination and oppression of all kinds, and for the firmer establishment of democratic rights and freedoms. A number of universal and regional Human Rights Conventions achieved recognition and ratification by many countries, and the ever-widening categories of those deemed to be in need of such protection were bound to arouse interest in the sufferings of innocent people who had been the victims of violent crime. At the same time, society in the developed world was becoming rapidly richer, and welfare arrangements were being steadily extended to victims of various forms of disability and disadvantage: in this climate some provision for the victims of crime could hardly be far behind. In addition, there was strong political pressure in Western societies to make more generous provision for the poor and to ensure a fairer distribution of society's resources. Given the ever-growing public expenditure on the enforcement of law and the punishment of criminals, the public was increasingly likely to be moved by an appeal to the apparent unfairness involved in devoting no comparable resources to relieve the plight of innocent victims of crime.

II

If it was this degree of public moral consensus which impelled some governments in the 1960s to make provision for compensation, the theoretical justification for doing so remained obscure. In 1961, for example, the UK government could find "no constitutional or social principle on which state compensation could be justified", and the British Home Office vigorously resisted any suggestion that the victim has a legal "right" to compensation. This did not prevent the same government from making arrangements to award such compensation and from setting up a quasi-judicial agency to administer them; but the same fear that to acknowledge a "right" to compensation would commit the government to meeting an unlimited number of claims in full, and thereby create an uncontrollable channel of public expenditure, lies behind its continuing reluctance to bring into force the statutory criminal-injuries compensation scheme established by the Criminal Justice Act, 1988. A similar lack of clarity characterises the wording of the European Convention. In the preamble the reasons given for the "necessity" of providing at least minimum provisions for compensation are "equity" and "social solidarity", but these reasons are not further elucidated. In the Explanatory Report (Council of Europe, 1984) a number of other arguments are listed, without comment; it is also stated that recent victim studies "have thrown light on victims' psychological and physical distress after a crime", which "points to the need to compensate the victim" (paras 6 and 7). Thus, even if there is now public consensus on the need to provide compensation, the justification for doing so remains both obscure and controversial.

III

Part of the difficulty resides in the notion of "compensation" itself. In Hebrew law the guiding principle for the assessment of criminal damages was the *lex talionis*, an eye for an eye and a tooth for a tooth. This was echoed in an early judgement of the US Supreme Court (*Monongahela Navigation Co.* v. *US*, 1893) which described compensation as the provision of a "full and perfect equivalent". The difficulty is, of course, that in the majority of cases perfect equivalence is unattainable. If you take my car and in using it damage it, then it *may* be sufficient compensation if you make good the damage and provide for the inconvenience. The relative ease of calculating adequate compensation in such a case is due to the fact that cars are generally regarded not as *ends* in themselves but as *means* of transport. If, however, you assault me in the process, then it is likely that the loss I suffer constitutes damage to things which I regard as intimately connected with the very sense of my life's having the value it does have, things such as bodily and psychological integrity. People desire good health in order to pursue their chosen ends; but equally the point of some activities is that they induce and help to maintain health. The same is true in respect of psychological well-being. Thus, in taking someone's property against their will – either by theft or, for that matter, by legally sanctioned confiscation – there may be losses in respect of mental and physical health which are not wholly compensated for by providing alternative instruments for the attainment of those goals for which mental and bodily health were the agent's means.

Similarly, physical damage or shock may render someone unfit for employment which is likely to be their sole or main source of income. If one compensates them for loss of earnings one has provided equivalent means in the sense of restoring financial powers. But this may fall short of adequate compensation if it neglects the fact that someone's employment may be a constituent feature of their life, not merely a means but an end in itself. To the extent that this has been denied them they have suffered a special kind of loss; one that is often deeper than the loss of income, for it affects their very sense of identity and thereby their idea of what makes their life a liveable one.

But the fact that it is seldom possible to compensate a victim of crime by providing an exact equivalent of the loss sustained does not mean that compensation is either useless or arbitrary. It is true that any provision of alternative goods may be inadequate or inappropriate, and that there may always remain what one may call an "*ineliminable residue of loss*". It is also true that the damage a person sustains may be mitigated by care and treatment and may eventually be healed. Nevertheless the very fact that compensation is provided may of itself be a source of help and satisfaction to the victim. At the very least, it represents an acknowledgement by society of undeserved loss or damage. Ideally, both the acknowledgement and the material reparation should be provided by the offender. But in practice this is seldom possible, and one of the strongest arguments for the state taking responsibility for compensation is that victims may thereby receive something of that which they have a right to expect but which in the normal way cannot be obtained from the offender.

IV

Mention of the offender at this point makes it necessary to distinguish between different consequences of liability for injury to another person. Civil law has traditionally provided for compensation in cases where the agents of injury to the interest of others are deemed to be at fault. An award of damages is the most well know form of compensation, though for reasons explored later, civil actions for personal injuries arising from the commission of crimes of violence are rare. In criminal law, on the other hand, the principal consequence is the sanctioning of the offender. The primary justification for judicial punishment has nothing to do with the individual victim; it is that the offender has broken the laws of society, and it is the responsibility of the state to punish the transgression, to deter further such offences and (where possible) to rehabilitate the offender. It is therefore not surprising that justifications for judicial penalties are concerned mainly with the offender and with the need to protect society from such offences: the rights or interests of the immediate victims play no part in the reasoning. So far as the criminal law is concerned, a victim is viewed simply as a citizen in whose person civil society itself has been offended against. But this does not necessarily mean that the state has no further responsibilities towards the victim. It is of the essence of any criminal justice system that the individual citizen ceases to have a right to personal revenge. A political society, it is often said, is one in which the state has a monopoly of coercive force. The individual may be imagined to have ceded to the state the duty of exacting retribution for unlawful injury, and once this is done the victim has no further claim on the offender. However, even if a victim has handed over to the state the responsibility for punishment, this does not altogether settle the matter of reparation. Where the offender is in a position to make restitution or offer compensation, this should be enforced by the courts. Where the offender is not apprehended, or has no means to pay, it is for the state to provide compensation.

But to bring the question within the scope of a general theory of punishment is to enter a notoriously difficult field. Traditional justifications for judicial punishment are of three sorts: *non-consequentialist*, *consequentialist*, and *contractualist*; arguing, respectively, that punishment is right (a) in itself, (b) on account of its beneficial effects (for society and/or the criminal) and (c) because it is implied by a social consensus. In practice penal policy is usually based on a combination of these; but it is important to distinguish them, and in fact they correspond to three main lines of traditional philosophical theory. Allowing for simplification, one may group the various social and political theories under three headings: *natural law theories*, which hold that the nature of human beings implies certain universal values for them; *consequentialist theories*, which argue that an action or policy is justified to the extent that it maximises the level and distribution of some given value within a defined community; and *contractualist theories*, which argue that the rightness or wrongness of policies depends upon whether they, and/or the institutions which establish and enforce them, have the support of the members of society.

This is not the place to discuss the merits of these competing theories. The important point to notice is that, so far as the judicial process is concerned, more than one of them is customarily invoked to support a particular sentencing policy (e.g., a deterrent element is consequentialist, a retributive element is non-consequentialist); and that different moral theories can be appealed to in support of similar moral claims or policies, e.g., a severer regime of punishment may be justified both because it is deterrent (consequentialist) and because it is deserved (non-consequentialist). It is thus not necessary to agree on the philosophical basis of all moral actions in order to be able to commend a particular policy on moral grounds. If it can be shown that more than one philosophical theory supports the proposal, there is a reasonable presumption that the proposed policy has moral justification.

V

These considerations have all arisen from the notion of *compensation*, and provide some basis for an argument that the State has an obligation to provide it. But before going further it is necessary to say something about the notion of *victims*. It is arguable that those who suffer grievous harm through accident or natural disaster are entitled to at least as much support as crime victims. That this is the public perception seems to be shown by the huge response to appeals on behalf of the victims of any particularly sensational natural disaster. On this view, victims of violent crime would simply be a particular category of those requiring public assistance, and there would be no question of *compensation* at all. It could be said, for instance, that the state might provide assistance to victims through an expanded national insurance scheme. Building on existing arrangements such a scheme could, but need not, make special provision for victims of crime as opposed to subjects of other misfortunes for which redress through the civil courts is, for whatever legitimate reason, unavailable. One reason for according special treatment for crime victims would be the presumption of a distinctive harm suffered by those who have been wronged. But equally a reason for not singling out this group might be the thought that it is a highly relative matter what constitutes crime, and so to attach special significance to this gives inappropiate emphasis to these misfortunes and stigmatises their victims. Furthermore, to treat crime-victims differently is, in effect, to compensate them for a loss additional to those shared with victims of accident or disease.

A second non-compensatory option would be for the state to provide the victim with the means of taking civil action against the offender, suing him or her for damages in respect of a tort. The rationale for this approach would be that when a criminal damage is inflicted two interests are affected: those of the society or the state, for which the remedy is punishment, and those of the immediate victim, for which the remedy is damages. On this view the residue calls for state treatment, not through compensation but by way of state provision of legal services, or of the means to secure them. In this regard the role of the state would be an enabling one again related to that which it already occupies with respect to the provision of health and social services.

Interesting as it may be, this second way of proceeding is inadequate in circumstances in which the offender is not apprehended, or disappears before civil action can proceed, or in which he or she lacks the means to provide damages. One could of course take the view that these possibilities are part of life's lottery and that the state has no further duty beyond that of punishing and providing the means for civil actions. But the application of such a policy would certainly be perceived as unfair to a large number of the victims of violent crime; and the claim that the government has no duty to compensate would be in defiance of the view, now commonly embodied in the practice of courts, that every punishment administered by the state should, where appropriate, include an element of reparation.

Yet even if victims of violent crime cannot be simply subsumed into the general category of victims of misfortune – even if they are "special" – there are certain respects in which the obligation which the state has towards them is similar to that which it has towards those who are disadvantaged in other ways. Various kinds of aid may be required and are available. The most urgent needs of the victim may be counselling, help from the police, legal advice or protection from the media.

None of this need be controversial: it is part of what government is now expected to do for any who suffer disadvantage through no fault of their own. Indeed some would argue that, if properly administered, this form of provision for victims is more beneficial than any monetary compensation. As we have seen, compensation in any particular case is not likely to be objectively quantifiable or in any real sense equivalent to the loss or damage sustained. Monetary values bear little relation to the personal impact of violence. On the other hand moral, psychological and financial support can be provided through the health and social services, and there is a strong case for saying that generous provision of these services for victims is a better use of public money than a system of monetary compensation that will seldom have any real equivalence with the hurt actually suffered. At present, partly perhaps for historical reasons, monetary compensation is given a far higher priority in public expenditure than the provision of social and psychological aid for victims. Simply on grounds of value for money, a strong case could be made out for reversing these priorities.

Yet, once it is granted that some compensation must be given to the victim, money remains the one practical means by which the state can provide it in any systematic way; further, as we noted earlier, the fact of compensation may be more significant to the victim than the amount, even though the amount must be perceived to be equitable in relation to other awards made to victims in similar circumstances. It remains to consider in more detail the arguments which are used to justify such awards.

VI

We have observed that different kinds of philosophical reasoning may be invoked to justify particular policies, and that this does not weaken the case for them; indeed, where arguments based on different premises support the same conclusion, the force of the argument may be strengthened. It will be convenient to list the arguments for a state obligation according to the broad philosophical categories of "consequentialist" (or forward looking) and "non-consequentialist" (or backward looking) and to note those which draw their strength from both (i.e., mixed theories).

Consequentialist

An element of reparation in the criminal system is necessary if individuals are to retain respect for the administration of justice and not take the law into their own hands, seek to recover their property by force, or commit acts of personal revenge. Also victims may be more ready to report offences and co-operate with the police and the courts if the successful outcome of a prosecution will strengthen their claim to compensation. This is presumably the sense of the Explanatory Report on the European Convention, when it speaks (para. 7) of the need "to quell the social conflict caused by the offence and make it easier to apply rational, effective crime policy".

Non-consequentialist

The European Convention includes "equity" among its arguments for the necessity of compensation. This can be understood in two ways. It may mean that it is unfair that victims should receive nothing from the state when substantial public expenditure is devoted to the apprehension, conviction and punishment of criminals; and also that it is unfair that help and relief are not given to victims of crime on a scale comparable to that given to sufferers from other forms of disadvantage or disability. If such a disposition of public funds is felt to be inequitable, it is arguably wrong in itself and ought to be rectified. It can also be argued (though not perhaps so plausibly) that every offence marks a failure by the state in its obligation to protect its citizens from unlawful attack, and therefore that the state owes something to the victim as compensation for this failure. Moreover, since human life and dignity are overriding social priorities, since compensation in various forms (from simple recognition to monetary reparation) can contribute to the continuance of quality of life and the restoration of dignity, and since only the state has the resources to provide such compensation, the damaging consequences of violent crime for the life and dignity of the victim lay a positive duty on government to respond with such means as are available.

But if it is recognised that government has a duty or an obligation, it may follow that the victim has a right to be compensated. This consequence has evidently alarmed politicians, who appear to have inferred that the exercise of this right would make victims legally entitled to whatever level of compensation a court or officials agency might determine, and that this would result in public expenditure outside political control. But this is to misunderstand the meaning of "rights". It is widely agreed that every citizen of this country has a right to health care and education. But to claim this right, applicants have to show that they meet the appropriate conditions (such as an illness that would benefit from treatment, or the standard of educational achievement qualifying for a particular course). Moreover, the right is to no more than a fair share of that which the state may reasonably be expected to provide within the limits of its economic circumstances. Similarly with a right to compensation. This is a right to an equitable share in such provision for compensation as the government can reasonably afford. It is not a blank cheque to be filled in by a Compensation Board.

Mixed theories

The second reason adopted in the European Convention for the necessity to compensate victims of violent crime is "social solidarity". The focus of concern is upon the common good and the idea that in the person of the victim a harm is done to society which he or she has no duty to bear alone. Accordingly compensation is a means by which the loss is distributed across society as a whole, so recognising the reality of social existence and deepening a sense of community. To promote such social solidarity is widely seen as a proper objective of government and is an aim shared by many organisations and agencies in the community. It may be seen both as something which is good as a means to the greater happiness and well-being of the citizens and also as something good in itself and a laudable aim of public policy.

A further argument under this heading, which has already been spelt out, derives from the theory of punishment. Judicial punishment should include some element of reparation to the victim; if this cannot be recovered from the offender, it becomes the duty of the government to supply it. This argument presupposes that the provision of reparation is good in itself; but it may also take into account the beneficial consequences for the victim of acknowledgement and compensation.

Finally, a government may be said to have assumed an obligation to maintain arrangements for compensation by ratifying the European Convention in 1990. This again may be justified by the beneficial consequences it is likely to have for citizens of European countries who suffer criminal injuries when abroad: but it may also be regarded as good in itself in so far as a government has an absolute duty to honour treaties into which it has entered in the name of its people. The philosophical theories on which these arguments are based may now be set out schematically as in the diagram.

THEORIES OF STATE COMPENSATION

BACKWARD-LOOKING NON-CONSEQUENTIALIST THEORIES			FORWARD-LOOKING CONSEQUENTIALIST THEORIES	
EQUALITY	SOCIAL DAMAGES for government failure	DUTY TOWARDS LIFE AND DIGNITY	MAINTENANCE OF LAW AND ORDER	SOCIAL ENHANCEMENT

MIXED THEORIES

LEGAL OBLIGATION (e.g., international convention)	SOCIAL SOLIDARITY	DUTY OF REPARATION

The diagram shows that these arguments depend for their theoretical justification on more than one philosophical theory. But, as was argued above, this does not by any means weaken their cumulative force. As in other issues of moral philosophy, similar moral claims may be supported by different moral theories: the resulting moral consensus is often more significant than the different routes by which it is reached. And where (as in the central column) the same conclusion is reached by both consequentialist and non-consequentialist reasoning, the force of the argument may be regarded as particularly strong. Not all the theories advanced, of course, are of equal weight. In particular, that of social maintenance and enhancement (i.e., that compensation increases social cohesion around respect for the law) is open to serious question on empirical grounds, and that of social damages (i.e., that the government has failed to provide protection) seems to presuppose the impossible condition that government should be able to protect all citizens from all criminal assaults. But taken together they amount to a formidable case, and any government today which sought to evade or reduce its responsibility for compensation would properly incur severe moral censure.

Note

1   The present essay is an edited version of that published in the *Journal of Applied Philosophy*, vol. 12 (1995). The latter itself derives from a longer paper which appears as *Appendix A* to *Compensating the Victim of Crime*, Report of an Independent Working Party (London: Victim Support, 1993).

References

The following is a brief list of writings relevant to the principles and policies of state compensation.

Ashworth, A., "Punishment and Compensation: Victims, Offenders and the State", *Oxford Journal of Legal Studies*, 6 (1986).

Cane, P., *Atiyah's Accidents, Compensation and the Law*, 5th edition (London: Weidenfeld & Nicolson, 1993).

Chapman, J. W. (ed.), *Compensatory Justice, Nomos, xxxiii* (New York: New York University Press, 1991).

Council of Europe, *Explanatory Report on the European Convention on the Compensation of Victims of Violent Crime* (Strasburg: Council of Europe, 1984).

Goodin, R. E., "Theories of Compensation", *Oxford Journal of Legal Studies*, 9 (1989); reprinted in Frey, R. G. and Morris, C. W. (eds), *Liability and Responsibility: Essays in Law and Morals* (Cambridge: Cambridge University Press, 1991).

MacCormick, N., "The Obligation of Reparation". *Proceedings of the Aristotelian Society*, 78 (1978); reprinted in N. MacCormick, *Legal Right and Social Democracy* (Oxford: Clarendon, 1982).

Miers, D., "The Responsibilities and the Rights of Victims of Crime", *Modern Law Review*, 55 (1992).

Montague, P., "Rights and Duties of Compensation", *Philosophy and Public Affairs*, 13 (1984).

Economic Justice

Philosophers have historically distinguished between three types of justice. In the previous section on PUNISHMENT, the authors discussed two of these: retributive and compensatory justice. In the current section, the authors focus on the third: distributive justice. Distributive justice concerns how we should distribute the products of social cooperation among the community's citizens. Some of the most important goods a society distributes are economic.

The first two selections articulate the most widely discussed theories of economic justice. The essay by Rawls outlines the economic implications of his theory of justice. Before I describe his economic views (captured in his "second principle of justice"), I must briefly mention his "first principle of justice," namely, that the first responsibility of government is to guarantee equal civil liberties for all citizens. According to Rawls, governments should protect liberties such as those granted in the *United States Constitution*: freedom of speech, freedom of religion, freedom of the press, etc. These liberties are essential to any just society; we cannot sacrifice them to increase economic well-being. Nor may we sacrifice any particular individual's civil liberties for the benefit of others, not even the majority. Rawls's emphasis on individual freedom is reminiscent of the views of several authors in the sections on DRUGS and FREE SPEECH, for example, John Stuart Mill.

After these individual liberties are secure, we may then settle on a system for distributing economic goods. He proposes that we adopt his "second principle of justice," namely, that the state should distribute economic goods to maximize the advantage of the least advantaged members of society. This principle will permit some people to have more economic goods than others, but only if their having more goods will promote the well-being of the least well-off members of society. By following this principle, we know that even the most disadvantaged members of society will have a tolerably decent life – the best life they could reasonably except.

Rawls's argument for these two principles has important theoretical implications, and is therefore worthy of mention. We should arrive at principles of justice from behind what he calls "the veil of ignorance." That is, we should ask not, "What principle of justice would

I adopt if I knew my talents, interests, and station in life?" but "What principles of justice would I adopt if I were ignorant of my talents, interests, and station in life?" He offers both practical and moral reasons for claiming that we should select principles of justice in this way. The practical reason is simple: if we ask the first question, we lose any chance for consensus. Each of us will, intentionally or unintentionally, strive to design principles that will benefit us, given our particular array of interests and talents. However, if we asked the second question, we would be likely to select principles of justice that promoted our interests, no matter what our specific interests and talents happened to be. Therefore, we would be more likely to identify principles on which all rational people (who go through this reasoning process) could agree.

Rawls also offers moral reasons for selecting principles from behind the veil of ignorance. Reasoning behind the veil of ignorance will lead us to minimize the influence of luck in determining peoples' life prospects. Rawls claims that the circumstances of one's birth – one's natural talents, social status, family influence, etc. – are matters of luck that should not unduly influence our chances in life. A central task of morality is to constrain the detrimental effects of luck.

Is he correct? That is clearly a theoretical question with profound consequences for many practical moral issues. Those who embrace a retributive theory of PUNISHMENT would probably sympathize with Rawls's claim. For if justice requires that we give people what they deserve, and what they deserve is determined by their freely chosen actions, then it is difficult to see why someone who was born intelligent deserves more than someone who was born retarded. We shall also see disagreements about the appropriate role of luck in the discussion of INTERNATIONAL JUSTICE AND WORLD HUNGER. Children in developed countries have better life prospects than children in third world countries for one reason alone: luck. I did not deserve to be born to parents who could provide for me, in a country with an educational system like the US; certainly I did not deserve it more than a poor child in Addis Ababa, Baghdad, or Jakarta. So why should I have a relatively cushy life, while they fight to stay alive, simply because of luck? Should luck play such a large role in determining our fates? Or should morality seek to limit luck's influence?

Nozick thinks not. The job of morality is not to eliminate the detrimental effects of luck. In fact, morality should not strive to achieve any particular economic distribution. That is not the job of justice. The state does not have the right to distribute economic goods. Particular individuals already own those goods. The role of a theory of economic justice is simply to set down rules that everyone should follow in acquiring and transferring economic goods. The ideal theory, according to Nozick, would go something like this: If someone acquires her goods justly, that is, by initially acquiring them fairly, or by receiving the goods, via transfer, from someone who justly owned them, then there is nothing else we need know; the distribution is just. What matters, according to Nozick, is not the final distribution, but the rules followed in determining that distribution.

Nozick further argues that we can only achieve and maintain an ideal distribution by constantly interfering with individual liberty. If people have liberty, then they will, through private transfers, inevitably alter the distribution so that it no longer satisfies the ideal – no matter what the ideal. Perhaps we can best understand Nozick's view, if we assume that he imports Mill's emphasis on individual liberty (FREE SPEECH and DRUGS) into the economic arena. For Nozick, all liberty – whether civil or economic – is created equal. If he is correct, that has important implications for other practical issues.

For instance, if we embrace Nozick's view about the sanctity of individual property rights, then individuals should be able to keep their property, even if, by so doing, other people die. Indeed, that is precisely the thrust of Arthur's arguments about WORLD HUN-GER. However, Wolf explicitly rejects Nozick's views about the pre-eminence of property rights.

Wolf claims that property rights are very important; in fact, he offers compelling arguments explaining why they are important. However, the arguments for property rights cannot, he claims, justify my having an over-abundance of economic goods while others, through no fault of their own, starve to death. On this view the rich have a stringent moral obligation to help the poor. The fact that the poor live in Pakistan or Peru rather than Peoria, Illinois, does not diminish our obligation to them. Distance, he argues, is morally irrelevant. The question about the moral relevance of distance was discussed earlier by Williams and Rachels (FAMILY AND FRIENDS).

Young rejects this entire way of describing and discussing the issue of justice. Although distribution is an important element of justice, it is not, she claims, the only or even the most important element. For instance, the state should provide educational and employment opportunities for all citizens. We cannot use a purely distributive model to adequately evaluate whether the state has provided for these fundamental needs. Distributive justice is concerned with handing out consumable goods in a fair and reasonable manner. However, equality of opportunity is not so much a matter of what we have, as what we do. The distributive paradigm simply ignores these crucial elements of justice.

Moreover, the "standard" ways of framing issues about justice mask the powerful role social institutions play not only in determining who gets what, but also in determining how we define and evaluate jobs and positions. Why do we describe some positions as professional jobs and other jobs as "white-collar"? Is there any intrinsic reason why physicians should make more money than astro-physicists, even if both positions require similar training, talent, and expertise? And how, exactly, do we best guarantee equality of opportunity?

The distributive paradigm does not give us a plausible response to any of these questions. So, Young argues, we should abandon the distributive paradigm, and focus instead on relationships of power, especially relationships of domination and oppression. Other authors raised these concerns earlier, for example, in the discussions of SEXUAL AND RACIAL DISCRIMINATION and AFFIRMATIVE ACTION.

Further Reading

Feinberg, J. 1980: *Rights, Justice, and the Bounds of Liberty*. Princeton, NJ: Princeton University Press.

Goodin, R. and Pettit, P. 1993: *A Companion to Contemporary Political Philosophy*. Oxford: Blackwell Publishers.

Locke, J. 1963: *Two Treatises of Government*, Peter Laslett (ed.). New York: Cambridge University Press.

Nozick, R. 1974: *Anarchy, State, and Utopia*. New York: Basic Books.

Rawls, J. 1970: *A Theory of Jusice*. Cambridge, MA: Harvard University Press.

Waldron, J. 1986: "Welfare and the Images of Charity." *Philosophical Quarterly*, 36: 463–82.

49

A Theory of Justice

John Rawls

The Main Idea of the Theory of Justice

My aim is to present a conception of justice which generalizes and carries to a higher level of abstraction the familiar theory of the social contract as found, say, in Locke, Rousseau, and Kant.[1] In order to do this we are not to think of the original contract as one to enter a particular society or to set up a particular form of government. Rather, the guiding idea is that the principles of justice for the basic structure of society are the object of the original agreement. They are the principles that free and rational persons concerned to further their own interests would accept in an initial position of equality as defining the fundamental terms of their association. These principles are to regulate all further agreements; they specify the kinds of social cooperation that can be entered into and the forms of government that can be established. This way of regarding the principles of justice I shall call justice as fairness.

Thus we are to imagine that those who engage in social cooperation choose together, in one joint act, the principles which are to assign basic rights and duties and to determine the division of social benefits. Men are to decide in advance how they are to regulate their claims against one another and what is to be the foundation charter of their society. Just as each person must decide by rational reflection what constitutes his good, that is, the system of ends which it is rational for him to pursue, so a group of persons must decide once and for all what is to count among them as just and unjust. The choice which rational men would make in this hypothetical situation of equal liberty, assuming for the present that this choice problem has a solution, determines the principles of justice.

In justice as fairness the original position of equality corresponds to the state of nature in the traditional theory of the social contract. This original position is not, of course, thought of as an actual historical state of affairs, much less as a primitive condition of culture. It is understood as a purely hypothetical situation characterized so as to lead to a certain conception of justice.[2] Among the essential features of this situation is that no one knows his place in society, his class position or social status, nor does any one know his fortune in the distribution of natural assets and abilities, his intelligence, strength, and the like. I shall even assume that the parties do not know their conceptions of the good or their special psychological propensities. The principles of justice are chosen behind a veil of ignorance. This ensures that no one is advantaged or disadvantaged in the choice of principles by the outcome of natural chance or the contingency of social circumstances. Since all are similarly situated and no one is able to design principles to favor his particular condition, the principles of justice are the result of a fair agreement or bargain. For given the circumstances of the original position, the symmetry of everyone's relations to each other, this initial situation is fair between individuals as moral persons, that is, as rational beings with their own ends and capable, I shall assume, of a sense of justice. The original position is, one might say, the appropriate initial status quo, and thus the fundamental agreements reached in it are fair. This explains the propriety of the name "justice as fairness": it conveys the idea that the principles of justice are agreed to in an initial situation that is fair. The name does not mean that the concepts of justice and fairness are the same, any more than the phrase "poetry as metaphor" means that the concepts of poetry and metaphor are the same.

Justice as fairness begins, as I have said, with one of the most general of all choices which persons might make together, namely, with the choice of the first principles of a conception of justice which is to regulate all subsequent criticism and reform of institutions. Then, having chosen a conception of justice, we can suppose that they are to choose a constitution and a legislature to enact laws, and so on, all in accordance with the principles of justice initially agreed upon. Our social situation is just if it is such that by this sequence of hypothetical agreements we would have contracted into the general system of rules which defines it. Moreover, assuming that the original position does determine a set of principles (that is, that a particular concept of justice would be chosen), it will then be true that whenever social institutions satisfy these principles those engaged in them can say to one another that they are cooperating on terms to which they would agree if they were free and equal persons whose relations with respect to one another were fair. They could all view their arrangements as meeting the stipulations which they would acknowledge in an initial situation that embodies widely accepted and reasonable constraints on the choice of principles. The general recognition of this fact would provide the basis for a public acceptance of the corresponding principles of justice. No society can, of course, be a scheme of cooperation which men enter voluntarily in a literal sense; each person finds himself placed at birth in some particular position in some particular society, and the nature of this position materially affects his life prospects. Yet a society satisfying the principles of justice as fairness comes as close as a society can to being a voluntary scheme, for it meets the principles which free and equal persons would assent to under circumstances that are fair. In this sense its members are autonomous and the obligations they recognize self-imposed.

One feature of justice as fairness is to think of the parties in the initial situation as rational and mutually disinterested. This does not mean that the parties are egoists, that is, individuals with only certain kinds of interests, say in wealth, prestige, and domination. But they are conceived as not taking an interest in one another's interests. They are to presume that even their spiritual aims may be opposed, in the way that the aims of those of different religions may be opposed. Moreover, the concept of rationality must be interpreted as far as possible in the narrow sense, standard in economic theory, of taking the most effective means to given ends. I shall modify this concept to some extent, as explained later, but one must try to avoid introducing into it any controversial ethical elements. The initial situation must be characterized by stipulations that are widely accepted.

In working out the conception of justice as fairness one main task clearly is to determine which principles of justice would be chosen in the original position. To do this we must describe this situation in some detail and formulate with care the problem of choice which it presents. These matters I shall take up later. It may be observed, however, that once the principles of justice are thought of as arising from an original agreement in a situation of equality, it is an open question whether the principle of utility would be acknowledged. Offhand it hardly seems likely that persons who view themselves as equals, entitled to press their claims upon one another, would agree to a principle which may require lesser life prospects for some simply for the sake of a greater sum of advantages enjoyed by others. Since each desires to protect his interests, his capacity to advance his conception of the good, no one has a reason to acquiesce in an enduring loss for himself in order to bring about a greater net balance of satisfaction. In the absence of strong and lasting benevolent impulses, a rational man would not accept a basic structure merely because it maximized the algebraic sum of advantages irrespective of its permanent effects on his own basic rights and interests. Thus it seems that the principle of utility is incompatible with the conception of social cooperation among equals for mutual advantage. It appears to be inconsistent with the idea of reciprocity implicit in the notion of a well-ordered society. Or, at any rate, so I shall argue.

I shall maintain instead that the persons in the initial situation would choose two rather different principles: the first requires equality in the assignment of basic rights and duties, while the second holds that social and economic inequalities, for example inequalities of wealth and authority, are just only if they result in compensating benefits for everyone, and in particular for the least advantaged members of society. These principles rule out justifying institutions on the grounds that the hardships of some are offset by a greater good in the aggregate. It may be expedient but it is not just that some should have less in order that others may prosper. But there is no injustice in the greater benefits earned by a few provided that the situation of persons not so fortunate is thereby improved. The intuitive idea is that since everyone's well-being depends upon a scheme of cooperation without which no one could have a satisfactory life, the division of advantages should be such as to draw forth the willing cooperation of everyone taking part in it, including those less well situated. Yet this can be expected only if reasonable terms are proposed. The two principles mentioned seem to be a fair agreement on the basis of which those better endowed, or more fortunate in their social position, neither of which we can be said to deserve, could expect the willing cooperation of others when some workable scheme is a necessary condition of the welfare of all.[3] Once we decide to look for a conception of justice that nullifies the accidents of natural endowment and the contingencies of social circumstance as counters in the quest for political and economic advantage, we are led to these principles. They express the result of leaving aside those aspects of the social world that seem arbitrary from a moral point of view.

The problem of the choice of principles, however, is extremely difficult. I do not expect the answer I shall suggest to be convincing to everyone. It is, therefore, worth noting from the outset that justice as fairness, like other contract views, consists of two parts: (1) an interpretation of the initial situation and of the problem of choice posed there, and (2) a set of principles which, it is argued, would be agreed to. One may accept the first part of the theory (or some variant thereof), but not the other, and conversely. The concept of the initial contractual situation may seem reasonable although the particular principles proposed are rejected. To be sure, I want to maintain that the most appropriate conception of this situation does lead to principles of justice contrary to utilitarianism and perfectionism, and therefore that the contract doctrine provides an alternative to these views. Still, one may dispute this contention even though one grants that the contractarian method is a useful way of studying ethical theories and of setting forth their underlying assumptions.

521

Justice as fairness is an example of what I have called a contract theory. Now there may be an objection to the term "contract" and related expressions, but I think it will serve reasonably well. Many words have misleading connotations which at first are likely to confuse. The terms "utility" and "utilitarianism" are surely no exception. They too have unfortunate suggestions which hostile critics have been willing to exploit; yet they are clear enough for those prepared to study utilitarian doctrine. The same should be true of the term "contract" applied to moral theories. As I have mentioned, to understand it one has to keep in mind that it implies a certain level of abstraction. In particular, the content of the relevant agreement is not to enter a given society or to adopt a given form of government, but to accept certain moral principles. Moreover, the undertakings referred to are purely hypothetical: a contract view holds that certain principles would be accepted in a well-defined initial situation.

The merit of the contract terminology is that it conveys the idea that principles of justice may be conceived as principles that would be chosen by rational persons, and that in this way conceptions of justice may be explained and justified. The theory of justice is a part, perhaps the most significant part, of the theory of rational choice. Furthermore, principles of justice deal with conflicting claims upon the advantages won by social cooperation; they apply to the relations among several persons or groups. The word "contract" suggests this plurality as well as the condition that the appropriate division of advantages must be in accordance with principles acceptable to all parties. The condition of publicity for principles of justice is also connoted by the contract phraseology. Thus, if these principles are the outcome of an agreement, citizens have a knowledge of the principles that others follow. It is characteristic of contract theories to stress the public nature of political principles. Finally there is the long tradition of the contract doctrine. Expressing the tie with this line of thought helps to define ideas and accords with natural piety. There are then several advantages in the use of the term "contract." With due precautions taken, it should not be misleading.

A final remark. Justice as fairness is not a complete contract theory. For it is clear that the contractarian idea can be extended to the choice of more or less an entire ethical system, that is, to a system including principles for all the virtues and not only for justice. Now for the most part I shall consider only principles of justice and others closely related to them; I make no attempt to discuss the virtues in a systematic way. Obviously if justice as fairness succeeds reasonably well, a next step would be to study the more general view suggested by the name "rightness as fairness." But even this wider theory fails to embrace all moral relationships, since it would seem to include only our relations with other persons and to leave out of account how we are to conduct ourselves toward animals and the rest of nature. I do not contend that the contract notion offers a way to approach these questions, which are certainly of the first importance; and I shall have to put them aside. We must recognize the limited scope of justice as fairness and of the general type of view that it exemplifies. How far its conclusions must be revised once these other matters are understood cannot be decided in advance.

The Original Position and Justification

I have said that the original position is the appropriate initial status quo which insures that the fundamental agreements reached in it are fair. This fact yields the name "justice as fairness." It is clear, then, that I want to say that one conception of justice is more reasonable than another, or justifiable with respect to it, if rational persons in the initial situation would choose its principles over those of the other for the role of justice. Conceptions of justice are to be ranked by their acceptability to persons so circumstanced. Understood in this way the question of justification is settled by working out a problem of deliberation: we have to ascertain which principles it would be rational to adopt given the contractual situation. This connects the theory of justice with the theory of rational choice.

If this view of the problem of justification is to succeed, we must, of course, describe in some detail the nature of this choice problem. A problem of rational decision has a definite answer only if we know the beliefs and interests of the parties, their relations with respect to one another, the alternatives between which they are to choose, the procedure whereby they make up their minds, and so on. As the circumstances are presented in different ways, correspondingly different principles are accepted. The concept of the original position, as I shall refer to it, is that of the most philosophically favored interpretation of this initial choice situation for the purposes of a theory of justice.

But how are we to decide what is the most favored interpretation? I assume, for one thing, that there is a broad measure of agreement that principles of justice should be chosen under certain conditions. To justify a particular description of the initial situation one shows that it incorporates these commonly shared presumptions. One argues from widely accepted but weak premises to more specific conclusions. Each of the presumptions should by itself be natural and plausible; some of them may seem innocuous or even trivial. The aim of the contract approach is to establish that taken together they impose significant bounds on acceptable principles of justice. The ideal outcome would be that these conditions determine a unique set of principles; but I shall be satisfied if they suffice to rank the main traditional conceptions of social justice.

One should not be misled, then, by the somewhat unusual conditions which characterize the original position. The idea here is simply to make vivid to ourselves the restrictions that it seems reasonable to impose on arguments for principles of justice, and therefore on these principles themselves. Thus it seems reasonable and generally acceptable that no one should be advantaged or disadvantaged by natural fortune or social circumstances in the choice of principles. It also seems widely agreed that it should be impossible to tailor principles to the circumstances of one's own case. We should ensure further that particular inclinations and aspirations, and persons' conceptions of their good, do not affect the principles adopted. The aim is to rule out those principles that it would be rational to propose for acceptance, however little the chance of success, only if one knew certain things that are irrelevant from the standpoint of justice. For example, if a man knew that he was wealthy, he might find it rational to advance the principle that various taxes for welfare measures be counted unjust; if he knew that he was poor, he would be most likely to propose the contrary principle. To represent the desired restrictions one imagines a situation in which everyone is deprived of this sort of information. One excludes the knowledge of those contingencies which sets men at odds and allows them to be guided by their prejudices. In this manner the veil of ignorance is arrived at in a natural way. This concept should cause no difficulty if we keep in mind the constraints on arguments that it is meant to express. At any time we can enter the original position, so to speak, simply by following a certain procedure, namely, by arguing for principles of justice in accordance with these restrictions.

It seems reasonable to suppose that the parties in the original position are equal. That is, all have the same rights in the procedure for choosing principles; each can make proposals, submit reasons for their acceptance, and so on. Obviously the purpose of these conditions is to represent equality between human beings as moral persons, as creatures having a conception of their good and capable of a sense of justice. The basis of equality is taken to be similar in these two respects. Systems of ends are not ranked in value; and each man is presumed to have the requisite ability to understand and to act upon whatever principles are adopted. Together with the veil of ignorance, these conditions define the principles of justice as those which rational persons concerned to advance their interests would consent to as equals when none are known to be advantaged or disadvantaged by social and natural contingencies.

There is, however, another side to justifying a particular description of the original position. This is to see if the principles which would be chosen match our considered convictions of justice or extend them in an acceptable way. We can note whether applying these principles would lead us to make the same judgments about the basic structure of society which we now make intuitively and in which we have the greatest confidence; or whether, in cases where our present judgments are in doubt and given with hesitation, these principles offer a resolution which we can affirm on reflection. There are questions which we feel sure must be answered in a certain way. For example, we are confident that religious intolerance and racial discrimination are unjust. We think that we have examined these things with care and have reached what we believe is an impartial judgment not likely to be distorted by an excessive attention to our own interests. These convictions are provisional fixed points which we presume any conceptions of justice must fit. But we have much less assurance as to what is the correct distribution of wealth and authority. Here we may be looking for a way to remove our doubts. We can check an interpretation of the initial situation, then, by the capacity of its principles to accommodate our firmest convictions and to provide guidance where guidance is needed.

In searching for the most favored description of this situation we work from both ends. We begin by describing it so that it represents generally shared and preferably weak conditions. We then see if these conditions are strong enough to yield a significant set of principles. If not, we look for further premises equally reasonable. But if so, and these principles match our considered convictions of justice, then so far well and good. But presumably there will be discrepancies. In this case we have a choice. We can either modify the account of the initial situation or we can revise our existing judgments, for even the judgments we take provisionally as fixed points are liable to revision. By going back and forth, sometimes altering the conditions of the contractual circumstances, at others withdrawing our judgments and conforming them to principle, I assume that eventually we shall find a description of the initial situation that both expresses reasonable conditions and yields principles which match our considered judgments duly pruned and adjusted. This state of affairs I refer to as reflective equilibrium.[4] It is an equilibrium because at last our principles and judgments coincide; and it is reflective since we know to what principles our judgments conform and the premises of their derivation. At the moment everything is in order. But this equilibrium is not necessarily stable. It is liable to be upset by further examination of the conditions which should be imposed on the contractual situation and by particular cases which may lead us to revise our judgments. Yet for the time being we have done what we can to render coherent and to justify our convictions of social justice. We have reached a conception of the original position.

I shall not, of course, actually work through this process. Still, we may think of the interpretation of the original position that I shall present as the result of such a hypothetical course of reflection. It represents the attempt to accommodate within one scheme both reasonable philosophical conditions on principles as well as our considered judgments of justice. In arriving at the favored interpretation of the initial situation there is no point at which an appeal is made to self-evidence in the traditional sense either of general conceptions or of particular convictions. I do not claim for the principles of justice proposed that they are necessary truths or derivable from such truths. A conception of justice cannot be deduced from self-evident premises or conditions on principles; instead, its justification is a matter of the mutual support of many considerations, of everything fitting together into one coherent view.

A final comment. We shall want to say that certain principles of justice are justified because they would be agreed to in an initial situation of equality. I have emphasized that this original position is purely hypothetical. It is natural to ask why, if this agreement is never actually entered into, we should take any interest in these principles, moral or otherwise. The answer is that the conditions embodied in the description of the original position are ones that we do in fact accept. Or if we do not, then perhaps we can be persuaded to do so by philosophical reflection. Each aspect of the contractual situation can be given supporting grounds. Thus what we shall do is to collect together into one conception a number of conditions on principles that we are ready upon due consideration to recognize as reasonable. These constraints express what we are prepared to regard as limits on fair terms of social cooperation. One way to look at the idea of the original position, therefore, is to see it as an expository device which sums up the meaning of these conditions and helps us to extract their consequences. On the other hand, this conception is also an intuitive notion that suggests its own elaboration, so that led on by it we are drawn to define more clearly the standpoint from which we can best interpret moral relationships. We need a conception that enables us to envision our objective from afar: the intuitive notion of the original position is to do this for us. . . .

Two Principles of Justice

I shall now state in a provisional form the two principles of justice that I believe would be chosen in the original position. In this section I wish to make only the most general comments, and therefore the first formulation of these principles is tentative. As we go on I shall run through several formulations and approximate step by step the final statement to be given much later [in the book]. I believe that doing this allows the exposition to proceed in a natural way.

The first statement of the two principles reads as follows.
First: each person is to have an equal right to the most extensive basic liberty compatible with a similar liberty for others.
Second: social and economic inequalities are to be arranged so that they are both (a) reasonably expected to be to everyone's advantage, and (b) attached to positions and offices open to all.

By way of general comment, these principles primarily apply, as I have said, to the basic structure of society. They are to govern the assignment of rights and duties and to regulate the distribution of social and economic advantages. As their formulation suggests, these principles presuppose that the social structure can be divided into two more or less distinct parts, the first principle applying to the one, the second to the other. They distinguish between those aspects of the social system that define and secure the equal liberties of citizenship and those that specify and establish social and economic inequalities. The basic liberties of citizens are roughly speaking, political liberty (the right to vote and to be eligible for public office) together with freedom of speech and assembly; liberty of conscience and freedom of thought; freedom of the person along with the right to hold (personal) property; and freedom from arbitrary arrest and seizure as defined by the concept of the rule of law. These liberties are all required to be equal by the first principle, since citizens of a just society are to have the same basic rights.

The second principle applies, in the first approximation, to the distribution of income and wealth and to the design of organizations that make use of differences in authority and responsibility, or chains of command. While the distribution of wealth and income need not be equal, it must be to everyone's advantage, and at the same time, positions of authority and offices of command must be accessible to all. One applies the second principle by holding positions open, and then, subject to this constraint, arranges social and economic inequalities so that everyone benefits.

These principles are to be arranged in a serial order with the first principle prior to the second. This ordering means that a departure from the institutions of equal liberty required by the first principle cannot be justified by, or compensated for, by greater social and economic advantages. The distribution of wealth and income, and the hierarchies of authority, must be consistent with both the liberties of equal citizenship and equality of opportunity.

It is clear that these principles are rather specific in their content, and their acceptance rests on certain assumptions that I must eventually try to explain and justify. A theory of justice depends upon a theory of society in ways that will become evident as we proceed. For the present, it should be observed that the two principles (and this holds for all formulations) are a special case of a more general conception of justice that can be expressed as follows.

> All social values – liberty and opportunity, income and wealth, and the bases of self-respect – are to be distributed equally unless an unequal distribution of any, or all, of these values is to everyone's advantage.

Injustice then, is simply inequalities that are not to the benefit of all. Of course, this conception is extremely vague and requires interpretation.

As a first step, suppose that the basic structure of society distributes certain primary goods, that is, things that every rational man is presumed to want. These goods normally have a use whatever a person's rational plan of life. For simplicity, assume that the chief primary goods at the disposition of society are rights and liberties, powers and opportunities, income and wealth. (Later on in Part Three the primary good of self-respect has a central place.) These are the social primary goods. Other primary goods such as health and vigor, intelligence and imagination, are natural goods; although their possession is influenced by the basic structure, they are not so directly under its control. Imagine, then, a hypothetical initial arrangement in which all the social primary goods are equally distributed: everyone has similar rights and duties, and income and wealth are evenly shared. This state of affairs provides a benchmark for judging improvements. If certain inequalities of wealth and organizational powers would make everyone better off than in this hypothetical starting situation, then they accord with the general conception.

Now it is possible, at least theoretically, that by giving up some of their fundamental liberties men are sufficiently compensated by the resulting social and economic gains. The general conception of justice imposes no restrictions on what sort of inequalities are permissible; it only requires that everyone's position be improved. We need not suppose anything so drastic as consenting to a condition of slavery. Imagine instead that men forgo certain political rights when the economic returns are significant and their capacity to influence the course of policy by the exercise of these rights would be marginal in any case. It is this kind of exchange which the two principles as stated rule out; being arranged in serial order they do not permit exchanges between basic liberties and economic and social gains. The serial ordering of principles expresses an underlying preference among primary social goods. When this preference is rational, so likewise is the choice of these principles in this order.

In developing justice as fairness I shall, for the most part, leave aside the general conception of justice and examine instead the special case of the two principles in serial order. The advantage of this procedure is that from the first the matter of priorities is recognized and an effort made to find principles to deal with it. One is led to attend throughout to the conditions under which the acknowledgement of the absolute weight of liberty with respect to social and economic advantages, as defined by the lexical order of the two principles, would be reasonable. Offhand, this ranking appears extreme and too special a case to be of much interest; but there is more justification for it than would appear at first sight. Or at any rate, so I shall maintain. Furthermore, the distinction between fundamental rights and liberties and economic and social benefits marks a difference among primary social goods that one should try to exploit. It suggests an important division in the social system. Of course, the distinctions drawn and the ordering proposed are bound to be at best only approximations. There are surely circumstances in which they fail. But it is essential to depict clearly the main lines of a reasonable concept of justice; and under many conditions anyway, the two principles in serial order may serve well enough. When necessary we can fall back on the more general conception.

The fact that the two principles apply to institutions has certain consequences. Several points illustrate this. First of all, the rights and liberties referred to by these principles are those which are defined by the public rules of the basic structure. Whether men are free is determined by the rights and duties established by the major institutions of society. Liberty is a certain pattern of social forms. The first principle simply requires that certain sorts of rules, those defining basic liberties, apply to everyone equally and that they allow the most extensive liberty compatible with a like liberty for all. The only reason for circumscribing the rights defining liberty and making men's freedom less extensive than it might otherwise be is that these equal rights as institutionally defined would interfere with one another.

Another thing to bear in mind is that when principles mention persons, or require that everyone gain from an inequality, the reference is to representative persons holding the various social positions, or offices, or whatever, established by the basic structure. Thus in applying the second principle I assume that it is possible to assign an expectation of well-being to representative individuals holding these positions. This expectation indicates their life prospects as viewed from their social station. In general, the expectations of representative persons depend upon the distribution of rights and duties throughout the basic structure. When this changes, expectations change. I assume, then, that expectations are connected: by raising the prospects of the representative man in one position we presumably increase or decrease the prospects of representative men in other positions. Since it applies to institutional forms, the second principle (or rather the first part of it) refers to the expectations of representative individuals. As I shall discuss below, neither principle applies to distributions of particular goods to particular individuals who may be identified by their proper names. The situation where someone is considering how to allocate certain commodities to needy persons who are known to him is not within the scope of the principles. They are meant to regulate basic institutional arrangements. We must not assume that there is much similarity from the standpoint of justice between an administrative allotment of goods to specific persons and the appropriate design of society. Our common-sense intuitions for the former may be a poor guide to the latter.

Now the second principle insists that each person benefit from permissible inequalities in the basic structure. This means that it must be reasonable for each relevant representative man defined by this structure, when he views it as a going concern, to prefer his prospects with the inequality to his prospects without it. One is not allowed to justify differences in income or organizational powers on the ground that the disadvantages of those in one position are outweighed by the greater advantages of those in another. Much less can infringements of liberty be counterbalanced in this way. Applied to the basic structure, the principle of utility would have us maximize the sum of expectations of representative men (weighted by the number of persons they represent, on the classical view); and this would permit us to compensate for the losses of some by the gains of others. Instead, the two principles require that everyone benefit from economic and social inequalities. It is obvious, however, that there are indefinitely many ways in which all may be advantaged when the initial arrangement of equality is taken as a benchmark. How then are we to choose among these possibilities? The principles must be specified so that they yield a determinate conclusion. I now turn to this problem. . . .

The Reasoning Leading to the Two Principles of Justice

In this section I take up the choice between the two principles of justice and the principle of average utility. Determining the rational preference between these two options is perhaps the central problem in developing the conception of justice as fairness as a viable alternative to the utilitarian tradition. I shall begin in this section by presenting some intuitive remarks favoring the two principles. I shall also discuss briefly the qualitative structure of the argument that needs to be made if the case for these principles is to be conclusive.

It will be recalled that the general conception of justice as fairness requires that all primary social goods be distributed equally unless an unequal distribution would be to everyone's advantage. No restrictions are placed on exchanges of these goods and therefore a lesser liberty can be compensated for by greater social and economic benefits. Now looking at the situation from the standpoint of one person selected arbitrarily, there is no way for him to win special advantages for himself. Nor, on the other hand, are there grounds for his acquiescing in special disadvantages. Since it is not reasonable for him to expect more than an equal share in the division of social goods, and since it is not rational for him to agree to less, the sensible thing for him to do is to acknowledge as the first principle of justice one requiring an equal distribution. Indeed, this principle is so obvious that we would expect it to occur to anyone immediately.

Thus, the parties start with a principle establishing equal liberty for all, including equality of opportunity, as well as an equal distribution of income and wealth. But there is no reason why this acknowledgment should be final. If there are inequalities in the basic structure that work to make everyone better off in comparison with the benchmark of initial equality, why not permit them? The immediate gain which a greater equality might allow can be regarded as intelligently invested in view of its future return. If, for example, these inequalities set up various incentives which succeed in eliciting more productive efforts, a person in the original position may look upon them as necessary to cover the costs of training and to encourage effective performance. One might think that ideally individuals should want to serve one another. But since the parties are assumed not to take an interest in one another's interests, their acceptance of these inequalities is only the acceptance of the relations in which men stand in the circumstances of justice. They have no grounds for complaining of one another's motives. A person in the original position would, therefore, concede the justice of these inequalities. Indeed, it would be shortsighted of him not to do so. He would hesitate to agree to these regularities only if he would be dejected by the bare knowledge or perception that others were better situated; and I have assumed that the parties decide as if they are not moved by envy. In order to make the principle regulating inequalities determinate, one looks at the system from the standpoint of the least advantaged representative person. Inequalities are permissible when they maximize, or at least all contribute to, the long-term expectations of the least fortunate group in society.

Now this general conception imposes no constraints on what sorts of inequalities are allowed, whereas the special conception, by putting the two principles in serial order (with the necessary adjustments in meaning), forbids exchanges between basic liberties and economic and social benefits. I shall not try to justify this ordering here. But roughly, the idea underlying this ordering is that if the parties assume that their basic liberties can be effectively exercised, they will not exchange a lesser liberty for an improvement in economic well-being. It is only when social conditions do not allow the effective establishment of these rights that one can concede their limitation; and these restrictions can be granted only to the extent that they are necessary to prepare the way for a free society. The denial of equal liberty can be defended only if it is necessary to raise the level of civilization so that in due course these freedoms can be enjoyed. Thus in adopting a serial order we are in effect making a special assumption in the original position, namely, that the parties know that the conditions of their society, whatever they are, admit the effective realization of the equal liberties. The serial ordering of the two principles of justice eventually comes to be reasonable if the general conception is consistently followed. This lexical ranking is the long-run tendency of the general view. For the most part I shall assume that the requisite circumstances for the serial order obtain.

It seems clear from these remarks that the two principles are at least a plausible conception of justice. The question, though, is how one is to argue for them more systematically. Now there are several things to do. One can work out their consequences for institutions and note their implications for fundamental social policy. In this way they are tested by a comparison with our considered judgments of justice. Part II is devoted to this. But one can also try to find arguments in their favor that are decisive from the standpoint of the original position. In order to see how this might be done, it is useful as a heuristic device to think of the two principles as the maximin solution to the problem of social justice. There is an analogy between the two principles and the maximin rule for choice under uncertainty.[6] This is evident from the fact that the two principles are those a person would choose for the design of a society in which his enemy is to assign him his place. The maximin rule tells us to rank alternatives by their worst possible outcomes: we are to adopt the alternative the worst outcome of which is superior to the worst outcomes of the others. The persons in the original position do not, of course, assume that their initial place in society is decided by a malevolent opponent. As I note below, they should not reason from false premises. The veil of ignorance does not violate this idea, since an absence of information is not misinformation. But that the two principles of justice would be chosen if the parties were forced to protect themselves against such a contingency explains the sense in which this conception is the maximin solution. And this analogy suggests that if the original position has been described so that it is rational for the parties to adopt the conservative attitude expressed by

	Circumstances		
Decisions	c_1	c_2	c_3
d_1	−7	8	12
d_2	−8	7	14
d_3	5	6	8

this rule, a conclusive argument can indeed be constructed for these principles. Clearly the maximin rule is not, in general, a suitable guide for choices under uncertainty. But it is attractive in situations marked by certain special features. My aim, then, is to show that a good case can be made for the two principles based on the fact that the original position manifests these features to the fullest possible degree, carrying them to the limit, so to speak.

Consider the gain-and-loss table shown here. It represents the gains and losses for a situation which is not a game of strategy. There is no one playing against the person making the decision; instead he is faced with several possible circumstances which may or may not obtain. Which circumstances happen to exist does not depend upon what the person choosing decides or whether he announces his moves in advance. The numbers in the table are monetary values (in hundreds of dollars) in comparison with some initial situation. The gain (g) depends upon the individual's decision (d) and the circumstances (c). Thus g = f (d, c). Assuming that there are three possible decisions and three possible circumstances, we might have this gain-and-loss table.

The maximin rule requires that we make the third decision. For in this case the worst that can happen is that one gains 500 dollars, which is better than the worst for the other actions. If we adopt one of these we may lose either 800 or 700 dollars. Thus, the choice of d_3 maximizes f (d, c) for that value of c, which for a given d, minimizes f. The term "maximin" means the *maximum minimorum*; and the rule directs our attention to the worst that can happen under any proposed course of action, and directs us to decide in the light of that.

Now there appear to be three chief features of situations that give plausibility to this unusual rule.[7] First, since the rule takes no account of the likelihoods of the possible circumstances, there must be some reason for sharply discounting estimates of these probabilities. Offhand, the most natural rule of choice would seem to be to compute the expectation of monetary gain for each decision and then to adopt the course of action with the highest prospect. (This expectation is defined as follows: let us suppose that g_{ij} represents the numbers in the gain-and-loss table, where i is the row index and j is the column index; and let p_j, j = 1, 2, 3, be the likelihoods of the circumstances, with $\Sigma p_j = 1$. Then the expectation for the ith decision is equal to $\Sigma p_j g_{ij}$.) Thus it must be, for example, that the situation is one in which a knowledge of likelihoods is impossible, or at best extremely insecure. In this case it is unreasonable not to be skeptical of probabilistic calculations unless there is no other way out, particularly if the decision is a fundamental one that needs to be justified to others.

The second feature that suggests the maximin rule is the following: the person choosing has a conception of the good such that he cares very little, if anything, for what he might gain above the minimum stipend that he can, in fact, be sure of by following the maximin rule. It is not worthwhile for him to take a chance for the sake of a further advantage, especially when it may turn out that he loses much that is important to him. This last provision brings in the third feature, namely, that the rejected alternatives have outcomes that one can hardly accept. The situation involves grave risks. Of course these features work most effectively in combination. The paradigm situation for following the maximin rule is when all three features are realized to the highest degree. This rule does not, then, generally apply, nor of course is it self-evident. Rather, it is a maxim, a rule of thumb, that comes into its own in special circumstances. Its application depends upon the qualitative structure of the possible gains and losses in relation to one's conception of the good, all this against a background in which it is reasonable to discount conjectural estimates of likelihoods.

It should be noted, as the comments on the gain-and-loss table say, that the entries in the table represent monetary values and not utilities. This difference is significant since for one thing computing expectations on the basis of such objective values is not the same thing as computing expected utility and may lead to different results. The essential point though is that in justice as fairness the parties do not know their conception of the good and cannot estimate their utility in the ordinary sense. In any case, we want to go behind de facto preferences generated by given conditions. Therefore expectations are based upon an index of primary goods and the parties make their choice accordingly. The entries in the example are in terms of money and not utility to indicate this aspect of the contract doctrine.

Now, as I have suggested, the original position has been defined so that it is a situation in which the maximin rule applies. In order to see this, let us review briefly the nature of this situation with these three special features in mind. To begin with, the veil of ignorance excludes all but the vaguest knowledge of likelihoods. The parties have no basis for determining the probable nature of their society, or their place in it. Thus they have strong reasons for being wary of probability calculations if any other course is open to them. They must also take into account the fact that their choice of principles should seem reasonable to others, in particular their descendants, whose rights will be deeply affected by it. There are further grounds for discounting that I shall mention as we go along. For the present it suffices to note that these considerations are strengthened by the fact that the parties know very little about the gain-and-loss table. Not only are they unable to conjecture the likelihoods of the various possible circumstances, they cannot say much about what the possible circumstances are, much less enumerate them and foresee the outcome of each alternative available. Those deciding are much more in the dark than the illustration by a numerical table suggests. It is for this reason that I have spoken of an analogy with the maximin rule.

Several kinds of arguments for the two principles of justice illustrate the second feature. Thus, if we can maintain that these principles provide a workable theory of social justice, and that they are compatible with reasonable demands of efficiency, then this conception guarantees a satisfactory minimum. There may be, on reflection, little reason for trying to do better. Thus much of the argument, especially in Part Two, is to show, by their application to the main questions of social justice, that the two principles are a satisfactory conception. These details have a philosophical purpose. Moreover, this line of thought is practically decisive if we can establish the priority of liberty, the lexical ordering of the two principles. For this priority implies that the persons in the original position have no desire to try for greater gains at the expense of the equal liberties. The minimum assured by the two principles in lexical order is not one that the parties wish to jeopardize for the sake of greater economic and social advantages.

Finally, the third feature holds if we can assume that other conceptions of justice may lead to institutions that the parties would find intolerable. For example, it has sometimes been held that under some conditions the utility principle (in either form) justifies, if not slavery or serfdom, at any rate serious infractions of liberty for the sake of greater social benefits. We need not consider here the truth of this claim, or the likelihood that the requisite conditions obtain. For the moment, this contention is only to illustrate the way in which conceptions of justice may allow for outcomes which the parties may not be able to accept. And having the ready alternative of the two principles of justice which secure a satisfactory minimum, it seems unwise, if not irrational, for them to take a chance that these outcomes are not realized. . . .

Notes

1   As the text suggests, I shall regard Locke's *Second Treatise of Government*, Rousseau's *The Social Contract*, and Kant's ethical works beginning with *The Foundations of the Metaphysics of Morals* as definitive of the contract tradition. For all of its greatness, Hobbes's *Leviathan* raises special problems. A general historical survey is provided by J. W. Gough, *The Social Contract*, 2nd edn (Oxford: Clarendon Press, 1957); and Otto Gierke, *Natural Law and the Theory of Society*, trans. with an introduction by Ernest Barker (Cambridge: Cambridge University Press, 1934). A presentation of the contract view as primarily an ethical theory is to be found in G. R. Grice, *The Grounds of Moral Judgment* (Cambridge: Cambridge University Press, 1967).

2   Kant is clear that the original agreement is hypothetical. See *The Metaphysics of Morals*, pt I (*Rechtslehre*), especially paragraphs 47, 52; and pt II of the essay "Concerning the Common Saying: This May Be True in Theory but It Does Not Apply in Practice," in *Kant's Political Writings*, ed. Hans Reiss and trans. H. B. Nisbet (Cambridge: Cambridge University Press, 1970), pp. 73–87. See Georges Vlachos, *La Pensée politique de Kant* (Paris: Presses Universitaires de France, 1962), pp. 326–35; and J. G. Murphy, *Kant: The Philosophy of Right* (London: Macmillan, 1970), pp. 109–12, 133–6, for a further discussion.

3   For the formulation of this intuitive idea I am indebted to Allan Gibbard.

4   The process of mutual adjustment of principles and considered judgments is not peculiar to moral philosophy. See Nelson Goodman, *Fact, Fiction, and Forecast* (Cambridge: MA: Harvard University Press, 1955), pp. 65–8, for parallel remarks concerning the justification of the principles of deductive and inductive inference.

5   For a similar view, see B. A. O. Williams, "The Idea of Equality," *Philosophy, Politics, and Society*, Second Series, ed. Peter Laslett and W. G. Runciman (Oxford: Basil Blackwell, 1962), p. 113.

6   An accessible discussion of this and other rules of choice under uncertainty can be found in W. J. Baumol, *Economic Theory and Operations Analysis*, 2nd edn (Englewood Cliffs, NJ: Prentice-Hall, 1965), chapter 24. Baumol gives a geometric interpretation of these rules, including the diagram used in paragraph 13 to illustrate the difference principle. See pp. 558–62. See also R. D. Luce and Howard Raiffa, *Games and Decisions* (New York: John Wiley and Sons, 1957), chapter XIII, for a fuller account.

7   Here I borrow from William Fellner, *Probability and Profit* (Homewood, IL: R. D. Irwin, 1965), pp. 140–2, where these features are noted.

50

The Entitlement Theory of Justice

Robert Nozick

The minimal state is the most extensive state that can be justified. Any state more extensive violates people's rights. Yet many persons have put forth reasons purporting to justify a more extensive state. It is impossible [here] to examine all the reasons that have been put forth. Therefore, I shall focus upon those generally acknowledged to be most weighty and influential, to see precisely wherein they fail. In this chapter we consider the claim that a more extensive state is justified, because necessary (or the best instrument) to achieve distributive justice . . .

The term "distributive justice" is not a neutral one. Hearing the term "distribution," most people presume that some thing or mechanism uses some principle or criterion to give out a supply of things. Into this process of distributing shares some error may have crept. So it is an open question, at least, whether *re*distribution should take place; whether we should do again what has already been done once, though poorly. However, we are not in the position of children who have been given portions of pie by someone who now makes last minute adjustments to rectify careless cutting. There is no *central* distribution, no person or group entitled to control all the resources, jointly deciding how they are to be doled out. What each person gets, he gets from others who give to him in exchange for something, or as a gift. In a free society, diverse persons control different resources, and new holdings arise out of the voluntary exchanges and actions of persons. There is no more a distributing or distribution of shares than there is a distributing of mates in a society in which persons choose whom they shall marry. The total result is the product of many individual decisions which the different individuals involved are entitled to make. Some uses of the term "distribution," it is true, do not imply a previous distributing appropriately judged by some criterion (for example, "probability distribution"): nevertheless, despite the title of this chapter, it would be best to use a terminology that clearly is neutral. We shall speak of people's holdings; a principle of justice in holdings describes (part of) what justice tells us (requires) about holdings. I shall state first what I take to be the correct view about justice in holdings, and then turn to the discussion of alternate views.

The subject of justice in holdings consists of three major topics. The first is the *original acquisition of holdings*, the appropriation of unheld things. This includes the issues of how unheld things may come to be held, the process, or processes, by which unheld things may come to be held, the things that may come to be held by these processes, the extent of what comes to be held by a particular process, and so on. We shall refer to the complicated truth about this topic, which we shall not formulate here, as the principle of justice in acquisition.

The second topic concerns the *transfer of holdings* from one person to another. By what processes may a person transfer holdings to another? How may a person acquire a holding from another who holds it? Under this topic come general descriptions of voluntary exchange, and gift and (on the other hand) fraud, as well as reference to particular conventional details fixed upon in a given society. The complicated truth about this subject (with placeholders for conventional details) we shall call the principle of justice in transfer. (And we shall suppose it also includes principles governing how a person may divest himself of a holding, passing it into an unheld state.)

If the world were wholly just, the following inductive definition would exhaustively cover the subject of justice in holdings.

1. A person who acquires a holding in accordance with the principle of justice in acquisition is entitled to that holding.
2. A person who acquires a holding in accordance with the principle of justice in transfer, from someone else entitled to the holding, is entitled to the holding.
3. No one is entitled to a holding except by (repeated) applications of 1 and 2.

The complete principle of distributive justice would say simply that a distribution is just if everyone is entitled to the holdings they possess under the distribution.

A distribution is just if it arises from another just distribution by legitimate means. The legitimate means of moving from one distribution to another are specified by the principle of justice in transfer. The legitimate first "moves" are specified by the principle of justice in acquisition.[1] Whatever arises from a just situation by just steps is itself just. The means of change specified by the principle of justice in transfer preserve justice. As correct rules of inference are truth-preserving, and any conclusion deduced via repeated application of such rules from only true premises is itself true, so the means of transition from one situation to another specified by the principle of justice in transfer are justice-preserving, and any situation actually arising from repeated transitions in accordance with the principle from a just situation is itself just. The parallel between justice-preserving transformations and truth-preserving transformations illuminates where it fails as well as where it holds. That a conclusion could have been deduced by truth-preserving means from premises that are true suffices to show its truth. That from a just situation a situation *could* have arisen via justice-preserving means does *not* suffice to show its justice. The fact that a thief's victims voluntarily *could* have presented him with gifts does not entitle the thief to his ill-gotten gains. Justice in holdings is historical; it depends upon what actually has happened. We shall return to this point later.

Not all actual situations are generated in accordance with the two principles of justice in holdings: the principle of justice in acquisition and the principle of justice in transfer. Some people steal from others, or defraud them, or enslave them, seizing their product and preventing them from living as they choose, or forcibly exclude others from competing in exchanges. None of these are permissible modes of transition from one situation to another. And some persons acquire holdings by means not sanctioned by the principle of justice in acquisition.

The existence of past injustice (previous violations of the first two principles of justice in holdings) raises the third major topic under justice in holdings: the rectification of injustice in holdings. If past injustice has shaped present holdings in various ways, some identifiable and some not, what now, if anything, ought to be done to rectify these injustices? What obligations do the performers of injustice have toward those whose position is worse than it would have been had the injustice not been done? Or, than it would have been had compensation been paid promptly? How, if at all, do things change if the beneficiaries and those made worse off are not the direct parties in the act of injustice, but, for example, their descendants? Is an injustice done to someone whose holding was itself based upon an unrectified injustice? How far back must one go in wiping clean the historical slate of injustices? What may victims of injustice permissibly do in order to rectify the injustices being done to them, including the many injustices done by persons acting through their government? I do not know of a thorough or theoretically sophisticated treatment of such issues. Idealizing greatly, let us suppose theoretical investigation will produce a principle of rectification. This principle uses historical information about previous situations and injustices done in them (as defined by the first two principles of justice and rights against interference), and information about the actual course of events that flowed from these injustices, until the present, and it yields a description (or descriptions) of holdings in the society. The principle of rectification presumably will make use of its best estimate of subjunctive information about what would have occurred (or a probability distribution over what might have occurred, using the expected value) if the injustice had not taken place. If the actual description of holdings turns out not to be one of the descriptions yielded by the principle, then one of the descriptions yielded must be realized.[2]

The general outlines of the theory of justice in holdings are that the holdings of a person are just if he is entitled to them by the principles of justice in acquisition and transfer, or by the principle of rectification of injustice (as specified by the first two principles). If each person's holdings are just, then the total set (distribution) of holdings is just. To turn these general outlines into a specific theory we would have to specify the details of each of the three principles of justice in holdings: the principle of acquisition of holdings, the principle of transfer of holdings, and the principle of rectification of violations of the first two principles. I shall not attempt that task here.

Historical principles and end-result principles

The general outlines of the entitlement theory illuminate the nature and defects of other conceptions of distributive justice. The entitlement theory of justice in distribution is *historical*; whether a distribution is just depends upon how it came about. In contrast, *current time-slice principles* of justice hold that the justice of a distribution is determined by how things are distributed (who has what) as judged by some *structural* principle(s) of just distribution. A utilitarian who judges between any two distributions by seeing which has the greater sum of utility and, if the sums tie, applies some fixed equality criterion to choose the more equal distribution, would hold a current time-slice principle of justice. As would someone who had a fixed schedule of trade-offs between the sum of happiness and equality. According to a current time-slice principle, all that needs to be looked at, in judging the justice of a distribution, is who ends up with what; in comparing any two distributions one need look only at the matrix presenting the distributions. No further information need be fed into a principle of justice. It is a consequence of such principles of justice that any two structurally identical distributions are equally just. (Two distributions are structurally identical if they present the same profile, but perhaps have different persons occupying the particular slots. My having ten and your having five, and my having five and your having ten are structurally identical distributions.) Welfare economics is the theory of current time-slice principles of justice. The subject is conceived as operating on matrices representing only current information about distribution. This, as well as some of the usual conditions (for example, the choice of distribution is invariant under relabeling of columns), guarantees that welfare economics will be a current time-slice theory, with all of its inadequacies.

Most persons do not accept current time-slice principles as constituting the whole story about distributive shares. They think it relevant in assessing the justice of a situation to consider not only the distribution it embodies, but also how that distribution came about. If some persons are in prison for murder or war crimes, we do not say that to assess the justice of the distribution in the society we must look only at what this person has, and that person has, and that person has, . . . at the current time. We think it relevant to ask whether someone did something so that he *deserved* to be punished, deserved to have a lower share. Most will agree to the relevance of further information with regard to punishments and penalties. Consider also desired things. One traditional socialist view is that workers are entitled to the product and full fruits of their labor; they have earned it; a distribution is unjust if it does not give the workers what they are entitled to. Such entitlements are based upon some past history. No socialist holding this view would find it comforting to be told that because the actual distribution A happens to coincide structurally with the one he desires D, A therefore is no less just than D; it differs only in that the "parasitic" owners of capital receive under A what the workers are entitled to under D, and the workers receive under A what the owners are entitled to under D, namely very little. This socialist rightly, in my view, holds onto the notions of earning, producing, entitlement, desert, and so forth, and he rejects current time-slice principles that look only to the structure of the resulting set of holdings. (The set of holdings resulting from what? Isn't it implausible that how holdings are produced and come to exist has no effect at all on who should hold what?) His mistake lies in his view of what entitlements arise out of what sorts of productive processes.

We construe the position we discuss too narrowly by speaking of *current* time-slice principles. Nothing is changed if structural principles operate upon a time sequence of current time-slice profiles and, for example, give someone more now to counterbalance the less he has had earlier. A utilitarian or an egalitarian or any mixture of the two over time will inherit the difficulties of his more myopic comrades. He is not helped by the fact that *some* of the information others consider relevant in assessing a distribution is reflected, unrecoverably, in past matrices. Henceforth, we shall refer to such unhistorical principles of distributive justice, including the current time-slice principles, as *end-result principles* or *end-state principles*.

In contrast to end-result principles of justice, *historical principles* of justice hold that past circumstances or actions of people can create differential entitlements or differential deserts to things. An injustice can be worked by moving from one distribution to another structurally identical one, for the second, in profile the same, may violate people's entitlements or deserts; it may not fit the actual history.

Patterning

The entitlement principles of justice in holdings that we have sketched are historical principles of justice. To better understand their precise character, we shall distinguish them from another subclass of the historical principles. Consider, as an example, the principle of distribution according to moral merit. This principle requires that total distributive shares vary directly with moral merit; no person should have a greater share than anyone whose moral merit is greater. (If moral merit could be not merely ordered but measured on an interval or ratio scale, stronger principles could be formulated.) Or consider the principle that results by substituting "usefulness to society" for "moral merit" in the previous principle. Or instead of "distribute according to moral merit," or "distribute according to usefulness to society," we might consider "distribute according to the weighted sum of moral merit, usefulness to society, and need," with the weights of the different dimensions equal. Let us call a principle of distribution *patterned* if it specifies that a distribution is to vary along with some natural dimension, weighted sum of natural dimensions, or lexicographic ordering of natural dimensions. And let us say a distribution is patterned if it accords with some patterned principle. (I speak of natural dimensions, admittedly without a general criterion for them, because for any set of holdings some artificial dimensions can be gimmicked up to vary along with the distribution of the set.) The principle of distribution in accordance with moral merit is a patterned historical principle, which specifies a patterned distribution. "Distribute according to IQ" is a patterned principle that looks to information not contained in distributional matrices. It is not historical, however, in that it does not look to any past actions creating differential entitlements to evaluate a distribution; it requires only distributional matrices whose columns are labeled by IQ scores. The distribution in a society, however, may be composed of such simple patterned distributions, without itself being simply patterned. Different sectors may operate different patterns, or some combination of patterns may operate in different proportions across a society. A distribution composed in this manner, from a small number of patterned distributions, we also shall term "patterned." And we extend the use of "pattern" to include the overall designs put forth by combinations of end-state principles.

Almost every suggested principle of distributive justice is patterned: to each according to his moral merit, or needs, or marginal product, or how hard he tries, or the weighted sum of the foregoing, and so on. The principle of entitlement we have sketched is *not* patterned.[3] There is no one natural dimension or weighted sum or combination of a small number of natural dimensions that yields the distributions generated in accordance with the principle of entitlement. The set of holdings that results when some persons receive their marginal products, others win at gambling, others receive a share of their mate's income, others receive gifts from foundations, others receive interest on loans, others receive gifts from admirers, others receive returns on investment, others make for themselves much of what they have, others find things, and so on, will not be patterned. Heavy strands of patterns will run through it; significant portions of the variance in holdings will be accounted for by pattern-variables. If most people most of the time choose to transfer some of their entitlements to others only in exchange for something from them, then a large part of what many people hold will vary with what they held that others wanted. More details are provided by the theory of marginal productivity. But gifts to relatives, charitable donations, bequests to children, and the like, are not best conceived, in the first instance, in this manner. Ignoring the strands of pattern, let us suppose for the moment that a distribution actually arrived at by the operation of the principle of entitlement is random with respect to any pattern.

Though the resulting set of holdings will be unpatterned, it will not be incomprehensible, for it can be seen as arising from the operation of a small number of principles. These principles specify how an initial distribution may arise (the principle of acquisition of holdings) and how distributions may be transformed into others (the principle of transfer of holdings). The process whereby the set of holdings is generated will be intelligible, though the set of holdings itself that results from this process will be unpatterned.

The writings of F. A. Hayek focus less than is usually done upon what patterning distributive justice requires. Hayek argues that we cannot know enough about each person's situation to distribute to each according to his moral merit (but would justice demand we do so if we did have this knowledge?); and he goes on to say, "our objection is against all attempts to impress upon society a deliberately chosen pattern of distribution, whether it be an order of equality or of inequality." However, Hayek concludes that in a free society there will be distribution in accordance with value rather than with moral merit; that is, in accordance with the perceived value of a person's actions and services to others. Despite his rejection of a patterned conception of distributive justice, Hayek himself suggests a pattern he thinks justifiable: distribution in accordance with the perceived benefits given to others, leaving room for the complaint that a free society does not realize exactly this pattern. Stating this patterned strand of a free capitalist society more precisely, we get "To each according to how much he benefits others who have the resources for benefiting those who benefit them." This will seem arbitrary unless some acceptable initial set of holdings is specified, or unless it is held that the operation of the system over time washes out any significant effects from the initial set of holdings. As an example of the latter, if almost anyone would have bought a car from Henry Ford, the supposition that it was an arbitrary matter who held the money then (and so bought) would not place Henry Ford's earnings under a cloud. In any event, *his* coming to hold it is not arbitrary. Distribution according to benefits to others *is* a major patterned strand in a free capitalist society, as Hayek correctly points out, but it is only a strand and does not constitute the whole pattern of a system of entitlements (namely, inheritance, gifts for arbitrary reasons, charity, and so on) or a standard that one should insist a society fit.

Will people tolerate for long a system yielding distributions that they believe are unpatterned? No doubt people will not long accept a distribution they believe is *unjust*. People want their society to be and to look just. But must the look of justice reside in a resulting pattern rather than in the underlying generating principles? We are in no position to conclude that the inhabitants of a society embodying an entitlement conception of justice in holdings will find it unacceptable. Still, it must be granted that were people's reasons for transferring some of their holdings to others always irrational or arbitrary, we would find this disturbing. (Suppose people always determined what holdings they would transfer, and to whom, by using a random device.) We feel more comfortable upholding the justice of an entitlement system if most of the transfers under it are done for reasons. This does not mean necessarily that all deserve what holdings they receive. It means only that there is a purpose or point to someone's transferring a holding to one person rather than to another; that usually we can see what the transferrer thinks he's gaining, what cause he thinks he's serving, what goals he thinks he's helping to achieve, and so forth. Since in a capitalist society people often transfer holdings to others in accordance with how much they perceive these others benefiting them, the fabric constituted by the individual transactions and transfers is largely reasonable and intelligible.[4] (Gifts to loved ones, bequests to children, charity to the needy also are nonarbitrary components of the fabric.) In stressing the large strand of distribution in accordance with benefit to others, Hayek shows the point of many transfers, and so shows that the system of transfer of entitlements is not just spinning its gears aimlessly. The system of entitlements is defensible when constituted by the individual aims of individual transactions. No overarching aim is needed, no distributional pattern is required.

To think that the task of a theory of distributive justice is to fill in the blank in "to each according to his ——" is to be predisposed to search for a pattern; and the separate treatment of "from each according to his ——" treats production and distribution as two separate and independent issues. On an entitlement view these are *not* two separate questions. Whoever makes something, having bought or contracted for all other held resources used in the process (transferring some of his holdings for these cooperating factors), is entitled to it. The situation is *not* one of something's getting made, and there being an open question of who is to get it. Things come into the world already attached to people having entitlements over them. From the point of view of the historical entitlement conception of justice in holdings, those who start afresh to complete "to each according to his ——" treat objects as if they appeared from nowhere, out of nothing. A complete theory of justice might cover this limit case as well; perhaps here is a use for the usual conceptions of distributive justice.

So entrenched are maxims of the usual form that perhaps we should present the entitlement conception as a competitor. Ignoring acquisition and rectification, we might say:

> From each according to what he chooses to do, to each according to what he makes for himself (perhaps with the contracted aid of others) and what others choose to do for him and choose to give him of what they've been given previously (under this maxim) and haven't yet expended or transferred.

This, the discerning reader will have noticed, has its defects as a slogan. So as a summary and great simplification (and not as a maxim with any independent meaning) we have:

> *From each as they choose, to each as they are chosen.*

How liberty upsets patterns

It is not clear how those holding alternative conceptions of distributive justice can reject the entitlement conception of justice in holdings. For suppose a distribution favored by one of these non-entitlement conceptions is realized. Let us suppose it is your favorite one and let us call this distribution D_1; perhaps everyone has an equal share, perhaps shares vary in accordance with some dimension you treasure. Now suppose that Wilt Chamberlain is greatly in demand by basketball teams, being a great gate attraction. (Also suppose contracts run only for a year, with players being free agents.) He signs the following sort of contract with a team: In each home game, twenty-five cents from the price of each ticket of admission goes to him. (We ignore the question of whether he is "gouging" the owners, letting them look out for themselves.) The season starts, and people cheerfully attend his team's games; they buy their tickets, each time dropping a separate twenty-five cents of their admission price into a special box with Chamberlain's name on it. They are excited about seeing him play; it is worth the total admission price to them. Let us suppose that in one season one million persons attend his home games, and Wilt Chamberlain winds up with $250,000, a much larger sum than the average income and larger even than anyone else has.

Is he entitled to this income? Is this new distribution D_2, unjust? If so, why? There is *no* question about whether each of the people was entitled to the control over the resources they held in D_1; because that was the distribution (your favorite) that (for the purposes of argument) we assumed was acceptable. Each of these persons *chose* to give twenty-five cents of their money to Chamberlain. They could have spent it on going to the movies, or on candy bars, or on copies of *Dissent* magazine, or of *Monthly Review*. But they all, at least one million of them, converged on giving it to Wilt Chamberlain in exchange for watching him play basketball. If D_1 was a just distribution, and people voluntarily moved from it to D_2, transferring parts of their shares they were given under D_1 (what was it for if not to do something with?), isn't D_2 also just? If the people were entitled to dispose of the resources to which they were entitled (under D_1), didn't this include their being entitled to give it to, or exchange it with, Wilt Chamberlain? Can anyone else complain on grounds of justice? Each other person already has his legitimate share under D_1. Under D_1, there is nothing that anyone has that anyone else has a claim of justice against. After someone transfers something to Wilt Chamberlain, third parties *still* have their legitimate shares; *their* shares are not changed. By what process could such a transfer among two persons give rise to a legitimate claim of distributive justice on a portion of what was transferred, by a third party who had no claim of justice on any holding of the others *before* the transfer?[5] To cut off objections irrelevant here, we might imagine the exchanges occurring in a socialist society, after hours. After playing whatever basketball he does in his daily work, or doing whatever other daily work he does, Wilt Chamberlain decides to put in *overtime* to earn additional money. (First his work quota is set; he works time over that.) Or imagine it is a skilled juggler people like to see, who puts on shows after hours.

Why might someone work overtime in a society in which it is assumed their needs are satisfied? Perhaps because they care about things other than needs. I like to write in books that I read, and to have easy access to books for browsing at odd hours. It would be very pleasant and convenient to have the resources of Widener Library in my back yard. No society, I assume, will provide such resources close to each person who would like them as part of his regular allotment (under D_1). Thus, persons either must do without some extra things that they want, or must be allowed to do something extra to get some of these things. On what basis could the inequalities that would eventuate be forbidden? Notice also that small factories would spring up in a socialist society, unless forbidden. I melt down some of my personal possessions (under D_1) and build a machine out of the material. I offer you, and others, a philosophy lecture once a week in exchange for your cranking the handle on my machine, whose products I exchange for yet other things, and so on. (The raw materials used by the machine are given to me by others who possess them under D_1, in exchange for hearing lectures.) Each person might participate to gain things over and above their allotment under D_1. Some persons even might want to leave their job in socialist industry and work full time in this private sector. I wish merely to note how private property even in means of production would occur in a socialist society that did not forbid people to use as they wished some of the resources they are given under the socialist distribution D_1. The socialist society would have to forbid capitalist acts between consenting adults.

The general point illustrated by the Wilt Chamberlain example and the example of the entrepreneur in a socialist society is that no end-state principle or distributional patterned principle of justice can be continuously realized without continuous interference with people's lives. Any favored pattern would be transformed into one unfavored by the principle, by people choosing to act in various ways; for example, by people exchanging goods and services with other people, or giving things to other people, things the transferrers are entitled to under the favored distributional pattern. To maintain a pattern one must either continually interfere to stop people from transferring resources as they wish to, or continually (or periodically) interfere to take from some persons resources that others for some reason chose to transfer to them. (But if some time limit is to be set on how long people may keep resources others voluntarily transfer to them, why let them keep these resources for *any* period of time? Why not have immediate confiscation?) It might be objected that all persons voluntarily will choose to refrain from actions which would upset the pattern. This presupposes unrealistically (1) that all will most want to maintain the pattern (are those who don't, to be "re-educated" or forced to undergo "self-criticism"?), (2) that each can gather enough information about his own actions and the ongoing activities of others to discover which of his actions will upset the pattern, and (3) that diverse and far-flung persons can coordinate their actions to dovetail into the pattern. Compare the manner in which the market is neutral among persons' desires, as it reflects and transmits widely scattered information via prices, and coordinates persons' activities.

It puts things perhaps a bit too strongly to say that every patterned (or end-state) principle is liable to be thwarted by the voluntary actions of the individual parties transferring some of their shares they receive under the principle. For perhaps some *very* weak patterns are not so thwarted. Any distributional pattern with any egalitarian component is overturnable by the voluntary actions of individual persons over time; as is every patterned condition with sufficient content so as actually to have been proposed as presenting the central core of distributive justice. Still, given the possibility that some weak conditions or patterns may not be unstable in this way, it would be better to formulate an explicit description of the kind of interesting and contentful patterns under discussion, and to prove a theorem about their instability. Since the weaker the patterning, the more likely it is that the entitlement system itself satisfies it, a plausible conjecture is that any patterning either is unstable or is satisfied by the entitlement system. . . .

Redistribution and property rights

Apparently, patterned principles allow people to choose to spend upon themselves, but not upon others, those resources they are entitled to (or rather, receive) under some favored distributional pattern D_1. For if each of several persons chooses to expend some of his D_1 resources upon one other person, then that other person will receive more than his D_1 share, disturbing the favored distributional pattern. Maintaining a distributional pattern is individualism with a vengeance! Patterned distributional principles do not give people what entitlement principles do, only better distributed. For they do not give the right to choose what to do with what one has; they do not give the right to choose to pursue an end involving (intrinsically, or as a means) the enhancement of another's position. To such views, families are disturbing; for within a family occur transfers that upset the favored distributional pattern. Either families themselves become units to which distribution takes place, the column occupiers (on what rationale?), or loving behavior is forbidden. We should note in passing the ambivalent position of radicals toward the family. Its loving relationships are seen as a model to be emulated and extended across the whole society, at the same time that it is denounced as a suffocating institution to be broken and condemned as a focus of parochial concerns that interfere with achieving radical goals. Need we say that it is not appropriate to enforce across the wider society the relationships of love and care appropriate within a family, relationships which are voluntarily undertaken?[6] Incidentally, love is an interesting instance of another relationship that is historical, in that (like justice) it depends upon what actually occurred. An adult may come to love another because of the other's characteristics; but it is the other person, and not the characteristics, that is loved. The love is not transferrable to someone else with the same characteristics, even to one who "scores" higher for these characteristics. And the love endures through changes of the characteristics that gave rise to it. One loves the particular person one actually encountered. Why love is historical, attaching to persons in this way and not to characteristics, is an interesting and puzzling question.

Proponents of patterned principles of distributive justice focus upon criteria for determining who is to receive holdings; they consider the reasons for which someone should have something, and also the total picture of holdings. Whether or not it is better to give than to receive, proponents of patterned principles ignore giving altogether. In considering the distribution of goods, income, and so forth, their theories are theories of recipient justice; they completely ignore any right a person might have to give something to someone. Even in exchanges where each party is simultaneously giver and recipient, patterned principles of justice focus only upon the recipient role and its supposed rights. Thus discussions tend to focus on whether people (should) have a right to inherit, rather than on whether people (should) have a right to bequeath or on whether persons who have a right to hold also have a right to choose that others hold in their place. I lack a good explanation of why the usual theories of distributive justice are so recipient oriented; ignoring givers and transferrers and their rights is of a piece with ignoring producers and their entitlements. But why is it *all* ignored?

Patterned principles of distributive justice necessitate *re*distributive activities. The likelihood is small that any actual freely-arrived-at set of holdings fits a given pattern; and the likelihood is nil that it will continue to fit the pattern as people exchange and give. From the point of view of an entitlement theory, redistribution is a serious matter indeed, involving, as it does, the violation of people's rights. (An exception is those takings that fall under the principle of the rectification of injustices.) From other points of view, also, it is serious.

Taxation of earnings from labor is on a par with forced labor.[7] Some persons find this claim obviously true: taking the earnings of n hours labor is like taking n hours from the person; it is like forcing the person to work n hours for another's purpose. Others find the claim absurd. But even these, *if* they object to forced labor, would oppose forcing unemployed hippies to work for the benefit of the needy.[8] And they would also object to forcing each person to work five extra hours each week for the benefit of the needy. But a system that takes five hours' wages in taxes does not seem to them like one that forces someone to work five hours, since it offers the person forced a wider range of choice in activities than does taxation in kind with the particular labor specified. (But we can imagine a gradation of systems of forced labor, from one that specifies a particular activity, to one that gives a choice among two activities, to . . . ; and so on up.) Furthermore, people envisage a system with something like a proportional tax on everything above the amount necessary for basic needs. Some think this does not force someone to work extra hours, since there is no fixed number of extra hours he is forced to work, and since he can avoid the tax entirely by earning only enough to cover his basic needs. This is a very uncharacteristic view of forcing for those who *also* think people are forced to do something *whenever* the alternatives they face are considerably worse. However, *neither* view is correct. The fact that others intentionally intervene, in violation of a side constraint against aggression, to threaten force to limit the alternatives, in this case to paying taxes or (presumably the worse alternative) bare subsistence, makes the taxation system one of forced labor and distinguishes it from other cases of limited choices which are not forcings.

The man who chooses to work longer to gain an income more than sufficient for his basic needs prefers some extra goods or services to the leisure and activities he could perform during the possible nonworking hours; whereas the man who chooses not to work the extra time prefers the leisure activities to the extra goods or services he could acquire by working more. Given this, if it would be illegitimate for a tax system to seize some of a man's leisure (forced labor) for the purpose of serving the needy, how can it be legitimate for a tax system to seize some of a man's goods for that purpose? Why should we treat the man whose happiness requires certain material goods or services differently from the man whose preferences and desires make such goods unnecessary for his happiness? Why should the man who prefers seeing a movie (and who has to earn money for a ticket) be open to the required call to aid the needy, while the person who prefers looking at a sunset (and hence need earn no extra money) is not? Indeed, isn't it surprising that redistributionists choose to ignore the man whose pleasures are so easily attainable without extra labor, while adding yet another burden to the poor unfortunate who must work for his pleasures? If anything, one would have expected the reverse. Why is the person with the nonmaterial or nonconsumption desire allowed to proceed unimpeded to his most favored feasible alternative, whereas the man whose pleasures or desires involve material things and who must work for extra money (thereby serving whomever considers his activities valuable enough to pay him) is constrained in what he can realize? Perhaps there is no difference in principle. And perhaps some think the answer concerns merely administrative convenience. (These questions and issues will not disturb those who think that forced labor to serve the needy or to realize some favored end-state pattern is acceptable.) In a fuller discussion we would have (and want) to extend our argument to include interest, entrepreneurial profits, and so on. Those who doubt that this extension can be carried through, and who draw the line here at taxation of income from labor, will have to state rather complicated patterned *historical* principles of distributive justice, since end-state principles would not distinguish *sources* of income in any way. It is enough for now to get away from end-state principles and to make clear how various patterned principles are dependent upon particular views about the sources or the illegitimacy or the lesser legitimacy of profits, interest, and so on; which particular views may well be mistaken.

What sort of right over others does a legally institutionalized end-state pattern give one? The central core of the notion of a property right in X, relative to which other parts of the notion are to be explained, is the right to determine what shall be done with X; the right to choose which of the constrained set of options concerning X shall be realized or attempted. The constraints are set by other principles or laws operating in the society; in our theory, by the Lockean rights people possess (under the minimal state). My property rights in my knife allow me to leave it where I will, but not in your chest. I may choose which of the acceptable options involving the knife is to be realized. This notion of property helps us to understand why earlier theorists spoke of people as having property in themselves and their labor. They viewed each person as having a right to decide what would become of himself and what he would do, and as having a right to reap the benefits of what he did.

This right of selecting the alternative to be realized from the constrained set of alternatives may be held by an *individual* or by a *group* with some procedure for reaching a joint decision; or the right may be passed back and forth, so that one year I decide what is to become of X, and the next year you do (with the alternative of destruction, perhaps, being excluded). Or, during the same time period, some types of decisions about X may be made by me, and others by you. And so on. We lack an adequate, fruitful, analytical apparatus for classifying the *types* of constraints on the set of options among which choices are to be made, and the *types* of ways decision powers can be held, divided, and amalgamated. A *theory* of property would, among other things, contain such a classification of constraints and decision modes, and from a small number of principles would follow a host of interesting statements about the *consequences* and effects of certain combinations of constraints and modes of decision.

When end-result principles of distributive justice are built into the legal structure of a society, they (as do most patterned principles) give each citizen an enforceable claim to some portion of the total social product; that is, to some portion of the sum total of the individually and jointly made products. This total product is produced by individuals laboring, using means of production others have saved to bring into existence, by people organizing production or creating means to produce new things or things in a new way. It is on this batch of individual activities that patterned distributional principles give each individual an enforceable claim. Each person has a claim to the activities and the products of other persons, independently of whether the other persons enter into particular relationships that give rise to these claims, and independently of whether they voluntarily take these claims upon themselves, in charity or in exchange for something.

Whether it is done through taxation on wages or on wages over a certain amount, or through seizure of profits, or through there being a big *social pot* so that it's not clear what's coming from where and what's going where, patterned principles of distributive justice involve appropriating the actions of other persons. Seizing the results of someone's labor is equivalent to seizing hours from him and directing him to carry on various activities. If people force you to do certain work, or unrewarded work, for a certain period of time, they decide what you are to do and what purposes your work is to serve apart from your decisions. This process whereby they take this decision from you makes them a *part-owner* of you; it gives them a property right in you. Just as having such partial control and power of decision, by right, over an animal or inanimate object would be to have a property right in it.

End-state and most patterned principles of distributive justice institute (partial) ownership by others of people and their actions and labor. These principles involve a shift from the classical liberals' notion of self-ownership to a notion of (partial) property rights in *other* people.

Considerations such as these confront end-state and other patterned conceptions of justice with the question of whether the actions necessary to achieve the selected pattern don't themselves violate moral side constraints. Any view holding that there are moral side constraints on actions, that not all moral considerations can be built into end states that are to be achieved, must face the possibility that some of its goals are not achievable by any morally permissible available means. An entitlement theorist will face such conflicts in a society that deviates from the principles of justice for the generation of holdings, if and only if the only actions available to realize the principles themselves violate some moral constraints. Since deviation from the first two principles of justice (in acquisition and transfer) will involve other persons' direct and aggressive intervention to violate rights, and since moral constraints will not exclude defensive or retributive action in such cases, the entitlement theorist's problem rarely will be pressing. And whatever difficulties he has in applying the principle of rectification to persons who did not themselves violate the first two principles are difficulties in balancing the conflicting considerations so as correctly to formulate the complex principle of rectification itself; he will not violate moral side constraints by applying the principle. Proponents of patterned conceptions of justice, however, often will face head-on clashes (and poignant ones if they cherish each party to the clash) between moral side constraints on how individuals may be treated and their patterned conception of justice that presents an end state or other pattern that *must* be realized.

May a person emigrate from a nation that has institutionalized some end-state or patterned distributional principle? For some principles (for example, Hayek's) emigration presents no theoretical problem. But for others it is a tricky matter. Consider a nation having a compulsory scheme of minimal social provision to aid the neediest (or one organized so as to maximize the position of the worst-off group); no one may opt out of participating in it. (None may say, "Don't compel me to contribute to others and don't provide for me via this compulsory mechanism if I am in need.") Everyone above a certain level is forced to contribute to aid the needy. But if emigration from the country were allowed, anyone could choose to move to another country that did not have compulsory social provision but otherwise was (as much as possible) identical. In such a case, the person's *only* motive for leaving would be to avoid participating in the compulsory scheme of social provision. And if he does leave, the needy in his initial country will receive no (compelled) help from him. What rationale yields the result that the person be permitted to emigrate, yet forbidden to stay and opt out of the compulsory scheme of social provision? If providing for the needy is of overriding importance, this does militate against allowing internal opting out; but it also speaks against allowing external emigration. (Would it also support, to some extent, the kidnapping of persons living in a place without compulsory social provision, who could be forced to make a contribution to the needy in your community?) Perhaps the crucial component of the position that allows emigration solely to avoid certain arrangements, while not allowing anyone internally to opt out of them, is a concern for fraternal feelings within the country. "We don't want anyone here who doesn't contribute, who doesn't care enough about the others to contribute." That concern, in this case, would have to be tied to the view that forced aiding tends to produce fraternal feelings between the aided and the aider (or perhaps merely to the view that the knowledge that someone or other voluntarily is not aiding produces unfraternal feelings).

Notes

1   Applications of the principle of justice in acquisition may also occur as part of the move from one distribution to another. You may find an unheld thing now and appropriate it. Acquisitions also are to be understood as included when, to simplify, I speak only of transitions by transfers.

2   If the principle of rectification of violations of the first two principles yields more than one description of holdings, then some choice must be made as to which of these is to be realized. Perhaps the sort of considerations about distributive justice and equality that I argue against play a legitimate role in *this* subsidiary choice. Similarly, there may be room for such considerations in deciding which otherwise arbitrary features a statute will embody, when such features are unavoidable because other considerations do not specify a precise line; yet a line must be drawn.

3   One might try to squeeze a patterned conception of distributive justice into the framework of the entitlement conception, by formulating a gimmicky obligatory "principle of transfer" that would lead to the pattern. For example, the principle that if one has more than the mean income one must transfer everything one holds above the mean to persons below the mean so as to bring them up to (but not over) the mean. We can formulate a criterion for a "principle of transfer" to rule out such obligatory transfers, or we can say that no correct principle of transfer, no principle of transfer in a free society will be like this. The former is probably the better course, though the latter also is true.

Alternatively, one might think to make the entitlement conception instantiate a pattern, by using matrix entries that express the relative strength of a person's entitlements as measured by some real-valued function. But even if the limitation to natural dimensions failed to exclude this function, the resulting edifice would *not* capture our system of entitlements to *particular* things.

4 We certainly benefit because great economic incentives operate to get others to spend much time and energy to figure out how to serve us by providing things we will want to pay for. It is not mere paradox mongering to wonder whether capitalism should be criticized for most rewarding and hence encouraging, not individualists like Thoreau who go about their own lives, but people who are occupied with serving others and winning them as customers. But to defend capitalism one need not think businessmen are the finest human types. (I do not mean to join here the general maligning of businessmen, either.) Those who think the finest should acquire the most can try to convince their fellows to transfer resources in accordance with *that* principle.

5 Might not a transfer have instrumental effects on a third party, changing his feasible options? (But what if the two parties to the transfer independently had used their holdings in this fashion?) I discuss this question below, but note here that this question concedes the point for distributions of ultimate intrinsic noninstrumental goods (pure utility experiences, so to speak) that are transferrable. It also could be objected that the transfer might make a third party more envious because it worsens his position relative to someone else. I find it incomprehensible how this can be thought to involve a claim of justice. . . .

Here and elsewhere in this chapter, a theory which incorporates elements of pure procedural justice might find what I say acceptable, *if* kept in its proper place; that is, if background institutions exist to ensure the satisfaction of certain conditions on distributive shares. But if these institutions are not themselves the sum or invisible-hand result of people's voluntary (nonaggressive) actions, the constraints they impose require justification. At no point does our argument assume any background institutions more extensive than those of the minimal night-watchman state, a state limited to protecting persons against murder, assault, theft, fraud, and so forth.

6 One indication of the stringency of Rawls's difference principle, which we attend to in the second part of this chapter, is its inappropriateness as a governing principle even within a family of individuals who love one another. Should a family devote its resources to maximizing the position of its least well off and least talented child, holding back the other children or using resources for their education and development only if they will follow a policy through their lifetimes of maximizing the position of their least fortunate sibling? Surely not. How then can this even be considered as the appropriate policy for enforcement in the wider society? (I discuss below what I think would be Rawls's reply: that some principles apply at the macro-level which do not apply to micro-situations.)

7 I am unsure as to whether the arguments I present below show that such taxation merely *is* forced labor; so that "is on a par with" means "is one kind of." Or alternatively, whether the arguments emphasize the great similarities between such taxation and forced labor, to show it is plausible and illuminating to view such taxation in the light of forced labor. This latter approach would remind one of how John Wisdom conceives of the claims of metaphysicians.

8 Nothing hangs on the fact that here and elsewhere I speak loosely of *needs*, since I go on, each time, to reject the criterion of justice which includes it. If, however, something did depend upon the notion, one would want to examine it more carefully. For a skeptical view, see Kenneth Minogue, *The Liberal Mind* (New York: Random House, 1963), pp. 103–12.

51

Displacing the Distributive Paradigm

Iris Marion Young

It was in general a mistake to make a fuss about so-called distribution *and put the principal stress on it. Any distribution whatever of the means of consumption is only a consequence of the distribution of the conditions of production themselves. The latter distribution, however, is a feature of the mode of production itself.*

Karl Marx

Thousands of buses converge on the city, and tens of thousands of people of diverse colors, ages, occupations, and life styles swarm onto the mall around the Washington Monument until the march begins. At midday people move into the streets, chanting, singing, waving wild papier-mâché missiles or effigies of government officials. Many carry signs or banners on which a simple slogan is inscribed: "Peace, Jobs, and Justice."

This scene has occurred many times in Washington, DC, in the last decade, and many more times in other US cities. What does "justice" mean in this slogan? In this context, as in many other political contexts today, I suggest that social justice means the elimination of institutionalized domination and oppression. Any aspect of social organization and practice relevant to domination and oppression is in principle subject to evaluation by ideals of justice.

Contemporary philosophical theories of justice, however, do not conceive justice so broadly. Instead, philosophical theories of justice tend to restrict the meaning of social justice to the morally proper distribution of benefits and burdens among society's members. In this essay I define and assess this distributive paradigm. While distributive issues are crucial to a satisfactory conception of justice, it is a mistake to reduce social justice to distribution.

I find two problems with the distributive paradigm. First, it tends to focus thinking about social justice on the allocation of material goods such as things, resources, income, and wealth, or on the distribution of social positions, especially jobs. This focus tends to ignore the social structure and institutional context that often help determine distributive patterns.

Of particular importance to the analyses that follow are issues of decision-making power and procedures, division of labor, and culture.

One might agree that defining justice in terms of distribution tends to bias thinking about justice toward issues concerning wealth, income, and other material goods, and that other issues such as decision-making power or the structure of the division of labor are as import-ant, and yet argue that distribution need not be restricted to material goods and resources. Theorists frequently consider issues of the distribution of such nonmaterial goods as power, opportunity, or self-respect. But this widening of the concept of distribution exhibits the second problem with the distributive paradigm. When metaphorically extended to nonmaterial social goods, the concept of distribution represents them as though they were static things, instead of a function of social relations and processes.

In criticizing distributively oriented theories I wish neither to reject distribution as unim-portant nor to offer a new positive theory to replace the distributive theories. I wish rather to displace talk of justice that regards persons as primarily possessors and consumers of goods to a wider context that also includes action, decisions about action, and provision of the means to develop and exercise capacities. The concept of social justice includes all aspects of institutional rules and relations insofar as they are subject to potential collective decision. The concepts of domination and oppression, rather than the concept of distribu-tion, should be the starting point for a conception of social justice. . . .

The Distributive Paradigm Presupposes and Obscures Institutional Context

Most theorizing about social justice focuses on the distribution of material resources, in-come, or positions of reward and prestige. Contemporary debates among theorists of justice, as Charles Taylor (1985) points out, are inspired largely by two practical issues. First, is the distribution of wealth and income in advanced capitalist countries just, and if not, does justice permit or even require the provision of welfare services and other redistributive measures? Second, is the pattern of the distribution of positions of high income and prestige just, and if not, are affirmative action policies just means to rectify that injustice? Nearly all writers who define justice in distributive terms identify questions of the equality or inequal-ity of wealth and income as the primary questions of social justice (see also Arthur and Shaw, 1978). They usually subsume the second set of questions, about the justice of the distribution of social positions, under the question of economic distribution, since "more desirable" positions usually correspond to those that yield higher income or greater access to resources.

Applied discussions of justice too usually focus on the distribution of material goods and resources. Discussions of justice in medical care, for example, usually focus on the allocation of medical resources such as treatment, sophisticated equipment, expensive procedures, and so on (e.g., Daniels, 1985, esp. chapters 3 and 4). Similarly, issues of justice enter discussion in environmental ethics largely through consideration of the impact that alternative policies might have on the distribution of natural and social resources among individuals and groups (see, e.g., Simon, 1984). . . .

The social context of welfare capitalist society helps account for this tendency to focus on the distribution of income and other resources. Public political dispute in welfare corporate society is largely restricted to issues of taxation, and the allocation of public funds among competing social interests. Public discussions of social injustice tend to revolve around inequalities of wealth and income, and the extent to which the state can or should mitigate the suffering of the poor.

There are certainly pressing reasons for philosophers to attend to these issues of the distribution of wealth and resources. In a society and world with vast differences in the amount of material goods to which individuals have access, where millions starve while others can have anything they want, any conception of justice must address the distribution of material goods. The immediate provision of basic material goods for people now suffering severe deprivation must be a first priority for any program that seeks to make the world more just. Such a call obviously entails considerations of distribution and redistribution.

But in contemporary American society, many public appeals to justice do not concern primarily the distribution of material goods. Citizens in a rural Massachusetts town organize against a decision to site a huge hazardous waste treatment plant in their town. Their leaflets convince people that state law has treated the community unjustly by denying them the option of rejecting the plant (Young, 1983). Citizens in an Ohio city are outraged at the announcement that a major employer is closing down its plant. They question the legitimacy of the power of private corporate decision-makers to throw half the city out of work without warning, and without any negotiation and consultation with the community. Discussion of possible compensation makes them snicker; the point is not simply that we are out of jobs and thus lack money, they claim, but that no private party should have the right to decide to decimate the local economy. Justice may require that former workers and other members of the community have the option of taking over and operating the plant themselves (Schweickart, 1984). These two cases concern not so much the justice of material distributions as the justice of decision-making power and procedures.

Black critics claim that the television industry is guilty of gross injustice in its depictions of Blacks. More often than not, Blacks are represented as criminals, hookers, maids, scheming dealers, or jiving connivers. Blacks rarely appear in roles of authority, glamour, or virtue. Arab Americans are outraged at the degree to which television and film present recognizable Arabs only as sinister terrorists or gaudy princes, and conversely that terrorists are almost always Arab. Such outrage at media stereotyping issues in claims about the injustice not of material distribution, but of cultural imagery and symbols.

In an age of burgeoning computer technology, organizations of clerical workers argue that no person should have to spend the entirety of her working day in front of a computer terminal typing in a set of mindless numbers at monitored high speeds. This claim about injustice concerns not the distribution of goods, for the claim would still be made if VDT operators earned $30,000 annually. Here the primary issues of justice concern the structure of the division of labor and a right to meaningful work.

There are many such claims about justice and injustice in our society which are not primarily about the distribution of income, resources, or positions. A focus on the distribution of material goods and resources inappropriately restricts the scope of justice, because it fails to bring social structures and institutional contexts under evaluation. Several writers make this claim about distributive theories specifically with regard to their inability to bring capitalist institutions and class relations under evaluation. In his classic paper, for example, Allen Wood (1972) argues that for Marx justice refers only to superstructural juridical relations of distribution, which are constrained by the underlying mode of production. Because they are confined to distribution, principles of justice cannot be used to evaluate the social relations of production themselves (cf. Wolff, 1977, pp. 199–208).

Other writers criticize distributive theories of justice, especially Rawls's (the first selection), for presupposing at the same time that they obscure the context of class inequality that the theories are unable to evaluate (Macpherson, 1973; Nielsen, 1978). A distributive conception of justice is unable to bring class relations into view and evaluate them, Evan Simpson suggests, because its individualism prevents an understanding of structural phenomena, the "macroscopic transfer emerging from a complicated set of individual actions" (Simpson, 1980, p. 497) which cannot be understood in terms of any particular individual actions or acquisitions.

Many who make this Marxist criticism of the distributive focus of theories of justice conclude that justice is a concept of bourgeois ideology and thus not useful for a socialist normative analysis. Others disagree, and this dispute has occupied much of the Marxist literature on justice. I will argue later that a criticism of the distributive paradigm does not entail abandoning or transcending the concept of justice. For the moment I wish to focus on the point on which both sides in this dispute agree, namely, that predominant approaches to justice tend to presuppose and uncritically accept the relations of production that define an economic system.

The Marxist analysis of the distributive paradigm provides a fruitful starting point, but it is both too narrow and too general. On the one hand, capitalist class relations are not the only phenomena of social structure or institutional context that the distributive paradigm fails to evaluate. Some feminists point out, for example, that contemporary theories of justice presuppose family structure, without asking how social relations involving sexuality, intimacy, childrearing, and household labor ought best to be organized (see Okin, 1986; Pateman, 1988, pp. 41–3). Like their forebears, contemporary liberal theorists of justice tend to presume that the units among which basic distributions take place are families, and that it is as family members, often heads of families, that individuals enter the public realm where justice operates (Nicholson, 1986, chapter 4). Thus they neglect issues of justice within families – for example, the issue of whether the traditional sexual division of labor still presupposed by much law and employment policy is just.

While the Marxist criticism is too narrow, it is also too vague. The claim that the distributive paradigm fails to bring class relations under evaluation is too general to make clear what specific nondistributive issues are at stake. While property is something distributed, for example, in the form of goods, land, buildings, or shares of stock, the legal relations that define entitlement, possible forms of title, and so on are not goods to be distributed. The legal framework consists of rules defining practices and rights to make decisions about the disposition of goods. Class domination is certainly enacted by agents deciding where to invest their capital – a distributive decision; but the social rules, rights, procedures, and influences that structure capitalist decision-making are not distributed goods. In order to understand and evaluate the institutional framework within which distributive issues arise, the ideas of "class" and "mode of production" must be concretized in terms of specific social processes and relations.

The general criticism I am making of the predominant focus on the distribution of wealth, income, and positions is that such a focus ignores and tends to obscure the institutional context within which those distributions take place, and which is often at least partly the cause of patterns of distribution of jobs or wealth. Institutional context should be understood in a broader sense than "mode of production." It includes any structures or practices, the rules and norms that guide them, and the language and symbols that mediate social interactions within them, in institutions of state, family, and civil society, as well as the workplace. These are relevant to judgments of justice and injustice insofar as they condition people's ability to participate in determining their actions and their ability to develop and exercise their capacities.

Many discussions of social justice not only ignore the institutional contexts within which distributions occur, but often presuppose specific institutional structures whose justice they fail to bring under evaluation. Some political theories, for example, tend to assume centralized legislative and executive institutions separated from the day-to-day lives of most people in the society, and state officials with the authority to make and enforce policy decisions. They take for granted such institutions of the modern state as bureaucracies and welfare agencies for implementing and enforcing tax schemes and administering services (see, e.g., Rawls, 1971, pp. 274–84). Issues of the just organization of government institutions, and just methods of political decision-making, rarely get raised.

To take a different kind of example, when philosophers ask about the just principles for allocating jobs and offices among persons, they typically assume a stratification of such positions. They assume a hierarchical division of labor in which some jobs and offices carry significant autonomy, decision-making power, authority, income, and access to resources, while others lack most of these attributes. Rarely do theorists explicitly ask whether such a definition and organization of social positions is just.

Many other examples of ways in which theorizing about justice frequently presupposes specific structural and institutional background conditions could be cited. In every case a clear understanding of these background conditions can reveal how they affect distribution – what there is to distribute, how it gets distributed, who distributes, and what the distributive outcome is. With Michael Walzer, my intention here is "to shift our attention from distribution itself to conception and creation: the naming of the goods, the giving of meaning, and the collective making" (Walzer, 1983, p. 7). I shall focus most of my discussion on three primary categories of nondistributive issues that distributive theories tend to ignore: decision-making structure and procedures, division of labor, and culture.

Decision-making issues include not only questions of who by virtue of their positions have the effective freedom or authority to make what sorts of decisions, but also the rules and procedures according to which decisions are made. Discussion of economic justice, for example, often deemphasizes the decision-making structures which are crucial determinants of economic relations. Economic domination in our society occurs not simply or primarily because some persons have more wealth and income than others, as important as this is. Economic domination derives at least as much from the corporate and legal structures and procedures that give some persons the power to make decisions about investment, production, marketing, employment, interest rates, and wages that affect millions of other people. Not all who make these decisions are wealthy or even privileged, but the decision-making structure operates to reproduce distributive inequality and the unjust constraints on people's lives that I name exploitation and marginalization. As Carol Gould (1988, pp. 133–4) points out, rarely do theories of justice take such structures as an explicit focus. In the chapters that follow I raise several specific issues of decision-making structure, and argue for democratic decision-making procedures as an element and condition of social justice.

Division of labor can be understood both distributively and nondistributively. As a distributive issue, division of labor refers to how pregiven occupations, jobs, or tasks are allocated among individuals or groups. As a nondistributive issue, on the other hand, division of labor concerns the definition of the occupations themselves. Division of labor as an institutional structure involves the range of tasks performed in a given position, the definition of the nature, meaning, and value of those tasks, and the relations of cooperation, conflict, and authority among positions. Feminist claims about the justice of a sexual division of labor, for example, have been posed both distributively and nondistributively. On the one hand, feminists have questioned the justice of a pattern of distribution of positions that finds a small proportion of women in the most prestigious jobs. On the other hand, they have also questioned the conscious or unconscious association of many occupations or jobs with masculine or feminine characteristics, such as instrumentality or affectivity, and this is not itself a distributive issue. . . .

Overextending the Concept of Distribution

The following objection might be made to my argument thus far. It may be true that philosophical discussions of justice tend to emphasize the distribution of goods and to ignore institutional issues of decision-making structure and culture. But this is not a necessary consequence of the distributive definition of justice. Theories of distributive justice can and should be applied to issues of social organization beyond the allocation of wealth, income, and resources. Indeed, this objection insists, many theorists explicitly extend the scope of distributive justice to such nonmaterial goods.

Rawls, for example, regards the subject of justice as "the way in which the major social institutions distribute fundamental rights and duties" (Rawls, 1971, p. 7), and for him this clearly includes rights and duties related to decision-making, social positions, power, and so on, as well as wealth or income. Similarly, David Miller specifies that "the 'benefits' the distribution of which a conception of justice evaluates should be taken to include intangible benefits such as prestige and self-respect" (Miller, 1976, p. 22). William Galston, finally, insists that "issues of justice involve not only the distribution of property or income, but also such non-material goods as productive tasks, opportunities for development, citizenship, authority, honor, and so on" (Galston, 1980, p. 6; cf. p. 116).

The distributive paradigm of justice may have a bias toward focusing on easily identifiable distributions, such as distributions of things, income, and jobs. Its beauty and simplicity, however, consist in its ability to accommodate any issue of justice, including those concerning culture, decision-making structures, and the division of labor. To do so the paradigm simply formulates the issue in terms of the distribution of some material or nonmaterial good among various agents. Any social value can be treated as some thing or aggregate of things that some specific agents possess in certain amounts, and alternative end-state patterns of distribution of that good among those agents can be compared. For example, neoclassical economists have developed sophisticated schemes for reducing all intentional action to a matter of maximizing a utility function in which the utility of all conceivable goods can be quantified and compared.

But this, in my view, is the main problem with the distributive paradigm: it does not recognize the limits to the application of a logic of distribution. Distributive theorists of justice agree that justice is the primary normative concept for evaluating all aspects of social institutions, but at the same time they identify the scope of justice with distribution. This entails applying a logic of distribution to social goods which are not material things or measurable quantities. Applying a logic of distribution to such goods produces a misleading conception of the issues of justice involved. It reifies aspects of social life that are better understood as a function of rules and relations than as things. And it conceptualizes social justice primarily in terms of end-state patterns, rather than focusing on social processes. This distributive paradigm implies a misleading or incomplete social ontology.

But why should issues of social ontology matter for normative theorizing about justice? Any normative claims about society make assumptions about the nature of society, often only implicitly. Normative judgments of justice are about something, and without a social ontology we do not know what they are about. The distributive paradigm implicitly assumes that social judgments are about what individual persons have, how much they have, and how that amount compares with what other persons have. This focus on possession tends to preclude thinking about what people are doing, according to what institutionalized rules, how their doings and havings are structured by institutionalized relations that constitute their positions, and how the combined effect of their doings has recursive effects on their lives. Before developing this argument further, let us look at some examples of the application of the distributive paradigm to three nonmaterial goods frequently discussed by theorists of justice: rights, opportunity, and self-respect.

I quoted Rawls earlier to the effect that justice concerns the distribution of "rights and duties," and talk of distributing rights is by no means limited to him. But what does distributing a right mean? One may talk about having a right to a distributive share of material things, resources, or income. But in such cases it is the good that is distributed, not the right. What can it mean to distribute rights that do not refer to resources or things, like the right of free speech, or the right of trial by jury? We can conceive of a society in which some persons are granted these rights while others are not, but this does not mean that some people have a certain "amount" or "portion" of a good while others have less. Altering the situation so that everyone has these rights, moreover, would not entail that the formerly privileged group gives over some of its right of free speech or trial by jury to the rest of society's members, on analogy with a redistribution of income.

Rights are not fruitfully conceived as possessions. Rights are relationships, not things; they are institutionally defined rules specifying what people can do in relation to one another. Rights refer to doing more than having, to social relationships that enable or constrain action.

Talk of distributing opportunities involves a similar confusion. If by opportunity we mean "chance," we can meaningfully talk of distributing opportunities, of some people having more opportunities than others, while some have none at all. When I go to the carnival I can buy three chances to knock over the kewpie doll, and my friend can buy six, and she will have more chances than I. Matters are rather different, however, with other opportunities. James Nickel (1988, p. 110) defines opportunities as "states of affairs that combine the absence of insuperable obstacles with the presences of means – internal or external – that give one a chance of overcoming the obstacles that remain." Opportunity in this sense is a condition of enablement, which usually involves a configuration of social rules and social relations, as well as an individual's self-conception and skills.

We may mislead ourselves by the fact that in ordinary language we talk about some people having "fewer" opportunities than others. When we talk that way, the opportunities sound like separable goods that can be increased or decreased by being given out or withheld, even though we know that opportunities are not allocated. Opportunity is a concept of enablement rather than possession; it refers to doing more than having. A person has opportunities if he or she is not constrained from doing things, and lives under the enabling conditions for doing them. Having opportunities in this sense certainly does often entail having material possessions, such as food, clothing, tools, land, or machines. Being enabled or constrained refers more directly, however, to the rules and practices that govern one's action, the way other people treat one in the context of specific social relations, and the broader structural possibilities produced by the confluence of a multitude of actions and practices. It makes no sense to speak of opportunities as themselves things possessed. Evaluating social justice according to whether persons have opportunities, therefore, must involve evaluating not a distributive outcome but the social structures that enable or constrain the individuals in relevant situations (cf. Simpson, 1980; Reiman, 1987).

Consider educational opportunity, for example. Providing educational opportunity certainly entails allocating specific material resources – money, buildings, books, computers, and so on – and there are reasons to think that the more resources, the wider the opportunities offered to children in an educational system. But education is primarily a process taking place in a complex context of social relations. In the cultural context of the United States, male children and female children, working-class children and middle-class children, Black children and white children often do not have equally enabling educational opportunities even when an equivalent amount of resources has been devoted to their education. This does not show that distribution is irrelevant to educational opportunity, only that opportunity has a wider scope than distribution.

Many writers on justice, to take a final example, not only regard self-respect as a primary good that all persons in a society must have if the society is to be just, but also talk of distributing self-respect. But what can it mean to distribute self-respect? Self-respect is not an entity or measurable aggregate, it cannot be parceled out of some stash, and above all it cannot be detached from persons as a separable attribute adhering to an otherwise unchanged substance. Self-respect names not some possession or attribute a person has, but her or his attitude toward her or his entire situation and life prospects. While Rawls does not speak of self-respect as something itself distributed, he does suggest that distributive arrangements provide the background conditions for self-respect (Rawls, 1971, pp. 148–50). It is certainly true that in many circumstances the possession of certain distributable material goods may be a condition of self-respect. Self-respect, however, also involves many nonmaterial conditions that cannot be reduced to distributive arrangements (cf. Howard, 1985).

People have or lack self-respect because of how they define themselves and how others regard them, because of how they spend their time, because of the amount of autonomy and decision-making power they have in their activities, and so on. Some of these factors can be conceptualized in distributive terms, but others cannot. Self-respect is at least as much a function of culture as it is of goods, for example, and in later chapters I shall discuss some elements of cultural imperialism that undermine the self-respect of many persons in our society. The point here is that none of the forms and not all of the conditions of self-respect can meaningfully be conceived as goods that individuals possess; they are rather relations and processes in which the actions of individuals are embedded.

These, then, are the general problems with extending the concept of distribution beyond material goods or measurable quantities to nonmaterial values. First, doing so reifies social relations and institutional rules. Something identifiable and assignable must be distributed. In accord with its implicit social ontology that gives primacy to substance over relations, moreover, the distributive paradigm tends to conceive of individuals as social atoms, logically prior to social relations and institutions. As Galston makes clear in the passage I quoted earlier (Galston, 1980, p. 112), conceiving justice as a distribution of goods among individuals involves analytically separating the individuals from those goods. Such an atomistic conception of the individual as a substance to which attributes adhere fails to appreciate that individual identities and capacities are in many respects themselves the products of social processes and relations. Societies do not simply distribute goods to persons who are what they are apart from society, but rather constitute individuals in their identities and capacities (Sandel, 1982; Taylor, 1985). In the distributive logic, however, there is little room for conceiving persons' enablement or constraint as a function of their relations to one another. . . . Such an atomistic social ontology ignores or obscures the importance of social groups for understanding issues of justice.

Secondly, the distributive paradigm must conceptualize all issues of justice in terms of patterns. It implies a static social ontology that ignores processes. In the distributive paradigm individuals or other agents lie as points in the social field, among whom larger or smaller packets of goods are assigned. One evaluates the justice of the pattern by comparing the size of the packages individuals have and comparing the total pattern to other possible patterns of assignment.

Robert Nozick (1974, the previous selection) argues that such a static or end-state approach to justice is inappropriately ahistorical. End-state approaches to justice, he argues, operate as though social goods magically appear and get distributed. They ignore the processes that create the goods and produce distributive patterns, which they find irrelevant for evaluating justice. For Nozick, only the process is relevant to evaluating distributions. If individuals begin with holdings they are justly entitled to, and undertake free exchanges, then the distributive outcomes are just, no matter what they are. This entitlement theory shares with other theories a possessively individualist social ontology. Society consists only of individuals with "holdings" of social goods which they augment or reduce through individual production and contractual exchange. The theory does not take into account structural effects of the actions of individuals that they cannot foresee or intend, and to which they might not agree if they could. Nevertheless, Nozick's criticism of end-state theories for ignoring social processes is apt. . . .

This identification of a weakness in traditional social theory can be applied to the distributive paradigm of justice. I disagree with Nozick that end-state patterns are irrelevant to questions of justice. Because they inhibit the ability of some people to live and be healthy, or grant some people resources that allow them to coerce others, some distributions must come into question no matter how they came about. Evaluating patterns of distribution is often an important starting point for questioning about justice. For many issues of social justice, however, what is important is not the particular pattern of distribution at a particular moment, but rather the reproduction of a regular distributive pattern over time.

For example, unless one begins with the assumption that all positions of high status, income, and decision-making power ought to be distributed in comparable numbers to women and men, finding that very few top corporate managers are women might not involve any question of injustice. It is in the context of a social change involving more acceptance of women in corporate management, and a considerable increase in the number of women who obtain degrees in business, that a question of injustice becomes most apparent here. Even though more women earn degrees in business, and in-house policies of some companies aim to encourage women's careers, a pattern of distribution of managerial positions that clusters women at the bottom and men at the top persists. Assuming that justice ultimately means equality for women, this pattern is puzzling, disturbing. We are inclined to ask: what's going on here? Why is this general pattern reproduced even in the face of conscious efforts to change it? Answering that question entails evaluation of a matrix of rules, attitudes, interactions, and policies as a social process that produces and reproduces that pattern. An adequate conception of justice must be able to understand and evaluate the processes as well as the patterns.

One might object that this account confuses the empirical issue of what causes a particular distribution with the normative issue of whether the distribution is just. As will be apparent, however, in the spirit of critical social theory I do not accept this division between empirical and normative social theory. While there is a distinction between empirical and normative statements and the kinds of reasons required for each, no normative theory meant to evaluate existing societies can avoid empirical inquiry, and no empirical investigation of social structures and relations can avoid normative judgments. Inquiry about social justice must consider the context and causes of actual distributions in order to make normative judgments about institutional rules and relations.

The pattern orientation of the distributive paradigm, then, tends to lead to abstraction from institutional rules and relations and a consequent failure to bring them into evaluation. For many aspects of social structure and institutional context cannot be brought into view without examining social processes and the unintended cumulative consequences of individual actions. Without a more temporal approach to social reality, a theory of justice cannot conceptualize exploitation, as a social process by which the labor of some unreciprocally supports the privilege of others. . . .

Defining Injustice as Domination and Oppression

Because distributive models of power, rights, opportunity, and self-respect work so badly, justice should not be conceived primarily on the model of the distribution of wealth, income, and other material goods. Theorizing about justice should explicitly limit the concept of distribution to material goods, like things, natural resources, or money. The scope of justice is wider than distributive issues. Though there may be additional nondistributive issues of justice, my concerns in this book focus on issues of decision-making, division of labor, and culture.

Political thought of the modern period greatly narrowed the scope of justice as it had been conceived by ancient and medieval thought. Ancient thought regarded justice as the virtue of society as a whole, the well-orderedness of institutions that foster individual virtue and promote happiness and harmony among citizens. Modern political thought abandoned the notion that there is a natural order to society that corresponds to the proper ends of human nature. Seeking to liberate the individual to define "his" own ends, modern political theory also restricted the scope of justice to issues of distribution and the minimal regulation of action among such self-defining individuals (Heller, 1987, chapter 2; cf. MacIntyre, 1981, chapter 17).

While I hardly intend to revert to a full-bodied Platonic conception of justice, I nevertheless think it is important to broaden the understanding of justice beyond its usual limits in contemporary philosophical discourse. Agnes Heller (1987, chapter 5) proposes one such broader conception in what she calls an incomplete ethico-political concept of justice. According to her conception, justice names not principles of distribution, much less some particular distributive pattern. This represents too narrow and substantive a way of reflecting on justice. Instead, justice names the perspectives, principles, and procedures for evaluating institutional norms and rules. Developing Habermas's communicative ethics, Heller suggests that justice is primarily the virtue of citizenship, of persons deliberating about problems and issues that confront them collectively in their institutions and actions, under conditions without domination or oppression, with reciprocity and mutual tolerance of difference. She proposes the following test of the justice of social or political norms:

> Every valid social and political norm and rule (every law) must meet the condition that the foreseeable consequences and side effects the general observance of that law (norm) exacts on the satisfaction of the needs of each and every individual would be accepted by everyone concerned, and that the claim of the norm to actualize the universal values of freedom and/or life could be accepted by each and every individual, regardless of the values to which they are committed. (Heller, 1987, pp. 240–41).

. . . I endorse and follow this general conception of justice derived from a conception of communicative ethics. The idea of justice here shifts from a focus on distributive patterns to procedural issues of participation in deliberation and decision-making. For a norm to be just, everyone who follows it must in principle have an effective voice in its consideration and be able to agree to it without coercion. For a social condition to be just, it must enable all to meet their needs and exercise their freedom; thus justice requires that all be able to express their needs.

As I understand it, the concept of justice coincides with the concept of the political. Politics includes all aspects of institutional organization, public action, social practices and habits, and cultural meanings insofar as they are potentially subject to collective evaluation and decision-making. Politics in this inclusive sense certainly concerns the policies and actions of government and the state, but in principle can also concern rules, practices, and actions in any other institutional context (cf. Mason, 1982, pp. 11–24).

The scope of justice, I have suggested, is much wider than distribution, and covers everything political in this sense. This coheres with the meaning of justice claims of the sort mentioned at the outset of this chapter. When people claim that a particular rule, practice, or cultural meaning is wrong and should be changed, they are often making a claim about social injustice. Some of these claims involve distributions, but many also refer to other ways in which social institutions inhibit or liberate persons. . . .

Persons certainly are possessors and consumers, and any conception of justice should presume the value of meeting material needs, living in a comfortable environment, and experiencing pleasures. Adding an image of people as doers and actors (Macpherson, 1973; Gintis and Bowles, 1986) helps to displace the distributive paradigm. As doers and actors, we seek to promote many values of social justice in addition to fairness in the distribution of goods: learning and using satisfying and expansive skills in socially recognized settings; participating in forming and running institutions, and receiving recognition for such participation; playing and communicating with others, and expressing our experience, feelings, and perspective on social life in contexts where others can listen. Certainly many distributive theorists of justice would recognize and affirm these values. The framework of distribution, however, leads to a deemphasizing of these values and a failure to inquire about the institutional conditions that promote them.

This, then, is how I understand the connection between justice and the values that constitute the good life. Justice is not identical with the concrete realization of these values in individual lives; justice, that is, is not identical with the good life as such. Rather, social justice concerns the degree to which a society contains and supports the institutional conditions necessary for the realization of these values. The values comprised in the good life can be reduced to two very general ones: (1) developing and exercising one's capacities and expressing one's experience (cf. Gould, 1988, chapter 2; Galston, 1980, pp. 61–9), and (2) participating in determining one's action and the conditions of one's action (cf. Young, 1979). These are universalist values, in the sense that they assume the equal moral worth of all persons, and thus justice requires their promotion for everyone. To these two general values correspond two social conditions that define injustice: oppression, the institutional constraint on self-development; and domination, the institutional constraint on self-determination.

Oppression consists in systematic institutional processes which prevent some people from learning and using satisfying and expansive skills in socially recognized settings, or institutionalized social processes which inhibit people's ability to play and communicate with others or to express their feelings and perspective on social life in contexts where others can listen. While the social conditions of oppression often include material deprivation or maldistribution, they also involve issues beyond distribution.

Domination consists in institutional conditions which inhibit or prevent people from participating in determining their actions or the conditions of their actions. Persons live within structures of domination if other persons or groups can determine without reciprocation the conditions of their action, either directly or by virtue of the structural consequences of their actions. Thorough social and political democracy is the opposite of domination.

References

Arthur, John and William Shaw (eds). 1978. *Justice and Economic Distribution* (Englewood Cliffs, NJ: Prentice-Hall).

Daniels, Norman. 1985. *Just Health Care* (Cambridge: Cambridge University Press).

Galston, William. 1980. *Justice and the Human Good* (Chicago: University of Chicago Press).

Gintis, Herbert and Samuel Bowles. 1986. *Capitalism and Democracy* (New York: Basic Books).

Gould, Carol. 1988. *Rethinking Democracy: Freedom and Political Cooperation in Politics, Economics, and Society* (Cambridge: Cambridge University Press).

Heller, Agnes. 1987. *Beyond Justice* (New York: Basic Books).

Howard, Michael. 1985. "Worker Control, Self-Respect, and Self-Esteem." *Philosophy Research Archives*, 10: 455–72.

MacIntyre, Alasdair. 1981. *After Virtue* (Notre Dame: University of Notre Dame Press).

Macpherson, C. B. 1973. *Democratic Theory: Essays in Retrieval* (Oxford: Oxford University Press).

Mason, Ronald. 1982. *Participatory and Workplace Democracy* (Carbondale: Southern Illinois University Press).

Miller, David. 1976. *Social Justice* (Oxford: Clarendon Press).

Nicholson, Linda. 1986. *Gender and History* (New York: Colombia University Press).

Nickel, James. 1988. "Equal Opportunity in a Pluralistic Society." In Ellen Frankel Paul, Fred D. Miller, Jeffrey Paul, and John Ahrens (eds), *Equal Opportunity* (Oxford: Blackwell).

Nielsen, Kai. 1978. "Class and Justice." In John Arthur and William Shaw (eds), *Justice and Economic Distribution* (Englewood Cliffs, NJ: Prentice-Hall).

Nozick, Robert. 1974. *Anarchy, State, and Utopia* (New York: Basic Books).

Okin, Susan. 1986. "Are our Theories of Justice Gender-Neutral?" In Robert Fullinwider and Claudia Mills (eds), *The Moral Foundations of Civil Rights* (Totowa, NJ: Rowman and Littlefield).

Pateman, Carole. 1988. *The Sexual Contract* (Stanford: Stanford University Press).

Rawls, John. 1971. *A Theory of Justice* (Cambridge: Harvard University Press).

Reiman, Jeffrey. 1987. "Exploitation, Force, and the Moral Assessment of Capitalism: Thoughts on Roemer and Cohen." *Philosophy and Public Affairs*, 16 (Winter): 3–41.

Sandel, Michael. 1982. *Liberalism and the Limits of Justice* (Cambridge: Cambridge University Press).

Schweickart, David. 1984. "Plant Relocations: A Philosophical Reflection." *Review of Radical Political Economics*, 16 (Winter): 32–51.

Simon, Robert. 1984. "Troubled Waters: Global Justice and Ocean Resources." In Tom Regan (ed.), *Earthbound* (New York: Random House).

Simpson, Evan. 1980. "The Subject of Justice." *Ethics*, 90 (July): 490–501.

Taylor, Charles. 1985. "The Nature and Scope of Distributive Justice." In *Philosophy and the Human Sciences* (Cambridge: Cambridge University Press).

Walzer, Michael. 1983. *Spheres of Justice* (New York: Basic Books).

Wolff, Robert Paul. 1977. *Understanding Rawls* (Princeton: Princeton University Press).

Wood, Allen. 1972. "The Marxian Critique of Justice." *Philosophy and Public Affairs*, 1 (Spring): 244–82.

Young, Iris. 1979. "Self-Determination as a Principle of Justice." *Philosophical Forum*, 11 (Fall): 172–82.

——. 1983. "Justice and Hazardous Waste." In Michael Bradie (ed.), *The Applied Turn in Contemporary Philosophy* (Bowling Green, OH: Applied Philosophy Program, Bowling Green State University).

52

Property Rights, Economic Inequalities, and International Obligations

Clark Wolf

I. Two Conceptions of Justice

Few moral concepts have inspired as much fervent praise and angry condemnation as the concept of property rights. Perhaps this is especially true in the United States and other relatively young countries, where many people can trace their ancestry back to landless immigrants who arrived with nothing, labored through lifetimes and generations to acquire property rights in land, and who often fought fiercely to defend those rights. Many people consequently feel that their own labor and the labor of their ancestors entitles them to what they now own, and that any effort to take their property from them, or to limit their right to do as they wish with what they rightfully own, must be excessive interference at least, or at worst, oppression and tyranny.

It is not difficult to understand how people come to feel this way. Property rights are closely related to our general right to liberty, the precious right to live our lives as we please without interference, at least where our choices don't harm others. Property rights are necessary for the existence of an economic market that makes mutually advantageous economic activity possible, and which is perhaps the most efficient institution possible for the production and distribution of goods and services. The notion that labor creates entitlement is as ancient as it is elemental, and it has seemed to many that there is something deeply natural about it. Wherever laborers have been forced to work without gaining any entitlement to the fruits of their labor, they have bitterly resented the injustice of their situation, and often have risen up to try to abolish the institutions they come to regard as the source of this injustice. This conception of justice, which focuses on property rights and the relationship between labor and entitlement, might be called "propertarianism."

It is clear that property rights are important from the moral point of view – at least their importance will not be questioned in my discussion here. But we may still ask what weight these rights have when they come in conflict with other morally significant considerations. For there is another conception of justice that may be just as universal and just as deeply embedded in our understandings and judgments. Jean-Jacques Rousseau expressed the core of this second conception well when he wrote:

> It is obviously contrary to the law of nature, however it may be defined, for a child to command an old man, for an imbecile to lead a wise man, and for a handful of people to gorge themselves on superfluities while the starving multitude lacks necessities. (Rousseau, 1992, pp. 868–9)

Even if we have doubts about Rousseau's claim that enormous disparity in wealth is "contrary to the law of nature" we may well share with Rousseau, and with many others throughout history, the sense that there is something seriously wrong in a world that contains both crawling destitution and extravagant overabundance. Rousseau put this notion in terms of the value of equality: this second conception of justice, egalitarianism, holds that societies are unjust if they are characterized by vast inequality in wealth or well-being.

These two conceptions of justice, propertarianism and egalitarianism, both have deep roots in philosophical traditions worldwide. Each of these conceptions of justice has been attributed to "nature": Rousseau believed that extreme inequalities violate laws of nature, while John Locke argued that labor-based property rights are natural rights. More interestingly, these conceptions of justice may not simply be artifacts of our culture, or dependent on the peculiarities of one philosophical tradition, for variations on these conceptions have been articulated by thoughtful people from different unrelated philosophical traditions, and people from widely different cultural backgrounds have found them attractive. They may not be "natural" in the sense that some have thought: rules assigning labor-based property rights, or proscribing radical inequalities may not be discoverable laws of nature in the way that laws of physics are laws of nature. But it may be that common properties of human beings, and common features of the human condition lead people to develop notions of property and equality, and to regard these notions as normative. In this sense, commitment to these conceptions of justice may be "natural."

But to say that these conceptions of justice may be natural in this sense is not necessarily an endorsement of them. It may be "natural" in this same sense, for people to become bitter and spiteful under certain circumstances, but that would not justify us in regarding bitterness and spite as moral virtues. People may have a "natural" propensity to be deceived by certain fallacious lines of reasoning, but such reasoning is nonetheless fallacious. A similar problem plagues these two "natural" conceptions of justice: unfortunately, they seem to be incompatible with one another. Over time, inequalities will emerge wherever private property rights are respected, since different people will labor differently, and (perhaps more importantly) different people will inherit different goods. Since it takes wealth to create wealth, these inequalities are likely to increase until the point is reached at which some are extravagantly wealthy while others are impoverished.

How should we regard inequalities that "naturally" arise in institutions that respect property rights? Those who regard equality as overridingly important are likely to say "so much the worse for property rights." Here is Rousseau's reaction:

> The first person who, having enclosed a plot of land, took it into his head to say "this is mine" and found people simple enough to believe him, was the true founder of civil society. What crimes, wars, murders, what miseries and horrors would the human race have been spared, had someone pulled up the stakes, filled in the ditch and cried out to his fellow men: "Do not listen to this impostor. You are lost if you forget that the fruits of the earth belong to all and the earth to no one!" (Rousseau, 1992, p. 877)

Without private property, individual people could not amass wealth, and without rich people, the great pernicious disparities whose existence Rousseau lamented could not come into existence. But those who take property rights seriously have found Rousseau's account excessively simplistic and one-sided. Voltaire wrote in the margin of Rousseau's essay, beside the passage quoted above: "What! He who has planted, sown, fenced in, has no right to the fruit of his labor!" And commenting on Rousseau's stake-pulling, ditch-filling savior of humankind, he scribbled "What! That unjust man, that thief, would have been the benefactor of mankind! That is the philosophy of the beggar who would like the rich to be robbed by the poor!" (Havens, 1966, p. 15). Like many readers, Voltaire regarded Rousseau's attack on the institution of private property outrageous, since it severed the link between labor and ownership. People have a right to things when they invest their labor into them. And if it is wrong to violate people's rights, then it is wrong to take from people what they rightfully own, even if this is the only way to gain equality. But even appreciation of Voltaire's argument may not undermine our sense that Rousseau was right to argue that something has gone deeply wrong when some are destitute and others have much more than they need. What is to be done if we can satisfy our sense that "radical inequality is unjust" only at the expense of our conviction that it is unjust to deprive people of property they rightfully hold?

The conflict between these alternative conceptions of justice has been the source of what may be the most vigorous disputes in political philosophy. Some writers simply start with one or the other conception, and expand it into a fully articulated theory of justice, without trying to account for the intuitions behind the alternative conception. Thus Robert Nozick (1974) starts with the intuitive appeal of individual rights and property rights in particular, while others like G. A. Cohen (1989) begin with the intuitive appeal of egalitarianism, and the moral repugnance of radical inequalities. In this paper, I hope to outline a middle way between these conflicting alternatives. I will argue that we can develop an account of justice that incorporates what each of these views gets right. The resultant view gives special weight to individual rights and property claims, but also preserves Rousseau's sense that some kinds of economic inequalities are incompatible with justice.

II. Property, Labor, and Entitlement

When an individual has a property right, she has a claim to do many different things. Ordinary property rights include the right to exclude others from using what one owns, the right to give away what one owns, and other prerogatives, claims, and powers. To understand these rights properly, we need to understand how people might initially acquire them. In this interest, it will be valuable to consider the most famous account of the creation and evolution of property rights as articulated by John Locke in his *Second Treatise of Government*.

Locke began with the assumption that individual persons have private property rights in their bodies and their labor. The earth and all its fruits, however, he viewed as the common property of all. So for Locke, a philosophical account of property rights must show how individuals could gain *private* property rights in what previously was held in common. According to Locke, it is necessity that justifies such exclusive appropriation:

> He that is nourished by the Acorns he picked up under an Oak, or the Apples he gathered from the trees in the wood has certainly appropriated them to himself. . . . And will any one say he

had no right to those Acorns or Apples he thus appropriated, because he had not the consent of all Mankind to make them his? . . . If such consent as that was necessary, Man would have starved, notwithstanding the Plenty God had given him. . . . The Grass my Horse has bit, the Turfs my Servant has cut; and the Ore I Have digg'd in any place where I have a right to them in common with others, become my *Property* without the assignation or consent of anybody. (Locke, 1963, pp. 329–30)

Private ownership is gained, according to Locke, when we mix our labor with resources that are initially held in common. By mixing what we own (our labor) with what we do not (Locke's acorns and apples), we come to have private property rights in those resources:

Whatsoever then [a person] removes out of the State that Nature hath provided, and left it in, he hath mixed his *Labour* with, and joyned it to something that is his own, and thereby makes it his *Property*. It being by him removed from the common state Nature placed it in, hath by this *labour* something annexed to it, that excludes the common right of other men. For this *Labour* being the unquestionable Property of the Labourer, no Man but he can have a right to what that is once joyned to, at least where there is enough, and as good left in common for others. (Locke, 1963, p. 329)

On Locke's view, Voltaire's gardener, who has planted, sown, and fenced in a garden, has property rights in the fruits of his labor as long as his activities do not unreasonably limit the opportunities of others: he must simply be careful to leave them "enough and as good" as he has himself appropriated.

Locke's initial assumptions may seem strange. What can it mean to say that individuals "own their bodies"? And how can one have property rights in something as intangible as labor? The easiest way to gain a sympathetic understanding of Locke's intent is to interpret these rights in terms of the obligations of others: a person's "property right" in her body is equivalent to the obligation that other people have not to harm her, and not to use her body without consent or permission. Most of us accept that people do have such obligations: this partly explains why assault and rape, for example, are morally reprehensible. Locke's notion that we have private property rights in our labor may initially seem more problematical. Labor is not a tangible object, and it may seem difficult to see how a person could own it. Once again, however, this notion is easier to accept if we interpret this right in terms of the moral obligations of others: My "property right in my labor" is equivalent to others' obligation not to force me to do what I do not freely choose to do. Again, most people accept the implicit moral judgment that it is morally wrong to gain others' help through threat and coercion. We need not interpret Locke's claim that *people have property rights in their own labor* to mean anything more than this. Critics of Locke often pejoratively argue that he is a "natural rights" theorist, and that his theory fails because there simply are no natural rights. But most of those who make this claim would agree that people have a moral obligation not to harm or use others, and not to gain their cooperation through coercion or threat. These obligations are all Locke needs to get his theory of property off the ground: if we do indeed have moral obligations not to harm others or to gain their cooperation through force or threat, then Locke's argument still has force.

Locke claims that there are limits on appropriation, since appropriators have an obligation not to harm or coerce others. If appropriation harms others, or seriously sets back their interests, then it cannot be justified. Locke expresses this restriction in his famous proviso, which stipulates that labor mixing creates private property rights *at least* where "enough and as good" is left for others. If appropriation unjustifiably sets back the interests of others, then it may be necessary to compensate them for their loss before one acquires a legitimate property right in the soil one has tilled or the trees one has nurtured. If such compensation is impossible, then one may have no right to appropriate at all.

Of course, current property rights did not originate in appropriation from an unowned heath or a commons, but usually through the violent extermination and expulsion of prior claimants. There were people in America long before European settlers arrived to carve out their claims and build their homes. Americans with European ancestors may be right in thinking that their forebears labored and fought for their property, but on Locke's view, the people they fought had prior claims. Effort and labor cannot validate claims on property that is stolen from others, so if the land we "own" was stolen from the Native Americans, then our property rights will not be legitimate in Locke's sense. If these current rights deserve moral respect, it cannot be because they arose through a justifiable process. Still, by discovering the limitations of ideal property rights, we may come to a better understanding of the limitations on our own more dubious claims.

III. Limitations on Property Rights: Necessity

What limitations are there on private property rights? Contemporary Lockean theories like that of Robert Nozick sometimes seem to imply that property rights are absolute and inviolable under any circumstances whatsoever. But even Nozick recognizes that rights of ownership do not include any claim to use one's property in ways that might be harmful to others, just as Locke includes identical restrictions on the circumstances of legitimate appropriation. The same restrictions that define the moral limitations of appropriation define limitations on the structure of our property rights, and the ways in which we are justified in using what we own. If, as Locke and Nozick agree, it would be wrong to appropriate when appropriation would harm others or unjustifiably set back their interests, then rights of ownership must also be limited rights: we have no right to use what we own in ways that would unjustifiably set back the interests of others. Unsurprisingly, such limitations on property rights are deeply entrenched in our legal institutions. It is not only immoral but also illegal to use one's property in ways that harm others.

Locke himself was concerned to examine circumstances in which appropriation itself could constitute a harm to others, and his proviso that "enough and as good" must be left for others is best understood as a prohibition on such harmful appropriation. Locke bases the right to appropriate on necessity: we *need* to be able to appropriate things to our own uses, else we would "Starve amid the Plenty" of the earth. But this reliance on necessity has implications for the limitations of the rights Locke defends: if our property rights depend, in the way that Locke argues, on people's need to satisfy basic, urgent needs, then these rights must be sensitive to the urgent needs of others.

In some contexts, this limitation on property rights is uncontroversial: If the only way I can save my life is to infringe your property rights, then it seems clear that I may legitimately do so. Joel Feinberg offers the following colorful example:

> Suppose that you are on a back-packing trip in the mountain country when an unanticipated blizzard strikes the area with such ferocity that your life is imperiled. Fortunately, you stumble onto an unoccupied cabin, locked and boarded up for the winter, clearly somebody else's private property. You smash in a window, enter, and huddle in a corner for three days until the storm abates. During this period, you help yourself to your unknown benefactor's food supply

and burn his wooden furniture in the fireplace to keep warm. Surely you are justified in doing all these things, and yet you have infringed the clear rights of another person. (Feinberg, 1980, p. 230)

Of course it is permissible to break into a cabin if this is the only way one can preserve one's life. The owner's property right simply includes no claim against those whose needs are urgent and desperate. The notion that property rights are limited, and include no claims against the extreme necessity of others is not an especially radical suggestion, nor is it merely a matter of concern for scholars of Locke's work. In fact, we have incorporated similar restrictions on property rights in our own legal system – a system which gives a central place to the legal and moral significance of property rights. For example, ownership of one's house does not justify one, either legally or morally, in expelling unwanted guests into dangerous inclement weather (see *Depue* v. *Flateau*). Nor does ownership of a dock justify one in casting off the mooring lines of a boat that pulls up to avoid being destroyed in a storm (see *Ploof* v. *Putnam*, and *Vincent* v. *Lake Erie Transportation Co.*).

But recognition of other kinds of necessity will be more controversial, and has much more far-reaching implications. For the notion that our property rights are limited by the urgent needs of others also implies that these rights must give way to the needs of those who are impoverished and needy in a more standard sense. If we own more than we need, our claim to surplus property must sometimes give way to the urgent needs of others. Locke expressed this limitation clearly and elegantly:

> God the Lord and Father of all has given no one of his Children such a Property, in his peculiar portion of the things of this world, but that he has given his needy Brother a right to the Surplusage of his Goods; so that it cannot be justly denied him, when his pressing Wants call for it. And therefore no Man could ever have a just Power over the Life of another, by Right of property in Land or Possessions; since 'twould always be a Sin in any Man of Estate, to let his Brother perish for want of affording him Relief out of his Plenty. As *Justice* gives each every Man a Title to the product of his honest Industry, and the fair Acquisitions of his Ancestors descended to him; so *Charity* gives every Man a Title to so much out of another's Plenty, as will keep him from extream want, where he has no means to subsist otherwise; and a Man can no more justly make use of another's necessity, to force him to become his Vassal, by withholding that Relief God requires him to afford to the wants of his Brother, than he that has more strength can seize upon a weaker, master him to his Obedience, and with a Dagger at his Throat, offer him Death or Slavery. (Locke, 1963, pp. 205–6)

While Locke here discusses property rights in theological terms, he understands the basis of these rights in terms of labor and the terms of legitimate appropriation discussed above. Those in need, Locke argues, are *entitled* to the surplus of those who own more than they need. Their claims on this "surplusage" simply outweigh the claims of those who own it. This surplusage cannot be "justly denied" to those who are in need. According to Locke, this aspect of charity is not separate from justice, but is one aspect of justice: to be uncharitable in this sense is to be unjust. Even libertarians like Robert Nozick allow that property rights may be limited, and "violable" when their violation is necessary to "avoid catastrophic moral horror" (Nozick, 1974, pp. 29–30). But surely few moral horrors could be more catastrophic than destitution and want, with their consequent effects on the lives of those whose urgent needs are left unmet. Nozick's account of property rights thus inherits the limitations of it's Lockean ancestor, and current accounts of property rights must also take these limitations into account.

The implications of these limitations are as clear as they are radical: if our property rights in excess of what we need to live decently include no claims against the urgent needs of others, and if there are others who are in urgent need, and whom we could help by giving to them from our surplus, then we *owe* our superabundance of property to those needy people. According to Locke, those who possess surplus but who uncharitably deny the needs of others have violated the principles that justified property rights in the first place.

IV.   Limitations on Property Rights: Mutuality

Consider a group of people, each of whom owns a house lot that includes marshland bordering a greater lake. Suppose that there is an obligation not to destroy the marsh, since it represents a biological and ecological resource in which many other people have a crucial interest. Destruction of the marsh would unjustifiably set back that interest, and thus would constitute a harm. Each landowner might have an interest in developing his or her portion of marsh by digging a narrow channel for a boat launch and by putting up a dock. If the marsh is large enough that no individual dock would destroy it, then building one dock will not violate the obligation not to destroy the marsh. But if each owner builds a dock, the marsh will be destroyed. In such circumstances, each person can justifiably say, "My development will not destroy the marsh." But it is not the case that each of them has the right to develop, since the total system of development rights would harm others. The moral of this story is that limitations on individual property rights are sometimes determined by the overall effects of the total system of rights. Just as initial acquisition is unjustified when it would harm others, the total system of appropriation is unjustified if others are harmed by it, even if no individual act that takes place within that system is harmful.

Like many recent economists and political theorists, Locke believed that the institution of property ownership is overwhelmingly beneficial rather than harmful. This institution makes larger economic markets possible, and results in a much larger total of social surplus that would not exist in alternate institutions. A larger social surplus means that society produces more of what people want and need. But if some are unable to participate in the market, and are excluded from the enjoyment of the surplus they create, they may have a valid complaint against the system that excludes them, and their interests may be set back by the institutions themselves. In such cases, if their interests are *unjustifiably* set back, those who are excluded may have a valid claim to receive compensation from those who enjoy the benefits of these institutions.

Obviously, it matters a great deal who *owns* the social surplus that markets create. If market institutions tend to concentrate resources and wealth in the hands of a few, while others are much worse off than they would have been under alternate institutions, then those who are worse off will have no reason to love or respect property rights. The argument that overall social surplus is larger than it would have been under alternate institutions will not impress those who are excluded in this way, and they may have no good reason to respect the institution that seems to work to their disadvantage. When a society ignores people's needs, who can blame the needy if they come to regard property rights, and the legal system that enforces them, as a form of oppressive exclusion? Banquo's murderer, in MacBeth III. i, explains his contempt for law and right: "I am one . . . whom the vile blows and buffets of the world have so incensed that I am reckless what I do to spite the world." If our society allows people to become destitute and desperate, and ignores the fundamental needs of those who are impoverished, we cannot be surprised when those who are in need lack "proper respect" for the rights of others.

But there is more to the problem than simple recognition that the desperate and the destitute will have no reason to respect rights to private property. The appropriate response to that worry might simply be to put up strong walls to defend ourselves and our property from them. More importantly, the existence of people whose destitution and unmet need are a consequence of our institution of private property itself would call into question the moral justification of that institution, and would implicitly call into question the justification of our claims on what we purport to own. We cannot properly respond to such needs by putting up more walls and protecting what we claim as our property. When we possess more than we need while others lack basic necessities, we have a positive obligation to aid those who are in need. Such an obligation is implicit in the moral justification of our claims to private property, since the validity of our rights depends on fulfillment of this obligation.

So far we have discussed the obligation to aid others as hypothetical: we have such an obligation if there are people whose interests are unjustifiably set back by the institutions from which we benefit, and if there is some effective way we can aid them. But it can be argued that we actually do have such obligations, since our institutions harm people in just this way. Recent economic studies have conclusively shown that famine and widespread destitution are not caused by material scarcity of food or goods. Surprisingly, local food availability and production has often increased in times of famine, as it did during the Bangladesh famine of 1974. Famine stricken regions often *export* food, since those who own it can usually get a better price elsewhere, and since those who need it cannot afford to purchase it. This is well documented, for example, in the case of the Irish famines of the 1840s, and that of the Ethiopian famine of 1973. (See Drèze and Sen, pp. 27–9, and Sen, 1994, p. 63.) In such circumstances, poverty and destitution are not caused by shortage, but result from a system of property entitlements that leaves those who are in need with no right to the resources they need. Typically, famine and destitution result from failures of entitlement, not from any real shortage of food, goods, or resources. In this important sense, they are a consequence of our system of property rights.

If we find that our institutions are harmful to others, how should we respond? Rousseau is often interpreted as recommending that we should abolish property rights entirely. Surely this was Voltaire's interpretation, which explains Voltaire's outrage at Rousseau's discussion of property in the *Essay on the Origins of Inequality*. Actually Rousseau's views on the redistribution of property were fairly conservative. In other writings, Rousseau defended property rights, and argued that extensive redistribution of property was undesirable because it would be socially disruptive and would often cause more harms than it would mend. In our own situation, it is unlikely that the elimination of the institution of private property would improve the circumstances of those who currently live in poverty. It is likely that efforts to eliminate property rights, or to coercively enforce equality, would leave people much worse off than they already are. Rather than abolishing the institution, we should see to it that the institution does not work to the disadvantage of others. This can be accomplished by providing those who are excluded with what they need, and by using the superfluous wealth of our society to aid those whose needs are at risk.

V. Property Rights and the Obligation to Aid: The Central Arguments

This discussion has included two central arguments: First, I have argued that property rights are limited rights, that include no claims against the urgent needs of others. Second,

I have argued that the justification of the institution of property is contingent, and depends on our ability to ensure that that system does not work to the disadvantage of others. Recognition that the institution of property rights, as it exists in our world, has grave costs for others, should not motivate us to eliminate the institution itself, but rather to recognize and fulfill our obligation to alleviate these costs by using the surplus that this institution creates to aid and improve the lives of those who are disadvantaged. Fulfillment of this obligation is required because our property rights are limited and do not entitle us to deny sustenance to those whose needs are urgent, but also because the justification of the institution of property itself depends on our ability to ensure that this institution does not make others worse off.

If these arguments are correct, they imply a weighty obligation for most of us. They imply an obligation not to use our excess wealth for our own enjoyment, but instead to use it to alleviate the urgent needs of others, and to help those who are excluded by the market to enter it and enjoy its benefits. Our obligation does not require us to aid others to the point of marginal utility – the point at which additional aid would cause as much disadvantage as it would alleviate. We have an obligation to do what we can without sacrificing the fundamental needs of ourselves and our families, or compromising our own ability to live a full and productive life. We have an obligation to aid others when their urgent needs represent weightier moral claims than our own. We may justly provide for our own basic needs and those of our families *first*, but we fail to meet our obligations if we provide ourselves or our families with luxuries while there are others who lack basic necessities (Rachels, 1989, p. 60).

Sometimes people argue that the world is too complex, and that we have no effective means to aid the destitute and desperate. But given the existence of effective aid organizations like OXFAM and Habitat for Humanity, among many others, it is self-deceptive for us to try to argue that there is no effective way for us to provide aid for those who are in need. Rather than simply providing food for the hungry, OXFAM and other effective organizations support agricultural and economic development projects that aim to provide people and communities with the opportunities and resources they need to become self-sufficient. Aid of this sort does not create a "culture of dependency" – on the contrary, it ultimately enables those who are impoverished to take care of themselves.

VI. What Counts as "Surplus"?

It is clear that fulfillment of our obligations to others would sharply curtail our consumption of luxury goods and excess consumer goods. But how much of what we consume constitutes "surplusage of goods," as Locke called it, or "superfluities" in the words of Rousseau? How weighty are our obligations to others, and what, in particular, do they require of us? In order to answer this question, we need an account of human needs, and an account of what it is to live a decent human life. We cannot provide such an account in this short essay, but it is clear that many of the things we own, consume, and buy constitute "surplusage" far beyond any reasonable conception of what people need in order to live well. We must determine what counts as surplus wealth from the larger perspective of the human condition worldwide, taking into account the effects that current resource consumption will have for members of future generations. Clearly it would be wrong for current generations to consume resources irresponsibly, leaving later generations unable to meet their needs, just as it would be wrong for those who are now well off to spend their excess wealth on superfluous consumption when there are so many who lack basic necessities.

From this perspective, what constitutes surplus consumption? Currently we who are citizens of the relatively wealthy countries who are members of the Organization for Economic Cooperation and Development (OECD) comprise 15 percent of the world's total population, but consume 73 percent of world output (Folbre, 1995, 10.11). The extent of inequalities within developed countries like the United States makes this disparity even more striking: the wealthiest 1 percent of American citizens hold roughly 37 percent of the nation's wealth, while the top 10 percent holds roughly 68 percent (Folbre, 1995, 1.2). Americans and Europeans spend enormous amounts of money on hair coloring, sports cars, sound recordings, and stylish clothing, while there are many in the world who cannot afford an adequately nutritious diet, and have little or no access to education or medical care. It seems clear that the world we live in contains the same disparities in wealth that Rousseau found so morally repugnant. We should find these disparities repugnant as well.

It is unlikely that we will be able to achieve unanimous agreement on just where the cut-off point between requirements and superfluities should lie: there may be disagreement, for example, about whether arts and music constitute fundamental needs, or essential elements of a human life, or whether they are expendable superfluities. But it is beyond question that the lifestyles enjoyed in America and Europe include many such luxuries and superfluities. There is nothing wrong with luxury or superfluity *as such*, but in a global context in which so many people lack basic necessities, it seems clear that our claims to these resources are simply outweighed by the needs of others. For most people, fulfillment of the obligations implicit in our property rights would clearly involve significant changes in lifestyle and consumption patterns.

VII.   Is Equality Valuable? Is Inequality Unjust?

These considerations bring us back to Rousseau's claims about inequality and disparity: his famous assertion that it is contrary to the law of nature for some people to "gorge themselves on superfluities" while others lack basic necessities. This is usually understood as a defense of equality, and it is certain the Rousseau took himself to be condemning inequality. But perhaps it is not inequality as such that is objectionable. Imagine an extremely wealthy society in which the worst off members are as well off as the Sultan of Brunei (currently the wealthiest person in the world, with holdings valued at about 37 billion US dollars). Suppose that this society is marked by radical inequalities: the very *best* off members of this society are so wealthy that their wealth makes the Sultan of Brunei's wealth tiny in comparison. If inequality is unjust in itself, then it would follow that this society must be seriously unjust.

But it's hard to work up much moral indignation about the situation of a person as wealthy as the Sultan of Brunei, even if he were the worst off member of a fabulously wealthy group. When even the worst off members of society are quite well off, inequalities don't seem unjust, or even significant from the moral point of view. Such considerations should lead us to conclude that it is not inequality that is morally repugnant, but the juxtaposition of crawling destitution and excessive affluence. The reason such disparities are unjust is now clear: the claims of those who have urgent unmet needs simply outweigh the claims of those who possess more than they need. What is objectionable is not inequality as such, but inequality combined with the extreme destitution and misery of those who are worst off. If everyone were adequately well off, if there were not people whose fundamental needs are unmet, then inequality would not be a problem, so we need not eliminate inequality in our efforts to make the world more just. Besides this, the elimination of inequality is probably not possible, and would surely require unacceptable curtailment of individual liberty.

It is appropriate to note an additional limitation on the argument I have offered: from the fact that we have obligations of charity, it does not immediately follow that others have a right to force us to fulfill those obligations. The question whether or not this aspect of charity may be enforced cannot be answered by arguments that explain the contents of our obligations. (On this point, see DenUyl, 1993; and Lomasky, 1995.) But there is a strong *prima facie* case in favor of the view that such obligations may indeed be legitimately enforced, perhaps through taxation for welfare support. If the claims of the needy take precedence over the competing claims of those who are well off, then welfare taxation cannot be said to violate the property rights of the well off. And if the claims of the needy are not preempted or defeated by any other claims, then their claims constitute welfare rights. We might therefore view legitimate welfare institutions as protections for the rights of the needy and the vulnerable. (See Buchanan, 1987; and Waldron, 1986.)

When amended with appropriate qualifications, both the propertarian conception of justice and the egalitarian conception share the implication that we have an obligation to do what we can to eliminate destitution and deprivation wherever they exist, and both imply that we have a weighty obligation to provide aid to those whose needs are urgent. We can, in the end, acknowledge the moral significance of property rights without relinquishing Rousseau's insight that some kinds of inequality are unjust when they include some who "gorge themselves on superfluities" while others lack basic necessities. But the only way we can do this is by acknowledging our own weighty obligation to aid others around the world who are desperate and destitute. If we fail to fulfill this obligation, then our own property claims are empty and illegitimate.

References

Buchanan, Allen: 1987. "Justice and Charity." *Ethics*, 97(3): 558–75.

Cohen, G. A.: 1989. "The Currency of Egalitarian Justice." *Ethics*, 99(4): 906–44.

DenUyl, Douglas J.: 1993. "The Right to Welfare and the Virtue of Charity," in Ellen Frankel Paul, Fred D. Miller Jr, and Jeffrey Paul (eds), *Altruism* (New York: Cambridge University Press).

Drèze, Jean, and Amartya Sen: 1989. *Hunger and Public Action* (Oxford: Clarendon Press).

Feinberg, Joel: 1980. *Rights, Justice, and the Bounds of Liberty* (Princeton NJ: Princeton University Press).

Folbre, Nancy: 1995. *The New Field Guide to the US Economy* (New York: The New Press).

Havens, George R.: 1966. *Voltaire's Marginalia on the Pages of Rousseau* (New York: Haskell House).

Locke, John: 1963. *Two Treatises of Government*, ed. Peter Laslett (New York: Cambridge University Press).

Lomasky, Loren: 1995. "Justice to Charity." *Social Philosophy and Policy*, 12(2): 32–53.

Nozick, Robert: 1974. *Anarchy, State, and Utopia* (New York: Basic Books).

Rachels, James: 1989. "Morality, Parents, and Children," in Hugh LaFollette and George Graham (eds), *Person to Person* (Philadelphia: Temple University Press).

Rousseau, Jean-Jacques: 1992. "Discourse on the Origins of Inequality," in Michael L. Morgan (ed.), *Classics of Moral and Political Theory* (Indianapolis, IN: Hackett).

Sen, Amartya: 1994. "Population and Reasoned Agency: Food, Fertility, and Economic Development," in Kerstin Lindahl-Kiessling and Hans Landberg, *Population, Economic*

Development, and the Environment (New York: Oxford University Press).

Waldron, Jeremy: 1986. "Welfare and the Images of Charity." *Philosophical Quarterly*, 36: 463–82.

Wolf, Clark: 1995. "Contemporary Property Rights, Lockean Provisos, and the Interests of Future Generations." *Ethics*, 105(4): 791–818.

Court Cases

Depue v. *Flateau*, 100 Minn. 209, 111 N.W. 1, 8 L.R.A.(N.S) 485.

Ploof v. *Putnam*, 81 Vt. 471, 71 A. 188.

Vincent v. *Lake Erie Transportation Co.*, 109 Minn. 456, 124 N.W. 221.

World Hunger and
International Justice

Do we have any obligations to, or moral responsibility for, people living in other countries? If so, are we responsible only for our political allies, or obligated only to countries we think can benefit us? Or are we also obligated to countries with which we have few – or even antagonistic – relations? Most people acknowledge that we are obligated not to harm others, even if they do not live within our country, and even if they are not our allies. Thus, I should not embezzle money from my boss – whether my boss is a foreigner or a fellow citizen. Are we obligated to do more than not harm foreigners? Should we also prevent harm to them? Must we, for example, feed starving children in Thailand or promote the economy of Zimbabwe? If so, how much should we help them, and under what circumstances?

For years, questions about the nature and extent of our obligations to people in other countries have been hotly debated in the United Nations, in the halls of Congress, and on talk shows. One currently pressing question is: should Western countries intervene in Bosnia to try to stop the "racial cleansing"? Two years ago we were asking: should we intervene in Rwanda to stop genocide? Some people claim that we should not intervene, that what happens in another country is just none of our business. Others advocate intervention, military or otherwise.

Although none of the authors in this section explicitly discuss military intervention, their arguments about our obligations (or our lack of them) to foreigners have clear implications for the propriety of such intervention. For instance, if we have no moral obligation to prevent harm to foreigners, then we should intervene only if we think it is in our national interest. On this view, entering the Gulf War was reasonable for us since we needed to protect the flow of cheap oil. It would have been silly, however, to have intervened simply to stop political aggression against Kuwait. Why should we endanger our soldiers to stop aggression against foreigners? On the other hand, if we have strong obligations or responsibilities to prevent harm, then we have one compelling reason for intervening, even if it is not in our best national interest. In short, questions about the scope of our obligations to our fellow citizens (ECONOMIC JUSTICE) are replicated in the international arena.

Consider the current debate in the United States about economic trade. I frequently hear people complain that although Japan wants to sell us her goods without having to face protective tariffs, she nonetheless erects such tariffs on (some) goods we wish to sell there. According to the conventional wisdom, this position is inconsistent, unfair. I suspect Goodin would agree. However, he claims that most Western countries are equally inconsistent in their relations with the rest of the world, and especially Third World countries. Why? We do not treat immigration and emigration similarly: although we let our citizens emigrate to Third World countries, we are reluctant to accept immigrants from those same countries. Moreover, whereas we welcome money from other countries, we are reluctant to accept their people. Perhaps there are good reasons for a country to have (relatively) closed borders. On that issue Goodin takes no stance. However, he does claim that whatever our policy, we must be consistent: if borders are to be closed, they should be closed both ways, for the same reasons, and to the same extent.

Of course, countries would economically benefit from placing heavier demands on other countries than they place on themselves. Countries with no moral scruples are likely to do just that. Goodin claims, though, that if we claim to be a moral country, we must demand of ourselves no less than we demand of others. Which brings us back to a different form of the question with which we began: how far do our moral obligations extend? And just how strong are these obligations?

Many people think those obligations extend at least this far and have at least this much strength: that we should feed starving children living in other countries. To decide if these suppositions are defensible, we must settle two important theoretical questions. First, are our obligations to foreigners as strong as our obligations to fellow citizens? Second, do we have obligations to prevent harm, as well as obligations not to do harm directly? Singer claims the answer to both is "Yes."

Let us look at each question in turn. First, Singer claims there is no fundamental difference between our obligations to someone near and to someone far away. It may be more difficult to help a foreigner than a neighbor. If so, we have a practical reason to favor the neighbor: our intervention is more likely to help. However, he argues, if we can help distant people (roughly) as effectively as we can help our neighbors, then we have the same general obligation – whatever it is – to both.

Questions about the precise scope of our moral obligations lie at the base of virtually every issue discussed in this volume. Most people recognize that they should care for their children and family. Nevertheless, exactly how much further do our obligations go? That issue, which first raised its head in the essays by Williams and Rachels (FAMILY AND FRIENDS), keeps cropping up, albeit in a different guise. In the previous section we discussed our obligations to fellow citizens. Here we are discussing obligations to citizens of other countries. Earlier we asked whether our obligations extend to non-human ANIMALS. In the following section, the authors will ask whether we are also obligated to the ENVIRONMENT.

The second theoretical issue likewise intersects virtually every issue in this book: the *act/omission* distinction. The act/omission distinction first appeared in the essays on EUTHANASIA, and has lurked in the background of most issues in this volume. Everyone acknowledges that we must make serious personal sacrifices to stop from actively harming others. For instance, I should crash my expensive car rather than run over a child who strays into the road in front of me.

However, many people claim that whereas I may have to make a considerable sacrifice so that I do not directly harm another, I need not make similar sacrifices to keep a comparable harm from occurring – unless, of course, I created the conditions that led to that harm. We can see the force of the act/omission distinction in the debate over world hunger. Those who think the distinction is morally significant, claim that whereas I should not kill a young child in a distant country simply to increase my wealth, I need not give up my wealth to keep that same child from starving to death.

Singer denies the moral force of this distinction. He claims not only that those of us in affluent nations have an obligation to feed the starving of the world, but that the obligation is sufficiently strong that we must be willing to make substantial sacrifices for them. Arthur disagrees. We are not morally required to make substantial (and perhaps not even minor) sacrifices to help others. After all, he says, each of us has a right to our life and our property. These rights are sufficiently strong to show that we may keep our property, even if that means others die of starvation.

Crocker rejects this entire way of describing the problem of world hunger. On his view it distorts the issues, leads us to ask the wrong questions, and prompts ineffective action. The debate, as standardly described, asks whether we (the affluent West) should give food or aid to them (the starving Third World). This question, though, incorrectly implies that the sources of world hunger are (a) starvation caused by famine, rather than chronic malnutrition, and (b) lack of food rather than lack of access to food.

They also prompt the wrong moral questions. By asking if we have an obligation to help, it is assumed that we are in no way responsible for the hunger. Yet, according to Crocker, we have often erected and maintained obstacles to the economic development of much of the world, obstacles that make hunger more likely. Were people in these countries allowed to (and occasionally given aid to empower them to) develop their ability to sustain themselves, then we would greatly reduce, if not eradicate, the problem of world hunger. Again we see how reconceptualizing a moral problem radically alters our understanding of that problem. We saw this maneuver earlier in Rothman's discussion of ABORTION, and in Harris's and Narayan's essay on AFFIRMATIVE ACTION.

Rolston also redefines the issue, although rather differently than does Crocker. Rolston asks what happens when we are forced to choose between feeding people and saving nature. Do people always win? Rolston says not. To assume that they do ignores (a) the long-term costs of damaging the environment, (b) the fact that many people deeply value nature for its own sake, and (c) that morality does not require that we abandon things we value simply to help others. To that extent, Rolston's argument parallels Arthur's: neither claims we should cavalierly ignore the starving. However, both claim that morality does not require that we abandon things we deeply value.

Rolston's claims about the relative value of humans and the environment deserves further exploration. The essays on the ENVIRONMENT, in the following section, should help us think more carefully about their comparative value.

Further Reading

Aiken, W. and LaFollette, H. 1996: *World Hunger and Morality*. Englewood Cliffs, NJ: Prentice-Hall.

Brown, P. and Shue, H. (eds) 1977: *Food Policy: The Responsibility of the United States in the Life and Death Choices*. New York: Free Press.

Drèze, J. and Sen, A. (eds) 1990: *The Political Economy of Hunger. Entitlement and Well-Being*. Oxford: Clarendon Press.

——1989: *Hunger and Public Action*. Oxford: Clarendon Press.

Food and Agricultural Organization (FAO) 1992: *World Food Supplies and Prevalence of Chronic Undernutrition in Developing Regions as Assessed in 1992*. Rome: FAO Press.

Nussbaum, M. and Sen, A. (eds) 1993: *The Quality of Life*. Oxford: Clarendon Press.

United Nations Children's Fund (UNICEF) 1993: *The State of the World's Children 1993*. Oxford: Oxford University Press.

53

Free Movement: If People were Money

Robert Goodin

In the penultimate year of the Reagan presidency, the United States expelled over a million illegal aliens and was decidedly bullish about it.[1] In the same year, the United States absorbed over two hundred billion dollars worth of direct foreign investment and was not even slightly sheepish about it.[2] Australia, Great Britain and, indeed, much of the civilized and semi-civilized world had been doing much the same, albeit in a little less dramatic fashion, for the past decade or in some cases much more.

The message is clear enough. Had immigrants been investments – had the people been money – their influx would have been welcomed with open arms. Instead, it was deeply resented and fiercely resisted. But why is there such a disparity in policy responses? Surely foreign penetration is foreign penetration, whatever form it takes. What makes the inflow of people so very different from the inflow of finance capital? This essay is devoted to exploring that question.

The Nature of Borders

The formal functions of international boundaries are purely juridical. They physically delimit the sphere of sovereignty. They define jurisdictions. They specify, literally, how far the writ of any given sovereign runs. Formally, frontiers merely mark the point at which one body of law gives way to another.

In practice, international borders reflect various other realities and serve various other ends, as well. Power politics being what they are, sovereigns' writs tend to run just as far as they are willing and able to press them. So, unsurprisingly, international boundaries have historically tended also to mark out a militarily defensible space, delimited by some substantially impenetrable physical barriers (the Alps, the Pyrenees or the English Channel).

Boundaries chosen purely for military purposes thus served – in the first instance, almost automatically – social functions as well. Insofar as international borders corresponded to relatively impenetrable physical barriers, they substantially impeded movement of all sorts.

It was hard to move anything – people or goods, just as surely as armies or cannons – across them. So the same thing that once kept out foreign princes also kept out foreigners quite generally, their persons as well as their commodities and their commercial influence. Devices designed to secure sovereign prerogatives also helped to secure a substantial measure of autarky in social and economic realms, as well.

Nowadays, however, physical barriers to the movement of people and more especially of money are not what they once were. Even for the economically destitute, hitching a ride across oceans or continents proves far from impossible. And money, of course, moves literally with the flick of the finger on the keyboard. What was once a given of nature has now become a matter of policy. It is now for us, collectively, to say how much movement we are prepared to allow across our borders.

How Open should Borders Be?

Let me begin by sketching the sorts of considerations that seem to figure most centrally in contemporary policy discussions over how open or closed borders should be, in general terms. Then, in subsequent sections, I shall raise further questions about the justifiability of making borders differentially open depending on what it is that is crossing them in which direction.

The case for free movement

At least within the Anglo–American democracies, the standard way of arguing for freer movement seems to be liberal–egalitarian in form.[3] The premises at work here are, essentially, two: one is egalitarianism; the other is universalism, which in the present context amounts principally to globalism. The first holds that distributions of life prospects ought to be roughly equal, or at least substantially more equal than they now are. The second holds that our focus, in making those comparisons, ought to be upon people in general rather than merely upon people living within some particular political jurisdiction.[4]

Within that logic, the concern for freer movement of people derives essentially from a perception of the limited scope of government-to-government capital transfers. Whether those programs take the form of foreign aid or foreign loans, or whether they are multilateral or bilateral, those programs as we now know them all seem simply incapable of changing the lives of people in recipient countries in any big way.

They have limited success largely because they have limited funds. Rich countries simply put too little into international transfer programs to make much difference. "The majority of aid," it is said, "is successful in terms of its own objectives."[5] And that may well be true. But, alas, reducing global inequality is only one among many objectives of most such programs – and a secondary one at that.

There is every reason to believe that a generously funded, well-targeted program of foreign assistance could help reduce global economic inequalities. We now know enough about how to organize aid programs to be pretty confident of accomplishing those goals, if only we were truly serious about them. The point is precisely that the richer nations are not now, and seem unlikely soon to become, deeply committed to goals of global redistribution.

In such circumstances, we are driven to rely instead upon decidedly second-best mechanisms of global redistribution. If we cannot move enough money to where the needy people are, then we will have to count on moving as many of the needy people as possible to where the money is. In these circumstances, if we really want people in poorer countries to enjoy life chances even remotely similar to those of people in richer countries, then the best way of ensuring that seems to be for the poor people themselves to move to the richer country. (Even then, the guarantee is less than iron-clad: much depends upon the skills of immigrants, the willingness of domestic employers to employ them, and the willingness of governments to apply the same labor and social security laws to them.)

Of course, there is likely to be even more political resistance to that policy than the other. Citizens of rich nations are likely to be even more reluctant to welcome lots of destitute foreigners into their country than they historically have been to ship substantial sums of money abroad to relieve their suffering.

But that, in a way, is precisely the political point underlying exercises in moral philosophy on this topic. The goal of such exercises is precisely to put rich countries on the spot. The aim is to argue that, if arguments for international distributive justice are valid and if rich countries do not want to give generously of their money to meet the demands that those arguments impose, then they are morally obliged to pay instead in a currency that they hold even dearer.

Morally, rich countries faced with strong moral arguments for global redistribution have only two options. Ideally, they should provide the poor with substantial sums of foreign aid; failing that, as a moral minimum they must alternatively be willing to admit substantial numbers of immigrants from the poorest countries. If that second alternative is politically even more unacceptable than the first, and if morally those are the only two options, and if people are capable of being moved by reflections upon morality at all, then perhaps citizens of the richer countries might, on second thought, take a more generous attitude toward foreign aid.

This point can – and politically should – be put just that sharply. If the rich countries do not want to let foreigners in, then the very least they must do is send much more money to compensate them for their being kept out. Those capital transfers really must be understood as compensation rather than as charity. They are merely the fair recompense for their being blocked from doing something (that is, moving to a richer country) that could, and quite probably would, have resulted in their earning that much more for themselves.

The case against free movement

That, or something like it, probably approximates the political logic underlying most arguments for freer movement of people and of money between the rich and poor nations of the world. Against those considerations, however, are arrayed others which argue for preserving or perhaps even increasing barriers to movement of both sorts.

Some of those arguments are inspired by what has recently been termed "communitarianism." On this view, different people and peoples are morally entitled – and perhaps are morally enjoined – to lead their own different lives in their own different ways, without undue influence from other people in other communities organized on different premises.[6] That leads quite naturally to the view that people's moral concern may legitimately stop with those physically near and emotionally dear to them.[7] The moral permissibility of closed borders follows obviously and straightforwardly from that logic.[8]

How important you think that argument for closed borders to be depends, though, upon how you assess the larger claims of communitarianism. And that, in turn, depends upon how you understand those claims in the first place. Roughly speaking, is their argument for "the rootedness of moral agents" a proposition about psychology or about ethics?

If it is the former, saying merely that everyone has to start someplace – grow up in some particular community and so on – then the claim is undoubtedly true but of doubtful relevance to moral assessment. Arguments of that sort might help explain people's natural prejudices; if the psychological forces at work are strong, perhaps such arguments might even serve to excuse people in acting on those prejudices. But it is in the nature of excuses that what is being excused remains morally wrong. There is nothing in the argument, thus understood, to lead us to suppose that it is morally worthy – positively desirable, as opposed to sadly excusable – for moral agents to confine their sympathies in such ways.

Sometimes communitarians seem to be claiming more, though. Sometimes they seem to say not only that it is psychologically understandable but also that it is morally desirable that people should root themselves in this way. Now, of course, if the psychological forces at work are so strong that that is the only way in which people can develop a moral sense at all – and, furthermore, having thus developed it they cannot widen it without losing it altogether – then it would indeed be desirable to develop a limited moral sense rather than none at all. All of that remains really very back-handed praise for narrow communitarian values, to be sure. But I simply cannot see how any stronger, positive moral claim for communitarianism might be grounded.

If communitarianism were true, it would provide a strong argument for closed borders. But the moral case for communitarianism itself seems to rest on relatively weak arguments, thus compromising in turn the communitarian case for closed borders. Furthermore, even if communitarian arguments were compelling, they would justify us in closing our borders only at the price of laying upon us an increased obligation to open our pocketbooks. Recall the structure of the argument for free movement developed above: if you are not going to send more capital to where the poor people are, you have to let poor people move to where the capital is. The converse is true, too. If communitarians are not going to let poor people move to where the money is, then they have to be prepared to send more of their communities' money as foreign aid to where the poor people are forced to remain.

There is another way of justifying closed borders, though. Rather than appealing to narrow communitarian values, this argument works in essentially universalistic terms. Closed borders do not fall nearly so automatically out of this argument. Instead, it treats them as a second-best stop-gap. On this argument, in the ideal world all borders would be open. It is only because we live in an imperfect world that we sometimes need closed borders to correct, control or contain those imperfections.

To elaborate, let me take as my text a passage from John Maynard Keynes. He begins his 1933 essay on "National Self-Sufficiency" by saying:

> I was brought up, like most Englishmen, to respect free trade not only as an economic doctrine which a rational and instructed person could not doubt but almost as a part of the moral law. . . . I thought England's years, to be both the explanation before man and the justification before heaven of her economic supremacy.

But contrary to all those natural inclinations, Keynes reports that he had latterly been convinced of the need for barriers to free trade. He explains the logic of this new position as follows:

> There is no prospect for the next generation of a uniformity of economic systems throughout the world. . . . We all need [therefore] to be as free as possible of interference from economic changes elsewhere in order to make our own favourite experiments towards the ideal social

republic of the future; and . . . deliberate movement towards greater national self-sufficiency and economic isolation will make our task easier . . .[9]

The logic of this second-best proposition seems impeccable. Every state, perhaps, ought to have a generous welfare state. Every state, perhaps, ought to pursue Keynes's proposed policies for driving the rate of interest to zero and, in that way, effectively nationalize the control of finance capital. But no country can pursue those options all on its own. A particularly generous welfare state will always be at risk of being swamped with immigrants, so long as it allows people to move in freely from abroad.[10] A state deliberately pushing down interest rates will always risk finding its policies foiled by capital flight, insofar as it allows free movement of capital out of the country.[11] Only by closing its borders to those sorts of movements can a country confidently pursue for itself, and by itself, ideals for which other nations of the world are not yet ready.

Closed borders might be justified, then, as a matter either of principle or of pragmatism. My own inclination is to say that, if they are going to be justified at all, it can only be in the latter way. However, I shall abstain from taking any position on the larger issue of which justification – if either – might truly warrant closing our borders, and to what extent. I shall instead mount a more limited plea for consistency across all our various policies touching on issues of trans-national movement.

The Demands of Consistency

How open overall we want our borders to be is an important question, and one that admits of diverse answers from diverse moral perspectives. That question is complicated enough. But the real question facing policy-makers is yet more complicated still.

We are typically confronted with proposals for borders to be differentially open. There are suggestions for borders to be more open to the movement of some things than to others. Thus, people tend to urge one policy for governing the import of computers and quite another for the import of explosives, one policy for admitting foreigners as individuals and quite another for admitting the same number of aliens all at the same time as part of one large group (refugees, for example).

Likewise, there are suggestions for borders to be more open to movement in one direction rather than another. Thus, for example, many are tempted to take a much more relaxed attitude toward exporting explosives than toward importing them, or to expelling a large group of political dissidents than to admitting a similarly large group of troublemakers from abroad.

That we typically do make such distinctions seems undeniable. Whether we are morally entitled to do so is, as always, a separate question. There may or may not be any good reasons for nations to have relatively closed borders. That is an open question. But on the face of things it would seem that if ethically valid reasons for closed borders can be found at all, then those reasons must presumably apply *systematically*. That is to say, they should presumably dictate that borders be closed to the same extent in all directions and for all purposes.

I shall say more about the nature, source and strength of this presumption in favor of symmetrical treatment shortly. First, though, let us see what would follow from this argument from consistency if it were to be sustained.

First, the systematic application of principles governing trans-boundary movement would apparently preclude any distinction according to the direction of movement. Whatever reason there is to keep something from coming into the country, consistency would seem to require us to impose the same prohibition upon that thing's going out.

Consider, in particular, the contrast between states' emigration and immigration policies. Consistency would seem to require us to judge the movement of people in both directions by the same standards, however harsh or lenient those may be. This symmetry manifests itself in several ways. Historically, perhaps the most widely discussed has been the pro-position – enshrined in the Magna Carta and in countless texts since – that citizens should have an equal right to leave and to return to their own country.[12] But by the same token, it seems ethically inconsistent on the face of things for countries (of NATO, for example) to mount a vigorous international campaign for the freedom (of, for example, Soviet Jews) to emigrate, while at the same time rigorously restricting the number of immigrants they will themselves accept.

The inconsistency at work there may be pragmatic rather than literally logical in form. Still, pragmatically, "in a world where all the inhabitable space is divided between states, . . . everyone needs to have his right of domicile formally recognized by one of those states."[13] And in light of that fact, it amounts to simple bad faith to insist that people be allowed to leave without any guarantee – a guarantee that could come only from our being prepared to act as the underwriter of last resort – that they will have someplace to which to go. The bad faith might not matter, in any practical sense, so long as someone else is willing to take in those whom we will not. But even if others' generosity saves us from having to face the consequences of our paradoxical stance, a lingering sense of bad faith in this matter remains.[14]

Secondly, the systematic application of principles governing trans-boundary movement would apparently preclude any disctinction according to the nature of the objects coming or going across the borders. Whatever reason we have for keeping out foreign objects of one sort, consistency would seem to require us to impose similar rules to keep out other objects of a similar sort, as well.

Consider, in particular, the contrast between the rules which states apply to the move-ment of people and to the movement of money across their borders. Consistency would seem to require states to judge the trans-national migration of people and of money – movement of human capital and of financial capital – by similar standards, equally harshly or equally leniently. It is, on the face of things, ethically inconsistent for some countries (until recently, perhaps, Poland) to run a blocked currency alongside open doors to emigra-tion. It is, on the face of things, equally inconsistent for other countries (of Africa, perhaps) to open their doors to skilled immigrants but refuse to permit direct overseas investment in certain sectors.

Contemporary Practice

These inconsistencies – if inconsistencies they truly be – seem absolutely rife in the contem-porary world. Different states have different worries and impose different rules in con-sequence. But whatever the particulars of those rules, whether or not a state is prepared to permit the movement of people depends crucially upon the direction in which they are proposing to move. States rarely decide issues governing emigration and immigration according to the same criteria.

It was not always so. For large parts of European history, it has been relatively easy for people to change their country of residence. The French Constitution of 1791 guarantees "liberté d' aller, de rester, de partir": coming, staying and going were all on a par.[15] Throughout the nineteenth century, it remained the conventional wisdom that movement should be easy in both directions. There was, in context, nothing wildly unrealistic about the resolution of an 1889 International Emigration Conference saying, "We affirm the right of the individual to come and go and dispose of his person and his destinies as he pleases."[16]

With the end of the First World War, though, came the regime of passports and visas.[17] So, by the time the Universal Declaration on Human Rights was signed in 1948, the right to emigrate and to immigrate were once again treated separately and quite differently. The text of Article 13(2) stipulates that "everyone has the right to leave any country, including his own," but implicitly it is only a national who enjoys a right "to return to his country."[18] The right to leave the country is thus deemed universal, the right to enter, restricted to nationals returning home. It is perfectly proper, we now seem to suppose, that immigration should be harder than emigration. But what principled grounds could be offered for supposing that that should be so?

By the same token, countries which are only too happy to borrow vast quantities of money from abroad are all too reluctant to allow very many people at all to immigrate from abroad. I have already quoted statistics on the United States, in that regard. Here is another way of looking at those same statistics. The extra forty billion dollars worth of direct foreign investment flowing into the US in 1987 amounted to just under 1/100th of its Gross National Product. The six hundred thousand new legal immigrants which the US admitted in the same year amounted to less than 1/4000th of its entire population.[19]

Why were US policy-makers wildly excited about the one – proportionately, the smaller – and so little perturbed by the other? Whatever harm foreign control might do to the fabric of American society, it is on the face of things simply not credible to suppose that a single migrant can do 40 times as much damage as putting control of the same proportion of the US economy in foreign hands.[20]

This apparent inconsistency is nowise confined to the United States, though. It is only the most notorious offender in recent years. The same inconsistency could easily enough be found in the way in which Australia is so very welcoming of Japanese money but not Japanese migrants, and/or in the way in which Britain is so very welcoming of the capital but not the persons of its Hong Kong subjects.

The Presumption of Symmetry

In framing rules for trans-national movements, what to treat differently and how differently to treat it depends upon what deeper theories we happen to embrace. In part, those are empirical theories concerning the causes and consequences of the movements in question. In important part, though, those are moral theories specifying which consequences to welcome and which to shun, which policy interventions to permit and which not.

Thus, in trying to defend against these charges of inconsistency, policy-makers will inevitably – if often only implicitly – be asserting the superiority of one moral theory over another. Differences between objects and between directions of movement which matter from the perspective of one moral theory, and which within it suffice to justify different treatment of two cases, do not from the perspective of another. Analogies that seem apt from one perspective seem false from another.

It must be admitted, though, that on almost any theory some sorts of differential treatment in these matters is almost bound to be permissible. That is only to be expected. It is absurd, on the face of things, to suppose that the same rules should apply to the movement of people as to cattle, gunpowder or microcomputers. Such diverse objects display obviously different properties. It is only reasonable that they should be treated differently, in rules governing their cross-border movements as in many other respects.

But it is one thing to say that some such distinctions will presumably prove justified. It is quite another to presume that differential treatment is permissible, prior to actually being offered any such justifications. Some distinctions will almost certainly prove justified, but not just any old distinctions.

Presumably justifications for differential treatment can sometimes – perhaps often – be found. Still, until adequate justification actually has been provided for any particular distinction, the presumption must remain on the side of treating all (presumptively like) cases alike. The burden of proving the moral merits of differential treatment must rest with those proposing it. Call this the principle of *no discrimination without justification*.[21]

This formulation might seem to make the case for consistent treatment of movements across borders too weak to be of much interest. It casts the case purely in terms of a presumption; and presumptions, by their nature, can always be rebutted. But how strong or weak this argument turns out to be depends upon how hard or easy it is to find good arguments for rebutting the presumption in question. If in the case of trans-boundary movements good arguments for differential treatment are thin on the ground – as clearly they are in so many other cases of differential treatment – then a mere presumption might in and of itself take us quite a long way toward firm policy conclusions.

Human Capital and Finance Capital

So many kinds of goods, so different in obviously important ways, flow across state borders that it is plainly unreasonable to expect that presumption of identical treatment to prevail in absolutely all cases of trans-boundary flows. Sometimes, though, that presumption does seem particularly robust.

Consider, for example, the problem of exporting hazardous products. Since human physiology is pretty standard across the world, products that are dangerous for Americans to use are probably dangerous for Indonesians as well. So if something is too hazardous to be used in or imported into one's own country, then surely it is right for there to be a strong presumption in favor of supposing that it is also too hazardous to be exported from one's own to other countries.[22] That presumption, like all presumptions, is in principle rebuttable. In practice, though, it seems awfully hard to rebut.

There is another analogy that seems on its face similarly robust, one between the movement of people and the movement of money. Both, in economic terms, are forms of capital. The movement of people shifts human capital – the physical and intellectual capacities embodied in human bodies. The movement of money shifts financial capital, and with it the productive capacities that are procurable in exchange for money.

Economically, there is good reason for seeing labor and capital as analogous. Overall, they complement one another as factors of production; at the margins, they substitute for one another in that capacity. The standard Cobb-Douglas production function mathematically represents output simply as a function of labor and capital inputs, and of those alone. In that equation, it takes some of each to produce anything at all: with zero labor inputs you get zero output, and likewise with zero capital inputs. But at the margins, the two are capable of substituting for one another: the more you have of one, the less you will need of the other to produce any given quantity of outputs.

What is true of labor and capital contributions to production in general seems particularly true of their trans-national flows in encouraging economic growth. The way in which the two substitute for one another in spurring growth in any particular industry is clear enough. So too is the way in which they can complement one another in developing basic infrastructure: to build railroads, for example, poor and underpopulated countries have historically needed in-flows of both capital and labor from abroad.[23]

For the purposes of economic modeling, it is clearly crucial to determine whether (or when) labor and capital complement or substitute for one another. For moral purposes, it is not so clear at all that we need to know is whether the sign of the coefficient linking them is positive or negative.

Consider an analogy from within a single national economy. We may well think that wages and profits ought, for the sake of consistency, to be taxed at the same rate, whatever the complicated economic interrelationships between those factors. No amount of evidence about whether higher wages lead to lower profits or to higher ones can alter the perceived requirements of fairness on that score.

Similarly, perhaps nothing morally follows from a determination of whether, in international flows, capital and labor substitute for one another or whether they complement one another. Be they economically substitutes or complements, morally it might nonetheless be argued that they are the same "kind" of thing and ought to be treated similarly in our rules governing their trans-national movements.

Perhaps the best reason for regarding them so is the simple fact that the distinctions drawn by those resisting that analogy are so strained and self-serving. They seem little more than cynical attempts on the parts of states to participate only in those aspects of a regime of free movement from which they themselves would benefit. The British, Americans, Australians and so on happily accept foreign money but only reluctantly accept unskilled (or even skilled) foreign peoples. The regimes of the old Eastern Bloc let money and people in but not out. Developing states admit human capital, in the form of skilled settlers, but not finance capital.

There are good reasons, of an understandably self-interested kind, for all those policies. The states in question suppose, probably quite rightly, that the sorts of trans-boundary movement that they shun would work to their detriment. But while self-interest makes their position comprehensible, it hardly makes it moral. Quite the contrary, when the clearest argument for a distinction is so transparently self-interested, there must be something like a double-presumption against that distinction, on moral grounds.

Notes

1 That is just under four times 1970 levels. See US Department of Commerce, *Statistical Abstract of the United States, 1989* (Washington, DC: Government Printing Office, 1989), table 296.

2 That is over seven times 1970 levels, even discounting for inflation, according to the *Statistical Abstract of the United States, 1989*, tables 1359 and 748.

3 See, e.g., the discussions in: Michael Teitelbaum, "Right versus Right: Immigration and Refugee Policy in the United States," *Foreign Affairs*, 59 (1980), 21–59; Anon., "Developments in the Law: Immigration Policy and the Rights of Aliens," *Harvard Law Review*, 96 (1983), 1286–1465; Joseph Carens, "Aliens and Citizens: The Case for Open Borders," *Review of Politics*,

49 (Spring 1987), 251–73; and Alan Dowty, *Closed Borders: The Contemporary Assault on Freedom of Movement* (New Haven, CT: Yale University Press, 1987).

4　Charles Beitz, *Political Theory and International Relations* (Princeton, NJ: Princeton University Press, 1979), part 3, and "Cosmopolitan Ideals and National Sentiment"; and Henry Shue, "The Burdens of Justice," *Journal of Philosophy*, 80 (1983), 591–600 and 600–8 respectively.

5　Robert Cassen et al., *Does Aid Work?* (Oxford: Clarendon Press, 1986), p. 294.

6　Michael J. Sandel, *Liberalism and the Limits of Justice* (Cambridge: Cambridge University Press, 1982); and Michael Walzer, *Spheres of Justice* (New York: Basic Books, 1983), chapter 2. Cf. Will Kymlicka, *Liberalism, Community and Culture* (Oxford: Clarendon Press, 1989).

7　David Miller, "The Ethical Significance of Nationality," *Ethics*, 98 (1988), 647–62; cf. Robert E. Goodin, "What is So Special about our Fellow Countrymen?" *Ethics*, 98 (1988), 663–86.

8　This is, certainly in its practical consequences and to some extent in its underlying logic as well, an echo of older concerns with the legitimate authority of sovereigns to command the loyalty of their subjects. For a discussion see Frederick G. Whelan, "Citizenship and the Right to Leave," *American Political Science Review*, 75 (1981), 63–83.

9　John Maynard Keynes, "National Self-Sufficiency," *Collected Writings*, ed. Donald Moggridge (London: Macmillan, 1982), vol. 21, pp. 233–46 at 233–4 and 241. See similarly James E. Meade's 1934 paper for the New Fabian Research Bureau, "The Exchange Policy of a Socialist Government," *Collected Papers*, ed. Susan Howson (London: Unwin Hyman, 1988), vol. 3, pp. 11–26.

10　Walzer, *Spheres of Justice*, chapter 2. Cf. Joseph Carens, "Immigration and the Welfare State," *Democracy and the Welfare State*, ed. Amy Gutmann (Princeton, NJ: Princeton University Press, 1988), pp. 207–30.

11　Keynes, "National Self-Sufficiency."

12　Magna Carta of 1215, chapter 42. See further Stig A. F. Jagerskiold, "Historical Aspects of the Right to Leave and to Return," *The Right to Leave and to Return*, ed. Karel Vasak and Sidney Liskofsky (New York: American Jewish Commission, 1976), pp. 3–20.

13　Maurice Cranston, "The Political and Philosophical Aspects of the Right to Leave and to Return," in Vasak and Liskofsky, ibid., pp. 21–35 at p. 28.

14　Recall in this connection the history of the Jews immediately prior to and during World War II: many countries demanded that Hitler let Jews flee but none were particularly prepared to admit them. See Bernard Wasserstein, *Britain and the Jews of Europe, 1939–45* (London: Institute of Jewish Affairs, 1979).

15　Quoted in Cranston, "The Political and Philosophical Aspects," p. 28.

16　Quoted in Brinley Thomas, *International Migration and Economic Development* (Paris: UNESCO, 1961), p. 9.

17　Guy S. Goodwin-Gill, *International Law and the Movement of Persons* (Oxford: Clarendon Press, 1978), chapter 2.

18　Reproduced in Ian Brownlie (ed.), *Basic Documents in International Law*, 3rd edn (Oxford: Clarendon Press, 1983), pp. 251–6 at 253; the International Covenant on Civil and Political Rights, Article 12, reproduces these propositions almost verbatim. Of course, Article 14 goes on to say that "everyone has the right to seek and enjoy in other countries asylum from persecutions" – at least insofar as they are for political crimes – but if the state denies them asylum then international law requires the refugees to leave.

19　*Statistical Abstract of the United States*, tables 1359, 685, 9, 2 and 46.

20　For those who prefer – rightly – to talk in terms of stocks rather than flows, here are the corresponding statistics. Foreign direct investment in the US in 1987 was 5.78 percent of GNP, whereas the foreign-born were (in 1980, the last year for which statistics are available) 6.22 percent of the entire US population. By that reckoning they are just about on a par – which still leaves us puzzling why there is such a disproportionate response to such proportionately similar phenomena.

21　This principle is, of course, standard in the literature on justice, equality and discrimination. See, e.g., William K. Frankena, "The Concept of Social Justice," *Social Justice*, ed. Richard B. Brandt (Englewood Cliffs, NJ:

Prentice-Hall, 1962), pp. 1–30; and Bernard Williams, "The Idea of Equality," *Philosophy, Politics and Society*, 2nd series, ed. P. Laslett and W. G. Runciman (Oxford: Blackwell, 1962), pp. 110–31.

22 Henry Shue, "Exporting Hazards," *Ethics*, 91 (1981), 579–606.

23 Simon Kuznets, *Modern Economic Growth* (New Haven: Yale University Press, 1966), pp. 40–56. "Latin-American economists with whom I have spoken have not infrequently stressed the reduced flow of international private investment as an important reason why even an underpopulated country such as Brazil cannot employ new European immigrants on the scale once possible"; Howard S. Ellis, "Are there Preferable Alternatives to International Migration as an Aid to Economic Development?" *Economics of International Migration*, ed. Brinley Thomas (London: Macmillan, 1958), pp. 347–64 at 354–5.

54

Famine, Affluence, and Morality

Peter Singer

As I write this, in November 1971, people are dying in East Bengal from lack of food, shelter, and medical care. The suffering and death that are occurring there now are not inevitable, not unavoidable in any fatalistic sense of the term. Constant poverty, a cyclone, and a civil war have turned at least nine million people into destitute refugees; nevertheless, it is not beyond the capacity of the richer nations to give enough assistance to reduce any further suffering to very small proportions. The decisions and actions of human beings can prevent this kind of suffering. Unfortunately, human beings have not made the necessary decisions. At the individual level, people have, with very few exceptions, not responded to the situation in any significant way. Generally speaking, people have not given large sums to relief funds; they have not written to their parliamentary representatives demanding increased government assistance; they have not demonstrated in the streets, held symbolic fasts, or done anything else directed toward providing the refugees with the means to satisfy their essential needs. At the government level, no government has given the sort of massive aid that would enable the refugees to survive for more than a few days. Britain, for instance, has given rather more than most countries. It has, to date, given £14,750,000. For comparative purposes, Britain's share of the nonrecoverable development costs of the Anglo-French Concorde project is already in excess of £275,000,000, and on present estimates will reach £440,000,000. The implication is that the British government values a supersonic transport more than thirty times as highly as it values the lives of the nine million refugees. Australia is another country which, on a per capita basis, is well up in the "aid to Bengal" table. Australia's aid, however, amounts to less than one-twelfth of the cost of Sydney's new opera house. The total amount given, from all sources, now stands at about £65,000,000. The estimated cost of keeping the refugees alive for one year is £464,000,000. Most of the refugees have now been in the camps for more than six months. The World Bank has said that India needs a minimum of £300,000,000 in assistance from other countries before the end of the year. It seems obvious that assistance on this scale will not be forthcoming. India will be forced to choose between letting the refugees starve or diverting funds from her own development program, which will mean that more of her own people will starve in the future.[1]

These are the essential facts about the present situation in Bengal. So far as it concerns us here, there is nothing unique about this situation except its magnitude. The Bengal emergency is just the latest and most acute of a series of major emergencies in various parts of the world, arising both from natural and from man-made causes. There are also many parts of the world in which people die from malnutrition and lack of food independent of any special emergency. I take Bengal as my example only because it is the present concern, and because the size of the problem has ensured that it has been given adequate publicity. Neither individuals nor governments can claim to be unaware of what is happening there.

What are the moral implications of a situation like this? In what follows, I shall argue that the way people in relatively affluent countries react to a situation like that in Bengal cannot be justified; indeed, the whole way we look at moral issues – our moral conceptual scheme – needs to be altered, and with it, the way of life that has come to be taken for granted in our society.

In arguing for this conclusion I will not, of course, claim to be morally neutral. I shall, however, try to argue for the moral position that I take, so that anyone who accepts certain assumptions, to be made explicit, will, I hope, accept my conclusion.

I begin with the assumption that suffering and death from lack of food, shelter, and medical care are bad. I think most people will agree about this, although one may reach the same view by different routes. I shall not argue for this view. People can hold all sorts of eccentric positions, and perhaps from some of them it would not follow that death by starvation is in itself bad. It is difficult, perhaps impossible, to refute such positions, and so for brevity I will henceforth take this assumption as accepted. Those who disagree need read no further.

My next point is this: if it is in our power to prevent something bad from happening, without thereby sacrificing anything of comparable moral importance, we ought, morally, to do it. By "without sacrificing anything of comparable moral importance" I mean without causing anything else comparably bad to happen, or doing something that is wrong in itself, or failing to promote some moral good, comparable in significance to the bad thing that we can prevent. This principle seems almost as uncontroversial as the last one. It requires us only to prevent what is bad, and to promote what is good, and it requires this of us only when we can do it without sacrificing anything that is, from the moral point of view, comparably important. I could even, as far as the application of my argument to the Bengal emergency is concerned, qualify the point so as to make it: if it is in our power to prevent something very bad from happening, without thereby sacrificing anything morally significant, we ought, morally, to do it. An application of this principle would be as follows: if I am walking past a shallow pond and see a child drowning in it, I ought to wade in and pull the child out. This will mean getting my clothes muddy, but this is insignificant, while the death of the child would presumably be a very bad thing.

The uncontroversial appearance of the principle just stated is deceptive. If it were acted upon, even in its qualified form, our lives, our society, and our world would be fundamentally changed. For the principle takes, firstly, no account of proximity or distance. It makes no moral difference whether the person I can help is a neighbor's child ten yards from me or a Bengali whose name I shall never know, ten thousand miles away. Secondly, the principle makes no distinction between cases in which I am the only person who could possibly do anything and cases in which I am just one among millions in the same position.

I do not think I need to say much in defense of the refusal to take proximity and distance into account. The fact that a person is physically near to us, so that we have personal contact with him, may make it more likely that we *shall* assist him, but this does not show that we *ought* to help him rather than another who happens to be further away. If we accept any principle of impartiality, universalizability, equality, or whatever, we cannot discriminate against someone merely because he is far away from us (or we are far away from him). Admittedly, it is possible that we are in a better position to judge what needs to be done to help a person near to us than one far away, and perhaps also to provide the assistance we judge to be necessary. If this were the case, it would be a reason for helping those near to us first. This may once have been a justification for being more concerned with the poor in one's town than with famine victims in India. Unfortunately for those who like to keep their moral responsibilities limited, instant communication and swift transportation have changed the situation. From the moral point of view, the development of the world into a "global village" has made an important, though still unrecognized, difference to our moral situation. Expert observers and supervisors, sent out by famine relief organizations or permanently stationed in famine-prone areas, can direct our aid to a refugee in Bengal almost as effectively as we could get it to someone in our own block. There would seem, therefore, to be no possible justification for discriminating on geographical grounds.

There may be a greater need to defend the second implication of my principle – that the fact that there are millions of other people in the same position, in respect to the Bengali refugees, as I am, does not make the situation significantly different from a situation in which I am the only person who can prevent something very bad from occurring. Again, of course, I admit that there is a psychological difference between the cases; one feels less guilty about doing nothing if one can point to others, similarly placed, who have also done nothing. Yet this can make no real difference to our moral obligations.[2] Should I consider that I am less obliged to pull the drowning child out of the pond if on looking around I see other people, no further away than I am, who have also noticed the child but are doing nothing? One has only to ask this question to see the absurdity of the view that numbers lessen obligation. It is a view that is an ideal excuse for inactivity; unfortunately most of the major evils – poverty, overpopulation, pollution – are problems in which everyone is almost equally involved.

The view that numbers do make a difference can be made plausible if stated in this way: if everyone in circumstances like mine gave £5 to the Bengal Relief Fund, there would be enough to provide food, shelter, and medical care for the refugees; there is no reason why I should give more than anyone else in the same circumstances as I am; therefore I have no obligation to give more than £5. Each premise in this argument is true, and the argument looks sound. It may convince us, unless we notice that it is based on a hypothetical premise, although the conclusion is not stated hypothetically. The argument would be sound if the conclusion were: if everyone in circumstances like mine were to give £5, I would have no obligation to give more than £5. If the conclusion were so stated, however, it would be obvious that the argument has no bearing on a situation in which it is not the case that everyone else gives £5. This, of course, is the actual situation. It is more or less certain that not everyone in circumstances like mine will give £5. So there will not be enough to provide the needed food, shelter, and medical care. Therefore by giving more than £5 I will prevent more suffering than I would if I gave just £5.

It might be thought that this argument has an absurd consequence. Since the situation appears to be that very few people are likely to give substantial amounts, it follows that I and everyone else in similar circumstances ought to give as much as possible, that is, at least up to the point at which by giving more one would begin to cause serious suffering for oneself and one's dependants – perhaps even beyond this point to the point of marginal utility, at which by giving more one would cause oneself and one's dependants as much suffering as one would prevent in Bengal. If everyone does this, however, there will be more than can be used for the benefit of the refugees, and some of the sacrifice will have been unnecessary. Thus, if everyone does what he ought to do, the result will not be as good as it would be if everyone did a little less than he ought to do, or if only some do all that they ought to do.

The paradox here arises only if we assume that the actions in question – sending money to the relief funds – are performed more or less simultaneously, and are also unexpected. For if it is to be expected that everyone is going to contribute something, then clearly each is not obliged to give as much as he would have been obliged to had others not been giving too. And if everyone is not acting more or less simultaneously, then those giving later will know how much more is needed, and will have no obligation to give more than is necessary to reach this amount. To say this is not to deny the principle that people in the same circumstances have the same obligations, but to point out that the fact that others have given, or may be expected to give, is a relevant circumstance: those giving after it has become known that many others are giving and those giving before are not in the same circumstances. So the seemingly absurd consequence of the principle I have put forward can occur only if people are in error about the actual circumstances – that is, if they think they are giving when others are not, but in fact they are giving when others are. The result of everyone doing what he really ought to do cannot be worse than the result of everyone doing less than he ought to do, although the result of everyone doing what he reasonably believes he ought to do could be.

If my argument so far has been sound, neither our distance from a preventable evil nor the number of other people who, in respect to that evil, are in the same situation as we are, lessens our obligation to mitigate or prevent that evil. I shall therefore take as established the principle I asserted earlier. As I have already said, I need to assert it only in its qualified form: if it is in our power to prevent something very bad from happening, without thereby sacrificing anything else morally significant, we ought, morally, to do it.

The outcome of this argument is that our traditional moral categories are upset. The traditional distinction between duty and charity cannot be drawn, or at least, not in the place we normally draw it. Giving money to the Bengal Relief Fund is regarded as an act of charity in our society. The bodies which collect money are known as "charities." These organizations see themselves in this way – if you send them a check, you will be thanked for your "generosity." Because giving money is regarded as an act of charity, it is not thought that there is anything wrong with not giving. The charitable man may be praised, but the man who is not charitable is not condemned. People do not feel in any way ashamed or guilty about spending money on new clothes or a new car instead of giving it to famine relief. (Indeed, the alternative does not occur to them.) This way of looking at the matter cannot be justified. When we buy new clothes not to keep ourselves warm but to look "well-dressed" we are not providing for any important need. We would not be sacrificing anything significant if we were to continue to wear our old clothes, and give the money to famine relief. By doing so, we would be preventing another person from starving. It follows from what I have said earlier that we ought to give money away, rather than spend it on clothes which we do not need to keep us warm. To do so is not charitable, or generous. Nor is it the kind of act which philosophers and theologians have called "supererogatory" – an act which it would be good to do, but not wrong not to do. On the contrary, we ought to give the money away, and it is wrong not to do so.

I am not maintaining that there are no acts which are charitable, or that there are no acts which it would be good to do but not wrong not to do. It may be possible to redraw the distinction between duty and charity in some other place. All I am arguing here is that the present way of drawing the distinction, which makes it an act of charity for a man living at the level of affluence which most people in the "developed nations" enjoy to give money to save someone else from starvation, cannot be supported. It is beyond the scope of my argument to consider whether the distinction should be redrawn or abolished altogether. There would be many other possible ways of drawing the distinction – for instance, one might decide that it is good to make other people as happy as possible, but not wrong not to do so.

Despite the limited nature of the revision in our moral conceptual scheme which I am proposing, the revision would, given the extent of both affluence and famine in the world today, have radical implications. These implications may lead to further objections, distinct from those I have already considered. I shall discuss two of these.

One objection to the position I have taken might be simply that it is too drastic a revision of our moral scheme. People do not ordinarily judge in the way I have suggested they should. Most people reserve their moral condemnation for those who violate some moral norm, such as the norm against taking another person's property. They do not condemn those who indulge in luxury instead of giving to famine relief. But given that I did not set out to present a morally neutral description of the way people make moral judgments, the way people do in fact judge has nothing to do with the validity of my conclusion. My conclusion follows from the principle which I advanced earlier, and unless that principle is rejected, or the arguments are shown to be unsound, I think the conclusion must stand, however strange it appears.

It might, nevertheless, be interesting to consider why our society, and most other societies, do judge differently from the way I have suggested they should. In a well-known article, J. O. Urmson suggests that the imperatives of duty, which tell us what we must do, as distinct from what it would be good to do but not wrong not to do, function so as to prohibit behavior that is intolerable if men are to live together in society.[3] This may explain the origin and continued existence of the present division between acts of duty and acts of charity. Moral attitudes are shaped by the needs of society, and no doubt society needs people who will observe the rules that make social existence tolerable. From the point of view of a particular society, it is essential to prevent violations of norms against killing, stealing, and so on. It is quite inessential, however, to help people outside one's own society.

If this is an explanation of our common distinction between duty and supererogation, however, it is not a justification of it. The moral point of view requires us to look beyond the interests of our own society. Previously, as I have already mentioned, this may hardly have been feasible, but it is quite feasible now. From the moral point of view, the prevention of the starvation of millions of people outside our society must be considered at least as pressing as the upholding of property norms within our society.

It has been argued by some writers, among them Sidgwick and Urmson, that we need to have a basic moral code which is not too far beyond the capacities of the ordinary man, for otherwise there will be a general breakdown of compliance with the moral code. Crudely stated, this argument suggests that if we tell people that they ought to refrain from murder and give everything they do not really need to famine relief, they will do neither, whereas if we tell them that they ought to refrain from murder and that it is good to give to famine relief but not wrong not to do so, they will at least refrain from murder. The issue here is: Where should we draw the line between conduct that is required and conduct that is good although not required, so as to get the best possible result? This would seem to be an empirical question, although a very difficult one. One objection to the Sidgwick–Urmson line of argument is that it takes insufficient account of the effect that moral standards can have on the decisions we make. Given a society in which a wealthy man who gives 5 percent of his income to famine relief is regarded as most generous, it is not surprising that a proposal that we all ought to give away half our incomes will be thought to be absurdly unrealistic. In a society which held that no man should have more than enough while others have less than they need, such a proposal might seem narrow-minded. What it is possible for a man to do and what he is likely to do are both, I think, very greatly influenced by what people around him are doing and expecting him to do. In any case, the possibility that by spreading the idea that we ought to be doing very much more than we are to relieve famine we shall bring about a general breakdown of moral behavior seems remote. If the stakes are an end to widespread starvation, it is worth the risk. Finally, it should be emphasized that these considerations are relevant only to the issue of what we should require from others, and not to what we ourselves ought to do.

The second objection to my attack on the present distinction between duty and charity is one which has from time to time been made against utilitarianism. It follows from some forms of utilitarian theory that we all ought, morally, to be working full time to increase the balance of happiness over misery. The position I have taken here would not lead to this conclusion in all circumstances, for if there were no bad occurrences that we could prevent without sacrificing something of comparable moral importance, my argument would have no application. Given the present conditions in many parts of the world, however, it does follow from my argument that we ought, morally, to be working full time to relieve great suffering of the sort that occurs as a result of famine or other disasters. Of course, mitigating circumstances can be adduced – for instance, that if we wear ourselves out through overwork, we shall be less effective than we would otherwise have been. Nevertheless, when all considerations of this sort have been taken into account, the conclusion remains: we ought to be preventing as much suffering as we can without sacrificing something else of comparable moral importance. This conclusion is one which we may be reluctant to face. I cannot see, though, why it should be regarded as a criticism of the position for which I have argued, rather than a criticism of our ordinary standards of behavior. Since most people are self-interested to some degree, very few of us are likely to do everything that we ought to do. It would, however, hardly be honest to take this as evidence that it is not the case that we ought to do it.

It may still be thought that my conclusions are so wildly out of line with what everyone else thinks and has always thought that there must be something wrong with the argument somewhere. In order to show that my conclusions, while certainly contrary to contemporary Western moral standards, would not have seemed so extraordinary at other times and in other places, I would like to quote a passage from a writer not normally thought of as a way-out radical, Thomas Aquinas.

> Now, according to the natural order instituted by divine providence, material goods are provided for the satisfaction of human needs. Therefore the division and appropriation of property, which proceeds from human law, must not hinder the satisfaction of man's necessity from such goods. Equally, whatever a man has in superabundance is owed, of natural right, to the poor for their sustenance. So Ambrosius says, and it is also to be found in the *Decretum Gratiani*: "The bread which you withhold belongs to the hungry; the clothing you shut away, to the naked; and the money you bury in the earth is the redemption and freedom of the penniless."[4]

I now want to consider a number of points, more practical than philosophical, which are relevant to the application of the moral conclusion we have reached. These points challenge not the idea that we ought to be doing all we can to prevent starvation, but the idea that giving away a great deal of money is the best means to this end.

It is sometimes said that overseas aid should be a government responsibility, and that therefore one ought not to give to privately run charities. Giving privately, it is said, allows the government and the noncontributing members of society to escape their responsibilities.

This argument seems to assume that the more people there are who give to privately organized famine relief funds, the less likely it is that the government will take over full responsibility for such aid. This assumption is unsupported, and does not strike me as at all plausible. The opposite view – that if no one gives voluntarily, a government will assume that its citizens are uninterested in famine relief and would not wish to be forced into giving aid – seems more plausible. In any case, unless there were a definite probability that by refusing to give one would be helping to bring about massive government assistance, people who do refuse to make voluntary contributions are refusing to prevent a certain amount of suffering without being able to point to any tangible beneficial consequence of their refusal. So the onus of showing how their refusal will bring about government action is on those who refuse to give.

I do not, of course, want to dispute the contention that governments of affluent nations should be giving many times the amount of genuine, no-strings-attached aid that they are giving now. I agree, too, that giving privately is not enough, and that we ought to be campaigning actively for entirely new standards for both public and private contributions to famine relief. Indeed, I would sympathize with someone who thought that campaigning was more important than giving oneself, although I doubt whether preaching what one does not practice would be very effective. Unfortunately, for many people the idea that "it's the government's responsibility" is a reason for not giving which does not appear to entail any political action either.

Another, more serious reason for not giving to famine relief funds is that until there is effective population control, relieving famine merely postpones starvation. If we save the Bengal refugees now, others, perhaps the children of these refugees, will face starvation in a few years' time. In support of this, one may cite the now well-known facts about the population explosion and the relatively limited scope for expanded production.

This point, like the previous one, is an argument against relieving suffering that is happening now, because of a belief about what might happen in the future; it is unlike the previous point in that very good evidence can be adduced in support of this belief about the future. I will not go into the evidence here. I accept that the earth cannot support indefinitely a population rising at the present rate. This certainly poses a problem for anyone who thinks it important to prevent famine. Again, however, one could accept the argument without drawing the conclusion that it absolves one from any obligation to do anything to prevent famine. The conclusion that should be drawn is that the best means of preventing famine, in the long run, is population control. It would then follow from the position reached earlier that one ought to be doing all one can to promote population control (unless one held that all forms of population control were wrong in themselves, or would have significantly bad consequences). Since there are organizations working specifically for population control, one would then support them rather than more orthodox methods of preventing famine.

A third point raised by the conclusion reached earlier relates to the question of just how much we all ought to be giving away. One possibility, which has already been mentioned, is that we ought to give until we reach the level of marginal utility – that is, the level at which, by giving more, I would cause as much suffering to myself or my dependants as I would relieve by my gift. This would mean, of course, that one would reduce oneself to very near the material circumstances of a Bengali refugee. It will be recalled that earlier I put forward both a strong and a moderate version of the principle of preventing bad occurrences. The strong version, which required us to prevent bad things from happening unless in doing so we would be sacrificing something of comparable moral significance, does seem to require reducing ourselves to the level of marginal utility. I should also say that the strong version seems to me to be the correct one. I proposed the more moderate version – that we should prevent bad occurrences unless, to do so, we had to sacrifice something morally significant – only in order to show that, even on this surely undeniable principle, a great change in our way of life is required. On the more moderate principle, it may not follow that we ought to reduce ourselves to the level of marginal utility, for one might hold that to reduce oneself and one's family to this level is to cause something significantly bad to happen. Whether this is so I shall not discuss, since, as I have said, I can see no good reason for holding the moderate version of the principle rather than the strong version. Even if we accepted the principle only in its moderate form, however, it should be clear that we would have to give away enough to ensure that the consumer society, dependent as it is on people spending on trivia rather than giving to famine relief, would slow down and perhaps disappear entirely. There are several reasons why this would be desirable in itself. The value and necessity of economic growth are now being questioned not only by conservationists, but by economists as well.[5] There is no doubt, too, that the consumer society has had a distorting effect on the goals and purposes of its members. Yet looking at the matter purely from the point of view of overseas aid, there must be a limit to the extent to which we should deliberately slow down our economy; for it might be the case that if we gave away, say, 40 percent of our Gross National Product, we would slow down the economy so much that in absolute terms we would be giving less than if we gave 25 percent of the much larger GNP that we would have if we limited our contribution to this smaller percentage.

I mention this only as an indication of the sort of factor that one would have to take into account in working out an ideal. Since Western societies generally consider 1 percent of the GNP an acceptable level for overseas aid, the matter is entirely academic. Nor does it affect the question of how much an individual should give in a society in which very few are giving substantial amounts.

It is sometimes said, though less often now than it used to be, that philosophers have no special role to play in public affairs, since most public issues depend primarily on an assessment of facts. On questions of fact, it is said, philosophers as such have no special expertise, and so it has been possible to engage in philosophy without committing oneself to any position on major public issues. No doubt there are some issues of social policy and foreign policy about which it can truly be said that a really expert assessment of the facts is required before taking sides or acting, but the issue of famine is surely not one of these. The facts about the existence of suffering are beyond dispute. Nor, I think, is it disputed that we can do something about it, either through orthodox methods of famine relief or through population control or both. This is therefore an issue on which philosophers are competent to take a position. The issue is one which faces everyone who has more money than he needs to support himself and his dependants, or who is in a position to take some sort of political action. These categories must include practically every teacher and student of philosophy in the universities of the Western world. If philosophy is to deal with matters that are relevant to both teachers and students, this is an issue that philosophers should discuss.

Discussion, though, is not enough. What is the point of relating philosophy to public (and personal) affairs if we do not take our conclusions seriously? In this instance, taking our conclusion seriously means acting upon it. The philosopher will not find it any easier than anyone else to alter his attitudes and way of life to the extent that, if I am right, is involved in doing everything that we ought to be doing. At the very least, though, one can make a start. The philosopher who does so will have to sacrifice some of the benefits of the consumer society, but he can find compensation in the satisfaction of a way of life in which theory and practice, if not yet in harmony, are at least coming together.

Postscript

The crisis in Bangladesh that spurred me to write the above article is now of historical interest only, but the world food crisis is, if anything, still more serious. The huge grain reserves that were then held by the United States have vanished. Increased oil prices have made both fertilizer and energy more expensive in developing countries, and have made it difficult for them to produce more food. At the same time, their population has continued to grow. Fortunately, as I write now, there is no major famine anywhere in the world; but poor people are still starving in several countries, and malnutrition remains very wide-spread. The need for assistance is, therefore, just as great as when I first wrote, and we can be sure that without it there will, again, be major famines.

The contrast between poverty and affluence that I wrote about is also as great as it was then. True, the affluent nations have experienced a recession, and are perhaps not as prosperous as they were in 1971. But the poorer nations have suffered as least as much from the recession, in reduced government aid (because if governments decide to reduce expenditure, they regard foreign aid as one of the expendable items, ahead of, for instance, defense or public construction projects) and in increased prices for goods and materials they need to buy. In any case, compared with the difference between the affluent nations and the poor nations, the whole recession was trifling; the poorest in the affluent nations remained incomparably better off than the poorest in the poor nations.

So the case for aid, on both a personal and a governmental level, remains as great now as it was in 1971, and I would not wish to change the basic argument that I put forward then.

There are, however, some matters of emphasis that I might put differently if I were to rewrite the article, and the most important of these concerns the population problem. I still think that, as I wrote then, the view that famine relief merely postpones starvation unless something is done to check population growth is not an argument against aid, it is only an argument against the *type* of aid that should be given. Those who hold this view have the same obligation to give to prevent starvation as those who do not; the difference is that they regard assisting population control schemes as a more effective way of preventing starvation in the long run. I would now, however, have given greater space to the discussion of the population problem; for I now think that there is a serious case for saying that if a country refuses to take any steps to slow the rate of its population growth, we should not give it aid. This is, of course, a very drastic step to take, and the choice it represents is a horrible choice to have to make; but if, after a dispassionate analysis of all the available information, we come to the conclusion that without population control we will not, in the long run, be able to prevent famine or other catastrophes, then it may be more humane in the long run to aid those countries that are prepared to take strong measures to reduce population growth, and to use our aid policy as a means of pressuring other countries to take similar steps.

It may be objected that such a policy involves an attempt to coerce a sovereign nation.

But since we are not under an obligation to give aid unless that aid is likely to be effective in reducing starvation or malnutrition, we are not under an obligation to give aid to countries that make no effort to reduce a rate of population growth that will lead to catastrophe. Since we do not force any nation to accept our aid, simply making it clear that we will not give aid where it is not going to be effective cannot properly be regarded as a form of coercion.

I should also make it clear that the kind of aid that will slow population growth is not just assistance with the setting up of facilities for dispensing contraceptives and performing sterilizations. It is also necessary to create the conditions under which people do not wish to have so many children. This will involve, among other things, providing greater economic security for people, particularly in their old age, so that they do not need the security of a large family to provide for them. Thus, the requirements of aid designed to reduce population growth and aid designed to eliminate starvation are by no means separate; they overlap, and the latter will often be a means to the former. The obligation of the affluent is, I believe, to do both. Fortunately, there are now many people in the foreign aid field, including those in the private agencies, who are aware of this.

One other matter that I should now put forward slightly differently is that my argument does, of course, apply to assistance with development, particularly agricultural development, as well as to direct famine relief. Indeed, I think the former is usually the better long-term investment. Although this was my view when I wrote the article, the fact that I started from a famine situation, where the need was for immediate food, has led some readers to suppose that the argument is only about giving food and not about other types of aid. This is quite mistaken, and my view is that the aid should be of whatever type is most effective.

On a more philosophical level, there has been some discussion of the original article which has been helpful in clarifying the issues and pointing to the areas in which more work on the argument is needed. In particular, as John Arthur has shown in "Rights and the Duty to Bring Aid" (included in this volume), something more needs to be said about the notion of "moral significance." The problem is that to give an account of this notion involves nothing less than a full-fledged ethical theory; and while I am myself inclined toward a utilitarian view, it was my aim in writing "Famine, Affluence, and Morality" to produce an argument which would appeal not only to utilitarians, but also to anyone who accepted the initial premises of the argument, which seemed to me likely to have a very wide acceptance. So I tried to get around the need to produce a complete ethical theory by allowing my readers to fill in their own version – within limits – of what is morally significant, and then see what the moral consequences are. This tactic works reasonably well with those who are prepared to agree that such matters as being fashionably dressed are not really of moral significance; but Arthur is right to say that people could take the opposite view without being obviously irrational. Hence, I do not accept Arthur's claim that the weak principle implies little or no duty of benevolence, for it will imply a significant duty of benevolence for those who admit, as I think most nonphilosophers and even off-guard philosophers will admit, that they spend considerable sums on items that by their own standards are of no moral significance. But I do agree that the weak principle is nonetheless too weak, because it makes it too easy for the duty of benevolence to be avoided.

On the other hand, I think the strong principle will stand, whether the notion of moral significance is developed along utilitarian lines, or once again left to the individual reader's own sincere judgment. In either case, I would argue against Arthur's view that we are morally entitled to give greater weight to our own interests and purposes simply because they are our own. This view seems to me contrary to the idea, now widely shared by moral philosophers, that some element of impartiality or universalizability is inherent in the very notion of a moral judgment. (For a discussion of the different formulations of this idea, and an indication of the extent to which they are in agreement, see R. M. Hare, "Rules of War and Moral Reasoning," *Philosophy and Public Affairs*, I, no. 2, 1972.) Granted, in normal circumstances, it may be better for everyone if we recognize that each of us will be primarily responsible for running our own lives and only secondarily responsible for others. This, however, is not a moral ultimate, but a secondary principle that derives from consideration of how a society may best order its affairs, given the limits of altruism in human beings. Such secondary principles are, I think, swept aside by the extreme evil of people starving to death.

Notes

1   There was also a third possibility: that India would go to war to enable the refugees to return to their lands. Since I wrote this paper, India has taken this way out. The situation is no longer that described above, but this does not affect my argument, as the next paragraph indicates.

2   In view of the special sense philosophers often give to the term, I should say that I use "obligation" simply as the abstract noun derived from "ought," so that "I have an obligation to" means no more, and no less, than "I ought to." This usage is in accordance with the definition of "ought" given by the *Shorter Oxford English Dictionary*: "the general verb to express duty or obligation." I do not think any issue of substance hangs on the way the term is used; sentences in which I use "obligation" could all be rewritten, although somewhat clumsily, as sentences in which a clause containing "ought" replaces the term "obligation."

3   J. O. Urmson, "Saints and Heroes," in *Essays in Moral Philosophy*, ed. Abraham I. Melden (Seattle: University of Washington Press, 1958), p. 214. For a related but significantly different view see also Henry Sidgwick, *The Methods of Ethics*, 7th edn (London: Dover Press, 1907), pp. 220–1, 492–3.

4   *Summa Theologica*, II–II, Question 66, Article 7, in *Aquinas, Selected Political Writings*, ed. A. P. d'Entrèves, trans. J. G. Dawson (Oxford: Basil Blackwell, 1948), p. 171.

5   See, for instance, John Kenneth Galbraith, *The New Industrial State* (Boston: Houghton Mifflin, 1967); and E. J. Mishan, *The Costs of Economic Growth* (New York: Praeger, 1967).

55

Rights and the Duty to Bring Aid

John Arthur

I

There is no doubt that the large and growing incidence of world hunger constitutes a major problem, both moral and practical, for the fortunate few who have surpluses of cheap food. Our habits regarding meat consumption exemplify the magnitude of the moral issue. Americans now consume about two and a half times the meat they did in 1950 (currently about 125 lbs per capita per year). Yet, meat is extremely inefficient as a source of food. Only a small portion of the total calories consumed by the animal remains to be eaten in the meat. As much as 95 percent of the food is lost by feeding and eating cattle rather than producing the grain for direct human consumption. Thus, the same amount of food consumed by Americans largely indirectly in meat form could feed one and a half billion persons on a (relatively meatless) Chinese diet. Much, if not all, of the world's food crisis could be resolved if Americans were simply to change their eating habits by moving toward direct consumption of grain and at the same time providing the surpluses for the hungry. Given this, plus the serious moral problems associated with animal suffering,[1] the overall case for vegetarianism seems strong.

I want to discuss here only one of these two related problems, the obligations of the affluent few to starving people. I begin by considering a recent article on the subject by Peter Singer, entitled "Famine, Affluence, and Morality" (reprinted in this volume).[2] I argue that Singer fails to establish the claim that such an obligation exists. This is the case for both the strong and weak interpretations of his view. I then go on to show that the role of rights needs to be given greater weight than utilitarian theories like Singer's allow. The rights of both the affluent and the starving are shown to be morally significant but not in themselves decisive, since obligations of benevolence can and often do override rights of others (e.g., property rights). Finally, I argue that under specific conditions the affluent are obligated not to exercise their rights to consume at the expense of others' lives.

II

Singer's argument is in two stages. First, he argues that two general moral principles are and ought to be accepted. Then he claims that the principles imply an obligation to eliminate starvation. The first principle is simply that "suffering and death from lack of food, shelter and medical care are bad."[3] This principle seems obviously true and I will have little to say about it. Some may be inclined to think that the existence of an evil in itself places an obligation on others, but that is, of course, the problem which Singer addresses. I take it that he is not begging the question in this obvious way and will argue from the existence of evil to the obligation of others to eliminate it. But how, exactly, does he establish the connection? It is the second principle which he thinks shows that connection.

The necessary link is provided by either of two versions of this principle. The first (strong) formulation which Singer offers of the second principle is as follows:

> if it is in our power to prevent something bad from happening, without thereby sacrificing anything of comparable moral importance, we ought, morally, to do it.[4]

The weaker principle simply substitutes for "comparable moral importance" the phrase "any moral significance." He goes on to develop these notions, saying that:

> By "without sacrificing anything of comparable moral importance" I mean without causing anything else comparably bad to happen, or doing something that is wrong in itself, or failing to promote some moral good, comparable in significance to the bad thing we can prevent.[5]

These remarks can be interpreted for the weaker principle by simply eliminating "comparable" in the statement.

One question is, of course, whether either of these two principles ought to be accepted. There are two ways in which this could be established. First, they could be shown, by philosophical argument, to follow from reasonably well established premises or from a general theory. Secondly, they might be justified because they are principles which underlie particular moral judgments the truth of which is accepted. Singer doesn't do either of these explicitly, although he seems to have the second in mind. He first speaks of what he takes to be the "uncontroversial appearance" of the principles. He then applies the principles to a similar case in which a drowning child requires help. Singer argues, in essence, that since the drowning is bad and it can be avoided without sacrificing something of moral significance, it is obligatory that the child be saved. He claims further that both the strong and weak versions are sufficient to establish the duty. Dirtying one's clothes, for example, is not of "moral significance" and so does not justify failure to act. The last part of his paper is devoted to the claim that the analogy between the case of the child and that of starving people is apt in that geographical distance and others' willingness to act are not acceptable excuses for inaction.

III

My concern here is not with these latter issues. Rather, I want to focus on the two versions of the second principle, discussing each in terms of (1) whether it is plausible, and (2) if true, whether it establishes the duty to provide aid. I will deal with the weak version first, arguing that it fails at step (2) in the argument.

This version reads, "if it is in our power to prevent something bad from happening without thereby sacrificing *anything* morally significant we ought morally to do it." Singer later claims that:

> Even if we accept the principle in its moderate form, however, it should be clear that we would have to give away enough to ensure that the consumer society, dependent as it is on people spending on trivia rather than giving to famine relief, would slow down and perhaps disappear entirely.[6]

The crucial idea of "morally significant" is left largely unanalyzed. Two examples are given: dirtying one's clothes and being "well dressed." Both are taken to be morally *insignificant*.

It could perhaps be argued against Singer that these things *are* morally significant. Both, for example, would be cases of decreasing aesthetic value, and if you think aesthetic values are intrinsic you might well dispute the claim that being "well dressed" is without moral significance. There is, however, a more serious objection to be raised. To see this, we need to distinguish between the possible value of the *fact* of being "well dressed" and the value of the *enjoyment* some persons receive and create by being "well dressed" (and, of course, the unhappiness avoided of being "badly dressed").

That such enjoyment and unhappiness are of some moral significance can be seen by the following case. Suppose it were possible that, by simply singing a chorus of "Dixie," you could eliminate all the unhappiness and embarrassment that some people experience at being badly dressed. Surely, doing that would be an act of moral significance. It would be good for you to do so, perhaps even wrong not to. Similarly, throwing mud on people's clothes, though not a great wrong, is surely not "without *any* moral significance."

It seems then, that the weak principle (while perhaps true) does not generally establish a duty to provide aid to starving people. Whether it does in specific instances depends on the nature of the cost to the person providing the aid. If *either* the loss to the giver is in itself valuable or the loss results in increased unhappiness or decreased happiness to someone, then the principle does not require that the burden be accepted.

(It is interesting to ask just how much giving *would* be required by this principle. If we can assume that givers would benefit in some minimal way by giving – and that they are reasonable – then perhaps the best answer is that the level of giving required is the level that is actually given. Otherwise, why would people *not* give more if there is no value to them in things they choose to keep?)

In addition to the moral significance of the costs that I just described, there is a further problem which will become particularly significant in considering the strong principle. For many people it is part of their moral sense that they and others have a special relationship to their own goals or projects. That is, in making one's choices a person may properly weigh the outcome that one desires more heavily than the goals that others may have. Often this is expressed as a right or entitlement.[7] Thus, for example, if P acquires some good (x) in a just social arrangement without violating others' rights, then P has a special title to x that P is entitled to weigh against the desires of others. P need not, in determining whether he ought to give x to another, overlook the fact that x is his; he acquired it fairly, and so has special say in what happens to it. If this is correct, it is a fact of some moral significance and thus would also block the inference from the weak principle to the obligation to give what one has to others. I will pursue this line of argument in the following section while considering the strong version of the principle.

IV

Many people, especially those inclined toward utilitarianism, would probably accept the preceding, believing that it is the stronger of the two principles that should be used. "After all," they might argue, "the real issue is the great *disparity* between the amount of good which could be produced by resources of the rich if applied to problems of starvation as against the small amount of good produced by the resources if spent on second cars and houses, fancy clothes etc." I will assume that the facts are just as the claim suggests. That is, I will assume that it can *not* be plausibly argued that there are, for example, artistic or cultural values which (1) would be lost by such redistribution of wealth and (2) are equal in value to the starvation which would be eliminated. Thus, if the strong principle is true, then it (unlike the weak version) would require radical changes in our common understanding of the duties of the wealthy to starving people.

But is it true, as Singer suggests, that "if it is in our power to prevent something bad from happening without thereby sacrificing something of comparable moral significance we ought morally to do it?" Here the problem with the meaning of "moral significance" is even more acute than in the weak version. All that was required for the weak principle was that we be able to distinguish courses of action that have moral significance from those that do not. Here, however, the moral significance of alternative acts must be both *recognized* and *weighed*. And how is this to be done, according to Singer? Unfortunately, he provides little help here, though this is crucial in evaluating his argument.

I will discuss one obvious interpretation of "comparable moral significance," argue it is inadequate, and then suggest what I take to be some of the factors an adequate theory would consider.

Assuming that giving aid is not "bad in itself," the only other facts which Singer sees as morally significant in evaluating obligations are the good or bad consequences of actions. Singer's strong version obviously resembles the act utilitarian principle. With respect to starvation, this interpretation is open to the objection raised at the end of section III above, since it takes no account of a variety of important factors, such as the apparent right to give added weight to one's own choices and interests, and to ownership. I now wish to look at this claim in more detail.

Consider the following examples of moral problems which I take to be fairly common. One obvious means by which you could aid others is with your body. Many of your extra organs (eye, kidney) could be given to another with the result that there would be more good than if you kept both. You wouldn't see as well or live as long, perhaps, but that is not of comparable significance to the benefit others would receive. Yet, surely the fact that it is your eye and you need it is not insignificant. Perhaps there could be cases where one is obligated to sacrifice one's health or sight, but what seems clear is that this is not true in every case where (slightly) more good would come of your doing so. Secondly, suppose a woman has a choice between remaining with her husband or leaving. As best she can determine, the morally relevant factors do not indicate which she should do (the consequences of each seem about equally good and there is no question of broken promises, deception, or whatever). But, suppose in addition to these facts, it is the case that by remaining with her husband the woman will be unable to pursue important aspects of the plan of life she has set for herself. Perhaps by remaining she will be forced to sacrifice a career which she wishes to pursue. If the *only* facts that are of moral significance are the consequences of her choice, then she ought, presumably, to flip a coin (assuming there is some feature of her staying that is of equal importance to the unhappiness at the loss of the career *she* will experience). Surely, though, the fact that some goals are ones *she* chooses for herself (assuming she doesn't violate the others' rights) is of significance. It is, after all, *her* life and *her* future and she is entitled to treat it that way. In neither of these cases is the person required to accept as equal to his or her own goals and well-being the welfare of even his or her family, much less the whole world. The fact that others may benefit even slightly more from their pursuing another course is not in itself sufficient to show they ought to act other than they choose. Servility, though perhaps not a vice, is certainly not an obligation that all must fulfill.[8]

The above goes part way, I think, in explaining the importance we place on allowing people maximal latitude in pursuing their goals. Rights or entitlements to things that are our own reflect important facts about people. Each of us has only one life and it is uniquely valuable to each of us. Your choices do not constitute my life, nor do mine yours. The purely utilitarian interpretation of "moral significance" provides for assigning no special weight to the goals and interests of individuals in making their choices. It provides no basis for saying that though there may be greater total good done by one course, still a person could be entitled for some reason to pursue another.

It seems, then, that determining whether giving aid to starving persons would be sacrificing something of comparable moral significance demands weighing the fact that the persons are entitled to give special weight to their own interests where their future or (fairly acquired) property is at issue. Exactly *how much* weight may be given is a question that I will consider shortly. The point here is that the question of the extent of the obligation to eliminate starvation has not been answered. My argument was that however "moral significance" is best understood, it is far too simple to suggest that *only* the total good produced is relevant. If providing quality education for one's children is a goal, then (assuming the resources were acquired fairly) the fact that it is a goal *itself* provides additional weight against other ways the resources might be used, including the one that maximizes the total good. Further, if the resources to be used for the purpose are legitimately owned, then that too is something that the parent is entitled to consider.

Returning to the case of the drowning child, the same point may be made. Suppose it is an important part of a person's way of life that he not interfere. Perhaps the passer-by believes God's will is being manifested in this particular incident and strongly values non-interference with God's working out of His plan. Surely, this is especially relevant to the question of whether the person is obligated to intervene, even when the greatest good would be promoted by intervention. When saying that a person is obligated to act in some way, the significance *to the person* of the act must not only be considered along with all the other features of the act, but is also of special moral significance in determining that person's duty. More, however, needs to be said here.

Suppose, for instance, that the case were like this: A passer-by sees a child drowning but fails to help, not for the sake of another important goal but rather out of lack of interest. Such situations are not at all uncommon, as when people fail to report violent crimes they observe in progress. I assume that anyone who fails to act in such circumstances is acting wrongly. As with the case of the utilitarian principle discussed earlier, the drowning child also represents a limiting case. In the former, *no* significance is assigned to the woman's choice by virtue of its being *hers*. Here, however, the interests of *others* are not weighed. An acceptable principle of benevolence would fall between the two limiting cases. The relative moral significance of alternative acts could then be determined by applying the principle, distinguishing acts which are obligatory from charitable ones.

In summary, I have argued that neither the strong nor the weak principle advanced by Singer provides an adequate solution to the issue of affluence and hunger. The essential problem is with his notion of "moral significance." I argued that the weak principle fails to show any obligations, given the normal conception of factors which possess such significance. I then argued that the strong principle (which is close to act utilitarianism) is mistaken. The basic objection to this principle is that it fails to take account of certain aspects of the situation which must be considered in any adequate formulation of the principle.

V

As I suggested earlier, a fully adequate formulation of the principle of benevolence depends on a general theory of right. Such a theory would not only include a principle of benevolence but also give account of the whole range of rights and duties and a means to weigh conflicting claims. In this section, I discuss some of the various problems associated with benevolence, obligation, and rights. In the final section, I offer what I believe to be an adequate principle of benevolence.

One view, which has been criticized recently by Judith Thomson,[9] suggests that whenever there is a duty or obligation there must be a corresponding right. I presume we want to say that in some cases (e.g., the drowning child) there is an obligation to benevolence, but does this also mean that the child has a *right* to be aided? Perhaps there is only a semantic point here regarding "right," but perhaps also there is a deeper disagreement.

I suggest that, whether we call it a "right" or not, there are important differences between obligations based on benevolence and other obligations. Two differences are significant. First, the person who has the obligation to save the drowning child did not *do anything* that created the situation. But, compare this case with a similar one of a lifeguard who fails to save someone. Here there is a clear sense in which the drowning victim may claim a right to have another do his utmost to save him. An agreement was reached whereby the lifeguard *accepted* the responsibility for the victim's welfare. The guard, in a sense, took on the goals of the swimmers as his own. To fail to aid is a special sort of injustice that the passer-by does not do. It seems clearly appropriate to speak of the lifeguard's failure to act as a case of a right being violated.

A second important point regarding the drowning child example and rights is that the passer-by is not *taking positive steps* in reference to the child. This can be contrasted with an action that might be taken to drown a child who would not otherwise die. Here, again, it is appropriate to describe this act as a violation of a right (to life). Other violations of rights also seem to require that one act, not merely fail to take action – for example, property rights (theft) and privacy rights (listening without leave). The drowning child and starvation cases are wrong not because of acts but the failure to act.

Thus, there are important differences between duties of benevolence and others where a right is obviously at issue. Cases of failing to aid are not (unlike right violations) either instances of positive actions that are taken or ones in which the rich or the passer-by has taken responsibility by a previous act. It does not follow from this, however, that strong obligations are not present to save other persons. Obviously, one ought to aid a drowning child (at least) in cases where there is no serious risk or cost to the passer-by. This is true even though there is no obvious right that the child has to be aided.

Furthermore, if saving a drowning child requires using someone's boat without their permission (a violation of property right), then it still ought to be done. Duties to bring aid can override duties not to violate rights. The best thing to say here is that, depending on the circumstances, duties to aid and not to violate rights can each outweigh the other. Where actions involve both violation of rights and failing to meet duties to aid (the lifeguard's failing to save), the obligation is stronger than either would be by itself. Describing the situation in this way implies that although there is a sense in which the boat owner, the affluent spender, and the passer-by have a right to fail to act, still they are obligated not to exercise that right because there is a stronger duty to give aid.

Some may be inclined to say, against this, that in fact the passer-by does not have such a right not to help. But this claim is ambiguous. If what is meant is that they ought to help, then I agree. There is, however, still a point in saying owners of food have the right to use the food as they see fit. It serves to emphasize that there is a moral difference between these cases and ones where the object of need is *not* legitimately owned by anyone (as, for example, if it's not another's boat but a log that the drowning child needs). To say that the property right is *lost* where the principle of benevolence overrides is to hide this difference, though it is morally significant.

Other people might be inclined to say about these situations that the point of saying someone has a right to their food, time, boat or whatever is that others ought not to intervene to force them to bring aid. A person defending this view might accept my claim that in fact the person ought to help. It might then be argued that because they are not violating a right of another (to be saved) and they have a (property) right to the good, others can't, through state authority, force them to bring aid.

This claim obviously raises a variety of questions in legal and political philosophy, and is outside the scope of the present paper. My position does not preclude good samaritan laws, nor are they implied. This is a further question which requires further argument. That one has a moral right to x, but is obligated for other reasons not to exercise the right, leaves open the issue of whether others either can or should make that person fulfill the obligation.

If what I have said is correct, two general points should be made about starvation. First, even though it may be that the affluent have a right to use resources to pursue their own goals, and not provide aid, they may also be strongly obligated not to exercise the right. This is because, in the circumstances, the duty to benevolence is overriding. The existence and extent of such an obligation can be determined only by discovering the relative weight of these conflicting principles. In the final section, I consider how this should be done.

Secondly, even if it is also true that the passer-by and the affluent do not violate a right of another in failing to help, it may still be the case that they strongly ought not to do so. Of course, their behavior could also be even worse than it is (by drowning the child or sending poisoned food to the hungry and thus violating their rights). All that shows, however, is that the failure to help is not the *most* morally objectionable course that can be imagined in the circumstances. This point hardly constitutes justification for failing to act.

VI

I argued earlier that neither Singer's weak principle nor the utilitarian one is what we are after. The former would imply (wrongly) little or no duty of benevolence, and the latter does not take seriously enough the rights and interests of the affluent. What is needed is a principle which we may use to determine the circumstances in which the needs of others create a duty to bring aid which is more stringent than the rights of the affluent to pursue their own interests and use their property as they desire.

The following principle, while similar to the utilitarian one, seems to be most adequate: "If it is in our power to prevent death of an innocent without sacrificing anything of *substantial* significance then we ought morally to do it." The problem, of course, is to determine exactly what is meant by "substantial significance." I assume there are no duties present that arise out of others' rights, as, for example, those of one's children to be provided for. Considerations of that sort would lead beyond the present paper. My concern here is limited to instances in which there is a question of bringing aid (where no obvious right to the aid is present) or using resources for other (preferred) ends.

There are two questions which are important in deciding whether what is being given up by the affluent is of substantial significance. First, we might specify *objectively* the needs which people have, and grant that the duty to bring aid is not present unless these needs have already been met. Included among the needs which are of substantial significance would be those things without which a person cannot continue to function physically – for example, food, clothing, health care, housing, and sufficient training to provide these for oneself.

It also, however, seems reasonable that certain psychological facts ought to be weighed before a person is obligated to help others meet their needs. For example, if you cannot have an even modestly happy life without some further good, then surely that, too, is something to which you are entitled. This suggests a second, *subjective* standard that should also be employed to determine whether something is of no substantial significance and so ought not be consumed at the expense of others' basic needs. The best way to put this, I believe, is to say that "if the lack of x would not affect the long-term happiness of a person, then x is of no substantial significance." By "long-term happiness" I mean to include anything which, if not acquired, will result in unhappiness over an extended period of one's life, not just something the lack of which is a source of momentary loss but soon forgotten. Thus, in a normal case, dirtying one's clothes to save a drowning child is of no substantial significance and so the duty of benevolence is overriding. If, however, selling some possession for famine relief would mean the person's life *really is* (for a long period) less happy, then the possessions are of substantial significance and so the person is not wrong in exercising the right of ownership instead of providing aid. If the possessions had been sold, it would have been an act of charity, not fulfillment of a duty. The same analysis can be provided for other choices we make – for example, how our time is spent and whether to donate organs. If doing so would result in your not seeing well and this would make your life less happy over time, then you are not obligated to do so.

If what I have said is correct, then duties of benevolence increase as one's dependence on possessions for living a happy life decreases. If a person's long-term happiness does not depend on (second?) cars and fancy clothes, then that person ought not to purchase those goods at the expense of others' basic needs being unfulfilled. Thus, depending on the psychological nature of persons, their duties of benevolence will vary.

The question of the actual effect of not buying a new car, house, clothes, or whatever on one's long-term happiness is of course a difficult one. My own feeling is that if the principle were to be applied honestly, those of us who are relatively affluent would discover that a substantial part of the resources and time we expend should be used to bring aid. The extent of the obligation must, finally, be determined by asking whether the lack of some good *really would* result in a need not being met or in a less happy life for its owner, and that is a question between each of us and our conscience.

In summary, I have argued that Singer's utilitarian principle is inadequate to establish the claim that acts to eliminate starvation are obligatory, but that such an obligation still exists.

The rights of both the affluent and the hungry are considered, and a principle is defended which clarifies the circumstances in which it is a duty and not merely charitable to provide aid to others whose basic needs are not being met.

Notes

1 Peter Singer, *Animal Liberation* (New York: New York Review of Books/Random House, 1975).

2 Peter Singer, "Famine, Affluence, and Morality," *Philosophy and Public Affairs*, I, no. 3 (Spring 1972).

3 Ibid., p. 586 (in this volume).

4 Ibid.

5 Ibid. I assume "importance" and "significance" are synonymous.

6 Ibid., p. 592 (in this volume).

7 In a recent book (*Anarchy, State, and Utopia*, New York: Basic Books, 1974), Robert Nozick argues that such rights are extensive against state authority.

8 For an argument that servility is wrong, see Thomas Hill, "Servility and Self-Respect," *The Monist*, VII, no. 4 (January 1973).

9 Judith Jarvis Thomson, "The Right to Privacy," *Philosophy and Public Affairs*, IV, no. 4 (Summer 1975).

56

Hunger, Capability, and Development

David A. Crocker[1]

World Hunger and Moral Obligation,[2] the predecessor of the present volume, illustrated and advanced the new philosophical movement called "applied ethics." The anthology's focus was salutary. The essays addressed the question of "what moral responsibility affluent nations (or those people in them) have to the starving masses." Among those arguing that nations do have a positive obligation to aid distant and hungry people, there were efforts to explore the nature, foundation, and limits of this obligation. It is now apparent, however, that this initial moral problematic needs to be recast and enlarged.

I argue that the philosophical discussion in WH, and innumerable subsequent texts and anthologies in applied ethics, committed what Whitehead called "the fallacy of misplaced concreteness."[3] Philosophers abstracted one part – famine and food aid – from the whole complex of hunger, poverty, and development, and proceeded to consider that part in isolation from other dimensions. We now need to redirect and then broaden our attention with respect to the complex causes, conditions, and cures of hunger. Otherwise, we will have an incomplete and distorted picture of both the facts and the values involved. Instead of philosophical preoccupation with the moral basis for aid from rich countries to famine victims in poor countries, emphasis should be shifted (1) from moral foundations to interpretative and strategic concepts, (2) from famine to persistent malnutrition, (3) from remedy to prevention, (4) from food availability to food entitlements, (5) from food and food entitlements to capabilities and a capabilities-based model of development. Overall, the progression I favor will take us from an ethics of aid to an ethics for development.

From Moral Foundations to Interpretative and Strategic Concepts

The moral problem of world hunger and the ethics of famine relief were among the first practical issues that philosophers tackled after John Rawls's pivotal 1971 study, *A Theory of Justice,*[4] convinced them that reflection on normative issues was part of the philosopher's task. Although Rawls himself limited ethical analysis to abstract principles of distributive justice, applied philosophical ethicists addressed the ethical and conceptual aspects of a variety of practical problems and policies. In the same year that Rawls's volume appeared, Peter Singer first wrote about famine in East Bengal (now Bangladesh)[5] and, more generally, about "the obligations of the affluent to those in danger of starvation."[6] In his 1974 *New York Times Magazine* article, "Philosophers are Back on the Job,"[7] Singer championed the philosophical turn to applied ethics, employing the ethics of famine relief as a leading example.

Philosophers were back on the job because, as John Dewey had urged fifty years earlier, "philosophy recovers itself when it ceases to be a device for dealing with the problems of philosophers and becomes a method, cultivated by philosophers, for dealing with the problems of men."[8] One of these human problems in the mid-seventies was whether or not affluent states and their citizens were in any way morally obligated to send food to famine victims in other countries. Is such aid morally required, permissible, or impermissible?

More than two decades later, however, many perceive the problem of "world hunger and moral obligation" differently. When we see pictures – whether in the media or on the cover of WH – of a starving child crouching on infertile soil, the question "Do we have a duty to help?" seems to many beside the point. Of course we should help, provided that such help will do genuine and sustainable good.[9] We should not take seriously those who insist that no action be taken until an argument is found to justify the view that the rich in the North should help the poor in the South. To be sure, there is a place for moral debate with respect to *how much* assistance morality requires us to give distant people, in light of our concomitant obligations to aid our families, friends, and compatriots.[10] And in some contexts – university seminar rooms, for instance – it can be valuable to consider whether we owe the foreign poor anything at all. But usually we see no good reason to doubt that we owe them *something*, if we can be reasonably sure that our help will alleviate their immediate misery and improve their long-term prospects. What challenges aid to distant peoples is not so much skepticism concerning moral foundations as pessimism about practical results.

Unfortunately, preoccupied as they were with the task of justifying aid to distant people, most philosophers evinced scant interest in institutional and practical issues. They seemed to believe that if they could resolve the foundational questions, the rest would be easy; the rational – on its own – would become real. Thus, although WH's editors did challenge their readers to consider "If one ought to help the hungry, how should one help?" (WH, 10), the volume's essays almost completely failed to address the best ways to diagnose and remedy the problem of world hunger.

It might be objected that analysis of the causes and cures of world hunger is a purely factual, empirical, or technical matter to which ethicists cannot contribute. Yet I would argue that facts and values cannot be so easily kept separate, for we discern ethically salient features of facts on the basis of our moral values.[11] Ethical reflection, whether the work of philosophers or non-philosophers, plays not only a critical and guiding role but also an interpretative role in relation to social reality and change. An ethic proposes norms for assessing present social institutions, envisaging future alternatives, and assigning moral obligations. An ethic, finally, provides a basis for deciding how agents should act in particular circumstances. What is equally important and frequently neglected, however, is that a normative vision also informs the ways we discern, describe, explain, and forecast social phenomena. How we "read" the situation, as well as how we describe and classify it, will be a function of our value commitments and even our moral sensitivities.[12] For instance, if we ask, "How is India doing?" we are seeking an empirical analysis of what is going on in that country. Yet alternative ethical perspectives will focus on distinct, though sometimes over-lapping, facts: hedonistic utilitarianism attends to pleasures and pains, preference utilitarianism selects preference satisfactions and dissatisfactions (or per capita productivity and consumption), human-rights approaches emphasize human-rights compliances and violations, and contractarians investigate the distributions of "social primary goods" such as income, wealth, liberties, and opportunities. In each case the ethic structures what counts as morally relevant information. One value of dialogue between different ethical perspectives is that we learn to see the world in new and different ways. Moreover, as Sherman says, "how to see becomes as much a matter of inquiry (*zetēsis*) as what to do."[13]

Amartya Sen, Martha Nussbaum, Jean Drèze, and others offer the capabilities ethic as the result of an inquiry about understanding and combatting world hunger and other deprivations. Capabilities theorists employ this ethic to appraise social institutions and guide policy-formation and actions.[14] To accomplish this task they defend explicit ethical principles and assign moral responsibilities.[15] The capabilities perspective, however, also yields distinctive ways of perceiving world hunger and understanding its empirical causes and attempted cures. With its emphasis on "the commodity commands [i.e., entitlements] and basic capabilities that people enjoy" (HPA, 273), the capabilities ethic interprets and supplies a rationale for broadening the investigative focus from food aid for famine victims to the most important (and modifiable) causes, conditions, consequences, and remedies of endemic hunger and other privations.[16] As Drèze and Sen argue, "seeing hunger as entitlement failure points to possible remedies as well as helping us to understand the forces that generate hunger and sustain it" (HPA, 24). In this essay I emphasize the interpretative contribution of the capabilities ethic and argue that this normative perspective helps justify a broader approach to world hunger.

In the mid-1990s, philosophical reflection on world hunger remains important. After Ethiopia, Kampuchea, Sudan, Somalia, and Rwanda, however, philosophers are appropriately less concerned with morally justifying aid to the distant hungry and more concerned with the conceptual and ethical dimensions of understanding hunger and with policies for successfully combatting it.

From Famine to Persistent Malnutrition

Philosophers, like policymakers and the public, typically pay excessive attention to famine and insufficient attention to persistent malnutrition.[17] Both famine and endemic malnutrition are forms of hunger in the sense of "an inadequacy in dietary intake relative to the kind and quantity of food required for growth, for activity, and for maintenance of good health."[18] Famine and chronic hunger, however, differ in character, causes, consequences, and cures. Famine is dramatic, "involving acute starvation and sharp increase in mortality" (HPA, 7). It makes a sensational topic for the evening news or fund-raising rock concerts. Chronic hunger, "involving sustained nutritional deprivation on a persistent basis," has deeper causes than famine and is less visible. Moreover, persistent hunger affects many more people[19] and is harder to eradicate than famine. The consequences of persistent hunger – severe incapacitation, chronic illness, and humiliation – may be worse than death. And chronic hunger is itself a killer, since weak or sickly persons are especially prone to deadly diseases. If we are concerned about the misery and mortality caused by famine, we should be even more exercised by the harms caused by persistent malnutrition.

Strategies to combat famine and persistent malnutrition also differ:

> To take one example [of diverse strategies in responding to transitory and endemic hunger], in the context of famine prevention the crucial need for speedy intervention and the scarcity of resources often call for a calculated reliance on existing distributional mechanisms (e.g., the operation of private trade stimulated by cash support to famine victims) to supplement the logistic capability of relief agencies. In the context of combatting chronic hunger, on the other hand, there is much greater scope for slower but none the less powerful avenues of action such as institution building, legal reforms, asset redistribution or provisioning in kind. (HPA, 7–8)

Famine and chronic malnutrition don't always go together. Nations – for instance, India since independence and Haiti in 1994 – can be free of famine and yet beset by endemic malnutrition. A country such as China can achieve a reasonably high level of nutritional well-being and yet be stricken by terrible famines. To be exclusively preoccupied with famine is to ignore food deprivation and misery in countries not prone to famine.

As important as is the distinction between these two types of hunger, we must neither exaggerate the differences nor fail to recognize certain linkages. Not only are famine and chronic malnutrition both forms of hunger, but they have certain causes and remedies in common. Both can be understood as what Drèze and Sen call "entitlement failures" and "capability failures" (of which more presently).

As with many other problems, a nation with the right sort of basic political, economic, and social institutions – for instance, stable families, infrastructure, certain kinds of markets, a democratic government, a free press, and nongovernmental organizations – can prevent and remedy both sorts of hunger, while a society without the right set of interlocking institutions is likely to experience one or the other if not both. Moreover, some of the best short-term and long-term approaches to famine prevention – remunerated public employment and, more generally, sustainable development – build on and often intensify effective efforts to address persistent malnutrition (HPA, 158). In contrast, the most common emergency action to combat famine – the herding of people into relief camps in order to dole out free food – jeopardizes long-term solutions by disrupting normal economic activities, upsetting family life, and creating breeding grounds for infectious diseases.

From Remedy to Prevention

Whether concerned with abrupt or chronic hunger, almost all the essays in WH emphasized the moral response to *existing* hunger problems rather than the prevention of *future* ones. Only Onora O'Neill clearly addressed the question of prefamine as well as famine policies (WH, 161–4). On the basis of an expanded conception of the duty not to kill others, O'Neill argued that we have a duty to adopt prefamine policies that ensure that famine is postponed as long as possible and is minimized in severity. Such prefamine policies must include both a population policy and a resources policy, for "a duty to try to postpone the advent and minimize the severity of famine is a duty on the one hand to minimize the number of persons there will be and on the other to maximize the means of subsistence" (WH, 163).

O'Neill's approach, however, unfortunately assumes that famines cannot be prevented altogether, only postponed and minimized. This supposition flies in the face of recent historical experience. Drèze and Sen summarize their findings on this point when they observe, "There is no real evidence to doubt that all famines in the modern world are preventable by human action; . . . many countries – even some very poor ones – manage consistently to prevent them" (HPA, 47). Nations that have successfully prevented impending famines (sometimes without outside help) include India (after independence), Cape Verde, Kenya, Zimbabwe, and Botswana (HPA, chapter 8).

It is also possible to prevent and reduce if not eliminate chronic hunger. We must combat that pessimism – a close cousin of complacency – that assures us that the hungry will always be with us – at least in the same absolute and relative numbers.[20] One of the great achievements of Drèze and Sen is to document, through detailed case studies of successes in fighting hunger, that "there is, in fact, little reason for presuming that the terrible problems of hunger and starvation in the world cannot be changed by human action" (HPA, 276). What is needed is a forward-looking perspective for short-term and long-term prevention of both types of hunger.

From Food Availability to Food Entitlements

Moral reflection on the prevention and relief of world hunger must be expanded from food productivity, availability, and distribution to what Sen calls food "entitlements." Popular images of famine relief emphasize policies that, in Garrett Hardin's words, "move food to the people" or "move people to food" (WH, 19). In either case, the assumption is that hunger is principally caused by lack of food. Chronic hunger, it is often believed, will be solved by greater agricultural productivity, and famine "relief" consists in getting food and starving people together. Much hunger, however, occurs even when people and ample food – even peak supplies – are in close proximity. For a starving person may have no access to or command over the food that is right next door.

In a country, region, and even village stricken by famine, there is often more than enough food for everyone to be adequately fed. Recent research makes it evident that since 1960 there has been sufficient food to feed all the world's people on a "near-vegetarian diet" and that "we are approaching a second threshold of improved diet sufficiency"[21] in which 10 percent of everyone's diet could consist of animal products. Accordingly, it is often said that the problem is one of distribution. This term, however, is ambiguous. But purely spatial redistribution is insufficient and may not be necessary. Sen reminds us that "people have perished in famines in sight of much food in shops."[22] What good distribution of food should mean is that people have effective access to or can acquire the food (whether presently nearby or far away). Hence, it is better to say that the problem of hunger, whether transitory or persistent, involves an "entitlement failure" in the sense that the hungry person is not able to acquire food or lacks command over food. What is crucial is not the mere food itself, nor the amount of food divided by the number of people in a given area, nor even the food transported to a stricken area. What is decisive is whether particular households and individuals have operative "entitlements" over food. The distinction between households and individuals is important, for households as units may have sufficient food for the nourishment of each family member, yet some members – usually women or female children – may starve due to entitlement failures.

We must be careful here, for Sen's use of the term "entitlement" has caused no little confusion and controversy. Unlike Robert Nozick's normative or prescriptive use of the term, Sen employs "entitlement" in a descriptive way – relatively free of moral endorsement or criticism – to refer to a person's actual or operative command, permitted by law (backed by state power) or custom, over certain commodities.[23] A person's entitlements will be a function of (i) that person's endowments, for instance, what goods or services she has to exchange for food, (ii) exchange opportunities, for instance, the going rate of exchange of work for food, (iii) legal claims against the state, for instance, rights to work, food stamps, or welfare, and (iv) nonlegal but socially approved and operative rules, for instance, the household "social discipline" that mandates that women eat after and less than men.[24]

Generally speaking, an entitlement to food would be the actual ability, whether *morally* justified or not, to acquire food by some legally or socially approved means – whether by producing it, trading for it, buying it, or receiving it in a government feeding program. A Hutu child separated from his family may be morally justified in stealing a meal from a Tutsi food supply center, but he has no legal claim or other social basis for effective access to the food. In Sen's sense, then, the child lacks an entitlement to that food.

To view hunger as an entitlement failure does not commit one to the position that hunger is never due to lack of food nor that it is always explained by the same set of causes. Rather, the entitlement theory of hunger directs one to examine the various links in a society's "food chain" – production, acquisition, and consumption – any of which can be dysfunctional and thereby result in an entitlement failure. A production failure, due to drought or pests, will result in an entitlement failure for those peasants "whose means of survival depend on food that they grow themselves."[25] Even when food is abundant and increasing in an area, landless laborers may starve because they have insufficient money to buy food, no job to get money, nothing of worth to trade for food, or no effective claim on their government or other group.

Conceiving hunger as an entitlement failure also yields ways of preventing impending famines and ways of remedying actual famines. What is needed is not only food but institutions that protect against entitlement failure and restore lost entitlements. Moving food to hungry people may not be necessary, for the food may already be physically present. The problem is that some people cannot gain access to it. Even worse, increasing food availability in a given area may increase the hunger problem. For instance, direct delivery of free food can send market food prices plummeting, thereby causing a disincentive for farmers to grow food. The result is a decline not only in their productivity but also in their own food entitlements. Moreover, even when necessary, food by itself is not sufficient to prevent or cure famine if people never had entitlements to food or lost what they had previously. And it may be that the best way to ensure that people have the ability to command food is to give them not food itself, but rather cash relief or cash for work. Such cash "may provide the ability to command food without directly giving the food."[26] It may also have the effect of increasing food availability, for the cash may "pull" private food traders into the area in order to meet the demand.

One deficiency of the "food availability" approach to hunger is that it is purely aggregative, that is, concerned solely with the amount of food in a given area summed over the number of people. Thus, it has inspired a simplistic and inconclusive debate between "Malthusian optimists," those who think that the answer to the "world food problem" is more food, and "Malthusian pessimists," those who think that *the* answer is fewer people.[27] Another – more deadly – consequence is that data concerning food output and availability often lull government officials and others into a false sense of food security and thereby prevent them from doing what they might to prevent or mitigate famine: "The focus on food per head and Malthusian optimism have literally killed millions."[28] In contrast, Sen's approach is dis-aggregative with respect to command over food on the part of vulnerable occupation groups, households, and, most important, individuals (see HPA, 30–31). It recognizes that although food is indispensable for famine prevention and remedy, much more than food is needed. According to the capabilities ethic, an approach to hunger that attended exclusively to food and entitlements to food would stop short of the fundamental goal – to reduce human deprivation and contribute to human well-being.

From Food and Food Entitlements to Capabilities and Development

Different moral theories understand human well-being and the good human life in diverse ways. Capabilities theorists choose valuable human "functionings" and capabilities to so function as the basis of their ethical outlook. They argue that these moral categories are superior to other candidates for *fundamental* concepts, such as resources or commodities, utilities, needs, or rights. Although these latter concepts do have a role in a complete moral theory and approach to world hunger, they refer to "moral furniture" that is in some sense secondary. Commodities are at best *means* to the end of valuable functions and ability to so function. Utilities are only one among several good functionings and may "muffle" and "mute" deprivations. Rights are not free-standing but are best defined in relation to valuable human functions and abilities to so function.[29]

What do capabilities theorists mean by the term *functionings*? A person's functionings consist of his or her physical and mental states ("beings") and activities ("doings"). The most important of these functionings, the failure of which constitutes poverty and the occurrence of which constitutes well-being, "vary from such elementary physical ones as being well-nourished, being adequately clothed and sheltered, avoiding preventable morbidity, etc., to more complex social achievements such as taking part in the life of the community, being able to appear in public without shame, and so on."[30] A person's *capabilities* are that set of functionings open to the person, given the person's personal characteristics ("endowment") as well as economic and social opportunities. An alternative formulation is that the general idea of capability refers "to the extent of freedom that people have in pursuing valuable activities or functionings" (HPA, 42).

Drèze and Sen give four reasons for expanding the perspective on hunger to include capabilities as well as food and entitlements: (i) individual variability, (ii) social variability, (iii) diverse means to nourishment, (iv) nourishment as a means to other good goals. Let us briefly consider each.

(i) *Individual variability*

The capabilities approach recommends itself because it makes sense of and insists on the distinction between food intake and being nourished or capable of being nourished. The focus is not on food in itself nor on food as merely ingested, but on food as a means to being well-nourished and being able to be well-nourished. Exclusive attention to food, food entitlement, and food intake neglects importantly diverse impacts that the same food can have on different human beings and on the same individual at different times. A particular woman at various stages of her life "requires" different amounts and types of food, depending on her age, her reproductive status, and her state of health. More generally, higher food intake at one time may compensate for lower or no intake at other times without it being true that the person is ever suffering from nutritional distress or malfunctioning.

Instead of identifying hungry people simply by a lack of food intake and mechanically monitoring individuals or dispensing food to them according to nutritional requirements, the focus should be on nutritional functioning and those "nutrition-related capabilities that are crucial to human well-being" (HPA, 14). A person's energy level, strength, weight and height (within average parameters that permit exceptions), the ability to be productive and the capacities to avoid morbidity and mortality – all valuable functionings or capabilities to function – should supplement and may be more significant with respect to nutritional well-being than the mere quantity of food or types of nutrients (HPA, 41).[31]

(ii) Social variability

In addition to differences in individual or communal biological or physical characteristics, the capabilities approach is sensitive to differences in socially acquired tastes and beliefs with respect to foods. That is, it recognizes that these tastes and beliefs can also block the conversion of food into nutritional functioning. Attempts to relieve hunger sometimes fail because hungry people are unable, for some reason, to eat nutritious food. Hungry people sometimes won't eat because the taste of available grain is too different from that to which they are accustomed. There is evidence that people who receive extra cash for food sometimes fail to improve their nutritional status, apparently because they choose to consume nutritionally deficient foods. If food is to make a difference in people's nutritional and wider well-being, it must be food that the individuals in question are generally willing and able to convert into nutritional functioning.[32] This is not to say that food habits cannot be changed. Rather, it underscores the importance of nutritional education and social criticism of certain food-consumption patterns. Even nutritious food to which people are entitled, however, will not by itself protect or restore nutritional well-being.

(iii) Diverse means to being well-nourished

If one goal of public action is to protect, restore, and promote nutritional well-being, we must realize that food is only one means of reaching this goal (HPA, 267). A preoccupation with food transfers as the way to address impending or actual hunger ignores the many other means that can serve and may even be necessary to achieve the end of being (able to be) well-nourished. These include "access to health care, medical facilities, elementary education, drinking water, and sanitary facilities" (HPA, 13).

To achieve nutritional well-being, a hungry parasite-stricken person needs not only food but also medicine to kill the parasites that cause the malabsorption of consumed food. A disease-enfeebled person who is too weak to eat requires medical care as well as food. A Rwandan youngster separated from its family in a refugee camp may be ignorant of what to eat and what not to eat. Without clean water, basic sanitation, and health education, recipients of nutritious food aid may succumb to malaria, cholera, dysentery, and typhoid before having the chance to be adequately nourished.

In particular situations, the best way to combat famine may not be to dispense food but to supply jobs for those who can work and cash for those who can't (HPA, 121). The evidence is impressive that an increase in the purchasing power of hungry people often pulls food into a famine area, as private traders find ways of meeting the increased demand (HPA, 88–93). Finally, famine and chronic hunger are prevented and reduced by long-term development strategies that protect and promote entitlements and valuable capabilities. In the next section, we will return to the hunger-fighting role of national development strategies and international development. At this juncture, the crucial point is that direct food delivery is only one means, and often not the best means, for fighting world hunger. The capabilities approach helpfully interprets and underscores that point when it insists that public action can and should employ an array of complementary strategies to achieve the end of nutritional well-being for all.

(iv) *Food as a means to other components of well-being*

The capabilities approach helps widen our vision to see that the food that hungry people command and consume can accomplish much more than to give them nutritional well-being. Nutritional well-being is only one element in human well-being; the overcoming of transitory or chronic hunger also enables people and their governments to protect and promote other ingredients of well-being. Being adequately nourished, for instance, contributes to healthy functioning that is both good in itself and indispensable to the ability to avoid premature death and fight off or recover from disease. Having nutritional well-being and good health, in turn, is crucial to acquiring and exercising other valuable capabilities such as being able to learn, think, deliberate, and choose as well as to be a good pupil, friend, householder, parent, worker, or citizen.

Because adequate food and food entitlements can have so many beneficial consequences in people's lives, creative development programs and projects find ways in which people can link food distribution/acquirement to other valuable activities. Pregnant and lactating women (and their infants) acquire food supplements in health clinics, for nutritional deficiencies affect fetal and infant development. Schoolchildren eat free or subsidized lunches at school, for hungry children don't learn as well and certain nutritional deficiencies result in visual and cognitive impairment.[33]

Nutritional well-being, then, is both constitutive of and a means to human well-being and personal development. And human development is the ultimate purpose of societal development. Hence, a more ample perspective on world hunger must include socioeconomic development as part of the cure. Just as the right kind of development is a large part of the answer to the various problems of population, so it is crucial to resolving the diverse problems of world hunger.[34]

In the capabilities approach to international development, the linkage between hunger alleviation and development is spelled out in the language of valuable capabilities and functionings. In this approach, a society's development is conceived as a process of change that protects, restores, strengthens, and expands people's valued and valuable capabilities.[35] Being able to be well-nourished and other nutrition-related capabilities are among the most important capabilities. Hence, a society striving to be developed will search for, establish, and maintain institutions and policies that attack and try to eradicate all forms of hunger and the poverty that causes hunger.[36] Even emergency measures to prevent, relieve, or extirpate famine must not undermine, and, if possible, should contribute to, long-term strategies that "may be used to reduce or eliminate failures of basic capabilities" (HPA, 16). Economic, political and other institutions, such as schools and the family, must be modified and development strategies elected in the light of the effect such changes will have on what all persons will be able to do and be.

From the Ethics of Aid to an Ethics for Development

Finally, the ethics of famine relief should be incorporated into an ethics for development. International development ethics evaluates the basic goals and appropriate strategies for morally desirable social change. No longer fixated on the stark options of earlier debates –

food aid versus no food aid, aid as duty versus aid as charity – it asks instead what kind of aid is morally defensible and, even more fundamentally, what sort of national and international development aid should foster.

As early as the mid-fifties, development economists had been examining the developmental impact of different kinds of food aid and trying to design famine relief that would contribute to rather than undermine long-term development goals.[37] Yet in the seventies, philosophers and others, such as Garrett Hardin, failed to refer to the nuanced debate that had been going on for more than twenty years. Furthermore, as one expert on food aid remarks, "many of them did not feel it important to become more than superficially familiar with the technical or institutional aspects of food production, distribution, or policy."[38] As happens all too often, the owl of Minerva – Hegel's image for the philosopher – "spreads its wings only with the falling of dusk" and comes on the scene too late to give "instruction as to what the world ought to be."[39]

Moreover, when philosophers did try to analyze development, they usually emphasized development *aid* that rich countries provided to poor countries, rather than the development *goals* that poor countries set and pursued for themselves. By the mid-eighties, however, ethicists became increasingly aware that they couldn't talk about morally justified or unjustified development aid from the outside without first talking about the recipient nation's own development philosophies, goals, strategies, leadership, and will.[40] One marked advantage of the capabilities ethic is that it puts its highest priority on a nation's intellectual and institutional capability for *self*-development without denying the role of international theoretical and practical help (see HPA, 273; and "Goods and People").

With respect to morally defensible "development paths," a new discipline – international development ethics – has emerged.[41] Development ethicists ask several related questions. What should count as development? Which should be the most fundamental principles to inform a country's choice of development goals and strategies? What moral issues emerge in development policymaking and practice? How should the burdens and benefits of good development be distributed? What role – if any – should more affluent societies and individuals play in the self-development of those less well off? What are the most serious national and international impediments to good development? Who should decide these questions and by what methods? To what extent, if any, do moral skepticism, political realism, and moral relativism pose a challenge to this boundary-crossing ethical inquiry?

This new discipline is being practiced in ways that sharply distinguish it from the earlier ethics of famine relief. First, development ethics is international in the triple sense that ethicists from diverse societies are trying to forge an international consensus about solutions to global problems. It has become evident that policy analysts and ethicists – whether from "developing" countries or "developed" countries – should not simply accept the operative or professed values implicit in a particular country's established development path. Rather, both cultural insiders and outsiders[42] should engage in an ongoing and critical dialogue that includes explicit ethical analysis, assessment, and construction with respect to universal development ends and generally appropriate means of national, regional, and planetary change. Rather than being predominantly if not exclusively the work of white North American males, as was the case in the initial ethics of famine relief, international development ethics is an inquiry that includes participants from a variety of nations, groups, and moral traditions seeking an international consensus about problems of international scope.[43]

Secondly, development ethics is interdisciplinary rather than exclusively philosophical. It eschews abstract ethical reflection and relates values to relevant facts in a variety of ways. Development ethicists, as we have seen in Drèze and Sen's work on hunger, evaluate (i) the normative assumptions of different development models, (ii) the empirical categories employed to interpret, explain, and forecast the facts, and (iii) development programs, strategies, and institutions.[44]

Finally, development ethics straddles the theory/practice distinction. Its practitioners include, as well as engage in dialogue with, policymakers and development activists. Instead of conducting a merely academic exercise, development theorists and development practitioners together assess the moral costs and benefits of current development policies, programs, and projects, and articulate alternative development visions.[45]

Famine, food aid, and the ethics of famine relief remain – as they were in the mid-seventies – pressing personal, national, and international challenges. Philosophers can play a role in meeting these challenges and thereby reducing world hunger. This goal is best achieved, however, when the questions of world hunger and moral obligation are reframed and widened. Since the best long-term cure for hunger is national and international development, we must put emergency food aid in a developmental perspective and incorporate an ethics of famine relief into an international development ethics. To avoid the fallacy of misplaced concreteness is not to eschew abstractions but to place them in their proper relations to each other and to the concrete world of facts and values.

Notes

1   I owe thanks to my colleagues at the Institute for Philosophy and Public Policy and the School of Public Affairs for illuminating discussions of these issues. Will Aiken, Arthur Evenchik, Hugh LaFollette, and James W. Nickel made valuable comments on earlier versions of the essay. I gratefully acknowledge support for this research from the National Endowment for the Humanities, Grant no. R0–22709–94. The views expressed are mine and not necessarily those of NEH.

2   William Aiken and Hugh LaFollette (eds), *World Hunger and Moral Obligation* (Englewood Cliffs, NJ: Prentice-Hall, 1977). Hereafter I cite this volume as WH.

3   Alfred North Whitehead, *Science and the Modern World* (New York: Macmillan, 1925), p. 200.

4   John Rawls, *A Theory of Justice* (Cambridge, MA: Belknap Press of Harvard University Press, 1971).

5   Peter Singer, "Famine, Affluence, and Morality," *Philosophy and Public Affairs*, 1 (1972), 229–43. Singer's initial essay, reproduced with a new "Postscript" in WH, was written in 1971 and first appeared in *Philosophy and Public Affairs* in 1972, the initial year of publication of what was to become the premier philosophical journal in applied ethics.

6   Peter Singer, "Reconsidering the Famine Relief Argument," in Peter G. Brown and Henry Shue (eds), *Food Policy: The Responsibility of the United States in the Life and Death Choices* (New York: Free Press, 1977), p. 36.

7   *New York Times Magazine*, July 7, 1974, 17–20.

8   "The Need for Recovery of Philosophy," in Richard J. Bernstein (ed.), *John Dewey: On Experience, Nature and Freedom* (New York: Liberal Arts Press, 1960), p. 67.

9   A 1995 study by the Program on International Policy Attitudes shows that 80 percent of those polled agreed that "the United States should be willing to share at least a small portion of its wealth with those in the world who are in great need." This belief does not seem to stem solely from a view of national interest. For 67 percent agreed that "as one of the world's rich nations, the United States has a moral responsibility toward poor nations to help them develop economically and improve their people's lives" and 77 percent rejected the idea that the US should give aid only when it serves the national interest. Although 87 percent believe that waste and corruption is rife in foreign aid programs, 55 percent said they would be willing to pay more taxes for foreign aid if

they knew that "most foreign aid was going to the poor people who really need it rather than to wasteful bureaucracies and corrupt governments." Steven Kull, "Americans and Foreign Aid: A Study of American Public Attitudes," Program of International Policy Attitudes, Center for International and Security Studies at Maryland, University of Maryland, 1, 4, 6.

10 See, for example, Catherine W. Wilson, "On Some Alleged Limitations to Moral Endeavor," *Journal of Philosophy*, 90 (1993), 275–89. It is beyond the scope of this paper to consider the best way to think about our general duty to assist others and our particular duty to aid the foreign needy.

11 I owe the idea of perceiving or discerning "ethical salience" to Nancy Sherman, *The Fabric of Character: Aristotle's Theory of Virtue* (Oxford: Clarendon Press, 1989), pp. 28–44. See also Martha Nussbaum, *Love's Knowledge: Essays on Philosophy and Literature* (New York and Oxford: Oxford University Press, 1990), especially chapters 2, 5.

12 For a discussion of how ethical principles constrain what counts as relevant and irrelevant factual information, see Amartya Sen, "Well-being, Agency, and Freedom: The Dewey Lectures 1984," *Journal of Philosophy*, 82 (1985), 169–84. Sherman discusses the way in which the agent's "reading of the circumstances" may be influenced by his or her moral or immoral character; see *Fabric*, p. 29.

13 Sherman, *Fabric*, p. 30.

14 See, for example, recent volumes in the World Institute for Development Economics Research (WIDER) series *Studies in Development Economics*; Jean Drèze and Amartya Sen, *Hunger and Public Action* (Oxford: Clarendon Press, 1989), hereafter cited in the text as HPA; Jean Drèze and Amartya Sen (eds), *The Political Economy of Hunger. Entitlement and Well-Being*, 3 volumes: Vol. 1, *Entitlement and Well-being*; Vol. 2, *Famine and Prevention*; Vol. 3, *Endemic Hunger* (Oxford: Clarendon Press, 1990); Martha C. Nussbaum and Amartya Sen (eds), *The Quality of Life* (Oxford: Clarendon Press, 1993). See also Keith Griffin and John Knight (eds), *Human Development and the International Development Strategy for the 1990s* (London:

Macmillan, 1989). For a bibliography of Sen and Nussbaum's extensive writings and an analysis of the "capabilities ethic" as a feature of the "capabilities approach" to development, see my essays: "Functioning and Capability: The Foundations of Sen's and Nussbaum's Development Ethic," *Political Theory*, 20 (November 1992), 584–612; "Functioning and Capability: The Foundations of Sen's and Nussbaum's Development Ethic, Part 2," in Martha Nussbaum and Jonathan Glover (eds), *Women, Culture, and Development* (New York: Oxford University Press/Clarendon Press, 1995); and *Florecimiento humano y desarrollo internacional: La nueva ética de capacidades humanas* (San José, Costa Rica: Instituto Tecnológico de Costa Rica, forthcoming). For an article that anticipates many of my arguments, but that I did not have an opportunity to read until after the present essay was completed, see George R. Lucas, Jr, "African Famine: New Economic and Ethical Perspectives," *Journal of Philosophy*, 87 (November 1990), 629–41.

15 See Amartya Sen, "The Right Not to be Hungry," in *Contemporary Philosophy: A New Survey*, Vol. II (The Hague: Martinus Nijhoff, 1982), pp. 343–60.

16 Just as one's focus can be too narrow, it can also be so broad as to be disabling. Blaming or praising such large formations as capitalism, socialism, or industrialism commits fallacies of hasty generalization and deters us from examining causes that are both specific and alterable in the short and medium run. I owe this point to James W. Nickel.

17 The editors of WH did distinguish the two types of hunger (WH, 1), but they themselves and the anthology's other contributors almost exclusively attended to the plight of famine victims rather than that of the chronically hungry.

18 Sara Millman and Robert W. Kates, "Toward Understanding Hunger," in Lucile F. Newman (ed.), *Hunger in History: Food Shortage, Poverty, and Deprivation* (Cambridge, MA: Basil Blackwell, 1990), p. 3.

19 In the fall of 1994, it is estimated that while 800 million people suffer from malnutrition, none suffer from famine. See *Hunger 1995: Causes of Hunger* (Silver Spring, MD: Bread

for the World Institute, 1994), p. 10. However, serious potential for famine exists in Rwanda and Afghanistan, and the US presence in Haiti has averted famine in a country with severe and widespread malnutrition.

20 Studies show that the number of chronically malnourished people in the world decreased from 976 million people in 1975 to 786 million in 1990 and that in the same period, due to a population increase of 1.1 billion, the proportion of hungry people in the developing world declined from 33 percent to 20 percent. See *Hunger 1995: Causes of Hunger*, pp. 10–11.

21 Robert W. Kates and Sara Millman, "On Ending Hunger: The Lessons of History," in *Hunger in History*, p. 404.

22 Amartya Sen, "The Food Problem: Theory and Practice," *Third World Quarterly*, 3 (July 1982), 454.

23 Sen states that "the entitlement of a person stands for the set of different alternative commodity bundles that the person can acquire through the use of the various legal channels of acquirement open to someone in his position" ("Food, Economics and Entitlements," in Drèze and Sen, *The Political Economy of Hunger*, Vol. 1, *Entitlement and Well-Being*, Oxford: Clarendon Press, 1990, p. 36).

24 See HPA, 10–1; Amartya Sen, *Inequality Reexamined* (New York: Russell Sage Foundation; Cambridge: Harvard University Press, 1992), pp. 149–50; and "Goods and People" in *Resources, Values, and Development* (Cambridge, MA: Harvard University Press, 1984); Charles Gore shows that Sen has gradually expanded his concept of entitlement to include nonlegal – primarily household – rules, but that Sen needs to go further in recognizing the ways in which "socially approved moral rules" may be extra-legal and even anti-legal. See Charles Gore, "Entitlement Relations and 'Unruly' Social Practices: A Comment on the Work of Amartya Sen," *Journal of Development Economics*, 29 (1993), 429–60.

25 Amartya Sen, "Food Entitlements and Economic Chains," in *Hunger in History*, p. 377.

26 Amartya Sen, "Food, Economics and Entitlements," in *The Political Economy of Hunger*, Vol. 1, *Entitlement and Well-Being*, p. 43.

27 Sen, "The Food Problem," 447–51. Cf. HPA, 24–5; and "Food, Economics, and Entitlements," 35–6.

28 Amartya Sen, "The Food Problem," 450. Cf. Amartya Sen, *Poverty and Famines: An Essay on Entitlement and Deprivation* (Oxford: Clarendon Press, 1981); and "Goods and People."

29 For a clarification and defense of these claims, see Sen and Nussbaum's writings and my analysis and evaluations of them in the essays referred to in n. 14.

30 Sen, *Inequality Reexamined*, p. 110.

31 For a more detailed and technical discussion of these issues by nutritionists who are sympathetic with the capabilities approach, see S. R. Osmani (ed.), *Nutrition and Poverty* (Oxford: Clarendon Press, 1992). See also Paul Streeten, *Thinking about Development* (Cambridge: Cambridge University Press, 1995).

32 A new strain of "miracle" rice, which promises enormous productivity gains, will be hybridized with local rice varieties in order to make it acceptable to regional tastes in different parts of the world.

33 Cf. John Osgood Field and Mitchel B. Wallerstein, "Beyond Humanitarianism: A Developmental Perspective on American Food Aid," in *Food Policy*, pp. 234–58.

34 See Amartya Sen, "Population: Delusion and Reality," *New York Review of Books*, 61 (September 22, 1994), 62–71; and "Goods and People."

35 See Amartya Sen, "Goods and People"; "Development: Which Way Now?" in *Resources, Values and Development* (Oxford: Blackwell; Cambridge, MA: Harvard University Press, 1984) pp. 485–508; "The Concept of Development," in Hollis Chenery and T. N. Srinivasan (eds), *Handbook of Development Economics*, vol. 1 (Amsterdam: North Holland, 1988), pp. 9–26; "Development as Capability Expansion," in Griffin and Knight (eds), *Human Development and the International Development Strategy for the 1990s*, pp. 41–58; Crocker, "Functioning and Capability," 584–8. See also United Nations Development Programme, *Human Development Report 1994* (New York and Oxford: Oxford University Press, 1994), p. 13: "The purpose of development is to create

an environment in which all people can expand their capabilities, and opportunities can be enlarged for both present and future generations."

36 For a detailed examination of institutions and policies – both national and international – that have proved successful in alleviating hunger and reducing poverty, see HPA, and Streeten, *Thinking about Development*.

37 For a good account, with full references, of controversies in the fifties, sixties, and seventies concerning US food aid and development policy, see Anne O. Krueger, Constantine Michalopoulos, and Vernon W. Ruttan, *Aid and Development* (Baltimore and London: Johns Hopkins University Press, 1989); Vernon W. Ruttan (ed.), *Why Food Aid?* (Baltimore and London: Johns Hopkins University Press, 1993), especially pp. 37–129.

38 Ruttan (ed.), *Why Food Aid?*, p. 66.

39 Georg W. F. Hegel, *Hegel's Philosophy of Right*, trans. T. M. Knox (Oxford: Oxford University Press, 1952), pp. 12–13.

40 See especially, Nigel Dower, *World Poverty: Challenge and Response* (York, UK: Ebor Press, 1983); Onora O'Neill, *Faces of Hunger: An Essay on Poverty, Justice, and Development* (London: Allen & Unwin, 1986); Jerome M. Segal, "What is Development?" Working Paper, DN-1 (College Park, MD: Institute for Philosophy and Public Policy, October 1986).

41 For philosophical accounts of development ethics, see David A. Crocker, "Toward Development Ethics," *World Development*, 19, no. 5 (1991), 457–83; and "Development Ethics and Development Theory-Practice," Discussion Paper CBPE 93-2 (College Station: Center for Biotechnology Policy and Ethics, Texas A&M University, 1993); and Nigel Dower, "What is Development? – A Philosopher's Answer," Centre for Development Studies Occasional Paper Series, 3 (Glasgow: University of Glasgow, 1988).

42 David A. Crocker, "Insiders and Outsiders in International Development Ethics,"

Ethics and International Affairs 5 (1991), 149–73.

43 See Godfrey Gunatilleke, Neelen Tiruchelvam, and Radhika Coomaraswamy (eds), *Ethical Dilemmas of Development in Asia* (Lexington, MA: Lexington Books, 1988); Kwame Gyekye, *The Unexamined Life: Philosophy and the African Experience* (Legon: Ghana Universities Press, 1988); Martha Nussbaum, "Aristotelian Social Democracy," in R. Bruce Douglass, Gerald R. Mara, and Henry S. Richardson (eds.), *Liberalism and the Good* (New York and London: Routledge, 1990), pp. 203–52; and Luis Camacho, *Ciencia y tecnología en el sub-desarrollo* (Cártago: Editorial Tecnológica de Costa Rica, 1993).

44 Since the early sixties, Denis Goulet has been addressing the ethical and value dimensions of development theory and practice. His new book, *Development Ethics: A Guide to Theory and Practice* (New York: Apex Books, forthcoming), treats development ethics from the perspective of a policy analyst and activist. Economist Paul Streeten, an architect of the basic human-needs strategy and currently a consultant with UNDP, has persistently addressed ethical issues in his work; see, for example, *Strategies for Human Development: Global Poverty and Unemployment* (Copenhagen: Handelshjskolens Forlag, 1994).

45 An early anticipation of an integrated approach to world hunger is Peter G. Brown and Henry Shue (eds), *Food Policy: The Responsibility of the United States in the Life and Death Choices* (New York: Free Press, 1977). This anthology, which appeared in the same year as WH, shared WH's deficiencies with respect to minority and international participation. *Food Policy's* contributors, however, included policy analysts and policymakers as well as a variety of academics. Moreover, the volume displayed an excellent balance – as a whole and in several individual essays – of moral, empirical, institutional, political, and policy analysis.

57

Feeding People versus Saving Nature?

Holmes Rolston III

A bumper sticker reads: Hungry loggers eat spotted owls. That seems to pinpoint an ethical issue, and often one where the humanist protagonist, taking high moral ground, intends to put the environmentalist on the defensive. You wouldn't let the Ethiopians starve to save some butterfly, would you? "Human beings are at the centre of concerns for sustainable development." So the *Rio Declaration* begins. Once this was to be an *Earth Charter*, but the developing nations were more interested in getting their poor fed: "All States and all people shall cooperate in the essential task of eradicating poverty as an indispensable requirement."[1] Can we fault them for putting poor people first?

We have to be circumspect. If, in the abstract, we are asked whether we should feed hungry people or save nature, most people will favor people; nature be damned. However, that question misrepresents the choices we actually face. Moral questions only make sense in context; asking the questions outside the context is invariably misleading. So before we can reasonably decide whether to favor people or nature, we must analyze the choices we face, in the actual context, with all its richness.

Humans win? Nature loses? We must not forget, of course, that humans do not really win if they sacrifice their life support system. "In order to achieve sustainable development, environmental protection shall constitute an integral part of the development process and cannot be considered in isolation from it."[2] After all, food has to be grown in some reasonably healthy natural system, and the clean water that the poor need is also good for fauna and flora. Extractive reserves, where people can hunt, gather medicinal plants, or nuts, or latex from rubber trees, leaving the forests healthy and largely intact, give people an incentive to conserve. Tourism can benefit the local poor as well as the wildlife. When possible, we should seek solutions that benefit both humans and nature. Practically, these are often the only kind likely to work; and, where possible, they will be most satisfying.

Yet there are times when we sacrifice nature for human development – most development requires that some nature be sacrificed. Most people think this is an acceptable trade-off. After all, people seem supremely important; and food is their most urgent need. People should always win, even if nature loses? Perhaps. Can we ever say that we ought save nature rather than feed people?

1. Feed People First? Do We? Ought We?

"Feed people first!" That has a ring of righteousness. In the biblical parable of the great judgement, Jesus welcomes the righteous to their reward. "I was hungry and you gave me food, I was thirsty and you gave me drink." Those who refused to help are damned (Matthew 2: 31–46). The vision of those in heaven is that "they shall hunger no more, neither thirst any more" (Revelation 7: 16). Jesus teaches his disciples to pray, "Give us this day our daily bread" (Matthew 6: 11). Food is such a basic value, if there is to be any ethics at all, surely food comes first.

Does it always? A woman washed Jesus's feet with expensive ointment. When the disciples complained that it should have been sold and given to the poor, Jesus replied, "you always have the poor with you." He commended her: "She has done a beautiful thing" (Matthew 26: 10–11). While the poor are a continuing concern, with whom Jesus demonstrated ample solidarity, if we did nothing else of value until there were no more poor, we would have to postpone everything else indefinitely. Christians would never have built a sanctuary with an organ and stained glass, but rather would always have given the poor their daily bread. Eradicating poverty is one vital goal, but at the same time, set this commendable ideal beside the plain fact that we all daily prefer other values. Every time we buy a Christmas gift, or go to a symphony concert, or take a college education, we spend money that might have helped to eradicate poverty. We mostly choose to do things we value more than feeding the hungry.

An ethicist may reply, yes, that is the fact of the matter. But no normative ought follows from the description of this behavior. We ought not to behave so. Such widespread behavior, however, engaged in almost universally by persons who regard themselves as being ethical, including readers of this article, is strong evidence that we in fact not only have these norms but think we ought to have them. To be sure, charity is appropriate, and we censure those who are wholly insensitive to the plight of others. Concern for the poor is indispensable, but we do not, and ought not, dispense with all these other values we pursue, while yet some people are starving.

If one were to advocate doing nothing else until no one in the world is hungry, this would paralyze civilization. People would not have invented writing, or smelted iron, or written music, or invented airplanes. Plato would not have written his dialogues, or Aquinas the *Summa Theologica*; Edison would not have discovered the electric light bulb. Einstein could not have discovered the theory of relativity, because he would have been working for Bread for the World. We both do and ought to devote ourselves to various worthy causes, while yet persons go hungry.

Our moral systems in fact do not teach us to feed the poor first. The Ten Commandments do not say that; the Golden Rule does not; Kant did not say that; nor does the utilitarian greatest good for the greatest number imply that. Eradicating poverty may be indispensable but not always prior to all other cultural values. It may not always be prior to conserving natural values either.

2. Choosing for People to Die

But food is absolutely vital. "Thou shalt not kill" is one of the commandments. Next to the evil of taking life is taking the sustenance for life. Is not saving nature, thereby preventing hunting, harvesting, or development by those who need the produce of that land to put food in their mouths, almost like killing? Surely one ought not to choose for someone else to die; everyone has a right to life. To fence out the hungry is choosing that people will die. That can't be right.

Or can it? In broader social policy we make many decisions that cause people to die. When in 1988 we increased the US national speed limit on rural Interstate highways from 55 to 65 miles per hour, we chose for 400 persons to die each year.[3] We decide against hiring more police, though if we did, some murders would be avoided. The city council spends that money on a new art museum, or to give schoolteachers a raise. Congress decides not to pass a national health-care program that would subsidize medical insurance for some who cannot otherwise afford it; and some, in result, fail to get timely medical care and die of preventable diseases.

We may decide to leave existing air pollution standards in place because it is expensive for industry to install new scrubbers, even though there is statistical evidence that a certain number of persons will contract diseases and die prematurely. All money budgeted for the National Endowment for the Humanities, and almost all that for the National Science Foundation, could be spent to prevent the deaths of babies from malnutrition. We do not know exactly who will die, but we know that some will; we often have reasonable estimates how many. The situation would be similar, should we choose to save nature rather than to feed people.

Wealthy and poverty-stricken nations alike put up borders across which the poor are forbidden to pass. Rich nations will not let them in; their own governments will not let them out. We may have misgivings about this on both sides, but if we believe in immigration laws at all, we, on the richer side of the border, think that protecting our lifestyle counts more than their betterment, even if they just want to be better fed. If we let anyone who pleased enter the United States, and gave them free passage, hundreds of millions would come. Already 30 percent of our population growth is by immigration, legal and illegal. Sooner or later we must fence them out, or face the loss of prosperity that we value. We may not think this is always right, but when one faces the escalating numbers that would swamp the United States, it seems sometimes right. Admitting refugees is humane, but it lets such persons flee their own national problems and does not contribute to any long-term solutions in the nations from which they emigrate. Meanwhile, people die as a result of such decisions.

Some of these choices address the question whether we ought to save nature if this causes people to die. Inside our US boundaries, we have a welfare system. Fortunately, we are wealthy enough to afford this as well as nature conservation. But if it came to this, we would think it wrong-headed to put animals (or art, or well-paid teachers) over starving people. Does that not show that, as domestic policy, we feed people first? Yet we let foreigners die, when we are not willing to open up our five hundred wilderness areas, nearly 100 million acres, to Cubans and Ethiopians.

3. Hunger and Social Justice

The welfare concept introduces another possibility, that the wealthy should be taxed to feed the poor. We should do that first, rather than losing our wildlife, or wilderness areas, or giving up art, or underpaying the teachers. In fact, there is a way greatly to relieve this tragedy. Few persons would need to go without enough if we could use the produce of the already domesticated landscape justly and charitably. It is better to try to fix this problem where it arises, within society, than to try to enlarge the sphere of society by the sacrifice of remnant natural values, by, say, opening up the wilderness areas to settlement. That only postpones the problem.

Peoples in the South (a code word for the lesser developed countries, or the poor) complain about the overconsumption by peoples in the North (the industrial rich), often legitimately so. But Brazil has within its own boundaries the most skewed income distribution in the world. The US ratio of personal income for the top 20 percent of people to the bottom 20 percent is 9 to 1; the ratio in Brazil is 26 to 1. Just 1 percent of Brazilians control 45 percent of the agricultural land. The biggest 20 landowners own more land between them than the 3.3 million smallest farmers. With the Amazon still largely undeveloped, there is already more arable land per person in Brazil than in the United States. The top 10 percent of Brazilians spend 51 percent of the national income.[4] This anthropocentric inequity ought to be put "at the center of concern" when we decide about saving nature versus feeding people.

Save the Amazon! No! The howler monkeys and toucans may delight tourists, but we ought not to save them if people need to eat. Such either–or choices mask how marginalized peoples are forced onto marginal lands; and those lands become easily stressed, both because the lands are by nature marginal for agriculture, range, and life support, and also because by human nature marginalized peoples find it difficult to plan for the long-range. They are caught up in meeting their immediate needs.

Prime agricultural lands can also be stressed to produce more and more, because there is a growing population to feed, or to grow an export crop, because there is an international debt to pay. Prime agricultural lands in southern Brazil, formerly used for growing food and worked by tenants who lived on these lands and ate their produce, as well as sending food into the cities, have been converted to growing coffee as an export crop, using mechanized farming, to help pay Brazil's massive debt, contracted by a military government since overthrown. Peoples forced off these lands were resettled in the Amazon basin, aided by development schemes fostered by the military government, resettled on lands really not suitable for agriculture. The integrity of the Amazon, to say nothing of the integrity of these peoples, is being sacrificed to cover for misguided loans. Meanwhile the wealthy in Brazil pay little or no income tax that might be used for such loan repayment.

The world is full enough of societies that have squandered their resources, inequitably distributed wealth, degraded their landscapes, and who will be tempted to jeopardize what natural values remain as an alternative to solving hard social problems. The decision about poor people over nature usually lies in the context of another decision, often a tacit one, to protect vested interests, wealthy people over poor people, wealthy people who are exploiting nature. En route to any conclusion such as let-people-starve, we regularly reach an if-then, go-to decision point in our logic, where before we face the people-over-nature choice we have to reaffirm or let stand the wealthy-over-poor choice.

In the more fortunate nations, we may distribute wealth more equitably, perhaps through taxes or minimum wage laws, or by labor unions, or educational opportunities, and we do have in place the welfare systems referred to earlier, refusing to let anyone starve. But lest we in the US seem too righteous, we also recall that we have such policies only domestically. The international picture puts this in a different light. There are two major blocs, the G-7 nations (the Group of 7, the big nations of North America, Europe, and Japan, "the North"), and the G-77 nations, once 77 but now including some 128 less developed nations, often south of the industrial North. The G-7 nations hold about one-fifth of the world's five

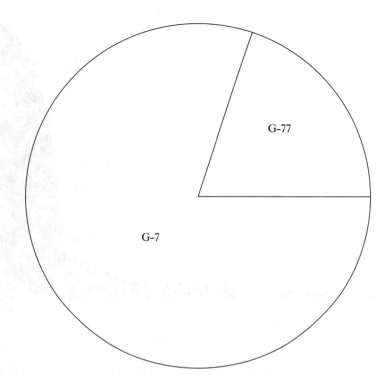

Figure 57.1   G-7/G-77 pie chart.

billion persons, and they produce and consume about four-fifths of all goods and services. The G-77 nations, with four-fifths of the world's people, produce and consume one-fifth. (See figure 57.1, which diagrams this as a sort of pie chart.) For every person added to the population of the North, twenty are added in the South. For every dollar of economic growth per person in the South, twenty dollars accrue in the North.[5]

The distribution problem is complex. Earth's natural resources are unevenly distributed by nature. Diverse societies have often taken different directions of development; they have different governments, ideologies, and religions; they have made different social choices, valued material prosperity differently. Typically, where there is agricultural and industrial development, people think of this as an impressive achievement. Pies have to be produced before they can be divided, and who has produced this pie? Who deserves the pie? People ought to get what they earn. Fairness nowhere commands rewarding all parties equally; justice is giving each his or her due. We treat equal equally; we treat unequals equitably, and that typically means unequal treatment proportionately to merit. There is nothing evidently unfair in the pie diagram, not, at least, until we have inquired about earnings. Some distribution patterns reflect achievement. Not all of the asymmetrical distribution is a result of social injustice.

Meanwhile, it is difficult to look at the distribution chart and not think that something is unfair. Is some of the richness on one side related to the poverty on the other? Regularly, the poor come off poorly when they bargain with the rich; and wealth that originates as impressive achievement can further accumulate through exploitation. Certainly many of the hungry people have worked just as hard as many of the rich.

Some will say that what the poorer nations need to do is to imitate the productive people.

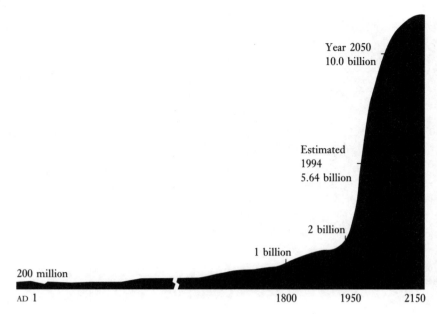

Figure 57.2   World Population Growth.

Unproductive people need to learn how to make more pie. Then they can feed themselves. Those in the G-7 nations who emphasize the earnings model tend to recommend to the G-77 nations that they produce more, often offering to help them produce by investments which can also be productive for the G-7 nations. Those in the G-77 nations do indeed wish to produce, but they also realize that the problem is one of sharing as well as producing. Meanwhile the growth graphs caution us that producing can be as much part of the problem as part of the solution. One way to think of the circular pie chart is that this is planet Earth, and we do not have any way of producing a bigger planet. We could, though, feed more people by sacrificing more nature.

Meanwhile too, any such decisions take place inside this 1/5-gets-4/5ths, 4/5ths-gets-1/5 picture. So it is not just the Brazilians, but all of us in the United States, Europe, and Japan as well that have to face an if-then, go-to decision point, reaffirming and/or letting stand the wealthy-over-poor division of the Earth's pie that we enjoy. This is what stings when we see the bumper-sticker ethical injunction: "Live simply that others may simply live."

4.   Escalating Human Populations

Consider human population growth (see figure 57.2). Not only have the numbers of persons grown, their expectations have grown, so that we must superimpose one exploding curve on top of another. A superficial reading of such a graph is that humans really start winning big in the twentieth century. There are lots of them, and they want, and many get, lots of things. If one is a moral humanist, this can seem a good thing. Wouldn't it be marvelous if all could get what they want, and none hunger and thirst any more?

But when we come to our senses, we realize that this kind of winning, if it keeps on escalating, is really losing. Humans will lose, and nature will be destroyed as well. Cultures have become consumptive, with ever-escalating insatiable desires, overlaid on ever-escalating population growth. Culture does not know how to say "Enough!" and that is not satisfactory. Feeding people always seems humane; but, by just feeding people, without attention to the larger social results, we could be feeding a kind of cancer, that is, an explosion of unregulated growth.

One can say that where there is a hungry mouth, one should put food into it. But when there are two mouths there in result the next day, and four the day after that, and sixteen the day after that, one needs a more complex answer. The population of Egypt was less than 3 million for over five millennia, fluctuating between 1.5 and 2.5 million, even into the 1800s. Today the population of Egypt is about 55 million. Egypt has to import more than half its food. The effects on nature, both on land health and on wildlife, have been adversely proportional.

If, in this picture, we look at individual persons, caught up in this uncontrolled growth, and if we try to save nature, some persons will go hungry. Surely that is a bad thing. Would anyone want to say that such persons ought not to sacrifice nature, if needs be, to alleviate such harm as best they can? From their perspective, they are only doing what humans have always done, making a resourceful use of nature to meet their own needs. Regardless of whether such persons ought to have been born, they have been born; and now that they are here, for better or worse, it is unlikely that they are going to adopt the heroic course of starving in order to save nature. Even if a person should do this for himself voluntarily, it would be wrong for a mother to impose starvation on her children. And it is wrong, and hypocritical, for us to impose starvation on them.

But here we face a time-bound truth, where too much of a good thing becomes a bad thing. We have to figure in where such persons are located on the population curve, and realize that a good thing when human numbers are manageable is no longer a good thing when such a person is really another cell of cancerous growth. That sounds cruel, and it is tragic, but it does not cease to be true for these reasons. For a couple to have two children may be a blessing; but the tenth child is a tragedy. When the child comes, one has to be as humane as possible, but one will only be making the best of a tragic situation, and if the tenth child is reared, and has ten children in turn, that will only multiply the tragedy. The quality of humans' lives deteriorates; the poor get poorer. Natural resources are further stressed; ecosystem health and integrity degenerate; and this compounds the losses again – a lose–lose situation. In a social system misfitted to its landscape, one's wins can only be temporary in a losing human ecology.

Even if there were an equitable distribution of wealth, the human population cannot go on escalating without people becoming all equally poor. Of the 90 million new people who will come on board planet Earth this year, 85 million will appear in the Third World, the countries least able to support such population growth. At the same time, the 5 million new people in the industrial countries will put as much strain on the environment as the 85 million new poor. There are three problems: overpopulation, overconsumption, and under-distribution. Sacrificing nature for development does not solve any of these problems, none at all. It only brings further loss. The poor, after a meal for a day or two, perhaps a decade or two, are soon hungry all over again, only now poorer still because their natural wealth is also gone.

To say that we ought always to feed the poor first commits a good-better-best fallacy. If feeding some humans is good, feeding more is better. And more. And more! Feeding all of them is best? That sounds right. We can hardly bring ourselves to say that anyone ought to starve. But we reach a point of diminishing returns, when the goods put at threat lead us to wonder. Once you agree that we ought always to feed people first, the existence of all other values is reduced to a contingency, to be promoted if and only if nobody can be fed by its sacrifice, value that can be permitted only when everyone has been lifted out of the bottomless pit of the poor. There can be no values above the poverty line. This is true of instrumental and intrinsic values in culture, and as well of instrumental and intrinsic values in nature.

5. When Nature Comes First

Humans now control 40 percent of the planet's land-based primary net productivity, that is, the basic plant growth which captures the energy on which everything else depends.[6] If the human population doubles, the capture will rise to 60–80 percent, and little habitat will remain for natural forms of life that cannot be accommodated after we have put people first. Humans do not use the lands they have domesticated effectively. A World Bank study found that 35 percent of the Earth's land has now become degraded.[7] Daniel Hillel, in a soils study, concludes, "Present yields are extremely low in many of the developing countries, and as they can be boosted substantially and rapidly, there should be no need to reclaim new land and to encroach further upon natural habitats."[8]

Africa is a case in point, and Madagascar epitomizes Africa's future. Its fauna and flora evolved independently from the mainland continent; there are 30 primates, all lemurs; the reptiles and amphibians are 90 percent endemic, including two-thirds of all the chameleons of the world, and 10,000 plant species, of which 80 percent are endemic. Humans came there about 1,500 years ago and, although there were some losses, they lived with the fauna and flora more or less intact until the twentieth century. Now an escalating population of impoverished Malagasy people rely heavily on slash-and-burn agriculture, and the forest cover is one-third of the original (27.6 million acres to 9.4 million acres), most of the loss occurring since 1950.[9] Madagascar is the most eroded nation on Earth, and little or none of the fauna and flora is safely conserved. The population is expanding at 3.2 percent a year; remaining forest is shrinking at 3 percent, almost all to provide for the expanding population. Are we to say that none ought to be conserved until after no person is hungry?

Tigers are sliding toward extinction. Populations have declined 95 percent in the twentieth century; the two main factors are loss of habitat and a ferocious black market in bones and other body parts used in traditional medicine, uses that are given no medical credence. Ranthambhore National Park in Rajasthan, India, is a tiger sanctuary; there were 40 tigers during the late 1980s, reduced in a few years by human pressures – illicit cattle grazing and poaching – to 20–25 tigers today. There are 200,000 Indians within three miles of the core of the park – more than double the population when the park was launched, 21 years ago. Most depend on wood from the 150 square miles of park to cook their food. They graze in and around the park some 150,000 head of scrawny cattle, buffalo, goats, and camels. The cattle impoverish habitat and carry diseases to the ungulates that are the tiger's prey base. In May 1993, a young tigress gave birth to four cubs; that month 316 babies were born in the villages surrounding the park.[10]

Hungry people will take what they need. So it is futile to think we can save tigers on habitat that hungry people could use. One will have to fix the hunger first, else one can save no nature. Yes, but what we are contending here is that sacrificing nature is no fix whatever for this hunger; it can at best alleviate it for a few years, after which the hunger will be back worse than ever. People have a right to access to the means of life? Yes, but the tigers have not threatened any such access. People did the overreproducing; they maldistribute resources between rich and poor. It cannot follow that the innocent tigers ought to be sacrificed of their access to the means of life to fix this people problem.

The tigers may be doomed, but ought they to be? Consider, for instance, that there are minimal reforestation efforts, or that cattle dung can be used for fuel with much greater efficiency than is being done, or that, in an experimental herd of jersey and holstein cattle there, the yield of milk increased to ten times that of the gaunt, free-ranging local cattle, and that a small group of dairy producers has increased milk production 1,000 percent in just thee years. In some moods we may insist that people are more important than tigers. But in other moods these majestic animals seem the casualties of human inabilities to manage themselves and their resources intelligently, a tragic story that leaves us wondering whether the tigers should always lose and the people win.

Ought we to save nature if this results in people going hungry? In people dying? Regrettably, sometimes, the answer is yes. In twenty years Africa's black rhinoceros population declined from 65,000 to 2,500, a loss of 97 percent; the species faces imminent extinction. Again, as with the tigers, there has been loss of habitat due to human population growth; but the primary direct cause is poaching, this time for horns. People cannot eat horns; but they can buy food with the money from selling them. Zimbabwe has a hard-line shoot-to-kill policy for poachers, and over 150 poachers have been killed.[11]

So Zimbabweans do not always put people first; they are willing to kill some, and to let others go hungry. Otherwise, there will be no rhinos at all. Always too, we must guard against inhumanity, and take care, so far as we can, that poachers have other alternatives for overcoming their poverty. Still, if it comes to this, the Zimbabwean policy is right. Given the fact that rhinos have been so precipitously reduced, given that the Zimbabwean population is escalating (the average married woman there *desires* to have six children),[12] one ought to put the black rhino as a species first.

What about ordinary people, who are not breaking any laws? Even when the multiple causal factors are known, and lamented, should we not factor out overpopulation, overconsumption, and maldistribution, none of which are the fault of the particular individuals who may wish to develop their lands? "I did not ask to be born; I am poor, not overconsuming; I am not the cause but rather the victim of the inequitable distribution of wealth. I only want enough to eat, is that not my right?" Human rights must include, if anything at all, the right to subsistence.

So even if particular persons are located at the wrong point on the global growth graph, even if they are willy-nilly part of a cancerous and consumptive society, even if there is some better social solution than the wrong one that is in fact happening, have they not a right that will override the conservation of natural value? Will it not just be a further wrong to them to deprive them of their right to what little they have? Can basic human rights ever be overridden by a society that wants to do better by conserving natural value?

This requires some weighing of the endangered natural values. If one concludes that the natural values at stake are quite high, and that the opportunities for development are low, because the envisioned development is inadvisable, then a possible answer is: No, there will be no development of these reserved areas, even if, with escalating populations, they become more poor. We are not always obligated to cover human mistakes with the sacrifice of natural values.

Does this violate human rights? Anywhere that there is legal zoning, persons are told what they may and may not do, in order to protect various social and natural values. Land ownership is limited when the rights of use conflict with the rights of other persons. One's rights are constrained by the harm one does to others, and we legislate to enforce this. Environmental policy may and ought to regulate the harms that people do on the lands on which they live, and it is perfectly appropriate to set aside conservation reserves to protect the cultural, ecological, scientific, economic, historical, aesthetic, religious, and other values people have at stake here, as well as for values that the fauna and flora have intrinsically in themselves. Indeed, unless there is such reserving of natural areas, counterbalancing the high pressures for development, there will be almost no conservation at all. Every person on Earth is told that he or she cannot develop some areas.

Persons are not told that they must starve, but they are told that they cannot save themselves from starving by sacrificing the nature set aside in reserves – not at least beyond the traditional kinds of uses that did leave the biodiversity on the landscape. If one is already residing in a location where development is constrained, this may seem unfair. Human rights to development, even by those who are poor, though they are to be taken quite seriously, are not everywhere absolute, but have to be weighed against the other values at stake. An individual sees at a local scale; the farmer wants only to graze cattle or plant crops on the now forested land. But environmental ethics sees that the actions of individuals cumulate and produce larger-scale changes that go on over the heads of these individuals. This ethic will regularly be constraining individuals in the interest of some larger ecological and social goods. That will regularly seem cruel, unfair to the individual caught in such constraints. This is the tragedy of the commons; individuals cannot see far enough ahead, under the pressures of the moment, to operate at intelligent ecological scales. Social policy must be set synoptically. This invokes both ecology and ethics, and blends them, if we are to respect life at all relevant scales.

These poor may not have so much a right to develop in any way they please, as a right to a more equitable distribution of the goods of the Earth that we, the wealthy, think we absolutely own.

Our traditional focus on individuals, and their rights, can blind us to how the mistakes (as well as the wisdom) of the parents can curse (and bless) the children, as the Ten Commandments put it, how "the iniquity of the fathers is visited upon the children to the third and fourth generation" (cf. Exodus 20: 5). All this has a deeply tragic dimension, made worse by the coupling of human foibles with ecological realities. We have little reason to think that misguided compassion that puts food into every hungry mouth, be the consequences whatever they may, will relieve the tragedy. We also have no reason to think that the problem will be solved without wise compassion, balancing a love for persons and a love for nature.

Ought we to feed people first, and save nature last? We never face so simple a question. The practical question is more complex:

- If persons widely demonstrate that they value many other worthwhile things over feeding the hungry (Christmas gifts, college educations, symphony concerts)
- and if developed countries, to protect what they value, post national boundaries across which the poor may not pass (immigration laws)
- and if there is unequal and unjust distribution of wealth, and if just redistribution to alleviate poverty is refused
- and if charitable redistribution of justified unequal distribution of wealth is refused
- and if one-fifth of the world continues to consume four-fifths of the production of goods and four-fifths consumes one-fifth

- and if escalating birthrates continue so that there are no real gains in alleviating poverty, only larger numbers of poor in the next generation
- and if low productivity on domesticated lands continues, and if the natural lands to be sacrificed are likely to be low in productivity
- and if significant natural values are at stake, including extinctions of species, then one ought not always to feed people first, but rather one ought sometimes to save nature.

Many of the "ands" in this conjunction can be replaced with "ors" and the statement will remain true, though we cannot say outside of particular contexts how many. The logic is not so much that of implication as of the weighing up of values and disvalues, natural and human, and of human rights and wrongs, past, present, and future.

Some will complain that all this is veiled cultural imperialism, the wealthy North imposing its new-found environmental values on the South, as if the South destroying its biodiversity were not also a form of cultural imperialism sacrificing nature. Our argument is really counter-imperialist: culture ought not always to triumph over nature, but ought at times to be constrained to solutions within culture, saving nature. Some will complain that it is easy to be generous about nature at somebody else's expense, to let their babies starve; but no one who so complains has availed himself or herself of the opportunities for generosity that he or she already has.

Some will protest that this risks becoming misanthropic and morally callous. The Ten Commandments order us not to kill, and saving nature can never justify what amounts to killing people. Yes, but there is another kind of killing here, one not envisioned at Sinai, where humans are superkilling species. Extinction kills forms (*species*) – not just individuals; it kills collectively, not just distributively. Killing a natural kind is the death of birth, not just of an individual life. The historical lineage is stopped forever. Preceding the Ten Commandments is the Noah myth, when nature was primordially put at peril as great as the actual threat today. There, God seems more concerned about species than about the humans who had then gone so far astray. In the covenant reestablished, the beasts are specifically included. "Keep them alive with you ... according to their kinds" (Genesis 6: 19–20). There is something ungodly about an ethic by which the late-coming *Homo sapiens* arrogantly regards the welfare of his own species as absolute, with the welfare of all the other five million species sacrificed to that. The commandment not to kill is as old as Cain and Abel, but the most archaic commandment of all is the divine, "Let the earth bring forth" (Genesis 1). Stopping that genesis is the most destructive event possible, and we humans have no right to do that. Saving nature is not always morally naive; it can deepen our understanding of the human place in the scheme of things entire, and of our duties on this majestic home planet.

Notes

1 *Rio Declaration on Environment and Development*, Principles 1, 5, UNCED document A/CONF. 151/26, vol. 1, pp. 15–25.

2 *Rio Declaration*, Principle 4.

3 Insurance Institute for Highway Safety (Arlington, Virginia), *Status Report*, vol. 29, no. 10 (September 10, 1994): 3.

4 Jonathan Power, 1992. "Despite Its Gifts, Brazil Is a Basket Case," *Miami Herald*, June 22, p. 10A.

5 The pie chart summarizes data in the *World Development Report 1991* (New York: Oxford University Press, 1991).

6 Peter M. Vitousek, Paul R. Ehrlich, Anne H. Ehrlich, and Pamela A. Matson, "Human Appropriation of the Products of

Biosynthesis," *BioScience*, 36 (1986): 368–73.

7 Robert Goodland, "The Case that the World has Reached Limits," in Robert Goodland, Herman E. Daly, and Salah El Serafy (eds), *Population, Technology, and Lifestyle* (Washington, DC: Island Press, 1992), pp. 3–22.

8 Daniel Hillel, *Out of the Earth* (New York: Free Press, Macmillan, 1991), p. 279.

9 E. O. Wilson, *The Diversity of Life* (Cambridge, MA: Harvard University Press, 1992), p. 267; Alison Jolly, *A World Like Our Own: Man and Nature in Madagascar* (New Haven: Yale University Press, 1980).

10 Geoffrey C. Ward, "The People and the Tiger," *Audubon*, 96, no. 4 (July–August 1994): 62–9.

11 Joel Berger and Carol Cunningham, "Active Intervention and Conservation: Africa's Pachyderm Problem," *Science*, 263 (1994): 1241–2.

12 John Bongaarts, "Population Policy Options in the Developing World," *Science*, 263 (1994): 771–6.

Environment

Most people understand the claim that we have obligations and responsibilities to other humans, even strangers – even if they disagree about the scope and strength of these obligations. Many people also understand the claim that we have obligations and responsibilities to animals – even if they think that our obligations to animals are considerably less stringent than our obligations to humans. However, the claim that we have substantial obligations to or responsibilities for the environment would befuddle many people.

Yet, to varying extents and in different ways, that is exactly what the authors in this section claim. Leopold, the father of the modern environmental movement, claims we must abandon the old anthropocentric (human-centered) conception of ethics and replace it with a non-anthropocentric (environment-centered) ethic. Historically most people thought ethics was concerned only about the needs and interests of humans (and then, only some humans!). Most people never questioned whether using the environment for our purposes was morally acceptable. Those few who worried about the environment, were worried only because they feared that by damaging the environment, we would ultimately harm ourselves (polluted water, radioactive waste, etc.). In short, if the environment had any value, its value was entirely instrumental. Nonetheless, these people were progressive for their time – most people at that time thought the environment was nothing more than an economic resource.

That, Leopold claims, must change. We must begin to see the land not as an economic utensil, but as something with intrinsic value (value in itself and not merely for us). Although Leopold's analysis suggests there is a profound difference between seeing the environment merely for our use, and seeing it as having some value on its own, Sterba claims that informed anthropocentric and non-anthropocentric ethics actually share a similar practical outlook. Specifically, although these competing views lead us to think about the environment differently, they typically give us the same practical guidance on particular environmental questions.

It is worth noting Sterba's implicit suggestion that ethical theory, though important, is not as important as many philosophers have thought. Sterba suggests that although theory is important, what ultimately matters is not one's theoretical commitments, but rather the specific practical advice that those commitments entail. The suggestion here, and elsewhere in Sterba's work, is that upon close examination, most theories yield the same practical advice. The precise role of ethical theory is itself a profoundly important theoretical issue. Sterba's analysis of these competing views of ethics also reintroduces two old theoretical friends: the act/omission distinction, and debates about the nature and importance of equality.

The last two papers in this section explicitly discuss the connection between environmental issues and other moral issues discussed in this volume. Warren makes conspicuous what many feminists have long claimed: that the concerns of feminism and the concerns of environmental ethicists are intertwined. A careful examination of environmental issues will explicate the oppression of women, while a study of feminism will help elucidate issues in environmental ethics.

What an anthropocentric environmental ethic and male domination of women have in common, she claims, is a commitment to hierarchical thinking. Generally men think they are superior to women and to nature, and thus, can legitimately dominate both. This is the key to understanding the exploitation of both women and nature. If men no longer dominated women, she claims, they would likely no longer dominate nature either. As a corollary, Warren proposes that feminism be reconceptualized not merely as a movement to liberate women, but as a movement to overcome all oppression. Of course, not all the authors in this book will agree with Warren, either about how women have been treated, or whether domination is always inappropriate. For instance, Fox (ANIMALS) defends the claim that we can exploit animals because we are superior to them. On the other hand, both Singer and Regan, in that same section, argued that being superior did not justify domination.

If we embrace ecofeminism, says Warren, we must abandon the standard Western understanding of ourselves and the world that emphasizes separateness, control, and domination. Ecofeminism, in contrast, stresses an appreciation of narrative and focuses our attention on relationships, caring, and sensitivity. All too often we make moral decisions in the abstract. Instead, she claims, we should be sensitive to the context in which problems arise and within which we must make decisions. Feminism does not deny the separateness of individuals. However, it conceives of individuals only in relation to others. In a true relationship, neither party strives to control or dominate the other, but rather, each seeks to appreciate and enhance the other.

Warren's claims about domination and narrative are intricately related to themes developed earlier by Bartky, Rothman, and Langton. Emotional exploitation, according to Bartky (FAMILY AND FRIENDS), is a form of domination prevalent in interpersonal relationships between men and women. The domination occurs, Bartky says, because men see themselves as superior to, more important than, women. Additionally, Rothman argues that we have misdescribed the ABORTION debate by erasing women from the moral equation. Thus, the standard debate focuses on the status of the fetus, rather than on a contextually rich narrative about the relationship between women and their fetuses. Finally, Langton argues that men's domination over women provides the relevant background that explains why we should understand pornography not as a form of FREE SPEECH, but as an authoritative silencing of women.

Although, in his recent preface, Callicott moderates the thrust of the original essay, that essay poses significant questions about the relationship between the moral standing of the environment as a whole, and the standing of ANIMALS within that environment. Those committed to animal rights, he claims, divide the biotic community into animals (especially "higher" animals) and the rest of nature. Having made this distinction, they are more concerned about animals than about the rest of the environment.

The proper focus of environmental ethics, however, is not for any particular creature, or even a species, but on sustaining the entire biotic community. Environmentalism is more concerned about the whole community than about any particular individual within that community. Additionally, whereas many in the animal-rights movement are primarily concerned about the treatment of domesticated animals, the environmentalist is more concerned about the treatment of wild animals.

Further Reading

Callicott, J. 1989: *In Defense of the Land Ethic: Essays in Environmental Philosophy*. Albany: State University of New York Press.

Dower, N. (ed.) 1989: *Ethics and the Environmental Concern*. Aldershot, UK: Avebury Press.

Regan, T. 1984: *Earthbound: New Introductory Essays in Environmental Ethics*. New York: Random House.

Rolston, H. 1986: *Philosophy Gone Wild: Essays in Environmental Ethics*. Buffalo, NY: Prometheus Books.

Sterba, J. (ed.) 1995: *Earth Ethics: Environmental Ethics, Animal Rights, and Practical Applications*. Englewood Cliffs, NJ: Prentice-Hall.

VanDeVeer, D. and Pierce, C. (eds) 1994: *The Environmental Ethics and Policy Book*. Belmont, CA: Wadsworth.

——1986: *People, Penguins, and Plastic Trees. Basic Issues in Environmental Ethics*. Belmont, CA: Wadsworth.

Wenz, P. 1996: *Nature's Keeper*. Philadelphia: Temple University Press.

58

The Land Ethic

Aldo Leopold

When god-like Odysseus returned from the wars in Troy, he hanged all on one rope a dozen slave-girls of his household whom he suspected of misbehavior during his absence.

This hanging involved no question of propriety. The girls were property. The disposal of property was then, as now, a matter of expediency, not of right and wrong.

Concepts of right and wrong were not lacking from Odysseus' Greece: witness the fidelity of his wife through the long years before at last his blackprowed galleys clove the wine-dark seas for home. The ethical structure of that day covered wives, but had not yet been extended to human chattels. During the three thousand years which have since elapsed, ethical criteria have been extended to many fields of conduct, with corresponding shrinkages in those judged by expediency only.

The Ethical Sequence

This extension of ethics, so far studied only by philosophers, is actually a process in ecological evolution. Its sequences may be described in ecological as well as in philosophical terms. An ethic, ecologically, is a limitation on freedom of action in the struggle for existence. An ethic, philosophically, is a differentiation of social from anti-social conduct. These are two definitions of one thing. The thing has its origin in the tendency of inter-dependent individuals or groups to evolve modes of co-operation. The ecologist calls these symbioses. Politics and economics are advanced symbioses in which the original free-for-all competition has been replaced, in part, by co-operative mechanisms with an ethical content.

The complexity of co-operative mechanisms has increased with population density, and with the efficiency of tools. It was simpler, for example, to define the anti-social uses of sticks and stones in the days of the mastodons than of bullets and billboards in the age of motors.

The first ethics dealt with the relation between individuals; the Mosaic Decalogue is an example. Later accretions dealt with the relation between the individual and society. The

Golden Rule tries to integrate the individual to society; democracy to integrate social organization to the individual.

There is as yet no ethic dealing with man's relation to land and to the animals and plants which grow upon it. Land, like Odysseus' slave-girls, is still property. The land-relation is still strictly economic, entailing privileges but not obligations.

The extension of ethics to this third element in human environment is, if I read the evidence correctly, an evolutionary possibility and an ecological necessity. It is the third step in a sequence. The first two have already been taken. Individual thinkers since the days of Ezekiel and Isaiah have asserted that the despoliation of land is not only inexpedient but wrong. Society, however, has not yet affirmed their belief. I regard the present conservation movement as the embryo of such an affirmation.

An ethic may be regarded as a mode of guidance for meeting ecological situations so new or intricate, or involving such deferred reactions, that the path of social expediency is not discernible to the average individual. Animal instincts are modes of guidance for the individual in meeting such situations. Ethics are possibly a kind of community instinct in-the-making.

The Community Concept

All ethics so far evolved rest upon a single premise: that the individual is a member of a community of interdependent parts. His instincts prompt him to compete for his place in the community, but his ethics prompt him also to co-operate (perhaps in order that there may be a place to compete for).

The land ethic simply enlarges the boundaries of the community to include soils, waters, plants, and animals, or collectively: the land.

This sounds simple: do we not already sing our love for and obligation to the land of the free and the home of the brave? Yes, but just what and whom do we love? Certainly not the soil, which we are sending helter-skelter downriver. Certainly not the waters, which we assume have no function except to turn turbines, float barges, and carry off sewage. Certainly not the plants, of which we exterminate whole communities without batting an eye. Certainly not the animals, of which we have already extirpated many of the largest and most beautiful species. A land ethic of course cannot prevent the alteration, management, and use of these "resources," but it does affirm their right to continued existence, and, at least in spots, their continued existence in a natural state.

In short, a land ethic changes the role of *Homo sapiens* from conqueror of the land-community to plain member and citizen of it. It implies respect for his fellow-members, and also respect for the community as such.

The Land Pyramid

An ethic to supplement and guide the economic relation to land presupposes the existence of some mental image of land as a biotic mechanism. We can be ethical only in relation to something we can see, feel, understand, love, or otherwise have faith in.

The image commonly employed in conservation education is "the balance of nature." For reasons too lengthy to detail here, this figure of speech fails to describe accurately what little we know about the land mechanism. A much truer image is the one employed in ecology:

the biotic pyramid. I shall first sketch the pyramid as a symbol of land, and later develop some of its implications in terms of land-use.

Plants absorb energy from the sun. This energy flows through a circuit called the biota, which may be represented by a pyramid consisting of layers. The bottom layer is the soil. A plant layer rests on the soil, an insect layer on the plants, a bird and rodent layer on the insects, and so on up through various animal groups to the apex layer, which consists of the larger carnivores.

The species of a layer are alike not in where they came from, or in what they look like, but rather in what they eat. Each successive layer depends on those below it for food and often for other services, and each in turn furnishes food and services to those above. Proceeding upward, each successive layer decreases in numerical abundance. Thus, for every carnivore there are hundreds of his prey, thousands of their prey, millions of insects, uncountable plants. The pyramidal form of the system reflects this numerical progression from apex to base. Man shares an intermediate layer with the bears, raccoons, and squirrels, which eat both meat and vegetables.

The lines of dependency for food and other services are called food chains. Thus soil–oak–deer–Indian is a chain that has now been largely converted to soil–corn–cow–farmer. Each species, including ourselves, is a link in many chains. The deer eats a hundred plants other than oak, and the cow a hundred plants other than corn. Both, then, are links in a hundred chains. The pyramid is a tangle of chains so complex as to seem disorderly, yet the stability of the system proves it to be a highly organized structure. Its functioning depends on the co-operation and competition of its diverse parts.

In the beginning, the pyramid of life was low and squat; the food chains short and simple. Evolution has added layer after layer, link after link. Man is one of thousands of accretions to the height and complexity of the pyramid. Science has given us many doubts, but it has given us at least one certainty: the trend of evolution is to elaborate and diversify the biota.

Land, then, is not merely soil; it is a fountain of energy flowing through a circuit of soils, plants, and animals. Food chains are the living channels which conduct energy upward; death and decay return it to the soil. The circuit is not closed; some energy is dissipated in decay, some is added by absorption from the air, some is stored in soils, peats, and long-lived forests; but it is a sustained circuit, like a slowly augmented revolving fund of life. There is always a net loss by downhill wash, but this is normally small and offset by the decay of rocks. It is deposited in the ocean and, in the course of geological time, raised to form new lands and new pyramids.

The velocity and character of the upward flow of energy depend on the complex structure of the plant and animal community, much as the upward flow of sap in a tree depends on its complex cellular organization. Without this complexity, normal circulation would presumably not occur. Structure means the characteristic numbers, as well as the characteristic kinds and functions, of the component species. This interdependence between the complex structure of the land and its smooth functioning as an energy unit is one of its basic attributes.

When a change occurs in one part of the circuit, many other parts must adjust themselves to it. Change does not necessarily obstruct or divert the flow of energy; evolution is a long series of self-induced changes, the net result of which has been to elaborate the flow mechanism and to lengthen the circuit. Evolutionary changes, however, are usually slow and local. Man's invention of tools has enabled him to make changes of unprecedented violence, rapidity, and scope.

One change is in the composition of floras and faunas. The larger predators are lopped off the apex of the pyramid; food chains, for the first time in history, become shorter rather than longer. Domesticated species from other lands are substituted for wild ones, and wild ones are moved to new habitats. In this world-wide pooling of faunas and floras, some species get out of bounds as pests and diseases, others are extinguished. Such effects are seldom intended or foreseen; they represent unpredicted and often untraceable readjustments in the structure. Agricultural science is largely a race between the emergence of new pests and the emergence of new techniques for their control.

Another change touches the flow of energy through plants and animals and its return to the soil. Fertility is the ability of soil to receive, store, and release energy. Agriculture, by overdrafts on the soil, or by too radical a substitution of domestic for native species in the superstructure, may derange the channels of flow or deplete storage. Soils depleted of their storage or of the organic matter which anchors it, wash away faster than they form. This is erosion.

Waters, like soil, are part of the energy circuit. Industry, by polluting waters or obstructing them with dams, may exclude the plants and animals necessary to keep energy in circulation.

Transportation brings about another basic change: the plants or animals grown in one region are now consumed and returned to the soil in another. Transportation taps the energy stored in rocks, and in the air, and uses it elsewhere; thus we fertilize the garden with nitrogen gleaned by the guano birds from the fishes of seas on the other side of the Equator. Thus the formerly localized and self-contained circuits are pooled on a world-wide scale.

The process of altering the pyramid for human occupation releases stored energy, and this often gives rise, during the pioneering period, to a deceptive exuberance of plant and animal life, both wild and tame. These releases of biotic capital tend to becloud or postpone the penalties of violence.

This thumbnail sketch of land as an energy circuit conveys three basic ideas:

1. That land is not merely soil.
2. That the native plants and animals kept the energy circuit open; others may or may not.
3. That man-made changes are of a different order than evolutionary changes, and have effects more comprehensive than is intended or foreseen.

These ideas, collectively, raise two basic issues: Can the land adjust itself to the new order? Can the desired alterations be accomplished with less violence?

Biotas seem to differ in their capacity to sustain violent conversion. Western Europe, for example, carries a far different pyramid than Caesar found there. Some large animals are lost; swampy forests have become meadows or plowland; many new plants and animals are introduced, some of which escape as pests; the remaining natives are greatly changed in distribution and abundance. Yet the soil is still there and, with the help of imported nutrients, still fertile; the waters flow normally; the new structure seems to function and to persist. There is no visible stoppage or derangement of the circuit.

Western Europe, then, has a resistant biota. Its inner processes are tough, elastic, resistant to strain. No matter how violent the alterations, the pyramid, so far, has developed some new *modus vivendi* which preserves its habitability for man, and for most of the other natives.

Japan seems to present another instance of radical conversion without disorganization.

Most other civilized regions, and some as yet barely touched by civilization, display various stages of disorganization, varying from initial symptoms to advanced wastage. In Asia Minor and North Africa diagnosis is confused by climatic changes, which may have been either the cause or the effect of advanced wastage. In the United States the degree of disorganization varies locally; it is worst in the Southwest, the Ozarks, and parts of the South, and least in New England and the Northwest. Better land-uses may still arrest it in the less advanced regions. In parts of Mexico, South America, South Africa, and Australia a violent and accelerating wastage is in progress, but I cannot assess the prospects.

This almost world-wide display of disorganization in the land seems to be similar to disease in an animal, except that it never culminates in complete disorganization or death. The land recovers, but at some reduced level of complexity, and with a reduced carrying capacity for people, plants, and animals. Many biotas currently regarded as "lands of opportunity" are in fact already subsisting on exploitative agriculture, i.e., they have already exceeded their sustained carrying capacity. Most of South America is overpopulated in this sense.

In arid regions we attempt to offset the process of wastage by reclamation, but it is only too evident that the prospective longevity of reclamation projects is often short. In our own West, the best of them may not last a century.

The combined evidence of history and ecology seems to support one general deduction: the less violent the man-made changes, the greater the probability of successful readjustment in the pyramid. Violence, in turn, varies with human population density; a dense population requires a more violent conversion. In this respect, North America has a better chance for permanence than Europe, if she can contrive to limit her density.

This deduction runs counter to our current philosophy, which assumes, because a small increase in density enriched human life, that an indefinite increase will enrich it indefinitely. Ecology knows of no density relationship that holds for indefinitely wide limits. All gains from density are subject to a law of diminishing returns.

Whatever may be the equation for men and land, it is improbable that we as yet know all its terms. Recent discoveries in mineral and vitamin nutrition reveal unsuspected dependencies in the up-circuit: incredibly minute quantities of certain substances determine the value of soils to plants, of plants to animals. What of the down-circuit? What of the vanishing species, the preservation of which we now regard as an esthetic luxury? They helped build the soil; in what unsuspected ways may they be essential to its maintenance? Professor Weaver proposes that we use prairie flowers to reflocculate the wasting soils of the dust bowl; who knows for what purpose cranes and condors, otters and grizzlies may some day be used?

The Outlook

It is inconceivable to me that an ethical relation to land can exist without love, respect, and admiration for land, and a high regard for its value. By value, I of course mean something far broader than mere economic value; I mean value in the philosophical sense.

Perhaps the most serious obstacle impeding the evolution of a land ethic is the fact that our educational and economic system is headed away from, rather than toward, an intense consciousness of land. Your true modern is separated from the land by many middlemen, and by innumerable physical gadgets. He has no vital relation to it; to him it is the space between cities, on which crops grow. Turn him loose for a day on the land, and if the spot does not happen to be a golf links or a "scenic" area, he is bored stiff. If crops could be raised by hydroponics instead of farming, it would suit him very well. Synthetic substitutes for wood, leather, wool, and other natural land products suit him better than the originals. In short, land is something he has "outgrown."

Almost equally serious as an obstacle to a land ethic is the attitude of the farmer for whom the land is still an adversary, or a taskmaster that keeps him in slavery. Theoretically, the mechanization of farming ought to cut the farmer's chains, but whether it really does is debatable.

One of the requisites for an ecological comprehension of land is an understanding of ecology, and this is by no means co-extensive with "education"; in fact, much higher education seems deliberately to avoid ecological concepts. An understanding of ecology does not necessarily originate in courses bearing ecological labels; it is quite as likely to be labeled geography, botany, agronomy, history, or economics. This is as it should be, but whatever the label, ecological training is scarce.

The case for a land ethic would appear hopeless but for the minority which is in obvious revolt against these "modern" trends.

The "key-log" which must be moved to release the evolutionary process for an ethic is simply this: quit thinking about decent land-use as solely an economic problem. Examine each question in terms of what is ethically and esthetically right, as well as what is economically expedient. A thing is right when it tends to preserve the integrity, stability, and beauty of the biotic community. It is wrong when it tends otherwise.

It of course goes without saying that economic feasibility limits the tether of what can or cannot be done for land. It always has and it always will. The fallacy the economic determinists have tied around our collective neck, and which we now need to cast off, is the belief that economics determines *all* land-use. This is simply not true. An innumerable host of actions and attitudes, comprising perhaps the bulk of all land relations, is determined by the land-user's tastes and predilections, rather than by his purse. The bulk of all land relations hinges on investments of time, forethought, skill, and faith rather than on investments of cash. As a land-user thinketh, so is he.

I have purposely presented the land ethic as a product of social evolution because nothing so important as an ethic is ever "written." Only the most superficial student of history supposes that Moses "wrote" the Decalogue; it evolved in the minds of a thinking community, and Moses wrote a tentative summary of it for a "seminar." I say tentative because evolution never stops.

The evolution of a land ethic is an intellectual as well as emotional process. Conservation is paved with good intentions which prove to be futile, or even dangerous, because they are devoid of critical understanding either of the land, or of economic land-use. I think it is a truism that as the ethical frontier advances from the individual to the community, its intellectual content increases.

The mechanism of operation is the same for any ethic: social approbation for right actions: social disapproval for wrong actions.

By and large, our present problem is one of attitudes and implements. We are remodeling the Alhambra with a steam-shovel, and we are proud of our yardage. We shall hardly relinquish the shovel, which after all has many good points, but we are in need of gentler and more objective criteria for its successful use.

Conservation as a Moral Issue

Thus far we have considered the problem of conservation of land purely as an economic issue. A false front of exclusively economic determinism is so habitual to Americans in discussing public questions that one must speak in the language of compound interest to get a hearing. In my opinion, however, one cannot round out a real understanding of the situation in the Southwest without likewise considering its moral aspects.

In past and more outspoken days conservation was put in terms of decency rather than dollars. Who cannot feel the moral scorn and contempt for poor craftsmanship in the voice of Ezekiel when he asks: *Seemeth it a small thing unto you to have fed upon good pasture, but ye must tread down with your feet the residue of your pasture? And to have drunk of the clear waters, but ye must foul the residue with your feet?*

In these two sentences may be found an epitome of the moral question involved. Ezekiel seems to scorn waste, pollution, and unnecessary damage as something unworthy – as something damaging not only to the reputation of the waster, but to the self-respect of the craft and the society of which he is a member. We might even draw from his words a broader concept – that the privilege of possessing the earth entails the responsibility of passing it on, the better for our use, not only to immediate posterity, but to the Unknown Future, the nature of which is not given us to know. It is possible that Ezekiel respected the soil, not only as a craftsman respects his material, but as a moral being respects a living thing.

Many of the world's most penetrating minds have regarded our so-called "inanimate nature" as a living thing, and probably many of us who have neither the time nor the ability to reason out conclusions on such matters by logical processes have felt intuitively that there existed between man and the earth a closer and deeper relation than would necessarily follow the mechanistic conception of the earth as our physical provider and abiding place.

Of course, in discussing such matters we are beset on all sides with the pitfalls of language. The very words *living thing* have an inherited and arbitrary meaning derived not from reality, but from human perceptions of human affairs. But we must use them for better or for worse.

A good expression of this conception of an organized animate nature is given by the Russian philosopher Onpensky, who presents the following analogy:

> Were we to observe, from the inside, one cubic centimetre of the human body, knowing nothing of the existence of the entire body and of man himself, then the phenomena going on in this little cube of flesh would seem like elemental phenomena in inanimate nature.

He then states that it is at least not impossible to regard the earth's parts – soil, mountains, rivers, atmosphere, etc. – as organs, or parts of organs, of a co-ordinated whole, each part with a definite function. And, if we could see this whole, as a whole, through a great period of time, we might perceive not only organs with co-ordinated functions, but possibly also that process of consumption and replacement which in biology we call the metabolism, or growth. In such a case we would have all the visible attributes of a living thing, which we do not now realize to be such because it is too big, and its life processes too slow. And there would also follow that invisible attribute – a soul, or consciousness – which not only Onpensky, but many philosophers of all ages, ascribe to all living things and aggregations thereof, including the "dead" earth.

There is not much discrepancy, except in language, between this conception of a living earth, and the conception of a dead earth, with enormously slow, intricate, and interrelated functions among its parts, as given us by physics, chemistry, and geology. The essential thing for present purposes is that both admit the interdependent functions of the elements. But "anything indivisible is a living being," says Onpensky. Possibly, in our intuitive perceptions, which may be truer than our science and less impeded by words than our philosophies, we realize the indivisibility of the earth – its soil, mountains, rivers, forests, climate, plants, and animals, and respect it collectively not only as a useful servant but as a living being, vastly less alive than ourselves in degree, but vastly greater than ourselves in time and space – a being that was old when the morning stars sang together, and, when the last of us has been gathered unto his fathers, will still be young.

Philosophy, then, suggests one reason why we cannot destroy the earth with moral impunity; namely, that the "dead" earth is an organism possessing a certain kind and degree of life, which we intuitively respect as such. Possibly, to most men of affairs, this reason is too intangible to either accept or reject as a guide to human conduct. But philosophy also offers another and more easily debatable question: was the earth made for man's use, or has man merely the privilege of temporarily possessing an earth made for other and inscrutable purposes? The question of what he can properly do with it must necessarily be affected by this question.

Most religions, insofar as I know, are premised squarely on the assumption that man is the end and purpose of creation, and that not only the dead earth, but all creatures thereon, exist solely for his use. The mechanistic or scientific philosophy does not start with this as a premise, but ends with it as a conclusion and hence may be placed in the same category for the purpose in hand. This high opinion of his own importance in the universe Jeanette Marks stigmatizes as "the great human impertinence." John Muir, in defense of rattlesnakes, protests: ". . . as if nothing that does not obviously make for the benefit of man had any right to exist; as if our ways were God's ways." But the noblest expression of this anthropomorphism is Bryant's "Thanatopsis":

> . . . The hills
> Rock-ribbed and ancient as the sun, – the vales
> Stretching in pensive quietness between;
> The venerable woods – rivers that move
> In majesty, and the complaining brooks
> That make the meadows green, and, poured round all
> Old oceans gray and melancholy waste, –
> *Are but the solemn decorations all*
> *Of the great tomb of man.*

Since most of mankind today profess either one of the anthropomorphic religions or the scientific school of thought which is likewise anthropomorphic, I will not dispute the point. It just occurs to me, however, in answer to the scientists, that God started his show a good many million years before he had any men for audience – a sad waste of both actors and music – and in answer to both, that it is just barely possible that God himself likes to hear birds sing and see flowers grow. But here again we encounter the insufficiency of words as symbols for realities.

Granting that the earth is for man – there is still a question: what man? Did not the cliff dwellers who tilled and irrigated these our valleys think that they were the pinnacle of creation – that these valleys were made for them? Undoubtedly. And then the Pueblos? Yes. And then the Spaniards? Not only thought so, but said so. And now we Americans? Ours beyond a doubt! (How happy a definition is that one of Hadley's which states, "Truth is that which prevails in the long run"!)

Five races – five cultures – have flourished here. We may truthfully say of our four predecessors that they left the earth alive, undamaged. Is it possibly a proper question for us to consider what the sixth shall say about us? If we are logically anthropomorphic, yes. We and

> . . . all that tread
> The globe are but a handful to the tribes
> That slumber in its bosom. Take the wings
> Of morning; pierce the Barcan wilderness
> Or lose thyself in the continuous woods
> Where rolls the Oregon, and hears no sound
> Save his own dashings – yet the dead are there,
> And millions in those solitudes, since first
> The flight of years began, have laid them down
> In their last sleep.

And so, in time, shall we. And if there be, indeed, a special nobility inherent in the human race – a special cosmic value, distinctive from and superior to all other life – by what token shall it be manifest?

By a society decently respectful of its own and all other life, capable of inhabiting the earth without defiling it? Or by a society like that of John Burrough's potato bug, which exterminated the potato, and thereby exterminated itself? As one or the other shall we be judged in "the derisive silence of eternity."

Thinking Like a Mountain

A deep chesty bawl echoes from rimrock to rimrock, rolls down the mountain, and fades into the far blackness of the night. It is an outburst of wild defiant sorrow, and of contempt for all the adversities of the world.

Every living thing (and perhaps many a dead one as well) pays heed to that call. To the deer it is a reminder of the way of all flesh, to the pine a forecast of midnight scuffles and of blood upon the snow, to the coyote a promise of gleanings to come, to the cowman a threat of red ink at the bank, to the hunter a challenge of fang against bullet. Yet behind these obvious and immediate hopes and fears there lies a deeper meaning, known only to the mountain itself. Only the mountain has lived long enough to listen objectively to the howl of a wolf.

Those unable to decipher the hidden meaning know nevertheless that it is there, for it is felt in all wolf country, and distinguishes that country from all other land. It tingles in the spine of all who hear wolves by night, or who scan their tracks by day. Even without sight or sound of wolf, it is implicit in a hundred small events: the midnight whinny of a pack horse, the rattle of rolling rocks, the bound of a fleeing deer, the way shadows lie under the spruces. Only the ineducable tyro can fail to sense the presence or absence of wolves, or the fact that mountains have a secret opinion about them.

My own conviction on this score dates from the day I saw a wolf die. We were eating lunch on a high rimrock, at the foot of which a turbulent river elbowed its way. We saw what we thought was a doe fording the torrent, her breast awash in white water. When she climbed the bank toward us and shook out her tail, we realized our error: it was a wolf. A half-dozen others, evidently grown pups, sprang from the willows and all joined in a welcoming mêlée of wagging tails and playful maulings. What was literally a pile of wolves writhed and tumbled in the center of an open flat at the foot of our rimrock.

In those days we had never heard of passing up a chance to kill a wolf. In a second we were pumping lead into the pack, but with more excitement than accuracy: how to aim a steep downhill shot is always confusing. When our rifles were empty, the old wolf was down, and a pup was dragging a leg into impassable slide-rocks.

We reached the old wolf in time to watch a fierce green fire dying in her eyes. I realized then, and have known ever since, that there was something new to me in those eyes — something known only to her and to the mountain. I was young then, and full of trigger-itch; I thought that because fewer wolves meant more deer, that no wolves would mean hunters' paradise. But after seeing the green fire die, I sensed that neither the wolf nor the mountain agreed with such a view.

Since then I have lived to see state after state extirpate its wolves. I have watched the face of many a newly wolfless mountain, and seen the south-facing slopes wrinkle with a maze of new deer trails. I have seen every edible bush and seedling browsed, first to anaemic desuetude, and then to death. I have seen every edible tree defoliated to the height of a saddlehorn. Such a mountain looks as if someone had given God a new pruning shears, and forbidden Him all other exercise. In the end the starved bones of the hoped-for deer herd, dead of its own too-much, bleach with the bones of the dead sage, or molder under the high-lined junipers.

I now suspect that just as a deer herd lives in mortal fear of its wolves, so does a mountain live in mortal fear of its deer. And perhaps with better cause, for while a buck pulled down by wolves can be replaced in two or three years, a range pulled down by too many deer may fail of replacement in as many decades.

So also with cows. The cowman who cleans his range of wolves does not realize that he is taking over the wolf's job of trimming the herd to fit the range. He has not learned to think like a mountain. Hence we have dustbowls, and rivers washing the future into the sea.

We all strive for safety, prosperity, comfort, long life, and dullness. The deer strives with his supple legs, the cowman with trap and poison, the statesman with pen, the most of us with machines, votes, and dollars, but it all comes to the same thing: peace in our time. A measure of success in this is all well enough, and perhaps is a requisite to objective thinking, but too much safety seems to yield only danger in the long run. Perhaps this is behind Thoreau's dictum: In wildness is the salvation of the world. Perhaps this is the hidden meaning in the howl of the wolf, long known among mountains, but seldom perceived among men.

59

Reconciling Anthropocentric and Nonanthropocentric Environmental Ethics

James P. Sterba

A central debate, if not the most central debate, in contemporary environmental ethics is between those who defend an anthropocentric ethics which holds that humans are superior overall to the members of other species, and those who defend a nonanthropocentric ethics which holds that the members of all species are equal. Here I propose to go some way toward resolving this debate by showing that when the most morally defensible versions of each of these perspectives are laid out, they do not lead to different practical requirements. In this way I hope to show how it is possible for defenders of anthropocentric and nonanthropocentric environmental ethics, despite their theoretical disagreement concerning whether humans are superior to members of other species, to agree on a common set of principles for achieving environmental justice.

I. Nonanthropocentric Environmental Ethics

Consider first the nonanthropocentric perspective. In support of this perspective, it can be argued that we have no non-question-begging grounds for regarding the members of any living species as superior to the members of any other. It allows that the members of species differ in a myriad of ways, but argues that these differences do not provide grounds for thinking that the members of any one species are superior to the members of any other. In particular, it denies that the differences between species provide grounds for thinking that humans are superior to the members of other species. Of course, the nonanthropocentric perspective recognizes that humans have distinctive traits which the members of other species lack, like rationality and moral agency. It just points out that the members of nonhuman species also have distinctive traits that humans lack, like the homing ability of pigeons, the speed of the cheetah, and the ruminative ability of sheep and cattle.

Nor will it do to claim that the distinctive traits that humans have are more valuable than the distinctive traits that members of other species possess because there is no non-question-begging standpoint from which to justify that claim. From a human standpoint, rationality and moral agency are more valuable than any of the distinctive traits found in nonhuman species, since, as humans, we would not be better off if we were to trade in those traits for the distinctive traits found in nonhuman species. Yet the same holds true of nonhuman species. Generally, pigeons, cheetahs, sheep and cattle would not be better off if they were to trade in their distinctive traits for the distinctive traits of other species.

Of course, the members of some species might be better off if they could retain the distinctive traits of their species while acquiring one or another of the distinctive traits possessed by some other species. For example, we humans might be better off if we could retain our distinctive traits while acquiring the ruminative ability of sheep and cattle. But many of the distinctive traits of species cannot be even imaginatively added to the members of other species without substantially altering the original species. For example, in order for the cheetah to acquire the distinctive traits possessed by humans, presumably it would have to be so transformed that its paws became something like hands to accommodate its human-like mental capabilities, thereby losing its distinctive speed, and ceasing to be a cheetah. So possessing distinctively human traits would not be good for the cheetah. And with the possible exception of our nearest evolutionary relatives, the same holds true for the members of other species: they would not be better off having distinctively human traits. Only in fairy tales and in the world of Disney can the members of nonhuman species enjoy a full array of distinctively human traits. So there would appear to be no non-question-begging perspective from which to judge that distinctively human traits are more valuable than the distinctive traits possessed by other species. Judged from a non-question-begging perspective, we would seemingly have to regard the members of all species as equals.

It might be useful at this point to make my argument even more explicit. Here is one way this could be done.

1. We should not aggress against any living being unless there are either self-evident or non-question-begging reasons for doing so. (It would be difficult to reject this principle given the various analogous principles we accept, such as the principle of formal equality: equals should be treated equally and unequals unequally.)
2. To treat humans as superior overall to other living beings is to aggress against them by sacrificing their basic needs to meet the nonbasic needs of humans. (Definition.)
3. Therefore, we should not treat humans as superior overall to other living beings unless we have either self-evident or non-question-begging reasons for doing so. (From 1 and 2.)
4. We do not have either self-evident or non-question-begging reasons for treating humans as superior overall to other living beings. (That we do not have any non-question-begging reasons for treating humans as superior overall to other living beings was established by the previous argument. That we do not have any self-evident reasons for doing so, I take it, is obvious.)
5. Therefore, we should not treat humans as superior overall to other living beings. (From 3 and 4.)
6. Not to treat humans as superior overall to other living beings is to treat them as equal overall to other living beings. (Definition.)
7. Therefore, we should treat humans as equal overall to other living beings. (From 5 and 6.)

Nevertheless, I want to go on to claim that regarding the members of all species as equals still allows for human preference in the same way that regarding all humans as equals still allows for self-preference.

First of all, human preference can be justified on grounds of defense. Thus, we have

> *A Principle of Human Defense*: Actions that defend oneself and other human beings against harmful aggression are permissible even when they necessitate killing or harming animals or plants.

This Principle of Human Defense allows us to defend ourselves and other human beings from harmful aggression first against our persons and the persons of other human beings that we are committed to or happen to care about and secondly against our justifiably held property and the justifiably held property of other human beings that we are committed to or happen to care about.

This principle is analogous to the principle of self-defense that applies in human ethics and permits actions in defense of oneself or other human beings against harmful human aggression. In the case of human aggression, however, it will sometimes be possible to effectively defend oneself and other human beings by first suffering the aggression and then securing adequate compensation later. Since, in the case of nonhuman aggression, this is unlikely to obtain, more harmful preventive actions such as killing a rabid dog or swatting a mosquito will be justified. There are simply more ways to effectively stop aggressive humans than there are to stop aggressive nonhumans.

Secondly, human preference can also be justified on grounds of preservation. Accordingly, we have

> *A Principle of Human Preservation*: Actions that are necessary for meeting one's basic needs or the basic needs of other human beings are permissible even when they require aggressing against the basic needs of animals and plants.

Now needs, in general, if not satisfied, lead to lacks or deficiencies with respect to various standards. The basic needs of humans, if not satisfied, lead to lacks or deficiencies with respect to a standard of a decent life. The basic needs of animals and plants, if not satisfied, lead to lacks or deficiencies with respect to a standard of a healthy life. The means necessary for meeting the basic needs of humans can vary widely from society to society. By contrast, the means necessary for meeting the basic needs of particular species of animals and plants are more invariant.

In human ethics, there is no principle that is strictly analogous to this Principle of Human Preservation. There is a principle of self-preservation in human ethics that permits actions that are necessary for meeting one's own basic needs or the basic needs of other people, even if this requires *failing to meet* (through an act of omission) the basic needs of still other people. For example, we can use our resources to feed ourselves and our family, even if this necessitates failing to meet the basic needs of people in Third World countries. But, in general, we don't have a principle that allows us to *aggress against* (through an act of commission) the basic needs of some people in order to meet our own basic needs or the basic needs of other people to whom we are committed or that we happen to care about. Actually, the closest we come to permitting aggressing against the basic needs of other people in order to meet our own basic needs or the basic needs of people to whom we are committed or that we happen to care about is our acceptance of the outcome of life-and-death struggles in lifeboat cases, where no one has an antecedent right to the available resources. For example, if you had to fight off others in order to secure the last place in a lifeboat for yourself or for a member of your family, we might say that you justifiably aggressed against the basic needs of those whom you fought to meet your own basic needs or the basic needs of the member of your family.

Nevertheless, our survival requires a principle of preservation that permits aggressing against the basic needs of at least some other living things whenever this is necessary to meet our own basic needs or the basic needs of other human beings. Here there are two possibilities. The first is a principle of preservation that allows us to aggress against the basic needs of both humans and nonhumans whenever it would serve our own basic needs or the basic needs of other human beings. The second is the principle, given above, that allows us to aggress against the basic needs of only nonhumans whenever it would serve our own basic needs or the basic needs of other human beings. The first principle does not express any general preference for the members of the human species, and thus it permits even cannibalism provided that it serves to meet our own basic needs or the basic needs of other human beings. In contrast, the second principle does express a degree of preference for the members of the human species in cases where their basic needs are at stake. Happily, this degree of preference for our own species is still compatible with the equality of all species because favoring the members of one's own species to this extent is characteristic of the members of nearly all species with which we interact and is thereby legitimated. The reason it is legitimated is that we would be required to sacrifice the basic needs of members of the human species only if the members of other species were making similar sacrifices for the sake of members of the human species. Notice that this is not an argument that since the members of other species aren't sacrificing for us, we don't have to sacrifice for them, but rather an argument that since the members of other species are not sacrificing for us, we don't have to sacrifice *our basic needs* for them. Now it may be objected that the members of most other species are incapable of making this kind of sacrifice. This is true for most species, but irrelevant here because to reasonably ask this much altruism from humans just requires comparable altruism from the members of other species benefiting those humans. Actually, this degree of altruism toward humans may be found in some species of domestic animals, for example, dogs and horses.

In addition, if we were to prefer consistently the basic needs of the members of other species whenever those needs conflicted with our own (or even if we do so half the time), given the characteristic behavior of the members of other species, we would soon be facing extinction, and, fortunately, we have no reason to think that we are morally required to bring about our own extinction. For these reasons, the degree of preference for our own species found in the above Principle of Human Preservation is justified, even if we were to adopt a nonanthropocentric perspective.

Nevertheless, preference for humans can go beyond bounds, and the bounds that are compatible with a nonanthropocentric perspective are expressed by the following:

> *A Principle of Disproportionality*: Actions that meet nonbasic or luxury needs of humans are prohibited when they aggress against the basic needs of animals and plants.

This principle is strictly analogous to the principle in human ethics mentioned previously that prohibits meeting some people's nonbasic or luxury needs by aggressing against the basic needs of other people.

Without a doubt, the adoption of such a principle with respect to nonhuman nature would significantly change the way we live our lives. Such a principle is required, however, if there is to be any substance to the claim that the members of all species are equal. We can no more consistently claim that the members of all species are equal and yet aggress against the basic needs of some animals or plants whenever this serves our own nonbasic or luxury needs, than we can consistently claim that all humans are equal and aggress against the basic needs of some other human beings whenever this serves our nonbasic or luxury needs. Consequently, if species equality is to mean anything, it must be the case that the basic needs of the members of nonhuman species are protected against aggressive actions which only serve to meet the nonbasic needs of humans, as required by the Principle of Disproportionality.

So while a nonanthropocentric perspective allows for a degree of preference for the members of the human species, it also significantly limits that preference.

To see why these limits on preference for the members of the human species are all that is required for recognizing the equality of species, we need to understand the equality of species by analogy with the equality of humans. We need to see that just as we claim that humans are equal but treat them differently, so too we can claim that all species are equal but treat them differently. In human ethics, there are various interpretations given to human equality that allow for different treatment of humans. In ethical egoism, everyone is *equally at liberty* to pursue his or her own interests, but this allows us to always prefer ourselves to others, who are understood to be like opponents in a competitive game. In libertarianism, everyone has an *equal right to liberty*, but although this imposes some limits on the pursuit of self-interest, it is said to allow us to refrain from helping others in severe need. In welfare liberalism, everyone has an *equal right to welfare and opportunity*, but this need not commit us to providing everyone with exactly the same resources. In socialism, everyone has an *equal right to self-development*, and although this may commit us to providing everyone with the same resources, it still sanctions some degree of self-preference. So just as there are these various ways to interpret human equality that still allow us to treat humans differently, there are various ways that we can interpret species equality that allow us to treat species differently.

Now one might interpret species equality in a very strong sense, analogous to the interpretation of equality found in socialism. But the kind of species equality that I have defended is more akin to the equality found in welfare liberalism or in libertarianism than it is to the equality found in socialism. In brief, this form of equality requires that we not aggress against the basic needs of the members of other species for the sake of the nonbasic needs of the members of our own species (the Principle of Disproportionality), but it permits us to aggress against the basic needs of the members of other species for the sake of the basic needs of the members of our own species (the Principle of Human Preservation), and also permits us to defend the basic and even the nonbasic needs of the members of our own species against harmful aggression by members of other species (the Principle of Human Defense). In this way, I have argued that we can accept the claim of species equality, while avoiding imposing an unreasonable sacrifice on the members of our own species.

II. Individualism and Holism

It might be objected here that I have not yet taken into account the conflict within a nonanthropocentric ethics between holists and individualists. According to holists, the good of a species or the good of an ecosystem or the good of the whole biotic community can trump the good of individual living things.[1] According to individualists, the good of each individual living thing must be respected.[2]

Now one might think that holists would require that we abandon my Principle of Human Preservation. Yet consider. Assuming that people's basic needs are at stake, how could it be morally objectionable for them to try to meet those needs, even if this were to harm nonhuman individuals, or species, or whole ecosystems, or even, to some degree, the whole biotic community? Of course, we can *ask* people in such conflict cases not to meet their basic needs in order to prevent harm to nonhuman individuals or species, ecosystems or the whole biotic community. But if people's basic needs are at stake, we cannot reasonably demand that they make such a sacrifice. We could demand, of course, that people do all that they reasonably can to keep such conflicts from arising in the first place, for, just as in human ethics, many severe conflicts of interest can be avoided simply by doing what is morally required early on. Nevertheless, when people's basic needs are at stake, the individualist perspective seems incontrovertible. We cannot reasonably require people to be saints.

At the same time, when people's basic needs are not at stake, we would be justified in acting on holistic grounds to prevent serious harm to nonhuman individuals, or species, or ecosystems, or the whole biotic community. Obviously, it will be difficult to know when our interventions will have this effect, but when we can be reasonably sure that they will, such interventions (e.g. culling elk herds in wolf-free ranges or preserving the habitat of endangered species) would be morally permissible, and maybe even morally required.[3] This shows that it is possible to agree with individualists when the basic needs of human beings are at stake, and to agree with holists when they are not.

Yet this combination of individualism and holism appears to conflict with the equality of species by imposing greater sacrifices on the members of nonhuman species than it does on the members of the human species. Fortunately, appearances are deceiving here. Although the proposed resolution only justifies imposing holism when people's basic needs are not at stake, it does not justify imposing individualism at all. Rather it would simply permit individualism when people's basic needs *are* at stake. Of course, we could impose holism under all conditions. But given that this would, in effect, involve going to war against people who are simply striving to meet their own basic needs in the only way they can, as permitted by the Principle of Human Preservation, intervention in such cases would not be justified. It would involve taking away the means of survival from people, even when these means are not required for one's own survival.

Nevertheless, this combination of individualism and holism may leave animal liberationists wondering about the further implications of this resolution for the treatment of animals. Obviously, a good deal of work has already been done on this topic. Initially, philosophers thought that humanism could be extended to include animal liberation and eventually environmental concern.[4] Then Baird Callicott argued that animal liberation and environmental concern were as opposed to each other as they were to humanism.[5] The resulting conflict Callicott called "a triangular affair." Agreeing with Callicott, Mark Sagoff contended that any attempt to link together animal liberation and environmental concern would lead to "a bad marriage and a quick divorce."[6] Yet more recently, such philosophers as Mary Ann Warren have tended to play down the opposition between animal liberation and environmental concern, and even Callicott now thinks he can bring the two back together again.[7] There are good reasons for thinking that such a reconciliation is possible.

Right off, it would be good for the environment if people generally, especially people in the First World, adopted a more vegetarian diet of the sort that animal liberationists are recommending. This is because a good portion of livestock production today consumes grains that could be more effectively used for direct human consumption. For example, 90 percent of the protein, 99 percent of the carbohydrate, and 100 percent of the fiber value of grain is wasted by cycling it through livestock, and currently 64 percent of the US grain crop is fed to livestock.[8] So by adopting a more vegetarian diet, people generally, and especially people in the First World, could significantly reduce the amount of farmland that has to be keep in production to feed the human population. This, in turn, could have beneficial effects on the whole biotic community by eliminating the amount of soil erosion and environmental pollutants that result from raising livestock. For example, it has been estimated that 85 percent of US topsoil lost from cropland, pasture, range land and forest land is directly associated with raising livestock.[9] So, in addition to preventing animal suffering, there are these additional reasons to favor a more vegetarian diet.

But even though a more vegetarian diet seems in order, it is not clear that the interests of farm animals would be well served if all of us became complete vegetarians. Sagoff assumes that in a completely vegetarian human world people would continue to feed farm animals as before.[10] But it is not clear that we would have any obligation to do so. Moreover, in a completely vegetarian human world, we would probably need about half of the grain we now feed livestock to meet people's nutritional needs, particularly in Second and Third World countries. There simply would not be enough grain to go around. And then there would be the need to conserve cropland for future generations. So in a completely vegetarian human world, it seems likely that the population of farm animals would be decimated, relegating many of the farm animals that remain to zoos. On this account, it would seem to be more in the interest of farm animals generally that they be maintained under healthy conditions, and then killed relatively painlessly and eaten, rather than that they not be maintained at all. So a completely vegetarian human world would not seem to serve the interest of farm animals.

Nor, it seems, would it be in the interest of wild species who no longer have their natural predators not to be hunted by humans. Of course, where possible, it may be preferable to reintroduce natural predators. But this may not always be possible because of the proximity of farm animals and human populations, and then if action is not taken to control the populations of wild species, disaster could result for the species and their environments. For example, deer, rabbits, squirrels, quails and ducks reproduce rapidly, and in the absence of predators can quickly exceed the carrying capacity of their environments. So it may be in the interest of certain wild species and their environments that humans intervene periodically to maintain a balance. Of course, there will be many natural environments where it is in the interest of the environment and the wild animals that inhabit it to be simply left alone. But here too animal liberation and environmental concern would not be in conflict. For these reasons, animal liberationists would have little reason to object to the proposed combination of individualism and holism within a nonanthropocentric environmental ethics.

III. Anthropocentric Environmental Ethics

Suppose, however, we were to reject the central contention of the nonanthropocentric perspective and deny that the members of all species are equal. We might claim, for example, that humans are superior because they, through culture, "realize a greater range of values" than members of nonhuman species, or we might claim that humans are superior in virtue of their "unprecedented capacity to create ethical systems that impart worth to other life-forms."[11] Or we might offer some other grounds for human superiority. Suppose, then, we adopt this anthropocentric perspective. What follows?

First of all, we will still need a principle of human defense. However, there is no need to adopt a different principle of human defense from the principle favored by a nonanthropocentric perspective. Whether we judge humans to be equal or superior to the members of other species, we will still want a principle that allows us to defend ourselves and other human beings from harmful aggression, even when this necessitates killing or harming animals or plants.

Secondly, we will also need a principle of human preservation. But here too there is no need to adopt a different principle from the principle of human preservation favored by a nonanthropocentric perspective. Whether we judge humans to be equal or superior to the members of other species, we will still want a principle that permits actions that are necessary for meeting our own basic needs or the basic needs of other human beings, even when this requires aggressing against the basic needs of animals and plants.

The crucial question is whether we will need a different principle of disproportionality. If we judge humans to be superior to the members of other species, will we still have grounds for protecting the basic needs of animals and plants against aggressive action to meet the nonbasic or luxury needs of humans?

Here it is important to distinguish between two degrees of preference that we noted earlier. First, we could prefer the basic needs of animals and plants over the nonbasic or luxury needs of humans when to do otherwise would involve *aggressing against* (by an act of commission) the basic needs of animals and plants. Secondly, we could prefer the basic needs of animals and plants over the nonbasic or luxury needs of humans when to do otherwise would involve simply *failing to meet* (by an act of omission) the basic needs of animals and plants.

Now in human ethics when the basic needs of some people are in conflict with the nonbasic or luxury needs of others, the distinction between failing to meet and aggressing against basic needs seems to have little moral force. In such conflict cases, both ways of not meeting basic needs are objectionable.

But in environmental ethics, whether we adopt an anthropocentric or a nonanthropocentric perspective, we would seem to have grounds for morally distinguishing between the two cases, favoring the basic needs of animals and plants when to do otherwise would involve *aggressing against* those needs in order to meet our own nonbasic or luxury needs, but not when it would involve simply *failing to meet* those needs in order to meet our own nonbasic or luxury needs. This degree of preference for the members of the human species would be compatible with the equality of species insofar as members of nonhuman species similarly fail to meet the basic needs of members of the human species where there is a conflict of interest.

Even so, this theoretical distinction would have little practical force since most of the ways that we have of preferring our own nonbasic needs over the basic needs of animals and plants actually involve aggressing against their basic needs to meet our own nonbasic or luxury needs rather than simply failing to meet their basic needs.

Yet even if most of the ways that we have of preferring our own nonbasic or luxury needs do involve aggressing against the basic needs of animals and plants, wouldn't human superiority provide grounds for preferring ourselves or other human beings in these ways? Or put another way, shouldn't human superiority have more theoretical and practical significance than I am allowing? Not, I claim, if we are looking for the most morally defensible position to take.

For consider: The claim that humans are superior to the members of other species, if it can be justified at all, is something like the claim that a person came in first in a race where others came in second, third, fourth, and so on. It would not imply that the members of other species are without intrinsic value. In fact, it would imply just the opposite – that the members of other species are also intrinsically valuable, although not as intrinsically valuable as humans, just as the claim that a person came in first in a race implies that the persons who came in second, third, fourth, and so on are also meritorious, although not as meritorious as the person who came in first.

This line of argument draws further support once we consider the fact that many animals and plants are superior to humans in one respect or another, e.g., the sense of smell of the wolf, or the acuity of sight of the eagle, or the survivability of the cockroach, or the photosynthetic power of plants. So any claim of human superiority must allow for the recognition of excellences in nonhuman species, even for some excellences that are superior to their corresponding human excellences. In fact, it demands that recognition.

Moreover, if the claim of human superiority is to have any moral force, it must rest on non-question-begging grounds. Accordingly, we must be able to give a non-question-begging response to the nonanthropocentric argument for the equality of species. Yet for any such argument to be successful, it would have to recognize the intrinsic value of the members of nonhuman species. Even if it could be established that human beings have greater intrinsic value, we would still have to recognize that nonhuman nature has intrinsic value as well. So the relevant question is: How are we going to recognize the presumably lesser intrinsic value of nonhuman nature?

Now if human needs, even nonbasic or luxury ones, are always preferred to even the basic needs of the members of nonhuman species, we would not be giving any recognition to the intrinsic value of nonhuman nature. But what if we allowed the nonbasic or luxury needs of humans to trump the basic needs of nonhuman nature half the time, and half the time we allowed the basic needs of nonhuman nature to trump the nonbasic or luxury needs of humans. Would that be enough? Certainly, it would be a significant advance over what we are presently doing. For what we are presently doing is meeting the basic needs of nonhuman nature, at best, only when it serves our own needs or the needs of those we are committed to or happen to care about, and that does not recognize the intrinsic value of nonhuman nature at all. A fifty–fifty arrangement would be an advance indeed. But it would not be enough.

The reason why it would not be enough is that the claim that humans are superior to nonhuman nature no more supports the practice of aggressing against the basic needs of nonhuman nature to satisfy our own nonbasic or luxury needs than the claim that a person came in first in a race would support the practice of aggressing against the basic needs of those who came in second, third, fourth, and so on to satisfy the nonbasic or luxury needs of the person who came in first. A higher degree of merit does not translate into a right of domination, and to claim a right to aggress against the basic needs of nonhuman nature in order to meet our own nonbasic or luxury needs is clearly to claim a right of domination. All that our superiority as humans would justify is not meeting the basic needs of nonhuman nature when this conflicts with our nonbasic or luxury needs. What it does not justify is aggressing against the basic needs of nonhuman nature when this conflicts with our nonbasic or luxury needs.

IV.   Objective and Subjective Value Theory

Now it might be objected that my argument so far presupposes an objective theory of value which regards things as valuable because of the qualities they actually have rather than a subjective theory of value which regards things as valuable simply because humans happen to value them. However, I contend that when both these theories are defensibly formulated, they will lead to the same practical requirements.

For consider: Suppose we begin with a subjective theory of value that regards things as valuable simply because humans value them. Of course, some things would be valued by humans instrumentally, others intrinsically, but, according to this theory, all things would have the value they have, if they have any value at all, simply because they are valued by humans either instrumentally or intrinsically.

One problem facing such a theory is: why should we think that humans alone determine the value that things have? For example, why not say that things are valuable because the members of other species value them? Why not say that grass is valuable because zebras value it, and that zebras are valuable because lions value them, and so on? Or why not say, assuming God exists, that things are valuable because God values them?

Nor would it do simply to claim that we authoritatively determine what is valuable for ourselves, that nonhuman species authoritatively determine what is valuable for themselves, and that God authoritatively determines what is valuable for the Godhead. For what others value should at least be relevant data when authoritatively determining what is valuable for ourselves.

Another problem for a subjective theory of value is that we probably would not want to say that just anything we happen to value determines what is valuable for ourselves. For surely we would want to say that at least some of the things that people value, especially people who are evil or deficient in certain ways, are not really valuable, even for them. Merely thinking that something is valuable doesn't make it so.

Suppose then we modified this subjective theory of value to deal with these problems. Let the theory claim that what is truly valuable for people is what they would value if they had all the relevant information (including, where it is relevant, the knowledge of what others would value) and reasoned correctly. Of course, there will be many occasions where we are unsure that ideal conditions have been realized, unsure, that is, that we have all the relevant information and have reasoned correctly. And even when we are sure that ideal conditions have been realized, we may not always be willing to act upon what we come to value due to weakness of will.

Nevertheless, when a subjective theory of value is formulated in this way, it will have the same practical requirements as an objective theory of value that is also defensibly formulated. For an objective theory of value holds that what is valuable is determined by the qualities things actually have. But in order for the qualities things actually have to be valuable in the sense of being capable of being valued, they must be accessible to us, at least under ideal conditions; that is, they must be the sort of qualities that we would value if we had all the relevant information and reasoned correctly. But this is just what is valuable according to our modified subjective theory of value. So once a subjective theory of value and an objective theory of value are defensibly formulated in the manner I propose, they will lead us to value the same things.

Now it is important to note here that with respect to some of the things we value intrinsically, such as animals and plants, our valuing them depends simply on our ability to discover the value that they actually have based on their qualities, whereas for other things that we value intrinsically, such as our aesthetic experiences and the objects that provided us with those experiences, the value that these things have depends significantly on the way we are constituted. So that if we were constituted differently, what we valued aesthetically would be different as well. Of course, the same holds true for some of the things that we value morally. For example, we morally value not killing human beings because of the way we are constituted. Constituted as we are, killing is usually bad for any human that we would kill. But suppose that we were constituted differently such that killing human beings was immensely pleasurable for those humans that we killed, following which they immediately sprang back to life asking us to kill them again. If human beings were constituted in this way, we would no longer morally value not killing. In fact, constituted in this new way, I think we would come to morally value *killing* and the relevant rule for us might be "Kill human beings as often as you can." But while such aesthetic and moral values are clearly dependent on the way we are constituted, they still are not anthropocentric in the sense that they imply human superiority. Such values can be recognized from both an anthropocentric and a nonanthropocentric perspective.

It might be objected, however, that while the intrinsic values of an environmental ethics need not be anthropocentric in the sense that they imply human superiority, these values must be anthropocentric in the sense that humans would reasonably come to hold them. This seems correct. However, appealing to this sense of anthropocentric, Eugene Hargrove has argued that not all living things would turn out to be intrinsically valuable as a non-anthropocentric environmental ethics maintains.[12] Hargrove cites as hypothetical examples of living things that would not turn out to be intrinsically valuable the creatures in the films *Alien* and *Aliens*. What is distinctive about these creatures in *Alien* and *Aliens* is that they require the deaths of many other living creatures, whomever they happen upon, to reproduce and survive as a species. Newly hatched, these creatures emerge from their eggs and immediately enter host organisms, which they keep alive and feed upon while they develop. When the creatures are fully developed, they explode out of the chest of their host organisms, killing their hosts with some fanfare. Hargrove suggests that if such creatures existed, we would not intrinsically value them because it would not be reasonable for us to do so.[13]

Following Paul Taylor, Hargrove assumes that to intrinsically value a creature is to recognize a negative duty not to destroy or harm that creature and a positive duty to protect it from being destroyed or harmed by others. Since Hargrove thinks that we would be loath to recognize any such duties with respect to such alien creatures, we would not consider them to be intrinsically valuable.

Surely it seems clear that we would seek to kill such alien creatures by whatever means are available to us, but why should that preclude our recognizing them as having intrinsic value any more than our seeking to kill any person who is engaged in lethal aggression against us would preclude our recognizing that person as having intrinsic value? To recognize something as having intrinsic value does not preclude destroying it to preserve other things that also have intrinsic value when there is good reason to do so. Furthermore, recognizing a prima facie negative duty not to destroy or harm something and a prima facie positive duty to protect it from being destroyed or harmed by others is perfectly consistent with recognizing an all-things-considered duty to destroy that thing when it is engaged in lethal aggression against us. Actually, all we are doing here is simply applying our Principle of Human Defense, and, as I have argued earlier, there is no reason to think that the application of this principle would preclude our recognizing the intrinsic value of every living being.

Still another objection that might be raised to my reconciliationist argument is that my view is too individualistic, as evidenced by the fact that my principles of environmental justice refer to individual humans, plants and animals but not specifically to species or ecosystems. Now, I would certainly agree with Paul Taylor that all individual living beings as well as species populations can be benefited or harmed and have a good of their own, and, hence, qualify as moral subjects.[14] But Taylor goes on to deny that species themselves are moral subjects with a good of their own, because he regards "species" as a class name, and classes, he contends, have no good of their own.[15] Yet here I would disagree with Taylor because species are unlike abstract classes in that they evolve, split, bud off new species, become endangered, go extinct, and have interests distinct from the interests of their members.[16] For example, a particular species of deer but not individual members of that species can have an interest in being preyed upon. Hence, species can be benefited and harmed and have a good of their own, and so should qualify on Taylor's view, as well as my own, as moral subjects. So, too, ecosystems should qualify as moral subjects since they can be benefited and harmed and have a good of their own, having features and interests not shared by their components.[17] Following Lawrence Johnson, we can go on to characterize moral subjects as living systems in a persistent state of low entropy sustained by metabolic processes for accumulating energy whose organic unity and self-identity is maintained in equilibrium by homeostatic feedback processes.[18]

Thus, modifying my view in order to take into account species and ecosystems requires the following changes in my first three principles of environmental justice:

> *A Principle of Human Defense*: Actions that defend oneself and other human beings against harmful aggression are permissible even when they necessitate killing or harming individual animals or plants or even destroying whole species or ecosystems.

> *A Principle of Human Preservation*: Actions that are necessary for meeting one's basic needs or the basic needs of other human beings are permissible even when they require aggressing against the basic needs of individual animals and plants or even of whole species or ecosystems.

> *A Principle of Disproportionality*: Actions that meet nonbasic or luxury needs of humans are prohibited when they aggress against the basic needs of individual animals and plants, or of whole species or ecosystems.

But while this modification is of theoretical interest since it allows that species and ecosystems as well as individuals count morally, it actually has little or no practical effect on the application of these principles. This is because, for the most part, the positive or negative impact the application of these principles would have on species and ecosystems is correspondingly reflected in the positive or negative impact the application of these principles would have on the individual members of those species or ecosystems. As a consequence, actions that are permitted or prohibited with respect to species and ecosystems according to the modified principles are already permitted or prohibited respectively through their correspondence with actions that are permitted or prohibited according to the unmodified principles.

However, this is not always the case. In fact, considerations about what benefits nonhuman species or subspecies as opposed to individuals of those species or subspecies have already figured in my previous argument. For example, I have argued for culling elk herds in wolf-free ranges, but this is primarily for the good of herds or species of elk and certainly not for the good of the particular elk who are being culled from those herds. Also I have argued that it would be for the good of farm animals generally that they be maintained under healthy conditions, and then killed relatively painlessly and eaten, rather than that they not be maintained at all. But clearly this is an argument about what would be good for existing flocks or herds, or species or subspecies of farm animals. It is not an argument about what would be good for the existing individual farm animals who would be killed relatively painlessly and eaten. Nevertheless, for the most part, because of the coincidence between the welfare of species and ecosystems and the welfare of individual members of those species and ecosystems, the two formulations of the first three principles turn out to be practically equivalent.

In sum, I have argued that whether we endorse an anthropocentric or a nonanthropocentric environmental ethics, we should favor a Principle of Human Defense, a Principle of Human Preservation, and a Principle of Disproportionality as I have interpreted them. In the past, failure to recognize the importance of a Principle of Human Defense and a Principle of Human Preservation has led philosophers to overestimate the amount of sacrifice required of humans.[19] By contrast, failure to recognize the importance of a Principle of Disproportionality has led philosophers to underestimate the amount of sacrifice required of humans.[20] I claim that taken together these three principles strike the right balance between concerns of human welfare and the welfare of nonhuman nature.

Notes

1 Aldo Leopold's view is usually interpreted as holistic in this sense. Leopold wrote "A thing is right when it tends to preserve the integrity, stability and beauty of the biotic community. It is wrong when it tends otherwise." See his *A Sand County Almanac* (Oxford, 1949).

2 For a defender of this view, see Paul Taylor, *Respect for Nature* (Princeton, 1987).

3 Where it is most likely to be morally required is where our negligent actions have caused the environmental problem in the first place.

4 Peter Singer's *Animal Liberation* (New York, 1975) inspired this view.

5 Baird Callicott, "Animal Liberation: A Triangular Affair," *Environmental Ethics* (1980), pp. 311–28.

6 Mark Sagoff, "Animal Liberation and Environmental Ethics: Bad Marriage, Quick Divorce," *Osgood Hall Law Journal* (1984), pp. 297–307.

7 Mary Ann Warren, "The Rights of the Nonhuman World," in *Environmental Philosophy*, edited by Robert Elliot and Arran Gare (London, 1983), pp. 109–34; and Baird Callicott, *In Defense of the Land Ethic* (Albany, 1989), chapter 3.

8 *Realities for the 90s* (Santa Cruz, 1991), p. 4.

9 Ibid., p. 5.

10 Mark Sagoff, "Animal Liberation," pp. 301–5.

11 Holmes Rolston, *Environmental Ethics* (Philadelphia, 1988), pp. 66–8; Murray Bookchin, *The Ecology of Freedom* (Montreal, 1991), p. xxxvi.

12 Eugene Hargrove, "Weak Anthropocentric Intrinsic Value," in *After Earth Day*, edited by Max Oelschlaeger (Denton, 1992), pp. 147ff.

13 Ibid., p. 151. Notice that there are at least two ways that X might intrinsically value Y. First, X might regard Y as good in itself for X or as an end in itself for X, by contrast with valuing Y instrumentally. Secondly, X might regard the good of Y as constraining the way that X can use Y. This second way of intrinsically valuing Y is the principal way we value human beings. It is the sense of value that Kantians are referring to when they claim that people should never be used as means only. Another way to put what I have been arguing is that we should extend this second way of intrinsically valuing to animals and plants.

14 Paul Taylor, *Respect for Nature*, pp. 68–71 and p. 17.

15 Ibid., pp. 68–71.

16 One way to think about species is as ongoing genetic lineages sequentially embodied in different organisms. See Lawrence Johnson, *A Morally Deep World* (New York: Cambridge University Press, 1991), p. 156; Holmes Rolston III, *Environmental Ethics*, chapter 4.

17 Ecosystems can be simple or complex, stable or unstable, and they can suffer total collapse.

18 Johnson, *A Morally Deep World*, chapter 6.

19 For example, in "Animal Liberation: A Triangular Affair," Baird Callicott had defended Edward Abbey's assertion that he would sooner shoot a man than a snake.

20 For example, Eugene Hargrove argues that from a traditional wildlife perspective, the lives of individual specimens of quite plentiful nonhuman species count for almost nothing at all. See chapter 4 of his *Foundations of Environmental Ethics* (Prentice-Hall, 1989).

60

The Power and the Promise of Ecological Feminism

Karen J. Warren

Introduction

Ecological feminism (ecofeminism) has begun to receive a fair amount of attention lately as an alternative feminist and environmental ethic. Since Françoise d'Eaubonne introduced the term *écoféminisme* in 1974 to bring attention to women's potential for bringing about an ecological revolution, the term has been used in a variety of ways. As I use the term in this paper, ecological feminism is the position that there are important connections – historical, experiential, symbolic, theoretical – between the domination of women and the domination of nature, an understanding of which is crucial to both feminism and environmental ethics. I argue that the promise and power of ecological feminism is that *it provides a distinctive framework both for reconceiving feminism and for developing an environmental ethic which takes seriously connections between the domination of women and the domination of nature*. I do so by discussing the nature of a feminist ethic and the ways in which ecofeminism provides a feminist and environmental ethic. I conclude that any feminist theory *and* any environmental ethic which fails to take seriously the twin and interconnected dominations of women and nature is at best incomplete and at worst simply inadequate.

Feminism, Ecological Feminism, and Conceptual Frameworks

Whatever else it is, feminism is at least the movement to end sexist oppression. It involves the elimination of any and all factors that contribute to the continued and systematic domination or subordination of women. While feminists disagree about the nature of and solutions to the subordination of women, all feminists agree that sexist oppression exists, is wrong, and must be abolished.

A "feminist issue" is any issue that contributes in some way to understanding the oppression of women. Equal rights, comparable pay for comparable work, and food production are feminist issues wherever and whenever an understanding of them contributes to an understanding of the continued exploitation or subjugation of women. Carrying water and searching for firewood are feminist issues wherever and whenever women's primary responsibility for these tasks contributes to their lack of full participation in decision making, income producing, or high status positions engaged in by men. What counts as a feminist issue, then, depends largely on context, particularly the historical and material conditions of women's lives.

Environmental degradation and exploitation are feminist issues because an understanding of them contributes to an understanding of the oppression of women. In India, for example, both deforestation and reforestation through the introduction of a monoculture-species tree (e.g., eucalyptus) intended for commercial production are feminist issues because the loss of indigenous forests and multiple species of trees has drastically affected rural Indian women's ability to maintain a subsistence household. Indigenous forests provide a variety of trees for food, fuel, fodder, household utensils, dyes, medicines, and income-generating uses, while monoculture-species forests do not. Although I do not argue for this claim here, a look at the global impact of environmental degradation on women's lives suggests important respects in which environmental degradation is a feminist issue.

Feminist philosophers claim that some of the most important feminist issues are *conceptual* ones: these issues concern how one conceptualizes such mainstay philosophical notions as reason and rationality, ethics, and what it is to be human. Ecofeminists extend this feminist philosophical concern to nature. They argue that, ultimately, some of the most important connections between the domination of women and the domination of nature are conceptual. To see this, consider the nature of conceptual frameworks.

A *conceptual framework* is a set of *basic* beliefs, values, attitudes, and assumptions which shape and reflect how one views oneself and one's world. It is a socially constructed lens through which we perceive ourselves and others. It is affected by such factors as gender, race, class, age, affectional orientation, nationality, and religious background.

Some conceptual frameworks are oppressive. An *oppressive conceptual framework* is one that explains, justifies, and maintains relationships of domination and subordination. When an oppressive conceptual framework is *patriarchal*, it explains, justifies, and maintains the subordination of women by men.

I have argued elsewhere that there are three significant features of oppressive conceptual frameworks: (1) value-hierarchical thinking, i.e., "up–down" thinking which places higher value, status, or prestige on what is "up" rather than on what is "down"; (2) value dualisms, i.e., disjunctive pairs in which the disjuncts are seen as oppositional (rather than as complementary) and exclusive (rather than as inclusive), and which place higher value (status, prestige) on one disjunct rather than the other (e.g., dualisms which give higher value or status to that which has historically been identified as "mind," "reason," and "male" than to that which has historically been identified as "body," "emotion," and "female"); and (3) logic of domination, i.e., a structure of argumentation which leads to a justification of subordination.

The third feature of oppressive conceptual frameworks is the most significant. A logic of domination is not *just* a logical structure. It also involves a substantive value system, since an ethical premise is needed to permit or sanction the "just" subordination of that which is subordinate. This justification typically is given on grounds of some alleged characteristic (e.g., rationality) which the dominant (e.g., men) have and the subordinate (e.g., women) lack.

Contrary to what many feminists and ecofeminists have said or suggested, there may be nothing *inherently* problematic about "hierarchical thinking" or even "value-hierarchical thinking" in contexts other than contexts of oppression. Hierarchical thinking is important in daily living for classifying data, comparing information, and organizing material. Taxonomies (e.g., plant taxonomies) and biological nomenclature seem to require *some* form of "hierarchical thinking." Even "value-hierarchical thinking" may be quite acceptable in certain contexts. (The same may be said of "value dualisms" in non-oppressive contexts.) For example, suppose it is true that what is unique about humans is our conscious capacity to radically reshape our social environments (or "societies"), as Murray Bookchin suggests. Then one could truthfully say that humans are better equipped to radically reshape their environments than are rocks or plants – a "value-hierarchical" way of speaking.

The problem is not simply *that* value-hierarchical thinking and value dualisms are used, but *the way* in which each has been used *in oppressive conceptual frameworks* to establish inferiority and to justify subordination.[1] It is the logic of domination, *coupled* with value-hierarchical thinking and value dualisms, which "justifies" subordination. What is explanatorily basic, then, about the nature of oppressive conceptual frameworks is the logic of domination.

For ecofeminism, that a logic of domination is explanatorily basic is important for at least three reasons. First, without a logic of domination, a description of similarities and differences would be just that – a description of similarities and differences. Consider the claim, "Humans are different from plants and rocks in that humans can (and plants and rocks cannot) consciously and radically reshape the communities in which they live; humans are similar to plants and rocks in that they are both members of an ecological community." Even if humans are "better" than plants and rocks with respect to the conscious ability of humans to radically transform communities, one does not *thereby* get any *morally* relevant distinction between humans and nonhumans, or an argument for the domination of plants and rocks by humans. To get *those* conclusions one needs to add at least two powerful assumptions, namely, (A2) and (A4) in argument A below:

(A1) Humans do, and plants and rocks do not, have the capacity to consciously and radically change the community in which they live.

(A2) Whatever has the capacity to consciously and radically change the community in which it lives is morally superior to whatever lacks this capacity.

(A3) Thus, humans are morally superior to plants and rocks.

(A4) For any X and Y, if X is morally superior to Y, then X is morally justified in subordinating Y.

(A5) Thus, humans are morally justified in subordinating plants and rocks.

Without the two assumptions that *humans are morally superior* to (at least some) nonhumans (A3), and that *superiority justifies subordination* (A4), all one has is some difference between humans and some nonhumans. This is true *even if* that difference is given in terms of superiority. Thus, it is the logic of domination (A4) which is the bottom line in ecofeminist discussions of oppression.

Second, ecofeminists argue that, at least in Western societies, the oppressive conceptual framework which sanctions the twin dominations of women and nature is a patriarchal one characterized by all three features of an oppressive conceptual framework. Many ecofeminists claim that, historically, within at least the dominant Western culture, a patriarchal conceptual framework has sanctioned the following argument B:

(B1) Women are identified with nature and the realm of the physical; men are identified with the "human" and the realm of the mental.

(B2) Whatever is identified with nature and the realm of the physical is inferior to ("below") whatever is identified with the "human" and the realm of the mental; or, conversely, the latter is superior to ("above") the former.

(B3)   Thus, women are inferior to ("below") men; or, conversely, men are superior to ("above") women.

(B4)   For any X and Y, if X is superior to Y, then X is justified in subordinating Y.

(B5)   Thus, men are justified in subordinating women.

If sound, argument B establishes *patriarchy*, i.e., the conclusion given at (B5) that the systematic domination of women by men is justified. But according to ecofeminists, (B5) is justified by just those three features of an oppressive conceptual framework identified earlier: value-hierarchical thinking, the assumption at (B2); value dualisms, the assumed dualism of the mental and the physical at (B1) and the assumed inferiority of the physical *vis-à-vis* the mental at (B2); and a logic of domination, the assumption at (B4), the same as the previous premise (A4). Hence, according to ecofeminists, insofar as an oppressive patriarchal conceptual framework has functioned historically (within at least dominant Western culture) to sanction the twin dominations of women and nature (argument B), both argument B and the patriarchal conceptual framework, from whence it comes, ought to be rejected.

Of course, the preceding does not identify which premises of B are false. What is the status of premises (B1) and (B2)? Most, if not all, feminists claim that (B1), and many ecofeminists claim that (B2), have been assumed or asserted within the dominant Western philosophical and intellectual tradition.[2] As such, these feminists assert, as a matter of historical fact, that the dominant Western philosophical tradition has assumed the truth of (B1) and (B2). Ecofeminists, however, either deny (B2) or do not affirm (B2). Furthermore, because some ecofeminists are anxious to deny any historical identification of women with nature, some ecofeminists deny (B1) when (B1) is used to support anything other than a strictly historical claim about what has been asserted or assumed to be true within patriarchal culture – e.g., when (B1) is used to assert that women properly are identified with the realm of nature and the physical.[3] Thus, from an ecofeminist perspective, (B1) and (B2) are properly viewed as problematic though historically sanctioned claims: they are problematic precisely because of the way they have functioned historically in a patriarchal conceptual framework and culture to sanction the dominations of women and nature.

What *all* ecofeminists agree about, then, is the way in which *the logic of domination* has functioned historically within patriarchy to sustain and justify the twin dominations of women and nature.[4] Since *all* feminists (and not just ecofeminists) oppose patriarchy, the conclusion given at (B5), all feminists (including ecofeminists) must oppose at least the logic of domination, premise (B4), on which argument B rests – whatever the truth-value status of (B1) and (B2) *outside* of a patriarchal context.

That *all* feminists must oppose the logic of domination shows the breadth and depth of the ecofeminist critique of B: it is a critique not only of the three assumptions on which this argument for the domination of women and nature rests, namely, the assumptions at (B1), (B2), and (B4); it is also a critique of patriarchal conceptual frameworks generally, i.e., of those oppressive conceptual frameworks which put men "up" and women "down," allege some way in which women are morally inferior to men, and use that alleged difference to justify the subordination of women by men. Therefore, ecofeminism is necessary to *any* feminist critique of patriarchy, and, hence, necessary to feminism (a point I discuss again later).

Third, ecofeminism clarifies why the logic of domination, and any conceptual framework which gives rise to it, must be abolished in order both to make possible a meaningful notion of difference which does not breed domination and to prevent feminism from becoming a "support" movement based primarily on shared experiences. In contemporary society, there is no one "woman's voice," no *woman* (or *human*) *simpliciter*: every woman (or human) is a woman (or human) of some race, class, age, affectional orientation, marital status, regional or national background, and so forth. Because there are no "monolithic experiences" that all women share, feminism must be a "solidarity movement" based on shared beliefs and interests rather than a "unity in sameness" movement based on shared experiences and shared victimization. In the words of Maria Lugones, "Unity – not to be confused with solidarity – is understood as conceptually tied to domination."

Ecofeminists insist that the sort of logic of domination used to justify the domination of humans by gender, racial or ethnic, or class status is also used to justify the domination of nature. Because eliminating a logic of domination is part of a feminist critique – whether a critique of patriarchy, white supremacist culture, or imperialism – ecofeminists insist that *naturism* is properly viewed as an integral part of any feminist solidarity movement to end sexist oppression and the logic of domination which conceptually grounds it.

Ecofeminism Reconceives Feminism

The discussion so far has focused on some of the oppressive conceptual features of patriarchy. As I use the phrase, the "logic of traditional feminism" refers to the location of the conceptual roots of sexist oppression, at least in Western societies, in an oppressive patriarchal conceptual framework characterized by a logic of domination. Insofar as other systems of oppression (e.g., racism, classism, ageism, heterosexism) are also conceptually maintained by a logic of domination, appeal to the logic of traditional feminism ultimately locates the basic conceptual interconnections among *all* systems of oppression in the logic of domination. It thereby explains at a *conceptual* level why the eradication of sexist oppression requires the eradication of the other forms of oppression. It is by clarifying this conceptual connection between systems of oppression that a movement to end sexist oppression – traditionally the special turf of feminist theory and practice – leads to a reconceiving of feminism as *a movement to end all forms of oppression.*

Suppose one agrees that the logic of traditional feminism requires the expansion of feminism to include other social systems of domination (e.g., racism and classism). What warrants the inclusion of nature in these "social systems of domination"? Why must the logic of traditional feminism include the abolition of "naturism" (i.e., the domination or oppression of nonhuman nature) among the "isms" feminism must confront? The conceptual justification for expanding feminism to include ecofeminism is twofold. One basis has already been suggested: by showing that the conceptual connections between the dual dominations of women and nature are located in an oppressive and, at least in Western societies, patriarchal conceptual framework characterized by a logic of domination, ecofeminism explains how and why feminism, conceived as a movement to end sexist oppression, must be expanded and reconceived as also a movement to end naturism. This is made explicit by the following argument C:

(C1)   Feminism is a movement to end sexism.
(C2)   But Sexism is conceptually linked with naturism (through an oppressive conceptual framework characterized by a logic of domination).
(C3)   Thus, Feminism is (also) a movement to end naturism.

Because, ultimately, these connections between sexism and naturism are conceptual – embedded in an oppressive conceptual framework – the logic of traditional feminism leads to the embracement of ecological feminism.

The other justification for reconceiving feminism to include ecofeminism has to do with the concepts of gender and nature. Just as conceptions of gender are socially constructed, so are conceptions of nature. Of course, the claim that women and nature are social constructions does not require anyone to deny that there are actual humans and actual trees, rivers, and plants. It simply implies that *how* women and nature are conceived is a matter of historical and social reality. These conceptions vary cross-culturally and by historical time period. As a result, any discussion of the "oppression or domination of nature" involves reference to historically specific forms of social domination of nonhuman nature by humans, just as discussion of the "domination of women" refers to historically specific forms of social domination of women by men. Although I do not argue for it here, an ecofeminist defense of the historical connections between the dominations of women and of nature, claims (B1) and (B2) in argument B, involves showing that within patriarchy the feminization of nature and the naturalization of women have been crucial to the historically successful subordinations of both.

If ecofeminism promises to reconceive traditional feminism in ways which include naturism as a legitimate feminist issue, does ecofeminism also promise to reconceive environmental ethics in ways which are feminist? I think so. This is the subject of the remainder of the paper.

Climbing from Ecofeminism to Environmental Ethics

Many feminists and some environmental ethicists have begun to explore the use of first-person narrative as a way of raising philosophically germane issues in ethics often lost or underplayed in mainstream philosophical ethics. Why is this so? What is it about narrative which makes it a significant resource for theory and practice in feminism and environmental ethics? Even if appeal to first-person narrative is a helpful literary device for describing ineffable experience or a legitimate social science methodology for documenting personal and social history, how is first-person narrative a valuable vehicle of argumentation for ethical decision making and theory building? One fruitful way to begin answering these questions is to ask them of a particular first-person narrative.

Consider the following first-person narrative about rock climbing:

> For my very first rock climbing experience, I chose a somewhat private spot, away from other climbers and on-lookers. After studying "the chimney," I focused all my energy on making it to the top. I climbed with intense determination, using whatever strength and skills I had to accomplish this challenging feat. By midway I was exhausted and anxious. I couldn't see what to do next – where to put my hands or feet. Growing increasingly more weary as I clung somewhat desperately to the rock, I made a move. It didn't work. I fell. There I was, dangling midair above the rocky ground below, frightened but terribly relieved that the belay rope had held me. I knew I was safe. I took a look up at the climb that remained. I was determined to make it to the top. With renewed confidence and concentration, I finished the climb to the top.
>
> On my second day of climbing, I rappelled down about 200 feet from the top of the Palisades at Lake Superior to just a few feet above the water level. I could see no one – not my belayer, not the other climbers, no one. I unhooked slowly from the rappel rope and took a deep cleansing breath. I looked all around me – really looked – and listened. I heard a cacophony of voices – birds, trickles of water on the rock before me, waves lapping against the rocks below. I closed my eyes and began to feel the rock with my hands – the cracks and crannies, the raised lichen and mosses, the almost imperceptible nubs that might provide a resting place for my

fingers and toes when I began to climb. At that moment I was bathed in serenity. I began to talk to the rock in an almost inaudible, child-like way, as if the rock were my friend. I felt an overwhelming sense of gratitude for what it offered me – a chance to know myself and the rock differently, to appreciate unforeseen miracles like the tiny flowers growing in the even tinier cracks in the rock's surface, and to come to know a sense of *being in relationship* with the natural environment. It felt as if the rock and I were silent conversational partners in a longstanding friendship. I realized then that I had come to care about this cliff which was so different from me, so unmovable and invincible, independent and seemingly indifferent to my presence. I wanted to be with the rock as I climbed. Gone was the determination to conquer the rock, to forcefully impose my will on it; I wanted simply to work respectfully with the rock as I climbed. And as I climbed, that is what I felt. I felt myself *caring* for this rock and feeling thankful that climbing provided the opportunity for me to know it and myself in this new way.

There are at least four reasons why use of such a first-person narrative is important to feminism and environmental ethics. First, such a narrative gives voice to a felt sensitivity often lacking in traditional analytical ethical discourse, namely, a sensitivity to conceiving of oneself as fundamentally "in relationship with" others, including the nonhuman environment. It is a modality which *takes relationships themselves seriously*. It thereby stands in contrast to a strictly reductionist modality that takes relationships seriously only or primarily because of the nature of the *relators* or parties to those relationships (e.g., relators conceived as moral agents, right holders, interest carriers, or sentient beings). In the rock-climbing narrative above, it is the climber's relationship with the rock she climbs which takes on special significance – which is itself a locus of value – in addition to whatever moral status or moral considerability she or the rock or any other parties to the relationship may also have.[5]

Second, such a first-person narrative gives expression to a variety of ethical attitudes and behaviors often overlooked or underplayed in mainstream Western ethics, e.g., the difference in attitudes and behaviors toward a rock when one is "making it to the top" and when one thinks of oneself as "friends with" or "caring about" the rock one climbs.[6] These different attitudes and behaviors suggest an ethically germane contrast between two different types of relationship humans or climbers may have toward a rock: an imposed conqueror-type relationship, and an emergent caring-type relationship. This contrast grows out of, and is faithful to, felt, lived experience.

The difference between conquering and caring attitudes and behaviors in relation to the natural environment provides a third reason why the use of first-person narrative is important to feminism and environmental ethics: it provides a way of conceiving of ethics and ethical meaning as *emerging out of* particular situations moral agents find themselves in, rather than as being *imposed on* those situations (e.g., as a derivation or instantiation of some predetermined abstract principle or rule). This emergent feature of narrative centralizes the importance of *voice*. When a multiplicity of cross-cultural *voices* are centralized, narrative is able to give expression to a range of attitudes, values, beliefs, and behaviors which may be overlooked or silenced by imposed ethical meaning and theory. As a reflection of and on felt, lived experiences, the use of narrative in ethics provides a stance from which ethical discourse can be held accountable to the historical, material, and social realities in which moral subjects find themselves.

Lastly, and for our purposes perhaps most importantly, the use of narrative has argumentative significance. Jim Cheney calls attention to this feature of narrative when he claims, "To contextualize ethical deliberation is, in some sense, to provide a narrative or story, from which the solution to the ethical dilemma emerges as the fitting conclusion." Narrative has argumentative force by suggesting *what counts* as an appropriate conclusion to an ethical situation. One ethical conclusion suggested by the climbing narrative is that what counts as a proper ethical attitude toward mountains and rocks is an attitude of respect and care (whatever that turns out to be or involve), not one of domination and conquest.

In an essay entitled "In and Out of Harm's Way: Arrogance and Love," feminist philosopher Marilyn Frye distinguishes between "arrogant" and "loving" perception as one way of getting at this difference in the ethical attitudes of care and conquest. Frye writes:

> The loving eye is a contrary of the arrogant eye.
>
> The loving eye knows the independence of the other. It is the eye of a seer who knows that nature is indifferent. It is the eye of one who knows that to know the seen, one must consult something other than one's own will and interests and fears and imagination. One must look at the thing. One must look and listen and check and question.
>
> The loving eye is one that pays a certain sort of attention. This attention can require a discipline but *not* a self-denial. The discipline is one of self-knowledge, knowledge of the scope and boundary of the self. . . . In particular, it is a matter of being able to tell one's own interests from those of others and of knowing where one's self leaves off and another begins. . . .
>
> The loving eye does not make the object of perception into something edible, does not try to assimilate it, does not reduce it to the size of the seer's desire, fear and imagination, and hence does not have to simplify. It knows the complexity of the other as something which will forever present new things to be known. The science of the loving eye would favor The Complexity Theory of Truth [in contrast to The Simplicity Theory of Truth] and presuppose The Endless Interestingness of the Universe.

According to Frye, the loving eye is not an invasive, coercive eye which annexes others to itself, but one which "knows the complexity of the other as something which will forever present new things to be known."

When one climbs a rock as a conqueror, one climbs with an arrogant eye. When one climbs with a loving eye, one constantly "must look and listen and check and question." One recognizes the rock as something very different, something perhaps totally indifferent to one's own presence, and finds in that difference joyous occasion for celebration. One knows "the boundary of the self," where the self – the "I," the climber – leaves off and the rock begins. There is no fusion of two into one, but a complement of two entities *acknowledged* as separate, different, independent, yet *in relationship*; they are in relationship *if only* because the loving eye is perceiving it, responding to it, noticing it, attending to it.

An ecofeminist perspective about both women and nature involves this shift in attitude from "arrogant perception" to "loving perception" of the nonhuman world. Arrogant perception of nonhumans by humans presupposes and maintains *sameness* in such a way that it expands the moral community to those beings who are thought to resemble (be like, similar to, or the same as) humans in some morally significant way. Any environmental movement or ethic based on arrogant perception builds a moral hierarchy of beings and assumes some common denominator of moral considerability in virtue of which like beings deserve similar treatment or moral consideration and unlike beings do not. Such environmental ethics are or generate a "unity in sameness." In contrast, "loving perception" presupposes and maintains *difference* – a distinction between the self and other, between human and at least some nonhumans – in such a way that perception of the other as other *is* an expression of love for one who/which is recognized at the outset as independent, dissimilar, different. As Maria Lugones says, in loving perception, "Love is seen not as fusion and erasure of difference but as incompatible with them." "Unity in sameness" alone is an *erasure of difference*.

"Loving perception" of the nonhuman natural world is an attempt to understand what it means *for humans* to care about the nonhuman world, a world *acknowledged* as being independent, different, perhaps even indifferent to humans. Humans *are* different from rocks in important ways, even if they are also both members of some ecological community. A moral community based on loving perception of oneself *in relationship with* a rock, or with the natural environment as a whole, is one which acknowledges and respects difference, whatever "sameness" also exists. The limits of loving perception are determined only by the limits of one's (e.g., a person's, a community's) ability to respond lovingly (or with appropriate care, trust, or friendship) – whether it is to other humans or to the nonhuman world and elements of it.

If what I have said so far is correct, then there are very different ways to climb a mountain and *how* one climbs it and *how* one narrates the experience of climbing it matter ethically. If one climbs with "arrogant perception," with an attitude of "conquer and control," one keeps intact the very sorts of thinking that characterize a logic of domination and an oppressive conceptual framework. Since the oppressive conceptual framework which sanctions the domination of nature is a patriarchal one, one also thereby keeps intact, even if unwittingly, a patriarchal conceptual framework. Because the dismantling of patriarchal conceptual frameworks is a feminist issue, *how* one climbs a mountain and *how* one narrates – or tells the story – about the experience of climbing also are *feminist issues*. In this way, ecofeminism makes visible why, at a conceptual level, environmental ethics is a feminist issue.

Conclusion

I have argued in this paper that ecofeminism provides a framework for a distinctively feminist and environmental ethics. Ecofeminism grows out of what is felt and theorized about connections between the domination of women and the domination of nature. As a contextualist ethic, ecofeminism refocuses environmental ethics on what nature might mean, morally speaking, *for* humans, and on how the relational attitudes of humans to others – humans as well as nonhumans – sculpt both what it is to be human and the nature and ground of human responsibilities to the nonhuman environment. Part of what this refocusing does is to take seriously the voices of women and other oppressed persons in the construction of that ethic.

A Sioux elder once told me a story about his son. He sent his seven-year-old son to live with the child's grandparents on a Sioux reservation so that he could "learn the Indian ways." Part of what the grandparents taught the son was how to hunt the four-leggeds of the forest. As I heard the story, the boy was taught, "to shoot your four-legged brother in his hind area, slowing it down but not killing it. Then, take the four legged's head in your hands, and look into his eyes. The eyes are where all the suffering is. Look into your brother's eyes and feel his pain. Then, take your knife and cut the four-legged under his chin, here, on his neck, so that he dies quickly. And as you do, ask your brother, the four-legged, for forgiveness for what you do. Offer also a prayer of thanks to your four-legged kin for offering his body to you just now, when you need food to eat and clothing to wear. And promise the four-legged that you will put yourself back into the earth when you die, to become nourishment for the earth, and for the sister flowers, and for the brother deer. It is appropriate that you should offer this blessing for the four-legged and, in due time, reciprocate in turn with your body in this way, as the four-legged gives life to you for your survival." As I reflect upon that story, I am struck by the power of the environmental ethic that grows out of and takes seriously narrative, context, and such values and relational attitudes as care, loving perception, and appropriate reciprocity, and doing what is appropriate in a given situation – however that notion of appropriateness eventually gets filled out. I am also struck by what one is able to see, once one begins to explore some of the historical and conceptual connections between the dominations of women and of nature. A *re-conceiving* and *re-visioning* of both feminism and environmental ethics, is, I think, the power and promise of ecofeminism.

Notes

1 It may be that in contemporary Western society, which is so thoroughly structured by categories of gender, race, class, age, and affectional orientation, that there simply is no meaningful notion of "value-hierarchical thinking" which does not function in an oppressive context. For purposes of this paper, I leave that question open.

2 Many feminists who argue for the historical point that claims (B1) and (B2) have been asserted or assumed to be true within the dominant Western philosophical tradition do so by discussion of that tradition's conceptions of reason, rationality, and science. For a sampling of the sorts of claims made within that context, see "Reason, Rationality, and Gender," ed. Nancy Tuana and Karen J. Warren, a special issue of the American Philosophical Association's *Newsletter on Feminism and Philosophy*, 88, no. 2 (March 1989): 17–71. Ecofeminists who claim that (B2) has been assumed to be true within the dominant Western philosophical tradition include: Gray, *Green Paradise Lost*; Griffin, *Woman and Nature: The Roaring Inside Her*; Merchant, *The Death of Nature*; Ruether, *New Woman/New Earth*. For a discussion of some of these ecofeminist historical accounts, see Plumwood, "Ecofeminism." While I agree that the historical connection between the domination of women and the domination of nature is a crucial one, I do not argue for that claim here.

3 Ecofeminists who deny (B1) when (B1) is *offered* as anything other than a true, descriptive, historical claim about patriarchal culture often do so on grounds that an objectionable sort of biological determinism, or at least harmful female sex gender stereotypes, underlie (B1). For a discussion of this "split" among those ecofeminists ("nature feminists")

who assert and those ecofeminists ("social feminists") who deny (B1) as anything other than a true historical claim about how women are described in patriarchal culture, see Griscom, "On Healing the Nature/History Split."

4 I make no attempt here to defend the historically sanctioned truth of these premises.

5 Suppose, as I think is the case, that a necessary condition for the existence of a moral relationship is that at least one party to the relationship is a moral being (leaving open for our purposes what counts as a "moral being"). If this is so, then the Mona Lisa cannot properly be said to have or stand in a moral relationship with the wall on which she hangs, and a wolf cannot have or properly be said to have or stand in a moral relationship with a moose. Such a necessary-condition account leaves open the question whether *both* parties to the relationship must be moral beings. My point here is simply that however one resolves *that* question, recognition of the relationships themselves as a locus of value is a recognition of a source of value that is different from and not reducible to the values of the "moral beings" in those relationships.

6 It is interesting to note that the image of being friends with the Earth is one which cytogeneticist Barbara McClintock uses when she describes the importance of having "a feeling for the organism," "listening to the material (in this case the corn plant)," in one's work as a scientist. See Evelyn Fox Keller, "Women, Science, and Popular Mythology," in *Machina Ex Dea: Feminist Perspectives on Technology*, ed. Joan Rothschild (New York: Pergamon Press, 1983); and Evelyn Fox Keller, *A Feeling For the Organism: The Life and Work of Barbara McClintock* (San Francisco: W. H. Freeman, 1983).

61

Animal Liberation: A Triangular Affair

J. Baird Callicott

Preface (1994)

I wrote "A Triangular Affair" to sharply distinguish environmental ethics from animal liberation/rights when the former seemed to be overshadowed by the latter. Back in the late 1970s and early 1980s, when the piece was conceived and composed, many people seemed to conflate the two. In my youthful zeal to draw attention to the then unheralded Leopold land ethic, I made a few remarks that in retrospect appear irresponsible.

Most important, I no longer think that the land ethic is misanthropic. "All ethics so far evolved." Leopold wrote, "rest upon a single premiss: that the individual is a member of a community of interdependent parts. . . . The land ethic simply enlarges the boundaries of the community to include soils, waters, plants, and animals, or collectively: the land." The biotic community and its correlative land ethic *does not replace* our several human communities and their correlative ethics – our duties and obligations to family and family members, to municipality and fellow-citizens, to country and countrymen, to humanity and human beings. Rather it *supplements* them. Hence the land ethic leaves our traditional human morality quite intact and pre-emptive.

Second in importance, I now think that we do in fact have duties and obligations – implied by the essentially communitarian premisses of the land ethic – to domestic animals, as well as to wild fellow-members of the biotic community and to the biotic community as a whole. Farm animals, work animals, and pets have long been members of what Mary Midgley calls the "mixed" community. They have entered into a kind of implicit social contract with us which lately we have abrogated. Think of it this way. Each of us belongs to several hierarchically ordered human communities, each with its peculiar set of duties and obligations: to various mixed human–animal domestic communities, with their peculiar sets of duties and obligations; and to the biotic community, with its peculiar set of duties and obligations (which in sum Leopold called the land ethic). The land ethic no more eclipses our moral responsibilities in regard to domestic animals than it does our moral responsibilities in regard to other people.

Further, I now think that a vegetarian diet is indicated by the land ethic, no less than by the animal welfare ethics. Rainforests are felled to make pasture for cattle. Better for the environment if we ate forest fruits instead of beef. Livestock ruin watercourses and grasslands. And raising field crops for animal feed increases soil erosion and ground-water depletion.

Finally, though certainly I still wish there were far more bears than actually there are, a target ratio of one bear for every two people seems a bit extravagant.

"A Triangular Affair" clearly distinguishes between holistic environmental ethics, on the one hand, and individualistic "moral humanism" and "humane moralism," on the other. And that remains a serviceable distinction. Moralists of every stripe, however, must make common cause against the forces that are often simultaneously destroying human, mixed, and biotic communities. The differences between human, humane, and environmental concerns are real, and sometimes conflictive. But just as often they are convergent and mutually reinforcing. And all our ethical concerns can be theoretically unified, I am convinced, by a communitarian moral philosophy, thus enabling conflicts, when they do arise, to be adjudicated rationally.

Environmental Ethics and Animal Liberation

Partly because it is so new to Western philosophy (or at least heretofore only scarcely represented), *environmental ethics* has no precisely fixed conventional definition in glossaries of philosophical terminology. Aldo Leopold, however, is universally recognized as the father or founding genius of recent environmental ethics. His "land ethic" has become a modern classic and may be treated as the standard example, the paradigm case, as it were, of what an environmental ethic is. *Environmental ethics* then can be defined ostensively by using Leopold's land ethic as the exemplary type. I do not mean to suggest that all environmental ethics should necessarily conform to Leopold's paradigm, but the extent to which an ethical system resembles Leopold's land ethic might be used, for want of anything better, as a criterion to measure the extent to which it is or is not of the environmental sort.

It is Leopold's opinion, and certainly an overall review of the prevailing traditions of Western ethics, both popular and philosophical, generally confirms it, that traditional Western systems of ethics have not accorded moral standing to nonhuman beings.[1] Animals and plants, soils and waters, which Leopold includes in his community of ethical beneficiaries, have traditionally enjoyed no moral standing, no rights, no respect, in sharp contrast to human persons whose rights and interests ideally must be fairly and equally considered if our actions are to be considered "ethical" or "moral." One fundamental and novel feature of the Leopold land ethic, therefore, is the extension of *direct* ethical considerability from people to nonhuman natural entities.

At first glance, the recent ethical movement usually labeled "animal liberation" or "animal rights" seems to be squarely and centrally a kind of environmental ethics.[2] The more uncompromising among the animal liberationists have demanded equal moral consideration on behalf of cows, pigs, chickens, and other apparently enslaved and oppressed nonhuman animals.[3] The theoreticians of this new hyper-egalitarianism have coined such terms as *speciesism* (on analogy with *racism* and *sexism*) and *human chauvinism* (on analogy with *male chauvinism*), and have made animal liberation seem, perhaps not improperly, the next and most daring development of political liberalism.[4] Aldo Leopold also draws upon metaphors of political liberalism when he tells us that his land ethic "changes the role of *Homo sapiens* from conqueror of the land community to plain member and citizen of it."[5] For animal liberationists it is as if the ideological battles for equal rights and equal consideration for women and for racial minorities have been all but won, and the next and greatest challenge is to purchase equality, first theoretically and then practically, for all (actually only *some*) animals, regardless of species. This more rhetorically implied than fully articulated historical progression of moral rights from fewer to greater numbers of "persons" (allowing that animals may also be persons), as advocated by animal liberationists, also parallels Leopold's scenario in "The Land Ethic" of the historical extension of "ethical criteria" to more and more "fields of conduct" and to larger and larger groups of people during the past three thousand or so years.[6] As Leopold develops it, the land ethic is a cultural "evolutionary possibility," the next "step in a sequence."[7] For Leopold, however, the next step is much more sweeping, much more inclusive than the animal liberationists envision, since it "enlarges the boundaries of the [moral] community to include soils, waters, [and] plants . . ." as well as animals.[8] Thus, the animal liberation movement *could* be construed as partitioning Leopold's perhaps undigestable and totally inclusive environmental ethic into a series of more assimilable stages: today animal rights, tomorrow equal rights for plants, and after that full moral standing for rocks, soil, and other earthy compounds, and perhaps sometime in the still more remote future, liberty and equality for water and other elementary bodies.

Put just this way, however, there is something jarring about such a graduated progression in the exfoliation of a more inclusive environmental ethic, something that seems absurd. A more or less reasonable case might be made for rights for some animals, but when we come to plants, soils, and waters, the frontier between plausibility and absurdity appears to have been crossed. Yet, there is no doubt that Leopold sincerely proposes that *land* (in his inclusive sense) be ethically regarded. The beech and chestnut, for example, have in his view as much "biotic right" to life as the wolf and the deer, and the effects of human actions on mountains and streams for Leopold is an ethical concern as genuine and serious as the comfort and longevity of brood hens.[9] In fact, Leopold to all appearances never considered the treatment of brood hens on a factory farm or steers in a feed lot to be a pressing moral issue. He seems much more concerned about the integrity of the farm *wood lot* and the effects of clear-cutting steep slopes on neighboring *streams*.

Animal liberationists put their ethic into practice (and display their devotion to it) by becoming vegetarians, and the moral complexities of vegetarianism have been thoroughly debated in the recent literature as an adjunct issue to animal rights.[10] (No one however has yet expressed, as among Butler's Erewhonians, qualms about eating plants, though such sentiments might be expected to be latently present, if the rights of plants are next to be defended.) Aldo Leopold, by contrast, did not even condemn hunting animals, let alone eating them, nor did he personally abandon hunting, for which he had had an enthusiasm since boyhood, upon becoming convinced that his ethical responsibilities extended beyond the human sphere.[11] There are several interpretations for this behavioral peculiarity. One is that Leopold did not see that his land ethic actually ought to prohibit hunting, cruelly killing, and eating animals. A corollary of this interpretation is that Leopold was so unperspicacious as deservedly to be thought stupid – a conclusion hardly comporting with the intellectual subtlety he usually evinces in most other respects. If not stupid, then perhaps Leopold was hypocritical. But if a hypocrite, we should expect him to conceal his proclivity for blood sports and flesh eating and to treat them as shameful vices to be indulged secretively. As it is, bound together between the same covers with "The Land Ethic" are his unabashed reminiscences of killing and consuming *game*.[12] This term (like *stock*) when used of animals, moreover, appears to be morally equivalent to referring to a sexually appealing young woman as a "piece" or to a strong, young black man as a "buck" – if animal rights, that is, are to be considered as on a par with women's rights and the rights of formerly enslaved races. A third interpretation of Leopold's approbation of regulated and disciplined sport hunting (and *a fortiori* meat eating) is that it is a form of human/animal behavior not inconsistent with the land ethic as he conceived it. A corollary of this interpretation is that Leopold's land ethic and the environmental ethic of the animal liberation movement rest upon very different theoretical foundations, and that they are thus two very different forms of environmental ethics.

The urgent concern of animal liberationists for the suffering of *domestic* animals, toward which Leopold manifests an attitude which can only be described as indifference, and the urgent concern of Leopold, on the other hand, for the disappearance of *species* of plants as well as animals and for soil erosion and stream pollution, appear to be symptoms not only of very different ethical perspectives, but of profoundly different cosmic visions as well. The neat similarities, noted at the beginning of this discussion, between the environmental ethic of the animal liberation movement and the classical Leopoldian land ethic appear in light of these observations to be rather superficial and to conceal substrata of thought and value which are not at all similar. The theoretical foundations of the animal liberation movement and those of the Leopoldian land ethic may even turn out not to be companionable, complementary, or mutually consistent. The animal liberationists may thus find themselves not only engaged in controversy with the many conservative philosophers upholding *apartheid* between man and "beast," but also faced with an unexpected dissent from another, very different, system of environmental ethics.[13] Animal liberation and animal rights may well prove to be a triangular rather than, as it has so far been represented in the philosophical community, a polar controversy.

Ethical Humanism and Humane Moralism

The orthodox response of "ethical humanism" (as this philosophical perspective may be styled) to the suggestion that nonhuman animals should be accorded moral standing is that such animals are not worthy of this high perquisite. Only human beings are rational, or capable of having interests, or possess *self*-awareness, or have linguistic abilities, or can represent the future, it is variously argued.[14] These essential attributes taken singly or in various combinations make people somehow exclusively deserving of moral consideration. The so-called "lower animals," it is insisted, lack the crucial qualification for ethical considerability and so may be treated (albeit humanely, according to some, so as not to brutalize man) as things or means, not as persons or as ends.[15]

The theoreticians of the animal liberation movement ("humane moralists" as they may be called) typically reply as follows.[16] Not all human beings qualify as worthy of moral regard, according to the various criteria specified. Therefore, by parity of reasoning, human persons who do not so qualify as moral patients may be treated, as animals often are, as mere things or means (e.g., used in vivisection experiments, disposed of if their existence is inconvenient, eaten, hunted, etc., etc.). But the ethical humanists would be morally outraged if irrational and inarticulate infants, for example, were used in painful or lethal medical experiments, or if severely retarded people were hunted for pleasure. Thus, the double-dealing, the hypocrisy, of ethical humanism appears to be exposed.[17] Ethical humanism, though claiming to discriminate between worthy and unworthy ethical patients on the basis of objective criteria impartially applied, turns out after all, it seems, to be *speciesism*, a philosophically indefensible prejudice (analogous to racial prejudice) against animals. The tails side of this argument is that some animals, usually the "higher" lower animals (cetaceans, other primates, etc.), as ethological studies seem to indicate, may meet the criteria specified for moral worth, although the ethical humanists, even so, are not prepared to grant them full dignity and the rights of persons. In short, the ethical humanists' various criteria for moral standing do not include all or only human beings, humane moralists argue, although in practice ethical humanism wishes to make the class of morally considerable beings coextensive with the class of human beings.

The humane moralists, for their part, insist upon *sentience* (*sensibility* would have been a more precise word choice) as the only relevant capacity a being need possess to enjoy full moral standing. If animals, they argue, are conscious entities who, though deprived of reason, speech, forethought or even *self*-awareness (however that may be judged), are capable of suffering, then their suffering should be as much a matter of ethical concern as that of our fellow human beings, or strictly speaking, as our very own. What, after all, has rationality or any of the other allegedly uniquely human capacities to do with ethical standing? Why, in other words, should beings who reason or use speech (etc.) qualify for moral status, and those who do not fail to qualify?[18] Isn't this just like saying that only persons with white skin should be free, or that only persons who beget and not those who bear should own property? The criterion seems utterly unrelated to the benefit for which it selects. On the other hand, the capacity to suffer is, it seems, a more relevant criterion for moral standing because – as Bentham and Mill, notable among modern philosophers, and Epicurus, among the ancients, aver – pain is evil, and its opposite, pleasure and freedom from pain, good. As moral agents (and this seems axiomatic), we have a duty to behave in such a way that the effect of our actions is to promote and procure good, so far as possible, and to reduce and minimize evil. That would amount to an obligation to produce pleasure and reduce pain. Now pain is pain wherever and by whomever it is suffered. As a *moral* agent, I should not consider my pleasure and pain to be of greater consequence in determining a course of action than that of other persons. Thus, by the same token, if animals suffer pain – and among philosophers only strict Cartesians would deny that they do – then we are morally obliged to consider their suffering as much an evil to be minimized by conscientious moral agents as human suffering.[19] Certainly actions of ours which contribute to the suffering of animals, such as hunting them, butchering and eating them, experimenting on them, etc., are on these assumptions morally reprehensible. Hence, a person who regards himself or herself as not aiming in life to live most selfishly, conveniently, or profitably, but rightly and in accord with practical principle, if convinced by these arguments, should, among other things, cease to eat the flesh of animals, to hunt them, to wear fur and leather clothing and bone ornaments and other articles made from the bodies of animals, to eat eggs and drink milk, if the animal producers of these commodities are retained under inhumane circumstances, and to patronize zoos (as sources of psychological if not physical torment of animals). On the other hand, since certain very simple animals are almost certainly insensible to pleasure and pain, they may and indeed should be treated as morally inconsequential. Nor is there any *moral* reason why trees should be respected or rivers or mountains or anything which is, though living or tributary to life processes, unconscious. The humane moralists, like the moral humanists, draw a firm distinction between those beings worthy of moral consideration and those not. They simply insist upon a different but quite definite cut-off point on the spectrum of natural entities, and accompany their criterion with arguments to show that it is more ethically defensible (granting certain assumptions) and more consistently applicable than that of the moral humanists.[20]

The First Principle of the Land Ethic

The fundamental principle of humane moralism, as we see, is Benthamic. Good is equivalent to pleasure and, more pertinently, evil is equivalent to pain. The presently booming controversy between moral humanists and humane moralists appears, when all the learned dust has settled, to be essentially internecine; at least, the lines of battle are drawn along familiar watersheds of the conceptual terrain.[21] A classical ethical theory, Bentham's, has been refitted and pressed into service to meet relatively new and unprecedented ethically relevant situations – the problems raised especially by factory farming and ever more exotic and frequently ill-conceived scientific research employing animal subjects. Then, those with Thomist, Kantian, Lockean, Moorean (etc.) ethical affiliation have heard the bugle and have risen to arms. It is no wonder that so many academic philosophers have been drawn into the fray. The issues have an apparent newness about them; moreover, they are socially and politically *avant garde*. But there is no serious challenge to cherished first principles.[22] Hence, without having to undertake any creative ethical reflection or exploration, or any reexamination of historical ethical theory, a fresh debate has been stirred up. The familiar historical positions have simply been retrenched, applied, and exercised.

But what about the third (and certainly minority) party to the animal liberation debate? What sort of reasonable and coherent moral theory would at once urge that animals (and plants and soils and waters) be included in the same class with people as beings to whom ethical consideration is owed and yet not object to some of them being slaughtered (whether painlessly or not) and eaten, others hunted, trapped, and in various other ways seemingly cruelly used? Aldo Leopold provides a concise statement of what might be called the categorical imperative or principal precept of the land ethic: "A thing is right when it tends to preserve the integrity, stability, and beauty of the biotic community. It is wrong when it tends otherwise."[23] What is especially note worthy, and that to which attention should be directed in this proposition, is the idea that the good of the biotic *community* is the ultimate measure of the moral value, the rightness or wrongness, of actions. Thus, to hunt and kill a white-tailed deer in certain districts may not only be ethically permissible, it might actually be a moral requirement, necessary to protect the local environment, taken as a whole, from the disintegrating effects of a cervid population explosion. On the other hand, rare and endangered animals like the lynx should be especially nurtured and preserved. The lynx, cougar, and other wild feline predators, from the neo-Benthamite perspective (if consistently and evenhandedly applied), should be regarded as merciless, wanton, and incorrigible murderers of their fellow creatures, who not only kill, it should be added, but cruelly toy with their victims, thus increasing the measure of pain in the world. From the perspective of the land ethic, predators generally should be nurtured and preserved as critically important members of the biotic communities to which they are native. Certain plants, similarly, may be overwhelmingly important to the stability, integrity, and beauty of biotic communities, while some animals, such as domestic sheep (allowed perhaps by egalitarian and humane herdspersons to graze freely and to reproduce themselves without being harvested for lamb and mutton) could be a pestilential threat to the natural floral community of a given locale. Thus, the land ethic is logically coherent in demanding at once that moral consideration be given to plants as well as to animals and yet in permitting animals to be killed, trees felled, and so on. In every case the effect upon ecological systems is the decisive factor in the determination of the ethical quality of actions. . . .

The Land Ethic and the Ecological Point of View

. . . Since ecology focuses upon the relationships between and among things, it inclines its students toward a more holistic vision of the world. Before the rather recent emergence of ecology as a science the landscape appeared to be, one might say, a collection of objects, some of them alive, some conscious, but all the same, an aggregate, a plurality of separate individuals. With this "atomistic" representation of things it is no wonder that moral issues might be understood as competing and mutually contradictory clashes of the "rights" of separate individuals, each separately pursuing its "interests." Ecology has made it possible to apprehend the same landscape as an articulate unity (without the least hint of mysticism or ineffability). Ordinary organic bodies have articulated and discernible parts (limbs, various organs, myriad cells); yet, because of the character of the network of relations among those parts, they form in a perfectly familiar sense a second-order whole. Ecology makes it possible to see land, similarly, as a unified system of integrally related parts, as, so to speak, a third-order organic whole.[24]

Another analogy that has helped ecologists to convey the particular holism which their science brings to reflective attention is that land is integrated as a human community is integrated. The various parts of the "biotic community" (individual animals and plants) depend upon one another *economically* so that the system as such acquires distinct characteristics of its own. Just as it is possible to characterize and define collectively peasant societies, agrarian communities, industrial complexes, capitalist, communist, and socialist economic systems, and so on, ecology characterizes and defines various biomes as desert, savanna, wetland, tundra, woodland, etc., communities, each with its particular "professions," "roles," or "niches."

Now we may think that among the duties we as moral agents have toward ourselves is the duty of self-preservation, which may be interpreted as a duty to maintain our own organic integrity. It is not uncommon in historical moral theory, further, to find that in addition to those peculiar responsibilities we have in relation both to ourselves and to other persons severally, we also have a duty to behave in ways that do not harm the fabric of society *per se*. The land ethic, in similar fashion, calls our attention to the recently discovered integrity – in other words, the unity – of the biota, and posits duties binding upon moral agents in relation to that whole. Whatever the strictly formal logical connections between the concept of a social community and moral responsibility, there appears to be a strong psychological bond between that idea and conscience. Hence, the representation of the natural environment as, in Leopold's terms, "one humming community" (or, less consistently in his discussion, a third-order organic being) brings into play, whether rationally or not, those stirrings of conscience which we feel in relation to delicately complex, functioning social and organic systems.[25]

The neo-Benthamite humane moralists have, to be sure, digested one of the metaphysical implications of modern biology. They insist that human beings must be understood continuously with the rest of organic nature. People are (and are only) animals, and much of the rhetorical energy of the animal liberation movement is spent in fighting a rear-guard action for this aspect of Darwinism against those philosophers who still cling to the dream of a special metaphysical status for people in the order of "creation." To this extent the animal liberation movement is biologically enlightened and argues from the taxonomical and evolu-tionary continuity of man and beast to moral standing for some nonhuman animals. Indeed, pain, in their view the very substance of evil, is something that is conspicuously common to people and other sensitive animals, something that we as people experience not in virtue of our metasimian cerebral capabilities, but because of our participation in a more gener-ally animal, limbic-based consciousness. *If* it is pain and suffering that is the ultimate evil besetting human life, and this not in virtue of our humanity but in virtue of our ani-mality, then it seems only fair to promote freedom from pain for those animals who share with us in this mode of experience and to grant them rights similar to ours as a means to this end.

Recent ethological studies of other primates, ceteceans, and so on, are not infrequently cited to drive the point home, but the biological information of the animal liberation move-ment seems to extend no further than this – the continuity of human with other animal life forms. The more recent ecological perspective especially seems to be ignored by humane moralists. The holistic outlook of ecology and the associated value premium conferred upon the biotic community, its beauty, integrity, and stability may simply not have penetrated the thinking of the animal liberationists, or it could be that to include it would involve an intolerable contradiction with the Benthamite foundations of their ethical theory. Bentham's view of the "interests of the community" was bluntly reductive. With his characteristic bluster, Bentham wrote, "The community is a fictitious *body* composed of the individual persons who are considered as constituting as it were its *members*. The interest of the community then is, what? – the sum of the interests of the several members who compose it."[26] Bentham's very simile – the community is like a body composed of members – gives the lie to his reduction of its interests to the sum of its parts taken severally. The interests of a person are not those of his or her cells summed up and averaged out. Our organic health and well-being, for example, require vigorous exercise and metabolic stimulation, which cause stress and often pain to various parts of the body and a more rapid turnover in the life cycle of our individual cells. For the sake of the person taken as a whole, some parts may be, as it were, unfairly sacrificed. On the level of social organization, the interests of society may not always coincide with the sum of the interests of its parts. Discipline, sacrifice, and individual restraint are often necessary in the social sphere to maintain social integrity as within the bodily organism. A society, indeed, is particularly vulnerable to disintegration when its members become preoccupied totally with their own particular interest, and ignore those distinct and independent interests of the community as a whole. One example, unfor-tunately, our own society, is altogether too close at hand to be examined with strict aca-demic detachment. The United States seems to pursue uncritically a social policy of reductive utilitarianism, aimed at promoting the happiness of all its members severally. Each special interest accordingly clamors more loudly to be satisfied while the community as a whole becomes noticeably more and more infirm economically, environmentally, and politically.

The humane moralists, whether or not they are consciously and deliberately following Bentham on this particular, nevertheless, in point of fact, are committed to the welfare of certain kinds of animals distributively or reductively in applying their moral concern for nonhuman beings.[27] They lament the treatment of animals, most frequently farm and laboratory animals, and plead the special interests of these beings. We might ask, from the perspective of the land ethic, what the effect upon the natural environment taken as a whole would be if domestic animals were actually liberated? There is, almost certainly, very little real danger that this might actually happen, but it would be instructive to speculate on the ecological consequences.

Ethical Holism

Before we take up this question, however, some points of interest remain to be considered on the matter of a holistic versus a reductive environmental ethic. To pit the one against the other as I have done without further qualification would be mistaken. A society is constituted by its members, an organic body by its cells, and the ecosystem by the plants, animals, minerals, fluids, and gases which compose it. One cannot affect a system as a whole without affecting at least some of its components. An environmental ethic which takes as its *summum bonum* the integrity, stability, and beauty of the biotic community is not conferring moral standing on something *else* besides plants, animals, soils, and waters. Rather, the former, the good of the community as a whole, serves as a standard for the assessment of the relative value and relative ordering of its constitutive parts and therefore provides a means of adjudicating the often mutually contradictory demands of the parts considered separately for *equal* consideration. If diversity does indeed contribute to stability (a classical "law" of ecology), then *specimens* of rare and endangered species, for example, have a *prima facie* claim to preferential consideration from the perspective of the land ethic. Animals of those species, which, like the honey bee, function in ways critically important to the economy of nature, moreover, would be granted a greater claim to moral attention than psychologically more complex and sensitive ones, say, rabbits and moles, which seem to be plentiful, globally distributed, reproductively efficient, and only routinely integrated into the natural economy. Animals and plants, mountains, rivers, seas, the atmosphere are the *immediate* practical beneficiaries of the land ethic. The well-being of the biotic community, the biosphere as a whole, cannot be logically separated from their survival and welfare.

Some suspicion may arise at this point that the land ethic is ultimately grounded in *human* interests, not in those of nonhuman natural entities. Just as we might prefer a sound and attractive house to one in the opposite condition, so the "goodness" of a whole, stable, and beautiful environment seems rather to be of the instrumental, not the autochthonous, variety. The question of ultimate value is a very sticky one for environmental as well as for all ethics and cannot be fully addressed here. It is my view that there can be no value apart from an evaluator, that all value is as it were in the eye of the beholder. The value that is attributed to the ecosystem, therefore, is humanly dependent or (allowing that other living things may take a certain delight in the well-being of the whole of things, or that the gods may) at least dependent upon some variety of morally and aesthetically sensitive consciousness. Granting this, however, there is a further, very crucial distinction to be drawn. It is possible that while things may only have value because we (or someone) values them, they may nonetheless be valued for themselves as well as for the contribution they might make to the realization of our (or someone's) interests. Children are valued for themselves by most parents. Money, on the other hand, has only an instrumental or indirect value. Which sort of value has the health of the biotic community and its members severally for Leopold and the land ethic? It is especially difficult to separate these two general sorts of value, the one of moral significance, the other merely selfish, when something that may be valued in *both ways at once* is the subject of consideration. Are pets, for example, well-treated, like children, for the sake of themselves, or, like mechanical appliances, because of the sort of services they provide their owners? Is a healthy biotic community something we value because we are so utterly and (to the biologically well-informed) so obviously dependent upon it not only for our happiness but for our very survival, or may we also perceive it disinterestedly as having an independent worth? Leopold insists upon a noninstrumental value for the biotic community and *mutatis mutandis* for its constituents. According to Leopold, collective enlightened self-interest on the part of human beings does not go far enough; the land ethic in his opinion (and no doubt this reflects his own moral intuitions) requires "love, respect, and admiration for land, and a high regard for its value." The land ethic, in Leopold's view, creates "obligations over and above self-interest." And "obligations have no meaning without conscience, and the problem we face is the extension of the social conscience from people to land."[28] If, in other words, any genuine ethic is possible, if it is possible to value *people* for the sake of themselves, then it is equally possible to value *land* in the same way.

Some indication of the genuinely biocentric value orientation of ethical environmentalism is indicated in what otherwise might appear to be gratuitous misanthropy. The biospheric perspective does not exempt *Homo sapiens* from moral evaluation in relation to the well-being of the community of nature taken as a whole. The preciousness of individual deer, as of any other specimen, is inversely proportional to the population of the species. Environmentalists, however reluctantly and painfully, do not omit to apply the same logic to their own kind. As omnivores, the population of human beings should, perhaps, be roughly twice that of bears, allowing for differences of size. A global population of more than four billion persons and showing no signs of an orderly decline presents an alarming prospect to humanists, but it is at present a global disaster (the more *per capita* prosperity, indeed, the more disastrous it appears) for the biotic community. If the land ethic were only a means of managing nature for the sake of man, misleadingly phrased in moral terminology, then man would be considered as having an ultimate value essentially different from that of his "resources." The extent of misanthropy in modern environmentalism thus may be taken as a measure of the degree to which it is biocentric. Edward Abbey in his enormously popular *Desert Solitaire* bluntly states that he would sooner shoot a man than a snake.[29] Abbey may not be simply depraved; this is perhaps only his way of dramatically making the point that the human population has become so disproportionate from the biological point of view that if one had to choose between a specimen of *Homo sapiens* and a specimen of a rare even if unattractive species, the choice would be moot. Among academicians, Garret Hardin, a human ecologist by discipline who has written extensively on ethics, environmental and otherwise, has shocked philosophers schooled in the preciousness of human life with his "lifeboat" and "survival" ethics and his "wilderness economics." In context of the latter, Hardin recommends limiting access to wilderness by criteria of hardiness and woodcraft and would permit no emergency roads or airborne rescue vehicles to violate the pristine purity of wilderness areas. If a wilderness adventurer should have a serious accident, Hardin recommends that he or she get out on his or her own or die in the attempt. Danger, from the strictly human-centered, psychological perspective, is part of the wilderness experience, Hardin argues, but in all probability his more important concern is to protect from mechanization the remnants of wild country that remain even if the price paid is the incidental loss of human life which, from the perspective once more of the biologist, is a commodity altogether too common in relation to wildlife and to wild landscapes.[30] . . .

. . . Modern systems of ethics have, it must be admitted, considered the principle of the equality of persons to be inviolable. This is true, for example, of both major schools of modern ethics, the utilitarian school going back to Bentham and Mill, and the deontological, originating with Kant. The land ethic manifestly does not accord equal moral worth to each and every member of the biotic community; the moral worth of individuals (including, n.b., human individuals) is relative, to be assessed in accordance with the particular relation of each to the collective entity which Leopold called "land."

There is, however, a classical Western ethic, with the best philosophical credentials, which assumes a similar holistic posture (with respect to the social moral sphere). I have in mind Plato's moral and social philosophy. Indeed, two of the same analogies figuring in the conceptual foundations of the Leopold land ethic appear in Plato's value theory.[31] From the ecological perspective, according to Leopold as I have pointed out, land is like an organic body or like a human society. According to Plato, body, soul, and society have similar structures and corresponding virtues.[32] The goodness of each is a function of its structure or organization and the relative value of the parts or constituents of each is calculated according to the contribution made to the integrity, stability, and beauty of each whole.[33] In the *Republic*, Plato, in the very name of virtue and justice, is notorious for, among other things, requiring infanticide for a child whose only offense was being born without the sanction of the state, making presents to the enemy of guardians who allow themselves to be captured alive in combat, and radically restricting the practice of medicine to the dressing of wounds and the curing of seasonal maladies on the principle that the infirm and chronically ill not only lead miserable lives but contribute nothing to the good of the polity.[34] Plato, indeed, seems to regard individual human life and certainly human pain and suffering with complete indifference. On the other hand, he shrinks from nothing so long as it seems to him to be in the interest of the community. Among the apparently inhuman recommendations that he makes to better the community are a program of eugenics involving a phony lottery (so that those whose natural desires are frustrated, while breeding proceeds from the best stock as in a kennel or stable, will blame chance, not the design of the rulers), the destruction of the pair bond and nuclear family (in the interests of greater military and bureaucratic efficiency and group solidarity), and the utter abolition of private property.[35]

When challenged with the complaint that he is ignoring individual human happiness (and the happiness of those belonging to the most privileged class at that), he replies that it is the well-being of the community as a whole, not that of any person or special class at which his legislation aims.[36] This principle is readily accepted, first of all, in our attitude toward the body, he reminds us – the separate interests of the parts of which we acknowledge to be subordinate to the health and well-being of the whole – and secondly, assuming that we accept his faculty psychology, in our attitude toward the soul – whose multitude of desires must be disciplined, restrained, and, in the case of some, altogether repressed in the interest of personal virtue and a well-ordered and morally responsible life.

Given these formal similarities to Plato's moral philosophy, we may conclude that the land ethic – with its holistic good and its assignment of differential values to the several parts of the environment irrespective of their intelligence, sensibility, degree of complexity, or any other characteristic discernible in the parts considered separately – is somewhat foreign to modern systems of ethical philosophy, but perfectly familiar in the broader context of classical Western ethical philosophy. If, therefore, Plato's system of public and private justice is properly an "ethical" system, then so is the land ethic in relation to environmental virtue and excellence.[37]

Reappraising Domesticity

Among the last philosophical remarks penned by Aldo Leopold before his untimely death in 1948 is the following: "Perhaps such a shift of values [as implied by the attempt to weld together the concepts of ethics and ecology] can be achieved by reappraising things unnatural, tame, and confined in terms or things natural, wild, and free."[38] John Muir, in a similar spirit of reappraisal, had noted earlier the difference between the wild mountain sheep of the Sierra and the ubiquitous domestic variety. The latter, which Muir described as "hooved locusts," were only, in his estimation, "half alive" in comparison with their natural and autonomous counterparts.[39] One of the more distressing aspects of the animal liberation movement is the failure of almost all its exponents to draw a sharp distinction between the very different plights (and rights) of wild and domestic animals.[40] But this distinction lies at the very center of the land ethic. Domestic animals are creations of man. They are living artifacts, but artifacts nevertheless, and they constitute yet another mode of extension of the works of man into the ecosystem. From the perspective of the land ethic a herd of cattle, sheep, or pigs is as much or more a ruinous blight on the landscape as a fleet of four-wheel drive off-road vehicles. There is thus something profoundly incoherent (and insensitive as well) in the complaint of some animal liberationists that the "natural behavior" of chickens and bobby calves is cruelly frustrated on factory farms. It would make almost as much sense to speak of the natural behavior of tables and chairs.

Here a serious disanalogy (which no one to my knowledge has yet pointed out) becomes clearly evident between the liberation of blacks from slavery (and more recently, from civil inequality) and the liberation of animals from a similar sort of subordination and servitude. Black slaves remained, as it were, metaphysically autonomous: they were by nature if not by convention free beings quite capable of living on their own. They could not be enslaved for more than a historical interlude, for the strength of the force of their freedom was too great. They could, in other words, be retained only by a continuous counterforce, and only temporarily. This is equally true of caged wild animals. African cheetas in American and European zoos are captive, not indentured, beings. But this is not true of cows, pigs, sheep, and chickens. They have been bred to docility, tractability, stupidity, and dependency. It is literally meaningless to suggest that they be liberated. It is, to speak in hyperbole, a logical impossibility.

Certainly it is a practical impossibility. Imagine what would happen if the people of the world became morally persuaded that domestic animals were to be regarded as oppressed and enslaved persons and accordingly *set free*. In one scenario we might imagine that like former American black slaves they would receive the equivalent of forty acres and a mule and be turned out to survive on their own. Feral cattle and sheep would hang around farm outbuildings waiting forlornly to be sheltered and fed, or would graze aimlessly through their abandoned and deteriorating pastures. Most would starve or freeze as soon as winter settled in. Reproduction which had been assisted over many countless generations by their former owners might be altogether impossible in the feral state for some varieties, and the care of infants would be an art not so much lost as never acquired. And so in a very short time, after much suffering and agony, these species would become abruptly extinct. Or, in another scenario beginning with the same simple emancipation from human association, survivors of the first massive die-off of untended livestock might begin to recover some of their remote wild ancestral genetic traits and become smaller, leaner, heartier, and smarter versions of their former selves. An actual contemporary example is afforded by the feral mustangs ranging over parts of the American West. In time such animals as these would become (just as the mustangs are now) competitors both with their former human masters and (with perhaps more tragic consequences) indigenous wildlife for food and living space.

Foreseeing these and other untoward consequences of immediate and unplanned liberation of livestock, a human population grown morally more perfect than at present might decide that they had a duty, accumulated over thousands of years, to continue to house and feed as before their former animal slaves (whom they had rendered genetically unfit to care for themselves), but not to butcher them or make other ill use of them, including frustrating their "natural" behavior, their right to copulate freely, reproduce, and enjoy the delights of being parents. People, no longer having meat to eat, would require more vegetables, cereals, and other plant foods, but the institutionalized animal incompetents would still consume all the hay and grains (and more since they would no longer be slaughtered) than they did formerly. This would require clearing more land and bringing it into agricultural production with further loss of wildlife habitat and ecological destruction. Another possible scenario might be a decision on the part of people not literally to liberate domestic animals but simply to cease to breed and raise them. When the last livestock have been killed and eaten (or permitted to die "natural" deaths), people would become vegetarians and domestic livestock species would thus be rendered deliberately extinct (just as they had been deliberately created). But there is surely some irony in an outcome in which the beneficiaries of a humane extension of conscience are destroyed in the process of being saved.[41]

The land ethic, it should be emphasized, as Leopold has sketched it, provides for the *rights* of nonhuman natural beings to a share in the life processes of the biotic community. The conceptual foundation of such rights, however, is less conventional than natural, based upon, as one might say, evolutionary and ecological entitlement. Wild animals and native plants have a particular place in nature, according to the land ethic, which domestic animals (because they are products of human art and represent an extended presence of human beings in the natural world) do not have. The land ethic, in sum, is as much opposed, though on different grounds, to commercial traffic in wildlife, zoos, the slaughter of whales and other marine mammals, etc., as is the humane ethic. Concern for animal (and plant) rights and well-being is as fundamental to the land ethic as to the humane ethic, but the difference between naturally evolved and humanly bred species is an essential consideration for the one, though not for the other.

The "shift of values" which results from our "reappraising things unnatural, tame, and confined in terms of things natural, wild, and free" is especially dramatic when we reflect upon the definitions of *good* and *evil* espoused by Bentham and Mill and uncritically accepted by their contemporary followers. Pain and pleasure seem to have nothing at all to do with good and evil if our appraisal is taken from the vantage point of ecological biology. Pain in particular is primarily information. In animals, it informs the central nervous system of stress, irritation, or trauma in outlying regions of the organism. A certain level of pain under optimal organic circumstances is indeed desirable as an indicator of exertion – of the degree of exertion needed to maintain fitness, to stay "in shape," and of a level of exertion beyond which it would be dangerous to go. An arctic wolf in pursuit of a caribou may experience pain in her feet or chest because of the rigors of the chase. There is nothing bad or wrong in that. Or, consider a case of injury. Suppose that a person in the course of a wilderness excursion sprains an ankle. Pain informs him or her of the injury and by its intensity the amount of further stress the ankle may endure in the course of getting to safety. Would it be better if pain were not experienced upon injury or, taking advantage of recent technology, anaesthetized? Pleasure appears to be, for the most part (unfortunately it is not always so) a reward accompanying those activities which contribute to organic maintenance, such as the pleasures associated with eating, drinking, grooming, and so on, or those which contribute to social solidarity like the pleasures of dancing, conversation, teasing, etc., or those which contribute to the continuation of the species, such as the pleasures of sexual activity and of being parents. The doctrine that life is the happier the freer it is from pain and that the happiest life conceivable is one in which there is continuous pleasure uninterrupted by pain is biologically preposterous. A living mammal which experienced no pain would be one which had a lethal dysfunction of the nervous system. The idea that pain is evil and ought to be minimized or eliminated is as primitive a notion as that of a tyrant who puts to death messengers bearing bad news on the supposition that thus his well-being and security is improved.[42]

More seriously still, the value commitments of the humane movement seem at bottom to betray a world-denying or rather a life-loathing philosophy. The natural world as actually constituted is one in which one being lives at the expense of others.[43] Each organism, in Darwin's metaphor, struggles to maintain its own organic integrity. The more complex animals seem to experience (judging from our own case, and reasoning from analogy) appropriate and adaptive psychological accompaniments to organic existence. There is a palpable passion for self-preservation. There are desire, pleasure in the satisfaction of desires, acute agony attending injury, frustration, and chronic dread of death. But these experiences are the psychological substance of living. To live *is* to be anxious about life, to feel pain and pleasure in a fitting mixture, and sooner or later to die. That is the way the system works. If nature as a whole is good, then pain and death are also good. Environmental ethics in general require people to play fair in the natural system. The neo-Benthamites have in a sense taken the uncourageous approach. People have attempted to exempt themselves from the life/death reciprocities of natural processes and from ecological limitations in the name of a prophylactic ethic of maximizing rewards (pleasure) and minimizing unwelcome information (pain). To be fair, the humane moralists seem to suggest that we should attempt to project the same values into the nonhuman animal world and to widen the charmed circle – no matter that it would be biologically unrealistic to do so or biologically ruinous if, per impossible, such an environmental ethic were implemented.

There is another approach, Rather than imposing our alienation from nature and natural processes and cycles of life on other animals, we human beings could reaffirm our participation in nature by accepting life as it is given without a sugar coating. Instead of imposing artificial legalities, rights, and so on on nature, we might take the opposite course and accept and affirm natural biological laws, principles, and limitations in the human personal and social spheres. Such appears to have been the posture toward life of tribal peoples in the past. The chase was relished with its dangers, rigors, and hardships as well as its rewards: animal flesh was respectfully consumed; a tolerance for pain was cultivated; virtue and magnanimity were prized; lithic, floral, and faunal spirits were worshipped; population was routinely optimized by sexual continency, abortion, infanticide, and stylized warfare; and other life forms, although certainly appropriated, were respected as fellow players in a magnificent and awesome, if not altogether idyllic, drama of life, It is impossible today to return to the symbiotic relationship of Stone Age man to the natural environment, but the ethos of this by far the longest era of human existence could be abstracted and integrated with a future human culture seeking a viable and mutually beneficial relationship with nature. Personal, social, and environmental *health* would, accordingly, receive a premium value rather than comfort, self-indulgent pleasure, and anaesthetic insulation from pain. Sickness would be regarded as a worse evil than death. The pursuit of health or wellness at the personal, social, and environmental levels would require self-discipline in the form of simple diet, vigorous exercise, conservation, and social responsibility.

Leopold's prescription for the realization and implementation of the land ethic – the reappraisal of things unnatural, tame, and confined in terms of things natural, wild, and free – does not stop, in other words, with a reappraisal of nonhuman domestic animals in terms of their wild (or willed) counterparts; the human ones should be similarly reappraised. This means, among other things, the reappraisal of the comparatively recent values and concerns of "civilized" *Homo sapiens* in terms of those of our "savage" ancestors.[44] Civilization has insulated and alienated us from the rigors and challenges of the natural environment. The hidden agenda of the humane ethic is the imposition of the anti-natural prophylactic ethos of comfort and soft pleasure on an even wider scale. The land ethic, on the other hand, requires a shrinkage, if at all possible, of the domestic sphere; it rejoices in a recrudescence of wilderness and a renaissance of tribal cultural experience.

The converse of those goods and evils, axiomatic to the humane ethic, may be illustrated and focused by the consideration of a single issue raised by the humane morality: a vegetarian diet. Savage people seem to have had, if the attitudes and values of surviving tribal cultures are representative, something like an intuitive grasp of ecological relationships and certainly a morally charged appreciation of eating. There is nothing more intimate than eating, more symbolic of the connectedness of life, and more mysterious. What we eat and how we eat is by no means an insignificant ethical concern.

From the ecological point of view, for human beings universally to become vegetarians is tantamount to a shift of trophic niche from omnivore with carnivorous preferences to herbivore. The shift is a downward one on the trophic pyramid, which in effect shortens those food chains terminating with man. It represents an increase in the efficiency of the conversion of solar energy from plant to human biomass, and thus, by bypassing animal intermediates, increases available food resources for human beings. The human population would probably, as past trends overwhelmingly suggest, expand in accordance with the potential thus afforded. The net result would be fewer nonhuman beings and more human beings, who, of course, have requirements of life far more elaborate than even those of domestic animals, requirements which would tax other "natural resources" (trees for shelter, minerals mined at the expense of topsoil and its vegetation, etc.) more than under present circumstances. A vegetarian human population is therefore *probably* ecologically catastrophic.

Meat eating as implied by the foregoing remarks may be more *ecologically* responsible than a wholly vegetable diet. Meat, however, purchased at the supermarket, externally packaged and internally laced with petrochemicals, fattened in feed lots, slaughtered impersonally, and, in general, mechanically processed from artificial insemination to microwave roaster, is an affront not only to physical metabolism and bodily health but to conscience as well. From the perspective of the land ethic, the immoral aspect of the factory farm has to do far less with the suffering and killing of nonhuman animals than with the monstrous transformation of living things from an organic to a mechanical mode of being. Animals, beginning with the Neolithic Revolution, have been debased through selective breeding, but they have nevertheless remained animals. With the Industrial Revolution an even more profound and terrifying transformation has overwhelmed them. They have become, in Ruth Harrison's most apt description, "animal machines." The very presence of animals, so emblematic of delicate, complex organic tissue, surrounded by machines, connected to machines, penetrated by machines in research laboratories or crowded together in space-age "production facilities" is surely the more real and visceral source of our outrage at vivisection and factory farming than the contemplation of the quantity of pain that these unfortunate beings experience. I wish to denounce as loudly as the neo-Benthamites this ghastly abuse of animal life, but also to stress that the pain and suffering of research and agribusiness animals is not greater than that endured by free-living wildlife as a consequence of predation, disease, starvation, and cold – indicating that there is something immoral about vivisection and factory farming which is not an ingredient in the natural lives and deaths of wild beings. That immoral something is the transmogrification of organic to mechanical processes.

Ethical vegetarianism to all appearances insists upon the human consumption of plants (in a paradoxical moral gesture toward those animals whose very existence is dependent upon human carnivorousness), even when the tomatoes are grown hydroponically, the lettuce generously coated with chlorinated hydrocarbons, the potatoes pumped up with chemical fertilizers, and the cereals stored with the help of chemical preservatives. The land ethic takes as much exception to the transmogrification of plants by mechanicochemical means as to that of animals. The important thing, I would think, is not to eat vegetables as opposed to animal flesh, but to resist factory farming in all its manifestations, including especially its liberal application of pesticides, herbicides, and chemical fertilizers to maximize the production of *vegetable* crops.

The land ethic, with its ecological perspective, helps us to recognize and affirm the organic integrity of self and the untenability of a firm distinction between self and environment. On the ethical question of what to eat, it answers, not vegetables instead of animals, but organically as opposed to mechanicochemically produced food. Purists like Leopold prefer, in his expression, to get their "meat from God," i.e., to hunt and consume wildlife and to gather wild plant foods, and thus to live within the parameters of the aboriginal human ecological niche.[45] Second best is eating from one's own orchard, garden, henhouse, pigpen, and barnyard. Third best is buying or bartering organic foods from one's neighbors and friends.

Conclusion

Philosophical controversy concerning animal liberation/rights has been most frequently represented as a polar dispute between traditional moral humanists and seemingly *avant garde* humane moralists. Further, animal liberation has been assumed to be closely allied with environmental ethics, possibly because in Leopold's classical formulation moral standing and indeed rights (of some unspecified sort) is accorded nonhuman beings, among them animals. The purpose of this discussion has been to distinguish sharply environmental ethics from the animal liberation/rights movement both in theory and practical application and to suggest, thereupon, that there is an under-represented, but very important, point of view respecting the problem of the moral status of nonhuman animals. The debate over animal liberation, in short, should be conceived as triangular, not polar, with land ethics or environmental ethics, the third and, in my judgment, the most creative, interesting, and practicable alternative. Indeed, from this third point of view moral humanism and humane moralism appear to have much more in common with one another than either have with environmental or land ethics. On reflection one might even be led to suspect that the noisy debate between these parties has served to drown out the much deeper challenge to "business-as-usual" ethical philosophy represented by Leopold and his exponents, and to keep ethical philosophy firmly anchored to familiar modern paradigms.

Moral humanism and humane moralism, to restate succinctly the most salient conclusions of this essay, are *atomistic* or distributive in their theory of moral value, while environmental ethics (again, at least, as set out in Leopold's outline) is *holistic* or collective. Modern ethical theory, in other words, has consistently located moral value in individuals and set out certain metaphysical reasons for including some individuals and excluding others. Humane moralism remains firmly within this modern convention and centers its attention on the competing criteria for moral standing and rights holding, while environmental ethics locates ultimate value in the "biotic community" and assigns differential moral value to the constitutive individuals relatively to that standard. This is perhaps the most fundamental theoretical difference between environmental ethics and the ethics of animal liberation.

Allied to this difference are many others. One of the more conspicuous is that in environmental ethics, plants are included within the parameters of the ethical theory as well as animals. Indeed, inanimate entities such as oceans and lakes, mountains, forests, and wetlands are assigned a greater value than individual animals and in a way quite different from systems which accord them moral considerability through a further multiplication of competing individual loci of value and holders of rights.

There are intractable practical differences between environmental ethics and the animal liberation movement. Very different moral obligations follow in respect, most importantly, to domestic animals, the principal beneficiaries of the humane ethic. Environmental ethics sets a very low priority on domestic animals as they very frequently contribute to the erosion of the integrity, stability, and beauty of the biotic communities into which they have been insinuated. On the other hand, animal liberation, if pursued at the practical as well as rhetorical level, would have ruinous consequences on plants, soils, and waters, consequences which could not be directly reckoned according to humane moral theory. As this last remark suggests, the animal liberation/animal rights movement is in the final analysis utterly unpracticable. An imagined society in which all animals capable of sensibility received equal consideration or held rights to equal consideration would be so ludicrous that it might be more appropriately and effectively treated in satire than in philosophical discussion. The land ethic, by contrast, even though its ethical purview is very much wider, is nevertheless eminently practicable, since, by reference to a single good, competing individual claims may be adjudicated and relative values and priorities assigned to the myriad components of the biotic community. This is not to suggest that the implementation of environmental ethics as social policy would be easy. Implementation of the land ethic would require discipline, sacrifice, retrenchment, and massive economic reform, tantamount to a virtual revolution in prevailing attitudes and life styles. Nevertheless, it provides a unified and coherent practical principle and thus a decision procedure at the practical level which a distributive or atomistic ethic may achieve only artificially and so imprecisely as to be practically indeterminate.

Notes

*The author expresses his appreciation to Richard A. Watson for helpful comments on the final version of this paper.

1   Aldo Leopold, *A Sand County Almanac* (New York: Oxford University Press, 1949), pp. 202–3. Some traditional Western systems of ethics, however, have accorded moral standing to nonhuman beings. The Pythagorean tradition did, followed by Empedocles of Acragas; Saint Francis of Assisi apparently believed in the animal soul; in modern ethics Jeremy Bentham's hedonistic utilitarian system is also an exception to the usual rule. John Passmore ("The Treatment of Animals," *Journal of the History of Ideas*, 36 [1975]: 196–218), provides a well–researched and eye–opening study of historical ideas about the moral status of animals in Western thought. Though exceptions to the prevailing attitudes have existed, they are exceptions indeed and represent but a small minority of Western religious and philosophical points of view.

2   The tag "animal-liberation" for this moral movement originates with Peter Singer whose book *Animal Liberation* (New York: New York Review, 1975) has been widely influential. "Animal rights" have been most persistently and unequivocally championed by Tom Regan in various articles, among them: "The Moral Basis of Vegetarianism,"

Canadian Journal of Philosophy, 5 (1975): 181–214; "Exploring the Idea of Animal Rights," in *Animal Rights: A Symposium*, eds D. Patterson and R. Ryder (London: Centaur, 1979); "Animal Rights, Human Wrongs," *Environmental Ethics*, 2 (1980): 99–120. A more complex and qualified position respecting animal rights has been propounded by Joel Feinberg, "The Rights of Animals and Unborn Generations," in *Philosophy and Environmental Crisis*, ed. William T. Blackstone (Athens: University of Georgia Press, 1974), pp. 43–68; and "Human Duties and Animal Rights," in *On the Fifth Day*, eds R. K. Morris and M. W. Fox (Washington: Acropolis Books, 1978), pp. 45–69. Lawrence Haworth ("Rights, Wrongs and Animals," *Ethics*, 88 [1978]: 95–105), in the context of the contemporary debate, claims limited rights on behalf of animals. S. R. L. Clark's *The Moral Status of Animals* (Oxford: Clarendon Press, 1975) has set out arguments which differ in some particulars from those of Singer, Regan, and Feinberg with regard to the moral considerability of some nonhuman animals. In this discussion, as a tribute to Singer, I use the term *animal liberation* generically to cover the several philosophical rationales for a humane ethic. Singer has laid particular emphasis on the inhumane usage of animals in agribusiness and scientific research. Two thorough professional studies from the humane perspective of these institutions are Ruth Harrison's *Animal Machines* (London: Stuart, 1964); and Richard Ryder's *Victims of Science* (London: Davis-Poynter, 1975), respectively.

3   Peter Singer and Tom Regan especially insist upon *equal* moral *consideration* for nonhuman animals. Equal moral *consideration* does not necessarily imply equal *treatment*, however, as Singer insists. Cf. Singer, *Animal Liberation*, pp. 3, 17–24; and Singer, "The Fable of the Fox and the Unliberated Animals," *Ethics*, 88 (1978): 119–20. Regan provides an especially clear summary of both his position and Singer's in "Animal Rights, Human Wrong," pp. 108–12.

4   We have Richard Ryder to thank for coining the term *speciesism*. See his *Speciesism: The Ethics of Vivisection* (Edinburgh: Scottish Society for the Prevention of Vivisection, 1974). Richard Routley introduced the term *human chauvinism* in "Is There a Need for a New, an Environmental Ethic?" *Proceedings of the Fifteenth World Congress of Philosophy*, 1 (1973): 205–10. Peter Singer ("All Animals Are Equal," in *Animal Rights and Human Obligations*, eds Tom Regan and Peter Singer [Englewood Cliffs, NJ: Prentice-Hall, 1976], pp. 148–62) developed the egalitarian comparison of speciesism with racism and sexism in detail. To extend the political comparison further, animal liberation is also a reformist and activist movement. We are urged to act, to become vegetarians, to boycott animal products, etc. The concluding paragraph of Regan's "Animal Rights, Human Wrongs," (p. 120) is especially zealously hortatory.

5   Leopold, *Sand County Almanac*, p. 204.

6   Ibid., pp. 201–3. A more articulate historical representation of the parallel expansion of legal rights appears in C. D. Stone's *Should Trees Have Standing?* (Los Altos: William Kaufman, 1972), pp. 3–10, however without specific application to animal liberation.

7   Leopold, *Sand County Almanac*, p. 203.

8   Ibid., p. 204.

9   Ibid., p. 221 (trees); pp. 129–33 (mountains); p. 209 (streams).

10   John Benson ("Duty and the Beast," *Philosophy*, 53 [1978]: 547–8) confesses that in the course of considering issues raised by Singer et al. he was "obliged to change my own diet as a result." An elaborate critical discussion is Philip E. Devine's "The Moral Basis of Vegetarianism" (*Philosophy*, 53 [1978]: 481–505).

11   For a biography of Leopold including particular reference to Leopold's career as a "sportsman," see Susan L. Flader, *Thinking Like a Mountain* (Columbia: University of Missouri Press, 1974).

12   See especially, Leopold, *Sand County Almanac*, pp. 54–8; 62–6; 120–2; 149–54; 177–87.

13   A most thorough and fully argued dissent is provided by John Rodman in "The Liberation of Nature," *Inquiry*, 20 (1977): 83–131. It is surprising that Singer, whose book is the subject of Rodman's extensive critical review, or some of Singer's philosophical

allies, has not replied to these very penetrating and provocative criticisms. Another less specifically targeted dissent is Paul Shepard's "Animal Rights and Human Rites" (*North American Review* [Winter 1974]: 35–41). More recently Kenneth Goodpaster ("From Egoism to Environmentalism," in *Ethics and Problems of the 21st Century*, eds K. Goodpaster and K. Sayre [Notre Dame: Notre Dame University Press, 1979], pp. 21–35) has expressed complaints about the animal liberation and animal rights movement in the name of environmental ethics. "The last thing we need," writes Goodpaster, "is simply another 'liberation movement'" (p. 29).

14 Singer, "All Animals Are Equal" (p. 159), uses the term *humanist* to convey a speciesist connotation. Rationality and future-conceiving capacities as criteria for rights holding have been newly revived by Michael E. Levin with specific reference to Singer in "Animal Rights Evaluated," *The Humanist* (July/August 1977): 12, 14–15. John Passmore, in *Man's Responsibility for Nature* (New York: Charles Scribner's Sons, 1974), cf. p. 116, has recently insisted upon having interest as a criterion for having rights and denied that nonhuman beings have interests. L. P. Francis and R. Norman ("Some Animals Are More Equal than Others," *Philosophy*, 53 [1978]: 507–27) have argued, again with specific reference to animal liberationists, that linguistic abilities are requisite for moral status. H. J. McCloskey ("The Right to Life," *Mind*, 84 [1975]: 410–13; and "Moral Rights and Animals," *Inquiry*, 22 [1979]: 23–54), adapting an idea of Kant's, defends *autonomy* as the main ingredient of human nature which entitles human beings to rights. Michael Fox ("Animal Liberation: A Critique," *Ethics*, 88 [1978]: 106–18) defends, among other exclusively human qualifications for rights holding, *self*-awareness. Richard A. Watson ("Self-Consciousness and the Rights of Nonhuman Animals and Nature," *Environmental Ethics*, 1 [1979]: 99–129) also defends self-consciousness as a criterion for rights holding, but allows that some nonhuman animals also possess it.

15 In addition to the historical figures, who are nicely summarized and anthologized in *Animal Rights and Human Obligations*, John Passmore has recently defended the reactionary notion that cruelty towards animals is morally reprehensible for reasons independent of any obligation or duties people have to animals as such (*Man's Responsibility*, cf. p. 117).

16 "Humane moralists" is perhaps a more historically accurate designation than "animal liberationists." John Rodman, "The Liberation of Nature" (pp. 88–9), has recently explored in a programmatic way the connection between the contemporary animal liberation/rights movements and the historical humane societies movement.

17 Tom Regan styles more precise formulations of this argument, "the argument from marginal cases," in "An Examination and Defense of One Argument Concerning Animal Rights," *Inquiry*, 22 (1979): 190. Regan directs our attention to Andrew Linzey, *Animal Rights* (London: SCM Press, 1976) as well as to Singer, *Animal Liberation*, for paradigmatic employment of this argument on behalf of moral standing for animals (p. 144).

18 A particularly lucid advocacy of this notion may be found in Feinberg, "Human Duties and Animal Rights," especially pp. 53ff.

19 Again, Feinberg in "Human Duties and Animal Rights" (pp. 57–9) expresses this point especially forcefully.

20 John Rodman's comment in "The Liberation of Nature" (p. 91) is worth repeating here since it has to all appearances received so little attention elsewhere: "If it would seem arbitrary . . . to find one species claiming a monopoly on intrinsic value by virtue of its allegedly exclusive possession of reason, free will, soul, or some other occult quality, would it not seem almost as arbitrary to find that same species claiming a monopoly of intrinsic value for itself and those species most resembling it (e.g. in type of nervous system and behavior) by virtue of their common and allegedly exclusive possession of sentience [i.e., sensibility]?" Goodpaster ("From Egoism to Environmentalism," p. 29) remarks that in modern moral philosophy "a fixation on egoism and a consequent loyalty to a model of moral sentiment or reason which in essence generalizes

or universalizes that egoism . . . makes it particularly inhospitable to our recent felt need for an environmental ethic. . . . For such an ethic does not readily admit of being reduced to 'humanism' – nor does it sit well with any class or generalization model of moral concern."

21 John Rodman, "The Liberation of Nature" (p. 95), comments: "Why do our 'new ethics' seem so old? . . . Because the attempt to produce a 'new ethics' by the process of 'extension' perpetuates the basic assumptions of the conventional modern paradigm, however much it fiddles with the boundaries." When the assumptions remain conventional, the boundaries are, in my view, scalar, but triangular when both positions are considered in opposition to the land ethic. The scalar relation is especially clear when two other positions, not specifically discussed in the text, the reverence-for-life ethic and pan-moralism, are considered. The reverence-for-life ethic (as I am calling it in deference to Albert Schweitzer) seems to be the next step on the scale after the humane ethic. William Frankena considers it so in "Ethics and the Environment," *Ethics and Problems of the 21st Century*, pp. 3–20. W. Murry Hunt ("Are *Mere Things* Morally Considerable," *Environmental Ethics*, 2 [1980]: 59–65) has gone a step past Schweitzer, and made the bold suggestion that *everything* should be accorded moral standing, pan-moralism. Hunt's discussion shows clearly that there is a similar logic ("slippery slope" logic) involved in taking each downward step, and thus a certain commonality of underlying assumptions among all the ethical types to which the land ethic stands in opposition. Hunt is not unaware that his suggestion may be interpreted as a *reductio ad absurdum* of the whole matter, but insists that that is not his intent. The land ethic is not part of this linear series of steps and hence may be represented as a point off the scale. The principal difference, as I explain below, is that the land ethic is collective or "holistic" while the others are distributive or "atomistic." Another relevant difference is that moral humanism, humane moralism, reverence-for-life ethics, and the limiting case, pan-moralism, either openly or implicitly espouse a pecking-order model of nature. The land ethic, founded upon an ecological model of nature emphasizing the contributing roles played by various species in the economy of nature, abandons the "higher"/"lower" ontological and axiological schema, in favor of a functional system of value. The land ethic, in other words, is inclined to establish value distinctions not on the basis of higher and lower order of being, but on the basis of the importance of organisms, minerals, and so on to the biotic community. Some bacteria, for example, may be of greater value to the health or economy of nature than dogs, and thus command more respect.

22 Rodman, "The Liberation of Nature" (p. 86), says in reference to Singer's humane ethic that "the weakness . . . lies in the limitation of its horizon to the late eighteenth and early nineteenth century Utilitarian humane movement [and] its failure to live up to its own noble declaration that 'philosophy ought to question the basic assumptions, of the age.' . . ."

23 Leopold, *Sand County Almanac*, pp. 224–5.

24 By "first," "second," and "third" order wholes I intend paradigmatically single cell organisms, multicell organisms, and bio-coenoses, respectively.

25 "Some Fundamentals of Conservation in the Southwest," composed in the 1920s but unpublished until it appeared last year (*Environmental Ethics*, 1 [1979]: 131–41), shows that the organic analogy, conceptually representing the nature of the whole resulting from ecological relationships, antedates the community analogy in Leopold's thinking, so far at least as its moral implications are concerned. "The Land Ethic" of *Sand County Almanac* employs almost exclusively the community analogy but a rereading of "The Land Ethic" in the light of "Some Fundamentals" reveals that Leopold did not entirely abandon the organic analogy in favor of the community analogy. For example, toward the end of "The Land Ethic" Leopold talks about "land health" and "land the collective organism" (p. 258). William Morton Wheeler, *Essays in Philosophical Biology* (New York: Russell and Russell, 1939); and Lewis Thomas, *Lives of a Cell* (New York: Viking Press, 1974), provide extended discussions

of holistic approaches to social, ethical, and environmental problems. Kenneth Goodpaster, almost alone among academic philosophers, has explored the possibility of a holistic environmental ethical system in "From Egoism to Environmentalism."

26 J. Bentham, *An Introduction to the Principles of Morals and Legislation* (Oxford: Oxford University Press, 1823), chapter 1, sec. 4.

27 This has been noticed and lamented by Alistair S. Gunn ("Why Should We Care about Rare Species?" *Environmental Ethics*, 2 [1980]: 36) who comments, "Environmentalism seems incompatible with the 'Western' obsession with individualism, which leads us to resolve questions about our treatment of animals by appealing to the essentially atomistic, competitive notion of rights. . . ." John Rodman, "The Liberation of Nature" (p. 89), says practically the same thing: "The moral atomism that focuses on individual animals and their subjective experiences does not seem well adapted to coping with ecological systems." Peter Singer has in fact actually stressed the individual focus of his humane ethic in "Not for Humans Only: The Place of Nonhumans in Environmental Issues" (*Ethics and Problems of the 21st Century*, pp. 191–206) as if it were a virtue! More revealingly, the only grounds that he can discover for moral concern over species, since species are *per se* not sensible entities (and that is the extent of his notion of an ethically relevant consideration), are anthropocentric grounds, human aesthetics, environmental integrity for humans, etc.

28 Leopold, *Sand County Almanac*, pp. 223 and 209.

29 Edward Abbey, *Desert Solitaire* (New York: Balantine Books, 1968), p. 20.

30 Garrett Hardin, "The Economics of Wilderness," *Natural History*, 78 [1969]: 173–7. Hardin is blunt: "Making great and spectacular efforts to save the life of an individual makes sense only when there is a shortage of people. I have not lately heard that there is a shortage of people" (p. 176).

31 In *Republic*, 5, Plato directly says that "the best governed state most nearly resembles an organism" (462D) and that there is no "greater evil for a state than the thing that distracts it and makes it many instead of

one, or a greater good than that which binds it together and makes it one" (462A). Goodpaster in "From Egoism to Environmentalism" (p. 30) has in a general way anticipated this connection: "The oft-repeated plea by some ecologists and environmentalists that our thinking needs to be less atomistic and more 'holistic' translates in the present context into a plea for a more embracing object of moral consideration. In a sense it represents a plea to return to the richer Greek conception of man by nature social and not intelligibly removable from his social and political context though it goes beyond the Greek conception in emphasizing that societies too need to be understood in a context, an ecological context, and that it is this larger whole that is the 'bearer of value.'"

32 See especially *Republic*, 4.444A–E.

33 For a particularly clear statement by Plato of the idea that the goodness of anything is a matter of the fitting order of the parts in relation to respective wholes see *Gorgias*, 503D–507A.

34 Cf. *Republic*, 5.461C (infanticide); 486A (disposition of captives); *Republic*, 3.405D–406E (medicine).

35 Cf. *Republic*, 5.459A–460E (eugenics, nonfamily life and child rearing); *Republic*, 3.416D–417B (private property).

36 Cf. *Republic*, 4.419A–421C; and *Republic*, 7.419D–521B.

37 After so much strident complaint has been registered here about the lack of freshness in self-proclaimed "new" environmental ethics (which turn out to be "old" ethics retreaded) there is surely an irony in comparing the (apparently brand new) Leopoldian land ethic to Plato's ethical philosophy. There is, however, an important difference. The humane moralists have simply revived and elaborated Bentham's historical application of hedonism to questions regarding the treatment of animals with the capacity of sensibility. There is nothing new but the revival and elaboration. Plato, on the other hand, never develops anything faintly resembling an *environmental* ethic. Plato never reached an ecological view of living nature. The wholes of his universe are body, soul, society, and cosmos. Plato is largely, if not exclusively,

concerned with moral problems involving individual human beings in a political context and he has the temerity to insist that the good of the whole transcends individual claims. (Even in the *Crito*, Plato is sympathetic to the city's claim to put *Socrates* to death however unjust the verdict against him.) Plato thus espouses a holistic ethic which is valuable as a (very different) paradigm to which the Leopoldian *land* ethic, which is also holistic but in relation to a very different whole, may be compared. It is interesting further that some (but not all) of the analogies which Plato finds useful to convey his holistic social values are also useful to Leopold in his effort to set out a land ethic.

38 Leopold, *Sand County Almanac*, p. ix.

39 See John Muir, "The Wild Sheep of California," *Overland Monthly*, 12 (1874): 359.

40 Roderick Nash (*Wilderness and the American Mind*, rev. edn [New Haven and London: Yale University Press, 1973], p. 2) suggests that the English word *wild* is ultimately derived from *will*. A wild being is thus a willed one – "self-willed, willful, or uncontrollable." The humane moralists' indifference to this distinction is rather dramatically represented in Regan's "Animal Rights, Human Wrongs" (pp. 99–104), which begins with a bid for the reader's sympathy through a vivid description of four concrete episodes of human cruelty toward animals. I suspect that Regan's intent is to give examples of four principal categories of animal abuse at the hands of man: whaling, traffic in zoo captives, questionable scientific experimentation involving unquestionable torture, and intensive meat production. But his illustrations, divided according to precepts central to land ethics, concern two episodes of wanton slaughter of *wild* animals, a blue whale and a gibbon, aggravated by the consideration that both are specimens of disappearing species, and two episodes of routine cruelty toward *domestic* animals, a "bobby calf" (destined to become veal) and a laboratory rabbit. The misery of the calf and the agony of the rabbit are, to be sure, reprehensible, from the perspective of the land ethic, for reasons I explain shortly, but it is, I think, a trivialization of the deeper environmental and ecological issues involved in modern whaling and wildlife traffic to discuss the exploita-

tion and destruction of blue whales and gibbon apes as if they are wrong for the same reasons that the treatment of laboratory rabbits and male dairy calves is wrong. The inhumane treatment of penned domestics should not be, I suggest, even discussed in the same context as whaling and wildlife traffic; it is a disservice to do so.

41 John Rodman. "The Liberation of Nature" (p. 101), castigates Singer for failing to consider what the consequences of human animal liberation might be. With tongue in cheek he congratulates Singer for taking a step toward the elimination of a more subtle evil, the genetic debasement of other animal beings, i.e., domestication *per se*.

42 A particularly strong statement of the ultimate value commitment of the neo-Benthamites is found in Feinberg's "Human Duties and Animal Rights" (p. 57) "We regard pain and suffering as an intrinsic evil . . . simply because they are pain and suffering. . . . The question 'What's wrong with pain anyway?' is never allowed to arise." I shall raise it. I herewith declare in all soberness that I see nothing wrong with pain. It is a marvelous method, honed by the evolutionary process, of conveying important organic information. I think it was the late Alan Watts who somewhere remarked that upon being asked if he did not think there was too much pain in the world replied, "No, I think there's just enough."

43 Paul Shepard, "Animal Rights and Human Rites" (p. 37), comments that "the humanitarian's projection onto nature of illegal murder and the rights of civilized people to safety not only misses the point but is exactly contrary to fundamental ecological reality: the structure of nature is a sequence of killings."

44 This matter has been ably and fully explored by Paul Shepard, *The Tender Carnivore and the Sacred Game* (New York: Scribner's Sons, 1973). A more empirical study has been carried out by Marshall Sahlins, *Stone Age Economics* (Chicago: Aldine/Atherton, 1972).

45 The expression "our meat from God" is found in Leopold, *Sand County Almanac*, p. viii. Leopold mentions "organic farming" as something intimately connected with the land ethic; in the same context he also speaks of "biotic farming" (p. 222).

18

Index